Get the eBook FREE!
(PDF, ePub, Kindle, and liveBook all included)

We believe that once you buy a book from us, you should be able to read it in any format we have available. To get electronic versions of this book at no additional cost to you, purchase and then register this book at the Manning website.

Go to https://www.manning.com/freebook and follow the instructions to complete your pBook registration.

That's it!
Thanks from Manning!

Praises from reviewers of *Pro ASP.NET Core 7, Tenth Edition*

If you're looking for breadth and depth coverage of ASP.NET Core development, this is the book for you.
—Greg White, Software Development Manager, PicoBrew Inc.

A must have book for the .NET developer/engineer.
—Foster Haines, Consultant, Foster's Website Company

The book for web development professionals.
—Renato Gentile, Solutions Architect, S3K S.p.A.

This book guides you as a beginner and will remain your for-ever reference book.
—Werner Nindl, Partner, Nova Advisory

An encyclopedic journey.
—Richard Young, IT Director, Design Synthesis, Inc

From tiny throw-away sites to large production websites, this book teaches all you need to know.
—Samuel Bosch, Team Lead, ILVO

By the end of this book you should be able to write code for real-world projects.
—Rich Yonts, Senior Software Engineer, Teradata

Pro ASP.NET Core 7

TENTH EDITION

ADAM FREEMAN

MANNING

SHELTER ISLAND

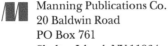
Manning Publications Co.
20 Baldwin Road
PO Box 761
Shelter Island, NY 11964

Development editor:	Marina Michaels
Technical editor:	Fabio Ferracchiati
Production editor:	Aleksandar Dragosavljević
Copy editor:	Katie Petito
Typesetter:	Tamara Švelić Sabljić
Cover designer:	Marija Tudor

ISBN 9781633437821
Printed in the United States of America

Dedicated to my lovely wife, Jacqui Griffyth.
(And also to Peanut.)

contents

5

Essential C# features   73

    23.1 Preparing for this chapter   632
          Running the example application   632

    23.2 Understanding Razor Pages   633
          Configuring Razor Pages   633 ▪ Creating a Razor Page   634

    23.3 Understanding Razor Pages routing   639
          Specifying a routing pattern in a Razor Page   640
          Adding routes for a Razor Page   642

    23.4 Understanding the Page model class   644
          *Using a code-behind class file   644 ▪ Understanding action
          results in Razor Pages   647 ▪ Handling multiple HTTP
          methods   651 ▪ Selecting a handler method   653*

    23.5 Understanding the Razor Page view   656
          *Creating a layout for Razor Pages   656 ▪ Using partial views
          in Razor Pages   658 ▪ Creating Razor Pages without page
          models   659*

          Summary   661

24   *Using view components*   662

    24.1 Preparing for this chapter   663
          *Dropping the database   666 ▪ Running the example
          application   666*

    24.2 Understanding view components   667

    24.3 Creating and using a view component   667
          Applying a view component   668

    24.4 Understanding view component results   671
          *Returning a partial view   672 ▪ Returning HTML
          fragments   675*

    24.5 Getting context data   678
          Providing context from the parent view using arguments   679
          Creating asynchronous view components   683

    24.6 Creating view components classes   685
          Creating a hybrid controller class   688

          Summary   690

preface

This is the 49th book I have written. I wrote my first book in 1996, and I would not have believed anyone who told me that I would still be writing over a quarter of a century later, or that books would become such an important part of my life.

I have a bookshelf on which I keep every book I have written. It is an act of pure self-indulgence, but I am proud of these books and what they represent. They span 2.5 meters on a single shelf (or 8 feet if you prefer) and they mark the chapters of my life: the book I wrote the year I married my beloved wife; the book I was writing when my father died; the book I finished while we moved house; the book I wrote after I retired. Each book reminds me of people and places going back 27 years.

Of all the books I have written, Pro ASP.NET Core is my favourite. This is the 10th edition, but I almost didn't write it at all. I had already written a book about ASP.NET Web Forms and found it to be a frustrating process, so I wasn't keen to write about the MVC framework and Microsoft's attempt to modernize their web development products. My wife persuaded me to accept the publisher's offer and I have never looked back. ASP.NET has evolved into ASP.NET Core, and each edition of this book has been a little bigger and a little more detailed.

This is a big and complicated book because ASP.NET Core is big and complicated. But I put a lot of effort into writing books that are easy to follow, even if the topics can be difficult to understand. As I write this preface and I think of you, my future reader, my hope is that the book you hold in your hand helps you with your career, makes your project easier to implement, or helps you move into a new and more exciting role.

There is something unique about receiving the first copies of a book, fresh from the printers. The process of getting a book into print takes just enough time for it to be a surprise when the box arrives at the door. Writing is an abstract process and writing about software especially so. The finished book feels like an idea made real. These days, ebooks are more popular and more convenient, but my heart will always beat with joy for the printed version. As you hold this book, I hope you feel some of that joy, and that this book plays some small part in helping you achieve something you will be proud of, whatever that may be.

about this book

Pro ASP.NET Core, Tenth Edition was written to help you build web applications using the latest version of .NET and ASP.NET Core. It begins with setting up the development environment and creating a simple web application, before moving on to creating a simple but realistic online store, and then diving into the detail of important ASP.NET Core features.

Who should read this book

This book is for experienced developers who are new to ASP.NET Core, or who are moving from an earlier version of ASP.NET, including legacy Web Forms.

How this book is organized: a roadmap

The book has four parts. The first part covers setting up the development environment, creating a simple web application, and using the development tools. There is also a primer on important C# features for readers who are moving from an earlier version of ASP.NET or ASP.NET Core. The rest of this part of the book contains the SportsStore example application, which shows how to create a basic but functional online store, and demonstrates how the many different ASP.NET Core features work together.

The second part of the book describes the key features of the ASP.NET Core platform. I explain how HTTP requests are processed, how to create and use middleware components, how to create routes, how to define and consume services, and how to work with Entity Framework Core. These chapters explain the foundations of ASP.NET Core, and understanding them is essential for effective ASP.NET Core development.

The third part of the book focuses on the ASP.NET features you will need every day, including HTTP request handling, creating RESTful web services, generating HTML responses, and receiving data from users.

The final part of this book describes advanced ASP.NET Core features, including using Blazor to create rich client-side applications, and using ASP.NET Core Identity to authenticate users.

About the code

This book contains many examples of source code both in numbered listings and in line with normal text. In both cases, the source code is formatted in a fixed-width font to separate it from ordinary text. Code is also in bold to highlight statements that have changed from previous listings.

The source code for every chapter in this book is available at https://github.com/manningbooks/pro-asp.net-core-7.

liveBook discussion forum

Purchase of *Pro ASP.NET Core 7, Tenth Edition* includes free access to liveBook, Manning's online reading platform. Using liveBook's exclusive discussion features, you can attach comments to the book globally or to specific sections or paragraphs. It's a snap to make notes for yourself, ask and answer technical questions, and receive help from the author and other users. To access the forum, go to https://livebook.manning.com/book/pro-aspdotnet-core-7-tenth-edition/discussion. You can also learn more about Manning's forums and the rules of conduct at https://livebook.manning.com/discussion.

Manning's commitment to our readers is to provide a venue where a meaningful dialogue between individual readers and between readers and the author can take place. It is not a commitment to any specific amount of participation on the part of the author, whose contribution to the forum remains voluntary (and unpaid). We suggest you try asking the author some challenging questions lest his interest stray! The forum and the archives of previous discussions will be accessible from the publisher's website as long as the book is in print.

about the author

ADAM FREEMAN is an experienced IT professional who started his career as a programmer. He has held senior positions in a range of companies, most recently serving as Chief Technology Officer and Chief Operating Officer of a global bank. He has written 49 programming books, focusing mostly on web application development. Now retired, he spends his time writing and trying to make furniture.

ABOUT THE TECHNICAL EDITOR

Fabio Claudio Ferracchiati is a senior consultant and a senior analyst/developer using Microsoft technologies. He works for TIM (www.telecomitalia.it). He is a Microsoft Certified Solution Developer for .NET, a Microsoft Certified Application Developer for .NET, a Microsoft Certified Professional, and a prolific author and technical reviewer. Over the past ten years, he's written articles for Italian and international magazines and coauthored more than ten books on a variety of computer topics.

about the cover illustration

The figure on the cover of *Pro ASP.NET Core 7, Tenth Edition* is "Turc en habit d'hiver," or "Turk in winter clothes," taken from a collection by Jacques Grasset de Saint-Sauveur, published in 1788. Each illustration is finely drawn and colored by hand.

In those days, it was easy to identify where people lived and what their trade or station in life was just by their dress. Manning celebrates the inventiveness and initiative of the computer business with book covers based on the rich diversity of regional culture centuries ago, brought back to life by pictures from collections such as this one.

Putting ASP.NET Core in context

1

This chapter covers

- Putting ASP.NET Core in context
- Understanding the role of the ASP.NET Core platform
- Putting the ASP.NET Core application frame works in context
- Understanding the structure of this book
- Getting support when something doesn't work

ASP.NET Core is Microsoft's web development platform. The original ASP.NET was introduced in 2002, and it has been through several reinventions and reincarnations to become ASP.NET Core 7, which is the topic of this book.

ASP.NET Core consists of a platform for processing HTTP requests, a series of principal frameworks for creating applications, and secondary utility frameworks that provide supporting features, as illustrated by figure 1.1.

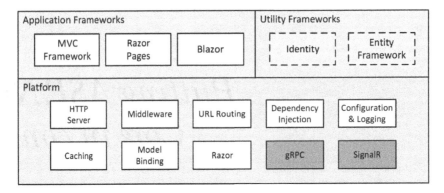

Figure 1.1   The structure of ASP.NET Core

Understanding .NET Core, .NET Framework, and .NET

If you have never worked for a large corporation, you might have the impression that Microsoft is a disciplined organization with a clear strategy and an army of programmers working together to deliver complex products like ASP.NET Core.

In reality, Microsoft is a chaotic collection of dysfunctional tribes that are constantly trying to undermine each other to get prestige and promotions. Products are released during lulls in the fighting, and successes are often entirely unexpected. This isn't unique to Microsoft—it is true of any large company—but it has a particular bearing on ASP.NET Core and the naming confusion that Microsoft has created.

Several years ago, the part of Microsoft responsible for ASP.NET created its own version of the .NET platform, allowing ASP.NET to be updated more often than the rest of .NET. *ASP.NET Core* and *.NET Core* were created, allowing cross-platform development, and using a subset of the original .NET APIs, many of which were specific to Windows. It was a painful transition, but it meant that web development could evolve independently of the "legacy" Windows-only development, which would continue under the renamed *.NET Framework*.

But no one wants to be in the "legacy" tribe because there is no glory in keeping the lights on at Microsoft. .NET Core was clearly the future and, one by one, the.NET groups at Microsoft argued that their technology and APIs should be part of .NET Core. The .NET Core APIs were gradually expanded, and the result was an incoherent mess, with half-hearted attempts to differentiate .NET Core and .NET Framework and standardize the APIs.

To clean up the mess, Microsoft has merged *.NET Core* and *.NET Framework* into *.NET*, dropping the *Core* part of the name. ".NET" is a name I like to think was chosen on the way out of the office on a holiday weekend but which I suspect is the result of many months of heated argument.

The problem with dropping *Core* from the name is that it cannot be carried out consistently. The name *ASP.NET Core* originally denoted the .NET Core version of ASP.NET, and going back to that name would be even more confusing.

(continued)

The result is that even Microsoft can't decide what name to use. You will see the term *ASP.NET Core* in a lot of the developer documentation—and that's the name I use in this book—but you will also see *ASP.NET Core in .NET*, especially in press releases and marketing material. It is not clear which name will win out, but until there is clarity, you should take care to determine whether you are using .NET Framework, .NET Core, or .NET.

1.1 Understanding the application frameworks

When you start using ASP.NET Core, it can be confusing to find that there are different application frameworks available. As you will learn, these frameworks are complementary and solve different problems, or, for some features, solve the same problems in different ways. Understanding the relationship between these frameworks means understanding the changing design patterns that Microsoft has supported, as I explain in the sections that follow.

1.1.1 Understanding the MVC Framework

The MVC Framework was introduced in the early ASP.NET, long before .NET Core and the newer .NET were introduced. The original ASP.NET relied on a development model called Web Forms, which re-created the experience of writing desktop applications but resulted in unwieldy web projects that did not scale well. The MVC Framework was introduced alongside Web Forms with a development model that embraced the character of HTTP and HTML, rather than trying to hide it.

MVC stands for Model-View-Controller, which is a design pattern that describes the shape of an application. The MVC pattern emphasizes *separation of concerns*, where areas of functionality are defined independently, which was an effective antidote to the indistinct architectures that Web Forms led to.

Early versions of the MVC Framework were built on the ASP.NET foundations that were originally designed for Web Forms, which led to some awkward features and workarounds. With the move to .NET Core, ASP.NET became ASP.NET Core, and the MVC Framework was rebuilt on an open, extensible, and cross-platform foundation.

The MVC Framework remains an important part of ASP.NET Core, but the way it is commonly used has changed with the rise of single-page applications (SPAs). In an SPA, the browser makes a single HTTP request and receives an HTML document that delivers a rich client, typically written in a JavaScript framework such as Angular or React. The shift to SPAs means that the clean separation that the MVC Framework was originally intended for is not as important, and the emphasis placed on following the MVC pattern is no longer essential, even though the MVC Framework remains useful (and is used to support SPAs through web services, as described in chapter 19).

Putting patterns in their place

Design patterns provoke strong reactions, as the emails I receive from readers will testify. A substantial proportion of the messages I receive are complaints that I have not applied a pattern correctly.

Patterns are just other people's solutions to the problems they encountered in other projects. If you find yourself facing the same problem, understanding how it has been solved before can be helpful. But that doesn't mean you have to follow the pattern exactly, or at all, as long as you understand the consequences. If a pattern is intended to make projects manageable, for example, and you choose to deviate from that pattern, then you must accept that your project may be more difficult to manage. But a pattern followed slavishly can be worse than no pattern at all, and no pattern is suited to every project.

My advice is to use patterns freely, adapt them as necessary, and ignore zealots who confuse patterns with commandments.

1.1.2   *Understanding Razor Pages*

One drawback of the MVC Framework is that it can require a lot of preparatory work before an application can start producing content. Despite its structural problems, one advantage of Web Forms was that simple applications could be created in a couple of hours.

Razor Pages takes the development ethos of Web Forms and implements it using the platform features originally developed for the MVC Framework. Code and content are mixed to form self-contained pages; this re-creates the speed of Web Forms development without some of the underlying technical problems (although scaling up complex projects can still be an issue).

Razor Pages can be used alongside the MVC Framework, which is how I tend to use them. I write the main parts of the application using the MVC Framework and use Razor Pages for the secondary features, such as administration and reporting tools. You can see this approach in chapters 7–11, where I develop a realistic ASP.NET Core application called SportsStore.

1.1.3   *Understanding Blazor*

The rise of JavaScript client-side frameworks can be a barrier for C# developers, who must learn a different—and somewhat idiosyncratic—programming language. I have come to love JavaScript, which is as fluid and expressive as C#. But it takes time and commitment to become proficient in a new programming language, especially one that has fundamental differences from C#.

Blazor attempts to bridge this gap by allowing C# to be used to write client-side applications. There are two versions of Blazor: Blazor Server and Blazor WebAssembly. Blazor Server relies on a persistent HTTP connection to the ASP.NET Core server, where the application's C# code is executed. Blazor WebAssembly goes one step further and executes the application's C# code in the browser. Neither version of Blazor is suited for all situations, as I explain in chapter 33, but they both give a sense of direction for the future of ASP.NET Core development.

1.1.4 Understanding the utility frameworks

Two frameworks are closely associated with ASP.NET Core but are not used directly to generate HTML content or data. Entity Framework Core is Microsoft's object-relational mapping (ORM) framework, which represents data stored in a relational database as .NET objects. Entity Framework Core can be used in any .NET application, and it is commonly used to access databases in ASP.NET Core applications.

ASP.NET Core Identity is Microsoft's authentication and authorization framework, and it is used to validate user credentials in ASP.NET Core applications and restrict access to application features.

I describe only the basic features of both frameworks in this book, focusing on the capabilities required by most ASP.NET Core applications. But these are both complex frameworks that are too large to describe in detail in what is already a large book about ASP.NET Core.

Topics for future editions

I don't have space in this book to cover every ASP.NET Core, Entity Framework Core, and ASP.NET Core Identity feature, so I have focused on those aspects that most projects require. If there are topics you think I should include in the next edition or in new deep-dive books, then please send me your suggestions at adam@adam-freeman.com.

1.1.5 Understanding the ASP.NET Core platform

The ASP.NET Core platform contains the low-level features required to receive and process HTTP requests and create responses. There is an integrated HTTP server, a system of middleware components to handle requests, and core features that the application frameworks depend on, such as URL routing and the Razor view engine.

Most of your development time will be spent with the application frameworks, but effective ASP.NET Core use requires an understanding of the powerful capabilities that the platform provides, without which the higher-level frameworks could not function. I demonstrate how the ASP.NET Core platform works in detail in part 2 of this book and explain how the features it provides underpin every aspect of ASP.NET Core development.

I have not described two notable platform features in this book: SignalR and gRPC. SignalR is used to create low-latency communication channels between applications. It provides the foundation for the Blazor Server framework that I describe in part 4 of this book, but SignalR is rarely used directly, and there are better alternatives for those few projects that need low-latency messaging, such as Azure Event Grid or Azure Service Bus.

gRPC is an emerging standard for cross-platform remote procedure calls (RPCs) over HTTP that was originally created by Google (the *g* in gRPC) and offers efficiency and scalability benefits. gRPC may be the future standard for web services, but it cannot be used in web applications because it requires low-level control of the HTTP messages that it sends, which browsers do not allow. (There is a browser library that allows gRPC to be used via a proxy server, but that undermines the benefits of using gRPC.) Until gRPC can be used in the browser, its inclusion in ASP.NET Core is of interest only for projects that use it for communication between back-end servers, such as in microservices development. I may cover gRPC in future editions of this book but not until it can be used in the browser.

1.2 Understanding this book

To get the most from this book, you should be familiar with the basics of web development, understand how HTML and CSS work, and have a working knowledge of C#. Don't worry if you haven't done any client-side development, such as JavaScript. The emphasis in this book is on C# and ASP.NET Core, and you will be able to pick up everything you need to know as you progress through the chapters. In chapter 5, I summarize the most important C# features for ASP.NET Core development.

1.2.1 What software do I need to follow the examples?

You need a code editor (either Visual Studio or Visual Studio Code), the .NET Core Software Development Kit, and SQL Server LocalDB. All are available for use from Microsoft without charge, and chapter 2 contains instructions for installing everything you need.

1.2.2 What platform do I need to follow the examples?

This book is written for Windows. I used Windows 10 Pro, but any version of Windows supported by Visual Studio, Visual Studio Code, and .NET Core should work. ASP.NET Core is supported on other platforms, but the examples in this book rely on the SQL Server LocalDB feature, which is specific to Windows. You can contact me at adam @adam-freeman.com if you are trying to use another platform, and I will give you some general pointers for adapting the examples, albeit with the caveat that I won't be able to provide detailed help if you get stuck.

1.2.3 What if I have problems following the examples?

The first thing to do is to go back to the start of the chapter and begin again. Most problems are caused by missing a step or not fully following a listing. Pay close attention to the emphasis in code listings, which highlights the changes that are required.

Next, check the errata/corrections list, which is included in the book's GitHub repository. Technical books are complex, and mistakes are inevitable, despite my best efforts and those of my editors. Check the errata list for the list of known errors and instructions to resolve them.

If you still have problems, then download the project for the chapter you are reading from the book's GitHub repository, https://github.com/manningbooks/pro-asp .net-core-7, and compare it to your project. I create the code for the GitHub repository by working through each chapter, so you should have the same files with the same contents in your project.

If you still can't get the examples working, then you can contact me at adam @adam-freeman.com for help. Please make it clear in your email which book you are reading and which chapter/example is causing the problem. Please remember that I get a lot of emails and that I may not respond immediately.

1.2.4 What if I find an error in the book?

You can report errors to me by email at adam@adam-freeman.com, although I ask that you first check the errata/corrections list for this book, which you can find in the book's GitHub repository at https://github.com/manningbooks/pro-asp.net-core-7, in case it has already been reported.

I add errors that are likely to cause confusion to readers, especially problems with example code, to the errata/corrections file on the GitHub repository, with a grateful acknowledgment to the first reader who reported them. I also publish a typos list, which contains less serious issues, which usually means errors in the text surrounding examples that are unlikely to prevent a reader from following or understanding the examples.

Errata bounty

Manning has agreed to give a free ebook to readers who are the first to report errors that make it onto the GitHub errata list for this book, which is for serious issues that will disrupt a reader's progress. Readers can select any Manning ebook, not just my books.

This is an entirely discretionary and experimental program. Discretionary means that only I decide which errors are listed in the errata and which reader is the first to make a report. Experimental means Manning may decide not to give away any more books at any time for any reason. There are no appeals, and this is not a promise or a contract or any kind of formal offer or competition. Or, put another way, this is a nice and informal way to say thank you and to encourage readers to report mistakes that I have missed when writing this book.

1.2.5 What does this book cover?

I have tried to cover the features that will be required by most ASP.NET Core projects. This book is split into four parts, each of which covers a set of related topics.

PART 1: INTRODUCING ASP.NET CORE

This part of the book introduces ASP.NET Core. In addition to setting up your development environment and creating your first application, you'll learn about the most important C# features for ASP.NET Core development and how to use the ASP.NET

Core development tools. Most of part 1 is given over to the development of a project called SportsStore, through which I show you a realistic development process from inception to deployment, touching on all the main features of ASP.NET Core and showing how they fit together—something that can be lost in the deep-dive chapters in the rest of the book.

PART 2: THE ASP.NET CORE PLATFORM

The chapters in this part of the book describe the key features of the ASP.NET Core platform. I explain how HTTP requests are processed, how to create and use middleware components, how to create routes, how to define and consume services, and how to work with Entity Framework Core. These chapters explain the foundations of ASP.NET Core, and understanding them is essential for effective ASP.NET Core development.

PART 3: ASP.NET CORE APPLICATIONS

The chapters in this part of the book explain how to create different types of applications, including RESTful web services and HTML applications using controllers and Razor Pages. These chapters also describe the features that make it easy to generate HTML, including the views, view components, and tag helpers.

PART 4: ADVANCED ASP.NET CORE FEATURES

The final part of the book explains how to create applications using Blazor Server, how to use the experimental Blazor WebAssembly, and how to authenticate users and authorize access using ASP.NET Core Identity.

1.2.6 *What doesn't this book cover?*

This book doesn't cover basic web development topics, such as HTML and CSS, and doesn't teach basic C# (although chapter 5 does describe C# features useful for ASP.NET Core development that may not be familiar to developers using older versions of .NET).

As much as I like to dive into the details in my books, not every ASP.NET Core feature is useful in mainstream development, and I have to keep my books to a printable size. When I decide to omit a feature, it is because I don't think it is important or because the same outcome can be achieved using a technique that I do cover.

As noted earlier, I have not described the ASP.NET Core support for SignalR and gRPC, and I note other features in later chapters that I don't describe, either because they are not broadly applicable or because there are better alternatives available. In each case, I explain why I have omitted a description and provide a reference to the Microsoft documentation for that topic.

1.2.7 *How do I contact the author?*

You can email me at adam@adam-freeman.com. It has been a few years since I first published an email address in my books. I wasn't entirely sure that it was a good idea, but I am glad that I did it. I have received emails from around the world, from readers working or studying in every industry, and—for the most part anyway—the emails are positive, polite, and a pleasure to receive.

I try to reply promptly, but I get a lot of email, and sometimes I get a backlog, especially when I have my head down trying to finish writing a book. I always try to help readers who are stuck with an example in the book, although I ask that you follow the steps described earlier in this chapter before contacting me.

While I welcome reader emails, there are some common questions for which the answers will always be no. I am afraid that I won't write the code for your new startup, help you with your college assignment, get involved in your development team's design dispute, or teach you how to program.

1.2.8 What if I really enjoyed this book?

Please email me at adam@adam-freeman.com and let me know. It is always a delight to hear from a happy reader, and I appreciate the time it takes to send those emails. Writing these books can be difficult, and those emails provide essential motivation to persist at an activity that can sometimes feel impossible.

1.2.9 What if this book has made me angry and I want to complain?

You can still email me at adam@adam-freeman.com, and I will still try to help you. Bear in mind that I can only help if you explain what the problem is and what you would like me to do about it. You should understand that sometimes the only outcome is to accept I am not the writer for you and that we will have closure only when you return this book and select another. I'll give careful thought to whatever has upset you, but after 25 years of writing books, I have come to understand that not everyone enjoys reading the books I like to write.

Summary

- ASP.NET Core is a cross-platform framework for creating web applications.
- The ASP.NET Core platform is a powerful foundation on which application frameworks have been built.
- The MVC Framework was the original ASP.NET Core framework. It is powerful and flexible but takes time to prepare.
- The Razor Pages framework is a newer addition, which requires less initial preparation but can be more difficult to manage in complex projects.
- Blazor is a framework that allows client-side applications to be written in C#, rather than JavaScript. There are versions of Blazor that execute the C# code within the ASP.NET Core server and entirely within the browser.

Part 1

Getting started

This chapter covers

- Installing the code editor and SDK required for ASP.NET Core development
- Creating a simple ASP.NET Core project
- Responding to HTTP requests using a combination of code and markup

The best way to appreciate a software development framework is to jump right in and use it. In this chapter, I explain how to prepare for ASP.NET Core development and how to create and run an ASP.NET Core application.

2.1 Choosing a code editor

Microsoft provides a choice of tools for ASP.NET Core development: Visual Studio and Visual Studio Code. Visual Studio is the traditional development environment for .NET applications, and it offers an enormous range of tools and features for developing all sorts of applications. But it can be resource-hungry and slow, and some of the features are so determined to be helpful they get in the way of development.

Visual Studio Code is a lightweight alternative that doesn't have the bells and whistles of Visual Studio but is perfectly capable of handling ASP.NET Core development.

All the examples in this book include instructions for both editors, and both Visual Studio and Visual Studio Code can be used without charge, so you can use whichever suits your development style.

If you are new to .NET development, then start with Visual Studio. It provides more structured support for creating the different types of files used in ASP.NET

Core development, which will help ensure you get the expected results from the code examples.

> **NOTE**   This book describes ASP.NET Core development for Windows. It is possible to develop and run ASP.NET Core applications on Linux and macOS, but most readers use Windows, and that is what I have chosen to focus on. Almost all the examples in this book rely on LocalDB, which is a Windows-only feature provided by SQL Server that is not available on other platforms. If you want to follow this book on another platform, then you can contact me using the email address in chapter 1, and I will try to help you get started.

2.1.1   *Installing Visual Studio*

ASP.NET Core 7 requires Visual Studio 2022. I use the free Visual Studio 2022 Community Edition, which can be downloaded from www.visualstudio.com. Run the installer, and you will see the prompt shown in figure 2.1.

Figure 2.1   Starting the Visual Studio installer

Click the Continue button, and the installer will download the installation files, as shown in figure 2.2.

Figure 2.2   Downloading the Visual Studio installer files

When the installer files have been downloaded, you will be presented with a set of installation options, grouped into workloads. Ensure that the "ASP.NET and web development" workload is checked, as shown in figure 2.3.

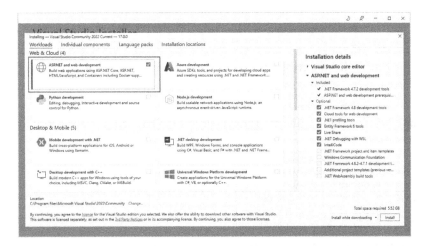

Figure 2.3 Selecting the workload

Select the "Individual components" section at the top of the window and ensure the SQL Server Express 2019 LocalDB option is checked, as shown in figure 2.4. This is the database component that I will be using to store data in later chapters.

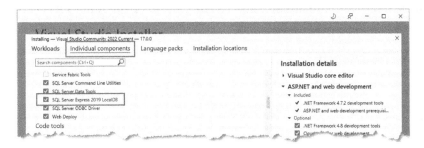

Figure 2.4 Ensuring LocalDB is installed

Click the Install button, and the files required for the selected workload will be downloaded and installed. To complete the installation, a reboot may be required.

NOTE You must also install the SDK, as described in the following section.

INSTALLING THE .NET SDK

The Visual Studio installer will install the .NET Software Development Kit (SDK), but it may not install the version required for the examples in this book. Go to https://dotnet.microsoft.com/download/dotnet-core/7.0 and download the installer for version 7.0.0 of the .NET SDK, which is the current release at the time of writing.

Run the installer; once the installation is complete, open a new PowerShell command prompt from the Windows Start menu and run the command shown in listing 2.1, which displays a list of the installed .NET SDKs.

Listing 2.1   Listing the Installed SDKs

```
dotnet --list-sdks
```

Here is the output from a fresh installation on a Windows machine that has not been used for .NET:

```
7.0.100 [C:\Program Files\dotnet\sdk]
```

If you have been working with different versions of .NET, you may see a longer list, like this one:

```
5.0.100 [C:\Program Files\dotnet\sdk]
6.0.100 [C:\Program Files\dotnet\sdk]
6.0.113 [C:\Program Files\dotnet\sdk]
6.0.202 [C:\Program Files\dotnet\sdk]
6.0.203 [C:\Program Files\dotnet\sdk]
7.0.100 [C:\Program Files\dotnet\sdk]
```

Regardless of how many entries there are, you must ensure there is one for the 7.0.1xx version, where the last two digits may differ.

2.1.2   *Installing Visual Studio Code*

If you have chosen to use Visual Studio Code, download the installer from https://code.visualstudio.com. No specific version is required, and you should select the current stable build. Run the installer and ensure you check the Add to PATH option, as shown in figure 2.5.

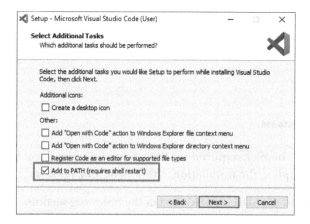

Figure 2.5   Configuring the Visual Studio Code installation

INSTALLING THE .NET SDK

The Visual Studio Code installer does not include the .NET SDK, which must be installed separately. Go to https://dotnet.microsoft.com/download/dotnet-core/7.0

and download the installer for version 7.0.0 of the .NET SDK. Run the installer; once the installation is complete, open a new PowerShell command prompt from the Windows Start menu and run the command shown in listing 2.2, which displays a list of the installed .NET SDKs.

Listing 2.2 Listing the Installed SDKs

```
dotnet --list-sdks
```

Here is the output from a fresh installation on a Windows machine that has not been used for .NET:

```
7.0.100 [C:\Program Files\dotnet\sdk]
```

If you have been working with different versions of .NET, you may see a longer list, like this one:

```
5.0.100 [C:\Program Files\dotnet\sdk]
6.0.100 [C:\Program Files\dotnet\sdk]
6.0.113 [C:\Program Files\dotnet\sdk]
6.0.202 [C:\Program Files\dotnet\sdk]
6.0.203 [C:\Program Files\dotnet\sdk]
7.0.100 [C:\Program Files\dotnet\sdk]
```

Regardless of how many entries there are, you must ensure there is one for the 7.0.1xx version, where the last two digits may differ.

INSTALLING SQL SERVER LOCALDB

The database examples in this book require LocalDB, which is a zero-configuration version of SQL Server that can be installed as part of the SQL Server Express edition, which is available for use without charge from https://www.microsoft.com/en-in/sql-server/sql-server-downloads. Download and run the Express edition installer and select the Custom option, as shown in figure 2.6.

Figure 2.6 Selecting the installation option for SQL Server

Once you have selected the Custom option, you will be prompted to select a download location for the installation files. Click the Install button, and the download will begin.

When prompted, select the option to create a new SQL Server installation, as shown in figure 2.7.

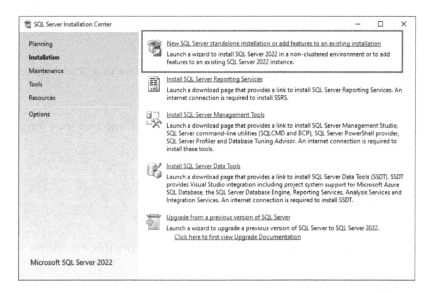

Figure 2.7   Selecting an installation option

Work through the installation process, selecting the default options as they are presented. When you reach the Feature Selection page, ensure that the LocalDB option is checked, as shown in figure 2.8. (You may want to uncheck the Machine Learning Services option, which is not used in this book and takes a long time to download and install.)

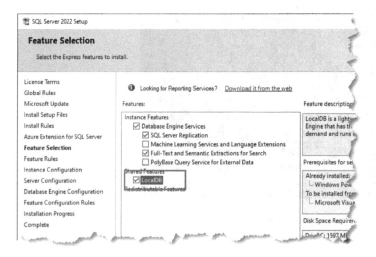

Figure 2.8   Selecting the LocalDB feature

On the Instance Configuration page, select the "Default instance" option, as shown in figure 2.9.

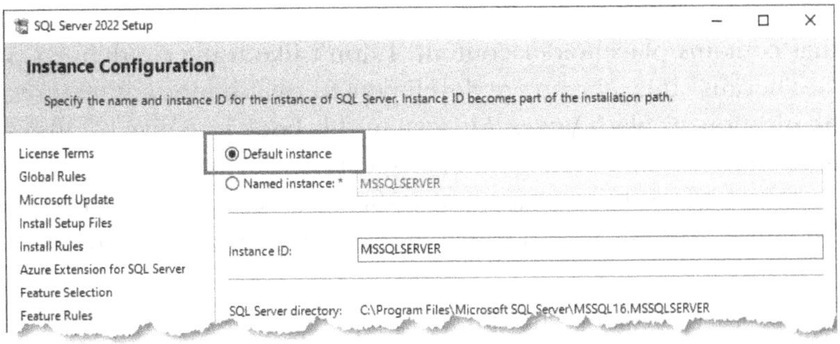

Figure 2.9   Configuring the database

Continue to work through the installation process, selecting the default values, and complete the installation.

2.2   *Creating an ASP.NET Core project*

The most direct way to create a project is to use the command line. Open a new Power-Shell command prompt from the Windows Start menu, navigate to the folder where you want to create your ASP.NET Core projects, and run the commands shown in listing 2.3.

> **TIP**   You can download the example project for this chapter—and for all the other chapters in this book—from https://github.com/manningbooks/pro-asp .net-core-7. See chapter 1 for how to get help if you have problems running the examples.

Listing 2.3   Creating a new project

```
dotnet new globaljson --sdk-version 7.0.100 --output FirstProject
dotnet new mvc --no-https --output FirstProject --framework net7.0
dotnet new sln -o FirstProject
dotnet sln FirstProject add FirstProject
```

The first command creates a folder named `FirstProject` and adds to it a file named `global.json`, which specifies the version of .NET that the project will use; this ensures you get the expected results when following the examples. The second command creates a new ASP.NET Core project. The .NET SDK includes a range of templates for starting new projects, and the `mvc` template is one of the options available for ASP.NET Core applications. This project template creates a project that is configured for the MVC Framework, which is one of the application types supported by ASP.NET Core. Don't be intimidated by the idea of choosing a framework, and don't worry if you have not heard of MVC—by the end of the book, you will understand the features that each offers and how they fit together. The remaining commands create a solution file, which allows multiple projects to be used together.

> **NOTE**   This is one of a small number of chapters in which I use a project template that contains placeholder content. I don't like using predefined project templates because they encourage developers to treat important features, such as authentication, as black boxes. My goal in this book is to give you the knowledge to understand and manage every aspect of your ASP.NET Core applications, and that's why I start with an empty ASP.NET Core project. This chapter is about getting started quickly, for which the mvc template is well-suited.

2.2.1   Opening the project using Visual Studio

Start Visual Studio and click the "Open a project or solution" button, as shown in figure 2.10.

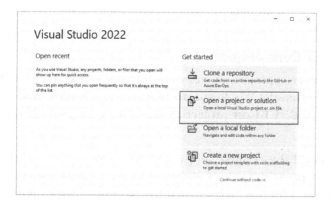

Figure 2.10   Opening the ASP.NET Core project

Navigate to the `FirstProject` folder, select the `FirstProject.sln` file, and click the Open button. Visual Studio will open the project and display its contents in the Solution Explorer window, as shown in figure 2.11. The files in the project were created by the project template.

Figure 2.11
Opening the project in Visual Studio

2.2.2   *Opening the project with Visual Studio Code*

Start Visual Studio Code and select File > Open Folder. Navigate to the `FirstProject` folder and click the Select Folder button. Visual Studio Code will open the project and display its contents in the Explorer pane, as shown in figure 2.12. (The default dark theme used in Visual Studio Code doesn't show well on the page, so I have changed to the light theme for the screenshots in this book.)

Figure 2.12   Opening the project in Visual Studio Code

Additional configuration is required the first time you open a .NET project in Visual Studio Code. The first step is to click the `Program.cs` file in the Explorer pane. This will trigger a prompt from Visual Studio Code to install the features required for C# development, as shown in figure 2.13. If you have not opened a C# project before, you will see a prompt that offers to install the required assets, also shown in figure 2.13.

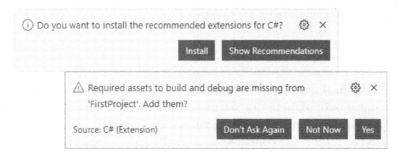

Figure 2.13   Installing Visual Studio Code C# features

Click the Install or Yes button, as appropriate, and Visual Studio Code will download and install the features required for .NET projects.

2.3   *Running the ASP.NET Core application*

Visual Studio and Visual Studio Code can both run projects directly, but I use the command line tools throughout this book because they are more reliable and work more consistently, helping to ensure you get the expected results from the examples.

When the project is created, a file named launchSettings.json is created in the Properties folder, and it is this file that determines which HTTP port ASP.NET Core will use to listen for HTTP requests. Open this file in your chosen editor and change the ports in the URLs it contains to 5000, as shown in listing 2.4.

Listing 2.4   Setting the Port in the launchSettings.json File in the Properties Folder

```
{
  "iisSettings": {
    "windowsAuthentication": false,
    "anonymousAuthentication": true,
    "iisExpress": {
      "applicationUrl": "http://localhost:5000",
      "sslPort": 0
    }
  },
  "profiles": {
    "FirstProject": {
      "commandName": "Project",
      "dotnetRunMessages": true,
      "launchBrowser": true,
      "applicationUrl": "http://localhost:5000",
      "environmentVariables": {
        "ASPNETCORE_ENVIRONMENT": "Development"
      }
    },
    "IIS Express": {
      "commandName": "IISExpress",
      "launchBrowser": true,
      "environmentVariables": {
        "ASPNETCORE_ENVIRONMENT": "Development"
      }
    }
  }
}
```

It is only the URL in the profiles section that affects the .NET command-line tools, but I have changed both of them to avoid any problems. Open a new PowerShell command prompt from the Windows Start menu; navigate to the FirstProject project folder, which is the folder that contains the FirstProject.csproj file; and run the command shown in listing 2.5.

Listing 2.5   Starting the example application

```
dotnet run
```

The dotnet run command compiles and starts the project. Once the application has started, open a new browser window and request http://localhost:5000, which will produce the response shown in figure 2.14.

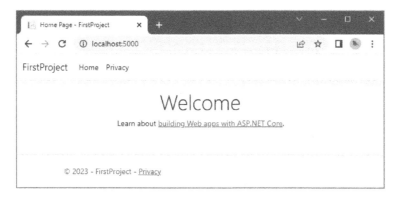

Figure 2.14 Running the example project

When you are finished, use Control+C to stop the ASP.NET Core application.

2.3.1 *Understanding endpoints*

In an ASP.NET Core application, incoming requests are handled by *endpoints*. The endpoint that produced the response in figure 2.14 is an *action*, which is a method that is written in C#. An action is defined in a *controller*, which is a C# class that is derived from the `Microsoft.AspNetCore.Mvc.Controller` class, the built-in controller base class.

Each public method defined by a controller is an action, which means you can invoke the action method to handle an HTTP request. The convention in ASP.NET Core projects is to put controller classes in a folder named `Controllers`, which was created by the template used to set up the project.

The project template added a controller to the `Controllers` folder to help jump-start development. The controller is defined in the class file named `HomeController.cs`. Controller classes contain a name followed by the word `Controller`, which means that when you see a file called `HomeController.cs`, you know that it contains a controller called `Home`, which is the default controller that is used in ASP.NET Core applications.

> **TIP** Don't worry if the terms *controller* and *action* don't make immediate sense. Just keep following the example, and you will see how the HTTP request sent by the browser is handled by C# code.

Find the `HomeController.cs` file in the Solution Explorer or Explorer pane and click it to open it for editing. You will see the following code:

```
using System.Diagnostics;
using Microsoft.AspNetCore.Mvc;
using FirstProject.Models;

namespace FirstProject.Controllers;

public class HomeController : Controller {
    private readonly ILogger<HomeController> _logger;
```

```
    public HomeController(ILogger<HomeController> logger) {
        _logger = logger;
    }

    public IActionResult Index() {
        return View();
    }

    public IActionResult Privacy() {
        return View();
    }

    [ResponseCache(Duration = 0, Location = ResponseCacheLocation.None,
        NoStore = true)]
    public IActionResult Error() {
        return View(new ErrorViewModel { RequestId = Activity.Current?.Id
            ?? HttpContext.TraceIdentifier });
    }
}
```

Using the code editor, replace the contents of the `HomeController.cs` file so that it matches listing 2.6. I have removed all but one of the methods, changed the result type and its implementation, and removed the `using` statements for unused namespaces.

Listing 2.6   Changing the HomeController.cs file in the Controllers folder

```
using Microsoft.AspNetCore.Mvc;

namespace FirstProject.Controllers {

    public class HomeController : Controller {

        public string Index() {
            return "Hello World";
        }
    }
}
```

The result is that the `Home` controller defines a single action, named `Index`. These changes don't produce a dramatic effect, but they make for a nice demonstration. I have changed the method named `Index` so that it returns the string `Hello World`. Using the PowerShell prompt, run the `dotnet run` command in the `FirstProject` folder again and use the browser to request http://localhost:5000. The configuration of the project created by the template in listing 2.3 means the HTTP request will be processed by the `Index` action defined by the `Home` controller. Put another way, the request will be processed by the `Index` method defined by the `HomeController` class. The `string` produced by the `Index` method is used as the response to the browser's HTTP request, as shown in figure 2.15.

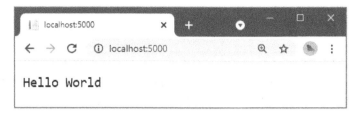

Figure 2.15 The output from the action method

2.3.2 Understanding routes

The ASP.NET Core *routing* system is responsible for selecting the endpoint that will handle an HTTP request. A *route* is a rule that is used to decide how a request is handled. When the project was created, a default rule was created to get started. You can request any of the following URLs, and they will be dispatched to the Index action defined by the Home controller:

- /
- /Home
- /Home/Index

So, when a browser requests http://yoursite/ or http://yoursite/Home, it gets back the output from HomeController's Index method. You can try this yourself by changing the URL in the browser. At the moment, it will be http://localhost:5000/. If you append /Home or /Home/Index to the URL and press Return, you will see the same Hello World result from the application.

2.3.3 Understanding HTML rendering

The output from the previous example wasn't HTML—it was just the string Hello World. To produce an HTML response to a browser request, I need a *view*, which tells ASP.NET Core how to process the result produced by the Index method into an HTML response that can be sent to the browser.

CREATING AND RENDERING A VIEW

The first thing I need to do is modify my Index action method, as shown in listing 2.7. The changes are shown in bold, which is a convention I follow throughout this book to make the examples easier to follow.

Listing 2.7 Rendering a view in the HomeController.cs file in the Controllers folder

```
using Microsoft.AspNetCore.Mvc;

namespace FirstProject.Controllers {

    public class HomeController : Controller {
```

```
        public ViewResult Index() {
            return View("MyView");
        }
    }
}
```

When I return a `ViewResult` object from an action method, I am instructing ASP.NET Core to *render* a view. I create the `ViewResult` by calling the `View` method, specifying the name of the view that I want to use, which is `MyView`.

Use Control+C to stop ASP.NET Core and then use the `dotnet run` command to compile and start it again. Use the browser to request http://localhost:5000, and you will see ASP.NET Core trying to find the view, as shown by the error message displayed in figure 2.16.

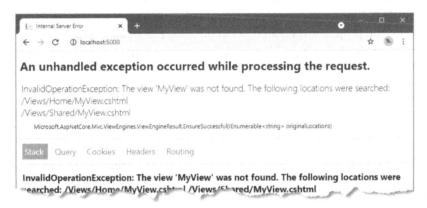

Figure 2.16   Trying to find a view

This is a helpful error message. It explains that ASP.NET Core could not find the view I specified for the action method and explains where it looked. Views are stored in the `Views` folder, organized into subfolders. Views that are associated with the `Home` controller, for example, are stored in a folder called `Views/Home`. Views that are not specific to a single controller are stored in a folder called `Views/Shared`. The template used to create the project added the `Home` and `Shared` folders automatically and added some placeholder views to get the project started.

If you are using Visual Studio, right-click the `Views/Home` folder in the Solution Explorer and select Add > New Item from the pop-up menu. Visual Studio will present you with a list of templates for adding items to the project. Locate the Razor View - Empty item, which can be found in the ASP.NET Core > Web > ASP.NET section, as shown in figure 2.17.

For Visual Studio, you may need to click the Show All Templates button before the list of templates is displayed. Set the name of the new file to `MyView.cshtml` and click the Add button. Visual Studio will add a file named `MyView.cshtml` to the `Views/Home` folder and will open it for editing. Replace the contents of the file with those shown in listing 2.8.

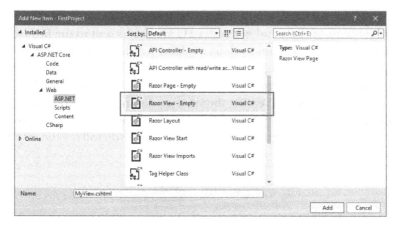

Figure 2.17 Selecting a Visual Studio item template

Visual Studio Code doesn't provide item templates. Instead, right-click the `Views/Home` folder in the file explorer pane and select New File from the pop-up menu. Set the name of the file to `MyView.cshtml` and press Return. The file will be created and opened for editing. Add the content shown in listing 2.8.

> **TIP** It is easy to end up creating the view file in the wrong folder. If you didn't end up with a file called `MyView.cshtml` in the `Views/Home` folder, then either drag the file into the correct folder or delete the file and try again.

Listing 2.8   The contents of the MyView.cshtml file in the Views/Home folder

```
@{
    Layout = null;
}

<!DOCTYPE html>

<html>
<head>
    <meta name="viewport" content="width=device-width" />
    <title>Index</title>
</head>
<body>
    <div>
        Hello World (from the view)
    </div>
</body>
</html>
```

The new contents of the view file are mostly HTML. The exception is the part that looks like this:

```
...
@{
    Layout = null;
}
...
```

This is an expression that will be interpreted by Razor, which is the component that processes the contents of views and generates HTML that is sent to the browser. Razor is a *view engine*, and the expressions in views are known as *Razor expressions.*

The Razor expression in listing 2.8 tells Razor that I chose not to use a layout, which is like a template for the HTML that will be sent to the browser (and which I describe in chapter 22). To see the effect of creating the view, use Control+C to stop ASP.NET Core if it is running and use the `dotnet run` command to compile and start the application again. Use a browser to request http://localhost:5000, and you will see the result shown in figure 2.18.

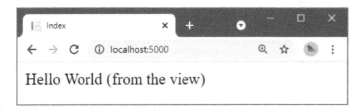

Figure 2.18   Rendering a view

When I first edited the `Index` action method, it returned a `string` value. This meant that ASP.NET Core did nothing except pass the string value as is to the browser. Now that the `Index` method returns a `ViewResult`, Razor is used to process a view and render an HTML response. Razor was able to locate the view because I followed the standard naming convention, which is to put view files in a folder whose name matched the controller that contains the action method. In this case, this meant putting the view file in the `Views/Home` folder, since the action method is defined by the `Home` controller.

I can return other results from action methods besides strings and `ViewResult` objects. For example, if I return a `RedirectResult`, the browser will be redirected to another URL. If I return an `HttpUnauthorizedResult`, I can prompt the user to log in. These objects are collectively known as *action results*. The action result system lets you encapsulate and reuse common responses in actions. I'll tell you more about them and explain the different ways they can be used in chapter 19.

ADDING DYNAMIC OUTPUT

The whole point of a web application is to construct and display *dynamic* output. The job of the action method is to construct data and pass it to the view so it can be used to create HTML content based on the data values. Action methods provide data to views by passing arguments to the `View` method, as shown in listing 2.9. The data provided to the view is known as the *view model.*

Listing 2.9   Using a view model in the HomeController.cs file in the Controllers folder

```
using Microsoft.AspNetCore.Mvc;

namespace FirstProject.Controllers {

    public class HomeController : Controller {
```

```
    public ViewResult Index() {
        int hour = DateTime.Now.Hour;
        string viewModel =
            hour < 12 ? "Good Morning" : "Good Afternoon";
        return View("MyView", viewModel);
    }
}
```

The view model in this example is a `string`, and it is provided to the view as the second argument to the `View` method. Listing 2.10 updates the view so that it receives and uses the view model in the HTML it generates.

Listing 2.10   Using a view model in the MyView.cshtml file in the Views/Home folder

```
@model string
@{
    Layout = null;
}

<!DOCTYPE html>

<html>
<head>
    <meta name="viewport" content="width=device-width" />
    <title>Index</title>
</head>
<body>
    <div>
        @Model World (from the view)
    </div>
</body>
</html>
```

The type of the view model is specified using the `@model` expression, with a lowercase m. The view model value is included in the HTML output using the `@Model` expression, with an uppercase M. (It can be difficult at first to remember which is lowercase and which is uppercase, but it soon becomes second nature.)

When the view is rendered, the view model data provided by the action method is inserted into the HTML response. Use Control+C to stop ASP.NET Core and use the `dotnet run` command to build and start it again. Use a browser to request http://localhost:5000, and you will see the output shown in figure 2.19 (although you may see the morning greeting if you are following this example before midday).

Figure 2.19   Generating dynamic content

2.3.4 *Putting the pieces together*

It is a simple result, but this example reveals all the building blocks you need to create a simple ASP.NET Core web application and to generate a dynamic response. The ASP.NET Core platform receives an HTTP request and uses the routing system to match the request URL to an endpoint. The endpoint, in this case, is the `Index` action method defined by the `Home` controller. The method is invoked and produces a `ViewResult` object that contains the name of a view and a view model object. The Razor view engine locates and processes the view, evaluating the `@Model` expression to insert the data provided by the action method into the response, which is returned to the browser and displayed to the user. There are, of course, many other features available, but this is the essence of ASP.NET Core, and it is worth bearing this simple sequence in mind as you read the rest of the book.

Summary

- ASP.NET Core development can be done with Visual Studio or Visual Studio Code, or you can choose your own code editor.
- Most code editors provide integrated code builds, but the most reliable way to get consistent results across tools and platforms is by using the `dotnet` command.
- ASP.NET Core relies on endpoints to process HTTP requests.
- Endpoints can be written entirely in C# or use HTML that has been annotated with code expressions.

Your first ASP.NET
Core application

This chapter covers

- Using ASP.NET Core to create an application that accepts RSVP responses
- Creating a simple data model
- Creating a controller and view that presents and processes a form
- Validating user data and displaying validation errors
- Applying CSS styles to the HTML generated by the application

Now that you are set up for ASP.NET Core development, it is time to create a simple application. In this chapter, you'll create a data-entry application using ASP.NET Core. My goal is to demonstrate ASP.NET Core in action, so I will pick up the pace a little and skip over some of the explanations as to how things work behind the scenes. But don't worry; I'll revisit these topics in-depth in later chapters.

3.1 Setting the scene

Imagine that a friend has decided to host a New Year's Eve party and that she has asked me to create a web app that allows her invitees to electronically RSVP. She has asked for these four key features:

- A home page that shows information about the party
- A form that can be used to RSVP
- Validation for the RSVP form, which will display a thank-you page
- A summary page that shows who is coming to the party

In this chapter, I create an ASP.NET Core project and use it to create a simple application that contains these features; once everything works, I'll apply some styling to improve the appearance of the finished application.

3.2   *Creating the project*

Open a PowerShell command prompt from the Windows Start menu, navigate to a convenient location, and run the commands in listing 3.1 to create a project named PartyInvites.

> **TIP**   You can download the example project for this chapter—and for all the other chapters in this book—from https://github.com/manningbooks/pro-asp .net-core-7. See chapter 1 for how to get help if you have problems running the examples.

Listing 3.1   Creating a new project

```
dotnet new globaljson --sdk-version 7.0.100 --output PartyInvites
dotnet new mvc --no-https --output PartyInvites --framework net7.0
dotnet new sln -o PartyInvites
dotnet sln PartyInvites add PartyInvites
```

These are the same commands I used to create the project in chapter 2. These commands ensure you get the right project starting point that uses the required version of .NET.

3.2.1   *Preparing the project*

Open the project (by opening the `PartyInvites.sln` file with Visual Studio or the `PartyInvites` folder in Visual Studio Code) and change the contents of the `launchSettings.json` file in the `Properties` folder, as shown in listing 3.2, to set the port that will be used to listen for HTTP requests.

Listing 3.2   Setting ports in the launchSettings.json file in the Properties folder

```
{
  "iisSettings": {
    "windowsAuthentication": false,
    "anonymousAuthentication": true,
    "iisExpress": {
      "applicationUrl": "http://localhost:5000",
      "sslPort": 0
    }
  },
  "profiles": {
    "PartyInvites": {
      "commandName": "Project",
```

```
      "dotnetRunMessages": true,
      "launchBrowser": true,
      "applicationUrl": "http://localhost:5000",
      "environmentVariables": {
        "ASPNETCORE_ENVIRONMENT": "Development"
      }
    },
    "IIS Express": {
      "commandName": "IISExpress",
      "launchBrowser": true,
      "environmentVariables": {
        "ASPNETCORE_ENVIRONMENT": "Development"
      }
    }
  }
}
```

Replace the contents of the `HomeController.cs` file in the `Controllers` folder with the code shown in listing 3.3.

Listing 3.3   The new contents of the HomeController.cs file in the Controllers folder

```
using Microsoft.AspNetCore.Mvc;

namespace PartyInvites.Controllers {
    public class HomeController : Controller {

        public IActionResult Index() {
            return View();
        }
    }
}
```

This provides a clean starting point for the new application, defining a single action method that selects the default view for rendering. To provide a welcome message to party invitees, open the `Index.cshtml` file in the `Views/Home` folder and replace the contents with those shown in listing 3.4.

Listing 3.4   Replacing the contents of the Index.cshtml file in the Views/Home folder

```
@{
    Layout = null;
}

<!DOCTYPE html>
<html>
<head>
    <meta name="viewport" content="width=device-width" />
    <title>Party!</title>
</head>
<body>
    <div>
        <div>
            We're going to have an exciting party.<br />
            (To do: sell it better. Add pictures or something.)
```

```
        </div>
     </div>
  </body>
  </html>
```

Run the command shown in listing 3.5 in the PartyInvites folder to compile and execute the project.

Listing 3.5 Compiling and running the project

```
dotnet watch
```

Once the project has started, a new browser window will be opened, and you will see the details of the party (well, the placeholder for the details, but you get the idea), as shown in figure 3.1.

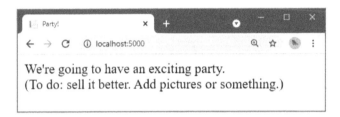

Figure 3.1
Adding to the
view HTML

Leave the `dotnet watch` command running. As you make changes to the project, you will see that the code is automatically recompiled and that changes are automatically displayed in the browser.

If you make a mistake following the examples, you may find that the `dotnet watch` command indicates that it can't automatically update the browser. If that happens, select the option to restart the application.

3.2.2 Adding a data model

The data model is the most important part of any ASP.NET Core application. The model is the representation of the real-world objects, processes, and rules that define the subject, known as the *domain*, of the application. The model, often referred to as a *domain model*, contains the C# objects (known as *domain objects*) that make up the universe of the application and the methods that manipulate them. In most projects, the job of the ASP.NET Core application is to provide the user with access to the data model and the features that allow the user to interact with it.

The convention for an ASP.NET Core application is that the data model classes are defined in a folder named `Models`, which was added to the project by the template used in listing 3.1.

I don't need a complex model for the PartyInvites project because it is such a simple application. I need just one domain class that I will call `GuestResponse`. This object will represent an RSVP from an invitee.

If you are using Visual Studio, right-click the `Models` folder and select Add > Class from the pop-up menu. Set the name of the class to `GuestResponse.cs` and click the

Add button. If you are using Visual Studio Code, right-click the `Models` folder, select New File, and enter `GuestResponse.cs` as the file name. Use the new file to define the class shown in listing 3.6.

> **Listing 3.6   The contents of the GuestResponse.cs file in the Models folder**

```
namespace PartyInvites.Models {

    public class GuestResponse {

        public string? Name { get; set; }
        public string? Email { get; set; }
        public string? Phone { get; set; }
        public bool? WillAttend { get; set; }
    }
}
```

Notice that all the properties defined by the `GuestResponse` class are nullable. I explain why this is important in the "Adding Validation" section later in the chapter.

Restarting the automatic build

You may see a warning produced by the `dotnet watch` command telling you that a hot reload cannot be applied. The `dotnet watch` command can't cope with every type of change, and some changes cause the automatic rebuild process to fail. You will see this prompt at the command line:

```
watch : Do you want to restart your app
    - Yes (y) / No (n) / Always (a) / Never (v)?
```

Press `a` to always rebuild the project. Microsoft makes frequent improvements to the `dotnet watch` command and so the actions that trigger this problem change.

3.2.3   *Creating a second action and view*

One of my application goals is to include an RSVP form, which means I need to define an action method that can receive requests for that form. A single controller class can define multiple action methods, and the convention is to group related actions in the same controller. Listing 3.7 adds a new action method to the `Home` controller. Controllers can return different result types, which are explained in later chapters.

> **Listing 3.7   Adding an action in the HomeController.cs file in the Controllers folder**

```
using Microsoft.AspNetCore.Mvc;

namespace PartyInvites.Controllers {
    public class HomeController : Controller {

        public IActionResult Index() {
            return View();
        }
```

```
        public ViewResult RsvpForm() {
            return View();
        }
    }
}
```

Both action methods invoke the `View` method without arguments, which may seem odd, but remember that the Razor view engine will use the name of the action method when looking for a view file, as explained in chapter 2. That means the result from the `Index` action method tells Razor to look for a view called `Index.cshtml`, while the result from the `RsvpForm` action method tells Razor to look for a view called `Rsvp-Form.cshtml`.

If you are using Visual Studio, right-click the `Views/Home` folder and select Add > New Item from the pop-up menu. Select the Razor View – Empty item, set the name to `RsvpForm.cshtml`, and click the Add button to create the file. Replace the contents with those shown in listing 3.8.

If you are using Visual Studio Code, right-click the `Views/Home` folder and select New File from the pop-up menu. Set the name of the file to `RsvpForm.cshtml` and add the contents shown in listing 3.8.

> **Listing 3.8   The contents of the RsvpForm.cshtml file in the Views/Home folder**

```
@{
    Layout = null;
}

<!DOCTYPE html>

<html>
<head>
    <meta name="viewport" content="width=device-width" />
    <title>RsvpForm</title>
</head>
<body>
    <div>
        This is the RsvpForm.cshtml View
    </div>
</body>
</html>
```

This content is just static HTML for the moment. Use the browser to request http://localhost:5000/home/rsvpform. The Razor view engine locates the `RsvpForm.cshtml` file and uses it to produce a response, as shown in figure 3.2.

**Figure 3.2
Rendering a
second view**

3.2.4 Linking action methods

I want to be able to create a link from the `Index` view so that guests can see the `Rsvp-Form` view without having to know the URL that targets a specific action method, as shown in listing 3.9.

> **Listing 3.9 Adding a link in the Index.cshtml file in the Views/Home folder**

```
@{
    Layout = null;
}

<!DOCTYPE html>
<html>
<head>
    <meta name="viewport" content="width=device-width" />
    <title>Party!</title>
</head>
<body>
    <div>
        <div>
            We're going to have an exciting party.<br />
            (To do: sell it better. Add pictures or something.)
        </div>
        <a asp-action="RsvpForm">RSVP Now</a>
    </div>
</body>
</html>
```

The addition to the listing is an `a` element that has an `asp-action` attribute. The attribute is an example of a *tag helper* attribute, which is an instruction for Razor that will be performed when the view is rendered. The `asp-action` attribute is an instruction to add an `href` attribute to the `a` element that contains a URL for an action method. I explain how tag helpers work in chapters 25–27, but this tag helper tells Razor to insert a URL for an action method defined by the same controller for which the current view is being rendered.

Use the browser to request http://localhost:5000, and you will see the link that the helper has created, as shown in figure 3.3.

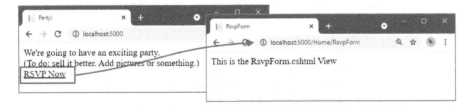

Figure 3.3 Linking between action methods

Roll the mouse over the RSVP Now link in the browser. You will see that the link points to http://localhost:5000/Home/RsvpForm.

There is an important principle at work here, which is that you should use the features provided by ASP.NET Core to generate URLs, rather than hard-code them into your views. When the tag helper created the `href` attribute for the `a` element, it inspected the configuration of the application to figure out what the URL should be. This allows the configuration of the application to be changed to support different URL formats without needing to update any views.

3.2.5   Building the form

Now that I have created the view and can reach it from the `Index` view, I am going to build out the contents of the `RsvpForm.cshtml` file to turn it into an HTML form for editing `GuestResponse` objects, as shown in listing 3.10.

> **Listing 3.10   Creating a form view in the RsvpForm.cshtml file in the Views/Home folder**

```
@model PartyInvites.Models.GuestResponse
@{
    Layout = null;
}

<!DOCTYPE html>

<html>
<head>
    <meta name="viewport" content="width=device-width" />
    <title>RsvpForm</title>
</head>
<body>
    <form asp-action="RsvpForm" method="post">
        <div>
            <label asp-for="Name">Your name:</label>
            <input asp-for="Name" />
        </div>
        <div>
            <label asp-for="Email">Your email:</label>
            <input asp-for="Email" />
        </div>
        <div>
            <label asp-for="Phone">Your phone:</label>
            <input asp-for="Phone" />
        </div>
        <div>
            <label asp-for="WillAttend">Will you attend?</label>
            <select asp-for="WillAttend">
                <option value="">Choose an option</option>
                <option value="true">Yes, I'll be there</option>
                <option value="false">No, I can't come</option>
            </select>
        </div>
        <button type="submit">Submit RSVP</button>
    </form>
</body>
</html>
```

The `@model` expression specifies that the view expects to receive a `GuestResponse` object as its view model. I have defined a `label` and `input` element for each property of the `GuestResponse` model class (or, in the case of the `WillAttend` property, a `select` element). Each element is associated with the model property using the `asp-for` attribute, which is another tag helper attribute. The tag helper attributes configure the elements to tie them to the view model object. Here is an example of the HTML that the tag helpers produce:

```
<p>
    <label for="Name">Your name:</label>
    <input type="text" id="Name" name="Name" value="">
</p>
```

The `asp-for` attribute on the `label` element sets the value of the `for` attribute. The `asp-for` attribute on the `input` element sets the `id` and `name` elements. This may not look especially useful, but you will see that associating elements with a model property offers additional advantages as the application functionality is defined.

Of more immediate use is the `asp-action` attribute applied to the `form` element, which uses the application's URL routing configuration to set the `action` attribute to a URL that will target a specific action method, like this:

```
<form method="post" action="/Home/RsvpForm">
```

As with the helper attribute I applied to the a element, the benefit of this approach is that when you change the system of URLs that the application uses, the content generated by the tag helpers will reflect the changes automatically.

Use the browser to request http://localhost:5000 and click the RSVP Now link to see the form, as shown in figure 3.4.

Figure 3.4   **Adding an HTML form to the application**

3.2.6   *Receiving form data*

I have not yet told ASP.NET Core what I want to do when the form is posted to the server. As things stand, clicking the Submit RSVP button just clears any values you have entered in the form. That is because the form posts back to the `RsvpForm` action method in the `Home` controller, which just renders the view again. To receive and process submitted form data, I am going to use an important feature of controllers. I will add a second `RsvpForm` action method to create the following:

- A method that responds to HTTP GET requests: A GET request is what a browser issues normally each time someone clicks a link. This version of the action will be responsible for displaying the initial blank form when someone first visits /Home/ RsvpForm.

- A method that responds to HTTP POST requests: The form element defined in listing 3.10 sets the method attribute to post, which causes the form data to be sent to the server as a POST request. This version of the action will be responsible for receiving submitted data and deciding what to do with it.

Handling GET and POST requests in separate C# methods helps to keep my controller code tidy since the two methods have different responsibilities. Both action methods are invoked by the same URL, but ASP.NET Core makes sure that the appropriate method is called, based on whether I am dealing with a GET or POST request. Listing 3.11 shows the changes to the HomeController class.

> **Listing 3.11   Adding a method in the HomeController.cs file in the Controllers folder**

```
using Microsoft.AspNetCore.Mvc;
using PartyInvites.Models;

namespace PartyInvites.Controllers {
    public class HomeController : Controller {

        public IActionResult Index() {
            return View();
        }

        [HttpGet]
        public ViewResult RsvpForm() {
            return View();
        }

        [HttpPost]
        public ViewResult RsvpForm(GuestResponse guestResponse) {
            // TODO: store response from guest
            return View();
        }
    }
}
```

I have added the HttpGet attribute to the existing RsvpForm action method, which declares that this method should be used only for GET requests. I then added an over-loaded version of the RsvpForm method, which accepts a GuestResponse object. I applied the HttpPost attribute to this method, which declares it will deal with POST requests. I explain how these additions to the listing work in the following sections. I also imported the PartyInvites.Models namespace—this is just so I can refer to the GuestResponse model type without needing to qualify the class name.

UNDERSTANDING MODEL BINDING

The first overload of the `RsvpForm` action method renders the same view as before—the `RsvpForm.cshtml` file—to generate the form shown in figure 3.4. The second overload is more interesting because of the parameter, but given that the action method will be invoked in response to an HTTP `POST` request and that the `GuestResponse` type is a C# class, how are the two connected?

The answer is *model binding*, a useful ASP.NET Core feature whereby incoming data is parsed and the key-value pairs in the HTTP request are used to populate properties of domain model types.

Model binding is a powerful and customizable feature that eliminates the grind of dealing with HTTP requests directly and lets you work with C# objects rather than dealing with individual data values sent by the browser. The `GuestResponse` object that is passed as the parameter to the action method is automatically populated with the data from the form fields. I dive into the details of model binding in chapter 28.

To demonstrate how model binding works, I need to do some preparatory work. One of the application goals is to present a summary page with details of who is attending the party, which means that I need to keep track of the responses that I receive. I am going to do this by creating an in-memory collection of objects. This isn't useful in a real application because the response data will be lost when the application is stopped or restarted, but this approach will allow me to keep the focus on ASP.NET Core and create an application that can easily be reset to its initial state. Later chapters will demonstrate persistent data storage.

Add a class file named `Repository.cs` to the `Models` folder and use it to define the class shown in listing 3.12.

> **Listing 3.12 The contents of the Repository.cs file in the Models folder**

```
namespace PartyInvites.Models {
    public static class Repository {
        private static List<GuestResponse> responses = new();

        public static IEnumerable<GuestResponse> Responses => responses;

        public static void AddResponse(GuestResponse response) {
            Console.WriteLine(response);
            responses.Add(response);
        }
    }
}
```

The `Repository` class and its members are `static`, which will make it easy for me to store and retrieve data from different places in the application. ASP.NET Core provides a more sophisticated approach for defining common functionality, called *dependency injection*, which I describe in chapter 14, but a static class is a good way to get started for a simple application like this one.

If you are using Visual Studio, saving the contents of the `Repository.cs` file will trigger a warning produced by the `dotnet watch` command telling you that a hot reload cannot be applied, which is the same warning described earlier in the chapter for Visual Studio Code users. You will see this prompt at the command line:

```
watch : Do you want to restart your app

    - Yes (y) / No (n) / Always (a) / Never (v)?
```

Press a to always rebuild the project.

STORING RESPONSES

Now that I have somewhere to store the data, I can update the action method that receives the HTTP POST requests, as shown in listing 3.13.

Listing 3.13   Updating an action in the HomeController.cs file in the Controllers folder

```
using Microsoft.AspNetCore.Mvc;
using PartyInvites.Models;

namespace PartyInvites.Controllers {
    public class HomeController : Controller {

        public IActionResult Index() {
            return View();
        }

        [HttpGet]
        public ViewResult RsvpForm() {
            return View();
        }

        [HttpPost]
        public ViewResult RsvpForm(GuestResponse guestResponse) {
            Repository.AddResponse(guestResponse);
            return View("Thanks", guestResponse);
        }
    }
}
```

Before the POST version of the RsvpForm method is invoked, the ASP.NET Core model binding feature extracts values from the HTML form and assigns them to the properties of the GuestResponse object. The result is used as the argument when the method is invoked to handle the HTTP request, and all I have to do to deal with the form data sent in a request is to work with the GuestResponse object that is passed to the action method—in this case, to pass it as an argument to the Repository. AddResponse method so t hat the response can be stored.

3.2.7   *Adding the Thanks view*

The call to the View method in the RsvpForm action method creates a ViewResult that selects a view called Thanks and uses the GuestResponse object created by the model binder as the view model. Add a Razor View named Thanks.cshtml to the Views/Home folder with the content shown in listing 3.14 to present a response to the user.

Listing 3.14   The contents of the Thanks.cshtml file in the Views/Home folder

```
@model PartyInvites.Models.GuestResponse
@{
    Layout = null;
}


<!DOCTYPE html>

<html>
<head>
    <meta name="viewport" content="width=device-width" />
    <title>Thanks</title>
</head>
<body>
    <div>
        <h1>Thank you, @Model?.Name!</h1>
        @if (Model?.WillAttend == true) {
            @:It's great that you're coming.
            @:The drinks are already in the fridge!
        } else {
            @:Sorry to hear that you can't make it,
            @:but thanks for letting us know.
        }
    </div>
    Click <a asp-action="ListResponses">here</a> to see who is coming.
</body>
</html>
```

The HTML produced by the `Thanks.cshtml` view depends on the values assigned to the `GuestResponse` view model provided by the `RsvpForm` action method. To access the value of a property in the domain object, I use an `@Model.<PropertyName>` expression. So, for example, to get the value of the `Name` property, I use the `@Model.Name` expression. Don't worry if the Razor syntax doesn't make sense—I explain it in more detail in chapter 21.

Now that I have created the `Thanks` view, I have a basic working example of handling a form. Use the browser to request http://localhost:5000, click the RSVP Now link, add some data to the form, and click the Submit RSVP button. You will see the response shown in figure 3.5 (although it will differ if your name is not Joe or you said you could not attend).

Figure 3.5   The Thanks view

3.2.8   *Displaying responses*

At the end of the `Thanks.cshtml` view, I added an `a` element to create a link to display the list of people who are coming to the party. I used the `asp-action` tag helper attribute to create a URL that targets an action method called `ListResponses`, like this:

```
...
Click <a asp-action="ListResponses">here</a> to see who is coming.
...
```

If you hover the mouse over the link that is displayed by the browser, you will see that it targets the `/Home/ListResponses` URL. This doesn't correspond to any of the action methods in the `Home` controller, and if you click the link, you will see a 404 Not Found error response.

To add an endpoint that will handle the URL, I need to add another action method to the `Home` controller, as shown in listing 3.15.

> **Listing 3.15   Adding an action in the HomeController.cs file in the Controllers folder**

```
using Microsoft.AspNetCore.Mvc;
using PartyInvites.Models;

namespace PartyInvites.Controllers {
    public class HomeController : Controller {

        public IActionResult Index() {
            return View();
        }

        [HttpGet]
        public ViewResult RsvpForm() {
            return View();
        }

        [HttpPost]
        public ViewResult RsvpForm(GuestResponse guestResponse) {
            Repository.AddResponse(guestResponse);
            return View("Thanks", guestResponse);
        }

        public ViewResult ListResponses() {
            return View(Repository.Responses
                .Where(r => r.WillAttend == true));
        }
    }
}
```

The new action method is called `ListResponses`, and it calls the `View` method, using the `Repository.Responses` property as the argument. This will cause Razor to render the default view, using the action method name as the name of the view file, and to use the data from the repository as the view model. The view model data is filtered using LINQ so that only positive responses are provided to the view.

Add a Razor View named `ListResponses.cshtml` to the `Views/Home` folder with the content shown in listing 3.16.

```
@model IEnumerable<PartyInvites.Models.GuestResponse>
@{
    Layout = null;
}

<!DOCTYPE html>

<html>
<head>
    <meta name="viewport" content="width=device-width" />
    <title>Responses</title>
</head>
<body>
    <h2>Here is the list of people attending the party</h2>
    <table>
        <thead>
            <tr><th>Name</th><th>Email</th><th>Phone</th></tr>
        </thead>
        <tbody>
            @foreach (PartyInvites.Models.GuestResponse r in Model!) {
                <tr>
                    <td>@r.Name</td>
                    <td>@r.Email</td>
                    <td>@r.Phone</td>
                </tr>
            }
        </tbody>
    </table>
</body>
</html>
```

Razor view files have the `.cshtml` file extension to denote a mix of C# code and HTML elements. You can see this in listing 3.16 where I have used an `@foreach` expression to process each of the `GuestResponse` objects that the action method passes to the view using the `View` method. Unlike a normal C# `foreach` loop, the body of a Razor `@foreach` expression contains HTML elements that are added to the response that will be sent back to the browser. In this view, each `GuestResponse` object generates a `tr` element that contains `td` elements populated with the value of an object property.

Use the browser to request http://localhost:5000, click the RSVP Now link, and fill in the form. Submit the form and then click the link to see a summary of the data that has been entered since the application was first started, as shown in figure 3.6. The view does not present the data in an appealing way, but it is enough for the moment, and I will address the styling of the application later in this chapter.

Figure 3.6   Showing a list of party attendees

3.2.9   *Adding validation*

I can now add data validation to the application. Without validation, users could enter nonsense data or even submit an empty form. In an ASP.NET Core application, validation rules are defined by applying attributes to model classes, which means the same validation rules can be applied in any form that uses that class. ASP.NET Core relies on attributes from the `System.ComponentModel.DataAnnotations` namespace, which I have applied to the `GuestResponse` class in listing 3.17.

> **Listing 3.17   Applying validation in the GuestResponse.cs file in the Models folder**

```
using System.ComponentModel.DataAnnotations;

namespace PartyInvites.Models {

    public class GuestResponse {

        [Required(ErrorMessage = "Please enter your name")]
        public string? Name { get; set; }

        [Required(ErrorMessage = "Please enter your email address")]
        [EmailAddress]
        public string? Email { get; set; }

        [Required(ErrorMessage = "Please enter your phone number")]
        public string? Phone { get; set; }

        [Required(ErrorMessage = "Please specify whether you'll attend")]
        public bool? WillAttend { get; set; }
    }
}
```

ASP.NET Core detects the attributes and uses them to validate data during the model-binding process.

As noted earlier, I used nullable types to define the `GuestResponse` properties. This is useful for denoting properties that may not be assigned values, but it has a special value for the `WillAttend` property because it allows the `Required` validation attribute to work. If I had used a regular non-nullable `bool`, the value I received through model-binding could be only `true` or `false`, and I would not be able to tell whether the user had selected a value. A nullable `bool` has three possible values: `true`, `false`, and `null`. The value of the `WillAttend` property will be `null` if the user has not selected a value, and this causes the `Required` attribute to report a validation error. This is a nice example of how ASP.NET Core elegantly blends C# features with HTML and HTTP.

I check to see whether there has been a validation problem using the `ModelState` `.IsValid` property in the action method that receives the form data, as shown in listing 3.18.

Listing 3.18   Checking for errors in the HomeController.cs file in the Controllers folder

```
using Microsoft.AspNetCore.Mvc;
using PartyInvites.Models;

namespace PartyInvites.Controllers {
    public class HomeController : Controller {

        public IActionResult Index() {
            return View();
        }

        [HttpGet]
        public ViewResult RsvpForm() {
            return View();
        }

        [HttpPost]
        public ViewResult RsvpForm(GuestResponse guestResponse) {
            if (ModelState.IsValid) {
                Repository.AddResponse(guestResponse);
                return View("Thanks", guestResponse);
            } else {
                return View();
            }
        }

        public ViewResult ListResponses() {
            return View(Repository.Responses
                .Where(r => r.WillAttend == true));
        }
    }
}
```

The `Controller` base class provides a property called `ModelState` that provides details of the outcome of the model binding process. If the `ModelState.IsValid` property returns `true`, then I know that the model binder has been able to satisfy the validation constraints I specified through the attributes on the `GuestResponse` class. When this happens, I render the `Thanks` view, just as I did previously.

If the `ModelState.IsValid` property returns `false`, then I know that there are validation errors. The object returned by the `ModelState` property provides details of each problem that has been encountered, but I don't need to get into that level of detail because I can rely on a useful feature that automates the process of asking the user to address any problems by calling the `View` method without any parameters.

When it renders a view, Razor has access to the details of any validation errors associated with the request, and tag helpers can access the details to display validation errors to the user. Listing 3.19 shows the addition of validation tag helper attributes to the `RsvpForm` view.

Listing 3.19   Adding a summary to the RsvpForm.cshtml file in the Views/Home folder

```
@model PartyInvites.Models.GuestResponse
@{
    Layout = null;
}


<!DOCTYPE html>

<html>
<head>
    <meta name="viewport" content="width=device-width" />
    <title>RsvpForm</title>
</head>
<body>
    <form asp-action="RsvpForm" method="post">
        <div asp-validation-summary="All"></div>
        <div>
            <label asp-for="Name">Your name:</label>
            <input asp-for="Name" />
        </div>
        <div>
            <label asp-for="Email">Your email:</label>
            <input asp-for="Email" />
        </div>
        <div>
            <label asp-for="Phone">Your phone:</label>
            <input asp-for="Phone" />
        </div>
        <div>
            <label asp-for="WillAttend">Will you attend?</label>
            <select asp-for="WillAttend">
                <option value="">Choose an option</option>
                <option value="true">Yes, I'll be there</option>
                <option value="false">No, I can't come</option>
            </select>
        </div>
        <button type="submit">Submit RSVP</button>
    </form>
</body>
</html>
```

The `asp-validation-summary` attribute is applied to a `div` element, and it displays a list of validation errors when the view is rendered. The value for the `asp-validation-summary` attribute is a value from an enumeration called `ValidationSummary`, which specifies what types of validation errors the summary will contain. I specified `All`, which is a good starting point for most applications, and I describe the other values and explain how they work in chapter 29.

To see how the validation summary works, run the application, fill out the `Name` field, and submit the form without entering any other data. You will see a summary of validation errors, as shown in figure 3.7.

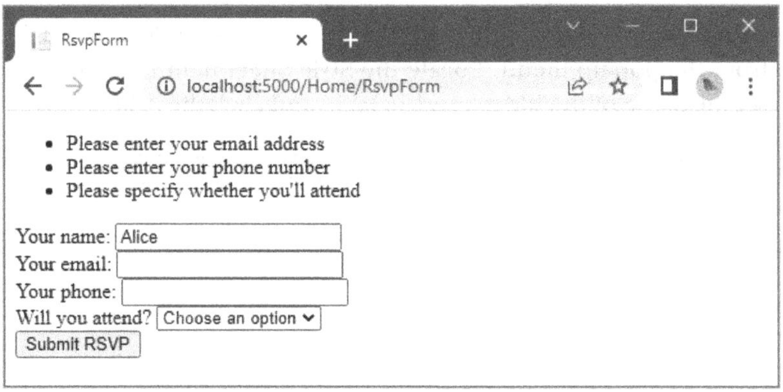

Figure 3.7   Displaying validation errors

The `RsvpForm` action method will not render the `Thanks` view until all the validation constraints applied to the `GuestResponse` class have been satisfied. Notice that the data entered in the `Name` field was preserved and displayed again when Razor rendered the view with the validation summary. This is another benefit of model binding, and it simplifies working with form data.

HIGHLIGHTING INVALID FIELDS

The tag helper attributes that associate model properties with elements have a handy feature that can be used in conjunction with model binding. When a model class property has failed validation, the helper attributes will generate slightly different HTML. Here is the `input` element that is generated for the Phone field when there is no validation error:

```
<input type="text" data-val="true"
    data-val-required="Please enter your phone number" id="Phone"
    name="Phone" value="">
```

For comparison, here is the same HTML element after the user has submitted the form without entering data into the text field (which is a validation error because I applied the `Required` attribute to the `Phone` property of the `GuestResponse` class):

```
<input type="text" class="input-validation-error"
    data-val="true" data-val-required="Please enter your phone number" id="Phone"
    name="Phone" value="">
```

I have highlighted the difference: the `asp-for` tag helper attribute added the `input` element to a class called `input-validation-error`. I can take advantage of this feature by creating a stylesheet that contains CSS styles for this class and the others that different HTML helper attributes use.

The convention in ASP.NET Core projects is that static content is placed into the `wwwroot` folder and organized by content type so that CSS stylesheets go into the `wwwroot/css` folder, JavaScript files go into the `wwwroot/js` folder, and so on.

> **TIP**   The project template used in listing 3.1 creates a `site.css` file in the `wwwroot/css` folder. You can ignore this file, which I don't use in this chapter.

If you are using Visual Studio, right-click the `wwwroot/css` folder and select Add > New Item from the pop-up menu. Locate the Style Sheet item template, as shown in figure 3.8; set the name of the file to `styles.css`; and click the Add button.

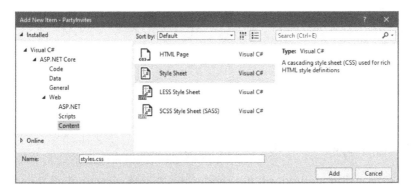

Figure 3.8   Creating a CSS stylesheet

If you are using Visual Studio Code, right-click the `wwwroot/css` folder, select New File from the pop-up menu, and use `styles.css` as the file name. Regardless of which editor you use, replace the contents of the file with the styles shown in listing 3.20.

Listing 3.20   The contents of the styles.css file in the wwwroot/css folder

```css
.field-validation-error {
    color: #f00;
}

.field-validation-valid {
    display: none;
}

.input-validation-error {
    border: 1px solid #f00;
    background-color: #fee;
}

.validation-summary-errors {
```

```
    font-weight: bold;
    color: #f00;
}

.validation-summary-valid {
    display: none;
}
```

To apply this stylesheet, I added a `link` element to the `head` section of the `RsvpForm` view, as shown in listing 3.21.

> **Listing 3.21 Applying a stylesheet in the RsvpForm.cshtml file in the Views/Home folder**

```
...
<head>
    <meta name="viewport" content="width=device-width" />
    <title>RsvpForm</title>
    <link rel="stylesheet" href="/css/styles.css" />
</head>
...
```

The `link` element uses the `href` attribute to specify the location of the stylesheet. Notice that the `wwwroot` folder is omitted from the URL. The default configuration for ASP.NET includes support for serving static content, such as images, CSS stylesheets, and JavaScript files, and it maps requests to the `wwwroot` folder automatically. With the application of the stylesheet, a more obvious validation error will be displayed when data is submitted that causes a validation error, as shown in figure 3.9.

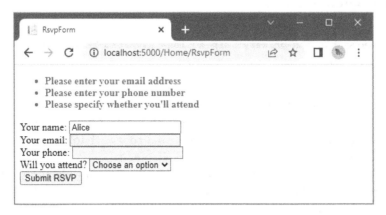

Figure 3.9 Automatically highlighted validation errors

3.2.10 *Styling the content*

All the functional goals for the application are complete, but the overall appearance of the application is poor. When you create a project using the `mvc` template, as I did for the example in this chapter, some common client-side development packages are installed. While I am not a fan of using template projects, I do like the client-side libraries that Microsoft has chosen. One of them is called Bootstrap, which is a good CSS framework originally developed by Twitter that has become a major open-source project and a mainstay of web application development.

STYLING THE WELCOME VIEW

The basic Bootstrap features work by applying classes to elements that correspond to CSS selectors defined in the files added to the `wwwroot/lib/bootstrap` folder. You can get full details of the classes that Bootstrap defines from http://getbootstrap.com, but you can see how I have applied some basic styling to the `Index.cshtml` view file in listing 3.22.

Listing 3.22   Adding Bootstrap to the Index.cshtml file in the Views/Home folder

```
@{
    Layout = null;
}


<!DOCTYPE html>

<html>
<head>
    <meta name="viewport" content="width=device-width" />
    <link rel="stylesheet" href="/lib/bootstrap/dist/css/bootstrap.css" />
    <title>Index</title>
</head>
<body>
    <div class="text-center m-2">
        <h3> We're going to have an exciting party!</h3>
        <h4>And YOU are invited!</h4>
        <a class="btn btn-primary" asp-action="RsvpForm">RSVP Now</a>
    </div>
</body>
</html>
```

I have added a `link` element whose `href` attribute loads the `bootstrap.css` file from the `wwwroot/lib/bootstrap/dist/css` folder. The convention is that third-party CSS and JavaScript packages are installed into the `wwwroot/lib` folder, and I describe the tool that is used to manage these packages in chapter 4.

Having imported the Bootstrap stylesheets, I need to style my elements. This is a simple example, so I need to use only a small number of Bootstrap CSS classes: `text-center`, `btn`, and `btn-primary`.

The `text-center` class centers the contents of an element and its children. The `btn` class styles a `button`, `input`, or a element as a pretty button, and the `btn-primary` class specifies which of a range of colors I want the button to be. You can see the effect by running the application, as shown in figure 3.10.

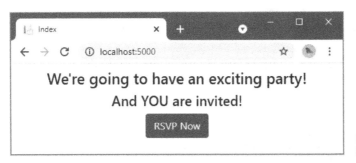

Figure 3.10
Styling a view

It will be obvious to you that I am not a web designer. In fact, as a child, I was excused from art lessons on the basis that I had absolutely no talent whatsoever. This had the happy result of making more time for math lessons but meant that my artistic skills have not developed beyond those of the average 10-year-old. For a real project, I would seek a professional to help design and style the content, but for this example, I am going it alone, and that means applying Bootstrap with as much restraint and consistency as I can muster.

STYLING THE FORM VIEW

Bootstrap defines classes that can be used to style forms. I am not going to go into detail, but you can see how I have applied these classes in listing 3.23.

> **Listing 3.23 Adding styles to the RsvpForm.cshtml file in the Views/Home folder**

```
@model PartyInvites.Models.GuestResponse
@{
    Layout = null;
}

<!DOCTYPE html>

<html>
<head>
    <meta name="viewport" content="width=device-width" />
    <title>RsvpForm</title>
    <link rel="stylesheet" href="/lib/bootstrap/dist/css/bootstrap.css" />
    <link rel="stylesheet" href="/css/styles.css" />
</head>
<body>
    <h5 class="bg-primary text-white text-center m-2 p-2">RSVP</h5>
    <form asp-action="RsvpForm" method="post" class="m-2">
        <div asp-validation-summary="All"></div>
        <div class="form-group">
            <label asp-for="Name" class="form-label">Your name:</label>
            <input asp-for="Name" class="form-control" />
        </div>
        <div class="form-group">
            <label asp-for="Email" class="form-label">Your email:</label>
            <input asp-for="Email"  class="form-control" />
        </div>
        <div class="form-group">
```

```
                <label asp-for="Phone" class="form-label">Your phone:</label>
                <input asp-for="Phone" class="form-control" />
            </div>
            <div class="form-group">
                <label asp-for="WillAttend" class="form-label">
                    Will you attend?
                </label>
                <select asp-for="WillAttend" class="form-select">
                    <option value="">Choose an option</option>
                    <option value="true">Yes, I'll be there</option>
                    <option value="false">No, I can't come</option>
                </select>
            </div>
            <button type="submit" class="btn btn-primary mt-3">
                Submit RSVP
            </button>
        </form>
    </body>
</html>
```

The Bootstrap classes in this example create a header, just to give structure to the layout. To style the form, I have used the `form-group` class, which is used to style the element that contains the `label` and the associated `input` or `select` element, which is assigned to the `form-control` class. You can see the effect of the styles in figure 3.11.

**Figure 3.11
Styling the
RsvpForm view**

STYLING THE THANKS VIEW

The next view file to style is `Thanks.cshtml`, and you can see how I have done this in listing 3.24, using CSS classes that are similar to the ones I used for the other views. To make an application easier to manage, it is a good principle to avoid duplicating code and markup wherever possible. ASP.NET Core provides several features to help reduce duplication, which I describe in later chapters. These features include Razor layouts (Chapter 22), partial views (Chapter 22), and view components (Chapter 24).

```
@model PartyInvites.Models.GuestResponse
@{
    Layout = null;
}

<!DOCTYPE html>

<html>
<head>
    <meta name="viewport" content="width=device-width" />
    <title>Thanks</title>
        <link rel="stylesheet"
            href="/lib/bootstrap/dist/css/bootstrap.css" />
</head>
<body class="text-center">
    <div>
        <h1>Thank you, @Model?.Name!</h1>
        @if (Model?.WillAttend == true) {
            @:It's great that you're coming.
            @:The drinks are already in the fridge!
        } else {
            @:Sorry to hear that you can't make it,
            @:but thanks for letting us know.
        }
    </div>
    Click <a asp-action="ListResponses">here</a> to see who is coming.
</body>
</html>
```

Figure 3.12 shows the effect of the styles.

Figure 3.12 Styling the Thanks view

STYLING THE LIST VIEW

The final view to style is `ListResponses`, which presents the list of attendees. Styling the content follows the same approach as used for the other views, as shown in listing 3.25.

Listing 3.25   Adding styles to the ListResponses.cshtml file in the Views/Home folder

```
@model IEnumerable<PartyInvites.Models.GuestResponse>
@{
    Layout = null;
}

<!DOCTYPE html>

<html>
<head>
    <meta name="viewport" content="width=device-width" />
    <title>Responses</title>
    <link rel="stylesheet" href="/lib/bootstrap/dist/css/bootstrap.css" />
</head>
<body>
    <div class="text-center p-2">
        <h2 class="text-center">
            Here is the list of people attending the party
        </h2>
        <table class="table table-bordered table-striped table-sm">
            <thead>
                <tr><th>Name</th><th>Email</th><th>Phone</th></tr>
            </thead>
            <tbody>
                @foreach (PartyInvites.Models.GuestResponse r in Model!) {
                    <tr>
                        <td>@r.Name</td>
                        <td>@r.Email</td>
                        <td>@r.Phone</td>
                    </tr>
                }
            </tbody>
        </table>
    </div>
</body>
</html>
```

Figure 3.13 shows the way that the table of attendees is presented. Adding these styles to the view completes the example application, which now meets all the development goals and has an improved appearance.

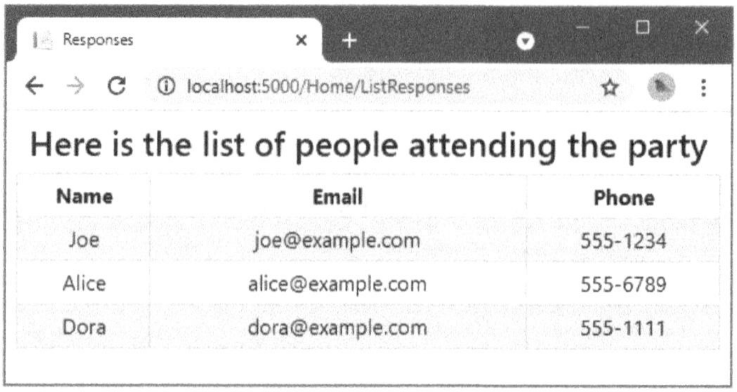

Figure 3.13
Styling the
ListResponses
view

Summary

- ASP.NET Core projects are created with the `dotnet new` command.
- Controllers define action methods that are used to handle HTTP requests.
- Views generate HTML content that is used to respond to HTTP requests.
- Views can contain HTML elements that are bound to data model properties.
- Model binding is the process by which request data is parsed and assigned to the properties of objects that are passed to action methods for processing.
- The data in the request can be subjected to validation and errors can be displayed to the user within the same HTML form that was used to submit the data.
- The HTML content generated by views can be styled using the same CSS features that are applied to static HTML content.

Using the
development tools

This chapter covers

- Using command-line tools to create an ASP.NET Core project
- Adding code and content to a project
- Building and running an ASP.NET Core project
- Using the hot reload feature
- Installing NuGet packages
- Installing tool packages
- Installing client-side packages
- Using the debugger

In this chapter, I introduce the tools that Microsoft provides for ASP.NET Core development and that are used throughout this book.

Unlike earlier editions of this book, I rely on the command-line tools provided by the .NET SDK and additional tool packages that Microsoft publishes. In part, I have done this to help ensure you get the expected results from the examples but also because the command-line tools provide access to all the features required for ASP. NET Core development, regardless of which editor/IDE you have chosen.

Visual Studio—and, to a lesser extent, Visual Studio Code—offers access to some of the tools through user interfaces, which I describe in this chapter, but Visual

Studio and Visual Studio Code don't support all the features that are required for ASP. NET Core development, so there are times that using the command line is inevitable.

As ASP.NET Core has evolved, I have gradually moved to using just the command-line tools, except for when I need to use a debugger (although, as I explain later in the chapter, this is a rare requirement). Your preferences may differ, especially if you are used to working entirely within an IDE, but my suggestion is to give the command-line tools a go. They are simple, concise, and predictable, which cannot be said for all the equivalent functionality provided by Visual Studio and Visual Studio Code. Table 4.1 provides a guide to the chapter.

Table 4.1   Chapter guide

Problem	Solution	Listing
Creating a project	Use the `dotnet new` commands.	1–3
Building and running projects	Use the `dotnet build` and `dotnet run` commands.	4–10
Adding packages to a project	Use the `dotnet add package` command.	11, 12
Installing tool commands	Use the `dotnet tool` command.	14, 15
Managing client-side packages	Use the `libman` command or the Visual Studio client-side package manager.	16–19

4.1   Creating ASP.NET Core projects

The .NET SDK includes a set of command-line tools for creating, managing, building, and running projects. Visual Studio provides integrated support for some of these tasks, but if you are using Visual Studio Code, then the command line is the only option.

I use the command-line tools throughout this book because they are simple and concise. The Visual Studio integrated support is awkward and makes it easy to unintentionally create a project with the wrong configuration, as the volume of emails from confused readers of earlier editions of this book has demonstrated.

> **TIP**   You can download the example project for this chapter—and for all the other chapters in this book—from https://github.com/manningbooks/pro-asp .net-core-7. See chapter 1 for how to get help if you have problems running the examples.

4.1.1   Creating a project using the command line

The `dotnet` command provides access to the .NET command-line features. The `dotnet new` command is used to create a new project, configuration file, or solution file. To see the list of templates available for creating new items, open a PowerShell command prompt and run the command shown in listing 4.1.

Listing 4.1   Listing the .NET templates

```
dotnet new --list
```

Each template has a short name that makes it easier to use. There are many templates available, but table 4.2 describes the ones that are most useful for creating ASP.NET Core projects.

Table 4.2   Useful ASP.NET Core project templates

Name	Description
web	This template creates a project that is set up with the minimum code and content required for ASP.NET Core development. This is the template I use for most of the chapters in this book.
mvc	This template creates an ASP.NET Core project configured to use the MVC Framework.
webapp	This template creates an ASP.NET Core project configured to use Razor Pages.
blazorserver	This template creates an ASP.NET Core project configured to use Blazor Server.
angular	This template creates an ASP.NET Core project that contains client-side features using the Angular JavaScript framework.
react	This template creates an ASP.NET Core project that contains client-side features using the React JavaScript framework.
reactredux	This template creates an ASP.NET Core project that contains client-side features using the React JavaScript framework and the popular Redux library.

There are also templates that create commonly required files used to configure projects, as described in table 4.3.

Understanding the limitations of project templates

The project templates described in table 4.2 are intended to help jump-start development by taking care of basic configuration settings and adding placeholder content.

These templates can give you a sense of rapid progress, but they contain assumptions about how a project should be configured and developed. If you don't understand the impact of those assumptions, you won't be able to get the results you require for the specific demands of your project.

The web template creates a project with the minimum configuration required for ASP.NET Core development. This is the project template I use for most of the examples in this book so that I can explain how each feature is configured and how the features can be used together.

Once you understand how ASP.NET Core works, the other project templates can be useful because you will know how to adapt them to your needs. But, while you are learning, I recommend sticking to the web template, even though it can take a little more effort to get results.

Table 4.3 The configuration item templates

Name	Description
globaljson	This template adds a `global.json` file to a project, specifying the version of .NET that will be used.
sln	This template creates a solution file, which is used to group multiple projects and is commonly used by Visual Studio. The solution file is populated with the `dotnet sln add` command, as shown in listing 4.2.
gitignore	This template creates a `.gitignore` file that excludes unwanted items from Git source control.

To create a project, open a new PowerShell command prompt and run the commands shown in listing 4.2.

Listing 4.2 Creating a new project

```
dotnet new globaljson --sdk-version 7.0.100 --output MySolution/MyProject
dotnet new web --no-https --output MySolution/MyProject --framework net7.0
dotnet new sln -o MySolution
dotnet sln MySolution add MySolution/MyProject
```

The first command creates a `MySolution/MyProject` folder that contains a `global.json` file, which specifies that the project will use .NET version 7. The top-level folder, named `MySolution`, is used to group multiple projects. The nested `MyProject` folder will contain a single project.

I use the `globaljson` template to help ensure you get the expected results when following the examples in this book. Microsoft is good at ensuring backward compatibility with .NET releases, but breaking changes do occur, and it is a good idea to add a `global.json` file to projects so that everyone in the development team is using the same version.

The second command creates the project using the `web` template, which I use for most of the examples in this book. As noted in table 4.3, this template creates a project with the minimum content required for ASP.NET Core development. Each template has its own set of arguments that influence the project that is created. The `--no-https` argument creates a project without support for HTTPS. (I explain how to use HTTPS in chapter 16.) The `--framework` argument selects the .NET runtime that will be used for the project.

The other commands create a solution file that references the new project. Solution files are a convenient way of opening multiple related files at the same time. A `MySolution.sln` file is created in the `MySolution` folder, and opening this file in Visual Studio will load the project created with the web template. This is not essential, but it stops Visual Studio from prompting you to create the file when you exit the code editor.

OPENING THE PROJECT

To open the project, start Visual Studio, select Open a Project or Solution, and open the `MySolution.sln` file in the `MySolution` folder. Visual Studio will open the solution file, discover the reference to the project that was added by the final command in listing 4.2, and open the project as well.

Visual Studio Code works differently. Start Visual Studio Code, select File > Open Folder, and navigate to the `MySolution` folder. Click Select Folder, and Visual Studio Code will open the project.

Although Visual Studio Code and Visual Studio are working with the same project, each displays the contents differently. Visual Studio Code shows you a simple list of files, ordered alphabetically, as shown on the left of figure 4.1. Visual Studio hides some files and nests others within related file items, as shown on the right of figure 4.1.

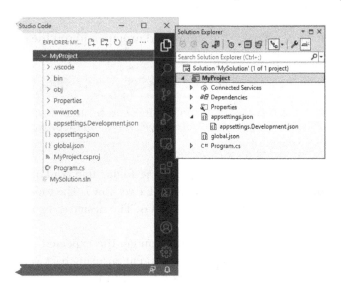

Figure 4.1   Opening a project in Visual Studio Code and Visual Studio

There are buttons at the top of the Visual Studio Solution Explorer that disable file nesting and show the hidden items in the project. When you open a project for the first time in Visual Studio Code, you may be prompted to add assets for building and debugging the project. Click the Yes button.

4.2   Adding code and content to projects

If you are using Visual Studio Code, then you add items to the project by right-clicking the folder that should contain the file and selecting New File from the pop-up menu (or selecting New Folder if you are adding a folder).

> **NOTE**   You are responsible for ensuring that the file extension matches the type of item you want to add; for example, an HTML file must be added with the `.html` extension. I give the complete file name and the name of the containing folder for every item added to a project throughout this book, so you will always know exactly what files you need to add.

Right-click the My Project item in the list of files and select New Folder from the pop-up menu. Set the name to `wwwroot`, which is where static content is stored in ASP.NET Core projects. Press Enter, and a folder named `wwwroot` will be added to the project. Right-click the new `wwwroot` folder, select New File, and set the name to `demo.html`. Press Enter to create the HTML file and add the content shown in listing 4.3.

Listing 4.3   The contents of the demo.html file in the wwwroot folder

```html
<!DOCTYPE html>
<html>
<head>
    <meta charset="utf-8" />
    <title></title>
</head>
<body>
    <h3>HTML File from MyProject</h3>
</body>
</html>
```

Visual Studio provides a more comprehensive approach that can be helpful, but only when used selectively. To create a folder, right-click the MyProject item in the Solution Explorer and select Add > New Folder from the pop-up menu. Set the name of the new item to `wwwroot` and press Enter; Visual Studio will create the folder.

Right-click the new wwwroot item in the Solution Explorer and select Add > New Item from the pop-up menu. Visual Studio will present you with an extensive selection of templates for adding items to the project. These templates can be searched using the text field in the top-right corner of the window or filtered using the categories on the left of the window. The item template for an HTML file is named HTML Page, as shown in figure 4.2.

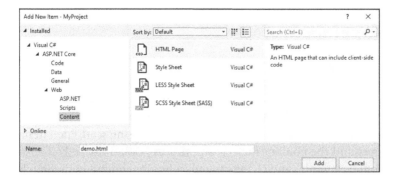

Figure 4.2   Adding an item to the example project

Enter `demo.html` in the Name field, click the Add button to create the new file, and replace the contents with the element shown in listing 4.3. (If you omit the file extension, Visual Studio will add it for you based on the item template you have selected. If you entered just `demo` into the Name field when you created the file, Visual Studio would have created a file with the `.html` extension because you had selected the HTML Page item template.)

4.2.1 *Understanding item scaffolding*

The item templates presented by Visual Studio can be useful, especially for C# classes where it sets the namespace and class name automatically. But Visual Studio also provides *scaffolded items,* which I recommend against using. The Add > New Scaffolded Item leads to a selection of items that guide you through a process to add more complex items. Visual Studio will also offer individual scaffolded items based on the name of the folder that you are adding an item to. For example, if you right-click a folder named `Views`, Visual Studio will helpfully add scaffolded items to the top of the menu, as shown in figure 4.3.

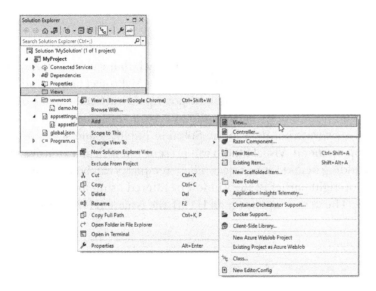

Figure 4.3 Scaffolded items in the Add menu

The `View` and `Controller` items are scaffolded, and selecting them will present you with choices that determine the content of the items you create.

Just like the project templates, I recommend against using scaffolded items, at least until you understand the content they create. In this book, I use only the Add > New Item menu for the examples and change the placeholder content immediately.

4.3 *Building and running projects*

The simplest way to build and run a project is to use the command-line tools. To prepare, add the statement shown in listing 4.4 to the `Program.cs` class file in the `MyProject` folder.

```
var builder = WebApplication.CreateBuilder(args);
var app = builder.Build();

app.MapGet("/", () => "Hello World!");

app.UseStaticFiles();

app.Run();
```

This statement adds support for responding to HTTP requests with static content in the wwwroot folder, such as the HTML file created in the previous section. (I explain this feature in more detail in chapter 15.)

Next, set the HTTP port that ASP.NET Core will use to receive HTTP requests, as shown in listing 4.5.

```
{
  "iisSettings": {
    "windowsAuthentication": false,
    "anonymousAuthentication": true,
    "iisExpress": {
      "applicationUrl": "http://localhost:5000",
      "sslPort": 0
    }
  },
  "profiles": {
    "MyProject": {
      "commandName": "Project",
      "dotnetRunMessages": true,
      "launchBrowser": true,
      "applicationUrl": "http://localhost:5000",
      "environmentVariables": {
        "ASPNETCORE_ENVIRONMENT": "Development"
      }
    },
    "IIS Express": {
      "commandName": "IISExpress",
      "launchBrowser": true,
      "environmentVariables": {
        "ASPNETCORE_ENVIRONMENT": "Development"
      }
    }
  }
}
```

To build the example project, run the command shown in listing 4.6 in the MyProject folder.

```
dotnet build
```

You can build and run the project in a single step by running the command shown in listing 4.7 in the `MyProject` folder.

```
dotnet run
```

The compiler will build the project and then start the integrated ASP.NET Core HTTP server to listen for HTTP requests on port 5000. You can see the contents of the static HTML file added to the project earlier in the chapter by opening a new browser window and requesting http://localhost:5000/demo.html, which produces the response shown in figure 4.4.

Figure 4.4   Running the example application

4.3.1   *Using the hot reload feature*

.NET has an integrated hot reload feature, which compiles and applies updates to applications on the fly. For ASP.NET Core applications, this means that changes to the project are automatically reflected in the browser without having to manually stop the ASP.NET Core application and use the `dotnet run` command. Use Control+C to stop ASP.NET Core if the application is still running from the previous section and run the command shown in listing 4.8 in the `MyProject` folder.

```
dotnet watch
```

The `dotnet watch` command opens a new browser window, which it does to ensure that the browser loads a small piece of JavaScript that opens an HTTP connection to the server that is used to handle reloading. (The new browser window can be disabled by setting the `launchBrowser` property shown in listing 4.5 to `false`, but you will have to perform a manual reload the first time you start or restart ASP.NET Core.) Use the browser to request http://localhost:5000/demo.html, and you will see the output shown on the left of figure 4.5.

The `dotnet watch` command monitors the project for changes. When a change is detected, the project is automatically recompiled, and the browser is reloaded. To see this process in action, make the change shown in listing 4.9 to the `demo.html` file in the `wwwroot` folder.

Listing 4.9 Changing the message in the demo.html file in the wwwroot folder

```html
<!DOCTYPE html>
<html>
<head>
    <meta charset="utf-8" />
    <title></title>
</head>
<body>
    <h3>New Message</h3>
</body>
</html>
```

When you save the changes to the HTML file, the `dotnet watch` tool will detect the change and automatically update the browser, as shown in figure 4.5.

Figure 4.5 The hot reload feature

The `dotnet watch` command is a clever feat of engineering, and it has good support for ASP.NET Core applications, allowing changes to be easily applied. But not all changes can be handled with a hot reload.

If you are using Visual Studio, right-click the MyProject item in the Solution Explorer, select Add > Class from the pop-up menu, and set the name of the new class file to `MyClass.cs`. When Visual Studio opens the file for editing, change the namespace as shown in listing 4.10.

Listing 4.10 Changing a namespace in the MyClass.cs file in the MyProject folder

```
namespace MyProject.MyNamespace {
    public class MyClass {
    }
}
```

If you are using Visual Studio Code, add a file named `MyClass.cs` to the `MyProject` folder with the content shown in listing 4.10.

Regardless of which editor you use, you will see output similar to the following when you save the class file:

```
watch : File changed: C:\MySolution\MyProject\MyClass.cs.
watch : Unable to apply hot reload because of a rude edit.
```

There are some changes that the `dotnet watch` command can't handle with a hot reload and the application is restarted instead. You may be prompted to accept the restart. The restart has little effect on the example application, but it means that the application state is lost, which can be frustrating when working on real projects.

But even though it isn't perfect, the hot reload feature is useful, especially when it comes to iterative adjustments to the HTML an application produces. I don't use it in most of the chapters in this book because the examples require many changes that are not handled with hot reloads and that can prevent changes from taking effect, but I do use it for my own non-book related development projects.

4.4 Managing packages

Most projects require additional features beyond those set up by the project templates, such as support for accessing databases or for making HTTP requests, neither of which is included in the standard ASP.NET Core packages added to the project by the template used to create the example project. In the sections that follow, I describe the tools available to manage the different types of packages that are used in ASP.NET Core development.

4.4.1 Managing NuGet packages

.NET packages are added to a project with the `dotnet add package` command. Use a PowerShell command prompt to run the command shown in listing 4.11 in the `MyProject` folder to add a package to the example project.

Listing 4.11   Adding a package to the example project

```
dotnet add package Microsoft.EntityFrameworkCore.SqlServer --version 7.0.0
```

This command installs version 7.0.0 of the `Microsoft.EntityFrameworkCore.SqlServer` package. The package repository for .NET projects is `nuget.org`, where you can search for the package and see the versions available. The package installed in listing 4.11, for example, is described at https://www.nuget.org/packages/Microsoft.EntityFrameworkCore.SqlServer/7.0.0. You can see the packages installed in a project by running the command shown in listing 4.12.

> **TIP**   The project file—which is the file with the `.csproj` extension—is used to keep track of the packages added to a project. You can examine this file by opening it for editing in Visual Studio Code or by right-clicking the project item in the Visual Studio Solution Explorer and selecting Edit Project File from the pop-up menu.

Listing 4.12   Listing the packages in a project

```
dotnet list package
```

This command produces the following output when it is run in the `MyProject` folder, showing the package added in listing 4.11:

```
Project 'MyProject' has the following package references
   [net7.0]:
   Top-level Package                               Requested   Resolved
   > Microsoft.EntityFrameworkCore.SqlServer       7.0.0       7.0.0
```

Packages are removed with the `dotnet remove package` command. To remove the package from the example project, run the command shown in listing 4.13 in the `MyProject` folder.

Listing 4.13   Removing a package from the example project

```
dotnet remove package Microsoft.EntityFrameworkCore.SqlServer
```

4.4.2   Managing tool packages

Tool packages install commands that can be used from the command line to perform operations on .NET projects. One common example is the Entity Framework Core tools package that installs commands that are used to manage databases in ASP.NET Core projects. Tool packages are managed using the `dotnet tool` command. To install the Entity Framework Core tools package, run the commands shown in listing 4.14.

Listing 4.14   Installing a tool package

```
dotnet tool uninstall --global dotnet-ef
dotnet tool install --global dotnet-ef --version 7.0.0
```

The first command removes the `dotnet-ef` package, which is named `dotnet-ef`. This command will produce an error if the package has not already been installed, but it is a good idea to remove existing versions before installing a package. The `dotnet tool install` command installs version 7.0.0 of the `dotnet-ef` package, which is the version I use in this book. The commands installed by tool packages are used through the `dotnet` command. To test the package installed in listing 4.14, run the command shown in listing 4.15 in the `MyProject` folder.

> **TIP**   The `--global` arguments in listing 4.14 mean the package is installed for global use and not just for a specific project. You can install tool packages into just one project, in which case the command is accessed with `dotnet tool run <command>`. The tools I use in this book are all installed globally.

Listing 4.15   Running a tool package command

```
dotnet ef --help
```

The commands added by this tool package are accessed using `dotnet ef`, and you will see examples in later chapters that rely on these commands.

4.4.3   Managing client-side packages

Client-side packages contain content that is delivered to the client, such as images, CSS stylesheets, JavaScript files, and static HTML. Client-side packages are added to ASP.NET Core using the Library Manager (LibMan) tool. To install the LibMan tool package, run the commands shown in listing 4.16.

Listing 4.16   Installing the LibMan tool package

```
dotnet tool uninstall --global Microsoft.Web.LibraryManager.Cli
dotnet tool install --global Microsoft.Web.LibraryManager.Cli
    --version 2.1.175
```

These commands remove any existing LibMan package and install the version that is used throughout this book. The next step is to initialize the project, which creates the file that LibMan uses to keep track of the client packages it installs. Run the command shown in listing 4.17 in the `MyProject` folder to initialize the example project.

Listing 4.17   Initializing the example project

```
libman init -p cdnjs
```

LibMan can download packages from different repositories. The `-p` argument in listing 4.17 specifies the repository at https://cdnjs.com, which is the most widely used. Once the project is initialized, client-side packages can be installed. To install the Bootstrap CSS framework that I use to style HTML content throughout this book, run the command shown in listing 4.18 in the `MyProject` folder.

Listing 4.18   Installing the Bootstrap CSS framework

```
libman install bootstrap@5.2.3 -d wwwroot/lib/bootstrap
```

The command installs version 5.2.3 of the Bootstrap package, which is known by the name `bootstrap` on the CDNJS repository. The `-d` argument specifies the location into which the package is installed. The convention in ASP.NET Core projects is to install client-side packages into the `wwwroot/lib` folder.

Once the package has been installed, add the classes shown in listing 4.19 to the elements in the `demo.html` file. This is how the features provided by the Bootstrap package are applied.

> **NOTE**   I don't get into the details of using the Bootstrap CSS framework in this book. See https://getbootstrap.com for the Bootstrap documentation.

Listing 4.19   Applying Bootstrap classes in the demo.html file in the wwwroot folder

```
<!DOCTYPE html>
<html>
<head>
    <meta charset="utf-8" />
    <title></title>
    <link href="/lib/bootstrap/css/bootstrap.min.css" rel="stylesheet" />
</head>
<body>
    <h3 class="bg-primary text-white text-center p-2">New Message</h3>
</body>
</html>
```

Start ASP.NET Core and request http://localhost:5000/demo.html, and you will see the styled content shown in figure 4.6.

Figure 4.6   Using a client-side package

4.5   Debugging projects

Visual Studio and Visual Studio Code both provide debuggers that can be used to control and inspect the execution of an ASP.NET Core application. Open the `Program.cs` file in the `MyProject` folder, and click this statement in the code editor:

```
...
app.MapGet("/", () => "Hello World!");
...
```

Select Debug > Toggle Breakpoint in Visual Studio or select Run > Toggle Breakpoint in Visual Studio Code. A breakpoint is shown as a red dot alongside the code statement, as shown in figure 4.7, and will interrupt execution and pass control to the user.

Figure 4.7   Setting a breakpoint

Start the project by selecting Debug > Start Debugging in Visual Studio or selecting Run > Start Debugging in Visual Studio Code. (Choose .NET if Visual Studio Code prompts you to select an environment and then select the Start Debugging menu item again.)

   The application will be started and continue normally until the statement to which the breakpoint is reached, at which point execution is halted. Execution can be controlled using the Debug or Run menu or the controls that Visual Studio and Visual Studio Code display. Both debuggers are packed with features—more so if you have a paid-for version of Visual Studio—and I don't describe them in depth in this book. The Visual Studio debugger is described at https://docs.microsoft.com/en-us/visual studio/debugger, and the Visual Studio Code debugger is described at https://code .visualstudio.com/docs/editor/debugging.

How I debug my code

Debuggers are powerful tools, but I rarely use them. In most situations, I prefer to add `Console.WriteLine` statements to my code to figure out what is going on, which I can easily do because I use the `dotnet run` command to run my projects from the command line. This is a rudimentary approach that works for me, not least because most of the errors in my code tend to be where statements are not being called because a condition in an `if` statement isn't effective. If I want to examine an object in detail, I tend to serialize it to JSON and pass the result to the `WriteLine` method.

This may seem like madness if you are a dedicated user of the debugger, but it has the advantage of being quick and simple. When I am trying to figure out why code isn't working, I want to explore and iterate quickly, and I find the amount of time taken to start the debugger to be a barrier. My approach is also reliable. The Visual Studio and Visual Studio Code debuggers are sophisticated, but they are not always entirely predictable, and .NET and ASP.NET Core change too quickly for the debugger features to have entirely settled down. When I am utterly confused by the behavior of some code, I want the simplest possible diagnostic tool, and that, for me, is a message written to the console.

I am not suggesting that this is the approach you should use, but it can be a good place to start when you are not getting the results you expect and you don't want to battle with the debugger to figure out why.

Summary

- ASP.NET Core projects are created with the `dotnet new` command.
- There are templates to jumpstart popular project types and to create common project items.
- The `dotnet build` command compiles a project.
- The `dotnet run` command builds and executes a project.
- The `dotnet watch` command builds and executes a project, and performs hot reloading when changes are detected.
- Packages are added to a project with the `dotnet add package` command.
- Tool packages are installing using the `dotnet tool install` command.
- Client-side packages are managed with the `libman` tool package.

Essential C# features

5

This chapter covers

- Using C# language features for ASP.NET Core development
- Dealing with null values and the null state analysis feature
- Creating objects concisely
- Adding features to classes without directly modifying them
- Expressing functions concisely
- Modifying interfaces without breaking implementation classes
- Defining asynchronous methods

In this chapter, I describe C# features used in web application development that are not widely understood or that often cause confusion. This is not a book about C#, however, so I provide only a brief example for each feature so that you can follow the examples in the rest of the book and take advantage of these features in your projects. Table 5.1 provides a guide to this chapter.

Table 5.1   Chapter guide

Problem	Solution	Listing
Reducing duplication in `using` statements	Use global or implicit `using` statements.	8–10
Managing null values	Use nullable and non-nullable types, which are managed with the null management operators.	11–20
Mixing static and dynamic values in strings	Use string interpolation.	21
Initializing and populate objects	Use the object and collection initializers and target-typed `new` expressions.	22–26
Assigning a value for specific types	Use pattern matching.	27, 28
Extending the functionality of a class without modifying it	Define an extension method.	29–36
Expressing functions and methods concisely	Use lambda expressions.	37–44
Defining a variable without explicitly declaring its type	Use the `var` keyword.	45–47
Modifying an interface without requiring changes in its implementation classes	Define a default implementation.	48–52
Performing work asynchronously	Use tasks or the `async`/`await` keywords.	53–55
Producing a sequence of values over time	Use an asynchronous enumerable.	56–59
Getting the name of a class or member	Use a `nameof` expression.	60, 61

5.1   Preparing for this chapter

To create the example project for this chapter, open a new PowerShell command prompt and run the commands shown in listing 5.1. If you are using Visual Studio and prefer not to use the command line, you can create the project using the process described in chapter 4.

> **TIP**   You can download the example project for this chapter—and for all the other chapters in this book—from https://github.com/manningbooks/pro-asp .net-core-7. See chapter 1 for how to get help if you have problems running the examples.

Listing 5.1   Creating the example project

```
dotnet new globaljson --sdk-version 7.0.100 --output LanguageFeatures
dotnet new web --no-https --output LanguageFeatures --framework net7.0
dotnet new sln -o LanguageFeatures
dotnet sln LanguageFeatures add LanguageFeatures
```

5.1.1 Opening the project

If you are using Visual Studio, select File > Open > Project/Solution, select the `LanguageFeatures.sln` file in the `LanguageFeatures` folder, and click the Open button to open the solution file and the project it references. If you are using Visual Studio Code, select File > Open Folder, navigate to the `LanguageFeatures` folder, and click the Select Folder button.

5.1.2 Enabling the MVC Framework

The `web` project template creates a project that contains a minimal ASP.NET Core configuration. This means the placeholder content that is added by the `mvc` template used in chapter 3 is not available and that extra steps are required to reach the point where the application can produce useful output. In this section, I make the changes required to set up the MVC Framework, which is one of the application frameworks supported by ASP.NET Core, as I explained in chapter 1. First, to enable the MVC framework, make the changes shown in listing 5.2 to the `Program.cs` file.

> **Listing 5.2   Enabling MVC in the Program.cs file in the LanguageFeatures folder**

```
var builder = WebApplication.CreateBuilder(args);

builder.Services.AddControllersWithViews();

var app = builder.Build();

//app.MapGet("/", () => "Hello World!");
app.MapDefaultControllerRoute();

app.Run();
```

I explain how to configure ASP.NET Core applications in part 2, but the two statements added in listing 5.2 provide a basic MVC framework setup using a default configuration.

5.1.3 Creating the application components

Now that the MVC framework is set up, I can add the application components that I will use to demonstrate important C# language features. As you create these components, you will see that the code editor underlines some expressions to warn you of potential problems. These are safe to ignore until the "Understanding Null State Analysis" section, where I explain their significance.

CREATING THE DATA MODEL

I started by creating a simple model class so that I can have some data to work with. I added a folder called `Models` and created a class file called `Product.cs` within it, which I used to define the class shown in listing 5.3.

Listing 5.3   The contents of the Product.cs file in the Models folder

```
namespace LanguageFeatures.Models {
    public class Product {

        public string Name { get; set; }
        public decimal? Price { get; set; }

        public static Product[] GetProducts() {

            Product kayak = new Product {
                Name = "Kayak", Price = 275M
            };

            Product lifejacket = new Product {
                Name = "Lifejacket", Price = 48.95M
            };

            return new Product[] { kayak, lifejacket, null };
        }
    }
}
```

The Product class defines Name and Price properties, and there is a static method
called GetProducts that returns a Product array. One of the elements contained
in the array returned by the GetProducts method is set to null, which I will use to
demonstrate some useful language features later in the chapter.

The Visual Studio and Visual Studio Code editors will highlight a problem with the
Name property. This is a deliberate error that I explain later in the chapter and which
should be ignored for now.

CREATING THE CONTROLLER AND VIEW

For the examples in this chapter, I use a simple controller class to demonstrate different language features. I created a Controllers folder and added to it a class file called
HomeController.cs, the contents of which are shown in listing 5.4.

Listing 5.4   The contents of the HomeController.cs file in the Controllers folder

```
using Microsoft.AspNetCore.Mvc;

namespace LanguageFeatures.Controllers {
    public class HomeController : Controller {

        public ViewResult Index() {
            return View(new string[] { "C#", "Language", "Features" });
        }
    }
}
```

The Index action method tells ASP.NET Core to render the default view and provides
it with an array of strings as its view model, which will be included in the HTML sent
to the client. To create the view, I added a Views/Home folder (by creating a Views

folder and then adding a `Home` folder within it) and added a Razor View called `Index`
`.cshtml`, the contents of which are shown in listing 5.5.

> **Listing 5.5   The contents of the Index.cshtml file in the Views/Home folder**

```
@model IEnumerable<string>
@{ Layout = null; }

<!DOCTYPE html>
<html>
<head>
    <meta name="viewport" content="width=device-width" />
    <title>Language Features</title>
</head>
<body>
    <ul>
        @foreach (string s in Model) {
            <li>@s</li>
        }
    </ul>
</body>
</html>
```

The code editor will highlight part of this file to denote a warning, which I explain
shortly.

5.1.4   Selecting the HTTP port

Change the HTTP port that ASP.NET Core uses to receive requests, as shown in listing
5.6.

> **Listing 5.6   Setting the HTTP port in the launchSettings.json file in the Properties
> folder**

```
{
  "iisSettings": {
    "windowsAuthentication": false,
    "anonymousAuthentication": true,
    "iisExpress": {
      "applicationUrl": "http://localhost:5000",
      "sslPort": 0
    }
  },
  "profiles": {
    "LanguageFeatures": {
      "commandName": "Project",
      "dotnetRunMessages": true,
      "launchBrowser": true,
      "applicationUrl": "http://localhost:5000",
      "environmentVariables": {
        "ASPNETCORE_ENVIRONMENT": "Development"
      }
    },
    "IIS Express": {
      "commandName": "IISExpress",
```

```
      "launchBrowser": true,
      "environmentVariables": {
        "ASPNETCORE_ENVIRONMENT": "Development"
      }
    }
  }
 }
}
```

5.1.5   Running the example application

Start ASP.NET Core by running the command shown in listing 5.7 in the `Language-Features` folder.

Listing 5.7   Running the example application

```
dotnet run
```

The output from the `dotnet run` command will include two build warnings, which I explain in the "Understanding Null State Analysis" section. Once ASP.NET Core has started, use a web browser to request http://localhost:5000, and you will see the output shown in figure 5.1.

Figure 5.1   Running the example application

Since the output from all the examples in this chapter is text, I will show the messages displayed by the browser like this:

```
C#
Language
Features
```

5.2   Understanding top-level statements

Top-level statements are intended to remove unnecessary code structure from class files. A project can contain one file that defines code statements outside of a namespace or a file. For ASP.NET Core applications, this feature is used to configure the application in the `Program.cs` file. Here is the content of the `Program.cs` file in the example application for this chapter:

```
var builder = WebApplication.CreateBuilder(args);

builder.Services.AddControllersWithViews();
```

```
var app = builder.Build();

//app.MapGet("/", () => "Hello World!");

app.MapDefaultControllerRoute();

app.Run();
```

If you have used earlier versions of ASP.NET Core, you will be familiar with the `Startup` class, which was used to configure the application. Top-level statements have allowed this process to be simplified, and all of the configuration statements are now defined in the `Program.cs` file.

The compiler will report an error if there is more than one file in a project with top-level statements, so the `Program.cs` file is the only place you will find them in an ASP.NET Core project.

5.3 *Understanding global using statements*

C# supports global `using` statements, which allow a `using` statement to be defined once but take effect throughout a project. Traditionally, each code file contains a series of `using` statements that declare dependencies on the namespaces that it requires. Listing 5.8 adds a `using` statement that provides access to the types defined in the `Models` namespace. (The code editor will highlight part of this code listing, which I explain in the "Understanding Null State Analysis" section.)

> Listing 5.8 Adding a statement in the HomeController.cs file in the Controllers folder

```
using Microsoft.AspNetCore.Mvc;
using LanguageFeatures.Models;

namespace LanguageFeatures.Controllers {
    public class HomeController : Controller {

        public ViewResult Index() {
            Product[] products = Product.GetProducts();
            return View(new string[] { products[0].Name });
        }
    }
}
```

To access the `Product` class, I added a `using` statement for the namespace that contains it, which is `LanguageFeatures.Models`. The code file already contains a `using` statement for the `Microsoft.AspNetCore.Mvc` namespace, which provides access to the `Controller` class, from which the `HomeController` class is derived.

In most projects, some namespaces are required throughout the application, such as those containing data model classes. This can result in a long list of `using` statements, duplicated in every code file. Global `using` statements address this problem by allowing `using` statements for commonly required namespaces to be defined in a single location. Add a code file named `GlobalUsings.cs` to the `LanguageFeatures` project with the content shown in listing 5.9.

Listing 5.9   The contents of the GlobalUsings.cs file in the LanguageFeatures folder

```
global using LanguageFeatures.Models;
global using Microsoft.AspNetCore.Mvc;
```

The `global` keyword is used to denote a global `using`. The statements in listing 5.9 make the `LanguageFeatures.Models` and `Microsoft.AspNetCore.Mvc` namespaces available throughout the application, which means they can be removed from the `HomeController.cs` file, as shown in listing 5.10.

Listing 5.10   Removing statements in the HomeController.cs file in the Controllers folder

```
//using Microsoft.AspNetCore.Mvc;
//using LanguageFeatures.Models;

namespace LanguageFeatures.Controllers {
    public class HomeController : Controller {

        public ViewResult Index() {
            Product[] products = Product.GetProducts();
            return View(new string[] { products[0].Name });
        }
    }
}
```

If you run the example, you will see the following results displayed in the browser window:

```
Kayak
```

You will receive warnings when compiling the project, which I explain in the "Understanding Null State Analysis" section.

> **NOTE**   Global `using` statements are a good idea, but I have not used them in this book because I want to make it obvious when I add a dependency to a new namespace.

5.3.1   Understanding implicit using statements

The ASP.NET Core project templates enable a feature named *implicit usings*, which define global `using` statements for these commonly required namespaces:

- `System`
- `System.Collections.Generic`
- `System.IO`
- `System.Linq`
- `System.Net.Http`
- `System.Net.Http.Json`
- `System.Threading`
- `System.Threading.Tasks`

- `Microsoft.AspNetCore.Builder`
- `Microsoft.AspNetCore.Hosting`
- `Microsoft.AspNetCore.Http`
- `Microsoft.AspNetCore.Routing`
- `Microsoft.Extensions.Configuration`
- `Microsoft.Extensions.DependencyInjection`
- `Microsoft.Extensions.Hosting`
- `Microsoft.Extensions.Logging`

`using` statements are not required for these namespaces, which are available throughout the application. These namespaces don't cover all of the ASP.NET Core features, but they do cover the basics, which is why no explicit `using` statements are required in the `Program.cs` file.

5.4 Understanding null state analysis

The editor and compiler warnings shown in earlier sections are produced because ASP.NET Core project templates enable *null state analysis*, in which the compiler identifies attempts to access references that may be unintentionally null, preventing null reference exceptions at runtime.

Open the `Product.cs` file, and the editor will display two warnings, as shown in figure 5.2. The figure shows how Visual Studio displays a warning, but Visual Studio Code is similar.

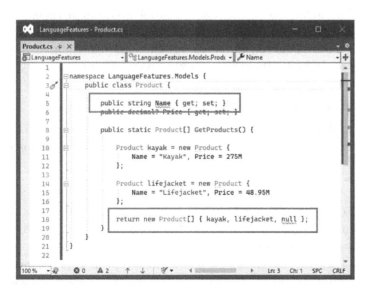

Figure 5.2 A null state analysis warning

When null state analysis is enabled, C# variables are divided into two groups: nullable and non-nullable. As their name suggests, nullable variables can be assigned the special value `null`. This is the behavior that most programmers are familiar with, and it is entirely up to the developer to guard against trying to use `null` references, which will trigger a `NullReferenceException`.

By contrast, non-nullable variables can never be `null`. When you receive a non-nullable variable, you don't have to guard against a `null` value because that is not a value that can ever be assigned.

A question mark (the `?` character) is appended to a type to denote a nullable type. So, if a variable's type is `string?`, for example, then it can be assigned any value `string` value or `null`. When attempting to access this variable, you should check to ensure that it isn't `null` before attempting to access any of the fields, properties, or methods defined by the `string` type.

If a variable's type is `string`, then it cannot be assigned `null` values, which means you can confidently access the features it provides without needing to guard against `null` references.

The compiler examines the code in the project and warns you when it finds statements that might break these rules. The most common issues are attempting to assign `null` to non-nullable variables and attempting to access members defined by nullable variables without checking to see if they are `null`. In the sections that follow, I explain the different ways that the warnings raised by the compiler in the example application can be addressed.

> **NOTE** Getting to grips with nullable and non-nullable types can be frustrating. A change in one code file can simply move a warning to another part of the application, and it can feel like you are chasing problems through a project. But it is worth sticking with null state analysis because null reference exceptions are the most common runtime error, and few programmers are disciplined enough to guard against null values without the compiler analysis feature.

5.4.1   *Ensuring fields and properties are assigned values*

The first warning in the `Product.cs` file is for the `Name` field, whose type is `string`, which is a non-nullable type (because it hasn't been annotated with a question mark).

```
...
public string Name { get; set; }
...
```

One consequence of using non-nullable types is that properties like `Name` must be assigned a value when a new instance of the enclosing class is created. If this were not the case, then the `Name` property would not be initialized and would be `null`. And this is a problem because we can't assign `null` to a non-nullable property, even indirectly.

The `required` keyword can be used to indicate that a value is required for a non-nullable type, as shown in listing 5.11.

Listing 5.11 Using the required keyword in the Product.cs file in the Models folder

```
namespace LanguageFeatures.Models {
    public class Product {

        public required string Name { get; set; }
        public decimal? Price { get; set; }

        public static Product[] GetProducts() {

            Product kayak = new Product {
                Name = "Kayak", Price = 275M
            };

            Product lifejacket = new Product {
                Name = "Lifejacket", Price = 48.95M
            };

            return new Product[] { kayak, lifejacket, null };
        }
    }
}
```

The compiler will check to make sure that a value is assigned to the property when a new instance of the containing type is created. The two `Product` objects used in the listing are created with a value for the `Name` field, which satisfies the demands of the `required` keyword. Listing 5.12 omits the `Name` value from one of `Product` objects.

Listing 5.12 Omitting a value in the Product.cs file in the Models folder

```
namespace LanguageFeatures.Models {
    public class Product {

        public required string Name { get; set; }
        public decimal? Price { get; set; }

        public static Product[] GetProducts() {

            Product kayak = new Product {
                Name = "Kayak", Price = 275M
            };

            Product lifejacket = new Product {
                //Name = "Lifejacket",
                Price = 48.95M
            };

            return new Product[] { kayak, lifejacket, null };
        }
    }
}
```

If you run the example, the build process will fail with this error:

```
Required member 'Product.Name' must be set in the object initializer or
attribute constructor.
```

This error—and the corresponding red line in the code editor—tell you that a value for the `Name` property is required but has not been provided.

5.4.2 *Providing a default value for non-nullable types*

The `required` keyword is a good way to denote a property that cannot be `null`, and which requires a value when an object is created. This approach can become cumbersome in situations where there may not always be a suitable data value available, because it requires the code wants to create the object to provide a fallback value and there is no good way to enforce consistency.

For these situations a default value can be used instead of the `required` keyword, as shown in listing 5.13.

Listing 5.13   Providing a default value in the Product.cs file in the Models folder

```
namespace LanguageFeatures.Models {
    public class Product {

        public string Name { get; set; } = string.Empty;
        public decimal? Price { get; set; }

        public static Product[] GetProducts() {

            Product kayak = new Product {
                Name = "Kayak", Price = 275M
            };

            Product lifejacket = new Product {
                //Name = "Lifejacket",
                Price = 48.95M
            };

            return new Product[] { kayak, lifejacket, null };
        }
    }
}
```

The default value in this example is the empty string. This value will be replaced for `Product` objects that are created with a `Name` value and ensures consistency for objects that are created without one.

5.4.3 *Using nullable types*

The remaining warning in the `Product.cs` file occurs because there is a mismatch between the type used for the result of the `GetProducts` method and the values that are used to initialize it:

```
...
return new Product[] { kayak, lifejacket, null };
...
```

The type of the array that is created is `Product[]`, which contains non-nullable `Product` references. But one of the values used to populate the array is `null`, which isn't allowed. Listing 5.14 changes the array type so that nullable values are allowed.

Listing 5.14 Using a nullable type in the Product.cs file in the Models folder

```
namespace LanguageFeatures.Models {
    public class Product {

        public string Name { get; set; } = string.Empty;
        public decimal? Price { get; set; }

        public static Product?[] GetProducts() {

            Product kayak = new Product {
                Name = "Kayak", Price = 275M
            };

            Product lifejacket = new Product {
                //Name = "Lifejacket",
                Price = 48.95M
            };

            return new Product?[] { kayak, lifejacket, null };
        }
    }
}
```

The type `Product?[]` denotes an array of `Product?` references, which means the result can include `null`. Notice that I had to make the same change to the result type declared by the `GetProducts` method because a `Product?[]` array cannot be used where a `Product[]` is expected.

Selecting the right nullable type

Care must be taken to apply the question mark correctly, especially when dealing with arrays and collections. A variable of type `Product?[]` denotes an array that can contain `Product` or `null` values but that won't be `null` itself:

```
...
Product?[] arr1 = new Product?[] { kayak, lifejacket, null }; // OK
Product?[] arr2 = null;                                       // Not OK
...
```

A variable of type `Product[]?` is an array that can hold only `Product` values and not `null` values, but the array itself may be `null`:

```
...
Product[]? arr1 = new Product?[] { kayak, lifejacket, null }; // Not OK
Product[]? arr2 = null;                                       // OK
...
```

A variable of type `Product?[]?` is an array that can contain `Product` or `null` values and that can itself be `null`:

```
...
Product?[]? arr1 = new Product?[] { kayak, lifejacket, null }; // OK
Product?[]? arr2 = null;                                       // Also OK
...
```

> *(continued)*
>
> Null state analysis is a useful feature, but that doesn't mean it is always easy to understand.

5.4.4   *Checking for null values*

I explained that dealing with null state analysis warnings can feel like chasing a problem through code, and you can see a simple example of this in the `HomeController.cs` file in the `Controllers` folder. In listing 5.14, I changed the type returned by the `GetProducts` method to allow `null` values, but that has created a mismatch in the `HomeController` class, which invokes that method and assigns the result to an array of non-nullable `Product` values:

```
...
Product[] products = Product.GetProducts();
...
```

This is easily resolved by changing the type of the `products` variable to match the type returned by the `GetProducts` method, as shown in listing 5.15.

> **Listing 5.15   Changing Type in the HomeController.cs File in the Controllers Folder**

```
namespace LanguageFeatures.Controllers {
    public class HomeController : Controller {

        public ViewResult Index() {
            Product?[] products = Product.GetProducts();
            return View(new string[] { products[0].Name });
        }
    }
}
```

This resolves one warning and introduces another, as shown in figure 5.3.

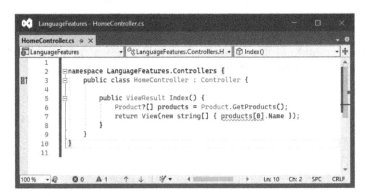

Figure 5.3   An additional null state analysis warning

The statement flagged by the compiler attempts to access the Name field of the element at index zero in the array, which might be null since the array type is Product?[]. Addressing this issue requires a check for null values, as shown in listing 5.16.

```
namespace LanguageFeatures.Controllers {
    public class HomeController : Controller {

        public ViewResult Index() {
            Product?[] products = Product.GetProducts();
            Product? p = products[0];
            string val;
            if (p != null) {
                val = p.Name;
            } else {
                val = "No value";
            }
            return View(new string[] { val });
        }
    }
}
```

This is an especially verbose way of avoiding a null, which I will refine shortly. But it demonstrates an important point, which is that the compiler can understand the effect of C# expressions when checking for a null reference. In listing 5.16, I use an if statement to see if a Product? variable is not null, and the compiler understands that the variable cannot be null within the scope of the if clause and doesn't generate a warning when I read the name field:

```
...
if (p != null) {
    val = p.Name;
} else {
    val = "No value";
}
...
```

The compiler has a sophisticated understanding of C# but doesn't always get it right, and I explain what to do when the compiler isn't able to accurately determine whether a variable is null in the "Overriding Null State Analysis" section.

USING THE NULL CONDITIONAL OPERATOR

The null conditional operator is a more concise way of avoiding member access for null values, as shown in listing 5.17.

```
namespace LanguageFeatures.Controllers {
    public class HomeController : Controller {

        public ViewResult Index() {
```

```
        Product?[] products = Product.GetProducts();

        string? val = products[0]?.Name;
        if (val != null) {
            return View(new string[] { val });
        }
        return View(new string[] { "No Value" });
    }
  }
}
```

The null conditional operator is a question mark applied before a member is accessed, like this:

```
...
string? val = products[0]?.Name;
...
```

The operator returns `null` if it is applied to a variable that is `null`. In this case, if the element at index zero of the products array is `null`, then the operator will return `null` and prevent an attempt to access the `Name` property, which would cause an exception. If `products[0]` isn't `null`, then the operator does nothing, and the expression returns the value assigned to the `Name` property. Applying the null conditional operator can return `null`, and its result must always be assigned to a nullable variable, such as the `string?` used in this example.

USING THE NULL-COALESCING OPERATOR

The null-coalescing operator is two question mark characters (`??`) and is used to provide a fallback value, often used in conjunction with the null conditional operator, as shown in listing 5.18.

> **Listing 5.18   Using the null-coalescing operator in the HomeController.cs file in the Controllers folder**

```
namespace LanguageFeatures.Controllers {
    public class HomeController : Controller {

        public ViewResult Index() {
            Product?[] products = Product.GetProducts();
            return View(new string[] { products[0]?.Name ?? "No Value" });
        }
    }
}
```

The `??` operator returns the value of its left-hand operand if it isn't `null`. If the left-hand operand is `null`, then the `??` operator returns the value of its right-hand operand. This behavior works well with the null conditional operator. If `products[0]` is null, then the `?` operator will return `null`, and the `??` operator will return `"No Value"`. If `products[0]` isn't `null`, then the result will be the value of its `Name` property. This is a more concise way of performing the same null checks shown in earlier examples.

NOTE The ? and ?? operators cannot always be used, and you will see examples in later chapters where I use an if statement to check for null values. One common example is when using the await/async keywords, which are described later in this chapter, and which do not integrate well with the null conditional operator.

5.4.5 Overriding null state analysis

The C# compiler has a sophisticated understanding of when a variable can be null, but it doesn't always get it right, and there are times when you have a better understanding of whether a null value can arise than the compiler. In these situations, the null-forgiving operator can be used to tell the compiler that a variable isn't null, regardless of what the null state analysis suggests, as shown in listing 5.19.

Listing 5.19 Using the null-forgiving operator in the HomeController.cs file in the Controllers folder

```
namespace LanguageFeatures.Controllers {
    public class HomeController : Controller {

        public ViewResult Index() {
            Product?[] products = Product.GetProducts();
            return View(new string[] { products[0]!.Name });
        }
    }
}
```

The null-forgiving operator is an exclamation mark and is used in this example to tell the compiler that products[0] isn't null, even though null state analysis has identified that it might be.

When using the ! operator, you are telling the compiler that you have better insight into whether a variable can be null, and, naturally, this should be done only when you are entirely confident that you are right.

5.4.6 Disabling null state analysis warnings

An alternative to the null-forgiving operator is to disable null state analysis warnings for a particular section of code or a complete code file, as shown in listing 5.20.

Listing 5.20 Disabling warnings in the HomeController.cs file in the Controllers folder

```
namespace LanguageFeatures.Controllers {
    public class HomeController : Controller {

        public ViewResult Index() {
            Product?[] products = Product.GetProducts();
            #pragma warning disable CS8602
            return View(new string[] { products[0].Name });
        }
    }
}
```

This listing uses a #pragma directive to suppress warning CS8602 (you can identify warnings in the output from the build process).

> **NOTE** .NET includes a set of advanced attributes that can be used to provide the compiler with guidance for null state analysis. These are not widely used and are encountered only in chapter 36 of this book because they are used by one part of the ASP.NET Core API. See https://docs.microsoft.com/en-us/dotnet/csharp/language-reference/attributes/nullable-analysis for details.

5.5   *Using string interpolation*

C# supports *string interpolation* to create formatted strings, which uses templates with variable names that are resolved and inserted into the output, as shown in listing 5.21.

> **Listing 5.21   Using string interpolation in the HomeController.cs file in the Controllers folder**

```
namespace LanguageFeatures.Controllers {
    public class HomeController : Controller {

        public ViewResult Index() {
            Product?[] products = Product.GetProducts();

            return View(new string[] {
                $"Name: {products[0]?.Name}, Price: { products[0]?.Price }"
            });
        }
    }
}
```

Interpolated strings are prefixed with the $ character and contain *holes*, which are references to values contained within the { and } characters. When the string is evaluated, the holes are filled in with the current values of the variables or constants that are specified.

> **TIP** String interpolation supports the string format specifiers, which can be applied within holes, so $"Price: {price:C2}" would format the price value as a currency value with two decimal digits, for example.

Start ASP.NET Core and request http://localhost:5000, and you will see a formatted string:

```
Name: Kayak, Price: 275
```

5.6   *Using object and collection initializers*

When I create an object in the static GetProducts method of the Product class, I use an *object initializer*, which allows me to create an object and specify its property values in a single step, like this:

```
...
Product kayak = new Product {
    Name = "Kayak", Price = 275M
```

```
};
...
```

This is another syntactic sugar feature that makes C# easier to use. Without this feature, I would have to call the `Product` constructor and then use the newly created object to set each of the properties, like this:

```
...
Product kayak = new Product();
kayak.Name = "Kayak";
kayak.Price = 275M;
...
```

A related feature is the *collection initializer*, which allows the creation of a collection and its contents to be specified in a single step. Without an initializer, creating a string array, for example, requires the size of the array and the array elements to be specified separately, as shown in listing 5.22.

Listing 5.22 Initializing an object in the HomeController.cs file in the Controllers folder

```
namespace LanguageFeatures.Controllers {

    public class HomeController : Controller {

        public ViewResult Index() {
            string[] names = new string[3];
            names[0] = "Bob";
            names[1] = "Joe";
            names[2] = "Alice";
            return View("Index", names);
        }
    }
}
```

Using a collection initializer allows the contents of the array to be specified as part of the construction, which implicitly provides the compiler with the size of the array, as shown in listing 5.23.

Listing 5.23 A collection initializer in the HomeController.cs file in the Controllers folder

```
namespace LanguageFeatures.Controllers {

    public class HomeController : Controller {

        public ViewResult Index() {
            return View("Index", new string[] { "Bob", "Joe", "Alice" });
        }
    }
}
```

The array elements are specified between the { and } characters, which allows for a more concise definition of the collection and makes it possible to define a collection inline within a method call. The code in listing 5.23 has the same effect as the code in listing 5.22. Restart ASP.NET Core and request http://localhost:5000, and you will see the following output in the browser window:

```
Bob
Joe
Alice
```

5.6.1   *Using an Index Initializer*

Recent versions of C# tidy up the way collections that use indexes, such as dictionaries, are initialized. Listing 5.24 shows the `Index` action rewritten to define a collection using the traditional C# approach to initializing a dictionary.

> **Listing 5.24   Initializing a dictionary in the HomeController.cs file in the Controllers folder**

```csharp
namespace LanguageFeatures.Controllers {

    public class HomeController : Controller {

        public ViewResult Index() {
            Dictionary<string, Product> products
                = new Dictionary<string, Product> {
                {
                    "Kayak",
                    new Product { Name = "Kayak", Price = 275M }
                },
                {
                    "Lifejacket",
                    new Product{ Name = "Lifejacket", Price = 48.95M }
                }
            };
            return View("Index", products.Keys);
        }
    }
}
```

The syntax for initializing this type of collection relies too much on the { and } characters, especially when the collection values are created using object initializers. The latest versions of C# support a more natural approach to initializing indexed collections that is consistent with the way that values are retrieved or modified once the collection has been initialized, as shown in listing 5.25.

> **Listing 5.25   Using collection initializer syntax in the HomeController.cs file in the Controllers folder**

```csharp
namespace LanguageFeatures.Controllers {

    public class HomeController : Controller {

        public ViewResult Index() {
            Dictionary<string, Product> products
                = new Dictionary<string, Product> {
                ["Kayak"] = new Product { Name = "Kayak", Price = 275M },
                ["Lifejacket"] = new Product { Name = "Lifejacket",
```

```
                    Price = 48.95M }
            };
            return View("Index", products.Keys);
        }
    }
}
```

The effect is the same—to create a dictionary whose keys are `Kayak` and `Lifejacket` and whose values are `Product` objects—but the elements are created using the index notation that is used for other collection operations. Restart ASP.NET Core and request http://localhost:5000, and you will see the following results in the browser:

```
Kayak
Lifejacket
```

5.7 *Using target-typed new expressions*

The example in listing 5.25 is still verbose and declares the collection type when defining the variable and creating an instance with the `new` keyword:

```
...
Dictionary<string, Product> products = new Dictionary<string, Product> {
    ["Kayak"] = new Product { Name = "Kayak", Price = 275M },
    ["Lifejacket"] = new Product { Name = "Lifejacket", Price = 48.95M }
};
...
```

This can be simplified using a target-typed `new` expression, as shown in listing 5.26.

> **Listing 5.26   Using a target-typed new expression in the HomeController.cs file in the Controllers folder**

```
namespace LanguageFeatures.Controllers {

    public class HomeController : Controller {

        public ViewResult Index() {
            Dictionary<string, Product> products = new () {
                ["Kayak"] = new Product { Name = "Kayak", Price = 275M },
                ["Lifejacket"] = new Product { Name = "Lifejacket",
                    Price = 48.95M }
            };
            return View("Index", products.Keys);
        }
    }
}
```

The type can be replaced with `new()` when the compiler can determine which type is required and constructor arguments are provided as arguments to the `new` method. Creating instances with the `new()` expression works only when the compiler can determine which type is required. Restart ASP.NET Core and request http://localhost:5000, and you will see the following results in the browser:

```
Kayak
Lifejacket
```

5.8   Pattern Matching

One of the most useful recent additions to C# is support for pattern matching, which can be used to test that an object is of a specific type or has specific characteristics. This is another form of syntactic sugar, and it can dramatically simplify complex blocks of conditional statements. The is keyword is used to perform a type test, as demonstrated in listing 5.27.

Listing 5.27   Testing a type in the HomeController.cs file in the Controllers folder

```
namespace LanguageFeatures.Controllers {

    public class HomeController : Controller {

        public ViewResult Index() {

            object[] data = new object[] { 275M, 29.95M,
                "apple", "orange", 100, 10 };
            decimal total = 0;
            for (int i = 0; i < data.Length; i++) {
                if (data[i] is decimal d) {
                    total += d;
                }
            }

            return View("Index", new string[] { $"Total: {total:C2}" });
        }
    }
}
```

The is keyword performs a type check and, if a value is of the specified type, will assign the value to a new variable, like this:

```
...
if (data[i] is decimal d) {
...
```

This expression evaluates as true if the value stored in data[i] is a decimal. The value of data[i] will be assigned to the variable d, which allows it to be used in subsequent statements without needing to perform any type conversions. The is keyword will match only the specified type, which means that only two of the values in the data array will be processed (the other items in the array are string and int values). If you run the application, you will see the following output in the browser window:

```
Total: $304.95
```

5.8.1   Pattern matching in switch statements

Pattern matching can also be used in switch statements, which support the when keyword for restricting when a value is matched by a case statement, as shown in listing 5.28.

Listing 5.28 Pattern matching in the HomeController.cs file in the Controllers folder

```
namespace LanguageFeatures.Controllers {

    public class HomeController : Controller {

        public ViewResult Index() {

            object[] data = new object[] { 275M, 29.95M,
                "apple", "orange", 100, 10 };
            decimal total = 0;
            for (int i = 0; i < data.Length; i++) {
                switch (data[i]) {
                    case decimal decimalValue:
                        total += decimalValue;
                        break;
                    case int intValue when intValue > 50:
                        total += intValue;
                        break;
                }
            }

            return View("Index", new string[] { $"Total: {total:C2}" });
        }
    }
}
```

To match any value of a specific type, use the type and variable name in the case statement, like this:

```
...
case decimal decimalValue:
...
```

This case statement matches any decimal value and assigns it to a new variable called decimalValue. To be more selective, the when keyword can be included, like this:

```
...
case int intValue when intValue > 50:
...
```

This case statement matches int values and assigns them to a variable called intValue, but only when the value is greater than 50. Restart ASP.NET Core and request http://localhost:5000, and you will see the following output in the browser window:

```
Total: $404.95
```

5.9   *Using extension methods*

Extension methods are a convenient way of adding methods to classes that you cannot modify directly, typically because they are provided by Microsoft or a third-party package. Listing 5.29 shows the definition of the ShoppingCart class, which I added to the Models folder in a class file called ShoppingCart.cs and which represents a collection of Product objects.

Listing 5.29   The contents of the ShoppingCart.cs file in the Models folder

```
namespace LanguageFeatures.Models {

    public class ShoppingCart {
        public IEnumerable<Product?>? Products { get; set; }
    }
}
```

This is a simple class that acts as a wrapper around a sequence of `Product` objects (I only need a basic class for this example). Note the type of the `Products` property, which denotes a nullable enumerable of nullable `Products`, meaning that the `Products` property may be `null` and that any sequence of elements assigned to the property may contain `null` values.

Suppose I need to be able to determine the total value of the `Product` objects in the `ShoppingCart` class, but I cannot modify the class because it comes from a third party, and I do not have the source code. I can use an extension method to add the functionality I need.

Add a class file named `MyExtensionMethods.cs` in the `Models` folder and use it to define the class shown in listing 5.30.

Listing 5.30   The contents of the MyExtensionMethods.cs file in the Models folder

```
namespace LanguageFeatures.Models {

    public static class MyExtensionMethods {

        public static decimal TotalPrices(this ShoppingCart cartParam) {
            decimal total = 0;
            if (cartParam.Products != null) {
                foreach (Product? prod in cartParam.Products) {
                    total += prod?.Price ?? 0;
                }
            }
            return total;
        }
    }
}
```

Extension methods are `static` and are defined in `static` classes. Listing 5.30 defines a single extension method named `TotalPrices`. The `this` keyword in front of the first parameter marks `TotalPrices` as an extension method. The first parameter tells .NET which class the extension method can be applied to—`ShoppingCart` in this case. I can refer to the instance of the `ShoppingCart` that the extension method has been applied to by using the `cartParam` parameter. This extension method enumerates the `Product` objects in the `ShoppingCart` and returns the sum of the `Product.Price` property values. Listing 5.31 shows how I apply the extension method in the `Home` controller's action method.

NOTE Extension methods do not let you break through the access rules that classes define for methods, fields, and properties. You can extend the functionality of a class by using an extension method but only using the class members that you had access to anyway.

> **Listing 5.31 Applying an extension method in the HomeController.cs file in the Controllers folder**

```
namespace LanguageFeatures.Controllers {
    public class HomeController : Controller {

        public ViewResult Index() {
            ShoppingCart cart
                = new ShoppingCart { Products = Product.GetProducts()};
            decimal cartTotal = cart.TotalPrices();
            return View("Index",
                new string[] { $"Total: {cartTotal:C2}" });
        }
    }
}
```
The key statement is this one:
```
...
decimal cartTotal = cart.TotalPrices();
...
```

I call the `TotalPrices` method on a `ShoppingCart` object as though it were part of the `ShoppingCart` class, even though it is an extension method defined by a different class altogether. .NET will find extension classes if they are in the scope of the current class, meaning that they are part of the same namespace or in a namespace that is the subject of a `using` statement. Restart ASP.NET Core and request http://localhost:5000, which will produce the following output in the browser window:
```
Total: $323.95
```

5.9.1 Applying extension methods to an interface

Extension methods can also be applied to an interface, which allows me to call the extension method on all the classes that implement the interface. Listing 5.32 shows the `ShoppingCart` class updated to implement the `IEnumerable<Product>` interface.

> **Listing 5.32 Implementing an interface in the ShoppingCart.cs file in the Models folder**

```
using System.Collections;

namespace LanguageFeatures.Models {

    public class ShoppingCart : IEnumerable<Product?> {
        public IEnumerable<Product?>? Products { get; set; }

        public IEnumerator<Product?> GetEnumerator() =>
                Products?.GetEnumerator()
                    ?? Enumerable.Empty<Product?>().GetEnumerator();
```

```
        IEnumerator IEnumerable.GetEnumerator() => GetEnumerator();
    }
}
```

I can now update the extension method so that it deals with IEnumerable<Product?>, as shown in listing 5.33.

Listing 5.33   Updating an extension method in the MyExtensionMethods.cs file in the
               Models folder

```
namespace LanguageFeatures.Models {

    public static class MyExtensionMethods {

        public static decimal TotalPrices(
                this IEnumerable<Product?> products) {
            decimal total = 0;
            foreach (Product? prod in products) {
                total += prod?.Price ?? 0;
            }
            return total;
        }
    }
}
```

The first parameter type has changed to IEnumerable<Product?>, which means the foreach loop in the method body works directly on Product? objects. The change to using the interface means that I can calculate the total value of the Product objects enumerated by any IEnumerable<Product?>, which includes instances of Shopping-Cart but also arrays of Product objects, as shown in listing 5.34.

Listing 5.34   Applying an extension method in the HomeController.cs file in the
               Controllers folder

```
namespace LanguageFeatures.Controllers {
    public class HomeController : Controller {

        public ViewResult Index() {
            ShoppingCart cart
                = new ShoppingCart { Products = Product.GetProducts()};

            Product[] productArray = {
                new Product {Name = "Kayak", Price = 275M},
                new Product {Name = "Lifejacket", Price = 48.95M}
            };

            decimal cartTotal = cart.TotalPrices();
            decimal arrayTotal = productArray.TotalPrices();

            return View("Index", new string[] {
                $"Cart Total: {cartTotal:C2}",
                $"Array Total: {arrayTotal:C2}" });
        }
    }
}
```

Restart ASP.NET Core and request http://localhost:5000, which will produce the following output in the browser, demonstrating that I get the same result from the extension method, irrespective of how the `Product` objects are collected:

```
Cart Total: $323.95
Array Total: $323.95
```

5.9.2 *Creating filtering extension methods*

The last thing I want to show you about extension methods is that they can be used to filter collections of objects. An extension method that operates on an `IEnumerable<T>` and that also returns an `IEnumerable<T>` can use the `yield` keyword to apply selection criteria to items in the source data to produce a reduced set of results. Listing 5.35 demonstrates such a method, which I have added to the `MyExtensionMethods` class.

> **Listing 5.35** **A filtering extension method in the MyExtensionMethods.cs file in the Models folder**

```
namespace LanguageFeatures.Models {

    public static class MyExtensionMethods {

        public static decimal TotalPrices(
                this IEnumerable<Product?> products) {
            decimal total = 0;
            foreach (Product? prod in products) {
                total += prod?.Price ?? 0;
            }
            return total;
        }

        public static IEnumerable<Product?> FilterByPrice(
                this IEnumerable<Product?> productEnum,
                decimal minimumPrice) {

            foreach (Product? prod in productEnum) {
                if ((prod?.Price ?? 0) >= minimumPrice) {
                    yield return prod;
                }
            }
        }
    }
}
```

This extension method, called `FilterByPrice`, takes an additional parameter that allows me to filter products so that `Product` objects whose `Price` property matches or exceeds the parameter are returned in the result. Listing 5.36 shows this method being used.

Listing 5.36   Using the filtering extension method in the HomeController.cs file in the Controllers folder

```
namespace LanguageFeatures.Controllers {
    public class HomeController : Controller {

        public ViewResult Index() {
            ShoppingCart cart
                = new ShoppingCart { Products = Product.GetProducts()};

            Product[] productArray = {
                new Product {Name = "Kayak", Price = 275M},
                new Product {Name = "Lifejacket", Price = 48.95M},
                new Product {Name = "Soccer ball", Price = 19.50M},
                new Product {Name = "Corner flag", Price = 34.95M}
            };

            decimal arrayTotal =
                productArray.FilterByPrice(20).TotalPrices();

            return View("Index",
                new string[] { $"Array Total: {arrayTotal:C2}" });
        }
    }
}
```

When I call the `FilterByPrice` method on the array of `Product` objects, only those that cost more than $20 are received by the `TotalPrices` method and used to calculate the total. If you run the application, you will see the following output in the browser window:

```
Total: $358.90
```

5.10   *Using lambda expressions*

Lambda expressions are a feature that causes a lot of confusion, not least because the feature they simplify is also confusing. To understand the problem that is being solved, consider the `FilterByPrice` extension method that I defined in the previous section. This method is written so that it can filter `Product` objects by price, which means I must create a second method if I want to filter by name, as shown in listing 5.37.

Listing 5.37   Adding a filter method in the MyExtensionMethods.cs file in the Models folder

```
namespace LanguageFeatures.Models {

    public static class MyExtensionMethods {

        public static decimal TotalPrices(
                this IEnumerable<Product?> products) {
            decimal total = 0;
            foreach (Product? prod in products) {
                total += prod?.Price ?? 0;
            }
```

```
                return total;
        }

        public static IEnumerable<Product?> FilterByPrice(
                this IEnumerable<Product?> productEnum,
                decimal minimumPrice) {

            foreach (Product? prod in productEnum) {
                if ((prod?.Price ?? 0) >= minimumPrice) {
                    yield return prod;
                }
            }
        }

        public static IEnumerable<Product?> FilterByName(
                this IEnumerable<Product?> productEnum,
                char firstLetter) {

            foreach (Product? prod in productEnum) {
                if (prod?.Name?[0] == firstLetter) {
                    yield return prod;
                }
            }
        }
    }
}
```

Listing 5.38 shows the use of both filter methods applied in the controller to create two different totals.

> **Listing 5.38   Using two filter methods in the HomeController.cs file in the Controllers folder**

```
namespace LanguageFeatures.Controllers {
    public class HomeController : Controller {

        public ViewResult Index() {
            ShoppingCart cart
                = new ShoppingCart { Products = Product.GetProducts() };

            Product[] productArray = {
                new Product {Name = "Kayak", Price = 275M},
                new Product {Name = "Lifejacket", Price = 48.95M},
                new Product {Name = "Soccer ball", Price = 19.50M},
                new Product {Name = "Corner flag", Price = 34.95M}
            };

            decimal priceFilterTotal =
                productArray.FilterByPrice(20).TotalPrices();
            decimal nameFilterTotal =
                productArray.FilterByName('S').TotalPrices();

            return View("Index", new string[] {
                $"Price Total: {priceFilterTotal:C2}",
                $"Name Total: {nameFilterTotal:C2}" });
```

```
        }
    }
}
```

The first filter selects all the products with a price of $20 or more, and the second filter selects products whose name starts with the letter *S*. You will see the following output in the browser window if you run the example application:

```
Price Total: $358.90
Name Total: $19.50
```

5.10.1 Defining functions

I can repeat this process indefinitely to create filter methods for every property and every combination of properties that I am interested in. A more elegant approach is to separate the code that processes the enumeration from the selection criteria. C# makes this easy by allowing functions to be passed around as objects. Listing 5.39 shows a single extension method that filters an enumeration of `Product` objects but that delegates the decision about which ones are included in the results to a separate function.

> **Listing 5.39   Creating a general filter method in the MyExtensionMethods.cs file in the Models folder**

```
namespace LanguageFeatures.Models {

    public static class MyExtensionMethods {

        public static decimal TotalPrices(
                this IEnumerable<Product?> products) {
            decimal total = 0;
            foreach (Product? prod in products) {
                total += prod?.Price ?? 0;
            }
            return total;
        }

        public static IEnumerable<Product?> FilterByPrice(
                this IEnumerable<Product?> productEnum,
                decimal minimumPrice) {

            foreach (Product? prod in productEnum) {
                if ((prod?.Price ?? 0) >= minimumPrice) {
                    yield return prod;
                }
            }
        }

        public static IEnumerable<Product?> Filter(
                this IEnumerable<Product?> productEnum,
                Func<Product?, bool> selector) {

            foreach (Product? prod in productEnum) {
                if (selector(prod)) {
                    yield return prod;
```

```
                    }
                }
            }
        }
    }
```

The second argument to the `Filter` method is a function that accepts a `Product?` object and that returns a `bool` value. The `Filter` method calls the function for each `Product?` object and includes it in the result if the function returns `true`. To use the `Filter` method, I can specify a method or create a stand-alone function, as shown in listing 5.40.

Listing 5.40 Using a function to filter objects in the HomeController.cs file in the Controllers folder

```
namespace LanguageFeatures.Controllers {
    public class HomeController : Controller {

        bool FilterByPrice(Product? p) {
            return (p?.Price ?? 0) >= 20;
        }

        public ViewResult Index() {
            ShoppingCart cart
                = new ShoppingCart { Products = Product.GetProducts()};

            Product[] productArray = {
                new Product {Name = "Kayak", Price = 275M},
                new Product {Name = "Lifejacket", Price = 48.95M},
                new Product {Name = "Soccer ball", Price = 19.50M},
                new Product {Name = "Corner flag", Price = 34.95M}
            };

            Func<Product?, bool> nameFilter = delegate (Product? prod) {
                return prod?.Name?[0] == 'S';
            };

            decimal priceFilterTotal = productArray
                .Filter(FilterByPrice)
                .TotalPrices();
            decimal nameFilterTotal = productArray
                .Filter(nameFilter)
                .TotalPrices();

            return View("Index", new string[] {
                $"Price Total: {priceFilterTotal:C2}",
                $"Name Total: {nameFilterTotal:C2}" });
        }
    }
}
```

Neither approach is ideal. Defining methods like `FilterByPrice` clutters up a class definition. Creating a `Func<Product?, bool>` object avoids this problem but uses an awkward syntax that is hard to read and hard to maintain. It is this issue that lambda expressions address by allowing functions to be defined in a more elegant and expressive way, as shown in listing 5.41.

> **Listing 5.41   Using a lambda expression in the HomeController.cs file in the Controllers folder**

```
namespace LanguageFeatures.Controllers {
    public class HomeController : Controller {

        //bool FilterByPrice(Product? p) {
        //    return (p?.Price ?? 0) >= 20;
        //}

        public ViewResult Index() {
            ShoppingCart cart
                = new ShoppingCart { Products = Product.GetProducts()};

            Product[] productArray = {
                new Product {Name = "Kayak", Price = 275M},
                new Product {Name = "Lifejacket", Price = 48.95M},
                new Product {Name = "Soccer ball", Price = 19.50M},
                new Product {Name = "Corner flag", Price = 34.95M}
            };

            //Func<Product?, bool> nameFilter = delegate (Product? prod) {
            //    return prod?.Name?[0] == 'S';
            //};

            decimal priceFilterTotal = productArray
                .Filter(p => (p?.Price ?? 0) >= 20)
                .TotalPrices();
            decimal nameFilterTotal = productArray
                .Filter(p => p?.Name?[0] == 'S')
                .TotalPrices();

            return View("Index", new string[] {
                $"Price Total: {priceFilterTotal:C2}",
                $"Name Total: {nameFilterTotal:C2}" });
        }
    }
}
```

The lambda expressions are shown in bold. The parameters are expressed without specifying a type, which will be inferred automatically. The => characters are read aloud as "goes to" and link the parameter to the result of the lambda expression. In my examples, a Product? parameter called p goes to a bool result, which will be true if the Price property is equal or greater than 20 in the first expression or if the Name property starts with *S* in the second expression. This code works in the same way as the separate method and the function delegate but is more concise and is—for most people—easier to read.

Other Forms for Lambda Expressions

I don't need to express the logic of my delegate in the lambda expression. I can as easily call a method, like this:

```
...
prod => EvaluateProduct(prod)
...
```

If I need a lambda expression for a delegate that has multiple parameters, I must wrap the parameters in parentheses, like this:

```
...
(prod, count) => prod.Price > 20 && count > 0
...
```

Finally, if I need logic in the lambda expression that requires more than one statement, I can do so by using braces ({ }) and finishing with a `return` statement, like this:

```
...
(prod, count) => {
    // ...multiple code statements...
    return result;
}
...
```

You do not need to use lambda expressions in your code, but they are a neat way of expressing complex functions simply and in a manner that is readable and clear. I like them a lot, and you will see them used throughout this book.

5.10.2 Using lambda expression methods and properties

Lambda expressions can be used to implement constructors, methods, and properties. In ASP.NET Core development, you will often end up with methods that contain a single statement that selects the data to display and the view to render. In listing 5.42, I have rewritten the `Index` action method so that it follows this common pattern.

> **Listing 5.42 Creating a common action pattern in the HomeController.cs file in the Controllers folder**

```
namespace LanguageFeatures.Controllers {
    public class HomeController : Controller {

        public ViewResult Index() {
            return View(Product.GetProducts().Select(p => p?.Name));
        }
    }
}
```

The action method gets a collection of `Product` objects from the static `Product` `.GetProducts` method and uses LINQ to project the values of the `Name` properties, which are then used as the view model for the default view. If you run the application, you will see the following output displayed in the browser window:

```
Kayak
```

There will be empty list items in the browser window as well because the `GetProducts` method includes a `null` reference in its results and one of the Product objects is created without a `Name` value, but that doesn't matter for this section of the chapter.

When a constructor or method body consists of a single statement, it can be rewritten as a lambda expression, as shown in listing 5.43.

Listing 5.43   A lambda action method in the HomeController.cs file in the Controllers folder

```
namespace LanguageFeatures.Controllers {
    public class HomeController : Controller {

        public ViewResult Index() =>
            View(Product.GetProducts().Select(p => p?.Name));
    }
}
```

Lambda expressions for methods omit the `return` keyword and use => (goes to) to associate the method signature (including its arguments) with its implementation. The `Index` method shown in listing 5.43 works in the same way as the one shown in listing 5.42 but is expressed more concisely. The same basic approach can also be used to define properties. Listing 5.44 shows the addition of a property that uses a lambda expression to the `Product` class.

Listing 5.44   A lambda property in the Product.cs file in the Models folder

```
namespace LanguageFeatures.Models {
    public class Product {

        public string Name { get; set; } = string.Empty;
        public decimal? Price { get; set; }

        public bool NameBeginsWithS => Name.Length > 0 && Name[0] == 'S';

        public static Product?[] GetProducts() {

            Product kayak = new Product {
                Name = "Kayak", Price = 275M
            };

            Product lifejacket = new Product {
                //Name = "Lifejacket",
                Price = 48.95M
            };

            return new Product?[] { kayak, lifejacket, null };
        }
    }
}
```

5.11 Using type inference and anonymous types

The `var` keyword allows you to define a local variable without explicitly specifying the variable type, as demonstrated by listing 5.45. This is called *type inference*, or *implicit typing*.

Listing 5.45   Using type inference in the HomeController.cs file in the Controllers folder

```
namespace LanguageFeatures.Controllers {
    public class HomeController : Controller {

        public ViewResult Index() {
            var names = new[] { "Kayak", "Lifejacket", "Soccer ball" };
            return View(names);
        }
    }
}
```

It is not that the `names` variable does not have a type; instead, I am asking the compiler to infer the type from the code. The compiler examines the array declaration and works out that it is a string array. Running the example produces the following output:

```
Kayak
Lifejacket
Soccer ball
```

5.11.1 Using anonymous types

By combining object initializers and type inference, I can create simple view model objects that are useful for transferring data between a controller and a view without having to define a class or struct, as shown in listing 5.46.

Listing 5.46   An anonymous type in the HomeController.cs file in the Controllers folder

```
namespace LanguageFeatures.Controllers {
    public class HomeController : Controller {

        public ViewResult Index() {
            var products = new[] {
                new { Name = "Kayak", Price = 275M },
                new { Name = "Lifejacket", Price = 48.95M },
                new { Name = "Soccer ball", Price = 19.50M },
                new { Name = "Corner flag", Price = 34.95M }
            };

            return View(products.Select(p => p.Name));
        }
    }
}
```

Each of the objects in the `products` array is an anonymously typed object. This does not mean that it is dynamic in the sense that JavaScript variables are dynamic. It just means that the type definition will be created automatically by the compiler. Strong typing is still enforced. You can get and set only the properties that have been defined in the initializer, for example. Restart ASP.NET Core and request http://localhost:5000, and you will see the following output in the browser window:

```
Kayak
Lifejacket
Soccer ball
Corner flag
```

The C# compiler generates the class based on the name and type of the parameters in the initializer. Two anonymously typed objects that have the same property names and types defined in the same order will be assigned to the same automatically generated class. This means that all the objects in the `products` array will have the same type because they define the same properties.

> **TIP**   I have to use the `var` keyword to define the array of anonymously typed objects because the type isn't created until the code is compiled, so I don't know the name of the type to use. The elements in an array of anonymously typed objects must all define the same properties; otherwise, the compiler can't work out what the array type should be.

To demonstrate this, I have changed the output from the example in listing 5.47 so that it shows the type name rather than the value of the `Name` property.

> **Listing 5.47   Displaying the type name in the HomeController.cs file in the Controllers folder**

```
namespace LanguageFeatures.Controllers {
    public class HomeController : Controller {

        public ViewResult Index() {
            var products = new[] {
                new { Name = "Kayak", Price = 275M },
                new { Name = "Lifejacket", Price = 48.95M },
                new { Name = "Soccer ball", Price = 19.50M },
                new { Name = "Corner flag", Price = 34.95M }
            };

            return View(products.Select(p => p.GetType().Name));
        }
    }
}
```

All the objects in the array have been assigned the same type, which you can see if you run the example. The type name isn't user-friendly but isn't intended to be used directly, and you may see a different name than the one shown in the following output:

```
<>f__AnonymousType0`2
<>f__AnonymousType0`2
<>f__AnonymousType0`2
<>f__AnonymousType0`2
```

5.12 *Using default implementations in interfaces*

C# provides the ability to define default implementations for properties and methods defined by interfaces. This may seem like an odd feature because an interface is intended to be a description of features without specifying an implementation, but this addition to C# makes it possible to update interfaces without breaking the existing implementations of them.

Add a class file named `IProductSelection.cs` to the `Models` folder and use it to define the interface shown in listing 5.48.

> **Listing 5.48   The contents of the IProductSelection.cs file in the Models folder**

```
namespace LanguageFeatures.Models {

    public interface IProductSelection {

        IEnumerable<Product>? Products { get; }
    }
}
```

Update the `ShoppingCart` class to implement the new interface, as shown in listing 5.49.

> **Listing 5.49   Implementing an interface in the ShoppingCart.cs file in the Models folder**

```
namespace LanguageFeatures.Models {

    public class ShoppingCart : IProductSelection {
        private List<Product> products = new();

        public ShoppingCart(params Product[] prods) {
            products.AddRange(prods);
        }

        public IEnumerable<Product>? Products { get => products; }
    }
}
```

Listing 5.50 updates the `Home` controller so that it uses the `ShoppingCart` class.

> **Listing 5.50   Using an interface in the HomeController.cs file in the Controllers folder**

```
namespace LanguageFeatures.Controllers {
    public class HomeController : Controller {

        public ViewResult Index() {
            IProductSelection cart = new ShoppingCart(
                new Product { Name = "Kayak", Price = 275M },
                new Product { Name = "Lifejacket", Price = 48.95M },
                new Product { Name = "Soccer ball", Price = 19.50M },
                new Product { Name = "Corner flag", Price = 34.95M }
            );
            return View(cart.Products?.Select(p => p.Name));
```

```
            }
        }
    }
```

This is the familiar use of an interface, and if you restart ASP.NET Core and request http://localhost:5000, you will see the following output in the browser:

```
Kayak
Lifejacket
Soccer ball
Corner flag
```

If I want to add a new feature to the interface, I must locate and update all the classes that implement it, which can be difficult, especially if an interface is used by other development teams in their projects. This is where the default implementation feature can be used, allowing new features to be added to an interface, as shown in listing 5.51.

> **Listing 5.51   Adding a feature in the IProductSelection.cs file in the Models folder**

```
namespace LanguageFeatures.Models {

    public interface IProductSelection {

        IEnumerable<Product>? Products { get; }

        IEnumerable<string>? Names => Products?.Select(p => p.Name);
    }
}
```

The listing defines a Names property and provides a default implementation, which means that consumers of the IProductSelection interface can use the Names property even if it isn't defined by implementation classes, as shown in listing 5.52.

> **Listing 5.52   Using a default implementation in the HomeController.cs file in the Controllers folder**

```
namespace LanguageFeatures.Controllers {
    public class HomeController : Controller {

        public ViewResult Index() {
            IProductSelection cart = new ShoppingCart(
                new Product { Name = "Kayak", Price = 275M },
                new Product { Name = "Lifejacket", Price = 48.95M },
                new Product { Name = "Soccer ball", Price = 19.50M },
                new Product { Name = "Corner flag", Price = 34.95M }
            );
            return View(cart.Names);
        }
    }
}
```

The ShoppingCart class has not been modified, but the Index method can use the default implementation of the Names property. Restart ASP.NET Core and request http://localhost:5000, and you will see the following output in the browser:

```
Kayak
Lifejacket
Soccer ball
Corner flag
```

5.13   *Using asynchronous methods*

Asynchronous methods perform work in the background and notify you when they are complete, allowing your code to take care of other business while the background work is performed. Asynchronous methods are an important tool in removing bottlenecks from code and allow applications to take advantage of multiple processors and processor cores to perform work in parallel.

In ASP.NET Core, asynchronous methods can be used to improve the overall performance of an application by allowing the server more flexibility in the way that requests are scheduled and executed. Two C# keywords—async and await—are used to perform work asynchronously.

5.13.1   *Working with tasks directly*

C# and .NET have excellent support for asynchronous methods, but the code has tended to be verbose, and developers who are not used to parallel programming often get bogged down by the unusual syntax. To create an example, add a class file called MyAsyncMethods.cs to the Models folder and add the code shown in listing 5.53.

> **Listing 5.53   The contents of the MyAsyncMethods.cs file in the Models folder**

```
namespace LanguageFeatures.Models {

    public class MyAsyncMethods {

        public static Task<long?> GetPageLength() {
            HttpClient client = new HttpClient();
            var httpTask = client.GetAsync("http://manning.com");
            return httpTask.ContinueWith((Task<HttpResponseMessage>
                    antecedent) => {
                return antecedent.Result.Content.Headers.ContentLength;
            });
        }
    }
}
```

This method uses a System.Net.Http.HttpClient object to request the contents of the Manning home page and returns its length. .NET represents work that will be done asynchronously as a Task. Task objects are strongly typed based on the result that the background work produces. So, when I call the HttpClient.GetAsync method, what I get back is a Task<HttpResponseMessage>. This tells me that the request will be performed in the background and that the result of the request will be an HttpResponseMessage object.

> **TIP**   When I use words like *background*, I am skipping over a lot of detail to make just the key points that are important to the world of ASP.NET Core. The .NET

support for asynchronous methods and parallel programming is excellent, and I encourage you to learn more about it if you want to create truly high-performing applications that can take advantage of multicore and multiprocessor hardware. You will see how ASP.NET Core makes it easy to create asynchronous web applications throughout this book as I introduce different features.

The part that most programmers get bogged down with is the *continuation*, which is the mechanism by which you specify what you want to happen when the task is complete. In the example, I have used the `ContinueWith` method to process the `HttpResponse-Message` object I get from the `HttpClient.GetAsync` method, which I do with a lambda expression that returns the value of a property that contains the length of the content I get from the Manning web server. Here is the continuation code:

```
...
return httpTask.ContinueWith((Task<HttpResponseMessage> antecedent) => {
    return antecedent.Result.Content.Headers.ContentLength;
});
...
```

Notice that I use the `return` keyword twice. This is the part that causes confusion. The first use of the `return` keyword specifies that I am returning a `Task<HttpResponse-Message>` object, which, when the task is complete, will `return` the length of the `ContentLength` header. The `ContentLength` header returns a `long?` result (a nullable long value), and this means the result of my `GetPageLength` method is `Task<long?>`, like this:

```
...
public static Task<long?> GetPageLength() {
...
```

Do not worry if this does not make sense—you are not alone in your confusion. It is for this reason that Microsoft added keywords to C# to simplify asynchronous methods.

5.13.2 *Applying the async and await keywords*

Microsoft introduced two keywords to C# that simplify using asynchronous methods like `HttpClient.GetAsync`. The keywords are `async` and `await`, and you can see how I have used them to simplify my example method in listing 5.54.

> **Listing 5.54 Using the async and await keywords in the MyAsyncMethods.cs file in the Models folder**

```
namespace LanguageFeatures.Models {

    public class MyAsyncMethods {

        public async static Task<long?> GetPageLength() {
            HttpClient client = new HttpClient();
            var httpMessage = await client.GetAsync("http://manning.com");
            return httpMessage.Content.Headers.ContentLength;
        }
    }
}
```

I used the await keyword when calling the asynchronous method. This tells the C# compiler that I want to wait for the result of the Task that the GetAsync method returns and then carry on executing other statements in the same method.

Applying the await keyword means I can treat the result from the GetAsync method as though it were a regular method and just assign the HttpResponseMessage object that it returns to a variable. Even better, I can then use the return keyword in the normal way to produce a result from another method—in this case, the value of the ContentLength property. This is a much more natural technique, and it means I do not have to worry about the ContinueWith method and multiple uses of the return keyword.

When you use the await keyword, you must also add the async keyword to the method signature, as I have done in the example. The method result type does not change—my example GetPageLength method still returns a Task<long?>. This is because await and async are implemented using some clever compiler tricks, meaning that they allow a more natural syntax, but they do not change what is happening in the methods to which they are applied. Someone who is calling my GetPageLength method still has to deal with a Task<long?> result because there is still a background operation that produces a nullable long—although, of course, that programmer can also choose to use the await and async keywords.

This pattern follows through into the controller, which makes it easy to write asynchronous action methods, as shown in listing 5.55.

NOTE You can also use the async and await keywords in lambda expressions, which I demonstrate in later chapters.

Listing 5.55 An asynchronous action method in the HomeController.cs file in the Controllers folder

```
namespace LanguageFeatures.Controllers {
    public class HomeController : Controller {

        public async Task<ViewResult> Index() {
            long? length = await MyAsyncMethods.GetPageLength();
            return View(new string[] { $"Length: {length}" });
        }
    }
}
```

I have changed the result of the Index action method to Task<ViewResult>, which declares that the action method will return a Task that will produce a ViewResult object when it completes, which will provide details of the view that should be rendered and the data that it requires. I have added the async keyword to the method's definition, which allows me to use the await keyword when calling the MyAsync-Methods.GetPathLength method. .NET takes care of dealing with the continuations, and the result is asynchronous code that is easy to write, easy to read, and easy to maintain. Restart ASP.NET Core and request http://localhost:5000, and you will see output similar to the following (although with a different length since the content of the Manning website changes often):

```
Length: 472922
```

5.13.3 *Using an asynchronous enumerable*

An asynchronous enumerable describes a sequence of values that will be generated over time. To demonstrate the issue that this feature addresses, listing 5.56 adds a method to the `MyAsyncMethods` class.

> **Listing 5.56   Adding a method in the MyAsyncMethods.cs file in the Models folder**

```
namespace LanguageFeatures.Models {

    public class MyAsyncMethods {

        public async static Task<long?> GetPageLength() {
            HttpClient client = new HttpClient();
            var httpMessage = await client.GetAsync("http://manning.com");
            return httpMessage.Content.Headers.ContentLength;
        }

        public static async Task<IEnumerable<long?>>
                GetPageLengths(List<string> output,
                    params string[] urls) {
            List<long?> results = new List<long?>();
            HttpClient client = new HttpClient();
            foreach (string url in urls) {
                output.Add($"Started request for {url}");
                var httpMessage = await client.GetAsync($"http://{url}");
                results.Add(httpMessage.Content.Headers.ContentLength);
                output.Add($"Completed request for {url}");
            }
            return results;
        }
    }
}
```

The `GetPageLengths` method makes HTTP requests to a series of websites and gets their length. The requests are performed asynchronously, but there is no way to feed the results back to the method's caller as they arrive. Instead, the method waits until all the requests are complete and then returns all the results in one go. In addition to the URLs that will be requested, this method accepts a `List<string>` to which I add messages in order to highlight how the code works. Listing 5.57 updates the `Index` action method of the `Home` controller to use the new method.

> **Listing 5.57   Using the new method in the HomeController.cs file in the Controllers folder**

```
namespace LanguageFeatures.Controllers {
    public class HomeController : Controller {
```

```
public async Task<ViewResult> Index() {
    List<string> output = new List<string>();
    foreach (long? len in await MyAsyncMethods.GetPageLengths(
            output,
            "manning.com", "microsoft.com", "amazon.com")) {
        output.Add($"Page length: { len}");
    }
    return View(output);
}
    }
}
```

The action method enumerates the sequence produced by the GetPageLengths method and adds each result to the List<string> object, which produces an ordered sequence of messages showing the interaction between the foreach loop in the Index method that processes the results and the foreach loop in the GetPageLengths method that generates them. Restart ASP.NET Core and request http:// localhost:5000, and you will see the following output in the browser (which may take several seconds to appear and may have different page lengths):

```
Started request for manning.com
Completed request for manning.com
Started request for microsoft.com
Completed request for microsoft.com
Started request for amazon.com
Completed request for amazon.com
Page length: 26973
Page length: 199526
Page length: 357777
```

You can see that the Index action method doesn't receive the results until all the HTTP requests have been completed. This is the problem that the asynchronous enumerable feature solves, as shown in listing 5.58.

> **Listing 5.58 Using an asynchronous enumerable in the MyAsyncMethods.cs file in the Models folder**

```
namespace LanguageFeatures.Models {

    public class MyAsyncMethods {

        public async static Task<long?> GetPageLength() {
            HttpClient client = new HttpClient();
            var httpMessage = await client.GetAsync("http://manning.com");
            return httpMessage.Content.Headers.ContentLength;
        }

        public static async IAsyncEnumerable<long?>
                GetPageLengths(List<string> output,
                    params string[] urls) {
            HttpClient client = new HttpClient();
            foreach (string url in urls) {
                output.Add($"Started request for {url}");
                var httpMessage = await client.GetAsync($"http://{url}");
```

```
                    output.Add($"Completed request for {url}");
                    yield return httpMessage.Content.Headers.ContentLength;
                }
            }
        }
}
```

The methods result is IAsyncEnumerable<long?>, which denotes an asynchronous sequence of nullable long values. This result type has special support in .NET Core and works with standard yield return statements, which isn't otherwise possible because the result constraints for asynchronous methods conflict with the yield keyword. Listing 5.59 updates the controller to use the revised method.

```
namespace LanguageFeatures.Controllers {
    public class HomeController : Controller {

        public async Task<ViewResult> Index() {
            List<string> output = new List<string>();
            await foreach (long? len in MyAsyncMethods.GetPageLengths(
                    output,
                    "manning.com", "microsoft.com", "amazon.com")) {
                output.Add($"Page length: { len}");
            }
            return View(output);
        }
    }
}
```

The difference is that the await keyword is applied before the foreach keyword and not before the call to the async method. Restart ASP.NET Core and request http://localhost:5000; once the HTTP requests are complete, you will see that the order of the response messages has changed, like this:

```
Started request for manning.com
Completed request for manning.com
Page length: 26973
Started request for microsoft.com
Completed request for microsoft.com
Page length: 199528
Started request for amazon.com
Completed request for amazon.com
Page length: 441398
```

The controller receives the next result in the sequence as it is produced. As I explain in chapter 19, ASP.NET Core has special support for using IAsyncEnumerable<T> results in web services, allowing data values to be serialized as the values in the sequence are generated.

5.14 Getting names

There are many tasks in web application development in which you need to refer to the name of an argument, variable, method, or class. Common examples include when you throw an exception or create a validation error when processing input from the user. The traditional approach has been to use a string value hard-coded with the name, as shown in listing 5.60.

> **Listing 5.60   Hard-coding a name in the HomeController.cs file in the Controllers folder**

```
namespace LanguageFeatures.Controllers {
    public class HomeController : Controller {

        public ViewResult Index() {
            var products = new[] {
                new { Name = "Kayak", Price = 275M },
                new { Name = "Lifejacket", Price = 48.95M },
                new { Name = "Soccer ball", Price = 19.50M },
                new { Name = "Corner flag", Price = 34.95M }
            };
            return View(products.Select(p =>
                $"Name: {p.Name}, Price: {p.Price}"));
        }
    }
}
```

The call to the LINQ `Select` method generates a sequence of strings, each of which contains a hard-coded reference to the `Name` and `Price` properties. Restart ASP.NET Core and request http://localhost:5000, and you will see the following output in the browser window:

```
Name: Kayak, Price: 275
Name: Lifejacket, Price: 48.95
Name: Soccer ball, Price: 19.50
Name: Corner flag, Price: 34.95
```

This approach is prone to errors, either because the name was mistyped or because the code was refactored and the name in the string isn't correctly updated. C# supports the `nameof` expression, in which the compiler takes responsibility for producing a name string, as shown in listing 5.61.

> **Listing 5.61   Using nameof expressions in the HomeController.cs file in the Controllers folder**

```
namespace LanguageFeatures.Controllers {
    public class HomeController : Controller {

        public ViewResult Index() {
            var products = new[] {
                new { Name = "Kayak", Price = 275M },
                new { Name = "Lifejacket", Price = 48.95M },
                new { Name = "Soccer ball", Price = 19.50M },
                new { Name = "Corner flag", Price = 34.95M }
```

```
    };
    return View(products.Select(p =>
    $"{nameof(p.Name)}: {p.Name}, {nameof(p.Price)}: {p.Price}"));
    }
  }
}
```

The compiler processes a reference such as p.Name so that only the last part is included in the string, producing the same output as in previous examples. There is IntelliSense support for nameof expressions, so you will be prompted to select references, and expressions will be correctly updated when you refactor code. Since the compiler is responsible for dealing with nameof, using an invalid reference causes a compiler error, which prevents incorrect or outdated references from escaping notice.

Summary

- Top-level statements allow code to be defined outside of a class, which can make ASP.NET Core configuration more concise.

- Global using statements take effect throughout a project so that namespaces don't have to be imported in individual C# files.

- Null state analysis ensures that null values are only assigned to nullable types and that values are read safely.

- String interpolation allows data values to be composed into strings.

- Object initialization patterns simplify the code required to create objects.

- Target-typed expressions omit the type name from the new statement.

- Pattern matching is used to execute code when a value has specific characteristics.

- Extension methods allow new functionality to be added to a type without needing to modify the class file.

- Lambda expressions are a concise way to express functions.

- Interfaces can be defined with default implementations, which means it is possible to modify the interface without breaking implementation classes.

- The async and await keywords are used to create asynchronous methods without needing to work directly with tasks and continuations.

Testing ASP.NET Core applications

6

This chapter covers

- Creating unit tests projects for ASP.NET Core application
- Writing and running unit tests
- Isolating application components for testing
- Simplifying component isolation with a mocking package

In this chapter, I demonstrate how to unit test ASP.NET Core applications. Unit testing is a form of testing in which individual components are isolated from the rest of the application so their behavior can be thoroughly validated. ASP.NET Core has been designed to make it easy to create unit tests, and there is support for a wide range of unit testing frameworks. I show you how to set up a unit test project and describe the process for writing and running tests. Table 6.1 provides a guide to the chapter.

Deciding whether to unit test

Being able to easily perform unit testing is one of the benefits of using ASP.NET Core, but it isn't for everyone, and I have no intention of pretending otherwise.

(continued)

I like unit testing, and I use it in my own projects, but not all of them and not as consistently as you might expect. I tend to focus on writing unit tests for features and functions that I know will be hard to write and likely will be the source of bugs in deployment. In these situations, unit testing helps structure my thoughts about how to best implement what I need. I find that just thinking about what I need to test helps produce ideas about potential problems, and that's before I start dealing with actual bugs and defects.

That said, unit testing is a tool and not a religion, and only you know how much testing you require. If you don't find unit testing useful or if you have a different methodology that suits you better, then don't feel you need to unit test just because it is fashionable. (However, if you *don't* have a better methodology and you are not testing at all, then you are probably letting users find your bugs, which is rarely ideal. You don't *have* to unit test, but you really should consider doing *some* testing of *some* kind.)

If you have not encountered unit testing before, then I encourage you to give it a try to see how it works. If you are not a fan of unit testing, then you can skip this chapter and move on to chapter 7, where I start to build a more realistic ASP.NET Core application.

Table 6.1 Chapter guide

Problem	Solution	Listing
Creating a unit test project	Use the `dotnet new` command with the project template for your preferred test framework.	8
Creating an XUnit test	Create a class with methods decorated with the `Fact` attribute and use the `Assert` class to inspect the test results.	10
Running unit tests	Use the Visual Studio or Visual Studio Code test runners or use the `dotnet test` command.	12
Isolating a component for testing	Create mock implementations of the objects that the component under test requires.	13–20

6.1   Preparing for this chapter

To prepare for this chapter, I need to create a simple ASP.NET Core project. Open a new PowerShell command prompt using the Windows Start menu, navigate to a convenient location, and run the commands shown in listing 6.1.

> **TIP**   You can download the example project for this chapter—and for all the other chapters in this book—from https://github.com/manningbooks/pro-asp .net-core-7. See chapter 1 for how to get help if you have problems running the examples.

```
dotnet new globaljson --sdk-version 7.0.100 --output Testing/SimpleApp
dotnet new web --no-https --output Testing/SimpleApp --framework net7.0
dotnet new sln -o Testing

dotnet sln Testing add Testing/SimpleApp
```

These commands create a new project named SimpleApp using the web template, which contains the minimal configuration for ASP.NET Core applications. The project folder is contained within a solution folder also called Testing.

6.1.1 Opening the project

If you are using Visual Studio, select File > Open > Project/Solution, select the Testing.sln file in the Testing folder, and click the Open button to open the solution file and the project it references. If you are using Visual Studio Code, select File > Open Folder, navigate to the Testing folder, and click the Select Folder button.

6.1.2 Selecting the HTTP port

Set the port on which ASP.NET Core will receive HTTP requests by editing the launchSettings.json file in the Properties folder, as shown in listing 6.2.

```
{
  "iisSettings": {
    "windowsAuthentication": false,
    "anonymousAuthentication": true,
    "iisExpress": {
      "applicationUrl": "http://localhost:5000",
      "sslPort": 0
    }
  },
  "profiles": {
    "SimpleApp": {
      "commandName": "Project",
      "dotnetRunMessages": true,
      "launchBrowser": true,
      "applicationUrl": "http://localhost:5000",
      "environmentVariables": {
        "ASPNETCORE_ENVIRONMENT": "Development"
      }
    },
    "IIS Express": {
      "commandName": "IISExpress",
      "launchBrowser": true,
      "environmentVariables": {
        "ASPNETCORE_ENVIRONMENT": "Development"
      }
    }
  }
}
```

6.1.3   *Enabling the MVC Framework*

As I explained in chapter 1, ASP.NET Core supports different application frameworks, but I am going to continue using the MVC Framework in this chapter. I introduce the other frameworks in the SportsStore application that I start to build in chapter 7, but for the moment, the MVC Framework gives me a foundation for demonstrating how to perform unit testing that is familiar from earlier examples. Add the statements shown in listing 6.3 to the `Program.cs` file in the `SimpleApp` folder.

> **Listing 6.3   Enabling the MVC Framework in the Program.cs file in the SimpleApp folder**

```
var builder = WebApplication.CreateBuilder(args);

builder.Services.AddControllersWithViews();

var app = builder.Build();

//app.MapGet("/", () => "Hello World!");
app.MapDefaultControllerRoute();

app.Run();
```

6.1.4   *Creating the application components*

Now that the MVC Framework is set up, I can add the application components that I will use to run tests.

CREATING THE DATA MODEL

I started by creating a simple model class so that I can have some data to work with. I added a folder called `Models` and created a class file called `Product.cs` within it, which I used to define the class shown in listing 6.4.

> **Listing 6.4   The contents of the Product.cs file in the Models folder**

```
namespace SimpleApp.Models {
    public class Product {

        public string Name { get; set; } = string.Empty;
        public decimal? Price { get; set; }

        public static Product[] GetProducts() {

            Product kayak = new Product {
                Name = "Kayak", Price = 275M
            };

            Product lifejacket = new Product {
                Name = "Lifejacket", Price = 48.95M
            };

            return new Product[] { kayak, lifejacket };
        }
    }
}
```

The Product class defines Name and Price properties, and there is a static method called GetProducts that returns a Products array.

CREATING THE CONTROLLER AND VIEW

For the examples in this chapter, I use a simple controller class to demonstrate different language features. I created a Controllers folder and added to it a class file called HomeController.cs, the contents of which are shown in listing 6.5.

> **Listing 6.5**   **The contents of the HomeController.cs file in the Controllers folder**

```
using Microsoft.AspNetCore.Mvc;
using SimpleApp.Models;

namespace SimpleApp.Controllers {
    public class HomeController : Controller {

        public ViewResult Index() {
            return View(Product.GetProducts());
        }
    }
}
```

The Index action method tells ASP.NET Core to render the default view and provides it with the Product objects obtained from the static Product.GetProducts method. To create the view for the action method, I added a Views/Home folder (by creating a Views folder and then adding a Home folder within it) and added a Razor View called Index.cshtml, with the contents shown in listing 6.6.

> **Listing 6.6**   **The contents of the Index.cshtml file in the Views/Home folder**

```
@using SimpleApp.Models
@model IEnumerable<Product>
@{ Layout = null; }

<!DOCTYPE html>
<html>
<head>
    <meta name="viewport" content="width=device-width" />
    <title>Simple App</title>
</head>
<body>
    <ul>
        @foreach (Product p in Model ?? Enumerable.Empty<Product>()) {
            <li>Name: @p.Name, Price: @p.Price</li>
        }
    </ul>
</body>
</html>
```

6.1.5   *Running the example application*

Start ASP.NET Core by running the command shown in listing 6.7 in the `SimpleApp` folder.

> **Listing 6.7   Running the example application**

```
dotnet run
```

Request http://localhost:5000, and you will see the output shown in figure 6.1.

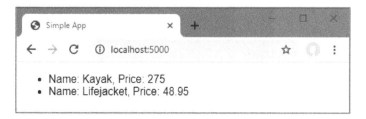

Figure 6.1   Running the example application

6.2   *Creating a unit test project*

For ASP.NET Core applications, you generally create a separate Visual Studio project to hold the unit tests, each of which is defined as a method in a C# class. Using a separate project means you can deploy your application without also deploying the tests. The .NET Core SDK includes templates for unit test projects using three popular test tools, as described in table 6.2.

Table 6.2   The unit test project tools

Name	Description
mstest	This template creates a project configured for the MS Test framework, which is produced by Microsoft.
nunit	This template creates a project configured for the NUnit framework.
xunit	This template creates a project configured for the XUnit framework.

These testing frameworks have largely the same feature set and differ only in how they are implemented and how they integrate into third-party testing environments. I recommend starting with XUnit if you do not have an established preference, largely because it is the test framework that I find easiest to work with.

The convention is to name the unit test project `<ApplicationName>.Tests`. Run the commands shown in listing 6.8 in the `Testing` folder to create the XUnit test project named `SimpleApp.Tests`, add it to the solution file, and create a reference between projects so the unit tests can be applied to the classes defined in the `SimpleApp` project.

Listing 6.8 Creating the unit test project

```
dotnet new xunit -o SimpleApp.Tests --framework net7.0
dotnet sln add SimpleApp.Tests
dotnet add SimpleApp.Tests reference SimpleApp
```

If you are using Visual Studio, you will be prompted to reload the solution, which will cause the new unit test project to be displayed in the Solution Explorer, alongside the existing project. You may find that Visual Studio Code doesn't build the new project. If that happens, select Terminal > Configure Default Build Task, select "build" from the list, and, if prompted, select .NET Core from the list of environments.

REMOVING THE DEFAULT TEST CLASS

The project template adds a C# class file to the test project, which will confuse the results of later examples. Either delete the `UnitTest1.cs` file from the `SimpleApp.Tests` folder using the Solution Explorer or File Explorer pane or run the command shown in listing 6.9 in the `Testing` folder.

Listing 6.9 Removing the default test class file

```
Remove-Item SimpleApp.Tests/UnitTest1.cs
```

6.3 Writing and running unit tests

Now that all the preparation is complete, I can write some tests. To get started, I added a class file called `ProductTests.cs` to the `SimpleApp.Tests` project and used it to define the class shown in listing 6.10. This is a simple class, but it contains everything required to get started with unit testing.

NOTE The `CanChangeProductPrice` method contains a deliberate error that I resolve later in this section.

Listing 6.10 The contents of the ProductTests.cs file in the SimpleApp.Tests folder

```
using SimpleApp.Models;
using Xunit;

namespace SimpleApp.Tests {

    public class ProductTests {

        [Fact]
        public void CanChangeProductName() {

            // Arrange
            var p = new Product { Name = "Test", Price = 100M };

            // Act
            p.Name = "New Name";

            //Assert
```

```
        Assert.Equal("New Name", p.Name);
    }

    [Fact]
    public void CanChangeProductPrice() {
        // Arrange
        var p = new Product { Name = "Test", Price = 100M };

        // Act
        p.Price = 200M;

        //Assert
        Assert.Equal(100M, p.Price);
    }
  }
}
```

There are two unit tests in the `ProductTests` class, each of which tests a behavior of the `Product` model class from the `SimpleApp` project. A test project can contain many classes, each of which can contain many unit tests.

Conventionally, the name of the test methods describes what the test does, and the name of the class describes what is being tested. This makes it easier to structure the tests in a project and to understand what the results of all the tests are when they are run by Visual Studio. The name `ProductTests` indicates that the class contains tests for the `Product` class, and the method names indicate that they test the ability to change the name and price of a `Product` object.

The `Fact` attribute is applied to each method to indicate that it is a test. Within the method body, a unit test follows a pattern called *arrange, act, assert* (A/A/A). *Arrange* refers to setting up the conditions for the test, *act* refers to performing the test, and *assert* refers to verifying that the result was the one that was expected.

The arrange and act sections of these tests are regular C# code, but the assert section is handled by xUnit.net, which provides a class called `Assert`, whose methods are used to check that the outcome of an action is the one that is expected.

> **TIP** The `Fact` attribute and the `Assert` class are defined in the `Xunit` namespace, for which there must be a `using` statement in every test class.

The methods of the `Assert` class are static and are used to perform different kinds of comparison between the expected and actual results. Table 6.3 shows the commonly used `Assert` methods.

Table 6.3   Commonly used xUnit.net assert methods

Name	Description
`Equal(expected, result)`	This method asserts that the result is equal to the expected outcome. There are overloaded versions of this method for comparing different types and for comparing collections. There is also a version of this method that accepts an additional argument of an object that implements the `IEqualityComparer<T>` interface for comparing objects.
`NotEqual(expected, result)`	This method asserts that the result is not equal to the expected outcome.
`True(result)`	This method asserts that the result is `true`.
`False(result)`	This method asserts that the result is `false`.
`IsType(expected, result)`	This method asserts that the result is of a specific type.
`IsNotType(expected, result)`	This method asserts that the result is not a specific type.
`IsNull(result)`	This method asserts that the result is `null`.
`IsNotNull(result)`	This method asserts that the result is not `null`.
`InRange(result, low, high)`	This method asserts that the result falls between `low` and `high`.
`NotInRange(result, low, high)`	This method asserts that the result falls outside `low` and `high`.
`Throws(exception, expression)`	This method asserts that the specified expression throws a specific exception type.

Each `Assert` method allows different types of comparison to be made and throws an exception if the result is not what was expected. The exception is used to indicate that a test has failed. In the tests in listing 6.10, I used the `Equal` method to determine whether the value of a property has been changed correctly.

```
...
Assert.Equal("New Name", p.Name);
...
```

6.3.1   *Running tests with the Visual Studio Test Explorer*

Visual Studio includes support for finding and running unit tests through the Test Explorer window, which is available through the Test > Test Explorer menu and is shown in figure 6.2.

> **TIP**   Build the solution if you don't see the unit tests in the Test Explorer window. Compilation triggers the process by which unit tests are discovered.

**Figure 6.2
The Visual Studio
Test Explorer**

Run the tests by clicking the Run All Tests button in the Test Explorer window (it is the button that shows two arrows and is the first button in the row at the top of the window). As noted, the `CanChangeProductPrice` test contains an error that causes the test to fail, which is clearly indicated in the test results shown in the figure.

6.3.2 Running tests with Visual Studio Code

Visual Studio Code detects tests and allows them to be run using the code lens feature, which displays details about code features in the editor. To run all the tests in the `ProductTests` class, click Run All Tests in the code editor when the unit test class is open, as shown in figure 6.3.

> **TIP** Close and reopen the `Testing` folder in Visual Studio Code if you don't see the code lens test features.

Figure 6.3   Running tests with the Visual Studio Code code lens feature

Visual Studio Code runs the tests using the command-line tools that I describe in the following section, and the results are displayed as text in a terminal window.

6.3.3 Running tests from the command line

To run the tests in the project, run the command shown in listing 6.11 in the `Testing` folder.

Listing 6.11   Running unit tests

```
dotnet test
```

The tests are discovered and executed, producing the following results, which show the deliberate error that I introduced earlier:

```
Starting test execution, please wait...
A total of 1 test files matched the specified pattern.
[xUnit.net 00:00:00.81]
    SimpleApp.Tests.ProductTests.CanChangeProductPrice [FAIL]
  Failed SimpleApp.Tests.ProductTests.CanChangeProductPrice [4 ms]
  Error Message:
   Assert.Equal() Failure
Expected: 100
Actual:   200
```

```
Stack Trace:
    at SimpleApp.Tests.ProductTests.CanChangeProductPrice() in
        C:\Testing\SimpleApp.Tests\ProductTests.cs:line 31
    at System.RuntimeMethodHandle.InvokeMethod(Object target, Void**
        arguments, Signature sig, Boolean isConstructor)
    at System.Reflection.MethodInvoker.Invoke(Object obj, IntPtr* args,
        BindingFlags invokeAttr)

Failed!  - Failed:     1, Passed:     1, Skipped:     0,
    Total:     2, Duration: 26 ms - SimpleApp.Tests.dll (net7.0)
```

6.3.4 Correcting the unit test

The problem with the unit test is with the arguments to the `Assert.Equal` method, which compares the test result to the original `Price` property value rather than the value it has been changed to. Listing 6.12 corrects the problem.

> **TIP** When a test fails, it is always a good idea to check the accuracy of the test before looking at the component it targets, especially if the test is new or has been recently modified.

Listing 6.12 Correcting a test in the ProductTests.cs file in the SimpleApp.Tests folder

```csharp
using SimpleApp.Models;
using Xunit;

namespace SimpleApp.Tests {

    public class ProductTests {

        [Fact]
        public void CanChangeProductName() {

            // Arrange
            var p = new Product { Name = "Test", Price = 100M };

            // Act
            p.Name = "New Name";

            //Assert
            Assert.Equal("New Name", p.Name);
        }

        [Fact]
        public void CanChangeProductPrice() {

            // Arrange
            var p = new Product { Name = "Test", Price = 100M };

            // Act
            p.Price = 200M;

            //Assert
```

```
        Assert.Equal(200M, p.Price);
    }
  }
}
```

Run the tests again, and you will see they all pass. If you are using Visual Studio, you can click the Run Failed Tests button, which will execute only the tests that failed, as shown in figure 6.4.

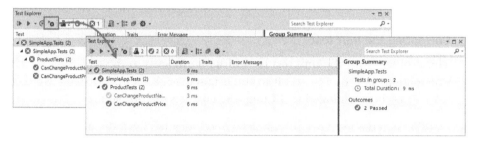

Figure 6.4   Running only failed tests

6.3.5   *Isolating components for unit testing*

Writing unit tests for model classes like `Product` is easy. Not only is the `Product` class simple, but it is self-contained, which means that when I perform an action on a `Product` object, I can be confident that I am testing the functionality provided by the `Product` class.

The situation is more complicated with other components in an ASP.NET Core application because there are dependencies between them. The next set of tests that I define will operate on the controller, examining the sequence of `Product` objects that are passed between the controller and the view.

When comparing objects instantiated from custom classes, you will need to use the xUnit.net `Assert.Equal` method that accepts an argument that implements the `IEqualityComparer<T>` interface so that the objects can be compared. My first step is to add a class file called `Comparer.cs` to the unit test project and use it to define the helper classes shown in listing 6.13.

Listing 6.13   The contents of the Comparer.cs file in the SimpleApp.Tests folder

```
using System;
using System.Collections.Generic;

namespace SimpleApp.Tests {

    public class Comparer {

        public static Comparer<U?> Get<U>(Func<U?, U?, bool> func) {
            return new Comparer<U?>(func);
        }
    }
```

```
    public class Comparer<T> : Comparer, IEqualityComparer<T> {
        private Func<T?, T?, bool> comparisonFunction;

        public Comparer(Func<T?, T?, bool> func) {
            comparisonFunction = func;
        }

        public bool Equals(T? x, T? y) {
            return comparisonFunction(x, y);
        }

        public int GetHashCode(T obj) {
            return obj?.GetHashCode() ?? 0;
        }
    }
}
```

These classes will allow me to create IEqualityComparer<T> objects using lambda expressions rather than having to define a new class for each type of comparison that I want to make. This isn't essential, but it will simplify the code in my unit test classes and make them easier to read and maintain.

Now that I can easily make comparisons, I can illustrate the problem of dependencies between components in the application. I added a new class called HomeControllerTests.cs to the SimpleApp.Tests folder and used it to define the unit test shown in listing 6.14.

Listing 6.14   The HomeControllerTests.cs file in the SimpleApp.Tests folder

```
using Microsoft.AspNetCore.Mvc;
using System.Collections.Generic;
using SimpleApp.Controllers;
using SimpleApp.Models;
using Xunit;

namespace SimpleApp.Tests {
    public class HomeControllerTests {

        [Fact]
        public void IndexActionModelIsComplete() {
            // Arrange
            var controller = new HomeController();
            Product[] products = new Product[]  {
                new Product { Name = "Kayak", Price = 275M },
                new Product { Name = "Lifejacket", Price = 48.95M}
            };

            // Act
            var model = (controller.Index() as ViewResult)?.ViewData.Model
                as IEnumerable<Product>;

            // Assert
            Assert.Equal(products, model,
                Comparer.Get<Product>((p1, p2) => p1?.Name == p2?.Name
```

```
                              && p1?.Price == p2?.Price));
                  }
              }
       }
```

The unit test creates an array of `Product` objects and checks that they correspond to the ones the `Index` action method provides as the view model. (Ignore the act section of the test for the moment; I explain the `ViewResult` class in chapters 21 and 22. For the moment, it is enough to know that I am getting the model data returned by the `Index` action method.)

The test passes, but it isn't a useful result because the `Product` data that I am testing is coming from the hardwired objects' `Product` class. I can't write a test to make sure that the controller behaves correctly when there are more than two `Product` objects, for example, or if the `Price` property of the first object has a decimal fraction. The overall effect is that I am testing the combined behavior of the `HomeController` and `Product` classes and only for the specific hardwired objects.

Unit tests are effective when they target small parts of an application, such as an individual method or class. What I need is the ability to isolate the `Home` controller from the rest of the application so that I can limit the scope of the test and rule out any impact caused by the repository.

ISOLATING A COMPONENT

The key to isolating components is to use C# interfaces. To separate the controller from the repository, I added a new class file called `IDataSource.cs` to the `Models` folder and used it to define the interface shown in listing 6.15.

> **Listing 6.15   The contents of the IDataSource.cs file in the SimpleApp/Models folder**

```
namespace SimpleApp.Models {
    public interface IDataSource {

        IEnumerable<Product> Products { get; }
    }
}
```

In listing 6.16, I have removed the static method from the `Product` class and created a new class that implements the `IDataSource` interface.

> **Listing 6.16   A data source in the Product.cs file in the SimpleApp/Models folder**

```
namespace SimpleApp.Models {
    public class Product {

        public string Name { get; set; } = string.Empty;
        public decimal? Price { get; set; }

        //public static Product[] GetProducts() {

        //     Product kayak = new Product {
        //          Name = "Kayak", Price = 275M
```

```
        //      };

        //      Product lifejacket = new Product {
        //          Name = "Lifejacket", Price = 48.95M
        //      };

        //      return new Product[] { kayak, lifejacket };
        //}
    }

    public class ProductDataSource : IDataSource {
        public IEnumerable<Product> Products =>
            new Product[] {
                new Product { Name = "Kayak", Price = 275M },
                new Product { Name = "Lifejacket", Price = 48.95M }
            };
    }
}
```

The next step is to modify the controller so that it uses the `ProductDataSource` class as the source for its data, as shown in listing 6.17.

> **TIP** ASP.NET Core supports a more elegant approach for solving this problem, known as *dependency injection*, which I describe in chapter 14. Dependency injection often causes confusion, so I isolate components in a simpler and more manual way in this chapter.

Listing 6.17 Adding a property in the HomeController.cs file in the Controllers folder

```
using Microsoft.AspNetCore.Mvc;
using SimpleApp.Models;

namespace SimpleApp.Controllers {
    public class HomeController : Controller {
        public IDataSource dataSource = new ProductDataSource();

        public ViewResult Index() {
            return View(dataSource.Products);
        }
    }
}
```

This may not seem like a significant change, but it allows me to change the data source the controller uses during testing, which is how I can isolate the controller. In listing 6.18, I have updated the controller unit tests so they use a special version of the repository.

Listing 6.18 Isolating the controller in the HomeControllerTests.cs file in the SimpleApp.Tests folder

```
using Microsoft.AspNetCore.Mvc;
using System.Collections.Generic;
using SimpleApp.Controllers;
using SimpleApp.Models;
```

```
using Xunit;

namespace SimpleApp.Tests {
    public class HomeControllerTests {

        class FakeDataSource : IDataSource {
            public FakeDataSource(Product[] data) => Products = data;
            public IEnumerable<Product> Products { get; set; }
        }

        [Fact]
        public void IndexActionModelIsComplete() {

            // Arrange
            Product[] testData = new Product[] {
                new Product { Name = "P1", Price = 75.10M },
                new Product { Name = "P2", Price = 120M },
                new Product { Name = "P3", Price = 110M }
            };
            IDataSource data = new FakeDataSource(testData);
            var controller = new HomeController();
            controller.dataSource = data;

            // Act
            var model = (controller.Index() as ViewResult)?.ViewData.Model
                as IEnumerable<Product>;

            // Assert
            Assert.Equal(data.Products, model,
                Comparer.Get<Product>((p1, p2) => p1?.Name == p2?.Name
                    && p1?.Price == p2?.Price));
        }
    }
}
```

I have defined a fake implementation of the IDataSource interface that lets me use any test data with the controller.

Understanding test-driven development

I have followed the most commonly used unit testing style in this chapter, in which an application feature is written and then tested to make sure it works as required. This is popular because most developers think about application code first and testing comes second (this is certainly the category that I fall into).

This approach is that it tends to produce unit tests that focus only on the parts of the application code that were difficult to write or that needed some serious debugging, leaving some aspects of a feature only partially tested or untested altogether.

An alternative approach is *Test-Driven Development* (TDD). There are lots of variations on TDD, but the core idea is that you write the tests for a feature before implementing the feature itself. Writing the tests first makes you think more carefully about the specification you are implementing and how you will know that a feature has been implemented correctly. Rather than diving into the implementation detail, TDD makes you consider what the measures of success or failure will be in advance.

(continued)

The tests that you write will all fail initially because your new feature will not be implemented. But as you add code to the application, your tests will gradually move from red to green, and all your tests will pass by the time that the feature is complete. TDD requires discipline, but it does produce a more comprehensive set of tests and can lead to more robust and reliable code.

6.3.6 Using a mocking package

It was easy to create a fake implementation for the IDataSource interface, but most classes for which fake implementations are required are more complex and cannot be handled as easily.

A better approach is to use a mocking package, which makes it easy to create fake—or mock—objects for tests. There are many mocking packages available, but the one I use (and have for years) is called Moq. To add Moq to the unit test project, run the command shown in listing 6.19 in the Testing folder.

NOTE The Moq package is added to the unit testing project and not the project that contains the application to be tested.

Listing 6.19 Installing the mocking package

```
dotnet add SimpleApp.Tests package Moq --version 4.18.4
```

6.3.7 Creating a mock object

I can use the Moq framework to create a fake IDataSource object without having to define a custom test class, as shown in listing 6.20.

Listing 6.20 Creating a mock object in the HomeControllerTests.cs file in the SimpleApp.Tests folder

```
using Microsoft.AspNetCore.Mvc;
using System.Collections.Generic;
using SimpleApp.Controllers;
using SimpleApp.Models;
using Xunit;
using Moq;

namespace SimpleApp.Tests {
    public class HomeControllerTests {

        //class FakeDataSource : IDataSource {
        //    public FakeDataSource(Product[] data) => Products = data;
        //    public IEnumerable<Product> Products { get; set; }
        //}
```

```
[Fact]
public void IndexActionModelIsComplete() {

    // Arrange
    Product[] testData = new Product[] {
        new Product { Name = "P1", Price = 75.10M },
        new Product { Name = "P2", Price = 120M },
        new Product { Name = "P3", Price = 110M }
    };
    var mock = new Mock<IDataSource>();
    mock.SetupGet(m => m.Products).Returns(testData);
    var controller = new HomeController();
    controller.dataSource = mock.Object;

    // Act
    var model = (controller.Index() as ViewResult)?.ViewData.Model
        as IEnumerable<Product>;

    // Assert
    Assert.Equal(testData, model,
        Comparer.Get<Product>((p1, p2) => p1?.Name == p2?.Name
            && p1?.Price == p2?.Price));
    mock.VerifyGet(m => m.Products, Times.Once);
    }
}
}
```

The use of Moq has allowed me to remove the fake implementation of the IData-Source interface and replace it with a few lines of code. I am not going to go into detail about the different features that Moq supports, but I will explain the way that I used Moq in the examples. (See https://github.com/Moq/moq4 for examples and documentation for Moq. There are also examples in later chapters as I explain how to unit test different types of components.)

The first step is to create a new instance of the Mock object, specifying the interface that should be implemented, like this:

```
...
var mock = new Mock<IDataSource>();
...
```

The Mock object I created will fake the IDataSource interface. To create an implementation of the Product property, I use the SetUpGet method, like this:

```
...
mock.SetupGet(m => m.Products).Returns(testData);
...
```

The SetupGet method is used to implement the getter for a property. The argument to this method is a lambda expression that specifies the property to be implemented, which is Products in this example. The Returns method is called on the result of the SetupGet method to specify the result that will be returned when the property value is read.

The `Mock` class defines an `Object` property, which returns the object that implements the specified interface with the behaviors that have been defined. I used the `Object` property to set the `dataSource` field defined by the `HomeController`, like this:

```
...
controller.dataSource = mock.Object;
...
```

The final Moq feature I used was to check that the `Products` property was called once, like this:

```
...
mock.VerifyGet(m => m.Products, Times.Once);
...
```

The `VerifyGet` method is one of the methods defined by the `Mock` class to inspect the state of the mock object when the test has completed. In this case, the `VerifyGet` method allows me to check the number of times that the `Products` property method has been read. The `Times.Once` value specifies that the `VerifyGet` method should throw an exception if the property has not been read exactly once, which will cause the test to fail. (The `Assert` methods usually used in tests work by throwing an exception when a test fails, which is why the `VerifyGet` method can be used to replace an `Assert` method when working with mock objects.)

The overall effect is the same as my fake interface implementation, but mocking is more flexible and more concise and can provide more insight into the behavior of the components under test.

Summary

- Unit tests are typically defined within a dedicated unit test project.
- A test framework simplifies writing unit tests by providing common features, such as assertions.
- Unit tests typically follow the arrange/act/assert pattern.
- Tests can be run within Visual Studio/Visual Studio Code or using the `dotnet test` command.
- Effective unit tests isolate and test individual components.
- Isolating components is simplified by mocking packages, such as Moq.

SportsStore:
A real application

This chapter covers

- Creating the SportsStore ASP.NET Core project
- Adding a data model and support for a database
- Displaying a basic product catalog
- Paginating data
- Styling content

In the previous chapters, I built quick and simple ASP.NET Core applications. I described ASP.NET Core patterns, the essential C# features, and the tools that good ASP.NET Core developers require. Now it is time to put everything together and build a simple but realistic e-commerce application.

My application, called SportsStore, will follow the classic approach taken by online stores everywhere. I will create an online product catalog that customers can browse by category and page, a shopping cart where users can add and remove products, and a checkout where customers can enter their shipping details. I will also create an administration area that includes create, read, update, and delete (CRUD) facilities for managing the catalog, and I will protect it so that only logged-in administrators can make changes.

My goal in this chapter and those that follow is to give you a sense of what real ASP.NET Core development is by creating as realistic an example as possible. I want to focus on ASP.NET Core, of course, so I have simplified the integration with external systems, such as the database, and omitted others entirely, such as payment processing.

You might find the going a little slow as I build up the levels of infrastructure I need, but the initial investment will result in maintainable, extensible, well-structured code with excellent support for unit testing.

Unit testing

I include sections on unit testing different components in the SportsStore application throughout the development process, demonstrating how to isolate and test different ASP.NET Core components.

I know that unit testing is not embraced by everyone. If you do not want to unit test, that is fine with me. To that end, when I have something to say that is purely about testing, I put it in a sidebar like this one. If you are not interested in unit testing, you can skip right over these sections, and the SportsStore application will work just fine. You do not need to do any kind of unit testing to get the technology benefits of ASP.NET Core, although, of course, support for testing is a key reason for adopting ASP.NET Core in many projects.

Most of the features I use for the SportsStore application have their own chapters later in the book. Rather than duplicate everything here, I tell you just enough to make sense of the example application and point you to another chapter for in-depth information.

I will call out each step needed to build the application so that you can see how the ASP.NET Core features fit together. You should pay particular attention when I create views. You will get some odd results if you do not follow the examples closely.

7.1 Creating the projects

I am going to start with a minimal ASP.NET Core project and add the features I require as they are needed. Open a new PowerShell command prompt from the Windows Start menu and run the commands shown in listing 7.1 to get started.

> **TIP** You can download the example project for this chapter—and for all the other chapters in this book—from https://github.com/manningbooks/pro-asp .net-core-7. See chapter 1 for how to get help if you have problems running the examples.

Listing 7.1 Creating the SportsStore project

```
dotnet new globaljson --sdk-version 7.0.100 --output SportsSln/SportsStore
dotnet new web --no-https --output SportsSln/SportsStore --framework net7.0
dotnet new sln -o SportsSln

dotnet sln SportsSln add SportsSln/SportsStore
```

These commands create a `SportsSln` solution folder that contains a `SportsStore` project folder created with the `web` project template. The `SportsSln` folder also contains a solution file, to which the `SportsStore` project is added.

I am using different names for the solution and project folders to make the examples easier to follow, but if you create a project with Visual Studio, the default is to use the same name for both folders. There is no "right" approach, and you can use whatever names suit your project.

7.1.1   Creating the unit test project

To create the unit test project, run the commands shown in listing 7.2 in the same location you used for the commands shown in listing 7.1.

Listing 7.2   Creating the unit test project

```
dotnet new xunit -o SportsSln/SportsStore.Tests --framework net7.0
dotnet sln SportsSln add SportsSln/SportsStore.Tests
dotnet add SportsSln/SportsStore.Tests reference SportsSln/SportsStore
```

I am going to use the Moq package to create mock objects. Run the command shown in listing 7.3 to install the Moq package into the unit testing project. Run this command from the same location as the commands in listing 7.2.

Listing 7.3   Installing the Moq package

```
dotnet add SportsSln/SportsStore.Tests package Moq --version 4.18.4
```

7.1.2   Opening the projects

If you are using Visual Studio Code, select File > Open Folder, navigate to the SportsSln folder, and click the Select Folder button. Visual Studio Code will open the folder and discover the solution and project files. When prompted, as shown in figure 7.1, click Yes to install the assets required to build the projects. Select SportsStore if Visual Studio Code prompts you to select the project to run.

If you are using Visual Studio, click the "Open a project or solution" button on the splash screen or select File > Open > Project/Solution. Select the SportsSln.sln file in the SportsSln folder and click the Open button to open the project.

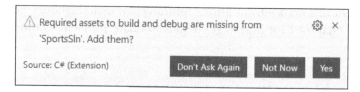

Figure 7.1   Adding assets in Visual Studio Code

7.1.3   Configuring the HTTP port

To configure the HTTP port that ASP.NET Core will use to listen for HTTP requests, make the changes shown in listing 7.4 to the launchSettings.json file in the SportsStore/Properties folder.

Listing 7.4 Setting the HTTP Port in the launchSettings.json File in the SportsStore/Properties Folder

```
{
  "iisSettings": {
    "windowsAuthentication": false,
    "anonymousAuthentication": true,
    "iisExpress": {
      "applicationUrl": "http://localhost:5000",
      "sslPort": 0
    }
  },
  "profiles": {
    "SportsStore": {
      "commandName": "Project",
      "dotnetRunMessages": true,
      "launchBrowser": true,
      "applicationUrl": "http://localhost:5000",
      "environmentVariables": {
        "ASPNETCORE_ENVIRONMENT": "Development"
      }
    },
    "IIS Express": {
      "commandName": "IISExpress",
      "launchBrowser": true,
      "environmentVariables": {
        "ASPNETCORE_ENVIRONMENT": "Development"
      }
    }
  }
}
```

7.1.4 Creating the application project folders

The next step is to create folders that will contain the application's components. Right-click the SportsStore item in the Visual Studio Solution Explorer or Visual Studio Code Explorer pane and select Add > New Folder or New Folder to create the set of folders described in table 7.1.

Table 7.1 The application project folders

Name	Description
Models	This folder will contain the data model and the classes that provide access to the data in the application's database.
Controllers	This folder will contain the controller classes that handle HTTP requests.
Views	This folder will contain all the Razor files, grouped into separate subfolders.
Views/Home	This folder will contain Razor files that are specific to the Home controller, which I create in the "Creating the Controller and View" section.
Views/Shared	This folder will contain Razor files that are common to all controllers.

7.1.5   *Preparing the services and the request pipeline*

The `Program.cs` file is used to configure the ASP.NET Core application. Apply the changes shown in listing 7.5 to the `Program.cs` file in the `SportsStore` project to configure the basic application features.

> **NOTE** The `Program.cs` file is an important ASP.NET Core feature. I describe it in detail in part 2.

Listing 7.5   Configuring the application in the Program.cs file in the SportsStore folder

```
var builder = WebApplication.CreateBuilder(args);

builder.Services.AddControllersWithViews();

var app = builder.Build();

//app.MapGet("/", () => "Hello World!");

app.UseStaticFiles();
app.MapDefaultControllerRoute();

app.Run();
```

The `builder.Services` property is used to set up objects, known as *services*, that can be used throughout the application and that are accessed through a feature called *dependency injection*, which I describe in chapter 14. The `AddControllersWithViews` method sets up the shared objects required by applications using the MVC Framework and the Razor view engine.

ASP.NET Core receives HTTP requests and passes them along a *request pipeline*, which is populated with middleware components registered using the `app` property. Each middleware component is able to inspect requests, modify them, generate a response, or modify the responses that other components have produced. The request pipeline is the heart of ASP.NET Core, and I describe it in detail in chapter 12, where I also explain how to create custom middleware components.

The `UseStaticFiles` method enables support for serving static content from the `wwwroot` folder and will be created later in the chapter.

One especially important middleware component provides the endpoint routing feature, which matches HTTP requests to the application features—known as *endpoints*—able to produce responses for them, a process I describe in detail in chapter 13. The endpoint routing feature is added to the request pipeline automatically, and the `MapDefaultControllerRoute` registers the MVC Framework as a source of endpoints using a default convention for mapping requests to classes and methods.

7.1.6 *Configuring the Razor view engine*

The Razor view engine is responsible for processing view files, which have the `.cshtml` extension, to generate HTML responses. Some initial preparation is required to configure Razor to make it easier to create views for the application.

Add a Razor View Imports file named `_ViewImports.cshtml` in the `Views` folder with the content shown in listing 7.6.

> **CAUTION** Pay close attention to the contents of this file. It is easy to make a mistake that causes the application to generate incorrect HTML content.

> **Listing 7.6   The contents of the _ViewImports.cshtml file in the SportsStore/Views folder**

```
@using SportsStore.Models
@addTagHelper *, Microsoft.AspNetCore.Mvc.TagHelpers
```

The `@using` statement will allow me to use the types in the `SportsStore.Models` namespace in views without needing to refer to the namespace. The `@addTagHelper` statement enables the built-in tag helpers, which I use later to create HTML elements that reflect the configuration of the SportsStore application and which I describe in detail in chapter 15. (You may see a warning or error displayed by the code editor for the contents of this file, but this will be resolved shortly and can be ignored.)

Add a Razor View Start file named `_ViewStart.cshtml` to the `SportsStore/Views` folder with the content shown in listing 7.7. (The file will already contain this expression if you create the file using the Visual Studio item template.)

> **Listing 7.7   The contents of the _ViewStart.cshtml file in the SportsStore/Views folder**

```
@{
    Layout = "_Layout";
}
```

The Razor View Start file tells Razor to use a layout file in the HTML that it generates, reducing the amount of duplication in views. To create the view, add a Razor layout named `_Layout.cshtml` to the `Views/Shared` folder, with the content shown in listing 7.8.

> **Listing 7.8   The contents of the _Layout.cshtml file in the SportsStore/Views/Shared folder**

```
<!DOCTYPE html>
<html>
<head>
    <meta name="viewport" content="width=device-width" />
    <title>SportsStore</title>
</head>
<body>
    <div>
        @RenderBody()
    </div>
</body>
</html>
```

This file defines a simple HTML document into which the contents of other views will be inserted by the @RenderBody expression. I explain how Razor expressions work in detail in chapter 21.

7.1.7   Creating the controller and view

Add a class file named HomeController.cs in the SportsStore/Controllers folder and use it to define the class shown in listing 7.9. This is a minimal controller that contains just enough functionality to produce a response.

> **Listing 7.9   The contents of the HomeController.cs file in the SportsStore/Controllers folder**

```
using Microsoft.AspNetCore.Mvc;

namespace SportsStore.Controllers {
    public class HomeController: Controller {

        public IActionResult Index() => View();

    }
}
```

The MapDefaultControllerRoute method used in listing 7.5 tells ASP.NET Core how to match URLs to controller classes. The configuration applied by that method declares that the Index action method defined by the Home controller will be used to handle requests.

The Index action method doesn't do anything useful yet and just returns the result of calling the View method, which is inherited from the Controller base class. This result tells ASP.NET Core to render the default view associated with the action method. To create the view, add a Razor View file named Index.cshtml to the Views/Home folder with the content shown in listing 7.10.

> **Listing 7.10   The contents of the Index.cshtml file in the SportsStore/Views/Home folder**

```
<h4>Welcome to SportsStore</h4>
```

7.1.8   Starting the data model

Almost all projects have a data model of some sort. Since this is an e-commerce application, the most obvious model I need is for a product. Add a class file named Product.cs to the Models folder and use it to define the class shown in listing 7.11.

> **Listing 7.11   The contents of the Product.cs file in the SportsStore/Models folder**

```
using System.ComponentModel.DataAnnotations.Schema;

namespace SportsStore.Models {

    public class Product {
```

```
        public long? ProductID { get; set; }

        public string Name { get; set; } = String.Empty;

        public string Description { get; set; } = String.Empty;

        [Column(TypeName = "decimal(8, 2)")]
        public decimal Price { get; set; }

        public string Category { get; set; } = String.Empty;
    }
}
```

The `Price` property has been decorated with the `Column` attribute to specify the SQL data type that will be used to store values for this property. Not all C# types map neatly onto SQL types, and this attribute ensures the database uses an appropriate type for the application data.

7.1.9 Checking and running the application

Before going any further, it is a good idea to make sure the application builds and runs as expected. Run the command shown in listing 7.12 in the `SportsStore` folder.

> **Listing 7.12 Running the example application**

```
dotnet run
```

Request http://localhost:5000, and you will see the response shown in figure 7.2.

Figure 7.2 Running the example application

7.2 Adding data to the application

Now that the SportsStore contains some basic setup and can produce a simple response, it is time to add some data so that the application has something more useful to display. The SportsStore application will store its data in a SQL Server LocalDB database, which is accessed using Entity Framework Core. Entity Framework Core is the Microsoft object-to-relational mapping (ORM) framework, and it is the most widely used method of accessing databases in ASP.NET Core projects.

> **CAUTION** If you did not install LocalDB when you prepared your development environment in chapter 2, you must do so now. The SportsStore application will not work without its database.

7.2.1 Installing the Entity Framework Core packages

The first step is to add Entity Framework Core to the project. Use a PowerShell command prompt to run the command shown in listing 7.13 in the `SportsStore` folder. If you receive an error asking you to specify a project, then delete the `SportsStore -Backup.csproj` file in the SportsStore folder and try again.

> **Listing 7.13   Adding the Entity Framework Core packages to the SportsStore project**

```
dotnet add package Microsoft.EntityFrameworkCore.Design --version 7.0.0
dotnet add package Microsoft.EntityFrameworkCore.SqlServer --version 7.0.0
```

These packages install Entity Framework Core and the support for using SQL Server. Entity Framework Core also requires a tools package, which includes the command-line tools required to prepare and create databases for ASP.NET Core applications. Run the commands shown in listing 7.14 to remove any existing version of the tools package, if there is one, and install the version used in this book. (Since this package is installed globally, you can run these commands in any folder.)

> **Listing 7.14   Installing the Entity Framework Core tool package**

```
dotnet tool uninstall --global dotnet-ef
dotnet tool install --global dotnet-ef --version 7.0.0
```

7.2.2 Defining the connection string

Configuration settings, such as database connection strings, are stored in JSON configuration files. To describe the connection to the database that will be used for the SportsStore data, add the entries shown in listing 7.15 to the `appsettings.json` file in the `SportsStore` folder.

The project also contains an `appsettings.Development.json` file that contains configuration settings that are used only in development. This file is displayed as nested within the `appsettings.json` file by Solution Explorer but is always visible in Visual Studio Code. I use only the `appsettings.json` file for the development of the SportsStore project, but I explain the relationship between the files and how they are both used in detail in chapter 15.

> **TIP**   Connection strings must be expressed as a single unbroken line, which is fine in the code editor but doesn't fit on the printed page and is the cause of the awkward formatting in listing 7.15. When you define the connection string in your own project, make sure that the value of the `SportsStoreConnection` item is on a single line.

> **Listing 7.15   Adding a configuration setting in the appsettings.json file in the SportsStore folder**

```
{
  "Logging": {
    "LogLevel": {
```

```
      "Default": "Information",
      "Microsoft.AspNetCore": "Warning"
    }
  },
  "AllowedHosts": "*",
  "ConnectionStrings": {
    "SportsStoreConnection": "Server=(localdb)\\MSSQLLocalDB;Database=
SportsStore;MultipleActiveResultSets=true"
  }
}
```

This configuration string specifies a LocalDB database called SportsStore and enables the multiple active result set (MARS) feature, which is required for some of the database queries that will be made by the SportsStore application using Entity Framework Core.

Pay close attention when you add the configuration setting. JSON data must be expressed exactly as shown in the listing, which means you must ensure you correctly quote the property names and values. You can download the configuration file from the GitHub repository if you have difficulty.

TIP Each database server requires its own connection string format. A helpful site for formulating connection strings is https://www.connectionstrings.com.

7.2.3 Creating the database context class

Entity Framework Core provides access to the database through a context class. Add a class file named StoreDbContext.cs to the Models folder and use it to define the class shown in listing 7.16.

Listing 7.16 The contents of the StoreDbContext.cs file in the SportsStore/Models folder

```csharp
using Microsoft.EntityFrameworkCore;

namespace SportsStore.Models {
    public class StoreDbContext : DbContext {

        public StoreDbContext(DbContextOptions<StoreDbContext> options)
            : base(options) { }

        public DbSet<Product> Products => Set<Product>();
    }
}
```

The DbContext base class provides access to the Entity Framework Core's underlying functionality, and the Products property will provide access to the Product objects in the database. The StoreDbContext class is derived from DbContext and adds the properties that will be used to read and write the application's data. There is only one property for now, which will provide access to Product objects.

7.2.4   Configuring Entity Framework Core

Entity Framework Core must be configured so that it knows the type of database to which it will connect, which connection string describes that connection, and which context class will present the data in the database. Listing 7.17 shows the required changes to the `Program.cs` file.

> **Listing 7.17   Configuring Entity Framework Core in the Program.cs file in the SportsStore folder**

```
using Microsoft.EntityFrameworkCore;
using SportsStore.Models;

var builder = WebApplication.CreateBuilder(args);

builder.Services.AddControllersWithViews();

builder.Services.AddDbContext<StoreDbContext>(opts => {
    opts.UseSqlServer(
        builder.Configuration["ConnectionStrings:SportsStoreConnection"]);
});

var app = builder.Build();

app.UseStaticFiles();
app.MapDefaultControllerRoute();

app.Run();
```

The `IConfiguration` interface provides access to the ASP.NET Core configuration system, which includes the contents of the `appsettings.json` file and which I describe in detail in chapter 15. Access to the configuration data is through the `builder.Configuration` property, which allows the database connection string to be obtained. Entity Framework Core is configured with the `AddDbContext` method, which registers the database context class and configures the relationship with the database. The `UseSQLServer` method declares that SQL Server is being used.

7.2.5   Creating a repository

The next step is to create a repository interface and implementation class. The repository pattern is one of the most widely used, and it provides a consistent way to access the features presented by the database context class. Not everyone finds a repository useful, but my experience is that it can reduce duplication and ensures that operations on the database are performed consistently. Add a class file named `IStoreRepository.cs` to the `Models` folder and use it to define the interface shown in listing 7.18.

> **Listing 7.18   The contents of the IStoreRepository.cs file in the SportsStore/Models folder**

```
namespace SportsStore.Models {
    public interface IStoreRepository {
```

```
    IQueryable<Product> Products { get; }
  }
}
```

This interface uses `IQueryable<T>` to allow a caller to obtain a sequence of `Product` objects. The `IQueryable<T>` interface is derived from the more familiar `IEnumerable<T>` interface and represents a collection of objects that can be queried, such as those managed by a database.

A class that depends on the `IStoreRepository` interface can obtain `Product` objects without needing to know the details of how they are stored or how the implementation class will deliver them.

Understanding IEnumerable<T> and IQueryable<T> interfaces

The `IQueryable<T>` interface is useful because it allows a collection of objects to be queried efficiently. Later in this chapter, I add support for retrieving a subset of `Product` objects from a database, and using the `IQueryable<T>` interface allows me to ask the database for just the objects that I require using standard LINQ statements and without needing to know what database server stores the data or how it processes the query. Without the `IQueryable<T>` interface, I would have to retrieve all of the `Product` objects from the database and then discard the ones that I don't want, which becomes an expensive operation as the amount of data used by an application increases. It is for this reason that the `IQueryable<T>` interface is typically used instead of `IEnumerable<T>` in database repository interfaces and classes.

However, care must be taken with the `IQueryable<T>` interface because each time the collection of objects is enumerated, the query will be evaluated again, which means that a new query will be sent to the database. This can undermine the efficiency gains of using `IQueryable<T>`. In such situations, you can convert the `IQueryable<T>` interface to a more predictable form using the `ToList` or `ToArray` extension method.

To create an implementation of the repository interface, add a class file named `EFStoreRepository.cs` in the `Models` folder and use it to define the class shown in listing 7.19.

Listing 7.19   The contents of the EFStoreRepository.cs file in the SportsStore/Models folder

```
namespace SportsStore.Models {
    public class EFStoreRepository : IStoreRepository {
        private StoreDbContext context;

        public EFStoreRepository(StoreDbContext ctx) {
            context = ctx;
        }

        public IQueryable<Product> Products => context.Products;
    }
}
```

I'll add additional functionality as I add features to the application, but for the moment, the repository implementation just maps the `Products` property defined by the `IStoreRepository` interface onto the `Products` property defined by the `StoreDbContext` class. The `Products` property in the context class returns a `DbSet` `<Product>` object, which implements the `IQueryable<T>` interface and makes it easy to implement the repository interface when using Entity Framework Core.

Earlier in the chapter, I explained that ASP.NET Core supports services that allow objects to be accessed throughout the application. One benefit of services is they allow classes to use interfaces without needing to know which implementation class is being used. I explain this in detail in chapter 14, but for the SportsStore chapters, it means that application components can access objects that implement the `IStoreRepository` interface without knowing that it is the `EFStoreRepository` implementation class they are using. This makes it easy to change the implementation class the application uses without needing to make changes to the individual components. Add the statement shown in listing 7.20 to the `Program.cs` file to create a service for the `IStoreRepository` interface that uses `EFStoreRepository` as the implementation class.

TIP   Don't worry if this doesn't make sense right now. This topic is one of the most confusing aspects of working with ASP.NET Core, and it can take a while to understand.

> **Listing 7.20   Creating the repository service in the Program.cs file in the SportsStore folder**

```
using Microsoft.EntityFrameworkCore;
using SportsStore.Models;

var builder = WebApplication.CreateBuilder(args);

builder.Services.AddControllersWithViews();

builder.Services.AddDbContext<StoreDbContext>(opts => {
    opts.UseSqlServer(
        builder.Configuration["ConnectionStrings:SportsStoreConnection"]);
});

builder.Services.AddScoped<IStoreRepository, EFStoreRepository>();

var app = builder.Build();

app.UseStaticFiles();
app.MapDefaultControllerRoute();

app.Run();
```

The `AddScoped` method creates a service where each HTTP request gets its own repository object, which is the way that Entity Framework Core is typically used.

7.2.6 Creating the database migration

Entity Framework Core can generate the schema for the database using the data model classes through a feature called *migrations*. When you prepare a migration, Entity Framework Core creates a C# class that contains the SQL commands required to prepare the database. If you need to modify your model classes, then you can create a new migration that contains the SQL commands required to reflect the changes. In this way, you don't have to worry about manually writing and testing SQL commands and can just focus on the C# model classes in the application.

Entity Framework Core commands are performed from the command line. Open a PowerShell command prompt and run the command shown in listing 7.21 in the `SportsStore` folder to create the migration class that will prepare the database for its first use.

Listing 7.21 Creating the database migration

```
dotnet ef migrations add Initial
```

When this command has finished, the SportsStore project will contain a `Migrations` folder. This is where Entity Framework Core stores its migration classes. One of the file names will be a timestamp followed by `_Initial.cs`, and this is the class that will be used to create the initial schema for the database. If you examine the contents of this file, you can see how the `Product` model class has been used to create the schema.

7.2.7 Creating seed data

To populate the database and provide some sample data, I added a class file called `SeedData.cs` to the `Models` folder and defined the class shown in listing 7.22.

Listing 7.22 The contents of the SeedData.cs file in the SportsStore/Models folder

```csharp
using Microsoft.EntityFrameworkCore;

namespace SportsStore.Models {

    public static class SeedData {

        public static void EnsurePopulated(IApplicationBuilder app) {
            StoreDbContext context = app.ApplicationServices
                .CreateScope().ServiceProvider
                .GetRequiredService<StoreDbContext>();

            if (context.Database.GetPendingMigrations().Any()) {
                context.Database.Migrate();
            }

            if (!context.Products.Any()) {
                context.Products.AddRange(
                    new Product {
                        Name = "Kayak", Description =
                            "A boat for one person",
```

```
                        Category = "Watersports", Price = 275
                    },
                    new Product {
                        Name = "Lifejacket",
                        Description = "Protective and fashionable",
                        Category = "Watersports", Price = 48.95m
                    },
                    new Product {
                        Name = "Soccer Ball",
                        Description = "FIFA-approved size and weight",
                        Category = "Soccer", Price = 19.50m
                    },
                    new Product {
                        Name = "Corner Flags",
                        Description =
                          "Give your playing field a professional touch",
                        Category = "Soccer", Price = 34.95m
                    },
                    new Product {
                        Name = "Stadium",
                        Description = "Flat-packed 35,000-seat stadium",
                        Category = "Soccer", Price = 79500
                    },
                    new Product {
                        Name = "Thinking Cap",
                        Description = "Improve brain efficiency by 75%",
                        Category = "Chess", Price = 16
                    },
                    new Product {
                        Name = "Unsteady Chair",
                        Description =
                          "Secretly give your opponent a disadvantage",
                        Category = "Chess", Price = 29.95m
                    },
                    new Product {
                        Name = "Human Chess Board",
                        Description = "A fun game for the family",
                        Category = "Chess", Price = 75
                    },
                    new Product {
                        Name = "Bling-Bling King",
                        Description = "Gold-plated, diamond-studded King",
                        Category = "Chess", Price = 1200
                    }
                );
                context.SaveChanges();
            }
        }
    }
}
```

The static `EnsurePopulated` method receives an `IApplicationBuilder` argument, which is the interface used in the `Program.cs` file to register middleware components to handle HTTP requests. `IApplicationBuilder` also provides access to the application's services, including the Entity Framework Core database context service.

The EnsurePopulated method obtains a StoreDbContext object through the IApplicationBuilder interface and calls the Database.Migrate method if there are any pending migrations, which means that the database will be created and prepared so that it can store Product objects. Next, the number of Product objects in the database is checked. If there are no objects in the database, then the database is populated using a collection of Product objects using the AddRange method and then written to the database using the SaveChanges method.

The final change is to seed the database when the application starts, which I have done by adding a call to the EnsurePopulated method from the Program.cs file, as shown in listing 7.23.

Listing 7.23 Seeding the database in the Program.cs file in the SportsStore folder

```
using Microsoft.EntityFrameworkCore;
using SportsStore.Models;

var builder = WebApplication.CreateBuilder(args);

builder.Services.AddControllersWithViews();

builder.Services.AddDbContext<StoreDbContext>(opts => {
    opts.UseSqlServer(
        builder.Configuration["ConnectionStrings:SportsStoreConnection"]);
});

builder.Services.AddScoped<IStoreRepository, EFStoreRepository>();

var app = builder.Build();

app.UseStaticFiles();
app.MapDefaultControllerRoute();

SeedData.EnsurePopulated(app);

app.Run();
```

Resetting the database

If you need to reset the database, then run this command in the SportsStore folder:

```
...
dotnet ef database drop --force --context StoreDbContext
...
```

Start ASP.NET Core, and the database will be re-created and seeded with data.

7.3   Displaying a list of products

As you have seen, the initial preparation work for an ASP.NET Core project can take some time. But the good news is that once the foundation is in place, the pace improves, and features are added more rapidly. In this section, I am going to create a controller and an action method that can display details of the products in the repository.

> **Using the Visual Studio scaffolding**
>
> As I noted in chapter 4, Visual Studio supports scaffolding to add items to a project.
>
> I don't use scaffolding in this book. The code and markup that the scaffolding generates are so generic as to be all but useless, and the scenarios that are supported are narrow and don't address common development problems. My goal in this book is not only to make sure you know how to create ASP.NET Core applications but also to explain how everything works behind the scenes, and that is harder to do when responsibility for creating components is handed to the scaffolding.
>
> If you are using Visual Studio, add items to the project by right-clicking a folder in the Solution Explorer, selecting Add > New Item from the pop-up menu, and then choosing an item template from the Add New Item window.
>
> You may find your development style to be different from mine, and you may find that you prefer working with the scaffolding in your own projects. That's perfectly reasonable, although I recommend you take the time to understand what the scaffolding does so you know where to look if you don't get the results you expect.

7.3.1   Preparing the controller

Add the statements shown in listing 7.24 to prepare the controller to display the list of products.

> **Listing 7.24   Preparing the controller in the HomeController.cs file in the SportsStore/ Controllers folder**

```
using Microsoft.AspNetCore.Mvc;
using SportsStore.Models;

namespace SportsStore.Controllers {
    public class HomeController : Controller {
        private IStoreRepository repository;

        public HomeController(IStoreRepository repo) {
            repository = repo;
        }

        public IActionResult Index() => View(repository.Products);
    }
}
```

When ASP.NET Core needs to create a new instance of the `HomeController` class to handle an HTTP request, it will inspect the constructor and see that it requires an object that implements the `IStoreRepository` interface. To determine what implementation class should be used, ASP.NET Core consults the configuration created in the `Program.cs` file, which tells it that `EFStoreRepository` should be used and that a new instance should be created for every request. ASP.NET Core creates a new `EFStoreRepository` object and uses it to invoke the `HomeController` constructor to create the controller object that will process the HTTP request.

This is known as *dependency injection*, and its approach allows the `HomeController` object to access the application's repository through the `IStoreRepository` interface without knowing which implementation class has been configured. I could reconfigure the service to use a different implementation class—one that doesn't use Entity Framework Core, for example—and dependency injection means that the controller will continue to work without changes.

NOTE   Some developers don't like dependency injection and believe it makes applications more complicated. That's not my view, but if you are new to dependency injection, then I recommend you wait until you have read chapter 14 before you make up your mind.

Unit test: repository access

I can unit test that the controller is accessing the repository correctly by creating a mock repository, injecting it into the constructor of the `HomeController` class, and then calling the `Index` method to get the response that contains the list of products. I then compare the `Product` objects I get to what I would expect from the test data in the mock implementation. See chapter 6 for details of how to set up unit tests. Here is the unit test I created for this purpose, in a class file called `HomeControllerTests.cs` that I added to the `SportsStore.Tests` project:

```
using System;
using System.Collections.Generic;
using System.Linq;
using Microsoft.AspNetCore.Mvc;
using Moq;
using SportsStore.Controllers;
using SportsStore.Models;
using Xunit;

namespace SportsStore.Tests {

    public class HomeControllerTests {

        [Fact]
        public void Can_Use_Repository() {
            // Arrange
            Mock<IStoreRepository> mock = new Mock<IStoreRepository>();
            mock.Setup(m => m.Products).Returns((new Product[] {
                new Product {ProductID = 1, Name = "P1"},
                new Product {ProductID = 2, Name = "P2"}
            }).AsQueryable<Product>());

            HomeController controller = new HomeController(mock.Object);
```

(continued)

```
            // Act
            IEnumerable<Product>? result =
                (controller.Index() as ViewResult)?.ViewData.Model
                    as IEnumerable<Product>;

            // Assert
            Product[] prodArray = result?.ToArray()
                ?? Array.Empty<Product>();
            Assert.True(prodArray.Length == 2);
            Assert.Equal("P1", prodArray[0].Name);
            Assert.Equal("P2", prodArray[1].Name);
        }
    }
}
```

It is a little awkward to get the data returned from the action method. The result is a
`ViewResult` object, and I have to cast the value of its `ViewData.Model` property to
the expected data type. I explain the different result types that can be returned by action
methods and how to work with them in part 2.

7.3.2   Updating the view

The `Index` action method in listing 7.24 passes the collection of `Product` objects from
the repository to the `View` method, which means these objects will be the view model
that Razor uses when it generates HTML content from the view. Make the changes
to the view shown in listing 7.25 to generate content using the `Product` view model
objects.

> **Listing 7.25   Using the product data in the Index.cshtml file in the SportsStore/**
> **Views/Home folder**

```
@model IQueryable<Product>

@foreach (var p in Model ?? Enumerable.Empty<Product>()) {
    <div>
        <h3>@p.Name</h3>
        @p.Description
        <h4>@p.Price.ToString("c")</h4>
    </div>
}
```

The `@model` expression at the top of the file specifies that the view expects to receive
a sequence of `Product` objects from the action method as its model data. I use an
`@foreach` expression to work through the sequence and generate a simple set of
HTML elements for each `Product` object that is received.

There is a quirk in the way that Razor Views work that means the model data is
always nullable, even when the type specified by the `@model` expression is not. For this
reason, I use the null-coalescing operator in the `@foreach` expression with an empty
enumeration.

The view doesn't know where the `Product` objects came from, how they were obtained, or whether they represent all the products known to the application. Instead, the view deals only with how details of each `Product` are displayed using HTML elements.

> **TIP** I converted the `Price` property to a string using the `ToString("c")` method, which renders numerical values as currency according to the culture settings that are in effect on your server. For example, if the server is set up as `en-US`, then `(1002.3).ToString("c")` will return `$1,002.30`, but if the server is set to `en-GB`, then the same method will return £1,002.30.

7.3.3 Running the application

Start ASP.NET Core and request http://localhost:5000 to see the list of products, which is shown in figure 7.3. This is the typical pattern of development for ASP.NET Core. An initial investment of time setting everything up is necessary, and then the basic features of the application snap together quickly.

Figure 7.3 Displaying a list of products

7.4 Adding pagination

You can see from figure 7.3 that the `Index.cshtml` view displays the products in the database on a single page. In this section, I will add support for pagination so that the view displays a smaller number of products on a page and so the user can move from page to page to view the overall catalog. To do this, I am going to add a parameter to the `Index` method in the `Home` controller, as shown in listing 7.26.

> **Listing 7.26 Adding pagination in the HomeController.cs file in the SportsStore/ Controllers folder**

```
using Microsoft.AspNetCore.Mvc;
using SportsStore.Models;

namespace SportsStore.Controllers {
    public class HomeController : Controller {
        private IStoreRepository repository;
```

```
        public int PageSize = 4;

        public HomeController(IStoreRepository repo) {
            repository = repo;
        }

        public ViewResult Index(int productPage = 1)
            => View(repository.Products
                .OrderBy(p => p.ProductID)
                .Skip((productPage - 1) * PageSize)
                .Take(PageSize));
    }
}
```

The PageSize field specifies that I want four products per page. I have added an optional parameter to the Index method, which means that if the method is called without a parameter, the call is treated as though I had supplied the value specified in the parameter definition, with the effect that the action method displays the first page of products when it is invoked without an argument. Within the body of the action method, I get the Product objects, order them by the primary key, skip over the products that occur before the start of the current page, and take the number of products specified by the PageSize field.

Unit test: pagination

I can unit test the pagination feature by mocking the repository, requesting a specific page from the controller, and making sure I get the expected subset of the data. Here is the unit test I created for this purpose and added to the HomeControllerTests.cs file in the SportsStore.Tests project:

```
using System;
using System.Collections.Generic;
using System.Linq;
using Microsoft.AspNetCore.Mvc;
using Moq;
using SportsStore.Controllers;
using SportsStore.Models;
using Xunit;

namespace SportsStore.Tests {

    public class HomeControllerTests {

        [Fact]
        public void Can_Use_Repository() {

            // ...statements omitted for brevity...
        }

        [Fact]
        public void Can_Paginate() {
            // Arrange
            Mock<IStoreRepository> mock = new Mock<IStoreRepository>();
```

(continued)

```
        mock.Setup(m => m.Products).Returns((new Product[] {
            new Product {ProductID = 1, Name = "P1"},
            new Product {ProductID = 2, Name = "P2"},
            new Product {ProductID = 3, Name = "P3"},
            new Product {ProductID = 4, Name = "P4"},
            new Product {ProductID = 5, Name = "P5"}
        }).AsQueryable<Product>());

        HomeController controller = new HomeController(mock.Object);
        controller.PageSize = 3;

        // Act
        IEnumerable<Product> result =
            (controller.Index(2) as ViewResult)?.ViewData.Model
                as IEnumerable<Product>
                    ?? Enumerable.Empty<Product>();

        // Assert
        Product[] prodArray = result.ToArray();
        Assert.True(prodArray.Length == 2);
        Assert.Equal("P4", prodArray[0].Name);
        Assert.Equal("P5", prodArray[1].Name);
    }
  }
}
```

You can see the new test follows the pattern of the existing one, relying on Moq to provide a known set of data with which to work.

7.4.1 Displaying page links

Restart ASP.NET Core and request http://localhost:5000, and you will see that there are now four items shown on the page, as shown in figure 7.4. If you want to view another page, you can append query string parameters to the end of the URL, like this:

`http://localhost:5000/?productPage=2`

Figure 7.4 Paging through data

Using these query strings, you can navigate through the catalog of products. There is no way for customers to figure out that these query string parameters exist, and even if there were, customers are not going to want to navigate this way. Instead, I need to render some page links at the bottom of each list of products so that customers can navigate between pages. To do this, I am going to create a *tag helper*, which generates the HTML markup for the links I require.

ADDING THE VIEW MODEL

To support the tag helper, I am going to pass information to the view about the number of pages available, the current page, and the total number of products in the repository. The easiest way to do this is to create a view model class, which is used specifically to pass data between a controller and a view. Create a `Models/ViewModels` folder in the `SportsStore` project, add to it a class file named `PagingInfo.cs`, and define the class shown in listing 7.27.

> **Listing 7.27   The contents of the PagingInfo.cs file in the SportsStore/Models/ ViewModels folder**

```
namespace SportsStore.Models.ViewModels {

    public class PagingInfo {
        public int TotalItems { get; set; }
        public int ItemsPerPage { get; set; }
        public int CurrentPage { get; set; }

        public int TotalPages =>
            (int)Math.Ceiling((decimal)TotalItems / ItemsPerPage);
    }
}
```

ADDING THE TAG HELPER CLASS

Now that I have a view model, it is time to create a tag helper class. Create a folder named `Infrastructure` in the SportsStore project and add to it a class file called `PageLinkTagHelper.cs`, with the code shown in listing 7.28. Tag helpers are a big part of ASP.NET Core development, and I explain how they work and how to use and create them in chapters 25–27.

> **TIP**   The `Infrastructure` folder is where I put classes that deliver the plumbing for an application but that are not related to the application's main functionality. You don't have to follow this convention in your own projects.

> **Listing 7.28   The contents of the PageLinkTagHelper.cs file in the SportsStore/ Infrastructure folder**

```
using Microsoft.AspNetCore.Mvc;
using Microsoft.AspNetCore.Mvc.Rendering;
using Microsoft.AspNetCore.Mvc.Routing;
using Microsoft.AspNetCore.Mvc.ViewFeatures;
```

```
using Microsoft.AspNetCore.Razor.TagHelpers;
using SportsStore.Models.ViewModels;

namespace SportsStore.Infrastructure {

    [HtmlTargetElement("div", Attributes = "page-model")]
    public class PageLinkTagHelper : TagHelper {
        private IUrlHelperFactory urlHelperFactory;

        public PageLinkTagHelper(IUrlHelperFactory helperFactory) {
            urlHelperFactory = helperFactory;
        }

        [ViewContext]
        [HtmlAttributeNotBound]
        public ViewContext? ViewContext { get; set; }

        public PagingInfo? PageModel { get; set; }

        public string? PageAction { get; set; }

        public override void Process(TagHelperContext context,
                TagHelperOutput output) {
            if (ViewContext != null && PageModel != null) {
                IUrlHelper urlHelper
                    = urlHelperFactory.GetUrlHelper(ViewContext);
                TagBuilder result = new TagBuilder("div");
                for (int i = 1; i <= PageModel.TotalPages; i++) {
                    TagBuilder tag = new TagBuilder("a");
                    tag.Attributes["href"] = urlHelper.Action(PageAction,
                        new { productPage = i });
                    tag.InnerHtml.Append(i.ToString());
                    result.InnerHtml.AppendHtml(tag);
                }
                output.Content.AppendHtml(result.InnerHtml);
            }
        }
    }
}
```

This tag helper populates a div element with a elements that correspond to pages of products. I am not going to go into detail about tag helpers now; it is enough to know that they are one of the most useful ways that you can introduce C# logic into your views. The code for a tag helper can look tortured because C# and HTML don't mix easily. But using tag helpers is preferable to including blocks of C# code in a view because a tag helper can be easily unit tested.

Most ASP.NET Core components, such as controllers and views, are discovered automatically, but tag helpers have to be registered. In listing 7.29, I have added a statement to the _ViewImports.cshtml file in the Views folder that tells ASP.NET Core to look for tag helper classes in the SportsStore project. I also added an @using expression so that I can refer to the view model classes in views without having to qualify their names with the namespace.

Listing 7.29   Registering a tag helper in the _ViewImports.cshtml file in the SportsStore/Views folder

```
@using SportsStore.Models
@using SportsStore.Models.ViewModels
@addTagHelper *, Microsoft.AspNetCore.Mvc.TagHelpers
@addTagHelper *, SportsStore
```

Unit test: creating page links

To test the `PageLinkTagHelper` tag helper class, I call the `Process` method with test data and provide a `TagHelperOutput` object that I inspect to see the HTML that is generated, as follows, which I defined in a new `PageLinkTagHelperTests.cs` file in the `SportsStore.Tests` project:

```
using System.Collections.Generic;
using System.Threading.Tasks;
using Microsoft.AspNetCore.Mvc;
using Microsoft.AspNetCore.Mvc.Rendering;
using Microsoft.AspNetCore.Mvc.Routing;
using Microsoft.AspNetCore.Razor.TagHelpers;
using Moq;
using SportsStore.Infrastructure;
using SportsStore.Models.ViewModels;
using Xunit;

namespace SportsStore.Tests {

    public class PageLinkTagHelperTests {

        [Fact]
        public void Can_Generate_Page_Links() {
            // Arrange
            var urlHelper = new Mock<IUrlHelper>();
            urlHelper.SetupSequence(x =>
                    x.Action(It.IsAny<UrlActionContext>()))
                .Returns("Test/Page1")
                .Returns("Test/Page2")
                .Returns("Test/Page3");

            var urlHelperFactory = new Mock<IUrlHelperFactory>();
            urlHelperFactory.Setup(f =>
                    f.GetUrlHelper(It.IsAny<ActionContext>()))
                    .Returns(urlHelper.Object);

            var viewContext = new Mock<ViewContext>();

            PageLinkTagHelper helper =
                    new PageLinkTagHelper(urlHelperFactory.Object) {
                        PageModel = new PagingInfo {
                            CurrentPage = 2,
                            TotalItems = 28,
                            ItemsPerPage = 10
                        },
```

(continued)

```
                    ViewContext = viewContext.Object,
                    PageAction = "Test"
                };

        TagHelperContext ctx = new TagHelperContext(
            new TagHelperAttributeList(),
            new Dictionary<object, object>(), "");

        var content = new Mock<TagHelperContent>();
        TagHelperOutput output = new TagHelperOutput("div",
            new TagHelperAttributeList(),
            (cache, encoder) => Task.FromResult(content.Object));

        // Act
        helper.Process(ctx, output);

        // Assert
        Assert.Equal(@"<a href=""Test/Page1"">1</a>"
            + @"<a href=""Test/Page2"">2</a>"
            + @"<a href=""Test/Page3"">3</a>",
             output.Content.GetContent());
    }
  }
}
```

The complexity in this test is in creating the objects that are required to create and use a tag helper. Tag helpers use `IUrlHelperFactory` objects to generate URLs that target different parts of the application, and I have used Moq to create an implementation of this interface and the related `IUrlHelper` interface that provides test data.

The core part of the test verifies the tag helper output by using a literal string value that contains double quotes. C# is perfectly capable of working with such strings, as long as the string is prefixed with @ and uses two sets of double quotes ("") in place of one set of double quotes. You must remember not to break the literal string into separate lines unless the string you are comparing to is similarly broken. For example, the literal I use in the test method has wrapped onto several lines because the width of a printed page is narrow. I have not added a newline character; if I did, the test would fail.

ADDING THE VIEW MODEL DATA

I am not quite ready to use the tag helper because I have yet to provide an instance of the `PagingInfo` view model class to the view. To do this, I added a class file called `ProductsListViewModel.cs` to the `Models/ViewModels` folder of the SportsStore project with the content shown in listing 7.30.

> **Listing 7.30 The contents of the ProductsListViewModel.cs file in the SportsStore/ Models/ViewModels folder**

```
namespace SportsStore.Models.ViewModels {

    public class ProductsListViewModel {
        public IEnumerable<Product> Products { get; set; }
```

```
        = Enumerable.Empty<Product>();
    public PagingInfo PagingInfo { get; set; } = new();
    }
}
```

I can update the `Index` action method in the `HomeController` class to use the `ProductsListViewModel` class to provide the view with details of the products to display on the page and with details of the pagination, as shown in listing 7.31.

> **Listing 7.31   Updating the action method in the HomeController.cs file in the Sports Store/Controllers folder**

```
using Microsoft.AspNetCore.Mvc;
using SportsStore.Models;
using SportsStore.Models.ViewModels;

namespace SportsStore.Controllers {
    public class HomeController : Controller {
        private IStoreRepository repository;
        public int PageSize = 4;

        public HomeController(IStoreRepository repo) {
            repository = repo;
        }

        public ViewResult Index(int productPage = 1)
            => View(new ProductsListViewModel {
                Products = repository.Products
                    .OrderBy(p => p.ProductID)
                    .Skip((productPage - 1) * PageSize)
                    .Take(PageSize),
                PagingInfo = new PagingInfo {
                    CurrentPage = productPage,
                    ItemsPerPage = PageSize,
                    TotalItems = repository.Products.Count()
                }
            });
    }
}
```

These changes pass a `ProductsListViewModel` object as the model data to the view.

Unit test: page model view data

I need to ensure that the controller sends the correct pagination data to the view. Here is the unit test I added to the `HomeControllerTests` class in the test project to make sure:

```
...
[Fact]
public void Can_Send_Pagination_View_Model() {

    // Arrange
    Mock<IStoreRepository> mock = new Mock<IStoreRepository>();
    mock.Setup(m => m.Products).Returns((new Product[] {
        new Product {ProductID = 1, Name = "P1"},
```

(continued)

```
      new Product {ProductID = 2, Name = "P2"},
      new Product {ProductID = 3, Name = "P3"},
      new Product {ProductID = 4, Name = "P4"},
      new Product {ProductID = 5, Name = "P5"}
   }).AsQueryable<Product>());

   // Arrange
   HomeController controller =
      new HomeController(mock.Object) { PageSize = 3 };

   // Act
   ProductsListViewModel result =
      controller.Index(2)?.ViewData.Model as ProductsListViewModel
         ?? new();

   // Assert
   PagingInfo pageInfo = result.PagingInfo;
   Assert.Equal(2, pageInfo.CurrentPage);
   Assert.Equal(3, pageInfo.ItemsPerPage);
   Assert.Equal(5, pageInfo.TotalItems);
   Assert.Equal(2, pageInfo.TotalPages);
}
...
```

I also need to modify the earlier unit tests to reflect the new result from the `Index` action method. Here are the revised tests:

```
...
[Fact]
public void Can_Use_Repository() {
   // Arrange
   Mock<IStoreRepository> mock = new Mock<IStoreRepository>();
   mock.Setup(m => m.Products).Returns((new Product[] {
      new Product {ProductID = 1, Name = "P1"},
      new Product {ProductID = 2, Name = "P2"}
   }).AsQueryable<Product>());

   HomeController controller = new HomeController(mock.Object);

   // Act
   ProductsListViewModel result =
      controller.Index()?.ViewData.Model as ProductsListViewModel
         ?? new();

   // Assert
   Product[] prodArray = result.Products.ToArray();
   Assert.True(prodArray.Length == 2);
   Assert.Equal("P1", prodArray[0].Name);
   Assert.Equal("P2", prodArray[1].Name);
}

[Fact]
public void Can_Paginate() {
   // Arrange
   Mock<IStoreRepository> mock = new Mock<IStoreRepository>();
```

(continued)

```
    mock.Setup(m => m.Products).Returns((new Product[] {
        new Product {ProductID = 1, Name = "P1"},
        new Product {ProductID = 2, Name = "P2"},
        new Product {ProductID = 3, Name = "P3"},
        new Product {ProductID = 4, Name = "P4"},
        new Product {ProductID = 5, Name = "P5"}
    }).AsQueryable<Product>());

    HomeController controller = new HomeController(mock.Object);
    controller.PageSize = 3;

    // Act
    ProductsListViewModel result =
        controller.Index(2)?.ViewData.Model as ProductsListViewModel
            ?? new();

    // Assert
    Product[] prodArray = result.Products.ToArray();
    Assert.True(prodArray.Length == 2);
    Assert.Equal("P4", prodArray[0].Name);
    Assert.Equal("P5", prodArray[1].Name);
}
...
```

I would usually create a common setup method, given the degree of duplication between these two test methods. However, since I am delivering the unit tests in individual sidebars like this one, I am going to keep everything separate so you can see each test on its own.

The view is currently expecting a sequence of Product objects, so I need to update the Index.cshtml file, as shown in listing 7.32, to deal with the new view model type.

Listing 7.32   Updating the Index.cshtml file in the SportsStore/Views/Home folder

```
@model ProductsListViewModel

@foreach (var p in Model.Products ?? Enumerable.Empty<Product>()) {
    <div>
        <h3>@p.Name</h3>
        @p.Description
        <h4>@p.Price.ToString("c")</h4>
    </div>
}
```

I have changed the @model directive to tell Razor that I am now working with a different data type. I updated the foreach loop so that the data source is the Products property of the model data.

DISPLAYING THE PAGE LINKS

I have everything in place to add the page links to the Index view. I created the view model that contains the paging information, updated the controller so that it passes this information to the view, and changed the `@model` directive to match the new model view type. All that remains is to add an HTML element that the tag helper will process to create the page links, as shown in listing 7.33.

Listing 7.33 Adding the pagination links in the Index.cshtml file in the SportsStore/Views/Home folder

```
@model ProductsListViewModel

@foreach (var p in Model.Products ?? Enumerable.Empty<Product>()) {
    <div>
        <h3>@p.Name</h3>
        @p.Description
        <h4>@p.Price.ToString("c")</h4>
    </div>
}

<div page-model="@Model.PagingInfo" page-action="Index"></div>
```

Restart ASP.NET Core and request http://localhost:5000, and you will see the new page links, as shown in figure 7.5. The style is still basic, which I will fix later in the chapter. What is important for the moment is that the links take the user from page to page in the catalog and allow for exploration of the products for sale. When Razor finds the `page-model` attribute on the `div` element, it asks the `PageLinkTagHelper` class to transform the element, which produces the set of links shown in the figure.

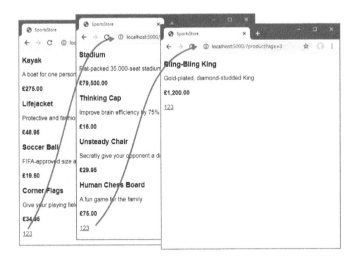

Figure 7.5 Displaying page navigation links

7.4.2 Improving the URLs

I have the page links working, but they still use the query string to pass page information to the server, like this:

```
http://localhost/?productPage=2
```

I can create URLs that are more appealing by creating a scheme that follows the pattern of *composable URLs*. A composable URL is one that makes sense to the user, like this one:

```
http://localhost/Page2
```

The ASP.NET Core routing feature makes it easy to change the URL scheme in an application. All I need to do is add a new route in the `Program.cs` file, as shown in listing 7.34.

> **Listing 7.34   Adding a new route in the Program.cs file in the SportsStore folder**

```
using Microsoft.EntityFrameworkCore;
using SportsStore.Models;

var builder = WebApplication.CreateBuilder(args);

builder.Services.AddControllersWithViews();

builder.Services.AddDbContext<StoreDbContext>(opts => {
    opts.UseSqlServer(
        builder.Configuration["ConnectionStrings:SportsStoreConnection"]);
});

builder.Services.AddScoped<IStoreRepository, EFStoreRepository>();

var app = builder.Build();

app.UseStaticFiles();
app.MapControllerRoute("pagination",
    "Products/Page{productPage}",
    new { Controller = "Home", action = "Index" });
app.MapDefaultControllerRoute();

SeedData.EnsurePopulated(app);

app.Run();
```

This is the only alteration required to change the URL scheme for product pagination. ASP.NET Core and the routing function are tightly integrated, so the application automatically reflects a change like this in the URLs used by the application, including those generated by tag helpers like the one I use to generate the page navigation links.

   Restart ASP.NET Core, request http://localhost:5000, and click one of the pagination links. The browser will navigate to a URL that uses the new URL scheme, as shown in figure 7.6.

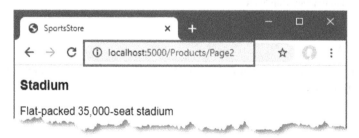

Figure 7.6
The new URL scheme displayed in the browser

7.5   Styling the content

I have built a great deal of infrastructure, and the basic features of the application are starting to come together, but I have not paid any attention to appearance. Even though this book is not about design or CSS, the SportsStore application design is so miserably plain that it undermines its technical strengths. In this section, I will put some of that right. I am going to implement a classic two-column layout with a header, as shown in figure 7.7.

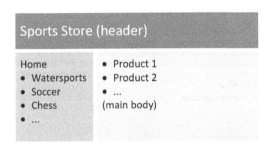

**Figure 7.7
The design
goal for the
SportsStore
application**

7.5.1   Installing the Bootstrap package

I am going to use the Bootstrap package to provide the CSS styles I will apply to the application. As explained in chapter 4, client-side packages are installed using LibMan. If you did not install the LibMan package when following the examples in chapter 4, use a PowerShell command prompt to run the commands shown in listing 7.35, which remove any existing LibMan package and install the version required for this book.

Listing 7.35   Installing the LibMan tool package

```
dotnet tool uninstall --global Microsoft.Web.LibraryManager.Cli
dotnet tool install --global Microsoft.Web.LibraryManager.Cli
    --version 2.1.175
```

Once you have installed LibMan, run the commands shown in listing 7.36 in the `SportsStore` folder to initialize the example project and install the Bootstrap package.

Listing 7.36   Initializing the example project

```
libman init -p cdnjs
libman install bootstrap@5.2.3 -d wwwroot/lib/bootstrap
```

7.5.2   Applying Bootstrap styles

Razor layouts provide common content so that it doesn't have to be repeated in multiple views. Add the elements shown in listing 7.37 to the `_Layout.cshtml` file in the `Views/Shared` folder to include the Bootstrap CSS stylesheet in the content sent to the browser and define a common header that will be used throughout the SportsStore application.

```
<!DOCTYPE html>
<html>
<head>
    <meta name="viewport" content="width=device-width" />
    <title>SportsStore</title>
    <link href="/lib/bootstrap/css/bootstrap.min.css" rel="stylesheet" />
</head>
<body>
    <div class="bg-dark text-white p-2">
        <span class="navbar-brand ml-2">SPORTS STORE</span>
    </div>
    <div class="row m-1 p-1">
        <div id="categories" class="col-3">
            Put something useful here later
        </div>
        <div class="col-9">
            @RenderBody()
        </div>
    </div>
</body>
</html>
```

Adding the Bootstrap CSS stylesheet to the layout means that I can use the styles it
defines in any of the views that rely on the layout. Listing 7.38 shows the styling
I applied to the Index.cshtml file.

```
@model ProductsListViewModel

@foreach (var p in Model.Products ?? Enumerable.Empty<Product>()) {
    <div class="card card-outline-primary m-1 p-1">
        <div class="bg-faded p-1">
            <h4>
                @p.Name
                <span class="badge rounded-pill bg-primary text-white"
                        style="float:right">
                    <small>@p.Price.ToString("c")</small>
                </span>
            </h4>
        </div>
        <div class="card-text p-1">@p.Description</div>
    </div>
}

<div page-model="@Model.PagingInfo" page-action="Index"
    page-classes-enabled="true" page-class="btn"
    page-class-normal="btn-outline-dark"
    page-class-selected="btn-primary" class="btn-group pull-right m-1">
</div>
```

I need to style the buttons generated by the `PageLinkTagHelper` class, but I don't want to hardwire the Bootstrap classes into the C# code because it makes it harder to reuse the tag helper elsewhere in the application or change the appearance of the buttons. Instead, I have defined custom attributes on the `div` element that specify the classes that I require, and these correspond to properties I added to the tag helper class, which are then used to style the `a` elements that are produced, as shown in listing 7.39.

Listing 7.39   Adding classes to elements in the PageLinkTagHelper.cs file in the SportsStore/Infrastructure folder

```csharp
using Microsoft.AspNetCore.Mvc;
using Microsoft.AspNetCore.Mvc.Rendering;
using Microsoft.AspNetCore.Mvc.Routing;
using Microsoft.AspNetCore.Mvc.ViewFeatures;
using Microsoft.AspNetCore.Razor.TagHelpers;
using SportsStore.Models.ViewModels;

namespace SportsStore.Infrastructure {

    [HtmlTargetElement("div", Attributes = "page-model")]
    public class PageLinkTagHelper : TagHelper {
        private IUrlHelperFactory urlHelperFactory;

        public PageLinkTagHelper(IUrlHelperFactory helperFactory) {
            urlHelperFactory = helperFactory;
        }

        [ViewContext]
        [HtmlAttributeNotBound]
        public ViewContext? ViewContext { get; set; }

        public PagingInfo? PageModel { get; set; }

        public string? PageAction { get; set; }

        public bool PageClassesEnabled { get; set; } = false;
        public string PageClass { get; set; } = String.Empty;
        public string PageClassNormal { get; set; } = String.Empty;
        public string PageClassSelected { get; set; } = String.Empty;

        public override void Process(TagHelperContext context,
                TagHelperOutput output) {
            if (ViewContext != null && PageModel != null) {
                IUrlHelper urlHelper
                    = urlHelperFactory.GetUrlHelper(ViewContext);
                TagBuilder result = new TagBuilder("div");
                for (int i = 1; i <= PageModel.TotalPages; i++) {
                    TagBuilder tag = new TagBuilder("a");
                    tag.Attributes["href"] = urlHelper.Action(PageAction,
                        new { productPage = i });
                    if (PageClassesEnabled) {
```

```
            tag.AddCssClass(PageClass);
            tag.AddCssClass(i == PageModel.CurrentPage
                ? PageClassSelected : PageClassNormal);
        }
        tag.InnerHtml.Append(i.ToString());
        result.InnerHtml.AppendHtml(tag);
    }
    output.Content.AppendHtml(result.InnerHtml);
        }
    }
  }
}
```

The values of the attributes are automatically used to set the tag helper property values, with the mapping between the HTML attribute name format (`page-class -normal`) and the C# property name format (`PageClassNormal`) taken into account. This allows tag helpers to respond differently based on the attributes of an HTML element, creating a more flexible way to generate content in an ASP.NET Core application.

Restart ASP.NET Core and request http://localhost:5000, and you will see the appearance of the application has been improved—at least a little, anyway—as illustrated by figure 7.8.

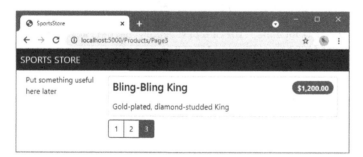

Figure 7.8   Applying styles to the SportsStore application

7.5.3   Creating a partial view

As a finishing flourish for this chapter, I am going to refactor the application to simplify the `Index.cshtml` view. I am going to create a *partial view*, which is a fragment of content that you can embed into another view, rather like a template. I describe partial views in detail in chapter 22, and they help reduce duplication when you need the same content to appear in different places in an application. Rather than copy and paste the same Razor markup into multiple views, you can define it once in a partial view. To create the partial view, I added a Razor View called `ProductSummary.cshtml` to the `Views/Shared` folder and added the markup shown in listing 7.40.

Listing 7.40 The contents of the ProductSummary.cshtml file in the SportsStore/ Views/Shared folder

```
@model Product

<div class="card card-outline-primary m-1 p-1">
    <div class="bg-faded p-1">
        <h4>
            @Model.Name
            <span class="badge rounded-pill bg-primary text-white"
                style="float:right">
                <small>@Model.Price.ToString("c")</small>
            </span>
        </h4>
    </div>
    <div class="card-text p-1">@Model.Description</div>
</div>
```

Now I need to update the `Index.cshtml` file in the `Views/Home` folder so that it uses the partial view, as shown in listing 7.41.

Listing 7.41 Using a partial view in the Index.cshtml file in the SportsStore/Views/ Home folder

```
@model ProductsListViewModel

@foreach (var p in Model.Products ?? Enumerable.Empty<Product>()) {
    <partial name="ProductSummary" model="p" />
}

<div page-model="@Model.PagingInfo" page-action="Index"
    page-classes-enabled="true" page-class="btn"
    page-class-normal="btn-outline-dark"
    page-class-selected="btn-primary" class="btn-group pull-right m-1">
</div>
```

I have taken the markup that was previously in the `@foreach` expression in the `Index.cshtml` view and moved it to the new partial view. I call the partial view using a `partial` element, using the `name` and `model` attributes to specify the name of the partial view and its view model. Using a partial view allows the same markup to be inserted into any view that needs to display a summary of a product.

Restart ASP.NET Core and request http://localhost:5000, and you will see that introducing the partial view doesn't change the appearance of the application; it just changes where Razor finds the content that is used to generate the response sent to the browser.

Summary

- The SportsStore ASP.NET Core project is created using the basic ASP.NET Core template.
- ASP.NET Core has close integration with Entity Framework Core, which is the .NET framework for working with relational data.
- Data can be paginated by including the page number in the request, either using the query string or the URL path and using the page when querying the database.
- The HTML content generated by ASP.NET Core can be styled using popular CSS frameworks, such as Bootstrap.

8 SportsStore: Navigation and cart

This chapter covers

- Navigating between product categories
- Correcting the pagination controls to support category navigation
- Using sessions to store data between requests
- Implementing a shopping cart using session data
- Displaying the shopping cart contents using Razor Pages

In this chapter, I continue to build out the SportsStore example app. I add support for navigating around the application and start building a shopping cart.

> **TIP** You can download the example project for this chapter—and for all the other chapters in this book—from https://github.com/manningbooks/pro-asp.net-core-7. See chapter 1 for how to get help if you have problems running the examples.

8.1 Adding navigation controls

The SportsStore application will be more useful if customers can navigate products by category. I will do this in three phases:

- Enhance the `Index` action method in the `HomeController` class so that it can filter the `Product` objects in the repository

- Revisit and enhance the URL scheme
- Create a category list that will go into the sidebar of the site, highlighting the current category and linking to others

8.1.1 *Filtering the product list*

I am going to start by enhancing the view model class, `ProductsListViewModel`, which I added to the `SportsStore` project in the previous chapter. I need to communicate the current category to the view to render the sidebar, and this is as good a place to start as any. Listing 8.1 shows the changes I made to the `ProductsListViewModel`.cs file in the `Models/ViewModels` folder.

> **Listing 8.1 Modifying the ProductsListViewModel.cs file in the SportsStore/Models/ViewModels folder**

```
namespace SportsStore.Models.ViewModels {

    public class ProductsListViewModel {
        public IEnumerable<Product> Products { get; set; }
            = Enumerable.Empty<Product>();
        public PagingInfo PagingInfo { get; set; } = new();
        public string? CurrentCategory { get; set; }
    }
}
```

I added a property called `CurrentCategory`. The next step is to update the `Home` controller so that the `Index` action method will filter `Product` objects by category and use the property I added to the view model to indicate which category has been selected, as shown in listing 8.2.

> **Listing 8.2. Supporting categories in the HomeController.cs file in the SportsStore/Controllers folder**

```
using Microsoft.AspNetCore.Mvc;
using SportsStore.Models;
using SportsStore.Models.ViewModels;

namespace SportsStore.Controllers {
    public class HomeController : Controller {
        private IStoreRepository repository;
        public int PageSize = 4;

        public HomeController(IStoreRepository repo) {
            repository = repo;
        }

        public ViewResult Index(string? category, int productPage = 1)
            => View(new ProductsListViewModel {
                Products = repository.Products
                    .Where(p => category == null ||
                        p.Category == category)
```

```
            .OrderBy(p => p.ProductID)
            .Skip((productPage - 1) * PageSize)
            .Take(PageSize),
        PagingInfo = new PagingInfo {
            CurrentPage = productPage,
            ItemsPerPage = PageSize,
            TotalItems = repository.Products.Count()
        },
        CurrentCategory = category
    });
    }
}
```

I made three changes to the action method. First, I added a parameter called category. This parameter is used by the second change in the listing, which is an enhancement to the LINQ query: if cat is not null, only those Product objects with a matching Category property are selected. The last change is to set the value of the Current-Category property I added to the ProductsListViewModel class. However, these changes mean that the value of PagingInfo.TotalItems is incorrectly calculated because it doesn't take the category filter into account. I will fix this later.

Unit test: updating existing tests

I changed the signature of the Index action method, which will prevent some of the existing unit test methods from compiling. To address this, I need to pass null as the first parameter to the Index method in those unit tests that work with the controller. For example, in the Can_Use_Repository test in the HomeControllerTests.cs file, the action section of the unit test becomes as follows:

```
...
[Fact]
public void Can_Use_Repository() {
    // Arrange
    Mock<IStoreRepository> mock = new Mock<IStoreRepository>();
    mock.Setup(m => m.Products).Returns((new Product[] {
        new Product {ProductID = 1, Name = "P1"},
        new Product {ProductID = 2, Name = "P2"}
    }).AsQueryable<Product>());

    HomeController controller = new HomeController(mock.Object);

    // Act
    ProductsListViewModel result =
        controller.Index(null)?.ViewData.Model
            as ProductsListViewModel ?? new();

    // Assert
    Product[] prodArray = result.Products.ToArray();
    Assert.True(prodArray.Length == 2);
    Assert.Equal("P1", prodArray[0].Name);
    Assert.Equal("P2", prodArray[1].Name);
}
...
```

(continued)

By using `null` for the `category` argument, I receive all the `Product` objects that the controller gets from the repository, which is the same situation I had before adding the new parameter. I need to make the same change to the `Can_Paginate` and `Can_Send_Pagination_View_Model` tests as well.

```
...
[Fact]
public void Can_Paginate() {
    // Arrange
    Mock<IStoreRepository> mock = new Mock<IStoreRepository>();
    mock.Setup(m => m.Products).Returns((new Product[] {
        new Product {ProductID = 1, Name = "P1"},
        new Product {ProductID = 2, Name = "P2"},
        new Product {ProductID = 3, Name = "P3"},
        new Product {ProductID = 4, Name = "P4"},
        new Product {ProductID = 5, Name = "P5"}
    }).AsQueryable<Product>());

    HomeController controller = new HomeController(mock.Object);
    controller.PageSize = 3;

    // Act
    ProductsListViewModel result =
        controller.Index(null, 2)?.ViewData.Model
            as ProductsListViewModel ?? new();

    // Assert
    Product[] prodArray = result.Products.ToArray();
    Assert.True(prodArray.Length == 2);
    Assert.Equal("P4", prodArray[0].Name);
    Assert.Equal("P5", prodArray[1].Name);
}

[Fact]
public void Can_Send_Pagination_View_Model() {

    // Arrange
    Mock<IStoreRepository> mock = new Mock<IStoreRepository>();
    mock.Setup(m => m.Products).Returns((new Product[] {
        new Product {ProductID = 1, Name = "P1"},
        new Product {ProductID = 2, Name = "P2"},
        new Product {ProductID = 3, Name = "P3"},
        new Product {ProductID = 4, Name = "P4"},
        new Product {ProductID = 5, Name = "P5"}
    }).AsQueryable<Product>());

    // Arrange
    HomeController controller =
        new HomeController(mock.Object) { PageSize = 3 };

    // Act
    ProductsListViewModel result =
        controller.Index(null, 2)?.ViewData.Model as
```

(continued)

```
        ProductsListViewModel ?? new();

    // Assert
    PagingInfo pageInfo = result.PagingInfo;
    Assert.Equal(2, pageInfo.CurrentPage);
    Assert.Equal(3, pageInfo.ItemsPerPage);
    Assert.Equal(5, pageInfo.TotalItems);
    Assert.Equal(2, pageInfo.TotalPages);
}
...
```

Keeping your unit tests synchronized with your code changes quickly becomes second nature when you get into the testing mindset.

To see the effect of the category filtering, start ASP.NET Core and select a category using the following URL:

```
http://localhost:5000/?category=soccer
```

You will see only the products in the `Soccer` category, as shown in figure 8.1.

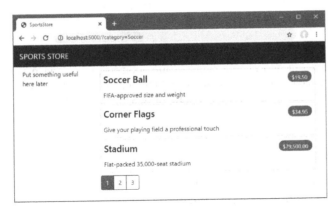

Figure 8.1 Using the query string to filter by category

Users won't want to navigate to categories using URLs, but you can see how small changes can have a big impact once the basic structure of an ASP.NET Core application is in place.

Unit Test: category filtering

I need a unit test to properly test the category filtering function to ensure that the filter can correctly generate products in a specified category. Here is the test method I added to the `HomeControllerTests` class:

```
...
[Fact]
public void Can_Filter_Products() {
```

(continued)

```
// Arrange
// - create the mock repository
Mock<IStoreRepository> mock = new Mock<IStoreRepository>();
mock.Setup(m => m.Products).Returns((new Product[] {
    new Product {ProductID = 1, Name = "P1", Category = "Cat1"},
    new Product {ProductID = 2, Name = "P2", Category = "Cat2"},
    new Product {ProductID = 3, Name = "P3", Category = "Cat1"},
    new Product {ProductID = 4, Name = "P4", Category = "Cat2"},
    new Product {ProductID = 5, Name = "P5", Category = "Cat3"}
}).AsQueryable<Product>());

// Arrange - create a controller and make the page size 3 items
HomeController controller = new HomeController(mock.Object);
controller.PageSize = 3;

// Action
Product[] result = (controller.Index("Cat2", 1)?.ViewData.Model
    as ProductsListViewModel ?? new()).Products.ToArray();

// Assert
Assert.Equal(2, result.Length);
Assert.True(result[0].Name == "P2" && result[0].Category == "Cat2");
Assert.True(result[1].Name == "P4" && result[1].Category == "Cat2");
}
...
```

This test creates a mock repository containing `Product` objects that belong to a range of categories. One specific category is requested using the action method, and the results are checked to ensure that the results are the right objects in the right order.

8.1.2   *Refining the URL scheme*

No one wants to see or use ugly URLs such as `/?category=Soccer`. To address this, I am going to change the routing configuration in the `Program.cs` file to create a more useful set of URLs, as shown in listing 8.3.

> **Listing 8.3   Changing the schema in the Program.cs file in the SportsStore folder**

```
using Microsoft.EntityFrameworkCore;
using SportsStore.Models;

var builder = WebApplication.CreateBuilder(args);

builder.Services.AddControllersWithViews();

builder.Services.AddDbContext<StoreDbContext>(opts => {
    opts.UseSqlServer(
        builder.Configuration["ConnectionStrings:SportsStoreConnection"]);
});

builder.Services.AddScoped<IStoreRepository, EFStoreRepository>();
```

```
var app = builder.Build();

app.UseStaticFiles();

app.MapControllerRoute("catpage",
    "{category}/Page{productPage:int}",
    new { Controller = "Home", action = "Index" });

app.MapControllerRoute("page", "Page{productPage:int}",
    new { Controller = "Home", action = "Index", productPage = 1 });

app.MapControllerRoute("category", "{category}",
    new { Controller = "Home", action = "Index", productPage = 1 });

app.MapControllerRoute("pagination",
    "Products/Page{productPage}",
    new { Controller = "Home", action = "Index", productPage = 1 });

app.MapDefaultControllerRoute();

SeedData.EnsurePopulated(app);

app.Run();
```

Table 8.1 describes the URL scheme that these routes represent. I explain the routing system in detail in chapter 13.

Table 8.1 Route summary

URL	Leads To
/	Lists the first page of products from all categories
/Page2	Lists the specified page (in this case, page 2), showing items from all categories
/Soccer	Shows the first page of items from a specific category (in this case, the Soccer category)
/Soccer/Page2	Shows the specified page (in this case, page 2) of items from the specified category (in this case, Soccer)

The ASP.NET Core routing system handles *incoming* requests from clients, but it also generates *outgoing* URLs that conform to the URL scheme and that can be embedded in web pages. By using the routing system both to handle incoming requests and to generate outgoing URLs, I can ensure that all the URLs in the application are consistent.

The IUrlHelper interface provides access to URL-generating functionality. I used this interface and the Action method it defines in the tag helper I created in the previous chapter. Now that I want to start generating more complex URLs, I need a way to receive additional information from the view without having to add extra properties to the tag helper class. Fortunately, tag helpers have a nice feature that allows properties with a common prefix to be received all together in a single collection, as shown in listing 8.4.

Listing 8.4   Prefixed values in the PageLinkTagHelper.cs file in the SportsStore/ Infrastructure folder

```
using Microsoft.AspNetCore.Mvc;
using Microsoft.AspNetCore.Mvc.Rendering;
using Microsoft.AspNetCore.Mvc.Routing;
using Microsoft.AspNetCore.Mvc.ViewFeatures;
using Microsoft.AspNetCore.Razor.TagHelpers;
using SportsStore.Models.ViewModels;

namespace SportsStore.Infrastructure {

    [HtmlTargetElement("div", Attributes = "page-model")]
    public class PageLinkTagHelper : TagHelper {
        private IUrlHelperFactory urlHelperFactory;

        public PageLinkTagHelper(IUrlHelperFactory helperFactory) {
            urlHelperFactory = helperFactory;
        }

        [ViewContext]
        [HtmlAttributeNotBound]
        public ViewContext? ViewContext { get; set; }

        public PagingInfo? PageModel { get; set; }

        public string? PageAction { get; set; }

        [HtmlAttributeName(DictionaryAttributePrefix = "page-url-")]
        public Dictionary<string, object> PageUrlValues { get; set; }
            = new Dictionary<string, object>();

        public bool PageClassesEnabled { get; set; } = false;
        public string PageClass { get; set; } = String.Empty;
        public string PageClassNormal { get; set; } = String.Empty;
        public string PageClassSelected { get; set; } = String.Empty;

        public override void Process(TagHelperContext context,
                TagHelperOutput output) {
            if (ViewContext != null && PageModel != null) {
            IUrlHelper urlHelper
                = urlHelperFactory.GetUrlHelper(ViewContext);
            TagBuilder result = new TagBuilder("div");
            for (int i = 1; i <= PageModel.TotalPages; i++) {
                TagBuilder tag = new TagBuilder("a");
                PageUrlValues["productPage"] = i;
                tag.Attributes["href"] = urlHelper.Action(PageAction,
                    PageUrlValues);
                if (PageClassesEnabled) {
                    tag.AddCssClass(PageClass);
                    tag.AddCssClass(i == PageModel.CurrentPage
                        ? PageClassSelected : PageClassNormal);
                }
                tag.InnerHtml.Append(i.ToString());
                result.InnerHtml.AppendHtml(tag);
```

```
                }
                output.Content.AppendHtml(result.InnerHtml);
            }
        }
    }
}
```

Decorating a tag helper property with the `HtmlAttributeName` attribute allows me to specify a prefix for attribute names on the element, which in this case will be `page-url-`. The value of any attribute whose name begins with this prefix will be added to the dictionary that is assigned to the `PageUrlValues` property, which is then passed to the `IUrlHelper.Action` method to generate the URL for the `href` attribute of the `a` elements that the tag helper produces.

In listing 8.5, I have added a new attribute to the `div` element that is processed by the tag helper, specifying the category that will be used to generate the URL. I have added only one new attribute to the view, but any attribute with the same prefix would be added to the dictionary.

> **Listing 8.5   Adding a attribute in the Index.cshtml file in the SportsStore/Views/ Home folder**

```
@model ProductsListViewModel

@foreach (var p in Model.Products ?? Enumerable.Empty<Product>()) {
    <partial name="ProductSummary" model="p" />
}

<div page-model="@Model.PagingInfo" page-action="Index"
     page-classes-enabled="true" page-class="btn"
     page-class-normal="btn-outline-dark"
     page-class-selected="btn-primary"
     page-url-category="@Model.CurrentCategory!"
     class="btn-group pull-right m-1">
</div>
```

I used the null-forgiving operator in the `page-url-category` expression so that I can pass a `null` value without receiving a compiler warning.

Prior to this change, the links generated for the pagination links looked like this:

`http://localhost:5000/Page1`

If the user clicked a page link like this, the category filter would be lost, and the application would present a page containing products from all categories. By adding the current category, taken from the view model, I generate URLs like this instead:

`http://localhost:5000/Chess/Page1`

When the user clicks this kind of link, the current category will be passed to the `Index` action method, and the filtering will be preserved. To see the effect of this change, start ASP.NET Core and request http://localhost:5000/chess, which will display just the products in the `Chess` category, as shown in figure 8.2.

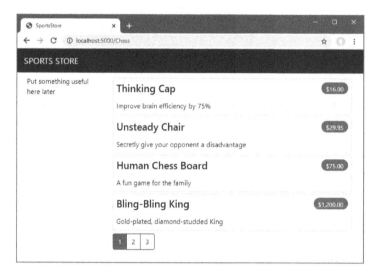

Figure 8.2
Filtering data by category

8.1.3   *Building a category navigation menu*

I need to provide users with a way to select a category that does not involve typing in URLs. This means presenting a list of the available categories and indicating which, if any, is currently selected.

ASP.NET Core has the concept of *view components*, which are perfect for creating items such as reusable navigation controls. A view component is a C# class that provides a small amount of reusable application logic with the ability to select and display Razor partial views. I describe view components in detail in chapter 24.

In this case, I will create a view component that renders the navigation menu and integrate it into the application by invoking the component from the shared layout. This approach gives me a regular C# class that can contain whatever application logic I need and that can be unit tested like any other class.

CREATING THE NAVIGATION VIEW COMPONENT

I created a folder called Components, which is the conventional home of view components, in the SportsStore project and added to it a class file named NavigationMenu-ViewComponent.cs, which I used to define the class shown in listing 8.6.

> **Listing 8.6   The contents of the NavigationMenuViewComponent.cs file in the SportsStore/Components folder**

```
using Microsoft.AspNetCore.Mvc;

namespace SportsStore.Components {

    public class NavigationMenuViewComponent : ViewComponent {

        public string Invoke() {
            return "Hello from the Nav View Component";
        }
    }
}
```

The view component's `Invoke` method is called when the component is used in a Razor view, and the result of the `Invoke` method is inserted into the HTML sent to the browser. I have started with a simple view component that returns a string, but I'll replace this with HTML shortly.

I want the category list to appear on all pages, so I am going to use the view component in the shared layout, rather than in a specific view. Within a view, view components are applied using a tag helper, as shown in listing 8.7.

> **Listing 8.7 Using a view component in the _Layout.cshtml file in the SportsStore/ Views/Shared folder**

```html
<!DOCTYPE html>
<html>
<head>
    <meta name="viewport" content="width=device-width" />
    <title>SportsStore</title>
    <link href="/lib/bootstrap/css/bootstrap.min.css" rel="stylesheet" />
</head>
<body>
    <div class="bg-dark text-white p-2">
        <span class="navbar-brand ml-2">SPORTS STORE</span>
    </div>
    <div class="row m-1 p-1">
        <div id="categories" class="col-3">
            <vc:navigation-menu />
        </div>
        <div class="col-9">
            @RenderBody()
        </div>
    </div>
</body>
</html>
```

I removed the placeholder text and replaced it with the `vc:navigation-menu` element, which inserts the view component. The element omits the `ViewComponent` part of the class name and hyphenates it, such that `vc:navigation-menu` specifies the `NavigationMenuViewComponent` class.

Restart ASP.NET Core and request http://localhost:5000, and you will see that the output from the `Invoke` method is included in the HTML sent to the browser, as shown in figure 8.3.

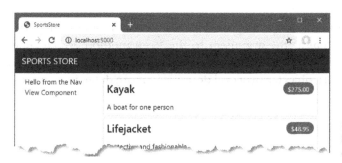

Figure 8.3 Using a view component

GENERATING CATEGORY LISTS

I can now return to the navigation view component and generate a real set of categories. I could build the HTML for the categories programmatically, as I did for the page tag helper, but one of the benefits of working with view components is they can render Razor partial views. That means I can use the view component to generate the list of categories and then use the more expressive Razor syntax to render the HTML that will display them. The first step is to update the view component, as shown in listing 8.8.

Listing 8.8   Adding categories in the NavigationMenuViewComponent.cs file in the SportsStore/Components folder

```
using Microsoft.AspNetCore.Mvc;
using SportsStore.Models;

namespace SportsStore.Components {

    public class NavigationMenuViewComponent : ViewComponent {
        private IStoreRepository repository;

        public NavigationMenuViewComponent(IStoreRepository repo) {
            repository = repo;
        }

        public IViewComponentResult Invoke() {
            return View(repository.Products
                .Select(x => x.Category)
                .Distinct()
                .OrderBy(x => x));
        }
    }
}
```

The constructor defined in listing 8.8 defines an `IStoreRepository` parameter. When ASP.NET Core needs to create an instance of the view component class, it will note the need to provide a value for this parameter and inspect the configuration in the `Program.cs` file to determine which implementation object should be used. This is the same dependency injection feature that I used in the controller in chapter 7, and it has the same effect, which is to allow the view component to access data without knowing which repository implementation will be used, a feature I describe in detail in chapter 14.

In the `Invoke` method, I use LINQ to select and order the set of categories in the repository and pass them as the argument to the `View` method, which renders the default Razor partial view, details of which are returned from the method using an `IViewComponentResult` object, a process I describe in more detail in chapter 24.

Unit test: generating the category list

The unit test for my ability to produce a category list is relatively simple. The goal is to create a list that is sorted in alphabetical order and contains no duplicates, and the simplest way to do this is to supply some test data that *does* have duplicate categories and that is *not* in order, pass this to the view component class, and assert that the data has been properly cleaned up. Here is the unit test, which I defined in a new class file called `NavigationMenuViewComponentTests.cs` in the `SportsStore.Tests` project:

```
using System.Collections.Generic;
using System.Linq;
using Microsoft.AspNetCore.Mvc.Rendering;
using Microsoft.AspNetCore.Mvc.ViewComponents;
using Moq;
using SportsStore.Components;
using SportsStore.Models;
using Xunit;

namespace SportsStore.Tests {

    public class NavigationMenuViewComponentTests {

        [Fact]
        public void Can_Select_Categories() {
            // Arrange
            Mock<IStoreRepository> mock = new Mock<IStoreRepository>();
            mock.Setup(m => m.Products).Returns((new Product[] {
                new Product {ProductID = 1, Name = "P1",
                    Category = "Apples"},
                new Product {ProductID = 2, Name = "P2",
                    Category = "Apples"},
                new Product {ProductID = 3, Name = "P3",
                    Category = "Plums"},
                new Product {ProductID = 4, Name = "P4",
                    Category = "Oranges"},
            }).AsQueryable<Product>());

            NavigationMenuViewComponent target =
                new NavigationMenuViewComponent(mock.Object);

            // Act = get the set of categories
            string[] results = ((IEnumerable<string>?)(target.Invoke()
                as ViewViewComponentResult)?.ViewData?.Model
                    ?? Enumerable.Empty<string>()).ToArray();

            // Assert
            Assert.True(Enumerable.SequenceEqual(new string[] { "Apples",
                "Oranges", "Plums" }, results));
        }
    }
}
```

I created a mock repository implementation that contains repeating categories and categories that are not in order. I assert that the duplicates are removed and that alphabetical ordering is imposed.

CREATING THE VIEW

Razor uses different conventions for locating views that are selected by view components. Both the default name of the view and the locations that are searched for the view are different from those used for controllers. To that end, I created the `Views/Shared/Components/NavigationMenu` folder in the SportsStore project and added to it a Razor View named `Default.cshtml`, to which I added the content shown in listing 8.9.

> **Listing 8.9   The contents of the Default.cshtml file in the SportsStore/Views/ Shared/Components/NavigationMenu folder**

```
@model IEnumerable<string>

<div class="d-grid gap-2">
    <a class="btn btn-outline-secondary"asp-action="Index"
        asp-controller="Home" asp-route-category="">
        Home
    </a>
    @foreach (string category in Model ?? Enumerable.Empty<string>()) {
        <a class="btn btn-outline-secondary"
            asp-action="Index" asp-controller="Home"
            asp-route-category="@category"
            asp-route-productPage="1">
            @category
        </a>
    }
</div>
```

This view uses one of the built-in tag helpers, which I describe in chapters 25–27, to create anchor elements whose `href` attribute contains a URL that selects a different product category.

Restart ASP.NET Core and request http://localhost:5000 to see the category navigation buttons. If you click a button, the list of items is updated to show only items from the selected category, as shown in figure 8.4.

Figure 8.4   Generating category links with a view component

HIGHLIGHTING THE CURRENT CATEGORY

There is no feedback to the user to indicate which category has been selected. It might be possible to infer the category from the items in the list, but some clear visual feedback seems like a good idea. ASP.NET Core components such as controllers and view components can receive information about the current request by asking for a context object. Most of the time, you can rely on the base classes that you use to create components to take care of getting the context object for you, such as when you use the `Controller` base class to create controllers.

The `ViewComponent` base class is no exception and provides access to context objects through a set of properties. One of the properties is called `RouteData`, which provides information about how the request URL was handled by the routing system.

In listing 8.10, I use the `RouteData` property to access the request data to get the value for the currently selected category. I could pass the category to the view by creating another view model class (and that's what I would do in a real project), but for variety, I am going to use the view bag feature, which allows unstructured data to be passed to a view alongside the view model object. I describe how this feature works in detail in chapter 22.

> **Listing 8.10** Passing the selected category in the NavigationMenuViewComponent.cs file in the SportsStore/Components folder

```csharp
using Microsoft.AspNetCore.Mvc;
using SportsStore.Models;

namespace SportsStore.Components {

    public class NavigationMenuViewComponent : ViewComponent {
        private IStoreRepository repository;

        public NavigationMenuViewComponent(IStoreRepository repo) {
            repository = repo;
        }

        public IViewComponentResult Invoke() {
            ViewBag.SelectedCategory = RouteData?.Values["category"];
            return View(repository.Products
                .Select(x => x.Category)
                .Distinct()
                .OrderBy(x => x));
        }
    }
}
```

Inside the `Invoke` method, I have dynamically assigned a `SelectedCategory` property to the `ViewBag` object and set its value to be the current category, which is obtained through the context object returned by the `RouteData` property. The `ViewBag` is a dynamic object that allows me to define new properties simply by assigning values to them.

Unit test: reporting the selected category

I can test that the view component correctly adds details of the selected category by reading the value of the ViewBag property in a unit test, which is available through the ViewViewComponentResult class. Here is the test, which I added to the NavigationMenuViewComponentTests class:

```
...
[Fact]
public void Indicates_Selected_Category() {

    // Arrange
    string categoryToSelect = "Apples";
    Mock<IStoreRepository> mock = new Mock<IStoreRepository>();
    mock.Setup(m => m.Products).Returns((new Product[] {
        new Product {ProductID = 1, Name = "P1", Category = "Apples"},
        new Product {ProductID = 4, Name = "P2", Category = "Oranges"},
    }).AsQueryable<Product>());

    NavigationMenuViewComponent target =
        new NavigationMenuViewComponent(mock.Object);
    target.ViewComponentContext = new ViewComponentContext {
        ViewContext = new ViewContext {
            RouteData = new Microsoft.AspNetCore.Routing.RouteData()
        }
    };
    target.RouteData.Values["category"] = categoryToSelect;

    // Action
    string? result = (string?)(target.Invoke()
        as ViewViewComponentResult)?.ViewData?["SelectedCategory"];

    // Assert
    Assert.Equal(categoryToSelect, result);
}
...
```

This unit test provides the view component with routing data through the View-ComponentContext property, which is how view components receive all their context data. The ViewComponentContext property provides access to view-specific context data through its ViewContext property, which in turn provides access to the routing information through its RouteData property. Most of the code in the unit test goes into creating the context objects that will provide the selected category in the same way that it would be presented when the application is running and the context data is provided by ASP.NET Core MVC.

Now that I am providing information about which category is selected, I can update the view selected by the view component and vary the CSS classes used to style the links so that the one representing the current category is distinct. Listing 8.11 shows the change I made to the Default.cshtml file.

Listing 8.11 Highlighting in the Default.cshtml file in the SportsStore/Views/Shared/Components/NavigationMenu folder

```
@model IEnumerable<string>

<div class="d-grid gap-2">
    <a class="btn btn-outline-secondary"asp-action="Index"
        asp-controller="Home" asp-route-category="">
        Home
    </a>
    @foreach (string category in Model ?? Enumerable.Empty<string>()) {
        <a class="btn @(category == ViewBag.SelectedCategory
                ? "btn-primary": "btn-outline-secondary")"
            asp-action="Index" asp-controller="Home"
            asp-route-category="@category"
            asp-route-productPage="1">
             @category
        </a>
    }
</div>
```

I have used a Razor expression within the `class` attribute to apply the `btn-primary` class to the element that represents the selected category and the `btn-secondary` class otherwise. These classes apply different Bootstrap styles and make the active button obvious, which you can see by restarting ASP.NET Core, requesting http://localhost:5000, and clicking one of the category buttons, as shown in figure 8.5.

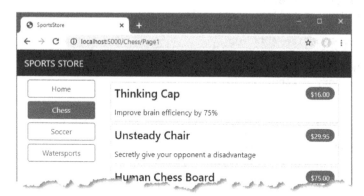

Figure 8.5 Highlighting the selected category

8.1.4 Correcting the page count

I need to correct the page links so that they work correctly when a category is selected. Currently, the number of page links is determined by the total number of products in the repository and not the number of products in the selected category. This means that the customer can click the link for page 2 of the `Chess` category and end up with an empty page because there are not enough chess products to fill two pages. You can see the problem in figure 8.6.

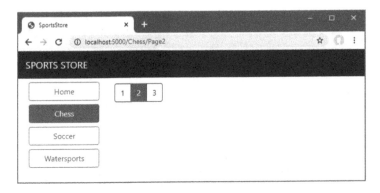

Figure 8.6   Displaying the wrong page links when a category is selected

I can fix this by updating the `Index` action method in the `Home` controller so that the pagination information takes the categories into account, as shown in listing 8.12.

Listing 8.12   Creating Category Pagination Data in the HomeController.cs File in the SportsStore/Controllers Folder

```
using Microsoft.AspNetCore.Mvc;
using SportsStore.Models;
using SportsStore.Models.ViewModels;

namespace SportsStore.Controllers {
    public class HomeController : Controller {
        private IStoreRepository repository;
        public int PageSize = 4;

        public HomeController(IStoreRepository repo) {
            repository = repo;
        }

        public ViewResult Index(string? category, int productPage = 1)
            => View(new ProductsListViewModel {
                Products = repository.Products
                    .Where(p => category == null
                        || p.Category == category)
                    .OrderBy(p => p.ProductID)
                    .Skip((productPage - 1) * PageSize)
                    .Take(PageSize),
                PagingInfo = new PagingInfo {
                    CurrentPage = productPage,
                    ItemsPerPage = PageSize,
                    TotalItems = category == null
                        ? repository.Products.Count()
                        : repository.Products.Where(e =>
                            e.Category == category).Count()
                },
                CurrentCategory = category
            });
    }
}
```

If a category has been selected, I return the number of items in that category; if not, I return the total number of products. Restart ASP.NET Core and request http://localhost:5000 to see the changes when a category is selected, as shown in figure 8.7.

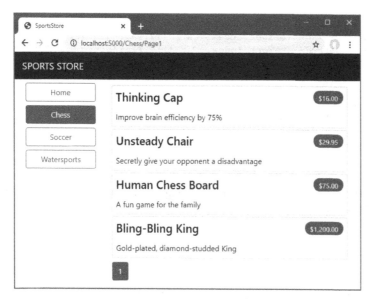

Figure 8.7   Displaying category-specific page counts

Unit test: category-specific product counts

Testing that I am able to generate the current product count for different categories is simple. I create a mock repository that contains known data in a range of categories and then call the `Index` action method requesting each category in turn. Here is the unit test method that I added to the `HomeControllerTests` class (you will need to import the `System` namespace for this test):

```
...
[Fact]
public void Generate_Category_Specific_Product_Count() {
    // Arrange
    Mock<IStoreRepository> mock = new Mock<IStoreRepository>();
    mock.Setup(m => m.Products).Returns((new Product[] {
        new Product {ProductID = 1, Name = "P1", Category = "Cat1"},
        new Product {ProductID = 2, Name = "P2", Category = "Cat2"},
        new Product {ProductID = 3, Name = "P3", Category = "Cat1"},
        new Product {ProductID = 4, Name = "P4", Category = "Cat2"},
        new Product {ProductID = 5, Name = "P5", Category = "Cat3"}
    }).AsQueryable<Product>());

    HomeController target = new HomeController(mock.Object);
    target.PageSize = 3;

    Func<ViewResult, ProductsListViewModel?> GetModel = result
```

(continued)

```
        => result?.ViewData?.Model as ProductsListViewModel;

    // Action
    int? res1 = GetModel(target.Index("Cat1"))?.PagingInfo.TotalItems;
    int? res2 = GetModel(target.Index("Cat2"))?.PagingInfo.TotalItems;
    int? res3 = GetModel(target.Index("Cat3"))?.PagingInfo.TotalItems;
    int? resAll = GetModel(target.Index(null))?.PagingInfo.TotalItems;

    // Assert
    Assert.Equal(2, res1);
    Assert.Equal(2, res2);
    Assert.Equal(1, res3);
    Assert.Equal(5, resAll);
}
...
```

Notice that I also call the `Index` method, specifying no category, to make sure I get the correct total count as well.

8.2   *Building the shopping cart*

The application is progressing nicely, but I cannot sell any products until I implement a shopping cart. In this section, I will create the shopping cart experience shown in figure 8.8. This will be familiar to anyone who has ever made a purchase online.

Figure 8.8   The basic shopping cart flow

An Add To Cart button will be displayed alongside each of the products in the catalog. Clicking this button will show a summary of the products the customer has selected so far, including the total cost. At this point, the user can click the Continue Shopping button to return to the product catalog or click the Checkout Now button to complete the order and finish the shopping session.

8.2.1   *Configuring Razor Pages*

So far, I have used the MVC Framework to define the SportsStore project features. For variety, I am going to use Razor Pages—another application framework supported by ASP.NET Core—to implement the shopping cart. Listing 8.13 configures the `Program.cs` file to enable Razor Pages in the SportsStore application.

Listing 8.13   Enabling Razor Pages in the Program.cs file in the SportsStore folder

```
using Microsoft.EntityFrameworkCore;
using SportsStore.Models;

var builder = WebApplication.CreateBuilder(args);

builder.Services.AddControllersWithViews();

builder.Services.AddDbContext<StoreDbContext>(opts => {
    opts.UseSqlServer(
        builder.Configuration["ConnectionStrings:SportsStoreConnection"]);
});

builder.Services.AddScoped<IStoreRepository, EFStoreRepository>();

builder.Services.AddRazorPages();

var app = builder.Build();

app.UseStaticFiles();

app.MapControllerRoute("catpage",
    "{category}/Page{productPage:int}",
    new { Controller = "Home", action = "Index" });

app.MapControllerRoute("page", "Page{productPage:int}",
    new { Controller = "Home", action = "Index", productPage = 1 });

app.MapControllerRoute("category", "{category}",
    new { Controller = "Home", action = "Index", productPage = 1 });

app.MapControllerRoute("pagination",
    "Products/Page{productPage}",
    new { Controller = "Home", action = "Index", productPage = 1 });

app.MapDefaultControllerRoute();
app.MapRazorPages();

SeedData.EnsurePopulated(app);

app.Run();
```

The AddRazorPages method sets up the services used by Razor Pages, and the Map-RazorPages method registers Razor Pages as endpoints that the URL routing system can use to handle requests.

Add a folder named Pages, which is the conventional location for Razor Pages, to the SportsStore project. Add a Razor View Imports file named _ViewImports .cshtml to the Pages folder with the content shown in listing 8.14. These expressions set the namespace that the Razor Pages will belong to and allow the SportsStore classes to be used in Razor Pages without needing to specify their namespace.

Listing 8.14   The _ViewImports.cshtml file in the SportsStore/Pages folder

```
@namespace SportsStore.Pages
@using Microsoft.AspNetCore.Mvc.RazorPages
@using SportsStore.Models
@using SportsStore.Infrastructure
@addTagHelper *, Microsoft.AspNetCore.Mvc.TagHelpers
```

Next, add a Razor View Start file named `_ViewStart.cshtml` to the `Pages` folder, with the content shown in listing 8.15. Razor Pages have their own configuration files, and this one specifies that the Razor Pages in the SportsStore project will use a layout file named `_CartLayout` by default.

Listing 8.15   The contents of the _ViewStart.cshtml file in the SportsStore/Pages folder

```
@{
    Layout = "_CartLayout";
}
```

Finally, to provide the layout the Razor Pages will use, add a Razor View named `_CartLayout.cshtml` to the `Pages` folder with the content shown in listing 8.16.

Listing 8.16   The contents of the _CartLayout.cshtml file in the SportsStore/Pages folder

```
<!DOCTYPE html>
<html>
<head>
    <meta name="viewport" content="width=device-width" />
    <title>SportsStore</title>
    <link href="/lib/bootstrap/css/bootstrap.min.css" rel="stylesheet" />
</head>
<body>
    <div class="bg-dark text-white p-2">
        <span class="navbar-brand ml-2">SPORTS STORE</span>
    </div>
    <div class="m-1 p-1">
        @RenderBody()
    </div>
</body>
</html>
```

8.2.2   Creating a Razor Page

If you are using Visual Studio, use the Razor Page template item and set the item name to `Cart.cshtml`. This will create a `Cart.cshtml` file and a `Cart.cshtml.cs` class file. Replace the contents of the file with those shown in listing 8.17. If you are using Visual Studio Code, just create a `Cart.cshtml` file with the content shown in listing 8.17.

Listing 8.17 The contents of the Cart.cshtml file in the SportsStore/Pages folder

```
@page

<h4>This is the Cart Page</h4>
```

Restart ASP.NET Core and request http://localhost:5000/cart to see the placeholder content from listing 8.17, which is shown in figure 8.9. Notice that I have not had to register the page and that the mapping between the /cart URL path and the Razor Page has been handled automatically.

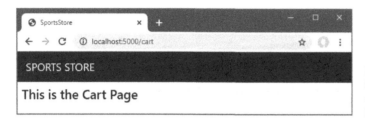

Figure 8.9 Placeholder content from a Razor Page

8.2.3 Creating the Add to Cart buttons

I have some preparation to do before I can implement the cart feature. First, I need to create the buttons that will add products to the cart. To prepare for this, I added a class file called `UrlExtensions.cs` to the `Infrastructure` folder and defined the extension method shown in listing 8.18.

Listing 8.18 The UrlExtensions.cs file in the SportsStore/Infrastructure folder

```
namespace SportsStore.Infrastructure {

    public static class UrlExtensions {

        public static string PathAndQuery(this HttpRequest request) =>
            request.QueryString.HasValue
                ? $"{request.Path}{request.QueryString}"
                : request.Path.ToString();
    }
}
```

The `PathAndQuery` extension method operates on the `HttpRequest` class, which ASP.NET Core uses to describe an HTTP request. The extension method generates a URL that the browser will be returned to after the cart has been updated, taking into account the query string, if there is one. In listing 8.19, I have added the namespace that contains the extension method to the view imports file so that I can use it in the partial view.

> **NOTE** This is the view imports file in the `Views` folder and not the one added to the `Pages` folder.

```
@using SportsStore.Models
@using SportsStore.Models.ViewModels
@using SportsStore.Infrastructure
@addTagHelper *, Microsoft.AspNetCore.Mvc.TagHelpers
@addTagHelper *, SportsStore
```

In listing 8.20, I have updated the partial view that describes each product so that it contains an Add To Cart button.

```
@model Product

<div class="card card-outline-primary m-1 p-1">
    <div class="bg-faded p-1">
        <h4>
            @Model.Name
            <span class="badge rounded-pill bg-primary text-white"
                style="float:right">
                <small>@Model.Price.ToString("c")</small>
            </span>
        </h4>
    </div>

    <form id="@Model.ProductID" asp-page="/Cart" method="post">
        <input type="hidden" asp-for="ProductID" />
        <input type="hidden" name="returnUrl"
            value="@ViewContext.HttpContext.Request.PathAndQuery()" />
        <span class="card-text p-1">
            @Model.Description
            <button type="submit" style="float:right"
                    class="btn btn-success btn-sm pull-right" >
                Add To Cart
            </button>
        </span>
    </form>

</div>
```

I have added a `form` element that contains hidden `input` elements specifying the `ProductID` value from the view model and the URL that the browser should be returned to after the cart has been updated. The `form` element and one of the `input` elements are configured using built-in tag helpers, which are a useful way of generating forms that contain model values and that target controllers or Razor Pages, as described in chapter 27. The other `input` element uses the extension method I created to set the return URL. I also added a `button` element that will submit the form to the application.

NOTE Notice that I have set the `method` attribute on the form element to `post`, which instructs the browser to submit the form data using an HTTP `POST` request. You can change this so that forms use the `GET` method, but you should think carefully about doing so. The HTTP specification requires that `GET` requests be *idempotent*, meaning that they must not cause changes, and adding a product to a cart is definitely a change.

8.2.4   Enabling sessions

I am going to store details of a user's cart using *session state*, which is data associated with a series of requests made by a user. ASP.NET provides a range of different ways to store session state, including storing it in memory, which is the approach that I am going to use. This has the advantage of simplicity, but it means that the session data is lost when the application is stopped or restarted. Enabling sessions requires adding services and middleware in the `Program.cs` file, as shown in listing 8.21.

> **Listing 8.21   Enabling sessions in the Program.cs file in the SportsStore folder**

```
using Microsoft.EntityFrameworkCore;
using SportsStore.Models;

var builder = WebApplication.CreateBuilder(args);

builder.Services.AddControllersWithViews();

builder.Services.AddDbContext<StoreDbContext>(opts => {
    opts.UseSqlServer(
        builder.Configuration["ConnectionStrings:SportsStoreConnection"]);
});

builder.Services.AddScoped<IStoreRepository, EFStoreRepository>();

builder.Services.AddRazorPages();
builder.Services.AddDistributedMemoryCache();
builder.Services.AddSession();

var app = builder.Build();

app.UseStaticFiles();
app.UseSession();

app.MapControllerRoute("catpage",
    "{category}/Page{productPage:int}",
    new { Controller = "Home", action = "Index" });

app.MapControllerRoute("page", "Page{productPage:int}",
    new { Controller = "Home", action = "Index", productPage = 1 });

app.MapControllerRoute("category", "{category}",
    new { Controller = "Home", action = "Index", productPage = 1 });

app.MapControllerRoute("pagination",
```

```
"Products/Page{productPage}",
new { Controller = "Home", action = "Index", productPage = 1 });
```

```
app.MapDefaultControllerRoute();
app.MapRazorPages();
```

```
SeedData.EnsurePopulated(app);
```

```
app.Run();
```

The `AddDistributedMemoryCache` method call sets up the in-memory data store. The `AddSession` method registers the services used to access session data, and the `Use-Session` method allows the session system to automatically associate requests with sessions when they arrive from the client.

8.2.5 *Implementing the cart feature*

Now that the preparations are complete, I can implement the cart features. I started by adding a class file called `Cart.cs` to the `Models` folder in the SportsStore project and used it to define the classes shown in listing 8.22.

> **Listing 8.22   The contents of the Cart.cs file in the SportsStore/Models folder**

```
namespace SportsStore.Models {

    public class Cart {

        public List<CartLine> Lines { get; set; } = new List<CartLine>();

        public void AddItem(Product product, int quantity) {
            CartLine? line = Lines
                .Where(p => p.Product.ProductID == product.ProductID)
                .FirstOrDefault();

            if (line == null) {
                Lines.Add(new CartLine {
                    Product = product,
                    Quantity = quantity
                });
            } else {
                line.Quantity += quantity;
            }
        }

        public void RemoveLine(Product product) =>
            Lines.RemoveAll(l => l.Product.ProductID
                == product.ProductID);

        public decimal ComputeTotalValue() =>
            Lines.Sum(e => e.Product.Price * e.Quantity);

        public void Clear() => Lines.Clear();
    }

    public class CartLine {
```

```
        public int CartLineID { get; set; }
        public Product Product { get; set; } = new();
        public int Quantity { get; set; }
    }
}
```

The Cart class uses the CartLine class, defined in the same file, to represent a product selected by the customer and the quantity the user wants to buy. I defined methods to add an item to the cart, remove a previously added item from the cart, calculate the total cost of the items in the cart, and reset the cart by removing all the items.

Unit test: testing the cart

The Cart class is relatively simple, but it has a range of important behaviors that must work properly. A poorly functioning cart would undermine the entire SportsStore application. I have broken down the features and tested them individually. I created a new unit test file called CartTests.cs in the SportsStore.Tests project to contain these tests.

The first behavior relates to when I add an item to the cart. If this is the first time that a given Product has been added to the cart, I want a new CartLine to be added. Here is the test, including the unit test class definition:

```
using System.Linq;
using SportsStore.Models;
using Xunit;

namespace SportsStore.Tests {

    public class CartTests {

        [Fact]
        public void Can_Add_New_Lines() {

            // Arrange - create some test products
            Product p1 = new Product { ProductID = 1, Name = "P1" };
            Product p2 = new Product { ProductID = 2, Name = "P2" };

            // Arrange - create a new cart
            Cart target = new Cart();

            // Act
            target.AddItem(p1, 1);
            target.AddItem(p2, 1);
            CartLine[] results = target.Lines.ToArray();

            // Assert
            Assert.Equal(2, results.Length);
            Assert.Equal(p1, results[0].Product);
            Assert.Equal(p2, results[1].Product);
        }
    }
}
```

(continued)

However, if the customer has already added a `Product` to the cart, I want to increment the quantity of the corresponding `CartLine` and not create a new one. Here is the test:

```
...
[Fact]
public void Can_Add_Quantity_For_Existing_Lines() {
    // Arrange - create some test products
    Product p1 = new Product { ProductID = 1, Name = "P1" };
    Product p2 = new Product { ProductID = 2, Name = "P2" };

    // Arrange - create a new cart
    Cart target = new Cart();

    // Act
    target.AddItem(p1, 1);
    target.AddItem(p2, 1);
    target.AddItem(p1, 10);
    CartLine[] results = (target.Lines ?? new())
        .OrderBy(c => c.Product.ProductID).ToArray();

    // Assert
    Assert.Equal(2, results.Length);
    Assert.Equal(11, results[0].Quantity);
    Assert.Equal(1, results[1].Quantity);
}
...
```

I also need to check that users can change their mind and remove products from the cart. This feature is implemented by the `RemoveLine` method. Here is the test:

```
...
[Fact]
public void Can_Remove_Line() {
    // Arrange - create some test products
    Product p1 = new Product { ProductID = 1, Name = "P1" };
    Product p2 = new Product { ProductID = 2, Name = "P2" };
    Product p3 = new Product { ProductID = 3, Name = "P3" };

    // Arrange - create a new cart
    Cart target = new Cart();
    // Arrange - add some products to the cart
    target.AddItem(p1, 1);
    target.AddItem(p2, 3);
    target.AddItem(p3, 5);
    target.AddItem(p2, 1);

    // Act
    target.RemoveLine(p2);

    // Assert
    Assert.Empty(target.Lines.Where(c => c.Product == p2));
    Assert.Equal(2, target.Lines.Count());
}
...
```

(continued)

The next behavior I want to test is the ability to calculate the total cost of the items in the cart. Here's the test for this behavior:

```
...
[Fact]
public void Calculate_Cart_Total() {
    // Arrange - create some test products
    Product p1 = new Product { ProductID = 1, Name = "P1", Price = 100M };
    Product p2 = new Product { ProductID = 2, Name = "P2", Price = 50M };

    // Arrange - create a new cart
    Cart target = new Cart();

    // Act
    target.AddItem(p1, 1);
    target.AddItem(p2, 1);
    target.AddItem(p1, 3);
    decimal result = target.ComputeTotalValue();

    // Assert
    Assert.Equal(450M, result);
}
...
```

The final test is simple. I want to ensure that the contents of the cart are properly removed when reset. Here is the test:

```
...
[Fact]
public void Can_Clear_Contents() {
    // Arrange - create some test products
    Product p1 = new Product { ProductID = 1, Name = "P1", Price = 100M };
    Product p2 = new Product { ProductID = 2, Name = "P2", Price = 50M };

    // Arrange - create a new cart
    Cart target = new Cart();

    // Arrange - add some items
    target.AddItem(p1, 1);
    target.AddItem(p2, 1);

    // Act - reset the cart
    target.Clear();

    // Assert
    Assert.Empty(target.Lines);
}
...
```

Sometimes, as in this case, the code required to test the functionality of a class is longer and more complex than the class itself. Do not let that put you off writing the unit tests. Defects in simple classes can have huge impacts, especially ones that play such an important role as `Cart` does in the example application.

DEFINING SESSION STATE EXTENSION METHODS

The session state feature in ASP.NET Core stores only int, string, and byte[] values. Since I want to store a Cart object, I need to define extension methods to the ISession interface, which provides access to the session state data to serialize Cart objects into JSON and convert them back. I added a class file called Session-Extensions.cs to the Infrastructure folder and defined the extension methods shown in listing 8.23.

Listing 8.23   The SessionExtensions.cs file in the SportsStore/Infrastructure folder

```
using System.Text.Json;

namespace SportsStore.Infrastructure {

    public static class SessionExtensions {

        public static void SetJson(this ISession session,
                string key, object value) {
            session.SetString(key, JsonSerializer.Serialize(value));
        }

        public static T? GetJson<T>(this ISession session, string key) {
            var sessionData = session.GetString(key);
            return sessionData == null
                ? default(T) : JsonSerializer.Deserialize<T>(sessionData);
        }
    }
}
```

These methods serialize objects into the JavaScript Object Notation format, making it easy to store and retrieve Cart objects.

COMPLETING THE RAZOR PAGE

The Cart Razor Page will receive the HTTP POST request that the browser sends when the user clicks an Add To Cart button. It will use the request form data to get the Product object from the database and use it to update the user's cart, which will be stored as session data for use by future requests. Listing 8.24 implements these features.

Listing 8.24   Handling requests in the Cart.cshtml file in the SportsStore/Pages folder

```
@page
@model CartModel

<h2>Your cart</h2>
<table class="table table-bordered table-striped">
    <thead>
        <tr>
            <th>Quantity</th>
            <th>Item</th>
            <th class="text-right">Price</th>
            <th class="text-right">Subtotal</th>
        </tr>
```

```
        </thead>
        <tbody>
            @foreach (var line in Model.Cart?.Lines
                        ?? Enumerable.Empty<CartLine>()) {
                <tr>
                    <td class="text-center">@line.Quantity</td>
                    <td class="text-left">@line.Product.Name</td>
                    <td class="text-right">
                        @line.Product.Price.ToString("c")
                    </td>
                    <td class="text-right">
                        @((line.Quantity * line.Product.Price).ToString("c"))
                    </td>
                </tr>
            }
        </tbody>
        <tfoot>
            <tr>
                <td colspan="3" class="text-right">Total:</td>
                <td class="text-right">
                    @Model.Cart?.ComputeTotalValue().ToString("c")
                </td>
            </tr>
        </tfoot>
</table>

<div class="text-center">
    <a class="btn btn-primary" href="@Model.ReturnUrl">
        Continue shopping
    </a>
</div>
```

Razor Pages allow HTML content, Razor expressions, and code to be combined in a single file, as I explain in chapter 23, but if you want to unit test a Razor Page, then you need to use a separate class file. If you are using Visual Studio, there will already be a class file named `Cart.cshtml.cs` in the `Pages` folder, which was created by the Razor Page template item. If you are using Visual Studio Code, you will need to create the class file separately. Use the class file, however it has been created, to define the class shown in listing 8.25.

Listing 8.25 The Cart.cshtml.cs file in the SportsStore/Pages folder

```
using Microsoft.AspNetCore.Mvc;
using Microsoft.AspNetCore.Mvc.RazorPages;
using SportsStore.Infrastructure;
using SportsStore.Models;

namespace SportsStore.Pages {

    public class CartModel : PageModel {
        private IStoreRepository repository;

        public CartModel(IStoreRepository repo) {
```

```
        repository = repo;
    }

    public Cart? Cart { get; set; }
    public string ReturnUrl { get; set; } = "/";

    public void OnGet(string returnUrl) {
        ReturnUrl = returnUrl ?? "/";
        Cart = HttpContext.Session.GetJson<Cart>("cart")
            ?? new Cart();
    }

    public IActionResult OnPost(long productId, string returnUrl) {
        Product? product = repository.Products
            .FirstOrDefault(p => p.ProductID == productId);
        if (product != null) {
            Cart = HttpContext.Session.GetJson<Cart>("cart")
                ?? new Cart();
            Cart.AddItem(product, 1);
            HttpContext.Session.SetJson("cart", Cart);
        }
        return RedirectToPage(new { returnUrl = returnUrl });
    }
}
}
```

The class associated with a Razor Page is known as its *page model class,* and it defines handler methods that are invoked for different types of HTTP requests, which update state before rendering the view. The page model class in listing 8.25, which is named CartModel, defines an OnPost handler method, which is invoked to handle HTTP POST requests. It does this by retrieving a Product from the database, retrieving the user's Cart from the session data, and updating its content using the Product. The modified Cart is stored, and the browser is redirected to the same Razor Page, which it will do using a GET request (which prevents reloading the browser from triggering a duplicate POST request).

The GET request is handled by the OnGet handler method, which sets the values of the ReturnUrl and Cart properties, after which the Razor content section of the page is rendered. The expressions in the HTML content are evaluated using the CartModel as the view model object, which means that the values assigned to the ReturnUrl and Cart properties can be accessed within the expressions. The content generated by the Razor Page details the products added to the user's cart and provides a button to navigate back to the point where the product was added to the cart.

The handler methods use parameter names that match the input elements in the HTML forms produced by the ProductSummary.cshtml view. This allows ASP.NET Core to associate incoming form POST variables with those parameters, meaning I do not need to process the form directly. This is known as *model binding* and is a powerful tool for simplifying development, as I explain in detail in chapter 28.

Understanding Razor Pages

Razor Pages can feel a little odd when you first start using them, especially if you have previous experience with the MVC Framework features provided by ASP.NET Core. But Razor Pages are complementary to the MVC Framework, and I find myself using them alongside controllers and views because they are well-suited to self-contained features that don't require the complexity of the MVC Framework. I describe Razor Pages in chapter 23 and show their use alongside controllers throughout part 3 and part 4 of this book.

The result is that the basic functions of the shopping cart are in place. First, products are listed along with a button to add them to the cart, which you can see by restarting ASP.NET Core and requesting http://localhost:5000, as shown in figure 8.10.

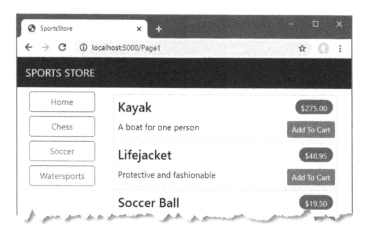

Figure 8.10
The Add To Cart buttons

Second, when the user clicks an Add To Cart button, the appropriate product is added to their cart, and a summary of the cart is displayed, as shown in figure 8.11. Clicking the Continue Shopping button returns the user to the product page they came from.

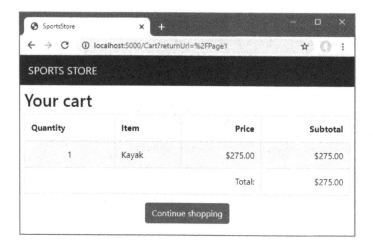

Figure 8.11
Displaying the contents of the shopping cart

Unit testing: razor pages

Testing Razor Pages can require a lot of mocking to create the context objects that the page model class requires. To test the behavior of the OnGet method defined by the CartModel class, I added a class file named CartPageTests.cs to the Sports-Store.Tests project and defined this test:

```
using Microsoft.AspNetCore.Http;
using Microsoft.AspNetCore.Mvc;
using Microsoft.AspNetCore.Mvc.RazorPages;
using Microsoft.AspNetCore.Routing;
using Moq;
using SportsStore.Models;
using SportsStore.Pages;
using System.Linq;
using System.Text;
using System.Text.Json;
using Xunit;

namespace SportsStore.Tests {

    public class CartPageTests {

        [Fact]
        public void Can_Load_Cart() {

            // Arrange
            // - create a mock repository
            Product p1 = new Product { ProductID = 1, Name = "P1" };
            Product p2 = new Product { ProductID = 2, Name = "P2" };
            Mock<IStoreRepository> mockRepo
                = new Mock<IStoreRepository>();
            mockRepo.Setup(m => m.Products).Returns((new Product[] {
                p1, p2
            }).AsQueryable<Product>());

            // - create a cart
            Cart testCart = new Cart();
            testCart.AddItem(p1, 2);
            testCart.AddItem(p2, 1);
            // - create a mock page context and session
            Mock<ISession> mockSession = new Mock<ISession>();
            byte[] data = Encoding.UTF8.GetBytes(
                    JsonSerializer.Serialize(testCart));
            mockSession.Setup(c =>
                c.TryGetValue(It.IsAny<string>(), out data!));
            Mock<HttpContext> mockContext = new Mock<HttpContext>();
            mockContext.SetupGet(c =>
                c.Session).Returns(mockSession.Object);

            // Action
            CartModel cartModel = new CartModel(mockRepo.Object) {
                PageContext = new PageContext(new ActionContext {
                    HttpContext = mockContext.Object,
                    RouteData = new RouteData(),
```

(continued)

```
                ActionDescriptor = new PageActionDescriptor()
            })
        };
        cartModel.OnGet("myUrl");

        //Assert
        Assert.Equal(2, cartModel.Cart?.Lines.Count());
        Assert.Equal("myUrl", cartModel.ReturnUrl);
    }
    }
}
```

I am not going to describe these unit tests in detail because there is a simpler way to perform these tests, which I explain in the next chapter. The complexity in this test is mocking the ISession interface so that the page model class can use extension methods to retrieve a JSON representation of a Cart object. The ISession interface only stores byte arrays, and getting and deserializing a string is performed by extension methods. Once the mock objects are defined, they can be wrapped in context objects and used to configure an instance of the page model class, which can be subjected to tests.

The process of testing the OnPost method of the page model class means capturing the byte array that is passed to the ISession interface mock and then deserializing it to ensure that it contains the expected content. Here is the unit test I added to the CartPageTests class:

```
...
[Fact]
public void Can_Update_Cart() {
    // Arrange
    // - create a mock repository
    Mock<IStoreRepository> mockRepo =
        new Mock<IStoreRepository>();
    mockRepo.Setup(m => m.Products).Returns((new Product[] {
        new Product { ProductID = 1, Name = "P1" }
    }).AsQueryable<Product>());

    Cart? testCart = new Cart();

    Mock<ISession> mockSession = new Mock<ISession>();
    mockSession.Setup(s =>
        s.Set(It.IsAny<string>(), It.IsAny<byte[]>()))
        .Callback<string, byte[]>((key, val) => {
        testCart = JsonSerializer.Deserialize<Cart>(
            Encoding.UTF8.GetString(val));
    });

    Mock<HttpContext> mockContext = new Mock<HttpContext>();
    mockContext.SetupGet(c =>
        c.Session).Returns(mockSession.Object);

    // Action
    CartModel cartModel = new CartModel(mockRepo.Object) {
        PageContext = new PageContext(new ActionContext {
            HttpContext = mockContext.Object,
            RouteData = new RouteData(),
```

(continued)

```
        ActionDescriptor = new PageActionDescriptor()
    })
};
cartModel.OnPost(1, "myUrl");

//Assert
Assert.Single(testCart.Lines);
Assert.Equal("P1", testCart.Lines.First().Product.Name);
Assert.Equal(1, testCart.Lines.First().Quantity);
}
...
```

Patience and a little experimentation are required to write effective unit tests, especially when the feature you are testing operates on the context objects that ASP.NET Core provides.

Summary

- The navigation controls include the selected category in the request URL, which is combined with the page number when querying the database.
- The View Bag allows data to be passed to views alongside the view model.
- Razor Pages are well-suited for simple self-contained features, like displaying the contents of a shopping cart.
- Sessions allow data to be associated with a series of related requests.

SportsStore: Completing the cart

This chapter covers

- Updating the shopping cart so that it persists itself as session data
- Creating a shopping cart summary widget using a view component
- Receiving and validating user data
- Displaying data validation errors to the user

In this chapter, I continue to build the SportsStore example app. In the previous chapter, I added the basic support for a shopping cart, and now I am going to improve on and complete that functionality.

> **TIP** You can download the example project for this chapter—and for all the other chapters in this book—from https://github.com/ManningBooks/pro-asp.net-core-7. See chapter 1 for how to get help if you have problems running the examples.

9.1 Refining the cart model with a service

I defined a `Cart` model class in the previous chapter and demonstrated how it can be stored using the session feature, allowing the user to build up a set of products for purchase. The responsibility for managing the persistence of the `Cart` class fell to the `Cart` Razor Page, which has to deal with getting and storing `Cart` objects as session data.

The problem with this approach is that I will have to duplicate the code that obtains and stores `Cart` objects in any other Razor Page or controller that uses them. In this section, I am going to use the services feature that sits at the heart of ASP.NET Core to simplify the way that `Cart` objects are managed, freeing individual components from needing to deal with the details directly.

Services are commonly used to hide details of how interfaces are implemented from the components that depend on them. But services can be used to solve lots of other problems as well and can be used to shape and reshape an application, even when you are working with concrete classes such as `Cart`.

9.1.1   Creating a storage-aware cart class

The first step in tidying up the way that the `Cart` class is used will be to create a subclass that is aware of how to store itself using session state. To prepare, I apply the `virtual` keyword to the `Cart` class, as shown in listing 9.1, so that I can override the members.

Listing 9.1   Applying the keyword in the Cart.cs file in the SportsStore/Models folder

```
namespace SportsStore.Models {

    public class Cart {

        public List<CartLine> Lines { get; set; } = new List<CartLine>();

        public virtual void AddItem(Product product, int quantity) {
            CartLine? line = Lines
                .Where(p => p.Product.ProductID == product.ProductID)
                .FirstOrDefault();

            if (line == null) {
                Lines.Add(new CartLine {
                    Product = product,
                    Quantity = quantity
                });
            } else {
                line.Quantity += quantity;
            }
        }

        public virtual void RemoveLine(Product product) =>
            Lines.RemoveAll(l =>
                l.Product.ProductID == product.ProductID);

        public decimal ComputeTotalValue() =>
            Lines.Sum(e => e.Product.Price * e.Quantity);

        public virtual void Clear() => Lines.Clear();
    }

    public class CartLine {
        public int CartLineID { get; set; }
        public Product Product { get; set; } = new();
```

```
        public int Quantity { get; set; }
    }
}
```

Next, I added a class file called `SessionCart.cs` to the `Models` folder and used it to define the class shown in listing 9.2.

> **Listing 9.2   The contents of the SessionCart.cs file in the SportsStore/Models folder**

```
using System.Text.Json.Serialization;
using SportsStore.Infrastructure;

namespace SportsStore.Models {

    public class SessionCart : Cart {

        public static Cart GetCart(IServiceProvider services) {
            ISession? session =
                services.GetRequiredService<IHttpContextAccessor>()
                    .HttpContext?.Session;
            SessionCart cart = session?.GetJson<SessionCart>("Cart")
                ?? new SessionCart();
            cart.Session = session;
            return cart;
        }

        [JsonIgnore]
        public ISession? Session { get; set; }

        public override void AddItem(Product product, int quantity) {
            base.AddItem(product, quantity);
            Session?.SetJson("Cart", this);
        }

        public override void RemoveLine(Product product) {
            base.RemoveLine(product);
            Session?.SetJson("Cart", this);
        }

        public override void Clear() {
            base.Clear();
            Session?.Remove("Cart");
        }
    }
}
```

The `SessionCart` class subclasses the `Cart` class and overrides the `AddItem`, `Remove-Line`, and `Clear` methods so they call the base implementations and then store the updated state in the session using the extension methods on the `ISession` interface. The static `GetCart` method is a factory for creating `SessionCart` objects and providing them with an `ISession` object so they can store themselves.

    Getting hold of the `ISession` object is a little complicated. I obtain an instance of the `IHttpContextAccessor` service, which provides me with access to an `HttpContext` object that, in turn, provides me with the `ISession`. This indirect approach is required because the session isn't provided as a regular service.

9.1.2   Registering the service

The next step is to create a service for the Cart class. My goal is to satisfy requests for Cart objects with SessionCart objects that will seamlessly store themselves. You can see how I created the service in listing 9.3.

Listing 9.3   Creating the cart service in the Program.cs file in the SportsStore folder

```
using Microsoft.EntityFrameworkCore;
using SportsStore.Models;

var builder = WebApplication.CreateBuilder(args);

builder.Services.AddControllersWithViews();

builder.Services.AddDbContext<StoreDbContext>(opts => {
    opts.UseSqlServer(
        builder.Configuration["ConnectionStrings:SportsStoreConnection"]);
});

builder.Services.AddScoped<IStoreRepository, EFStoreRepository>();

builder.Services.AddRazorPages();
builder.Services.AddDistributedMemoryCache();
builder.Services.AddSession();
builder.Services.AddScoped<Cart>(sp => SessionCart.GetCart(sp));
builder.Services.AddSingleton<IHttpContextAccessor,
    HttpContextAccessor>();

var app = builder.Build();

app.UseStaticFiles();
app.UseSession();

app.MapControllerRoute("catpage",
    "{category}/Page{productPage:int}",
    new { Controller = "Home", action = "Index" });

app.MapControllerRoute("page", "Page{productPage:int}",
    new { Controller = "Home", action = "Index", productPage = 1 });

app.MapControllerRoute("category", "{category}",
    new { Controller = "Home", action = "Index", productPage = 1 });

app.MapControllerRoute("pagination",
    "Products/Page{productPage}",
    new { Controller = "Home", action = "Index", productPage = 1 });

app.MapDefaultControllerRoute();
app.MapRazorPages();

SeedData.EnsurePopulated(app);

app.Run();
```

The `AddScoped` method specifies that the same object should be used to satisfy related requests for `Cart` instances. How requests are related can be configured, but by default, it means that any `Cart` required by components handling the same HTTP request will receive the same object.

Rather than provide the `AddScoped` method with a type mapping, as I did for the repository, I have specified a lambda expression that will be invoked to satisfy `Cart` requests. The expression receives the collection of services that have been registered and passes the collection to the `GetCart` method of the `SessionCart` class. The result is that requests for the `Cart` service will be handled by creating `SessionCart` objects, which will serialize themselves as session data when they are modified.

I also added a service using the `AddSingleton` method, which specifies that the same object should always be used. The service I created tells ASP.NET Core to use the `HttpContextAccessor` class when implementations of the `IHttpContextAccessor` interface are required. This service is required so I can access the current session in the `SessionCart` class.

9.1.3 *Simplifying the cart Razor Page*

The benefit of creating this kind of service is that it allows me to simplify the code where `Cart` objects are used. In listing 9.4, I have reworked the page model class for the `Cart` Razor Page to take advantage of the new service.

> **Listing 9.4 Using the service in the Cart.cshtml.cs file in the SportsStore/Pages folder**

```
using Microsoft.AspNetCore.Mvc;
using Microsoft.AspNetCore.Mvc.RazorPages;
using SportsStore.Infrastructure;
using SportsStore.Models;

namespace SportsStore.Pages {

    public class CartModel : PageModel {
        private IStoreRepository repository;

        public CartModel(IStoreRepository repo, Cart cartService) {
            repository = repo;
            Cart = cartService;
        }

        public Cart Cart { get; set; }
        public string ReturnUrl { get; set; } = "/";

        public void OnGet(string returnUrl) {
            ReturnUrl = returnUrl ?? "/";
            //Cart = HttpContext.Session.GetJson<Cart>("cart")
            //    ?? new Cart();
        }

        public IActionResult OnPost(long productId, string returnUrl) {
            Product? product = repository.Products
```

```
                .FirstOrDefault(p => p.ProductID == productId);
            if (product != null) {
                Cart.AddItem(product, 1);
            }
            return RedirectToPage(new { returnUrl = returnUrl });
        }
    }
}
```

The page model class indicates that it needs a `Cart` object by declaring a constructor argument, which has allowed me to remove the statements that load and store sessions from the handler methods. The result is a simpler page model class that focuses on its role in the application without having to worry about how `Cart` objects are created or persisted. And, since services are available throughout the application, any component can get hold of the user's cart using the same technique.

Updating the unit tests

The simplification of the `CartModel` class in listing 9.4 requires a corresponding change to the unit tests in the `CartPageTests.cs` file in the unit test project so that the `Cart` is provided as a constructor argument and not accessed through the context objects. Here is the change to the test for reading the cart:

```
...
[Fact]
public void Can_Load_Cart() {

    // Arrange
    // - create a mock repository
    Product p1 = new Product { ProductID = 1, Name = "P1" };
    Product p2 = new Product { ProductID = 2, Name = "P2" };
    Mock<IStoreRepository> mockRepo = new Mock<IStoreRepository>();
    mockRepo.Setup(m => m.Products).Returns((new Product[] {
        p1, p2
    }).AsQueryable<Product>());

    // - create a cart
    Cart testCart = new Cart();
    testCart.AddItem(p1, 2);
    testCart.AddItem(p2, 1);

    // Action
    CartModel cartModel = new CartModel(mockRepo.Object, testCart);
    cartModel.OnGet("myUrl");

    //Assert
    Assert.Equal(2, cartModel.Cart.Lines.Count());
    Assert.Equal("myUrl", cartModel.ReturnUrl);
}
...
```

I applied the same change to the unit test that checks changes to the cart:

```
(continued)
...
[Fact]
public void Can_Update_Cart() {
    // Arrange
    // - create a mock repository
    Mock<IStoreRepository> mockRepo = new Mock<IStoreRepository>();
    mockRepo.Setup(m => m.Products).Returns((new Product[] {
        new Product { ProductID = 1, Name = "P1" }
    }).AsQueryable<Product>());

    Cart testCart = new Cart();

    // Action
    CartModel cartModel = new CartModel(mockRepo.Object, testCart);
    cartModel.OnPost(1, "myUrl");

    //Assert
    Assert.Single(testCart.Lines);
    Assert.Equal("P1", testCart.Lines.First().Product.Name);
    Assert.Equal(1, testCart.Lines.First().Quantity);
}
...
```

Using services simplifies the testing process and makes it much easier to provide the class being tested with its dependencies.

9.2 Completing the cart functionality

Now that I have introduced the Cart service, it is time to complete the cart functionality by adding two new features. The first will allow the customer to remove an item from the cart. The second feature will display a summary of the cart at the top of the page.

9.2.1 Removing items from the cart

To remove items from the cart, I need to add a Remove button to the content rendered by the Cart Razor Page that will submit an HTTP POST request. The changes are shown in listing 9.5.

> **Listing 9.5 Removing cart items in the Cart.cshtml file in the SportsStore/Pages folder**

```
@page
@model CartModel

<h2>Your cart</h2>
<table class="table table-bordered table-striped">
    <thead>
        <tr>
            <th>Quantity</th>
            <th>Item</th>
```

```
                <th class="text-right">Price</th>
                <th class="text-right">Subtotal</th>
                <th></th>
            </tr>
        </thead>
        <tbody>
            @foreach (var line in Model.Cart?.Lines
                    ?? Enumerable.Empty<CartLine>()) {
                <tr>
                    <td class="text-center">@line.Quantity</td>
                    <td class="text-left">@line.Product.Name</td>
                    <td class="text-right">
                        @line.Product.Price.ToString("c")
                    </td>
                    <td class="text-right">
                        @((line.Quantity * line.Product.Price).ToString("c"))
                    </td>
                    <td class="text-center">
                        <form asp-page-handler="Remove" method="post">
                            <input type="hidden" name="ProductID"
                                value="@line.Product.ProductID" />
                            <input type="hidden" name="returnUrl"
                                value="@Model?.ReturnUrl" />
                            <button type="submit"
                                    class="btn btn-sm btn-danger">
                                Remove
                            </button>
                        </form>
                    </td>
                </tr>
            }
        </tbody>
        <tfoot>
            <tr>
                <td colspan="3" class="text-right">Total:</td>
                <td class="text-right">
                    @Model.Cart?.ComputeTotalValue().ToString("c")
                </td>
            </tr>
        </tfoot>
    </table>

<div class="text-center">
    <a class="btn btn-primary" href="@Model.ReturnUrl">
        Continue shopping
    </a>
</div>
```

The button requires a new handler method in the page model class that will receive the request and modify the cart, as shown in listing 9.6.

> **Listing 9.6   Removing an item in the Cart.cshtml.cs file in the SportsStore/Pages folder**

```
using Microsoft.AspNetCore.Mvc;
using Microsoft.AspNetCore.Mvc.RazorPages;
```

```
using SportsStore.Infrastructure;
using SportsStore.Models;

namespace SportsStore.Pages {

    public class CartModel : PageModel {
        private IStoreRepository repository;

        public CartModel(IStoreRepository repo, Cart cartService) {
            repository = repo;
            Cart = cartService;
        }

        public Cart Cart { get; set; }
        public string ReturnUrl { get; set; } = "/";

        public void OnGet(string returnUrl) {
            ReturnUrl = returnUrl ?? "/";
        }

        public IActionResult OnPost(long productId, string returnUrl) {
            Product? product = repository.Products
                .FirstOrDefault(p => p.ProductID == productId);
            if (product != null) {
                Cart.AddItem(product, 1);
            }
            return RedirectToPage(new { returnUrl = returnUrl });
        }

        public IActionResult OnPostRemove(long productId,
                string returnUrl) {
            Cart.RemoveLine(Cart.Lines.First(cl =>
                cl.Product.ProductID == productId).Product);
            return RedirectToPage(new { returnUrl = returnUrl });
        }
    }
}
```

The new HTML content defines an HTML form. The handler method that will receive the request is specified with the `asp-page-handler` tag helper attribute, like this:

```
...
<form asp-page-handler="Remove" method="post">
...
```

The specified name is prefixed with `On` and given a suffix that matches the request type so that a value of `Remove` selects the `OnPostRemove` handler method. The handler method uses the value it receives to locate the item in the cart and remove it.

Restart ASP.NET Core and request http://localhost:5000. Click the Add To Cart buttons to add items to the cart and then click a Remove button. The cart will be updated to remove the item you specified, as shown in figure 9.1.

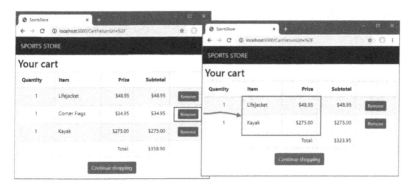

Figure 9.1 Removing items from the shopping cart

9.2.2 Adding the cart summary widget

I may have a functioning cart, but there is an issue with the way it is integrated into the interface. Customers can tell what is in their cart only by viewing the cart summary screen. And they can view the cart summary screen only by adding a new item to the cart.

To solve this problem, I am going to add a widget that summarizes the contents of the cart and that can be clicked to display the cart contents throughout the application. I will do this in much the same way that I added the navigation widget—as a view component whose output I can include in a Razor layout.

ADDING THE FONT AWESOME PACKAGE

As part of the cart summary, I am going to display a button that allows the user to check out. Rather than display the word *checkout* in the button, I want to use a cart symbol. Since I have no artistic skills, I am going to use the Font Awesome package, which is an excellent set of open source icons that are integrated into applications as fonts, where each character in the font is a different image. You can learn more about Font Awesome, including inspecting the icons it contains, at https://fontawesome.com.

To install the client-side package, use a PowerShell command prompt to run the command shown in listing 9.7 in the SportsStore project.

> **Listing 9.7 Installing the icon package**

```
libman install font-awesome@6.2.1 -d wwwroot/lib/font-awesome
```

CREATING THE VIEW COMPONENT CLASS AND VIEW

I added a class file called `CartSummaryViewComponent.cs` in the `Components` folder and used it to define the view component shown in listing 9.8.

Listing 9.8   The CartSummaryViewComponent.cs file in the SportsStore/
Components folder

```
using Microsoft.AspNetCore.Mvc;
using SportsStore.Models;

namespace SportsStore.Components {

    public class CartSummaryViewComponent : ViewComponent {
        private Cart cart;

        public CartSummaryViewComponent(Cart cartService) {
            cart = cartService;
        }

        public IViewComponentResult Invoke() {
            return View(cart);
        }
    }
}
```

This view component can take advantage of the service that I created earlier in the
chapter to receive a `Cart` object as a constructor argument. The result is a simple view
component class that passes on the `Cart` to the `View` method to generate the fragment
of HTML that will be included in the layout. To create the view for the component, I
created the `Views/Shared/Components/CartSummary` folder and added to it a Razor
View named `Default.cshtml` with the content shown in listing 9.9.

Listing 9.9   The Default.cshtml file in the Views/Shared/Components/
CartSummary folder

```
@model Cart

<div class="">
    @if (Model.Lines.Count() > 0) {
            <small class="navbar-text">
                <b>Your cart:</b>
                @Model.Lines.Sum(x => x.Quantity) item(s)
                @Model.ComputeTotalValue().ToString("c")
            </small>
    }
    <a class="btn btn-sm btn-secondary navbar-btn" asp-page="/Cart"
        asp-route-returnurl=
            "@ViewContext.HttpContext.Request.PathAndQuery()">
        <i class="fa fa-shopping-cart"></i>
    </a>
</div>
```

The view displays a button with the Font Awesome cart icon and, if there are items in
the cart, provides a snapshot that details the number of items and their total value.
Now that I have a view component and a view, I can modify the layout so that the cart
summary is included in the responses generated by the `Home` controller, as shown in
listing 9.10.

```
<!DOCTYPE html>
<html>
<head>
    <meta name="viewport" content="width=device-width" />
    <title>SportsStore</title>
    <link href="/lib/bootstrap/css/bootstrap.min.css" rel="stylesheet" />
    <link href="/lib/font-awesome/css/all.min.css" rel="stylesheet" />
</head>
<body>
    <div class="bg-dark text-white p-2">
        <div class="container-fluid">
            <div class="row">
                <div class="col navbar-brand">SPORTS STORE</div>
                <div class="col-6 navbar-text text-end">
                    <vc:cart-summary />
                </div>
            </div>
        </div>
    </div>
    <div class="row m-1 p-1">
        <div id="categories" class="col-3">
            <vc:navigation-menu />
        </div>
        <div class="col-9">
            @RenderBody()
        </div>
    </div>
</body>
</html>
```

You can see the cart summary by starting the application. When the cart is empty, only
the checkout button is shown. If you add items to the cart, then the number of items
and their combined cost are shown, as illustrated in figure 9.2. With this addition, customers know what is in their cart and have an obvious way to check out from the store.

Figure 9.2   Displaying a summary of the cart

9.3 Submitting orders

I have now reached the final customer feature in SportsStore: the ability to check out and complete an order. In the following sections, I will extend the data model to provide support for capturing the shipping details from a user and add the application support to process those details.

9.3.1 Creating the model class

I added a class file called Order.cs to the Models folder and used it to define the class shown in listing 9.11. This is the class I will use to represent the shipping details for a customer.

> Listing 9.11 The contents of the Order.cs file in the SportsStore/Models folder

```
using System.ComponentModel.DataAnnotations;
using Microsoft.AspNetCore.Mvc.ModelBinding;

namespace SportsStore.Models {

    public class Order {

        [BindNever]
        public int OrderID { get; set; }
        [BindNever]
        public ICollection<CartLine> Lines { get; set; }
            = new List<CartLine>();

        [Required(ErrorMessage = "Please enter a name")]
        public string? Name { get; set; }

        [Required(ErrorMessage = "Please enter the first address line")]
        public string? Line1 { get; set; }
        public string? Line2 { get; set; }
        public string? Line3 { get; set; }

        [Required(ErrorMessage = "Please enter a city name")]
        public string? City { get; set; }

        [Required(ErrorMessage = "Please enter a state name")]
        public string? State { get; set; }

        public string? Zip { get; set; }

        [Required(ErrorMessage = "Please enter a country name")]
        public string? Country { get; set; }

        public bool GiftWrap { get; set; }
    }
}
```

I am using the validation attributes from the System.ComponentModel.Data-Annotations namespace, just as I did in chapter 3. I describe validation further in chapter 29.

I also use the `BindNever` attribute, which prevents the user from supplying values for these properties in an HTTP request. This is a feature of the model binding system, which I describe in chapter 28, and it stops ASP.NET Core using values from the HTTP request to populate sensitive or important model properties.

9.3.2 Adding the checkout process

The goal is to reach the point where users can enter their shipping details and submit an order. To start, I need to add a Checkout button to the cart view, as shown in listing 9.12.

> **Listing 9.12 Adding a button in the Cart.cshtml file in the SportsStore/Pages folder**

```
...
<div class="text-center">
    <a class="btn btn-primary" href="@Model.ReturnUrl">
        Continue shopping
    </a>
    <a class="btn btn-primary" asp-action="Checkout"
            asp-controller="Order">
        Checkout
    </a>
</div>
...
```

This change generates a link that I have styled as a button and that, when clicked, calls the `Checkout` action method of the `Order` controller, which I create in the following section. To show how Razor Pages and controllers can work together, I am going to handle the order processing in a controller and then return to a Razor Page at the end of the process. To see the Checkout button, restart ASP.NET Core, request http://localhost:5000, and click one of the Add To Cart buttons. The new button is shown as part of the cart summary, as shown in figure 9.3.

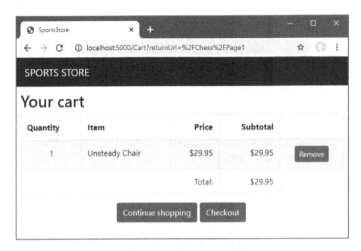

Figure 9.3 The Checkout button

9.3.3   Creating the controller and view

I now need to define the controller that will deal with the order. I added a class file called `OrderController.cs` to the `Controllers` folder and used it to define the class shown in listing 9.13.

Listing 9.13   The OrderController.cs file in the SportsStore/Controllers folder

```
using Microsoft.AspNetCore.Mvc;
using SportsStore.Models;

namespace SportsStore.Controllers {

    public class OrderController : Controller {

        public ViewResult Checkout() => View(new Order());
    }
}
```

The `Checkout` method returns the default view and passes a new `Order` object as the view model. To create the view, I created the `Views/Order` folder and added to it a Razor View called `Checkout.cshtml` with the markup shown in listing 9.14.

Listing 9.14   The Checkout.cshtml file in the SportsStore/Views/Order folder

```
@model Order

<h2>Check out now</h2>
<p>Please enter your details, and we'll ship your goods right away!</p>

<form asp-action="Checkout" method="post">
    <h3>Ship to</h3>
    <div class="form-group">
        <label>Name:</label>
        <input asp-for="Name" class="form-control" />
    </div>
    <h3>Address</h3>
    <div class="form-group">
        <label>Line 1:</label>
        <input asp-for="Line1" class="form-control" />
    </div>
    <div class="form-group">
        <label>Line 2:</label>
        <input asp-for="Line2" class="form-control" />
    </div>
    <div class="form-group">
        <label>Line 3:</label>
        <input asp-for="Line3" class="form-control" />
    </div>
    <div class="form-group">
        <label>City:</label>
        <input asp-for="City" class="form-control" />
    </div>
    <div class="form-group">
        <label>State:</label>
        <input asp-for="State" class="form-control" />
```

```
    </div>
    <div class="form-group">
        <label>Zip:</label>
        <input asp-for="Zip" class="form-control" />
    </div>
    <div class="form-group">
        <label>Country:</label>
        <input asp-for="Country" class="form-control" />
    </div>
    <h3>Options</h3>
    <div class="checkbox">
        <label>
            <input asp-for="GiftWrap" /> Gift wrap these items
        </label>
    </div>
    <div class="text-center">
        <input class="btn btn-primary" type="submit"
            value="Complete Order" />
    </div>
</form>
```

For each of the properties in the model, I have created a label and input elements to capture the user input, styled with Bootstrap, and configured using a tag helper. The asp-for attribute on the input elements is handled by a built-in tag helper that generates the type, id, name, and value attributes based on the specified model property, as described in chapter 27.

You can see the form, shown in figure 9.4, by restarting ASP.NET Core, requesting http://localhost:5000, adding an item to the basket, and clicking the Checkout button. Or, more directly, you can request http://localhost:5000/order/checkout.

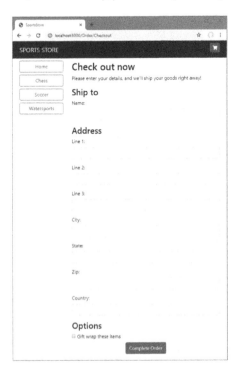

**Figure 9.4
The shipping
details form**

9.3.4 Implementing order processing

I will process orders by writing them to the database. Most e-commerce sites would not simply stop there, of course, and I have not provided support for processing credit cards or other forms of payment. But I want to keep things focused on ASP.NET Core, so a simple database entry will do.

EXTENDING THE DATABASE

Adding a new kind of model to the database is simple because of the initial setup I went through in chapter 7. First, I added a new property to the database context class, as shown in listing 9.15.

> **Listing 9.15 Adding a property in the StoreDbContext.cs file in the SportsStore/ Models folder**

```
using Microsoft.EntityFrameworkCore;

namespace SportsStore.Models {
    public class StoreDbContext : DbContext {

        public StoreDbContext(DbContextOptions<StoreDbContext> options)
            : base(options) { }

        public DbSet<Product> Products => Set<Product>();
        public DbSet<Order> Orders => Set<Order>();
    }
}
```

This change is enough for Entity Framework Core to create a database migration that will allow `Order` objects to be stored in the database. To create the migration, use a PowerShell command prompt to run the command shown in listing 9.16 in the `SportsStore` folder.

> **Listing 9.16 Creating a migration**

```
dotnet ef migrations add Orders
```

This command tells Entity Framework Core to take a new snapshot of the application data model, work out how it differs from the previous database version, and generate a new migration called `Orders`. The new migration will be applied automatically when the application starts because the `SeedData` calls the `Migrate` method provided by Entity Framework Core.

> **Resetting the database**
>
> When you are making frequent changes to the model, there will come a point when your migrations and your database schema get out of sync. The easiest thing to do is delete the database and start over. However, this applies only during development, of course, because you will lose any data you have stored. Run this command to delete the database:
>
> ```
> dotnet ef database drop --force --context StoreDbContext
> ```

(continued)

Once the database has been removed, run the following command from the Sports-
Store folder to re-create the database and apply the migrations you have created by
running the following command:

```
dotnet ef database update --context StoreDbContext
```

The migrations will also be applied by the SeedData class if you just start the application. Either way, the database will be reset so that it accurately reflects your data model
and allows you to return to developing your application.

CREATING THE ORDER REPOSITORY

I am going to follow the same pattern I used for the product repository to provide
access to the Order objects. I added a class file called IOrderRepository.cs to the
Models folder and used it to define the interface shown in listing 9.17.

> **Listing 9.17   The IOrderRepository.cs file in the SportsStore/Models folder**

```
namespace SportsStore.Models {

    public interface IOrderRepository {

        IQueryable<Order> Orders { get; }
        void SaveOrder(Order order);
    }
}
```

To implement the order repository interface, I added a class file called EFOrder-
Repository.cs to the Models folder and defined the class shown in listing 9.18.

> **Listing 9.18   The EFOrderRepository.cs File in the SportsStore/Models folder**

```
using Microsoft.EntityFrameworkCore;

namespace SportsStore.Models {

    public class EFOrderRepository : IOrderRepository {
        private StoreDbContext context;

        public EFOrderRepository(StoreDbContext ctx) {
            context = ctx;
        }

        public IQueryable<Order> Orders => context.Orders
                            .Include(o => o.Lines)
                            .ThenInclude(l => l.Product);

        public void SaveOrder(Order order) {
            context.AttachRange(order.Lines.Select(l => l.Product));
            if (order.OrderID == 0) {
                context.Orders.Add(order);
```

```
        }
        context.SaveChanges();
    }
  }
}
```

This class implements the `IOrderRepository` interface using Entity Framework Core, allowing the set of `Order` objects that have been stored to be retrieved and allowing for orders to be created or changed.

Understanding the order repository

Entity Framework Core requires instruction to load related data if it spans multiple tables. In listing 9.18, I used the `Include` and `ThenInclude` methods to specify that when an `Order` object is read from the database, the collection associated with the `Lines` property should also be loaded along with each `Product` object associated with each collection object.

```
. . .
public IQueryable<Order> Orders => context.Orders
    .Include(o => o.Lines)
    .ThenInclude(l => l.Product);
. . .
```

This ensures that I receive all the data objects that I need without having to perform separate queries and then assemble the data myself.

An additional step is also required when I store an `Order` object in the database. When the user's cart data is de-serialized from the session store, new objects are created that are not known to Entity Framework Core, which then tries to write all the objects into the database. For the `Product` objects associated with an `Order`, this means that Entity Framework Core tries to write objects that have already been stored, which causes an error. To avoid this problem, I notify Entity Framework Core that the objects exist and shouldn't be stored in the database unless they are modified, as follows:

```
. . .
context.AttachRange(order.Lines.Select(l => l.Product));
. . .
```

This ensures that Entity Framework Core won't try to write the de-serialized `Product` objects that are associated with the `Order` object.

In listing 9.19, I have registered the order repository as a service in the `Program.cs` file.

Listing 9.19   Registering the service in the Program.cs file in the SportsStore folder

```
using Microsoft.EntityFrameworkCore;
using SportsStore.Models;

var builder = WebApplication.CreateBuilder(args);

builder.Services.AddControllersWithViews();
```

```
builder.Services.AddDbContext<StoreDbContext>(opts => {
    opts.UseSqlServer(
        builder.Configuration["ConnectionStrings:SportsStoreConnection"]);
});

builder.Services.AddScoped<IStoreRepository, EFStoreRepository>();
builder.Services.AddScoped<IOrderRepository, EFOrderRepository>();

builder.Services.AddRazorPages();
builder.Services.AddDistributedMemoryCache();
builder.Services.AddSession();
builder.Services.AddScoped<Cart>(sp => SessionCart.GetCart(sp));
builder.Services.AddSingleton<IHttpContextAccessor,
    HttpContextAccessor>();

var app = builder.Build();

app.UseStaticFiles();
app.UseSession();

app.MapControllerRoute("catpage",
    "{category}/Page{productPage:int}",
    new { Controller = "Home", action = "Index" });

app.MapControllerRoute("page", "Page{productPage:int}",
    new { Controller = "Home", action = "Index", productPage = 1 });

app.MapControllerRoute("category", "{category}",
    new { Controller = "Home", action = "Index", productPage = 1 });

app.MapControllerRoute("pagination",
    "Products/Page{productPage}",
    new { Controller = "Home", action = "Index", productPage = 1 });

app.MapDefaultControllerRoute();
app.MapRazorPages();

SeedData.EnsurePopulated(app);

app.Run();
```

9.3.5 *Completing the order controller*

To complete the `OrderController` class, I need to modify the constructor so that it receives the services it requires to process an order and add an action method that will handle the HTTP form `POST` request when the user clicks the Complete Order button. Listing 9.20 shows both changes.

> **Listing 9.20   Completing the controller in the OrderController.cs file in the SportsStore/Controllers folder**

```
using Microsoft.AspNetCore.Mvc;
using SportsStore.Models;

namespace SportsStore.Controllers {
```

```
public class OrderController : Controller {
    private IOrderRepository repository;
    private Cart cart;

    public OrderController(IOrderRepository repoService,
            Cart cartService) {
        repository = repoService;
        cart = cartService;
    }

    public ViewResult Checkout() => View(new Order());

    [HttpPost]
    public IActionResult Checkout(Order order) {
        if (cart.Lines.Count() == 0) {
            ModelState.AddModelError("",
                "Sorry, your cart is empty!");
        }
        if (ModelState.IsValid) {
            order.Lines = cart.Lines.ToArray();
            repository.SaveOrder(order);
            cart.Clear();
            return RedirectToPage("/Completed",
                new { orderId = order.OrderID });
        } else {
            return View();
        }
    }
}
```

The Checkout action method is decorated with the HttpPost attribute, which means that it will be used to handle POST requests—in this case, when the user submits the form.

In chapter 8, I use the ASP.NET Core model binding feature to receive simple data values from the request. This same feature is used in the new action method to receive a completed Order object. When a request is processed, the model binding system tries to find values for the properties defined by the Order class. This works on a best-effort basis, which means I may receive an Order object lacking property values if there is no corresponding data item in the request.

To ensure I have the data I require, I applied validation attributes to the Order class. ASP.NET Core checks the validation constraints that I applied to the Order class and provides details of the result through the ModelState property. I can see whether there are any problems by checking the ModelState.IsValid property. I call the Model-State.AddModelError method to register an error message if there are no items in the cart. I will explain how to display such errors shortly, and I have much more to say about model binding and validation in chapters 28 and 29.

Unit test: order processing

To perform unit testing for the `OrderController` class, I need to test the behavior of the `POST` version of the `Checkout` method. Although the method looks short and simple, the use of model binding means that a lot is going on behind the scenes that needs to be tested.

I want to process an order only if there are items in the cart *and* the customer has provided valid shipping details. Under all other circumstances, the customer should be shown an error. Here is the first test method, which I defined in a class file called `Order-ControllerTests.cs` in the `SportsStore.Tests` project:

```
using Microsoft.AspNetCore.Mvc;
using Moq;
using SportsStore.Controllers;
using SportsStore.Models;
using Xunit;

namespace SportsStore.Tests {

    public class OrderControllerTests {

        [Fact]
        public void Cannot_Checkout_Empty_Cart() {
            // Arrange - create a mock repository
            Mock<IOrderRepository> mock = new Mock<IOrderRepository>();
            // Arrange - create an empty cart
            Cart cart = new Cart();
            // Arrange - create the order
            Order order = new Order();
            // Arrange - create an instance of the controller
            OrderController target =
                new OrderController(mock.Object, cart);

            // Act
            ViewResult? result = target.Checkout(order) as ViewResult;

            // Assert - check that the order hasn't been stored
            mock.Verify(m => m.SaveOrder(It.IsAny<Order>()), Times.Never);
            // Assert - check that the method is returning the default view
            Assert.True(string.IsNullOrEmpty(result?.ViewName));
            // Assert - check I am passing an invalid model to the view
            Assert.False(result?.ViewData.ModelState.IsValid);
        }
    }
}
```

This test ensures that I cannot check out with an empty cart. I check this by ensuring that the `SaveOrder` of the mock `IOrderRepository` implementation is never called, that the view the method returns is the default view (which will redisplay the data entered by customers and give them a chance to correct it), and that the model state being passed to the view has been marked as invalid. This may seem like a belt-and-braces set of assertions, but I need all three to be sure that I have the right behavior. The next test method works in much the same way but injects an error into the view model to simulate a problem reported by the model binder (which would happen in production when the customer enters invalid shipping data):

(continued)
```
...
[Fact]
public void Cannot_Checkout_Invalid_ShippingDetails() {

    // Arrange - create a mock order repository
    Mock<IOrderRepository> mock = new Mock<IOrderRepository>();
    // Arrange - create a cart with one item
    Cart cart = new Cart();
    cart.AddItem(new Product(), 1);
    // Arrange - create an instance of the controller
    OrderController target = new OrderController(mock.Object, cart);
    // Arrange - add an error to the model
    target.ModelState.AddModelError("error", "error");

    // Act - try to checkout
    ViewResult? result = target.Checkout(new Order()) as ViewResult;

    // Assert - check that the order hasn't been passed stored
    mock.Verify(m => m.SaveOrder(It.IsAny<Order>()), Times.Never);
    // Assert - check that the method is returning the default view
    Assert.True(string.IsNullOrEmpty(result?.ViewName));
    // Assert - check that I am passing an invalid model to the view
    Assert.False(result?.ViewData.ModelState.IsValid);
}
...
```

Having established that an empty cart or invalid details will prevent an order from being processed, I need to ensure that I process orders when appropriate. Here is the test:

```
...
[Fact]
public void Can_Checkout_And_Submit_Order() {
    // Arrange - create a mock order repository
    Mock<IOrderRepository> mock = new Mock<IOrderRepository>();
    // Arrange - create a cart with one item
    Cart cart = new Cart();
    cart.AddItem(new Product(), 1);
    // Arrange - create an instance of the controller
    OrderController target = new OrderController(mock.Object, cart);

    // Act - try to checkout
    RedirectToPageResult? result =
            target.Checkout(new Order()) as RedirectToPageResult;

    // Assert - check that the order has been stored
    mock.Verify(m => m.SaveOrder(It.IsAny<Order>()), Times.Once);
    // Assert - check the method is redirecting to the Completed action
    Assert.Equal("/Completed", result?.PageName);
}
...
```

I did not need to test that I can identify valid shipping details. This is handled for me automatically by the model binder using the attributes applied to the properties of the Order class.

9.3.6 *Displaying validation errors*

ASP.NET Core uses the validation attributes applied to the `Order` class to validate user data, but I need to make a simple change to display any problems. This relies on another built-in tag helper that inspects the validation state of the data provided by the user and adds warning messages for each problem that has been discovered. Listing 9.21 shows the addition of an HTML element that will be processed by the tag helper to the `Checkout.cshtml` file.

> **Listing 9.21 Adding a validation summary to the Checkout.cshtml file in the SportsStore/Views/Order folder**

```
@model Order

<h2>Check out now</h2>
<p>Please enter your details, and we'll ship your goods right away!</p>

<div asp-validation-summary="All" class="text-danger"></div>

<form asp-action="Checkout" method="post">
    <h3>Ship to</h3>
    <div class="form-group">
        <label>Name:</label>
        <input asp-for="Name" class="form-control" />
    </div>
    <h3>Address</h3>
    <div class="form-group">
        <label>Line 1:</label>
        <input asp-for="Line1" class="form-control" />
    </div>
    <div class="form-group">
        <label>Line 2:</label>
        <input asp-for="Line2" class="form-control" />
    </div>
    <div class="form-group">
        <label>Line 3:</label>
        <input asp-for="Line3" class="form-control" />
    </div>
    <div class="form-group">
        <label>City:</label>
        <input asp-for="City" class="form-control" />
    </div>
    <div class="form-group">
        <label>State:</label>
        <input asp-for="State" class="form-control" />
    </div>
    <div class="form-group">
        <label>Zip:</label>
        <input asp-for="Zip" class="form-control" />
    </div>
    <div class="form-group">
        <label>Country:</label>
        <input asp-for="Country" class="form-control" />
```

```
        </div>
        <h3>Options</h3>
        <div class="checkbox">
            <label>
                <input asp-for="GiftWrap" /> Gift wrap these items
            </label>
        </div>
        <div class="text-center">
            <input class="btn btn-primary" type="submit"
                value="Complete Order" />
        </div>
</form>
```

With this simple change, validation errors are reported to the user. To see the effect, restart ASP.NET Core, request http://localhost:5000/Order/Checkout, and click the Complete Order button without filling out the form. ASP.NET Core will process the form data, detect that the required values were not found, and generate the validation errors shown in figure 9.5.

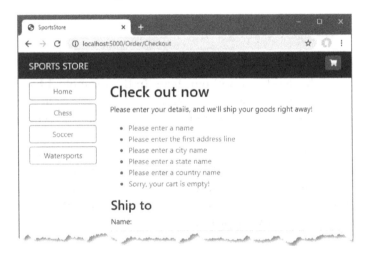

Figure 9.5 Displaying validation messages

TIP   The data submitted by the user is sent to the server before it is validated, which is known as *server-side validation* and for which ASP.NET Core has excellent support. The problem with server-side validation is that the user isn't told about errors until after the data has been sent to the server and processed and the result page has been generated—something that can take a few seconds on a busy server. For this reason, server-side validation is usually complemented by *client-side validation*, where JavaScript is used to check the values that the user has entered before the form data is sent to the server. I describe client-side validation in chapter 29.

9.3.7 Displaying a summary page

To complete the checkout process, I am going to create a Razor Page that displays a thank-you message with a summary of the order. Add a Razor Page named `Completed` `.cshtml` to the `Pages` folder with the contents shown in listing 9.22.

> **Listing 9.22   The contents of the Completed.cshtml file in the SportsStore/Pages folder**

```
@page

<div class="text-center">
    <h2>Thanks!</h2>
    <p>Thanks for placing order #@OrderId</p>
    <p>We'll ship your goods as soon as possible.</p>
    <a class="btn btn-primary" asp-controller="Home">Return to Store</a>
</div>

@functions {

    [BindProperty(SupportsGet = true)]
    public string? OrderId { get; set; }
}
```

Although Razor Pages usually have page model classes, they are not a requirement, and simple features can be developed without them. In this example, I have defined a property named `OrderId` and decorated it with the `BindProperty` attribute, which specifies that a value for this property should be obtained from the request by the model binding system.

Now customers can go through the entire process, from selecting products to checking out. If they provide valid shipping details (and have items in their cart), they will see the summary page when they click the Complete Order button, as shown in figure 9.6.

Notice the way the application moves between controllers and Razor Pages. The application features that ASP.NET Core provides are complementary and can be mixed freely in projects.

Figure 9.6   The completed order summary view

Summary

- Representations of user data can be written to persist themselves as session data.

- View components are used to present content that is not directly related to the view model for the current response, such as a summary of a shopping cart.

- View components can access services via dependency injection to get the data they require.

- User data can be received using HTTP POST requests, which are transformed into C# objects by model binding.

- ASP.NET Core provides integrated support for validating user data and displaying details of validation problems to the user.Revisit and enhance the URL scheme

- Create a category list that will go into the sidebar of the site, highlighting the current category and linking to others

SportsStore: Administration

In this chapter, I continue to build the SportsStore application to give the site administrator a way to manage orders and products. In this chapter, I use Blazor to create administration features. Blazor combines client-side JavaScript code with server-side code executed by ASP.NET Core, connected by a persistent HTTP connection. I describe Blazor in detail in chapters 32–35, but it is important to understand that the Blazor model is not suited to all projects. (I use Blazor Server in this chapter, which is a supported part of the ASP.NET Core platform. There is also Blazor Web-Assembly, which is, at the time of writing, experimental and runs entirely in the browser. I describe Blazor WebAssembly in chapter 36.)

> **TIP** You can download the example project for this chapter—and for all the other chapters in this book—from https://github.com/manningbooks/pro-asp.net-core-7. See chapter 1 for how to get help if you have problems running the examples.

10.1 Preparing Blazor Server

The first step is to enable the services and middleware for Blazor, as shown in listing 10.1.

Listing 10.1 Enabling Blazor in the Program.cs file in the SportsStore folder

```
using Microsoft.EntityFrameworkCore;
using SportsStore.Models;

var builder = WebApplication.CreateBuilder(args);

builder.Services.AddControllersWithViews();

builder.Services.AddDbContext<StoreDbContext>(opts => {
    opts.UseSqlServer(
        builder.Configuration["ConnectionStrings:SportsStoreConnection"]);
});

builder.Services.AddScoped<IStoreRepository, EFStoreRepository>();
builder.Services.AddScoped<IOrderRepository, EFOrderRepository>();

builder.Services.AddRazorPages();
builder.Services.AddDistributedMemoryCache();
builder.Services.AddSession();
builder.Services.AddScoped<Cart>(sp => SessionCart.GetCart(sp));
builder.Services.AddSingleton<IHttpContextAccessor,
    HttpContextAccessor>();
builder.Services.AddServerSideBlazor();

var app = builder.Build();

app.UseStaticFiles();
app.UseSession();

app.MapControllerRoute("catpage",
    "{category}/Page{productPage:int}",
    new { Controller = "Home", action = "Index" });

app.MapControllerRoute("page", "Page{productPage:int}",
    new { Controller = "Home", action = "Index", productPage = 1 });

app.MapControllerRoute("category", "{category}",
    new { Controller = "Home", action = "Index", productPage = 1 });

app.MapControllerRoute("pagination",
    "Products/Page{productPage}",
    new { Controller = "Home", action = "Index", productPage = 1 });

app.MapDefaultControllerRoute();
app.MapRazorPages();
app.MapBlazorHub();
app.MapFallbackToPage("/admin/{*catchall}", "/Admin/Index");

SeedData.EnsurePopulated(app);

app.Run();
```

The `AddServerSideBlazor` method creates the services that Blazor uses, and the `MapBlazorHub` method registers the Blazor middleware components. The final addition is to finesse the routing system to ensure that Blazor works seamlessly with the rest of the application.

10.1.1 Creating the imports file

Blazor requires its own imports file to specify the namespaces that it uses. Create the `Pages/Admin` folder and add to it a file named `_Imports.razor` with the content shown in listing 10.2. (If you are using Visual Studio, you can use the Razor Components template to create this file.)

> **NOTE** The conventional location for Blazor files is within the `Pages` folder, but Blazor files can be defined anywhere in the project. In part 4, for example, I used a folder named `Blazor` to help emphasize which features were provided by Blazor and which by Razor Pages.

Listing 10.2   The _Imports.razor file in the SportsStore/Pages/Admin folder

```
@using Microsoft.AspNetCore.Components
@using Microsoft.AspNetCore.Components.Forms
@using Microsoft.AspNetCore.Components.Routing
@using Microsoft.AspNetCore.Components.Web
@using Microsoft.EntityFrameworkCore
@using SportsStore.Models
```

The first four `@using` expressions are for the namespaces required for Blazor. The last two expressions are for convenience in the examples that follow because they will allow me to use Entity Framework Core and the classes in the `Models` namespace.

10.1.2 Creating the startup Razor Page

Blazor relies on a Razor Page to provide the initial content to the browser, which includes the JavaScript code that connects to the server and renders the Blazor HTML content. Add a Razor Page named `Index.cshtml` to the `Pages/Admin` folder with the contents shown in listing 10.3.

Listing 10.3   The Index.cshtml File in the SportsStore/Pages/Admin Folder

```
@page "/admin"
@{ Layout = null; }

<!DOCTYPE html>
<html>
<head>
    <title>SportsStore Admin</title>
    <link href="/lib/bootstrap/css/bootstrap.min.css" rel="stylesheet" />
    <base href="/" />
</head>
<body>
```

```
    <component type="typeof(Routed)" render-mode="Server" />
    <script src="/_framework/blazor.server.js"></script>
</body>
</html>
```

The `component` element is used to insert a Razor Component in the output from the Razor Page. Razor Components are the confusingly named Blazor building blocks, and the `component` element applied in listing 10.3 is named `Routed` and will be created shortly. The Razor Page also contains a `script` element that tells the browser to load the JavaScript file that Blazor Server uses. Requests for this file are intercepted by the Blazor Server middleware, and you don't need to explicitly add the JavaScript file to the project.

10.1.3 *Creating the routing and layout components*

Add a Razor Component named `Routed.razor` to the `Pages/Admin` folder and add the content shown in listing 10.4.

> **Listing 10.4   The Routed.razor File in the SportsStore/Pages/Admin Folder**

```
<Router AppAssembly="typeof(Program).Assembly">
    <Found>
        <RouteView RouteData="@context"
            DefaultLayout="typeof(AdminLayout)" />
    </Found>
    <NotFound>
        <h4 class="bg-danger text-white text-center p-2">
            No Matching Route Found
        </h4>
    </NotFound>
</Router>
```

The content of this component is described in detail in part 4 of this book, but, for this chapter, it is enough to know that the component will use the browser's current URL to locate a Razor Component that can be displayed to the user. If no matching component can be found, then an error message is displayed.

Blazor has its own system of layouts. To create the layout for the administration tools, add a Razor Component named `AdminLayout.razor` to the `Pages/Admin` folder with the content shown in listing 10.5.

> **Listing 10.5   The AdminLayout.razor File in the SportsStore/Pages/Admin Folder**

```
@inherits LayoutComponentBase

<div class="bg-info text-white p-2">
    <span class="navbar-brand ml-2">SPORTS STORE Administration</span>
</div>
<div class="container-fluid">
    <div class="row p-2">
        <div class="col-3">
            <div class="d-grid gap-1">
                <NavLink class="btn btn-outline-primary"
```

```
                            href="/admin/products"
                            ActiveClass="btn-primary text-white"
                            Match="NavLinkMatch.Prefix">
                    Products
                </NavLink>
                <NavLink class="btn btn-outline-primary"
                            href="/admin/orders"
                            ActiveClass="btn-primary text-white"
                            Match="NavLinkMatch.Prefix">
                    Orders
                </NavLink>
            </div>
        </div>
        <div class="col">
            @Body
        </div>
    </div>
</div>
```

Blazor uses Razor syntax to generate HTML but introduces its own directives and features. This layout renders a two-column display with Product and Order navigation buttons, which are created using `NavLink` elements. These elements apply a built-in Razor Component that changes the URL without triggering a new HTTP request, which allows Blazor to respond to user interaction without losing the application state.

10.1.4 *Creating the Razor Components*

To complete the initial setup, I need to add the components that will provide the administration tools, although they will contain placeholder messages at first. Add a Razor Component named `Products.razor` to the `Pages/Admin` folder with the content shown in listing 10.6.

Listing 10.6.   The Products.razor File in the SportsStore/Pages/Admin Folder

```
@page "/admin/products"
@page "/admin"

<h4>This is the products component</h4>
```

The `@page` directives specify the URLs for which this component will be displayed, which are `/admin/products` and `/admin`. Next, add a Razor Component named `Orders.razor` to the `Pages/Admin` folder with the content shown in listing 10.7.

Listing 10.7.   The Orders.razor File in the SportsStore/Pages/Admin Folder

```
@page "/admin/orders"

<h4>This is the orders component</h4>
```

10.1.5 *Checking the Blazor setup*

To make sure that Blazor is working correctly, start ASP.NET Core and request http://localhost:5000/admin. This request will be handled by the `Index` Razor Page in the

`Pages/Admin` folder, which will include the Blazor JavaScript file in the content it sends to the browser. The JavaScript code will open a persistent HTTP connection to the ASP.NET Core server, and the initial Blazor content will be rendered, as shown in figure 10.1.

NOTE   Microsoft has not released tools for testing Razor Components, which is why there are no unit testing examples in this chapter.

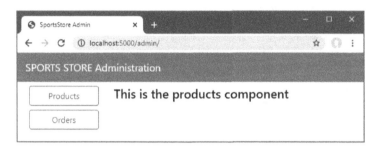

Figure 10.1   The Blazor application

Click the Orders button, and content generated by the `Orders` Razor Component will be displayed, as shown in figure 10.2. Unlike the other ASP.NET Core application frameworks I used in earlier chapters, the new content is displayed without a new HTTP request being sent, even though the URL displayed by the browser changes.

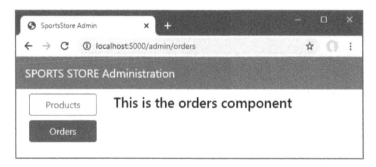

Figure 10.2   Navigating in the Blazor application

10.2   *Managing orders*

Now that Blazor has been set up and tested, I am going to start implementing administration features. In the previous chapter, I added support for receiving orders from customers and storing them in a database. In this section, I am going to create a simple administration tool that will let me view the orders that have been received and mark them as shipped.

10.2.1 Enhancing the model

The first change I need to make is to enhance the data model so that I can record which orders have been shipped. Listing 10.8 shows the addition of a new property to the Order class, which is defined in the Order.cs file in the Models folder.

> **Listing 10.8   Adding a property in the Order.cs file in the SportsStore/Models folder**

```
using System.ComponentModel.DataAnnotations;
using Microsoft.AspNetCore.Mvc.ModelBinding;

namespace SportsStore.Models {

    public class Order {

        [BindNever]
        public int OrderID { get; set; }
        [BindNever]
        public ICollection<CartLine> Lines { get; set; }
            = new List<CartLine>();

        [Required(ErrorMessage = "Please enter a name")]
        public string? Name { get; set; }

        [Required(ErrorMessage = "Please enter the first address line")]
        public string? Line1 { get; set; }
        public string? Line2 { get; set; }
        public string? Line3 { get; set; }

        [Required(ErrorMessage = "Please enter a city name")]
        public string? City { get; set; }

        [Required(ErrorMessage = "Please enter a state name")]
        public string? State { get; set; }

        public string? Zip { get; set; }

        [Required(ErrorMessage = "Please enter a country name")]
        public string? Country { get; set; }

        public bool GiftWrap { get; set; }

        [BindNever]
        public bool Shipped { get; set; }
    }
}
```

This iterative approach of extending and adapting the data model to support different features is typical of ASP.NET Core development. In an ideal world, you would be able to completely define the data model at the start of the project and just build the application around it, but that happens only for the simplest of projects, and, in practice, iterative development is to be expected as the understanding of what is required develops and evolves.

Entity Framework Core migrations make this process easier because you don't have to manually keep the database schema synchronized to the model class by writing your own SQL commands. To update the database to reflect the addition of the `Shipped` property to the `Order` class, open a new PowerShell window and run the command shown in listing 10.9 in the SportsStore project.

Listing 10.9 Creating a new migration

```
dotnet ef migrations add ShippedOrders
```

The migration will be applied automatically when the application is started and the `SeedData` class calls the `Migrate` method provided by Entity Framework Core.

10.2.2 *Displaying orders to the administrator*

I am going to display two tables, one of which shows the orders waiting to be shipped and the other the shipped orders. Each order will be presented with a button that changes the shipping state. This is not entirely realistic because orders processing is typically more complex than simply updating a field in the database, but integration with warehouse and fulfillment systems is well beyond the scope of this book.

To avoid duplicating code and content, I am going to create a Razor Component that displays a table without knowing which category of order it is dealing with. Add a Razor Component named `OrderTable.razor` to the `Pages/Admin` folder with the content shown in listing 10.10.

Listing 10.10 The OrderTable.razor file in the SportsStore/Pages/Admin folder

```
<table class="table table-sm table-striped table-bordered">
    <thead>
        <tr><th colspan="5" class="text-center">@TableTitle</th></tr>
    </thead>
    <tbody>
        @if (Orders?.Count() > 0) {
            @foreach (Order o in Orders) {
                <tr>
                    <td>@o.Name</td>
                    <td>@o.Zip</td>
                    <th>Product</th>
                    <th>Quantity</th>
                    <td>
                        <button class="btn btn-sm btn-danger"
                        @onclick="@(e =>
                                OrderSelected.InvokeAsync(o.OrderID))">
                            @ButtonLabel
                        </button>
                    </td>
                </tr>
                @foreach (CartLine line in o.Lines) {
                    <tr>
                        <td colspan="2"></td>
                        <td>@line.Product.Name</td>
```

```
                    <td>@line.Quantity</td>
                    <td></td>
                </tr>
            }
        }
    } else {
        <tr><td colspan="5" class="text-center">No Orders</td></tr>
    }
    </tbody>
</table>

@code {

    [Parameter]
    public string TableTitle { get; set; } = "Orders";

    [Parameter]
    public IEnumerable<Order> Orders { get; set; }
        = Enumerable.Empty<Order>();

    [Parameter]
    public string ButtonLabel { get; set; } = "Ship";

    [Parameter]
    public EventCallback<int> OrderSelected { get; set; }
}
```

Razor Components, as the name suggests, rely on the Razor approach to annotated HTML elements. The view part of the component is supported by the statements in the @code section. The @code section in this component defines four properties that are decorated with the Parameter attribute, which means the values will be provided at runtime by the parent component, which I will create shortly. The values provided for the parameters are used in the view section of the component to display details of a sequence of Order objects.

Blazor adds expressions to the Razor syntax. The view section of this component includes this button element, which has an @onclick attribute:

```
...
<button class="btn btn-sm btn-danger"
        @onclick="@(e => OrderSelected.InvokeAsync(o.OrderID))">
    @ButtonLabel
</button>
...
```

This tells Blazor how to react when the user clicks the button. In this case, the expression tells Razor to call the InvokeAsync method of the OrderSelected property. This is how the table will communicate with the rest of the Blazor application and will become clearer as I build out additional features.

TIP   I describe Blazor in-depth in part 4 of this book, so don't worry if the Razor Components in this chapter do not make immediate sense. The purpose of the SportsStore example is to show the overall development process, even if individual features are not understood.

The next step is to create a component that will get the `Order` data from the database and use the `OrderTable` component to display it to the user. Remove the placeholder content in the `Orders` component and replace it with the code and content shown in listing 10.11.

**Listing 10.11 The revised contents of the Orders.razor file in the SportsStore/
Pages/Admin folder**

```
@page "/admin/orders"
@inherits OwningComponentBase<IOrderRepository>

<OrderTable TableTitle="Unshipped Orders" Orders="UnshippedOrders"
        ButtonLabel="Ship" OrderSelected="ShipOrder" />
<OrderTable TableTitle="Shipped Orders" Orders="ShippedOrders"
        ButtonLabel="Reset" OrderSelected="ResetOrder" />
<button class="btn btn-info" @onclick="@(e => UpdateData())">
    Refresh Data
</button>

@code {

    public IOrderRepository Repository => Service;

    public IEnumerable<Order> AllOrders { get; set; }
        = Enumerable.Empty<Order>();
    public IEnumerable<Order> UnshippedOrders { get; set; }
        = Enumerable.Empty<Order>();
    public IEnumerable<Order> ShippedOrders { get; set; }
        = Enumerable.Empty<Order>();

    protected async override Task OnInitializedAsync() {
        await UpdateData();
    }

    public async Task UpdateData() {
        AllOrders = await Repository.Orders.ToListAsync();
        UnshippedOrders = AllOrders.Where(o => !o.Shipped);
        ShippedOrders = AllOrders.Where(o => o.Shipped);
    }

    public void ShipOrder(int id) => UpdateOrder(id, true);
    public void ResetOrder(int id) => UpdateOrder(id, false);

    private void UpdateOrder(int id, bool shipValue) {
        Order? o = Repository.Orders.FirstOrDefault(o => o.OrderID == id);
        if (o != null) {
            o.Shipped = shipValue;
            Repository.SaveOrder(o);
        }
    }
}
```

Blazor Components are not like the other application framework building blocks used for the user-facing sections of the SportsStore application. Instead of dealing with individual requests, components can be long-lived and deal with multiple user interactions over a longer period. This requires a different style of development, especially when it comes to dealing with data using Entity Framework Core. The `@inherits` expression ensures that this component gets its own repository object, which ensures its operations are separate from those performed by other components displayed to the same user. And to avoid repeatedly querying the database—which can be a serious problem in Blazor, as I explain in part 4—the repository is used only when the component is initialized, when Blazor invokes the `OnInitializedAsync` method, or when the user clicks a Refresh Data button.

To display its data to the user, the `OrderTable` component is used, which is applied as an HTML element, like this:

```
...
<OrderTable TableTitle="Unshipped Orders"
    Orders="UnshippedOrders" ButtonLabel="Ship"
    OrderSelected="ShipOrder" />
...
```

The values assigned to the `OrderTable` element's attributes are used to set the properties decorated with the `Parameter` attribute in listing 10.10. In this way, a single component can be configured to present two different sets of data without the need to duplicate code and content.

The `ShipOrder` and `ResetOrder` methods are used as the values for the `Order-Selected` attributes, which means they are invoked when the user clicks one of the buttons presented by the `OrderTable` component, updating the data in the database through the repository.

To see the new features, restart ASP.NET Core, request http://localhost:5000, and create an order. Once you have at least one order in the database, request http://localhost:5000/admin/orders, and you will see a summary of the order you created displayed in the Unshipped Orders table. Click the Ship button, and the order will be updated and moved to the Shipped Orders table, as shown in figure 10.3.

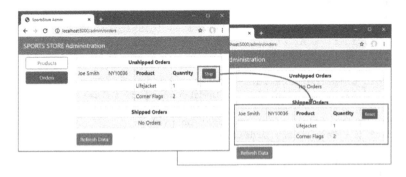

Figure 10.3 Administering orders

10.3 Adding catalog management

The convention for managing more complex collections of items is to present the user with two interfaces: a *list* interface and an *edit* interface, as shown in figure 10.4.

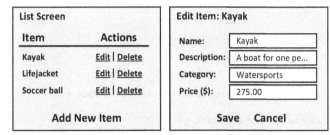

Figure 10.4 Sketch of a CRUD UI for the product catalog

Together, these interfaces allow a user to create, read, update, and delete items in the collection. Collectively, these actions are known as *CRUD*. In this section, I will implement these interfaces using Blazor.

TIP Developers need to implement CRUD so often that Visual Studio scaffolding includes scenarios for creating CRUD controllers or Razor Pages. But, like all Visual Studio scaffolding, I think it is better to learn how to create these features directly, which is why I demonstrate CRUD operations for all the ASP.NET Core application frameworks in later chapters.

10.3.1 Expanding the repository

The first step is to add features to the repository that will allow `Product` objects to be created, modified, and deleted. Listing 10.12 adds new methods to the `IStore-Repository` interface.

Listing 10.12 Adding methods in the IStoreRepository.cs file in the SportsStore/ Models folder

```
namespace SportsStore.Models {
    public interface IStoreRepository {

        IQueryable<Product> Products { get; }

        void SaveProduct(Product p);
        void CreateProduct(Product p);
        void DeleteProduct(Product p);
    }
}
```

Listing 10.13 adds implementations of these methods to the Entity Framework Core repository class.

Listing 10.13   Implementing methods in the EFStoreRepository.cs file in the SportsStore/Models folder

```
namespace SportsStore.Models {
    public class EFStoreRepository : IStoreRepository {
        private StoreDbContext context;

        public EFStoreRepository(StoreDbContext ctx) {
            context = ctx;
        }

        public IQueryable<Product> Products => context.Products;

        public void CreateProduct(Product p) {
            context.Add(p);
            context.SaveChanges();
        }

        public void DeleteProduct(Product p) {
            context.Remove(p);
            context.SaveChanges();
        }

        public void SaveProduct(Product p) {
            context.SaveChanges();
        }
    }
}
```

10.3.2 Applying validation attributes to the data model

I want to validate the values the user provides when editing or creating `Product` objects, just as I did for the customer checkout process. In listing 10.14, I have added validation attributes to the `Product` data model class.

Listing 10.14   Adding validation in the Product.cs file in the SportsStore/Models folder

```
using System.ComponentModel.DataAnnotations.Schema;
using System.ComponentModel.DataAnnotations;

namespace SportsStore.Models {

    public class Product {

        public long? ProductID { get; set; }

        [Required(ErrorMessage = "Please enter a product name")]
        public string Name { get; set; } = String.Empty;

        [Required(ErrorMessage = "Please enter a description")]
        public string Description { get; set; } = String.Empty;

        [Required]
        [Range(0.01, double.MaxValue,
            ErrorMessage = "Please enter a positive price")]
        [Column(TypeName = "decimal(8, 2)")]
```

```
        public decimal Price { get; set; }

        [Required(ErrorMessage = "Please specify a category")]
        public string Category { get; set; } = String.Empty;
    }
}
```

Blazor uses the same approach to validation as the rest of ASP.NET Core but, as you will see, applies it in a different way to deal with the more interactive nature of Razor Components.

10.3.3 Creating the list component

I am going to start by creating the table that will present the user with a table of products and the links that will allow them to be inspected and edited. Replace the contents of the `Products.razor` file with those shown in listing 10.15.

> **Listing 10.15   The revised contents of the Products.razor file in the SportsStore/ Pages/Admin folder**

```
@page "/admin/products"
@page "/admin"
@inherits OwningComponentBase<IStoreRepository>

<table class="table table-sm table-striped table-bordered">
    <thead>
        <tr>
            <th>ID</th>
            <th>Name</th>
            <th>Category</th>
            <th>Price</th>
            <td />
        </tr>
    </thead>
    <tbody>
        @if (ProductData?.Count() > 0) {
            @foreach (Product p in ProductData) {
                <tr>
                    <td>@p.ProductID</td>
                    <td>@p.Name</td>
                    <td>@p.Category</td>
                    <td>@p.Price.ToString("c")</td>
                    <td>
                        <NavLink class="btn btn-info btn-sm"
                          href="@GetDetailsUrl(p.ProductID ?? 0)">
                            Details
                        </NavLink>
                        <NavLink class="btn btn-warning btn-sm"
                          href="@GetEditUrl(p.ProductID ?? 0)">
                            Edit
                        </NavLink>
                    </td>
                </tr>
            }
        } else {
            <tr>
                <td colspan="5" class="text-center">No Products</td>
```

```
            </tr>
        }
    </tbody>
</table>

<NavLink class="btn btn-primary" href="/admin/products/create">
    Create
</NavLink>

@code {

    public IStoreRepository Repository => Service;

    public IEnumerable<Product> ProductData { get; set; }
        = Enumerable.Empty<Product>();

    protected async override Task OnInitializedAsync() {
        await UpdateData();
    }

    public async Task UpdateData() {
        ProductData = await Repository.Products.ToListAsync();
    }

    public string GetDetailsUrl(long id) =>
        $"/admin/products/details/{id}";
    public string GetEditUrl(long id) =>
        $"/admin/products/edit/{id}";
}
```

The component presents each `Product` object in the repository in a table row with
`NavLink` components that will navigate to the components that will provide a detailed
view and an editor. There is also a button that navigates to the component that will
allow new `Product` objects to be created and stored in the database. Restart ASP.NET
Core and request http://localhost:5000/admin/products, and you will see the content shown in figure 10.5, although none of the buttons presented by the `Products`
component work currently because I have yet to create the components they target.

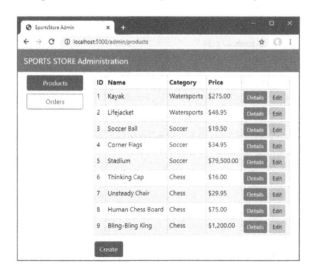

**Figure 10.5
Presenting a
list of products**

10.3.4 Creating the detail component

The job of the detail component is to display all the fields for a single `Product` object. Add a Razor Component named `Details.razor` to the `Pages/Admin` folder with the content shown in listing 10.16.

> **Listing 10.16. The Details.razor file in the SportsStore/Pages/Admin folder**

```
@page "/admin/products/details/{id:long}"
@inherits OwningComponentBase<IStoreRepository>

<h3 class="bg-info text-white text-center p-1">Details</h3>

<table class="table table-sm table-bordered table-striped">
    <tbody>
        <tr><th>ID</th><td>@Product?.ProductID</td></tr>
        <tr><th>Name</th><td>@Product?.Name</td></tr>
        <tr><th>Description</th><td>@Product?.Description</td></tr>
        <tr><th>Category</th><td>@Product?.Category</td></tr>
        <tr><th>Price</th><td>@Product?.Price.ToString("C")</td></tr>
    </tbody>
</table>

<NavLink class="btn btn-warning" href="@EditUrl">Edit</NavLink>
<NavLink class="btn btn-secondary" href="/admin/products">Back</NavLink>

@code {

    [Inject]
    public IStoreRepository? Repository { get; set; }

    [Parameter]
    public long Id { get; set; }

    public Product? Product { get; set; }

    protected override void OnParametersSet() {
        Product =
            Repository?.Products.FirstOrDefault(p => p.ProductID == Id);
    }

    public string EditUrl => $"/admin/products/edit/{Product?.ProductID}";
}
```

The component uses the `Inject` attribute to declare that it requires an implementation of the `IStoreRepository` interface, which is one of the ways that Blazor provides access to the application's services. The value of the `Id` property will be populated from the URL that has been used to navigate to the component, which is used to retrieve the `Product` object from the database. To see the detail view, restart ASP.NET Core, request http://localhost:5000/admin/products, and click one of the Details buttons, as shown in figure 10.6.

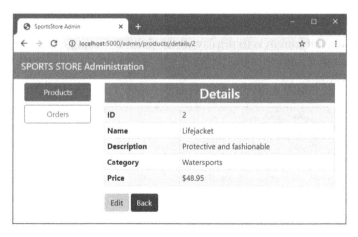

Figure 10.6   Displaying details of a product

10.3.5 *Creating the editor component*

The operations to create and edit data will be handled by the same component. Add a Razor Component named `Editor.razor` to the `Pages/Admin` folder with the content shown in listing 10.17.

Listing 10.17.   The Editor.razor file in the SportsStore/Pages/Admin folder

```
@page "/admin/products/edit/{id:long}"
@page "/admin/products/create"
@inherits OwningComponentBase<IStoreRepository>

<style>
    div.validation-message { color: rgb(220, 53, 69); font-weight: 500 }
</style>

<h3 class="bg-@ThemeColor text-white text-center p-1">
    @TitleText a Product
</h3>
<EditForm Model="Product" OnValidSubmit="SaveProduct">
    <DataAnnotationsValidator />
    @if(Product.ProductID.HasValue && Product.ProductID.Value != 0) {
        <div class="form-group">
            <label>ID</label>
            <input class="form-control" disabled
                value="@Product.ProductID" />
        </div>
    }
    <div class="form-group">
        <label>Name</label>
        <ValidationMessage For="@(() => Product.Name)" />
        <InputText class="form-control" @bind-Value="Product.Name" />
    </div>
    <div class="form-group">
```

```
        <label>Description</label>
        <ValidationMessage For="@(() => Product.Description)" />
        <InputText class="form-control"
            @bind-Value="Product.Description" />
    </div>
    <div class="form-group">
        <label>Category</label>
        <ValidationMessage For="@(() => Product.Category)" />
        <InputText class="form-control" @bind-Value="Product.Category" />
    </div>
    <div class="form-group">
        <label>Price</label>
        <ValidationMessage For="@(() => Product.Price)" />
        <InputNumber class="form-control" @bind-Value="Product.Price" />
    </div>
    <div class="mt-2">
        <button type="submit" class="btn btn-@ThemeColor">Save</button>
        <NavLink class="btn btn-secondary" href="/admin/products">
            Cancel
        </NavLink>
    </div>
</EditForm>

@code {

    public IStoreRepository Repository => Service;

    [Inject]
    public NavigationManager? NavManager { get; set; }

    [Parameter]
    public long Id { get; set; } = 0;

    public Product Product { get; set; } = new Product();

    protected override void OnParametersSet() {
        if (Id != 0) {
            Product = Repository.Products
                .FirstOrDefault(p => p.ProductID == Id) ?? new();
        }
    }

    public void SaveProduct() {
        if (Id == 0) {
            Repository.CreateProduct(Product);
        } else {
            Repository.SaveProduct(Product);
        }
        NavManager?.NavigateTo("/admin/products");
    }

    public string ThemeColor => Id == 0 ? "primary" : "warning";
    public string TitleText => Id == 0 ? "Create" : "Edit";
}
```

Blazor provides a set of built-in Razor Components that are used to display and validate forms, which is important because the browser can't submit data using a POST request in a Blazor Component. The EditForm component is used to render a Blazor-friendly form, and the InputText and InputNumber components render input elements that accept string and number values and that automatically update a model property when the user makes a change.

Data validation is integrated into these built-in components, and the OnValid-Submit attribute on the EditForm component is used to specify a method that is invoked only if the data entered into the form conforms to the rules defined by the validation attributes.

Blazor also provides the NavigationManager class, which is used to programmatically navigate between components without triggering a new HTTP request. The Editor component uses NavigationManager, which is obtained as a service, to return to the Products component after the database has been updated.

To see the editor, restart ASP.NET Core, request http://localhost:5000/admin, and click the Create button. Click the Save button without filling out the form fields, and you will see the validation errors that Blazor produces automatically, as shown in figure 10.7. Fill out the form and click Save again, and you will see the product you created displayed in the table, also as shown in figure 10.7.

Figure 10.7   Using the Editor component

Click the Edit button for one of the products, and the same component will be used to edit the selected Product object's properties. Click the Save button, and any changes you made—if they pass validation—will be stored in the database, as shown in figure 10.8.

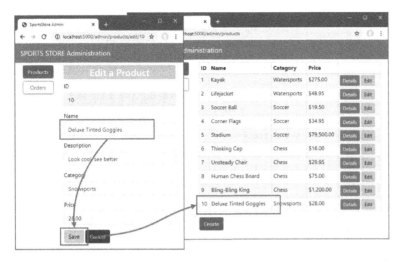

Figure 10.8 Editing products

10.3.6 Deleting products

The final CRUD feature is deleting products, which is easily implemented in the `Products` component, as shown in listing 10.18.

> **Listing 10.18 Adding delete support in the Products.razor file in the SportsStore/ Pages/Admin folder**

```
@page "/admin/products"
@page "/admin"
@inherits OwningComponentBase<IStoreRepository>

<table class="table table-sm table-striped table-bordered">
    <thead>
        <tr>
            <th>ID</th>
            <th>Name</th>
            <th>Category</th>
            <th>Price</th>
            <td />
        </tr>
    </thead>
    <tbody>
        @if (ProductData?.Count() > 0) {
            @foreach (Product p in ProductData) {
                <tr>
                    <td>@p.ProductID</td>
                    <td>@p.Name</td>
                    <td>@p.Category</td>
                    <td>@p.Price.ToString("c")</td>
                    <td>
                        <NavLink class="btn btn-info btn-sm"
                          href="@GetDetailsUrl(p.ProductID ?? 0)">
```

```
                        Details
                    </NavLink>
                    <NavLink class="btn btn-warning btn-sm"
                     href="@GetEditUrl(p.ProductID ?? 0)">
                        Edit
                    </NavLink>
                    <button class="btn btn-danger btn-sm"
                            @onclick="@(e => DeleteProduct(p))">
                        Delete
                    </button>
                </td>
            </tr>
        }
    } else {
        <tr>
            <td colspan="5" class="text-center">No Products</td>
        </tr>
    }
    </tbody>
</table>

<NavLink class="btn btn-primary" href="/admin/products/create">
    Create
</NavLink>

@code {

    public IStoreRepository Repository => Service;

    public IEnumerable<Product> ProductData { get; set; }
        = Enumerable.Empty<Product>();

    protected async override Task OnInitializedAsync() {
        await UpdateData();
    }

    public async Task UpdateData() {
        ProductData = await Repository.Products.ToListAsync();
    }

    public async Task DeleteProduct(Product p) {
        Repository.DeleteProduct(p);
        await UpdateData();
    }

    public string GetDetailsUrl(long id) =>
        $"/admin/products/details/{id}";
    public string GetEditUrl(long id) =>
        $"/admin/products/edit/{id}";
}
```

The new button element is configured with the @onclick attribute, which invokes the
DeleteProduct method. The selected Product object is removed from the database,
and the data displayed by the component is updated. Restart ASP.NET Core, request
http://localhost:5000/admin/products, and click a Delete button to remove an object
from the database, as shown in figure 10.9.

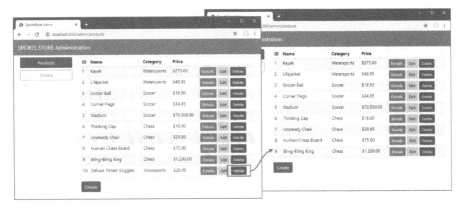

Figure 10.9   Deleting objects from the database

Summary

- Blazor creates ASP.NET Core applications that use JavaScript to respond to user interaction, handled by C# code running in the ASP.NET Core server.
- Blazor functionality is created using Razor Components, which have a similar syntax to Razor Pages and views.
- Requests are directed to components using the @page directive.
- The lifecycle of repository objects is aligned the to the component lifecycle using the @inherits OwningComponentBase<T> expression.
- Blazor provides built-in components for common tasks, such as receiving user input, defining layouts, and navigating between pages.

SportsStore:
Security and deployment

This chapter covers

- Authenticating users with ASP.NET Core Identity
- Authorizing user access to ASP.NET Core resources
- Preparing and publishing an application
- Creating a Docker container image for the SportsStore application

Authentication and authorization are provided by the ASP.NET Core Identity system, which integrates neatly into the ASP.NET Core platform and the individual application frameworks. In the sections that follow, I will create a basic security setup that allows one user, called Admin, to authenticate and access the administration features in the application. ASP.NET Core Identity provides many more features for authenticating users and authorizing access to application features and data, and you can find more information in chapters 37 and 38, where I show you how to create and manage user accounts and how to perform authorization using roles. But, as I noted previously, ASP.NET Core Identity is a large framework in its own right, and I cover only the basic features in this book.

My goal in this chapter is just to get enough functionality in place to prevent customers from being able to access the sensitive parts of the SportsStore application and, in doing so, give you a flavor of how authentication and authorization fit into an ASP.NET Core application.

> **TIP** You can download the example project for this chapter—and for all the other chapters in this book—from https://github.com/manningbooks/pro-asp .net-core-7. See chapter 1 for how to get help if you have problems running the examples.

11.1 Creating the Identity database

The ASP.NET Identity system is endlessly configurable and extensible and supports lots of options for how its user data is stored. I am going to use the most common, which is to store the data using Microsoft SQL Server accessed using Entity Framework Core.

11.1.1 Installing the Identity package for Entity Framework Core

To add the package that contains the ASP.NET Core Identity support for Entity Framework Core, use a PowerShell command prompt to run the command shown in listing 11.1 in the `SportsStore` folder.

Listing 11.1 Installing the Entity Framework Core package

```
dotnet add package Microsoft.AspNetCore.Identity.EntityFrameworkCore
    --version 7.0.0
```

11.1.2 Creating the context class

I need to create a database context file that will act as the bridge between the database and the Identity model objects it provides access to. I added a class file called `AppIdentityDbContext.cs` to the `Models` folder and used it to define the class shown in listing 11.2.

Listing 11.2 The AppIdentityDbContext.cs file in the SportsStore/Models folder

```
using Microsoft.AspNetCore.Identity;
using Microsoft.AspNetCore.Identity.EntityFrameworkCore;
using Microsoft.EntityFrameworkCore;

namespace SportsStore.Models {

    public class AppIdentityDbContext : IdentityDbContext<IdentityUser> {

        public AppIdentityDbContext(
                DbContextOptions<AppIdentityDbContext> options)
            : base(options) { }
    }
}
```

The `AppIdentityDbContext` class is derived from `IdentityDbContext`, which provides Identity-specific features for Entity Framework Core. For the type parameter, I used the `IdentityUser` class, which is the built-in class used to represent users.

11.1.3 Defining the connection string

The next step is to define the connection string for the database. Listing 11.3 shows the addition of the connection string to the `appsettings.json` file of the SportsStore project, which follows the same format as the connection string that I defined for the product database.

> **Listing 11.3   Defining a connection string in the appsettings.json file in the SportsStore folder**

```
{
  "Logging": {
    "LogLevel": {
      "Default": "Information",
      "Microsoft.AspNetCore": "Warning"
    }
  },
  "AllowedHosts": "*",
  "ConnectionStrings": {
    "SportsStoreConnection": "Server=(localdb)\\MSSQLLocalDB;Database=
SportsStore;MultipleActiveResultSets=true",
    "IdentityConnection": "Server=(localdb)\\MSSQLLocalDB;Database=Identity
;MultipleActiveResultSets=true"
  }
}
```

Remember that the connection string has to be defined in a single unbroken line in the `appsettings.json` file and is shown across multiple lines in the listing only because of the fixed width of a book page. The addition in the listing defines a connection string called `IdentityConnection` that specifies a LocalDB database called `Identity`.

11.1.4 Configuring the application

Like other ASP.NET Core features, Identity is configured in the `Program.cs` file. Listing 11.4 shows the additions I made to set up Identity in the SportsStore project, using the context class and connection string defined previously.

> **Listing 11.4   Configuring identity in the Program.cs file in the SportsStore folder**

```
using Microsoft.EntityFrameworkCore;
using SportsStore.Models;
using Microsoft.AspNetCore.Identity;

var builder = WebApplication.CreateBuilder(args);

builder.Services.AddControllersWithViews();

builder.Services.AddDbContext<StoreDbContext>(opts => {
    opts.UseSqlServer(
        builder.Configuration["ConnectionStrings:SportsStoreConnection"]);
});
```

```
builder.Services.AddScoped<IStoreRepository, EFStoreRepository>();
builder.Services.AddScoped<IOrderRepository, EFOrderRepository>();

builder.Services.AddRazorPages();
builder.Services.AddDistributedMemoryCache();
builder.Services.AddSession();
builder.Services.AddScoped<Cart>(sp => SessionCart.GetCart(sp));
builder.Services.AddSingleton<IHttpContextAccessor,
    HttpContextAccessor>();
builder.Services.AddServerSideBlazor();

builder.Services.AddDbContext<AppIdentityDbContext>(options =>
    options.UseSqlServer(
        builder.Configuration["ConnectionStrings:IdentityConnection"]));
builder.Services.AddIdentity<IdentityUser, IdentityRole>()
    .AddEntityFrameworkStores<AppIdentityDbContext>();

var app = builder.Build();

app.UseStaticFiles();
app.UseSession();

app.UseAuthentication();
app.UseAuthorization();

app.MapControllerRoute("catpage",
    "{category}/Page{productPage:int}",
    new { Controller = "Home", action = "Index" });

app.MapControllerRoute("page", "Page{productPage:int}",
    new { Controller = "Home", action = "Index", productPage = 1 });

app.MapControllerRoute("category", "{category}",
    new { Controller = "Home", action = "Index", productPage = 1 });

app.MapControllerRoute("pagination",
    "Products/Page{productPage}",
    new { Controller = "Home", action = "Index", productPage = 1 });

app.MapDefaultControllerRoute();
app.MapRazorPages();
app.MapBlazorHub();
app.MapFallbackToPage("/admin/{*catchall}", "/Admin/Index");

SeedData.EnsurePopulated(app);

app.Run();
```

In the listing, I extended the Entity Framework Core configuration to register the context class and used the `AddIdentity` method to set up the Identity services using the built-in classes to represent users and roles. I called the `UseAuthentication` and `UseAuthorization` methods to set up the middleware components that implement the security policy.

11.1.5 *Creating and applying the database migration*

The basic configuration is in place, and it is time to use the Entity Framework Core migrations feature to define the schema and apply it to the database. Open a new command prompt or PowerShell window and run the command shown in listing 11.5 in the SportsStore folder to create a new migration for the Identity database.

Listing 11.5   Creating the identity migration

```
dotnet ef migrations add Initial --context AppIdentityDbContext
```

The important difference from previous database commands is that I have used the -context argument to specify the name of the context class associated with the database that I want to work with, which is AppIdentityDbContext. When you have multiple databases in the application, it is important to ensure that you are working with the right context class.

Once Entity Framework Core has generated the initial migration, run the command shown in listing 11.6 in the SportsStore folder to create the database and apply the migration.

Listing 11.6   Applying the identity migration

```
dotnet ef database update --context AppIdentityDbContext
```

The result is a new LocalDB database called Identity that you can inspect using the Visual Studio SQL Server Object Explorer.

11.1.6 *Defining the seed data*

I am going to explicitly create the Admin user by seeding the database when the application starts. I added a class file called IdentitySeedData.cs to the Models folder and defined the static class shown in listing 11.7.

Listing 11.7   The IdentitySeedData.cs file in the SportsStore/Models folder

```
using Microsoft.AspNetCore.Identity;
using Microsoft.EntityFrameworkCore;

namespace SportsStore.Models {

    public static class IdentitySeedData {
        private const string adminUser = "Admin";
        private const string adminPassword = "Secret123$";

        public static async void EnsurePopulated(
            IApplicationBuilder app) {

            AppIdentityDbContext context = app.ApplicationServices
                .CreateScope().ServiceProvider
                .GetRequiredService<AppIdentityDbContext>();
            if (context.Database.GetPendingMigrations().Any()) {
                context.Database.Migrate();
            }
```

```
                UserManager<IdentityUser> userManager =
                    app.ApplicationServices
                    .CreateScope().ServiceProvider
                    .GetRequiredService<UserManager<IdentityUser>>();

                IdentityUser? user =
                    await userManager.FindByNameAsync(adminUser);
                if (user == null) {
                    user = new IdentityUser("Admin");
                    user.Email = "admin@example.com";
                    user.PhoneNumber = "555-1234";
                    await userManager.CreateAsync(user, adminPassword);
                }
            }
        }
    }
}
```

This code ensures the database is created and up-to-date and uses the `UserManager<T>` class, which is provided as a service by ASP.NET Core Identity for managing users, as described in chapter 38. The database is searched for the `Admin` user account, which is created—with a password of `Secret123$`—if it is not present. Do not change the hard-coded password in this example because Identity has a validation policy that requires passwords to contain a number and range of characters. See chapter 38 for details of how to change the validation settings.

> **CAUTION** Hard-coding the details of an administrator account is often required so that you can log into an application once it has been deployed and start administering it. When you do this, you must remember to change the password for the account you have created. See chapter 38 for details of how to change passwords using Identity. See chapter 15 for how to keep sensitive data, such as default passwords, out of source code control.

To ensure that the Identity database is seeded when the application starts, I added the statement shown in listing 11.8 to the `Program.cs` file.

Listing 11.8 Seeding the identity database in the Program.cs file in the SportsStore folder

```
using Microsoft.AspNetCore.Identity;
using Microsoft.EntityFrameworkCore;
using SportsStore.Models;

var builder = WebApplication.CreateBuilder(args);

builder.Services.AddControllersWithViews();

builder.Services.AddDbContext<StoreDbContext>(opts => {
    opts.UseSqlServer(
        builder.Configuration["ConnectionStrings:SportsStoreConnection"]);
});

builder.Services.AddScoped<IStoreRepository, EFStoreRepository>();
builder.Services.AddScoped<IOrderRepository, EFOrderRepository>();
```

```
builder.Services.AddRazorPages();
builder.Services.AddDistributedMemoryCache();
builder.Services.AddSession();
builder.Services.AddScoped<Cart>(sp => SessionCart.GetCart(sp));
builder.Services.AddSingleton<IHttpContextAccessor,
    HttpContextAccessor>();
builder.Services.AddServerSideBlazor();

builder.Services.AddDbContext<AppIdentityDbContext>(options =>
    options.UseSqlServer(
        builder.Configuration["ConnectionStrings:IdentityConnection"]));
builder.Services.AddIdentity<IdentityUser, IdentityRole>()
    .AddEntityFrameworkStores<AppIdentityDbContext>();

var app = builder.Build();

app.UseStaticFiles();
app.UseSession();

app.UseAuthentication();
app.UseAuthorization();

app.MapControllerRoute("catpage",
    "{category}/Page{productPage:int}",
    new { Controller = "Home", action = "Index" });

app.MapControllerRoute("page", "Page{productPage:int}",
    new { Controller = "Home", action = "Index", productPage = 1 });

app.MapControllerRoute("category", "{category}",
    new { Controller = "Home", action = "Index", productPage = 1 });

app.MapControllerRoute("pagination",
    "Products/Page{productPage}",
    new { Controller = "Home", action = "Index", productPage = 1 });

app.MapDefaultControllerRoute();
app.MapRazorPages();
app.MapBlazorHub();
app.MapFallbackToPage("/admin/{*catchall}", "/Admin/Index");

SeedData.EnsurePopulated(app);
IdentitySeedData.EnsurePopulated(app);

app.Run();
```

Deleting and re-creating the ASP.NET Core Identity database

If you need to reset the Identity database, then run the following command:

```
dotnet ef database drop --force --context AppIdentityDbContext
```

Restart the application, and the database will be re-created and populated with seed data.

11.2 *Adding a conventional administration feature*

In chapter 10, I used Blazor to create the administration features so that I could demonstrate a wide range of ASP.NET Core features in the SportsStore project. Although Blazor is useful, it is not suitable for all projects—as I explain in part 4—and most projects are likely to use controllers or Razor Pages for their administration features. I describe the way that ASP.NET Core Identity works with all the application frameworks in chapter 38, but just to provide a balance to the all-Blazor tools created in chapter 10, I am going to create a Razor Page that will display the list of users in the ASP.NET Core Identity database. I describe how to manage the Identity database in more detail in chapter 38, and this Razor Page is just to add a sensitive feature to the SportsStore application that isn't created with Blazor. Add a Razor Page named `IdentityUsers` `.cshtml` to the `SportsStore/Pages/Admin` folder with the contents shown in listing 11.9.

> **Listing 11.9   The IdentityUsers.cshtml file in the SportsStore/Pages/Admin folder**

```
@page
@model IdentityUsersModel
@using Microsoft.AspNetCore.Identity

<h3 class="bg-primary text-white text-center p-2">Admin User</h3>

<table class="table table-sm table-striped table-bordered">
    <tbody>
        <tr><th>User</th><td>@Model.AdminUser?.UserName</td></tr>
        <tr><th>Email</th><td>@Model.AdminUser?.Email</td></tr>
        <tr><th>Phone</th><td>@Model.AdminUser?.PhoneNumber</td></tr>
    </tbody>
</table>

@functions {

    public class IdentityUsersModel : PageModel {
        private UserManager<IdentityUser> userManager;

        public IdentityUsersModel(UserManager<IdentityUser> mgr) {
            userManager = mgr;
        }

        public IdentityUser? AdminUser { get; set; } = new();

        public async Task OnGetAsync() {
            AdminUser = await userManager.FindByNameAsync("Admin");
        }
    }
}
```

Restart ASP.NET Core and request http://localhost:5000/admin/identityusers to see the content generated by the Razor Page, which is shown in figure 11.1.

Figure 11.1 A Razor Page administration feature

11.3 Applying a basic authorization policy

Now that I have configured ASP.NET Core Identity, I can apply an authorization policy to the parts of the application that I want to protect. I am going to use the most basic authorization policy possible, which is to allow access to any authenticated user. Although this can be a useful policy in real applications as well, there are also options for creating finer-grained authorization controls, as described in chapters 37 and 38, but since the SportsStore application has only one user, distinguishing between anonymous and authenticated requests is sufficient.

For controllers and Razor pages, the `Authorize` attribute is used to restrict access, as shown in listing 11.10.

> **Listing 11.10 Restricting access in the IdentityUsers.cshtml file in the SportsStore/ Pages/Admin folder**

```
@page
@model IdentityUsersModel
@using Microsoft.AspNetCore.Identity
@using Microsoft.AspNetCore.Authorization

<h3 class="bg-primary text-white text-center p-2">Admin User</h3>

<table class="table table-sm table-striped table-bordered">
    <tbody>
        <tr><th>User</th><td>@Model.AdminUser?.UserName</td></tr>
        <tr><th>Email</th><td>@Model.AdminUser?.Email</td></tr>
        <tr><th>Phone</th><td>@Model.AdminUser?.PhoneNumber</td></tr>
    </tbody>
</table>

@functions {

    [Authorize]
    public class IdentityUsersModel : PageModel {
        private UserManager<IdentityUser> userManager;
```

```
        public IdentityUsersModel(UserManager<IdentityUser> mgr) {
            userManager = mgr;
        }

        public IdentityUser? AdminUser { get; set; } = new();

        public async Task OnGetAsync() {
            AdminUser = await userManager.FindByNameAsync("Admin");
        }
    }
}
```

When there are only authorized and unauthorized users, the `Authorize` attribute can be applied to the Razor Page that acts as the entry point for the Blazor part of the application, as shown in listing 11.11.

> **Listing 11.11   Applying authorization in the Index.cshtml file in the SportsStore/Pages/Admin folder**

```
@page "/admin"
@{ Layout = null; }
@using Microsoft.AspNetCore.Authorization
@attribute [Authorize]

<!DOCTYPE html>
<html>
<head>
    <title>SportsStore Admin</title>
    <link href="/lib/bootstrap/css/bootstrap.min.css" rel="stylesheet" />
    <base href="/" />
</head>
<body>
    <component type="typeof(Routed)" render-mode="Server" />
    <script src="/_framework/blazor.server.js"></script>
</body>
</html>
```

Since this Razor Page has been configured without a page model class, I can apply the attribute with an `@attribute` expression.

11.4   Creating the account controller and views

When an unauthenticated user sends a request that requires authorization, the user is redirected to the /Account/Login URL, which the application can use to prompt the user for their credentials. In chapters 38 and 39, I show you how to handle authentication using Razor Pages, so, for variety, I am going to use controllers and views for SportsStore. In preparation, I added a view model to represent the user's credentials by adding a class file called LoginModel.cs to the Models/ViewModels folder and using it to define the class shown in listing 11.12.

```
using System.ComponentModel.DataAnnotations;

namespace SportsStore.Models.ViewModels {

    public class LoginModel {

        public required string Name { get; set; }

        public required string Password { get; set; }

        public string ReturnUrl { get; set; } = "/";
    }
}
```

The Name and Password properties have been decorated with the Required attribute, which uses model validation to ensure that values have been provided. Next, I added a class file called AccountController.cs to the Controllers folder and used it to define the controller shown in listing 11.13. This is the controller that will respond to requests to the /Account/Login URL.

```
using Microsoft.AspNetCore.Authorization;
using Microsoft.AspNetCore.Identity;
using Microsoft.AspNetCore.Mvc;
using SportsStore.Models.ViewModels;

namespace SportsStore.Controllers {

    public class AccountController : Controller {
        private UserManager<IdentityUser> userManager;
        private SignInManager<IdentityUser> signInManager;

        public AccountController(UserManager<IdentityUser> userMgr,
                SignInManager<IdentityUser> signInMgr) {
            userManager = userMgr;
            signInManager = signInMgr;
        }

        public ViewResult Login(string returnUrl) {
            return View(new LoginModel {
                Name = string.Empty, Password = string.Empty,
                ReturnUrl = returnUrl
            });
        }

        [HttpPost]
        [ValidateAntiForgeryToken]
        public async Task<IActionResult> Login(LoginModel loginModel) {
            if (ModelState.IsValid) {
                IdentityUser? user =
                    await userManager.FindByNameAsync(loginModel.Name);
```

```
                if (user != null) {
                    await signInManager.SignOutAsync();
                    if ((await signInManager.PasswordSignInAsync(user,
                        loginModel.Password, false, false)).Succeeded) {
                            return Redirect(loginModel?.ReturnUrl
                                ?? "/Admin");
                    }
                }
                ModelState.AddModelError("", "Invalid name or password");
            }
            return View(loginModel);
        }

        [Authorize]
        public async Task<RedirectResult> Logout(string returnUrl = "/") {
            await signInManager.SignOutAsync();
            return Redirect(returnUrl);
        }
    }
}
```

When the user is redirected to the /Account/Login URL, the GET version of the Login action method renders the default view for the page, providing a view model object that includes the URL to which the browser should be redirected if the authentication request is successful.

Authentication credentials are submitted to the POST version of the Login method, which uses the UserManager<IdentityUser> and SignInManager<IdentityUser> services that have been received through the controller's constructor to authenticate the user and log them into the system. I explain how these classes work in chapters 37 and 38, but for now, it is enough to know that if there is an authentication failure, then I create a model validation error and render the default view; however, if authentication is successful, then I redirect the user to the URL that they want to access before they are prompted for their credentials.

> **CAUTION** In general, using client-side data validation is a good idea. It offloads some of the work from your server and gives users immediate feedback about the data they are providing. However, you should not be tempted to perform authentication at the client, as this would typically involve sending valid credentials to the client so they can be used to check the username and password that the user has entered, or at least trusting the client's report of whether they have successfully authenticated. Authentication should always be done at the server.

To provide the Login method with a view to render, I created the Views/Account folder and added a Razor View file called Login.cshtml with the contents shown in listing 11.14.

```
@model LoginModel
@{
    Layout = null;
}
<!DOCTYPE html>
<html>
<head>
    <meta name="viewport" content="width=device-width" />
    <title>SportsStore</title>
    <link href="/lib/bootstrap/css/bootstrap.min.css" rel="stylesheet" />
</head>
<body>
    <div class="bg-dark text-white p-2">
        <span class="navbar-brand ml-2">SPORTS STORE</span>
    </div>
    <div class="m-1 p-1">
        <div class="text-danger" asp-validation-summary="All"></div>

        <form asp-action="Login" asp-controller="Account" method="post">
            <input type="hidden" asp-for="ReturnUrl" />
            <div class="form-group">
                <label asp-for="Name"></label>
                <input asp-for="Name" class="form-control" />
            </div>
            <div class="form-group">
                <label asp-for="Password"></label>
                <input asp-for="Password" type="password"
                    class="form-control" />
            </div>
            <button class="btn btn-primary mt-2" type="submit">
                Log In
            </button>
        </form>
    </div>
</body>
</html>
```

The final step is a change to the shared administration layout to add a button that will log out the current user by sending a request to the Logout action, as shown in listing 11.15. This is a useful feature that makes it easier to test the application, without which you would need to clear the browser's cookies to return to the unauthenticated state.

```
@inherits LayoutComponentBase

<div class="bg-info text-white p-2">
    <div class="container-fluid">
        <div class="row">
            <div class="col">
                <span class="navbar-brand ml-2">
```

```
                    SPORTS STORE Administration
                </span>
            </div>
            <div class="col-2 text-right">
                <a class="btn btn-sm btn-primary" href="/account/logout">
                    Log Out
                </a>
            </div>
        </div>
    </div>
</div>
<div class="container-fluid">
    <div class="row p-2">
        <div class="col-3">
            <div class="d-grid gap-1">
                <NavLink class="btn btn-outline-primary"
                        href="/admin/products"
                        ActiveClass="btn-primary text-white"
                        Match="NavLinkMatch.Prefix">
                    Products
                </NavLink>
                <NavLink class="btn btn-outline-primary"
                        href="/admin/orders"
                        ActiveClass="btn-primary text-white"
                        Match="NavLinkMatch.Prefix">
                    Orders
                </NavLink>
            </div>
        </div>
        <div class="col">
            @Body
        </div>
    </div>
</div>
```

11.5 *Testing the security policy*

Everything is in place, and you can test the security policy by restarting ASP.NET Core and requesting http://localhost:5000/admin or http://localhost:5000/admin/identityusers.

Since you are presently unauthenticated and you are trying to target an action that requires authorization, your browser will be redirected to the /Account/Login URL. Enter Admin and Secret123$ as the name and password and submit the form. The Account controller will check the credentials you provided with the seed data added to the Identity database and—assuming you entered the right details—authenticate you and redirect you to the URL you requested, to which you now have access. Figure 11.2 illustrates the process.

Figure 11.2   **The administration authentication/authorization process**

11.6   *Preparing ASP.NET Core for deployment*

In this section, I will prepare SportsStore and create a container that can be deployed into production. There is a wide range of deployment models available for ASP.NET Core applications, but I have picked Docker containers because they can be run on most hosting platforms or be deployed into a private data center. This is not a complete guide to deployment, but it will give you a sense of the process to prepare an application.

11.6.1   *Configuring error handling*

At the moment, the application is configured to use the developer-friendly error pages, which provide helpful information when a problem occurs. This is not information that end users should see, so I added a Razor Page named `Error.cshtml` to the `Pages` folder with the content shown in listing 11.16.

Listing 11.16   The contents of the Error.cshtml file in the Pages folder

```
@page "/error"
@{
    Layout = null;
}
<!DOCTYPE html>
<html>
<head>
    <meta name="viewport" content="width=device-width" />
    <link href="/lib/bootstrap/css/bootstrap.min.css" rel="stylesheet" />
    <title>Error</title>
</head>
<body class="text-center">
    <h2 class="text-danger">Error.</h2>
    <h3 class="text-danger">
        An error occurred while processing your request
    </h3>
</body>
</html>
```

This kind of error page is the last resort, and it is best to keep it as simple as possible and not to rely on shared views, view components, or other rich features. In this case, I have disabled shared layouts and defined a simple HTML document that explains that there has been an error, without providing any information about what has happened.

In listing 11.17, I have reconfigured the application so that the Error page is used for unhandled exceptions when the application is in the production environment. I have also set the locale, which is required when deploying to a Docker container. The locale I have chosen is en-US, which represents the language and currency conventions of English as it is spoken in the United States.

> **Listing 11.17** **Configuring error handling in the Program.cs file in the SportsStore folder**

```
using Microsoft.AspNetCore.Identity;
using Microsoft.EntityFrameworkCore;
using SportsStore.Models;

var builder = WebApplication.CreateBuilder(args);

builder.Services.AddControllersWithViews();

builder.Services.AddDbContext<StoreDbContext>(opts => {
    opts.UseSqlServer(
        builder.Configuration["ConnectionStrings:SportsStoreConnection"]);
});

builder.Services.AddScoped<IStoreRepository, EFStoreRepository>();
builder.Services.AddScoped<IOrderRepository, EFOrderRepository>();

builder.Services.AddRazorPages();
builder.Services.AddDistributedMemoryCache();
builder.Services.AddSession();
builder.Services.AddScoped<Cart>(sp => SessionCart.GetCart(sp));
builder.Services.AddSingleton<IHttpContextAccessor,
    HttpContextAccessor>();
builder.Services.AddServerSideBlazor();

builder.Services.AddDbContext<AppIdentityDbContext>(options =>
    options.UseSqlServer(
        builder.Configuration["ConnectionStrings:IdentityConnection"]));
builder.Services.AddIdentity<IdentityUser, IdentityRole>()
    .AddEntityFrameworkStores<AppIdentityDbContext>();

var app = builder.Build();

if (app.Environment.IsProduction()) {
    app.UseExceptionHandler("/error");
}

app.UseRequestLocalization(opts => {
    opts.AddSupportedCultures("en-US")
    .AddSupportedUICultures("en-US")
    .SetDefaultCulture("en-US");
});
```

```
app.UseStaticFiles();
app.UseSession();

app.UseAuthentication();
app.UseAuthorization();

app.MapControllerRoute("catpage",
    "{category}/Page{productPage:int}",
    new { Controller = "Home", action = "Index" });

app.MapControllerRoute("page", "Page{productPage:int}",
    new { Controller = "Home", action = "Index", productPage = 1 });

app.MapControllerRoute("category", "{category}",
    new { Controller = "Home", action = "Index", productPage = 1 });

app.MapControllerRoute("pagination",
    "Products/Page{productPage}",
    new { Controller = "Home", action = "Index", productPage = 1 });

app.MapDefaultControllerRoute();
app.MapRazorPages();
app.MapBlazorHub();
app.MapFallbackToPage("/admin/{*catchall}", "/Admin/Index");

SeedData.EnsurePopulated(app);
IdentitySeedData.EnsurePopulated(app);

app.Run();
```

As I explain in chapter 12, the `IWebHostEnvironment` interface describes the environment in which the application is running. The changes mean that the `UseExceptionHandler` method is called when the application is in production, but the developer-friendly error pages are used otherwise.

11.6.2 *Creating the production configuration settings*

The JSON configuration files that are used to define settings such as connection strings can be created so they apply only when the application is in a specific environment, such as development, staging, or production. The template I used to create the SportsStore project in chapter 7 created the `appsettings.json` and `appsettings.Development.json` files, which are intended to be the default settings that are overridden with those that are specific for development. I am going to take the reverse approach for this chapter and define a file that contains just those settings that are specific to production. Add a JSON file named `appsettings.Production.json` to the `SportsStore` folder with the content shown in listing 11.18.

CAUTION   Do not use these connection strings in real projects. You must correctly describe the connection to your production database, which is unlikely to be the same as the ones in the listing.

Listing 11.18 The appsettings.Production.json file in the SportsStore folder

```
{
  "ConnectionStrings": {
    "SportsStoreConnection": "Server=sqlserver;Database=SportsStore;
➥MultipleActiveResultSets=true;User=sa;Password=MyDatabaseSecret123;
➥Encrypt=False",
    "IdentityConnection": "Server=sqlserver;Database=Identity;
➥MultipleActiveResultSets=true;User=sa;Password=MyDatabaseSecret123;
➥Encrypt=False"
  }
}
```

These connection strings, each of which is defined on a single line, describe connections to SQL Server running on `sqlserver`, which is another Docker container running SQL Server. For simplicity, I have disabled encryption for the connections to the database.

11.6.3 Creating the Docker image

In the sections that follow, I configure and create the Docker image for the application that can be deployed into a container environment such as Microsoft Azure or Amazon Web Services. Bear in mind that containers are only one style of deployment and there are many others available if this approach does not suit you.

> **NOTE** Bear in mind that I am going to connect to a database running on the development machine, which is not how most real applications are configured. Be sure to configure the database connection strings and the container networking settings to match your production environment.

INSTALLING DOCKER DESKTOP

Go to https://docker.com and download and install the Docker Desktop package. Follow the installation process, reboot your Windows machine, and run the command shown in listing 11.19 to check that Docker has been installed and is in your path. (The Docker installation process seems to change often, which is why I have not been more specific about the process.)

> **NOTE** You will have to create an account on Docker.com to download the installer.

Listing 11.19 Checking the Docker Desktop installation

```
docker --version
```

CREATING THE DOCKER CONFIGURATION FILES

Docker is configured using a file named `Dockerfile`. There is no Visual Studio item template for this file, so use the Text File template to add a file named `Dockerfile .text` to the project and then rename the file to `Dockerfile`. If you are using Visual

Studio Code, you can just create a file named `Dockerfile` without the extension. Use the configuration settings shown in listing 11.20 as the contents for the new file.

Creating container images without Docker files.

Microsoft has introduced features in .NET for creating application images without needing a Dockerfile, with the details of the configuration specified in the CSPROJ file instead. This is an interesting idea, but my view is that the configuration of the image is too important to leave to automated tools, and is something that should be understood by the developer because misconfiguration can impact seriously the performance of the application. For this reason, I have created a Dockerfile in this chapter, and this is what I do in my own projects. You can learn more about this feature at https://devblogs .microsoft.com/dotnet/announcing-builtin-container-support-for-the-dotnet-sdk.

Listing 11.20   The contents of the Dockerfile File in the SportsStore folder

```
FROM mcr.microsoft.com/dotnet/aspnet:7.0

COPY /bin/Release/net7.0/publish/ SportsStore/

ENV ASPNETCORE_ENVIRONMENT Production
ENV Logging__Console__FormatterName=Simple

EXPOSE 5000
WORKDIR /SportsStore
ENTRYPOINT ["dotnet", "SportsStore.dll",  "--urls=http://0.0.0.0:5000"]
```

These instructions copy the SportsStore application into a Docker image and configure its execution. Next, create a file called `docker-compose.yml` with the content shown in listing 11.21. Visual Studio doesn't have a template for this type of file, but if you select the Text File template and enter the complete file name, it will create the file. Visual Studio Code users can simply create a file named `docker-compose.yml`.

> **NOTE**   The configuration file in listing 11.21 is used by Docker Compose, which creates containers and lets them work together. Docker Compose has been eclipsed by Kubernetes, which has become the most popular choice for deploying containers into production. Kubernetes is incredibly complex, however, and Docker Compose remains a good choice for working with simple applications, especially during development and testing.

Listing 11.21   The contents of the docker-compose.yml file in the SportsStore folder

```
version: "3"
services:
    sportsstore:
        build: .
        ports:
            - "5000:5000"
```

```
    environment:
        - ASPNETCORE_ENVIRONMENT=Production
    depends_on:
        - sqlserver
sqlserver:
    image: "mcr.microsoft.com/mssql/server"
    environment:
        SA_PASSWORD: "MyDatabaseSecret123"
        ACCEPT_EULA: "Y"
```

The YML files are especially sensitive to formatting and indentation, and it is important to create this file exactly as shown. If you have problems, then use the `docker -compose.yml` file from the GitHub repository for this book.

PUBLISHING AND IMAGING THE APPLICATION

Prepare the SportsStore application by using a PowerShell prompt to run the command shown listing 11.22 in the `SportsStore` folder.

> **Listing 11.22   Preparing the application**

```
dotnet publish -c Release
```

Next, run the command shown in listing 11.23 to create the Docker image for the SportsStore application. This command will take some time to complete the first time it is run because it will download the Docker images for ASP.NET Core.

> **Listing 11.23   Performing the Docker build**

```
docker-compose build
```

The first time you run this command, you may be prompted to allow Docker to use the network, as shown in figure 11.3.

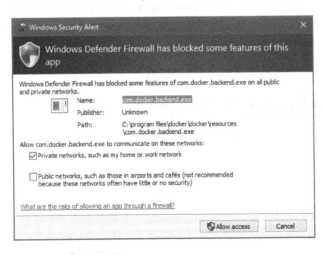

**Figure 11.3
Granting
network access**

Click the Allow button, return to the PowerShell prompt, use Control+C to terminate the Docker containers, and run the command in listing 11.23 again.

11.6.4 Running the containerized application

Run the command shown in listing 11.24 in the `SportsStore` folder to start the Docker containers for SQL Server.

Listing 11.24   Starting the database container

```
docker-compose up sqlserver
```

This command will take some time to complete the first time it is run because it will download the Docker images for SQL Server. You will see a large amount of output as SQL Server starts up. Once the database is running, use a separate command prompt to run the command shown in listing 11.25 to start the container for the SportsStore application.

Listing 11.25   Starting the SportsStore container

```
docker-compose up sportsstore
```

The application will be ready when you see output like this:

```
...
sportsstore_1  | info: Microsoft.Hosting.Lifetime[0]
sportsstore_1  |       Now listening on: http://0.0.0.0:5000
sportsstore_1  | info: Microsoft.Hosting.Lifetime[0]
sportsstore_1  |       Application started. Press Ctrl+C to shut down.
sportsstore_1  | info: Microsoft.Hosting.Lifetime[0]
sportsstore_1  |       Hosting environment: Production
sportsstore_1  | info: Microsoft.Hosting.Lifetime[0]
sportsstore_1  |       Content root path: /SportsStore
...
```

Open a new browser window and request http://localhost:5000, and you will receive a response from the containerized version of SportsStore, as shown in figure 11.4, which is now ready for deployment. Use Control+C at the PowerShell command prompts to terminate the Docker containers.

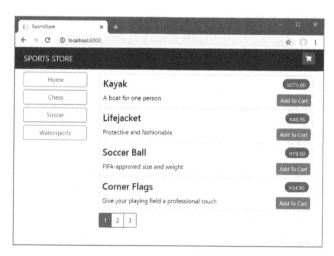

Figure 11.4 Running the SportsStore application in a container

Summary

- ASP.NET Core applications use ASP.NET Core Identity for user authentication and have built-in support for enforcing authorization using attributes.
- Applications are published to prepare them for deployment, using the `dotnet publish` command, specifying the environment name to ensure the correct configuration settings are used.
- Applications can be deployed into containers, which can be used on most hosting platforms or hosted locally within a data center.

Part 2

Understanding the ASP.NET Core platform

This chapter covers

- Understanding the basic structure of an ASP.NET Core application
- Understanding the HTTP request processing pipeline and middleware components
- Creating custom middleware components

The ASP.NET Core platform is the foundation for creating web applications; it provides the features that make it possible to use frameworks like MVC and Blazor. In this chapter, I explain how the basic ASP.NET Core features work, describe the purpose of the files in an ASP.NET Core project, and explain how the ASP.NET Core request pipeline is used to process HTTP requests and demonstrate the different ways that it can be customized.

Don't worry if not everything in this chapter makes immediate sense or appears to apply to the applications you intend to create. The features I describe in this chapter are the underpinnings for everything that ASP.NET Core does, and understanding how they work helps provide a context for understanding the features that you will use daily, as well as giving you the knowledge you need to diagnose problems when you don't get the behavior you expect. Table 12.1 puts the ASP.NET Core platform in context.

Table 12.1   Putting the ASP.NET Core platform in context

Question	Answer
What is it?	The ASP.NET Core platform is the foundation on which web applications are built and provides features for processing HTTP requests.
Why is it useful?	The ASP.NET Core platform takes care of the low-level details of web applications so that developers can focus on features for the end user.
How is it used?	The key building blocks are services and middleware components, both of which can be created using top-level statements in the `Program.cs` file.
Are there any pitfalls or limitations?	The use of the `Program.cs` file can be confusing, and close attention must be paid to the order of the statements it contains.
Are there any alternatives?	The ASP.NET Core platform is required for ASP.NET Core applications, but you can choose not to work with the platform directly and rely on just the higher-level ASP.NET Core features, which are described in later chapters.

Table 12.2 provides a guide to the chapter.

Table 12.2   Chapter guide

Problem	Solution	Listing
Creating a middleware component	Call the `Use` or `UseMiddleware` method to add a function or class to the request pipeline.	6–8
Modifying a response	Write a middleware component that uses the return pipeline path.	9
Preventing other components from processing a request	Short-circuit the request pipeline or create terminal middleware.	10, 12–14
Using different sets of middleware	Create a pipeline branch.	11
Configuring middleware components	Use the options pattern.	15–18

12.1   *Preparing for this chapter*

To prepare for this chapter, I am going to create a new project named Platform, using the template that provides the minimal ASP.NET Core setup. Open a new PowerShell command prompt from the Windows Start menu and run the commands shown in listing 12.1.

TIP You can download the example project for this chapter—and for all the other chapters in this book—from https://github.com/manningbooks/pro-asp .net-core-7. See chapter 1 for how to get help if you have problems running the examples.

```
dotnet new globaljson --sdk-version 7.0.100 --output Platform
dotnet new web --no-https --output Platform --framework net7.0
dotnet new sln -o Platform
dotnet sln Platform add Platform
```

If you are using Visual Studio, open the `Platform.sln` file in the `Platform` folder. If you are using Visual Studio Code, open the `Platform` folder. Click the Yes button when prompted to add the assets required for building and debugging the project.

Open the `launchSettings.json` file in the `Properties` folder and change the ports that will be used to handle HTTP requests, as shown in listing 12.2.

```
{
  "iisSettings": {
    "windowsAuthentication": false,
    "anonymousAuthentication": true,
    "iisExpress": {
      "applicationUrl": "http://localhost:5000",
      "sslPort": 0
    }
  },
  "profiles": {
    "Platform": {
      "commandName": "Project",
      "dotnetRunMessages": true,
      "launchBrowser": true,
      "applicationUrl": "http://localhost:5000",
      "environmentVariables": {
        "ASPNETCORE_ENVIRONMENT": "Development"
      }
    },
    "IIS Express": {
      "commandName": "IISExpress",
      "launchBrowser": true,
      "environmentVariables": {
        "ASPNETCORE_ENVIRONMENT": "Development"
      }
    }
  }
}
```

12.1.1 *Running the example application*

To start the application, run the command shown in listing 12.3 in the `Platform` folder.

> **Listing 12.3 Starting the example application**

```
dotnet run
```

Open a new browser window and use it to request http://localhost:5000. You will see the output shown in figure 12.1.

Figure 12.1 Running the example application

12.2 *Understanding the ASP.NET Core platform*

To understand ASP.NET Core, it is helpful to focus on just the key features: the request pipeline, middleware, and services. Understanding how these features fit together—even without going into detail—provides useful context for understanding the contents of the ASP.NET Core project and the shape of the ASP.NET Core platform.

12.2.1 *Understanding middleware and the request pipeline*

The purpose of the ASP.NET Core platform is to receive HTTP requests and send responses to them, which ASP.NET Core delegates to *middleware components*. Middleware components are arranged in a chain, known as the *request pipeline.*

When a new HTTP request arrives, the ASP.NET Core platform creates an object that describes it and a corresponding object that describes the response that will be sent in return. These objects are passed to the first middleware component in the chain, which inspects the request and modifies the response. The request is then passed to the next middleware component in the chain, with each component inspecting the request and adding to the response. Once the request has made its way through the pipeline, the ASP.NET Core platform sends the response, as illustrated in figure 12.2.

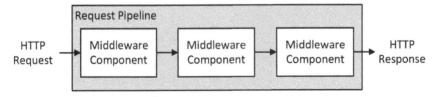

Figure 12.2 The ASP.NET Core request pipeline

Some components focus on generating responses for requests, but others are there to provide supporting features, such as formatting specific data types or reading and writing cookies. ASP.NET Core includes middleware components that solve common problems, as described in chapters 15 and 16, and I show how to create custom middleware components later in this chapter. If no response is generated by the middleware components, then ASP.NET Core will return a response with the HTTP 404 Not Found status code.

12.2.2   Understanding services

Services are objects that provide features in a web application. Any class can be used as a service, and there are no restrictions on the features that services provide. What makes services special is that they are managed by ASP.NET Core, and a feature called *dependency injection* makes it possible to easily access services anywhere in the application, including middleware components.

Dependency injection can be a difficult topic to understand, and I describe it in detail in chapter 14. For now, it is enough to know that there are objects that are managed by the ASP.NET Core platform that can be shared by middleware components, either to coordinate between components or to avoid duplicating common features, such as logging or loading configuration data, as shown in figure 12.3.

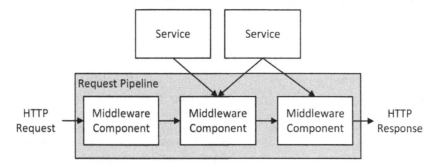

Figure 12.3   Services in the ASP.NET Core platform

As the figure shows, middleware components use only the services they require to do their work. As you will learn in later chapters, ASP.NET Core provides some basic services that can be supplemented by additional services that are specific to an application.

12.3   Understanding the ASP.NET Core project

The web template produces a project with just enough code and configuration to start the ASP.NET Core runtime with some basic services and middleware components. Figure 12.4 shows the files added to the project by the template.

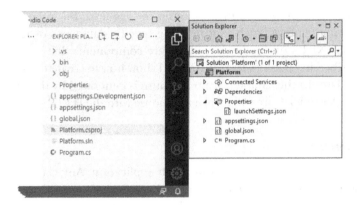

Figure 12.4
The files in the
example project

Visual Studio and Visual Studio Code take different approaches to displaying files and folders. Visual Studio hides items that are not commonly used by the developer and nests related items together, while Visual Studio Code shows everything.

This is why the two project views shown in the figure are different: Visual Studio has hidden the `bin` and `obj` folders and nested the `appsettings.Development.json` file within the `appsettings.json` file. The buttons at the top of the Solution Explorer window can be used to prevent nesting and to show all the files in the project.

Although there are few files in the project, they underpin ASP.NET Core development and are described in table 12.3.

Table 12.3   The files and folders in the Example project

Name	Description
`appsettings.json`	This file is used to configure the application, as described in chapter 15.
`appsettings.Development.json`	This file is used to define configuration settings that are specific to development, as explained in chapter 15.
`bin`	This folder contains the compiled application files. Visual Studio hides this folder.
`global.json`	This file is used to select a specific version of the .NET Core SDK.
`Properties/launchSettings.json`	This file is used to configure the application when it starts.
`obj`	This folder contains the intermediate output from the compiler. Visual Studio hides this folder.
`Platform.csproj`	This file describes the project to the .NET Core tools, including the package dependencies and build instructions, as described in the "Understanding the Project File" section. Visual Studio hides this file, but it can be edited by right-clicking the project item in the Solution Explorer and selecting Edit Project File from the pop-up menu.
`Platform.sln`	This file is used to organize projects. Visual Studio hides this folder.
`Program.cs`	This file is the entry point for the ASP.NET Core platform and is used to configure the platform, as described in the "Understanding the Entry Point" section

12.3.1 *Understanding the entry point*

The `Program.cs` file contains the code statements that are executed when the application is started and that are used to configure the ASP.NET platform and the individual frameworks it supports. Here is the content of the `Program.cs` file in the example project:

```
var builder = WebApplication.CreateBuilder(args);
var app = builder.Build();

app.MapGet("/", () => "Hello World!");

app.Run();
```

This file contains only top-level statements. The first statement calls the `Web-Application.CreateBuilder` and assigns the result to a variable named `builder`:

```
...
var builder = WebApplication.CreateBuilder(args);
...
```

This method is responsible for setting up the basic features of the ASP.NET Core platform, including creating services responsible for configuration data and logging, both of which are described in chapter 15. This method also sets up the HTTP server, named Kestrel, that is used to receive HTTP requests.

The result from the `CreateBuilder` method is a `WebApplicationBuilder` object, which is used to register additional services, although none are defined at present. The `WebApplicationBuilder` class defines a `Build` method that is used to finalize the initial setup:

```
...
var app = builder.Build();
...
```

The result of the `Build` method is a `WebApplication` object, which is used to set up middleware components. The template has set up one middleware component, using the `MapGet` extension method:

```
...
app.MapGet("/", () => "Hello World!");
...
```

`MapGet` is an extension method for the `IEndpointRouteBuilder` interface, which is implemented by the `WebApplication` class, and which sets up a function that will handle HTTP requests with a specified URL path. In this case, the function responds to requests for the default URL path, which is denoted by `/`, and the function responds to all requests by returning a simple `string` response, which is how the output shown in figure 12.1 was produced.

Most projects need a more sophisticated set of responses, and Microsoft provides middleware as part of ASP.NET Core that deals with the most common features required by web applications, which I describe in chapters 15 and 16. You can also create your own middleware, as described in the "Creating Custom Middleware" section, when the built-in features don't suit your requirements.

The final statement in the `Program.cs` file calls the `Run` method defined by the `WebApplication` class, which starts listening to HTTP requests.

Even though the function used with the `MapGet` method returns a string, ASP.NET Core is clever enough to create a valid HTTP response that will be understood by browsers. While ASP.NET Core is still running, open a new PowerShell command prompt and run the command shown in listing 12.4 to send an HTTP request to the ASP.NET Core server.

> **Listing 12.4   Sending an HTTP Request**

```
(Invoke-WebRequest http://localhost:5000).RawContent
```

The output from this command shows that the response sent by ASP.NET Core contains an HTTP status code and the set of basic headers, like this:

```
HTTP/1.1 200 OK
Transfer-Encoding: chunked
Content-Type: text/plain; charset=utf-8
Date: Wed, 14 Dec 2022 08:09:13 GMT
Server: Kestrel
```

12.3.2 *Understanding the project file*

The `Platform.csproj` file, known as the *project file*, contains the information that .NET Core uses to build the project and keep track of dependencies. Here is the content that was added to the file by the Empty template when the project was created:

```
<Project Sdk="Microsoft.NET.Sdk.Web">

  <PropertyGroup>
    <TargetFramework>net7.0</TargetFramework>
    <Nullable>enable</Nullable>
    <ImplicitUsings>enable</ImplicitUsings>
  </PropertyGroup>

</Project>
```

The `csproj` file is hidden when using Visual Studio; you can edit it by right-clicking the Platform project item in the Solution Explorer and selecting Edit Project File from the pop-up menu.

The project file contains XML elements that describe the project to MSBuild, the Microsoft build engine. MSBuild can be used to create complex build processes and is described in detail at https://docs.microsoft.com/en-us/visualstudio/msbuild/msbuild.

There is no need to edit the project file directly in most projects. The most common change to the file is to add dependencies on other .NET packages, but these are typically added using the command-line tools or the interface provided by Visual Studio.

To add a package to the project using the command line, open a new PowerShell command prompt, navigate to the `Platform` project folder (the one that contains the `csproj` file), and run the command shown in listing 12.5.

Listing 12.5   Adding a package to the project

```
dotnet add package Swashbuckle.AspNetCore --version 6.4.0
```

This command adds the `Swashbuckle.AspNetCore` package to the project. You will see this package used in chapter 20, but for now, it is the effect of the `dotnet add package` command that is important.

The new dependency will be shown in the `Platform.csproj` file:

```
<Project Sdk="Microsoft.NET.Sdk.Web">

  <PropertyGroup>
    <TargetFramework>net7.0</TargetFramework>
    <Nullable>enable</Nullable>
    <ImplicitUsings>enable</ImplicitUsings>
  </PropertyGroup>

  <ItemGroup>
    <PackageReference Include="Swashbuckle.AspNetCore" Version="6.4.0" />
  </ItemGroup>

</Project>
```

12.4   Creating custom middleware

As mentioned, Microsoft provides various middleware components for ASP.NET Core that handle the features most commonly required by web applications. You can also create your own middleware, which is a useful way to understand how ASP.NET Core works, even if you use only the standard components in your projects. The key method for creating middleware is `Use`, as shown in listing 12.6.

Listing 12.6   Creating custom middleware in the Program.cs file in the Platform folder

```
var builder = WebApplication.CreateBuilder(args);
var app = builder.Build();

app.Use(async (context, next) => {
    if (context.Request.Method == HttpMethods.Get
            && context.Request.Query["custom"] == "true") {
        context.Response.ContentType = "text/plain";
        await context.Response.WriteAsync("Custom Middleware \n");
    }
    await next();
});

app.MapGet("/", () => "Hello World!");

app.Run();
```

The `Use` method registers a middleware component that is typically expressed as a lambda function that receives each request as it passes through the pipeline (there is another method used for classes, as described in the next section).

The arguments to the lambda function are an `HttpContext` object and a function that is invoked to tell ASP.NET Core to pass the request to the next middleware component in the pipeline.

The `HttpContext` object describes the HTTP request and the HTTP response and provides additional context, including details of the user associated with the request. Table 12.4 describes the most useful members provided by the `HttpContext` class, which is defined in the `Microsoft.AspNetCore.Http` namespace.

Table 12.4   Useful HttpContext members

Name	Description
Connection	This property returns a `Connection-Info` object that provides information about the network connection underlying the HTTP request, including details of local and remote IP addresses and ports.
Request	This property returns an `HttpRequest` object that describes the HTTP request being processed.
RequestServices	This property provides access to the services available for the request, as described in chapter 14.
Response	This property returns an `HttpResponse` object that is used to create a response to the HTTP request.
Session	This property returns the session data associated with the request. The session data feature is described in chapter 16.
User	This property returns details of the user associated with the request, as described in chapters 37 and 38.
Features	This property provides access to request features, which allow access to the low-level aspects of request handling. See chapter 16 for an example of using a request feature.

The ASP.NET Core platform is responsible for processing the HTTP request to create the `HttpRequest` object, which means that middleware and endpoints don't have to worry about the raw request data. Table 12.5 describes the most useful members of the `HttpRequest` class.

Table 12.5   Useful HttpRequest members

Name	Description
Body	This property returns a stream that can be used to read the request body.
ContentLength	This property returns the value of the `Content-Length` header.
ContentType	This property returns the value of the `Content-Type` header.
Cookies	This property returns the request cookies.
Form	This property returns a representation of the request body as a form.
Headers	This property returns the request headers.
IsHttps	This property returns `true` if the request was made using HTTPS.
Method	This property returns the HTTP verb—also known as the HTTP method—used for the request.
Path	This property returns the path section of the request URL.
Query	This property returns the query string section of the request URL as key-value pairs.

The `HttpResponse` object describes the HTTP response that will be sent back to the client when the request has made its way through the pipeline. Table 12.6 describes the most useful members of the `HttpResponse` class. The ASP.NET Core platform makes dealing with responses as easy as possible, sets headers automatically, and makes it easy to send content to the client.

Table 12.6   Useful HttpResponse members

Name	Description
ContentLength	This property sets the value of the `Content-Length` header.
ContentType	This property sets the value of the `Content-Type` header.
Cookies	This property allows cookies to be associated with the response.
HasStarted	This property returns `true` if ASP.NET Core has started to send the response headers to the client, after which it is not possible to make changes to the status code or headers.
Headers	This property allows the response headers to be set.
StatusCode	This property sets the status code for the response.
WriteAsync(data)	This asynchronous method writes a data string to the response body.
Redirect(url)	This method sends a redirection response.

When creating custom middleware, the `HttpContext`, `HttpRequest`, and `Http-Response` objects are used directly, but, as you will learn in later chapters, this isn't usually required when using the higher-level ASP.NET Core features such as the MVC Framework and Razor Pages.

The middleware function I defined in listing 12.6 uses the `HttpRequest` object to check the HTTP method and query string to identify GET requests that have a `custom` parameter in the query string whose value is `true`, like this:

```
...
if (context.Request.Method == HttpMethods.Get
    && context.Request.Query["custom"] == "true") {
...
```

The `HttpMethods` class defines static strings for each HTTP method. For GET requests with the expected query string, the middleware function uses the `ContentType` property to set the `Content-Type` header and uses the `WriteAsync` method to add a string to the body of the response.

```
...
context.Response.ContentType = "text/plain";
await context.Response.WriteAsync("Custom Middleware \n");
...
```

Setting the `Content-Type` header is important because it prevents the subsequent middleware component from trying to set the response status code and headers. ASP.NET Core will always try to make sure that a valid HTTP response is sent, and this can lead to the response headers or status code being set after an earlier component has already written content to the response body, which produces an exception (because the headers have to be sent to the client before the response body can begin).

> **NOTE**   In this part of the book, all the examples send simple string results to the browser. In part 3, I show you how to create web services that return JSON data and introduce the different ways that ASP.NET Core can produce HTML results.

The second argument to the middleware is the function conventionally named `next` that tells ASP.NET Core to pass the request to the next component in the request pipeline.

```
...
if (context.Request.Method == HttpMethods.Get
        && context.Request.Query["custom"] == "true") {
    context.Response.ContentType = "text/plain";
    await context.Response.WriteAsync("Custom Middleware \n");
}
await next();
...
```

No arguments are required when invoking the next middleware component because ASP.NET Core takes care of providing the component with the `HttpContext` object and its own `next` function so that it can process the request. The `next` function is asynchronous, which is why the `await` keyword is used and why the lambda function is defined with the `async` keyword.

TIP   You may encounter middleware that calls `next.Invoke()` instead of `next()`. These are equivalent, and `next()` is provided as a convenience by the compiler to produce concise code.

Start ASP.NET Core using the `dotnet run` command and use a browser to request http://localhost:5000/?custom=true. You will see that the new middleware function writes its message to the response before passing on the request to the next middleware component, as shown in figure 12.5. Remove the query string, or change `true` to `false`, and the middleware component will pass on the request without adding to the response.

Figure 12.5   Creating custom middleware

12.4.1 Defining middleware using a class

Defining middleware using lambda functions is convenient, but it can lead to a long and complex series of statements in the `Program.cs` file and makes it hard to reuse middleware in different projects. Middleware can also be defined using classes, which keeps the code outside of the `Program.cs` file. To create a middleware class, add a class file named `Middleware.cs` to the `Platform` folder, with the content shown in listing 12.7.

Listing 12.7   The contents of the Middleware.cs file in the Platform folder

```
namespace Platform {

    public class QueryStringMiddleWare {
        private RequestDelegate next;

        public QueryStringMiddleWare(RequestDelegate nextDelegate) {
            next = nextDelegate;
        }

        public async Task Invoke(HttpContext context) {
            if (context.Request.Method == HttpMethods.Get
                    && context.Request.Query["custom"] == "true") {
                if (!context.Response.HasStarted) {
                    context.Response.ContentType = "text/plain";
                }
```

```
                    await context.Response.WriteAsync("Class Middleware \n");
                }
                await next(context);
            }
        }
    }
}
```

Middleware classes receive a `RequestDelegate` object as a constructor parameter, which is used to forward the request to the next component in the pipeline. The `Invoke` method is called by ASP.NET Core when a request is received and is given an `HttpContext` object that provides access to the request and response, using the same classes that lambda function middleware receives. The `RequestDelegate` returns a `Task`, which allows it to work asynchronously.

One important difference in class-based middleware is that the `HttpContext` object must be used as an argument when invoking the `RequestDelegate` to forward the request, like this:

```
...
await next(context);
...
```

Class-based middleware components are added to the pipeline with the `Use-Middleware` method, which accepts the middleware as a type argument, as shown in listing 12.8.

> **Listing 12.8   Adding class-based middleware in the Program.cs file in the Platform folder**

```
var builder = WebApplication.CreateBuilder(args);
var app = builder.Build();

app.Use(async (context, next) => {
    if (context.Request.Method == HttpMethods.Get
            && context.Request.Query["custom"] == "true") {
        context.Response.ContentType = "text/plain";
        await context.Response.WriteAsync("Custom Middleware \n");
    }
    await next();
});

app.UseMiddleware<Platform.QueryStringMiddleWare>();

app.MapGet("/", () => "Hello World!");

app.Run();
```

When the ASP.NET Core is started, the `QueryStringMiddleware` class will be instantiated, and its `Invoke` method will be called to process requests as they are received.

> **CAUTION**   A single middleware object is used to handle all requests, which means that the code in the `Invoke` method must be thread-safe.

Use the `dotnet run` command to start ASP.NET Core and use a browser to request http://localhost:5000/?custom=true. You will see the output from both middleware components, as shown in figure 12.6.

Figure 12.6 Using a class-based middleware component

12.4.2 *Understanding the return pipeline path*

Middleware components can modify the HTTPResponse object after the next function has been called, as shown by the new middleware in listing 12.9.

Listing 12.9 Adding new middleware in the Program.cs file in the Platform folder

```
var builder = WebApplication.CreateBuilder(args);
var app = builder.Build();

app.Use(async (context, next) => {
    await next();
    await context.Response
        .WriteAsync($"\nStatus Code: { context.Response.StatusCode}");
});

app.Use(async (context, next) => {
    if (context.Request.Method == HttpMethods.Get
            && context.Request.Query["custom"] == "true") {
        context.Response.ContentType = "text/plain";
        await context.Response.WriteAsync("Custom Middleware \n");
    }
    await next();
});

app.UseMiddleware<Platform.QueryStringMiddleWare>();

app.MapGet("/", () => "Hello World!");

app.Run();
```

The new middleware immediately calls the next method to pass the request along the pipeline and then uses the WriteAsync method to add a string to the response body. This may seem like an odd approach, but it allows middleware to make changes to the response before and after it is passed along the request pipeline by defining statements before and after the next function is invoked, as illustrated by figure 12.7.

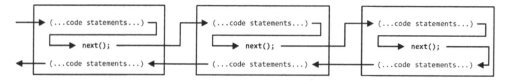

Figure 12.7   Passing requests and responses through the ASP.NET Core pipeline

Middleware can operate before the request is passed on, after the request has been processed by other components, or both. The result is that several middleware components collectively contribute to the response that is produced, each providing some aspect of the response or providing some feature or data that is used later in the pipeline.

Start ASP.NET Core using the `dotnet run` command and use a browser to request http://localhost:5000, which will produce output that includes the content from the new middleware component, as shown in figure 12.8.

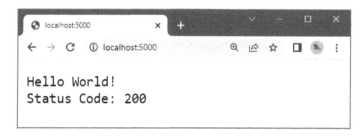

Figure 12.8   Modifying a response in the return path

> **NOTE**   Middleware components must not change the response status code or headers once ASP.NET Core has started to send the response to the client. Check the `HasStarted` property, described in table 12.6, to avoid exceptions.

12.4.3 Short-Circuiting the request pipeline

Components that generate complete responses can choose not to call the `next` function so that the request isn't passed on. Components that don't pass on requests are said to *short-circuit* the pipeline, which is what the new middleware component shown in listing 12.10 does for requests that target the `/short` URL.

Listing 12.10   Short-Circuiting the pipeline in the Program.cs file in the Platform folder

```
var builder = WebApplication.CreateBuilder(args);
var app = builder.Build();

app.Use(async (context, next) => {
    await next();
    await context.Response
```

```
            .WriteAsync($"\nStatus Code: { context.Response.StatusCode}");
});

app.Use(async (context, next) => {
    if (context.Request.Path == "/short") {
        await context.Response
            .WriteAsync($"Request Short Circuited");
    } else {
        await next();
    }
});

app.Use(async (context, next) => {
    if (context.Request.Method == HttpMethods.Get
            && context.Request.Query["custom"] == "true") {
        context.Response.ContentType = "text/plain";
        await context.Response.WriteAsync("Custom Middleware \n");
    }
    await next();
});

app.UseMiddleware<Platform.QueryStringMiddleWare>();

app.MapGet("/", () => "Hello World!");

app.Run();
```

The new middleware checks the `Path` property of the `HttpRequest` object to see whether the request is for the `/short` URL; if it is, it calls the `WriteAsync` method without calling the `next` function. To see the effect, restart ASP.NET Core and use a browser to request http://localhost:5000/short?custom=true, which will produce the output shown in figure 12.9.

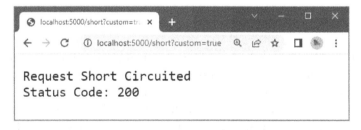

Figure 12.9 Short-circuiting the request pipeline

Even though the URL has the query string parameter that is expected by the next component in the pipeline, the request isn't forwarded, so that subsequent middleware doesn't get used. Notice, however, that the previous component in the pipeline has added its message to the response. That's because the short-circuiting only prevents components further along the pipeline from being used and doesn't affect earlier components, as illustrated in figure 12.10.

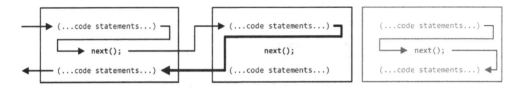

Figure 12.10   Short-circuiting the request pipeline

12.4.4 Creating pipeline branches

The `Map` method is used to create a section of pipeline that is used to process requests for specific URLs, creating a separate sequence of middleware components, as shown in listing 12.11.

> **Listing 12.11   Creating a pipeline branch in the Program.cs file in the Platform folder**

```
var builder = WebApplication.CreateBuilder(args);
var app = builder.Build();

app.Map("/branch", branch => {

    branch.UseMiddleware<Platform.QueryStringMiddleWare>();

    branch.Use(async (HttpContext context, Func<Task> next) => {
        await context.Response.WriteAsync($"Branch Middleware");
    });
});

app.UseMiddleware<Platform.QueryStringMiddleWare>();

app.MapGet("/", () => "Hello World!");

app.Run();
```

The first argument to the `Map` method specifies the string that will be used to match URLs. The second argument is the branch of the pipeline, to which middleware components are added with the `Use` and `UseMiddleware` methods.

The statements in listing 12.11 create a branch that is used for URLs that start with /branch and that pass requests through the `QueryStringMiddleware` class defined in listing 12.7 and a middleware lambda expression that adds a message to the response. Figure 12.11 shows the effect of the branch on the request pipeline.

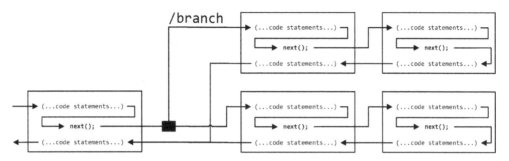

Figure 12.11 Adding a branch to the request pipeline

When a URL is matched by the Map method, it follows the branch. In this example, the final component in the middleware branch doesn't invoke the next delegate, which means that requests do not pass through the middleware components on the main path through the pipeline.

The same middleware can be used in different parts of the pipeline, which can be seen in listing 12.11, where the QueryStringMiddleWare class is used in both the main part of the pipeline and the branch.

To see the different ways that requests are handled, restart ASP.NET Core and use a browser to request the http://localhost:5000/?custom=true URL, which will be handled on the main part of the pipeline and will produce the output shown on the left of figure 12.12. Navigate to http://localhost:5000/branch?custom=true, and the request will be forwarded to the middleware in the branch, producing the output shown on the right in figure 12.12.

Figure 12.12 The effect of branching the request pipeline

Branching with a predicate

ASP.NET Core also supports the MapWhen method, which can match requests using a predicate, allowing requests to be selected for a pipeline branch on criteria other than just URLs.

The arguments to the MapWhen method are a predicate function that receives an Http-Context and that returns true for requests that should follow the branch, and a function that receives an IApplicationBuilder object representing the pipeline branch,

(continued)

to which middleware is added. Here is an example of using the `MapWhen` method to branch the pipeline:

```
...
app.MapWhen(context => context.Request.Query.Keys.Contains("branch"),
    branch => {
        // ...add middleware components here...
});
...
```

The predicate function returns `true` to branch for requests whose query string contains a parameter named `branch`. A cast to the `IApplicationBuilder` interface is not required because there only one `MapWhen` extension method has been defined.

12.4.5 *Creating terminal middleware*

Terminal middleware never forwards requests to other components and always marks the end of the request pipeline. There is a terminal middleware component in the `Program.cs` file, as shown here:

```
...
branch.Use(async (context, next) => {
    await context.Response.WriteAsync($"Branch Middleware");
});
...
```

ASP.NET Core supports the `Run` method as a convenience feature for creating terminal middleware, which makes it obvious that a middleware component won't forward requests and that a deliberate decision has been made not to call the `next` function. In listing 12.12, I have used the `Run` method for the terminal middleware in the pipeline branch.

> **Listing 12.12   Using the run method in the Program.cs file in the Platform folder**

```
var builder = WebApplication.CreateBuilder(args);
var app = builder.Build();

((IApplicationBuilder)app).Map("/branch", branch => {

    branch.UseMiddleware<Platform.QueryStringMiddleWare>();

    branch.Run(async (context) => {
        await context.Response.WriteAsync($"Branch Middleware");
    });
});

app.UseMiddleware<Platform.QueryStringMiddleWare>();

app.MapGet("/", () => "Hello World!");

app.Run();
```

The middleware function passed to the Run method receives only an HttpContext object and doesn't have to define a parameter that isn't used. Behind the scenes, the Run method is implemented through the Use method, and this feature is provided only as a convenience.

CAUTION Middleware added to the pipeline after a terminal component will never receive requests. ASP.NET Core won't warn you if you add a terminal component before the end of the pipeline.

Class-based components can be written so they can be used as both regular and terminal middleware, as shown in listing 12.13.

Listing 12.13 Adding terminal support in the Middleware.cs file in the Platform folder

```
namespace Platform {

    public class QueryStringMiddleWare {
        private RequestDelegate? next;

        public QueryStringMiddleWare() {
            // do nothing
        }

        public QueryStringMiddleWare(RequestDelegate nextDelegate) {
            next = nextDelegate;
        }

        public async Task Invoke(HttpContext context) {
            if (context.Request.Method == HttpMethods.Get
                    && context.Request.Query["custom"] == "true") {
                if (!context.Response.HasStarted) {
                    context.Response.ContentType = "text/plain";
                }
                await context.Response.WriteAsync("Class Middleware\n");
            }
            if (next != null) {
                await next(context);
            }
        }
    }
}
```

The component will forward requests only when the constructor has been provided with a non-null value for the nextDelegate parameter. listing 12.14 shows the application of the component in both standard and terminal forms.

Listing 12.14 Applying middleware in the Program.cs file in the Platform folder

```
var builder = WebApplication.CreateBuilder(args);
var app = builder.Build();

((IApplicationBuilder)app).Map("/branch", branch => {
    branch.Run(new Platform.QueryStringMiddleWare().Invoke);
```

```
});

app.UseMiddleware<Platform.QueryStringMiddleWare>();

app.MapGet("/", () => "Hello World!");

app.Run();
```

There is no equivalent to the `UseMiddleware` method for terminal middleware, so the `Run` method must be used by creating a new instance of the middleware class and selecting its `Invoke` method. Using the `Run` method doesn't alter the output from the middleware, which you can see by restarting ASP.NET Core and navigating to the http://localhost:5000/branch?custom=true URL, which produces the content shown in figure 12.13.

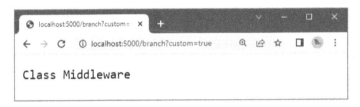

Figure 12.13.   Using the Run method to create terminal middleware

12.5   *Configuring middleware*

There is a common pattern for configuring middleware that is known as the *options pattern* and that is used by some of the built-in middleware components described in later chapters.

The starting point is to define a class that contains the configuration options for a middleware component. Add a class file named `MessageOptions.cs` to the `Platform` folder with the code shown in listing 12.15.

Listing 12.15   The contents of the MessageOptions.cs file in the Platform folder

```
namespace Platform {

    public class MessageOptions {

        public string CityName { get; set; } = "New York";
        public string CountryName{ get; set; } = "USA";
    }
}
```

The `MessageOptions` class defines properties that detail a city and a country. In listing 12.16, I have used the options pattern to create a custom middleware component that relies on the `MessageOptions` class for its configuration. I have also removed some of the middleware from previous examples for brevity.

```
using Microsoft.Extensions.Options;
using Platform;

var builder = WebApplication.CreateBuilder(args);

builder.Services.Configure<MessageOptions>(options => {
    options.CityName = "Albany";
});

var app = builder.Build();

app.MapGet("/location", async (HttpContext context,
    IOptions<MessageOptions> msgOpts) => {
        Platform.MessageOptions opts = msgOpts.Value;
        await context.Response.WriteAsync($"{opts.CityName}, "
            + opts.CountryName);
    });

app.MapGet("/", () => "Hello World!");

app.Run();
```

The options are set up using the `Services.Configure` method defined by the `Web-ApplicationBuilder` class, using a generic type parameter like this:

```
...
builder.Services.Configure<MessageOptions>(options => {
    options.CityName = "Albany";
});
...
```

This statement creates options using the `MessageOptions` class and changes the value of the `CityName` property. When the application starts, the ASP.NET Core platform will create a new instance of the `MessageOptions` class and pass it to the function supplied as the argument to the `Configure` method, allowing the default option values to be changed.

The options will be available as a service, which means this statement must appear before the call to the `Build` method is called, as shown in the listing.

Middleware components can access the configuration options by defining a parameter for the function that handles the request, like this:

```
...
app.MapGet("/location", async (HttpContext context,
    IOptions<MessageOptions> msgOpts) => {
        Platform.MessageOptions opts = msgOpts.Value;
        await context.Response.WriteAsync($"{opts.CityName}, "
            + opts.CountryName);
    });
...
```

Some of the extension methods used to register middleware components will accept any function to handle requests. When a request is processed, the ASP.NET

Core platform inspects the function to find parameters that require services, which allows the middleware component to use the configuration options in the response it generates:

```
...
app.MapGet("/location", async (HttpContext context,
    IOptions<MessageOptions> msgOpts) => {
        Platform.MessageOptions opts = msgOpts.Value;
        await context.Response.WriteAsync($"{opts.CityName}, "
            + opts.CountryName);
    });
...
```

This is an example of dependency injection, which I describe in detail in chapter 14. For now, however, you can see how the middleware component uses the options pattern by restarting ASP.NET Core and using a browser to request http://localhost:5000/location, which will produce the response shown in figure 12.14.

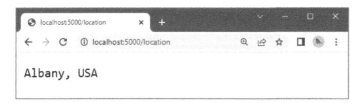

Figure 12.14   Using the options pattern

12.5.1 *Using the options pattern with class-based middleware*

The options pattern can also be used with class-based middleware and is applied in a similar way. Add the statements shown in listing 12.17 to the `Middleware.cs` file to define a class-based middleware component that uses the `MessageOptions` class for configuration.

Listing 12.17   Defining middleware in the Middleware.cs file in the Platform folder

```
using Microsoft.Extensions.Options;

namespace Platform {

    public class QueryStringMiddleWare {
        private RequestDelegate? next;

        // ...statements omitted for brevity...
    }

    public class LocationMiddleware {
        private RequestDelegate next;
        private MessageOptions options;

        public LocationMiddleware(RequestDelegate nextDelegate,
```

```
        IOptions<MessageOptions> opts) {
    next = nextDelegate;
    options = opts.Value;
}

public async Task Invoke(HttpContext context) {
    if (context.Request.Path == "/location") {
        await context.Response
            .WriteAsync($"{options.CityName}, "
                + options.CountryName);
    } else {
        await next(context);
    }
}
```

The `LocationMiddleware` class defines an `IOptions<MessageOptions>` constructor parameter, which can be used in the `Invoke` method to access the options settings.

Listing 12.18 reconfigures the request pipeline to replace the lambda function middleware component with the class from listing 12.17.

> **Listing 12.18 Using class-based middleware in the Program.cs file in the Platform folder**

```
//using Microsoft.Extensions.Options;
using Platform;

var builder = WebApplication.CreateBuilder(args);

builder.Services.Configure<MessageOptions>(options => {
    options.CityName = "Albany";
});

var app = builder.Build();

app.UseMiddleware<LocationMiddleware>();

app.MapGet("/", () => "Hello World!");

app.Run();
```

When the `UseMiddleware` statement is executed, the `LocationMiddleware` constructor is inspected, and its `IOptions<MessageOptions>` parameter will be resolved using the object created with the `Services.Configure` method. This is done using the dependency injection feature that is described in chapter 14, but the immediate effect is that the options pattern can be used to easily configure class-based middleware. Restart ASP.NET Core and request http://localhost:5000/location to test the new middleware, which will produce the same output as shown in figure 12.14.

Summary

- ASP.NET Core uses a pipeline to process HTTP requests.
- Each request is passed to a series of middleware components for processing.
- Once the request has reached the end of the pipeline, the same middleware components are able to inspect and modify the response before it is sent.
- Middleware components can choose not to forward requests to the next component in the pipeline, known as "short-circuiting."
- ASP.NET Core can be configured to use different sequences of middleware components to handle different request URLs.
- Middleware is configured using the options pattern, which is a simple and consistent approach used throughout ASP.NET Core.

Using URL routing

The URL routing feature makes it easier to generate responses by consolidating the processing and matching of request URLs. In this chapter, I explain how the ASP .NET Core platform supports URL routing, show its use, and explain why it can be preferable to creating custom middleware components. Table 13.1 puts URL routing in context.

> **NOTE** This chapter focuses on URL routing for the ASP.NET Core platform. See part 3 for details of how the higher-level parts of ASP.NET Core build on the features described in this chapter.

Table 13.1   Putting URL routing in context

Question	Answer
What is it?	URL routing consolidates the processing and matching of URLs, allowing components known as *endpoints* to generate responses.
Why is it useful?	URL routing obviates the need for each middleware component to process the URL to see whether the request will be handled or passed along the pipeline. The result is more efficient and easier to maintain.
How is it used?	The URL routing middleware components are added to the request pipeline and configured with a set of routes. Each route contains a URL path and a delegate that will generate a response when a request with the matching path is received.
Are there any pitfalls or limitations?	It can be difficult to define the set of routes matching all the URLs supported by a complex application.
Are there any alternatives?	URL routing is optional, and custom middleware components can be used instead.

Table 13.2 provides a guide to the chapter.

Table 13.2   Chapter guide

Problem	Solution	Listing
Handling requests for a specific set of URLs	Define a route with a pattern that matches the required URLs.	1–7
Extracting values from URLs	Use segment variables.	8–11, 15
Generating URLs	Use the link generator to produce URLs from routes.	12–14, 16
Matching URLs with different numbers of segments	Use optional segments or catchall segments in the URL routing pattern.	17–19
Restricting matches	Use constraints in the URL routing pattern.	20–22, 24–27
Matching requests that are not otherwise handled	Define fallback routes.	23
Seeing which endpoint will handle a request	Use the routing context data.	28

13.1   *Preparing for this chapter*

In this chapter, I continue to use the `Platform` project from chapter 12. To prepare for this chapter, add a file called `Population.cs` to the `Platform` folder with the code shown in listing 13.1.

> **TIP**   You can download the example project for this chapter—and for all the other chapters in this book—from https://github.com/manningbooks/pro-asp .net-core-7. See chapter 1 for how to get help if you have problems running the examples.

Listing 13.1   The contents of the Population.cs file in the Platform folder

```
namespace Platform {
    public class Population {
        private RequestDelegate? next;

        public Population() { }

        public Population(RequestDelegate nextDelegate) {
            next = nextDelegate;
        }

        public async Task Invoke(HttpContext context) {
            string[] parts = context.Request.Path.ToString()
                .Split("/", StringSplitOptions.RemoveEmptyEntries);
            if (parts.Length == 2 && parts[0] == "population") {
                string city = parts[1];
                int? pop = null;
                switch (city.ToLower()) {
                    case "london":
                        pop = 8_136_000;
                        break;
                    case "paris":
                        pop = 2_141_000;
                        break;
                    case "monaco":
                        pop = 39_000;
                        break;
                }
                if (pop.HasValue) {
                    await context.Response
                        .WriteAsync($"City: {city}, Population: {pop}");
                    return;
                }
            }
            if (next != null) {
                await next(context);
            }
        }
    }
}
```

This middleware component responds to requests for /population/<city> where
<city> is london, paris, or monaco. The middleware component splits up the URL
path string, checks that it has the expected length, and uses a switch statement to
determine if it is a request for a URL that it can respond to. A response is generated if
the URL matches the pattern the middleware is looking for; otherwise, the request is
passed along the pipeline.

Add a class file named Capital.cs to the Platform folder with the code shown in
listing 13.2.

Listing 13.2   The contents of the Capital.cs file in the Platform folder

```
namespace Platform {
    public class Capital {
        private RequestDelegate? next;

        public Capital() { }

        public Capital(RequestDelegate nextDelegate) {
            next = nextDelegate;
        }

        public async Task Invoke(HttpContext context) {
            string[] parts = context.Request.Path.ToString()
                .Split("/", StringSplitOptions.RemoveEmptyEntries);
            if (parts.Length == 2 && parts[0] == "capital") {
                string? capital = null;
                string country = parts[1];
                switch (country.ToLower()) {
                    case "uk":
                        capital = "London";
                        break;
                    case "france":
                        capital = "Paris";
                        break;
                    case "monaco":
                        context.Response.Redirect(
                            $"/population/{country}");
                        return;
                }
                if (capital != null) {
                    await context.Response.WriteAsync(
                        $"{capital} is the capital of {country}");
                    return;
                }
            }
            if (next != null) {
                await next(context);
            }
        }
    }
}
```

This middleware component is looking for requests for /capital/<country>, where
<country> is uk, france, or monaco. The capital cities of the United Kingdom and
France are displayed, but requests for Monaco, which is a city and a state, are redirected to /population/monaco.

Listing 13.3 replaces the middleware examples from the previous chapter and adds
the new middleware components to the request pipeline.

Listing 13.3   **Replacing the contents of the Program.cs file in the Platform folder**

```
using Platform;

var builder = WebApplication.CreateBuilder(args);
var app = builder.Build();

app.UseMiddleware<Population>();
app.UseMiddleware<Capital>();
app.Run(async (context) => {
    await context.Response.WriteAsync("Terminal Middleware Reached");
});

app.Run();
```

Start ASP.NET Core by running the command shown in listing 13.4 in the `Platform` folder.

Listing 13.4   **Starting the ASP.NET Core Runtime**

```
dotnet run
```

Navigate to http://localhost:5000/population/london, and you will see the output on the left side of figure 13.1. Navigate to http://localhost:5000/capital/france to see the output from the other middleware component, which is shown on the right side of figure 13.1.

Figure 13.1   **Running the example application**

13.1.1 *Understanding URL routing*

Each middleware component decides whether to act on a request as it passes along the pipeline. Some components are looking for a specific header or query string value, but most components—especially terminal and short-circuiting components—are trying to match URLs.

Each middleware component has to repeat the same set of steps as the request works its way along the pipeline. You can see this in the middleware defined in the previous section, where both components go through the same process: split up the URL, check the number of parts, inspect the first part, and so on.

This approach is far from ideal. It is inefficient because the same set of operations is repeated by each middleware component to process the URL. It is difficult to maintain because the URL that each component is looking for is hidden in its code. It breaks easily because changes must be carefully worked through in multiple places. For example, the `Capital` component redirects requests to a URL whose path starts with `/population`, which is handled by the `Population` component. If the `Population` component is revised to support the `/size` URL instead, then this change must also be reflected in the `Capital` component. Real applications can support complex sets of URLs and working changes fully through individual middleware components can be difficult.

URL routing solves these problems by introducing middleware that takes care of matching request URLs so that components, called *endpoints,* can focus on responses. The mapping between endpoints and the URLs they require is expressed in a *route.* The routing middleware processes the URL, inspects the set of routes, and finds the endpoint to handle the request, a process known as *routing.*

13.1.2   *Adding the routing middleware and defining an endpoint*

The routing middleware is added using two separate methods: `UseRouting` and `UseEndpoints`. The `UseRouting` method adds the middleware responsible for processing requests to the pipeline. The `UseEndpoints` method is used to define the routes that match URLs to endpoints. URLs are matched using patterns that are compared to the path of request URLs, and each route creates a relationship between one URL pattern and one endpoint. Listing 13.5 shows the use of the routing middleware and contains a simple route.

> **TIP**   I explain why there are two methods for routing in the "Accessing the endpoint in a middleware component" section.

Listing 13.5   Using the routing middleware in the Program.cs file in the Platform folder

```
using Platform;

var builder = WebApplication.CreateBuilder(args);

var app = builder.Build();

app.UseMiddleware<Population>();
app.UseMiddleware<Capital>();

app.UseRouting();

#pragma warning disable ASP0014

app.UseEndpoints(endpoints => {
    endpoints.MapGet("routing", async context => {
        await context.Response.WriteAsync("Request Was Routed");
    });
});

app.Run(async (context) => {
    await context.Response.WriteAsync("Terminal Middleware Reached");
});

app.Run();
```

There are no arguments to the UseRouting method. The UseEndpoints method receives a function that accepts an IEndpointRouteBuilder object and uses it to create routes using the extension methods described in table 13.3.

The code in listing 13.5 contains a #pragma directive that prevents a compiler warning, which I explain in the next section.

TIP There are also extension methods that set up endpoints for other parts of ASP.NET Core, such as the MVC Framework, as explained in part 3.

Table 13.3 The IEndpointRouteBuilder extension methods

Name	Description
MapGet(pattern, endpoint)	This method routes HTTP GET requests that match the URL pattern to the endpoint.
MapPost(pattern, endpoint)	This method routes HTTP POST requests that match the URL pattern to the endpoint.
MapPut(pattern, endpoint)	This method routes HTTP PUT requests that match the URL pattern to the endpoint.
MapDelete(pattern, endpoint)	This method routes HTTP DELETE requests that match the URL pattern to the endpoint.
MapMethods(pattern, methods, endpoint)	This method routes requests made with one of the specified HTTP methods that match the URL pattern to the endpoint.
Map(pattern, endpoint)	This method routes all HTTP requests that match the URL pattern to the endpoint.

Endpoints are defined using RequestDelegate, which is the same delegate used by conventional middleware, so endpoints are asynchronous methods that receive an HttpContext object and use it to generate a response. This means that the features described in chapter 12 for middleware components can also be used in endpoints.

Restart ASP.NET Core and use a browser to request http://localhost:5000/routing to test the new route. When matching a request, the routing middleware applies the route's URL pattern to the path section of the URL. The path is separated from the hostname by the / character, as shown in figure 13.2.

Path

Figure 13.2 The URL path

The path in the URL matches the pattern specified in the route.

```
. . .
endpoints.MapGet("routing", async context => {
. . .
```

URL patterns are conventionally expressed without a leading / character, which isn't part of the URL path. When the request URL path matches the URL pattern, the request will be forwarded to the endpoint function, which generates the response shown in figure 13.3.

Figure 13.3   Using an endpoint to generate a response

The routing middleware short-circuits the pipeline when a route matches a URL so that the response is generated only by the route's endpoint. The request isn't forwarded to other endpoints or middleware components that appear later in the request pipeline.

If the request URL isn't matched by any route, then the routing middleware passes the request to the next middleware component in the request pipeline. To test this behavior, request the http://localhost:5000/notrouted URL, whose path doesn't match the pattern in the route defined in listing 13.5.

The routing middleware can't match the URL path to a route and forwards the request, which reaches the terminal middleware, producing the response shown in figure 13.4.

Figure 13.4   Requesting a URL for which there is no matching route

Endpoints generate responses in the same way as the middleware components demonstrated in earlier chapters: they receive an `HttpContext` object that provides access to the request and response through `HttpRequest` and `HttpResponse` objects. This means that any middleware component can also be used as an endpoint. Listing 13.6 adds a route that uses the `Capital` and `Population` middleware components as endpoints.

Listing 13.6 Using components as endpoints in the Program.cs file in the Platform folder

```
using Platform;

var builder = WebApplication.CreateBuilder(args);

var app = builder.Build();

//app.UseMiddleware<Population>();
//app.UseMiddleware<Capital>();

app.UseRouting();

#pragma warning disable ASP0014

app.UseEndpoints(endpoints => {
    endpoints.MapGet("routing", async context => {
        await context.Response.WriteAsync("Request Was Routed");
    });
    endpoints.MapGet("capital/uk", new Capital().Invoke);
    endpoints.MapGet("population/paris", new Population().Invoke);
});

app.Run(async (context) => {
    await context.Response.WriteAsync("Terminal Middleware Reached");
});

app.Run();
```

Using middleware components like this is awkward because I need to create new instances of the classes to select the Invoke method as the endpoint. The URL patterns used by the routes support only some of the URLs that the middleware components support, but it is useful to understand that endpoints rely on features that are familiar from earlier chapters. To test the new routes, restart ASP.NET Core and use a browser to request http://localhost:5000/capital/uk and http://localhost:5000/population/paris, which will produce the results shown in figure 13.5.

Figure 13.5 Using middleware components as endpoints

13.1.3 Simplifying the pipeline configuration

I demonstrated the use of the UseRouting and UseEndpoints method because I wanted to emphasize that routing builds on the standard pipeline features and is implemented using regular middleware components.

However, as part of a drive to simplify the configuration of ASP.NET Core applications, Microsoft automatically applies the `UseRouting` and `UseEndpoints` methods to the request pipeline, which means that the methods described in table 13.3 can be used directly on the `WebApplication` object returned by the `WebApplication` `.CreateBuilder` method, as shown in listing 13.7.

When you call the `UseEndpoints` method, the C# code analyzer generates a warning that suggests registering routes at the top level of the `Program.cs` file.

Listing 13.7   Simplifying the code in the Program.cs file in the Platform folder

```
using Platform;

var builder = WebApplication.CreateBuilder(args);

var app = builder.Build();

app.UseRouting();

//#pragma warning disable ASP0014

//app.UseEndpoints(endpoints => {
//    endpoints.MapGet("routing", async context => {
//        await context.Response.WriteAsync("Request Was Routed");
//    });
//    endpoints.MapGet("capital/uk", new Capital().Invoke);
//    endpoints.MapGet("population/paris", new Population().Invoke);
//});

app.MapGet("routing", async context => {
    await context.Response.WriteAsync("Request Was Routed");
});
app.MapGet("capital/uk", new Capital().Invoke);
app.MapGet("population/paris", new Population().Invoke);

//app.Run(async (context) => {
//    await context.Response.WriteAsync("Terminal Middleware Reached");
//});

app.Run();
```

The `WebApplication` class implements the `IEndpointRouteBuilder` interface, which means that endpoints can be created more concisely. Behind the scenes, the routing middleware is still responsible for matching requests and selecting routes.

Restart ASP.NET Core and use a browser to request http://localhost:5000/capital/ uk and http://localhost:5000/population/paris, which will produce the results shown in figure 13.5.

Avoiding the direct route registration pitfall

Notice that I have removed the terminal middleware component from the pipeline. In the previous example, the routing middleware I added to the pipeline explicitly would forward

(continued)

requests along the pipeline only if none of the routes matched. Defining routes directly, as in listing 13.7, changes this behavior so that requests are always forwarded, which means the terminal middleware will be used for every request.

I show you an alternative to the terminal middleware that is part of the URL routing system in the "Defining Fallback Routes" section, but it is important to understand that using the simplified pipeline configuration doesn't just reduce the amount of code in the `Program.cs` file and can alter the way that requests are processed.

13.1.4 *Understanding URL patterns*

Using middleware components as endpoints shows that URL routing builds on the standard ASP.NET Core platform features. Although the URLs that the application handles can be seen by examining the routes, not all of the URLs understood by the `Capital` and `Population` classes are routed, and there have been no efficiency gains since the URL is processed once by the routing middleware to select the route and again by the `Capital` or `Population` class to extract the data values they require.

Making improvements requires understanding more about how URL patterns are used. When a request arrives, the routing middleware processes the URL to extract the segments from its path, which are the sections of the path separated by the / character, as shown in figure 13.6.

Figure 13.6 The URL segments

The routing middleware also extracts the segments from the URL routing pattern, as shown in figure 13.7.

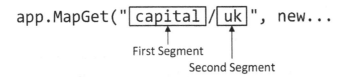

Figure 13.7 The URL pattern segments

To route a request, the segments from the URL pattern are compared to those from the request to see whether they match. The request is routed to the endpoint if its path contains the same number of segments and each segment has the same content as those in the URL pattern, as summarized in table 13.4.

Table 13.4   Matching URL segments

URL Path	Description
/capital	No match—too few segments
/capital/europe/uk	No match—too many segments
/name/uk	No match—first segment is not capital
/capital/uk	Matches

13.1.5 *Using segment variables in URL patterns*

The URL pattern used in listing 13.7 uses *literal segments,* also known as *static segments,* which match requests using fixed strings. The first segment in the pattern will match only those requests whose path has capital as the first segment, for example, and the second segment in the pattern will match only those requests whose second segment is uk. Put these together, and you can see why the route matches only those requests whose path is /capital/uk.

Segment variables, also known as *route parameters,* expand the range of path segments that a pattern segment will match, allowing more flexible routing. Segment variables are given a name and are denoted by curly braces (the { and } characters), as shown in listing 13.8.

Listing 13.8   Using segment variables in the Program.cs file in the Platform folder

```
using Platform;

var builder = WebApplication.CreateBuilder(args);

var app = builder.Build();

app.MapGet("{first}/{second}/{third}", async context => {
    await context.Response.WriteAsync("Request Was Routed\n");
    foreach (var kvp in context.Request.RouteValues) {
        await context.Response
            .WriteAsync($"{kvp.Key}: {kvp.Value}\n");
    }
});
app.MapGet("capital/uk", new Capital().Invoke);
app.MapGet("population/paris", new Population().Invoke);

app.Run();
```

The URL pattern {first}/{second}/{third} matches URLs whose path contains three segments, regardless of what those segments contain. When a segment variable is used, the routing middleware provides the endpoint with the contents of the URL path segment they have matched. This content is available through the HttpRequest .RouteValues property, which returns a RouteValuesDictionary object. Table 13.5 describes the most useful RouteValuesDictionary members.

TIP There are reserved words that cannot be used as the names for segment variables: `action`, `area`, `controller`, `handler`, and `page`.

Table 13.5 Useful RouteValuesDictionary members

Name	Description
`[key]`	The class defines an indexer that allows values to be retrieved by key.
`Keys`	This property returns the collection of segment variable names.
`Values`	This property returns the collection of segment variable values.
`Count`	This property returns the number of segment variables.
`ContainsKey(key)`	This method returns `true` if the route data contains a value for the specified key.

The `RouteValuesDictionary` class is enumerable, which means that it can be used in a `foreach` loop to generate a sequence of `KeyValuePair<string, object>` objects, each of which corresponds to the name of a segment variable and the corresponding value extracted from the request URL. The endpoint in listing 13.8 enumerates the `HttpRequest.RouteValues` property to generate a response that lists the names and values of the segment variables matched by the URL pattern.

The names of the segment variables are `first`, `second`, and `third`, and you can see the values extracted from the URL by restarting ASP.NET Core and requesting any three-segment URL, such as http://localhost:5000/apples/oranges/cherries, which produces the response shown in figure 13.8.

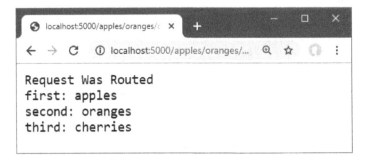

Figure 13.8 Using segment variables

Understanding route selection

When processing a request, the middleware finds all the routes that can match the request and gives each a score, and the route with the lowest score is selected to handle the route. The scoring process is complex, but the effect is that the most specific route receives the request. This means literal segments are given preference over segment

(continued)

variables and that segment variables with constraints are given preference over those without (constraints are described in the "Constraining Segment Matching" section later in this chapter). The scoring system can produce surprising results, and you should check to make sure that the URLs supported by your application are matched by the routes you expect.

If two routes have the same score, meaning they are equally suited to routing the request, then an exception will be thrown, indicating an ambiguous routing selection. See the "Avoiding Ambiguous Route Exceptions" section later in the chapter for details of how to avoid ambiguous routes.

REFACTORING MIDDLEWARE INTO AN ENDPOINT

Endpoints usually rely on the routing middleware to provide specific segment variables, rather than enumerating all the segment variables. By relying on the URL pattern to provide a specific value, I can refactor the `Capital` and `Population` classes to depend on the route data, as shown in listing 13.9.

Listing 13.9   Depending on the route data in the Capital.cs file in the Platform folder

```
namespace Platform {
    public class Capital {

        public static async Task Endpoint(HttpContext context) {
            string? capital = null;
            string? country
                = context.Request.RouteValues["country"] as string;
            switch ((country ?? "").ToLower()) {
                case "uk":
                    capital = "London";
                    break;
                case "france":
                    capital = "Paris";
                    break;
                case "monaco":
                    context.Response.Redirect($"/population/{country}");
                    return;
            }
            if (capital != null) {
                await context.Response
                    .WriteAsync($"{capital} is the capital of {country}");
            } else {
                context.Response.StatusCode
                    = StatusCodes.Status404NotFound;
            }
        }
    }
}
```

Middleware components can be used as endpoints, but the opposite isn't true once there is a dependency on the data provided by the routing middleware. In listing 13.9,

I used the route data to get the value of a segment variable named `country` through the indexer defined by the `RouteValuesDictionary` class.

```
...
string country = context.Request.RouteValues["country"] as string;
...
```

The indexer returns an `object` value that is cast to a `string` using the `as` keyword. The listing removes the statements that pass the request along the pipeline, which the routing middleware handles on behalf of endpoints.

The use of the segment variable means that requests may be routed to the endpoint with values that are not supported, so I added a statement that returns a 404 status code for countries the endpoint doesn't understand.

I also removed the constructors and replaced the `Invoke` instance method with a `static` method named `Endpoint`, which better fits with the way that endpoints are used in routes. Listing 13.10 applies the same set of changes to the `Population` class, transforming it from a standard middleware component into an endpoint that depends on the routing middleware to process URLs.

> **Listing 13.10   Depending on route data in the Population.cs file in the Platform folder**

```
namespace Platform {
    public class Population {

        public static async Task Endpoint(HttpContext context) {
            string? city = context.Request.RouteValues["city"] as string;
            int? pop = null;
            switch ((city ?? "").ToLower()) {
                case "london":
                    pop = 8_136_000;
                    break;
                case "paris":
                    pop = 2_141_000;
                    break;
                case "monaco":
                    pop = 39_000;
                    break;
            }
            if (pop.HasValue) {
                await context.Response
                    .WriteAsync($"City: {city}, Population: {pop}");
            } else {
                context.Response.StatusCode
                    = StatusCodes.Status404NotFound;
            }
        }
    }
}
```

The change to static methods tidies up the use of the endpoints when defining routes, as shown in listing 13.11.

Listing 13.11   Updating routes in the Program.cs file in the Platform folder

```
using Platform;

var builder = WebApplication.CreateBuilder(args);

var app = builder.Build();

app.MapGet("{first}/{second}/{third}", async context => {
    await context.Response.WriteAsync("Request Was Routed\n");
    foreach (var kvp in context.Request.RouteValues) {
        await context.Response
            .WriteAsync($"{kvp.Key}: {kvp.Value}\n");
    }
});

app.MapGet("capital/{country}", Capital.Endpoint);
app.MapGet("population/{city}", Population.Endpoint);

app.Run();
```

The new routes match URLs whose path has two segments, the first of which is `capital` or `population`. The contents of the second segment are assigned to the segment variables named `country` and `city`, allowing the endpoints to support the full set of URLs that were handled at the start of the chapter, without the need to process the URL directly. To test the new routes, restart ASP.NET Core and request http://localhost:5000/capital/uk and http://localhost:5000/population/london, which will produce the responses shown in figure 13.9.

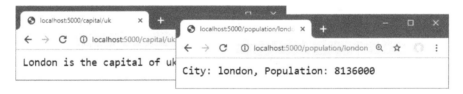

Figure 13.9   Using segment variables in endpoints

These changes address two of the problems I described at the start of the chapter. Efficiency has improved because the URL is processed only once by the routing middleware and not by multiple components. And it is easier to see the URLs that each endpoint supports because the URL patterns show how requests will be matched.

13.1.6   *Generating URLs from routes*

The final problem was the difficulty in making changes. The `Capital` endpoint still has a hardwired dependency on the URL that the `Population` endpoint supports. To break this dependency, the routing system allows URLs to be generated by supplying data values for segment variables. The first step is to assign a name to the route that will be the target of the URL that is generated, as shown in listing 13.12.

Listing 13.12 Naming a route in the Program.cs file in the Platform folder

```
using Platform;

var builder = WebApplication.CreateBuilder(args);

var app = builder.Build();

app.MapGet("{first}/{second}/{third}", async context => {
    await context.Response.WriteAsync("Request Was Routed\n");
    foreach (var kvp in context.Request.RouteValues) {
        await context.Response
            .WriteAsync($"{kvp.Key}: {kvp.Value}\n");
    }
});

app.MapGet("capital/{country}", Capital.Endpoint);
app.MapGet("population/{city}", Population.Endpoint)
    .WithMetadata(new RouteNameMetadata("population"));

app.Run();
```

The `WithMetadata` method is used on the result from the `MapGet` method to assign metadata to the route. The only metadata required for generating URLs is a name, which is assigned by passing a new `RouteNameMetadata` object, whose constructor argument specifies the name that will be used to refer to the route. The effect of the change in the listing is to assign the route the name `population`.

TIP Naming routes helps to avoid links being generated that target a route other than the one you expect, but they can be omitted, in which case the routing system will try to find the best matching route.

In listing 13.13, I have revised the `Capital` endpoint to remove the direct dependency on the /population URL and rely on the routing features to generate a URL.

Listing 13.13 Generating a URL in the Capital.cs file in the Platform folder

```
namespace Platform {
    public class Capital {

        public static async Task Endpoint(HttpContext context) {
            string? capital = null;
            string? country
                = context.Request.RouteValues["country"] as string;
            switch ((country ?? "").ToLower()) {
                case "uk":
                    capital = "London";
                    break;
                case "france":
                    capital = "Paris";
                    break;
                case "monaco":
                    LinkGenerator? generator =
```

```
                    context.RequestServices.GetService<LinkGenerator>();
                string? url = generator?.GetPathByRouteValues(context,
                    "population", new { city = country });
                if (url != null) {
                    context.Response.Redirect(url);
                }
                return;
            }
            if (capital != null) {
                await context.Response
                    .WriteAsync($"{capital} is the capital of {country}");
            } else {
                context.Response.StatusCode
                    = StatusCodes.Status404NotFound;
            }
        }
    }
}
```

URLs are generated using the `LinkGenerator` class. You can't just create a new `Link-Generator` instance; one must be obtained using the dependency injection feature that is described in chapter 14. For this chapter, it is enough to know that this statement obtains the `LinkGenerator` object that the endpoint will use:

```
...
LinkGenerator? generator =
    context.RequestServices.GetService<LinkGenerator>();
...
```

The `LinkGenerator` class provides the `GetPathByRouteValues` method, which is used to generate the URL that will be used in the redirection.

```
...
generator?.GetPathByRouteValues(context, "population",
    new { city = country });
...
```

The arguments to the `GetPathByRouteValues` method are the endpoint's `Http-Context` object, the name of the route that will be used to generate the link, and an object that is used to provide values for the segment variables. The `GetPathByRouteValues` method returns a URL that will be routed to the `Population` endpoint, which can be confirmed by restarting ASP.NET Core and requesting the http://localhost:5000/capital/monaco URL. The request will be routed to the `Capital` endpoint, which will generate the URL and use it to redirect the browser, producing the result shown in figure 13.10.

Figure 13.10   Generating a URL

The benefit of this approach is that the URL is generated from the URL pattern in the named route, which means a change in the URL pattern is reflected in the generated URLs, without the need to make changes to endpoints. To demonstrate, listing 13.14 changes the URL pattern.

Listing 13.14   Changing a URL pattern in the Program.cs file in the Platform folder

```
using Platform;

var builder = WebApplication.CreateBuilder(args);

var app = builder.Build();

app.MapGet("{first}/{second}/{third}", async context => {
    await context.Response.WriteAsync("Request Was Routed\n");
    foreach (var kvp in context.Request.RouteValues) {
        await context.Response
            .WriteAsync($"{kvp.Key}: {kvp.Value}\n");
    }
});

app.MapGet("capital/{country}", Capital.Endpoint);
app.MapGet("size/{city}", Population.Endpoint)
    .WithMetadata(new RouteNameMetadata("population"));

app.Run();
```

The name assigned to the route is unchanged, which ensures that the same endpoint is targeted by the generated URL. To see the effect of the new pattern, restart ASP.NET Core and request the http://localhost:5000/capital/monaco URL again. The redirection is to a URL that is matched by the modified pattern, as shown in figure 13.11. This feature addresses the final problem that I described at the start of the chapter, making it easy to change the URLs that an application supports.

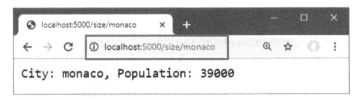

Figure 13.11   Changing the URL pattern

URL routing and areas

The URL routing system supports a feature called *areas*, which allows separate sections of the application to have their own controllers, views, and Razor Pages. I have not described the areas feature in this book because it is not widely used, and when it is used, it tends to cause more problems than it solves. If you want to break up an application, then I recommend creating separate projects.

13.2   *Managing URL matching*

The previous section introduced the basic URL routing features, but most applications require more work to ensure that URLs are routed correctly, either to increase or to restrict the range of URLs that are matched by a route. In the sections that follow, I show you the different ways that URL patterns can be adjusted to fine-tune the matching process.

13.2.1   *Matching multiple values from a single URL segment*

Most segment variables correspond directly to a segment in the URL path, but the routing middleware is able to perform more complex matches, allowing a single segment to be matched to a variable while discarding unwanted characters. Listing 13.15 defines a route that matches only part of a URL segment to a variable.

> Listing 13.15   Matching part of a segment in the Program.cs file in the Platform folder

```
using Platform;

var builder = WebApplication.CreateBuilder(args);

var app = builder.Build();

app.MapGet("files/{filename}.{ext}", async context => {
    await context.Response.WriteAsync("Request Was Routed\n");
    foreach (var kvp in context.Request.RouteValues) {
        await context.Response
            .WriteAsync($"{kvp.Key}: {kvp.Value}\n");
    }
});

app.MapGet("capital/{country}", Capital.Endpoint);
app.MapGet("size/{city}", Population.Endpoint)
    .WithMetadata(new RouteNameMetadata("population"));

app.Run();
```

A URL pattern can contain as many segment variables as you need, as long as they are separated by a static string. The requirement for a static separator is so the routing middleware knows where the content for one variable ends and the content for the next starts. The pattern in listing 13.15 matches segment variables named `filename` and `ext`, which are separated by a period; this pattern is often used by process file names. To see how the pattern matches URLs, restart ASP.NET Core and request the http://localhost:5000/files/myfile.txt URL, which will produce the response shown in figure 13.12.

Figure 13.12 Matching multiple values from a single path segment

---

Avoiding the complex pattern mismatching pitfall

The order of the segment variables in figure 13.12 shows that pattern segments that contain multiple variables are matched from right to left. This isn't important most of the time, because endpoints can't rely on a specific key order, but it does show that complex URL patterns are handled differently, which reflects the difficulty in matching them.

In fact, the matching process is so difficult that there can be unexpected matching failures. The specific failures change with each release of ASP.NET Core as the matching process is adjusted to address problems, but the adjustments often introduce new issues. At the time of writing, there is a problem with URL patterns where the content that should be matched by the first variable also appears as a literal string at the start of a segment. This is easier to understand with an example, as shown here:

```
...
app.MapGet("example/red{color}", async context => {
...
```

This pattern has a segment that begins with the literal string `red`, followed by a segment variable named `color`. The routing middleware will correctly match the pattern against the URL path `example/redgreen`, and the value of the `color` route variable will be `green`. However, the URL path `example/redredgreen` won't match because the matching process confuses the position of the literal content with the first part of the content that should be assigned to the `color` variable. This problem may be fixed by the time you read this book, but there will be other issues with complex patterns. It is a good idea to keep URL patterns as simple as possible and make sure you get the matching results you expect.

13.2.2 *Using default values for segment variables*

Patterns can be defined with default values that are used when the URL doesn't contain a value for the corresponding segment, increasing the range of URLs that a route can match. Listing 13.16 shows the use of default values in a pattern.

Listing 13.16   Using Default Values in the Program.cs File in the Platform Folder

```
using Platform;

var builder = WebApplication.CreateBuilder(args);

var app = builder.Build();

app.MapGet("files/{filename}.{ext}", async context => {
    await context.Response.WriteAsync("Request Was Routed\n");
    foreach (var kvp in context.Request.RouteValues) {
        await context.Response
            .WriteAsync($"{kvp.Key}: {kvp.Value}\n");
    }
});

app.MapGet("capital/{country=France}", Capital.Endpoint);
app.MapGet("size/{city}", Population.Endpoint)
    .WithMetadata(new RouteNameMetadata("population"));

app.Run();
```

Default values are defined using an equal sign and the value to be used. The default value in the listing uses the value `France` when there is no second segment in the URL path. The result is that the range of URLs that can be matched by the route increases, as described in table 13.6.

Table 13.6   Matching URLs

URL Path	Description
/	No match—too few segments
/city	No match—first segment isn't `capital`
/capital	Matches, `country` variable is France
/capital/uk	Matches, `country` variable is `uk`
/capital/europe/italy	No match—too many segments

To test the default value, restart ASP.NET Core and navigate to http://localhost:5000/capital, which will produce the result shown in figure 13.13.

Figure 13.13   Using a default value for a segment variable

13.2.3 *Using optional segments in a URL Pattern*

Default values allow URLs to be matched with fewer segments, but the use of the default value isn't obvious to the endpoint. Some endpoints define their own responses to deal with URLs that omit segments, for which *optional segments* are used. To prepare, listing 13.17 updates the Population endpoint so that it uses a default value when no city value is available in the routing data.

Listing 13.17 Using a default value in the Population.cs file in the Platform folder

```
namespace Platform {
    public class Population {

        public static async Task Endpoint(HttpContext context) {
            string city = context.Request.RouteValues["city"]
                as string ?? "london";
            int? pop = null;
            switch (city.ToLower()) {
                case "london":
                    pop = 8_136_000;
                    break;
                case "paris":
                    pop = 2_141_000;
                    break;
                case "monaco":
                    pop = 39_000;
                    break;
            }
            if (pop.HasValue) {
                await context.Response
                    .WriteAsync($"City: {city}, Population: {pop}");
            } else {
                context.Response.StatusCode
                    = StatusCodes.Status404NotFound;
            }
        }
    }
}
```

The change uses london as the default value because there is no city segment variable available. Listing 13.18 updates the route for the Population endpoint to make the second segment optional.

Listing 13.18 Using an optional segment in the Program.cs file in the Platform folder

```
using Platform;

var builder = WebApplication.CreateBuilder(args);

var app = builder.Build();

app.MapGet("files/{filename}.{ext}", async context => {
    await context.Response.WriteAsync("Request Was Routed\n");
```

```
    foreach (var kvp in context.Request.RouteValues) {
        await context.Response
            .WriteAsync($"{kvp.Key}: {kvp.Value}\n");
    }
});

app.MapGet("capital/{country=France}", Capital.Endpoint);
app.MapGet("size/{city?}", Population.Endpoint)
    .WithMetadata(new RouteNameMetadata("population"));

app.Run();
```

Optional segments are denoted with a question mark (the ? character) after the variable name and allow the route to match URLs that don't have a corresponding path segment, as described in table 13.7.

Table 13.7   Matching URLs

URL Path	Description
/	No match—too few segments.
/city	No match—first segment isn't `size`.
/size	Matches. No value for the `city` variable is provided to the endpoint.
/size/paris	Matches, `city` variable is `paris`.
/size/europe/italy	No match—too many segments.

To test the optional segment, restart ASP.NET Core and navigate to http://localhost:5000/size, which will produce the response shown in figure 13.14.

Figure 13.14   Using an optional segment

13.2.4 *Using a catchall segment variable*

Optional segments allow a pattern to match shorter URL paths. A *catchall* segment does the opposite and allows routes to match URLs that contain more segments than the pattern. A catchall segment is denoted with an asterisk before the variable name, as shown in listing 13.19.

Listing 13.19 Using a catchall segment in the Program.cs file in the Platform folder

```
using Platform;

var builder = WebApplication.CreateBuilder(args);

var app = builder.Build();

app.MapGet("{first}/{second}/{*catchall}", async context => {
    await context.Response.WriteAsync("Request Was Routed\n");
    foreach (var kvp in context.Request.RouteValues) {
        await context.Response
            .WriteAsync($"{kvp.Key}: {kvp.Value}\n");
    }
});

app.MapGet("capital/{country=France}", Capital.Endpoint);
app.MapGet("size/{city?}", Population.Endpoint)
    .WithMetadata(new RouteNameMetadata("population"));

app.Run();
```

The new pattern contains two-segment variables and a catchall, and the result is that the route will match any URL whose path contains two or more segments. There is no upper limit to the number of segments that the URL pattern in this route will match, and the contents of any additional segments are assigned to the segment variable named `catchall`. Restart ASP.NET Core and navigate to http://localhost:5000/one/two/three/four, which produces the response shown in figure 13.15.

> **TIP** Notice that the segments captured by the catchall are presented in the form *segment/ segment/ segment* and that the endpoint is responsible for processing the string to break out the individual segments.

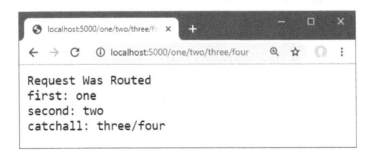

Figure 13.15 Using a catchall segment variable

13.2.5 *Constraining segment matching*

Default values, optional segments, and catchall segments all increase the range of URLs that a route will match. Constraints have the opposite effect and restrict matches. This can be useful if an endpoint can deal only with specific segment contents or if you want to differentiate matching closely related URLs for different endpoints. Constraints are applied by a colon (the : character) and a constraint type after a segment variable name, as shown in listing 13.20.

> **Listing 13.20   Applying constraints in the Program.cs file in the Platform folder**

```
using Platform;

var builder = WebApplication.CreateBuilder(args);

var app = builder.Build();

app.MapGet("{first:int}/{second:bool}", async context => {
    await context.Response.WriteAsync("Request Was Routed\n");
    foreach (var kvp in context.Request.RouteValues) {
        await context.Response
            .WriteAsync($"{kvp.Key}: {kvp.Value}\n");
    }
});

app.MapGet("capital/{country=France}", Capital.Endpoint);
app.MapGet("size/{city?}", Population.Endpoint)
    .WithMetadata(new RouteNameMetadata("population"));

app.Run();
```

This example constrains the first segment variable so it will match only the path segments that can be parsed to an `int` value, and it constrains the second segment so it will match only the path segments that can be parsed to a `bool`. Values that don't match the constraints won't be matched by the route. Table 13.8 describes the URL pattern constraints.

> **NOTE**   Some of the constraints match types whose format can differ based on locale. The routing middleware doesn't handle localized formats and will match only those values that are expressed in the invariant culture format.

Table 13.8   The URL pattern constraints

Constraint	Description
alpha	This constraint matches the letters *a* to *z* (and is case-insensitive).
bool	This constraint matches `true` and `false` (and is case-insensitive).
datetime	This constraint matches `DateTime` values, expressed in the nonlocalized invariant culture format.
decimal	This constraint matches `decimal` values, formatted in the nonlocalized invariant culture.
double	This constraint matches `double` values, formatted in the nonlocalized invariant culture.
file	This constraint matches segments whose content represents a file name, in the form `name.ext`. The existence of the file is not validated.
float	This constraint matches `float` values, formatted in the nonlocalized invariant culture.
guid	This constraint matches `GUID` values.
int	This constraint matches `int` values.
length(len)	This constraint matches path segments that have the specified number of characters.
length(min, max)	This constraint matches path segments whose length falls between the lower and upper values specified.
long	This constraint matches `long` values.
max(val)	This constraint matches path segments that can be parsed to an `int` value that is less than or equal to the specified value.
maxlength(len)	This constraint matches path segments whose length is equal to or less than the specified value.
min(val)	This constraint matches path segments that can be parsed to an `int` value that is more than or equal to the specified value.
minlength(len)	This constraint matches path segments whose length is equal to or more than the specified value.
nonfile	This constraint matches segments that do not represent a file name, i.e., values that would not be matched by the `file` constraint.
range(min, max)	This constraint matches path segments that can be parsed to an `int` value that falls between the inclusive range specified.
regex(expression)	This constraint applies a regular expression to match path segments.

To test the constraints, restart ASP.NET Core and request http://localhost:5000/100/ true, which is a URL whose path segments conform to the constraints in listing 13.20 and that produces the result shown on the left side of figure 13.16. Request http:// localhost:5000/apples/oranges, which has the right number of segments but contains values that don't conform to the constraints. None of the routes matches the request, which is forwarded to the terminal middleware, as shown on the right of figure 13.16.

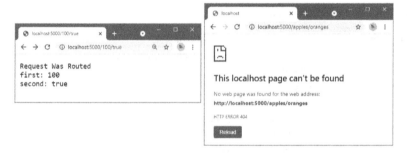

Figure 13.16   Testing constraints

Constraints can be combined to further restrict matching, as shown in listing 13.21.

Listing 13.21   Combining URL pattern constraints in the Program.cs file in the Platform folder

```
using Platform;

var builder = WebApplication.CreateBuilder(args);

var app = builder.Build();

app.MapGet("{first:alpha:length(3)}/{second:bool}", async context => {
    await context.Response.WriteAsync("Request Was Routed\n");
    foreach (var kvp in context.Request.RouteValues) {
        await context.Response
            .WriteAsync($"{kvp.Key}: {kvp.Value}\n");
    }
});

app.MapGet("capital/{country=France}", Capital.Endpoint);
app.MapGet("size/{city?}", Population.Endpoint)
    .WithMetadata(new RouteNameMetadata("population"));

app.Run();
```

The constraints are combined, and only path segments that can satisfy all the constraints will be matched. The combination in listing 13.21 constrains the URL pattern so that the first segment will match only three alphabetic characters. To test the pattern, restart ASP.NET Core and request http://localhost:5000/dog/true, which will produce the output shown in figure 13.17. Requesting the URL http://localhost:5000/dogs/true won't match the route because the first segment contains four characters.

**Figure 13.17
Combining
constraints**

CONSTRAINING MATCHING TO A SPECIFIC SET OF VALUES

The `regex` constraint applies a regular expression, which provides the basis for one of the most commonly required restrictions: matching only a specific set of values. In listing 13.22, I have applied the regex constraint to the routes for the `Capital` endpoint, so it will receive requests only for the values it can process.

> #### Listing 13.22 Matching specific values in the Program.cs file in the Platform folder

```
using Platform;

var builder = WebApplication.CreateBuilder(args);

var app = builder.Build();

app.MapGet("{first:alpha:length(3)}/{second:bool}", async context => {
    await context.Response.WriteAsync("Request Was Routed\n");
    foreach (var kvp in context.Request.RouteValues) {
        await context.Response
            .WriteAsync($"{kvp.Key}: {kvp.Value}\n");
    }
});

app.MapGet("capital/{country:regex(^uk|france|monaco$)}",
    Capital.Endpoint);
app.MapGet("size/{city?}", Population.Endpoint)
    .WithMetadata(new RouteNameMetadata("population"));

app.Run();
```

The route will match only those URLs with two segments. The first segment must be `capital`, and the second segment must be `uk`, `france`, or `monaco`. Regular expressions are case-insensitive, which you can confirm by restarting ASP.NET Core and requesting http://localhost:5000/capital/UK, which will produce the result shown in figure 13.18.

> **TIP** You may find that your browser requests /capital/uk, with a lowercase `uk`. If this happens, clear your browser history, and try again.

Figure 13.18. Matching specific values with a regular expression

13.2.6 Defining fallback routes

Fallback routes direct a request to an endpoint only when no other route matches a request. Fallback routes prevent requests from being passed further along the request pipeline by ensuring that the routing system will always generate a response, as shown in listing 13.23.

Listing 13.23   Using a fallback route in the Program.cs file in the Platform folder

```
using Platform;

var builder = WebApplication.CreateBuilder(args);

var app = builder.Build();

app.MapGet("{first:alpha:length(3)}/{second:bool}", async context => {
    await context.Response.WriteAsync("Request Was Routed\n");
    foreach (var kvp in context.Request.RouteValues) {
        await context.Response
            .WriteAsync($"{kvp.Key}: {kvp.Value}\n");
    }
});

app.MapGet("capital/{country:regex(^uk|france|monaco$)}",
    Capital.Endpoint);
app.MapGet("size/{city?}", Population.Endpoint)
    .WithMetadata(new RouteNameMetadata("population"));

app.MapFallback(async context => {
    await context.Response.WriteAsync("Routed to fallback endpoint");
});

app.Run();
```

The `MapFallback` method creates a route that will be used as a last resort and that will match any request. Table 13.9 describes the methods for creating fallback routes. (There are also methods for creating fallback routes that are specific to other parts of ASP.NET Core and that are described in part 3.)

Table 13.9. The methods for creating fallback routes

Name	Description
MapFallback(endpoint)	This method creates a fallback that routes requests to an endpoint.
MapFallbackToFile(path)	This method creates a fallback that routes requests to a file.

With the addition of the route in listing 13.23, the routing middleware will handle all requests, including those that match none of the regular routes. Restart ASP.NET Core and navigate to a URL that won't be matched by any of the routes, such as http://localhost:5000/notmatched, and you will see the response shown in figure 13.19.

Figure 13.19.   Using a fallback route

13.3   *Advanced routing features*

The routing features described in the previous sections address the needs of most projects, especially since they are usually accessed through higher-level features such as the MVC Framework, described in part 3. There are some advanced features for projects that have unusual routing requirements, which I describe in the following sections.

13.3.1   *Creating custom constraints*

If the constraints described in table 13.8 are not sufficient, you can define your own custom constraints by implementing the IRouteConstraint interface. To create a custom constraint, add a file named CountryRouteConstraint.cs to the Platform folder and add the code shown in listing 13.24.

> **Listing 13.24   The contents of the CountryRouteConstraint.cs file in the Platform folder**

```
namespace Platform {

    public class CountryRouteConstraint : IRouteConstraint {
        private static string[] countries = { "uk", "france", "monaco" };

        public bool Match(HttpContext? httpContext, IRouter? route,
                string routeKey, RouteValueDictionary values,
                RouteDirection routeDirection) {
            string segmentValue = values[routeKey] as string ?? "";
            return Array.IndexOf(countries, segmentValue.ToLower()) > -1;
        }
    }
}
```

The IRouteConstraint interface defines the Match method, which is called to allow a constraint to decide whether a request should be matched by the route. The parameters for the Match method provide the HttpContext object for the request, the route, the name of the segment, the segment variables extracted from the URL, and whether the request is to check for an incoming or outgoing URL. The Match method returns true if the constraint is satisfied by the request and false if it is not. The constraint in listing 13.24 defines a set of countries that are compared to the value of the segment variable to which the constraint has been applied. The constraint is satisfied if the segment matches one of the countries. Custom constraints are set up using the options pattern, as shown in listing 13.25. (The options pattern is described in chapter 12.)

Listing 13.25   Using a custom constraint in the Program.cs file in the Platform folder

```
using Platform;

var builder = WebApplication.CreateBuilder(args);

builder.Services.Configure<RouteOptions>(opts => {
    opts.ConstraintMap.Add("countryName",
        typeof(CountryRouteConstraint));
});

var app = builder.Build();

app.MapGet("capital/{country:countryName}", Capital.Endpoint);

app.MapGet("capital/{country:regex(^uk|france|monaco$)}",
    Capital.Endpoint);
app.MapGet("size/{city?}", Population.Endpoint)
    .WithMetadata(new RouteNameMetadata("population"));

app.MapFallback(async context => {
    await context.Response.WriteAsync("Routed to fallback endpoint");
});

app.Run();
```

The options pattern is applied to the `RouteOptions` class, which defines the `ConstraintMap` property. Each constraint is registered with a key that allows it to be applied in URL patterns. In listing 13.25, the key for the `CountryRouteConstraint` class is `countryName`, which allows me to constrain a route like this:

```
...
endpoints.MapGet("capital/{country:countryName}", Capital.Endpoint);
...
```

Requests will be matched by this route only when the first segment of the URL is `capital` and the second segment is one of the countries defined in listing 13.24.

13.3.2 *Avoiding ambiguous route exceptions*

When trying to route a request, the routing middleware assigns each route a score. As explained earlier in the chapter, precedence is given to more specific routes, and route selection is usually a straightforward process that behaves predictably, albeit with the occasional surprise if you don't think through and test the full range of URLs the application will support.

If two routes have the same score, the routing system can't choose between them and throws an exception, indicating that the routes are ambiguous. In most cases, the best approach is to modify the ambiguous routes to increase specificity by introducing literal segments or a constraint. There are some situations where that won't be possible, and some extra work is required to get the routing system to work as intended. Listing 13.26 replaces the routes from the previous example with two new routes that are ambiguous, but only for some requests.

Listing 13.26   Defining ambiguous routes in the Program.cs file in the Platform folder

```
using Platform;

var builder = WebApplication.CreateBuilder(args);

builder.Services.Configure<RouteOptions>(opts => {
    opts.ConstraintMap.Add("countryName",
        typeof(CountryRouteConstraint));
});

var app = builder.Build();

app.Map("{number:int}", async context => {
    await context.Response.WriteAsync("Routed to the int endpoint");
});
app.Map("{number:double}", async context => {
    await context.Response
        .WriteAsync("Routed to the double endpoint");
});

app.MapFallback(async context => {
    await context.Response.WriteAsync("Routed to fallback endpoint");
});

app.Run();
```

These routes are ambiguous only for some values. Only one route matches URLs where the first path segment can be parsed to a double, but both routes match for where the segment can be parsed as an `int` or a `double`. To see the issue, restart ASP.NET Core and request http://localhost:5000/23.5. The path segment `23.5` can be parsed to a `double` and produces the response shown on the left side of figure 13.20. Request http://localhost:5000/23, and you will see the exception shown on the right of figure 13.20. The segment `23` can be parsed as both an `int` and a `double`, which means that the routing system cannot identify a single route to handle the request.

Figure 13.20   An occasionally ambiguous routing configuration

For these situations, preference can be given to a route by defining its order relative to other matching routes, as shown in listing 13.27.

Listing 13.27   Breaking route ambiguity in the Program.cs file in the Platform folder

```
using Platform;

var builder = WebApplication.CreateBuilder(args);

builder.Services.Configure<RouteOptions>(opts => {
    opts.ConstraintMap.Add("countryName",
        typeof(CountryRouteConstraint));
});

var app = builder.Build();

app.Map("{number:int}", async context => {
    await context.Response.WriteAsync("Routed to the int endpoint");
}).Add(b => ((RouteEndpointBuilder)b).Order = 1);

app.Map("{number:double}", async context => {
    await context.Response
        .WriteAsync("Routed to the double endpoint");
}).Add(b => ((RouteEndpointBuilder)b).Order = 2);

app.MapFallback(async context => {
    await context.Response.WriteAsync("Routed to fallback endpoint");
});

app.Run();
```

The process is awkward and requires a call to the `Add` method, casting to a `Route-EndpointBuilder` and setting the value of the `Order` property. Precedence is given to the route with the lowest `Order` value, which means that these changes tell the routing system to use the first route for URLs that both routes can handle. Restart ASP.NET Core and request the http://localhost:5000/23 URL again, and you will see that the first route handles the request, as shown in figure 13.21.

Figure 13.21   Avoiding ambiguous routes

13.3.3   *Accessing the endpoint in a middleware component*

As earlier chapters demonstrated, not all middleware generates responses. Some components provide features used later in the request pipeline, such as the session middleware, or enhance the response in some way, such as status code middleware.

One limitation of the normal request pipeline is that a middleware component at the start of the pipeline can't tell which of the later components will generate a response. The routing middleware does something different.

As I demonstrated at the start of the chapter, routing is set up by calling the Use-Routing and UseEndpoints methods, either explicitly or relying on the ASP.NET Core platform to call them during startup.

Although routes are registered in the UseEndpoints method, the selection of a route is done in the UseRouting method, and the endpoint is executed to generate a response in the UseEndpoints method. Any middleware component that is added to the request pipeline between the UseRouting method and the UseEndpoints method can see which endpoint has been selected before the response is generated and alter its behavior accordingly.

In listing 13.28, I have added a middleware component that adds different messages to the response based on the route that has been selected to handle the request.

> **Listing 13.28 Adding a middleware component in the Program.cs file in the Platform folder**

```
using Platform;

var builder = WebApplication.CreateBuilder(args);

builder.Services.Configure<RouteOptions>(opts => {
    opts.ConstraintMap.Add("countryName",
        typeof(CountryRouteConstraint));
});

var app = builder.Build();

app.Use(async (context, next) => {
    Endpoint? end = context.GetEndpoint();
    if (end != null) {
        await context.Response
            .WriteAsync($"{end.DisplayName} Selected \n");
    } else {
        await context.Response.WriteAsync("No Endpoint Selected \n");
    }
    await next();
});

app.Map("{number:int}", async context => {
    await context.Response.WriteAsync("Routed to the int endpoint");
}).WithDisplayName("Int Endpoint")
    .Add(b => ((RouteEndpointBuilder)b).Order = 1);

app.Map("{number:double}", async context => {
    await context.Response
        .WriteAsync("Routed to the double endpoint");
}).WithDisplayName("Double Endpoint")
    .Add(b => ((RouteEndpointBuilder)b).Order = 2);
```

```
app.MapFallback(async context => {
    await context.Response.WriteAsync("Routed to fallback endpoint");
});
```

```
app.Run();
```

The `GetEndpoint` extension method on the `HttpContext` class returns the endpoint that has been selected to handle the request, described through an `Endpoint` object. The `Endpoint` class defines the properties described in table 13.10.

> **CAUTION** There is also a `SetEndpoint` method that allows the endpoint chosen by the routing middleware to be changed before the response is generated. This should be used with caution and only when there is a compelling need to interfere with the normal route selection process.

Table 13.10   The properties defined by the Endpoint class

Name	Description
`DisplayName`	This property returns the display name associated with the endpoint, which can be set using the `WithDisplayName` method when creating a route.
`Metadata`	This property returns the collection of metadata associated with the endpoint.
`RequestDelegate`	This property returns the delegate that will be used to generate the response.

To make it easier to identify the endpoint that the routing middleware has selected, I used the `WithDisplayName` method to assign names to the routes in listing 13.28. The new middleware component adds a message to the response reporting the endpoint that has been selected. Restart ASP.NET Core and request the http://localhost:5000/23 URL to see the output from the middleware that shows the endpoint has been selected between the two methods that add the routing middleware to the request pipeline, as shown in figure 13.22.

Figure 13.22   Determining the endpoint

Summary

- Routes allow an endpoint to match request with a URL pattern.
- URL patterns can match variable segments whose values can be read by the endpoint.
- URL patterns can contain optional segments that match URLs when they are present.
- Matching URLs can be controlled using constraints.
- Routes can be used to generate URLs that can be included in responses, ensuring that subsequent requests target a given endpoint.

Using dependency injection

14

This chapter covers

- Understanding how dependency injection allows components to access shared services
- Configuring services lifecycles to control when services are instantiated
- Understanding how to define and access services using dependency injection

Services are objects that are shared between middleware components and endpoints. There are no restrictions on the features that services can provide, but they are usually used for tasks that are needed in multiple parts of the application, such as logging or database access.

The ASP.NET Core *dependency injection* feature is used to create and consume services. This topic causes confusion and can be difficult to understand. In this chapter, I describe the problems that dependency injection solves and explain how dependency injection is supported by the ASP.NET Core platform. Table 14.1 puts dependency injection in context.

Table 14.1. Putting dependency injection in context

Question	Answer
What is it?	Dependency injection makes it easy to create loosely coupled components, which typically means that components consume functionality defined by interfaces without having any firsthand knowledge of which implementation classes are being used.
Why is it useful?	Dependency injection makes it easier to change the behavior of an application by changing the components that implement the interfaces that define application features. It also results in components that are easier to isolate for unit testing.
How is it used?	The `Program.cs` file is used to specify which implementation classes are used to deliver the functionality specified by the interfaces used by the application. Services can be explicitly requested through the `IServiceProvider` interface or by declaring constructor or method parameters.
Are there any pitfalls or limitations?	There are some differences in the way that middleware components and endpoints are handled and the way that services with different lifecycles are accessed.
Are there any alternatives?	You don't have to use dependency injection in your code, but it is helpful to know how it works because it is used by the ASP.NET Core platform to provide features to developers.

Table 14.2 provides a guide to the chapter.

Table 14.2. Chapter guide

Problem	Solution	Listing
Obtaining a service in a handler function defined in the `Program.cs` file	Add a parameter to the handler function.	15
Obtaining a service in a middleware component	Define a constructor parameter.	16, 30–32
Obtaining a service in an endpoint	Get an `IServiceProvider` object through the context objects.	17
Instantiating a class that has constructor dependencies	Use the `ActivatorUtilities` class.	18–20
Defining services that are instantiated for every dependency	Define transient services.	21–25
Defining services that are instantiated for every request	Define scoped services.	26–29
Accessing configuration services before the `Build` method is called in the `Program.cs` file	Use the properties defined by the `WebApplicationBuilder` class.	33
Managing service instantiation	Use a service factory.	34, 35
Defining multiple implementations for a service	Define multiple services with the same scope and consume them through the `GetServices` method.	36–38
Using services that support generic type parameters	Use a service with an unbound type.	39

14.1   *Preparing for this chapter*

In this chapter, I continue to use the `Platform` project from chapter 13. New classes are required to prepare for this chapter. Start by creating the `Platform/Services` folder and add to it a class file named `IResponseFormatter.cs`, with the code shown in listing 14.1.

> **TIP**   You can download the example project for this chapter—and for all the other chapters in this book—from https://github.com/manningbooks/pro-asp .net-core-7. See chapter 1 for how to get help if you have problems running the examples.

Listing 14.1   The contents of the IResponseFormatter.cs file in the Services folder

```
namespace Platform.Services {
    public interface IResponseFormatter {

        Task Format(HttpContext context, string content);
    }
}
```

The `IResponseFormatter` interface defines a single method that receives an `Http-Context` object and a `string`. To create an implementation of the interface, add a class called `TextResponseFormatter.cs` to the `Platform/Services` folder with the code shown in listing 14.2.

Listing 14.2   The contents of the TextResponseFormatter.cs file in the Services folder

```
namespace Platform.Services {
    public class TextResponseFormatter : IResponseFormatter {
        private int responseCounter = 0;

        public async Task Format(HttpContext context, string content) {
            await context.Response.
                WriteAsync($"Response {++responseCounter}:\n{content}");
        }
    }
}
```

The `TextResponseFormatter` class implements the interface and writes the content to the response as a simple string with a prefix to make it obvious when the class is used.

14.1.1   *Creating a middleware component and an endpoint*

Some of the examples in this chapter show how features are applied differently when using middleware and endpoints. Add a file called `WeatherMiddleware.cs` to the `Platform` folder with the code shown in listing 14.3.

Listing 14.3   The contents of the WeatherMiddleware.cs file in the Platform folder

```
namespace Platform {
    public class WeatherMiddleware {
```

```
        private RequestDelegate next;

        public WeatherMiddleware(RequestDelegate nextDelegate) {
            next = nextDelegate;
        }

        public async Task Invoke(HttpContext context) {
            if (context.Request.Path == "/middleware/class") {
                await context.Response
                  .WriteAsync("Middleware Class: It is raining in London");
            } else {
                await next(context);
            }
        }
    }
}
```

To create an endpoint that produces a similar result to the middleware component, add a file called `WeatherEndpoint.cs` to the `Platform` folder with the code shown in listing 14.4.

> **Listing 14.4 The contents of the WeatherEndpoint.cs file in the Platform folder**

```
namespace Platform {
    public class WeatherEndpoint {

        public static async Task Endpoint(HttpContext context) {
            await context.Response
                .WriteAsync("Endpoint Class: It is cloudy in Milan");
        }
    }
}
```

14.1.2 Configuring the request pipeline

Replace the contents of the `Program.cs` file with those shown in listing 14.5. The classes defined in the previous section are applied alongside a lambda function that produce similar results.

> **Listing 14.5 Replacing the contents of the Program.cs file in the Platform folder**

```
using Platform;
using Platform.Services;

var builder = WebApplication.CreateBuilder(args);

var app = builder.Build();

app.UseMiddleware<WeatherMiddleware>();

app.MapGet("endpoint/class", WeatherEndpoint.Endpoint);

IResponseFormatter formatter = new TextResponseFormatter();
app.MapGet("endpoint/function", async context => {
    await formatter.Format(context,
```

```
        "Endpoint Function: It is sunny in LA");
});
```

```
app.Run();
```

Start the application by opening a new PowerShell command prompt, navigating to the `Platform` project folder, and running the command shown in listing 14.6.

> **Listing 14.6   Starting the ASP.NET Core Runtime**

```
dotnet run
```

Use a browser to request http://localhost:5000/endpoint/function, and you will see the response shown in figure 14.1. Each time you reload the browser, the counter shown in the response will be incremented.

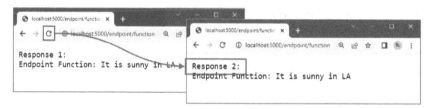

Figure 14.1 Running the example application

14.2 *Understanding service location and tight coupling*

To understand dependency injection, it is important to start with the two problems it solves. In the sections that follow, I describe both problems addressed by dependency injection.

Taking a view on dependency injection

Dependency injection is one of the topics that readers contact me about most often. About half of the emails complain that I am "forcing" DI upon them. Oddly, the other half are complaints that I did not emphasize the benefits of DI strongly enough and other readers may not have realized how useful it can be.

Dependency injection can be a difficult topic to understand, and its value is contentious. DI can be a useful tool, but not everyone likes it—or needs it.

DI offers limited benefit if you are not doing unit testing or if you are working on a small, self-contained, and stable project. It is still helpful to understand how DI works because DI is used to access some important ASP.NET Core features described in earlier chapters, but you don't always need to embrace DI in the custom classes you write. There are alternative ways of creating shared features—two of which I describe in the following sections—and using these is perfectly acceptable if you don't like DI.

I rely on DI in my applications because I find that projects often go in unexpected directions, and being able to easily replace a component with a new implementation can save me a lot of tedious and error-prone changes. I'd rather put in some effort at the start of the project than do a complex set of edits later.

> **(continued)**
>
> But I am not dogmatic about dependency injection and nor should you be. Dependency injection solves a problem that doesn't arise in every project, and only you can determine whether you need DI for your project.

14.2.1 Understanding the service location problem

Most projects have features that need to be used in different parts of the application, which are known as *services*. Common examples include logging tools and configuration settings but can extend to any shared feature, including the `TextResponseFormatter` class that is defined in listing 14.2 and to handle requests by the middleware component and the lambda function.

Each `TextResponseFormatter` object maintains a counter that is included in the response sent to the browser, and if I want to incorporate the same counter into the responses generated by other endpoints, I need to have a way to make a single `TextResponseFormatter` object available in such a way that it can be easily found and consumed at every point where responses are generated.

There are many ways to make services locatable, but there are two main approaches, aside from the one that is the main topic of this chapter. The first approach is to create an object and use it as a constructor or method argument to pass it to the part of the application where it is required. The other approach is to add a `static` property to the service class that provides direct access to the shared instance, as shown in listing 14.7. This is known as the *singleton pattern*, and it was a common approach before the widespread use of dependency injection.

Listing 14.7 A singleton in the TextResponseFormatter.cs file in the Services folder

```
namespace Platform.Services {
    public class TextResponseFormatter : IResponseFormatter {
        private int responseCounter = 0;
        private static TextResponseFormatter? shared;

        public async Task Format(HttpContext context, string content) {
            await context.Response.
                WriteAsync($"Response {++responseCounter}:\n{content}");
        }

        public static TextResponseFormatter Singleton {
            get {
                if (shared == null) {
                    shared = new TextResponseFormatter();
                }
                return shared;
            }
        }
    }
}
```

This is a basic implementation of the singleton pattern, and there are many variations that pay closer attention to issues such as safe concurrent access. What's important for this chapter is that the changes in listing 14.7 rely on the consumers of the `Text-ResponseFormatter` service obtaining a shared object through the static `Singleton` property, as shown in listing 14.8.

Listing 14.8   Using a singleton in the WeatherEndpoint.cs file in the Platform folder

```
using Platform.Services;

namespace Platform {
    public class WeatherEndpoint {

        public static async Task Endpoint(HttpContext context) {
            await TextResponseFormatter.Singleton.Format(context,
                "Endpoint Class: It is cloudy in Milan");
        }
    }
}
```

Listing 14.9 makes the same change to the lambda function in the `Program.cs` file.

Listing 14.9   Using a service in the Program.cs file in the Platform folder

```
using Platform;
using Platform.Services;

var builder = WebApplication.CreateBuilder(args);

var app = builder.Build();

app.UseMiddleware<WeatherMiddleware>();

app.MapGet("endpoint/class", WeatherEndpoint.Endpoint);

IResponseFormatter formatter = TextResponseFormatter.Singleton;
app.MapGet("endpoint/function", async context => {
    await formatter.Format(context,
        "Endpoint Function: It is sunny in LA");
});

app.Run();
```

The singleton pattern allows me to share a single `TextResponseFormatter` object so it is used by two endpoints, with the effect that a single counter is incremented by requests for two different URLs.

To see the effect of the singleton pattern, restart ASP.NET Core and request the http://localhost:5000/endpoint/class and http://localhost:5000/endpoint/function URLs. A single counter is updated for both URLs, as shown in figure 14.2.

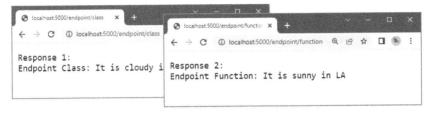

Figure 14.2 Implementing the singleton pattern to create a shared service

The singleton pattern is simple to understand and easy to use, but the knowledge of how services are located is spread throughout the application, and all service classes and service consumers need to understand how to access the shared object. This can lead to variations in the singleton pattern as new services are created and creates many points in the code that must be updated when there is a change. This pattern can also be rigid and doesn't allow any flexibility in how services are managed because every consumer always shares a single service object.

14.2.2 Understanding the tightly coupled components problem

Although I defined an interface in listing 14.1, the way that I have used the singleton pattern means that consumers are always aware of the implementation class they are using because that's the class whose static property is used to get the shared object. If I want to switch to a different implementation of the IResponseFormatter interface, I must locate every use of the service and replace the existing implementation class with the new one. There are patterns to solve this problem, too, such as the *type broker* pattern, in which a class provides access to singleton objects through their interfaces. Add a class file called TypeBroker.cs to the Platform/Services folder and use it to define the code shown in listing 14.10.

Listing 14.10   The contents of the TypeBroker.cs file in the Services folder

```
namespace Platform.Services {
    public static class TypeBroker {
        private static IResponseFormatter formatter
            = new TextResponseFormatter();

        public static IResponseFormatter Formatter => formatter;
    }
}
```

The Formatter property provides access to a shared service object that implements the IResponseFormatter interface. Consumers of the service need to know that the TypeBroker class is responsible for selecting the implementation that will be used, but this pattern means that service consumers can work through interfaces rather than concrete classes, as shown in listing 14.11.

Listing 14.11   Using a type broker in the WeatherEndpoint.cs file in the Platform folder

```
using Platform.Services;

namespace Platform {
    public class WeatherEndpoint {

        public static async Task Endpoint(HttpContext context) {
            await TypeBroker.Formatter.Format(context,
                "Endpoint Class: It is cloudy in Milan");
        }
    }
}
```

Listing 14.12 makes the same change to the lambda function so that both uses of the IResponseFormatter interface get their implementation objects from the type broker.

Listing 14.12   Using a type broker in the Program.cs file in the Platform folder

```
using Platform;
using Platform.Services;

var builder = WebApplication.CreateBuilder(args);

var app = builder.Build();

app.UseMiddleware<WeatherMiddleware>();

app.MapGet("endpoint/class", WeatherEndpoint.Endpoint);

IResponseFormatter formatter = TypeBroker.Formatter;
app.MapGet("endpoint/function", async context => {
    await formatter.Format(context,
        "Endpoint Function: It is sunny in LA");
});

app.Run();
```

This approach makes it easy to switch to a different implementation class by altering just the TypeBroker class and prevents service consumers from creating dependencies on a specific implementation. It also means that service classes can focus on the features they provide without having to deal with how those features will be located. To demonstrate, add a class file called HtmlResponseFormatter.cs to the Platform/Services folder with the code shown in listing 14.13.

Listing 14.13   The contents of the HtmlResponseFormatter.cs file in the Services folder

```
namespace Platform.Services {
    public class HtmlResponseFormatter : IResponseFormatter {

        public async Task Format(HttpContext context, string content) {
            context.Response.ContentType = "text/html";
```

```
await context.Response.WriteAsync($@"
    <!DOCTYPE html>
    <html lang=""en"">
    <head><title>Response</title></head>
    <body>
        <h2>Formatted Response</h2>
        <span>{content}</span>
    </body>
    </html>");
        }
    }
}
```

This implementation of the `IResponseFormatter` sets the `ContentType` property of the `HttpResponse` object and inserts the content into an HTML template string. To use the new formatter class, I only need to change the `TypeBroker`, as shown in listing 14.14.

> **Listing 14.14 changing the TypeBroker.cs file in the Platform/Services folder**

```
namespace Platform.Services {
    public static class TypeBroker {
        private static IResponseFormatter formatter
            = new HtmlResponseFormatter();

        public static IResponseFormatter Formatter => formatter;
    }
}
```

To confirm the new formatter works, restart ASP.NET Core and request http://localhost:5000/endpoint/function, which will produce the result shown in figure 14.3.

Figure 14.3 Using a different service implementation class

14.3 *Using dependency injection*

Dependency injection provides an alternative approach to providing services that tidy up the rough edges that arise in the singleton and type broker patterns, and is integrated with other ASP.NET Core features. Listing 14.15 shows the use of ASP.NET Core dependency injection to replace the type broker from the previous section.

Listing 14.15   Using dependency injection in the Program.cs file in the Platform folder

```
using Platform;
using Platform.Services;

var builder = WebApplication.CreateBuilder(args);

builder.Services.AddSingleton<IResponseFormatter,
    HtmlResponseFormatter>();

var app = builder.Build();

app.UseMiddleware<WeatherMiddleware>();

app.MapGet("endpoint/class", WeatherEndpoint.Endpoint);

//IResponseFormatter formatter = TypeBroker.Formatter;
app.MapGet("endpoint/function",
    async (HttpContext context, IResponseFormatter formatter) => {
        await formatter.Format(context,
            "Endpoint Function: It is sunny in LA");
});

app.Run();
```

Services are registered using extension methods defined by the `IServiceCollection` interface, an implementation of which is obtained using the `WebApplication-Builder.Services` property. In the listing, I used an extension method to create a service for the `IResponseFormatter` interface:

```
...
builder.Services.AddSingleton<IResponseFormatter, HtmlResponseFormatter>();
...
```

The `AddSingleton` method is one of the extension methods available for services and tells ASP.NET Core that a single object should be used to satisfy all demands for the service (the other extension methods are described in the "Using Service Lifecycles" section). The interface and the implementation class are specified as generic type arguments. To consume the service, I added parameters to the functions that handle requests, like this:

```
...
async (HttpContext context, IResponseFormatter formatter) => {
...
```

Many of the methods that are used to register middleware or create endpoints will accept any function, which allows parameters to be defined for the services that are required to produce a response. One consequence of this feature is that the C# compiler can't determine the parameter types, which is why I had to specify them in the listing.

The new parameter declares a dependency on the `IResponseFormatter` interface, and the function is said to depend on the interface. Before the function is invoked to handle a request, its parameters are inspected, the dependency is detected, and the application's services are inspected to determine whether it is possible to resolve the dependency.

The call to the `AddSingleton` method told the dependency injection system that a dependency on the `IResponseFormatter` interface can be resolved with an `Html-ResponseFormatter` object. The object is created and used as an argument to invoke the handler function. Because the object that resolves the dependency is provided from outside the function that uses it, it is said to have been *injected*, which is why the process is known as *dependency injection*.

14.3.1 Using a Service with a Constructor Dependency

Defining a service and consuming it in the same code file may not seem impressive, but once a service is defined, it can be used almost anywhere in an ASP.NET Core application. Listing 14.16 declares a dependency on the `IResponseFormatter` interface in the middleware class defined at the start of the chapter.

> Listing 14.16 A dependency in the WeatherMiddleware.cs file in the Platform folder

```
using Platform.Services;

namespace Platform {
    public class WeatherMiddleware {
        private RequestDelegate next;
        private IResponseFormatter formatter;

        public WeatherMiddleware(RequestDelegate nextDelegate,
                IResponseFormatter respFormatter) {
            next = nextDelegate;
            formatter = respFormatter;
        }

        public async Task Invoke(HttpContext context) {
            if (context.Request.Path == "/middleware/class") {
                await formatter.Format(context,
                    "Middleware Class: It is raining in London");
            } else {
                await next(context);
            }
        }
    }
}
```

To declare the dependency, I added a constructor parameter. To see the result, restart ASP.NET Core and request the http://localhost:5000/middleware/class URL, which will produce the response shown in figure 14.4.

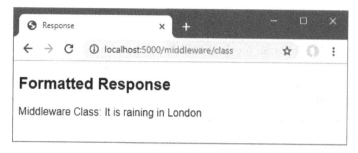

Figure 14.4 Declaring a dependency in a middleware class

When the request pipeline is being set up, the ASP.NET Core platform reaches the statement in the Program.cs file that adds the WeatherMiddleware class as a component.

```
...
app.UseMiddleware<WeatherMiddleware>();
...
```

The platform understands it needs to create an instance of the WeatherMiddleware class and inspects the constructor. The dependency on the IResponseFormatter interface is detected, the services are inspected to see if the dependency can be resolved, and the shared service object is used when the constructor is invoked.

There are two important points to understand about this example. The first is that WeatherMiddleware doesn't know which implementation class will be used to resolve its dependency on the IResponseFormatter interface—it just knows that it will receive an object that conforms to the interface through its constructor parameter. Second, the WeatherMiddleware class doesn't know how the dependency is resolved—it just declares a constructor parameter and relies on ASP.NET Core to figure out the details. This is a more elegant approach than my implementations of the singleton and type broker patterns earlier in the chapter, and I can change the implementation class used to resolve the service by changing the generic type parameters used in the Program.cs file.

14.3.2 *Getting services from the HttpContext object*

ASP.NET Core does a good job of supporting dependency injection as widely as possible but there will be times when you are not working directly with the ASP.NET Core API and won't have a way to declare your service dependencies directly.

Services can be accessed through the HttpContext object, which is used to represent the current request and response, as shown in listing 14.17. You may find that you receive an HttpContext object even if you are working with third-party code that acts as an intermediary to ASP.NET Core and which doesn't allow you to resolve services.

> **NOTE** This example is a demonstration of a common problem but ASP.NET Core does support dependency injection for endpoint delegates.

Listing 14.17 Using the HttpContext in the WeatherEndpoint.cs file in the Platform folder

```
using Platform.Services;

namespace Platform {
    public class WeatherEndpoint {

        public static async Task Endpoint(HttpContext context) {
            IResponseFormatter formatter = context.RequestServices
                .GetRequiredService<IResponseFormatter>();
            await formatter.Format(context,
                "Endpoint Class: It is cloudy in Milan");
        }
    }
}
```

The `HttpContext.RequestServices` property returns an object that implements the `IServiceProvider` interfaces, which provides access to the services that have been configured in the `Program.cs` file. The `Microsoft.Extensions.Dependency-Injection` namespace contains extension methods for the `IServiceProvider` interface that allow individual services to be obtained, as described in table 14.3.

Table 14.3 The IServiceProvider extension methods for obtaining services

Name	Description
`GetService<T>()`	This method returns a service for the type specified by the generic type parameter or `null` if no such service has been defined.
`GetService(type)`	This method returns a service for the type specified or `null` if no such service has been defined.
`GetRequiredService<T>()`	This method returns a service specified by the generic type parameter and throws an exception if a service isn't available.
`GetRequiredService(type)`	This method returns a service for the type specified and throws an exception if a service isn't available.

When the `Endpoint` method is invoked in listing 14.17, the `GetRequiredService<T>` method is used to obtain an `IResponseFormatter` object, which is used to format the response. To see the effect, restart ASP.NET Core and use the browser to request http://localhost:5000/endpoint/class, which will produce the formatted response shown in figure 14.5.

Figure 14.5 Using a service in an endpoint class

USING THE ACTIVATION UTILITY CLASS

I defined static methods for endpoint classes in chapter 13 because it makes them easier to use when creating routes. But for endpoints that require services, it can often be easier to use a class that can be instantiated because it allows for a more generalized approach to handling services. Listing 14.18 revises the endpoint with a constructor and removes the `static` keyword from the `Endpoint` method.

> **Listing 14.18   Revising the endpoint in the WeatherEndpoint.cs file in the Platform folder**

```
using Platform.Services;

namespace Platform {
    public class WeatherEndpoint {
        private IResponseFormatter formatter;

        public WeatherEndpoint(IResponseFormatter responseFormatter) {
            formatter = responseFormatter;
        }

        public async Task Endpoint(HttpContext context) {
            await formatter.Format(context,
                "Endpoint Class: It is cloudy in Milan");
        }
    }
}
```

The most common use of dependency injection in ASP.NET Core applications is in class constructors. Injection through methods, such as performed for middleware classes, is a complex process to re-create, but there are some useful built-in tools that take care of inspecting constructors and resolving dependencies using services. Create a file called `EndpointExtensions.cs` to the `Services` folder with the content shown in listing 14.19.

> **Listing 14.19   The contents of the EndpointExtensions.cs file in the Services folder**

```
using System.Reflection;

namespace Microsoft.AspNetCore.Builder {
```

```
public static class EndpointExtensions {

    public static void MapEndpoint<T>(this IEndpointRouteBuilder app,
            string path, string methodName = "Endpoint") {

        MethodInfo? methodInfo = typeof(T).GetMethod(methodName);
        if (methodInfo?.ReturnType != typeof(Task)) {
            throw new System.Exception("Method cannot be used");
        }
        T endpointInstance =
            ActivatorUtilities.CreateInstance<T>(app.ServiceProvider);
        app.MapGet(path, (RequestDelegate)methodInfo
            .CreateDelegate(typeof(RequestDelegate),
                endpointInstance));
    }
}
}
```

The `MapEndpoint` extension method accepts a generic type parameter that specifies the endpoint class that will be used. The other arguments are the path that will be used to create the route and the name of the endpoint class method that processes requests.

A new instance of the endpoint class is created, and a delegate to the specified method is used to create a route. Like any code that uses .NET reflection, the extension method in listing 14.19 can be difficult to read, but this is the key statement for this chapter:

```
...
T endpointInstance =
    ActivatorUtilities.CreateInstance<T>(app.ServiceProvider);
...
```

The `ActivatorUtilities` class, defined in the `Microsoft.Extensions.Dependency-Injection` namespace, provides methods for instantiating classes that have dependencies declared through their constructor. Table 14.4 shows the most useful `ActivatorUtilities` methods.

Table 14.4 The ActivatorUtilities methods

Name	Description
`CreateInstance<T>(services, args)`	This method creates a new instance of the class specified by the type parameter, resolving dependencies using the services and additional (optional) arguments.
`CreateInstance(services, type, args)`	This method creates a new instance of the class specified by the parameter, resolving dependencies using the services and additional (optional) arguments.
`GetServiceOrCreateInstance<T>(services, args)`	This method returns a service of the specified type, if one is available, or creates a new instance if there is no service.
`GetServiceOrCreateInstance(services, type, args)`	This method returns a service of the specified type, if one is available, or creates a new instance if there is no service.

These methods make it easy to instantiate classes that declare constructor dependencies. Both methods resolve constructor dependencies using services through an `IServiceProvider` object and an optional array of arguments that are used for dependencies that are not services. These methods make it easy to apply dependency injection to custom classes, and the use of the `CreateInstance` method results in an extension method that can create routes with endpoint classes that consume services. Listing 14.20 uses the new extension method to create a route.

> **Listing 14.20   Creating a route in the Program.cs file in the Platform folder**

```
using Platform;
using Platform.Services;

var builder = WebApplication.CreateBuilder(args);

builder.Services.AddSingleton<IResponseFormatter,
    HtmlResponseFormatter>();

var app = builder.Build();

app.UseMiddleware<WeatherMiddleware>();

//app.MapGet("endpoint/class", WeatherEndpoint.Endpoint);
app.MapEndpoint<WeatherEndpoint>("endpoint/class");

app.MapGet("endpoint/function",
    async (HttpContext context, IResponseFormatter formatter) => {
        await formatter.Format(context,
            "Endpoint Function: It is sunny in LA");
});

app.Run();
```

To confirm that requests are routed to the endpoint, restart ASP.NET Core and request the http://localhost:5000/endpoint/class URL, which should produce the same response as shown in figure 14.5.

14.4   *Using Service Lifecycles*

When I created the service in the previous section, I used the `AddSingleton` extension method, like this:

```
...
builder.Services.AddSingleton<IResponseFormatter, HtmlResponseFormatter>();
...
```

The `AddSingleton` method produces a service that is instantiated the first time it is used to resolve a dependency and is then reused for each subsequent dependency. This means that any dependency on the `IResponseFormatter` object will be resolved using the same `HtmlResponseFormatter` object.

Singletons are a good way to get started with services, but there are some problems for which they are not suited, so ASP.NET Core supports *scoped* and *transient* services, which give different lifecycles for the objects that are created to resolve dependencies. Table 14.5 describes the set of methods used to create services. There are versions of these methods that accept types as conventional arguments, as demonstrated in the "Using Unbound Types in Services" section, later in this chapter.

Table 14.5. The extension methods for creating services

Name	Description
`AddSingleton<T, U>()`	This method creates a single object of type U that is used to resolve all dependencies on type T.
`AddTransient<T, U>()`	This method creates a new object of type U to resolve each dependency on type T.
`AddScoped<T, U>()`	This method creates a new object of type U that is used to resolve dependencies on T within a single scope, such as request.

There are versions of the methods in Table 14.5 that have a single type argument, which allows a service to be created that solves the service location problem without addressing the tightly coupled issue. You can see an example of this type of service in chapter 24, where I share a simple data source that isn't accessed through an interface.

14.4.1 Creating transient services

The `AddTransient` method does the opposite of the `AddSingleton` method and creates a new instance of the implementation class for every dependency that is resolved. To create a service that will demonstrate the use of service lifecycles, add a file called `GuidService.cs` to the `Platform/Services` folder with the code shown in listing 14.21.

Listing 14.21   The contents of the GuidService.cs file in the Services folder

```
namespace Platform.Services {

    public class GuidService : IResponseFormatter {
        private Guid guid = Guid.NewGuid();

        public async Task Format(HttpContext context, string content) {
            await context.Response.WriteAsync($"Guid: {guid}\n{content}");
        }
    }
}
```

The `Guid` struct generates a unique identifier, which will make it obvious when a different instance is used to resolve a dependency on the `IResponseFormatter` interface. In listing 14.22, I have changed the statement that creates the `IResponseFormatter` service to use the `AddTransient` method and the `GuidService` implementation class.

Listing 14.22   Creating a transient service in the Program.cs file in the Platform folder

```
using Platform;
using Platform.Services;

var builder = WebApplication.CreateBuilder(args);

builder.Services.AddTransient<IResponseFormatter, GuidService>();

var app = builder.Build();

app.UseMiddleware<WeatherMiddleware>();

app.MapEndpoint<WeatherEndpoint>("endpoint/class");

app.MapGet("endpoint/function",
    async (HttpContext context, IResponseFormatter formatter) => {
        await formatter.Format(context,
            "Endpoint Function: It is sunny in LA");
});

app.Run();
```

If you restart ASP.NET Core and request the http://localhost:5000/endpoint/
function URL, you will receive the responses similar to the ones shown in figure 14.6.
Each response will be shown with a different GUID value, confirming that transient
service objects have been used to resolve the dependency on the `IResponseFormatter`
service.

Figure 14.6   Using transient services

14.4.2 Avoiding the transient service reuse pitfall

There is a pitfall when using transient services, which you can see by requesting http://
localhost:5000/middleware/class and clicking the reload button. Unlike the previous
example, the same GUID value is shown in every response, as shown in figure 14.7.

Figure 14.7   The same GUID values appearing in responses

New service objects are created only when dependencies are resolved, not when services are used. The components and endpoints in the example application have their dependencies resolved only when the application starts and the top-level statements in the `Program.cs` file are executed. Each receives a separate service object, which is then reused for every request that is processed.

To address this issue, I have to ensure that the dependency is resolved every time the `Invoke` method is called, as shown in listing 14.23.

```
using Platform.Services;

namespace Platform {
    public class WeatherMiddleware {
        private RequestDelegate next;
        //private IResponseFormatter formatter;

        public WeatherMiddleware(RequestDelegate nextDelegate) {
            next = nextDelegate;
            //formatter = respFormatter;
        }

        public async Task Invoke(HttpContext context,
                IResponseFormatter formatter) {
            if (context.Request.Path == "/middleware/class") {
                await formatter.Format(context,
                    "Middleware Class: It is raining in London");
            } else {
                await next(context);
            }
        }
    }
}
```

The ASP.NET Core platform will resolve dependencies declared by the `Invoke` method every time a request is processed, which ensures that a new transient service object is created.

The `ActivatorUtilities` class doesn't deal with resolving dependencies for methods. The simplest way of solving this issue for endpoints is to explicitly request services when each request is handled, which is the approach I used earlier when showing how services are used. It is also possible to enhance the extension method to request services on behalf of an endpoint, as shown in listing 14.24.

```
using System.Reflection;

namespace Microsoft.AspNetCore.Builder {

    public static class EndpointExtensions {

        public static void MapEndpoint<T>(this IEndpointRouteBuilder app,
```

```
                string path, string methodName = "Endpoint") {
            MethodInfo? methodInfo = typeof(T).GetMethod(methodName);
            if (methodInfo?.ReturnType != typeof(Task)) {
                throw new System.Exception("Method cannot be used");
            }
            T endpointInstance =
                ActivatorUtilities.CreateInstance<T>(app.ServiceProvider);

            ParameterInfo[] methodParams = methodInfo!.GetParameters();

            app.MapGet(path, context =>
                (Task)methodInfo.Invoke(endpointInstance,
                  methodParams.Select(p =>
                    p.ParameterType == typeof(HttpContext) ? context
                      : app.ServiceProvider.GetService(p.ParameterType))
                    .ToArray())!);
        }
    }
}
```

The code in listing 14.24 isn't as efficient as the approach taken by the ASP.NET Core platform for middleware components. All the parameters defined by the method that handles requests are treated as services to be resolved, except for the `HttpContext` parameter. A route is created with a delegate that resolves the services for every request and invokes the method that handles the request. Listing 14.25 revises the `Weather-Endpoint` class to move the dependency on `IResponseFormatter` to the `Endpoint` method so that a new service object will be received for every request.

Listing 14.25   Moving the dependency in the Platform/WeatherEndpoint.cs file

```
using Platform.Services;

namespace Platform {
    public class WeatherEndpoint {
        //private IResponseFormatter formatter;

        //public WeatherEndpoint(IResponseFormatter responseFormatter) {
        //    formatter = responseFormatter;
        //}

        public async Task Endpoint(HttpContext context,
                IResponseFormatter formatter) {
            await formatter.Format(context,
                "Endpoint Class: It is cloudy in Milan");
        }
    }
}
```

The changes in listing 14.23 to listing 14.25 ensure that the transient service is resolved for every request, which means that a new `GuidService` object is created and every response contains a unique ID.

Restart ASP.NET Core, navigate to http://localhost:5000/endpoint/class, and click the browser's reload button. Each time you reload, a new request is sent to ASP.NET

Core, and the component or endpoint that handles the request receives a new service object, such that a different GUID is shown in each response, as shown in figure 14.8.

Figure 14.8 Using a transient service

14.4.3 Using scoped services

Scoped services strike a balance between singleton and transient services. Within a scope, dependencies are resolved with the same object. A new scope is started for each HTTP request, which means that a service object will be shared by all the components that handle that request. To prepare for a scoped service, listing 14.26 changes the `WeatherMiddleware` class to declare three dependencies on the same service.

Listing 14.26 Adding dependencies in the Platform/WeatherMiddleware.cs file

```
using Platform.Services;

namespace Platform {
    public class WeatherMiddleware {
        private RequestDelegate next;

        public WeatherMiddleware(RequestDelegate nextDelegate) {
            next = nextDelegate;
        }

        public async Task Invoke(HttpContext context,
                IResponseFormatter formatter1,
                IResponseFormatter formatter2,
                IResponseFormatter formatter3) {
            if (context.Request.Path == "/middleware/class") {
                await formatter1.Format(context, string.Empty);
                await formatter2.Format(context, string.Empty);
                await formatter3.Format(context, string.Empty);
            } else {
                await next(context);
            }
        }
    }
}
```

Declaring several dependencies on the same service isn't required in real projects, but it is useful for this example because each dependency is resolved independently. Since the `IResponseFormatter` service was created with the `AddTransient` method, each dependency is resolved with a different object. Restart ASP.NET Core and request http://localhost:5000/middleware/class, and you will see that a different GUID is used for each of the three messages written to the response, as shown in figure 14.9. When you reload the browser, a new set of three GUIDs is displayed.

Figure 14.9 Resolving dependencies on a transient service

Listing 14.27 changes the `IResponseFormatter` service to use the scoped lifecycle with the `AddScoped` method.

> **TIP** You can create scopes through the `CreateScope` extension method for the `IServiceProvider` interface. The result is an `IServiceProvider` that is associated with a new scope and that will have its own implementation objects for scoped services.

Listing 14.27   Using a scoped service in the Program.cs file in the Platform folder

```
using Platform;
using Platform.Services;

var builder = WebApplication.CreateBuilder(args);

builder.Services.AddScoped<IResponseFormatter, GuidService>();

var app = builder.Build();

app.UseMiddleware<WeatherMiddleware>();

app.MapEndpoint<WeatherEndpoint>("endpoint/class");

app.MapGet("endpoint/function",
    async (HttpContext context, IResponseFormatter formatter) => {
        await formatter.Format(context,
            "Endpoint Function: It is sunny in LA");
});

app.Run();
```

Restart ASP.NET Core and request http://localhost:5000/middleware/class again, and you will see that the same GUID is used to resolve all three dependencies declared by the middleware component, as shown in figure 14.10. When the browser is reloaded, the HTTP request sent to ASP.NET Core creates a new scope and a new service object.

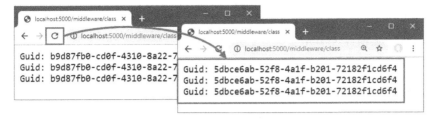

Figure 14.10 Using a scoped service

AVOIDING THE SCOPED SERVICE VALIDATION PITFALL

Service consumers are unaware of the lifecycle that has been selected for singleton and transient services: they declare a dependency or request a service and get the object they require.

Scoped services can be used only within a scope. A new scope is created automatically for each request that was received. Requesting a scoped service outside of a scope causes an exception. To see the problem, request http://localhost:5000/endpoint/class, which will generate the exception response shown in figure 14.11.

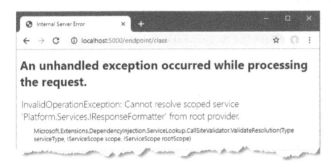

Figure 14.11 Requesting a scoped service

The extension method that configures the endpoint resolves services through an `IServiceProvider` object obtained from the routing middleware, like this:

```
...
app.ServiceProvider.GetService(p.ParameterType))
...
```

ACCESSING SCOPED SERVICES THROUGH THE CONTEXT OBJECT

The `HttpContext` class defines a `RequestServices` property that returns an `IServiceProvider` object that allows access to scoped services, as well as singleton and transient services. This fits well with the most common use of scoped services, which is to use a single service object for each HTTP request. Listing 14.28 revises the endpoint extension method so that dependencies are resolved using the services provided through the `HttpContext`.

```
using System.Reflection;

namespace Microsoft.AspNetCore.Builder {

    public static class EndpointExtensions {

        public static void MapEndpoint<T>(this IEndpointRouteBuilder app,
                string path, string methodName = "Endpoint") {

            MethodInfo? methodInfo = typeof(T).GetMethod(methodName);
            if (methodInfo?.ReturnType != typeof(Task)) {
                throw new System.Exception("Method cannot be used");
            }
            T endpointInstance =
                ActivatorUtilities.CreateInstance<T>(app.ServiceProvider);

            ParameterInfo[] methodParams = methodInfo!.GetParameters();

            app.MapGet(path, context =>
                (Task)methodInfo.Invoke(endpointInstance,
                  methodParams.Select(p =>
                    p.ParameterType == typeof(HttpContext) ? context
                      : context.RequestServices
                        .GetService(p.ParameterType))
                    .ToArray())!);
        }
    }
}
```

Using the HttpContext.RequestServices property ensures that services are resolved within the scope of the current HTTP request, which ensures that endpoints don't use scoped services inappropriately.

Creating new handlers for each request

Notice that the ActivatorUtilities.CreateInstance<T> method is still used to create an instance of the endpoint class in listing 14.28.

This presents a problem because it requires endpoint classes to know the lifecycles of the services on which they depend. The WeatherEndpoint class depends on the IResponseFormatter service and must know that a dependency can be declared only through the Endpoint method and not the constructor.

To remove the need for this knowledge, a new instance of the endpoint class can be created to handle each request, as shown in listing 14.29, which allows constructor and method dependencies to be resolved without needing to know which services are scoped.

```
using System.Reflection;

namespace Microsoft.AspNetCore.Builder {
```

```
public static class EndpointExtensions {

    public static void MapEndpoint<T>(this IEndpointRouteBuilder app,
            string path, string methodName = "Endpoint") {

        MethodInfo? methodInfo = typeof(T).GetMethod(methodName);
        if (methodInfo?.ReturnType != typeof(Task)) {
            throw new System.Exception("Method cannot be used");
        }
        //T endpointInstance =
        //ActivatorUtilities.CreateInstance<T> (app.ServiceProvider);

        ParameterInfo[] methodParams = methodInfo!.GetParameters();

        app.MapGet(path, context => {
            T endpointInstance =
                ActivatorUtilities.CreateInstance<T>
                    (context.RequestServices);
            return (Task)methodInfo.Invoke(endpointInstance!,
                methodParams.Select(p =>
                p.ParameterType == typeof(HttpContext)
                ? context
                : context.RequestServices.GetService(p.ParameterType))
                    .ToArray())!;
        });
    }
}
}
```

This approach requires a new instance of the endpoint class to handle each request, but it ensures that no knowledge of service lifecycles is required.

Restart ASP.NET Core and request http://localhost:5000/endpoint/class. The scoped service will be obtained from the context, producing the responses shown in figure 14.12.

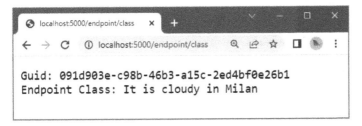

Figure 14.12 Using scoped services in lambda functions

Accessing scoped services when configuring the request pipeline

If you require a scoped service to configure the application in the `Program.cs` file, then you can create a new scope and then request the service, like this:

(continued)

```
...
app.Services.CreateScope().ServiceProvider
    .GetRequiredService<MyScopedService>();
...
```

The `CreateScope` method creates a scope that allows scoped services to be accessed. If you try to obtain a scoped service without creating a scope, then you will receive an exception.

14.5   *Other dependency injection features*

In the sections that follow, I describe some additional features available when using dependency injection. These are not required for all projects, but they are worth understanding because they provide context for how dependency injection works and can be helpful when the standard features are not quite what a project requires.

14.5.1   *Creating dependency chains*

When a class is instantiated to resolve a service dependency, its constructor is inspected, and any dependencies on services are resolved. This allows one service to declare a dependency on another service, creating a chain that is resolved automatically. To demonstrate, add a class file called `TimeStamping.cs` to the `Platform/Services` folder with the code shown in listing 14.30.

> **Listing 14.30   The contents of the TimeStamping.cs file in the Services folder**

```
namespace Platform.Services {

    public interface ITimeStamper {
        string TimeStamp { get; }
    }

    public class DefaultTimeStamper : ITimeStamper {

        public string TimeStamp {
            get => DateTime.Now.ToShortTimeString();
        }
    }
}
```

The class file defines an interface named `ITimeStamper` and an implementation class named `DefaultTimeStamper`. Next, add a file called `TimeResponseFormatter.cs` to the `Platform/Services` folder with the code shown in listing 14.31.

> **Listing 14.31   The contents of the TimeResponseFormatter.cs file in the Services folder**

```
namespace Platform.Services {
    public class TimeResponseFormatter : IResponseFormatter {
        private ITimeStamper stamper;
```

```
        public TimeResponseFormatter(ITimeStamper timeStamper) {
            stamper = timeStamper;
        }

        public async Task Format(HttpContext context, string content) {
            await context.Response.WriteAsync($"{stamper.TimeStamp}: "
                + content);
        }
    }
}
```

The TimeResponseFormatter class is an implementation of the IResponseFormatter interface that declares a dependency on the ITimeStamper interface with a constructor parameter. Listing 14.32 defines services for both interfaces in the Program.cs file.

NOTE Services don't need to have the same lifecycle as their dependencies, but you can end up with odd effects if you mix lifecycles. Lifecycles are applied only when a dependency is resolved, which means that if a scoped service depends on a transient service, for example, then the transient object will behave as though it was assigned the scoped lifecycle.

> **Listing 14.32 Configuring services in the Program.cs file in the Platform folder**

```
using Platform;
using Platform.Services;

var builder = WebApplication.CreateBuilder(args);

builder.Services.AddScoped<IResponseFormatter, TimeResponseFormatter>();
builder.Services.AddScoped<ITimeStamper, DefaultTimeStamper>();

var app = builder.Build();

app.UseMiddleware<WeatherMiddleware>();

app.MapEndpoint<WeatherEndpoint>("endpoint/class");

app.MapGet("endpoint/function",
    async (HttpContext context, IResponseFormatter formatter) => {
        await formatter.Format(context,
            "Endpoint Function: It is sunny in LA");
});

app.Run();
```

When a dependency on the IResponseFormatter service is resolved, the Time-ResponseFormatter constructor will be inspected, and its dependency on the ITime-Stamper service will be detected. A DefaultTimeStamper object will be created and injected into the TimeResponseFormatter constructor, which allows the original dependency to be resolved. To see the dependency chain in action, restart ASP. NET Core and request http://localhost:5000/endpoint/class, and you will see the timestamp generated by the `DefaultTimeStamper` class included in the response produced by the `TimeResponseFormatter` class, as shown in figure 14.13.

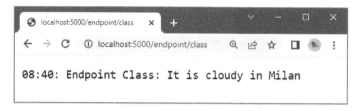

Figure 14.13   Creating a chain of dependencies

14.5.2   Accessing services in the Program.cs file

A common requirement is to use the application's configuration settings to alter the set of services that are created in the `Program.cs` file. This presents a problem because the configuration is presented as a service and services cannot normally be accessed until after the `WebApplicationBuilder.Build` method is invoked.

To address this issue, the `WebApplication` and `WebApplicationBuilder` classes define properties that provide access to the built-in services that provide access to the application configuration, as described in table 14.6.

Table 14.6   The WebApplication and WebApplicationBuilder properties for configuration services

Name	Description
`IConfiguration`	This property returns an implementation of the `IConfiguration` interface, which provides access to the application's configuration settings, as described in chapter 15. `Configuration`.
`Environment`	This property returns an implementation of the `IWebHostEnvironment` interface, which provides information about the environment in which the application is being executed and whose principal use is to determine if the application is configured for development or deployment, as described in chapter 15.

These services are described in chapter 15, but what's important for this chapter is that they can be used to customize which services are configured in the `Program.cs` file, as shown in listing 14.33.

Listing 14.33   Accessing configuration data in the Program.cs file in the Platform folder

```
using Platform;
using Platform.Services;

var builder = WebApplication.CreateBuilder(args);

IWebHostEnvironment env = builder.Environment;
```

```
if (env.IsDevelopment()) {
    builder.Services.AddScoped<IResponseFormatter,
        TimeResponseFormatter>();
    builder.Services.AddScoped<ITimeStamper, DefaultTimeStamper>();
} else {
    builder.Services.AddScoped<IResponseFormatter,
        HtmlResponseFormatter>();
}

var app = builder.Build();

app.UseMiddleware<WeatherMiddleware>();

app.MapEndpoint<WeatherEndpoint>("endpoint/class");

app.MapGet("endpoint/function",
    async (HttpContext context, IResponseFormatter formatter) => {
        await formatter.Format(context,
            "Endpoint Function: It is sunny in LA");
});

app.Run();
```

This example uses the `Environment` property to get an implementation of the `IWebHostEnvironment` interface and uses its `IsDevelopment` extension method to decide which services are set up for the application.

14.5.3 *Using service factory functions*

Factory functions allow you to take control of the way that service implementation objects are created, rather than relying on ASP.NET Core to create instances for you. There are factory versions of the `AddSingleton`, `AddTransient`, and `AddScoped` methods, all of which are used with a function that receives an `IServiceProvider` object and returns an implementation object for the service.

One use for factory functions is to define the implementation class for a service as a configuration setting, which is read through the `IConfguration` service. This requires the `WebApplicationBuilder` properties described in the previous section. Listing 14.34 adds a factory function for the `IResponseFormatter` service that gets the implementation class from the configuration data.

Listing 14.34 **Using a factory function in the Program.cs file in the Platform folder**

```
using Platform;
using Platform.Services;

var builder = WebApplication.CreateBuilder(args);

//IWebHostEnvironment env = builder.Environment;
IConfiguration config = builder.Configuration;

builder.Services.AddScoped<IResponseFormatter>(serviceProvider => {
    string? typeName = config["services:IResponseFormatter"];
    return (IResponseFormatter)ActivatorUtilities
        .CreateInstance(serviceProvider, typeName == null
```

```
                    ? typeof(GuidService) : Type.GetType(typeName, true)!);
});
builder.Services.AddScoped<ITimeStamper, DefaultTimeStamper>();

var app = builder.Build();

app.UseMiddleware<WeatherMiddleware>();

app.MapEndpoint<WeatherEndpoint>("endpoint/class");

app.MapGet("endpoint/function",
    async (HttpContext context, IResponseFormatter formatter) => {
        await formatter.Format(context,
            "Endpoint Function: It is sunny in LA");
});

app.Run();
```

The factory function reads a value from the configuration data, which is converted into a type and passed to the `ActivatorUtilities.CreateInstance` method. Listing 14.35 adds a configuration setting to the `appsettings.Development.json` file that selects the `HtmlResponseFormatter` class as the implementation for the `IResponseFormatter` service. The JSON configuration file is described in detail in chapter 15.

> **Listing 14.35   A setting in the appsettings.Development.json file in the Platform folder**

```
{
  "Logging": {
    "LogLevel": {
      "Default": "Information",
      "Microsoft.AspNetCore": "Warning"
    }
  },
  "services": {
    "IResponseFormatter": "Platform.Services.HtmlResponseFormatter"
  }
}
```

When a dependency on the `IResponseFormatter` service is resolved, the factory function creates an instance of the type specified in the configuration file. Restart ASP.NET Core and request the http://localhost:5000/endpoint/class URL, which will produce the response shown in figure 14.14.

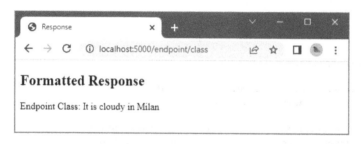

Figure 14.14   Using a service factory

14.5.4 *Creating services with multiple implementations*

Services can be defined with multiple implementations, which allows a consumer to select an implementation that best suits a specific problem. This is a feature that works best when the service interface provides insight into the capabilities of each implementation class. To provide information about the capabilities of the `IResponse-Formatter` implementation classes, add the default property shown in listing 14.36 to the interface.

> **Listing 14.36 Adding a property in the IResponseFormatter.cs file in the Services folder**

```
namespace Platform.Services {
    public interface IResponseFormatter {

        Task Format(HttpContext context, string content);

        public bool RichOutput => false;
    }
}
```

This `RichOutput` property will be `false` for implementation classes that don't override the default value. To ensure there is one implementation that returns `true`, add the property shown in listing 14.37 to the `HtmlResponseFormatter` class.

> **Listing 14.37 Overriding in the HtmlResponseFormatter.cs file in the Services folder**

```
namespace Platform.Services {
    public class HtmlResponseFormatter : IResponseFormatter {

        public async Task Format(HttpContext context, string content) {
            context.Response.ContentType = "text/html";
            await context.Response.WriteAsync($@"
                <!DOCTYPE html>
                <html lang=""en"">
                <head><title>Response</title></head>
                <body>
                    <h2>Formatted Response</h2>
                    <span>{content}</span>
                </body>
                </html>");
        }

        public bool RichOutput => true;
    }
}
```

Listing 14.38 registers multiple implementations for the `IResponseFormatter` service, which is done by making repeated calls to the `Add<lifecycle>` method. The listing also replaces the existing request pipeline with two routes that demonstrate how the service can be used.

```
//using Platform;
using Platform.Services;

var builder = WebApplication.CreateBuilder(args);

//IConfiguration config = builder.Configuration;

//builder.Services.AddScoped<IResponseFormatter>(serviceProvider => {
//     string? typeName = config["services:IResponseFormatter"];
//     return (IResponseFormatter)ActivatorUtilities
//         .CreateInstance(serviceProvider, typeName == null
//             ? typeof(GuidService) : Type.GetType(typeName, true)!);
//});
//builder.Services.AddScoped<ITimeStamper, DefaultTimeStamper>();

builder.Services.AddScoped<IResponseFormatter, TextResponseFormatter>();
builder.Services.AddScoped<IResponseFormatter, HtmlResponseFormatter>();
builder.Services.AddScoped<IResponseFormatter, GuidService>();

var app = builder.Build();

//app.UseMiddleware<WeatherMiddleware>();

//app.MapEndpoint<WeatherEndpoint>("endpoint/class");

//app.MapGet("endpoint/function",
//     async (HttpContext context, IResponseFormatter formatter) => {
//         await formatter.Format(context,
//             "Endpoint Function: It is sunny in LA");
//});

app.MapGet("single", async context => {
    IResponseFormatter formatter = context.RequestServices
        .GetRequiredService<IResponseFormatter>();
    await formatter.Format(context, "Single service");
});

app.MapGet("/", async context => {
    IResponseFormatter formatter = context.RequestServices
        .GetServices<IResponseFormatter>().First(f => f.RichOutput);
    await formatter.Format(context, "Multiple services");
});

app.Run();
```

The AddScoped statements register three services for the IResponseFormatter interface, each with a different implementation class. The route for the /single URL uses
the IServiceProvider.GetRequiredService<T> method to request a service, like
this:

```
...
context.RequestServices.GetRequiredService<IResponseFormatter>();
...
```

This is a service consumer that is unaware that there are multiple implementations available. The service is resolved using the most recently registered implementation, which is the `GuidService` class. Restart ASP.NET Core and request http://localhost:5000/single, and you will see the output on the left side of figure 14.15.

The other endpoint is a service consumer that is aware that multiple implementations may be available and that requests the service using the `IServiceProvider.GetServices<T>` method.

```
...
context.RequestServices.GetServices<IResponseFormatter>()
    .First(f => f.RichOutput);
...
```

This method returns an `IEnumerable<IResponseFormatter>` that enumerates the available implementations. These are filtered using the LINQ `First` method to select an implementation whose `RichOutput` property returns `true`. If you request http://localhost:5000, you will see the output on the right of figure 14.15, showing that the endpoint has selected the service implementation that best suits its needs.

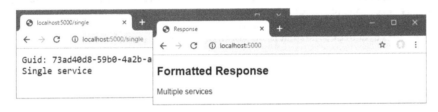

Figure 14.15 Using multiple service implementations

14.5.5 *Using unbound types in services*

Services can be defined with generic type parameters that are bound to specific types when the service is requested, as shown in listing 14.39.

Listing 14.39. Using an unbound type in the Program.cs file in the Platform folder

```
//using Platform.Services;

var builder = WebApplication.CreateBuilder(args);

//builder.Services.AddScoped<IResponseFormatter, TextResponseFormatter>();
//builder.Services.AddScoped<IResponseFormatter, HtmlResponseFormatter>();
//builder.Services.AddScoped<IResponseFormatter, GuidService>();

builder.Services.AddSingleton(typeof(ICollection<>), typeof(List<>));

var app = builder.Build();

//app.MapGet("single", async context => {
//    IResponseFormatter formatter = context.RequestServices
//        .GetRequiredService<IResponseFormatter>();
```

```
//    await formatter.Format(context, "Single service");
//});

//app.MapGet("/", async context => {
//    IResponseFormatter formatter = context.RequestServices
//        .GetServices<IResponseFormatter>().First(f => f.RichOutput);
//    await formatter.Format(context, "Multiple services");
//});

app.MapGet("string", async context => {
    ICollection<string> collection = context.RequestServices
        .GetRequiredService<ICollection<string>>();
    collection.Add($"Request: {DateTime.Now.ToLongTimeString()}");
    foreach (string str in collection) {
        await context.Response.WriteAsync($"String: {str}\n");
    }
});

app.MapGet("int", async context => {
    ICollection<int> collection
        = context.RequestServices.GetRequiredService<ICollection<int>>();
    collection.Add(collection.Count() + 1);
    foreach (int val in collection) {
        await context.Response.WriteAsync($"Int: {val}\n");
    }
});

app.Run();
```

This feature relies on the versions of the AddSingleton, AddScoped, and Add-
Transient methods that accept types as conventional arguments and cannot be
performed using generic type arguments. The service in listing 14.39 is created with
unbound types, like this:

```
...
services.AddSingleton(typeof(ICollection<>), typeof(List<>));
...
```

When a dependency on an ICollection<T> service is resolved, a List<T> object
will be created so that a dependency on ICollection<string>, for example, will be
resolved using a List<string> object. Rather than require separate services for each
type, the unbound service allows mappings for all generic types to be created.

The two endpoints in listing 14.39 request ICollection<string> and
ICollection<int> services, each of which will be resolved with a different
List<T> object. To target the endpoints, restart ASP.NET Core and request http://
localhost:5000/string and http://localhost:5000/int. The service has been defined
as a singleton, which means that the same List<string> and List<int> objects will
be used to resolve all requests for ICollection<string> and ICollection<int>.
Each request adds a new item to the collection, which you can see by reloading the web
browser, as shown in figure 14.16.

Figure 14.16   Using a singleton service with an unbound type

Summary

- Dependency injection allows application components to declare dependencies on services by defining constructor parameters.
- Services can be defined with a type, an object, or a factory function.
- The scope of a service determines when services are instantiated and how they are shared between components.
- Dependency injection is integrated into the ASP.NET Core request pipeline.

Using the platform
features, part 1

This chapter covers

- Understanding the built-in features provided by ASP.NET Core
- Accessing the application configuration
- Storing secrets outside of the project folder
- Logging messages
- Generating static content and using client-side packages

ASP.NET Core includes a set of built-in services and middleware components that provide features that are commonly required by web applications. In this chapter, I describe three of the most important and widely used features: application configuration, logging, and serving static content. In chapter 16, I continue to describe the platform features, focusing on the more advanced built-in services and middleware. Table 15.1 puts the chapter in context.

Table 15.1 Putting platform features in context

Question	Answer
What are they?	The platform features deal with common web application requirements, such as configuration, logging, static files, sessions, authentication, and database access.
Why are they useful?	Using these features means you don't have to re-create their functionality in your own projects.
How are they used?	The built-in middleware components are added to the request pipeline using extension methods whose name starts with `Use`. Services are set up using methods that start with `Add`.
Are there any pitfalls or limitations?	The most common problems relate to the order in which middleware components are added to the request pipeline. Middleware components form a chain along which requests pass, as described in chapter 12.
Are there any alternatives?	You don't have to use any of the services or middleware components that ASP.NET Core provides.

Table 15.2 provides a guide to the chapter.

Table 15.2 Chapter guide

Problem	Solution	Listing
Accessing the configuration data	Use the `IConfiguration` service.	4–8
Setting the application environment	Use the launch settings file.	9–11
Determining the application environment	Use the `IWebHostEnvironment` service.	12
Keeping sensitive data outside of the project	Create user secrets.	13–17
Logging messages	Use the `ILogger<T>` service.	18–27
Delivering static content	Enable the static content middleware.	28–31
Delivering client-side packages	Install the package with LibMan and deliver it with the static content middleware.	32–35

15.1 Preparing for this chapter

In this chapter, I continue to use the Platform project created in chapter 14. To prepare for this chapter, update the `Program.cs` file to remove middleware and services, as shown in listing 15.1.

Listing 15.1   **The contents of the Program.cs file in the Platform folder**

```
var builder = WebApplication.CreateBuilder(args);

var app = builder.Build();

app.MapGet("/", async context => {
    await context.Response.WriteAsync("Hello World!");
});

app.Run();
```

One of the main topics in this chapter is configuration data. Replace the contents of the `appsettings.Development.json` file with the contents of listing 15.2 to remove the setting added in chapter 14.

Listing 15.2   **The contents of the appsettings.Development.json file in the Platform folder**

```
{
  "Logging": {
    "LogLevel": {
      "Default": "Debug",
      "System": "Information",
      "Microsoft": "Information"
    }
  }
}
```

Start the application by opening a new PowerShell command prompt, navigating to the `Platform` project folder, and running the command shown in listing 15.3.

> **TIP**   You can download the example project for this chapter—and for all the other chapters in this book—from https://github.com/manningbooks/pro-asp .net-core-7. See chapter 1 for how to get help if you have problems running the examples.

Listing 15.3   **Starting the ASP.NET Core runtime**

```
dotnet run
```

Open a new browser tab and navigate to http://localhost:5000; you will see the content shown in figure 15.1.

Figure 15.1   Running the example application

15.2 Using the configuration service

One of the built-in features provided by ASP.NET Core is access to the application's configuration settings, which is presented as a service.

The main source of configuration data is the `appsettings.json` file. The `appsettings.json` file created by the template used in chapter 12 contains the following settings:

```
{
  "Logging": {
    "LogLevel": {
      "Default": "Information",
      "Microsoft.AspNetCore": "Warning"
    }
  },
  "AllowedHosts": "*"
}
```

The configuration service will process the JSON configuration file and create nested configuration sections that contain individual settings. For the `appsettings.json` file in the example application, the configuration service will create a `Logging` configuration section that contains a `LogLevel` section. The `LogLevel` section will contain settings for `Default` and `Microsoft.AspnetCore`. There will also be an `AllowedHosts` setting that isn't part of a configuration section and whose value is an asterisk (the * character).

The configuration service doesn't understand the meaning of the configuration sections or settings in the `appsettings.json` file and is just responsible for processing the JSON data file and merging the configuration settings with the values obtained from other sources, such as environment variables or command-line arguments. The result is a hierarchical set of configuration properties, as shown in figure 15.2.

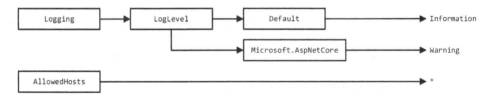

Figure 15.2   The hierarchy of configuration properties in the appsettings.json file

15.2.1 Understanding the environment configuration file

Most projects contain more than one JSON configuration file, allowing different settings to be defined for different parts of the development cycle. There are three predefined environments, named `Development`, `Staging`, and `Production`, each of which corresponds to a commonly used phase of development. During startup, the configuration service looks for a JSON file whose name includes the current environment. The default environment is `Development`, which means the configuration service will load the `appsettings.Development.json` file and use its contents to supplement the contents of the main `appsettings.json` file.

> **NOTE**   The Visual Studio Solution Explorer nests the `appsettings.Development.json` file in the `appsettings.json` item. You can expand the `appsettings.json` file to see and edit the nested entries or click the button at the top of the Solution Explorer that disables the nesting feature.

Here are the configuration settings added to the `appsettings.Development.json` file in listing 15.2:

```
{
  "Logging": {
    "LogLevel": {
      "Default": "Debug",
      "System": "Information",
      "Microsoft": "Information"
    }
  }
}
```

Where the same setting is defined in both files, the value in the `appsettings.Development.json` file will replace the one in the `appsettings.json` file, which means that the contents of the two JSON files will produce the hierarchy of configuration settings shown in figure 15.3.

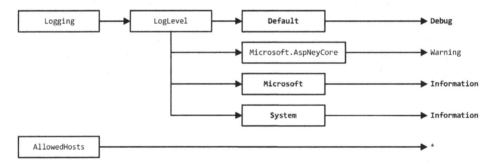

Figure 15.3   Merging JSON configuration settings

The effect of the additional configuration settings is to increase the detail level of logging messages, which I describe in more detail in the "Using the Logging Service" section.

15.2.2 Accessing configuration settings

The configuration data is accessed through a service. If you only require the configuration data to configure middleware, then the dependency on the configuration service can be declared using a parameter, as shown in listing 15.4.

Listing 15.4 Accessing configuration data in the Program.cs file in the Platform folder

```
var builder = WebApplication.CreateBuilder(args);

var app = builder.Build();

app.MapGet("config", async (HttpContext context,
        IConfiguration config) => {
    string? defaultDebug = config["Logging:LogLevel:Default"];
    await context.Response
        .WriteAsync($"The config setting is: {defaultDebug}");
});

app.MapGet("/", async context => {
    await context.Response.WriteAsync("Hello World!");
});

app.Run();
```

Configuration data is provided through the `IConfiguration` interface; this interface is defined in the `Microsoft.Extensions.Configuration` namespace and provides an API for navigating through the configuration hierarchy and reading configuration settings. Configuration settings can be read by specifying the path through the configuration sections, like this:

```
...
string? defaultDebug = config["Logging:LogLevel:Default"];
...
```

This statement reads the value of the `Default` setting, which is defined in the `LogLevel` section of the `Logging` part of the configuration. The names of the configuration sections and the configuration settings are separated by colons (the : character).

The value of the configuration setting read in listing 15.4 is used to provide a result for a middleware component that handles the `/config` URL. Restart ASP.NET Core using Control+C at the command prompt and run the command shown in listing 15.5 in the `Platform` folder.

Listing 15.5 Starting the ASP.NET Core platform

```
dotnet run
```

Once the runtime has restarted, navigate to the http://localhost:5000/config URL, and you will see the value of the configuration setting displayed in the browser tab, as shown in figure 15.4.

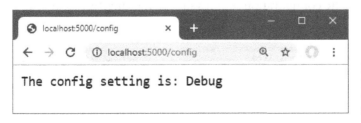

Figure 15.4 Reading configuration data

15.2.3 Using the configuration data in the Program.cs file

As noted in chapter 14, the WebApplication and WebApplicationBuilder classes provide a Configuration property that can be used to obtain an implementation of the IConfiguration interface, which is useful when using configuration data to configure an application's services. Listing 15.6 shows both uses of configuration data.

> **Listing 15.6   Configuring services and pipeline in the Program.cs file in the Platform folder**

```
var builder = WebApplication.CreateBuilder(args);

var servicesConfig = builder.Configuration;
// - use configuration settings to set up services

var app = builder.Build();

var pipelineConfig = app.Configuration;
// - use configuration settings to set up pipeline

app.MapGet("config", async (HttpContext context,
        IConfiguration config) => {
    string? defaultDebug = config["Logging:LogLevel:Default"];
    await context.Response
        .WriteAsync($"The config setting is: {defaultDebug}");
});

app.MapGet("/", async context => {
    await context.Response.WriteAsync("Hello World!");
});

app.Run();
```

This may seem like an unnecessary step because there is so little code in the Program .cs file in this example application, which makes it obvious that the configuration service isn't replaced. It isn't always as obvious in a real project, where services can be defined in groups by methods defined outside of the Program.cs file, making it difficult to see if these methods alter the IConfiguration service.

15.2.4 Using configuration data with the options pattern

In chapter 12, I described the options pattern, which is a useful way to configure middleware components. A helpful feature provided by the IConfiguration service is the ability to create options directly from configuration data.

To prepare, add the configuration settings shown in listing 15.7 to the appsettings .json file.

> **Listing 15.7   Adding configuration data in the appsettings.json file in the Platform folder**

```
{
  "Logging": {
    "LogLevel": {
```

```
      "Default": "Information",
      "Microsoft.AspNetCore": "Warning"
    }
  },
  "AllowedHosts": "*",
  "Location": {
    "CityName": "Buffalo"
  }
}
```

The `Location` section of the configuration file can be used to provide options pattern values, as shown in listing 15.8.

> **Listing 15.8 Using configuration data in the Program.cs file in the Platform folder**

```
using Platform;

var builder = WebApplication.CreateBuilder(args);

var servicesConfig = builder.Configuration;
builder.Services.Configure<MessageOptions>(
    servicesConfig.GetSection("Location"));

var app = builder.Build();

var pipelineConfig = app.Configuration;
// - use configuration settings to set up pipeline

app.UseMiddleware<LocationMiddleware>();

app.MapGet("config", async (HttpContext context,
        IConfiguration config) => {
    string? defaultDebug = config["Logging:LogLevel:Default"];
    await context.Response
        .WriteAsync($"The config setting is: {defaultDebug}");
});

app.MapGet("/", async context => {
    await context.Response.WriteAsync("Hello World!");
});

app.Run();
```

The configuration data is obtained using the `GetSection` method and passed to the `Configure` method when the options are created. The configuration values in the selected section are inspected and used to replace the default values with the same names in the options class. To see the effect, restart ASP.NET Core and use the browser to navigate to the http://localhost:5000/location URL. You will see the results shown in figure 15.5, where the `CityName` option is taken from the configuration data and the `CountryName` option is taken from the default value in the options class.

Figure 15.5   Using configuration data in the options pattern

15.2.5 *Understanding the launch settings file*

The `launchSettings.json` file in the `Properties` folder contains the configuration settings for starting the ASP.NET Core platform, including the TCP ports that are used to listen for HTTP and HTTPS requests and the environment used to select the additional JSON configuration files.

> **TIP**   Visual Studio often hides the `Properties` folder. If you can't see the folder, click the Show All Files button at the top of the Solution Explorer to reveal the folder and the `launchSettings.json` file.

Here is the content added to the `launchSettings.json` file when the project was created and then edited to set the HTTP ports:

```
{
  "iisSettings": {
    "windowsAuthentication": false,
    "anonymousAuthentication": true,
    "iisExpress": {
      "applicationUrl": "http://localhost:5000",
      "sslPort": 0
    }
  },
  "profiles": {
    "Platform": {
      "commandName": "Project",
      "dotnetRunMessages": true,
      "launchBrowser": true,
      "applicationUrl": "http://localhost:5000",
      "environmentVariables": {
        "ASPNETCORE_ENVIRONMENT": "Development"
      }
    },
    "IIS Express": {
      "commandName": "IISExpress",
      "launchBrowser": true,
      "environmentVariables": {
        "ASPNETCORE_ENVIRONMENT": "Development"
      }
    }
  }
}
```

The iisSettings section is used to configure the HTTP and HTTPS ports used when the ASP.NET Core platform is started through IIS Express, which is how older versions of ASP.NET Core were deployed.

The profiles section describes a series of launch profiles, which define configuration settings for different ways of running the application. The Platform section defines the configuration used by the dotnet run command. The IIS Express section defines the configuration used when the application is used with IIS Express.

Both profiles contain an environmentVariables section, which is used to define environment variables that are added to the application's configuration data. There is only one environment variable defined by default: ASPNETCORE_ENVIRONMENT.

During startup, the value of the ASPNETCORE_ENVIRONMENT setting is used to select the additional JSON configuration file so that a value of Development, for example, will cause the appsettings.Development.json file to be loaded.

When the application is started within Visual Studio Code, ASPNETCORE_ENVIRONMENT is set in a different file. Select Run > Open Configurations to open the launch.json file in the .vscode folder, which is created when a project is edited with Visual Studio Code. Here is the default configuration for the example project, showing the current ASPNETCORE_ENVIRONMENT value, with the comments removed for brevity:

```
{
    "version": "0.2.0",
    "configurations": [
        {

            "name": ".NET Core Launch (web)",
            "type": "coreclr",
            "request": "launch",
            "preLaunchTask": "build",
            "program": "${workspaceFolder}/bin/Debug/net7.0/Platform.dll",
            "args": [],
            "cwd": "${workspaceFolder}",
            "stopAtEntry": false,
            "serverReadyAction": {
                "action": "openExternally",
                "pattern": "\\bNow listening on:\\s+(https?://\\S+)"
            },
            "env": {
                "ASPNETCORE_ENVIRONMENT": "Development"
            },
            "sourceFileMap": {
                "/Views": "${workspaceFolder}/Views"
            }
        },
        {

            "name": ".NET Core Attach",
            "type": "coreclr",
            "request": "attach"
        }
    ]
}
```

To display the value of the ASPNETCORE_ENVIRONMENT setting, add the statements to the middleware component that responds to the /config URL, as shown in listing 15.9.

> **Listing 15.9   Displaying the configuration in the Program.cs file in the Platform folder**

```
using Platform;

var builder = WebApplication.CreateBuilder(args);

var servicesConfig = builder.Configuration;
builder.Services.Configure<MessageOptions>(
    servicesConfig.GetSection("Location"));

var app = builder.Build();

var pipelineConfig = app.Configuration;

app.UseMiddleware<LocationMiddleware>();

app.MapGet("config", async (HttpContext context,
        IConfiguration config) => {
    string? defaultDebug = config["Logging:LogLevel:Default"];
    await context.Response
        .WriteAsync($"The config setting is: {defaultDebug}");
    string? environ = config["ASPNETCORE_ENVIRONMENT"];
    await context.Response.WriteAsync($"\nThe env setting is: {environ}");
});

app.MapGet("/", async context => {
    await context.Response.WriteAsync("Hello World!");
});

app.Run();
```

Restart ASP.NET Core and navigate to http://localhost:5000/config, and you will see the value of the ASPNETCORE_ENVIRONMENT setting, as shown in figure 15.6.

Figure 15.6   Displaying the environment configuration setting

To see the effect that the ASPNETCORE_ENVIRONMENT setting has on the overall configuration, change the value in the launchSettings.json file, as shown in listing 15.10.

Listing 15.10 Changing the launchSettings.json file in the Platform/Properties folder

```json
{
  "iisSettings": {
    "windowsAuthentication": false,
    "anonymousAuthentication": true,
    "iisExpress": {
      "applicationUrl": "http://localhost:5000",
      "sslPort": 0
    }
  },
  "profiles": {
    "Platform": {
      "commandName": "Project",
      "dotnetRunMessages": true,
      "launchBrowser": true,
      "applicationUrl": "http://localhost:5000",
      "environmentVariables": {
        "ASPNETCORE_ENVIRONMENT": "Production"
      }
    },
    "IIS Express": {
      "commandName": "IISExpress",
      "launchBrowser": true,
      "environmentVariables": {
        "ASPNETCORE_ENVIRONMENT": "Development"
      }
    }
  }
}
```

If you are using Visual Studio, you can change the environment variables by selecting Debug > Launch Profiles. The settings for each launch profile are displayed, and there is support for changing the value of the ASPNETCORE_ENVIRONMENT variable, as shown in figure 15.7.

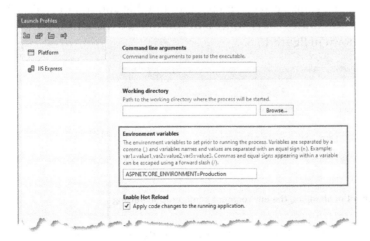

**Figure 15.7
Changing an
environment variable
using Visual Studio**

If you are using Visual Studio Code, select Run > Open Configurations and change the value in the env section, as shown in listing 15.11.

Listing 15.11   Changing the launch.json file in the Platform/.vscode folder

```
{
    "version": "0.2.0",
    "configurations": [
        {
            "name": ".NET Core Launch (web)",
            "type": "coreclr",
            "request": "launch",
            "preLaunchTask": "build",
            "program": "${workspaceFolder}/bin/Debug/net7.0/Platform.dll",
            "args": [],
            "cwd": "${workspaceFolder}",
            "stopAtEntry": false,
            "serverReadyAction": {
                "action": "openExternally",
                "pattern": "\\bNow listening on:\\s+(https?://\\S+)"
            },
            "env": {
                "ASPNETCORE_ENVIRONMENT": "Production"
            },
            "sourceFileMap": {
                "/Views": "${workspaceFolder}/Views"
            }
        },
        {
            "name": ".NET Core Attach",
            "type": "coreclr",
            "request": "attach"
        }
    ]
}
```

Save the changes to the property page or configuration file and restart ASP.NET Core. Navigate to http://localhost:5000/config, and you will see the effect of the environment change, as shown in figure 15.8.

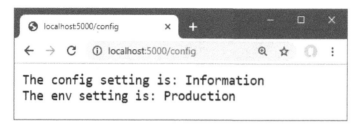

Figure 15.8   The effect of changing the environment configuration setting

Notice that both configuration values displayed in the browser have changed. The appsettings.Development.json file is no longer loaded, and there is no `appsettings.Production.json` file in the project, so only the configuration settings in the `appsettings.json` file are used.

15.2.6 *Using the environment service*

The ASP.NET Core platform provides the `IWebHostEnvironment` service for determining the current environment, which avoids the need to get the configuration setting manually. The `IWebHostEnvironment` service defines the property and methods shown in table 15.3. The methods are extension methods that are defined in the `Microsoft.Extensions.Hosting` namespace.

Table 15.3 The IWebHostEnvironment extension methods

Name	Description
`EnvironmentName`	This property returns the current environment.
`IsDevelopment()`	This method returns `true` when the `Development` environment has been selected.
`IsStaging()`	This method returns `true` when the `Staging` environment has been selected.
`IsProduction()`	This method returns `true` when the `Production` environment has been selected.
`IsEnvironment(env)`	This method returns `true` when the environment specified by the argument has been selected.

If you need to access the environment when setting up services, then you can use the `WebApplicationBuilder.Environment` property. If you need to access the environment when configuring the pipeline, you can use the `WebApplication.Environment` property. If you need to access the environment within a middleware component or endpoint, then you can define a `IWebHostEnvironment` parameter. All three approaches are shown in listing 15.12.

Listing 15.12 Accessing the environment in the Program.cs file in the Platform folder

```
using Platform;

var builder = WebApplication.CreateBuilder(args);

var servicesConfig = builder.Configuration;
builder.Services.Configure<MessageOptions>(
    servicesConfig.GetSection("Location"));

var servicesEnv = builder.Environment;
// - use environment to set up services

var app = builder.Build();

var pipelineConfig = app.Configuration;
// - use configuration settings to set up pipeline

var pipelineEnv = app.Environment;
```

```
// - use envirionment to set up pipeline

app.UseMiddleware<LocationMiddleware>();

app.MapGet("config", async (HttpContext context,
        IConfiguration config, IWebHostEnvironment env) => {
    string? defaultDebug = config["Logging:LogLevel:Default"];
    await context.Response
        .WriteAsync($"The config setting is: {defaultDebug}");
    await context.Response
        .WriteAsync($"\nThe env setting is: {env.EnvironmentName}");
});

app.MapGet("/", async context => {
    await context.Response.WriteAsync("Hello World!");
});

app.Run();
```

Restart ASP.NET Core and use a browser to request http://localhost:5000/config, which produces the output shown in figure 15.8.

15.2.7 Storing user secrets

During development, it is often necessary to use sensitive data to work with the services that an application depends on. This data can include API keys, database connection passwords, or default administration accounts, and it is used both to access services and to reinitialize them to test application changes with a fresh database or user configuration.

If the sensitive data is included in the C# classes or JSON configuration files, it will be checked into the source code version control repository and become visible to all developers and to anyone else who can see the code—which may mean visible to the world for projects that have open repositories or repositories that are poorly secured.

The user secrets service allows sensitive data to be stored in a file that isn't part of the project and won't be checked into version control, allowing each developer to have sensitive data that won't be accidentally exposed through a version control check-in.

STORING USER SECRETS

The first step is to prepare the file that will be used to store sensitive data. Run the command shown in listing 15.13 in the Platform folder.

> **Listing 15.13   Initializing user secrets**

```
dotnet user-secrets init
```

This command adds an element to the Platform.csproj project file that contains a unique ID for the project that will be associated with the secrets on each developer machine. Next, run the commands shown in listing 15.14 in the Platform folder.

Listing 15.14 Storing a user secret

```
dotnet user-secrets set "WebService:Id" "MyAccount"
dotnet user-secrets set "WebService:Key" "MySecret123$"
```

Each secret has a key and a value, and related secrets can be grouped together by using a common prefix, followed by a colon (the : character), followed by the secret name. The commands in listing 15.14 create related Id and Key secrets that have the Web-Service prefix.

After each command, you will see a message confirming that a secret has been added to the secret store. To check the secrets for the project, use the command prompt to run the command shown in listing 15.15 in the Platform folder.

Listing 15.15 Listing the user secrets

```
dotnet user-secrets list
```

This command produces the following output:

```
WebService:Key = MySecret123$
WebService:Id = MyAccount
```

Behind the scenes, a JSON file has been created in the %APPDATA%\Microsoft\User-Secrets folder (or the ~/.microsoft/usersecrets folder for Linux) to store the secrets. Each project has its own folder (whose name corresponds to the unique ID created by the init command in listing 15.13).

> **TIP** If you are using Visual Studio, you can create and edit the JSON file directly by right-clicking the project in the Solution Explorer and selecting Manage User Secrets from the pop-up menu.

READING USER SECRETS

User secrets are merged with the normal configuration settings and accessed in the same way. In listing 15.16, I have added a statement that displays the secrets to the middleware component that handles the /config URL.

Listing 15.16 Using user secrets in the Program.cs file in the Platform folder

```
using Platform;

var builder = WebApplication.CreateBuilder(args);

var servicesConfig = builder.Configuration;
builder.Services.Configure<MessageOptions>(
    servicesConfig.GetSection("Location"));

var servicesEnv = builder.Environment;
// - use environment to set up services

var app = builder.Build();

var pipelineConfig = app.Configuration;
```

```
// - use configuration settings to set up pipeline

var pipelineEnv = app.Environment;
// - use envirionment to set up pipeline

app.UseMiddleware<LocationMiddleware>();

app.MapGet("config", async (HttpContext context,
        IConfiguration config, IWebHostEnvironment env) => {
    string? defaultDebug = config["Logging:LogLevel:Default"];
    await context.Response
        .WriteAsync($"The config setting is: {defaultDebug}");
    await context.Response
        .WriteAsync($"\nThe env setting is: {env.EnvironmentName}");
    string? wsID = config["WebService:Id"];
    string? wsKey = config["WebService:Key"];
    await context.Response.WriteAsync($"\nThe secret ID is: {wsID}");
    await context.Response.WriteAsync($"\nThe secret Key is: {wsKey}");
});

app.MapGet("/", async context => {
    await context.Response.WriteAsync("Hello World!");
});

app.Run();
```

User secrets are loaded only when the application is set to the Development environment. Edit the launchSettings.json file to change the environment to Development, as shown in listing 15.17.

> **Listing 15.17   Changing the launchSettings.json file in the Platform/Properties folder**

```
{
  "iisSettings": {
    "windowsAuthentication": false,
    "anonymousAuthentication": true,
    "iisExpress": {
      "applicationUrl": "http://localhost:5000",
      "sslPort": 0
    }
  },
  "profiles": {
    "Platform": {
      "commandName": "Project",
      "dotnetRunMessages": true,
      "launchBrowser": true,
      "applicationUrl": "http://localhost:5000",
      "environmentVariables": {
        "ASPNETCORE_ENVIRONMENT": "Development"
      }
    },
    "IIS Express": {
      "commandName": "IISExpress",
      "launchBrowser": true,
      "environmentVariables": {
```

```
        "ASPNETCORE_ENVIRONMENT": "Development"
      }
    }
  }
}
```

Save the changes, restart the ASP.NET Core runtime using the `dotnet run` command, and request the http://localhost:5000/config URL to see the user secrets, as shown in figure 15.9.

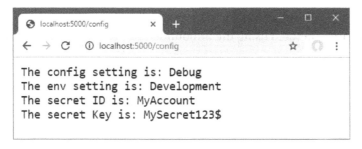

Figure 15.9   Displaying user secrets

15.3   Using the logging service

ASP.NET Core provides a logging service that can be used to record messages that describe the state of the application to track errors, monitor performance, and help diagnose problems.

Log messages are sent to logging providers, which are responsible for forwarding messages to where they can be seen, stored, and processed. There are built-in providers for basic logging, and there is a range of third-party providers available for feeding messages into logging frameworks that allow messages to be collated and analyzed.

Three of the built-in providers are enabled by default: the console provider, the debug provider, and the `EventSource` provider. The debug provider forwards messages so they can be processed through the `System.Diagnostics.Debug` class, and the `EventSource` provider forwards messages for event tracing tools, such as `PerfView` (https://github.com/Microsoft/perfview). I use the console provider in this chapter because it is simple and doesn't require any additional configuration to display logging messages.

> **TIP**   You can see the list of providers available and instructions for enabling them at https://docs.microsoft.com/en-us/aspnet/core/fundamentals/logging.

15.3.1   Generating logging messages

To prepare for this section, listing 15.18 reconfigures the application to remove the services, middleware, and endpoints from the previous section.

Listing 15.18   Configuring the application in the Program.cs file in the Platform folder

```
using Platform;

var builder = WebApplication.CreateBuilder(args);

var app = builder.Build();

app.MapGet("population/{city?}", Population.Endpoint);

app.Run();
```

Logging messages are generated using the unbounded `ILogger<>` service, as shown in listing 15.19.

Listing 15.19   Generating logging messages in the Population.cs file in the Platform folder

```
namespace Platform {
    public class Population {

        public static async Task Endpoint(HttpContext context,
                ILogger<Population> logger) {
            logger.LogDebug("Started processing for {path}",
                context.Request.Path);
            string city = context.Request.RouteValues["city"]
                as string ?? "london";
            int? pop = null;
            switch (city.ToLower()) {
                case "london":
                    pop = 8_136_000;
                    break;
                case "paris":
                    pop = 2_141_000;
                    break;
                case "monaco":
                    pop = 39_000;
                    break;
            }
            if (pop.HasValue) {
                await context.Response
                    .WriteAsync($"City: {city}, Population: {pop}");
            } else {
                context.Response.StatusCode
                    = StatusCodes.Status404NotFound;
            }
            logger.LogDebug("Finished processing for {path}",
                context.Request.Path);
        }
    }
}
```

The logging service groups log messages together based on the category assigned to messages. Log messages are written using the `ILogger<T>` interface, where the generic parameter `T` is used to specify the category. The convention is to use the type of the class that generates the messages as the category type, which is why listing 15.19 declares a dependency on the service using `Population` for the type argument, like this:

```
...
public static async Task Endpoint(HttpContext context,
    ILogger<Population> logger) {
...
```

This ensures that log messages generated by the `Endpoint` method will be assigned the category `Population`. Log messages are created using the extension methods shown in table 15.4.

Table 15.4 The ILogger<T> extension methods

Name	Description
LogTrace	This method generates a `Trace`-level message, used for low-level debugging `during` development.
LogDebug	This method generates a `Debug`-level message, used for low-level debugging during development or production problem resolution.
LogInformation	This method generates an `Information`-level message, used to provide information about the general state of the application.
LogWarning	This method generates a `Warning`-level message, used to record unexpected, but minor, problems that are unlikely to disrupt the application.
LogError	This method generates an `Error`-level message, used to record exceptions or errors that are not handled by the application.
LogCritical	This method generates a `Critical`-level message, used to record serious failures.

Log messages are assigned a level that reflects their importance and detail. The levels range from `Trace`, for detailed diagnostics, to `Critical`, for the most important information that requires an immediate response. There are overloaded versions of each method that allow log messages to be generated using strings or exceptions. In listing 15.19, I used the `LogDebug` method to generate logging messages when a request is handled.

```
...
logger.LogDebug("Started processing for {path}", context.Request.Path);
...
```

The result is log messages at the `Debug` level that are generated when the response is started and completed. To see the log messages, restart ASP.NET Core and use a browser to request http://localhost:5000/population. Look at the console output, and you will see the log messages in the output from ASP.NET Core, like this:

```
Building...
info: Microsoft.Hosting.Lifetime[14]
      Now listening on: http://localhost:5000
```

```
info: Microsoft.Hosting.Lifetime[0]
      Application started. Press Ctrl+C to shut down.
info: Microsoft.Hosting.Lifetime[0]
      Hosting environment: Development
info: Microsoft.Hosting.Lifetime[0]
      Content root path: C:\Platform
dbug: Platform.Population[0]
      Started processing for /population
dbug: Platform.Population[0]
      Finished processing for /population
```

LOGGING MESSAGES IN THE PROGRAM.CS FILE

The `Logger<>` service is useful for logging in classes but isn't suited to logging in the `Program.cs` file, where top-level statements are used to configure the application. The simplest approach is to use the `ILogger` returned by the `Logger` property defined by the `WebApplication` class, as shown in listing 15.20.

> **Listing 15.20   Logging in the Program.cs file in the Platform folder**

```
using Platform;

var builder = WebApplication.CreateBuilder(args);

var app = builder.Build();

app.Logger.LogDebug("Pipeline configuration starting");

app.MapGet("population/{city?}", Population.Endpoint);

app.Logger.LogDebug("Pipeline configuration complete");

app.Run();
```

The `ILogger` interface defines all the methods described in table 15.4. Start ASP.NET Core, and you will see the logging messages in the startup output, like this:

```
Building...
dbug: Platform[0]
      Pipeline configuration starting
dbug: Platform[0]
      Pipeline configuration complete
info: Microsoft.Hosting.Lifetime[14]
      Now listening on: http://localhost:5000
info: Microsoft.Hosting.Lifetime[0]
      Application started. Press Ctrl+C to shut down.
info: Microsoft.Hosting.Lifetime[0]
      Hosting environment: Development
info: Microsoft.Hosting.Lifetime[0]
      Content root path: C:\Platform
```

The category for logging messages generated using the `ILogger` provided by the `WebApplication` class is the name of the application, which is `Platform` for this example. If you want to generate log messages with a different category, which can be useful in lambda functions, for example, then you can use the `ILoggerFactory` interface, which is available as a service, and call the `CreateLogger` method to obtain an `ILogger` for a specified category, as shown in listing 15.21.

Listing 15.21 Creating a logger in the Program.cs file in the Platform folder

```
using Platform;

var builder = WebApplication.CreateBuilder(args);

var app = builder.Build();

var logger = app.Services
    .GetRequiredService<ILoggerFactory>().CreateLogger("Pipeline");

logger.LogDebug("Pipeline configuration starting");

app.MapGet("population/{city?}", Population.Endpoint);

logger.LogDebug("Pipeline configuration complete");

app.Run();
```

Restart ASP.NET Core, and you will see the following messages in the output produced as the application starts:

```
Building...
dbug: Pipeline[0]
      Pipeline configuration starting
dbug: Pipeline[0]
      Pipeline configuration complete
info: Microsoft.Hosting.Lifetime[14]
      Now listening on: http://localhost:5000
info: Microsoft.Hosting.Lifetime[0]
      Application started. Press Ctrl+C to shut down.
info: Microsoft.Hosting.Lifetime[0]
      Hosting environment: Development
info: Microsoft.Hosting.Lifetime[0]
      Content root path: C:\Platform
```

15.3.2 Logging messages with attributes

An alternative approach to generating log messages is to use the `LoggerMessage` attribute, as shown in listing 15.22.

Listing 15.22 Using the attribute in the Population.cs file in the Platform folder

```
namespace Platform {
    public partial class Population {

        public static async Task Endpoint(HttpContext context,
                ILogger<Population> logger) {
            //logger.LogDebug("Started processing for {path}",
            //    context.Request.Path);
            StartingResponse(logger, context.Request.Path);
            string city = context.Request.RouteValues["city"]
                as string ?? "london";
```

```
                int? pop = null;
                switch (city.ToLower()) {
                    case "london":
                        pop = 8_136_000;
                        break;
                    case "paris":
                        pop = 2_141_000;
                        break;
                    case "monaco":
                        pop = 39_000;
                        break;
                }
                if (pop.HasValue) {
                    await context.Response
                        .WriteAsync($"City: {city}, Population: {pop}");
                } else {
                    context.Response.StatusCode
                        = StatusCodes.Status404NotFound;
                }
                logger.LogDebug("Finished processing for {path}",
                    context.Request.Path);
            }

        [LoggerMessage(0, LogLevel.Debug, "Starting response for {path}")]
        public static partial void StartingResponse(ILogger logger,
            string path);
    }
}
```

The `LoggerMessage` attribute is applied to `partial` methods, which must be defined
in `partial` classes. When the application is compiled, the attribute generates the
implementation for the method to which it is applied, resulting in logging, which
Microsoft says offers better performance than the other techniques described in this
section. Full details of how this feature works can be found at https://docs.microsoft
.com/en-us/dotnet/core/extensions/logger-message-generator.

> **NOTE** I do not doubt Microsoft's assertion that using the `LoggerMessage` attri-
> bute is faster, but I doubt it matters for most projects. Use the attribute if you
> find this approach easier to understand and maintain, but don't rush to adopt
> it just for the sake of a performance gain unless you have an application that
> doesn't meet its performance goals and you are sure that logging performance
> is contributing to the problem. I am confident that this will never be the case for
> most projects because of the nature of most web applications, but please get in
> touch if you find yourself in this position because I am always willing to have my
> assumptions proven wrong.

Start ASP.NET Core and use a browser to request http://localhost:5000/population,
and the output will include the following log messages:

```
dbug: Platform.Population[0]
      Starting response for /population
dbug: Platform.Population[0]
      Finished processing for /population
```

15.3.3 *Configuring minimum logging levels*

Earlier in this chapter, I showed you the default contents of the `appsettings.json` and `appsettings.Development.json` files and explained how they are merged to create the application's configuration settings. The settings in the JSON file are used to configure the logging service, which ASP.NET Core provides to record messages about the state of the application.

The `Logging:LogLevel` section of the `appsettings.json` file is used to set the minimum level for logging messages. Log messages that are below the minimum level are discarded. The `appsettings.json` file contains the following levels:

```
...
"Default": "Information",
"Microsoft.AspNetCore": "Warning"
...
```

The category for the log messages—which is set using the generic type argument or using a string—is used to select a minimum filter level.

For the log messages generated by the `Population` class, for example, the category will be `Platform.Population`, which means that they can be matched directly by adding a `Platform.Population` entry to the `appsettings.json` file or indirectly by specifying just the `Platform` namespace. Any category for which there is no minimum log level is matched by the `Default` entry, which is set to `Information`.

It is common to increase the detail of the log messages displayed during development, which is why the levels in the `appsettings.Development.json` file specify more detailed logging levels, like this:

```
...
"Default": "Debug",
"System": "Information",
"Microsoft": "Information"
...
```

When the application is configured for the `Development` environment, the default logging level is `Debug`. The levels for the `System` and `Microsoft` categories are set to `Information`, which affects the logging messages generated by ASP.NET Core and the other packages and frameworks provided by Microsoft.

You can tailor the logging levels to focus the log on those parts of the application that are of interest by setting a level to `Trace`, `Debug`, `Information`, `Warning`, `Error`, or `Critical`. Logging messages can be disabled for a category using the `None` value.

Listing 15.23 sets the level to `Debug` for the `Microsoft.AspNetCore` setting, which will increase the default level of detail and will have the effect of displaying debug-level messages generated by ASP.NET Core.

> **TIP** If you are using Visual Studio, you may have to expand the `appsettings.json` item in the Solution Explorer to see the `appsettings.Development.json` file.

> **Listing 15.23   Configuring the appsettings.Development.json file in the Platform folder**

```
{
  "Logging": {
    "LogLevel": {
      "Default": "Debug",
      "System": "Information",
      "Microsoft": "Information",
      "Microsoft.AspNetCore": "Debug"
    }
  }
}
```

Restart ASP.NET Core and request the http://localhost:5000/population URL, and you will see a series of messages from the different ASP.NET Core components. You can reduce the detail by being more specific about the namespace for which messages are required, as shown in listing 15.24.

> **Listing 15.24   Configuring the appsettings.Development.json file in the Platform folder**

```
{
  "Logging": {
    "LogLevel": {
      "Default": "Debug",
      "System": "Information",
      "Microsoft": "Information",
      "Microsoft.AspNetCore": "Warning",
      "Microsoft.AspNetCore.Routing": "Debug"
    }
  }
}
```

The changes return the `Microsoft.AspNetCore` category to `Warning` and set the `Microsoft.AspNetCore.Routing` category to `Debug`, which increases the detail level for logging messages by the components responsible for routing. Restart ASP.NET Core and request http://localhost:5000/population again, and you will see fewer messages overall, but still see those that report how the request was matched to a route:

```
...
dbug: Microsoft.AspNetCore.Routing.Matching.DfaMatcher[1001]
      1 candidate(s) found for the request path '/population'
dbug: Microsoft.AspNetCore.Routing.Matching.DfaMatcher[1005]
      Endpoint 'HTTP: GET population/{city?} =>
        Endpoint' with route pattern 'population/{city?}' is valid
        for the request path '/population'
dbug: Microsoft.AspNetCore.Routing.EndpointRoutingMiddleware[1]
      Request matched endpoint 'HTTP: GET population/{city?} => Endpoint'
info: Microsoft.AspNetCore.Routing.EndpointMiddleware[0]
      Executing endpoint 'HTTP: GET population/{city?} => Endpoint'
dbug: Platform.Population[0]
      Starting response for /population
dbug: Platform.Population[0]
      Finished processing for /population
info: Microsoft.AspNetCore.Routing.EndpointMiddleware[1]
      Executed endpoint 'HTTP: GET population/{city?} => Endpoint'
...
```

If you are having trouble figuring out a routing scheme, then these messages can be helpful in figuring out what the application is doing with requests.

15.3.4 Logging HTTP requests and responses

ASP.NET Core includes built-in middleware for generating log messages that describe the HTTP requests received by an application and the responses it produces. Listing 15.25 adds the HTTP logging middleware to the request pipeline.

> **Listing 15.25   Adding logging middleware in the Program.cs file in the Platform folder**

```
using Platform;

var builder = WebApplication.CreateBuilder(args);

var app = builder.Build();

app.UseHttpLogging();

//var logger = app.Services
//   .GetRequiredService<ILoggerFactory>().CreateLogger("Pipeline");

//logger.LogDebug("Pipeline configuration starting");

app.MapGet("population/{city?}", Population.Endpoint);

//logger.LogDebug("Pipeline configuration complete");

app.Run();
```

The `UseHttpLogging` method adds a middleware component that generates logging messages that describe the HTTP requests and responses. These log messages are generated with the `Microsoft.AspNetCore.HttpLogging.HttpLoggingMiddleware` category and the `Information` severity, which I have enabled in listing 15.26.

> **Listing 15.26   Logging in the appsettings.Development.json file in the Platform folder**

```
{
  "Logging": {
    "LogLevel": {
      "Default": "Debug",
      "System": "Information",
      "Microsoft": "Information",
      "Microsoft.AspNetCore": "Warning",
      "Microsoft.AspNetCore.HttpLogging.HttpLoggingMiddleware":
          "Information"
    }
  }
}
```

Restart ASP.NET Core and request http://localhost:5000/population, and you will see logging messages that describe the HTTP request sent by the browser and the response the application produces, similar to the following:

```
...
info: Microsoft.AspNetCore.HttpLogging.HttpLoggingMiddleware[1]
      Request:
      Protocol: HTTP/1.1
      Method: GET
      Scheme: http
      PathBase:
      Path: /population
      Accept: text/html,application/xhtml+xml,application/xml;q=0.9,
          image/avif,image/webp,image/apng,*/*;q=0.8,
          application/signed-exchange;v=b3;q=0.9
      Connection: keep-alive
      Host: localhost:5000
      User-Agent: Mozilla/5.0 (Windows NT 10.0; Win64; x64)
          AppleWebKit/537.36 (KHTML, like Gecko)
          Chrome/94.0.4606.71 Safari/537.36
      Accept-Encoding: gzip, deflate, br
      Accept-Language: en-GB,en-US;q=0.9,en;q=0.8
      Cache-Control: [Redacted]
      Cookie: [Redacted]
      Upgrade-Insecure-Requests: [Redacted]
      sec-ch-ua: [Redacted]
      sec-ch-ua-mobile: [Redacted]
      sec-ch-ua-platform: [Redacted]
      Sec-Fetch-Site: [Redacted]
      Sec-Fetch-Mode: [Redacted]
      Sec-Fetch-User: [Redacted]
      Sec-Fetch-Dest: [Redacted]
dbug: Platform.Population[0]
      Starting response for /population
dbug: Platform.Population[0]
      Finished processing for /population
info: Microsoft.AspNetCore.HttpLogging.HttpLoggingMiddleware[2]
      Response:
      StatusCode: 200
      Date: [Redacted]
      Server: [Redacted]
      Transfer-Encoding: chunked
...
```

The details of the HTTP request and response logging messages can be configured
using the AddHttpLogging method, as shown in listing 15.27.

> **Listing 15.27   HTTP logging messages in the Program.cs file in the Platform folder**

```
using Platform;
using Microsoft.AspNetCore.HttpLogging;

var builder = WebApplication.CreateBuilder(args);

builder.Services.AddHttpLogging(opts => {
    opts.LoggingFields = HttpLoggingFields.RequestMethod
        | HttpLoggingFields.RequestPath
        | HttpLoggingFields.ResponseStatusCode;
});
```

```
var app = builder.Build();

app.UseHttpLogging();

app.MapGet("population/{city?}", Population.Endpoint);

app.Run();
```

This method selects the fields and headers that are included in the logging message. The configuration in listing 15.27 selects the method and path from the HTTP request and the status code from the response. See https://docs.microsoft.com/en-us/aspnet/core/fundamentals/http-logging for the complete set of configuration options for HTTP logging.

Restart ASP.NET Core and request http://localhost:5000/population, and you will see the selected details in the output:

```
...
info: Microsoft.AspNetCore.HttpLogging.HttpLoggingMiddleware[1]
      Request:
      Method: GET
      PathBase:
      Path: /population
dbug: Platform.Population[0]
      Starting response for /population
dbug: Platform.Population[0]
      Finished processing for /population
info: Microsoft.AspNetCore.HttpLogging.HttpLoggingMiddleware[2]
      Response:
      StatusCode: 200
...
```

> **NOTE** ASP.NET Core also provides middleware that will generate log messages in the W3C format. See https://docs.microsoft.com/en-us/aspnet/core/fundamentals/w3c-logger for details.

15.4 Using static content and client-side packages

Most web applications rely on a mix of dynamically generated and static content. The dynamic content is generated by the application based on the user's identity and actions, such as the contents of a shopping cart or the detail of a specific product and is generated fresh for each request. I describe the different ways that dynamic content can be created using ASP.NET Core in part 3.

Static content doesn't change and is used to provide images, CSS stylesheets, JavaScript files, and anything else on which the application relies but which doesn't have to be generated for every request. The conventional location for static content in an ASP.NET Core project is the wwwroot folder.

To prepare static content to use in the examples for this section, create the Platform/wwwroot folder and add to it a file called static.html, with the content shown in listing 15.28. You can create the file with the HTML Page template if you are using Visual Studio.

Listing 15.28   The contents of the static.html file in the wwwroot folder

```
<!DOCTYPE html>
<html lang="en">
<head>
    <title>Static Content</title>
</head>
<body>
    <h3>This is static content</h3>
</body>
</html>
```

The file contains a basic HTML document with just the basic elements required to display a message in the browser.

15.4.1   *Adding the static content middleware*

ASP.NET Core provides a middleware component that handles requests for static content, which is added to the request pipeline in listing 15.29.

Listing 15.29   Adding middleware in the Program.cs file in the Platform folder

```
using Platform;
using Microsoft.AspNetCore.HttpLogging;

var builder = WebApplication.CreateBuilder(args);

builder.Services.AddHttpLogging(opts => {
    opts.LoggingFields = HttpLoggingFields.RequestMethod
        | HttpLoggingFields.RequestPath
        | HttpLoggingFields.ResponseStatusCode;
});

var app = builder.Build();

app.UseHttpLogging();

app.UseStaticFiles();

app.MapGet("population/{city?}", Population.Endpoint);

app.Run();
```

The UseStaticFiles extension method adds the static file middleware to the request pipeline. This middleware responds to requests that correspond to the names of disk files and passes on all other requests to the next component in the pipeline. This middleware is usually added close to the start of the request pipeline so that other components don't handle requests that are for static files.

Restart ASP.NET Core and navigate to http://localhost:5000/static.html. The static file middleware will receive the request and respond with the contents of the static .html file in the wwwroot folder, as shown in figure 15.10.

Figure 15.10   Serving static content

The middleware component returns the content of the requested file and sets the response headers, such as `Content-Type` and `Content-Length`, that describe the content to the browser.

CHANGING THE DEFAULT OPTIONS FOR THE STATIC CONTENT MIDDLEWARE

When the `UseStaticFiles` method is invoked without arguments, the middleware will use the `wwwroot` folder to locate files that match the path of the requested URL.

This behavior can be adjusted by passing a `StaticFileOptions` object to the `UseStaticFiles` method. Table 15.5 describes the properties defined by the `StaticFileOptions` class.

Table 15.5   The properties defined by the StaticFileOptions class

Name	Description
ContentTypeProvider	This property is used to get or set the `IContentType-Provider` object that is responsible for producing the MIME type for a file. The default implementation of the interface uses the file extension to determine the content type and supports the most common file types.
DefaultContentType	This property is used to set the default content type if the `IContentTypeProvider` cannot determine the type of the file.
FileProvider	This property is used to locate the content for requests, as shown in the listing below.
OnPrepareResponse	This property can be used to register an action that will be invoked before the static content response is generated.
RequestPath	This property is used to specify the URL path that the middleware will respond to, as shown in the following listing.
ServeUnknownFileTypes	By default, the static content middleware will not serve files whose content type cannot be determined by the `IContentTypeProvider`. This behavior is changed by setting this property to `true`.

The `FileProvider` and `RequestPath` properties are the most commonly used. The `FileProvider` property is used to select a different location for static content, and the `RequestPath` property is used to specify a URL prefix that denotes requests for static context. Listing 15.30 uses both properties to configure the static file middleware.

TIP There is also a version of the UseStaticFiles method that accepts a single string argument, which is used to set the RequestPath configuration property. This is a convenient way of adding support for URLs without needing to create an options object.

Listing 15.30   Configuring the static files in the Program.cs file in the Platform folder

```
using Platform;
using Microsoft.AspNetCore.HttpLogging;
using Microsoft.Extensions.FileProviders;

var builder = WebApplication.CreateBuilder(args);

builder.Services.AddHttpLogging(opts => {
    opts.LoggingFields = HttpLoggingFields.RequestMethod
        | HttpLoggingFields.RequestPath
        | HttpLoggingFields.ResponseStatusCode;
});

var app = builder.Build();

app.UseHttpLogging();

app.UseStaticFiles();

var env = app.Environment;
app.UseStaticFiles(new StaticFileOptions {
    FileProvider = new
        PhysicalFileProvider($"{env.ContentRootPath}/staticfiles"),
    RequestPath = "/files"
});

app.MapGet("population/{city?}", Population.Endpoint);

app.Run();
```

Multiple instances of the middleware component can be added to the pipeline, each of which handles a separate mapping between URLs and file locations. In the listing, a second instance of the static files middleware is added to the request pipeline so that requests for URLs that start with /files will be handled using files from a folder named staticfiles. Reading files from the folder is done with an instance of the Physical-FileProvider class, which is responsible for reading disk files. The PhysicalFile-Provider class requires an absolute path to work with, which I based on the value of the ContentRootPath property defined by the IWebHostEnvironment interface, which is the same interface used to determine whether the application is running in the Development or Production environment.

To provide content for the new middleware component to use, create the Platform/staticfiles folder and add to it an HTML file named hello.html with the content shown in listing 15.31.

> **Listing 15.31   The contents of the hello.html file in the Platform/staticfiles folder**

```
<!DOCTYPE html>
<html lang="en">
<head>
    <title>Static Content</title>
</head>
<body>
    <h3>This is additional static content</h3>
</body>
</html>
```

Restart ASP.NET Core and use the browser to request the http://localhost:5000/files/ hello.html URL. Requests for URLs that begin with /files and that correspond to files in the staticfiles folder are handled by the new middleware, as shown in figure 15.11.

Figure 15.11   Configuring the static files middleware

15.4.2   Using client-side packages

Most web applications rely on client-side packages to support the content they generate, using CSS frameworks to style content or JavaScript packages to create rich functionality in the browser. Microsoft provides the Library Manager tool, known as LibMan, for downloading and managing client-side packages.

PREPARING THE PROJECT FOR CLIENT-SIDE PACKAGES

Use the command prompt to run the commands shown in listing 15.32, which remove any existing LibMan package and install the version required by this chapter as a global .NET Core tool.

> **Listing 15.32   Installing LibMan**

```
dotnet tool uninstall --global Microsoft.Web.LibraryManager.Cli
dotnet tool install --global Microsoft.Web.LibraryManager.Cli
    --version 2.1.175
```

The next step is to create the LibMan configuration file, which specifies the repository that will be used to get client-side packages and the directory into which packages will be downloaded. Open a PowerShell command prompt and run the command shown in listing 15.33 in the Platform folder.

```
libman init -p cdnjs
```

The -p argument specifies the provider that will get packages. I have used cdnjs, which selects cdnjs.com. The other option is unpkg, which selects unpkg.com. If you don't have existing experience with package repositories, then you should start with the cdnjs option.

The command in listing 15.33 creates a file named libman.json in the Platform folder; the file contains the following settings:

```
...
{
  "version": "1.0",
  "defaultProvider": "cdnjs",
  "libraries": []
}
...
```

If you are using Visual Studio, you can create and edit the libman.json file directly by selecting Project > Manage Client-Side Libraries.

INSTALLING CLIENT-SIDE PACKAGES

Packages are installed from the command line. Run the command shown in listing 15.34 in the Platform folder to install the Bootstrap package.

```
libman install bootstrap@5.2.3 -d wwwroot/lib/bootstrap
```

The required version is separated from the package name by the @ character, and the -d argument is used to specify where the package will be installed. The wwwroot/lib folder is the conventional location for installing client-side packages in ASP.NET Core projects.

USING A CLIENT-SIDE PACKAGE

Once a client-side package has been installed, its files can be referenced by script or link HTML elements or by using the features provided by the higher-level ASP.NET Core features described in later chapters.

For simplicity in this chapter, listing 15.35 adds a link element to the static HTML file created earlier in this section.

```
<!DOCTYPE html>
<html lang="en">
<head>
    <link rel="stylesheet" href="/lib/bootstrap/css/bootstrap.min.css" />
    <title>Static Content</title>
</head>
<body>
```

```
    <h3 class="p-2 bg-primary text-white">This is static content</h3>
</body>
</html>
```

Restart ASP.NET Core and request http://localhost:5000/static.html. When the browser receives and processes the contents of the `static.html` file, it will encounter the `link` element and send an HTTP request to the ASP.NET Core runtime for the `/lib/bootstrap/css/bootstrap.min.css` URL. The original static file middleware component will receive this request, determine that it corresponds to a file in the `wwwroot` folder, and return its contents, providing the browser with the Bootstrap CSS stylesheet. The Bootstrap styles are applied through the classes to which the `h3` element has been assigned, producing the result shown in figure 15.12.

Figure 15.12 Using a client-side package

Summary

- The ASP.NET Core platform includes features for common tasks, must of which are presented as services.
- The configuration service provides access to the application configuration, which includes the contents of the `appsettings.json` file and environment variables.
- The configuration data is typically used with the options service to configure the services available through dependency injection.
- The user secrets feature is used to store sensitive data outside of the project folder, so they are not committed into a version control code repository.
- The logging service is used to generate log messages, with different severity levels and with options for sending the log messages to different handlers.
- ASP.NET Core includes middleware for serving static content and a tool for adding packages that will be delivered as static content to the project.

Using the platform
features, part 2

In this chapter, I continue to describe the basic features provided by the ASP.NET Core platform. I explain how cookies are used and how the user's consent for tracking cookies is managed. I describe how sessions provide a robust alternative to basic cookies, how to use and enforce HTTPS requests, how to deal with errors, and how to filter requests based on the `Host` header. Table 16.1 provides a guide to the chapter.

Table 16.1 Chapter guide

Problem	Solution	Listing
Using cookies	Use the context objects to read and write cookies.	1-3
Managing cookie consent	Use the consent middleware.	4-6
Storing data across requests	Use sessions.	7, 8
Securing HTTP requests	Use the HTTPS middleware.	9-13
Restrict the number of requests handled by the application	Use the rate limiting middleware	14
Handling errors	Use the error and status code middleware.	15-20
Restricting a request with the host header	Set the `AllowedHosts` configuration setting.	21

16.1 *Preparing for this chapter*

In this chapter, I continue to use the `Platform` project from chapter 15. To prepare for this chapter, replace the contents of the `Program.cs` file with the contents of listing 16.1, which removes the middleware and services from the previous chapter.

> **TIP**   You can download the example project for this chapter—and for all the other chapters in this book—from https://github.com/manningbooks/proasp .net-core-7. See chapter 1 for how to get help if you have problems running the examples.

Listing 16.1   Replacing the contents of the Program.cs file in the Platform folder

```
var builder = WebApplication.CreateBuilder(args);

var app = builder.Build();

app.MapFallback(async context =>
    await context.Response.WriteAsync("Hello World!"));

app.Run();
```

Start the application by opening a new PowerShell command prompt, navigating to the folder that contains the `Platform.csproj` file, and running the command shown in listing 16.2.

Listing 16.2   Starting the ASP.NET Core runtime

```
dotnet run
```

Open a new browser window and use it to request http://localhost:5000, which will produce the response shown in figure 16.1.

**Figure 16.1
Running the
example
application**

16.2 Using cookies

Cookies are small amounts of text added to responses that the browser includes in subsequent requests. Cookies are important for web applications because they allow features to be developed that span a series of HTTP requests, each of which can be identified by the cookies that the browser sends to the server.

ASP.NET Core provides support for working with cookies through the `HttpRequest` and `HttpResponse` objects that are provided to middleware components. To demonstrate, listing 16.3 changes the routing configuration in the example application to add endpoints that implement a counter.

Listing 16.3   Using cookies in the Program.cs file in the Platform folder

```
var builder = WebApplication.CreateBuilder(args);

var app = builder.Build();

app.MapGet("/cookie", async context => {
    int counter1 =
        int.Parse(context.Request.Cookies["counter1"] ?? "0") + 1;
    context.Response.Cookies.Append("counter1", counter1.ToString(),
        new CookieOptions {
            MaxAge = TimeSpan.FromMinutes(30)
        });
    int counter2 =
        int.Parse(context.Request.Cookies["counter2"] ?? "0") + 1;
    context.Response.Cookies.Append("counter2", counter2.ToString(),
        new CookieOptions {
            MaxAge = TimeSpan.FromMinutes(30)
        });
    await context.Response
        .WriteAsync($"Counter1: {counter1}, Counter2: {counter2}");
});

app.MapGet("clear", context => {
    context.Response.Cookies.Delete("counter1");
    context.Response.Cookies.Delete("counter2");
    context.Response.Redirect("/");
    return Task.CompletedTask;
});

app.MapFallback(async context =>
    await context.Response.WriteAsync("Hello World!"));

app.Run();
```

The new endpoints rely on cookies called `counter1` and `counter2`. When the `/cookie` URL is requested, the middleware looks for the cookies and parses the values to an `int`. If there is no cookie, a fallback zero is used.

```
...
int counter1 = int.Parse(context.Request.Cookies["counter1"] ?? "0") + 1;
...
```

Cookies are accessed through the `HttpRequest.Cookies` property, where the name of the cookie is used as the key. The value retrieved from the cookie is incremented and used to set a cookie in the response, like this:

```
...
context.Response.Cookies.Append("counter1", counter1.ToString(),
    new CookieOptions {
        MaxAge = TimeSpan.FromMinutes(30)
});
...
```

Cookies are set through the `HttpResponse.Cookies` property and the `Append` method creates or replaces a cookie in the response. The arguments to the `Append` method are the name of the cookie, its value, and a `CookieOptions` object, which is used to configure the cookie. The `CookieOptions` class defines the properties described in table 16.2, each of which corresponds to a cookie field.

> **NOTE** Cookies are sent in the response header, which means that cookies can be set only before the response body is written, after which any changes to the cookies are ignored.

Table 16.2 The CookieOptions properties

Name	Description
Domain	This property specifies the hosts to which the browser will send the cookie. By default, the cookie will be sent only to the host that created the cookie.
Expires	This property sets the expiry for the cookie.
HttpOnly	When `true`, this property tells the browser not to include the `cookie` in requests made by JavaScript code.
IsEssential	This property is used to indicate that a cookie is essential, as described in the "Managing Cookie Consent" section.
MaxAge	This property specifies the number of seconds until the cookie expires. Older browsers do not support cookies with this setting.
Path	This property is used to set a URL path that must be present in the request before the cookie will be sent by the browser.
SameSite	This property is used to specify whether the cookie should be included in cross-site requests. The values are `Lax`, `Strict`, and `None` (which is the default value).
Secure	When `true`, this property tells the browser to send the cookie using HTTPS only.

The only cookie option set in listing 16.3 is `MaxAge`, which tells the browser that the cookies expire after 30 minutes. The middleware in listing 16.3 deletes the cookies when the /clear URL is requested, which is done using the `HttpResponse.Cookie.Delete` method, after which the browser is redirected to the / URL.

```
...
app.MapGet("clear", context => {
    context.Response.Cookies.Delete("counter1");
    context.Response.Cookies.Delete("counter2");
    context.Response.Redirect("/");
    return Task.CompletedTask;
});
...
```

Restart ASP.NET Core and navigate to http://localhost:5000/cookie. The response will contain cookies that are included in subsequent requests, and the counters will be incremented each time the browser is reloaded, as shown in figure 16.2. A request for http://localhost:5000/clear will delete the cookies, and the counters will be reset.

Figure 16.2 Using a cookie

16.2.1 Enabling cookie consent checking

The EU General Data Protection Regulation (GDPR) requires the user's consent before nonessential cookies can be used. ASP.NET Core provides support for obtaining consent and preventing nonessential cookies from being sent to the browser when consent has not been granted. The options pattern is used to create a policy for cookies, which is applied by a middleware component, as shown in listing 16.4.

> **CAUTION** Cookie consent is only one part of GDPR. See https://en.wikipedia.org/wiki/General_Data_Protection_Regulation for a good overview of the regulations.

> **Listing 16.4 Enabling cookie consent in the Program.cs file in the Platform folder**

```
var builder = WebApplication.CreateBuilder(args);

builder.Services.Configure<CookiePolicyOptions>(opts => {
    opts.CheckConsentNeeded = context => true;
});

var app = builder.Build();

app.UseCookiePolicy();
```

```
app.MapGet("/cookie", async context => {
    int counter1 =
        int.Parse(context.Request.Cookies["counter1"] ?? "0") + 1;
    context.Response.Cookies.Append("counter1", counter1.ToString(),
        new CookieOptions {
            MaxAge = TimeSpan.FromMinutes(30),
            IsEssential = true
        });
    int counter2 =
        int.Parse(context.Request.Cookies["counter2"] ?? "0") + 1;
    context.Response.Cookies.Append("counter2", counter2.ToString(),
        new CookieOptions {
            MaxAge = TimeSpan.FromMinutes(30)
        });
    await context.Response
        .WriteAsync($"Counter1: {counter1}, Counter2: {counter2}");
});

app.MapGet("clear", context => {
    context.Response.Cookies.Delete("counter1");
    context.Response.Cookies.Delete("counter2");
    context.Response.Redirect("/");
    return Task.CompletedTask;
});

app.MapFallback(async context =>
    await context.Response.WriteAsync("Hello World!"));

app.Run();
```

The options pattern is used to configure a `CookiePolicyOptions` object, which sets the overall policy for cookies in the application using the properties described in table 16.3.

Table 16.3. The CookiePolicyOptions properties

Name	Description
CheckConsentNeeded	This property is assigned a function that receives an `HttpContext` object and returns `true` if it represents a request for which cookie consent is required. The function is called for every request, and the default function always returns `false`.
ConsentCookie	This property returns an object that is used to configure the cookie sent to the browser to record the user's cookie consent.
HttpOnly	This property sets the default value for the `HttpOnly` property, as described in table 16.2.
MinimumSameSitePolicy	This property sets the lowest level of security for the `SameSite` property, as described in table 16.2.
Secure	This property sets the default value for the `Secure` property, as described in table 16.2.

To enable consent checking, I assigned a new function to the `CheckConsentNeeded` property that always returns `true`. The function is called for every request that ASP

.NET Core receives, which means that sophisticated rules can be defined to select the requests for which consent is required. For this application, I have taken the most cautious approach and required consent for all requests.

The middleware that enforces the cookie policy is added to the request pipeline using the UseCookiePolicy method. The result is that only cookies whose IsEssential property is true will be added to responses. Listing 16.4 sets the IsEssential property on cookie1 only, and you can see the effect by restarting ASP.NET Core, requesting http://localhost:5000/cookie, and reloading the browser. Only the counter whose cookie is marked as essential updates, as shown in figure 16.3.

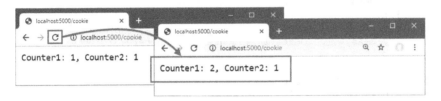

Figure 16.3 Using cookie consent

16.2.2 *Managing cookie consent*

Unless the user has given consent, only cookies that are essential to the core features of the web application are allowed. Consent is managed through a *request feature*, which provides middleware components with access to the implementation details of how requests and responses are handled by ASP.NET Core. Features are accessed through the HttpRequest.Features property, and each feature is represented by an interface whose properties and methods deal with one aspect of low-level request handling.

Features deal with aspects of request handling that rarely need to be altered, such as the structure of responses. The exception is the management of cookie consent, which is handled through the ITrackingConsentFeature interface, which defines the methods and properties described in table 16.4.

Table 16.4. The ITrackingConsentFeature members

Name	Description
CanTrack	This property returns true if nonessential cookies can be added to the current request, either because the user has given consent or because consent is not required.
CreateConsentCookie()	This method returns a cookie that can be used by JavaScript clients to indicate consent.
GrantConsent()	Calling this method adds a cookie to the response that grants consent for nonessential cookies.
HasConsent	This property returns true if the user has given consent for nonessential cookies.
IsConsentNeeded	This property returns true if consent for nonessential cookies is required for the current request.
WithdrawConsent()	This method deletes the consent cookie.

To deal with consent, add a class file named `ConsentMiddleware.cs` to the `Platform` folder and the code shown in listing 16.5. Managing cookie consent can be done using lambda expressions, but I have used a class in this example to keep the `Program.cs` method uncluttered.

> **Listing 16.5** The contents of the ConsentMiddleware.cs file in the Platform folder

```
using Microsoft.AspNetCore.Http.Features;

namespace Platform {
    public class ConsentMiddleware {
        private RequestDelegate next;

        public ConsentMiddleware(RequestDelegate nextDelgate) {
            next = nextDelgate;
        }

        public async Task Invoke(HttpContext context) {
            if (context.Request.Path == "/consent") {
                ITrackingConsentFeature? consentFeature
                    = context.Features.Get<ITrackingConsentFeature>();
                if (consentFeature != null) {
                    if (!consentFeature.HasConsent) {
                        consentFeature.GrantConsent();
                    } else {
                        consentFeature.WithdrawConsent();
                    }
                    await context.Response.WriteAsync(
                        consentFeature.HasConsent ? "Consent Granted \n"
                            : "Consent Withdrawn\n");
                }
            } else {
                await next(context);
            }
        }
    }
}
```

Request features are obtained using the `Get` method, where the generic type argument specifies the feature interface that is required, like this:

```
...
ITrackingConsentFeature? consentFeature
    = context.Features.Get<ITrackingConsentFeature>();
...
```

Using the properties and methods described in table 16.4, the new middleware component responds to the `/consent` URL to determine and change the cookie consent. Listing 16.6 adds the new middleware to the request pipeline.

> **Listing 16.6** Adding middleware in the Program.cs file in the Platform folder

```
var builder = WebApplication.CreateBuilder(args);

builder.Services.Configure<CookiePolicyOptions>(opts => {
```

```
    opts.CheckConsentNeeded = context => true;
});

var app = builder.Build();

app.UseCookiePolicy();
app.UseMiddleware<Platform.ConsentMiddleware>();

app.MapGet("/cookie", async context => {
```

// ...statments omitted for brevity...

To see the effect, restart ASP.NET Core and request http://localhost:5000/consent and then http://localhost:5000/cookie. When consent is granted, nonessential cookies are allowed, and both the counters in the example will work, as shown in figure 16.4. Repeat the process to withdraw consent, and you will find that only the counter whose cookie has been denoted as essential works.

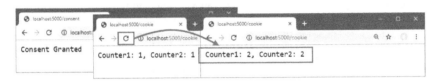

Figure 16.4 Managing cookie consent

16.3   *Using sessions*

The example in the previous section used cookies to store the application's state data, providing the middleware component with the data required. The problem with this approach is that the contents of the cookie are stored at the client, where it can be manipulated and used to alter the behavior of the application.

A better approach is to use the ASP.NET Core session feature. The session middleware adds a cookie to responses, which allows related requests to be identified and which is also associated with data stored at the server.

When a request containing the session cookie is received, the session middleware component retrieves the server-side data associated with the session and makes it available to other middleware components through the HttpContext object. Using sessions means that the application's data remains at the server and only the identifier for the session is sent to the browser.

16.3.1 *Configuring the session service and middleware*

Setting up sessions requires configuring services and adding a middleware component to the request pipeline. Listing 16.7 adds the statements to the Program.cs file to set up sessions for the example application and removes the endpoints from the previous section.

Listing 16.7 Configuring sessions in the Program.cs file in the Platform folder

```
var builder = WebApplication.CreateBuilder(args);

builder.Services.AddDistributedMemoryCache();

builder.Services.AddSession(opts => {
    opts.IdleTimeout = TimeSpan.FromMinutes(30);
    opts.Cookie.IsEssential = true;
});

var app = builder.Build();

app.UseSession();

app.MapFallback(async context =>
    await context.Response.WriteAsync("Hello World!"));

app.Run();
```

When you use sessions, you must decide how to store the associated data. ASP.NET Core provides three options for session data storage, each of which has its own method to register a service, as described in table 16.5.

Table 16.5 The session storage methods

Name	Description
AddDistributedMemoryCache	This method sets up an in-memory cache. Despite the name, the cache is not distributed and is responsible only for storing data for the instance of the ASP.NET Core runtime where it is created.
AddDistributedSqlServerCache	This method sets up a cache that stores data in SQL Server and is available when the Microsoft .Extensions.Caching.SqlServer package is installed. This cache is used in chapter 17.
AddStackExchangeRedisCache	This method sets up a Redis cache and is available when the Microsoft.Extensions.Caching .Redis package is installed.

Caching is described in detail in chapter 17, but for this chapter, I used the in-memory cache:

```
...
builder.Services.AddDistributedMemoryCache();
...
```

Despite its name, the cache service created by the AddDistributedMemoryCache method isn't distributed and stores the session data for a single instance of the ASP. NET Core runtime. If you scale an application by deploying multiple instances of the runtime, then you should use one of the other caches, such as the SQL Server cache, which is demonstrated in chapter 17.

The next step is to use the options pattern to configure the session middleware, like this:

```
...
builder.Services.AddSession(opts => {
    opts.IdleTimeout = TimeSpan.FromMinutes(30);
    opts.Cookie.IsEssential = true;
});
...
```

Table 16.6 shows that the options class for sessions is `SessionOptions` and describes the key properties it defines.

Table 16.6   Properties defined by the SessionOptions class

Name	Description
Cookie	This property is used to configure the session cookie.
IdleTimeout	This property is used to configure the time span after which a session expires.

The `Cookie` property returns an object that can be used to configure the session cookie. Table 16.7 describes the most useful cookie configuration properties for session data.

Table 16.7   Cookie configuration properties

Name	Description
HttpOnly	This property specifies whether the browser will prevent the cookie from being included in HTTP requests sent by JavaScript code. This property should be set to `true` for projects that use a JavaScript application whose requests should be included in the session. The default value is `true`.
IsEssential	This property specifies whether the cookie is required for the application to function and should be used even when the user has specified that they don't want the application to use cookies. The default value is `false`. See the "Managing Cookie Consent" section for more details.
SecurityPolicy	This property sets the security policy for the cookie, using a value from the `CookieSecurePolicy` enum. The values are `Always` (which restricts the cookie to HTTPS requests), `SameAsRequest` (which restricts the cookie to HTTPS if the original request was made using HTTPS), and `None` (which allows the cookie to be used on HTTP and HTTPS requests). The default value is `None`.

The options set in listing 16.7 allow the session cookie to be included in requests started by JavaScript and flag the cookie as essential so that it will be used even when the user has expressed a preference not to use cookies (see the "Managing Cookie Consent" section for more details about essential cookies). The `IdleTimeout` option has been set so that sessions expire if no request containing the sessions cookie is received for 30 minutes.

CAUTION The session cookie isn't denoted as essential by default, which can cause problems when cookie consent is used. Listing 16.7 sets the `IsEssential` property to `true` to ensure that sessions always work. If you find sessions don't work as expected, then this is the likely cause, and you must either set `IsEssential` to `true` or adapt your application to deal with users who don't grant consent and won't accept session cookies.

The final step is to add the session middleware component to the request pipeline, which is done with the `UseSession` method. When the middleware processes a request that contains a session cookie, it retrieves the session data from the cache and makes it available through the `HttpContext` object, before passing the request along the request pipeline and providing it to other middleware components. When a request arrives without a session cookie, a new session is started, and a cookie is added to the response so that subsequent requests can be identified as being part of the session.

16.3.2 Using session data

The session middleware provides access to details of the session associated with a request through the `Session` property of the `HttpContext` object. The `Session` property returns an object that implements the `ISession` interface, which provides the methods shown in table 16.8 for accessing session data.

Table 16.8 Useful ISession methods and extension methods

Name	Description
`Clear()`	This method removes all the data in the session.
`CommitAsync()`	This asynchronous method commits changed session data to the cache.
`GetString(key)`	This method retrieves a string value using the specified key.
`GetInt32(key)`	This method retrieves an integer value using the specified key.
`Id`	This property returns the unique identifier for the session.
`IsAvailable`	This returns `true` when the session data has been loaded.
`Keys`	This enumerates the keys for the session data items.
`Remove(key)`	This method removes the value associated with the specified key.
`SetString(key,val)`	This method stores a string using the specified key.
`SetInt32(key, val)`	This method stores an integer using the specified key.

Session data is stored in key-value pairs, where the keys are strings and the values are strings or integers. This simple data structure allows session data to be stored easily by each of the caches listed in table 16.5. Applications that need to store more complex data can use serialization, which is the approach I took for the SportsStore. Listing 16.8 uses session data to re-create the counter example.

> **Listing 16.8   Using session data in the Program.cs file in the Platform folder**

```
var builder = WebApplication.CreateBuilder(args);

builder.Services.AddDistributedMemoryCache();

builder.Services.AddSession(opts => {
    opts.IdleTimeout = TimeSpan.FromMinutes(30);
    opts.Cookie.IsEssential = true;
});

var app = builder.Build();

app.UseSession();

app.MapGet("/session", async context => {
    int counter1 = (context.Session.GetInt32("counter1") ?? 0) + 1;
    int counter2 = (context.Session.GetInt32("counter2") ?? 0) + 1;
    context.Session.SetInt32("counter1", counter1);
    context.Session.SetInt32("counter2", counter2);
    await context.Session.CommitAsync();
    await context.Response
        .WriteAsync($"Counter1: {counter1}, Counter2: {counter2}");
});

app.MapFallback(async context =>
    await context.Response.WriteAsync("Hello World!"));

app.Run();
```

The `GetInt32` method is used to read the values associated with the keys `counter1` and `counter2`. If this is the first request in a session, no value will be available, and the null-coalescing operator is used to provide an initial value. The value is incremented and then stored using the `SetInt32` method and used to generate a simple result for the client.

The use of the `CommitAsync` method is optional, but it is good practice to use it because it will throw an exception if the session data can't be stored in the cache. By default, no error is reported if there are caching problems, which can lead to unpredictable and confusing behavior.

All changes to the session data must be made before the response is sent to the client, which is why I read, update, and store the session data before calling the `Response`
`.WriteAsync` method in listing 16.8.

Notice that the statements in listing 16.8 do not have to deal with the session cookie, detect expired sessions, or load the session data from the cache. All this work is done automatically by the session middleware, which presents the results through the `HttpContext.Session` property. One consequence of this approach is that the `HttpContext.Session` property is not populated with data until after the session middleware has processed a request, which means that you should attempt to access session data only in middleware or endpoints that are added to the request pipeline after the UseSession method is called.

Restart ASP.NET Core and navigate to the http://localhost:5000/session URL, and you will see the value of the counter. Reload the browser, and the counter values will be incremented, as shown in figure 16.5. The sessions and session data will be lost when ASP.NET Core is stopped because I chose the in-memory cache. The other storage options operate outside of the ASP.NET Core runtime and survive application restarts.

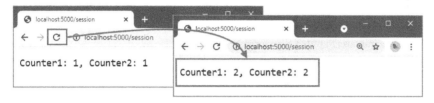

Figure 16.5 Using session data

16.4 Working with HTTPS connections

Users increasingly expect web applications to use HTTPS connections, even for requests that don't contain or return sensitive data. ASP.NET Core supports both HTTP and HTTPS connections and provides middleware that can force HTTP clients to use HTTPS.

> **HTTPS vs. SSL vs. TLS**
>
> HTTPS is the combination of HTTP and the Transport Layer Security (TLS) or Secure Sockets Layer (SSL). TLS has replaced the obsolete SSL protocol, but the term SSL has become synonymous with secure networking and is often used to refer to TLS. If you are interested in security and cryptography, then the details of HTTPS are worth exploring, and https://en.wikipedia.org/wiki/HTTPS is a good place to start.

16.4.1 Enabling HTTPS connections

HTTPS is enabled and configured in the launchSettings.json file in the Properties folder, as shown in listing 16.9.

> **Listing 16.9   Changes in the launchSettings.json file in the Platform/Properties folder**

```
{
  "iisSettings": {
    "windowsAuthentication": false,
    "anonymousAuthentication": true,
    "iisExpress": {
      "applicationUrl": "http://localhost:5000",
```

```
      "sslPort": 0
    }
  },
  "profiles": {
    "Platform": {
      "commandName": "Project",
      "dotnetRunMessages": true,
      "launchBrowser": true,
      "applicationUrl": "http://localhost:5000;https://localhost:5500",
      "environmentVariables": {
        "ASPNETCORE_ENVIRONMENT": "Development"
      }
    },
    "IIS Express": {
      "commandName": "IISExpress",
      "launchBrowser": true,
      "environmentVariables": {
        "ASPNETCORE_ENVIRONMENT": "Development"
      }
    }
  }
}
```

The new `applicationUrl` setting sets the URLs to which the application will respond, and HTTPS is enabled by adding an HTTPS URL to the configuration setting. Note that the URLs are separated by a semicolon and no spaces are allowed.

The .NET Core runtime includes a test certificate that is used for HTTPS requests. Run the commands shown in listing 16.10 in the `Platform` folder to regenerate and trust the test certificate.

Listing 16.10   Regenerating the Development Certificates

```
dotnet dev-certs https --clean
dotnet dev-certs https --trust
```

Select Yes to the prompts to delete the existing certificate that has already been trusted and select Yes to trust the new certificate, as shown in figure 16.6.

Figure 16.6 Regenerating the HTTPS certificate

16.4.2 Detecting HTTPS requests

Requests made using HTTPS can be detected through the `HttpRequest.IsHttps` property. In listing 16.11, I added a message to the fallback response that reports whether a request is made using HTTPS.

Listing 16.11 Detecting HTTPS in the Program.cs file in the Platform folder

```
var builder = WebApplication.CreateBuilder(args);

builder.Services.AddDistributedMemoryCache();

builder.Services.AddSession(opts => {
    opts.IdleTimeout = TimeSpan.FromMinutes(30);
    opts.Cookie.IsEssential = true;
});

var app = builder.Build();

app.UseSession();

app.MapGet("/session", async context => {
    int counter1 = (context.Session.GetInt32("counter1") ?? 0) + 1;
    int counter2 = (context.Session.GetInt32("counter2") ?? 0) + 1;
    context.Session.SetInt32("counter1", counter1);
    context.Session.SetInt32("counter2", counter2);
    await context.Session.CommitAsync();
    await context.Response
        .WriteAsync($"Counter1: {counter1}, Counter2: {counter2}");
});

app.MapFallback(async context => {
    await context.Response
        .WriteAsync($"HTTPS Request: {context.Request.IsHttps} \n");
    await context.Response.WriteAsync("Hello World!");
});

app.Run();
```

To test HTTPS, restart ASP.NET Core and navigate to http://localhost:5000. This is a regular HTTP request and will produce the result shown on the left of figure 16.7. Next, navigate to https://localhost:5500, paying close attention to the URL scheme, which is https and not http, as it has been in previous examples. The new middleware will detect the HTTPS connection and produce the output on the right of figure 16.7.

Figure 16.7 Detecting an HTTPS request

16.4.3 Enforcing HTTPS requests

ASP.NET Core provides a middleware component that enforces the use of HTTPS by sending a redirection response for requests that arrive over HTTP. Listing 16.12 adds this middleware to the request pipeline.

Listing 16.12   Enforcing HTTPS in the Program.cs file in the Platform folder

```
var builder = WebApplication.CreateBuilder(args);

builder.Services.AddDistributedMemoryCache();

builder.Services.AddSession(opts => {
    opts.IdleTimeout = TimeSpan.FromMinutes(30);
    opts.Cookie.IsEssential = true;
});

var app = builder.Build();

app.UseHttpsRedirection();
app.UseSession();

app.MapGet("/session", async context => {
    int counter1 = (context.Session.GetInt32("counter1") ?? 0) + 1;
    int counter2 = (context.Session.GetInt32("counter2") ?? 0) + 1;
    context.Session.SetInt32("counter1", counter1);
    context.Session.SetInt32("counter2", counter2);
    await context.Session.CommitAsync();
    await context.Response
        .WriteAsync($"Counter1: {counter1}, Counter2: {counter2}");
});

app.MapFallback(async context => {
    await context.Response
        .WriteAsync($"HTTPS Request: {context.Request.IsHttps} \n");
    await context.Response.WriteAsync("Hello World!");
});

app.Run();
```

The UseHttpsRedirection method adds the middleware component, which appears at the start of the request pipeline so that the redirection to HTTPS occurs before any other component can short-circuit the pipeline and produce a response using regular HTTP.

Configuring HTTPS redirection

The options pattern can be used to configure the HTTPS redirection middleware, by calling the AddHttpsRedirection method like this:

```
...
builder.Services.AddHttpsRedirection(opts => {
```

(continued)
```
    opts.RedirectStatusCode = StatusCodes.Status307TemporaryRedirect;
    opts.HttpsPort = 443;
});
...
```

The only two configuration options are shown in this fragment, which sets the status code used in the redirection response, and the port to which the client is redirected, overriding the value that is loaded from the configuration files. Specifying the HTTPS port can be useful when deploying the application, but care should be taken when changing the redirection status code.

Restart ASP.NET Core and request http://localhost:5000, which is the HTTP URL for the application. The HTTPS redirection middleware will intercept the request and redirect the browser to the HTTPS URL, as shown in figure 16.8.

TIP Modern browsers often hide the URL scheme, which is why you should pay attention to the port number that is displayed. To display the URL scheme in the figure, I had to click the URL bar so the browser would display the full URL.

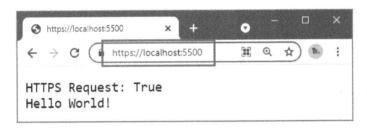

Figure 16.8
Forcing HTTPS
requests

16.4.4 Enabling HTTP strict transport security

One limitation of HTTPS redirection is that the user can make an initial request using HTTP before being redirected to a secure connection, presenting a security risk.

The HTTP Strict Transport Security (HSTS) protocol is intended to help mitigate this risk and works by including a header in responses that tells browsers to use HTTPS only when sending requests to the web application's host. After an HSTS header has been received, browsers that support HSTS will send requests to the application using HTTPS even if the user specifies an HTTP URL. Listing 16.13 shows the addition of the HSTS middleware to the request pipeline.

Listing 16.13 Enabling HSTS in the Program.cs file in the Platform folder

```
var builder = WebApplication.CreateBuilder(args);

builder.Services.AddDistributedMemoryCache();

builder.Services.AddSession(opts => {
```

```
        opts.IdleTimeout = TimeSpan.FromMinutes(30);
        opts.Cookie.IsEssential = true;
});

builder.Services.AddHsts(opts => {
    opts.MaxAge = TimeSpan.FromDays(1);
    opts.IncludeSubDomains = true;
});

var app = builder.Build();

if (app.Environment.IsProduction()) {
    app.UseHsts();
}

app.UseHttpsRedirection();
app.UseSession();

app.MapGet("/session", async context => {
    int counter1 = (context.Session.GetInt32("counter1") ?? 0) + 1;
    int counter2 = (context.Session.GetInt32("counter2") ?? 0) + 1;
    context.Session.SetInt32("counter1", counter1);
    context.Session.SetInt32("counter2", counter2);
    await context.Session.CommitAsync();
    await context.Response
        .WriteAsync($"Counter1: {counter1}, Counter2: {counter2}");
});

app.MapFallback(async context => {
    await context.Response
        .WriteAsync($"HTTPS Request: {context.Request.IsHttps} \n");
    await context.Response.WriteAsync("Hello World!");
});

app.Run();
```

The middleware is added to the request pipeline using the UseHsts method. The HSTS middleware can be configured with the AddHsts method, using the properties described in table 16.9.

Table 16.9 The HSTS configuration properties

Name	Description
ExcludeHosts	This property returns a List<string> that contains the hosts for which the middleware won't send an HSTS header. The defaults exclude localhost and the loopback addresses for IP version 4 and version 6.
IncludeSubDomains	When true, the browser will apply the HSTS setting to subdomains. The default value is false.
MaxAge	This property specifies the period for which the browser should make only HTTPS requests. The default value is 30 days.
Preload	This property is set to true for domains that are part of the HSTS preload scheme. The domains are hard-coded into the browser, which avoids the initial insecure request and ensures that only HTTPS is used. See hstspreload.org for more details.

HSTS is disabled during development and enabled only in production, which is why the UseHsts method is called only for that environment.

```
...
if (app.Environment.IsProduction()) {
    app.UseHsts();
}
...
```

HSTS must be used with care because it is easy to create a situation where clients cannot access the application, especially when nonstandard ports are used for HTTP and HTTPS.

If the example application is deployed to a server named myhost, for example, and the user requests http://myhost:5000, the browser will be redirected to https://myhost:5500 and sent the HSTS header, and the application will work as expected. But the next time the user requests http://myhost:5000, they will receive an error stating that a secure connection cannot be established.

This problem arises because some browsers take a simplistic approach to HSTS and assume that HTTP requests are handled on port 80 and HTTPS requests on port 443.

When the user requests http://myhost:5000, the browser checks its HSTS data and sees that it previously received an HSTS header for myhost. Instead of the HTTP URL that the user entered, the browser sends a request to https://myhost:5000. ASP.NET Core doesn't handle HTTPS on the port it uses for HTTP, and the request fails. The browser doesn't remember or understand the redirection it previously received for port 5001.

This isn't an issue where port 80 is used for HTTP and 443 is used for HTTPS. The URL http://myhost is equivalent to http://myhost:80, and https://myhost is equivalent to https://myhost:443, which means that changing the scheme targets the right port.

Once a browser has received an HSTS header, it will continue to honor it for the duration of the header's MaxAge property. When you first deploy an application, it is a good idea to set the HSTS MaxAge property to a relatively short duration until you are confident that your HTTPS infrastructure is working correctly, which is why I have set MaxAge to one day in listing 16.13. Once you are sure that clients will not need to make HTTP requests, you can increase the MaxAge property. A MaxAge value of one year is commonly used.

> **TIP** If you are testing HSTS with Google Chrome, you can inspect and edit the list of domains to which HSTS is applied by navigating to chrome://net-internals/#hsts.

16.5 Using rate limits

ASP.NET Core includes middleware components that limit the rate at which requests are processed, which can be a good way to ensure that a large number of requests doesn't overwhelm the application. The .NET framework provides a general API for rate limiting, which is integrated into ASP.NET Core through extension methods used in the `Program.cs` file. Listing 16.14 defines a rate limit and applies it to an endpoint.

CAUTION   Use this feature with caution. Once a rate limit has been reached, ASP.NET Core rejects HTTP requests with an error until capacity becomes available again, which can confuse clients and users alike.

> **Listing 16.14   Defining a rate limit in the Program.cs file in the Platform folder**

```
using Microsoft.AspNetCore.RateLimiting;

var builder = WebApplication.CreateBuilder(args);

builder.Services.AddDistributedMemoryCache();

builder.Services.AddSession(opts => {
    opts.IdleTimeout = TimeSpan.FromMinutes(30);
    opts.Cookie.IsEssential = true;
});

builder.Services.AddHsts(opts => {
    opts.MaxAge = TimeSpan.FromDays(1);
    opts.IncludeSubDomains = true;
});

builder.Services.AddRateLimiter(opts => {
    opts.AddFixedWindowLimiter("fixedWindow", fixOpts => {
        fixOpts.PermitLimit = 1;
        fixOpts.QueueLimit = 0;
        fixOpts.Window = TimeSpan.FromSeconds(15);
    });
});

var app = builder.Build();

if (app.Environment.IsProduction()) {
    app.UseHsts();
}

app.UseHttpsRedirection();

app.UseRateLimiter();

app.UseSession();

app.MapGet("/session", async context => {
    int counter1 = (context.Session.GetInt32("counter1") ?? 0) + 1;
    int counter2 = (context.Session.GetInt32("counter2") ?? 0) + 1;
    context.Session.SetInt32("counter1", counter1);
    context.Session.SetInt32("counter2", counter2);
    await context.Session.CommitAsync();
    await context.Response
        .WriteAsync($"Counter1: {counter1}, Counter2: {counter2}");
}).RequireRateLimiting("fixedWindow");
```

```
app.MapFallback(async context => {
    await context.Response
        .WriteAsync($"HTTPS Request: {context.Request.IsHttps} \n");
    await context.Response.WriteAsync("Hello World!");
});
```

```
app.Run();
```

The `AddRateLimiter` extension method is used to configure rate limiting, which is done using the options pattern. In this example, I have used the `AddFixedWindow-Limiter` method to create a rate-limiting policy that limits the number of requests that will be handled in a specified duration. The `AddFixedWindowLimiter` method is one of four extension methods that are available for rate limiting, described in table 16.10. Full details of how each of these rate limits works can be found at https://learn.microsoft.com/en-us/aspnet/core/performance/rate-limit.

Table 16.10 The rate limiting extension methods

Name	Description
`AddFixedWindowLimiter`	This method creates a rate limiter that allows a specified number of requests in a fixed period.
`AddSlidingWindowLimiter`	This method creates a rate limiter that allows a specified number of requests in a fixed period, with the addition of a sliding window to smooth the rate limits.
`AddTokenBucketLimiter`	This method creates a rate limiter that maintains a pool of tokens that are allocated to requests. Requests can be allocated different amounts of tokens, and requests are only handled when there are sufficient free tokens in the pool.
`AddConcurrencyLimiter`	This method creates a rate limiter that allows a specific number of concurrent requests.

This is the least flexible of the time-based rate limiters, but it is the easiest to demonstrate and test:

```
...
opts.AddFixedWindowLimiter("fixedWindow", fixOpts => {
    fixOpts.PermitLimit = 1;
    fixOpts.QueueLimit = 0;
    fixOpts.Window = TimeSpan.FromSeconds(15);
});
...
```

Each extension method is configured with an instance of its own options class, but they all share the most important properties. The `PermitLimit` property is used to specify the maximum number of requests, and the `QueueLimit` property is used to specify the maximum number of requests that will be queued waiting for available capacity. If there is no available capacity and no available slots in the queue, then requests will be rejected. The combination of properties is given a name, which is used to apply the rate limit to endpoints.

These options are supplemented by additional properties which are specific to each rate limiter. In the case of the `AddFixedWindowLimiter` method, the `Window` property is used to specify the duration to which the rate is applied.

In listing 16.14, I specified a `PermitLimit` of 1, a `QueueLimit` of 0, and a `Window` of 15 seconds. This means that one request will be accepted every 15 seconds, without any queue, meaning that any additional requests will be rejected. This rate limit is assigned the name `fixedWindow`.

The rate limiting middleware is added to the pipeline using the `UseRateLimiter` method and applied to an endpoint with the `RequireRateLimiting` method. An application can define multiple rate limits and so a name is used to select the rate limit that is required:

```
...
}).RequireRateLimiting("fixedWindow");
...
```

Endpoints can be con configured with different rate limits, or no rate limit, and each rate limit will be managed independently.

Applying rate limits to controllers and pages

ASP.NET Core provides extension methods to configure rate limits for controllers, described in chapter 19, and Razor Pages, which are described in chapter 23.

It can be difficult to test rate limits effectively because browsers will often apply their own restrictions on the requests they send. Microsoft provides recommendations for testing tools at https://learn.microsoft.com/en-us/aspnet/core/performance/rate-limit#testing-endpoints-with-rate-limiting, but a policy as simple as the one defined in listing 16.14 is easy to test.

Restart ASP.NET Core and request https://localhost:5500/session. Click the Reload button within 15 seconds, and the new request will exceed the rate limit and ASP.NET Core will respond with a 503 status code, as shown in figure 16.9. Wait until the 15-second period has elapsed and click the Reload button again; the rate limit should reset and the request will be processed normally.

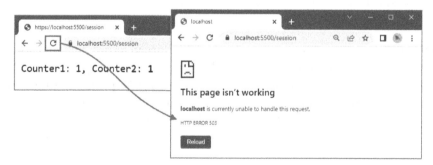

Figure 16.9 The effect of a rate limit.

16.6 Handling exceptions and errors

When the request pipeline is created, the `WebApplicationBuilder` class uses the development environment to enable middleware that handles exceptions by producing HTTP responses that are helpful to developers. Here is a fragment of code from the `WebApplicationBuilder` class:

```
...
if (context.HostingEnvironment.IsDevelopment()) {
    app.UseDeveloperExceptionPage();
}
...
```

The `UseDeveloperExceptionPage` method adds the middleware component that intercepts exceptions and presents a more useful response. To demonstrate the way that exceptions are handled, listing 16.15 replaces the middleware and endpoints used in earlier examples with a new component that deliberately throws an exception.

> ### Listing 16.15 Adding Middleware in the Program.cs File in the Platform Folder

```
var builder = WebApplication.CreateBuilder(args);

var app = builder.Build();

app.Run(context => {
    throw new Exception("Something has gone wrong");
});

app.Run();
```

Restart ASP.NET Core and navigate to http://localhost:5000 to see the response that the middleware component generates, which is shown in figure 16.10. The page presents a stack trace and details about the request, including details of the headers and cookies it contained.

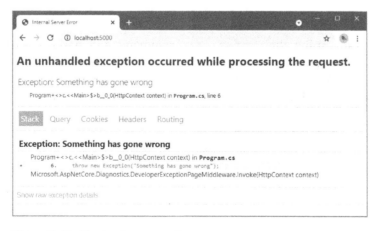

Figure 16.10 The developer exception page

16.6.1 *Returning an HTML error response*

When the developer exception middleware is disabled, as it will be when the application is in production, ASP.NET Core deals with unhandled exceptions by sending a response that contains just an error code. Listing 16.16 changes the environment to production.

> **Listing 16.16   Changes in the launchSettings.json file in the Platform/Properties folder**

```
{
  "iisSettings": {
    "windowsAuthentication": false,
    "anonymousAuthentication": true,
    "iisExpress": {
      "applicationUrl": "http://localhost:5000",
      "sslPort": 0
    }
  },
  "profiles": {
    "Platform": {
      "commandName": "Project",
      "dotnetRunMessages": true,
      "launchBrowser": true,
      "applicationUrl": "http://localhost:5000;https://localhost:5500",
      "environmentVariables": {
        "ASPNETCORE_ENVIRONMENT": "Production"
      }
    },
    "IIS Express": {
      "commandName": "IISExpress",
      "launchBrowser": true,
      "environmentVariables": {
        "ASPNETCORE_ENVIRONMENT": "Development"
      }
    }
  }
}
```

Start ASP.NET Core using the `dotnet run` command and navigate to http://localhost:5000. The response you see will depend on your browser because ASP.NET Core has only provided it with a response containing status code 500, without any content to display. Figure 16.11 shows how this is handled by Google Chrome.

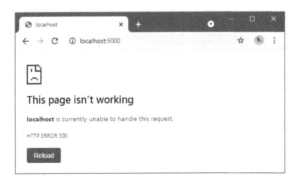

**Figure 16.11
Returning an
error response**

As an alternative to returning just status codes, ASP.NET Core provides middleware that intercepts unhandled exceptions and sends a redirection to the browser instead, which can be used to show a friendlier response than the raw status code. The exception redirection middleware is added with the `UseExceptionHandler` method, as shown in listing 16.17.

Listing 16.17 Returning an error response in the Program.cs file in the Platform folder

```
var builder = WebApplication.CreateBuilder(args);

var app = builder.Build();

if (!app.Environment.IsDevelopment()) {
    app.UseExceptionHandler("/error.html");
    app.UseStaticFiles();
}

app.Run(context => {
    throw new Exception("Something has gone wrong");
});

app.Run();
```

When an exception is thrown, the exception handler middleware will intercept the response and redirect the browser to the URL provided as the argument to the `UseExceptionHandler` method. For this example, the redirection is to a URL that will be handled by a static file, so the `UseStaticFiles` middleware has also been added to the pipeline.

To add the file that the browser will receive, create an HTML file named `error.html` in the `wwwroot` folder and add the content shown in listing 16.18.

Listing 16.18 The contents of the error.html file in the Platform/wwwroot folder

```html
<!DOCTYPE html>
<html lang="en">
<head>
    <link rel="stylesheet" href="/lib/bootstrap/css/bootstrap.min.css" />
    <title>Error</title>
</head>
<body class="text-center">
    <h3 class="p-2">Something went wrong...</h3>
    <h6>You can go back to the <a href="/">homepage</a> and try again</h6>
</body>
</html>
```

Restart ASP.NET Core and navigate to http://localhost:5000 to see the effect of the new middleware. Instead of the raw status code, the browser will be sent the content of the `/error.html` URL, as shown in figure 16.12.

**Figure 16.12
Displaying an
HTML error**

There are versions of the `UseExceptionHandler` method that allow more complex responses to be composed, but my advice is to keep error handling as simple as possible because you can't anticipate all of the problems an application may encounter, and you run the risk of encountering another exception when trying to handle the one that triggered the handler, resulting in a confusing response or no response at all.

16.6.2 *Enriching status code responses*

Not all error responses will be the result of uncaught exceptions. Some requests cannot be processed for reasons other than software defects, such as requests for URLs that are not supported or that require authentication. For this type of problem, redirecting the client to a different URL can be problematic because some clients rely on the error code to detect problems. You will see examples of this in later chapters when I show you how to create and consume RESTful web applications.

ASP.NET Core provides middleware that adds user-friendly content to error responses without requiring redirection. This preserves the error status code while providing a human-readable message that helps users make sense of the problem.

The simplest approach is to define a string that will be used as the body for the response. This is more awkward than simply pointing at a file, but it is a more reliable technique, and as a rule, simple and reliable techniques are preferable when handling errors. To create the string response for the example project, add a class file named `ResponseStrings.cs` to the `Platform` folder with the code shown in listing 16.19.

> **Listing 16.19   The contents of the ResponseStrings.cs file in the Platform folder**

```
namespace Platform {

    public static class Responses {

        public static string DefaultResponse = @"
        <!DOCTYPE html>
            <html lang=""en"">
            <head>
                <link rel=""stylesheet""
                    href=""/lib/bootstrap/css/bootstrap.min.css"" />
                <title>Error</title>
            </head>
            <body class=""text-center"">
                <h3 class=""p-2"">Error {0}</h3>
                <h6>
```

```
            You can go back to the <a href=""/"">homepage</a>
                and try again
        </h6>
    </body>
</html>";
    }
}
```

The `Responses` class defines a `DefaultResponse` property to which I have assigned a multiline string containing a simple HTML document. There is a placeholder—{0}— into which the response status code will be inserted when the response is sent to the client.

Listing 16.20 adds the status code middleware to the request pipeline and adds a new middleware component that will return a 404 status code, indicating that the requested URL was not found.

Listing 16.20   Adding middleware in the Program.cs file in the Platform folder

```
var builder = WebApplication.CreateBuilder(args);

var app = builder.Build();

if (!app.Environment.IsDevelopment()) {
    app.UseExceptionHandler("/error.html");
    app.UseStaticFiles();
}

app.UseStatusCodePages("text/html", Platform.Responses.DefaultResponse);

app.Use(async (context, next) => {
    if (context.Request.Path == "/error") {
        context.Response.StatusCode = StatusCodes.Status404NotFound;
        await Task.CompletedTask;
    } else {
        await next();
    }
});

app.Run(context => {
    throw new Exception("Something has gone wrong");
});

app.Run();
```

The `UseStatusCodePages` method adds the response-enriching middleware to the request pipeline. The first argument is the value that will be used for the response's `Content-Type` header, which is `text/html` in this example. The second argument is the string that will be used as the body of the response, which is the HTML string from listing 16.19.

The custom middleware component sets the `HttpResponse.StatusCode` property to specify the status code for the response, using a value defined by the `StatusCode` class. Middleware components are required to return a `Task`, so I have used the `Task` `.CompletedTask` property because there is no work for this middleware component to do.

To see how the 404 status code is handled, restart ASP.NET Core and request http:// localhost:5000/error. The status code middleware will intercept the result and add the content shown in figure 16.13 to the response. The string used as the second argument to `UseStatusCodePages` is interpolated using the status code to resolve the placeholder.

Figure 16.13 Using the status code middleware

The status code middleware responds only to status codes between 400 and 600 and doesn't alter responses that already contain content, which means you won't see the response in the figure if an error occurs after another middleware component has started to generate a response. The status code middleware won't respond to unhandled exceptions because exceptions disrupt the flow of a request through the pipeline, meaning that the status code middleware isn't given the opportunity to inspect the response before it is sent to the client. As a result, the `UseStatusCodePages` method is typically used in conjunction with the `UseExceptionHandler` or `UseDeveloper-ExceptionPage` method.

> **NOTE** There are two related methods, `UseStatusCodePagesWithRedirects` and `UseStatusCodePagesWithReExecute`, which work by redirecting the client to a different URL or by rerunning the request through the pipeline with a different URL. In both cases, the original status code may be lost.

16.7 *Filtering requests using the host header*

The HTTP specification requires requests to include a `Host` header that specifies the hostname the request is intended for, which makes it possible to support virtual servers where one HTTP server receives requests on a single port and handles them differently based on the hostname that was requested.

The default set of middleware that is added to the request pipeline by the `Program` class includes middleware that filters requests based on the `Host` header so that only requests that target a list of approved hostnames are handled and all other requests are rejected.

The default configuration for the `Hosts` header middleware is included in the `appsettings.json` file, as follows:

```
...
{
  "Logging": {
    "LogLevel": {
      "Default": "Information",
      "Microsoft.AspNetCore": "Warning"
    }
  },
  "AllowedHosts": "*",
  "Location": {
    "CityName": "Buffalo"
  }
}
...
```

The `AllowedHosts` configuration property is added to the JSON file when the project is created, and the default value accepts requests regardless of the `Host` header value. You can change the configuration by editing the JSON file. The configuration can also be changed using the options pattern, as shown in listing 16.21.

NOTE The middleware is added to the pipeline by default, but you can use the `UseHostFiltering` method if you need to add the middleware explicitly.

Listing 16.21 Configuring host filtering in the Program.cs file in the Platform folder

```
using Microsoft.AspNetCore.HostFiltering;

var builder = WebApplication.CreateBuilder(args);

builder.Services.Configure<HostFilteringOptions>(opts => {
    opts.AllowedHosts.Clear();
    opts.AllowedHosts.Add("*.example.com");
});

var app = builder.Build();

if (!app.Environment.IsDevelopment()) {
    app.UseExceptionHandler("/error.html");
    app.UseStaticFiles();
}

app.UseStatusCodePages("text/html", Platform.Responses.DefaultResponse);

app.Use(async (context, next) => {
    if (context.Request.Path == "/error") {
        context.Response.StatusCode = StatusCodes.Status404NotFound;
        await Task.CompletedTask;
    } else {
        await next();
    }
});
```

```
app.Run(context => {
    throw new Exception("Something has gone wrong");
});
```

```
app.Run();
```

The `HostFilteringOptions` class is used to configure the host filtering middleware using the properties described in table 16.11.

Table 16.11 The HostFilteringOptions properties

Name	Description
AllowedHosts	This property returns a `List<string>` that contains the domains for which requests are allowed. Wildcards are allowed so that `*.example.com` accepts all names in the `example.com` domain and `*` accepts all header values.
AllowEmptyHosts	When `false`, this property tells the middleware to reject requests that do not contain a `Host` header. The default value is `true`.
IncludeFailureMessage	When `true`, this property includes a message in the response that indicates the reason for the error. The default value is `true`.

In listing 16.21, I called the `Clear` method to remove the wildcard entry that has been loaded from the `appsettings.json` file and then called the `Add` method to accept all hosts in the `example.com` domain. Requests sent from the browser to localhost will no longer contain an acceptable `Host` header. You can see what happens by restarting ASP. NET Core and using the browser to request http://localhost:5000. The `Host` header middleware checks the `Host` header in the request, determines that the request host-name doesn't match the `AllowedHosts` list, and terminates the request with the 400 status code, which indicates a bad request. Figure 16.14 shows the error message.

**Figure 16.14
A request
rejected based
on the Host
header**

Summary

- ASP.NET Core provides support for adding cookies to responses and reading those cookies when the client includes them in subsequent requests.
- Sessions allow related requests to be identified to provide continuity across requests.
- ASP.NET Core supports HTTPS requests and can be configured to disallow regular HTTP requests.
- Limits can be applied to the rate of requests handled by endpoints.

Working with data

This chapter covers

- Caching data values or complete responses using ASP.NET Core
- Working with Entity Framework Core to access data in a relational database

All the examples in the earlier chapters in this part of the book have generated fresh responses for each request, which is easy to do when dealing with simple strings or small fragments of HTML. Most real projects deal with data that is expensive to produce and needs to be used as efficiently as possible. In this chapter, I describe the features that ASP.NET Core provides for caching data and caching entire responses. I also show you how to create and configure the services required to access data in a database using Entity Framework Core. Table 17.1 puts the ASP.NET Core features for working with data in context.

NOTE The examples in this chapter rely on the SQL Server LocalDB feature that was installed in chapter 2. You will encounter errors if you have not installed LocalDB and the required updates.

Table 17.1 Putting the ASP.NET Core data features in context

Question	Answer
What are they?	The features described in this chapter allow responses to be produced using data that has been previously created, either because it was created for an earlier request or because it has been stored in a database.
Why are they useful?	Most web applications deal with data that is expensive to re-create for every request. The features in this chapter allow responses to be produced more efficiently and with fewer resources.
How are they used?	Data values are cached using a service. Responses are cached by a middleware component based on the `Cache-Control` header. Databases are accessed through a service that translates LINQ queries into SQL statements.
Are there any pitfalls or limitations?	For caching, it is important to test the effect of your cache policy before deploying the application to ensure you have found the right balance between efficiency and responsiveness. For Entity Framework Core, it is important to pay attention to the queries sent to the database to ensure that they are not retrieving large amounts of data that is processed and then discarded by the application.
Are there any alternatives?	All the features described in this chapter are optional. You can elect not to cache data or responses or to use an external cache. You can choose not to use a database or to access a database using a framework other than Entity Framework Core.

Table 17.2 provides a guide to the chapter.

Table 17.2 Chapter guide

Problem	Solution	Listing
Caching data values	Set up a cache service and use it in endpoints and middleware components to store data values.	3–6
Creating a persistent cache	Use the database-backed cache.	7–13
Caching entire responses	Enable the response or output caching middleware.	14-19
Storing application data	Use Entity Framework Core.	20-26, 29-31
Creating a database schema	Create and apply migrations.	27, 28
Accessing data in endpoints	Consume the database context service.	32
Including all request details in logging messages	Enable the sensitive data logging feature.	33

17.1   *Preparing for this chapter*

In this chapter, I continue to use the Platform project from chapter 16. To prepare for this chapter, replace the contents of the Program.cs file with the code shown in listing 17.1.

> **TIP**   You can download the example project for this chapter—and for all the other chapters in this book—from https://github.com/manningbooks/pro-asp .net-core-7. See chapter 1 for how to get help if you have problems running the examples.

Listing 17.1   Replacing the contents of the Program.cs file in the Platform folder

```
var builder = WebApplication.CreateBuilder(args);

var app = builder.Build();

app.MapGet("/", async context => {
    await context.Response.WriteAsync("Hello World!");
});

app.Run();
```

Start the application by opening a new PowerShell command prompt, navigating to the Platform project folder (which contains the Platform.csproj file), and running the command shown in listing 17.2.

Listing 17.2   Starting the ASP.NET Core runtime

```
dotnet run
```

Open a new browser tab, navigate to https://localhost:5000, and you will see the content shown in figure 17.1.

Figure 17.1   Running the example application

17.2   *Caching data*

In most web applications, there will be some items of data that are relatively expensive to generate but are required repeatedly. The exact nature of the data is specific to each project, but repeatedly performing the same set of calculations can increase the resources required to host the application. To represent an expensive response, add a class file called SumEndpoint.cs to the Platform folder with the code shown in listing 17.3.

Listing 17.3 The contents of the SumEndpoint.cs file in the Platform folder

```
namespace Platform {

    public class SumEndpoint {

        public async Task Endpoint(HttpContext context) {
            int count;
            int.TryParse((string?)context.Request.RouteValues["count"],
                out count);
            long total = 0;
            for (int i = 1; i <= count; i++) {
                total += i;
            }
            string totalString = $"({DateTime.Now.ToLongTimeString()}) "
                + total;
            await context.Response.WriteAsync(
                $"({DateTime.Now.ToLongTimeString()}) Total for {count}"
                + $" values:\n{totalString}\n");
        }
    }
}
```

Listing 17.4 creates a route that uses the endpoint, which is applied using the `Map-Endpoint` extension methods created in chapter 14.

Listing 17.4 Adding an endpoint in the Program.cs file in the Platform folder

```
var builder = WebApplication.CreateBuilder(args);

var app = builder.Build();

app.MapEndpoint<Platform.SumEndpoint>("/sum/{count:int=1000000000}");

app.MapGet("/", async context => {
    await context.Response.WriteAsync("Hello World!");
});

app.Run();
```

Restart ASP.NET Core and use a browser to request http://localhost:5000/sum. The endpoint will sum 1,000,000,000 integer values and produce the result shown in figure 17.2.

Reload the browser window, and the endpoint will repeat the calculation. Both the timestamps change in the response, as shown in the figure, indicating that every part of the response was produced fresh for each request.

> **TIP** You may need to increase or decrease the default value for the route parameter based on the capabilities of your machine. Try to find a value that takes two or three seconds to produce the result—just long enough that you can tell when the calculation is being performed but not so long that you can step out for coffee while it happens.

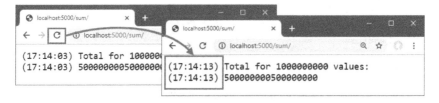

Figure 17.2   An expensive response

17.2.1 Caching data values

ASP.NET Core provides a service that can be used to cache data values through the `IDistributedCache` interface. Listing 17.5 revises the endpoint to declare a dependency on the service and use it to cache calculated values.

Listing 17.5   Using the cache service in the SumEndpoint.cs file in the Platform folder

```
using Microsoft.Extensions.Caching.Distributed;

namespace Platform {

    public class SumEndpoint {

        public async Task Endpoint(HttpContext context,
                IDistributedCache cache) {
            int count;
            int.TryParse((string?)context.Request.RouteValues["count"],
                out count);
            string cacheKey = $"sum_{count}";
            string? totalString = await cache.GetStringAsync(cacheKey);
            if (totalString == null) {
                long total = 0;
                for (int i = 1; i <= count; i++) {
                    total += i;
                }
                totalString = $"({DateTime.Now.ToLongTimeString()}) "
                    + total;
                await cache.SetStringAsync(cacheKey, totalString,
                    new DistributedCacheEntryOptions {
                        AbsoluteExpirationRelativeToNow =
                            TimeSpan.FromMinutes(2)
                    });
            }
            await context.Response.WriteAsync(
                $"({DateTime.Now.ToLongTimeString()}) Total for {count}"
                + $" values:\n{totalString}\n");
        }
    }
}
```

The cache service can store only byte arrays, which can be restrictive but allows for a range of `IDistributedCache` implementations to be used. There are extension methods available that allow strings to be used, which is a more convenient way of caching most data. Table 17.3 describes the most useful methods for using the cache.

Table 17.3 Useful IDistributedCache methods

Name	Description
GetString(key)	This method returns the cached string associated with the specified key, or null if there is no such item.
GetStringAsync(key)	This method returns a Task<string> that produces the cached string associated with the key, or null if there is no such item.
SetString(key, value, options)	This method stores a string in the cache using the specified key. The cache entry can be configured with an optional DistributedCacheEntryOptions object.
SetStringAsync(key, value, options)	This method asynchronously stores a string in the cache using the specified key. The cache entry can be configured with an optional Distributed-CacheEntryOptions object.
Refresh(key)	This method resets the expiry interval for the value associated with the key, preventing it from being flushed from the cache.
RefreshAsync(key)	This method asynchronously resets the expiry interval for the value associated with the key, preventing it from being flushed from the cache.
Remove(key)	This method removes the cached item associated with the key.
RemoveAsync(key)	This method asynchronously removes the cached item associated with the key.

By default, entries remain in the cache indefinitely, but the SetString and SetString-Async methods accept an optional DistributedCacheEntryOptions argument that is used to set an expiry policy, which tells the cache when to eject the item. Table 17.4 shows the properties defined by the DistributedCacheEntryOptions class.

Table 17.4 The DistributedCacheEntryOptions properties

Name	Description
AbsoluteExpiration	This property is used to specify an absolute expiry date.
AbsoluteExpirationRelativeToNow	This property is used to specify a relative expiry date.
SlidingExpiration	This property is used to specify a period of inactivity, after which the item will be ejected from the cache if it hasn't been read.

In listing 17.5, the endpoint uses the `GetStringAsync` to see whether there is a cached result available from a previous request. If there is no cached value, the endpoint performs the calculation and caches the result using the `SetStringAsync` method, with the `AbsoluteExpirationRelativeToNow` property to tell the cache to eject the item after two minutes.

```
...
await cache.SetStringAsync(cacheKey, totalStr,
    new DistributedCacheEntryOptions {
        AbsoluteExpirationRelativeToNow = TimeSpan.FromMinutes(2)
    });
...
```

The next step is to set up the cache service, as shown in listing 17.6.

Listing 17.6   Adding a service in the Program.cs file in the Platform folder

```
var builder = WebApplication.CreateBuilder(args);

builder.Services.AddDistributedMemoryCache(opts => {
    opts.SizeLimit = 200;
});

var app = builder.Build();

app.MapEndpoint<Platform.SumEndpoint>("/sum/{count:int=1000000000}");

app.MapGet("/", async context => {
    await context.Response.WriteAsync("Hello World!");
});

app.Run();
```

`AddDistributedMemoryCache` is the same method I used in chapter 16 to provide the data store for session data. This is one of the three methods used to select an implementation for the `IDistributedCache` service, as described in table 17.5.

Table 17.5   The cache service implementation methods

Name	Description
AddDistributedMemoryCache	This method sets up an in-memory cache.
AddDistributedSqlServerCache	This method sets up a cache that stores data in SQL Server and is available when the `Microsoft.Extensions.Caching.SqlServer` package is installed. See the "Caching Responses" section for details.
AddStackExchangeRedisCache	This method sets up a Redis cache and is available when the `Microsoft.Extensions.Caching.Redis` package is installed.

Listing 17.6 uses the `AddDistributedMemoryCache` method to create an in-memory cache as the implementation for the `IDistributedCache` service. This cache is

configured using the `MemoryDistributedCacheOptions` class, whose most useful properties are described in table 17.6.

Table 17.6 Useful MemoryCacheOptions properties

Name	Description
ExpirationScanFrequency	This property is used to set a `TimeSpan` that determines how often the cache scans for expired items.
SizeLimit	This property specifies the maximum number of items in the cache. When the size is reached, the cache will eject items.
CompactionPercentage	This property specifies the percentage by which the size of the cache is reduced when `SizeLimit` is reached.

The statement in listing 17.6 uses the `SizeLimit` property to restrict the cache to 200 items. Care must be taken when using an in-memory cache to find the right balance between allocating enough memory for the cache to be effective without exhausting server resources.

To see the effect of the cache, restart ASP.NET Core and request the http://localhost:5000/sum URL. Reload the browser, and you will see that only one of the timestamps will change, as shown in figure 17.3. This is because the cache has provided the calculation response, which allows the endpoint to produce the result without having to repeat the calculation.

Figure 17.3. Caching data values

If you wait for two minutes and then reload the browser, then both timestamps will change because the cached result will have been ejected, and the endpoint will have to perform the calculation to produce the result.

17.2.2 Using a shared and persistent data cache

The cache created by the `AddDistributedMemoryCache` method isn't distributed, despite the name. The items are stored in memory as part of the ASP.NET Core process, which means that applications that run on multiple servers or containers don't share cached data. It also means that the contents of the cache are lost when ASP.NET Core is stopped.

The `AddDistributedSqlServerCache` method stores the cache data in a SQL Server database, which can be shared between multiple ASP.NET Core servers and which stores the data persistently.

The first step is to create a database that will be used to store the cached data. You can store the cached data alongside the application's other data, but for this chapter, I am going to use a separate database, which will be named `CacheDb`. You can create the database using Azure Data Studio or SQL Server Management Studio, both of which are available for free from Microsoft. Databases can also be created from the command line using `sqlcmd`. Open a new PowerShell command prompt and run the command shown in listing 17.7 to connect to the LocalDB server.

> **TIP**   The `sqlcmd` tool should have been installed as part of the Visual Studio workload or as part of the SQL Server Express installation. If it has not been installed, then you can download an installer from https://docs.microsoft.com/en-us/sql/tools/sqlcmd-utility.

Listing 17.7   Connecting to the database server

```
sqlcmd -S "(localdb)\MSSQLLocalDB"
```

Pay close attention to the argument that specifies the database. There is one backslash, which is followed by `MSSQLLocalDB`. It can be hard to spot the repeated letters: **MS-SQL-LocalDB** (but without the hyphens).

When the connection has been established, you will see a `1>` prompt. Enter the commands shown in listing 17.8 and press the Enter key after each command.

> **CAUTION**   If you are using Visual Studio, you must apply the updates for SQL Server described in chapter 2. The version of SQL Server that is installed by default when you install Visual Studio cannot create LocalDB databases.

Listing 17.8   Creating the database

```
CREATE DATABASE CacheDb
GO
```

If no errors are reported, then enter `exit` and press Enter to terminate the connection.

> **TIP**   If you need to reset the cache database, use the command in listing 17.7 to open a connection and use the command `DROP DATABASE CacheDB`. You can then re-create the database using the commands in listing 17.8.

Run the commands shown in listing 17.9 to install the package required to create a cache.

Listing 17.9   Installing the SQL cache package

```
dotnet tool uninstall --global dotnet-sql-cache
dotnet tool install --global dotnet-sql-cache --version 7.0.0
```

The first command removes any existing version of the `dotnet-sql-cache` package, and the second command installs the version required for the examples in this book. The next step is to run the command shown in listing 17.10 to create a table in the new database, using the command installed by the `dotnet-sql-cache` package.

Listing 17.10 Creating the cache database table

```
dotnet sql-cache create "Server=(localdb)\MSSQLLocalDB;Database=CacheDb"
dbo DataCache
```

The arguments for this command are the connection string that specifies the database, the schema, and the name of the table that will be used to store the cached data. Enter the command on a single line and press Enter. It will take a few seconds for the tool to connect to the database. If the process is successful, you will see the following message:

```
Table and index were created successfully.
```

CREATING THE PERSISTENT CACHE SERVICE

Now that the database is ready, I can create the service that will use it to store cached data. To add the NuGet package required for SQL Server caching support, open a new PowerShell command prompt, navigate to the `Platform` project folder, and run the command shown in listing 17.11. (If you are using Visual Studio, you can add the package by selecting Project > Manage NuGet Packages.)

Listing 17.11 Adding a package to the project

```
dotnet add package Microsoft.Extensions.Caching.SqlServer --version 7.0.0
```

The next step is to define a connection string, which describes the database connection in the JSON configuration file, as shown in listing 17.12.

> **NOTE** The cache created by the `AddDistributedSqlServerCache` method is distributed, meaning that multiple applications can use the same database and share cache data. If you are deploying the same application to multiple servers or containers, all instances will be able to share cached data. If you are sharing a cache between different applications, then you should pay close attention to the keys you use to ensure that applications receive the data types they expect.

Listing 17.12 A connection string in the appsettings.json file in the Platform folder

```
{
  "Logging": {
    "LogLevel": {
      "Default": "Information",
      "Microsoft.AspNetCore": "Warning"
    }
  },
  "AllowedHosts": "*",
  "Location": {
    "CityName": "Buffalo"
  },
```

```
"ConnectionStrings": {
  "CacheConnection": "Server=(localdb)\\MSSQLLocalDB;Database=CacheDb"
  }
}
```

Notice that the connection string uses two backslash characters (\\) to escape the character in the JSON file. Listing 17.13 changes the implementation for the cache service to use SQL Server with the connection string from listing 17.12.

Listing 17.13   Using a persistent data cache in the Program.cs file in the Platform folder

```
var builder = WebApplication.CreateBuilder(args);

//builder.Services.AddDistributedMemoryCache(opts => {
//    opts.SizeLimit = 200;
//});

builder.Services.AddDistributedSqlServerCache(opts => {
    opts.ConnectionString
        = builder.Configuration["ConnectionStrings:CacheConnection"];
    opts.SchemaName = "dbo";
    opts.TableName = "DataCache";
});

var app = builder.Build();

app.MapEndpoint<Platform.SumEndpoint>("/sum/{count:int=1000000000}");

app.MapGet("/", async context => {
    await context.Response.WriteAsync("Hello World!");
});

app.Run();
```

The IConfiguration service is used to access the connection string from the application's configuration data. The cache service is created using the Add-DistributedSqlServerCache method and is configured using an instance of the SqlServerCacheOptions class, whose most useful properties are described in table 17.7.

Table 17.7.   Useful SqlServerCacheOptions properties

Name	Description
ConnectionString	This property specifies the connection string, which is conventionally stored in the JSON configuration file and accessed through the IConfiguration service.
SchemaName	This property specifies the schema name for the cache table.
TableName	This property specifies the name of the cache table.
ExpiredItemsDeletionInterval	This property specifies how often the table is scanned for expired items. The default is 30 minutes.
DefaultSlidingExpiration	This property specifies how long an item remains unread in the cache before it expires. The default is 20 minutes.

The listing uses the `ConnectionString`, `SchemaName`, and `TableName` properties to configure the cache middleware to use the database table. Restart ASP.NET Core and use a browser to request the http://localhost:5000/sum URL. There is no change in the response produced by the application, which is shown in figure 17.4, but you will find that the cached responses are persistent and will be used even when you restart ASP.NET Core.

Caching session-specific data values

When you use the `IDistributedCache` service, the data values are shared between all requests. If you want to cache different data values for each user, then you can use the session middleware described in chapter 16. The session middleware relies on the `IDistributedCache` service to store its data, which means that session data will be stored persistently and available to a distributed application when the `AddDistributedSqlServerCache` method is used.

17.3　Caching responses

An alternative to caching individual data items is to cache entire responses, which can be a useful approach if a response is expensive to compose and is likely to be repeated. Caching responses requires the addition of a service and a middleware component, as shown in listing 17.14.

> **Listing 17.14　Configuring Caching in the Program.cs File in the Platform Folder**

```
using Platform.Services;

var builder = WebApplication.CreateBuilder(args);

builder.Services.AddDistributedSqlServerCache(opts => {
    opts.ConnectionString
        = builder.Configuration["ConnectionStrings:CacheConnection"];
    opts.SchemaName = "dbo";
    opts.TableName = "DataCache";
});

builder.Services.AddResponseCaching();
builder.Services.AddSingleton<IResponseFormatter,
    HtmlResponseFormatter>();

var app = builder.Build();

app.UseResponseCaching();

app.MapEndpoint<Platform.SumEndpoint>("/sum/{count:int=1000000000}");

app.MapGet("/", async context => {
    await context.Response.WriteAsync("Hello World!");
});

app.Run();
```

The AddResponseCaching method is used to set up the service used by the cache. The middleware component is added with the UseResponseCaching method, which should be called before any endpoint or middleware that needs its responses cached.

I have also defined the IResponseFormatter service, which I used to explain how dependency injection works in chapter 14. Response caching is used only in certain circumstances, and, as I explain shortly, demonstrating the feature requires an HTML response.

> **NOTE**   The response caching feature does not use the IDistributedCache service. Responses are cached in memory and are not distributed.

In listing 17.15, I have updated the SumEndpoint class so that it requests response caching instead of caching just a data value.

Listing 17.15   Using response caching in the SumEndpoint.cs file in the Platform folder

```
//using Microsoft.Extensions.Caching.Distributed;
using Platform.Services;

namespace Platform {

    public class SumEndpoint {

        public async Task Endpoint(HttpContext context,
                IResponseFormatter formatter, LinkGenerator generator) {

            int count;
            int.TryParse((string?)context.Request.RouteValues["count"],
                out count);
            long total = 0;
            for (int i = 1; i <= count; i++) {
                total += i;
            }
            string totalString = $"({DateTime.Now.ToLongTimeString()}) "
                + total;

            context.Response.Headers["Cache-Control"]
                = "public, max-age=120";

            string? url = generator.GetPathByRouteValues(context, null,
                new { count = count });

            await formatter.Format(context,
                $"<div>({DateTime.Now.ToLongTimeString()}) Total for "
                + $"{count} values:</div><div>{totalString}</div>"
                + $"<a href={url}>Reload</a>");
        }
    }
}
```

Some of the changes to the endpoint enable response caching, but others are just to demonstrate that it is working. For enabling response caching, the important statement is the one that adds a header to the response, like this:

```
...
context.Response.Headers["Cache-Control"] = "public, max-age=120";
...
```

The `Cache-Control` header is used to control response caching. The middleware will only cache responses that have a `Cache-Control` header that contains the `public` directive. The `max-age` directive is used to specify the period that the response can be cached for, expressed in seconds. The `Cache-Control` header used in listing 17.15 enables caching and specifies that responses can be cached for two minutes.

Enabling response caching is simple, but checking that it is working requires care. When you reload the browser window or press Return in the URL bar, browsers will include a `Cache-Control` header in the request that sets the `max-age` directive to zero, which bypasses the response cache and causes a new response to be generated by the endpoint. The only reliable way to request a URL without the `Cache-Control` header is to navigate using an HTML anchor element, which is why the endpoint in listing 17.15 uses the `IResponseFormatter` service to generate an HTML response and uses the `LinkGenerator` service to create a URL that can be used in the anchor element's `href` attribute.

To check the response cache, restart ASP.NET Core and use the browser to request http://localhost:5000/sum. Once the response has been generated, click the Reload link to request the same URL. You will see that neither of the timestamps in the response change, indicating that the entire response has been cached, as shown in figure 17.4.

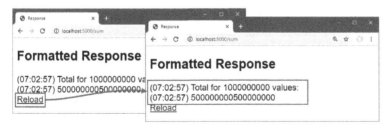

Figure 17.4 Caching responses

The `Cache-Control` header can be combined with the `Vary` header to provide fine-grained control over which requests are cached. See https://developer.mozilla.org/en-US/docs/Web/HTTP/Headers/Cache-Control and https://developer.mozilla.org/en-US/docs/Web/HTTP/Headers/Vary for details of the features provided by both headers.

Compressing responses

ASP.NET Core includes middleware that will compress responses for browsers that have indicated they can handle compressed data. The middleware is added to the pipeline with the `UseResponseCompression` method. Compression is a trade-off between the server resources required for compression and the bandwidth required to deliver content to the client, and it should not be switched on without testing to determine the performance impact.

17.4   *Caching output*

The use of the `Cache-Control` header follows the intended design of HTTP but limits the benefits of caching responses. ASP.NET Core includes an alternative approach to caching, known as *output caching*, which overcomes these problems and provides a more configurable—albeit complex—set of features. Caching is applied to endpoints and to prepare for this example, I need to update the code written in chapter 14 so that it produces a result on which the caching extension method can be invoked, as shown in listing 17.16.

> **NOTE**   The output cache feature is more comprehensive than response caching but has its own limitations. There is an API for implementing persistent cache storage, for example, but no default implementation. The distributed cache used in earlier examples can't be used because output caching requires careful locking of cached data.

> **Listing 17.16   A result in the EndpointExtensions.cs file in the Platform/Services folder**

```
using System.Reflection;

namespace Microsoft.AspNetCore.Builder {

    public static class EndpointExtensions {

        public static IEndpointConventionBuilder MapEndpoint<T>(
                this IEndpointRouteBuilder app,
                string path, string methodName = "Endpoint") {

            MethodInfo? methodInfo = typeof(T).GetMethod(methodName);
            if (methodInfo?.ReturnType != typeof(Task)) {
                throw new System.Exception("Method cannot be used");
            }

            ParameterInfo[] methodParams = methodInfo!.GetParameters();

            return app.MapGet(path, context => {
                T endpointInstance =
                    ActivatorUtilities.CreateInstance<T>
                        (context.RequestServices);
                return (Task)methodInfo.Invoke(endpointInstance!,
                    methodParams.Select(p =>
                    p.ParameterType == typeof(HttpContext)
                    ? context
                    : context.RequestServices.GetService(p.ParameterType))
                        .ToArray())!;
            });
        }
    }
}
```

This change alters the `MapEndpoint<T>` extension method to produce an implementation of the `IEndpointConventionBuilder` interface, which is the result produced by the built-in `MapGet` method and the other methods used to create endpoints. Listing 17.17 replaces the response caching from the previous section with output caching.

```
using Platform.Services;

var builder = WebApplication.CreateBuilder(args);

//builder.Services.AddDistributedSqlServerCache(opts => {
//      opts.ConnectionString
//          = builder.Configuration["ConnectionStrings:CacheConnection"];
//      opts.SchemaName = "dbo";
//      opts.TableName = "DataCache";
//});

builder.Services.AddOutputCache();

//builder.Services.AddResponseCaching();
builder.Services.AddSingleton<IResponseFormatter,
    HtmlResponseFormatter>();

var app = builder.Build();

//app.UseResponseCaching();
app.UseOutputCache();

app.MapEndpoint<Platform
    .SumEndpoint>("/sum/{count:int=1000000000}")
    .CacheOutput();

app.MapGet("/", async context => {
    await context.Response.WriteAsync("Hello World!");
});

app.Run();
```

This is the simplest output caching configuration, and it is applied in three parts. First, the `AddOutputCache` method is called to set up the services required for caching. Second, the `UseOutputCache` method is called to register the caching middleware, which will short-circuit the pipeline where requests are received that can be handled using cached content. The final step enables caching for a specific endpoint, which is done using the `CacheOutput` extension method:

```
...
app.MapEndpoint<Platform
    .SumEndpoint>("/sum/{count:int=1000000000}")
    .CacheOutput();
...
```

This extension method enables caching for the sum endpoint. The final step is to update the endpoint so that it doesn't set the caching header, as shown in listing 17.18.

```
//using Microsoft.Extensions.Caching.Distributed;
using Platform.Services;

namespace Platform {

    public class SumEndpoint {

        public async Task Endpoint(HttpContext context,
                IResponseFormatter formatter, LinkGenerator generator) {

            int count;
            int.TryParse((string?)context.Request.RouteValues["count"],
                out count);
            long total = 0;
            for (int i = 1; i <= count; i++) {
                total += i;
            }
            string totalString = $"({DateTime.Now.ToLongTimeString()}) "
                + total;

            //context.Response.Headers["Cache-Control"]
            //     = "public, max-age=120";

            string? url = generator.GetPathByRouteValues(context, null,
                new { count = count });

            await formatter.Format(context,
                $"<div>({DateTime.Now.ToLongTimeString()}) Total for "
                + $"{count} values:</div><div>{totalString}</div>"
                + $"<a href={url}>Reload</a>");
        }
    }
}
```

The endpoint doesn't need to manage the caching of its content directly, which means that the cache settings can be altered without needing to change the code that generates responses.

The configuration used in listing 17.18 applies the default caching policy, which caches content for one minute and caches only HTTP GET or HEAD requests that produce HTTP 200 responses, and which are not authenticated or set cookies.

To check the output cache, restart ASP.NET Core and use the browser to request http://localhost:5000/sum. You will see the same output as in earlier examples, but now the cache is applied when the browser is reloaded and not just when the user clicks on the link, as shown in figure 17.5.

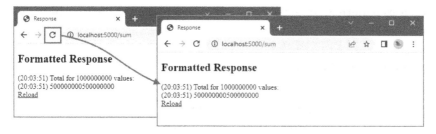

Figure 17.5. Output caching applies to all requests for a given URL

17.4.1 Defining a custom cache policy

The output caching feature supports custom caching policies and allows different policies to be applied to endpoints. Caching policies are defined using the options pattern, as shown in listing 17.19.

> **Listing 17.19   A custom configuration in the Program.cs file in the Platform folder**

```
using Platform.Services;

var builder = WebApplication.CreateBuilder(args);

builder.Services.AddOutputCache(opts => {
    opts.AddBasePolicy(policy => {
        policy.Cache();
        policy.Expire(TimeSpan.FromSeconds(10));
    });
    opts.AddPolicy("30sec", policy => {
        policy.Cache();
        policy.Expire(TimeSpan.FromSeconds(30));
    });
});

builder.Services.AddSingleton<IResponseFormatter,
    HtmlResponseFormatter>();

var app = builder.Build();

app.UseOutputCache();

app.MapEndpoint<Platform
    .SumEndpoint>("/sum/{count:int=1000000000}")
    .CacheOutput();

app.MapEndpoint<Platform
    .SumEndpoint>("/sum30/{count:int=1000000000}")
    .CacheOutput("30sec");

app.MapGet("/", async context => {
    await context.Response.WriteAsync("Hello World!");
});

app.Run();
```

The options pattern is applied to an `OutputCacheOptions` object, whose most useful methods are described in table 17.8.

Table 17.8 Useful OutputCacheOptions methods

Name	Description
AddBasePolicy	This method is used to define the default policy
AddPolicy	This method is used to create a policy that can be applied to specific endpoints.

The methods described in table 17.8 define policies using the methods defined by the `OutputCachePolicyBuilder` class. The basic methods are described in table 17.9.

Table 17.9 The basic OutputCachePolicyBuilder methods

Name	Description
Expire	This method sets the expiry interval for cached output, expressed as a `TimeSpan`.
SetLocking	This method is used to enable or disable locking in the cache. Locking is enabled by default and should only be disabled with caution since it can lead to unexpected behavior.
NoCache	This method disables caching in the policy.
Cache	This method enables caching in the policy.

The policies in listing 17.19 use the `Cache` and `Expire` methods. The `AddBasePolicy` method is used to change the cache duration for the default policy. The `AddPolicy` method is used to create a new cache policy named `30sec`, which caches output for 30 seconds:

```
...
opts.AddPolicy("30sec", policy => {
    policy.Cache();
    policy.Expire(TimeSpan.FromSeconds(30));
});
...
```

The name given to a policy created with the `AddPolicy` method is used to apply the policy to an endpoint, like this:

```
...
app.MapEndpoint<Platform
    .SumEndpoint>("/sum30/{count:int=1000000000}")
    .CacheOutput("30sec");
...
```

The result is that requests to the `/sum` URL are cached using the default policy, while requests to the `/sum30` URL are cached using the `30sec` policy, causing the output from the endpoints to be cached for a different duration.

17.5   Using Entity Framework Core

Not all data values are produced directly by the application, and most projects will need to access data in a database. Entity Framework Core is well-integrated into the ASP.NET Core platform, with good support for creating a database from C# classes and for creating C# classes to represent an existing database. In the sections that follow, I demonstrate the process for creating a simple data model, using it to create a database, and querying that database in an endpoint.

Working with Entity Framework Core

The most common complaint about Entity Framework Core is poor performance. When I review projects that have Entity Framework Core performance issues, the problem is almost always because the development team has treated Entity Framework Core as a black box and has not paid attention to the SQL queries that are sent to the database. Not all LINQ features can be translated into SQL, and the most common problem is a query that retrieves large amounts of data from the database, which is then discarded after it has been reduced to produce a single value.

Using Entity Framework Core requires a good understanding of SQL and ensuring that the LINQ queries made by the application are translated into efficient SQL queries. There are rare applications that have high-performance data requirements that cannot be met by Entity Framework Core, but that isn't the case for most typical web applications.

That is not to say that Entity Framework Core is perfect. It has its quirks and requires an investment in time to become proficient. If you don't like the way that Entity Framework Core works, then you may prefer to use an alternative, such as Dapper (https://dapperlib.github.io/Dapper). But if your issue is that queries are not being performed fast enough, then you should spend some time exploring how those queries are being processed, which you can do using the techniques described in the remainder of the chapter.

17.5.1 Installing Entity Framework Core

Entity Framework Core requires a global tool package that is used to manage databases from the command line and to manage packages for the project that provides data access. To install the tools package, open a new PowerShell command prompt and run the commands shown in listing 17.20.

Listing 17.20   Installing the Entity Framework Core Global Tool Package

```
dotnet tool uninstall --global dotnet-ef
dotnet tool install --global dotnet-ef --version 7.0.0
```

The first command removes any existing version of the `dotnet-ef` package, and the second command installs the version required for the examples in this book. This package provides the `dotnet ef` commands that you will see in later examples. To ensure the package is working as expected, run the command shown in listing 17.21.

Listing 17.21   Testing the Entity Framework Core Global Tool

```
dotnet ef --help
```

This command shows the help message for the global tool and produces the following output:

```
Entity Framework Core .NET Command-line Tools 7.0.0
Usage: dotnet ef [options] [command]
Options:
  --version           Show version information
  -h|--help           Show help information
  -v|--verbose        Show verbose output.
  --no-color          Don't colorize output.
  --prefix-output     Prefix output with level.
Commands:
  database    Commands to manage the database.
  dbcontext   Commands to manage DbContext types.
  migrations  Commands to manage migrations.
Use "dotnet ef [command] --help" for more information about a command.
```

Entity Framework Core also requires packages to be added to the project. If you are using Visual Studio Code or prefer working from the command line, navigate to the `Platform` project folder (the folder that contains the `Platform.csproj` file) and run the commands shown in listing 17.22.

Listing 17.22   Adding Entity Framework Core Packages to the Project

```
dotnet add package Microsoft.EntityFrameworkCore.Design --version 7.0.0
dotnet add package Microsoft.EntityFrameworkCore.SqlServer --version 7.0.0
```

17.5.2 *Creating the data model*

For this chapter, I am going to define the data model using C# classes and use Entity Framework Core to create the database and schema. Create the `Platform/Models` folder and add to it a class file called `Calculation.cs` with the contents shown in listing 17.23.

Listing 17.23   The contents of the Calculation.cs file in the Platform/Models folder

```
namespace Platform.Models {

    public class Calculation {
        public long Id { get; set; }
        public int Count { get; set; }
        public long Result { get; set; }
    }
}
```

You can see more complex data models in other chapters, but for this example, I am going to keep with the theme of this chapter and model the calculation performed in earlier examples. The `Id` property will be used to create a unique key for each object stored in the database, and the `Count` and `Result` properties will describe a calculation and its result.

Entity Framework Core uses a context class that provides access to the database. Add a file called `CalculationContext.cs` to the `Platform/Models` folder with the content shown in listing 17.24.

Listing 17.24 **The CalculationContext.cs file in the Platform/Models folder**

```
using Microsoft.EntityFrameworkCore;

namespace Platform.Models {

    public class CalculationContext : DbContext {

        public CalculationContext(
            DbContextOptions<CalculationContext> opts) : base(opts) { }

        public DbSet<Calculation> Calculations => Set<Calculation>();
    }
}
```

The `CalculationContext` class defines a constructor that is used to receive an options object that is passed on to the base constructor. The `Calculations` property provides access to the `Calculation` objects that Entity Framework Core will retrieve from the database.

17.5.3 *Configuring the database service*

Access to the database is provided through a service, as shown in listing 17.25.

Listing 17.25 **Configuring the data service in the Program.cs file in the Platform folder**

```
using Platform.Services;
using Platform.Models;
using Microsoft.EntityFrameworkCore;

var builder = WebApplication.CreateBuilder(args);

builder.Services.AddOutputCache(opts => {
    opts.AddBasePolicy(policy => {
        policy.Cache();
        policy.Expire(TimeSpan.FromSeconds(10));
    });
    opts.AddPolicy("30sec", policy => {
        policy.Cache();
        policy.Expire(TimeSpan.FromSeconds(30));
    });
});

builder.Services.AddSingleton<IResponseFormatter,
    HtmlResponseFormatter>();

builder.Services.AddDbContext<CalculationContext>(opts => {
    opts.UseSqlServer(
        builder.Configuration["ConnectionStrings:CalcConnection"]);
});
```

```
var app = builder.Build();

app.UseOutputCache();

app.MapEndpoint<Platform
    .SumEndpoint>("/sum/{count:int=1000000000}")
    .CacheOutput();

app.MapEndpoint<Platform
    .SumEndpoint>("/sum30/{count:int=1000000000}")
    .CacheOutput("30sec");

app.MapGet("/", async context => {
    await context.Response.WriteAsync("Hello World!");
});

app.Run();
```

The `AddDbContext` method creates a service for an Entity Framework Core context class. The method receives an options object that is used to select the database provider, which is done with the `UseSqlServer` method. The `IConfiguration` service is used to get the connection string for the database, which is defined in listing 17.26.

> **Listing 17.26   A connection string in the appsettings.json file in the Platform folder**

```
{
  "Logging": {
    "LogLevel": {
      "Default": "Information",
      "Microsoft.AspNetCore": "Warning",
      "Microsoft.EntityFrameworkCore": "Information"
    }
  },
  "AllowedHosts": "*",
  "Location": {
    "CityName": "Buffalo"
  },
  "ConnectionStrings": {
    "CacheConnection": "Server=(localdb)\\MSSQLLocalDB;Database=CacheDb",
    "CalcConnection": "Server=(localdb)\\MSSQLLocalDB;Database=CalcDb"
  }
}
```

The listing also sets the logging level for the `Microsoft.EntityFrameworkCore` category, which will show the SQL statements that are used by Entity Framework Core to query the database.

> **TIP** Set the `MultipleActiveResultSets` option to `True` for connection strings that will be used to make queries with multiple result sets. You can see an example of this option set in the connection strings for the SportsStore project in chapter 7.

17.5.4 *Creating and applying the database migration*

Entity Framework Core manages the relationship between data model classes and the database using a feature called *migrations*. When changes are made to the model classes, a new migration is created that modifies the database to match those changes. To create the initial migration, which will create a new database and prepare it to store `Calculation` objects, open a new PowerShell command prompt, navigate to the folder that contains the `Platform.csproj` file, and run the command shown in listing 17.27.

Listing 17.27   Creating a migration

```
dotnet ef migrations add Initial
```

The `dotnet ef` commands relate to Entity Framework Core. The command in listing 17.27 creates a new migration named `Initial`, which is the name conventionally given to the first migration for a project. You will see that a `Migrations` folder has been added to the project and that it contains class files whose statements prepare the database so that it can store the objects in the data model. To apply the migration, run the command shown in listing 17.28 in the `Platform` project folder.

Listing 17.28   Applying a migration

```
dotnet ef database update
```

This command executes the commands in the migration and uses them to prepare the database, which you can see in the SQL statements written to the command prompt.

17.5.5 *Seeding the database*

Most applications require some seed data, especially during development. Entity Framework Core does provide a database seeding feature, but it is of limited use for most projects because it doesn't allow data to be seeded where the database allocates unique keys to the objects it stores. This is an important feature in most data models because it means the application doesn't have to worry about allocating unique key values.

A more flexible approach is to use the regular Entity Framework Core features to add seed data to the database. Create a file called `SeedData.cs` in the `Platform/Models` folder with the code shown in listing 17.29.

Listing 17.29   The contents of the SeedData.cs file in the Platform/Models folder

```
using Microsoft.EntityFrameworkCore;

namespace Platform.Models {
    public class SeedData {
        private CalculationContext context;
        private ILogger<SeedData> logger;

        private static Dictionary<int, long> data
            = new Dictionary<int, long>() {
```

```
                {1, 1}, {2, 3}, {3, 6}, {4, 10}, {5, 15},
                {6, 21}, {7, 28}, {8, 36}, {9, 45}, {10, 55}
        };

        public SeedData(CalculationContext dataContext,
                ILogger<SeedData> log) {
            context = dataContext;
            logger = log;
        }

        public void SeedDatabase() {
            context.Database.Migrate();
            if (context.Calculations?.Count() == 0) {
                logger.LogInformation("Preparing to seed database");
                context.Calculations.AddRange(
                        data.Select(kvp => new Calculation() {
                            Count = kvp.Key, Result = kvp.Value
                        }));
                context.SaveChanges();
                logger.LogInformation("Database seeded");
            } else {
                logger.LogInformation("Database not seeded");
            }
        }
    }
}
```

The `SeedData` class declares constructor dependencies on the `CalculationContext` and `ILogger<T>` types, which are used in the `SeedDatabase` method to prepare the database. The context's `Database.Migrate` method is used to apply any pending migrations to the database, and the `Calculations` property is used to store new data using the `AddRange` method, which accepts a sequence of `Calculation` objects.

The new objects are stored in the database using the `SaveChanges` method. To use the `SeedData` class, make the changes shown in listing 17.30 to the `Program.cs` file.

> **Listing 17.30**   **Enabling database seeding in the Program.cs file in the Platform folder**

```
using Microsoft.EntityFrameworkCore;
using Platform.Models;
using Platform.Services;

var builder = WebApplication.CreateBuilder(args);

builder.Services.AddOutputCache(opts => {
    opts.AddBasePolicy(policy => {
        policy.Cache();
        policy.Expire(TimeSpan.FromSeconds(10));
    });
    opts.AddPolicy("30sec", policy => {
        policy.Cache();
        policy.Expire(TimeSpan.FromSeconds(30));
    });
});
```

```
builder.Services.AddSingleton<IResponseFormatter,
    HtmlResponseFormatter>();

builder.Services.AddDbContext<CalculationContext>(opts => {
    opts.UseSqlServer(
        builder.Configuration["ConnectionStrings:CalcConnection"]);
});

builder.Services.AddTransient<SeedData>();

var app = builder.Build();

app.UseOutputCache();

app.MapEndpoint<Platform
    .SumEndpoint>("/sum/{count:int=1000000000}")
    .CacheOutput();

app.MapEndpoint<Platform
    .SumEndpoint>("/sum30/{count:int=1000000000}")
    .CacheOutput("30sec");

app.MapGet("/", async context => {
    await context.Response.WriteAsync("Hello World!");
});

bool cmdLineInit = (app.Configuration["INITDB"] ?? "false") == "true";
if (app.Environment.IsDevelopment() || cmdLineInit) {
    var seedData = app.Services.GetRequiredService<SeedData>();
    seedData.SeedDatabase();
}
if (!cmdLineInit) {
    app.Run();
}
```

I create a service for the `SeedData` class, which means that it will be instantiated, and its dependencies will be resolved, which is more convenient than working directly with the class constructor.

If the hosting environment is `Development`, the database will be seeded automatically as the application starts. It can also be useful to seed the database explicitly, especially when setting up the application for staging or production testing. This statement checks for a configuration setting named `INITDB`:

```
...
bool cmdLineInit = (app.Configuration["INITDB"] ?? "false") == "true";
...
```

This setting can be supplied on the command line to seed the database, after which the application will terminate because the `Run` method, which starts listening for HTTP requests, is never called.

To seed the database, open a new PowerShell command prompt, navigate to the project folder, and run the command shown in listing 17.31.

```
dotnet run INITDB=true
```

The application will start, and the database will be seeded with the results for the ten calculations defined by the SeedData class, after which the application will terminate. During the seeding process, you will see the SQL statements that are sent to the database, which check to see whether there are any pending migrations, count the number of rows in the table used to store Calculation data, and, if the table is empty, add the seed data.

> **NOTE** If you need to reset the database, you can use the dotnet ef database drop --force command. You can then use dotnet run INITDB=true to re-create and seed the database again.

17.5.6 *Using data in an endpoint*

Endpoints and middleware components access Entity Framework Core data by declaring a dependency on the context class and using its DbSet<T> properties to perform LINQ queries. The LINQ queries are translated into SQL and sent to the database. The row data received from the database is used to create data model objects that are used to produce responses. Listing 17.32 updates the SumEndpoint class to use Entity Framework Core.

```
//using Platform.Services;
using Platform.Models;

namespace Platform {

    public class SumEndpoint {

        public async Task Endpoint(HttpContext context,
            CalculationContext dataContext) {

            int count;
            int.TryParse((string?)context.Request.RouteValues["count"],
                out count);

            long total = dataContext.Calculations?
                .FirstOrDefault(c => c.Count == count)?.Result ?? 0;
            if (total == 0) {
                for (int i = 1; i <= count; i++) {
                    total += i;
                }
                dataContext.Calculations?.Add(new() {
                    Count = count, Result = total
                });
                await dataContext.SaveChangesAsync();
            }
```

```
        string totalString = $"({DateTime.Now.ToLongTimeString()}) "
            + total;

        await context.Response.WriteAsync(
            $"({DateTime.Now.ToLongTimeString()}) Total for {count}"
            + $" values:\n{totalString}\n");
        }
    }
}
```

The endpoint uses the LINQ `FirstOrDefault` to search for a stored `Calculation` object for the calculation that has been requested like this:

```
...
dataContext.Calculations?
    .FirstOrDefault(c => c.Count == count)?.Result ?? 0;
...
```

If an object has been stored, it is used to prepare the response. If not, then the calculation is performed, and a new `Calculation` object is stored by these statements:

```
...
dataContext.Calculations?.Add(new () { Count = count, Result = total});
await dataContext.SaveChangesAsync();
...
```

The `Add` method is used to tell Entity Framework Core that the object should be stored, but the update isn't performed until the `SaveChangesAsync` method is called. To see the effect of the changes, restart ASP.NET Core MVC (without the `INITDB` argument if you are using the command line) and request the http://localhost:5000/sum/10 URL. This is one of the calculations with which the database has been seeded, and you will be able to see the query sent to the database in the logging messages produced by the application.

```
...
Executing DbCommand [Parameters=[@__count_0='?' (DbType = Int32)],
    CommandType='Text', CommandTimeout='30']
SELECT TOP(1) [c].[Id], [c].[Count], [c].[Result]
    FROM [Calculations] AS [c]
    WHERE [c].[Count] = @__count_0
...
```

If you request http://localhost:5000/sum/100, the database will be queried, but no result will be found. The endpoint performs the calculation and stores the result in the database before producing the result shown in figure 17.6.

Figure 17.6   Performing a calculation

Once a result has been stored in the database, subsequent requests for the same URL will be satisfied using the stored data. You can see the SQL statement used to store the data in the logging output produced by Entity Framework Core.

```
...
Executing DbCommand [Parameters=[@p0='?' (DbType = Int32),
    @p1='?' (DbType = Int64)],
        CommandType='Text', CommandTimeout='30']
SET NOCOUNT ON;
INSERT INTO [Calculations] ([Count], [Result])
VALUES (@p0, @p1);
SELECT [Id]
FROM [Calculations]
WHERE @@ROWCOUNT = 1 AND [Id] = scope_identity();
...
```

> **NOTE**   Notice that the data retrieved from the database is not cached and that each request leads to a new SQL query. Depending on the frequency and complexity of the queries you require, you may want to cache data values or responses using the techniques described earlier in the chapter.

ENABLING SENSITIVE DATA LOGGING

Entity Framework Core doesn't include parameter values in the logging messages it produces, which is why the logging output contains question marks, like this:

```
...
Executing DbCommand [Parameters=[@__count_0='?' (DbType = Int32)],
    CommandType='Text', CommandTimeout='30']
...
```

The data is omitted as a precaution to prevent sensitive data from being stored in logs. If you are having problems with queries and need to see the values sent to the database, then you can use the EnableSensitiveDataLogging method when configuring the database context, as shown in listing 17.33.

Listing 17.33   Sensitive data logging in the Program.cs file in the Platform folder

```
...
builder.Services.AddDbContext<CalculationContext>(opts => {
    opts.UseSqlServer(
        builder.Configuration["ConnectionStrings:CalcConnection"]);
    opts.EnableSensitiveDataLogging(true);
});
...
```

Restart ASP.NET Core MVC and request the http://localhost:5000/sum/100 URL again. When the request is handled, Entity Framework Core will include parameter values in the logging message it creates to show the SQL query, like this:

```
...
Executed DbCommand (40ms) [Parameters=[@__count_0='100'],
    CommandType='Text', CommandTimeout='30']
SELECT TOP(1) [c].[Id], [c].[Count], [c].[Result]
```

```
FROM [Calculations] AS [c]
WHERE [c].[Count] = @__count_0
...
```

This is a feature that should be used with caution because logs are often accessible by people who would not usually have access to the sensitive data that applications handle, such as credit card numbers and account details.

Summary

- ASP.NET Core provides support for caching individual data values, which can be accessed by endpoints.

- Entire responses can be cached, which means that requests are serviced from the cache without using the endpoint.

- ASP.NET Core provides two different middleware components for caching responses. The response cache requires a header to be set and only uses cached responses for some requests. The output cache is more complex, but more comprehensive, and uses cached responses more widely.

- Entity Framework Core provides access to relational data. Entity Framework Core is configured as a service and consumed by endpoints via dependency injection. Entity Framework Core can be used to create a database from a set of model classes and is queried using LINQ.

Part 3

Creating the
example project

This chapter covers

- Creating an ASP.NET Core project
- Creating a simple data model
- Adding Entity Framework Core to the ASP.NET Core project
- Creating and applying an Entity Framework Core migration
- Adding the Bootstrap CSS package to the project
- Defining a simple request pipeline configuration

In this chapter, you will create the example project used throughout this part of the book. The project contains a simple data model, a client-side package for formatting HTML content, and a simple request pipeline.

18.1 *Creating the project*

Open a new PowerShell command prompt and run the commands shown in listing 18.1.

> **TIP** You can download the example project for this chapter—and for all the other chapters in this book—from https://github.com/manningbooks/pro-asp .net-core-7. See chapter 1 for how to get help if you have problems running the examples.

Listing 18.1 Creating the project

```
dotnet new globaljson --sdk-version 7.0.100 --output WebApp
dotnet new web --no-https --output WebApp --framework net7.0
dotnet new sln -o WebApp
dotnet sln WebApp add WebApp
```

If you are using Visual Studio, open the `WebApp.sln` file in the `WebApp` folder. If you are using Visual Studio Code, open the `WebApp` folder. Click the Yes button when prompted to add the assets required for building and debugging the project, as shown in figure 18.1.

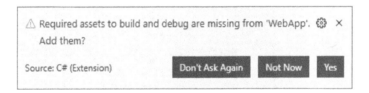

Figure 18.1 Adding project assets

Open the `launchSettings.json` file in the `WebApp/Properties` folder, change the HTTP port, and disable automatic browser launching, as shown in listing 18.2.

Listing 18.2 Setting the port in the launchSettings.json file in the Properties folder

```
{
  "iisSettings": {
    "windowsAuthentication": false,
    "anonymousAuthentication": true,
    "iisExpress": {
      "applicationUrl": "http://localhost:5000",
      "sslPort": 0
    }
  },
  "profiles": {
    "WebApp": {
      "commandName": "Project",
      "dotnetRunMessages": true,
      "launchBrowser": false,
      "applicationUrl": "http://localhost:5000",
      "environmentVariables": {
        "ASPNETCORE_ENVIRONMENT": "Development"
```

```
      }
    },
    "IIS Express": {
      "commandName": "IISExpress",
      "launchBrowser": true,
      "environmentVariables": {
        "ASPNETCORE_ENVIRONMENT": "Development"
      }
    }
  }
}
```

18.2 Adding a data model

A data model helps demonstrate the different ways that web applications can be built using ASP.NET Core, showing how complex responses can be composed and how data can be submitted by the user. In the sections that follow, I create a simple data model and use it to create the database schema that will be used to store the application's data.

18.2.1 Adding NuGet packages to the project

The data model will use Entity Framework Core to store and query data in a SQL Server LocalDB database. To add the NuGet packages for Entity Framework Core, use a PowerShell command prompt to run the commands shown in listing 18.3 in the `WebApp` project folder.

Listing 18.3   Adding packages to the project

```
dotnet add package Microsoft.EntityFrameworkCore.Design --version 7.0.0
dotnet add package Microsoft.EntityFrameworkCore.SqlServer --version 7.0.0
```

If you are using Visual Studio, you can add the packages by selecting Project > Manage NuGet Packages. Take care to choose the correct version of the packages to add to the project.

If you have not followed the examples in earlier chapters, you will need to install the global tool package that is used to create and manage Entity Framework Core migrations. Run the commands shown in listing 18.4 to remove any existing version of the package and install the version required for this book. (You can skip these commands if you installed this version of the tools package in earlier chapters.)

Listing 18.4   Installing a global tool package

```
dotnet tool uninstall --global dotnet-ef
dotnet tool install --global dotnet-ef --version 7.0.0
```

18.2.2 Creating the data model

The data model for this part of the book will consist of three related classes: `Product`, `Supplier`, and `Category`. Create a new folder named `Models` and add to it a class file named `Category.cs`, with the contents shown in listing 18.5.

Listing 18.5   The contents of the Category.cs file in the Models folder

```
namespace WebApp.Models {
    public class Category {

        public long CategoryId { get; set; }
        public required string Name { get; set; }

        public IEnumerable<Product>? Products { get; set; }

    }
}
```

Add a class called `Supplier.cs` to the `Models` folder and use it to define the class shown in listing 18.6.

Listing 18.6   The contents of the Supplier.cs file in the Models folder

```
namespace WebApp.Models {
    public class Supplier {

        public long SupplierId { get; set; }
        public required string Name { get; set; }
        public required string City { get; set; }

        public IEnumerable<Product>? Products { get; set; }

    }
}
```

Next, add a class named `Product.cs` to the `Models` folder and use it to define the class shown in listing 18.7.

Listing 18.7   The contents of the Product.cs file in the Models folder

```
using System.ComponentModel.DataAnnotations.Schema;

namespace WebApp.Models {
    public class Product {

        public long ProductId { get; set; }

        public required string Name { get; set; }
        [Column(TypeName = "decimal(8, 2)")]
        public decimal Price { get; set; }

        public long CategoryId { get; set; }
        public Category? Category { get; set; }

        public long SupplierId { get; set; }
        public Supplier? Supplier { get; set; }

    }
}
```

Each of the three data model classes defines a key property whose value will be allocated by the database when new objects are stored. There are also navigation properties that will be used to query for related data so that it will be possible, for example, to query for all the products in a specific category.

The `Price` property has been decorated with the `Column` attribute, which specifies the precision of the values that will be stored in the database. There isn't a one-to-one mapping between C# and SQL numeric types, and the `Column` attribute tells Entity Framework Core which SQL type should be used in the database to store `Price` values. In this case, the `decimal(8, 2)` type will allow a total of eight digits, including two following the decimal point.

To create the Entity Framework Core context class that will provide access to the database, add a file called `DataContext.cs` to the `Models` folder and add the code shown in listing 18.8.

Listing 18.8   The contents of the DataContext.cs file in the Models folder

```
using Microsoft.EntityFrameworkCore;

namespace WebApp.Models {
    public class DataContext : DbContext {

        public DataContext(DbContextOptions<DataContext> opts)
            : base(opts) { }

        public DbSet<Product> Products => Set<Product>();
        public DbSet<Category> Categories => Set<Category>();
        public DbSet<Supplier> Suppliers => Set<Supplier>();
    }
}
```

The context class defines properties that will be used to query the database for `Product`, `Category`, and `Supplier` data.

18.2.3 *Preparing the seed data*

Add a class called `SeedData.cs` to the `Models` folder and add the code shown in listing 18.9 to define the seed data that will be used to populate the database.

Listing 18.9   The contents of the SeedData.cs file in the Models folder

```
using Microsoft.EntityFrameworkCore;

namespace WebApp.Models {
    public static class SeedData {

        public static void SeedDatabase(DataContext context) {
            context.Database.Migrate();
            if (context.Products.Count() == 0
                    && context.Suppliers.Count() == 0
                    && context.Categories.Count() == 0) {

                Supplier s1 = new Supplier
                    { Name = "Splash Dudes", City = "San Jose"};
                Supplier s2 = new Supplier
                    { Name = "Soccer Town", City = "Chicago"};
                Supplier s3 = new Supplier
                    { Name = "Chess Co", City = "New York"};
```

```
Category c1 = new Category { Name = "Watersports" };
Category c2 = new Category { Name = "Soccer" };
Category c3 = new Category { Name = "Chess" };

context.Products.AddRange(
    new Product {  Name = "Kayak", Price = 275,
        Category = c1, Supplier = s1},
    new Product {  Name = "Lifejacket", Price = 48.95m,
        Category = c1, Supplier = s1},
    new Product {  Name = "Soccer Ball", Price = 19.50m,
        Category = c2, Supplier = s2},
    new Product {  Name = "Corner Flags", Price = 34.95m,
        Category = c2, Supplier = s2},
    new Product {  Name = "Stadium", Price = 79500,
        Category = c2, Supplier = s2},
    new Product {  Name = "Thinking Cap", Price = 16,
        Category = c3, Supplier = s3},
    new Product {  Name = "Unsteady Chair", Price = 29.95m,
        Category = c3, Supplier = s3},
    new Product {  Name = "Human Chess Board", Price = 75,
        Category = c3, Supplier = s3},
    new Product {  Name = "Bling-Bling King", Price = 1200,
        Category = c3, Supplier = s3}
    );
    context.SaveChanges();
        }
    }
  }
}
```

The static `SeedDatabase` method ensures that all pending migrations have been applied to the database. If the database is empty, it is seeded with categories, suppliers, and products. Entity Framework Core will take care of mapping the objects into the tables in the database, and the key properties will be assigned automatically when the data is stored.

18.2.4 Configuring EF Core services and middleware

Make the changes to the `Program.cs` file shown in listing 18.10, which configure Entity Framework Core and set up the `DataContext` services that will be used throughout this part of the book to access the database.

> Listing 18.10   Services and middleware in the Program.cs file in the WebApp folder

```
using Microsoft.EntityFrameworkCore;
using WebApp.Models;

var builder = WebApplication.CreateBuilder(args);

builder.Services.AddDbContext<DataContext>(opts => {
    opts.UseSqlServer(builder.Configuration[
        "ConnectionStrings:ProductConnection"]);
    opts.EnableSensitiveDataLogging(true);
});
```

```
var app = builder.Build();

app.MapGet("/", () => "Hello World!");

var context = app.Services.CreateScope().ServiceProvider
    .GetRequiredService<DataContext>();
SeedData.SeedDatabase(context);

app.Run();
```

The `DataContext` service is scoped, which means that I have to create a scope to get the service required by the `SeedDatabase` method.

To define the connection string that will be used for the application's data, add the configuration settings shown in listing 18.11 in the `appsettings.json` file. The connection string should be entered on a single line.

> **Listing 18.11 A connection string in the appsettings.json file in the WebApp folder**

```
{
  "Logging": {
    "LogLevel": {
      "Default": "Information",
      "Microsoft.AspNetCore": "Warning",
      "Microsoft.EntityFrameworkCore": "Information"
    }
  },
  "AllowedHosts": "*",
  "ConnectionStrings": {
    "ProductConnection": "Server=(localdb)\\MSSQLLocalDB;Database=Products;
MultipleActiveResultSets=True"
  }
}
```

In addition to the connection string, listing 18.11 sets the logging detail for Entity Framework Core so that the SQL queries sent to the database are logged.

18.2.5 *Creating and applying the migration*

To create the migration that will set up the database schema, use a PowerShell command prompt to run the command shown in listing 18.12 in the `WebApp` project folder.

> **Listing 18.12 Creating an Entity Framework Core migration**

```
dotnet ef migrations add Initial
```

Once the migration has been created, apply it to the database using the command shown in listing 18.13.

> **Listing 18.13 Applying the migration to the database**

```
dotnet ef database update
```

The logging messages displayed by the application will show the SQL commands that are sent to the database.

> **NOTE**   If you need to reset the database, then run the `dotnet ef database drop --force` command and then the command in listing 18.13.

18.3   *Adding the CSS framework*

Later chapters will demonstrate the different ways that HTML responses can be generated. Run the commands shown in listing 18.14 to remove any existing version of the LibMan package and install the version used in this book. (You can skip these commands if you installed this version of LibMan in earlier chapters.)

> **Listing 18.14   Installing the LibMan tool package**

```
dotnet tool uninstall --global Microsoft.Web.LibraryManager.Cli
dotnet tool install --global Microsoft.Web.LibraryManager.Cli
    --version 2.1.175
```

To add the Bootstrap CSS framework so that the HTML responses can be styled, run the commands shown in listing 18.15 in the `WebApp` project folder.

> **Listing 18.15   Installing the Bootstrap CSS framework**

```
libman init -p cdnjs
libman install bootstrap@5.2.3 -d wwwroot/lib/bootstrap
```

18.4   *Configuring the request pipeline*

To define a simple middleware component that will be used to make sure the example project has been set up correctly, add a class file called `TestMiddleware.cs` to the `WebApp` folder and add the code shown in listing 18.16.

> **Listing 18.16   The contents of the TestMiddleware.cs file in the WebApp folder**

```
using WebApp.Models;

namespace WebApp {
    public class TestMiddleware {
        private RequestDelegate nextDelegate;

        public TestMiddleware(RequestDelegate next) {
            nextDelegate = next;
        }

        public async Task Invoke(HttpContext context,
                DataContext dataContext) {
            if (context.Request.Path == "/test") {
                await context.Response.WriteAsync($"There are "
                    + dataContext.Products.Count() + " products\n");
                await context.Response.WriteAsync("There are "
                    + dataContext.Categories.Count() + " categories\n");
                await context.Response.WriteAsync($"There are "
                    + dataContext.Suppliers.Count() + " suppliers\n");
            } else {
```

```
                    await nextDelegate(context);
            }
        }
    }
}
```

Add the middleware component to the request pipeline, as shown in listing 18.17.

Listing 18.17   A middleware component in the Program.cs file in the WebApp folder

```
using Microsoft.EntityFrameworkCore;
using WebApp.Models;

var builder = WebApplication.CreateBuilder(args);

builder.Services.AddDbContext<DataContext>(opts => {
    opts.UseSqlServer(builder.Configuration[
        "ConnectionStrings:ProductConnection"]);
    opts.EnableSensitiveDataLogging(true);
});

var app = builder.Build();

app.UseMiddleware<WebApp.TestMiddleware>();

app.MapGet("/", () => "Hello World!");

var context = app.Services.CreateScope().ServiceProvider
    .GetRequiredService<DataContext>();
SeedData.SeedDatabase(context);

app.Run();
```

18.5 Running the example application

Start the application by running the command shown in listing 18.18 in the WebApp project folder.

Listing 18.18   Running the example application

```
dotnet run
```

Use a new browser tab and request http://localhost:5000/test, and you will see the response shown in figure 18.2.

Figure 18.2 Running the example application

Creating RESTful
web services

Web services accept HTTP requests and generate responses that contain data. In this chapter, I explain how the features provided by the MVC Framework, which is an integral part of ASP.NET Core, can be used to build on the capabilities described in part 2 to create web services.

The nature of web services means that some of the examples in this chapter are tested using command-line tools provided by PowerShell, and it is important to enter the commands exactly as shown. Chapter 20 introduces more sophisticated tools for working with web services, but the command-line approach is better suited to following examples in a book chapter, even if they can feel a little awkward as you type them in. Table 19.1 puts RESTful web services in context.

Table 19.1 Putting RESTful web services in context

Question	Answer
What are they?	Web services provide access to an application's data, typically expressed in the JSON format.
Why are they useful?	Web services are most often used to provide rich client-side applications with data.
How are they used?	The combination of the URL and an HTTP method describes an operation that is handled by an endpoint, or an action method defined by a controller.
Are there any pitfalls or limitations?	There is no widespread agreement about how web services should be implemented, and care must be taken to produce just the data the client expects.
Are there any alternatives?	There are several different approaches to providing clients with data, although RESTful web services are the most common.

Table 19.2 provides a guide to the chapter.

Table 19.2 Chapter guide

Problem	Solution	Listing
Defining a web service	Define endpoints in the `Program.cs` file or create a controller with action methods that correspond to the operations that you require.	3–13
Generating data sequences over time	Use the `IAsyncEnumerable<T>` response, which will prevent the request thread from blocking while results are generated.	14
Preventing request values from being used for sensitive data properties	Use a binding target to restrict the model binding process to only safe properties.	15–17
Expressing nondata outcomes	Use action results to describe the response that ASP. NET Core should send.	18–23
Validating data	Use the ASP.NET Core model binding and model validation features.	24–26
Automatically validating requests	Use the `ApiController` attribute.	27
Omitting null values from data responses	Map the data objects to filter out properties or configure the JSON serializer to ignore `null` properties.	28–32
Apply a rate limit	Use the `EnableRateLimiting` and `DisableRateLimiting`.	33, 34

19.1 *Preparing for this chapter*

In this chapter, I continue to use the WebApp project created in chapter 18. To prepare for this chapter, drop the database by opening a new PowerShell command prompt, navigating to the folder that contains the `WebApp.csproj` file, and running the command shown in listing 19.1.

TIP   You can download the example project for this chapter—and for all the other chapters in this book—from https://github.com/manningbooks/pro-asp .net-core-7. See chapter 1 for how to get help if you have problems running the examples.

Listing 19.1   Dropping the database

```
dotnet ef database drop --force
```

Start the application by running the command shown in listing 19.2 in the project folder.

Listing 19.2   Starting the example application

```
dotnet run
```

Request the URL http://localhost:5000/test once ASP.NET Core has started, and you will see the response shown in figure 19.1.

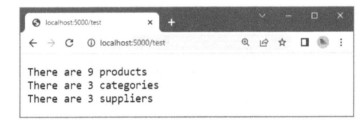

Figure 19.1 Running the example application

19.2 *Understanding RESTful web services*

Web services respond to HTTP requests with data that can be consumed by clients, such as JavaScript applications. There are no hard-and-fast rules for how web services should work, but the most common approach is to adopt the Representational State Transfer (REST) pattern. There is no authoritative specification for REST, and there is no consensus about what constitutes a RESTful web service, but there are some common themes that are widely used for web services. The lack of a detailed specification leads to endless disagreement about what REST means and how RESTful web services should be created, all of which can be safely ignored if the web services you create work for your projects.

19.2.1 *Understanding request URLs and methods*

The core premise of REST—and the only aspect for which there is broad agreement—is that a web service defines an API through a combination of URLs and HTTP methods such as GET and POST, which are also known as the HTTP *verbs*. The method specifies the type of operation, while the URL specifies the data object or objects that the operation applies to.

As an example, here is a URL that might identify a `Product` object in the example application:

`/api/products/1`

This URL may identify the `Product` object that has a value of `1` for its `ProductId` property. The URL identifies the `Product`, but it is the HTTP method that specifies what should be done with it. Table 19.3 lists the HTTP methods that are commonly used in web services and the operations they conventionally represent.

Table 19.3. **HTTP methods and operations**

HTTP Method	Description
GET	This method is used to retrieve one or more data objects.
POST	This method is used to create a new object.
PUT	This method is used to update an existing object.
PATCH	This method is used to update part of an existing object.
DELETE	This method is used to delete an object.

19.2.2 *Understanding JSON*

Most RESTful web services format the response data using the JavaScript Object Notation (JSON) format. JSON has become popular because it is simple and easily consumed by JavaScript clients. JSON is described in detail at www.json.org, but you don't need to understand every aspect of JSON to create web services because ASP.NET Core provides all the features required to create JSON responses.

Understanding the alternatives to RESTful web services

REST isn't the only way to design web services, and there are some popular alternatives. *GraphQL* is most closely associated with the React JavaScript framework, but it can be used more widely. Unlike REST web services, which provide specific queries through individual combinations of a URL and an HTTP method, GraphQL provides access to all an application's data and lets clients query for just the data they require in the format they require. GraphQL can be complex to set up—and can require more sophisticated clients—but the result is a more flexible web service that puts the developers of the client in control of the data they consume. GraphQL isn't supported directly by ASP.NET Core, but there are .NET implementations available. See https://graphql.org for more detail.

A new alternative is gRPC, a full remote procedure call framework that focuses on speed and efficiency. At the time of writing, gRPC cannot be used in web browsers, such as by the Angular or React framework, because browsers don't provide the fine-grained access that gRPC requires to formulate its HTTP requests.

19.3   Creating a web service using the minimal API

As you learn about the facilities that ASP.NET Core provides for web services, it can be easy to forget they are built on the features described in part 2. To create a simple web service, add the statements shown in listing 19.3 to the `Program.cs` file.

> **Listing 19.3   Creating a web service in the Program.cs file in the Platform folder**

```
using Microsoft.EntityFrameworkCore;
using WebApp.Models;
using System.Text.Json;

var builder = WebApplication.CreateBuilder(args);

builder.Services.AddDbContext<DataContext>(opts => {
    opts.UseSqlServer(builder.Configuration[
        "ConnectionStrings:ProductConnection"]);
    opts.EnableSensitiveDataLogging(true);
});

var app = builder.Build();

const string BASEURL = "api/products";

app.MapGet($"{BASEURL}/{{id}}", async (HttpContext context,
        DataContext data) => {
    string? id = context.Request.RouteValues["id"] as string;
    if (id != null) {
        Product? p = data.Products.Find(long.Parse(id));
        if (p == null) {
            context.Response.StatusCode = StatusCodes.Status404NotFound;
        } else {
            context.Response.ContentType = "application/json";
            await context.Response
                .WriteAsync(JsonSerializer.Serialize<Product>(p));
        }
    }
});

app.MapGet(BASEURL, async (HttpContext context, DataContext data) => {
    context.Response.ContentType = "application/json";
    await context.Response.WriteAsync(JsonSerializer
        .Serialize<IEnumerable<Product>>(data.Products));
});

app.MapPost(BASEURL, async (HttpContext context, DataContext data) => {
    Product? p = await
        JsonSerializer.DeserializeAsync<Product>(context.Request.Body);
    if (p != null) {
        await data.AddAsync(p);
        await data.SaveChangesAsync();
        context.Response.StatusCode = StatusCodes.Status200OK;
    }
});
```

```
app.MapGet("/", () => "Hello World!");

var context = app.Services.CreateScope().ServiceProvider
    .GetRequiredService<DataContext>();
SeedData.SeedDatabase(context);

app.Run();
```

The same API that I used to register endpoints in earlier chapters can be used to create a web service, using only features that you have seen before. The `MapGet` and `MapPost` methods are used to create three routes, all of which match URLs that start with `/api`, which is the conventional prefix for web services.

The endpoint for the first route receives a value from a segment variable that is used to locate a single `Product` object in the database. The endpoint for the second route retrieves all the `Product` objects in the database. The third endpoint handles POST requests and reads the request body to get a JSON representation of a new object to add to the database.

There are better ASP.NET Core features for creating web services, which you will see shortly, but the code in listing 19.3 shows how the HTTP method and the URL can be combined to describe an operation, which is the key concept in creating web services.

To test the web service, restart ASP.NET Core and request http://localhost:5000/api/products/1. The request will be matched by the first route defined in listing 19.3 and will produce the response shown on the left of figure 19.2. Next, request http://localhost:5000/api/products, which will be matched by the second route and produce the response shown on the right of figure 19.2.

> **NOTE** The responses shown in the figure contain `null` values for the `Supplier` and `Category` properties because the LINQ queries do not include related data. See chapter 20 for details.

Figure 19.2   Web service response

Testing the third route requires a different approach because it isn't possible to send HTTP POST requests using the browser. Open a new PowerShell command prompt and run the command shown in listing 19.4. It is important to enter the command exactly as shown because the `Invoke-RestMethod` command is fussy about the syntax of its arguments.

> **TIP** You may receive an error when you use the `Invoke-RestMethod` or `Invoke-WebRequest` command to test the examples in this chapter if you have not performed the initial setup for Microsoft Edge. The problem can be fixed by running the browser and selecting the initial configurations you require.

Listing 19.4   Sending a POST request

```
Invoke-RestMethod http://localhost:5000/api/products -Method POST -Body
(@{ Name="Swimming Goggles"; Price=12.75; CategoryId=1; SupplierId=1} |
ConvertTo-Json) -ContentType "application/json"
```

The command sends an HTTP POST command that is matched by the third route defined in listing 19.3. The body of the request is a JSON-formatted object that is parsed to create a `Product`, which is then stored in the database. The JSON object included in the request contains values for the `Name`, `Price`, `CategoryId`, and `SupplierId` properties. The unique key for the object, which is associated with the `ProductId` property, is assigned by the database when the object is stored. Use the browser to request the http://localhost:5000/api/products URL again, and you will see that the JSON response contains the new object, as shown in figure 19.3.

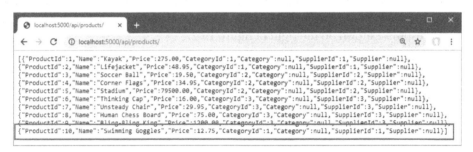

Figure 19.3   Storing new data using the web service

19.4   *Creating a web service using a controller*

The drawback of using individual endpoints to create a web service is that each endpoint has to duplicate a similar set of steps to produce a response: get the Entity Framework Core service so that it can query the database, set the `Content-Type` header for the response, serialize the objects into JSON, and so on. As a result, web services created with endpoints are difficult to understand and awkward to maintain, and the `Program.cs` file quickly becomes unwieldy.

A more elegant and robust approach is to use a *controller*, which allows a web service to be defined in a single class. Controllers are part of the MVC Framework, which builds on the ASP.NET Core platform and takes care of handling data in the same way that endpoints take care of processing URLs.

The rise and fall of the MVC pattern in ASP.NET Core

The MVC Framework is an implementation of the Model-View-Controller pattern, which describes one way to structure an application. The examples in this chapter use two of the three pillars of the pattern: a data model (the *M* in MVC) and controllers (the *C* in MVC). chapter 21 provides the missing piece and explains how views can be used to create HTML responses using Razor.

The MVC pattern was an important step in the evolution of ASP.NET and allowed the platform to break away from the Web Forms model that predated it. Web Forms applications were easy to start but quickly became difficult to manage and hid details of HTTP requests and responses from the developer. By contrast, the adherence to the MVC pattern provided a strong and scalable structure for applications written with the MVC Framework and hid nothing from the developer. The MVC Framework revitalized ASP.NET and provided the foundation for what became ASP.NET Core, which dropped support for Web Forms and focused solely on using the MVC pattern.

As ASP.NET Core evolved, other styles of web application have been embraced, and the MVC Framework is only one of the ways that applications can be created. That doesn't undermine the utility of the MVC pattern, but it doesn't have the central role that it used to in ASP.NET Core development, and the features that used to be unique to the MVC Framework can now be accessed through other approaches, such as Razor Pages and Blazor.

A consequence of this evolution is that understanding the MVC pattern is no longer a prerequisite for effective ASP.NET Core development. If you are interested in understanding the MVC pattern, then https://en.wikipedia.org/wiki/Model-view-controller is a good place to start. But for this book, understanding how the features provided by the MVC Framework build on the ASP.NET Core platform is all the context that is required.

19.4.1 Enabling the MVC Framework

The first step to creating a web service using a controller is to configure the MVC framework, which requires a service and an endpoint, as shown in listing 19.5. This listing also removes the endpoints defined in the previous section.

Listing 19.5 Enabling the MVC Framework in the Program.cs File in the WebApp folder

```
using Microsoft.EntityFrameworkCore;
using WebApp.Models;

var builder = WebApplication.CreateBuilder(args);

builder.Services.AddDbContext<DataContext>(opts => {
    opts.UseSqlServer(builder.Configuration[
        "ConnectionStrings:ProductConnection"]);
    opts.EnableSensitiveDataLogging(true);
});

builder.Services.AddControllers();

var app = builder.Build();
```

```
app.MapControllers();

app.MapGet("/", () => "Hello World!");

var context = app.Services.CreateScope().ServiceProvider
    .GetRequiredService<DataContext>();
SeedData.SeedDatabase(context);

app.Run();
```

The `AddControllers` method defines the services that are required by the MVC framework, and the `MapControllers` method defines routes that will allow controllers to handle requests. You will see other methods used to configure the MVC framework used in later chapters, which provide access to different features, but the methods used in listing 19.5 are the ones that configure the MVC framework for web services.

19.4.2 Creating a controller

Controllers are classes whose methods, known as *actions*, can process HTTP requests. Controllers are discovered automatically when the application is started. The basic discovery process is simple: any public class whose name ends with `Controller` is a controller, and any `public` method a controller defines is an action. To demonstrate how simple a controller can be, create the `WebApp/Controllers` folder and add to it a file named `ProductsController.cs` with the code shown in listing 19.6.

> **TIP** Controllers are conventionally defined in the `Controllers` folder, but they can be defined anywhere in the project and will still be discovered.

> **Listing 19.6   The contents of the ProductsController.cs file in the Controllers folder**

```
using Microsoft.AspNetCore.Mvc;
using WebApp.Models;

namespace WebApp.Controllers {

    [Route("api/[controller]")]
    public class ProductsController : ControllerBase {

        [HttpGet]
        public IEnumerable<Product> GetProducts() {
            return new Product[] {
                new Product() { Name = "Product #1" },
                new Product() { Name = "Product #2" },
            };
        }

        [HttpGet("{id}")]
        public Product GetProduct() {
            return new Product() {
                ProductId = 1, Name = "Test Product"
            };
        }
    }
}
```

The `ProductsController` class meets the criteria that the MVC framework looks for in a controller. It defines public methods named `GetProducts` and `GetProduct`, which will be treated as actions.

UNDERSTANDING THE BASE CLASS

Controllers are derived from the `ControllerBase` class, which provides access to features provided by the MVC Framework and the underlying ASP.NET Core platform. Table 19.4 describes the most useful properties provided by the `ControllerBase` class.

> **NOTE** Although controllers are typically derived from the `ControllerBase` or `Controller` classes (described in chapter 21), this is just convention, and the MVC Framework will accept any class whose name ends with `Controller`, that is derived from a class whose name ends with `Controller`, or that has been decorated with the `Controller` attribute. Apply the `NonController` attribute to classes that meet these criteria but that should not receive HTTP requests.

Table 19.4   Useful ControllerBase properties

Name	Description
`HttpContext`	This property returns the `HttpContext` object for the current request.
`ModelState`	This property returns details of the data validation process, as demonstrated in the "Validating Data" section later in the chapter and described in detail in chapter 29.
`Request`	This property returns the `HttpRequest` object for the current request.
`Response`	This property returns the `HttpResponse` object for the current response.
`RouteData`	This property returns the data extracted from the request URL by the routing middleware, as described in chapter 13.
`User`	This property returns an object that describes the user associated with the current request, as described in chapter 38.

A new instance of the controller class is created each time one of its actions is used to handle a request, which means the properties in table 19.4 describe only the current request.

UNDERSTANDING THE CONTROLLER ATTRIBUTES

The HTTP methods and URLs supported by the action methods are determined by the combination of attributes that are applied to the controller. The URL for the controller is specified by the `Route` attribute, which is applied to the class, like this:

```
...
[Route("api/[controller]")]
public class ProductsController: ControllerBase {
...
```

The [controller] part of the attribute argument is used to derive the URL from the name of the controller class. The Controller part of the class name is dropped, which means that the attribute in listing 19.6 sets the URL for the controller to /api/products.

Each action is decorated with an attribute that specifies the HTTP method that it supports, like this:

```
...
[HttpGet]
public Product[] GetProducts() {
...
```

The name given to action methods doesn't matter in controllers used for web services. There are other uses for controllers, described in chapter 21, where the name does matter, but for web services, it is the HTTP method attributes and the route patterns that are important.

The HttpGet attribute tells the MVC framework that the GetProducts action method will handle HTTP GET requests. Table 19.5 describes the full set of attributes that can be applied to actions to specify HTTP methods.

Table 19.5   The HTTP method attributes

Name	Description
HttpGet	This attribute specifies that the action can be invoked only by HTTP requests that use the GET verb.
HttpPost	This attribute specifies that the action can be invoked only by HTTP requests that use the POST verb.
HttpDelete	This attribute specifies that the action can be invoked only by HTTP requests that use the DELETE verb.
HttpPut	This attribute specifies that the action can be invoked only by HTTP requests that use the PUT verb.
HttpPatch	This attribute specifies that the action can be invoked only by HTTP requests that use the PATCH verb.
HttpHead	This attribute specifies that the action can be invoked only by HTTP requests that use the HEAD verb.
AcceptVerbs	This attribute is used to specify multiple HTTP verbs.

The attributes applied to actions to specify HTTP methods can also be used to build on the controller's base URL.

```
...
[HttpGet("{id}")]
public Product GetProduct() {
...
```

This attribute tells the MVC framework that the GetProduct action method handles GET requests for the URL pattern api/products/{id}. During the discovery process, the attributes applied to the controller are used to build the set of URL patterns that the controller can handle, summarized in table 19.6.

TIP When writing a controller, it is important to ensure that each combination of the HTTP method and URL pattern that the controller supports is mapped to only one action method. An exception will be thrown when a request can be handled by multiple actions because the MVC Framework is unable to decide which to use.

Table 19.6   The URL patterns

HTTP Method	URL Pattern	Action Method Name
GET	`api/products`	`GetProducts`
GET	`api/products/{id}`	`GetProduct`

You can see how the combination of attributes is equivalent to the `MapGet` methods I used for the same URL patterns when I used endpoints to create a web service earlier in the chapter.

GET and POST: Pick the right one

The rule of thumb is that GET requests should be used for all read-only information retrieval, while POST requests should be used for any operation that changes the application state. In standards-compliance terms, GET requests are for *safe* interactions (having no side effects besides information retrieval), and POST requests are for *unsafe* interactions (making a decision or changing something). These conventions are set by the World Wide Web Consortium (W3C), at https://www.rfc-editor.org/rfc/rfc9110.html.

GET requests are *addressable*: all the information is contained in the URL, so it's possible to bookmark and link to these addresses. Do not use GET requests for operations that change state. Many web developers learned this the hard way in 2005 when Google Web Accelerator was released to the public. This application prefetched all the content linked from each page, which is legal within the HTTP because GET requests should be safe. Unfortunately, many web developers had ignored the HTTP conventions and placed simple links to "delete item" or "add to shopping cart" in their applications. Chaos ensued.

UNDERSTANDING ACTION METHOD RESULTS

One of the main benefits provided by controllers is that the MVC Framework takes care of setting the response headers and serializing the data objects that are sent to the client. You can see this in the results defined by the action methods, like this:

```
...
[HttpGet("{id}")]
public Product GetProduct() {
...
```

When I used an endpoint, I had to work directly with the JSON serializer to create a string that can be written to the response and set the `Content-Type` header to tell the client that the response contained JSON data. The action method returns a `Product` object, which is processed automatically.

To see how the results from the action methods are handled, restart ASP.NET Core and request http://localhost:5000/api/products, which will produce the response shown on the left of figure 19.4, which is produced by the GetProducts action method. Next, request http://localhost:5000/api/products/1, which will be handled by the GetProduct method and produce the result shown on the right side of figure 19.4.

Figure 19.4   Using a controller

USING DEPENDENCY INJECTION IN CONTROLLERS

A new instance of the controller class is created each time one of its actions is used to handle a request. The application's services are used to resolve any dependencies the controller declares through its constructor and any dependencies that the action method defines. This allows services that are required by all actions to be handled through the constructor while still allowing individual actions to declare their own dependencies, as shown in listing 19.7.

Listing 19.7   Using services in the ProductsController.cs file in the Controllers folder

```
using Microsoft.AspNetCore.Mvc;
using WebApp.Models;

namespace WebApp.Controllers {

    [Route("api/[controller]")]
    public class ProductsController : ControllerBase {
        private DataContext context;

        public ProductsController(DataContext ctx) {
            context = ctx;
        }

        [HttpGet]
        public IEnumerable<Product> GetProducts() {
            return context.Products;
        }

        [HttpGet("{id}")]
        public Product? GetProduct([FromServices]
                ILogger<ProductsController> logger) {
            logger.LogInformation("GetProduct Action Invoked");
            return context.Products
                .OrderBy(p => p.ProductId).FirstOrDefault();
        }
    }
}
```

The constructor declares a dependency on the `DataContext` service, which provides access to the application's data. The services are resolved using the request scope, which means that a controller can request all services, without needing to understand their lifecycle.

The Entity Framework Core context service lifecycle

A new Entity Framework Core context object is created for each controller. Some developers will try to reuse context objects as a perceived performance improvement, but this causes problems because data from one query can affect subsequent queries. Behind the scenes, Entity Framework Core efficiently manages the connections to the database, and you should not try to store or reuse context objects outside of the controller for which they are created.

The `GetProducts` action method uses the `DataContext` to request all the `Product` objects in the database. The `GetProduct` method also uses the `DataContext` service, but it declares a dependency on `ILogger<T>`, which is the logging service described in chapter 15. Dependencies that are declared by action methods must be decorated with the `FromServices` attribute, like this:

```
...
public Product GetProduct([FromServices]
    ILogger<ProductsController> logger)
...
```

By default, the MVC Framework attempts to find values for action method parameters from the request URL, and the `FromServices` attribute overrides this behavior. The `FromServices` attribute can often be omitted, and ASP.NET Core will try to resolve parameters using dependency injection, but this doesn't work for all parameter types, and I prefer to use the attribute to clearly denote that the value for the parameter will be provided by dependency injection.

To see the use of the services in the controller, restart ASP.NET Core and request http://localhost:5000/api/products/1, which will produce the response shown in figure 19.5. You will also see the following logging message in the application's output:

```
...
info: WebApp.Controllers.ProductsController[0]
      GetProduct Action Invoked
...
```

Figure 19.5 Using services in a controller

CAUTION   One consequence of the controller lifecycle is that you can't rely on side effects caused by methods being called in a specific sequence. So, for example, I can't assign the `ILogger<T>` object received by the `GetProduct` method in listing 19.7 to a property that can be read by the `GetProducts` action in later requests. Each controller object is used to handle one request, and only one action method will be invoked by the MVC Framework for each object.

USING MODEL BINDING TO ACCESS ROUTE DATA

In the previous section, I noted that the MVC Framework uses the request URL to find values for action method parameters, a process known as *model binding*. Model binding is described in detail in chapter 28, but listing 19.8 shows a simple example.

Listing 19.8   Model binding in the ProductsController.cs file in the Controllers folder

```csharp
using Microsoft.AspNetCore.Mvc;
using WebApp.Models;

namespace WebApp.Controllers {

    [Route("api/[controller]")]
    public class ProductsController : ControllerBase {
        private DataContext context;

        public ProductsController(DataContext ctx) {
            context = ctx;
        }

        [HttpGet]
        public IEnumerable<Product> GetProducts() {
            return context.Products;
        }

        [HttpGet("{id}")]
        public Product? GetProduct(long id,
                [FromServices] ILogger<ProductsController> logger) {
            logger.LogDebug("GetProduct Action Invoked");
            return context.Products.Find(id);
        }
    }
}
```

The listing adds a `long` parameter named `id` to the `GetProduct` method. When the action method is invoked, the MVC Framework injects the value with the same name from the routing data, automatically converting it to a `long` value, which is used by the action to query the database using the LINQ `Find` method. The result is that the action method responds to the URL, which you can see by restarting ASP.NET Core and requesting http://localhost:5000/api/products/5, which will produce the response shown in figure 19.6.

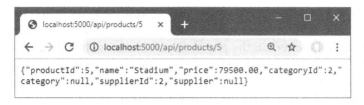

**Figure 19.6
Using model
binding in an
action**

MODEL BINDING FROM THE REQUEST BODY

The model binding feature can also be used on the data in the request body, which
allows clients to send data that is easily received by an action method. Listing 19.9 adds
a new action method that responds to POST requests and allows clients to provide a
JSON representation of the `Product` object in the request body.

Listing 19.9   Adding an action in the ProductsController.cs file in the Controllers folder

```
using Microsoft.AspNetCore.Mvc;
using WebApp.Models;

namespace WebApp.Controllers {

    [Route("api/[controller]")]
    public class ProductsController : ControllerBase {
        private DataContext context;

        public ProductsController(DataContext ctx) {
            context = ctx;
        }

        [HttpGet]
        public IEnumerable<Product> GetProducts() {
            return context.Products;
        }

        [HttpGet("{id}")]
        public Product? GetProduct(long id,
                [FromServices] ILogger<ProductsController> logger) {
            logger.LogDebug("GetProduct Action Invoked");
            return context.Products.Find(id);
        }

        [HttpPost]
        public void SaveProduct([FromBody] Product product) {
            context.Products.Add(product);
            context.SaveChanges();
        }
    }
}
```

The new action relies on two attributes. The `HttpPost` attribute is applied to the action
method and tells the MVC Framework that the action can process POST requests. The
`FromBody` attribute is applied to the action's parameter, and it specifies that the value

for this parameter should be obtained by parsing the request body. When the action method is invoked, the MVC Framework will create a new `Product` object and populate its properties with the values in the request body. The model binding process can be complex and is usually combined with data validation, as described in chapter 29, but for a simple demonstration, restart ASP.NET Core, open a new PowerShell command prompt, and run the command shown in listing 19.10.

```
Invoke-RestMethod http://localhost:5000/api/products -Method POST -Body  (@
{ Name="Soccer Boots"; Price=89.99; CategoryId=2; SupplierId=2} |
ConvertTo-Json) -ContentType "application/json"
```

Once the command has executed, use a web browser to request http://localhost:5000/api/products, and you will see the new object that has been stored in the database, as shown in figure 19.7.

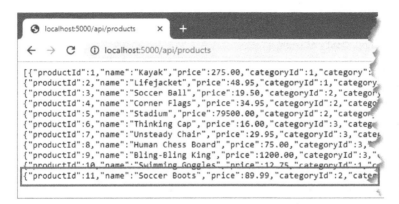

Figure 19.7 Storing new data using a controller

ADDING ADDITIONAL ACTIONS

Now that the basic features are in place, I can add actions that allow clients to replace and delete `Product` objects using the HTTP PUT and DELETE methods, as shown in listing 19.11.

```csharp
using Microsoft.AspNetCore.Mvc;
using WebApp.Models;

namespace WebApp.Controllers {

    [Route("api/[controller]")]
    public class ProductsController : ControllerBase {
        private DataContext context;

        public ProductsController(DataContext ctx) {
            context = ctx;
        }
```

```
[HttpGet]
public IEnumerable<Product> GetProducts() {
    return context.Products;
}

[HttpGet("{id}")]
public Product? GetProduct(long id,
        [FromServices] ILogger<ProductsController> logger) {
    logger.LogDebug("GetProduct Action Invoked");
    return context.Products.Find(id);
}

[HttpPost]
public void SaveProduct([FromBody] Product product) {
    context.Products.Add(product);
    context.SaveChanges();
}

[HttpPut]
public void UpdateProduct([FromBody] Product product) {
    context.Products.Update(product);
    context.SaveChanges();
}

[HttpDelete("{id}")]
public void DeleteProduct(long id) {
    context.Products.Remove(new Product() {
        ProductId = id, Name = string.Empty
    });
    context.SaveChanges();
}
    }
}
```

The UpdateProduct action is similar to the SaveProduct action and uses model binding to receive a Product object from the request body. The DeleteProduct action receives a primary key value from the URL and uses it to create a Product that has a value for the ProductId property, which is required because Entity Framework Core works only with objects, but web service clients typically expect to be able to delete objects using just a key value. (The empty string is assigned to the Name property, to which the required keyword has been applied and without which a Product object cannot be created. Entity Framework Core ignores the empty string when identifying the data to delete).

Restart ASP.NET Core and then use a different PowerShell command prompt to run the command shown in listing 19.12, which tests the UpdateProduct action.

Listing 19.12 Updating an object

```
Invoke-RestMethod http://localhost:5000/api/products -Method PUT -Body   (@{
ProductId=1; Name="Green Kayak"; Price=275; CategoryId=1; SupplierId=1} |
ConvertTo-Json) -ContentType "application/json"
```

The command sends an HTTP PUT request whose body contains a replacement object. The action method receives the object through the model binding feature

and updates the database. Next, run the command shown in listing 19.13 to test the
`DeleteProduct` action.

> **Listing 19.13   Deleting an object**

```
Invoke-RestMethod http://localhost:5000/api/products/2 -Method DELETE
```

This command sends an HTTP DELETE request, which will delete the object whose
`ProductId` property is 2. To see the effect of the changes, use the browser to request
http://localhost:5000/api/products, which will send a GET request that is handled by
the `GetProducts` action and produce the response shown in figure 19.8.

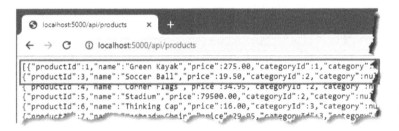

**Figure 19.8
Updating
and deleting
objects**

19.5   *Improving the web service*

The controller in listing 19.11 re-creates the functionality provided by the separate
endpoints, but there are still improvements that can be made, as described in the following sections.

Supporting cross-origin requests

If you are supporting third-party JavaScript clients, you may need to enable support for
cross-origin requests (CORS). Browsers protect users by only allowing JavaScript code to
make HTTP requests within the same origin, which means to URLs that have the same
scheme, host, and port as the URL used to load the JavaScript code. CORS loosens
this restriction by performing an initial HTTP request to check that the server will allow
requests originating from a specific URL, helping prevent malicious code using your service without the user's consent.

ASP.NET Core provides a built-in service that handles CORS, which is enabled by adding
the following statement to the `Program.cs` file:

```
...
builder.Services.AddCors();
...
```

The options pattern is used to configure CORS with the `CorsOptions` class defined in
the `Microsoft.AspNetCore.Cors.Infrastructure` namespace. See https://
docs.microsoft.com/en-gb/aspnet/core/security/cors for details.

19.5.1 *Using asynchronous actions*

The ASP.NET Core platform processes each request by assigning a thread from a pool. The number of requests that can be processed concurrently is limited to the size of the pool, and a thread can't be used to process any other request while it is waiting for an action to produce a result.

Actions that depend on external resources can cause a request thread to wait for an extended period. A database server, for example, may have its own concurrency limits and may queue up queries until they can be executed. The ASP.NET Core request thread is unavailable to process any other requests until the database produces a result for the action, which then produces a response that can be sent to the HTTP client.

This problem can be addressed by defining asynchronous actions, which allow ASP. NET Core threads to process other requests when they would otherwise be blocked, increasing the number of HTTP requests that the application can process simultaneously. Listing 19.14 revises the controller to use asynchronous actions.

NOTE Asynchronous actions don't produce responses any quicker, and the benefit is only to increase the number of requests that can be processed concurrently.

Listing 19.14 Async actions in the ProductsController.cs file in the Controllers folder

```
using Microsoft.AspNetCore.Mvc;
using WebApp.Models;

namespace WebApp.Controllers {

    [Route("api/[controller]")]
    public class ProductsController : ControllerBase {
        private DataContext context;

        public ProductsController(DataContext ctx) {
            context = ctx;
        }

        [HttpGet]
        public IAsyncEnumerable<Product> GetProducts() {
            return context.Products.AsAsyncEnumerable();
        }

        [HttpGet("{id}")]
        public async Task<Product?> GetProduct(long id) {
            return await context.Products.FindAsync(id);
        }

        [HttpPost]
        public async Task SaveProduct([FromBody] Product product) {
            await context.Products.AddAsync(product);
            await context.SaveChangesAsync();
        }

        [HttpPut]
        public async Task UpdateProduct([FromBody] Product product) {
```

```
            context.Update(product);
            await context.SaveChangesAsync();
        }

        [HttpDelete("{id}")]
        public async Task DeleteProduct(long id) {
            context.Products.Remove(new Product() {
                ProductId = id, Name = string.Empty
            });
            await context.SaveChangesAsync();
        }
    }
}
```

Entity Framework Core provides asynchronous versions of some methods, such as
`FindAsync`, `AddAsync,` and `SaveChangesAsync`, and I have used these with the `await`
keyword. Not all operations can be performed asynchronously, which is why the
`Update` and `Remove` methods are unchanged within the `UpdateProduct` and `Delete-`
`Product` actions.

For some operations—including LINQ queries to the database—the `IAsync-`
`Enumerable<T>` interface can be used, which denotes a sequence of objects that should
be enumerated asynchronously and prevents the ASP.NET Core request thread from
waiting for each object to be produced by the database, as explained in chapter 5.

There is no change to the responses produced by the controller, but the threads that
ASP.NET Core assigns to process each request are not necessarily blocked by the action
methods.

19.5.2 *Preventing over-binding*

Some of the action methods use the model binding feature to get data from the request
body so that it can be used to perform database operations. There is a problem with
the `SaveProduct` action, which can be seen by using a PowerShell prompt to run the
command shown in listing 19.15.

Listing 19.15   Saving a product

```
Invoke-RestMethod http://localhost:5000/api/products -Method POST -Body  (@
⇨{ ProductId=100; Name="Swim Buoy"; Price=19.99; CategoryId=1;
⇨SupplierId=1} | ConvertTo-Json) -ContentType "application/json"
```

This command fails with an error. Unlike the command that was used to test the POST
method, this command includes a value for the `ProductId` property. When Entity
Framework Core sends the data to the database, the following exception is thrown:

```
. . .
Microsoft.Data.SqlClient.SqlException (0x80131904): Cannot insert explicit
value for identity column in table 'Products' when IDENTITY_INSERT
is set to OFF.
. . .
```

By default, Entity Framework Core configures the database to assign primary key values
when new objects are stored. This means the application doesn't have to worry about
keeping track of which key values have already been assigned and allows multiple

applications to share the same database without the need to coordinate key alloca-
tion. The `Product` data model class needs a `ProductId` property, but the model binding process doesn't understand the significance of the property and adds any values
that the client provides to the objects it creates, which causes the exception in the
`SaveProduct` action method.

This is known as *over-binding*, and it can cause serious problems when a client provides values that the developer didn't expect. At best, the application will behave unexpectedly, but this technique has been used to subvert application security and grant
users more access than they should have.

The safest way to prevent over-binding is to create separate data model classes that
are used only for receiving data through the model binding process. Add a class file
named `ProductBindingTarget.cs` to the `WebApp/Models` folder and use it to define
the class shown in listing 19.16.

> **Listing 19.16   The ProductBindingTarget.cs file in the WebApp/Models folder**

```
namespace WebApp.Models {
    public class ProductBindingTarget {

        public required string Name { get; set; }

        public decimal Price { get; set; }

        public long CategoryId { get; set; }

        public long SupplierId { get; set; }

        public Product ToProduct() => new Product() {
            Name = this.Name, Price = this.Price,
            CategoryId = this.CategoryId, SupplierId = this.SupplierId
        };
    }
}
```

The `ProductBindingTarget` class defines only the properties that the application
wants to receive from the client when storing a new object. The `ToProduct` method
creates a `Product` that can be used with the rest of the application, ensuring that the
client can provide properties only for the `Name`, `Price`, `CategoryId`, and `SupplierId`
properties. Listing 19.17 uses the binding target class in the `SaveProduct` action to
prevent over-binding.

> **Listing 19.17   A binding target in the ProductsController.cs file in the Controllers folder**

```
...
[HttpPost]
public async Task SaveProduct([FromBody] ProductBindingTarget target) {
    await context.Products.AddAsync(target.ToProduct());
    await context.SaveChangesAsync();
}
...
```

Restart ASP.NET Core and repeat the command from listing 19.15, and you will see the response shown in figure 19.9. The client has included the `ProductId` value, but it is ignored by the model binding process, which discards values for read-only properties. (You may see a different value for the `ProductId` property when you run this example depending on the changes you made to the database before running the command.)

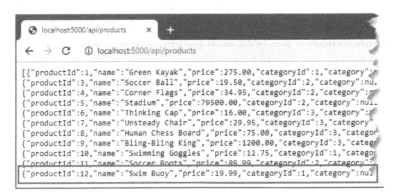

Figure 19.9 Discarding unwanted data values

19.5.3 Using action results

ASP.NET Core sets the status code for responses automatically, but you won't always get the result you desire, in part because there are no firm rules for RESTful web services, and the assumptions that Microsoft makes may not match your expectations. To see an example, use a PowerShell command prompt to run the command shown in listing 19.18, which sends a GET request to the web service.

Listing 19.18 Sending a GET request

```
Invoke-WebRequest http://localhost:5000/api/products/1000 | Select-Object
  StatusCode
```

The `Invoke-WebRequest` command is similar to the `Invoke-RestMethod` command used in earlier examples but makes it easier to get the status code from the response. The URL requested in listing 19.18 will be handled by the `GetProduct` action method, which will query the database for an object whose `ProductId` value is `1000`, and the command produces the following output:

```
StatusCode
----------
       204
```

There is no matching object in the database, which means that the `GetProduct` action method returns `null`. When the MVC Framework receives `null` from an action method, it returns the 204 status code, which indicates a successful request that has produced no data. Not all web services behave this way, and a common alternative is to return a 404 response, indicating not found.

Similarly, the `SaveProducts` action will return a 200 response when it stores an object, but since the primary key isn't generated until the data is stored, the client doesn't know what key value was assigned.

NOTE There is no right or wrong when it comes to these kinds of web service implementation details, and you should pick the approaches that best suit your project and personal preferences. This section is an example of how to change the default behavior and not a direction to follow any specific style of web service.

Action methods can direct the MVC Framework to send a specific response by returning an object that implements the `IActionResult` interface, which is known as an *action result*. This allows the action method to specify the type of response that is required without having to produce it directly using the `HttpResponse` object.

The `ControllerBase` class provides a set of methods that are used to create action result objects, which can be returned from action methods. Table 19.7 describes the most useful action result methods.

Table 19.7   Useful ControllerBase action result methods

Name	Description
`Ok`	The `IActionResult` returned by this method produces a 200 OK status code and sends an optional data object in the response body.
`NoContent`	The `IActionResult` returned by this method produces a 204 NO CONTENT status code.
`BadRequest`	The `IActionResult` returned by this method produces a 400 BAD REQUEST status code. The method accepts an optional model state object that describes the problem to the client, as demonstrated in the "Validating Data" section.
`File`	The `IActionResult` returned by this method produces a 200 OK response, sets the `Content-Type` header to the specified type, and sends the specified file to the client.
`NotFound`	The `IActionResult` returned by this method produces a 404 NOT FOUND status code.
`Redirect` `RedirectPermanent`	The `IActionResult` returned by these methods redirects the client to a spaecified URL.
`RedirectToRoute` `RedirectToRoutePermanent`	The `IActionResult` returned by these methods redirects the client to the specified URL that is created using the routing system, using convention routing, as described in the "Redirecting Using Route Values" sidebar.
`LocalRedirect` `LocalRedirectPermanent`	The `IActionResult` returned by these methods redirects the client to the specified URL that is local to the application.
`RedirectToAction` `RedirectToActionPermanent`	The `IActionResult` returned by these methods redirects the client to an action method. The URL for the redirection is created using the URL routing system.
`RedirectToPage` `RedirectToPagePermanent`	The `IActionResult` returned by these methods redirects the client to a Razor Page, described in chapter 23.
`StatusCode`	The `IActionResult` returned by this method produces a response with a specific status code.

When an action method returns an object, it is equivalent to passing the object to the Ok method and returning the result. When an action returns null, it is equivalent to returning the result from the NoContent method. Listing 19.19 revises the behavior of the GetProduct and SaveProduct actions so they use the methods from table 19.7 to override the default behavior for web service controllers.

Listing 19.19   Action results in the ProductsController.cs file in the Controllers folder

```
using Microsoft.AspNetCore.Mvc;
using WebApp.Models;

namespace WebApp.Controllers {

    [Route("api/[controller]")]
    public class ProductsController : ControllerBase {
        private DataContext context;

        public ProductsController(DataContext ctx) {
            context = ctx;
        }

        [HttpGet]
        public IAsyncEnumerable<Product> GetProducts() {
            return context.Products.AsAsyncEnumerable();
        }

        [HttpGet("{id}")]
        public async Task<IActionResult> GetProduct(long id) {
            Product? p = await context.Products.FindAsync(id);
            if (p == null) {
                return NotFound();
            }
            return Ok(p);
        }

        [HttpPost]
        public async Task<IActionResult>
                SaveProduct([FromBody] ProductBindingTarget target) {
            Product p = target.ToProduct();
            await context.Products.AddAsync(p);
            await context.SaveChangesAsync();
            return Ok(p);
        }

        [HttpPut]
        public async Task UpdateProduct([FromBody] Product product) {
            context.Update(product);
            await context.SaveChangesAsync();
        }

        [HttpDelete("{id}")]
        public async Task DeleteProduct(long id) {
            context.Products.Remove(new Product() {
                ProductId = id, Name = string.Empty
```

```
        });
        await context.SaveChangesAsync();
    }
  }
}
```

Restart ASP.NET Core and repeat the command from listing 19.18, and you will see an exception, which is how the `Invoke-WebRequest` command responds to error status codes, such as the 404 Not Found returned by the `GetProduct` action method.

To see the effect of the change to the `SaveProduct` action method, use a PowerShell command prompt to run the command shown in listing 19.20, which sends a POST request to the web service.

Listing 19.20 Sending a POST request

```
Invoke-RestMethod http://localhost:5000/api/products -Method POST -Body
➡(@{Name="Boot Laces"; Price=19.99; CategoryId=2; SupplierId=2} |
➡ConvertTo-Json) -ContentType "application/json"
```

The command will produce the following output, showing the values that were parsed from the JSON data received from the web service:

```
productId  : 13
name       : Boot Laces
price      : 19.99
categoryId : 2
category   :
supplierId : 2
supplier   :
```

PERFORMING REDIRECTIONS

Many of the action result methods in table 19.7 relate to redirections, which redirect the client to another URL. The most basic way to perform a redirection is to call the `Redirect` method, as shown in listing 19.21.

TIP The `LocalRedirect` and `LocalRedirectPermanent` methods throw an exception if a controller tries to perform a redirection to any URL that is not local. This is useful when you are redirecting to URLs provided by users, where an *open redirection attack* is attempted to redirect another user to an untrusted site.

Listing 19.21 Redirecting in the ProductsController.cs file in the Controllers folder

```
using Microsoft.AspNetCore.Mvc;
using WebApp.Models;

namespace WebApp.Controllers {

    [Route("api/[controller]")]
    public class ProductsController : ControllerBase {
        private DataContext context;

        public ProductsController(DataContext ctx) {
```

```
        context = ctx;
    }

    // ...other action methods omitted for brevity...

    [HttpGet("redirect")]
    public IActionResult Redirect() {
        return Redirect("/api/products/1");
    }
    }
}
```

The redirection URL is expressed as a `string` argument to the `Redirect` method, which produces a temporary redirection. Restart ASP.NET Core and use a PowerShell command prompt to run the command shown in listing 19.22, which sends a GET request that will be handled by the new action method.

Listing 19.22   Testing redirection

```
Invoke-RestMethod http://localhost:5000/api/products/redirect
```

The `Invoke-RestMethod` command will receive the redirection response from the web service and send a new request to the URL it is given, producing the following response:

```
productId   : 1
name        : Green Kayak
price       : 275.00
categoryId  : 1
category    :
supplierId  : 1
supplier    :
```

REDIRECTING TO AN ACTION METHOD

You can redirect to another action method using the `RedirectToAction` method (for temporary redirections) or the `RedirectToActionPermanent` method (for permanent redirections). Listing 19.23 changes the `Redirect` action method so that the client will be redirected to another action method defined by the controller.

Listing 19.23   Redirecting in the ProductsController.cs file in the Controllers folder

```
...
[HttpGet("redirect")]
public IActionResult Redirect() {
    return RedirectToAction(nameof(GetProduct), new { Id = 1 });
}
...
```

The action method is specified as a string, although the `nameof` expression can be used to select an action method without the risk of a typo. Any additional values required to create the route are supplied using an anonymous object. Restart ASP.NET Core and use a PowerShell command prompt to repeat the command in listing 19.22. The routing system will be used to create a URL that targets the specified action method, producing the following response:

```
productId   : 1
name        : Green Kayak
price       : 275.00
categoryId  : 1
category    :
supplierId  : 1
supplier    :
```

If you specify only an action method name, then the redirection will target the current controller. There is an overload of the `RedirectToAction` method that accepts action and controller names.

Redirecting using route values

The `RedirectToRoute` and `RedirectToRoutePermanent` methods redirect the client to a URL that is created by providing the routing system with values for segment variables and allowing it to select a route to use. This can be useful for applications with complex routing configurations, and caution should be used because it is easy to create a redirection to the wrong URL. Here is an example of redirection with the `Redirect-ToRoute` method:

```
...
[HttpGet("redirect")]
public IActionResult Redirect() {
    return RedirectToRoute(new {
        controller = "Products", action = "GetProduct", Id = 1
    });
}
...
```

The set of values in this redirection relies on convention routing to select the controller and action method. Convention routing is typically used with controllers that produce HTML responses, as described in chapter 21.

19.5.4 Validating data

When you accept data from clients, you must assume that a lot of the data will be invalid and be prepared to filter out values that the application can't use. The data validation features provided for MVC Framework controllers are described in detail in chapter 29, but for this chapter, I am going to focus on only one problem: ensuring that the client provides values for the properties that are required to store data in the database. The first step in model binding is to apply attributes to the properties of the data model class, as shown in listing 19.24.

> **Listing 19.24 Attributes in the ProductBindingTarget.cs file in the Models folder**

```
using System.ComponentModel.DataAnnotations;

namespace WebApp.Models {
    public class ProductBindingTarget {
```

```
    [Required]
    public required string Name { get; set; }

    [Range(1, 1000)]
    public decimal Price { get; set; }

    [Range(1, long.MaxValue)]
    public long CategoryId { get; set; }

    [Range(1, long.MaxValue)]
    public long SupplierId { get; set; }

    public Product ToProduct() => new Product() {
        Name = this.Name, Price = this.Price,
        CategoryId = this.CategoryId, SupplierId = this.SupplierId
    };
  }
}
```

The `Required` attribute denotes properties for which the client must provide a value and can be applied to properties that are assigned `null` when there is no value in the request. The `Range` attribute requires a value between upper and lower limits and is used for primitive types that will default to zero when there is no value in the request.

NOTE   The `Required` attribute could be omitted from the `Name` property because ASP.NET Core will infer the validation constraint from the `required` keyword. This is a useful feature, but I like to use the `Required` attribute for consistency and to make it obvious that the validation constraint was intentional.

Listing 19.25 updates the `SaveProduct` action to perform validation before storing the object that is created by the model binding process, ensuring that only objects that contain values for all four properties decorated with the validation attributes are accepted.

Listing 19.25   Validation in the ProductsController.cs file in the Controllers folder

```
...
[HttpPost]
public async Task<IActionResult>
      SaveProduct([FromBody] ProductBindingTarget target) {
    if (ModelState.IsValid) {
        Product p = target.ToProduct();
        await context.Products.AddAsync(p);
        await context.SaveChangesAsync();
        return Ok(p);
    }
    return BadRequest(ModelState);
}
...
```

The `ModelState` property is inherited from the `ControllerBase` class, and the `IsValid` property returns `true` if the model binding process has produced data that meets the validation criteria. If the data received from the client is valid, then the action result from the `Ok` method is returned. If the data sent by the client fails the validation check, then the `IsValid` property will be `false`, and the action result from the `BadRequest` method is used instead. The `BadRequest` method accepts the object returned by the `ModelState` property, which is used to describe the validation errors to the client. (There is no standard way to describe validation errors, so the client may rely only on the 400 status code to determine that there is a problem.)

To test the validation, restart ASP.NET Core and use a new PowerShell command prompt to run the command shown in listing 19.26.

Listing 19.26 Testing validation

```
Invoke-WebRequest http://localhost:5000/api/products -Method POST -Body
➥ (@{Name="Boot Laces"} | ConvertTo-Json) -ContentType "application/json"
```

The command will throw an exception that shows the web service has returned a 400 Bad Request response. Details of the validation errors are not shown because neither the `Invoke-WebRequest` command nor the `Invoke-RestMethod` command provides access to error response bodies. Although you can't see it, the body contains a JSON object that has properties for each data property that has failed validation, like this:

```
{
 "Price":["The field Price must be between 1 and 1000."],
 "CategoryId":["The field CategoryId must be between 1
    and 9.223372036854776E+18."],
 "SupplierId":["The field SupplierId must be between 1
    and 9.223372036854776E+18."]
}
```

You can see examples of working with validation messages in chapter 29 where the validation feature is described in detail.

19.5.5 *Applying the API controller attribute*

The `ApiController` attribute can be applied to web service controller classes to change the behavior of the model binding and validation features. The use of the `FromBody` attribute to select data from the request body and explicitly check the `ModelState.IsValid` property is not required in controllers that have been decorated with the `ApiController` attribute. Getting data from the body and validating data are required so commonly in web services that they are applied automatically when the attribute is used, restoring the focus of the code in the controller's action to dealing with the application features, as shown in listing 19.27.

Listing 19.27 The ProductsController.cs file in the Controllers folder

```
using Microsoft.AspNetCore.Mvc;
using WebApp.Models;

namespace WebApp.Controllers {

    [ApiController]
```

```
[Route("api/[controller]")]
public class ProductsController : ControllerBase {
    private DataContext context;

    public ProductsController(DataContext ctx) {
        context = ctx;
    }

    [HttpGet]
    public IAsyncEnumerable<Product> GetProducts() {
        return context.Products.AsAsyncEnumerable();
    }

    [HttpGet("{id}")]
    public async Task<IActionResult> GetProduct(long id) {
        Product? p = await context.Products.FindAsync(id);
        if (p == null) {
            return NotFound();
        }
        return Ok(p);
    }

    [HttpPost]
    public async Task<IActionResult>
            SaveProduct(ProductBindingTarget target) {
        Product p = target.ToProduct();
        await context.Products.AddAsync(p);
        await context.SaveChangesAsync();
        return Ok(p);
    }

    [HttpPut]
    public async Task UpdateProduct(Product product) {
        context.Update(product);
        await context.SaveChangesAsync();
    }

    [HttpDelete("{id}")]
    public async Task DeleteProduct(long id) {
        context.Products.Remove(new Product() {
            ProductId = id, Name = string.Empty
        });
        await context.SaveChangesAsync();
    }

    [HttpGet("redirect")]
    public IActionResult Redirect() {
        return RedirectToAction(nameof(GetProduct), new { Id = 1 });
    }
}
```

Using the `ApiController` attribute is optional, but it helps produce concise web service controllers.

19.5.6 *Omitting Null properties*

The final change I am going to make in this chapter is to remove the null values from the data returned by the web service. The data model classes contain navigation properties that are used by Entity Framework Core to associate related data in complex queries, as explained in chapter 20. For the simple queries that are performed in this chapter, no values are assigned to these navigation properties, which means that the client receives properties for which values are never going to be available. To see the problem, use a PowerShell command prompt to run the command shown in listing 19.28.

Listing 19.28 Sending a GET request

```
Invoke-WebRequest http://localhost:5000/api/products/1 |
Select-Object Content
```

The command sends a GET request and displays the body of the response from the web service, producing the following output:

```
Content
-------
{"productId":1,"name":"Green Kayak","price":275.00,
 "categoryId":1,"category":null,"supplierId":1,"supplier":null}
```

The request was handled by the GetProduct action method, and the category and supplier values in the response will always be null because the action doesn't ask Entity Framework Core to populate these properties.

PROJECTING SELECTED PROPERTIES

The first approach is to return just the properties that the client requires. This gives you complete control over each response, but it can become difficult to manage and confusing for client developers if each action returns a different set of values. Listing 19.29 shows how the Product object obtained from the database can be projected so that the navigation properties are omitted.

Listing 19.29 Omit properties in the ProductsController.cs file in the Controllers folder

```
...
[HttpGet("{id}")]
public async Task<IActionResult> GetProduct(long id) {
    Product? p = await context.Products.FindAsync(id);
    if (p == null) {
        return NotFound();
    }
    return Ok(new {
        p.ProductId, p.Name, p.Price, p.CategoryId, p.SupplierId
    });
}
...
```

The properties that the client requires are selected and added to an object that is passed to the Ok method. Restart ASP.NET Core and run the command from listing

19.28, and you will receive a response that omits the navigation properties and their null values, like this:

```
Content
-------
{"productId":1,"name":"Green Kayak","price":275.00,
 "categoryId":1,"supplierId":1}
```

CONFIGURING THE JSON SERIALIZER

The JSON serializer can be configured to omit properties when it serializes objects. One way to configure the serializer is with the JsonIgnore attribute, as shown in listing 19.30.

> **Listing 19.30   Configuring the serializer in the Product.cs file in the Models folder**

```
using System.ComponentModel.DataAnnotations.Schema;
using System.Text.Json.Serialization;

namespace WebApp.Models {
    public class Product {

        public long ProductId { get; set; }

        public required string Name { get; set; }
        [Column(TypeName = "decimal(8, 2)")]
        public decimal Price { get; set; }

        public long CategoryId { get; set; }
        public Category? Category { get; set; }

        public long SupplierId { get; set; }

        [JsonIgnore(Condition = JsonIgnoreCondition.WhenWritingNull)]
        public Supplier? Supplier { get; set; }
    }
}
```

The Condition property is assigned a JsonIgnoreCondition value, as described in table 19.8.

Table 19.8   The values defined by the JsonIgnoreCondition enum

Name	Description
Always	The property will always be ignored when serializing an object.
Never	The property will always be included when serializing an object.
WhenWritingDefault	The property will be ignored if the value is null or the default value for the property type.
WhenWritingNull	The property will be ignored if the value is null.

The JsonIgnore attribute has been applied using the WhenWritingNull value, which means that the Supplier property will be ignored if its value is null. Listing 19.31 updates the controller to use the Product class directly in the GetProduct action method.

```
...
[HttpGet("{id}")]
public async Task<IActionResult> GetProduct(long id) {
    Product? p = await context.Products.FindAsync(id);
    if (p == null) {
        return NotFound();
    }
    return Ok(p);
}
...
```

Restart ASP.NET Core and run the command from listing 19.28, and you will receive a response that omits the supplier property, like this:

```
Content
-------
{"productId":1,"name":"Green Kayak","price":275.00,"categoryId":1,
    "category":null,
 "supplierId":1}
```

The attribute has to be applied to model classes and is useful when a small number of properties should be ignored, but this can be difficult to manage for more complex data models. A general policy can be defined for serialization using the options pattern, as shown in listing 19.32.

```
using Microsoft.EntityFrameworkCore;
using WebApp.Models;
using Microsoft.AspNetCore.Mvc;
using System.Text.Json.Serialization;

var builder = WebApplication.CreateBuilder(args);

builder.Services.AddDbContext<DataContext>(opts => {
    opts.UseSqlServer(builder.Configuration[
        "ConnectionStrings:ProductConnection"]);
    opts.EnableSensitiveDataLogging(true);
});

builder.Services.AddControllers();

builder.Services.Configure<JsonOptions>(opts => {
    opts.JsonSerializerOptions.DefaultIgnoreCondition
        = JsonIgnoreCondition.WhenWritingNull;
});
```

```
var app = builder.Build();

app.MapControllers();

app.MapGet("/", () => "Hello World!");

var context = app.Services.CreateScope().ServiceProvider
    .GetRequiredService<DataContext>();
SeedData.SeedDatabase(context);

app.Run();
```

The JSON serializer is configured using the `JsonSerializerOptions` property of the `JsonOptions` class, and `null` values are managed using the `DefaultIgnoreCondition` property, which is assigned one of the `JsonIgnoreCondition` values described in table 19.8. (The `Always` value does not make sense when using the options pattern and will cause an exception when ASP.NET Core is started.)

This configuration change affects all JSON responses and should be used with caution, especially if your data model classes use `null` values to impart information to the client. To see the effect of the change, restart ASP.NET Core and use a browser to request http://localhost:5000/api/products, which will produce the response shown in figure 19.10.

TIP The `JsonIgnore` attribute can be used to override the default policy, which is useful if you need to include `null` or default values for a particular property.

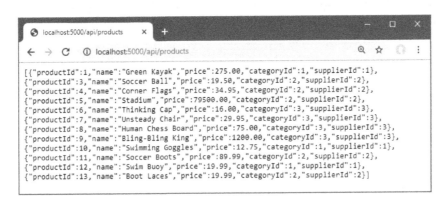

Figure 19.10   Configuring the JSON serializer

19.5.7 Applying a rate limit

In chapter 16, I demonstrated the rate limiting feature and showed you how it is applied to individual endpoints. This feature also works for controllers, using an attribute to select the rate limit that will be applied. In preparation, listing 19.33 defines a rate limiting policy and enables rate limits on controllers.

Listing 19.33   Rate limits in the Program.cs file in the WebApp folder

```
using Microsoft.EntityFrameworkCore;
using WebApp.Models;
using Microsoft.AspNetCore.Mvc;
using System.Text.Json.Serialization;
using Microsoft.AspNetCore.RateLimiting;

var builder = WebApplication.CreateBuilder(args);

builder.Services.AddDbContext<DataContext>(opts => {
    opts.UseSqlServer(builder.Configuration[
        "ConnectionStrings:ProductConnection"]);
    opts.EnableSensitiveDataLogging(true);
});

builder.Services.AddControllers();

builder.Services.AddRateLimiter(opts => {
    opts.AddFixedWindowLimiter("fixedWindow", fixOpts => {
        fixOpts.PermitLimit = 1;
        fixOpts.QueueLimit = 0;
        fixOpts.Window = TimeSpan.FromSeconds(15);
    });
});

builder.Services.Configure<JsonOptions>(opts => {
    opts.JsonSerializerOptions.DefaultIgnoreCondition
        = JsonIgnoreCondition.WhenWritingNull;
});

var app = builder.Build();

app.UseRateLimiter();
app.MapControllers();

app.MapGet("/", () => "Hello World!");

var context = app.Services.CreateScope().ServiceProvider
    .GetRequiredService<DataContext>();
SeedData.SeedDatabase(context);

app.Run();
```

This listing sets up the same policy I used in chapter 16, which limits requests to one every 15 seconds with no queue. Listing 19.34 applies the policy to the controller using the EnableRateLimiting and DisableRateLimiting attributes.

> **NOTE**   You can apply a single rate limiting policy to all controllers by calling app.MapControllers().RequireRateLimiting("fixedWindow"). This policy can be overridden for specific controllers and actions using the Enable-RateLimiting and DisableRateLimiting attributes.

```
using Microsoft.AspNetCore.Mvc;
using WebApp.Models;
using Microsoft.AspNetCore.RateLimiting;

namespace WebApp.Controllers {

    [ApiController]
    [Route("api/[controller]")]
    [EnableRateLimiting("fixedWindow")]
    public class ProductsController : ControllerBase {
        private DataContext context;

        public ProductsController(DataContext ctx) {
            context = ctx;
        }

        [HttpGet]
        public IAsyncEnumerable<Product> GetProducts() {
            return context.Products.AsAsyncEnumerable();
        }

        [HttpGet("{id}")]
        [DisableRateLimiting]
        public async Task<IActionResult> GetProduct(long id) {
            Product? p = await context.Products.FindAsync(id);
            if (p == null) {
                return NotFound();
            }
            return Ok(p);
        }

        // ...other action methods omitted for brevity...
    }
}
```

The EnableRateLimiting attribute is used to apply a rate limiting policy to the controller, specifying the name of the policy as an argument. This policy will apply to all of the action methods defined by the controller, except the GetProduct method, to which the DisableRateLimiting attribute has been applied and to which no limits will be enforced.

Restart ASP.NET Core and use a browser to request http://localhost:5000/api/products. Click the browser's reload button and you will exceed the request limit and see a 503 error, as shown in figure 19.11. You can request the URL http://localhost:5000/api/products/1 as often as you wish without producing an error.

Figure 19.11 An error caused by a rate limit

Summary

- RESTful web services use the HTTP method and URL to specify an operation to perform. Web services can be created using top-level statements but using controller scales is better for most projects.

- The base class for controllers defines properties that access the request data.

- Action methods are decorated with attributes to specify the HTTP methods they accept.

- ASP.NET Core will perform model binding to extract data from the request and pass it to an action method as an object.

- Care must be taken to receive only the data that is required from the user.

- Data validation can be performed on the data that is produced by model binding, ensuring that clients provide data in a way the ASP.NET Core application can work with.

- The rate limiting features described in chapter 16 can also be applied to web services.

Advanced web
service features

This chapter covers

- Managing related data in web service results
- Supporting the PATCH method to make selective changes
- Formatting content produced by web services
- Caching the output from web services
- Generating documentation that describes a web service

In this chapter, I describe advanced features that can be used to create RESTful web services. I explain how to deal with related data in Entity Framework Core queries, how to add support for the HTTP PATCH method, how to use content negotiations, and how to use OpenAPI to describe your web services. Table 20.1 puts this chapter in context.

Table 20.1   Putting advanced web service features in context

Question	Answer
What are they?	The features described in this chapter provide greater control over how ASP.NET Core web services work, including managing the data sent to the client and the format used for that data.
Why are they useful?	The default behaviors provided by ASP.NET Core don't meet the needs of every project, and the features described in this chapter allow web services to be reshaped to fit specific requirements.
How are they used?	The common theme for the features in this chapter is altering the responses produced by action methods.
Are there any pitfalls or limitations?	It can be hard to decide how to implement web services, especially if they are consumed by third-party clients. The behavior of a web service becomes fixed as soon as clients start using a web service, which means that careful thought is required when using the features described in this chapter.
Are there any alternatives?	The features described in this chapter are optional, and you can rely on the default behaviors of ASP.NET Core web services.

Table 20.2 provides a guide to the chapter.

Table 20.2   Chapter guide

Problem	Solution	Listing
Using relational data	Use the `Include` and `ThenInclude` methods in LINQ queries.	4
Breaking circular references	Explicitly set navigation properties to `null`.	5
Allowing clients to selectively update data	Support the HTTP PATCH method.	6–9
Supporting a range of response data types	Support content formatting and negotiation.	10–24
Cache output	Use the output caching middleware and the `OutputCache` attribute.	25, 26
Documenting a web service	Use OpenAPI to describe the web service.	27–29

20.1   Preparing for this chapter

This chapter uses the WebApp project created in chapter 18 and modified in chapter 19. To prepare for this chapter, add a file named `SuppliersController.cs` to the `WebApp/Controllers` folder with the content shown in listing 20.1.

TIP   You can download the example project for this chapter—and for all the other chapters in this book—from https://github.com/manningbooks/pro-asp .net-core-7. See chapter 1 for how to get help if you have problems running the examples.

> **Listing 20.1   The contents of the SuppliersController.cs file in the Controllers folder**

```
using Microsoft.AspNetCore.Mvc;
using WebApp.Models;

namespace WebApp.Controllers {

    [ApiController]
    [Route("api/[controller]")]
    public class SuppliersController : ControllerBase {
        private DataContext context;

        public SuppliersController(DataContext ctx) {
            context = ctx;
        }

        [HttpGet("{id}")]
        public async Task<Supplier?> GetSupplier(long id) {
            return await context.Suppliers.FindAsync(id);
        }
    }
}
```

The controller extends the `ControllerBase` class, declares a dependency on the `DataContext` service, and defines an action named `GetSupplier` that handles GET requests for the `/api/[controller]/{id}` URL pattern.

20.1.1 Dropping the database

Open a new PowerShell command prompt, navigate to the folder that contains the `WebApp.csproj` file, and run the command shown in listing 20.2 to drop the database.

> **Listing 20.2   Dropping the database**

```
dotnet ef database drop --force
```

20.1.2 Running the example application

Once the database has been dropped, use the PowerShell command prompt to run the command shown in listing 20.3.

> **Listing 20.3   Running the example application**

```
dotnet run
```

The database will be seeded as part of the application startup. Once ASP.NET Core is running, use a web browser to request http://localhost:5000/api/suppliers/1, which will produce the response shown in figure 20.1.

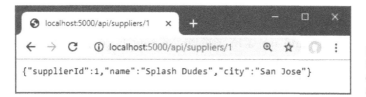

**Figure 20.1
Running the
example
application**

The response shows the `Supplier` object whose primary key matches the last segment of the request URL. In chapter 19, the JSON serializer was configured to ignore properties with `null` values, which is why the response doesn't include the navigation property defined by the `Supplier` data model class.

20.2 *Dealing with related data*

Although this isn't a book about Entity Framework Core, there is one aspect of querying for data that most web services encounter. The data model classes defined in chapter 18 include navigation properties, which Entity Framework Core can populate by following relationships in the database when the `Include` method is used, as shown in listing 20.4.

> **Listing 20.4 Related data in the SuppliersController.cs file in the Controllers folder**

```
using Microsoft.AspNetCore.Mvc;
using WebApp.Models;
using Microsoft.EntityFrameworkCore;

namespace WebApp.Controllers {

    [ApiController]
    [Route("api/[controller]")]
    public class SuppliersController : ControllerBase {
        private DataContext context;

        public SuppliersController(DataContext ctx) {
            context = ctx;
        }

        [HttpGet("{id}")]
        public async Task<Supplier?> GetSupplier(long id) {
            return await context.Suppliers
                .Include(s => s.Products)
                .FirstAsync(s => s.SupplierId == id);
        }
    }
}
```

The `Include` method tells Entity Framework Core to follow a relationship in the database and load the related data. In this case, the `Include` method selects the `Products` navigation property defined by the `Supplier` class, which causes Entity Framework

Core to load the `Product` objects associated with the selected `Supplier` and assign them to the `Products` property.

Restart ASP.NET Core and use a browser to request http://localhost:5000/api/suppliers/1, which will target the `GetSupplier` action method. The request fails, and you will see the exception shown in figure 20.2.

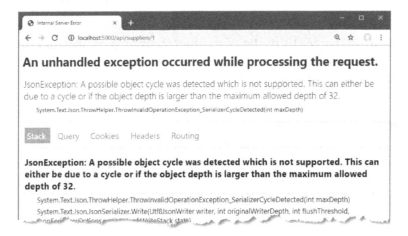

Figure 20.2   An exception caused by querying for related data

The JSON serializer has reported an "object cycle," which means there is a circular reference in the data that is being serialized for the response.

Looking at the code in listing 20.4, you might struggle to see why using the `Include` method has created a circular reference. The problem is caused by an Entity Framework Core feature that attempts to minimize the amount of data read from the database but that causes problems in ASP.NET Core applications.

When Entity Framework Core creates objects, it populates navigation properties with objects that have already been created by the same database context. This can be a useful feature in some kinds of applications, such as desktop apps, where a database context object has a long life and is used to make many requests over time. It isn't useful for ASP.NET Core applications, where a new context object is created for each HTTP request.

Entity Framework Core queries the database for the `Product` objects associated with the selected `Supplier` and assigns them to the `Supplier.Products` navigation property. The problem is that Entity Framework Core then looks at each `Product` object it has created and uses the query response to populate the `Product.Supplier` navigation property as well. For an ASP.NET Core application, this is an unhelpful step to take because it creates a circular reference between the navigation properties of the `Supplier` and `Product` objects, as shown in figure 20.3.

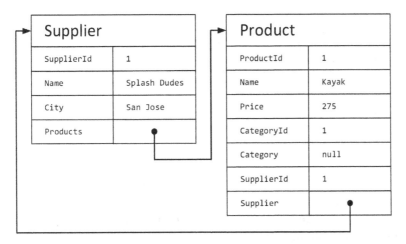

Figure 20.3 Understanding how Entity Framework Core uses related data

When the `Supplier` object is returned by the controller's action method, the JSON serializer works its way through the properties and follows the references to the `Product` objects, each of which has a reference back to the `Supplier` object, which it follows in a loop until the maximum depth is reached and the exception shown in figure 20.2 is thrown.

20.2.1 *Breaking circular references in related data*

There is no way to stop Entity Framework Core from creating circular references in the data it loads in the database. Preventing the exception means presenting the JSON serializer with data that doesn't contain circular references, which is most easily done by altering the objects after they have been created by Entity Framework Core and before they are serialized, as shown in listing 20.5.

Listing 20.5 References in the SuppliersController.cs file in the Controllers folder

```
using Microsoft.AspNetCore.Mvc;
using WebApp.Models;
using Microsoft.EntityFrameworkCore;

namespace WebApp.Controllers {

    [ApiController]
    [Route("api/[controller]")]
    public class SuppliersController : ControllerBase {
        private DataContext context;

        public SuppliersController(DataContext ctx) {
            context = ctx;
        }

        [HttpGet("{id}")]
        public async Task<Supplier?> GetSupplier(long id) {
```

```
Supplier supplier = await context.Suppliers
    .Include(s => s.Products)
    .FirstAsync(s => s.SupplierId == id);
if (supplier.Products != null) {
    foreach (Product p in supplier.Products) {
        p.Supplier = null;
    };
}
return supplier;
    }
  }
}
```

The `foreach` loop sets the `Supplier` property of each `Product` object to `null`, which breaks the circular references. Restart ASP.NET Core and request http://localhost:5000/api/suppliers/1 to query for a supplier and its related products, which produces the response shown in figure 20.4.

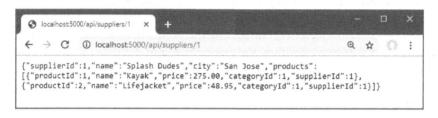

Figure 20.4 Querying for related data

20.3   *Supporting the HTTP PATCH method*

For simple data types, edit operations can be handled by replacing the existing object using the PUT method, which is the approach I took in chapter 19. Even if you only need to change a single property value in the `Product` class, for example, it isn't too much trouble to use a PUT method and include the values for all the other `Product` properties, too.

Not all data types are as easy to work with, either because they define too many properties or because the client has received values only for selected properties. The solution is to use a PATCH request, which sends just the changes to the web service rather than a complete replacement object.

20.3.1 *Understanding JSON Patch*

ASP.NET Core has support for working with the JSON Patch standard, which allows changes to be specified in a uniform way. The JSON Patch standard allows for a complex set of changes to be described, but for this chapter, I am going to focus on just the ability to change the value of a property.

I am not going to go into the details of the JSON Patch standard, which you can read at https://tools.ietf.org/html/rfc6902, but the client is going to send the web service JSON data like this in its HTTP PATCH requests:

```
[
  { "op": "replace", "path": "Name", "value": "Surf Co"},
  { "op": "replace", "path": "City", "value": "Los Angeles"},
]
```

A JSON Patch document is expressed as an array of operations. Each operation has an `op` property, which specifies the type of operation, and a `path` property, which specifies where the operation will be applied.

For the example application—and, in fact, for most applications—only the `replace` operation is required, which is used to change the value of a property. This JSON Patch document sets new values for the `Name` and `City` properties. The properties defined by the `Supplier` class not mentioned in the JSON Patch document will not be modified.

20.3.2 *Installing and configuring the JSON Patch package*

Support for JSON Patch isn't installed when a project is created with the Empty template. To install the JSON Patch package, open a new PowerShell command prompt, navigate to the folder that contains the `WebApp.csproj` file, and run the command shown in listing 20.6. If you are using Visual Studio, you can install the package by selecting Project > Manage NuGet Packages.

Listing 20.6 Installing the JSON Patch package

```
dotnet add package Microsoft.AspNetCore.Mvc.NewtonsoftJson --version 7.0.0
```

The Microsoft implementation of JSON Patch relies on the third-party Newtonsoft JSON.NET serializer. Add the statements shown in listing 20.7 to the `Program.cs` file to enable the JSON.NET serializer.

Listing 20.7 Enabling the serializer in the Program.cs file in the WebApp folder

```
using Microsoft.EntityFrameworkCore;
using WebApp.Models;
using Microsoft.AspNetCore.Mvc;
//using System.Text.Json.Serialization;
using Microsoft.AspNetCore.RateLimiting;

var builder = WebApplication.CreateBuilder(args);

builder.Services.AddDbContext<DataContext>(opts => {
    opts.UseSqlServer(builder.Configuration[
        "ConnectionStrings:ProductConnection"]);
    opts.EnableSensitiveDataLogging(true);
});

builder.Services.AddControllers().AddNewtonsoftJson();

builder.Services.AddRateLimiter(opts => {
    opts.AddFixedWindowLimiter("fixedWindow", fixOpts => {
        fixOpts.PermitLimit = 1;
        fixOpts.QueueLimit = 0;
        fixOpts.Window = TimeSpan.FromSeconds(15);
```

```
        });
    });

    //builder.Services.Configure<JsonOptions>(opts => {
    //    opts.JsonSerializerOptions.DefaultIgnoreCondition
    //        = JsonIgnoreCondition.WhenWritingNull;
    //});

    builder.Services.Configure<MvcNewtonsoftJsonOptions>(opts => {
        opts.SerializerSettings.NullValueHandling
            = Newtonsoft.Json.NullValueHandling.Ignore;
    });

    var app = builder.Build();

    app.UseRateLimiter();

    app.MapControllers();

    app.MapGet("/", () => "Hello World!");

    var context = app.Services.CreateScope().ServiceProvider
        .GetRequiredService<DataContext>();
    SeedData.SeedDatabase(context);

    app.Run();
```

The `AddNewtonsoftJson` method enables the JSON.NET serializer, which replaces the standard ASP.NET Core serializer. The JSON.NET serializer has its own configuration class, `MvcNewtonsoftJsonOptions`, which is applied through the options pattern. Listing 20.7 sets the `NullValueHandling` value, which tells the serializer to discard properties with `null` values.

> **TIP**   See https://www.newtonsoft.com/json for details of the other configuration options available for the JSON.NET serializer.

20.3.3 *Defining the action method*

To add support for the PATCH method, add the action method shown in listing 20.8 to the `SuppliersController` class.

> **Listing 20.8   Adding an action in the SuppliersController.cs file in the Controllers folder**

```
using Microsoft.AspNetCore.Mvc;
using WebApp.Models;
using Microsoft.EntityFrameworkCore;
using Microsoft.AspNetCore.JsonPatch;

namespace WebApp.Controllers {

    [ApiController]
    [Route("api/[controller]")]
    public class SuppliersController : ControllerBase {
```

```
    private DataContext context;

    public SuppliersController(DataContext ctx) {
        context = ctx;
    }

    [HttpGet("{id}")]
    public async Task<Supplier?> GetSupplier(long id) {
        Supplier supplier = await context.Suppliers
            .Include(s => s.Products)
            .FirstAsync(s => s.SupplierId == id);
        if (supplier.Products != null) {
            foreach (Product p in supplier.Products) {
                p.Supplier = null;
            };
        }
        return supplier;
    }

    [HttpPatch("{id}")]
    public async Task<Supplier?> PatchSupplier(long id,
            JsonPatchDocument<Supplier> patchDoc) {
        Supplier? s = await context.Suppliers.FindAsync(id);
        if (s != null) {
            patchDoc.ApplyTo(s);
            await context.SaveChangesAsync();
        }
        return s;
    }
}
}
```

The action method is decorated with the `HttpPatch` attribute, which denotes that it will handle HTTP PATCH requests. The model binding feature is used to process the JSON Patch document through a `JsonPatchDocument<T>` method parameter. The `JsonPatchDocument<T>` class defines an `ApplyTo` method, which applies each operation to an object. The action method in listing 20.8 retrieves a `Supplier` object from the database, applies the JSON PATCH, and stores the modified object.

Restart ASP.NET Core and use a separate PowerShell command prompt to run the command shown in listing 20.9, which sends an HTTP PATCH request with a JSON PATCH document that changes the value of the `City` property to `Los Angeles`.

Listing 20.9 Sending an HTTP PATCH request

```
Invoke-RestMethod http://localhost:5000/api/suppliers/1 -Method PATCH
➥ -ContentType "application/json" -Body '[{"op":"replace","path":"City",
➥ "value":"Los Angeles"}]'
```

The `PatchSupplier` action method returns the modified `Supplier` object as its result, which is serialized and sent to the client in the HTTP response. You can also see the effect of the change by using a web browser to request http://localhost:5000/suppliers/1, which produces the response shown in figure 20.5.

Figure 20.5   Updating using a PATCH request

20.4   *Understanding content formatting*

The web service examples so far have produced JSON results, but this is not the only data format that action methods can produce. The content format selected for an action result depends on four factors: the formats that the client will accept, the formats that the application can produce, the content policy specified by the action method, and the type returned by the action method. Figuring out how everything fits together can be daunting, but the good news is that the default policy works just fine for most applications, and you only need to understand what happens behind the scenes when you need to make a change or when you are not getting results in the format that you expect.

20.4.1   *Understanding the default content policy*

The best way to get acquainted with content formatting is to understand what happens when neither the client nor the action method applies any restrictions to the formats that can be used. In this situation, the outcome is simple and predictable.

1   If the action method returns a `string`, the string is sent unmodified to the client, and the `Content-Type` header of the response is set to `text/plain`.

2   For all other data types, including other simple types such as `int`, the data is formatted as JSON, and the `Content-Type` header of the response is set to `application/json`.

Strings get special treatment because they cause problems when they are encoded as JSON. When you encode other simple types, such as the C# `int` value 2, then the result is a quoted string, such as `"2"`. When you encode a string, you end up with two sets of quotes so that `"Hello"` becomes `""Hello""`. Not all clients cope well with this double encoding, so it is more reliable to use the `text/plain` format and sidestep the issue entirely. This is rarely an issue because few applications send `string` values; it is more common to send objects in the JSON format. To see the default policy, add a class file named `ContentController.cs` to the `WebApps/Controllers` folder with the code shown in listing 20.10.

```
using Microsoft.AspNetCore.Mvc;
using Microsoft.EntityFrameworkCore;
using WebApp.Models;

namespace WebApp.Controllers {

    [ApiController]
    [Route("/api/[controller]")]
    public class ContentController : ControllerBase {
        private DataContext context;

        public ContentController(DataContext dataContext) {
            context = dataContext;
        }

        [HttpGet("string")]
        public string GetString() => "This is a string response";

        [HttpGet("object")]
        public async Task<Product> GetObject() {
            return await context.Products.FirstAsync();
        }
    }
}
```

The controller defines actions that return string and object results. Restart ASP.NET Core and use a separate PowerShell prompt to run the command shown in listing 20.11; this command sends a request that invokes the `GetString` action method, which returns a string.

```
Invoke-WebRequest http://localhost:5000/api/content/string | select
@{n='Content-Type';e={ $_.Headers."Content-Type" }}, Content
```

This command sends a GET request to the `/api/content/string` URL and processes the response to display the `Content-Type` header and the content from the response. The command produces the following output, which shows the `Content-Type` header for the response:

```
Content-Type              Content
------------              -------
text/plain; charset=utf-8 This is a string response
```

Next, run the command shown in listing 20.12, which sends a request that will be handled by the `GetObject` action method.

```
Invoke-WebRequest http://localhost:5000/api/content/object | select
@{n='Content-Type';e={ $_.Headers."Content-Type" }}, Content
```

This command produces the following output, formatted for clarity, that shows that the response has been encoded as JSON:

```
Content-Type                    Content
------------                    -------
application/json; charset=utf-8 {"productId":1,"name":"Kayak",
    "price":275.00,"categoryId":1,"supplierId":1}
```

20.4.2 *Understanding content negotiation*

Most clients include an `Accept` header in a request, which specifies the set of formats that they are willing to receive in the response, expressed as a set of MIME types. Here is the `Accept` header that Google Chrome sends in requests:

```
Accept: text/html,application/xhtml+xml,application/xml;q=0.9,image/avif,
    image/webp,image/apng,*/*;q=0.8,application/signed-exchange;v=b3;q=0.9
```

This header indicates that Chrome can handle the HTML and XHTML formats (XHTML is an XML-compliant dialect of HTML), XML, and the AVIF, WEBP, and APNG formats. Chrome also supports the `application/signed-exchange`, which is the data type used for signed exchanges, which allow the origin of content to be validated regardless of how it has been delivered.

The `q` values in the header specify relative preference, where the value is 1.0 by default. Specifying a `q` value of 0.9 for `application/xml` tells the server that Chrome will accept XML data but prefers to deal with HTML or XHTML. The `*/*` item tells the server that Chrome will accept any format, but its `q` value specifies that it is the lowest preference of the specified types. Putting this together means that the `Accept` header sent by Chrome provides the server with the following information:

1 Chrome prefers to receive HTML or XHTML data and AVIF, WEBP, and APNG images.

2 If those formats are not available, then the next most preferred format is XML or a signed exchange.

3 If none of the preferred formats is available, then Chrome will accept any format.

You might assume from this that you can change the format produced by the ASP.NET Core application by setting the `Accept` header, but it doesn't work that way—or, rather, it doesn't work that way just yet because there is some preparation required.

To see what happens when the `Accept` header is changed, use a PowerShell prompt to run the command shown in listing 20.13, which sets the `Accept` header to tell ASP.NET Core that the client is willing to receive only XML data.

> **Listing 20.13 Requesting XML data**

```
Invoke-WebRequest http://localhost:5000/api/content/object
    -Headers @{Accept="application/xml"} | select @{n='Content-Type';e={
    $_.Headers."Content-Type" }}, Content
```

Here are the results, which show that the application has sent an `application/json` response:

```
Content-Type                    Content
------------                    -------
application/json; charset=utf-8 {"productId":1,"name":"Kayak",
 "price":275.00,"categoryId":1,"supplierId":1}
```

Including the `Accept` header has no effect on the format, even though the ASP.NET Core application sent the client a format that it hasn't specified. The problem is that, by default, the MVC Framework is configured to only use JSON. Rather than return an error, the MVC Framework sends JSON data in the hope that the client can process it, even though it was not one of the formats specified by the request `Accept` header.

ENABLING XML FORMATTING

For content negotiation to work, the application must be configured so there is some choice in the formats that can be used. Although JSON has become the default format for web applications, the MVC Framework can also support encoding data as XML, as shown in listing 20.14.

> **TIP** You can create your own content format by deriving from the `Microsoft` `.AspNetCore.Mvc.Formatters.OutputFormatter` class. This is rarely used because creating a custom data format isn't a useful way of exposing the data in your application, and the most common formats—JSON and XML—are already implemented.

Listing 20.14 Enabling XML formatting in the Program.cs file in the WebApp folder

```
using Microsoft.EntityFrameworkCore;
using WebApp.Models;
using Microsoft.AspNetCore.Mvc;
using Microsoft.AspNetCore.RateLimiting;

var builder = WebApplication.CreateBuilder(args);

builder.Services.AddDbContext<DataContext>(opts => {
    opts.UseSqlServer(builder.Configuration[
        "ConnectionStrings:ProductConnection"]);
    opts.EnableSensitiveDataLogging(true);
});

builder.Services.AddControllers()
    .AddNewtonsoftJson().AddXmlDataContractSerializerFormatters();

builder.Services.AddRateLimiter(opts => {
    opts.AddFixedWindowLimiter("fixedWindow", fixOpts => {
        fixOpts.PermitLimit = 1;
        fixOpts.QueueLimit = 0;
        fixOpts.Window = TimeSpan.FromSeconds(15);
    });
});

builder.Services.Configure<MvcNewtonsoftJsonOptions>(opts => {
    opts.SerializerSettings.NullValueHandling
        = Newtonsoft.Json.NullValueHandling.Ignore;
});
```

```
var app = builder.Build();

app.UseRateLimiter();

app.MapControllers();

app.MapGet("/", () => "Hello World!");

var context = app.Services.CreateScope().ServiceProvider
    .GetRequiredService<DataContext>();
SeedData.SeedDatabase(context);

app.Run();
```

The XML Serializer has some limitations, including the inability to deal with Entity
Framework Core navigation properties because they are defined through an interface.
To create an object that can be serialized, listing 20.15 uses `ProductBindingTarget`
defined in chapter 19.

> **Listing 20.15   Creating an object in the ContentController.cs file in the Controllers folder**

```
using Microsoft.AspNetCore.Mvc;
using Microsoft.EntityFrameworkCore;
using WebApp.Models;

namespace WebApp.Controllers {

    [ApiController]
    [Route("/api/[controller]")]
    public class ContentController : ControllerBase {
        private DataContext context;

        public ContentController(DataContext dataContext) {
            context = dataContext;
        }

        [HttpGet("string")]
        public string GetString() => "This is a string response";

        [HttpGet("object")]
        public async Task<ProductBindingTarget> GetObject() {
            Product p = await context.Products.FirstAsync();
            return new ProductBindingTarget() {
                Name = p.Name, Price = p.Price, CategoryId = p.CategoryId,
                SupplierId = p.SupplierId
            };
        }
    }
}
```

When the MVC Framework had only the JSON format available, it had no choice but
to encode responses as JSON. Now that there is a choice, you can see the content negotiation process working more fully. Restart ASP.NET Core MVC and run the command
in listing 20.13 again to request XML data, and you will see the following output (from
which I have omitted the namespace attributes for brevity):

```
Content-Type                    Content
------------                    -------
application/xml; charset=utf-8 <ProductBindingTarget>
                                 <Name>Kayak</Name>
                                 <Price>275.00</Price>
                                 <CategoryId>1</CategoryId>
                                 <SupplierId>1</SupplierId>
                               </ProductBindingTarget>
```

FULLY RESPECTING ACCEPT HEADERS

The MVC Framework will always use the JSON format if the `Accept` header contains `*/*`, indicating any format, even if there are other supported formats with a higher preference. This is an odd feature that is intended to deal with requests from browsers consistently, although it can be a source of confusion. Run the command shown in listing 20.16 to send a request with an `Accept` header that requests XML but will accept any other format if XML isn't available.

Listing 20.16   Requesting an XML response with a fallback

```
Invoke-WebRequest http://localhost:5000/api/content/object -Headers
@{Accept="application/xml,*/*;q=0.8"} | select @{n='Content-Type';
e={ $_.Headers."Content-Type" }}, Content
```

Even though the `Accept` header tells the MVC Framework that the client prefers XML, the presence of the `*/*` fallback means that a JSON response is sent. A related problem is that a JSON response will be sent when the client requests a format that the MVC Framework hasn't been configured to produce, which you can see by running the command shown in listing 20.17.

Listing 20.17   Requesting a PNG response

```
Invoke-WebRequest http://localhost:5000/api/content/object -Headers
@{Accept="img/png"} | select @{n='Content-Type';e={ $_.Headers.
"Content-Type" }}, Content
```

The commands in listing 20.16 and listing 20.17 both produce this response:

```
Content-Type                    Content
------------                    -------
application/json; charset=utf-8 {"name":"Kayak","price":275.00,
                                 "categoryId":1,"supplierId":1}
```

In both cases, the MVC Framework returns JSON data, which may not be what the client is expecting. Two configuration settings are used to tell the MVC Framework to respect the `Accept` setting sent by the client and not send JSON data by default. To change the configuration, add the statements shown in listing 20.18 to the `Program.cs` file.

Listing 20.18   Configuring negotiation in the Program.cs file in the WebApp folder

```
using Microsoft.EntityFrameworkCore;
using WebApp.Models;
using Microsoft.AspNetCore.Mvc;
```

```
using Microsoft.AspNetCore.RateLimiting;

var builder = WebApplication.CreateBuilder(args);

builder.Services.AddDbContext<DataContext>(opts => {
    opts.UseSqlServer(builder.Configuration[
        "ConnectionStrings:ProductConnection"]);
    opts.EnableSensitiveDataLogging(true);
});

builder.Services.AddControllers()
    .AddNewtonsoftJson().AddXmlDataContractSerializerFormatters();

builder.Services.AddRateLimiter(opts => {
    opts.AddFixedWindowLimiter("fixedWindow", fixOpts => {
        fixOpts.PermitLimit = 1;
        fixOpts.QueueLimit = 0;
        fixOpts.Window = TimeSpan.FromSeconds(15);
    });
});

builder.Services.Configure<MvcNewtonsoftJsonOptions>(opts => {
    opts.SerializerSettings.NullValueHandling
        = Newtonsoft.Json.NullValueHandling.Ignore;
});

builder.Services.Configure<MvcOptions>(opts => {
    opts.RespectBrowserAcceptHeader = true;
    opts.ReturnHttpNotAcceptable = true;
});

var app = builder.Build();

app.UseRateLimiter();

app.MapControllers();

app.MapGet("/", () => "Hello World!");

var context = app.Services.CreateScope().ServiceProvider
    .GetRequiredService<DataContext>();
SeedData.SeedDatabase(context);

app.Run();
```

The options pattern is used to set the properties of an MvcOptions object. Setting RespectBrowserAcceptHeader to true disables the fallback to JSON when the Accept header contains */*. Setting ReturnHttpNotAcceptable to true disables the fallback to JSON when the client requests an unsupported data format.

Restart ASP.NET Core and repeat the command from listing 20.16. Instead of a JSON response, the format preferences specified by the Accept header will be respected, and an XML response will be sent. Repeat the command from listing 20.17, and you will receive a response with the 406 status code.

```
...
Invoke-WebRequest : The remote server returned an error:
    (406) Not Acceptable.
...
```

Sending a 406 code indicates there is no overlap between the formats the client can handle and the formats that the MVC Framework can produce, ensuring that the client doesn't receive a data format it cannot process.

20.4.3 *Specifying an action result format*

The data formats that the MVC Framework can use for an action method result can be constrained using the `Produces` attribute, as shown in listing 20.19.

> **TIP** The `Produces` attribute is an example of a filter, which allows attributes to alter requests and responses. See chapter 30 for more details.

> Listing 20.19 Data formats in the ContentController.cs file in the Controllers folder

```
using Microsoft.AspNetCore.Mvc;
using Microsoft.EntityFrameworkCore;
using WebApp.Models;

namespace WebApp.Controllers {

    [ApiController]
    [Route("/api/[controller]")]
    public class ContentController : ControllerBase {
        private DataContext context;

        public ContentController(DataContext dataContext) {
            context = dataContext;
        }

        [HttpGet("string")]
        public string GetString() => "This is a string response";

        [HttpGet("object")]
        [Produces("application/json")]
        public async Task<ProductBindingTarget> GetObject() {
            Product p = await context.Products.FirstAsync();
            return new ProductBindingTarget() {
                Name = p.Name, Price = p.Price, CategoryId = p.CategoryId,
                SupplierId = p.SupplierId
            };
        }
    }
}
```

The argument for the attribute specifies the format that will be used for the result from the action, and more than one type can be specified. The `Produces` attribute restricts the types that the MVC Framework will consider when processing an `Accept` header. To see the effect of the `Produces` attribute, use a PowerShell prompt to run the command shown in listing 20.20.

> **Listing 20.20   Requesting data**

```
Invoke-WebRequest http://localhost:5000/api/content/object -Headers
@{Accept="application/xml,application/json;q=0.8"} | select
@{n='Content-Type';e={ $_.Headers."Content-Type" }}, Content
```

The `Accept` header tells the MVC Framework that the client prefers XML data but will accept JSON. The `Produces` attribute means that XML data isn't available as the data format for the `GetObject` action method and so the JSON serializer is selected, which produces the following response:

```
Content-Type                 Content
------------                 -------
application/json; charset=utf-8 {"name":"Kayak","price":275.00,
                                 "categoryId":1,"supplierId":1}
```

20.4.4 Requesting a format in the URL

The `Accept` header isn't always under the control of the programmer who is writing the client. In such situations, it can be helpful to allow the data format for the response to be requested using the URL. This feature is enabled by decorating an action method with the `FormatFilter` attribute and ensuring there is a `format` segment variable in the action method's route, as shown in listing 20.21.

> **Listing 20.21   Formatting in the ContentController.cs file in the Controllers folder**

```csharp
using Microsoft.AspNetCore.Mvc;
using Microsoft.EntityFrameworkCore;
using WebApp.Models;

namespace WebApp.Controllers {

    [ApiController]
    [Route("/api/[controller]")]
    public class ContentController : ControllerBase {
        private DataContext context;

        public ContentController(DataContext dataContext) {
            context = dataContext;
        }

        [HttpGet("string")]
        public string GetString() => "This is a string response";

        [HttpGet("object/{format?}")]
        [FormatFilter]
        [Produces("application/json", "application/xml")]
        public async Task<ProductBindingTarget> GetObject() {
            Product p = await context.Products.FirstAsync();
            return new ProductBindingTarget() {
                Name = p.Name, Price = p.Price, CategoryId = p.CategoryId,
                SupplierId = p.SupplierId
            };
        }
    }
}
```

The `FormatFilter` attribute is an example of a filter, which is an attribute that can modify requests and responses, as described in chapter 30. This filter gets the value of the `format` segment variable from the route that matched the request and uses it to override the `Accept` header sent by the client. I have also expanded the range of types specified by the `Produces` attribute so that the action method can return both JSON and XML responses.

Each data format supported by the application has a shorthand: `xml` for XML data, and `json` for JSON data. When the action method is targeted by a URL that contains one of these shorthand names, the `Accept` header is ignored, and the specified format is used. To see the effect, restart ASP.NET Core and use the browser to request http://localhost:5000/api/content/object/json   and   http://localhost:5000/api/content/object/xml, which produce the responses shown in figure 20.6.

Figure 20.6   Requesting data formats in the URL

20.4.5 Restricting the formats received by an action method

Most content formatting decisions focus on the data formats the ASP.NET Core application sends to the client, but the same serializers that deal with results are used to deserialize the data sent by clients in request bodies. The deserialization process happens automatically, and most applications will be happy to accept data in all the formats they are configured to send. The example application is configured to send JSON and XML data, which means that clients can send JSON and XML data in requests.

The `Consumes` attribute can be applied to action methods to restrict the data types it will handle, as shown in listing 20.22.

> **Listing 20.22   Adding actions in the ContentController.cs file in the Controllers folder**

```
using Microsoft.AspNetCore.Mvc;
using Microsoft.EntityFrameworkCore;
using WebApp.Models;

namespace WebApp.Controllers {

    [ApiController]
    [Route("/api/[controller]")]
    public class ContentController : ControllerBase {
        private DataContext context;
```

```
        public ContentController(DataContext dataContext) {
            context = dataContext;
        }

        [HttpGet("string")]
        public string GetString() => "This is a string response";

        [HttpGet("object/{format?}")]
        [FormatFilter]
        [Produces("application/json", "application/xml")]
        public async Task<ProductBindingTarget> GetObject() {
            Product p = await context.Products.FirstAsync();
            return new ProductBindingTarget() {
                Name = p.Name, Price = p.Price, CategoryId = p.CategoryId,
                SupplierId = p.SupplierId
            };
        }

        [HttpPost]
        [Consumes("application/json")]
        public string SaveProductJson(ProductBindingTarget product) {
            return $"JSON: {product.Name}";
        }

        [HttpPost]
        [Consumes("application/xml")]
        public string SaveProductXml(ProductBindingTarget product) {
            return $"XML: {product.Name}";
        }
    }
}
```

The new action methods are decorated with the Consumes attribute, restricting the data types that each can handle. The combination of attributes means that HTTP POST attributes whose Content-Type header is application/json will be handled by the SaveProductJson action method. HTTP POST requests whose Content-Type header is application/xml will be handled by the SaveProductXml action method. Restart ASP.NET Core and use a PowerShell command prompt to run the command shown in listing 20.23 to send JSON data to the example application.

> **Listing 20.23   Sending JSON data**

```
Invoke-RestMethod http://localhost:5000/api/content -Method POST -Body
⇒ (@{ Name="Swimming Goggles"; Price=12.75; CategoryId=1; SupplierId=1} |
⇒ ConvertTo-Json) -ContentType "application/json"
```

The request is automatically routed to the correct action method, which produces the following response:

```
JSON: Swimming Goggles
```

Run the command shown in listing 20.24 to send XML data to the example application.

Listing 20.24 Sending XML data

```
Invoke-RestMethod http://localhost:5000/api/content -Method POST -Body
"<ProductBindingTarget xmlns=`"http://schemas.datacontract.org/2004/07/
WebApp.Models`"> <CategoryId>1</CategoryId><Name>Kayak</Name><Price>
275.00</Price> <SupplierId>1</SupplierId></ProductBindingTarget>"
 -ContentType "application/xml"
```

The request is routed to the `SaveProductXml` action method and produces the following response:

```
XML: Kayak
```

The MVC Framework will send a `415 - Unsupported Media Type` response if a request is sent with a `Content-Type` header that doesn't match the data types that the application supports.

20.4.6 *Caching output*

In chapter 7, I demonstrated the output caching middleware, which allows caching policies to be defined and applied to endpoints. This feature can be extended to controllers using attributes, allowing fine-grained control over how responses from controllers are cached. To prepare, listing 20.25 configures the example application to set up a caching policy.

Listing 20.25 Configuring caching in the Program.cs file in the WebApp folder

```
using Microsoft.EntityFrameworkCore;
using WebApp.Models;
using Microsoft.AspNetCore.Mvc;
using Microsoft.AspNetCore.RateLimiting;

var builder = WebApplication.CreateBuilder(args);

// ...statements omitted for brevity...

builder.Services.Configure<MvcOptions>(opts => {
    opts.RespectBrowserAcceptHeader = true;
    opts.ReturnHttpNotAcceptable = true;
});

builder.Services.AddOutputCache(opts => {
    opts.AddPolicy("30sec", policy => {
        policy.Cache();
        policy.Expire(TimeSpan.FromSeconds(30));
    });
});

var app = builder.Build();

app.UseRateLimiter();
app.UseOutputCache();
app.MapControllers();

app.MapGet("/", () => "Hello World!");
```

```
var context = app.Services.CreateScope().ServiceProvider
    .GetRequiredService<DataContext>();
SeedData.SeedDatabase(context);

app.Run();
```

This configuration creates an output caching policy named `30sec`, which caches content for 30 seconds. The caching policy is applied to the controller using the `Output-Cache` attribute, as shown in listing 20.26.

> **Listing 20.26 Caching in the ContentController.cs file in the WebApp/Controllers folder**

```
using Microsoft.AspNetCore.Mvc;
using Microsoft.AspNetCore.OutputCaching;
using Microsoft.EntityFrameworkCore;
using WebApp.Models;

namespace WebApp.Controllers {

    [ApiController]
    [Route("/api/[controller]")]
    public class ContentController : ControllerBase {
        private DataContext context;

        public ContentController(DataContext dataContext) {
            context = dataContext;
        }

        [HttpGet("string")]
        [OutputCache(PolicyName = "30sec")]
        [Produces("application/json")]
        public string GetString() =>
            $"{DateTime.Now.ToLongTimeString()} String response";


        // ...other actions omitted for brevity...
    }
}
```

The `OutputCache` attribute can be applied to the entire controller, which causes the responses for all action methods, or applied to individual actions. The attribute accepts a policy name as an argument or can be used to create a custom policy. The attribute in listing 20.26 has been applied a single action and applies the policy created in listing 20.25. (I added the `Produces` attribute to force a JSON response, which is not required for caching but makes the response easier to see in the browser window).

Restart ASP.NET Core and use a browser to request http://localhost:5000/api/content/string. Reload the browser and you will see the same time displayed, illustrating that output is cached for 30 seconds, as shown in figure 20.7.

Figure 20.7 Cached output from a controller action

20.5 *Documenting and exploring web services*

When you are responsible for developing both the web service and its client, the purpose of each action and its results are obvious and are usually written at the same time. If you are responsible for a web service that is consumed by third-party developers, then you may need to provide documentation that describes how the web service works. The OpenAPI specification, which is also known as Swagger, describes web services in a way that can be understood by other programmers and consumed programmatically. In this section, I demonstrate how to use OpenAPI to describe a web service and show you how to fine-tune that description.

20.5.1 *Resolving action conflicts*

The OpenAPI discovery process requires a unique combination of the HTTP method and URL pattern for each action method. The process doesn't support the `Consumes` attribute, so a change is required to the `ContentController` to remove the separate actions for receiving XML and JSON data, as shown in listing 20.27.

> **Listing 20.27 Removing actions in the ContentController.cs file in the Controllers folder**

```
using Microsoft.AspNetCore.Mvc;
using Microsoft.AspNetCore.OutputCaching;
using Microsoft.EntityFrameworkCore;
using WebApp.Models;

namespace WebApp.Controllers {

    [ApiController]
    [Route("/api/[controller]")]
    public class ContentController : ControllerBase {
        private DataContext context;

        // ...methods omitted for brevity...

        [HttpPost]
        [Consumes("application/json")]
        public string SaveProductJson(ProductBindingTarget product) {
            return $"JSON: {product.Name}";
        }
```

```
//[HttpPost]
//[Consumes("application/xml")]
//public string SaveProductXml(ProductBindingTarget product) {
//    return $"XML: {product.Name}";
//}
    }
}
```

Commenting out one of the action methods ensures that each remaining action has a unique combination of HTTP method and URL.

20.5.2 *Installing and configuring the Swashbuckle package*

The Swashbuckle package is the most popular ASP.NET Core implementation of the OpenAPI specification and will automatically generate a description for the web services in an ASP.NET Core application. The package also includes tools that consume that description to allow the web service to be inspected and tested.

Open a new PowerShell command prompt, navigate to the folder that contains the WebApp.csproj file, and run the commands shown in listing 20.28 to install the NuGet package.

> **Listing 20.28   Adding a package to the project**

```
dotnet add package Swashbuckle.AspNetCore --version 6.4.0
```

Add the statements shown in listing 20.29 to the Program.cs file to add the services and middleware provided by the Swashbuckle package.

> **Listing 20.29   Configuring Swashbuckle in the Program.cs file in the WebApp folder**

```
using Microsoft.EntityFrameworkCore;
using WebApp.Models;
using Microsoft.AspNetCore.Mvc;
using Microsoft.AspNetCore.RateLimiting;
using Microsoft.OpenApi.Models;

var builder = WebApplication.CreateBuilder(args);

builder.Services.AddDbContext<DataContext>(opts => {
    opts.UseSqlServer(builder.Configuration[
        "ConnectionStrings:ProductConnection"]);
    opts.EnableSensitiveDataLogging(true);
});

builder.Services.AddControllers()
    .AddNewtonsoftJson().AddXmlDataContractSerializerFormatters();

builder.Services.AddRateLimiter(opts => {
    opts.AddFixedWindowLimiter("fixedWindow", fixOpts => {
        fixOpts.PermitLimit = 1;
        fixOpts.QueueLimit = 0;
        fixOpts.Window = TimeSpan.FromSeconds(15);
    });
});
```

```
builder.Services.Configure<MvcNewtonsoftJsonOptions>(opts => {
    opts.SerializerSettings.NullValueHandling
        = Newtonsoft.Json.NullValueHandling.Ignore;
});

builder.Services.Configure<MvcOptions>(opts => {
    opts.RespectBrowserAcceptHeader = true;
    opts.ReturnHttpNotAcceptable = true;
});

builder.Services.AddOutputCache(opts => {
    opts.AddPolicy("30sec", policy => {
        policy.Cache();
        policy.Expire(TimeSpan.FromSeconds(30));
    });
});

builder.Services.AddSwaggerGen(c => {
    c.SwaggerDoc("v1", new OpenApiInfo {
        Title = "WebApp", Version = "v1"
    });
});

var app = builder.Build();

app.UseRateLimiter();
app.UseOutputCache();
app.MapControllers();

app.MapGet("/", () => "Hello World!");

app.UseSwagger();
app.UseSwaggerUI(options => {
    options.SwaggerEndpoint("/swagger/v1/swagger.json", "WebApp");
});

var context = app.Services.CreateScope().ServiceProvider
    .GetRequiredService<DataContext>();
SeedData.SeedDatabase(context);

app.Run();
```

There are two features set up by the statements in listing 20.29. The feature generates an OpenAPI description of the web services that the application contains. You can see the description by restarting ASP.NET Core and using the browser to request the URL http://localhost:5000/swagger/v1/swagger.json, which produces the response shown in figure 20.8. The OpenAPI format is verbose, but you can see each URL that the web service controllers support, along with details of the data each expects to receive and the range of responses that it will generate.

```
{
  "openapi": "3.0.1",
  "info": {
    "title": "WebApp",
    "version": "v1"
  },
  "paths": {
    "/api/Categories/{id}": {
      "get": {
        "tags": [
          "Categories"
        ],
        "parameters": [
          {
            "name": "id",
            "in": "path",
            "required": true,
            "schema": {
              "type": "integer",
              "format": "int64"
            }
          }
```

Figure 20.8   The OpenAPI description of the web service

The second feature is a UI that consumes the OpenAPI description of the web service and presents the information in a more easily understood way, along with support for testing each action. Use the browser to request http://localhost:5000/swagger, and you will see the interface shown in figure 20.9. You can expand each action to see details, including the data that is expected in the request and the different responses that the client can expect.

**Figure 20.9
The OpenAPI
explorer
interface**

20.5.3 Fine-Tuning the API description

Relying on the API discovery process can produce a result that doesn't truly capture the web service. You can see this by examining the entry in the Products section that describes GET requests matched by the `/api/Products/{id}` URL pattern. Expand this item and examine the response section, and you will see there is only one status code response that will be returned, as shown in figure 20.10.

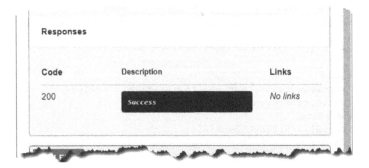

Figure 20.10   The data formats listed in the OpenAPI web service description

The API discovery process makes assumptions about the responses produced by an action method and doesn't always reflect what can really happen. In this case, the `GetProduct` action method in the `ProductsController` class can return another response that the discovery process hasn't detected.

```
...
[HttpGet("{id}")]
[DisableRateLimiting]
public async Task<IActionResult> GetProduct(long id) {
    Product? p = await context.Products.FindAsync(id);
    if (p == null) {
        return NotFound();
    }
    return Ok(p);
}
...
```

If a third-party developer attempts to implement a client for the web service using the OpenAPI data, they won't be expecting the 404 - Not Found response that the action sends when it can't find an object in the database.

RUNNING THE API ANALYZER

ASP.NET Core includes an analyzer that inspects web service controllers and highlights problems like the one described in the previous section. To enable the analyzer, add the elements shown in listing 20.30 to the `WebApp.csproj` file. (If you are using Visual Studio, right-click the WebApp project item in the Solution Explorer and select Edit Project File from the pop-up menu.)

Listing 20.30   Enabling the analyzer in the WebApp.csproj file in the WebApp folder

```
<Project Sdk="Microsoft.NET.Sdk.Web">

  <PropertyGroup>
    <TargetFramework>net7.0</TargetFramework>
```

```
        <Nullable>enable</Nullable>
        <ImplicitUsings>enable</ImplicitUsings>
    </PropertyGroup>

    <ItemGroup>
        <PackageReference Include="Microsoft.AspNetCore.Mvc.NewtonsoftJson"
                                    Version="7.0.0" />
        <PackageReference Include="Microsoft.EntityFrameworkCore.Design"
                                    Version="7.0.0">
            <IncludeAssets>
                        runtime; build; native; contentfiles; analyzers;
                        buildtransitive
            </IncludeAssets>
            <PrivateAssets>all</PrivateAssets>
        </PackageReference>
        <PackageReference Include="Microsoft.EntityFrameworkCore.SqlServer"
                                    Version="7.0.0" />
        <PackageReference Include="Swashbuckle.AspNetCore" Version="6.4.0" />
    </ItemGroup>

    <PropertyGroup>
        <IncludeOpenAPIAnalyzers>true</IncludeOpenAPIAnalyzers>
    </PropertyGroup>

</Project>
```

If you are using Visual Studio, you will see any problems detected by the API analyzer shown in the controller class file, as shown in figure 20.11.

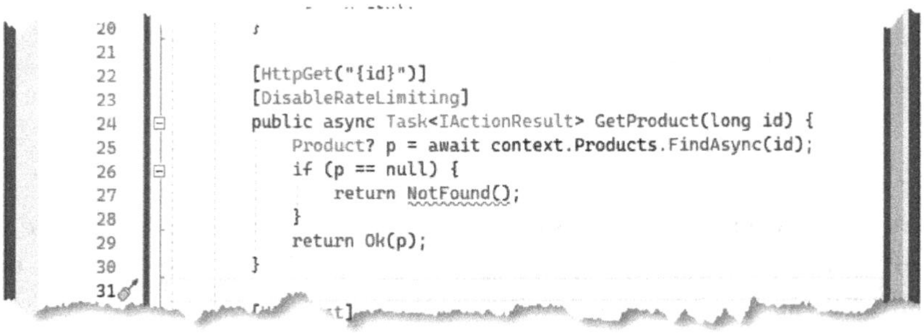

```
20                      {
21
22                      [HttpGet("{id}")]
23                      [DisableRateLimiting]
24                      public async Task<IActionResult> GetProduct(long id) {
25                          Product? p = await context.Products.FindAsync(id);
26                          if (p == null) {
27                              return NotFound();
28                          }
29                          return Ok(p);
30                      }
31
```

Figure 20.11   A problem detected by the API analyzer

If you are using Visual Studio Code, you will see warning messages when the project is compiled, either using the `dotnet build` command or when it is executed using the `dotnet run` command. When the project is compiled, you will see this message that describes the issue in the `ProductController` class:

```
Controllers\ProductsController.cs(27,24): warning API1000:
    Action method returns undeclared status code '404'.
[C:\WebApp\WebApp.csproj]
    1 Warning(s)
    0 Error(s)
```

DECLARING THE ACTION METHOD RESULT TYPE

To fix the problem detected by the analyzer, the `ProducesResponseType` attribute can be used to declare each of the response types that the action method can produce, as shown in listing 20.31.

> **Listing 20.31 Declaring results in the ProductsController.cs file in the Controllers folder**

```
...
[HttpGet("{id}")]
[DisableRateLimiting]
[ProducesResponseType(StatusCodes.Status200OK)]
[ProducesResponseType(StatusCodes.Status404NotFound)]
public async Task<IActionResult> GetProduct(long id) {
    Product? p = await context.Products.FindAsync(id);
    if (p == null) {
        return NotFound();
    }
    return Ok(p);
}
...
```

Restart ASP.NET Core and use a browser to request http://localhost:5000/swagger, and you will see the description for the action method has been updated to reflect the 404 response, as shown in figure 20.12.

Figure 20.12 Reflecting all the status codes produced by an action method

Summary

- The Entity Framework Core-related data feature can cause serialization problems when used in web service results.
- Cycles in object data must be broken before serialization.
- The PATCH method is used to specify fine-grained changes to data and is supported by ASP.NET Core.
- ASP.NET Core uses JSON to serialize data by default but supports a content negotiation process that allows clients to specify the formats they can accept.
- The output from web services can be cached, using the caching middleware that can be applied to any endpoint.
- Documentation for a web service can be generated using the OpenAPI specification.

21
Using controllers with views, part I

This chapter covers

- Using controllers with views to programmatically generate HTML content
- Using the Razor view syntax to mix code and markup
- Selecting a view in an action method
- Using view models to pass data from an action to a view

In this chapter, I introduce the *Razor view engine*, which is responsible for generating HTML responses that can be displayed directly to the user (as opposed to the JSON and XML responses, which are typically consumed by other applications). *Views* are files that contain C# expressions and HTML fragments that are processed by the view engine to generate HTML responses. I show how views work, explain how they are used in action methods, and describe the different types of C# expressions they contain. In chapter 22, I describe some of the other features that views support. Table 21.1 puts Razor views in context.

Table 21.1 Putting Razor Views in context

Question	Answer
What are they?	Views are files that contain a mix of static HTML content and C# expressions.
Why are they useful?	Views are used to create HTML responses for HTTP requests. The C# expressions are evaluated and combined with the HTML content to create a response.
How are they used?	The `View` method defined by the `Controller` class creates an action response that uses a view.
Are there any pitfalls or limitations?	It can take a little time to get used to the syntax of view files and the way they combine code and content.
Are there any alternatives?	There are third-party view engines that can be used in ASP.NET Core MVC, but their use is limited.

Table 21.2 provides a guide to the chapter

Table 21.2 Chapter guide

Problem	Solution	Listing
Enabling views	Use the `AddControllersWithViews` and `MapControllerRoute` methods to set up the required services and endpoints.	4, 6
Returning an HTML response from a controller action method	Use the `View` method to create a `ViewResult`.	5
Creating dynamic HTML content	Create a Razor View that uses expressions for dynamic content.	7, 8, 19, 20
Selecting a view by name	Provide the view name as an argument to the `View` method.	9, 10
Creating a view that can be used by multiple controllers	Create a shared view.	11–13
Specifying a model type for a view	Use an `@model` expression.	14–18
Allow for null view model values	Use a nullable type in the `@model` expression	19–21
Generating content selectively	Use `@if`, `@switch`, or `@foreach` expressions.	22–28
Including C# code in a view	Use a code block.	29

21.1 *Preparing for this chapter*

This chapter uses the `WebApp` project from chapter 20. To prepare for this chapter, replace the contents of the `Program.cs` file with the statements shown in listing 21.1, which removes some of the services and middleware used in earlier chapters.

TIP You can download the example project for this chapter—and for all the other chapters in this book—from https://github.com/manningbooks/pro-asp .net-core-7. See chapter 1 for how to get help if you have problems running the examples.

Listing 21.1 Replacing the contents of the Program.cs file in the WebApp folder

```
using Microsoft.EntityFrameworkCore;
using WebApp.Models;

var builder = WebApplication.CreateBuilder(args);

builder.Services.AddDbContext<DataContext>(opts => {
    opts.UseSqlServer(builder.Configuration[
        "ConnectionStrings:ProductConnection"]);
    opts.EnableSensitiveDataLogging(true);
});

builder.Services.AddControllers();

var app = builder.Build();

app.UseStaticFiles();
app.MapControllers();

var context = app.Services.CreateScope().ServiceProvider
    .GetRequiredService<DataContext>();
SeedData.SeedDatabase(context);

app.Run();
```

21.1.1 Dropping the database

Open a new PowerShell command prompt, navigate to the folder that contains the WebApp.csproj file, and run the command shown in listing 21.2 to drop the database.

Listing 21.2 Dropping the database

```
dotnet ef database drop --force
```

21.1.2 Running the example application

Use the PowerShell command prompt to run the command shown in listing 21.3.

Listing 21.3 Running the example application

```
dotnet watch
```

The database will be seeded as part of the application startup. Once ASP.NET Core is running, use a web browser to request http://localhost:5000/api/products, which will produce the response shown in figure 21.1.

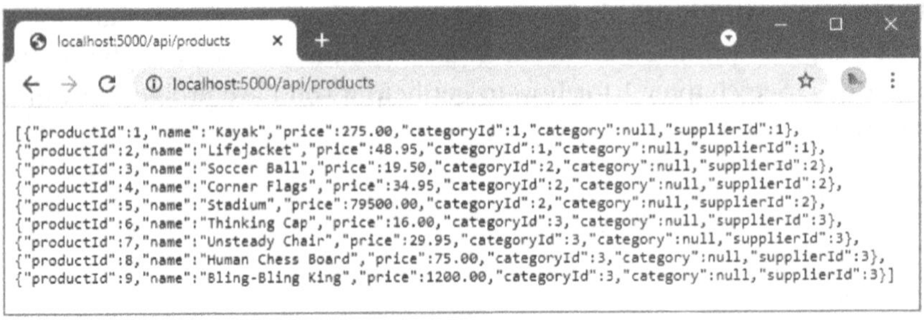

Figure 21.1   Running the example application

This chapter uses `dotnet watch`, rather than the `dotnet run` command used in earlier chapters. The `dotnet watch` command is useful when working with views because changes are pushed to the browser automatically. At some point, however, you will make a change that cannot be processed by the `dotnet watch` command, and you will see a message like this at the command prompt:

```
watch : Unable to apply hot reload because of a rude edit.
watch : Do you want to restart your app - Yes (y) / No (n) /
    Always (a) / Never (v)?
```

The point at which this arises depends on the editor you have chosen, but when this happens, select the `Always` option so that the application will always be restarted when a reload cannot be performed.

21.2   Getting started with views

I started this chapter with a web service controller to demonstrate the similarity with a controller that uses views. It is easy to think about web service and view controllers as being separate, but it is important to understand that the same underlying features are used for both types of response. In the sections that follow, I configure the application to support HTML applications and repurpose the `Home` controller so that it produces an HTML response.

21.2.1   Configuring the application

The first step is to configure ASP.NET Core to enable HTML responses, as shown in listing 21.4.

> **Listing 21.4   Changing the configuration in the Program.cs file in the WebApp folder**

```
using Microsoft.EntityFrameworkCore;
using WebApp.Models;

var builder = WebApplication.CreateBuilder(args);

builder.Services.AddDbContext<DataContext>(opts => {
    opts.UseSqlServer(builder.Configuration[
        "ConnectionStrings:ProductConnection"]);
    opts.EnableSensitiveDataLogging(true);
```

```
});

builder.Services.AddControllersWithViews();

var app = builder.Build();

app.UseStaticFiles();
app.MapControllers();
app.MapControllerRoute("Default",
    "{controller=Home}/{action=Index}/{id?}");

var context = app.Services.CreateScope().ServiceProvider
    .GetRequiredService<DataContext>();
SeedData.SeedDatabase(context);

app.Run();
```

HTML responses are created using views, which are files containing a mix of HTML elements and C# expressions. The AddControllers method I used in chapter 19 to enable the MVC Framework only supports web service controllers. To enable support for views, the AddControllersWithViews method is used.

The second change is the addition of the MapControllerRoute method in the end-point routing configuration. Controllers that generate HTML responses don't use the same routing attributes that are applied to web service controllers and rely on a feature named *convention routing*, which I describe in the next section.

21.2.2 Creating an HTML controller

Controllers for HTML applications are similar to those used for web services but with some important differences. To create an HTML controller, add a class file named HomeController.cs to the Controllers folder with the statements shown in listing 21.5.

> **Listing 21.5 The contents of the HomeController.cs file in the Controllers folder**

```
using Microsoft.AspNetCore.Mvc;
using WebApp.Models;

namespace WebApp.Controllers {

    public class HomeController : Controller {
        private DataContext context;

        public HomeController(DataContext ctx) {
            context = ctx;
        }

        public async Task<IActionResult> Index(long id = 1) {
            return View(await context.Products.FindAsync(id));
        }
    }
}
```

The base class for HTML controllers is `Controller`, which is derived from the `ControllerBase` class used for web service controllers and provides additional methods that are specific to working with views.

```
...
public class HomeController: Controller {
...
```

Action methods in HTML controllers return objects that implement the `IAction-Result` interface, which is the same result type used in chapter 19 to return specific status code responses. The `Controller` base class provides the `View` method, which is used to select a view that will be used to create a response.

```
...
return View(await context.Products.FindAsync(id));
...
```

> **TIP**   Notice that the controller in listing 21.5 hasn't been decorated with attributes. The `ApiController` attribute is applied only to web service controllers and should not be used for HTML controllers. The `Route` and HTTP method attributes are not required because HTML controllers rely on convention-based routing, which was configured in listing 21.4 and which is introduced shortly.

The `View` method creates an instance of the `ViewResult` class, which implements the `IActionResult` interface and tells the MVC Framework that a view should be used to produce the response for the client. The argument to the `View` method is called the *view model* and provides the view with the data it needs to generate a response.

There are no views for the MVC Framework to use at the moment, but if you restart ASP.NET Core and use a browser to request http://localhost:5000, you will see an error message that shows how the MVC Framework responds to the `ViewResult` it received from the `Index` action method, as shown in figure 21.2.

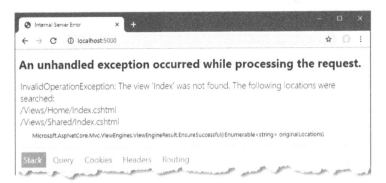

Figure 21.2   Using a view result

Behind the scenes, there are two important conventions at work, which are described in the following sections.

NOTE Two features can expand the range of search locations. The search will include the /Pages/Shared folder if the project uses Razor Pages, as explained in chapter 23.

UNDERSTANDING CONVENTION ROUTING

HTML controllers rely on *convention routing* instead of the Route attribute. The convention in this term refers to the use of the controller class name and the action method name used to configure the routing system, which was done in listing 21.5 by adding this statement to the endpoint routing configuration:

```
...
app.MapControllerRoute("Default",
    "{controller=Home}/{action=Index}/{id?}");
...
```

The route that this statement sets up matches two- and three-segment URLs. The value of the first segment is used as the name of the controller class, without the Controller suffix, so that Home refers to the HomeController class. The second segment is the name of the action method, and the optional third segment allows action methods to receive a parameter named id. Default values are used to select the Index action method on the Home controller for URLs that do not contain all the segments. This is such a common convention that the same routing configuration can be set up without having to specify the URL pattern, as shown in listing 21.6.

> **Listing 21.6 The default routing convention in the Program.cs file in the WebApp folder**

```
using Microsoft.EntityFrameworkCore;
using WebApp.Models;

var builder = WebApplication.CreateBuilder(args);

builder.Services.AddDbContext<DataContext>(opts => {
    opts.UseSqlServer(builder.Configuration[
        "ConnectionStrings:ProductConnection"]);
    opts.EnableSensitiveDataLogging(true);
});

builder.Services.AddControllersWithViews();

var app = builder.Build();

app.UseStaticFiles();
app.MapControllers();
app.MapDefaultControllerRoute();

var context = app.Services.CreateScope().ServiceProvider
    .GetRequiredService<DataContext>();
SeedData.SeedDatabase(context);

app.Run();
```

The MapDefaultControllerRoute method avoids the risk of mistyping the URL pattern and sets up the convention-based routing. I have configured one route in this chapter, but an application can define as many routes as it needs, and later chapters expand the routing configuration to make examples easier to follow.

> **TIP**   The MVC Framework assumes that any `public` method defined by an HTML controller is an action method and that action methods support all HTTP methods. If you need to define a method in a controller that is not an action, you can make it `private` or, if that is not possible, decorate the method with the `NonAction` attribute. You can restrict an action method to support specific HTTP methods by applying attributes so that the `HttpGet` attribute denotes an action that handles GET requests, the `HttpPost` method denotes an action that handles POST requests, and so on.

UNDERSTANDING THE RAZOR VIEW CONVENTION

When the `Index` action method defined by the `Home` controller is invoked, it uses the value of the `id` parameter to retrieve an object from the database and passes it to the `View` method.

```
...
public async Task<IActionResult> Index(long id = 1) {
    return View(await context.Products.FindAsync(id));
}
...
```

When an action method invokes the `View` method, it creates a `ViewResult` that tells the MVC Framework to use the default convention to locate a view. The Razor view engine looks for a view with the same name as the action method, with the addition of the `cshtml` file extension, which is the file type used by the Razor view engine. Views are stored in the `Views` folder, grouped by the controller they are associated with. The first location searched is the `Views/Home` folder, since the action method is defined by the `Home` controller (the name of which is taken by dropping `Controller` from the name of the controller class). If the `Index.cshtml` file cannot be found in the `Views/Home` folder, then the `Views/Shared` folder is checked, which is the location where views that are shared between controllers are stored.

While most controllers have their own views, views can also be shared so that common functionality doesn't have to be duplicated, as demonstrated in the "Using Shared Views" section.

The exception response in figure 21.2 shows the result of both conventions. The routing conventions are used to process the request using the `Index` action method defined by the `Home` controller, which tells the Razor view engine to use the view search convention to locate a view. The view engine uses the name of the action method and controller to build its search pattern and checks for the `Views/Home/Index.cshtml` and `Views/Shared/Index.cshtml` files.

21.2.3 Creating a Razor View

To provide the MVC Framework with a view to display, create the `Views/Home` folder and add to it a file named `Index.cshtml` with the content shown in listing 21.7. If you are using Visual Studio, create the view by right-clicking the `Views/Home` folder, selecting Add > New Item from the pop-up menu, and selecting the Razor View - Empty item in the ASP.NET Core > Web category, as shown in figure 21.3.

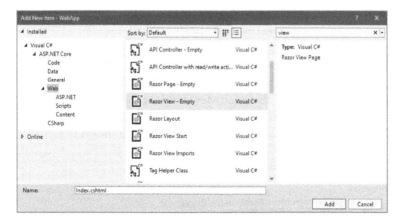

Figure 21.3 Creating a view using Visual Studio

TIP There is a menu item for creating views in the Add popup menu, but this relies on the Visual Studio scaffolding feature, which adds template content to create different types of view. I don't rely on the scaffolding in this book and instead show you how to create views from scratch.

Listing 21.7 The contents of the Index.cshtml file in the Views/Home folder

```
<!DOCTYPE html>
<html>
<head>
    <link href="/lib/bootstrap/css/bootstrap.min.css" rel="stylesheet" />
</head>
<body>
    <h6 class="bg-primary text-white text-center m-2 p-2">
        Product Table
    </h6>
    <div class="m-2">
        <table class="table table-sm table-striped table-bordered">
            <tbody>
                <tr><th>Name</th><td>@Model.Name</td></tr>
                <tr>
                    <th>Price</th>
                    <td>@Model.Price.ToString("c")</td>
                </tr>
            </tbody>
        </table>
    </div>
</body>
</html>
```

The view file contains standard HTML elements that are styled using the Bootstrap CSS framework, which is applied through the `class` attribute. The key view feature is the ability to generate content using C# expressions, like this:

```
...
<tr><th>Name</th><td>@Model.Name</td></tr>
<tr><th>Price</th><td>@Model.Price.ToString("c")</td></tr>
...
```

I explain how these expressions work in the "Understanding the Razor Syntax" section, but for now, it is enough to know that these expressions insert the value of the `Name` and `Price` properties from the `Product` view model passed to the `View` method by the action method in listing 21.5. Restart ASP.NET Core and use a browser to request http://localhost:5000, and you will see the HTML response shown in figure 21.4.

Figure 21.4
A view response

MODIFYING A RAZOR VIEW

The `dotnet watch` command detects and recompiles Razor Views automatically, meaning that the ASP.NET Core runtime doesn't have to be restarted when views are edited. To demonstrate the recompilation process, listing 21.8 adds new elements to the `Index` view.

> **Listing 21.8   Adding Elements in the Index.cshtml File in the Views/Home Folder**

```
<!DOCTYPE html>
<html>
<head>
    <link href="/lib/bootstrap/css/bootstrap.min.css" rel="stylesheet" />
</head>
<body>
    <h6 class="bg-primary text-white text-center m-2 p-2">
        Product Table
    </h6>
    <div class="m-2">
        <table class="table table-sm table-striped table-bordered">
            <tbody>
                <tr><th>Name</th><td>@Model.Name</td></tr>
                <tr>
                    <th>Price</th>
                    <td>@Model.Price.ToString("c")</td>
                </tr>
                <tr><th>Category ID</th><td>@Model.CategoryId</td></tr>
            </tbody>
        </table>
    </div>
</body>
</html>
```

Save the changes to the view; the change will be detected, and the browser will be automatically reloaded to display the change, as shown in figure 21.5.

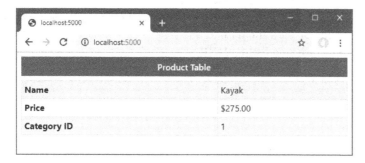

Figure 21.5
Modifying a
Razor View

21.2.4 Selecting a View by name

The action method in listing 21.5 relies entirely on convention, leaving Razor to select the view that is used to generate the response. Action methods can select a view by providing a name as an argument to the `View` method, as shown in listing 21.9.

Listing 21.9   Selecting a view in the HomeController.cs file in the Controllers folder

```
using Microsoft.AspNetCore.Mvc;
using WebApp.Models;

namespace WebApp.Controllers {

    public class HomeController : Controller {
        private DataContext context;

        public HomeController(DataContext ctx) {
            context = ctx;
        }

        public async Task<IActionResult> Index(long id = 1) {
            Product? prod = await context.Products.FindAsync(id);
            if (prod?.CategoryId == 1) {
                return View("Watersports", prod);
            } else {
                return View(prod);
            }
        }
    }
}
```

The action method selects the view based on the `CategoryId` property of the `Product` object that is retrieved from the database. If the `CategoryId` is 1, the action method invokes the `View` method with an additional argument that selects a view named `Watersports`.

```
...
return View("Watersports", prod);
...
```

Notice that the action method doesn't specify the file extension or the location for the view. It is the job of the view engine to translate `Watersports` into a view file.

If you save the `HomeController.cs` file, `dotnet watch` will detect the change and reload the browser, which will cause an error because the view file doesn't exist. To create the view, add a Razor View file named `Watersports.cshtml` to the `Views/Home` folder with the content shown in listing 21.10.

```
<!DOCTYPE html>
<html>
<head>
    <link href="/lib/bootstrap/css/bootstrap.min.css" rel="stylesheet" />
</head>
<body>
    <h6 class="bg-secondary text-white text-center m-2 p-2">
        Watersports
    </h6>
    <div class="m-2">
        <table class="table table-sm table-striped table-bordered">
            <tbody>
                <tr><th>Name</th><td>@Model.Name</td></tr>
                <tr>
                    <th>Price</th>
                    <td>@Model.Price.ToString("c")</td>
                </tr>
                <tr><th>Category ID</th><td>@Model.CategoryId</td></tr>
            </tbody>
        </table>
    </div>
</body>
</html>
```

The new view follows the same pattern as the `Index` view but has a different title above the table. Save the change and request http://localhost:5000/home/index/1 and http://localhost:5000/home/index/4. The action method selects the `Watersports` view for the first URL and the default view for the second URL, producing the two responses shown in figure 21.6.

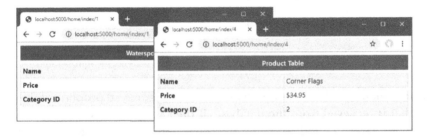

Figure 21.6   Selecting views

USING SHARED VIEWS

When the Razor view engine locates a view, it looks in the `Views/[controller]` folder and then the `Views/Shared` folder. This search pattern means that views that contain common content can be shared between controllers, avoiding duplication. To see how this process works, add a Razor View file named `Common.cshtml` to the `Views/Shared` folder with the content shown in listing 21.11.

Listing 21.11 The contents of the Common.cshtml file in the Views/Shared folder

```
<!DOCTYPE html>
<html>
<head>
    <link href="/lib/bootstrap/css/bootstrap.min.css" rel="stylesheet" />
</head>
<body>
    <h6 class="bg-secondary text-white text-center m-2 p-2">
        Shared View
    </h6>
</body>
</html>
```

Next, add an action method to the `Home` controller that uses the new view, as shown in listing 21.12.

Listing 21.12 Adding an action in the HomeController.cs file in the Controllers folder

```
using Microsoft.AspNetCore.Mvc;
using WebApp.Models;

namespace WebApp.Controllers {

    public class HomeController : Controller {
        private DataContext context;

        public HomeController(DataContext ctx) {
            context = ctx;
        }

        public async Task<IActionResult> Index(long id = 1) {
            Product? prod = await context.Products.FindAsync(id);
            if (prod?.CategoryId == 1) {
                return View("Watersports", prod);
            } else {
                return View(prod);
            }
        }

        public IActionResult Common() {
            return View();
        }
    }
}
```

The new action relies on the convention of using the method name as the name of the view. When a view doesn't require any data to display to the user, the `View` method can be called without arguments. Next, create a new controller by adding a class file named `SecondController.cs` to the `Controllers` folder, with the code shown in listing 21.13.

Listing 21.13   The contents of the SecondController.cs file in the Controllers folder

```
using Microsoft.AspNetCore.Mvc;

namespace WebApp.Controllers {

    public class SecondController : Controller {

        public IActionResult Index() {
            return View("Common");
        }
    }
}
```

The new controller defines a single action, named `Index`, which invokes the `View` method to select the `Common` view. Wait for the application to be built and navigate to http://localhost:5000/home/common and http://localhost:5000/second, both of which will render the `Common` view, producing the responses shown in figure 21.7.

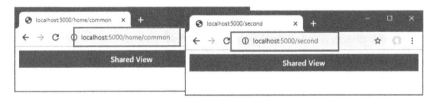

Figure 21.7   Using a shared view

Specifying a view location

The Razor view engine will look for a controller-specific view before a shared view. You can change this behavior by specifying the complete path to a view file, which can be useful if you want to select a shared view that would otherwise be ignored because there is a controller-specific view with the same name.

```
...
public IActionResult Index() {
    return View("/Views/Shared/Common.cshtml");
}
...
```

When specifying the view, the path relative to the project folder must be specified, starting with the / character. Notice that the full name of the file, including the file extension, is used.

This is a technique that should be used sparingly because it creates a dependency on a specific file, rather than allowing the view engine to select the file.

21.3 Working with Razor Views

Razor Views contain HTML elements and C# expressions. Expressions are mixed in with the HTML elements and denoted with the @ character, like this:

```
...
<tr><th>Name</th><td>@Model.Name</td></tr>
...
```

When the view is used to generate a response, the expressions are evaluated, and the results are included in the content sent to the client. This expression gets the name of the Product view model object provided by the action method and produces output like this:

```
...
<tr><th>Name</th><td>Corner Flags</td></tr>
...
```

This transformation can seem like magic, but Razor is simpler than it first appears. Razor Views are converted into C# classes that inherit from the RazorPage class, which are then compiled like any other C# class.

Seeing the compiled output from Razor Views

By default, Razor Views are compiled directly into a DLL, and the generated C# classes are not written to the disk during the build process. You can see the generated classes, by adding the following setting to the WebApp.csproj file, which is accessed in Visual Studio by right-clicking the WebApp item in the Solution Explorer and selecting Edit Project File from the pop-up menu:

```
...
<PropertyGroup>
    <EmitCompilerGeneratedFiles>true</EmitCompilerGeneratedFiles>
</PropertyGroup>
...
```

Save the project file and build the project using the dotnet build command. The C# files generated from the Razor Views will be written to the obj/Debug/net7.0/generated folder. You may have to dig around in the subfolders to find specific files.

The view from listing 21.10, for example, would be transformed into a class like this:

```
namespace AspNetCoreGeneratedDocument {

    using System;
    using System.Collections.Generic;
    using System.Linq;
    using System.Threading.Tasks;
    using Microsoft.AspNetCore.Mvc;
    using Microsoft.AspNetCore.Mvc.Rendering;
    using Microsoft.AspNetCore.Mvc.ViewFeatures;

    internal sealed class Views_Home_Watersports : RazorPage<dynamic> {

        public async override Task ExecuteAsync() {
            WriteLiteral("<!DOCTYPE html>\r\n<html>\r\n");
```

```
            WriteLiteral("<link href=\"");
            WriteLiteral("/lib/bootstrap/css/bootstrap.min.css\"");
            WriteLiteral("rel=\"stylesheet\" />\r\n");
            HeadTagHelper = CreateTagHelper<TagHelpers.HeadTagHelper>();
            __tagHelperExecutionContext.Add(HeadTagHelper);
            Write(__tagHelperExecutionContext.Output);
            WriteLiteral("\r\n");
            __tagHelperExecutionContext =
                    __tagHelperScopeManager.Begin("body",
                TagMode.StartTagAndEndTag, "76ad69...", async() => {
                WriteLiteral("<h6 class=\"bg-secondary text-white ");
                WriteLiteral("text-center m-2 p-2\">Watersports</h6>\n");
                WriteLiteral("<div class=\"m-2\"><table class=\"table ");
                WriteLiteral("table-sm table-striped table-bordered\">");
                WriteLiteral("<tbody>\r\n <tr>");
                WriteLiteral("<th>Name</th><td>");
                Write(Model.Name);
                WriteLiteral("</td></tr>\r\n<tr><th>Price</th><td>");
                Write(Model.Price.ToString("c"));
                WriteLiteral("</td></tr>\r\n<tr><th>Category ID</th><td>");
                Write(Model.CategoryId);
                WriteLiteral("</td></tr>\r\n</tbody>\r\n</table>\r\n");
                WriteLiteral("</div>\r\n");
            });
            BodyTagHelper = CreateTagHelper<TagHelpers.BodyTagHelper>();
            __tagHelperExecutionContext.Add(BodyTagHelper);
            Write(__tagHelperExecutionContext.Output);
            WriteLiteral("\r\n</html>\r\n");
        }


        public IModelExpressionProvider ModelExpressionProvider
            { get; private set; }
        public IUrlHelper Url { get; private set; }
        public IViewComponentHelper Component { get; private set; }
        public IJsonHelper Json { get; private set; }
        public IHtmlHelper<dynamic> Html { get; private set; }
    }
}
```

This class is a simplification of the code that is generated so that I can focus on the features that are most important for this chapter. The first point to note is that the class generated from the view inherits from the RazorPage<T> class.

```
...
internal sealed class Views_Home_Watersports : RazorPage<dynamic> {
...
```

Table 21.3 describes the most useful properties and methods defined by RazorPage<T>.

Caching responses

Responses from views can be cached by applying the ResponseCache attribute to action methods (or to the controller class, which caches the responses from all the action methods). See chapter 17 for details of how response caching is enabled.

Table 21.3 Useful RazorPage<T> members

Name	Description
Context	This property returns the HttpContext object for the current request.
ExecuteAsync()	This method is used to generate the output from the view.
Layout	This property is used to set the view layout, as described in chapter 22.
Model	This property returns the view model passed to the View method by the action.
RenderBody()	This method is used in layouts to include content from a view, as described in chapter 22.
RenderSection()	This method is used in layouts to include content from a section in a view, as described in chapter 22.
TempData	This property is used to access the temp data feature, which is described in chapter 22.
ViewBag	This property is used to access the view bag, which is described in chapter 22.
ViewContext	This property returns a ViewContext object that provides context data.
ViewData	This property returns the view data, which I used for unit testing controllers in the SportsStore application.
Write(str)	This method writes a string, which will be safely encoded for use in HTML.
WriteLiteral(str)	This method writes a string without encoding it for safe use in HTML.

The expressions in the view are translated into calls to the Write method, which encodes the result of the expression so that it can be included safely in an HTML document. The WriteLiteral method is used to deal with the static HTML regions of the view, which don't need further encoding. The result is a fragment like this from the CSHTML file:

```
...
<tr><th>Name</th><td>@Model.Name</td></tr>
...
```

This is converted into a series of C# statements like these in the ExecuteAsync method:

```
...
WriteLiteral("<th>Name</th><td>");
Write(Model.Name);
WriteLiteral("</td></tr>");
...
```

When the ExecuteAsync method is invoked, the response is generated with a mix of the static HTML and the expressions contained in the view. The results from evaluating the expressions are written to the response, producing HTML like this:

```
...
<th>Name</th><td>Kayak</td></tr>
...
```

In addition to the properties and methods inherited from the `RazorPage<T>` class, the generated view class defines the properties described in table 21.4, some of which are used for features described in later chapters.

Table 21.4   The additional View properties

Name	Description
Component	This property returns a helper for working with view components, which is accessed through the `vc` tag helper described in chapter 25.
Html	This property returns an implementation of the `IHtml-Helper` interface. This property is used to manage HTML encoding, as described in chapter 22.
Json	This property returns an implementation of the `IJson-Helper` interface, which is used to encode data as JSON, as described in chapter 22.
ModelExpressionProvider	This property provides access to expressions that select properties from the model, which is used through tag helpers, described in chapters 25–27.
Url	This property returns a helper for working with URLs, as described in chapter 26.

21.3.1 Setting the view model type

The generated class for the `Watersports.cshtml` file is derived from `RazorPage<T>`, but Razor doesn't know what type will be used by the action method for the view model, so it has selected `dynamic` as the generic type argument. This means that the `@Model` expression can be used with any property or method name, which is evaluated at runtime when a response is generated. To demonstrate what happens when a nonexistent member is used, add the content shown in listing 21.14 to the `Watersports.cshtml` file.

Listing 21.14   Adding content in the Watersports.cshtml file in the Views/Home folder

```
<!DOCTYPE html>
<html>
<head>
    <link href="/lib/bootstrap/css/bootstrap.min.css" rel="stylesheet" />
</head>
<body>
    <h6 class="bg-secondary text-white text-center m-2 p-2">
        Watersports
    </h6>
    <div class="m-2">
```

```
        <table class="table table-sm table-striped table-bordered">
            <tbody>
                <tr><th>Name</th><td>@Model.Name</td></tr>
                <tr>
                    <th>Price</th>
                    <td>@Model.Price.ToString("c")</td>
                </tr>
                <tr><th>Category ID</th><td>@Model.CategoryId</td></tr>
                <tr><th>Tax Rate</th><td>@Model.TaxRate</td></tr>
            </tbody>
        </table>
    </div>
</body>
</html>
```

Use a browser to request http://localhost:5000, and you will see the exception shown in figure 21.8. You may need to start ASP.NET Core to see this error because the `dotnet watch` command can be confused when it is unable to load the compiled view.

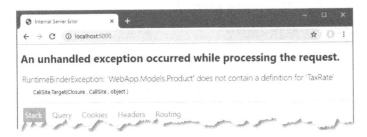

Figure 21.8 Using a nonexistent property in a view expression

To check expressions during development, the type of the `Model` object can be specified using the `model` keyword, as shown in listing 21.15.

TIP It is easy to get the two terms confused. `Model`, with an uppercase `M`, is used in expressions to access the view model object provided by the action method, while `model`, with a lowercase `m`, is used to specify the type of the view model.

Listing 21.15 Declaring the type in the Watersports.cshtml file in the Views/Home folder

```
@model WebApp.Models.Product
<!DOCTYPE html>
<html>
<head>
    <link href="/lib/bootstrap/css/bootstrap.min.css" rel="stylesheet" />
</head>
<body>
    <h6 class="bg-secondary text-white text-center m-2 p-2">
        Watersports
    </h6>
    <div class="m-2">
        <table class="table table-sm table-striped table-bordered">
```

```
            <tbody>
                <tr><th>Name</th><td>@Model.Name</td></tr>
                <tr>
                    <th>Price</th>
                    <td>@Model.Price.ToString("c")</td>
                </tr>
                <tr><th>Category ID</th><td>@Model.CategoryId</td></tr>
                <tr><th>Tax Rate</th><td>@Model.TaxRate</td></tr>
            </tbody>
        </table>
    </div>
</body>
</html>
```

An error warning will appear in the editor after a few seconds, as Visual Studio or Visual Studio Code checks the view in the background, as shown in figure 21.9. When the `dotnet watch` command is used, an error will be displayed in the browser, also shown in figure 21.9. The compiler will also report an error if you build the project or use the `dotnet build` or `dotnet run` command.

Figure 21.9   An error warning in a view file

When the C# class for the view is generated, the view model type is used as the generic type argument for the base class, like this:

```
...
internal sealed class Views_Home_Watersports :
RazorPage<WebApp.Models.Product> {
...
```

Specifying a view model type allows Visual Studio and Visual Studio Code to suggest property and method names as you edit views. Replace the nonexistent property with the one shown in listing 21.16.

Listing 21.16   Using a property in the Watersports.cshtml file in the Views/Home folder

```
@model WebApp.Models.Product
<!DOCTYPE html>
<html>
<head>
    <link href="/lib/bootstrap/css/bootstrap.min.css" rel="stylesheet" />
</head>
<body>
```

```
        <h6 class="bg-secondary text-white text-center m-2 p-2">
            Watersports
        </h6>
        <div class="m-2">
            <table class="table table-sm table-striped table-bordered">
                <tbody>
                    <tr><th>Name</th><td>@Model.Name</td></tr>
                    <tr>
                        <th>Price</th>
                        <td>@Model.Price.ToString("c")</td>
                    </tr>
                    <tr><th>Category ID</th><td>@Model.CategoryId</td></tr>
                    <tr><th>Supplier ID</th><td>@Model.SupplierId</td></tr>
                </tbody>
            </table>
        </div>
    </body>
</html>
```

As you type, the editor will prompt you with the possible member names defined by the view model class, as shown in figure 21.10. This figure shows the Visual Studio code editor, but Visual Studio Code has a comparable feature.

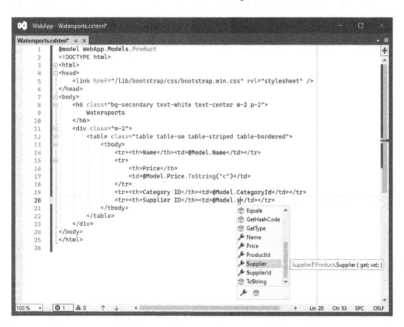

Figure 21.10   Editor suggestions when using a view model type

USING A VIEW IMPORTS FILE

When I declared the view model object at the start of the `Watersports.cshtml` file, I had to include the namespace that contains the class, like this:

```
. . .
@model WebApp.Models.Product
. . .
```

By default, all types that are referenced in a Razor View must be qualified with a namespace. This isn't a big deal when the only type reference is for the model object, but it can make a view more difficult to read when writing more complex Razor expressions such as the ones I describe later in this chapter.

You can specify a set of namespaces that should be searched for types by adding a *view imports* file to the project. The view imports file is placed in the `Views` folder and is named `_ViewImports.cshtml`.

> **NOTE**   Files in the `Views` folder whose names begin with an underscore (the `_` character) are not returned to the user, which allows the file name to differentiate between views that you want to render and the files that support them. View imports files and layouts (which I describe shortly) are prefixed with an underscore.

If you are using Visual Studio, right-click the `Views` folder in the Solution Explorer, select Add > New Item from the pop-up menu, and select the Razor View Imports template from the ASP.NET Core category, as shown in figure 21.11.

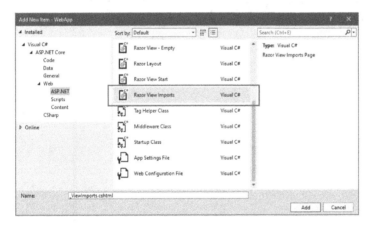

Figure 21.11   Creating a view imports file

Visual Studio will automatically set the name of the file to `_ViewImports.cshtml`, and clicking the Add button will create the file, which will be empty. If you are using Visual Studio Code, simply select the `Views` folder and add a new file called `_ViewImports.cshtml`. Regardless of which editor you used, add the expression shown listing 21.17.

> **Listing 21.17   The contents of the _ViewImports.cshtml file in the Views folder**

```
@using WebApp.Models
```

The namespaces that should be searched for classes used in Razor Views are specified using the `@using` expression, followed by the namespace. In listing 21.17, I have added an entry for the `WebApp.Models` namespace that contains the view model class used in the `Watersports.cshtml` view.

Now that the namespace is included in the view imports file, I can remove the namespace from the view, as shown in listing 21.18.

> **TIP** You can also add an `@using` expression to individual view files, which allows types to be used without namespaces in a single view.

Listing 21.18 Changing type in the Watersports.cshtml file in the Views/Home folder

```
@model Product
<!DOCTYPE html>
<html>
<head>
    <link href="/lib/bootstrap/css/bootstrap.min.css" rel="stylesheet" />
</head>
<body>
    <h6 class="bg-secondary text-white text-center m-2 p-2">
        Watersports
    </h6>
    <div class="m-2">
        <table class="table table-sm table-striped table-bordered">
            <tbody>
                <tr><th>Name</th><td>@Model.Name</td></tr>
                <tr>
                    <th>Price</th>
                    <td>@Model.Price.ToString("c")</td>
                </tr>
                <tr><th>Category ID</th><td>@Model.CategoryId</td></tr>
                <tr><th>Supplier ID</th><td>@Model.SupplierId</td></tr>
            </tbody>
        </table>
    </div>
</body>
</html>
```

Save the view file and use a browser to request http://localhost:5000, and you will see the response shown in figure 21.12.

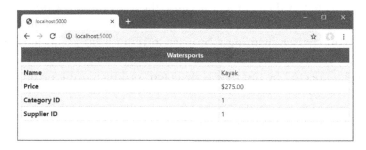

Figure 21.12 Using a view imports file

21.3.2 *Understanding the view model type pitfall*

There is a pitfall waiting for the unwary, which is that the object passed to the `View` method to set the view model isn't type checked before it is used. Here is the definition of the `View` method in the `Controller` class:

```
...
public virtual ViewResult View(object? model) {
    return View(viewName: null, model: model);
}
...
```

When the `@model` expression is used to set the view model type, it changes the base class for the view, and allows the expressions in the view to be checked by the compiler, but it doesn't prevent a controller from using an object with a completely different as the view model. As a simple demonstration, listing 21.19 defines an action method that uses the `Watersports` view but doesn't use the `Product` model type the view expects.

> **Listing 21.19   Adding an action in the HomeController.cs file in the Controllers folder**

```
using Microsoft.AspNetCore.Mvc;
using WebApp.Models;

namespace WebApp.Controllers {

    public class HomeController : Controller {
        private DataContext context;

        public HomeController(DataContext ctx) {
            context = ctx;
        }

        // ...other actions omitted for brevity...

        public IActionResult WrongModel() {
            return View("Watersports", "Hello, World!");
        }
    }
}
```

This mistake isn't detected by the compiler because the `WrongModel` action method is able to pass any object to the `View` method. The problem will only become apparent at runtime, which you can see by using a browser to request http://localhost:5000/home/wrongmodel. When the view is rendered, the mismatch between type of view model and the type expected by the view is detected, producing the error shown in figure 21.13.

Figure 21.13
A view model
type mismatch

UNDERSTANDING THE NULLABLE TYPE PITFALL

A complete type mismatch produces the kind of error shown in figure 21.13. This kind of problem is easy to detect and fix because the error is displayed as soon as the action method is invoked. There is, however, a more subtle mismatch, which can be harder to detect because it doesn't always produce an error. To help illustrate the issue, listing 21.20 sets the view model type in the `Index` view.

> **Listing 21.20 Setting the model type in the Index.cshtml file in the Views/Home folder**

```
@model Product
<!DOCTYPE html>
<html>
<head>
    <link href="/lib/bootstrap/css/bootstrap.min.css" rel="stylesheet" />
</head>
<body>
    <h6 class="bg-primary text-white text-center m-2 p-2">
        Product Table
    </h6>
    <div class="m-2">
        <table class="table table-sm table-striped table-bordered">
            <tbody>
                <tr><th>Name</th><td>@Model.Name</td></tr>
                <tr>
                    <th>Price</th>
                    <td>@Model.Price.ToString("c")</td>
                </tr>
                <tr><th>Category ID</th><td>@Model.CategoryId</td></tr>
            </tbody>
        </table>
    </div>
</body>
</html>
```

Restart ASP.NET Core and use a browser to request two URLs: http://localhost:5000/home/index/1 and http://localhost:5000/home/index/100. These URLs target the same action method, which renders the same view, but the second one produces an error, as shown in figure 21.14.

Figure 21.14   An error caused by a view model type mismatch

This issue arises when an action method uses a nullable type as the view model, which is how I wrote the Index action method in the Home controller in listing 21.9:

```
...
public async Task<IActionResult> Index(long id = 1) {
    Product? prod = await context.Products.FindAsync(id);
    if (prod?.CategoryId == 1) {
        return View("Watersports", prod);
    } else {
        return View(prod);
    }
}
...
```

The result of the LINQ query is a nullable Product, which allows for queries for which there is no data in the database. The action method passes on the result to the View method without filtering out the null values, which mean that requests for which the database contains data work, because they product a Product object, but requests for which there is no data fail, because they produce a null value.

One way to deal with this is to ensure that the action method doesn't pass null values to the View method. But another approach is to update the view so that expects a nullable view model type, as shown in listing 21.21.

Listing 21.21   Changing type in the Index.cshtml file in the Views/Home folder

```
@model Product?
<!DOCTYPE html>
<html>
<head>
    <link href="/lib/bootstrap/css/bootstrap.min.css" rel="stylesheet" />
</head>
<body>
    <h6 class="bg-primary text-white text-center m-2 p-2">
        Product Table
    </h6>
    <div class="m-2">
        <table class="table table-sm table-striped table-bordered">
            <tbody>
                <tr><th>Name</th><td>@Model?.Name</td></tr>
                <tr>
                    <th>Price</th>
                    <td>@Model?.Price.ToString("c")</td>
```

```
            </tr>
            <tr><th>Category ID</th><td>@Model?.CategoryId</td></tr>
          </tbody>
        </table>
      </div>
    </body>
</html>
```

The listing changes the view model type to `Product?`, which is a nullable type. This change requires the use of the null conditional operator to safely deal with null values, like this:

```
...
<tr><th>Name</th><td>@Model?.Name</td></tr>
...
```

This technique is useful when you want to render the view even when the action method produces a null value. Save the changes to the view and use the browser to request http://localhost:5000/home/index/100. The view will be rendered without an exception, but the null conditional operator will produce an empty table, because the null values the operator produces are discarded, as shown in figure 21.15.

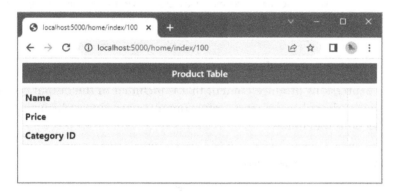

Figure 21.15   Using a nullable view model type

21.4   Understanding the Razor syntax

The Razor compiler separates the static fragments of HTML from the C# expressions, which are then handled separately in the generated class file. There are several types of expression that can be included in views, which I describe in the sections that follow.

21.4.1   Understanding directives

Directives are expressions that give instructions to the Razor view engine. The `@model` expression is a directive, for example, that tells the view engine to use a specific type for the view model, while the `@using` directive tells the view engine to import a namespace. Table 21.5 describes the most useful Razor directives.

Table 21.5   Useful Razor directives

Name	Description
@model	This directive specifies the type of the view model.
@using	This directive imports a namespace.
@page	This directive denotes a Razor Page, described in chapter 23.
@section	This directive denotes a layout section, as described in chapter 22.
@addTagHelper	This directive adds tag helpers to a view, as described in chapter 25.
@namespace	This directive sets the namespace for the C# class generated from a view.
@functions	This directive adds C# properties and methods to the C# class generated from a view and is commonly used in Razor Pages, as described in chapter 23.
@attribute	This directive adds an attribute to the C# class generated from a view. I use this feature to apply authorization restrictions in chapter 38.
@implements	This directive declares that the C# class generated from a view implements an interface. This feature is demonstrated in chapter 36.
@inherits	This directive sets the base class for the C# class generated from a view. This feature is demonstrated in chapter 36.
@inject	This directive provides a view with direct access to a service through dependency injection. This feature is demonstrated in chapter 23.

21.4.2 Understanding content expressions

Razor content expressions produce content that is included in the output generated by a view. Table 21.6 describes the most useful content expressions, which are demonstrated in the sections that follow.

Table 21.6   Useful Razor content expressions

Name	Description
@<expression>	This is the basic Razor expression, which is evaluated, and the result it produces is inserted into the response.
@if	This expression is used to select regions of content based on the result of an expression. See the "Using Conditional Expressions" section for examples.
@switch	This expression is used to select regions of content based on the result of an expression. See the "Using Conditional Expressions" section for examples.
@foreach	This expression generates the same region of content for each element in a sequence. See the "Enumerating Sequences" for examples.
@{ ... }	This expression defines a code block. See the "Using Razor Code Blocks" section for an example.
@:	This expression denotes a section of content that is not enclosed in HTML elements. See the "Using Conditional Expressions" section for an example.
@try	This expression is used to catch exceptions.
@await	This expression is used to perform an asynchronous operation, the result of which is inserted into the response. See chapter 24 for examples.

21.4.3 *Setting element content*

The simplest expressions are evaluated to produce a single value that is used as the content for an HTML element in the response sent to the client. The most common type of expression inserts a value from the view model object, like these expressions from the `Watersports.cshtml` view file:

```
...
<tr><th>Name</th><td>@Model.Name</td></tr>
<tr><th>Price</th><td>@Model.Price.ToString("c")</td></tr>
...
```

This type of expression can read property values or invoke methods, as these examples demonstrate. Views can contain more complex expressions, but these need to be enclosed in parentheses so that the Razor compiler can differentiate between the code and static content, as shown in listing 21.22.

> **Listing 21.22   Expressions in the Watersports.cshtml file in the Views/Home folder**

```
@model Product
<!DOCTYPE html>
<html>
<head>
    <link href="/lib/bootstrap/css/bootstrap.min.css" rel="stylesheet" />
</head>
<body>
    <h6 class="bg-secondary text-white text-center m-2 p-2">
        Watersports
    </h6>
    <div class="m-2">
        <table class="table table-sm table-striped table-bordered">
            <tbody>
                <tr><th>Name</th><td>@Model.Name</td></tr>
                <tr>
                    <th>Price</th>
                    <td>@Model.Price.ToString("c")</td>
                </tr>
                <tr><th>Tax</th><td>@Model.Price * 0.2m</td></tr>
                <tr><th>Tax</th><td>@(Model.Price * 0.2m)</td></tr>
            </tbody>
        </table>
    </div>
</body>
</html>
```

Use a browser to request http://localhost:5000; the response, shown in figure 21.16, shows why parentheses are important.

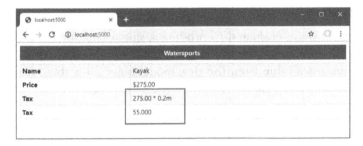

Figure 21.16   Expressions with and without parentheses

The Razor View compiler matches expressions conservatively and has assumed that the asterisk and the numeric value in the first expression are static content. This problem is avoided by parentheses for the second expression.

21.4.4   Setting attribute values

An expression can be used to set the values of element attributes, as shown in listing 21.23.

> **Listing 21.23   Setting Attributes in the Watersports.cshtml File in the Views/Home Folder**

```
@model Product
<!DOCTYPE html>
<html>
<head>
    <link href="/lib/bootstrap/css/bootstrap.min.css" rel="stylesheet" />
</head>
<body>
    <h6 class="bg-secondary text-white text-center m-2 p-2">
        Watersports
    </h6>
    <div class="m-2">
        <table class="table table-sm table-striped table-bordered"
                data-id="@Model.ProductId">
            <tbody>
                <tr><th>Name</th><td>@Model.Name</td></tr>
                <tr>
                    <th>Price</th>
                    <td>@Model.Price.ToString("c")</td>
                </tr>
                <tr><th>Tax</th><td>@Model.Price * 0.2m</td></tr>
                <tr><th>Tax</th><td>@(Model.Price * 0.2m)</td></tr>
            </tbody>
        </table>
    </div>
</body>
</html>
```

I used the Razor expressions to set the value for a `data` attribute on the `table` element.

TIP　Data attributes, which are attributes whose names are prefixed by `data-`, have been an informal way of creating custom attributes for many years and were made part of the formal standard as part of HTML5. They are most often applied so that JavaScript code can locate specific elements or so that CSS styles can be more narrowly applied.

If you request http://localhost:5000 and look at the HTML source that is sent to the browser, you will see that Razor has set the values of the attribute, like this:

```
...
<table class="table table-sm table-striped table-bordered" data-id="1">
    <tbody>
        <tr><th>Name</th><td>Kayak</td></tr>
        <tr><th>Price</th><td>$275.00</td></tr>
        <tr><th>Tax</th><td>275.00 * 0.2m</td></tr>
        <tr><th>Tax</th><td>55.000</td></tr>
    </tbody>
</table>
...
```

21.4.5 *Using conditional expressions*

Razor supports conditional expressions, which means that the output can be tailored based on the view model. This technique is at the heart of Razor and allows you to create complex and fluid responses from views that are simple to read and maintain. In listing 21.24, I have added a conditional statement to the `Watersports` view.

Listing 21.24　An if expression in the Watersports.cshtml file in the Views/Home folder

```
@model Product
<!DOCTYPE html>
<html>
<head>
    <link href="/lib/bootstrap/css/bootstrap.min.css" rel="stylesheet" />
</head>
<body>
    <h6 class="bg-secondary text-white text-center m-2 p-2">
        Watersports
    </h6>
    <div class="m-2">
        <table class="table table-sm table-striped table-bordered"
                data-id="@Model.ProductId">
            <tbody>
                @if (Model.Price > 200) {
                        <tr><th>Name</th><td>Luxury @Model.Name</td></tr>
                } else {
                        <tr><th>Name</th><td>Basic @Model.Name</td></tr>
                }
                <tr>
                    <th>Price</th>
                    <td>@Model.Price.ToString("c")</td>
                </tr>
                <tr><th>Tax</th><td>@Model.Price * 0.2m</td></tr>
```

```
        <tr><th>Tax</th><td>@(Model.Price * 0.2m)</td></tr>
      </tbody>
    </table>
  </div>
</body>
</html>
```

The @ character is followed by the `if` keyword and a condition that will be evaluated at runtime. The `if` expression supports optional `else` and `elseif` clauses and is terminated with a close brace (the } character). If the condition is met, then the content in the `if` clause is inserted into the response; otherwise, the content in the `else` clause is used instead.

Notice that the @ prefix isn't required to access a `Model` property in the condition.

```
...
@if (Model.Price > 200) {
...
```

But the @ prefix is required inside the `if` and `else` clauses, like this:

```
...
<tr><th>Name</th><td>Luxury @Model.Name</td></tr>
...
```

To see the effect of the conditional statement, use a browser to request http://localhost:5000/home/index/1 and http://localhost:5000/home/index/2. The conditional statement will produce different HTML elements for these URLs, as shown in figure 21.17.

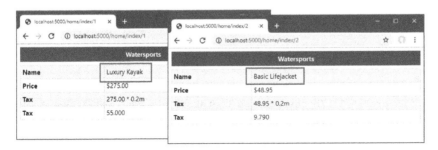

Figure 21.17 Using a conditional statement

Razor also supports @switch expressions, which can be a more concise way of handling multiple conditions, as shown in listing 21.25.

Listing 21.25 A switch in the Watersports.cshtml file in the Views/Home folder

```
@model Product
<!DOCTYPE html>
<html>
<head>
    <link href="/lib/bootstrap/css/bootstrap.min.css" rel="stylesheet" />
</head>
<body>
```

```
    <h6 class="bg-secondary text-white text-center m-2 p-2">
        Watersports
    </h6>
    <div class="m-2">
        <table class="table table-sm table-striped table-bordered"
               data-id="@Model.ProductId">
            <tbody>
                @switch (Model.Name) {
                    case "Kayak":
                        <tr><th>Name</th><td>Small Boat</td></tr>
                        break;
                    case "Lifejacket":
                        <tr><th>Name</th><td>Flotation Aid</td></tr>
                        break;
                    default:
                        <tr><th>Name</th><td>@Model.Name</td></tr>
                        break;
                }
                <tr>
                    <th>Price</th>
                    <td>@Model.Price.ToString("c")</td>
                </tr>
                <tr><th>Tax</th><td>@Model.Price * 0.2m</td></tr>
                <tr><th>Tax</th><td>@(Model.Price * 0.2m)</td></tr>
            </tbody>
        </table>
    </div>
</body>
</html>
```

Conditional expressions can lead to the same blocks of content being duplicated for each result clause. In the `switch` expression, for example, each `case` clause differs only in the content of the `td` element, while the `tr` and `th` elements remain the same. To remove this duplication, conditional expressions can be used within an element, as shown in listing 21.26.

Listing 21.26 Setting content in the Watersports.cshtml file in the Views/Home folder

```
@model Product
<!DOCTYPE html>
<html>
<head>
    <link href="/lib/bootstrap/css/bootstrap.min.css" rel="stylesheet" />
</head>
<body>
    <h6 class="bg-secondary text-white text-center m-2 p-2">
        Watersports
    </h6>
    <div class="m-2">
        <table class="table table-sm table-striped table-bordered"
               data-id="@Model.ProductId">
            <tbody>
                <tr><th>Name</th><td>
                    @switch (Model.Name) {
                        case "Kayak":
                            @:Small Boat
```

```
                                      break;
                        case "Lifejacket":
                            @:Flotation Aid
                            break;
                        default:
                            @Model.Name
                            break;
                    }
                </td></tr>
                <tr>
                    <th>Price</th>
                    <td>@Model.Price.ToString("c")</td>
                </tr>
                <tr><th>Tax</th><td>@Model.Price * 0.2m</td></tr>
                <tr><th>Tax</th><td>@(Model.Price * 0.2m)</td></tr>
            </tbody>
        </table>
    </div>
</body>
</html>
```

The Razor compiler needs help with literal values that are not enclosed in HTML elements, requiring the @: prefix, like this:

```
...
@:Small Boat
...
```

The compiler copes with HTML elements because it detects the open tag, but this additional help is required for text content. To see the effect of the switch statement, use a web browser to request http://localhost:5000/home/index/2, which produces the response shown in figure 21.18.

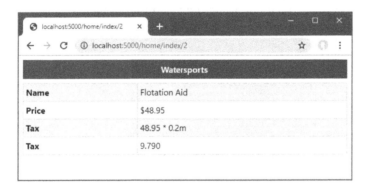

Figure 21.18   Using a switch expression with literal content

21.4.6 *Enumerating sequences*

The Razor @foreach expression generates content for each object in an array or a collection, which is a common requirement when processing data. Listing 21.27 adds an action method to the Home controller that produces a sequence of objects.L

Listing 21.27 Adding an action in the HomeController.cs file in the Controllers folder

```
using Microsoft.AspNetCore.Mvc;
using WebApp.Models;

namespace WebApp.Controllers {

    public class HomeController : Controller {
        private DataContext context;

        public HomeController(DataContext ctx) {
            context = ctx;
        }

        public async Task<IActionResult> Index(long id = 1) {
            Product? prod = await context.Products.FindAsync(id);
            if (prod?.CategoryId == 1) {
                return View("Watersports", prod);
            } else {
                return View(prod);
            }
        }

        public IActionResult Common() {
            return View();
        }

        public IActionResult WrongModel() {
            return View("Watersports", "Hello, World!");
        }

        public IActionResult List() {
            return View(context.Products);
        }
    }
}
```

The new action is called `List`, and it provides its view with the sequence of `Product` objects obtained from the Entity Framework Core data context. Add a Razor View file named `List.cshtml` to the `Views/Home` folder and add the content shown in listing 21.28.

Listing 21.28 The contents of the List.cshtml file in the Views/Home folder

```
@model IEnumerable<Product>
<!DOCTYPE html>
<html>
<head>
    <link href="/lib/bootstrap/css/bootstrap.min.css" rel="stylesheet" />
</head>
<body>
    <h6 class="bg-secondary text-white text-center m-2 p-2">Products</h6>
    <div class="m-2">
        <table class="table table-sm table-striped table-bordered">
```

```
            <thead>
                <tr><th>Name</th><th>Price</th></tr>
            </thead>
            <tbody>
                @foreach (Product p in Model) {
                    <tr><td>@p.Name</td><td>@p.Price</td></tr>
                }
            </tbody>
        </table>
    </div>
</body>
</html>
```

The `foreach` expression follows the same format as the C# `foreach` statement, and
I used the `??` operator to fall back to an empty collection when the model is `null`. In
the example, the variable `p` is assigned each object in the sequence provided by the
action method. The content within the expression is duplicated for each object and
inserted into the response after the expressions it contains are evaluated. In this case,
the content in the `foreach` expression generates a table row with cells that have their
own expressions.

```
...
<td>@p.Name</td><td>@p.Price</td>
...
```

Restart ASP.NET Core so that the new action method will be available and use a
browser to request http://localhost:5000/home/list, which produces the result shown
in figure 21.19, showing how the `foreach` expression populates a table body.

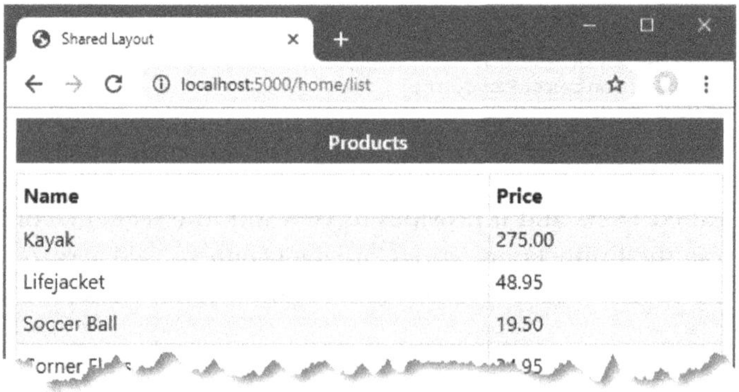

Figure 21.19   Using a foreach expression

21.4.7   Using Razor code blocks

Code blocks are regions of C# content that do not generate content but that can be
useful to perform tasks that support the expressions that do. Listing 21.29 adds a code
block that calculates an average value.

TIP The most common use of code blocks is to select a layout, which is described in chapter 22.

Listing 21.29 Using a code block in the List.cshtml file in the Views/Home folder

```
@model IEnumerable<Product>
@{
    decimal average = Model.Average(p => p.Price);
}
<!DOCTYPE html>
<html>
<head>
    <link href="/lib/bootstrap/css/bootstrap.min.css" rel="stylesheet" />
</head>
<body>
    <h6 class="bg-secondary text-white text-center m-2 p-2">Products</h6>
    <div class="m-2">
        <table class="table table-sm table-striped table-bordered">
            <thead>
                <tr><th>Name</th><th>Price</th></tr>
            </thead>
            <tbody>
                @foreach (Product p in Model) {
                    <tr>
                        <td>@p.Name</td><td>@p.Price</td>
                        <td>@((p.Price / average * 100).ToString("F1"))
                            % of average
                        </td>
                    </tr>
                }
            </tbody>
        </table>
    </div>
</body>
</html>
```

The code block is denoted by @{ and } and contains standard C# statements. The code block in listing 21.29 uses LINQ to calculate a value that is assigned to a variable named average, which is used in an expression to set the contents of a table cell, avoiding the need to repeat the average calculation for each object in the view model sequence. Use a browser to request http://localhost:5000/home/list, and you will see the response shown in figure 21.20.

NOTE Code blocks can become difficult to manage if they contain more than a few statements. For more complex tasks, consider using the view bag, described in chapter 22, or adding a nonaction method to the controller.

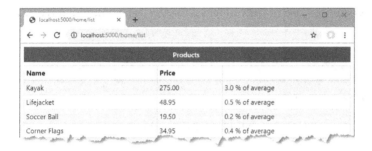

Figure 21.20   Using a code block

Summary

- Razor views are files that combine HTML and code expressions.
- Views are compiled into C# classes whose methods are invoked to generate HTML content.
- Views are selected as results in action methods, optionally passing data that will be used to generate the HTML result.
- Views can be defined with a view model, which allows the code expressions in the view to be type-checked.

Using controllers with
views, part II

This chapter covers

- Using the view bag and temp data to pass data from an action to a view
- Using layouts to define common content
- Using partial views to define reusable sections of content
- Encoding data within views

In this chapter, I describe more of the features provided by Razor Views. I show you how to pass additional data to a view using the view bag and how to use layouts and layout sections to reduce duplication. I also explain how the results from expressions are encoded and how to disable the encoding process. Table 22.1 provides a guide to the chapter.

Table 22.1 Chapter guide

Problem	Solution	Listing
Providing unstructured data to a view	Use the view bag.	5, 6
Providing temporary data to a view	Use temp data.	7, 8
Using the same content in multiple views	Use a layout.	9–12, 15–18
Selecting the default layout for views	Use a view start file.	13, 14
Interleaving unique and common content	Use layout sections.	19–24
Creating reusable sections of content	Use a partial view.	25–29
Inserting HTML into a response using a Razor expression	Encode the HTML.	30–32
Including JSON in a view	Use the JSON encoder.	33

22.1 Preparing for this chapter

This chapter uses the WebApp project from chapter 21. To prepare for this chapter, replace the contents of the `HomeController.cs` file with the code shown in listing 22.1.

> **TIP**   You can download the example project for this chapter—and for all the other chapters in this book—from https://github.com/manningbooks/pro-asp .net-core-7. See chapter 1 for how to get help if you have problems running the examples.

Listing 22.1   The contents of the HomeController.cs file in the Controllers folder

```
using Microsoft.AspNetCore.Mvc;
using WebApp.Models;

namespace WebApp.Controllers {

    public class HomeController : Controller {
        private DataContext context;

        public HomeController(DataContext ctx) {
            context = ctx;
        }

        public async Task<IActionResult> Index(long id = 1) {
            return View(await context.Products.FindAsync(id));
        }

        public IActionResult List() {
            return View(context.Products);
        }
    }
}
```

One of the features used in this chapter requires the session feature, which was described in chapter 16. To enable sessions, add the statements shown in listing 22.2 to the `Program.cs` file.

Listing 22.2   Enabling sessions in the Program.cs file in the WebApp folder

```
using Microsoft.EntityFrameworkCore;
using WebApp.Models;

var builder = WebApplication.CreateBuilder(args);

builder.Services.AddDbContext<DataContext>(opts => {
    opts.UseSqlServer(builder.Configuration[
        "ConnectionStrings:ProductConnection"]);
    opts.EnableSensitiveDataLogging(true);
});

builder.Services.AddControllersWithViews();

builder.Services.AddDistributedMemoryCache();
builder.Services.AddSession(options => {
    options.Cookie.IsEssential = true;
});

var app = builder.Build();

app.UseStaticFiles();
app.UseSession();
app.MapControllers();
app.MapDefaultControllerRoute();

var context = app.Services.CreateScope().ServiceProvider
    .GetRequiredService<DataContext>();
SeedData.SeedDatabase(context);

app.Run();
```

22.1.1 Dropping the database

Open a new PowerShell command prompt, navigate to the folder that contains the `WebApp.csproj` file, and run the command shown in listing 22.3 to drop the database.

Listing 22.3   Dropping the database

```
dotnet ef database drop --force
```

22.1.2 Running the example application

Once the database has been dropped, use the PowerShell command prompt to run the command shown in listing 22.4.

> **Listing 22.4 Running the example application**

```
dotnet watch
```

The database will be seeded as part of the application startup. Once ASP.NET Core is running, use a web browser to request http://localhost:5000, which will produce the response shown in figure 22.1.

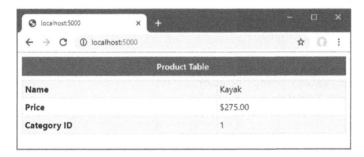

Figure 22.1 Running the example application

As noted in chapter 21, the `dotnet watch` command is useful when working with views, but when you make a change that cannot be handled without restarting ASP. NET Core, you will see a message like this at the command prompt:

```
watch : Unable to apply hot reload because of a rude edit.
watch : Do you want to restart your app - Yes (y) / No (n) /
    Always (a) / Never (v)?
```

The point at which this arises depends on the editor you have chosen, but when this happens, select the `Always` option so that the application will always be restarted when a reload cannot be performed.

22.2 Using the view bag

Action methods provide views with data to display with a view model, but sometimes additional information is required. Action methods can use the *view bag* to provide a view with extra data, as shown in listing 22.5.

> **Listing 22.5 Using the view bag in the HomeController.cs file in the Controllers folder**

```
using Microsoft.AspNetCore.Mvc;
using WebApp.Models;
using Microsoft.EntityFrameworkCore;

namespace WebApp.Controllers {

    public class HomeController : Controller {
        private DataContext context;

        public HomeController(DataContext ctx) {
            context = ctx;
        }
```

```
        public async Task<IActionResult> Index(long id = 1) {
            ViewBag.AveragePrice =
                await context.Products.AverageAsync(p => p.Price);
            return View(await context.Products.FindAsync(id));
        }

        public IActionResult List() {
            return View(context.Products);
        }
    }
}
```

The `ViewBag` property is inherited from the `Controller` base class and returns a `dynamic` object. This allows action methods to create new properties just by assigning values to them, as shown in the listing. The values assigned to the `ViewBag` property by the action method are available to the view through a property also called `ViewBag`, as shown in listing 22.6.

> **Listing 22.6 Using the view bag in the Index.cshtml file in the Views/Home folder**

```
@model Product?
<!DOCTYPE html>
<html>
<head>
    <link href="/lib/bootstrap/css/bootstrap.min.css" rel="stylesheet" />
</head>
<body>
    <h6 class="bg-primary text-white text-center m-2 p-2">
        Product Table
    </h6>
    <div class="m-2">
        <table class="table table-sm table-striped table-bordered">
            <tbody>
                <tr><th>Name</th><td>@Model?.Name</td></tr>
                <tr>
                    <th>Price</th>
                    <td>
                        @Model?.Price.ToString("c")
                        (@ (((Model?.Price / ViewBag.AveragePrice)
                                * 100).ToString("F2"))% of average price)
                    </td>
                </tr>
                <tr><th>Category ID</th><td>@Model?.CategoryId</td></tr>
            </tbody>
        </table>
    </div>
</body>
</html>
```

The `ViewBag` property conveys the object from the action to the view, alongside the view model object. In the listing, the action method queries for the average of the `Product.Price` properties in the database and assigns it to a view bag property named `AveragePrice`, which the view uses in an expression. Use a browser to request http://localhost:5000, which produces the response shown in figure 22.2.

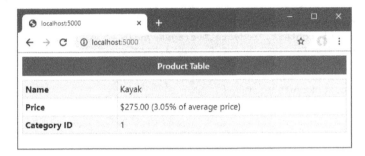

Figure 22.2   Using the view bag

When to use the view bag

The view bag works best when it is used to provide the view with small amounts of supplementary data without having to create new view model classes for each action method. The problem with the view bag is that the compiler cannot check the use of the properties on dynamic objects, much like views that don't use an @model expression. It can be difficult to judge when a new view model class should be used, and my rule of thumb is to create a new view model class when the same view bag property is used by multiple actions or when an action method adds more than two or three properties to the view bag.

22.3   Using temp data

The temp data feature allows a controller to preserve data from one request to another, which is useful when performing redirections. Temp data is stored using a cookie unless session state is enabled when it is stored as session data. Unlike session data, temp data values are marked for deletion when they are read and removed when the request has been processed.

Add a class file called CubedController.cs to the WebApp/Controllers folder and use it to define the controller shown in listing 22.7.

Listing 22.7   The contents of the CubedController.cs file in the Controllers folder

```
using Microsoft.AspNetCore.Mvc;

namespace WebApp.Controllers {
    public class CubedController: Controller {

        public IActionResult Index() {
            return View("Cubed");
        }

        public IActionResult Cube(double num) {
            TempData["value"] = num.ToString();
```

```
            TempData["result"] = Math.Pow(num, 3).ToString();
            return RedirectToAction(nameof(Index));
        }
    }
}
```

The `Cubed` controller defines an `Index` method that selects a view named `Cubed`. There is also a `Cube` action, which relies on the model binding process to obtain a value for its `num` parameter from the request (a process described in detail in chapter 28). The `Cubed` action method performs its calculation and stores the `num` value and the calculation result using `TempData` property, which returns a dictionary that is used to store key-value pairs. Since the temp data feature is built on top of the sessions feature, only values that can be serialized to strings can be stored, which is why I convert both double values to strings in listing 22.7. Once the values are stored as temp data, the `Cube` method performs a redirection to the `Index` method. To provide the controller with a view, add a Razor View file named `Cubed.cshtml` to the `WebApp/Views/Shared` folder with the content shown in listing 22.8.

> **Listing 22.8　The contents of the Cubed.cshtml file in the Views/Shared folder**

```
<!DOCTYPE html>
<html>
<head>
    <link href="/lib/bootstrap/css/bootstrap.min.css" rel="stylesheet" />
</head>
<body>
    <h6 class="bg-secondary text-white text-center m-2 p-2">Cubed</h6>
    <form method="get" action="/cubed/cube" class="m-2">
        <div class="form-group">
            <label>Value</label>
            <input name="num" class="form-control"
            value="@(TempData["value"])" />
        </div>
        <button class="btn btn-primary mt-1" type="submit">
            Submit
        </button>
    </form>
    @if (TempData["result"] != null) {
            <div class="bg-info text-white m-2 p-2">
                The cube of @TempData["value"] is @TempData["result"]
            </div>
    }
</body>
</html>
```

The base class used for Razor Views provides access to the temp data through a `TempData` property, allowing values to be read within expressions. In this case, temp data is used to set the content of an `input` element and display a results summary. Reading a temp data value doesn't remove it immediately, which means that values can be read repeatedly in the same view. It is only once the request has been processed that the marked values are removed.

To see the effect, use a browser to navigate to http://localhost:5000/cubed, enter a value into the form field, and click the Submit button. The browser will send a request that will set the temp data and trigger the redirection. The temp data values are preserved for the new request, and the results are displayed to the user. But reading the data values marks them for deletion, and if you reload the browser, the contents of the input element and the results summary are no longer displayed, as shown in figure 22.3.

TIP The object returned by the TempData property provides a Peek method, which allows you to get a data value without marking it for deletion, and a Keep method, which can be used to prevent a previously read value from being deleted. The Keep method doesn't protect a value forever. If the value is read again, it will be marked for removal once more. Use session data if you want to store items so that they won't be removed when the request is processed.

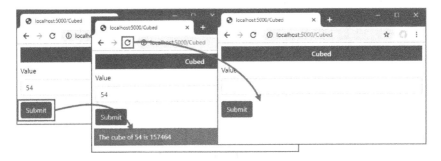

Figure 22.3   Using temp data

Using the temp data attribute

Controllers can define properties that are decorated with the TempData attribute, which is an alternative to using the TempData property, like this:

```
using Microsoft.AspNetCore.Mvc;

namespace WebApp.Controllers {
    public class CubedController: Controller {

        public IActionResult Index() {
            return View("Cubed");
        }

        public IActionResult Cube(double num) {
            Value = num.ToString();
            Result = Math.Pow(num, 3).ToString();
            return RedirectToAction(nameof(Index));
        }

        [TempData]
```

(continued)

```
        public string? Value { get; set; }


        [TempData]
        public string? Result { get; set; }
    }
}
```

The values assigned to these properties are automatically added to the temp data store, and there is no difference in the way they are accessed in the view. My preference is to use the `TempData` dictionary to store values because it makes the intent of the action method obvious to other developers. However, both approaches are entirely valid, and choosing between them is a matter of preference.

22.4   Working with layouts

The views in the example application contain duplicate elements that deal with setting up the HTML document, defining the `head` section, loading the Bootstrap CSS file, and so on. Razor supports *layouts*, which consolidate common content in a single file that can be used by any view.

Layouts are typically stored in the `Views/Shared` folder because they are usually used by the action methods of more than one controller. If you are using Visual Studio, right-click the `Views/Shared` folder, select Add > New Item from the pop-up menu, and choose the Razor Layout template, as shown in figure 22.4. Make sure the name of the file is `_Layout.cshtml` and click the Add button to create the new file. Replace the content added to the file by Visual Studio with the elements shown in listing 22.9.

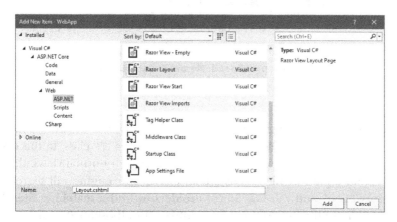

Figure 22.4   Creating a layout

If you are using Visual Studio Code, create a file named `_Layout.cshtml` in the `Views/Shared` folder and add the content shown in listing 22.9.

Listing 22.9   The contents of the _Layout.cshtml file in the Views/Shared folder

```
<!DOCTYPE html>
<html>
<head>
    <link href="/lib/bootstrap/css/bootstrap.min.css" rel="stylesheet" />
</head>
<body>
    <h6 class="bg-primary text-white text-center m-2 p-2">Shared View</h6>
    @RenderBody()
</body>
</html>
```

The layout contains the common content that will be used by multiple views. The content that is unique to each view is inserted into the response by calling the `RenderBody` method, which is inherited by the `RazorPage<T>` class, as described in chapter 21. Views that use layouts can focus on just their unique content, as shown in listing 22.10.

Listing 22.10   Using a layout in the Index.cshtml file in the Views/Home folder

```
@model Product?
@{
    Layout = "_Layout";
}
<div class="m-2">
    <table class="table table-sm table-striped table-bordered">
        <tbody>
            <tr><th>Name</th><td>@Model?.Name</td></tr>
            <tr>
                <th>Price</th>
                <td>
                    @Model?.Price.ToString("c")
                    (@(((Model?.Price / ViewBag.AveragePrice)
                            * 100).ToString("F2"))% of average price)
                </td>
            </tr>
            <tr><th>Category ID</th><td>@Model?.CategoryId</td></tr>
        </tbody>
    </table>
</div>
```

The layout is selected by adding a code block, denoted by the `@{` and `}` characters, that sets the `Layout` property inherited from the `RazorPage<T>` class. In this case, the `Layout` property is set to the name of the layout file. As with normal views, the layout is specified without a path or file extension, and the Razor engine will search in the `/Views/[controller]` and `/Views/Shared` folders to find a matching file. Restart ASP.NET Core and use the browser to request http://localhost:5000, and you will see the response shown in figure 22.5.

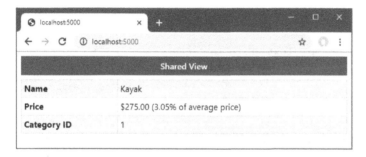

Figure 22.5   Using a layout

22.4.1   Configuring layouts using the view bag

The view can provide the layout with data values, allowing the common content provided by the view to be customized. The view bag properties are defined in the code block that selects the layout, as shown in listing 22.11.

Listing 22.11   Setting a property in the Index.cshtml file in the Views/Home folder

```
@model Product?
@{
    Layout = "_Layout";
    ViewBag.Title = "Product Table";
}
<div class="m-2">
    <table class="table table-sm table-striped table-bordered">
        <tbody>
            <tr><th>Name</th><td>@Model?.Name</td></tr>
            <tr>
                <th>Price</th>
                <td>
                    @Model?.Price.ToString("c")
                    (@(((Model?.Price / ViewBag.AveragePrice)
                            * 100).ToString("F2"))% of average price)
                </td>
            </tr>
            <tr><th>Category ID</th><td>@Model?.CategoryId</td></tr>
        </tbody>
    </table>
</div>
```

The view sets a `Title` property, which can be used in the layout, as shown in listing 22.12.

Listing 22.12   Using a property in the _Layout.cshtml file in the Views/Shared folder

```
<!DOCTYPE html>
<html>
<head>
    <title>@ViewBag.Title</title>
```

```
    <link href="/lib/bootstrap/css/bootstrap.min.css" rel="stylesheet" />
</head>
<body>
    <h6 class="bg-primary text-white text-center m-2 p-2">
        @(ViewBag.Title ?? "Layout")
    </h6>
    @RenderBody()
</body>
</html>
```

The `Title` property is used to set the content of the `title` element and `h6` element in the `body` section. Layouts cannot rely on view bag properties being defined, which is why the expression in the `h6` element provides a fallback value if the view doesn't define a `Title` property. To see the effect of the view bag property, use a browser to request http://localhost:5000, which produces the response shown in figure 22.6.

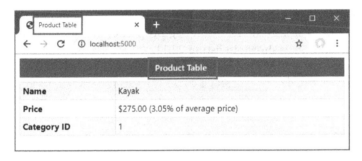

Figure 22.6   Using a view bag property to configure a layout

---

Understanding view bag precedence

The values defined by the view take precedence if the same view bag property is defined by the view and the action method. If you want to allow the action to override the value defined in the view, then use a statement like this in the view code block:

```
...
@{
    Layout = "_Layout";
    ViewBag.Title = ViewBag.Title ?? "Product Table";
}
...
```

This statement will set the value for the `Title` property only if it has not already been defined by the action method.

22.4.2   Using a view start file

Instead of setting the `Layout` property in every view, you can add a *view start* file to the project that provides a default `Layout` value. If you are using Visual Studio, right-click the `Views` folder item in the Solution Explorer, select Add > New Item, and locate the

Razor View Start template, as shown in figure 22.7. Make sure the name of the file is
`_ViewStart.cshtml` and click the Add button to create the file, which will have the
content shown in listing 22.13.

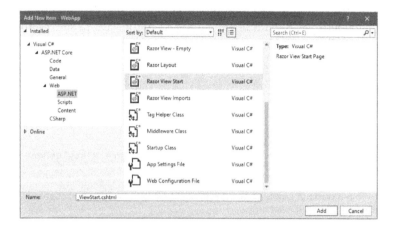

Figure 22.7   Creating a view start file

If you are using Visual Studio Code, then add a file named `_ViewStart.cshtml` to the
`Views` folder and add the content shown in listing 22.13.

Listing 22.13   The contents of the _ViewStart.cshtml file in the Views folder

```
@{
    Layout = "_Layout";
}
```

The file sets the `Layout` property, and the value will be used as the default. Listing
22.14 simplifies the `Common.cshtml` file, leaving just content that is unique to the view.

Listing 22.14   Removing content in the Common.cshtml file in the Views/Shared folder

```
<h6 class="bg-secondary text-white text-center m-2 p-2">Shared View</h6>
```

The view doesn't define a view model type and doesn't need to set the `Layout` property
because the project contains a view start file. The result is that the content in listing
22.14 will be added to the `body` section of the HTML content of the response. Use a
browser to navigate to http://localhost:5000/second, and you will see the response in
figure 22.8.

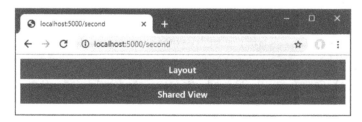

**Figure 22.8
Using a view
start file**

22.4.3 *Overriding the default layout*

There are two situations where you may need to define a Layout property in a view even when there is a view start file in the project. In the first situation, a view requires a different layout from the one specified by the view start file. To demonstrate, add a Razor layout file named _ImportantLayout.cshtml to the Views/Shared folder with the content shown in listing 22.15.

> **Listing 22.15 The _ImportantLayout.cshtml file in the Views/Shared folder**

```
<!DOCTYPE html>
<html>
<head>
    <title>@ViewBag.Title</title>
    <link href="/lib/bootstrap/css/bootstrap.min.css" rel="stylesheet" />
</head>
<body>
    <h3 class="bg-warning text-white text-center p-2 m-2">Important</h3>
    @RenderBody()
</body>
</html>
```

In addition to the HTML document structure, this file contains a header element that displays Important in large text. Views can select this layout by assigning its name to the Layout property, as shown in listing 22.16.

> **TIP** If you need to use a different layout for all the actions of a single controller, then add a view start file to the Views/[controller] folder that selects the view you require. The Razor engine will use the layout specified by the controller-specific view start file.

> **Listing 22.16 Using a specific layout in the Index.cshtml file in the Views/Home folder**

```
@model Product?
@{
    Layout = "_ImportantLayout";
    ViewBag.Title = "Product Table";
}
<div class="m-2">
    <table class="table table-sm table-striped table-bordered">
        <tbody>
            <tr><th>Name</th><td>@Model?.Name</td></tr>
            <tr>
                <th>Price</th>
                <td>
                    @Model?.Price.ToString("c")
                    (@(((Model?.Price / ViewBag.AveragePrice)
                        * 100).ToString("F2"))% of average price)
                </td>
            </tr>
            <tr><th>Category ID</th><td>@Model?.CategoryId</td></tr>
        </tbody>
    </table>
</div>
```

The `Layout` value in the view start file is overridden by the value in the view, allowing different layouts to be applied. Restart ASP.NET Core and use a browser to request http://localhost:5000, and the response will be produced using the new layout, as shown in figure 22.9.

Selecting a layout programmatically

The value that a view assigns to the `Layout` property can be the result of an expression that allows layouts to be selected by the view, similar to the way that action methods can select views. Here is an example that selects the layout based on a property defined by the view model object:

```
...
@model Product?
@{
    Layout = Model.Price > 100 ? "_ImportantLayout" : "_Layout";
    ViewBag.Title = "Product Table";
}
...
```

The layout named `_ImportantLayout` is selected when the value of the view model object's `Price` property is greater than 100; otherwise, `_Layout` is used.

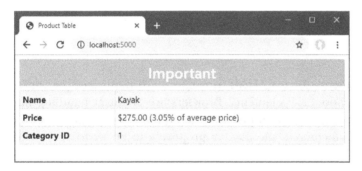

Figure 22.9 Specifying a layout in a view

The second situation where a `Layout` property can be needed is when a view contains a complete HTML document and doesn't require a layout at all. To see the problem, open a new PowerShell command prompt and run the command shown in listing 22.17.

Listing 22.17 Sending an HTTP request

```
Invoke-WebRequest http://localhost:5000/home/list |
    Select-Object -expand Content
```

This command sends an HTTP GET request whose response will be produced using the `List.cshtml` file in the `Views/Home` folder. This view contains a complete HTML document, which is combined with the content in the view specified by the view start file, producing a malformed HTML document, like this:

```
<!DOCTYPE html>
<html>
<head>
    <title></title>
    <link href="/lib/bootstrap/css/bootstrap.min.css" rel="stylesheet" />
</head>
<body>
    <h6 class="bg-primary text-white text-center m-2 p-2">Layout</h6>
    <!DOCTYPE html>
<html>
<head>
    <link href="/lib/bootstrap/css/bootstrap.min.css" rel="stylesheet" />
</head>
<body>
    <h6 class="bg-secondary text-white text-center m-2 p-2">Products</h6>
    <div class="m-2">
        <table class="table table-sm table-striped table-bordered">
            <thead><tr><th>Name</th><th>Price</th></tr></thead>
            <tbody>

                <!-- ...table rows omitted for brevity... >

            </tbody>
        </table>
    </div>
</body>
</html>
</body>
</html>
```

The structural elements for the HTML document are duplicated, so there are two html, head, body, and link elements. Browsers are adept at handling malformed HTML but don't always cope with poorly structured content. Where a view contains a complete HTML document, the Layout property can be set to null, as shown in listing 22.18.

> **Listing 22.18   Disabling layouts in the List.cshtml file in the Views/Home folder**

```
@model IEnumerable<Product>
@{
    Layout = null;
    decimal average = Model.Average(p => p.Price);
}
<!DOCTYPE html>
<html>
<head>
    <link href="/lib/bootstrap/css/bootstrap.min.css" rel="stylesheet" />
</head>
<body>
    <h6 class="bg-secondary text-white text-center m-2 p-2">Products</h6>
    <div class="m-2">
        <table class="table table-sm table-striped table-bordered">
```

```
        <thead>
            <tr><th>Name</th><th>Price</th></tr>
        </thead>
        <tbody>
            @foreach (Product p in Model) {
                <tr>
                    <td>@p.Name</td><td>@p.Price</td>
                    <td>@((p.Price / average * 100).ToString("F1"))
                        % of average
                    </td>
                </tr>
            }
        </tbody>
    </table>
</div>
</body>
</html>
```

Save the view and run the command shown in listing 22.17 again, and you will see that the response contains only the elements in the view and that the layout has been disabled.

```
<!DOCTYPE html>
<html>
<head>
    <link href="/lib/bootstrap/css/bootstrap.min.css" rel="stylesheet" />
</head>
<body>
    <h6 class="bg-secondary text-white text-center m-2 p-2">Products</h6>
    <div class="m-2">
        <table class="table table-sm table-striped table-bordered">
            <thead><tr><th>Name</th><th>Price</th></tr></thead>
            <tbody>
                <!-- ...table rows omitted for brevity... >

            </tbody>
        </table>
    </div>
</body>
</html>
```

22.4.4 *Using layout sections*

The Razor View engine supports the concept of *sections*, which allow you to provide regions of content within a layout. Razor sections give greater control over which parts of the view are inserted into the layout and where they are placed. To demonstrate the sections feature, I have edited the /Views/Home/Index.cshtml file, as shown in listing 22.19. The browser will display an error when you save the changes in this listing, which will be resolved when you make corresponding changes in the next listing.

> **Listing 22.19**   **Defining sections in the Index.cshtml file in the Views/Home folder**

```
@model Product?
@{
    Layout = "_Layout";
```

```
    ViewBag.Title = "Product Table";
}


@section Header {
    Product Information
}


<tr><th>Name</th><td>@Model?.Name</td></tr>
<tr>
    <th>Price</th>
    <td>@Model?.Price.ToString("c")</td>
</tr>
<tr><th>Category ID</th><td>@Model?.CategoryId</td></tr>

@section Footer {
    @(((Model?.Price / ViewBag.AveragePrice)
            * 100).ToString("F2"))% of average price
}
```

Sections are defined using the Razor `@section` expression followed by a name for the section. Listing 22.19 defines sections named `Header` and `Footer`, and sections can contain the same mix of HTML content and expressions, just like the main part of the view. Sections are applied in a layout with the `@RenderSection` expression, as shown in listing 22.20.

> **Listing 22.20   Using sections in the _Layout.cshtml file in the Views/Shared folder**

```
<!DOCTYPE html>
<html>
<head>
    <title>@ViewBag.Title</title>
    <link href="/lib/bootstrap/css/bootstrap.min.css" rel="stylesheet" />
</head>
<body>
    <div class="bg-info text-white m-2 p-1">
        This is part of the layout
    </div>

    <h6 class="bg-primary text-white text-center m-2 p-2">
        @RenderSection("Header")
    </h6>

    <div class="bg-info text-white m-2 p-1">
        This is part of the layout
    </div>

    <div class="m-2">
        <table class="table table-sm table-striped table-bordered">
            <tbody>
                @RenderBody()
            </tbody>
        </table>
    </div>
```

```
    <div class="bg-info text-white m-2 p-1">
        This is part of the layout
    </div>

    <h6 class="bg-primary text-white text-center m-2 p-2">
        @RenderSection("Footer")
    </h6>

    <div class="bg-info text-white m-2 p-1">
        This is part of the layout
    </div>
</body>
</html>
```

When the layout is applied, the `RenderSection` expression inserts the content of the specified section into the response. The regions of the view that are not contained within a section are inserted into the response by the `RenderBody` method. To see how the sections are applied, use a browser to request http://localhost:5000, which provides the response shown in figure 22.10.

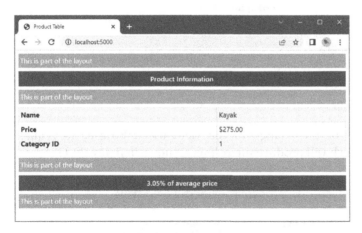

Figure 22.10 Using sections in a layout

> **NOTE** A view can define only the sections that are referred to in the layout. The view engine throws an exception if you define sections in the view for which there is no corresponding `@RenderSection` expression in the layout.

Sections allow views to provide fragments of content to the layout without specifying how they are used. As an example, listing 22.21 redefines the layout to consolidate the body and sections into a single HTML table.

Listing 22.21 Using a table in the _Layout.cshtml file in the Views/Shared folder

```
<!DOCTYPE html>
<html>
<head>
```

```
    <title>@ViewBag.Title</title>
    <link href="/lib/bootstrap/css/bootstrap.min.css" rel="stylesheet" />
</head>
<body>
    <div class="m-2">
        <table class="table table-sm table-striped table-bordered">
            <thead>
                <tr>
                    <th class="bg-primary text-white text-center"
                            colspan="2">
                        @RenderSection("Header")
                    </th>
                </tr>
            </thead>
            <tbody>
                @RenderBody()
            </tbody>
            <tfoot>
                <tr>
                    <th class="bg-primary text-white text-center"
                            colspan="2">
                        @RenderSection("Footer")
                    </th>
                </tr>
            </tfoot>
        </table>
    </div>
</body>
</html>
```

To see the effect of the change to the view, use a browser to request http://
localhost:5000, which will produce the response shown in figure 22.11.

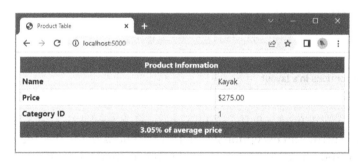

Figure 22.11   Changing how sections are displayed in a layout

USING OPTIONAL LAYOUT SECTIONS

By default, a view must contain all the sections for which there are `RenderSection`
calls in the layout, and an exception will be thrown if the layout requires a section that
the view hasn't defined. Listing 22.22 adds a call to the `RenderSection` method that
requires a section named `Summary`.

Listing 22.22 Adding a section in the _Layout.cshtml file in the Views/Shared folder

```html
<!DOCTYPE html>
<html>
<head>
    <title>@ViewBag.Title</title>
    <link href="/lib/bootstrap/css/bootstrap.min.css" rel="stylesheet" />
</head>
<body>
    <div class="m-2">
        <table class="table table-sm table-striped table-bordered">
            <thead>
                <tr>
                    <th class="bg-primary text-white text-center"
                            colspan="2">
                        @RenderSection("Header")
                    </th>
                </tr>
            </thead>
            <tbody>
                @RenderBody()
            </tbody>
            <tfoot>
                <tr>
                    <th class="bg-primary text-white text-center"
                            colspan="2">
                        @RenderSection("Footer")
                    </th>
                </tr>
            </tfoot>
        </table>
    </div>
    @RenderSection("Summary")
</body>
</html>
```

Restart ASP.NET Core and use a browser to request http://localhost:5000, and you will see the exception shown in figure 22.12. You may have to restart the `dotnet watch` command to see this error.

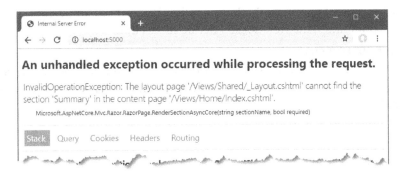

Figure 22.12 Attempting to render a nonexistent view section

There are two ways to solve this problem. The first is to create an optional section, which will be rendered only if it is defined by the view. Optional sections are created by passing a second argument to the RenderSection method, as shown in listing 22.23.

Listing 22.23   An optional section in the _Layout.cshtml file in the Views/Shared folder

```
<!DOCTYPE html>
<html>
<head>
    <title>@ViewBag.Title</title>
    <link href="/lib/bootstrap/css/bootstrap.min.css" rel="stylesheet" />
</head>
<body>
    <div class="m-2">
        <table class="table table-sm table-striped table-bordered">
            <thead>
                <tr>
                    <th class="bg-primary text-white text-center"
                            colspan="2">
                        @RenderSection("Header", false)
                    </th>
                </tr>
            </thead>
            <tbody>
                @RenderBody()
            </tbody>
            <tfoot>
                <tr>
                    <th class="bg-primary text-white text-center"
                            colspan="2">
                        @RenderSection("Footer", false)
                    </th>
                </tr>
            </tfoot>
        </table>
    </div>
    @RenderSection("Summary", false)
</body>
</html>
```

The second argument specifies whether a section is required, and using false prevents an exception when the view doesn't define the section.

TESTING FOR LAYOUT SECTIONS

The IsSectionDefined method is used to determine whether a view defines a specified section and can be used in an if expression to render fallback content, as shown in listing 22.24.

Listing 22.24   Checking a section in the _Layout.cshtml file in the Views/Shared folder

```
<!DOCTYPE html>
<html>
<head>
    <title>@ViewBag.Title</title>
```

```
        <link href="/lib/bootstrap/css/bootstrap.min.css" rel="stylesheet" />
</head>
<body>
    <div class="m-2">
        <table class="table table-sm table-striped table-bordered">
            <thead>
                <tr>
                    <th class="bg-primary text-white text-center"
                            colspan="2">
                        @RenderSection("Header", false)
                    </th>
                </tr>
            </thead>
            <tbody>
                @RenderBody()
            </tbody>
            <tfoot>
                <tr>
                    <th class="bg-primary text-white text-center"
                            colspan="2">
                        @RenderSection("Footer", false)
                    </th>
                </tr>
            </tfoot>
        </table>
    </div>
    @if (IsSectionDefined("Summary")) {
        @RenderSection("Summary", false)
    } else {
        <div class="bg-info text-center text-white m-2 p-2">
            This is the default summary
        </div>
    }
</body>
</html>
```

The `IsSectionDefined` method is invoked with the name of the section you want to check and returns `true` if the view defines that section. In the example, I used this helper to render fallback content when the view does not define the `Summary` section. To see the fallback content, use a browser to request http://localhost:5000, which produces the response shown in figure 22.13.

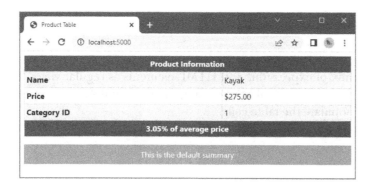

Figure 22.13 Displaying fallback content for a view section

22.5   *Using partial views*

You will often need to use the same set of HTML elements and expressions in several different places. *Partial views* are views that contain fragments of content that will be included in other views to produce complex responses without duplication.

22.5.1   *Enabling partial views*

Partial views are applied using a feature called *tag helpers*, which are described in detail in chapter 25; tag helpers are configured in the view imports file, which was added to the project in chapter 21. To enable the feature required for partial views, add the statement shown in listing 22.25 to the _ViewImports.cshtml file.

> **Listing 22.25   Enabling tag helpers in the _ViewImports.cshtml file in the Views folder**

```
@using WebApp.Models
@addTagHelper *, Microsoft.AspNetCore.Mvc.TagHelpers
```

22.5.2   *Creating a partial view*

Partial views are just regular CSHTML files, and it is only the way they are used that differentiates them from standard views. If you are using Visual Studio, right-click the Views/Home folder, select Add > New Item, and use the Razor View template to create a file named _RowPartial.cshtml. Once the file has been created, replace the contents with those shown in listing 22.26. If you are using Visual Studio Code, add a file named _RowPartial.cshtml to the Views/Home folder and add to it the content shown in listing 22.26.

> **TIP** Visual Studio provides some tooling support for creating prepopulated partial views, but the simplest way to create a partial view is to create a regular view using the Razor View item template.

> **Listing 22.26   The contents of the _RowPartial.cshtml file in the Views/Home folder**

```
@model Product

<tr>
    <td>@Model.Name</td>
    <td>@Model.Price</td>
</tr>
```

The model expression is used to define the view model type for the partial view, which contains the same mix of expressions and HTML elements as regular views. The content of this partial view creates a table row, using the Name and Price properties of a Product object to populate the table cells.

22.5.3 *Applying a partial view*

Partial views are applied by adding a `partial` element in another view or layout. In listing 22.27, I have added the element to the `List.cshtml` file so the partial view is used to generate the rows in the table.

Listing 22.27   Using a partial view in the List.cshtml file in the Views/Home folder

```
@model IEnumerable<Product>
@{
    Layout = null;
    decimal average = Model.Average(p => p.Price);
}
<!DOCTYPE html>
<html>
<head>
    <link href="/lib/bootstrap/css/bootstrap.min.css" rel="stylesheet" />
</head>
<body>
    <h6 class="bg-secondary text-white text-center m-2 p-2">Products</h6>
    <div class="m-2">
        <table class="table table-sm table-striped table-bordered">
            <thead>
                <tr><th>Name</th><th>Price</th></tr>
            </thead>
            <tbody>
                @foreach (Product p in Model) {
                    <partial name="_RowPartial" model="p" />
                }
            </tbody>
        </table>
    </div>
</body>
</html>
```

The attributes applied to the `partial` element control the selection and configuration of the partial view, as described in table 22.2.

Table 22.2   The partial element attributes

Name	Description
`name`	This property specifies the name of the partial view, which is located using the same search process as regular views.
`model`	This property specifies the value that will be used as the view model object for the partial view.
`for`	This property is used to define an expression that selects the view model object for the partial view, as explained next.
`view-data`	This property is used to provide the partial view with additional data.

The `partial` element in listing 22.27 uses the `name` attribute to select the `_Row-Partial` view and the `model` attribute to select the `Product` object that will be used as the view model object. The `partial` element is applied within the `@foreach` expression, which means that it will be used to generate each row in the table, which you can see by using a browser to request http://localhost:5000/home/list to produce the response shown in figure 22.14.

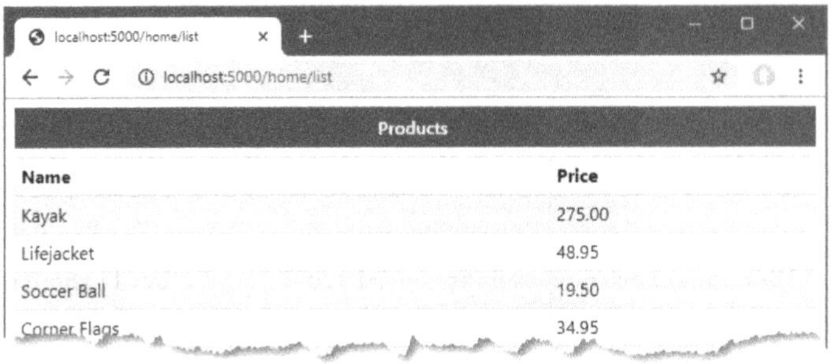

Figure 22.14   Using a partial view

SELECTING THE PARTIAL VIEW MODEL USING AN EXPRESSION

The `for` attribute is used to set the partial view's model using an expression that is applied to the view's model, which is a feature more easily demonstrated than described. Add a partial view named `_CellPartial.cshtml` to the `Views/Home` folder with the content shown in listing 22.28.

Listing 22.28   The contents of the _CellPartial.cshtml file in the Views/Home folder

```
@model string

<td class="bg-info text-white">@Model</td>
```

This partial view has a string view model object, which it uses as the contents of a table cell element; the table cell element is styled using the Bootstrap CSS framework. In listing 22.29, I have added a `partial` element to the `_RowPartial.cshtml` file that uses the `_CellPartial` partial view to display the table cell for the name of the `Product` object.

Listing 22.29   Using a partial in the _RowPartial.cshtml file in the Views/Home folder

```
@model Product

<tr>
    <partial name="_CellPartial" for="Name" />
    <td>@Model.Price</td>
</tr>
```

The `for` attribute selects the `Name` property as the model for the `_CellPartial` partial view. To see the effect, use a browser to request http://localhost:5000/home/list, which will produce the response shown in figure 22.15.

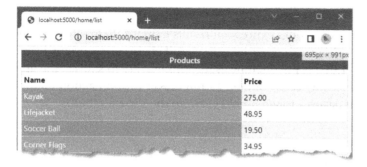

Figure 22.15 Selecting a model property for use in a partial view

Using templated delegates

Templated delegates are an alternative way of avoiding duplication in a view. Templated delegates are defined in a code block, like this:

```
...
@{
    Func<Product, object> row
        = @<tr><td>@item.Name</td><td>@item.Price</td></tr>;
}
...
```

The template is a function that accepts a `Product` input object and returns a dynamic result. Within the template expression, the input object is referred to as `item` in expressions. The templated delegate is invoked as a method expression to generate content.

```
...
<tbody>
    @foreach (Product p in Model) {
        @row(p)
    }
</tbody>
...
```

I find this feature awkward and prefer using partial views, although this is a matter of preference and habit rather than any objective problems with the way that templated delegates work.

22.6 Understanding content-encoding

Razor Views provide two useful features for encoding content. The HTML content-encoding feature ensures that expression responses don't change the structure of the response sent to the browser, which is an important security feature. The JSON encoding feature encodes an object as JSON and inserts it into the response, which can be a useful debugging feature and can also be useful when providing data to JavaScript applications. Both encoding features are described in the following sections.

22.6.1 Understanding HTML encoding

The Razor View engine encodes expression results to make them safe to include in an HTML document without changing its structure. This is an important feature when dealing with content that is provided by users, who may try to subvert the application or accidentally enter dangerous content. Listing 22.30 adds an action method to the Home controller that passes a fragment of HTML to the `View` method.

> **Listing 22.30   Adding an action in the HomeController.cs file in the Controllers folder**

```
using Microsoft.AspNetCore.Mvc;
using WebApp.Models;
using Microsoft.EntityFrameworkCore;

namespace WebApp.Controllers {

    public class HomeController : Controller {
        private DataContext context;

        public HomeController(DataContext ctx) {
            context = ctx;
        }

        public async Task<IActionResult> Index(long id = 1) {
            ViewBag.AveragePrice =
                await context.Products.AverageAsync(p => p.Price);
            return View(await context.Products.FindAsync(id));
        }

        public IActionResult List() {
            return View(context.Products);
        }

        public IActionResult Html() {
            return View((object)"This is a <h3><i>string</i></h3>");
        }
    }
}
```

The new action passes a string that contains HTML elements. To create the view for the new action method, add a Razor View file named `Html.cshtml` to the `Views/Home` folder with the content shown in listing 22.31.

> **TIP**   Notice that I cast the string passed to the `View` method as an object, without which the string is assumed to be the name of a view and not the view model object.

```
@model string
@{
    Layout = null;
}
<!DOCTYPE html>
<html>
<head>
    <link href="/lib/bootstrap/css/bootstrap.min.css" rel="stylesheet" />
</head>
<body>
    <div class="bg-secondary text-white text-center m-2 p-2">
        @Model
    </div>
</body>
</html>
```

Save the file and use a browser to request http://localhost:5000/home/html. The response, which is shown on the left of figure 22.16, shows how the potentially dangerous characters in the view model string have been escaped.

To include the result of an expression without safe encoding, you can invoke the `Html.Raw` method. The `Html` property is one of the properties added to the generated view class, described in chapter 21, which returns an object that implements the `IHtmlHelper` interface, as shown in listing 22.32.

```
@model string
@{
    Layout = null;
}
<!DOCTYPE html>
<html>
<head>
    <link href="/lib/bootstrap/css/bootstrap.min.css" rel="stylesheet" />
</head>
<body>
    <div class="bg-secondary text-white text-center m-2 p-2">
        @Html.Raw(Model)
    </div>
</body>
</html>
```

Save the changes, and you will see that the view model string is passed on without being encoded and is then interpreted by the browser as part of the HTML document, as shown on the right of figure 22.16.

Figure 22.16   HTML result encoding

CAUTION   Do not disable safe encoding unless you are entirely confident that no malicious content will be passed to the view. Careless use of this feature presents a security risk to your application and your users.

22.6.2   *Understanding JSON encoding*

The Json property, which is added to the class generated from the view, as described in chapter 21, can be used to encode an object as JSON. The most common use for JSON data is in RESTful web services, as described in earlier chapters, but I find the Razor JSON encoding feature useful as a debugging aid when I don't get the output I expect from a view. Listing 22.33 adds a JSON representation of the view model object to the output produced by the Index.cshtml view.

Listing 22.33   Using JSON encoding in the Index.cshtml file in the Views/Home folder

```
@model Product?
@{
    Layout = "_Layout";
    ViewBag.Title = "Product Table";
}

@section Header {
    Product Information
}

<tr><th>Name</th><td>@Model?.Name</td></tr>
<tr>
    <th>Price</th>
    <td>@Model?.Price.ToString("c")</td>
</tr>
<tr><th>Category ID</th><td>@Model?.CategoryId</td></tr>

@section Footer {
    @(((Model?.Price / ViewBag.AveragePrice)
            * 100).ToString("F2"))% of average price
}

@section Summary {
    <div class="bg-info text-white m-2 p-2">
        @Json.Serialize(Model)
    </div>
}
```

The `Json` property returns an implementation of the `IJsonHelper` interface, whose `Serialize` method produces a JSON representation of an object. Use a browser to request http://localhost:5000, and you will see the response shown in figure 22.17, which includes JSON in the `Summary` section of the view.

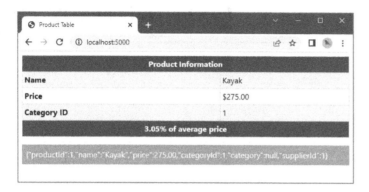

Figure 22.17   Encoding an expression result as JSON

Summary

- The view bag is used to pass unstructured data to a view, in addition to the view model.
- Temp data is similar to the view bag but is deleted once the data values have been read.
- Layouts define common content, such as the header of an HTML document.
- The default layout can be specified by creating a view start file.
- Layouts can contain sections, which can be optional or mandatory.
- Partial views define sections of content that can be reused within views.

Using Razor Pages

In this chapter, I introduce how to use Razor Pages, which is a simpler approach to generating HTML content, intended to capture some of the enthusiasm for the legacy ASP.NET Web Pages framework. I explain how Razor Pages work, explain how they differ from the controllers and views approach taken by the MVC Framework, and show you how they fit into the wider ASP.NET Core platform.

The process of explaining how Razor Pages work can minimize the differences from the controllers and views described in earlier chapters. You might form the impression that Razor Pages are just MVC-lite and dismiss them, which would be a shame. Razor Pages are interesting because of the developer experience and not the way they are implemented.

My advice is to give Razor Pages a chance, especially if you are an experienced MVC developer. Although the technology used will be familiar, the process of creating application features is different and is well-suited to small and tightly focused features that don't require the scale and complexity of controllers and views. I have been using the MVC Framework since it was first introduced, and I admit to ignoring the early releases of Razor Pages. Now, however, I find myself mixing Razor Pages and the MVC Framework in most projects, much as I did in the SportsStore example in part 1. Table 23.1 puts Razor Pages in context.

Table 23.1 Putting Razor Pages in context

Question	Answer
What are they?	Razor Pages are a simplified way of generating HTML responses.
Why are they useful?	The simplicity of Razor Pages means you can start getting results sooner than with the MVC Framework, which can require a relatively complex preparation process. Razor Pages are also easier for less experienced web developers to understand because the relationship between the code and content is more obvious.
How are they used?	Razor Pages associate a single view with the class that provides it with features and use a file-based routing system to match URLs.
Are there any pitfalls or limitations?	Razor Pages are less flexible than the MVC Framework, which makes them unsuitable for complex applications. Razor Pages can be used only to generate HTML responses and cannot be used to create RESTful web services.
Are there any alternatives?	The MVC Framework's approach of controllers and views can be used instead of Razor Pages.

Table 23.2 provides a guide to the chapter.

Table 23.2 Chapter guide

Problem	Solution	Listing
Enabling Razor Pages	Use `AddRazorPages` and `MapRazor-Pages` to set up the required services and middleware.	3
Creating a self-contained endpoint	Create a Razor Page.	4, 26, 27
Routing requests to a Razor Page	Use the name of the page or specify a route using the `@page` directive.	5–8
Providing logic to support the view section of a Razor Page	Use a page model class.	9–12
Creating results that are not rendered using the view section of a Razor Page	Define a handler method that returns an action result.	13–15
Handling multiple HTTP methods	Define handlers in the page model class.	16–18
Avoiding duplication of content	Use a layout or a partial view.	19–25

23.1   *Preparing for this chapter*

This chapter uses the WebApp project from chapter 22. Open a new PowerShell command prompt, navigate to the folder that contains the `WebApp.csproj` file, and run the command shown in listing 23.1 to drop the database.

> **TIP**   You can download the example project for this chapter—and for all the other chapters in this book—from https://github.com/manningbooks/pro-asp .net-core-7. See chapter 1 for how to get help if you have problems running the examples.

Listing 23.1   Dropping the database

```
dotnet ef database drop --force
```

23.1.1   *Running the example application*

Once the database has been dropped, use the PowerShell command prompt to run the command shown in listing 23.2.

Listing 23.2   Running the example application

```
dotnet run
```

The database will be seeded as part of the application startup. Once ASP.NET Core is running, use a web browser to request http://localhost:5000, which will produce the response shown in figure 23.1.

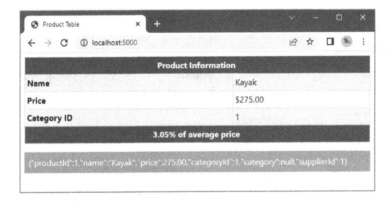

Figure 23.1   Running the example application

The `dotnet watch` command can be useful with Razor Pages development, but it doesn't handle the initial configuration of the services and middleware or changes to the routing configuration, which is why I have returned to the `dotnet run` command in this chapter.

23.2 Understanding Razor Pages

As you learn how Razor Pages work, you will see they share functionality with the MVC Framework. In fact, Razor Pages are typically described as a simplification of the MVC Framework—which is true—but that doesn't give any sense of why Razor Pages can be useful.

The MVC Framework solves every problem in the same way: a controller defines action methods that select views to produce responses. It is a solution that works because it is so flexible: the controller can define multiple action methods that respond to different requests, the action method can decide which view will be used as the request is being processed, and the view can depend on private or shared partial views to produce its response.

Not every feature in web applications needs the flexibility of the MVC Framework. For many features, a single action method will be used to handle a wide range of requests, all of which are dealt with using the same view. Razor Pages offer a more focused approach that ties together markup and C# code, sacrificing flexibility for focus.

But Razor Pages have limitations. Razor Pages tend to start out focusing on a single feature but slowly grow out of control as enhancements are made. And, unlike MVC controllers, Razor Pages cannot be used to create web services.

You don't have to choose just one model because the MVC Framework and Razor Pages coexist, as demonstrated in this chapter. This means that self-contained features can be easily developed with Razor Pages, leaving the more complex aspects of an application to be implemented using the MVC controllers and actions.

In the sections that follow, I show you how to configure and use Razor Pages, and then I explain how they work and demonstrate the common foundation they share with MVC controllers and actions.

23.2.1 Configuring Razor Pages

To prepare the application for Razor Pages, statements must be added to the `Program.cs` file to set up services and configure the endpoint routing system, as shown in listing 23.3.

> **Listing 23.3 Configuring the application in the Program.cs file in the WebApp folder**

```
using Microsoft.EntityFrameworkCore;
using WebApp.Models;

var builder = WebApplication.CreateBuilder(args);

builder.Services.AddDbContext<DataContext>(opts => {
    opts.UseSqlServer(builder.Configuration[
        "ConnectionStrings:ProductConnection"]);
    opts.EnableSensitiveDataLogging(true);
});

builder.Services.AddControllersWithViews();
```

```
builder.Services.AddRazorPages();

builder.Services.AddDistributedMemoryCache();
builder.Services.AddSession(options => {
    options.Cookie.IsEssential = true;
});

var app = builder.Build();

app.UseStaticFiles();
app.UseSession();
app.MapControllers();
app.MapDefaultControllerRoute();
app.MapRazorPages();

var context = app.Services.CreateScope().ServiceProvider
    .GetRequiredService<DataContext>();
SeedData.SeedDatabase(context);

app.Run();
```

The AddRazorPages method sets up the service that is required to use Razor Pages, and the MapRazorPages method creates the routing configuration that matches URLs to pages, which is explained later in the chapter.

23.2.2 Creating a Razor Page

Razor Pages are defined in the Pages folder. If you are using Visual Studio, create the WebApp/Pages folder, right-click it in the Solution Explorer, select Add > New Item from the pop-up menu, and select the Razor Page template, as shown in figure 23.2. Set the Name field to Index.cshtml and click the Add button to create the file and replace the contents of the file with those shown in listing 23.4.

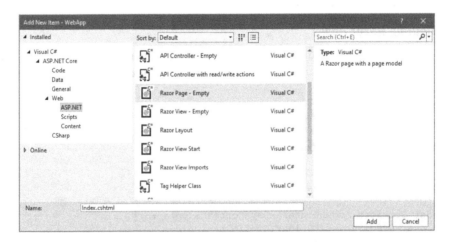

Figure 23.2   Creating a Razor Page

If you are using Visual Studio Code, create the WebApp/Pages folder and add to it a new file named Index.cshtml with the content shown in listing 23.4.

Listing 23.4 The contents of the Index.cshtml file in the Pages folder

```
@page
@model IndexModel
@using Microsoft.AspNetCore.Mvc.RazorPages
@using WebApp.Models;

<!DOCTYPE html>
<html>
<head>
    <link href="/lib/bootstrap/css/bootstrap.min.css" rel="stylesheet" />
</head>
<body>
    <div class="bg-primary text-white text-center m-2 p-2">
        @Model.Product?.Name
    </div>
</body>
</html>

@functions {

    public class IndexModel : PageModel {
        private DataContext context;

        public Product? Product { get; set; }

        public IndexModel(DataContext ctx) {
            context = ctx;
        }

        public async Task OnGetAsync(long id = 1) {
            Product = await context.Products.FindAsync(id);
        }
    }
}
```

Razor Pages use the Razor syntax that I described in chapters 21 and 22, and Razor Pages even use the same CSHTML file extension. But there are some important differences.

The @page directive must be the first thing in a Razor Page, which ensures that the file is not mistaken for a view associated with a controller. But the most important difference is that the @functions directive is used to define the C# code that supports the Razor content in the same file. I explain how Razor Pages work shortly, but to see the output generated by the Razor Page, restart ASP.NET Core and use a browser to request http://localhost:5000/index, which produces the response shown in figure 23.3.

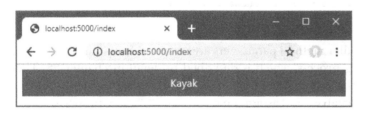

**Figure 23.3
Using a Razor
Page**

UNDERSTANDING THE URL ROUTING CONVENTION

URL routing for Razor Pages is based on the file name and location, relative to the Pages folder. The Razor Page in listing 23.4 is in a file named Index.cshtml, in the Pages folder, which means that it will handle requests for the /index. The routing convention can be overridden, as described in the "Understanding Razor Pages Routing" section, but, by default, it is the location of the Razor Page file that determines the URLs that it responds to.

UNDERSTANDING THE PAGE MODEL

In a Razor Page, the @model directive is used to select a *page model* class, rather than identifying the type of the object provided by an action method. The @model directive in listing 23.4 selects the IndexModel class.

```
...
@model IndexModel
...
```

The page model is defined within the @functions directive and is derived from the PageModel class, like this:

```
...
@functions {
    public class IndexModel: PageModel {
...
```

When the Razor Page is selected to handle an HTTP request, a new instance of the page model class is created, and dependency injection is used to resolve any dependencies that have been declared using constructor parameters, using the features described in chapter 14. The IndexModel class declares a dependency on the DataContext service created in chapter 18, which allows it to access the data in the database.

```
...
public IndexModel(DataContext ctx) {
    context = ctx;
}
...
```

After the page model object has been created, a handler method is invoked. The name of the handler method is On, followed by the HTTP method for the request so that the OnGet method is invoked when the Razor Page is selected to handle an HTTP GET request. Handler methods can be asynchronous, in which case a GET request will invoke the OnGetAsync method, which is the method implemented by the IndexModel class.

```
...
public async Task OnGetAsync(long id = 1) {
    Product = await context.Products.FindAsync(id);
}
...
```

Values for the handler method parameters are obtained from the HTTP request using the model binding process, which is described in detail in chapter 28. The OnGet-Async method receives the value for its id parameters from the model binder, which it uses to query the database and assign the result to its Product property.

UNDERSTANDING THE PAGE VIEW

Razor Pages use the same mix of HTML fragments and code expressions to generate content, which defines the view presented to the user. The page model's methods and properties are accessible in the Razor Page through the @Model expression. The Product property defined by the IndexModel class is used to set the content of an HTML element, like this:

```
...
<div class="bg-primary text-white text-center m-2 p-2">
    @Model.Product?.Name
</div>
...
```

The @Model expression returns an IndexModel object, and this expression reads the Name property of the object returned by the Product property.

The null conditional operator (?) isn't required for the Model property because it will always be assigned an instance of the page model class and cannot be null. The properties defined by the page model class can be null, however, which is why I have used the operator for the Product property in the Razor expression:

```
...
<div class="bg-primary text-white text-center m-2 p-2">
    @Model.Product?.Name
</div>
...
```

UNDERSTANDING THE GENERATED C# CLASS

Behind the scenes, Razor Pages are transformed into C# classes, just like regular Razor views. Here is a simplified version of the C# class that is produced from the Razor Page in listing 23.4:

```
namespace AspNetCoreGeneratedDocument {

    using System;
    using System.Collections.Generic;
    using System.Linq;
    using System.Threading.Tasks;
    using Microsoft.AspNetCore.Mvc;
    using Microsoft.AspNetCore.Mvc.Rendering;
    using Microsoft.AspNetCore.Mvc.ViewFeatures;
    using Microsoft.AspNetCore.Mvc.RazorPages;
    using WebApp.Models;

    internal sealed class Pages_Index :
            Microsoft.AspNetCore.Mvc.RazorPages.Page {

        public async override global::System.Threading.Tasks.Task
                ExecuteAsync() {
            WriteLiteral("\r\n<!DOCTYPE html>\r\n<html>\r\n");
            __tagHelperExecutionContext =
                __tagHelperScopeManager.Begin("head",
                    TagMode.StartTagAndEndTag, "7d534...",
                    async() => {
```

```
                WriteLiteral("\r\n<link href=\"" +
                    "/lib/bootstrap/css/bootstrap.min.css\"" +
                    "rel=\"stylesheet\" />\r\n");
            });
        HeadTagHelper = CreateTagHelper<TagHelpers.HeadTagHelper>();
        __tagHelperExecutionContext.Add(HeadTagHelper);
        Write(__tagHelperExecutionContext.Output);
        WriteLiteral("\r\n");
        __tagHelperExecutionContext =
            __tagHelperScopeManager.Begin("body",
                TagMode.StartTagAndEndTag, "7d534...", async() => {
            WriteLiteral("\r\n<div class=\"bg-primary text-white " +
                "text-center m-2 p-2\">");
            Write(Model.Product?.Name);
            WriteLiteral("</div>\r\n");
        });
        BodyTagHelper = CreateTagHelper<TagHelpers.BodyTagHelper>();
        __tagHelperExecutionContext.Add(BodyTagHelper);
        Write(__tagHelperExecutionContext.Output);
        WriteLiteral("\r\n</html>\r\n\r\n");
    }

    public class IndexModel: PageModel {
        private DataContext context;

        public Product? Product { get; set; }

        public IndexModel(DataContext ctx) {
            context = ctx;
        }

        public async Task OnGetAsync(long id = 1) {
            Product = await context.Products.FindAsync(id);
        }
    }

    public IModelExpressionProvider ModelExpressionProvider
        { get; private set; }
    public IUrlHelper Url { get; private set; }
    public IViewComponentHelper Component { get; private set; }
    public IJsonHelper Json { get; private set; }
    public IHtmlHelper<IndexModel> Html { get; private set; }
    public ViewDataDictionary<IndexModel> ViewData =>
        (ViewDataDictionary<IndexModel>)PageContext?.ViewData;
    public IndexModel Model => ViewData.Model;
    }
}
```

If you compare this code with the equivalent shown in chapter 21, you can see how Razor Pages rely on the same features used by the MVC Framework. The HTML fragments and view expressions are transformed into calls to the WriteLiteral and Write methods.

TIP The process for seeing the generated C# classes for Razor Pages is the same as for regular Razor Views, as described in chapter 21.

23.3 Understanding Razor Pages routing

Razor Pages rely on the location of the CSHTML file for routing so that a request for http://localhost:5000/index is handled by the `Pages/Index.cshtml` file. Adding a more complex URL structure for an application is done by adding folders whose names represent the segments in the URL you want to support. As an example, create the `WebApp/Pages/Suppliers` folder and add to it a Razor Page named `List.cshtml` with the contents shown in listing 23.5.

> **Listing 23.5 The contents of the List.cshtml file in the Pages/Suppliers folder**

```
@page
@model ListModel
@using Microsoft.AspNetCore.Mvc.RazorPages
@using WebApp.Models;

<!DOCTYPE html>
<html>
<head>
    <link href="/lib/bootstrap/css/bootstrap.min.css" rel="stylesheet" />
</head>
<body>
    <h5 class="bg-primary text-white text-center m-2 p-2">Suppliers</h5>
    <ul class="list-group m-2">
        @foreach (string s in Model.Suppliers) {
            <li class="list-group-item">@s</li>
        }
    </ul>
</body>
</html>

@functions {

    public class ListModel : PageModel {
        private DataContext context;

        public IEnumerable<string> Suppliers { get; set; }
            = Enumerable.Empty<string>();

        public ListModel(DataContext ctx) {
            context = ctx;
        }

        public void OnGet() {
            Suppliers = context.Suppliers.Select(s => s.Name);
        }
    }
}
```

The new page model class defines a `Suppliers` property that is set to the sequence of `Name` values for the `Supplier` objects in the database. The database operation in this example is synchronous, so the page model class defined the `OnGet` method, rather than `OnGetAsync`. The supplier names are displayed in a list using an `@foreach` expression. To use the new Razor Page, restart ASP.NET Core and use a browser to request http://localhost:5000/suppliers/list, which produces the response shown in figure 23.4. The path segments of the request URL correspond to the folder and file name of the `List.cshtml` Razor Page.

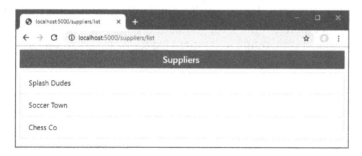

Figure 23.4   Using a folder structure to route requests

Understanding the default URL handling

The `MapRazorPages` method sets up a route for the default URL for the `Index.cshtml` Razor Page, following a similar convention used by the MVC Framework. It is for this reason that the first Razor Page added to a project is usually called `Index.cshtml`. However, when the application mixes Razor Pages and the MVC Framework together, the default route defined by Razor Pages takes precedence because it was created with a lower order (route ordering is described in chapter 13). This means a request http://localhost:5000 is handled by the `Index.cshtml` Razor Page in the example project and not the `Index` action on the `Home` controller.

If you want the MVC framework to handle the default URL, then you can change the order assigned to the Razor Pages routes, like this:

```
...
app.MapRazorPages().Add(b => ((RouteEndpointBuilder)b).Order = 2);
...
```

The Razor Pages routes are created with an `Order` of 0, which gives them precedence over the MVC routes, which are created with an `Order` of 1. Assigning an `Order` of 2 gives the MVC framework routes precedence.

In my own projects, where I mix Razor Pages and MVC controllers, I tend to rely on the MVC Framework to handle the default URL, and I avoid creating the `Index.cshtml` Razor Page to avoid confusion.

23.3.1 Specifying a routing pattern in a Razor Page

Using the folder and file structure to perform routing means there are no segment variables for the model binding process to use. Instead, values for the request handler methods are obtained from the URL query string, which you can see by using a browser to request http://localhost:5000/index?id=2, which produces the response shown in figure 23.5.

Figure 23.5 Using a query string parameter

The query string provides a parameter named `id`, which the model binding process uses to satisfy the `id` parameter defined by the `OnGetAsync` method in the `Index` Razor Page.

```
...
public async Task OnGetAsync(long id = 1) {
...
```

I explain how model binding works in detail in chapter 28, but for now, it is enough to know that the query string parameter in the request URL is used to provide the `id` argument when the `OnGetAsync` method is invoked, which is used to query the database for a product.

The `@page` directive can be used with a routing pattern, which allows segment variables to be defined, as shown in listing 23.6.

> **Listing 23.6 Defining a segment variable in the Index.cshtml file in the Pages folder**

```
@page "{id:long?}"
@model IndexModel
@using Microsoft.AspNetCore.Mvc.RazorPages
@using WebApp.Models;

<!DOCTYPE html>
<html>
<head>
    <link href="/lib/bootstrap/css/bootstrap.min.css" rel="stylesheet" />
</head>
<body>
    <div class="bg-primary text-white text-center m-2 p-2">
        @Model.Product?.Name
    </div>
</body>
</html>

@functions {

    // ...statements omitted for brevity...
}
```

All the URL pattern features that are described in chapter 13 can be used with the `@page` directive. The route pattern used in listing 23.6 adds an optional segment variable named `id`, which is constrained so that it will match only those segments that can be parsed to a `long` value. To see the change, restart ASP.NET Core and use a browser to request http://localhost:5000/index/4, which produces the response shown on the left of figure 23.6.

The @page directive can also be used to override the file-based routing convention for a Razor Page, as shown in listing 23.7.

> **Listing 23.7 Changing the route in the List.cshtml file in the Pages/Suppliers folder**

```
@page "/lists/suppliers"
@model ListModel
@using Microsoft.AspNetCore.Mvc.RazorPages
@using WebApp.Models;

<!DOCTYPE html>
<html>
<head>
    <link href="/lib/bootstrap/css/bootstrap.min.css" rel="stylesheet" />
</head>
<body>
    <h5 class="bg-primary text-white text-center m-2 p-2">Suppliers</h5>
    <ul class="list-group m-2">
        @foreach (string s in Model.Suppliers) {
            <li class="list-group-item">@s</li>
        }
    </ul>
</body>
</html>

@functions {

    // ...statements omitted for brevity...
}
```

The directive changes the route for the List page so that it matches URLs whose path is /lists/suppliers. To see the effect of the change, restart ASP.NET Core and request http://localhost:5000/lists/suppliers, which produces the response shown on the right of figure 23.6.

Figure 23.6 Changing routes using the @page directive

23.3.2 Adding routes for a Razor Page

Using the @page directive replaces the default file-based route for a Razor Page. If you want to define multiple routes for a page, then configuration statements can be added to the Program.cs file, as shown in listing 23.8.

> **Listing 23.8   Adding Razor Page routes in the Program.cs file in the WebApp folder**

```
using Microsoft.EntityFrameworkCore;
using WebApp.Models;
using Microsoft.AspNetCore.Mvc.RazorPages;

var builder = WebApplication.CreateBuilder(args);

builder.Services.AddDbContext<DataContext>(opts => {
    opts.UseSqlServer(builder.Configuration[
        "ConnectionStrings:ProductConnection"]);
    opts.EnableSensitiveDataLogging(true);
});

builder.Services.AddControllersWithViews();
builder.Services.AddRazorPages();

builder.Services.AddDistributedMemoryCache();
builder.Services.AddSession(options => {
    options.Cookie.IsEssential = true;
});

builder.Services.Configure<RazorPagesOptions>(opts => {
    opts.Conventions.AddPageRoute("/Index", "/extra/page/{id:long?}");
});

var app = builder.Build();

app.UseStaticFiles();
app.UseSession();
app.MapControllers();
app.MapDefaultControllerRoute();
app.MapRazorPages();

var context = app.Services.CreateScope().ServiceProvider
    .GetRequiredService<DataContext>();
SeedData.SeedDatabase(context);

app.Run();
```

The options pattern is used to add additional routes for a Razor Page using the
RazorPageOptions class. The AddPageRoute extension method is called on the
Conventions property to add a route for a page. The first argument is the path to the
page, without the file extension and relative to the Pages folder. The second argument is the URL pattern to add to the routing configuration. To test the new route,
restart ASP.NET Core and use a browser to request http://localhost:5000/extra/
page/2, which is matched by the URL pattern added in listing 23.8 and produces the
response shown on the left of figure 23.7. The route added in listing 23.8 supplements
the route defined by the @page attribute, which you can test by requesting http://
localhost:5000/index/2, which will produce the response shown on the right of figure
23.7.

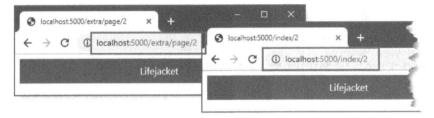

Figure 23.7   Adding a route for a Razor Page

23.4   Understanding the Page model class

Page models are derived from the `PageModel` class, which provides the link between the rest of ASP.NET Core and the view part of the Razor Page. The `PageModel` class provides methods for managing how requests are handled and properties that provide context data, the most useful of which are described in table 23.3. I have listed these properties for completeness, but they are not often required in Razor Page development, which focuses more on selecting the data that is required to render the view part of the page.

Table 23.3   Selected PageModel properties for context data

Name	Description
HttpContext	This property returns an `HttpContext` object, described in chapter 12.
ModelState	This property provides access to the model binding and validation features described in chapters 28 and 29.
PageContext	This property returns a `PageContext` object that provides access to many of the same properties defined by the `PageModel` class, along with additional information about the current page selection.
Request	This property returns an `HttpRequest` object that describes the current HTTP request, as described in chapter 12.
Response	This property returns an `HttpResponse` object that represents the current response, as described in chapter 12.
RouteData	This property provides access to the data matched by the routing system, as described in chapter 13.
TempData	This property provides access to the temp data feature, which is used to store data until it can be read by a subsequent request. See chapter 22 for details.
User	This property returns an object that describes the user associated with the request, as described in chapter 38.

23.4.1   Using a code-behind class file

The `@functions` directive allows the page-behind class and the Razor content to be defined in the same file, which is a development approach used by popular client-side frameworks, such as React or Vue.js.

Defining code and markup in the same file is convenient but can become difficult to manage for more complex applications. Razor Pages can also be split into separate view and code files, which is similar to the MVC examples in previous chapters and is reminiscent of ASP.NET Web Pages, which defined C# classes in files known as *code-behind files.* The first step is to remove the page model class from the CSHTML file, as shown in listing 23.9. I have also removed the @using expressions, which are no longer required.

> **Listing 23.9 Removing the Page model class in the Index.cshtml file in the Pages folder**

```
@page "{id:long?}"
@model WebApp.Pages.IndexModel

<!DOCTYPE html>
<html>
<head>
    <link href="/lib/bootstrap/css/bootstrap.min.css" rel="stylesheet" />
</head>
<body>
    <div class="bg-primary text-white text-center m-2 p-2">
        @Model.Product?.Name
    </div>
</body>
</html>
```

The @model expression has been modified to specify the namespace of the page model, which wasn't required previously because the @functions expression defined the IndexModel class within the namespace of the view. When defining the separate page model class, I define the class in the WebApp.Pages namespace. This isn't a requirement, but it makes the C# class consistent with the rest of the application.

The convention for naming Razor Pages code-behind files is to append the .cs file extension to the name of the view file. If you are using Visual Studio, the code-behind file was created by the Razor Page template when the Index.cshtml file was added to the project. Expand the Index.cshtml item in the Solution Explorer, and you will see the code-behind file, as shown in figure 23.8. Open the file for editing and replace the contents with the statements shown in listing 23.10.

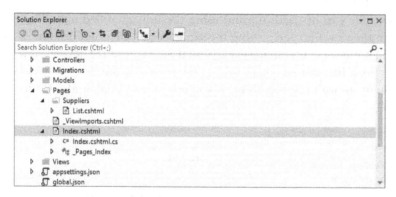

Figure 23.8 Revealing the code-behind file in the Visual Studio Solution Explorer

If you are using Visual Studio Code, add a file named `Index.cshtml.cs` to the `WebApp/Pages` folder with the content shown in listing 23.10.

> **Listing 23.10   The contents of the Index.cshtml.cs file in the Pages folder**

```
using Microsoft.AspNetCore.Mvc.RazorPages;
using WebApp.Models;

namespace WebApp.Pages {
    public class IndexModel : PageModel {
        private DataContext context;

        public Product? Product { get; set; }

        public IndexModel(DataContext ctx) {
            context = ctx;
        }

        public async Task OnGetAsync(long id = 1) {
            Product = await context.Products.FindAsync(id);
        }
    }
}
```

Restart ASP.NET Core and request http://localhost:5000/index to ensure the code-behind file is used, producing the response shown in figure 23.9.

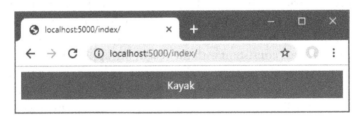

Figure 23.9   Using a code-behind file

ADDING A VIEW IMPORTS FILE

A view imports file can be used to avoid using the fully qualified name for the page model class in the view file, performing the same role as the one I used in chapter 22 for the MVC Framework. If you are using Visual Studio, use the Razor View Imports template to add a file named `_ViewImports.cshtml` to the `WebApp/Pages` folder, with the content shown in listing 23.11. If you are using Visual Studio Code, add the file directly.

> **Listing 23.11   The contents of the _ViewImports.cshtml file in the Pages folder**

```
@namespace WebApp.Pages
@using WebApp.Models
```

The `@namespace` directive sets the namespace for the C# class that is generated by a view, and using the directive in the view imports file sets the default namespace for all the Razor Pages in the application, with the effect that the view and its page model class are in the same namespace and the @model directive does not require a fully qualified type, as shown in listing 23.12.

Listing 23.12 Removing the namespace in the Index.cshtml file in the Pages folder

```
@page "{id:long?}"
@model IndexModel

<!DOCTYPE html>
<html>
<head>
    <link href="/lib/bootstrap/css/bootstrap.min.css" rel="stylesheet" />
</head>
<body>
    <div class="bg-primary text-white text-center m-2 p-2">
        @Model.Product?.Name
    </div>
</body>
</html>
```

Restart ASP.NET Core and use the browser to request http://localhost:5000/index. There is no difference in the response produced by the Razor Page, which is shown in figure 23.9.

23.4.2 Understanding action results in Razor Pages

Although it is not obvious, Razor Page handler methods use the same IActionResult interface to control the responses they generate. To make page model classes easier to develop, handler methods have an implied result that displays the view part of the page. Listing 23.13 makes the result explicit.

Listing 23.13 Using an explicit result in the Index.cshtml.cs file in the Pages folder

```
using Microsoft.AspNetCore.Mvc.RazorPages;
using WebApp.Models;
using Microsoft.AspNetCore.Mvc;

namespace WebApp.Pages {
    public class IndexModel : PageModel {
        private DataContext context;

        public Product? Product { get; set; }

        public IndexModel(DataContext ctx) {
            context = ctx;
        }

        public async Task<IActionResult> OnGetAsync(long id = 1) {
            Product = await context.Products.FindAsync(id);
            return Page();
        }
    }
}
```

The Page method is inherited from the PageModel class and creates a PageResult object, which tells the framework to render the view part of the page. Unlike the View method used in MVC action methods, the Razor Pages Page method doesn't accept arguments and always renders the view part of the page that has been selected to handle the request.

The PageModel class provides other methods that create different action results to produce different outcomes, as described in table 23.4.

Table 23.4   The PageModel action result methods

Name	Description
Page()	This IActionResult returned by this method produces a 200 OK status code and renders the view part of the Razor Page.
NotFound()	The IActionResult returned by this method produces a 404 NOT FOUND status code.
BadRequest(state)	The IActionResult returned by this method produces a 400 BAD REQUEST status code. The method accepts an optional model state object that describes the problem to the client, as demonstrated in chapter 19.
File(name, type)	The IActionResult returned by this method produces a 200 OK response, sets the Content-Type header to the specified type, and sends the specified file to the client.
Redirect(path) RedirectPermanent(path)	The IActionResult returned by these methods produces 302 FOUND and 301 MOVED PERMANENTLY responses, which redirect the client to the specified URL.
RedirectToAction(name) RedirectToActionPermanent(name)	The IActionResult returned by these methods produces 302 FOUND and 301 MOVED PERMANENTLY responses, which redirect the client to the specified action method. The URL used to redirect the client is produced using the routing features described in chapter 13.
RedirectToPage(name) RedirectToPagePermanent(name)	The IActionResult returned by these methods produce 302 FOUND and 301 MOVED PERMANENTLY responses that redirect the client to another Razor Page. If no name is supplied, the client is redirected to the current page.
StatusCode(code)	The IActionResult returned by this method produces a response with the specific status code.

USING AN ACTION RESULT

Except for the Page method, the methods in table 23.4 are the same as those available in action methods. However, care must be taken with these methods because sending a status code response is unhelpful in Razor Pages because they are used only when a client expects the content of the view.

Instead of using the NotFound method when requested data cannot be found, for example, a better approach is to redirect the client to another URL that can display an HTML message for the user. The redirection can be to a static HTML file, to another Razor Page, or to an action defined by a controller. Add a Razor Page named `NotFound.cshtml` to the `Pages` folder and add the content shown in listing 23.14.

Listing 23.14 The contents of the NotFound.cshtml file in the Pages folder

```
@page "/noid"
@model NotFoundModel
@using Microsoft.AspNetCore.Mvc.RazorPages
@using WebApp.Models;

<!DOCTYPE html>
<html>
<head>
    <link href="/lib/bootstrap/css/bootstrap.min.css" rel="stylesheet" />
    <title>Not Found</title>
</head>
<body>
    <div class="bg-primary text-white text-center m-2 p-2">
        No Matching ID
    </div>
    <ul class="list-group m-2">
        @foreach (Product p in Model.Products) {
                <li class="list-group-item">
                    @p.Name (ID: @p.ProductId)
                </li>
        }
    </ul>
</body>
</html>

@functions {

    public class NotFoundModel : PageModel {
        private DataContext context;

        public IEnumerable<Product> Products { get; set; }
            = Enumerable.Empty<Product>();

        public NotFoundModel(DataContext ctx) {
            context = ctx;
        }

        public void OnGetAsync(long id = 1) {
            Products = context.Products;
        }
    }
}
```

The `@page` directive overrides the route convention so that this Razor Page will handle the `/noid` URL path. The page model class uses an Entity Framework Core context object to query the database and displays a list of the product names and key values that are in the database.

In listing 23.15, I have updated the handle method of the `IndexModel` class to redirect the user to the `NotFound` page when a request is received that doesn't match a `Product` object in the database.

```
using Microsoft.AspNetCore.Mvc.RazorPages;
using WebApp.Models;
using Microsoft.AspNetCore.Mvc;

namespace WebApp.Pages {
    public class IndexModel : PageModel {
        private DataContext context;

        public Product? Product { get; set; }

        public IndexModel(DataContext ctx) {
            context = ctx;
        }

        public async Task<IActionResult> OnGetAsync(long id = 1) {
            Product = await context.Products.FindAsync(id);
            if (Product == null) {
                return RedirectToPage("NotFound");
            }
            return Page();
        }
    }
}
```

The `RedirectToPage` method produces an action result that redirects the client to a different Razor Page. The name of the target page is specified without the file extension, and any folder structure is specified relative to the `Pages` folder. To test the redirection, restart ASP.NET Core and request http://localhost:5000/index/500, which provides a value of 500 for the `id` segment variable and does not match anything in the database. The browser will be redirected and produce the result shown in figure 23.10.

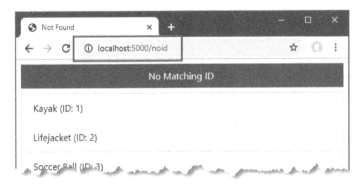

Figure 23.10   Redirecting to a different Razor Page

Notice that the routing system is used to produce the URL to which the client is redirected, which uses the routing pattern specified with the @page directive. In this example, the argument to the RedirectToPage method was NotFound, but this has been translated into a redirection to the /noid path specified by the @page directive in listing 23.14.

23.4.3 Handling multiple HTTP methods

Razor Pages can define handler methods that respond to different HTTP methods. The most common combination is to support the GET and POST methods that allow users to view and edit data. To demonstrate, add a Razor Page called Editor.cshtml to the Pages folder and add the content shown in listing 23.16.

> **NOTE** I have kept this example as simple as possible, but there are excellent ASP.NET Core features for creating HTML forms and for receiving data when it is submitted, as described in chapter 31.

Listing 23.16 The contents of the Editor.cshtml file in the Pages folder

```
@page "{id:long}"
@model EditorModel

<!DOCTYPE html>
<html>
<head>
    <link href="/lib/bootstrap/css/bootstrap.min.css" rel="stylesheet" />
</head>
<body>
    <div class="bg-primary text-white text-center m-2 p-2">Editor</div>
    <div class="m-2">
        <table class="table table-sm table-striped table-bordered">
            <tbody>
                <tr><th>Name</th><td>@Model.Product?.Name</td></tr>
                <tr><th>Price</th><td>@Model.Product?.Price</td></tr>
            </tbody>
        </table>
        <form method="post">
            @Html.AntiForgeryToken()
            <div class="form-group">
                <label>Price</label>
                <input name="price" class="form-control"
                        value="@Model.Product?.Price" />
            </div>
            <button class="btn btn-primary mt-2" type="submit">
                Submit
            </button>
        </form>
    </div>
</body>
</html>
```

The elements in the Razor Page view create a simple HTML form that presents the user with an input element containing the value of the `Price` property for a `Product` object. The `form` element is defined without an action attribute, which means the browser will send a POST request to the Razor Page's URL when the user clicks the Submit button.

> **NOTE**   The `@Html.AntiForgeryToken()` expression in listing 23.16 adds a hidden form field to the HTML form that ASP.NET Core uses to guard against cross-site request forgery (CSRF) attacks. I explain how this feature works in chapter 27, but for this chapter, it is enough to know that POST requests that do not contain this form field will be rejected.

If you are using Visual Studio, expand the `Editor.cshtml` item in the Solution Explorer to reveal the `Editor.cshtml.cs` class file and replace its contents with the code shown in listing 23.17. If you are using Visual Studio Code, add a file named `Editor.cshtml.cs` to the `WebApp/Pages` folder and use it to define the class shown in listing 23.17.

Listing 23.17   The contents of the Editor.cshtml.cs file in the Pages folder

```
using Microsoft.AspNetCore.Mvc;
using Microsoft.AspNetCore.Mvc.RazorPages;
using WebApp.Models;

namespace WebApp.Pages {
    public class EditorModel : PageModel {
        private DataContext context;

        public Product? Product { get; set; }

        public EditorModel(DataContext ctx) {
            context = ctx;
        }

        public async Task OnGetAsync(long id) {
            Product = await context.Products.FindAsync(id);
        }

        public async Task<IActionResult> OnPostAsync(long id,
                decimal price) {
            Product? p = await context.Products.FindAsync(id);
            if (p != null) {
                p.Price = price;
            }
            await context.SaveChangesAsync();
            return RedirectToPage();
        }
    }
}
```

The page model class defines two handler methods, and the name of the method tells the Razor Pages framework which HTTP method each handles. The `OnGetAsync` method is used to handle GET requests, which it does by locating a `Product`, whose details are displayed by the view.

The `OnPostAsync` method is used to handle POST requests, which will be sent by the browser when the user submits the HTML form. The parameters for the `OnPostAsync` method are obtained from the request so that the `id` value is obtained from the URL route and the `price` value is obtained from the form. (The model binding feature that extracts data from forms is described in chapter 28.)

> ### Understanding the POST Redirection
>
> Notice that the last statement in the `OnPostAsync` method invokes the `Redirect-ToPage` method without an argument, which redirects the client to the URL for the Razor Page. This may seem odd, but the effect is to tell the browser to send a GET request to the URL it used for the POST request. This type of redirection means that the browser won't resubmit the POST request if the user reloads the browser, preventing the same action from being accidentally performed more than once.

To see how the page model class handles different HTTP methods, restart ASP.NET Core and use a browser to navigate to http://localhost:5000/editor/1. Edit the field to set the price to 100 and click the Submit button. The browser will send a POST request that is handled by the `OnPostAsync` method. The database will be updated, and the browser will be redirected so that the updated data is displayed, as shown in figure 23.11.

Figure 23.11   Handling multiple HTTP methods

23.4.4 Selecting a handler method

The page model class can define multiple handler methods, allowing the request to select a method using a `handler` query string parameter or routing segment variable. To demonstrate this feature, add a Razor Page file named `HandlerSelector.cshtml` to the `Pages` folder with the content shown in listing 23.18.

Listing 23.18   The contents of the HandlerSelector.cshtml file in the Pages folder

```
@page
@model HandlerSelectorModel
@using Microsoft.AspNetCore.Mvc.RazorPages
@using Microsoft.EntityFrameworkCore

<!DOCTYPE html>
<html>
<head>
    <link href="/lib/bootstrap/css/bootstrap.min.css" rel="stylesheet" />
</head>
<body>
    <div class="bg-primary text-white text-center m-2 p-2">Selector</div>
    <div class="m-2">
        <table class="table table-sm table-striped table-bordered">
            <tbody>
                <tr><th>Name</th><td>@Model.Product?.Name</td></tr>
                <tr><th>Price</th><td>@Model.Product?.Price</td></tr>
                <tr>
                    <th>Category</th>
                    <td>@Model.Product?.Category?.Name</td>
                </tr>
                <tr>
                    <th>Supplier</th>
                    <td>@Model.Product?.Supplier?.Name</td>
                </tr>
            </tbody>
        </table>
        <a href="/handlerselector" class="btn btn-primary">Standard</a>
        <a href="/handlerselector?handler=related"
                class="btn btn-primary">
            Related
        </a>
    </div>
</body>
</html>

@functions {

    public class HandlerSelectorModel : PageModel {
        private DataContext context;

        public Product? Product { get; set; }

        public HandlerSelectorModel(DataContext ctx) {
            context = ctx;
        }

        public async Task OnGetAsync(long id = 1) {
            Product = await context.Products.FindAsync(id);
        }

        public async Task OnGetRelatedAsync(long id = 1) {
            Product = await context.Products
                .Include(p => p.Supplier)
```

```
            .Include(p => p.Category)
            .FirstOrDefaultAsync(p => p.ProductId == id);
        if (Product != null && Product.Supplier != null) {
            Product.Supplier.Products = null;
        }
        if (Product != null && Product.Category != null) {
            Product.Category.Products = null;
        }
    }
  }
}
```

The page model class in this example defines two handler methods: `OnGetAsync` and `OnGetRelatedAsync`. The `OnGetAsync` method is used by default, which you can see by restarting ASP.NET Core and using a browser to request http://localhost:5000/handlerselector. The handler method queries the database and presents the result to the user, as shown on the left of figure 23.12.

One of the anchor elements rendered by the page targets a URL with a handler query string parameter, like this:

```
...
<a href="/handlerselector?handler=related" class="btn btn-primary">
    Related
</a>
...
```

The name of the handler method is specified without the `On[method]` prefix and without the `Async` suffix so that the `OnGetRelatedAsync` method is selected using a handler value of `related`. This alternative handler method includes related data in its query and presents additional data to the user, as shown on the right of figure 23.12.

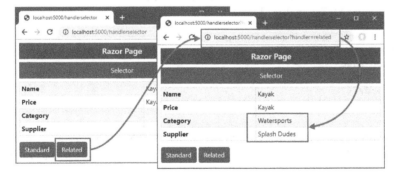

Figure 23.12 Selecting handler methods

Using rate limiting and output caching

In chapters 19 and 21, I demonstrated the use of the ASP.NET Core attributes for applying rate limits and output caching to controllers. These attributes can also be applied to page model classes, providing Razor Pages with the same features available in the MVC Framework.

23.5   *Understanding the Razor Page view*

The view part of a Razor Page uses the same syntax and has the same features as the views used with controllers. Razor Pages can use the full range of expressions and features such as sessions, temp data, and layouts. Aside from the use of the @page directive and the page model classes, the only differences are a certain amount of duplication to configure features such as layouts and partial views, as described in the sections that follow.

23.5.1   *Creating a layout for Razor Pages*

Layouts for Razor Pages are created in the same way as for controller views but in the Pages/Shared folder. If you are using Visual Studio, create the Pages/Shared folder and add to it a file named _Layout.cshtml using the Razor Layout template with the contents shown in listing 23.19. If you are using Visual Studio Code, create the Pages/Shared folder, create the _Layout.cshtml file in the new folder, and add the content shown in listing 23.19.

> **NOTE** Layouts can be created in the same folder as the Razor Pages that use them, in which case they will be used in preference to the files in the Shared folder.

> **Listing 23.19**   The contents of the _Layout.cshtml file in the Pages/Shared folder

```
<!DOCTYPE html>
<html>
<head>
    <link href="/lib/bootstrap/css/bootstrap.min.css" rel="stylesheet" />
    <title>@ViewBag.Title</title>
</head>
<body>
    <h5 class="bg-secondary text-white text-center m-2 p-2">
        Razor Page
    </h5>
    @RenderBody()
</body>
</html>
```

The layout doesn't use any features that are specific to Razor Pages and contains the same elements and expressions used in chapter 22 when I created a layout for the controller views.

Next, use the Razor View Start template to add a file named _ViewStart.cshtml to the Pages folder. Visual Studio will create the file with the content shown in listing 23.20. If you are using Visual Studio Code, create the _ViewStart.cshtml file and add the content shown in listing 23.20.

> **Listing 23.20**   The contents of the _ViewStart.cshtml file in the Pages folder

```
@{
    Layout = "_Layout";
}
```

The C# classes generated from Razor Pages are derived from the `Page` class, which provides the `Layout` property used by the view start file, which has the same purpose as the one used by controller views. In listing 23.21, I have updated the `Index` page to remove the elements that will be provided by the layout.

```
@page "{id:long?}"
@model IndexModel

<div class="bg-primary text-white text-center m-2 p-2">
    @Model.Product?.Name
</div>
```

Using a view start file applies the layout to all pages that don't override the value assigned to the `Layout` property. In listing 23.22, I have added a code block to the `Editor` page so that it doesn't use a layout.

```
@page "{id:long}"
@model EditorModel
@{
    Layout = null;
}

<!DOCTYPE html>
<html>
<head>
    <link href="/lib/bootstrap/css/bootstrap.min.css" rel="stylesheet" />
</head>
<body>

    <! ...elements omitted for brevity ... />

</body>
</html>
```

Restart ASP.NET Core and use a browser to request http://localhost:5000/index, and you will see the effect of the new layout, which is shown on the left of figure 23.13. Use the browser to request http://localhost:5000/editor/1, and you will receive content that is generated without the layout, as shown on the right of figure 23.13.

**Figure 23.13
Using a layout in
Razor Pages**

23.5.2 *Using partial views in Razor Pages*

Razor Pages can use partial views so that common content isn't duplicated. The example in this section relies on the tag helpers feature, which I describe in detail in chapter 25. For this chapter, add the directive shown in listing 23.23 to the view imports file, which enables the custom HTML element used to apply partial views.

> **Listing 23.23   Enabling tag helpers in the _ViewImports.cshtml file in the Pages folder**

```
@namespace WebApp.Pages
@using WebApp.Models
@addTagHelper *, Microsoft.AspNetCore.Mvc.TagHelpers
```

Next, add a Razor view named `_ProductPartial.cshtml` in the `Pages/Shared` folder and add the content shown in listing 23.24.

> **Listing 23.24   The _ProductPartial.cshtml File in the Pages/Shared Folder**

```
@model Product

<div class="m-2">
    <table class="table table-sm table-striped table-bordered">
        <tbody>
            <tr><th>Name</th><td>@Model?.Name</td></tr>
            <tr><th>Price</th><td>@Model?.Price</td></tr>
        </tbody>
    </table>
</div>
```

Notice there is nothing specific to Razor Pages in the partial view. Partial views use the `@model` directive to receive a view model object and do not use the `@page` directive or have page models, both of which are specific to Razor Pages. This allows Razor Pages to share partial views with MVC controllers, as described in the sidebar.

> #### Understanding the partial method search path
>
> The Razor view engine starts looking for a partial view in the same folder as the Razor Page that uses it. If there is no matching file, then the search continues in each parent directory until the `Pages` folder is reached. For a partial view used by a Razor Page defined in the `Pages/App/Data` folder, for example, the view engine looks in the `Pages/App/Data` folder, the `Page/App` folder, and then the `Pages` folder. If no file is found, the search continues to the `Pages/Shared` folder and, finally, to the `Views/Shared` folder.
>
> The last search location allows partial views defined for use with controllers to be used by Razor Pages, which is a useful feature for avoiding duplicate content in applications where MVC controllers and Razor Pages are both used.

Partial views are applied using the `partial` element, as shown in listing 23.25, with the `name` attribute specifying the name of the view and the `model` attribute providing the view model.

CAUTION Partial views receive a view model through their @model directive and not a page model. It is for this reason that the value of the model attribute is Model.Product and not just Model.

Listing 23.25 Using a partial view in the Index.cshtml file in the Pages folder

```
@page "{id:long?}"
@model IndexModel

<div class="bg-primary text-white text-center m-2 p-2">
    @Model.Product?.Name
</div>
<partial name="_ProductPartial" model="Model.Product" />
```

When the Razor Page is used to handle a response, the contents of the partial view are incorporated into the response. Restart ASP.NET Core and use a browser to request http://localhost:5000/index, and the response includes the table defined in the partial view, as shown in figure 23.14.

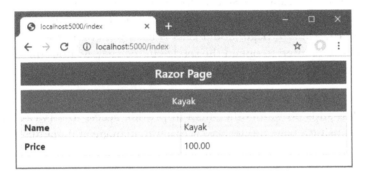

Figure 23.14 Using a partial view

23.5.3 Creating Razor Pages without page models

If a Razor Page is simply presenting data to the user, the result can be a page model class that simply declares a constructor dependency to set a property that is consumed in the view. To understand this pattern, add a Razor Page named Data.cshtml to the WebApp/Pages folder with the content shown in listing 23.26.

Listing 23.26 The contents of the Data.cshtml file in the Pages folder

```
@page
@model DataPageModel
@using Microsoft.AspNetCore.Mvc.RazorPages

<h5 class="bg-primary text-white text-center m-2 p-2">Categories</h5>
<ul class="list-group m-2">
    @foreach (Category c in Model.Categories) {
        <li class="list-group-item">@c.Name</li>
```

```
        }
    </ul>

    @functions {

        public class DataPageModel : PageModel {
            private DataContext context;

            public IEnumerable<Category> Categories { get; set; }
                = Enumerable.Empty<Category>();

            public DataPageModel(DataContext ctx) {
                context = ctx;
            }

            public void OnGet() {
                Categories = context.Categories;
            }
        }
    }
}
```

The page model in this example doesn't transform data, perform calculations, or do
anything other than giving the view access to the data through dependency injection.
To avoid this pattern, where a page model class is used only to access a service, the
@inject directive can be used to obtain the service in the view, without the need for a
page model, as shown in listing 23.27.

> **CAUTION**   The @inject directive should be used sparingly and only when the
> page model class adds no value other than to provide access to services. In all
> other situations, using a page model class is easier to manage and maintain.

> **Listing 23.27   Accessing a service in the Data.cshtml file in the Pages folder**

```
@page
@inject DataContext context;

<h5 class="bg-primary text-white text-center m-2 p-2">Categories</h5>
<ul class="list-group m-2">
    @foreach (Category c in context.Categories) {
        <li class="list-group-item">@c.Name</li>
    }
</ul>
```

The @inject expression specifies the service type and the name by which the service is
accessed. In this example, the service type is DataContext, and the name by which it is
accessed is context. Within the view, the @foreach expression generates elements for
each object returned by the DataContext.Categories properties. Since there is no
page model in this example, I have removed the @model and @using directives. Restart
ASP.NET Core and use a browser to navigate to http://localhost:5000/data, and you
will see the response shown in figure 23.15.

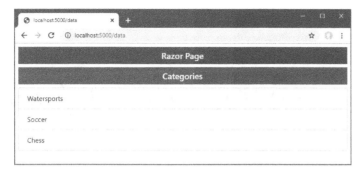

Figure 23.15   Using a Razor Page without a page model

Summary

- Razor Pages combines markup and code to generate HTML responses without the setup required by the MVC Framework.
- Razor Pages use the same syntax as regular Razor views, with additional expressions to define the page model.
- The page model is usually embedded within the markup using the `@functions` expression but can be defined in a separate C# class file.
- The routes supported by Razor Pages are defined using the `@page` expression.
- Razor Pages can use regular Razor features, such as layouts, view start files, and partial views.

Using view components

This chapter covers

- Using view components to generate content that is orthogonal to the main purpose of the application
- Applying view components in views
- Passing data to view components from the parent view
- Using partial views to generate HTML content
- Creating classes that are controllers and view components

I describe *view components* in this chapter, which are classes that provide action-style logic to support partial views; this means view components provide complex content to be embedded in views while allowing the C# code that supports it to be easily maintained. Table 24.1 puts view components in context.

Table 24.1 Putting view components in context

Question	Answer
What are they?	View components are classes that provide application logic to support partial views or to inject small fragments of HTML or JSON data into a parent view.
Why are they useful?	Without view components, it is hard to create embedded functionality such as shopping baskets or login panels in a way that is easy to maintain.
How are they used?	View components are typically derived from the `View-Component` class and are applied in a parent view using the custom `vc` HTML element or the `@await Component.InvokeAsync` expression.
Are there any pitfalls or limitations?	View components are a simple and predictable feature. The main pitfall is not using them and trying to include application logic within views where it is difficult to test and maintain.
Are there any alternatives?	You could put the data access and processing logic directly in a partial view, but the result is difficult to work with and hard to maintain.

Table 24.2 provides a guide to the chapter.

Table 24.2 Chapter guide

Problem	Solution	Listing
Creating a reusable unit of code and content	Define a view component.	7–13
Creating a response from a view component	Use one of the `IViewComponentResult` implementation classes.	14–18
Getting context data	Use the properties inherited from the base class or use the parameters of the `Invoke` or `InvokeAsync` method.	19–25
Generating view component responses asynchronously	Override the `InvokeAsync` method.	26–28
Integrating a view component into another endpoint	Create a hybrid controller or Razor Page.	29–36

24.1 Preparing for this chapter

This chapter uses the WebApp project from chapter 23. To prepare for this chapter, add a class file named `City.cs` to the `WebApp/Models` folder with the content shown in listing 24.1.

TIP   You can download the example project for this chapter—and for all the other chapters in this book—from https://github.com/manningbooks/pro-asp .net-core-7. See chapter 1 for how to get help if you have problems running the examples.

```
namespace WebApp.Models {

    public class City {
        public string? Name { get; set; }
        public string? Country { get; set; }
        public int? Population { get; set; }
    }
}
```

Add a class named `CitiesData.cs` to the `WebApp/Models` folder with the content shown in listing 24.2.

```
namespace WebApp.Models {

    public class CitiesData {

        private List<City> cities = new List<City> {
            new City {
                Name = "London",
                Country = "UK",
                Population = 8539000
            },
            new City {
                Name = "New York",
                Country = "USA",
                Population = 8406000
            },
            new City {
                Name = "San Jose",
                Country = "USA",
                Population = 998537
            },
            new City {
                Name = "Paris",
                Country = "France",
                Population = 2244000
            }
        };

        public IEnumerable<City> Cities => cities;

        public void AddCity(City newCity) {
            cities.Add(newCity);
        }
    }
}
```

The `CitiesData` class provides access to a collection of `City` objects and provides an `AddCity` method that adds a new object to the collection. Add the statement shown in listing 24.3 to the `Program.cs` file to create a service for the `CitiesData` class.

Listing 24.3   Defining a service in the Program.cs file in the WebApp folder

```
using Microsoft.EntityFrameworkCore;
using WebApp.Models;
using Microsoft.AspNetCore.Mvc.RazorPages;

var builder = WebApplication.CreateBuilder(args);

builder.Services.AddDbContext<DataContext>(opts => {
    opts.UseSqlServer(builder.Configuration[
        "ConnectionStrings:ProductConnection"]);
    opts.EnableSensitiveDataLogging(true);
});

builder.Services.AddControllersWithViews();
builder.Services.AddRazorPages();

builder.Services.AddDistributedMemoryCache();
builder.Services.AddSession(options => {
    options.Cookie.IsEssential = true;
});

builder.Services.Configure<RazorPagesOptions>(opts => {
    opts.Conventions.AddPageRoute("/Index", "/extra/page/{id:long?}");
});

builder.Services.AddSingleton<CitiesData>();

var app = builder.Build();

app.UseStaticFiles();
app.UseSession();
app.MapControllers();
app.MapDefaultControllerRoute();
app.MapRazorPages();

var context = app.Services.CreateScope().ServiceProvider
    .GetRequiredService<DataContext>();
SeedData.SeedDatabase(context);

app.Run();
```

The new statement uses the `AddSingleton` method to create a `CitiesData` service. There is no interface/implementation separation in this service, which I have created to easily distribute a shared `CitiesData` object. Add a Razor Page named `Cities` `.cshtml` to the `WebApp/Pages` folder and add the content shown in listing 24.4.

Listing 24.4   The contents of the Cities.cshtml file in the Pages folder

```
@page
@inject CitiesData Data

<div class="m-2">
    <table class="table table-sm table-striped table-bordered">
        <tbody>
            @foreach (City c in Data.Cities) {
                <tr>
                    <td>@c.Name</td>
                    <td>@c.Country</td>
                    <td>@c.Population</td>
                </tr>
            }
        </tbody>
    </table>
</div>
```

24.1.1 Dropping the database

Open a new PowerShell command prompt, navigate to the folder that contains the `WebApp.csproj` file, and run the command shown in listing 24.5 to drop the database.

Listing 24.5   Dropping the database

```
dotnet ef database drop --force
```

24.1.2 Running the example application

Use the PowerShell command prompt to run the command shown in listing 24.6.

Listing 24.6   Running the example application

```
dotnet run
```

The database will be seeded as part of the application startup. Once ASP.NET Core is running, use a web browser to request http://localhost:5000/cities, which will produce the response shown in figure 24.1.

Figure 24.1 Running the example application

24.2 Understanding view components

Applications commonly need to embed content in views that isn't related to the main purpose of the application. Common examples include site navigation tools and authentication panels that let the user log in without visiting a separate page.

The data for this type of feature isn't part of the model data passed from the action method or page model to the view. It is for this reason that I have created two sources of data in the example project: I am going to display some content generated using `City` data, which isn't easily done in a view that receives data from the Entity Framework Core repository and the `Product`, `Category`, and `Supplier` objects it contains.

Partial views are used to create reusable markup that is required in views, avoiding the need to duplicate the same content in multiple places in the application. Partial views are a useful feature, but they just contain fragments of HTML and Razor directives, and the data they operate on is received from the parent view. If you need to display different data, then you run into a problem. You could access the data you need directly from the partial view, but this breaks the development model and produces an application that is difficult to understand and maintain. Alternatively, you could extend the view models used by the application so that it includes the data you require, but this means you have to change every action method, which makes it hard to isolate the functionality of action methods for effective maintenance and testing.

This is where view components come in. A view component is a C# class that provides a partial view with the data that it needs, independently from the action method or Razor Page. In this regard, a view component can be thought of as a specialized action or page, but one that is used only to provide a partial view with data; it cannot receive HTTP requests, and the content that it provides will always be included in the parent view.

24.3 Creating and using a view component

A view component is any class whose name ends with `ViewComponent` and that defines an `Invoke` or `InvokeAsync` method or any class that is derived from the `ViewComponent` base class or that has been decorated with the `ViewComponent` attribute. I demonstrate the use of the attribute in the "Getting Context Data" section, but the other examples in this chapter rely on the base class.

View components can be defined anywhere in a project, but the convention is to group them in a folder named `Components`. Create the `WebApp/Components` folder and add to it a class file named `CitySummary.cs` with the content shown in listing 24.7.

> **Listing 24.7 The contents of the CitySummary.cs file in the Components folder**

```
using Microsoft.AspNetCore.Mvc;
using WebApp.Models;

namespace WebApp.Components {

    public class CitySummary : ViewComponent {
        private CitiesData data;

        public CitySummary(CitiesData cdata) {
```

```
            data = cdata;
        }

        public string Invoke() {
            return $"{data.Cities.Count()} cities, "
            + $"{data.Cities.Sum(c => c.Population)} people";
        }
    }
}
```

View components can take advantage of dependency injection to receive the services they require. In this example, the view component declares a dependency on the CitiesData class, which is then used in the Invoke method to create a string that contains the number of cities and the population total.

24.3.1 Applying a view component

View components can be applied in two different ways. The first technique is to use the Component property that is added to the C# classes generated from views and Razor Pages. This property returns an object that implements the IViewComponentHelper interface, which provides the InvokeAsync method. Listing 24.8 uses this technique to apply the view component in the Index.cshtml file in the Views/Home folder.

> **Listing 24.8   Using a view component in the Index.cshtml file in the Views/Home folder**

```
@model Product?
@{
    Layout = "_Layout";
    ViewBag.Title = "Product Table";
}

@section Header {
    Product Information
}

<tr><th>Name</th><td>@Model?.Name</td></tr>
<tr>
    <th>Price</th>
    <td>@Model?.Price.ToString("c")</td>
</tr>
<tr><th>Category ID</th><td>@Model?.CategoryId</td></tr>

@section Footer {
    @(((Model?.Price / ViewBag.AveragePrice)
            * 100).ToString("F2"))% of average price
}

@section Summary {
    <div class="bg-info text-white m-2 p-2">
        @await Component.InvokeAsync("CitySummary")
    </div>
}
```

View components are applied using the Component.InvokeAsync method, using the name of the view component class as the argument. The syntax for this technique can be confusing. View component classes define either an `Invoke` or `InvokeAsync` method, depending on whether their work is performed synchronously or asynchronously. But the `Component.InvokeAsync` method is always used, even to apply view components that define the `Invoke` method and whose operations are entirely synchronous.

To add the namespace for the view components to the list that are included in views, I added the statement shown in listing 24.9 to the `_ViewImports.cshtml` file in the `Views` folder.

> **Listing 24.9   Adding a namespace in the _ViewImports.cshtml file in the Views folder**

```
@using WebApp.Models
@addTagHelper *, Microsoft.AspNetCore.Mvc.TagHelpers
@using WebApp.Components
```

Restart ASP.NET Core and use a browser to request http://localhost:5000/home/index/1, which will produce the result shown in figure 24.2.

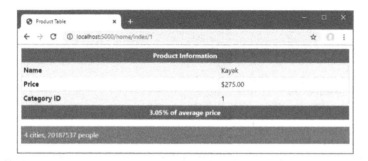

Figure 24.2
Using a view
component

APPLYING VIEW COMPONENTS USING A TAG HELPER

Razor Views and Pages can contain tag helpers, which are custom HTML elements that are managed by C# classes. I explain how tag helpers work in detail in chapter 25, but view components can be applied using an HTML element that is implemented as a tag helper. To enable this feature, add the directive shown in listing 24.10 to the `_ViewImports.cshtml` file in the `Views` folder.

> **NOTE**   View components can be used only in controller views or Razor Pages and cannot be used to handle requests directly.

> **Listing 24.10   Adding tag helper in the _ViewImports.cshtml file in the Views folder**

```
@using WebApp.Models
@addTagHelper *, Microsoft.AspNetCore.Mvc.TagHelpers
@using WebApp.Components
@addTagHelper *, WebApp
```

The new directive adds tag helper support for the example project, which is specified by name, and which is `WebApp` for this example. In listing 24.11, I have used the custom HTML element to apply the view component.

```
@model Product?
@{
    Layout = "_Layout";
    ViewBag.Title = "Product Table";
}

@section Header {
    Product Information
}

<tr><th>Name</th><td>@Model?.Name</td></tr>
<tr>
    <th>Price</th>
    <td>@Model?.Price.ToString("c")</td>
</tr>
<tr><th>Category ID</th><td>@Model?.CategoryId</td></tr>

@section Footer {
    @(((Model?.Price / ViewBag.AveragePrice)
            * 100).ToString("F2"))% of average price
}

@section Summary {
    <div class="bg-info text-white m-2 p-2">
        <vc:city-summary />
    </div>
}
```

The tag for the custom element is `vc`, followed by a colon, followed by the name of the view component class, which is transformed into kebab-case. Each capitalized word in the class name is converted to lowercase and separated by a hyphen so that `CitySummary` becomes `city-summary`, and the `CitySummary` view component is applied using the `vc:city-summary` element.

APPLYING VIEW COMPONENTS IN RAZOR PAGES

Razor Pages use view components in the same way, either through the `Component` property or through the custom HTML element. Since Razor Pages have their own view imports file, a separate `@addTagHelper` directive is required, as shown in listing 24.12.

```
@namespace WebApp.Pages
@using WebApp.Models
@addTagHelper *, Microsoft.AspNetCore.Mvc.TagHelpers
@addTagHelper *, WebApp
```

Listing 24.13 applies the `CitySummary` view component to the `Data` page.

Listing 24.13   Using a view component in the Data.cshtml file in the Pages folder

```
@page
@inject DataContext context;

<h5 class="bg-primary text-white text-center m-2 p-2">Categories</h5>
<ul class="list-group m-2">
    @foreach (Category c in context.Categories) {
        <li class="list-group-item">@c.Name</li>
    }
</ul>

<div class="bg-info text-white m-2 p-2">
    <vc:city-summary />
</div>
```

Use a browser to request http://localhost:5000/data, and you will see the response shown in figure 24.3, which displays the city data alongside the categories in the database.

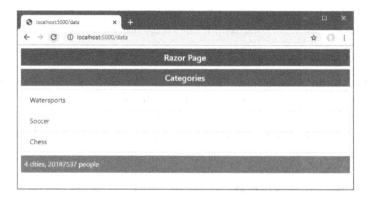

Figure 24.3   Using a view component in a Razor Page

24.4   *Understanding view component results*

The ability to insert simple string values into a view or page isn't especially useful, but fortunately, view components are capable of much more. More complex effects can be achieved by having the `Invoke` or `InvokeAsync` method return an object that implements the `IViewComponentResult` interface. There are three built-in classes that implement the `IViewComponentResult` interface, and they are described in table 24.3, along with the convenience methods for creating them provided by the `View-Component` base class. I describe the use of each result type in the sections that follow.

Table 24.3   The built-in IViewComponentResult implementation classes

Name	Description
ViewViewComponentResult	This class is used to specify a Razor View, with optional view model data. Instances of this class are created using the `View` method.
ContentViewComponentResult	This class is used to specify a text result that will be safely encoded for inclusion in an HTML document. Instances of this class are created using the `Content` method.
HtmlContentViewComponentResult	This class is used to specify a fragment of HTML that will be included in the HTML document without further encoding. There is no `ViewComponent` method to create this type of result.

There is special handling for two result types. If a view component returns a `string`, then it is used to create a `ContentViewComponentResult` object, which is what I relied on in earlier examples. If a view component returns an `IHtmlContent` object, then it is used to create an `HtmlContentViewComponentResult` object.

24.4.1   *Returning a partial view*

The most useful response is the awkwardly named `ViewViewComponentResult` object, which tells Razor to render a partial view and include the result in the parent view. The `ViewComponent` base class provides the `View` method for creating `ViewViewComponentResult` objects, and four versions of the method are available, described in table 24.4.

Table 24.4   The ViewComponent.View methods

Name	Description
View()	Using this method selects the default view for the view component and does not provide a view model.
View(model)	Using the method selects the default view and uses the specified object as the view model.
View(viewName)	Using this method selects the specified view and does not provide a view model.
View(viewName, model)	Using this method selects the specified view and uses the specified object as the view model.

These methods correspond to those provided by the `Controller` base class and are used in much the same way. To create a view model class that the view component can use, add a class file named `CityViewModel.cs` to the `WebApp/Models` folder and use it to define the class shown in listing 24.14.

Listing 24.14   **The contents of the CityViewModel.cs file in the Models folder**

```
namespace WebApp.Models {

    public class CityViewModel {
        public int? Cities { get; set; }
        public int? Population { get; set; }
    }
}
```

Listing 24.15 modifies the `Invoke` method of the `CitySummary` view component so it uses the `View` method to select a partial view and provides view data using a `CityView-Model` object.

Listing 24.15   **Selecting a view in the CitySummary.cs file in the Components folder**

```
using Microsoft.AspNetCore.Mvc;
using WebApp.Models;

namespace WebApp.Components {

    public class CitySummary : ViewComponent {
        private CitiesData data;

        public CitySummary(CitiesData cdata) {
            data = cdata;
        }

        public IViewComponentResult Invoke() {
            return View(new CityViewModel {
                Cities = data.Cities.Count(),
                Population = data.Cities.Sum(c => c.Population)
            });
        }
    }
}
```

There is no view available for the view component currently, but the error message this produces reveals the locations that are searched. Restart ASP.NET Core and use a browser to request http://localhost:5000/home/index/1 to see the locations that are searched when the view component is used with a controller. Request http://localhost:5000/data to see the locations searched when a view component is used with a Razor Page. Figure 24.4 shows both responses.

Figure 24.4   **The search locations for view component views**

Razor searches for a view named `Default.cshtml` when a view component invokes the `View` method without specifying a name. If the view component is used with a controller, then the search locations are as follows:

- `/Views/[controller]/Components/[viewcomponent]/Default.cshtml`
- `/Views/Shared/Components/[viewcomponent]/Default.cshtml`
- `/Pages/Shared/Components/[viewcomponent]/Default.cshtml`

When the `CitySummary` component is rendered by a view selected through the `Home` controller, for example, `[controller]` is `Home` and `[viewcomponent]` is `CitySummary`, which means the first search location is `/Views/Home/Components/CitySummary/Default.cshtml`. If the view component is used with a Razor Page, then the search locations are as follows:

- `/Pages/Components/[viewcomponent]/Default.cshtml`
- `/Pages/Shared/Components/[viewcomponent]/Default.cshtml`
- `/Views/Shared/Components/[viewcomponent]/Default.cshtml`

If the search paths for Razor Pages do not include the page name but a Razor Page is defined in a subfolder, then the Razor view engine will look for a view in the `Components/[viewcomponent]` folder, relative to the location in which the Razor Page is defined, working its way up the folder hierarchy until it finds a view or reaches the `Pages` folder.

> **TIP** Notice that view components used in Razor Pages will find views defined in the `Views/Shared/Components` folder and that view components defined in controllers will find views in the `Pages/Shared/Components` folder. This means you don't have to duplicate views when a view component is used by controllers and Razor Pages.

Create the `WebApp/Views/Shared/Components/CitySummary` folder and add to it a Razor View named `Default.cshtml` with the content shown in listing 24.16.

> **Listing 24.16 The Default.cshtml file in the Views/Shared/Components/ CitySummary folder**

```
@model CityViewModel

<table class="table table-sm table-bordered text-white bg-secondary">
    <thead>
        <tr><th colspan="2">Cities Summary</th></tr>
    </thead>
    <tbody>
        <tr>
            <td>Cities:</td>
            <td class="text-right">
                @Model?.Cities
            </td>
```

```
        </tr>
        <tr>
            <td>Population:</td>
            <td class="text-right">
                @Model?.Population?.ToString("#,###")
            </td>
        </tr>
    </tbody>
</table>
```

Views for view components are similar to partial views and use the @model directive to set the type of the view model object. This view receives a CityViewModel object from its view component, which is used to populate the cells in an HTML table. Restart ASP.NET Core and a browser to request http://localhost:5000/home/index/1 and http://localhost:5000/data, and you will see the view incorporated into the responses, as shown in figure 24.5.

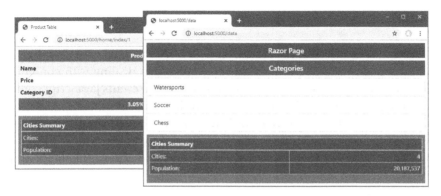

Figure 24.5   Using a view with a view component

24.4.2   *Returning HTML fragments*

The ContentViewComponentResult class is used to include fragments of HTML in the parent view without using a view. Instances of the ContentViewComponentResult class are created using the Content method inherited from the ViewComponent base class, which accepts a string value. Listing 24.17 demonstrates the use of the Content method.

> **TIP** In addition to the Content method, the Invoke method can return a string, which will be automatically converted to a ContentViewComponentResult. This is the approach I took in the view component when it was first defined.

Listing 24.17   Using the content method in the CitySummary.cs file in the Components folder

```
using Microsoft.AspNetCore.Mvc;
using WebApp.Models;

namespace WebApp.Components {

    public class CitySummary : ViewComponent {
        private CitiesData data;

        public CitySummary(CitiesData cdata) {
            data = cdata;
        }

        public IViewComponentResult Invoke() {
            return Content("This is a <h3><i>string</i></h3>");
        }
    }
}
```

The string received by the `Content` method is encoded to make it safe to include in an HTML document. This is particularly important when dealing with content that has been provided by users or external systems because it prevents JavaScript content from being embedded into the HTML generated by the application.

In this example, the `string` that I passed to the `Content` method contains some basic HTML tags. Restart ASP.NET Core and use a browser to request http://localhost:5000/home/index/1. The response will include the encoded HTML fragment, as shown in figure 24.6.

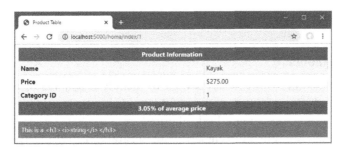

Figure 24.6   Returning an encoded HTML fragment using a view component

If you look at the HTML that the view component produced, you will see that the angle brackets have been replaced so that the browser doesn't interpret the content as HTML elements, as follows:

```
...
<div class="bg-info text-white m-2 p-2">
    This is a &lt;h3&gt;&lt;i&gt;string&lt;/i&gt;&lt;/h3&gt;
</div>
...
```

You don't need to encode content if you trust its source and want it to be interpreted as HTML. The Content method always encodes its argument, so you must create the HtmlContentViewComponentResult object directly and provide its constructor with an HtmlString object, which represents a string that you know is safe to display, either because it comes from a source that you trust or because you are confident that it has already been encoded, as shown in listing 24.18.

Listing 24.18   Returning a fragment in the CitySummary.cs file in the Components folder

```
using Microsoft.AspNetCore.Mvc;
using WebApp.Models;
using Microsoft.AspNetCore.Mvc.ViewComponents;
using Microsoft.AspNetCore.Html;

namespace WebApp.Components {

    public class CitySummary : ViewComponent {
        private CitiesData data;

        public CitySummary(CitiesData cdata) {
            data = cdata;
        }

        public IViewComponentResult Invoke() {
            return new HtmlContentViewComponentResult(
                new HtmlString("This is a <h3><i>string</i></h3>"));
        }
    }
}
```

This technique should be used with caution and only with sources of content that cannot be tampered with and that perform their own encoding. Restart ASP.NET Core and use a browser to request http://localhost:5000/home/index/1, and you will see the response isn't encoded and is interpreted as HTML elements, as shown in figure 24.7.

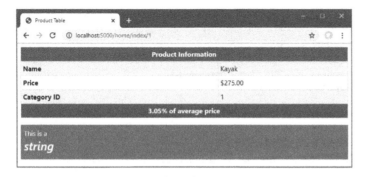

Figure 24.7   Returning an unencoded HTML fragment using a view component

24.5   *Getting context data*

Details about the current request and the parent view are provided to a view component through properties defined by the `ViewComponent` base class, as described in table 24.5.

Table 24.5   The ViewComponentContext properties

Name	Description
HttpContext	This property returns an `HttpContext` object that describes the current request and the response that is being prepared.
Request	This property returns an `HttpRequest` object that describes the current HTTP request.
User	This property returns an `IPrincipal` object that describes the current user, as described in chapters 37 and 38.
RouteData	This property returns a `RouteData` object that describes the routing data for the current request.
ViewBag	This property returns the `dynamic` view bag object, which can be used to pass data between the view component and the view, as described in chapter 22.
ModelState	This property returns a `ModelStateDictionary`, which provides details of the model binding process, as described in chapter 29.
ViewData	This property returns a `ViewDataDictionary`, which provides access to the view data provided for the view component.

The context data can be used in whatever way helps the view component do its work, including varying the way that data is selected or rendering different content or views. It is hard to devise a representative example of using context data in a view component because the problems it solves are specific to each project. In listing 24.19, I check the route data for the request to determine whether the routing pattern contains a controller segment variable, which indicates a request that will be handled by a controller and view.

> **Listing 24.19   Using request data in the CitySummary.cs file in the Components folder**

```
using Microsoft.AspNetCore.Mvc;
using WebApp.Models;
using Microsoft.AspNetCore.Mvc.ViewComponents;
using Microsoft.AspNetCore.Html;

namespace WebApp.Components {

    public class CitySummary : ViewComponent {
        private CitiesData data;

        public CitySummary(CitiesData cdata) {
            data = cdata;
        }

        public string Invoke() {
```

```
        if (RouteData.Values["controller"] != null) {
            return "Controller Request";
        } else {
            return "Razor Page Request";
        }
    }
  }
}
```

Restart ASP.NET Core and use a browser to request http://localhost:5000/home/ index/1 and http://localhost:5000/data, and you will see that the view component alters its output, as shown in figure 24.8.

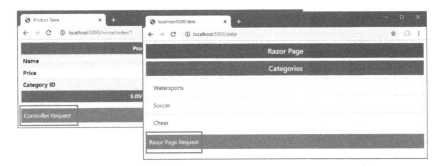

Figure 24.8 Using context data in a view component

24.5.1 *Providing context from the parent view using arguments*

Parent views can provide additional context data to view components, providing them with either data or guidance about the content that should be produced. The context data is received through the Invoke or InvokeAsync method, as shown in listing 24.20.

Listing 24.20 Receiving a value in the CitySummary.cs file in the Components folder

```
using Microsoft.AspNetCore.Mvc;
using WebApp.Models;
using Microsoft.AspNetCore.Mvc.ViewComponents;
using Microsoft.AspNetCore.Html;

namespace WebApp.Components {

    public class CitySummary : ViewComponent {
        private CitiesData data;

        public CitySummary(CitiesData cdata) {
            data = cdata;
        }

        public IViewComponentResult Invoke(string themeName) {
            ViewBag.Theme = themeName;
            return View(new CityViewModel {
                Cities = data.Cities.Count(),
```

```
                    Population = data.Cities.Sum(c => c.Population)
                });
            }
        }
    }
}
```

The `Invoke` method defines a `themeName` parameter that is passed on to the partial view using the view bag, which was described in chapter 22. Listing 24.21 updates the `Default` view to use the received value to style the content it produces.

```
@model CityViewModel

<table class="table table-sm table-bordered text-white bg-@ViewBag.Theme">
    <thead>
        <tr><th colspan="2">Cities Summary</th></tr>
    </thead>
    <tbody>
        <tr>
            <td>Cities:</td>
            <td class="text-right">
                @Model?.Cities
            </td>
        </tr>
        <tr>
            <td>Population:</td>
            <td class="text-right">
                @Model?.Population?.ToString("#,###")
            </td>
        </tr>
    </tbody>
</table>
```

A value for all parameters defined by a view component's `Invoke` or `InvokeAsync` method must always be provided. Listing 24.22 provides a value for `themeName` parameter in the view selected by the `Home` controller.

> **TIP** The view component will not be used if you do not provide values for all the parameters it defines, but no error message is displayed. If you don't see any content from a view component, then the likely cause is a missing parameter value.

```
@model Product?
@{
    Layout = "_Layout";
    ViewBag.Title = "Product Table";
}

@section Header {
    Product Information
}
```

```
<tr><th>Name</th><td>@Model?.Name</td></tr>
<tr>
    <th>Price</th>
    <td>@Model?.Price.ToString("c")</td>
</tr>
<tr><th>Category ID</th><td>@Model?.CategoryId</td></tr>

@section Footer {
    @(((Model?.Price / ViewBag.AveragePrice)
            * 100).ToString("F2"))% of average price
}

@section Summary {
    <div class="bg-info text-white m-2 p-2">
        <vc:city-summary theme-name="secondary" />
    </div>
}
```

The name of each parameter is expressed an attribute using kebab-case so that the
`theme-name` attribute provides a value for the `themeName` parameter. Listing 24.23 sets
a value in the `Data.cshtml` Razor Page.

Listing 24.23 Supplying a value in the Data.cshtml file in the Pages folder

```
@page
@inject DataContext context;

<h5 class="bg-primary text-white text-center m-2 p-2">Categories</h5>
<ul class="list-group m-2">
    @foreach (Category c in context.Categories) {
        <li class="list-group-item">@c.Name</li>
    }
</ul>

<div class="bg-info text-white m-2 p-2">
    <vc:city-summary theme-name="danger" />
</div>
```

Restart ASP.NET Core and use a browser to request http://localhost:5000/home/
index/1 and http://localhost:5000/data. The view component is provided with different values for the `themeName` parameter, producing the responses shown in figure
24.9.

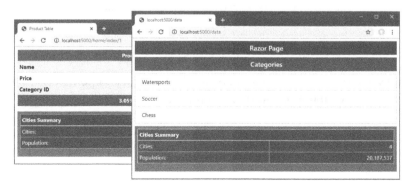

**Figure 24.9
Using context
data in a view
component**

Providing values using the component helper

If you prefer applying view components using the `Component.InvokeAsync` helper, then you can provide context using method arguments, like this:

```
...
<div cla"s="bg-info text-white m-2 p-2">
    @await Component.InvokeAsync("CitySummary",
        new { themeName= "danger" })
</div>
...
```

The first argument to the `InvokeAsync` method is the name of the view component class. The second argument is an object whose names correspond to the parameters defined by the view component.

USING A DEFAULT PARAMETER VALUE

Default values can be defined for the `Invoke` method parameters, as shown in listing 24.24, which provides a fallback if the parent view doesn't provide a value.

> **Listing 24.24   A default value in the CitySummary.cs file in the Components folder**

```
using Microsoft.AspNetCore.Mvc;
using WebApp.Models;
using Microsoft.AspNetCore.Mvc.ViewComponents;
using Microsoft.AspNetCore.Html;

namespace WebApp.Components {

    public class CitySummary : ViewComponent {
        private CitiesData data;

        public CitySummary(CitiesData cdata) {
            data = cdata;
        }

        public IViewComponentResult Invoke(string themeName="success") {
            ViewBag.Theme = themeName;
            return View(new CityViewModel {
                Cities = data.Cities.Count(),
                Population = data.Cities.Sum(c => c.Population)
            });
        }
    }
}
```

The default value is `success`, and it will be used if the view component is applied without a `theme-name` attribute, as shown in Listing 24.25.

Listing 24.25 Omitting the attribute in the Data.cshtml file in the Pages folder

```
@page
@inject DataContext context;

<h5 class="bg-primary text-white text-center m-2 p-2">Categories</h5>
<ul class="list-group m-2">
    @foreach (Category c in context.Categories) {
        <li class="list-group-item">@c.Name</li>
    }
</ul>

<div class="bg-info text-white m-2 p-2">
    <vc:city-summary />
</div>
```

Restart ASP.NET Core and use a browser to request http://localhost:5000/data. The default value is used to select the theme, as shown in figure 24.10.

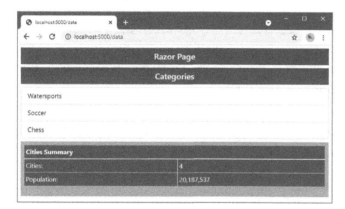

**Figure 24.10
Using a
default value**

24.5.2 Creating asynchronous view components

All the examples so far in this chapter have been synchronous view components, which can be recognized because they define the `Invoke` method. If your view component relies on asynchronous APIs, then you can create an asynchronous view component by defining an `InvokeAsync` method that returns a `Task`. When Razor receives the `Task` from the `InvokeAsync` method, it will wait for it to complete and then insert the result into the main view. To create a new component, add a class file named `PageSize.cs` to the `Components` folder and use it to define the class shown in listing 24.26.

Listing 24.26 The contents of the PageSize.cs file in the Components folder

```
using Microsoft.AspNetCore.Mvc;

namespace WebApp.Components {

    public class PageSize : ViewComponent {

        public async Task<IViewComponentResult> InvokeAsync() {
```

```
            HttpClient client = new HttpClient();
            HttpResponseMessage response
                = await client.GetAsync("http://microsoft.com");
            return View(response.Content.Headers.ContentLength);
        }
    }
}
```

The `InvokeAsync` method uses the `async` and `await` keywords to consume the asynchronous API provided by the `HttpClient` class and get the length of the content returned by sending a GET request to `microsoft.com`. The length is passed to the `View` method, which selects the default partial view associated with the view component.

Create the `Views/Shared/Components/PageSize` folder and add to it a Razor View named `Default.cshtml` with the content shown in listing 24.27.

> **Listing 24.27   The Default.cshtml file in the Views/Shared/Components/PageSize folder**

```
@model long
<div class="m-1 p-1 bg-light text-dark">Page size: @Model</div>
```

The final step is to use the component, which I have done in the `Index` view used by the `Home` controller, as shown in listing 24.28. No change is required in the way that asynchronous view components are used.

> **Listing 24.28   Using an asynchronous component in the Index.cshtml file in the Views/Home folder**

```
@model Product?
@{
    Layout = "_Layout";
    ViewBag.Title = "Product Table";
}

@section Header {
    Product Information
}

<tr><th>Name</th><td>@Model?.Name</td></tr>
<tr>
    <th>Price</th>
    <td>@Model?.Price.ToString("c")</td>
</tr>
<tr><th>Category ID</th><td>@Model?.CategoryId</td></tr>

@section Footer {
    @(((Model?.Price / ViewBag.AveragePrice)
            * 100).ToString("F2"))% of average price
}

@section Summary {
    <div class="bg-info text-white m-2 p-2">
        <vc:city-summary theme-name="secondary" />
        <vc:page-size />
    </div>
}
```

Restart ASP.NET Core and use a browser to request http://localhost:5000/home/ index/1, which will produce a response that includes the size of the Microsoft home page, as shown in figure 24.11. At the time of writing, the response sent by the Microsoft website is a concise message used for requests that don't include a browser user-agent header, but you may see a different response.

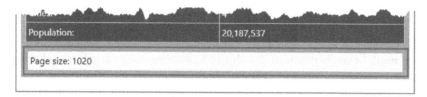

Figure 24.11 Using an asynchronous component

24.6 *Creating view components classes*

View components often provide a summary or snapshot of functionality that is handled in-depth by a controller or Razor Page. For a view component that summarizes a shopping basket, for example, there will often be a link that targets a controller that provides a detailed list of the products in the basket and that can be used to check out and complete the purchase.

In this situation, you can create a class that is a view component as well as a controller or Razor Page. If you are using Visual Studio, expand the `Cities.cshtml` item in the Solution Explorer to show the `Cities.cshtml.cs` file and replace its contents with those shown in listing 24.29. If you are using Visual Studio Code, add a file named `Cities.cshtml.cs` to the `Pages` folder with the content shown in listing 24.29.

Listing 24.29 The contents of the Cities.cshtml.cs file in the Pages folder

```
using Microsoft.AspNetCore.Mvc;
using Microsoft.AspNetCore.Mvc.RazorPages;
using Microsoft.AspNetCore.Mvc.ViewComponents;
using Microsoft.AspNetCore.Mvc.ViewFeatures;
using WebApp.Models;

namespace WebApp.Pages {

    [ViewComponent(Name = "CitiesPageHybrid")]
    public class CitiesModel : PageModel {

        public CitiesModel(CitiesData cdata) {
            Data = cdata;
        }

        public CitiesData? Data { get; set; }

        [ViewComponentContext]
        public ViewComponentContext Context { get; set; } = new();

        public IViewComponentResult Invoke() {
```

```
                    return new ViewViewComponentResult() {
                        ViewData = new ViewDataDictionary<CityViewModel>(
                            Context.ViewData,
                            new CityViewModel {
                                Cities = Data?.Cities.Count(),
                                Population = Data?.Cities.Sum(c => c.Population)
                            })
                    };
                }
            }
        }
```

This page model class is decorated with the `ViewComponent` attribute, which allows it to be used as a view component. The `Name` argument specifies the name by which the view component will be applied. Since a page model cannot inherit from the `View-Component` base class, a property whose type is `ViewComponentContext` is decorated with the `ViewComponentContext` attribute, which signals that it should be assigned an object that defines the properties described in table 24.5 before the `Invoke` or `InvokeAsync` method is invoked. The `View` method isn't available, so I have to create a `ViewViewComponentResult` object, which relies on the context object received through the decorated property. Listing 24.30 updates the view part of the page to use the new page model class.

> **Listing 24.30   Updating the view in the Cities.cshtml file in the Pages folder**

```
@page
@model WebApp.Pages.CitiesModel

<div class="m-2">
    <table class="table table-sm table-striped table-bordered">
        <tbody>
            @foreach (City c in Model.Data?.Cities ??
                        Enumerable.Empty<City>()) {
                <tr>
                    <td>@c.Name</td>
                    <td>@c.Country</td>
                    <td>@c.Population</td>
                </tr>
            }
        </tbody>
    </table>
</div>
```

The changes update the directives to use the page model class. To create the view for the hybrid view component, create the `Pages/Shared/Components/CitiesPageHybrid` folder and add to it a Razor View named `Default.cshtml` with the content shown in listing 24.31.

> **Listing 24.31   The Default.cshtml file in the Pages/Shared/Components/
> CitiesPageHybrid folder**

```
@model CityViewModel

<table class="table table-sm table-bordered text-white bg-dark">
```

```
<thead><tr><th colspan="2">Hybrid Page Summary</th></tr></thead>
<tbody>
    <tr>
        <td>Cities:</td>
        <td class="text-right">@Model?.Cities</td>
    </tr>
    <tr>
        <td>Population:</td>
        <td class="text-right">
            @Model?.Population?.ToString("#,###")
        </td>
    </tr>
</tbody>
</table>
```

Listing 24.32 applies the view component part of the hybrid class in another page.

Listing 24.32   Using a view component in the Data.cshtml file in the Pages folder

```
@page
@inject DataContext context;

<h5 class="bg-primary text-white text-center m-2 p-2">Categories</h5>
<ul class="list-group m-2">
    @foreach (Category c in context.Categories) {
        <li class="list-group-item">@c.Name</li>
    }
</ul>



<div class="bg-info text-white m-2 p-2">
    <vc:cities-page-hybrid />
</div>
```

Hybrids are applied just like any other view component. Restart ASP.NET Core and request http://localhost:5000/cities and http://localhost:5000/data. Both URLs are processed by the same class. For the first URL, the class acts as a page model; for the second URL, the class acts as a view component. Figure 24.12 shows the output for both URLs.

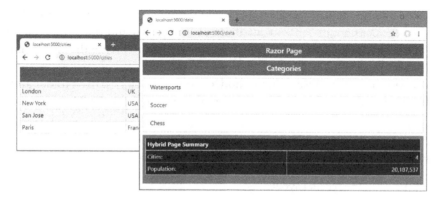

Figure 24.12   A hybrid page model and view component class

24.6.1 *Creating a hybrid controller class*

The same technique can be applied to controllers. Add a class file named
`CitiesController.cs` to the `Controllers` folder and add the statements shown in
listing 24.33.

> **Listing 24.33   The contents of the CitiesController.cs file in the Controllers folder**

```
using Microsoft.AspNetCore.Mvc;
using Microsoft.AspNetCore.Mvc.ViewComponents;
using Microsoft.AspNetCore.Mvc.ViewFeatures;
using WebApp.Models;

namespace WebApp.Controllers {

    [ViewComponent(Name = "CitiesControllerHybrid")]
    public class CitiesController : Controller {
        private CitiesData data;

        public CitiesController(CitiesData cdata) {
            data = cdata;
        }

        public IActionResult Index() {
            return View(data.Cities);
        }

        public IViewComponentResult Invoke() {
            return new ViewViewComponentResult() {
                ViewData = new ViewDataDictionary<CityViewModel>(
                    ViewData,
                    new CityViewModel {
                        Cities = data.Cities.Count(),
                        Population = data.Cities.Sum(c => c.Population)
                    })
            };
        }
    }
}
```

A quirk in the way that controllers are instantiated means that a property decorated
with the `ViewComponentContext` attribute isn't required and the `ViewData` property
inherited from the `Controller` base class can be used to create the view component
result.

   To provide a view for the action method, create the `Views/Cities` folder and add to
it a file named `Index.cshtml` with the content shown in listing 24.34.

> **Listing 24.34   The contents of the Index.cshtml file in the Views/Cities folder**

```
@model IEnumerable<City>
@{
    Layout = "_ImportantLayout";
}

<div class="m-2">
```

```
    <table class="table table-sm table-striped table-bordered">
        <tbody>
            @foreach (City c in Model) {
                <tr>
                    <td>@c.Name</td>
                    <td>@c.Country</td>
                    <td>@c.Population</td>
                </tr>
            }
        </tbody>
    </table>
</div>
```

To provide a view for the view component, create the `Views/Shared/Components/`
`CitiesControllerHybrid` folder and add to it a Razor View named `Default.cshtml`
with the content shown in listing 24.35.

> **Listing 24.35   The Default.cshtml file in the Views/Shared/Components/**
> **CitiesControllerHybrid folder**

```
@model CityViewModel

<table class="table table-sm table-bordered text-white bg-dark">
    <thead><tr><th colspan="2">Hybrid Controller Summary</th></tr></thead>
    <tbody>
        <tr>
            <td>Cities:</td>
            <td class="text-right">@Model.Cities</td>
        </tr>
        <tr>
            <td>Population:</td>
            <td class="text-right">
                @Model.Population?.ToString("#,###")
            </td>
        </tr>
    </tbody>
</table>
```

Listing 24.36 applies the hybrid view component in the `Data.cshtml` Razor Page,
replacing the hybrid class created in the previous section.

> **Listing 24.36   Applying the view component in the Data.cshtml file in the Pages folder**

```
@page
@inject DataContext context;

<h5 class="bg-primary text-white text-center m-2 p-2">Categories</h5>
<ul class="list-group m-2">
    @foreach (Category c in context.Categories) {
        <li class="list-group-item">@c.Name</li>
    }
</ul>

<div class="bg-info text-white m-2 p-2">
    <vc:cities-controller-hybrid />
</div>
```

Restart ASP.NET Core and use a browser to request http://localhost:5000/cities/index and http://localhost:5000/data. For the first URL, the class in listing 24.36 is used as a controller; for the second URL, the class is used as a view component. Figure 24.13 shows the responses for both URLs.

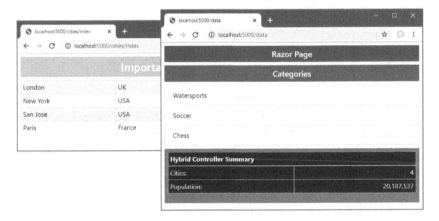

Figure 24.13   A hybrid controller and view component class

Summary

- View components are self-contained and generate content that isn't related to the main purpose of the application.
- View components are C# classes that are derived from `ViewComponent` and whose `Invoke` method is called to generate content.
- View components are applied using the `Component` property, which returns a helper or using the `vc` tag helper.
- View components can use partial views to generate HTML content.
- View components can receive data from the view in which they are applied and can use standard platform features such as dependency injection.

Using tag helpers

Tag helpers are C# classes that transform HTML elements in a view or page. Common uses for tag helpers include generating URLs for forms using the application's routing configuration, ensuring that elements of a specific type are styled consistently, and replacing custom shorthand elements with commonly used fragments of content. In this chapter, I describe how tag helpers work and how custom tag helpers are created and applied. In chapter 26, I describe the built-in tag helpers, and in chapter 27, I use tag helpers to explain how HTML forms are created. Table 25.1 puts tag helpers in context.

Table 25.1   Putting tag helpers in context

Question	Answer
What are they?	Tag helpers are classes that manipulate HTML elements, either to change them in some way, to supplement them with additional content, or to replace them entirely with new content.
Why are they useful?	Tag helpers allow view content to be generated or transformed using C# logic, ensuring that the HTML sent to the client reflects the state of the application.
How are they used?	The HTML elements to which tag helpers are applied are selected based on the name of the class or with the `HTMLTargetElement` attribute. When a view is rendered, elements are transformed by tag helpers and included in the HTML sent to the client.
Are there any pitfalls or limitations?	It can be easy to get carried away and generate complex sections of HTML content using tag helpers, which is something that is more readily achieved using view components, described in chapter 24.
Are there any alternatives?	You don't have to use tag helpers, but they make it easy to generate complex HTML in ASP.NET Core applications.

Table 25.2 provides a guide to the chapter.

Table 25.2   Chapter guide

Problem	Solution	Listing
Creating a tag helper	Define a class that is derived from the `TagHelper` class.	1–7
Controlling the scope of a tag helper	Alter the range of elements specified by the `HtmlTargetElement` attribute.	8–11
Creating custom HTML elements that are replaced with content	Use shorthand elements.	12, 13
Creating elements programmatically	Use the `TagBuilder` class.	14
Controlling where content is inserted	Use the prepend and append features.	15–18
Getting context data	Use the context object.	19, 20
Operating on the view model or page model	Use a model expression.	21–25
Creating coordinating tag helpers	Use the `Items` property.	26, 27
Suppressing content	Use the `SuppressOutput` method.	28, 29
Defining tag helper as services	Create tag helper components.	30–33

25.1   *Preparing for this chapter*

This chapter uses the WebApp project from chapter 24. To prepare for this chapter, replace the contents of the `Program.cs` file with those in listing 25.1, removing some of the configuration statements used in earlier chapters.

TIP You can download the example project for this chapter—and for all the other chapters in this book—from https://github.com/manningbooks/pro-asp .net-core-7. See chapter 1 for how to get help if you have problems running the examples.

```
using Microsoft.EntityFrameworkCore;
using WebApp.Models;

var builder = WebApplication.CreateBuilder(args);

builder.Services.AddDbContext<DataContext>(opts => {
    opts.UseSqlServer(builder.Configuration[
        "ConnectionStrings:ProductConnection"]);
    opts.EnableSensitiveDataLogging(true);
});
builder.Services.AddControllersWithViews();
builder.Services.AddRazorPages();
builder.Services.AddSingleton<CitiesData>();

var app = builder.Build();

app.UseStaticFiles();
app.MapControllers();
app.MapDefaultControllerRoute();
app.MapRazorPages();

var context = app.Services.CreateScope().ServiceProvider
    .GetRequiredService<DataContext>();
SeedData.SeedDatabase(context);

app.Run();
```

Next, replace the contents of the Index.cshtml file in the Views/Home folder with the content shown in listing 25.2.

```
@model Product?
@{
    Layout = "_SimpleLayout";
}

<table class="table table-striped table-bordered table-sm">
    <thead>
        <tr>
            <th colspan="2">Product Summary</th>
        </tr>
    </thead>
    <tbody>
        <tr><th>Name</th><td>@Model?.Name</td></tr>
        <tr><th>Price</th><td>@Model?.Price.ToString("c")</td></tr>
```

```
        <tr><th>Category ID</th><td>@Model?.CategoryId</td></tr>
    </tbody>
</table>
```

The view in listing 25.2 relies on a new layout. Add a Razor View file named _SimpleLayout.cshtml in the Views/Shared folder with the content shown in listing 25.3.

```
<!DOCTYPE html>
<html>
<head>
    <title>@ViewBag.Title</title>
    <link href="/lib/bootstrap/css/bootstrap.min.css" rel="stylesheet" />
</head>
<body>
    <div class="m-2">
        @RenderBody()
    </div>
</body>
</html>
```

25.1.1 Dropping the database

Open a new PowerShell command prompt, navigate to the folder that contains the WebApp.csproj file, and run the command shown in listing 25.4 to drop the database.

```
dotnet ef database drop --force
```

25.1.2 Running the example application

Use the PowerShell command prompt to run the command shown in listing 25.5.

```
dotnet run
```

Use a browser to request http://localhost:5000/home, which will produce the response shown in figure 25.1.

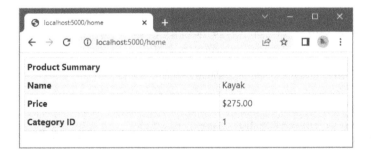

Figure 25.1   Running the example application

25.2   Creating a tag helper

The best way to understand tag helpers is to create one, which reveals how they operate and how they fit into an ASP.NET Core application. In the sections that follow, I go through the process of creating and applying a tag helper that will set the Bootstrap CSS classes for a `tr` element so that an element like this:

```
...
<tr bg-color="primary">
    <th colspan="2">Product Summary</th>
</tr>
...
```

will be transformed into this:

```
...
<tr class="bg-primary text-white text-center">
    <th colspan="2">Product Summary</th>
</tr>
...
```

The tag helper will recognize the `tr-color` attribute and use its value to set the `class` attribute on the element sent to the browser. This isn't the most dramatic—or useful— transformation, but it provides a foundation for explaining how tag helpers work.

25.2.1   Defining the tag helper class

Tag helpers can be defined anywhere in the project, but it helps to keep them together because they need to be registered before they can be used. Create the `WebApp/ TagHelpers` folder and add to it a class file named `TrTagHelper.cs` with the code shown in listing 25.6.

> **Listing 25.6   The contents of the TrTagHelper.cs file in the TagHelpers folder**

```
using Microsoft.AspNetCore.Razor.TagHelpers;

namespace WebApp.TagHelpers {

    public class TrTagHelper: TagHelper {

        public string BgColor { get; set; } = "dark";
        public string TextColor { get; set; } = "white";

        public override void Process(TagHelperContext context,
                TagHelperOutput output) {
            output.Attributes.SetAttribute("class",
                $"bg-{BgColor} text-center text-{TextColor}");
        }
    }
}
```

Tag helpers are derived from the `TagHelper` class, which is defined in the `Microsoft .AspNetCore.Razor.TagHelpers` namespace. The `TagHelper` class defines a `Process` method, which is overridden by subclasses to implement the behavior that transforms elements.

The name of the tag helper combines the name of the element it transforms followed by `TagHelper`. In the case of the example, the class name `TrTagHelper` indicates this is a tag helper that operates on `tr` elements. The range of elements to which a tag helper can be applied can be broadened or narrowed using attributes, as described later in this chapter, but the default behavior is defined by the class name.

> **TIP** Asynchronous tag helpers can be created by overriding the `ProcessAsync` method instead of the `Process` method, but this isn't required for most helpers, which tend to make small and focused changes to HTML elements. You can see an example of an asynchronous tag helper in the "Advanced Tag Helper Features" section.

RECEIVING CONTEXT DATA

Tag helpers receive information about the element they are transforming through an instance of the `TagHelperContext` class, which is received as an argument to the `Process` method and which defines the properties described in table 25.3.

Table 25.3   The TagHelperContext properties

Name	Description
AllAttributes	This property returns a read-only dictionary of the attributes applied to the element being transformed, indexed by name and by index.
Items	This property returns a dictionary that is used to coordinate between tag helpers, as described in the "Coordinating Between Tag Helpers" section.
UniqueId	This property returns a unique identifier for the element being transformed.

Although you can access details of the element's attributes through the `AllAttributes` dictionary, a more convenient approach is to define a property whose name corresponds to the attribute you are interested in, like this:

```
...
public string BgColor { get; set; } = "dark";
public string TextColor { get; set; } = "white";
...
```

When a tag helper is being used, the properties it defines are inspected and assigned the value of any whose name matches attributes applied to the HTML element. As part of this process, the attribute value will be converted to match the type of the C# property so that `bool` properties can be used to receive `true` and `false` attribute values and so `int` properties can be used to receive numeric attribute values such as 1 and 2.

Properties for which there are no corresponding HTML element attributes are not set, which means you should check to ensure that you are not dealing with `null` or provide default values, which is the approach taken in listing 25.6.

The name of the attribute is automatically converted from the default HTML style, `bg-color`, to the C# style, `BgColor`. You can use any attribute prefix except `asp-` (which

Microsoft uses) and `data-` (which is reserved for custom attributes that are sent to the client). The example tag helper will be configured using `bg-color` and `text-color` attributes, which will provide values for the `BgColor` and `TextColor` properties and be used to configure the `tr` element in the `Process` method, as follows:

```
...
output.Attributes.SetAttribute("class",
    $"bg-{BgColor} text-center text-{TextColor}");
...
```

> **TIP** Using the HTML attribute name for tag helper properties doesn't always lead to readable or understandable classes. You can break the link between the name of the property and the attribute it represents using the `HtmlAttributeName` attribute, which can be used to specify the HTML attribute that the property represents.

PRODUCING OUTPUT

The `Process` method transforms an element by configuring the `TagHelperOutput` object that is received as an argument. The `TagHelperOuput` object starts by describing the HTML element as it appears in the view and is modified through the properties and methods described in table 25.4.

Table 25.4 The TagHelperOutput properties and methods

Name	Description
`TagName`	This property is used to get or set the tag name for the output element.
`Attributes`	This property returns a dictionary containing the attributes for the output element.
`Content`	This property returns a `TagHelperContent` object that is used to set the content of the element.
`GetChildContentAsync()`	This asynchronous method provides access to the content of the element that will be transformed, as demonstrated in the "Creating Shorthand Elements" section.
`PreElement`	This property returns a `TagHelperContext` object that is used to insert content in the view before the output element. See the "Prepending and Appending Content and Elements" section.
`PostElement`	This property returns a `TagHelperContext` object that is used to insert content in the view after the output element. See the "Prepending and Appending Content and Elements" section.
`PreContent`	This property returns a `TagHelperContext` object that is used to insert content before the output element's content. See the "Prepending and Appending Content and Elements" section.
`PostContent`	This property returns a `TagHelperContext` object that is used to insert content after the output element's content. See the "Prepending and Appending Content and Elements" section.
`TagMode`	This property specifies how the output element will be written, using a value from the `TagMode` enumeration. See the "Creating Shorthand Elements" section.
`SupressOuput()`	Calling this method excludes an element from the view. See the "Suppressing the Output Element" section.

In the `TrTagHelper` class, I used the `Attributes` dictionary to add a `class` attribute to the HTML element that specifies Bootstrap styles, including the value of the `BgColor` and `TextColor` properties. The effect is that the background color for `tr` elements can be specified by setting `bg-color` and `text-color` attributes to Bootstrap names, such as `primary`, `info`, and `danger`.

25.2.2 Registering tag helpers

Tag helper classes must be registered with the `@addTagHelper` directive before they can be used. The set of views or pages to which a tag helper can be applied depends on where the `@addTagHelper` directive is used.

For a single view or page, the directive appears in the CSHTML file itself. To make a tag helper available more widely, it can be added to the view imports file, which is defined in the `Views` folder for controllers and the `Pages` folder for Razor Pages.

I want the tag helpers that I create in this chapter to be available anywhere in the application, which means that the `@addTagHelper` directive is added to the `_ViewImports.cshtml` files in the `Views` and `Pages` folders. The vc element used in chapter 24 to apply view components is a tag helper, which is why the directive required to enable tag helpers is already in the `_ViewImports.cshtml` file.

```
@using WebApp.Models
@addTagHelper *, Microsoft.AspNetCore.Mvc.TagHelpers
@using WebApp.Components
@addTagHelper *, WebApp
```

The first part of the argument specifies the names of the tag helper classes, with support for wildcards, and the second part specifies the name of the assembly in which they are defined. This `@addTagHelper` directive uses the wildcard to select all namespaces in the `WebApp` assembly, with the effect that tag helpers defined anywhere in the project can be used in any controller view. There is an identical statement in the Razor Pages `_ViewImports.cshtml` file in the `Pages` folder.

```
@namespace WebApp.Pages
@using WebApp.Models
@addTagHelper *, Microsoft.AspNetCore.Mvc.TagHelpers
@addTagHelper *, WebApp
```

The other `@addTagHelper` directive enables the built-in tag helpers that Microsoft provides, which are described in chapter 26.

25.2.3 Using a tag helper

The final step is to use the tag helper to transform an element. In listing 25.7, I have added the attribute to the `tr` element, which will apply the tag helper.

> Listing 25.7   Using a tag helper in the Index.cshtml file in the Views/Home folder

```
@model Product?
@{
    Layout = "_SimpleLayout";
}
```

```
<table class="table table-striped table-bordered table-sm">
    <thead>
        <tr bg-color="info" text-color="white">
            <th colspan="2">Product Summary</th>
        </tr>
    </thead>
    <tbody>
        <tr><th>Name</th><td>@Model?.Name</td></tr>
        <tr><th>Price</th><td>@Model?.Price.ToString("c")</td></tr>
        <tr><th>Category ID</th><td>@Model?.CategoryId</td></tr>
    </tbody>
</table>
```

Restart ASP.NET Core and use a browser to request http://localhost:5000/home, which produces the response shown in figure 25.2.

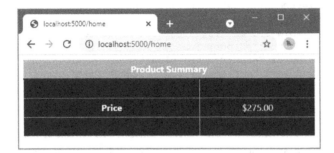

Figure 25.2
Using a tag
helper

The `tr` element to which the attributes were applied in listing 25.7 has been transformed, but that isn't the only change shown in the figure. By default, tag helpers apply to all elements of a specific type, which means that all the `tr` elements in the view have been transformed using the default values defined in the tag helper class, since no attributes were defined. (The reason that some table rows show no text is because of the Bootstrap `table-striped` class, which applies different styles to alternate rows.)

In fact, the problem is more serious because the `@addTagHelper` directives in the view import files mean that the example tag helper is applied to all `tr` elements used in any view rendered by controllers and Razor Pages. Use a browser to request http://localhost:5000/cities, for example, and you will see the `tr` elements in the response from the `Cities` Razor Page have also been transformed, as shown in figure 25.3.

Figure 25.3
Unexpectedly
modifying elements
with a tag helper

25.2.4 *Narrowing the scope of a tag helper*

The range of elements that are transformed by a tag helper can be controlled using the HtmlTargetElement element, as shown in listing 25.8.

> **Listing 25.8   Narrowing scope in the TrTagHelper.cs file in the TagHelpers folder**

```
using Microsoft.AspNetCore.Razor.TagHelpers;

namespace WebApp.TagHelpers {

    [HtmlTargetElement("tr", Attributes = "bg-color,text-color",
        ParentTag = "thead")]
    public class TrTagHelper : TagHelper {

        public string BgColor { get; set; } = "dark";
        public string TextColor { get; set; } = "white";

        public override void Process(TagHelperContext context,
                TagHelperOutput output) {
            output.Attributes.SetAttribute("class",
                $"bg-{BgColor} text-center text-{TextColor}");
        }
    }
}
```

The HtmlTargetElement attribute describes the elements to which the tag helper applies. The first argument specifies the element type and supports the additional named properties described in table 25.5.

Table 25.5   The HtmlTargetElement properties

Name	Description
Attributes	This property is used to specify that a tag helper should be applied only to elements that have a given set of attributes, supplied as a comma-separated list. An attribute name that ends with an asterisk will be treated as a prefix so that bg-* will match bg-color, bg-size, and so on.
ParentTag	This property is used to specify that a tag helper should be applied only to elements that are contained within an element of a given type.
TagStructure	This property is used to specify that a tag helper should be applied only to elements whose tag structure corresponds to the given value from the TagStructure enumeration, which defines Unspecified, NormalOrSelfClosing, and WithoutEndTag.

The Attributes property supports CSS attribute selector syntax so that [bg-color] matches elements that have a bg-color attribute, [bg-color=primary] matches elements that have a bg-color attribute whose value is primary, and [bg-color^=p] matches elements with a bg-color attribute whose value begins with p. The attribute applied to the tag helper in listing 25.8 matches `tr` elements with both `bg-color` and `text-color` attributes that are children of a `thead` element. Restart ASP.NET Core and use a browser to request http://localhost:5000/home/index/1, and you will see the scope of the tag helper has been narrowed, as shown in figure 25.4.

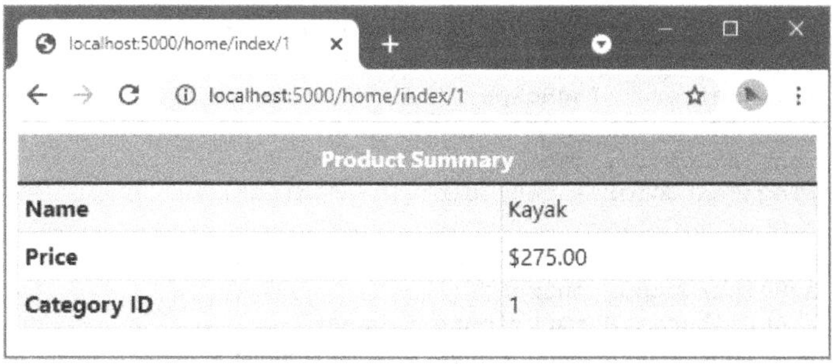

Figure 25.4 Narrowing the scope of a tag helper

25.2.5 *Widening the scope of a tag helper*

The `HtmlTargetElement` attribute can also be used to widen the scope of a tag helper so that it matches a broader range of elements. This is done by setting the attribute's first argument to an asterisk (the * character), which matches any element. Listing 25.9 changes the attribute applied to the example tag helper so that it matches any element that has `bg-color` and `text-color` attributes.

Listing 25.9   Widening scope in the TrTagHelper.cs file in the TagHelpers folder

```
using Microsoft.AspNetCore.Razor.TagHelpers;

namespace WebApp.TagHelpers {

    [HtmlTargetElement("*", Attributes = "bg-color,text-color")]
    public class TrTagHelper : TagHelper {

        public string BgColor { get; set; } = "dark";
        public string TextColor { get; set; } = "white";

        public override void Process(TagHelperContext context,
                TagHelperOutput output) {
            output.Attributes.SetAttribute("class",
                $"bg-{BgColor} text-center text-{TextColor}");
        }
    }
}
```

Care must be taken when using the asterisk because it is easy to match too widely and select elements that should not be transformed. A safer middle ground is to apply the `HtmlTargetElement` attribute for each type of element, as shown in listing 25.10.

Listing 25.10   Balancing scope in the TrTagHelper.cs file in the TagHelpers folder

```
using Microsoft.AspNetCore.Razor.TagHelpers;

namespace WebApp.TagHelpers {

    [HtmlTargetElement("tr", Attributes = "bg-color,text-color")]
    [HtmlTargetElement("td", Attributes = "bg-color")]
    public class TrTagHelper : TagHelper {

        public string BgColor { get; set; } = "dark";
        public string TextColor { get; set; } = "white";

        public override void Process(TagHelperContext context,
                TagHelperOutput output) {
            output.Attributes.SetAttribute("class",
                $"bg-{BgColor} text-center text-{TextColor}");
        }
    }
}
```

Each instance of the attribute can use different selection criteria. This tag helper matches `tr` elements with `bg-color` and `text-color` attributes and matches `td` elements with `bg-color` attributes. Listing 25.11 adds an element to be transformed to the `Index` view to demonstrate the revised scope.

Listing 25.11   Adding attributes in the Index.cshtml file in the Views/Home folder

```
@model Product?
@{
    Layout = "_SimpleLayout";
}

<table class="table table-striped table-bordered table-sm">
    <thead>
        <tr bg-color="info" text-color="white">
            <th colspan="2">Product Summary</th>
        </tr>
    </thead>
    <tbody>
        <tr><th>Name</th><td>@Model?.Name</td></tr>
        <tr>
            <th>Price</th>
            <td bg-color="dark">@Model?.Price.ToString("c")</td>
        </tr>
        <tr><th>Category ID</th><td>@Model?.CategoryId</td></tr>
    </tbody>
</table>
```

Restart ASP.NET Core and use a browser to request http://localhost:5000/home/index/1. The response will contain two transformed elements, as shown in figure 25.5.

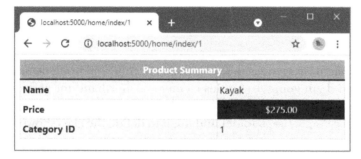

Figure 25.5   Managing the scope of a tag helper

Ordering tag helper execution

If you need to apply multiple tag helpers to an element, you can control the sequence in which they execute by setting the `Order` property, which is inherited from the `TagHelper` base class. Managing the sequence can help minimize the conflicts between tag helpers, although it is still easy to encounter problems.

25.3   Advanced tag helper features

The previous section demonstrated how to create a basic tag helper, but that just scratches the surface of what's possible. In the sections that follow, I show more advanced uses for tag helpers and the features they provide.

25.3.1   Creating shorthand elements

Tag helpers are not restricted to transforming the standard HTML elements and can also be used to replace custom elements with commonly used content. This can be a useful feature for making views more concise and making their intent more obvious. To demonstrate, listing 25.12 replaces the `thead` element in the `Index` view with a custom HTML element.

Listing 25.12   Adding a custom element in the Index.cshtml file in the Views/Home folder

```
@model Product?
@{
    Layout = "_SimpleLayout";
}

<table class="table table-striped table-bordered table-sm">
    <tablehead bg-color="dark">Product Summary</tablehead>
    <tbody>
        <tr><th>Name</th><td>@Model?.Name</td></tr>
        <tr>
            <th>Price</th>
            <td bg-color="dark">@Model?.Price.ToString("c")</td>
```

```
        </tr>
        <tr><th>Category ID</th><td>@Model?.CategoryId</td></tr>
    </tbody>
</table>
```

The `tablehead` element isn't part of the HTML specification and won't be understood by browsers. Instead, I am going to use this element as shorthand for generating the `thead` element and its content for the HTML table. Add a class named `TableHead-TagHelper.cs` to the `TagHelpers` folder and use it to define the class shown in listing 25.13.

> **TIP** When dealing with custom elements that are not part of the HTML specification, you must apply the `HtmlTargetElement` attribute and specify the element name, as shown in listing 25.13. The convention of applying tag helpers to elements based on the class name works only for standard element names.

> **Listing 25.13   The contents of TableHeadTagHelper.cs file in the TagHelpers folder**

```
using Microsoft.AspNetCore.Razor.TagHelpers;

namespace WebApp.TagHelpers {

    [HtmlTargetElement("tablehead")]
    public class TableHeadTagHelper : TagHelper {

        public string BgColor { get; set; } = "light";

        public override async Task ProcessAsync(TagHelperContext context,
                TagHelperOutput output) {

            output.TagName = "thead";
            output.TagMode = TagMode.StartTagAndEndTag;
            output.Attributes.SetAttribute("class",
                $"bg-{BgColor} text-white text-center");

            string content =
                (await output.GetChildContentAsync()).GetContent();
            output.Content.SetHtmlContent(
                $"<tr><th colspan=\"2\">{content}</th></tr>");
        }
    }
}
```

This tag helper is asynchronous and overrides the `ProcessAsync` method so that it can access the existing content of the elements it transforms. The `ProcessAsync` method uses the properties of the `TagHelperOuput` object to generate a completely different element: the `TagName` property is used to specify a `thead` element, the `TagMode` property is used to specify that the element is written using start and end tags, the `Attributes.SetAttribute` method is used to define a `class` attribute, and the `Content` property is used to set the element content.

The existing content of the element is obtained through the asynchronous `GetChildContentAsync` method, which returns a `TagHelperContent` object. This is the same object that is returned by the `TagHelperOutput.Content` property and allows the content of the element to be inspected and changed using the same type, through the methods described in table 25.6.

Table 25.6 Useful TagHelperContent methods

Name	Description
`GetContent()`	This method returns the contents of the HTML element as a string.
`SetContent(text)`	This method sets the content of the output element. The `string` argument is encoded so that it is safe for inclusion in an HTML element.
`SetHtmlContent(html)`	This method sets the content of the output element. The `string` argument is assumed to be safely encoded. Use with caution.
`Append(text)`	This method safely encodes the specified `string` and adds it to the content of the output element.
`AppendHtml(html)`	This method adds the specified `string` to the content of the output element without performing any encoding. Use with caution.
`Clear()`	This method removes the content of the output element.

In listing 25.13, the existing content of the element is read through the `GetContent` element and then set using the `SetHtmlContent` method. The effect is to wrap the existing content in the transformed element in `tr` and `th` elements.

Restart ASP.NET Core and navigate to http://localhost:5000/home/index/1, and you will see the effect of the tag helper, which is shown in figure 25.6.

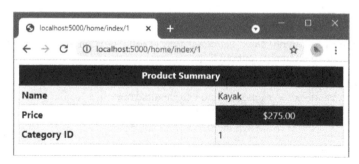

**Figure 25.6
Using a shorthand
element**

The tag helper transforms this shorthand element:

```
...
<tablehead bg-color="dark">Product Summary</tablehead>
...
```

into these elements:

```
...
<thead class="bg-dark text-white text-center">
    <tr>
```

```
        <th colspan="2">Product Summary</th>
    </tr>
</thead>
...
```

Notice that the transformed elements do not include the `bg-color` attribute. Attributes matched to properties defined by the tag helper are removed from the output element and must be explicitly redefined if they are required.

25.3.2 *Creating elements programmatically*

When generating new HTML elements, you can use standard C# string formatting to create the content you require, which is the approach I took in listing 25.13. This works, but it can be awkward and requires close attention to avoid typos. A more robust approach is to use the `TagBuilder` class, which is defined in the `Microsoft .AspNetCore.Mvc.Rendering` namespace and allows elements to be created in a more structured manner. The `TagHelperContent` methods described in table 25.6 accept `TagBuilder` objects, which makes it easy to create HTML content in tag helpers, as shown in listing 25.14.

> **Listing 25.14 HTML elements in the TableHeadTagHelper.cs file in the TagHelpers folder**

```
using Microsoft.AspNetCore.Razor.TagHelpers;
using Microsoft.AspNetCore.Mvc.Rendering;

namespace WebApp.TagHelpers {

    [HtmlTargetElement("tablehead")]
    public class TableHeadTagHelper: TagHelper {

        public string BgColor { get; set; } = "light";

        public override async Task ProcessAsync(TagHelperContext context,
                TagHelperOutput output) {

            output.TagName = "thead";
            output.TagMode = TagMode.StartTagAndEndTag;
            output.Attributes.SetAttribute("class",
                $"bg-{BgColor} text-white text-center");

            string content =
                (await output.GetChildContentAsync()).GetContent();

            TagBuilder header = new TagBuilder("th");
            header.Attributes["colspan"] = "2";
            header.InnerHtml.Append(content);

            TagBuilder row = new TagBuilder("tr");
            row.InnerHtml.AppendHtml(header);

            output.Content.SetHtmlContent(row);
        }
    }
}
```

This example creates each new element using a `TagBuilder` object and composes them to produce the same HTML structure as the string-based version in listing 25.13.

25.3.3 Prepending and appending content and elements

The `TagHelperOutput` class provides four properties that make it easy to inject new content into a view so that it surrounds an element or the element's content, as described in table 25.7. In the sections that follow, I explain how you can insert content around and inside the target element.

Table 25.7   The TagHelperOutput properties for appending context and elements

Name	Description
PreElement	This property is used to insert elements into the view before the target element.
PostElement	This property is used to insert elements into the view after the target element.
PreContent	This property is used to insert content into the target element, before any existing content.
PostContent	This property is used to insert content into the target element, after any existing content.

INSERTING CONTENT AROUND THE OUTPUT ELEMENT

The first `TagHelperOuput` properties are `PreElement` and `PostElement`, which are used to insert elements into the view before and after the output element. To demonstrate the use of these properties, add a class file named `ContentWrapperTagHelper.cs` to the `WebApp/TagHelpers` folder with the content shown in listing 25.15.

Listing 25.15   The contents of the WrapperTagHelper.cs file in the TagHelpers folder

```
using Microsoft.AspNetCore.Mvc.Rendering;
using Microsoft.AspNetCore.Razor.TagHelpers;

namespace WebApp.TagHelpers {

    [HtmlTargetElement("*", Attributes = "[wrap=true]")]
    public class ContentWrapperTagHelper: TagHelper {

        public override void Process(TagHelperContext context,
                TagHelperOutput output) {
            TagBuilder elem = new TagBuilder("div");
            elem.Attributes["class"] = "bg-primary text-white p-2 m-2";
            elem.InnerHtml.AppendHtml("Wrapper");

            output.PreElement.AppendHtml(elem);
            output.PostElement.AppendHtml(elem);
        }
    }
}
```

This tag helper transforms elements that have a wrap attribute whose value is true, which it does using the PreElement and PostElement properties to add a div element before and after the output element. Listing 25.16 adds an element to the Index view that is transformed by the tag helper.

```
@model Product?
@{
    Layout = "_SimpleLayout";
}

<div class="m-2" wrap="true">Inner Content</div>

<table class="table table-striped table-bordered table-sm">
    <tablehead bg-color="dark">Product Summary</tablehead>
    <tbody>
        <tr><th>Name</th><td>@Model?.Name</td></tr>
        <tr>
            <th>Price</th>
            <td bg-color="dark">@Model?.Price.ToString("c")</td>
        </tr>
        <tr><th>Category ID</th><td>@Model?.CategoryId</td></tr>
    </tbody>
</table>
```

Restart ASP.NET Core and use a browser to request http://localhost:5000/home/index/1. The response includes the transformed element, as shown in figure 25.7.

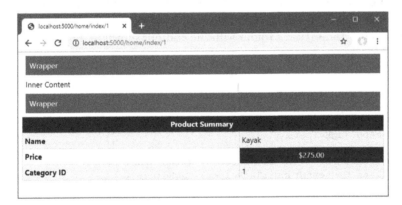

Figure 25.7   Inserting content around the output element

If you examine the HTML sent to the browser, you will see that this element:

```
...
<div class="m-2" wrap="true">Inner Content</div>
...
```

has been transformed into these elements:

```
...
<div class="bg-primary text-white p-2 m-2">Wrapper</div>
<div class="m-2" wrap="true">Inner Content</div>
<div class="bg-primary text-white p-2 m-2">Wrapper</div>
...
```

Notice that the `wrap` attribute has been left on the output element. This is because I didn't define a property in the tag helper class that corresponds to this attribute. If you want to prevent attributes from being included in the output, then define a property for them in the tag helper class, even if you don't use the attribute value.

INSERTING CONTENT INSIDE THE OUTPUT ELEMENT

The `PreContent` and `PostContent` properties are used to insert content inside the output element, surrounding the original content. To demonstrate this feature, add a class file named `HighlightTagHelper.cs` to the `TagHelpers` folder and use it to define the tag helper shown in listing 25.17.

> **Listing 25.17 The contents of the HighlightTagHelper.cs file in the TagHelpers folder**

```
using Microsoft.AspNetCore.Razor.TagHelpers;

namespace WebApp.TagHelpers {

    [HtmlTargetElement("*", Attributes = "[highlight=true]")]
    public class HighlightTagHelper: TagHelper {

        public override void Process(TagHelperContext context,
                TagHelperOutput output) {

            output.PreContent.SetHtmlContent("<b><i>");
            output.PostContent.SetHtmlContent("</i></b>");
        }
    }
}
```

This tag helper inserts `b` and `i` elements around the output element's content. Listing 25.18 adds the wrap attribute to one of the table cells in the `Index` view.

> **Listing 25.18 Adding an attribute in the Index.cshtml file in the Views/Home folder**

```
@model Product?
@{
    Layout = "_SimpleLayout";
}

<div class="m-2" wrap="true">Inner Content</div>

<table class="table table-striped table-bordered table-sm">
    <tablehead bg-color="dark">Product Summary</tablehead>
    <tbody>
        <tr><th>Name</th><td highlight="true">@Model?.Name</td></tr>
        <tr>
            <th>Price</th>
            <td bg-color="dark">@Model?.Price.ToString("c")</td>
```

```
        </tr>
        <tr><th>Category ID</th><td>@Model?.CategoryId</td></tr>
    </tbody>
</table>
```

Restart ASP.NET Core and use a browser to request http://localhost:5000/home/
index/1. The response includes the transformed element, as shown in figure 25.8.

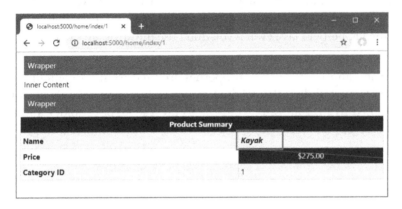

Figure 25.8   Inserting content inside an element

If you examine the HTML sent to the browser, you will see that this element:

```
...
<td highlight="true">@Model?.Name</td>
...
```

has been transformed into these elements:

```
...
<td highlight="true"><b><i>Kayak</i></b></td>
...
```

25.3.4 *Getting view context data*

A common use for tag helpers is to transform elements so they contain details of the
current request or the view model/page model, which requires access to context data.
To create this type of tag helper, add a file named `RouteDataTagHelper.cs` to the
`TagHelpers` folder, with the content shown in listing 25.19.

Listing 25.19   The contents of the RouteDataTagHelper.cs file in the TagHelpers folder

```
using Microsoft.AspNetCore.Mvc.Rendering;
using Microsoft.AspNetCore.Mvc.ViewFeatures;
using Microsoft.AspNetCore.Razor.TagHelpers;

namespace WebApp.TagHelpers {

    [HtmlTargetElement("div", Attributes = "[route-data=true]")]
    public class RouteDataTagHelper : TagHelper {

        [ViewContext]
```

```
[HtmlAttributeNotBound]
public ViewContext Context { get; set; } = new();

public override void Process(TagHelperContext context,
        TagHelperOutput output) {

    output.Attributes.SetAttribute("class", "bg-primary m-2 p-2");

    TagBuilder list = new TagBuilder("ul");
    list.Attributes["class"] = "list-group";
    RouteValueDictionary rd = Context.RouteData.Values;
    if (rd.Count > 0) {
        foreach (var kvp in rd) {
            TagBuilder item = new TagBuilder("li");
            item.Attributes["class"] = "list-group-item";
            item.InnerHtml.Append($"{kvp.Key}: {kvp.Value}");
            list.InnerHtml.AppendHtml(item);
        }
        output.Content.AppendHtml(list);
    } else {
        output.Content.Append("No route data");
    }
}
```

The tag helper transforms div elements that have a route-data attribute whose value is true and populates the output element with a list of the segment variables obtained by the routing system.

To get the route data, I added a property called Context and decorated it with two attributes, like this:

```
...
[ViewContext]
[HtmlAttributeNotBound]
public ViewContext Context { get; set; } = new();
...
```

The ViewContext attribute denotes that the value of this property should be assigned a ViewContext object when a new instance of the tag helper class is created, which provides details of the view that is being rendered, including the routing data, as described in chapter 13.

The HtmlAttributeNotBound attribute prevents a value from being assigned to this property if there is a matching attribute defined on the div element. This is good practice, especially if you are writing tag helpers for other developers to use.

TIP Tag helpers can declare dependencies on services in their constructors, which are resolved using the dependency injection feature described in chapter 14.

Listing 25.20 adds an element to the Home controller's Index view that will be transformed by the new tag helper.

```
@model Product?
@{
    Layout = "_SimpleLayout";
}

<div route-data="true"></div>

<table class="table table-striped table-bordered table-sm">
    <tablehead bg-color="dark">Product Summary</tablehead>
    <tbody>
        <tr><th>Name</th><td highlight="true">@Model?.Name</td></tr>
        <tr>
            <th>Price</th>
            <td bg-color="dark">@Model?.Price.ToString("c")</td>
        </tr>
        <tr><th>Category ID</th><td>@Model?.CategoryId</td></tr>
    </tbody>
</table>
```

Restart ASP.NET Core and use a browser to request http://localhost:5000/home/
index/1. The response will include a list of the segment variables the routing system
has matched, as shown in figure 25.9.

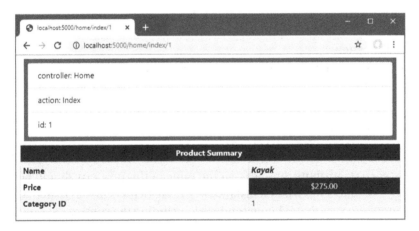

Figure 25.9 Displaying context data with a tag helper

25.3.5 *Working with model expressions*

Tag helpers can operate on the view model, tailoring the transformations they perform or the output they create. To see how this feature works, add a class file named
ModelRowTagHelper.cs to the TagHelpers folder, with the code shown in listing
25.21.

Listing 25.21   **The contents of the ModelRowTagHelper.cs file in the TagHelpers folder**

```
using Microsoft.AspNetCore.Mvc.Rendering;
using Microsoft.AspNetCore.Mvc.ViewFeatures;
using Microsoft.AspNetCore.Razor.TagHelpers;

namespace WebApp.TagHelpers {

    [HtmlTargetElement("tr", Attributes = "for")]
    public class ModelRowTagHelper : TagHelper {

        public string Format { get; set; } = "";
        public ModelExpression? For { get; set; }

        public override void Process(TagHelperContext context,
                TagHelperOutput output) {

            output.TagMode = TagMode.StartTagAndEndTag;

            TagBuilder th = new TagBuilder("th");
            th.InnerHtml.Append(For?.Name ?? String.Empty);
            output.Content.AppendHtml(th);

            TagBuilder td = new TagBuilder("td");
            if (Format != null &&
                    For?.Metadata.ModelType == typeof(decimal)) {
                td.InnerHtml.Append(((decimal)For.Model)
                    .ToString(Format));
            } else {
                td.InnerHtml.Append(For?.Model.ToString()
                    ?? String.Empty);
            }
            output.Content.AppendHtml(td);
        }
    }
}
```

This tag helper transforms `tr` elements that have a `for` attribute. The important part of this tag helper is the type of the `For` property, which is used to receive the value of the `for` attribute.

```
...
public ModelExpression? For { get; set; }
...
```

The `ModelExpression` class is used when you want to operate on part of the view model, which is most easily explained by jumping forward and showing how the tag helper is applied in the view, as shown in listing 25.22.

> **NOTE** The `ModelExpression` feature can be used only on view models or page models. It cannot be used on variables that are created within a view, such as with a `@foreach` expression.

```
@model Product
@{
    Layout = "_SimpleLayout";
}

<div route-data="true"></div>

<table class="table table-striped table-bordered table-sm">
    <tablehead bg-color="dark">Product Summary</tablehead>
    <tbody>
        <tr for="Name" />
        <tr for="Price" format="c" />
        <tr for="CategoryId" />
    </tbody>
</table>
```

The value of the `for` attribute is the name of a property defined by the view model class. When the tag helper is created, the type of the `For` property is detected and assigned a `ModelExpression` object that describes the selected property.

Notice that I have changed the view model type in listing 25.22. This is important because the `ModelExpression` feature works on non-nullable types. This is a useful feature, but it presents the problems with null values that I described in chapter 21.

I am not going to describe the `ModelExpression` class in any detail because any introspection on types leads to endless lists of classes and properties. Further, ASP.NET Core provides a useful set of built-in tag helpers that use the view model to transform elements, as described in chapter 26, which means you don't need to create your own.

For the example tag helper, I use three basic features that are worth describing. The first is to get the name of the model property so that I can include it in the output element, like this:

```
...
th.InnerHtml.Append(For?.Name ?? String.Empty);
...
```

The `Name` property returns the name of the model property. The second feature is to get the type of the model property so that I can determine whether to format the value, like this:

```
...
if (Format != null && For?.Metadata.ModelType == typeof(decimal)) {
...
```

The third feature is to get the value of the property so that it can be included in the response.

```
...
td.InnerHtml.Append(For?.Model.ToString() ?? String.Empty);
...
```

Restart ASP.NET Core and use a browser to request http://localhost:5000/home/index/2, and you will see the response shown in figure 25.10.

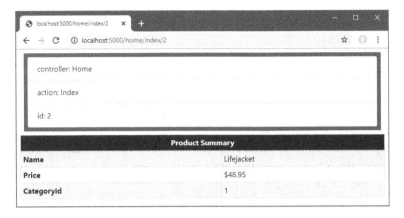

Figure 25.10   Using the view model in a tag helper

WORKING WITH THE PAGE MODEL

Tag helpers with model expressions can be applied in Razor Pages, although the expression that selects the property must account for the way that the `Model` property returns the page model class. Listing 25.23 applies the tag helper to the `Editor` Razor Page, whose page model defines a `Product` property.

Listing 25.23   Applying a tag helper in the Editor.cshtml file in the Pages folder

```
@page "{id:long}"
@model EditorModel
@{
    Layout = null;
}

<!DOCTYPE html>
<html>
<head>
    <link href="/lib/bootstrap/css/bootstrap.min.css" rel="stylesheet" />
</head>
<body>
    <div class="bg-primary text-white text-center m-2 p-2">Editor</div>
    <div class="m-2">
        <table class="table table-sm table-striped table-bordered">
            <tbody>
                <tr for="Product.Name" />
                <tr for="Product.Price" format="c" />
            </tbody>
        </table>
        <form method="post">
            @Html.AntiForgeryToken()
            <div class="form-group">
                <label>Price</label>
                <input name="price" class="form-control"
                    value="@Model.Product?.Price" />
            </div>
```

```
            <button class="btn btn-primary mt-2" type="submit">
                Submit
            </button>
        </form>
    </div>
</body>
</html>
```

The value for the `for` attribute selects the nested properties through the `Product` property, which provides the tag helper with the `ModelExpression` it requires.

Model expressions cannot be used with the null conditional operator, which presents a problem for this example because the type of the `Product` property is `Product?`. Listing 25.24 changes the property type to `Product` and assigns a default value. (I demonstrate a different way of resolving this issue in chapter 27.)

> **Listing 25.24   Changing a property type in the Editor.cshtml.cs file in the Pages folder**

```
using Microsoft.AspNetCore.Mvc;
using Microsoft.AspNetCore.Mvc.RazorPages;
using WebApp.Models;

namespace WebApp.Pages {
    public class EditorModel : PageModel {
        private DataContext context;

        public Product Product { get; set; }
            = new() { Name = string.Empty };

        public EditorModel(DataContext ctx) {
            context = ctx;
        }

        public async Task OnGetAsync(long id) {
            Product = await context.Products.FindAsync(id)
                ?? new() { Name = string.Empty };
        }

        public async Task<IActionResult> OnPostAsync(long id,
                decimal price) {
            Product? p = await context.Products.FindAsync(id);
            if (p != null) {
                p.Price = price;
            }
            await context.SaveChangesAsync();
            return RedirectToPage();
        }
    }
}
```

Restart ASP.NET Core and a browser to request http://localhost:5000/editor/1 to see the response from the page, which is shown on the left of figure 25.11.

Figure 25.11 Using a model expression tag helper with a Razor Page

One consequence of the page model is that the `ModelExpression.Name` property will return `Product.Name`, for example, instead of just `Name`. Listing 25.25 updates the tag helper so that it will display just the last part of the model expression name.

> **NOTE** This example is intended to highlight the effect of the page model on model expressions. Instead of displaying just the last part of the name, a more flexible approach is to add support for another attribute that allows the display value to be overridden as needed.

Listing 25.25 Handling names in the ModelRowTagHelper.cs file in the TagHelpers folder

```
using Microsoft.AspNetCore.Mvc.Rendering;
using Microsoft.AspNetCore.Mvc.ViewFeatures;
using Microsoft.AspNetCore.Razor.TagHelpers;

namespace WebApp.TagHelpers {

    [HtmlTargetElement("tr", Attributes = "for")]
    public class ModelRowTagHelper : TagHelper {

        public string Format { get; set; } = "";
        public ModelExpression? For { get; set; }

        public override void Process(TagHelperContext context,
                TagHelperOutput output) {

            output.TagMode = TagMode.StartTagAndEndTag;

            TagBuilder th = new TagBuilder("th");
            th.InnerHtml.Append(For?.Name.Split(".").Last()
                ?? String.Empty);
            output.Content.AppendHtml(th);

            TagBuilder td = new TagBuilder("td");
            if (Format != null &&
                    For?.Metadata.ModelType == typeof(decimal)) {
                td.InnerHtml.Append(((decimal)For.Model)
                    .ToString(Format));
            } else {
```

```
                    td.InnerHtml.Append(For?.Model.ToString()
                        ?? String.Empty);
                }
                output.Content.AppendHtml(td);
            }
        }
    }
}
```

Restart ASP.NET Core and use a browser to request http://localhost:5000/editor/1;
you will see the revised response, which is shown on the right of figure 25.11.

25.3.6 *Coordinating between tag helpers*

The `TagHelperContext.Items` property provides a dictionary used by tag helpers
that operate on elements and those that operate on their descendants. To demonstrate
the use of the `Items` collection, add a class file named `CoordinatingTagHelpers.cs`
to the `WebApp/TagHelpers` folder and add the code shown in listing 25.26.

> **Listing 25.26   The CoordinatingTagHelpers.cs file in the TagHelpers folder**

```
using Microsoft.AspNetCore.Razor.TagHelpers;

namespace WebApp.TagHelpers {

    [HtmlTargetElement("tr", Attributes = "theme")]
    public class RowTagHelper : TagHelper {

        public string Theme { get; set; } = String.Empty;

        public override void Process(TagHelperContext context,
                TagHelperOutput output) {
            context.Items["theme"] = Theme;
        }
    }

    [HtmlTargetElement("th")]
    [HtmlTargetElement("td")]
    public class CellTagHelper : TagHelper {

        public override void Process(TagHelperContext context,
                TagHelperOutput output) {

            if (context.Items.ContainsKey("theme")) {
                output.Attributes.SetAttribute("class",
                    $"bg-{context.Items["theme"]} text-white");
            }
        }
    }
}
```

The first tag helper operates on `tr` elements that have a `theme` attribute. Coordinating
tag helpers can transform their own elements, but this example simply adds the value
of the `theme` attribute to the `Items` dictionary so that it is available to tag helpers that
operate on elements contained within the `tr` element. The second tag helper operates
on `th` and `td` elements and uses the `theme` value from the `Items` dictionary to set the
Bootstrap style for its output elements.

Listing 25.27 adds elements to the `Home` controller's `Index` view that apply the coordinating tag helpers.

> **NOTE** Notice that I have added the `th` and `td` elements that are transformed in listing 25.27, instead of relying on a tag helper to generate them. Tag helpers are not applied to elements generated by other tag helpers and affect only the elements defined in the view.

Listing 25.27 Applying a tag helper in the Index.cshtml file in the Views/Home folder

```
@model Product
@{
    Layout = "_SimpleLayout";
}

<div route-data="true"></div>

<table class="table table-striped table-bordered table-sm">
    <tablehead bg-color="dark">Product Summary</tablehead>
    <tbody>
        <tr theme="primary">
            <th>Name</th><td>@Model?.Name</td>
        </tr>
        <tr theme="secondary">
            <th>Price</th><td>@Model?.Price.ToString("c")</td>
        </tr>
        <tr theme="info">
            <th>Category</th><td>@Model?.CategoryId</td>
        </tr>
    </tbody>
</table>
```

Restart ASP.NET Core and use a browser to request http://localhost:5000/home, which produces the response shown in figure 25.12. The value of the `theme` element has been passed from one tag helper to another, and a color theme is applied without needing to define attributes on each of the elements that is transformed.

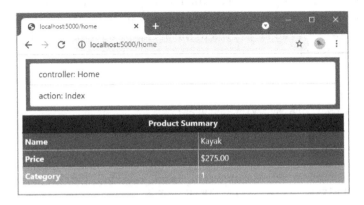

Figure 25.12 Coordination between tag helpers

25.3.7 *Suppressing the output element*

Tag helpers can be used to prevent an element from being included in the HTML response by calling the SuppressOuput method on the TagHelperOutput object that is received as an argument to the Process method. In listing 25.28, I have added an element to the Home controller's Index view that should be displayed only if the Price property of the view model exceeds a specified value.

> **Listing 25.28   Adding an element in the Index.cshtml file in the Views/Home folder**

```
@model Product
@{
    Layout = "_SimpleLayout";
}

<div show-when-gt="500" for="Price">
    <h5 class="bg-danger text-white text-center p-2">
        Warning: Expensive Item
    </h5>
</div>

<table class="table table-striped table-bordered table-sm">
    <tablehead bg-color="dark">Product Summary</tablehead>
    <tbody>
        <tr theme="primary">
            <th>Name</th><td>@Model?.Name</td>
        </tr>
        <tr theme="secondary">
            <th>Price</th><td>@Model?.Price.ToString("c")</td>
        </tr>
        <tr theme="info">
            <th>Category</th><td>@Model?.CategoryId</td>
        </tr>
    </tbody>
</table>
```

The show-when-gt attribute specifies the value above which the div element should be displayed, and the for property selects the model property that will be inspected. To create the tag helper that will manage the elements, including the response, add a class file named SelectiveTagHelper.cs to the WebApp/TagHelpers folder with the code shown in listing 25.29.

> **Listing 25.29   The contents of the SelectiveTagHelper.cs file in the TagHelpers folder**

```
using Microsoft.AspNetCore.Mvc.ViewFeatures;
using Microsoft.AspNetCore.Razor.TagHelpers;

namespace WebApp.TagHelpers {

    [HtmlTargetElement("div", Attributes = "show-when-gt, for")]
    public class SelectiveTagHelper : TagHelper {

        public decimal ShowWhenGt { get; set; }
```

```
public ModelExpression? For { get; set; }

public override void Process(TagHelperContext context,
        TagHelperOutput output) {

    if (For?.Model.GetType() == typeof(decimal)
            && (decimal)For.Model <= ShowWhenGt) {
        output.SuppressOutput();
    }
}
}
}
```

The tag helper uses the model expression to access the property and calls the
`SuppressOutput` method unless the threshold is exceeded. To see the effect, restart
ASP.NET Core and use a browser to request http://localhost:5000/home/index/1
and http://localhost:5000/home/index/5. The value for the `Price` property of the
`Product` selected by the first URL is less than the threshold, so the element is sup-
pressed. The value for the `Price` property of the `Product` selected by the second
URL is more than the threshold, so the element is displayed. figure 25.13 shows both
responses.

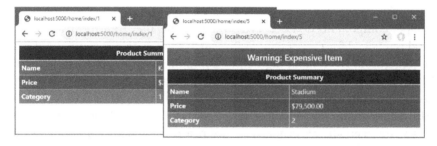

Figure 25.13 Suppressing output elements

25.4 Using tag helper components

Tag helper components provide an alternative approach to applying tag helpers as services.
This feature can be useful when you need to set up tag helpers to support another service or middleware component, which is typically the case for diagnostic tools or functionality that has both a client-side component and a server-side component, such as
Blazor, which is described in part 4. In the sections that follow, I show you how to create
and apply tag helper components.

25.4.1 Creating a tag helper component

Tag helper components are derived from the `TagHelperComponent` class, which provides a similar API to the `TagHelper` base class used in earlier examples. To create a
tag helper component, add a class file called `TimeTagHelperComponent.cs` in the
`TagHelpers` folder with the content shown in listing 25.30.

Listing 25.30   The TimeTagHelperComponent.cs file in the TagHelpers folder

```
using Microsoft.AspNetCore.Mvc.Rendering;
using Microsoft.AspNetCore.Razor.TagHelpers;

namespace WebApp.TagHelpers {

    public class TimeTagHelperComponent : TagHelperComponent {

        public override void Process(TagHelperContext context,
                TagHelperOutput output) {

            string timestamp = DateTime.Now.ToLongTimeString();

            if (output.TagName == "body") {
                TagBuilder elem = new TagBuilder("div");
                elem.Attributes.Add("class",
                    "bg-info text-white m-2 p-2");
                elem.InnerHtml.Append($"Time: {timestamp}");
                output.PreContent.AppendHtml(elem);
            }
        }
    }
}
```

Tag helper components do not specify the elements they transform, and the `Process` method is invoked for every element for which the tag helper component feature has been configured. By default, tag helper components are applied to transform `head` and `body` elements. This means that tag helper component classes must check the `TagName` property of the output element to ensure they perform only their intended transformations. The tag helper component in listing 25.30 looks for `body` elements and uses the `PreContent` property to insert a `div` element containing a timestamp before the rest of the element's content.

TIP   I show you how to increase the range of elements handled by tag helper components in the next section.

Tag helper components are registered as services that implement the `ITagHelper-Component` interface, as shown in listing 25.31.

Listing 25.31   Registering a component in the Program.cs file in the WebApp folder

```
using Microsoft.EntityFrameworkCore;
using WebApp.Models;
using Microsoft.AspNetCore.Razor.TagHelpers;
using WebApp.TagHelpers;

var builder = WebApplication.CreateBuilder(args);

builder.Services.AddDbContext<DataContext>(opts => {
    opts.UseSqlServer(builder.Configuration[
        "ConnectionStrings:ProductConnection"]);
```

```
            opts.EnableSensitiveDataLogging(true);
});
builder.Services.AddControllersWithViews();
builder.Services.AddRazorPages();
builder.Services.AddSingleton<CitiesData>();
builder.Services.AddTransient<ITagHelperComponent,
    TimeTagHelperComponent>();

var app = builder.Build();

app.UseStaticFiles();
app.MapControllers();
app.MapDefaultControllerRoute();
app.MapRazorPages();

var context = app.Services.CreateScope().ServiceProvider
    .GetRequiredService<DataContext>();
SeedData.SeedDatabase(context);

app.Run();
```

The AddTransient method is used to ensure that each request is handled using its own instance of the tag helper component class. To see the effect of the tag helper component, restart ASP.NET Core and use a browser to request http://localhost:5000/home. This response—and all other HTML responses from the application—contain the content generated by the tag helper component, as shown in figure 25.14.

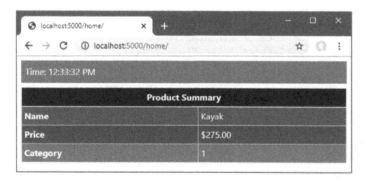

**Figure 25.14
Using a tag helper
component**

25.4.2 *Expanding tag helper component element selection*

By default, only the head and body elements are processed by the tag helper components, but additional elements can be selected by creating a class derived from the terribly named TagHelperComponentTagHelper class. Add a class file named Table-FooterTagHelperComponent.cs to the TagHelpers folder and use it to define the classes shown in listing 25.32.

Listing 25.32   The TableFooterTagHelperComponent.cs file in the TagHelpers folder

```
using Microsoft.AspNetCore.Mvc.Razor.TagHelpers;
using Microsoft.AspNetCore.Mvc.Rendering;
using Microsoft.AspNetCore.Razor.TagHelpers;

namespace WebApp.TagHelpers {

    [HtmlTargetElement("table")]
    public class TableFooterSelector : TagHelperComponentTagHelper {

        public TableFooterSelector(ITagHelperComponentManager mgr,
            ILoggerFactory log) : base(mgr, log) { }
    }

    public class TableFooterTagHelperComponent : TagHelperComponent {

        public override void Process(TagHelperContext context,
                TagHelperOutput output) {

            if (output.TagName == "table") {
                TagBuilder cell = new TagBuilder("td");
                cell.Attributes.Add("colspan", "2");
                cell.Attributes.Add("class",
                    "bg-dark text-white text-center");
                cell.InnerHtml.Append("Table Footer");
                TagBuilder row = new TagBuilder("tr");
                row.InnerHtml.AppendHtml(cell);
                TagBuilder footer = new TagBuilder("tfoot");
                footer.InnerHtml.AppendHtml(row);
                output.PostContent.AppendHtml(footer);
            }
        }
    }
}
```

The `TableFooterSelector` class is derived from `TagHelperComponentTagHelper`, and it is decorated with the `HtmlTargetElement` attribute that expands the range of elements processed by the application's tag helper components. In this case, the attribute selects `table` elements.

The `TableFooterTagHelperComponent` class, defined in the same file, is a tag helper component that transforms `table` elements by adding a `tfoot` element, which represents a table footer.

CAUTION   Bear in mind that when you create a new `TagHelperComponent` `TagHelper`, all the tag helper components will receive the elements selected by the `HtmlTargetAttribute` element.

The tag helper component must be registered as a service to receive elements for transformation, but the tag helper component tag helper (which is one of the worst naming choices I have seen for some years) is discovered and applied automatically. Listing 25.33 adds the tag helper component service.

Listing 25.33 Registering a component in the Program.cs file in the WebApp folder

```
...
builder.Services.AddControllersWithViews();
builder.Services.AddRazorPages();
builder.Services.AddSingleton<CitiesData>();
builder.Services.AddTransient<ITagHelperComponent,
    TimeTagHelperComponent>();
builder.Services.AddTransient<ITagHelperComponent,
    TableFooterTagHelperComponent>();
...
```

Restart ASP.NET Core and use a browser to request a URL that renders a table, such as http://localhost:5000/home or http://localhost:5000/cities. Each table will contain a table footer, as shown in figure 25.15.

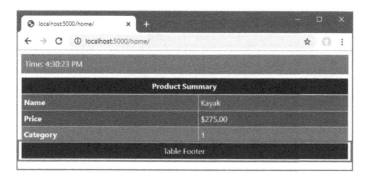

Figure 25.15 Expanding tag helper component element selection

Summary

- Tag helpers are C# classes that transform HTML elements in a response or replace a shorthand element with standard HTML content.
- Tag helpers can be configured using attributes, which are received through a `TagHelperContext` object.
- Tag helpers must be registered in the view imports file using the `@addTagHelper` directive.
- The scope of a tag helper can be controlled with the `HTMLTargetElement` attribute, which allows the elements that are transformed to be specified precisely.
- Tag helpers can use model expressions to generate content for the view model of the view to which they are applied.
- Tag helpers can be registered as services for dependency injection, using the tag helper component function.

Using the built-in
tag helpers

This chapter covers

- Creating anchor elements that target actions and Razor Pages
- Managing JavaScript and CSS files
- Working with image elements
- Caching fragments of content
- Generating content based on the hosting environment

ASP.NET Core provides a set of built-in tag helpers that apply the most commonly required element transformations. In this chapter, I explain those tag helpers that deal with anchor, `script`, `link`, and image elements, as well as features for caching content and selecting content based on the environment. In chapter 27, I describe the tag helpers that support HTML forms. Table 26.1 puts the built-in tag helpers in context.

Table 26.1 Putting the built-in tag helpers in context

Question	Answer
What are they?	The built-in tag helpers perform commonly required transformations on HTML elements.
Why are they useful?	Using the built-in tag helpers means you don't have to create custom helpers using the techniques in chapter 25.
How are they used?	The tag helpers are applied using attributes on standard HTML elements or through custom HTML elements.
Are there any pitfalls or limitations?	No, these tag helpers are well-tested and easy to use. Unless you have unusual needs, using these tag helpers is preferable to custom implementation.
Are there any alternatives?	These tag helpers are optional, and their use is not required.

Table 26.2 provides a guide to the chapter.

Table 26.2 Chapter guide

Problem	Solution	Listing
Creating elements that target endpoints	Use the anchor element tag helper attributes.	7, 8
Including JavaScript files in a response	Use the JavaScript tag helper attributes.	9–13
Including CSS files in a response	Use the CSS tag helper attributes.	14, 15
Managing image caching	Use the image tag helper attributes.	16
Caching sections of a view	Use the caching tag helper.	17–21
Varying content based on the application environment	Use the environment tag helper.	22

26.1 *Preparing for this chapter*

This chapter uses the WebApp project from chapter 25. To prepare for this chapter, comment out the statements that register the tag component helpers, as shown in listing 26.1.

> **TIP** You can download the example project for this chapter—and for all the other chapters in this book—from https://github.com/manningbooks/pro-asp .net-core-7. See chapter 1 for how to get help if you have problems running the examples.

Listing 26.1   The contents of the Program.cs file in the WebApp folder

```
using Microsoft.EntityFrameworkCore;
using WebApp.Models;
//using Microsoft.AspNetCore.Razor.TagHelpers;
//using WebApp.TagHelpers;

var builder = WebApplication.CreateBuilder(args);

builder.Services.AddDbContext<DataContext>(opts => {
    opts.UseSqlServer(builder.Configuration[
        "ConnectionStrings:ProductConnection"]);
    opts.EnableSensitiveDataLogging(true);
});
builder.Services.AddControllersWithViews();
builder.Services.AddRazorPages();
builder.Services.AddSingleton<CitiesData>();
//builder.Services.AddTransient<ITagHelperComponent,
//    TimeTagHelperComponent>();
//builder.Services.AddTransient<ITagHelperComponent,
//    TableFooterTagHelperComponent>();

var app = builder.Build();

app.UseStaticFiles();
app.MapControllers();
app.MapDefaultControllerRoute();
app.MapRazorPages();

var context = app.Services.CreateScope().ServiceProvider
    .GetRequiredService<DataContext>();
SeedData.SeedDatabase(context);

app.Run();
```

Next, update the _RowPartial.cshtml partial view in the Views/Home folder, making the changes shown in listing 26.2.

Listing 26.2   Making changes in the _RowPartial.cshtml file in the Views/Home folder

```
@model Product

<tr>
    <td>@Model.Name</td>
    <td>@Model.Price.ToString("c")</td>
    <td>@Model.CategoryId</td>
    <td>@Model.SupplierId</td>
    <td></td>
</tr>
```

Replace the contents of the List.cshtml file in the Views/Home folder, which applies a layout and adds additional columns to the table rendered by the view, as shown in listing 26.3.

Listing 26.3 Making changes in the List.cshtml file in the Views/Home folder

```
@model IEnumerable<Product>
@{ Layout = "_SimpleLayout"; }

<h6 class="bg-secondary text-white text-center m-2 p-2">Products</h6>
<div class="m-2">
    <table class="table table-sm table-striped table-bordered">
        <thead>
            <tr>
                <th>Name</th><th>Price</th>
                <th>Category</th><th>Supplier</th><th></th>
            </tr>
        </thead>
        <tbody>
            @foreach (Product p in Model) {
                <partial name="_RowPartial" model="p" />
            }
        </tbody>
    </table>
</div>
```

26.1.1 Adding an image file

One of the tag helpers described in this chapter provides services for images. I created the `wwwroot/images` folder and added an image file called `city.png`. This is a public domain panorama of the New York City skyline, as shown in figure 26.1.

Figure 26.1   Adding an image to the project

This image file is included in the source code for this chapter, which is available in the GitHub repository for this book. You can substitute your own image if you don't want to download the example project.

26.1.2 Installing a client-side package

Some of the examples in this chapter demonstrate the tag helper support for working with JavaScript files, for which I use the jQuery package. Use a PowerShell command prompt to run the command shown in listing 26.4 in the project folder, which contains the `WebApp.csproj` file.

Listing 26.4   Installing a package

```
libman install jquery@3.6.3 -d wwwroot/lib/jquery
```

26.1.3 Dropping the database

Open a new PowerShell command prompt, navigate to the folder that contains the `WebApp.csproj` file, and run the command shown in listing 26.5 to drop the database.

Listing 26.5   Dropping the database

```
dotnet ef database drop --force
```

26.1.4 Running the example application

Use the PowerShell command prompt to run the command shown in listing 26.6.

Listing 26.6   Running the example application

```
dotnet run
```

Use a browser to request http://localhost:5000/home/list, which will display a list of products, as shown in figure 26.2.

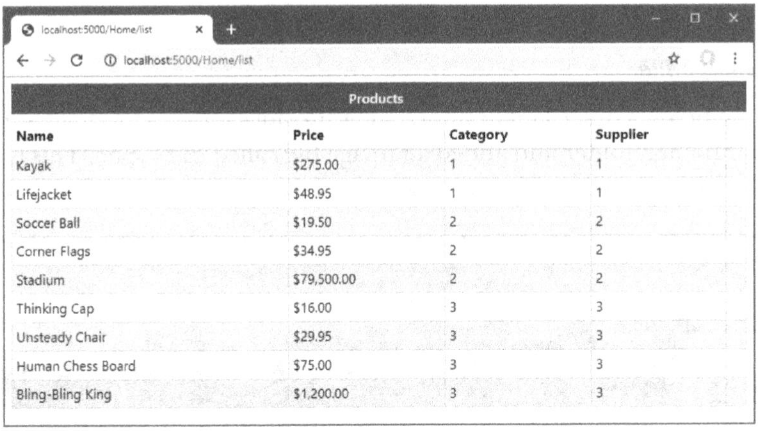

Figure 26.2   Running the example application

26.2   Enabling the built-in tag helpers

The built-in tag helpers are all defined in the `Microsoft.AspNetCore.Mvc.Tag-Helpers` namespace and are enabled by adding an `@addTagHelpers` directive to individual views or pages or, as in the case of the example project, to the view imports file. Here is the required directive from the `_ViewImports.cshtml` file in the `Views` folder, which enables the built-in tag helpers for controller views:

```
@using WebApp.Models
@addTagHelper *, Microsoft.AspNetCore.Mvc.TagHelpers
@using WebApp.Components
@addTagHelper *, WebApp
```

Here is the corresponding directive in the `_ViewImports.cshtml` file in the `Pages` folder, which enables the built-in tag helpers for Razor Pages:

```
@namespace WebApp.Pages
@using WebApp.Models
@addTagHelper *, Microsoft.AspNetCore.Mvc.TagHelpers
@addTagHelper *, WebApp
```

These directives were added to the example project in chapter 24 to enable the view components feature.

26.3 *Transforming anchor elements*

The a element is the basic tool for navigating around an application and sending GET requests to the application. The AnchorTagHelper class is used to transform the href attributes of a elements so they target URLs generated using the routing system, which means that hard-coded URLs are not required and a change in the routing configuration will be automatically reflected in the application's anchor elements. Table 26.3 describes the attributes the AnchorTagHelper class supports.

Table 26.3   The built-in tag helper attributes for anchor elements

Name	Description
asp-action	This attribute specifies the action method that the URL will target.
asp-controller	This attribute specifies the controller that the URL will target. If this attribute is omitted, then the URL will target the controller or page that rendered the current view.
asp-page	This attribute specifies the Razor Page that the URL will target.
asp-page-handler	This attribute specifies the Razor Page handler function that will process the request, as described in chapter 23.
asp-fragment	This attribute is used to specify the URL fragment (which appears after the # character).
asp-host	This attribute specifies the name of the host that the URL will target.
asp-protocol	This attribute specifies the protocol that the URL will use.
asp-route	This attribute specifies the name of the route that will be used to generate the URL.
asp-route-*	Attributes whose name begins with asp-route- are used to specify additional values for the URL so that the asp-route-id attribute is used to provide a value for the id segment to the routing system.
asp-all-route-data	This attribute provides values used for routing as a single value, rather than using individual attributes.

The AnchorTagHelper is simple and predictable and makes it easy to generate URLs in a elements that use the application's routing configuration. Listing 26.7 adds an anchor element that uses attributes from the table to create a URL that targets another action defined by the Home controller.

Listing 26.7 Transforming an element in the Views/Home/_RowPartial.cshtml file

```
@model Product

<tr>
    <td>@Model.Name</td>
    <td>@Model.Price.ToString("c")</td>
    <td>@Model.CategoryId</td>
    <td>@Model.SupplierId</td>
    <td>
        <a asp-action="index" asp-controller="home"
            asp-route-id="@Model?.ProductId"
                class="btn btn-sm btn-info text-white">
            Select
        </a>
    </td>
</tr>
```

The `asp-action` and `asp-controller` attributes specify the name of the action method and the controller that defines it. Values for segment variables are defined using `asp-route-[name]` attributes, such that the `asp-route-id` attribute provides a value for the `id` segment variable that is used to provide an argument for the action method selected by the `asp-action` attribute.

> **TIP** The `class` attributes added to the anchor elements in listing 26.7 apply Bootstrap CSS Framework styles that give the elements the appearance of buttons. This is not a requirement for using the tag helper.

To see the anchor element transformations, restart ASP.NET Core and use a browser to request http://localhost:5000/home/list, which will produce the response shown in figure 26.3.

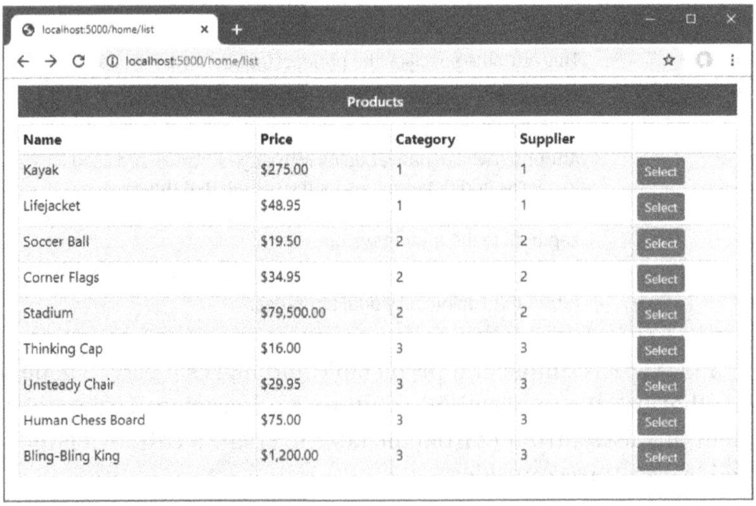
localhost:5000/home/list
localhost:5000/home/list
Products
Name
Price
Category
Supplier
Kayak
$275.00
1
1
Select
Lifejacket
$48.95
1
1
Select
Soccer Ball
$19.50
2
2
Select
Corner Flags
$34.95
2
2
Select
Stadium
$79,500.00
2
2
Select
Thinking Cap
$16.00
3
3
Select
Unsteady Chair
$29.95
3
3
Select
Human Chess Board
$75.00
3
3
Select
Bling-Bling King
$1,200.00
3
3
Select

Figure 26.3 Transforming anchor elements

If you examine the `Select` anchor elements, you will see that each `href` attribute includes the `ProductId` value of the `Product` object it relates to, like this:

```
...
<a class="btn btn-sm btn-info text-white" href="/Home/index/3">Select</a>
...
```

In this case, the value provided by the `asp-route-id` attribute means the default URL cannot be used, so the routing system has generated a URL that includes segments for the controller and action name, as well as a segment that will be used to provide a parameter to the action method. Clicking the anchor elements will send an HTTP GET request that targets the `Home` controller's `Index` method.

26.3.1 *Using anchor elements for Razor Pages*

The `asp-page` attribute is used to specify a Razor Page as the target for an anchor element's `href` attribute. The path to the page is prefixed with the `/` character, and values for route segments defined by the `@page` directive are defined using `asp-route`-`[name]` attributes. Listing 26.8 adds an anchor element that targets the `List` page defined in the `Pages/Suppliers` folder.

> **NOTE**　The `asp-page-handler` attribute can be used to specify the name of the page model handler method that will process the request.

> **Listing 26.8　Targeting a Razor Page in the List.cshtml file in the Views/Home folder**

```
@model IEnumerable<Product>
@{ Layout = "_SimpleLayout"; }

<h6 class="bg-secondary text-white text-center m-2 p-2">Products</h6>
<div class="m-2">
    <table class="table table-sm table-striped table-bordered">
        <thead>
            <tr>
                <th>Name</th><th>Price</th>
                <th>Category</th><th>Supplier</th><th></th>
            </tr>
        </thead>
        <tbody>
            @foreach (Product p in Model) {
                <partial name="_RowPartial" model="p" />
            }
        </tbody>
    </table>
    <a asp-page="/suppliers/list" class="btn btn-secondary">Suppliers</a>
</div>
```

Restart ASP.NET Core and a browser to request http://localhost:5000/home/list, and you will see the anchor element, which is styled to appear as a button. If you examine the HTML sent to the client, you will see the anchor element has been transformed like this:

```
...
<a class="btn btn-secondary" href="/lists/suppliers">Suppliers</a>
...
```

This URL used in the `href` attribute reflects the `@page` directive, which has been used to override the default routing convention in this page. Click the element, and the browser will display the Razor Page, as shown in figure 26.4.

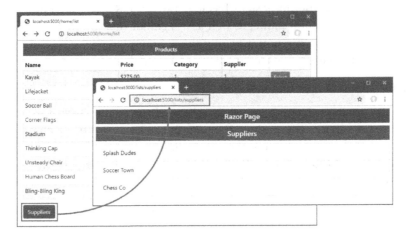

Figure 26.4   Targeting a Razor Page with an anchor element

Generating URLs (and NOT LINKS)

The tag helper generates URLs only in anchor elements. If you need to generate a URL, rather than a link, then you can use the `Url` property, which is available in controllers, page models, and views. This property returns an object that implements the `IUrlHelper` interface, which provides a set of methods and extension methods that generate URLs. Here is a Razor fragment that generates a URL in a view:

```
...
<div>@Url.Page("/suppliers/list")</div>
...
```

This fragment produces a `div` element whose content is the URL that targets the `/Suppliers/List` Razor Page. The same interface is used in controllers or page model classes, such as with this statement:

```
...
string url = Url.Action("List", "Home");
...
```

The statement generates a URL that targets the `List` action on the `Home` controller and assigns it to the `string` variable named `url`.

26.4 Using the JavaScript and CSS tag helpers

ASP.NET Core provides tag helpers that are used to manage JavaScript files and CSS stylesheets through the `script` and `link` elements. As you will see in the sections that follow, these tag helpers are powerful and flexible but require close attention to avoid creating unexpected results.

26.4.1 Managing JavaScript files

The `ScriptTagHelper` class is the built-in tag helper for `script` elements and is used to manage the inclusion of JavaScript files in views using the attributes described in table 26.4, which I describe in the sections that follow.

Table 26.4 The built-in tag helper attributes for script elements

Name	Description
asp-src-include	This attribute is used to specify JavaScript files that will be included in the view.
asp-src-exclude	This attribute is used to specify JavaScript files that will be excluded from the view.
asp-append-version	This attribute is used for cache busting, as described in the "Understanding Cache Busting" sidebar.
asp-fallback-src	This attribute is used to specify a fallback JavaScript file to use if there is a problem with a content delivery network.
asp-fallback-src-include	This attribute is used to select JavaScript files that will be used if there is a content delivery network problem.
asp-fallback-src-exclude	This attribute is used to exclude JavaScript files to present their use when there is a content delivery network problem.
asp-fallback-test	This attribute is used to specify a fragment of JavaScript that will be used to determine whether JavaScript code has been correctly loaded from a content delivery network.

SELECTING JAVASCRIPT FILES

The `asp-src-include` attribute is used to include JavaScript files in a view using globbing patterns. Globbing patterns support a set of wildcards that are used to match files, and table 26.5 describes the most common globbing patterns.

Table 26.5   Common globbing patterns

Pattern	Example	Description
?	js/src?.js	This pattern matches any single character except /. The example matches any file contained in the js directory whose name is src, followed by any character, followed by .js, such as js/src1.js and js/srcX.js but not js/src123.js or js/mydir/src1.js.
*	js/*.js	This pattern matches any number of characters except /. The example matches any file contained in the js directory with the .js file extension, such as js/src1.js and js/src123.js but not js/mydir/src1.js.
**	js/**/*.js	This pattern matches any number of characters including /. The example matches any file with the .js extension that is contained within the js directory or any subdirectory, such as /js/src1.js and /js/mydir/src1.js.

Globbing is a useful way of ensuring that a view includes the JavaScript files that the application requires, even when the exact path to the file changes, which usually happens when the version number is included in the file name or when a package adds additional files.

Listing 26.9 uses the asp-src-include attribute to include all the JavaScript files in the wwwroot/lib/jquery folder, which is the location of the jQuery package installed with the command in listing 26.4.

> **Listing 26.9   Selecting files in the _SimpleLayout.cshtml file in the Views/Shared folder**

```
<!DOCTYPE html>
<html>
<head>
    <title>@ViewBag.Title</title>
    <link href="/lib/bootstrap/css/bootstrap.min.css" rel="stylesheet" />
    <script asp-src-include="lib/jquery/**/*.js"></script>
</head>
<body>
    <div class="m-2">
        @RenderBody()
    </div>
</body>
</html>
```

Patterns are evaluated within the wwwroot folder, and the pattern I used locates any file with the js file extension, regardless of its location within the wwwroot folder; this means that any JavaScript package added to the project will be included in the HTML sent to the client.

Restart ASP.NET Core and a browser to request http://localhost:5000/home/list and examine the HTML sent to the browser. You will see the single script element in the layout has been transformed into a script element for each JavaScript file, like this:

```
...
<head>
  <title></title>
  <link href="/lib/bootstrap/css/bootstrap.min.css" rel="stylesheet">
  <script src="/lib/jquery/jquery.js"></script>
  <script src="/lib/jquery/jquery.min.js"></script>
  <script src="/lib/jquery/jquery.slim.js"></script>
  <script src="/lib/jquery/jquery.slim.min.js"></script>
</head>
...
```

If you are using Visual Studio, you may not have realized that the jQuery packages contain so many JavaScript files because Visual Studio hides them in the Solution Explorer. To reveal the full contents of the client-side package folders, you can either expand the individual nested entries in the Solution Explorer window or disable file nesting by clicking the button at the top of the Solution Explorer window, as shown in figure 26.5. (Visual Studio Code does not nest files.)

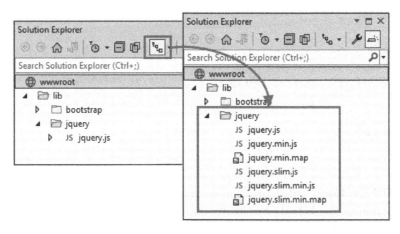

Figure 26.5   Disabling file nesting in the Visual Studio Solution Explorer

Understanding source maps

JavaScript files are minified to make them smaller, which means they can be delivered to the client faster and using less bandwidth. The minification process removes all the whitespace from the file and renames functions and variables so that meaningful names such as `myHelpfullyNamedFunction` will be represented by a smaller number of characters, such as `x1`. When using the browser's JavaScript debugger to track down problems in your minified code, names like `x1` make it almost impossible to follow progress through the code.

The files that have the `map` file extension are *source maps*, which browsers use to help debug minified code by providing a map between the minified code and the developer-readable, unminified source file. When you open the browser's F12 developer tools, the browser will automatically request source maps and use them to help debug the application's client-side code.

NARROWING THE GLOBBING PATTERN

No application would require all the files selected by the pattern in listing 26.9. Many packages include multiple JavaScript files that contain similar content, often removing less popular features to save bandwidth. The jQuery package includes the `jquery.slim.js` file, which contains the same code as the `jquery.js` file but without the features that handle asynchronous HTTP requests and animation effects.

Each of these files has a counterpart with the `min.js` file extension, which denotes a minified file. Minification reduces the size of a JavaScript file by removing all whitespace and renaming functions and variables to use shorter names.

Only one JavaScript file is required for each package and if you only require the minified versions, which will be the case in most projects, then you can restrict the set of files that the globbing pattern matches, as shown in listing 26.10.

Listing 26.10   Selecting files in the _SimpleLayout.cshtml file in the Views/Shared folder

```
<!DOCTYPE html>
<html>
<head>
    <title>@ViewBag.Title</title>
    <link href="/lib/bootstrap/css/bootstrap.min.css" rel="stylesheet" />
    <script asp-src-include="lib/jquery/**/*.min.js"></script>
</head>
<body>
    <div class="m-2">
        @RenderBody()
    </div>
</body>
</html>
```

Restart ASP.NET Core and a browser to request http://localhost:5000/home/list again and examine the HTML sent by the application. You will see that only the minified files have been selected.

```
...
<head>
  <title></title>
  <link href="/lib/bootstrap/css/bootstrap.min.css" rel="stylesheet">
  <script src="/lib/jquery/jquery.min.js"></script>
  <script src="/lib/jquery/jquery.slim.min.js"></script>
</head>
...
```

Narrowing the pattern for the JavaScript files has helped, but the browser will still end up with the normal and slim versions of jQuery and the bundled and unbundled versions of the Bootstrap JavaScript files. To narrow the selection further, I can include `slim` in the pattern, as shown in listing 26.11.

Listing 26.11   Narrowing the focus in the Views/Shared/_SimpleLayout.cshtml file

```
<!DOCTYPE html>
<html>
<head>
```

```
    <title>@ViewBag.Title</title>
    <link href="/lib/bootstrap/css/bootstrap.min.css" rel="stylesheet" />
    <script asp-src-include="lib/jquery**/*slim.min.js"></script>
</head>
<body>
    <div class="m-2">
        @RenderBody()
    </div>
</body>
</html>
```

Restart ASP.NET Core and use the browser to request http://localhost:5000/home/
list and examine the HTML the browser receives. The `script` element has been transformed like this:

```
...
<head>
  <title></title>
  <link href="/lib/bootstrap/css/bootstrap.min.css" rel="stylesheet">
  <script src="/lib/jquery/jquery.slim.min.js"></script>
</head>
...
```

Only one version of the jQuery file will be sent to the browser while preserving the flexibility for the location of the file.

Excluding files

Narrowing the pattern for the JavaScript files helps when you want to select a file whose
name contains a specific term, such as `slim`. It isn't helpful when the file you want
doesn't have that term, such as when you want the full version of the minified file.
Fortunately, you can use the `asp-src-exclude` attribute to remove files from the list
matched by the `asp-src-include` attribute, as shown in listing 26.12.

> **Listing 26.12 Excluding files in the _SimpleLayout.cshtml file in the Views/Shared**
> **folder**

```
<!DOCTYPE html>
<html>
<head>
    <title>@ViewBag.Title</title>
    <link href="/lib/bootstrap/css/bootstrap.min.css" rel="stylesheet" />
    <script asp-src-include="/lib/jquery/**/*.min.js"
        asp-src-exclude="**.slim.**">
    </script>
</head>
<body>
    <div class="m-2">
        @RenderBody()
    </div>
</body>
</html>
```

If you restart ASP.NET Core and use the browser to request http://localhost:5000/
home/list and examine the HTML response, you will see that the `script` element
links only to the full minified version of the jQuery library, like this:

```
...
<head>
    <title></title>
    <link href="/lib/bootstrap/css/bootstrap.min.css" rel="stylesheet">
    <script src="/lib/jquery/jquery.min.js"></script>
</head>
...
```

Understanding cache busting

Static content, such as images, CSS stylesheets, and JavaScript files, is often cached to stop requests for content that rarely changes from reaching the application servers. Caching can be done in different ways: the browser can be told to cache content by the server, the application can use cache servers to supplement the application servers, or the content can be distributed using a content delivery network. Not all caching will be under your control. Large corporations, for example, often install caches to reduce their bandwidth demands since a substantial percentage of requests tend to go to the same sites or applications.

One problem with caching is that clients don't immediately receive new versions of static files when you deploy them because their requests are still being serviced by previously cached content. Eventually, the cached content will expire, and the new content will be used, but that leaves a period where the dynamic content generated by the application's controllers is out of step with the static content being delivered by the caches. This can lead to layout problems or unexpected application behavior, depending on the content that has been updated.

Addressing this problem is called *cache busting*. The idea is to allow caches to handle static content but immediately reflect any changes that are made at the server. The tag helper classes support cache busting by adding a query string to the URLs for static content that includes a checksum that acts as a version number. For JavaScript files, for example, the `ScriptTagHelper` class supports cache busting through the `asp-append-version` attribute, like this:

```
...
<script asp-src-include="/lib/jquery/**/*.min.js"
    asp-src-exclude="**.slim.**" asp-append-version="true">
</script>
...
```

Enabling the cache busting feature produces an element like this in the HTML sent to the browser:

```
...
<script src="/lib/jquery/jquery.min.js?v=_xUj3OJU5yExlq6GSYGSHk7tPXikyn">
</script>
...
```

The same version number will be used by the tag helper until you change the contents of the file, such as by updating a JavaScript library, at which point a different checksum will be calculated. The addition of the version number means that each time you change the file, the client will request a different URL, which caches treat as a request for new content that cannot be satisfied with the previously cached content and pass on to the application server. The content is then cached as normal until the next update, which produces another URL with a different version.

WORKING WITH CONTENT DELIVERY NETWORKS

Content delivery networks (CDNs) are used to offload requests for application content to servers that are closer to the user. Rather than requesting a JavaScript file from your servers, the browser requests it from a hostname that resolves to a geographically local server, which reduces the amount of time required to load files and reduces the amount of bandwidth you have to provision for your application. If you have a large, geographically disbursed set of users, then it can make commercial sense to sign up to a CDN, but even the smallest and simplest application can benefit from using the free CDNs operated by major technology companies to deliver common JavaScript packages, such as jQuery.

For this chapter, I am going to use CDNJS, which is the same CDN used by the Library Manager tool to install client-side packages in the ASP.NET Core project. You can search for packages at https://cdnjs.com; for jQuery 3.6.3, which is the package and version installed in listing 26.4, there are six CDNJS URLs, all of which are accessible via HTTPS.

- `cdnjs.cloudflare.com/ajax/libs/jquery/3.6.3/jquery.js`

- `cdnjs.cloudflare.com/ajax/libs/jquery/3.6.3/jquery.min.js`

- `cdnjs.cloudflare.com/ajax/libs/jquery/3.6.3/jquery.min.map`

- `cdnjs.cloudflare.com/ajax/libs/jquery/3.6.3/jquery.slim.js`

- `cdnjs.cloudflare.com/ajax/libs/jquery/3.6.3/jquery.slim.min.js`

- `cdnjs.cloudflare.com/ajax/libs/jquery/3.6.3/jquery.slim.min.map`

These URLs provide the regular JavaScript file, the minified JavaScript file, and the source map for the minified file for both the full and slim versions of jQuery.

The problem with CDNs is that they are not under your organization's control, and that means they can fail, leaving your application running but unable to work as expected because the CDN content isn't available. The `ScriptTagHelper` class provides the ability to fall back to local files when the CDN content cannot be loaded by the client, as shown in listing 26.13.

> **Listing 26.13   CDN fallback in the _SimpleLayout.cshtml file in the Views/Shared folder**

```
<!DOCTYPE html>
<html>
<head>
    <title>@ViewBag.Title</title>
    <link href="/lib/bootstrap/css/bootstrap.min.css" rel="stylesheet" />
    <script src=
      "https://cdnjs.cloudflare.com/ajax/libs/jquery/3.6.0/jquery.min.js"
        asp-fallback-src="/lib/jquery/jquery.min.js"
        asp-fallback-test="window.jQuery">
    </script>
</head>
<body>
    <div class="m-2">
```

```
        @RenderBody()
    </div>
</body>
</html>
```

The `src` attribute is used to specify the CDN URL. The `asp-fallback-src` attribute is used to specify a local file that will be used if the CDN is unable to deliver the file specified by the regular `src` attribute. To figure out whether the CDN is working, the `asp-fallback-test` attribute is used to define a fragment of JavaScript that will be evaluated at the browser. If the fragment evaluates as `false`, then the fallback files will be requested.

> **TIP**   The `asp-fallback-src-include` and `asp-fallback-src-exclude` attributes can be used to select the local files with globbing patterns. However, given that CDN `script` elements select a single file, I recommend using the `asp -fallback-src` attribute to select the corresponding local file, as shown in the example.

Restart ASP.NET Core and a browser to request http://localhost:5000/home/list, and you will see that the HTML response contains two `script` elements, like this:

```
...
<head>
    <title></title>
    <link href="/lib/bootstrap/css/bootstrap.min.css" rel="stylesheet" />
    <script src=
      "https://cdnjs.cloudflare.com/ajax/libs/jquery/3.6.0/jquery.min.js">
    </script>
    <script>
        (window.jQuery||document.write(
          "\u003Cscript src=\u0022/lib/jquery/jquery.min.js\u0022\
            u003E\u003C/script\u003E"));
    </script>
</head>
...
```

The first `script` element requests the JavaScript file from the CDN. The second `script` element evaluates the JavaScript fragment specified by the `asp-fallback -test` attribute, which checks to see whether the first `script` element has worked. If the fragment evaluates to `true`, then no action is taken because the CDN worked. If the fragment evaluates to `false`, a new `script` element is added to the HTML document that instructs the browser to load the JavaScript file from the fallback URL.

It is important to test your fallback settings because you won't find out if they fail until the CDN has stopped working and your users cannot access your application. The simplest way to check the fallback is to change the name of the file specified by the `src` attribute to something that you know doesn't exist (I append the word FAIL to the file name) and then look at the network requests that the browser makes using the F12 developer tools. You should see an error for the CDN file followed by a request for the fallback file.

CAUTION   The CDN fallback feature relies on browsers loading and executing the contents of `script` elements synchronously and in the order in which they are defined. There are a number of techniques in use to speed up JavaScript loading and execution by making the process asynchronous, but these can lead to the fallback test being performed before the browser has retrieved a file from the CDN and executed its contents, resulting in requests for the fallback files even when the CDN is working perfectly and defeating the use of a CDN in the first place. Do not mix asynchronous script loading with the CDN fallback feature.

26.4.2 Managing CSS stylesheets

The `LinkTagHelper` class is the built-in tag helper for `link` elements and is used to manage the inclusion of CSS style sheets in a view. This tag helper supports the attributes described in table 26.6, which I demonstrate in the following sections.

Table 26.6.   The built-in tag helper attributes for link elements

Name	Description
`asp-href-include`	This attribute is used to select files for the `href` attribute of the output element.
`asp-href-exclude`	This attribute is used to exclude files from the `href` attribute of the output element.
`asp-append-version`	This attribute is used to enable cache busting, as described in the "Understanding Cache Busting" sidebar.
`asp-fallback-href`	This attribute is used to specify a fallback file if there is a problem with a CDN.
`asp-fallback-href-include`	This attribute is used to select files that will be used if there is a CDN problem.
`asp-fallback-href-exclude`	This attribute is used to exclude files from the set that will be used when there is a CDN problem.
`asp-fallback-href-test-class`	This attribute is used to specify the CSS class that will be used to test the CDN.
`asp-fallback-href-test-property`	This attribute is used to specify the CSS property that will be used to test the CDN.
`asp-fallback-href-test-value`	This attribute is used to specify the CSS value that will be used to test the CDN.

SELECTING STYLESHEETS

The `LinkTagHelper` shares many features with the `ScriptTagHelper`, including support for globbing patterns to select or exclude CSS files so they do not have to be specified individually. Being able to accurately select CSS files is as important as it is for JavaScript files because stylesheets can come in regular and minified versions and support source maps. The popular Bootstrap package, which I have been using to style

HTML elements throughout this book, includes its CSS stylesheets in the `wwwroot/lib/bootstrap/css` folder. These will be visible in Visual Studio Code, but you will have to expand each item in the Solution Explorer or disable nesting to see them in the Visual Studio Solution Explorer, as shown in figure 26.6.

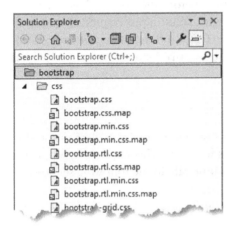

Figure 26.6
The Bootstrap
CSS files

The `bootstrap.css` file is the regular stylesheet, the `bootstrap.min.css` file is the minified version, and the `bootstrap.css.map` file is a source map. The other files contain subsets of the CSS features to save bandwidth in applications that don't use them.

Listing 26.14 replaces the regular `link` element in the layout with one that uses the `asp-href-include` and `asp-href-exclude` attributes. (I removed the `script` element for jQuery, which is no longer required.)

Listing 26.14   Selecting a stylesheet in the Views/Shared/_SimpleLayout.cshtml file

```
<!DOCTYPE html>
<html>
<head>
    <title>@ViewBag.Title</title>
    <link asp-href-include="/lib/bootstrap/css/*.min.css"
        asp-href-exclude=
        "**/*-reboot*,**/*-grid*,**/*-utilities*, **/*.rtl.*"
        rel="stylesheet" />
</head>
<body>
    <div class="m-2">
        @RenderBody()
    </div>
</body>
</html>
```

The same attention to detail is required as when selecting JavaScript files because it is easy to generate `link` elements for multiple versions of the same file or files that you don't want. Restart ASP.NET Core and use a browser to request http://localhost:5000/

home/list. Inspect the HTML received by the browser, and you will see that there is one `link` element, like this:

```
...
<head>
    <title></title>
    <link rel="stylesheet" href="/lib/bootstrap/css/bootstrap.min.css" />
</head>
...
```

WORKING WITH CONTENT DELIVERY NETWORKS

The `LinkTag` helper class provides a set of attributes for falling back to local content when a CDN isn't available, although the process for testing to see whether a stylesheet has loaded is more complex than testing for a JavaScript file. Listing 26.15 uses the CDNJS URL for the Bootstrap CSS stylesheet. (The CDN URL is too long to fit on the printed page, but should be on a single line in the code file).

Listing 26.15   Using a CDN for CSS in the Views/Shared/_SimpleLayout.cshtml file

```
<!DOCTYPE html>
<html>
<head>
    <title>@ViewBag.Title</title>
    <link href="https://cdnjs.cloudflare.com/ajax/libs/bootstrap/5.2.3/
css/bootstrap.min.css"
        asp-fallback-href="/lib/bootstrap/css/bootstrap.min.css"
        asp-fallback-test-class="btn"
        asp-fallback-test-property="display"
        asp-fallback-test-value="inline-block"
        rel="stylesheet" />
</head>
<body>
    <div class="m-2">
        @RenderBody()
    </div>
</body>
</html>
```

The `href` attribute is used to specify the CDN URL, and I have used the `asp-fallback -href` attribute to select the file that will be used if the CDN is unavailable. Testing whether the CDN works, however, requires the use of three different attributes and an understanding of the CSS classes defined by the CSS stylesheet that is being used.

Use a browser to request http://localhost:5000/home/list and examine the HTML elements in the response. You will see that the `link` element from the layout has been transformed into three separate elements, like this:

```
...
<head>
        <title></title>
        <link href="https://cdnjs.cloudflare.com/.../bootstrap.min.css"
            rel="stylesheet"/>
        <meta name="x-stylesheet-fallback-test" content="" class="btn" />
        <script>
          !function(a,b,c,d){var e,f=document,
```

```
        g=f.getElementsByTagName("SCRIPT"),
        h=g[g.length1].previousElementSibling,
        i=f.defaultView&&f.defaultView.getComputedStyle ?
        f.defaultView.getComputedStyle(h) : h.currentStyle;
        if(i&&i[a]!==b)for(e=0;e<c.length;e++)
            f.write('<link href="'+c[e]+'" '+d+"/>")}(
                "display","inline-block",
                ["/lib/bootstrap/css/bootstrap.min.css"],
                "rel=\u0022stylesheet\u0022 ");
    </script>
</head>
...
```

To make the transformation easier to understand, I have formatted the JavaScript code and shortened the URL.

The first element is a regular `link` whose `href` attribute specifies the CDN file. The second element is a `meta` element, which specifies the class from the `asp-fallback` `-test-class` attribute in the view. I specified the `btn` class in the listing, which means that an element like this is added to the HTML sent to the browser:

```
<meta name="x-stylesheet-fallback-test" content="" class="btn">
```

The CSS class that you specify must be defined in the stylesheet that will be loaded from the CDN. The `btn` class that I specified provides the basic formatting for Bootstrap button elements.

The `asp-fallback-test-property` attribute is used to specify a CSS property that is set when the CSS class is applied to an element, and the `asp-fallback-test-value` attribute is used to specify the value that it will be set to.

The `script` element created by the tag helper contains JavaScript code that adds an element to the specified class and then tests the value of the CSS property to determine whether the CDN stylesheet has been loaded. If not, a `link` element is created for the fallback file. The Bootstrap `btn` class sets the `display` property to `inline-block`, and this provides the test to see whether the browser has been able to load the Bootstrap stylesheet from the CDN.

> **TIP** The easiest way to figure out how to test for third-party packages like Bootstrap is to use the browser's F12 developer tools. To determine the test in listing 26.15, I assigned an element to the `btn` class and then inspected it in the browser, looking at the individual CSS properties that the class changes. I find this easier than trying to read through long and complex style sheets.

26.5   *Working with image elements*

The `ImageTagHelper` class is used to provide cache busting for images through the `src` attribute of `img` elements, allowing an application to take advantage of caching while ensuring that modifications to images are reflected immediately. The `Image-TagHelper` class operates in `img` elements that define the `asp-append-version` attribute, which is described in table 26.7 for quick reference.

Table 26.7   The built-in tag helper attribute for image elements

Name	Description
asp-append-version	This attribute is used to enable cache busting, as described in the "Understanding Cache Busting" sidebar.

In listing 26.16, I have added an `img` element to the shared layout for the city skyline image that I added to the project at the start of the chapter. I have also reset the `link` element to use a local file for brevity.

Listing 26.16   **Adding an image in the Views/Shared/_SimpleLayout.cshtml file**

```
<!DOCTYPE html>
<html>
<head>
    <title>@ViewBag.Title</title>
    <link href="/lib/bootstrap/css/bootstrap.min.css" rel="stylesheet" />
</head>
<body>
    <div class="m-2">
        <img src="/images/city.png" asp-append-version="true"
            class="m-2" />
        @RenderBody()
    </div>
</body>
</html>
```

Restart ASP.NET Core and a browser to request http://localhost:5000/home/list, which will produce the response shown in figure 26.7.

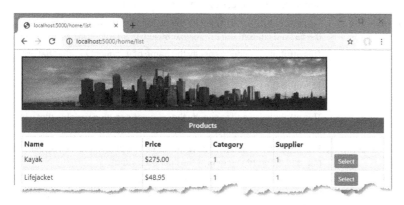

Figure 26.7   Using an image

Examine the HTML response, and you will see that the URL used to request the image file includes a version checksum, like this:

```
...
<img src="/images/city.png?v=KaMNDSZFAJufRcRDpKhOK_IIPNc7E" class="m-2">
...
```

The addition of the checksum ensures that any changes to the file will pass through any caches, avoiding stale content.

26.6   *Using the data cache*

The `CacheTagHelper` class allows fragments of content to be cached to speed up rendering of views or pages. The content to be `cached` is denoted using the `cache` element, which is configured using the attributes shown in table 26.8.

> **NOTE**   Caching is a useful tool for reusing sections of content so they don't have to be generated for every request. But using caching effectively requires careful thought and planning. While caching can improve the performance of an application, it can also create odd effects, such as users receiving stale content, multiple caches containing different versions of content, and update deployments that are broken because content cached from the previous version of the application is mixed with content from the new version. Don't enable caching unless you have a clearly defined performance problem to resolve, and make sure you understand the impact that caching will have.

Table 26.8   The built-in tag helper attributes for cache elements

Name	Description
enabled	This `bool` attribute is used to control whether the contents of the `cache` element are cached. Omitting this attribute enables caching.
expires-on	This attribute is used to specify an absolute time at which the cached content will expire, expressed as a `DateTime` value.
expires-after	This attribute is used to specify a relative time at which the cached content will expire, expressed as a `TimeSpan` value.
expires-sliding	This attribute is used to specify the period since it was last used when the cached content will expire, expressed as a `TimeSpan` value.
vary-by-header	This attribute is used to specify the name of a request header that will be used to manage different versions of the cached content.
vary-by-query	This attribute is used to specify the name of a query string key that will be used to manage different versions of the cached content.
vary-by-route	This attribute is used to specify the name of a routing variable that will be used to manage different versions of the cached content.
vary-by-cookie	This attribute is used to specify the name of a cookie that will be used to manage different versions of the cached content.
vary-by-user	This `bool` attribute is used to specify whether the name of the authenticated user will be used to manage different versions of the cached content.
vary-by	This attribute is evaluated to provide a key used to manage different versions of the content.
priority	This attribute is used to specify a relative priority that will be taken into account when the memory cache runs out of space and purges unexpired cached content.

Listing 26.17 replaces the `img` element from the previous section with content that contains timestamps.

```
<!DOCTYPE html>
<html>
<head>
    <title>@ViewBag.Title</title>
    <link href="/lib/bootstrap/css/bootstrap.min.css" rel="stylesheet" />
</head>
<body>
    <div class="m-2">
        <h6 class="bg-primary text-white m-2 p-2">
            Uncached timestamp: @DateTime.Now.ToLongTimeString()
        </h6>
        <cache>
            <h6 class="bg-primary text-white m-2 p-2">
                Cached timestamp: @DateTime.Now.ToLongTimeString()
            </h6>
        </cache>
        @RenderBody()
    </div>
</body>
</html>
```

The `cache` element is used to denote a region of content that should be cached and has been applied to one of the `h6` elements that contains a timestamp. Restart ASP. NET Core and a browser to request http://localhost:5000/home/list, and both timestamps will be the same. Reload the browser, and you will see that the cached content is used for one of the `h6` elements and the timestamp doesn't change, as shown in figure 26.8.

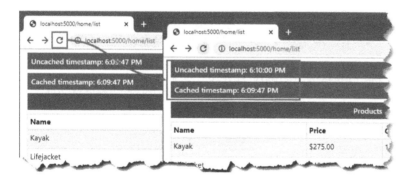

Figure 26.8   Using the caching tag helper

Using distributed caching for content

The cache used by the `CacheTagHelper` class is memory-based, which means that its capacity is limited by the available RAM and that each application server maintains

(continued)

a separate cache. Content will be ejected from the cache when there is a shortage of capacity available, and the entire contents are lost when the application is stopped or restarted.

The `distributed-cache` element can be used to store content in a shared cache, which ensures that all application servers use the same data and that the cache survives restarts. The `distributed-cache` element is configured with the same attributes as the cache element, as described in table 26.8. See chapter 17 for details of setting up a distributed cache.

26.6.1 Setting cache expiry

The `expires-*` attributes allow you to specify when cached content will expire, expressed either as an absolute time or as a time relative to the current time, or to specify a duration during which the cached content isn't requested. In listing 26.18, I have used the `expires-after` attribute to specify that the content should be cached for 15 seconds.

> **Listing 26.18   Setting expiry in the _SimpleLayout.cshtml file in the Views/ Shared folder**

```
<!DOCTYPE html>
<html>
<head>
    <title>@ViewBag.Title</title>
    <link href="/lib/bootstrap/css/bootstrap.min.css" rel="stylesheet" />
</head>
<body>
    <div class="m-2">
        <h6 class="bg-primary text-white m-2 p-2">
            Uncached timestamp: @DateTime.Now.ToLongTimeString()
        </h6>
        <cache expires-after="@TimeSpan.FromSeconds(15)">
            <h6 class="bg-primary text-white m-2 p-2">
                Cached timestamp: @DateTime.Now.ToLongTimeString()
            </h6>
        </cache>
        @RenderBody()
    </div>
</body>
</html>
```

Restart ASP.NET Core and use a browser to request http://localhost:5000/home/list and then reload the page. After 15 seconds the cached content will expire, and a new section of content will be created.

SETTING A FIXED EXPIRY POINT

You can specify a fixed time at which cached content will expire using the `expires-on` attribute, which accepts a `DateTime` value, as shown in listing 26.19.

Listing 26.19 Setting expiry in the _SimpleLayout.cshtml file in the Views/ Shared folder

```
<!DOCTYPE html>
<html>
<head>
    <title>@ViewBag.Title</title>
    <link href="/lib/bootstrap/css/bootstrap.min.css" rel="stylesheet" />
</head>
<body>
    <div class="m-2">
        <h6 class="bg-primary text-white m-2 p-2">
            Uncached timestamp: @DateTime.Now.ToLongTimeString()
        </h6>
        <cache expires-on="@DateTime.Parse("2100-01-01")">
            <h6 class="bg-primary text-white m-2 p-2">
                Cached timestamp: @DateTime.Now.ToLongTimeString()
            </h6>
        </cache>
        @RenderBody()
    </div>
</body>
</html>
```

I have specified that that data should be cached until the year 2100. This isn't a useful caching strategy since the application is likely to be restarted before the next century starts, but it does illustrate how you can specify a fixed point in the future rather than expressing the expiry point relative to the moment when the content is cached.

SETTING A LAST-USED EXPIRY PERIOD

The `expires-sliding` attribute is used to specify a period after which content is expired if it hasn't been retrieved from the cache. In listing 26.20, I have specified a sliding expiry of 10 seconds.

Listing 26.20 Sliding expiry in the _SimpleLayout.cshtml file in the Views/ Shared folder

```
<!DOCTYPE html>
<html>
<head>
    <title>@ViewBag.Title</title>
    <link href="/lib/bootstrap/css/bootstrap.min.css" rel="stylesheet" />
</head>
<body>
    <div class="m-2">
        <h6 class="bg-primary text-white m-2 p-2">
            Uncached timestamp: @DateTime.Now.ToLongTimeString()
        </h6>
        <cache expires-sliding="@TimeSpan.FromSeconds(10)">
            <h6 class="bg-primary text-white m-2 p-2">
                Cached timestamp: @DateTime.Now.ToLongTimeString()
            </h6>
```

```
        </cache>
        @RenderBody()
    </div>
</body>
</html>
```

You can see the effect of the `express-sliding` attribute by restarting ASP.NET Core and requesting http://localhost:5000/home/list and periodically reloading the page. If you reload the page within 10 seconds, the cached content will be used. If you wait longer than 10 seconds to reload the page, then the cached content will be discarded, the view component will be used to generate new content, and the process will begin anew.

USING CACHE VARIATIONS

By default, all requests receive the same cached content. The `CacheTagHelper` class can maintain different versions of cached content and use them to satisfy different types of HTTP requests, specified using one of the attributes whose name begins with `vary-by`. Listing 26.21 shows the use of the `vary-by-route` attribute to create cache variations based on the `action` value matched by the routing system.

Listing 26.21   Variation in the _SimpleLayout.cshtml file in the Views/Shared folder

```
<!DOCTYPE html>
<html>
<head>
    <title>@ViewBag.Title</title>
    <link href="/lib/bootstrap/css/bootstrap.min.css" rel="stylesheet" />
</head>
<body>
    <div class="m-2">
        <h6 class="bg-primary text-white m-2 p-2">
            Uncached timestamp: @DateTime.Now.ToLongTimeString()
        </h6>
        <cache expires-sliding="@TimeSpan.FromSeconds(10)"
                vary-by-route="action">
            <h6 class="bg-primary text-white m-2 p-2">
                Cached timestamp: @DateTime.Now.ToLongTimeString()
            </h6>
        </cache>
        @RenderBody()
    </div>
</body>
</html>
```

If you restart ASP.NET Core and use two browser tabs to request http://localhost:5000/home/index and http://localhost:5000/home/list, you will see that each window receives its own cached content with its own expiration, since each request produces a different `action` routing value.

> **TIP**   If you are using Razor Pages, then you can achieve the same effect using `page` as the value matched by the routing system.

26.7   Using the hosting environment tag helper

The `EnvironmentTagHelper` class is applied to the custom `environment` element and determines whether a region of content is included in the HTML sent to the browser-based on the hosting environment, which I described in chapters 15 and 16. The `environment` element relies on the `names` attribute, which I have described in table 26.9.

Table 26.9   The built-in tag helper attribute for environment elements

Name	Description
names	This attribute is used to specify a comma-separated list of hosting environment names for which the content contained within the `environment` element will be included in the HTML sent to the client.

In listing 26.22, I have added `environment` elements to the shared layout including different content in the view for the development and production hosting environments.

Listing 26.22   Using environment in the Views/Shared/_SimpleLayout.cshtml file

```
<!DOCTYPE html>
<html>
<head>
    <title>@ViewBag.Title</title>
    <link href="/lib/bootstrap/css/bootstrap.min.css" rel="stylesheet" />
</head>
<body>
    <div class="m-2">
        <environment names="development">
            <h2 class="bg-info text-white m-2 p-2">
                This is Development
            </h2>
        </environment>
        <environment names="production">
            <h2 class="bg-danger text-white m-2 p-2">
                This is Production
            </h2>
        </environment>
        @RenderBody()
    </div>
</body>
</html>
```

The `environment` element checks the current hosting environment name and either includes the content it contains or omits it (the `environment` element itself is always omitted from the HTML sent to the client). Figure 26.9 shows the output for the development and production environments. (See chapter 15 for details of how to set the environment.)

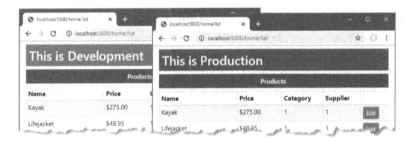

Figure 26.9 Managing content using the hosting environment

Summary

- The built-in tag helpers are enabled using the view imports files.
- The `AnchorTagHelper` class transforms anchor elements to target action methods or Razor Pages.
- The `ScriptTagHelper` and `LinkTagHelper` classes transform `script` and `link` elements, using local files or those provided by a content delivery network.
- The `ImageTagHelper` class transforms `img` elements, introducing cache-busting values to file names.
- The `CacheTagHelper` class is used to cache fragments of content.
- The `EnvironmentTagHelper` class incorporates content into the response for specific hosting environments.

Using the forms
tag helpers

This chapter covers

- Using ASP.NET Core tag helpers to transform form elements
- Transforming input elements and formatting their contents
- Generating label elements from model properties
- Generating select and option elements
- Protecting forms against cross-site request forgery

In this chapter, I describe the built-in tag helpers that are used to create HTML forms. These tag helpers ensure forms are submitted to the correct action or page handler method and that elements accurately represent specific model properties. Table 27.1 puts the form tag helpers in context.

Table 27.1　Putting form tag helpers in context

Question	Answer
What are they?	These built-in tag helpers transform HTML form elements.
Why are they useful?	These tag helpers ensure that HTML forms reflect the application's routing configuration and data model.
How are they used?	Tag helpers are applied to HTML elements using `asp-*` attributes.
Are there any pitfalls or limitations?	These tag helpers are reliable and predictable and present no serious issues.
Are there any alternatives?	You don't have to use tag helpers and can define forms without them if you prefer.

Table 27.2 provides a guide to the chapter.

Table 27.2　Chapter guide

Problem	Solution	Listing
Specifying how a form will be submitted	Use the form tag helper attributes.	10–13
Transforming `input` elements	Use the input tag helper attributes.	14–22
Transforming `label` elements	Use the label tag helper attributes.	23
Populating `select` elements	Use the select tag helper attributes.	24–26
Transforming text areas	Use the text area tag helper attributes.	27
Protecting against cross-site request forgery	Enable the anti-forgery feature.	28–32

27.1　Preparing for this chapter

This chapter uses the WebApp project from chapter 26. To prepare for this chapter, replace the contents of the _SimpleLayout.cshtml file in the Views/Shared folder with those shown in listing 27.1.

> **TIP**　You can download the example project for this chapter—and for all the other chapters in this book—from https://github.com/manningbooks/pro-asp .net-core-7. See chapter 1 for how to get help if you have problems running the examples.

Listing 27.1   The contents of the _SimpleLayout.cshtml file in the Views/Shared folder

```
<!DOCTYPE html>
<html>
<head>
    <title>@ViewBag.Title</title>
    <link href="/lib/bootstrap/css/bootstrap.min.css" rel="stylesheet" />
</head>
<body>
    <div class="m-2">
        @RenderBody()
    </div>
</body>
</html>
```

This chapter uses controller views and Razor Pages to present similar content. To differentiate more readily between controllers and pages, add the route shown in listing 27.2 to the `Program.cs` file.

Listing 27.2   Adding a route in the Program.cs file in the WebApp folder

```
using Microsoft.EntityFrameworkCore;
using WebApp.Models;

var builder = WebApplication.CreateBuilder(args);

builder.Services.AddDbContext<DataContext>(opts => {
    opts.UseSqlServer(builder.Configuration[
        "ConnectionStrings:ProductConnection"]);
    opts.EnableSensitiveDataLogging(true);
});
builder.Services.AddControllersWithViews();
builder.Services.AddRazorPages();
builder.Services.AddSingleton<CitiesData>();

var app = builder.Build();

app.UseStaticFiles();
//app.MapControllers();
//app.MapDefaultControllerRoute();
app.MapControllerRoute("forms",
    "controllers/{controller=Home}/{action=Index}/{id?}");
app.MapRazorPages();

var context = app.Services.CreateScope().ServiceProvider
    .GetRequiredService<DataContext>();
SeedData.SeedDatabase(context);

app.Run();
```

The new route introduces a static path segment that makes it obvious that a URL targets a controller.

27.1.1 *Dropping the database*

Open a new PowerShell command prompt, navigate to the folder that contains the `WebApp.csproj` file, and run the command shown in listing 27.3 to drop the database.

Listing 27.3   Dropping the database

```
dotnet ef database drop --force
```

27.1.2 *Running the example application*

Use the PowerShell command prompt to run the command shown in listing 27.4.

Listing 27.4   Running the example application

```
dotnet run
```

Use a browser to request http://localhost:5000/controllers/home/list, which will display a list of products, as shown in figure 27.1.

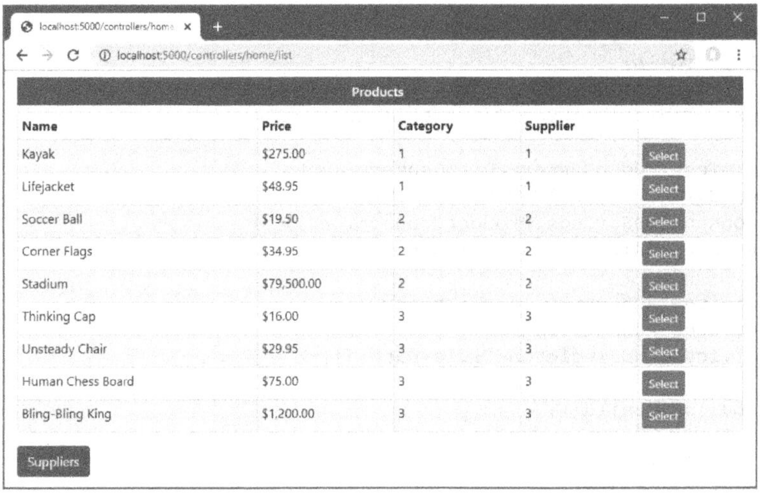

Figure 27.1   Running the example application

27.2   *Understanding the form handling pattern*

Most HTML forms exist within a well-defined pattern, shown in figure 27.2. First, the browser sends an HTTP GET request, which results in an HTML response containing a form, making it possible for the user to provide the application with data. The user clicks a button that submits the form data with an HTTP POST request, which allows the application to receive and process the user's data. Once the data has been processed, a response is sent that redirects the browser to a URL that confirms the user's actions.

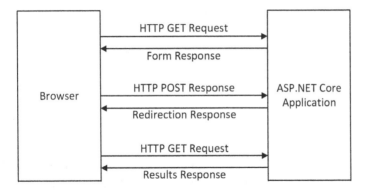

Figure 27.2 The HTML Post/Redirect/Get pattern

This is known as the Post/Redirect/Get pattern, and the redirection is important because it means the user can click the browser's reload button without sending another POST request, which can lead to inadvertently repeating an operation.

In the sections that follow, I show how to follow the pattern with controllers and Razor Pages. I start with a basic implementation of the pattern and then demonstrate improvements using tag helpers and, in chapter 28, the model binding feature.

27.2.1 Creating a controller to handle forms

Controllers that handle forms are created by combining features described in earlier chapters. Add a class file named `FormController.cs` to the `Controllers` folder with the code shown in listing 27.5.

> **Listing 27.5 The contents of the FormController.cs file in the Controllers folder**

```
using Microsoft.AspNetCore.Mvc;
using WebApp.Models;

namespace WebApp.Controllers {

    public class FormController : Controller {
        private DataContext context;

        public FormController(DataContext dbContext) {
            context = dbContext;
        }

        public async Task<IActionResult> Index(long id = 1) {
            return View("Form", await context.Products.FindAsync(id)
                ?? new () { Name = string.Empty });
        }

        [HttpPost]
        public IActionResult SubmitForm() {
            foreach (string key in
                    Request.Form.Keys.Where(k => !k.StartsWith("_"))) {
```

```
            TempData[key] = string.Join(", ",
                (string?)Request.Form[key]);
        }
        return RedirectToAction(nameof(Results));
    }

    public IActionResult Results() {
        return View();
    }
}
}
```

The `Index` action method selects a view named `Form`, which will render an HTML form to the user. When the user submits the form, it will be received by the `Submit-Form` action, which has been decorated with the `HttpPost` attribute so that it can only receive HTTP POST requests. This action method processes the HTML form data available through the `HttpRequest.Form` property so that it can be stored using the temp data feature. The temp data feature can be used to pass data from one request to another but can be used only to store simple data types. Each form data value is presented as a string array, which I convert to a single comma-separated string for storage. The browser is redirected to the `Results` action method, which selects the default view.

TIP   Only form data values whose name doesn't begin with an underscore are displayed. I explain why in the "Using the Anti-forgery Feature" section, later in this chapter.

To provide the controller with views, create the `Views/Form` folder and add to it a Razor View file named `Form.cshtml` with the content shown in listing 27.6.

Listing 27.6   The contents of the Form.cshtml file in the Views/Form folder

```
@model Product
@{ Layout = "_SimpleLayout"; }

<h5 class="bg-primary text-white text-center p-2">HTML Form</h5>

<form action="/controllers/form/submitform" method="post">
    <div class="form-group">
        <label>Name</label>
        <input class="form-control" name="Name" value="@Model.Name" />
    </div>
    <button type="submit" class="btn btn-primary mt-2">Submit</button>
</form>
```

This view contains a simple HTML form that is configured to submit its data to the `SubmitForm` action method using a POST request. The form contains an `input` element whose value is set using a Razor expression. Next, add a Razor View named `Results.cshtml` to the `Views/Form` folder with the content shown in listing 27.7.

```
@{ Layout = "_SimpleLayout"; }

<table class="table table-striped table-bordered table-sm">
    <thead>
        <tr class="bg-primary text-white text-center">
            <th colspan="2">Form Data</th>
        </tr>
    </thead>
    <tbody>
        @foreach (string key in TempData.Keys) {
            <tr>
                <th>@key</th>
                <td>@TempData[key]</td>
            </tr>
        }
    </tbody>
</table>
<a class="btn btn-primary" asp-action="Index">Return</a>
```

This view displays the form data back to the user. I'll show you how to process form data in more useful ways in chapter 31, but for this chapter the focus is on creating the forms, and seeing the data contained in the form is enough to get started.

Restart ASP.NET Core and use a browser to request http://localhost:5000/controllers/form to see the HTML form. Enter a value into the text field and click Submit to send a POST request, which will be handled by the `SubmitForm` action. The form data will be stored as temp data, and the browser will be redirected, producing the response shown in figure 27.3.

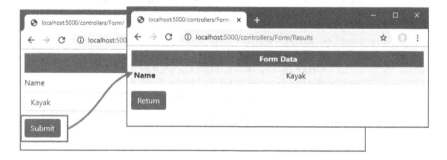

Figure 27.3   Using a controller to render and process an HTML form

27.2.2 Creating a Razor Page to handle forms

The same pattern can be implemented using Razor Pages. One page is required to render and process the form data, and a second page displays the results. Add a Razor Page named `FormHandler.cshtml` to the `Pages` folder with the contents shown in listing 27.8.

```
@page "/pages/form/{id:long?}"
@model FormHandlerModel
@using Microsoft.AspNetCore.Mvc.RazorPages

<div class="m-2">
    <h5 class="bg-primary text-white text-center p-2">HTML Form</h5>
    <form action="/pages/form" method="post">
        <div class="form-group">
            <label>Name</label>
            <input class="form-control" name="Name"
                    value="@Model.Product?.Name" />
        </div>
        <button type="submit" class="btn btn-primary mt-2">Submit</button>
    </form>
</div>

@functions {

    [IgnoreAntiforgeryToken]
    public class FormHandlerModel : PageModel {
        private DataContext context;

        public FormHandlerModel(DataContext dbContext) {
            context = dbContext;
        }

        public Product? Product { get; set; }

        public async Task OnGetAsync(long id = 1) {
            Product = await context.Products.FindAsync(id);
        }

        public IActionResult OnPost() {
            foreach (string key in Request.Form.Keys
                    .Where(k => !k.StartsWith("_"))) {
                TempData[key] = string.Join(", ",
                    (string?)Request.Form[key]);
            }
            return RedirectToPage("FormResults");
        }
    }
}
```

The OnGetAsync handler methods retrieves a Product from the database, which is used by the view to set the value for the input element in the HTML form. The form is configured to send an HTTP POST request that will be processed by the OnPost handler method. The form data is stored as temp data, and the browser is sent a redirection to a form named FormResults. To create the page to which the browser will be redirected, add a Razor Page named FormResults.cshtml to the Pages folder with the content shown in listing 27.9.

> **TIP** The page model class in listing 27.8 is decorated with the `IgnoreAnti forgeryToken` attribute, which is described in the "Using the Anti-forgery Feature" section.

Listing 27.9 The contents of the FormResults.cshtml file in the Pages folder

```
@page "/pages/results"

<div class="m-2">
    <table class="table table-striped table-bordered table-sm">
        <thead>
            <tr class="bg-primary text-white text-center">
                <th colspan="2">Form Data</th>
            </tr>
        </thead>
        <tbody>
            @foreach (string key in TempData.Keys) {
                <tr>
                    <th>@key</th>
                    <td>@TempData[key]</td>
                </tr>
            }
        </tbody>
    </table>
    <a class="btn btn-primary" asp-page="FormHandler">Return</a>
</div>
```

No code is required for this page, which accesses temp data directly and displays it in a table. Restart ASP.NET Core and use a browser to navigate to http://localhost:5000/ pages/form, enter a value into the text field, and click the Submit button. The form data will be processed by the `OnPost` method defined in listing 27.9, and the browser will be redirected to /pages/results, which displays the form data, as shown in figure 27.4.

> **TIP** If you receive a `RuntimeBinderException` exception that tells you that `System.Dynamic.DynamicObject` does not contain a definition for `Title`, then you need to clear your browser's cookies, start ASP.NET Core, and try again.

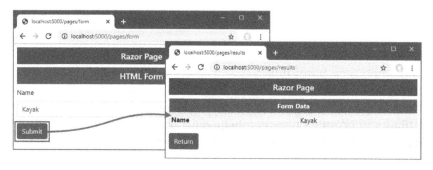

Figure 27.4 Using Razor Pages to render and process an HTML form

27.3   *Using tag helpers to improve HTML forms*

The examples in the previous section show the basic mechanisms for dealing with HTML forms, but ASP.NET Core includes tag helpers that transform form elements. In the sections that follow, I describe the tag helpers and demonstrate their use.

27.3.1   *Working with form elements*

The `FormTagHelper` class is the built-in tag helper for `form` elements and is used to manage the configuration of HTML forms so that they target the right action or page handler without the need to hard-code URLs. This tag helper supports the attributes described in table 27.3.

Table 27.3   The built-in tag helper attributes for form elements

Name	Description
asp-controller	This attribute is used to specify the `controller` value to the routing system for the `action` attribute URL. If omitted, then the controller rendering the view will be used.
asp-action	This attribute is used to specify the action method for the `action` value to the routing system for the `action` attribute URL. If omitted, then the action rendering the view will be used.
asp-page	This attribute is used to specify the name of a Razor Page.
asp-page-handler	This attribute is used to specify the name of the handler method that will be used to process the request. You can see an example of this attribute in the SportsStore application in chapter 9.
asp-route-*	Attributes whose name begins with `asp-route-` are used to specify additional values for the action attribute URL so that the `asp-route-id` attribute is used to provide a value for the `id` segment to the routing system.
asp-route	This attribute is used to specify the name of the route that will be used to generate the URL for the `action` attribute.
asp-antiforgery	This attribute controls whether anti-forgery information is added to the view, as described in the "Using the Anti-forgery Feature" section.
asp-fragment	This attribute specifies a fragment for the generated URL.

SETTING THE FORM TARGET

The `FormTagHelper` transforms `form` elements so they target an action method or Razor Page without the need for hard-coded URLs. The attributes supported by this tag helper work in the same way as for anchor elements, described in chapter 26, and use attributes to provide values that help generate URLs through the ASP.NET Core routing system. Listing 27.10 modifies the `form` element in the `Form` view to apply the tag helper.

NOTE If a `form` element is defined without a `method` attribute, then the tag helper will add one with the `post` value, meaning that the form will be submitted using an HTTP POST request. This can lead to surprising results if you omitted the `method` attribute because you expect the browser to follow the HTML5 specification and send the form using an HTTP GET request. It is a good idea to always specify the `method` attribute so that it is obvious how the form should be submitted.

Listing 27.10 Using a tag helper in the Form.cshtml file in the Views/Form folder

```
@model Product
@{  Layout = "_SimpleLayout"; }

<h5 class="bg-primary text-white text-center p-2">HTML Form</h5>

<form asp-action="submitform" method="post">
    <div class="form-group">
        <label>Name</label>
        <input class="form-control" name="Name" value="@Model.Name" />
    </div>
    <button type="submit" class="btn btn-primary mt-2">Submit</button>
</form>
```

The `asp-action` attribute is used to specify the name of the action that will receive the HTTP request. The routing system is used to generate the URLs, just as for the anchor elements described in chapter 26. The `asp-controller` attribute has not been used in listing 27.10, which means the controller that rendered the view will be used in the URL.

The `asp-page` attribute is also used to select a Razor Page as the target for the form, as shown in listing 27.11.

Listing 27.11 Setting the form target in the FormHandler.cshtml file in the Pages folder

```
...
<div class="m-2">
    <h5 class="bg-primary text-white text-center p-2">HTML Form</h5>
    <form asp-page="FormHandler" method="post">
        <div class="form-group">
            <label>Name</label>
            <input class="form-control" name="Name"
                value="@Model.Product?.Name" />
        </div>
        <button type="submit" class="btn btn-primary mt-2">Submit</button>
    </form>
</div>
...
```

Restart ASP.NET Core, use a browser to navigate to http://localhost:5000/controllers/ form, and examine the HTML received by the browser; you will see that the tag helper has added the `action` attribute to the `form` element like this:

```
...
<form method="post" action="/controllers/Form/submitform">
...
```

The routing system is used to generate a URL that will target the specified action method, which means that changes to the routing configuration will be reflected automatically in the form URL. Request http://localhost:5000/pages/form, and you will see that the `form` element has been transformed to target the page URL, like this:

```
...
<form method="post" action="/pages/form">
...
```

27.3.2 *Transforming form buttons*

The buttons that send forms can be defined outside of the `form` element. In these situations, the button has a `form` attribute whose value corresponds to the `id` attribute of the form element it relates to and a `formaction` attribute that specifies the target URL for the form.

The tag helper will generate the `formaction` attribute through the `asp-action`, `asp-controller`, or `asp-page` attributes, as shown in listing 27.12.

> **Listing 27.12   Transforming a button in the Form.cshtml file in the Views/Form folder**

```
@model Product
@{  Layout = "_SimpleLayout"; }

<h5 class="bg-primary text-white text-center p-2">HTML Form</h5>

<form asp-action="submitform" method="post" id="htmlform">
    <div class="form-group">
        <label>Name</label>
        <input class="form-control" name="Name" value="@Model.Name" />
    </div>
    <button type="submit" class="btn btn-primary mt-2">Submit</button>
</form>

<button form="htmlform" asp-action="submitform"
        class="btn btn-primary mt-2">
    Submit (Outside Form)
</button>
```

The value of the `id` attribute added to the `form` element is used by the `button` as the value of the `form` attribute, which tells the browser which form to submit when the button is clicked. The attributes described in table 27.3 are used to identify the target for the form, and the tag helper will use the routing system to generate a URL when the view is rendered. Listing 27.13 applies the same technique to the Razor Page.

> **Listing 27.13   Transforming a button in the FormHandler.cshtml file in the Pages folder**

```
...
<div class="m-2">
    <h5 class="bg-primary text-white text-center p-2">HTML Form</h5>
```

```
<form asp-page="FormHandler" method="post" id="htmlform">
    <div class="form-group">
        <label>Name</label>
        <input class="form-control" name="Name"
            value="@Model.Product?.Name" />
    </div>
    <button type="submit" class="btn btn-primary mt-2">Submit</button>
</form>
<button form="htmlform" asp-page="FormHandler"
        class="btn btn-primary mt-2">
    Submit (Outside Form)
</button>
</div>
...
```

Restart ASP.NET Core, use a browser to request http://localhost:5000/controllers/ form or http://localhost:5000/pages/form, and inspect the HTML sent to the browser. You will see the `button` element outside of the form has been transformed like this:

```
...
<button form="htmlform" class="btn btn-primary mt-2"
        formaction="/controller/Form/submitform">
    Submit (Outside Form)
</button>
...
```

Clicking the button submits the form, just as for a button that is defined within the form element, as shown in figure 27.5.

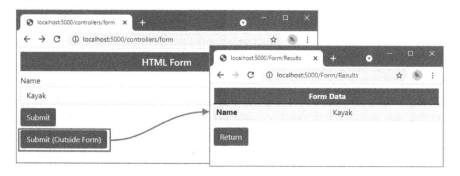

Figure 27.5   Defining a button outside of a form element

27.4   *Working with input elements*

The `input` element is the backbone of HTML forms and provides the main means by which a user can provide an application with unstructured data. The `InputTagHelper` class is used to transform `input` elements so they reflect the data type and format of the view model property they are used to gather, using the attributes described in table 27.4.

Table 27.4   The built-in tag helper attributes for input elements

Name	Description
asp-for	This attribute is used to specify the view model property that the input element represents.
asp-format	This attribute is used to specify a format used for the value of the view model property that the input element represents.

The asp-for attribute is set to the name of a view model property, which is then used to set the name, id, type, and value attributes of the input element. Listing 27.14 modifies the input element in the controller view to use the asp-for attribute.

Listing 27.14   Configuring an input element in the Form.cshtml file in the Views/Form folder

```
@model Product
@{  Layout = "_SimpleLayout"; }

<h5 class="bg-primary text-white text-center p-2">HTML Form</h5>

<form asp-action="submitform" method="post" id="htmlform">
    <div class="form-group">
        <label>Name</label>
        <input class="form-control" asp-for="Name" />
    </div>
    <button type="submit" class="btn btn-primary mt-2">Submit</button>
</form>

<button form="htmlform" asp-action="submitform"
        class="btn btn-primary mt-2">
    Submit (Outside Form)
</button>
```

This tag helper uses a model expression, described in chapter 25, which is why the value for the asp-for attribute is specified without the @ character. If you restart ASP. NET Core and inspect the HTML the application returns when using a browser to request http://localhost:5000/controllers/form, you will see the tag helper has transformed the input element like this:

```
...
<div class="form-group">
    <label>Name</label>
    <input class="form-control" type="text" data-val="true"
        data-val-required="The Name field is required." id="Name"
        name="Name" value="Kayak">
</div>
...
```

The values for the id and name attributes are obtained through the model expression, ensuring that you don't introduce typos when creating the form. The other attributes are more complex and are described in the sections that follow or in chapter 29, where I explain the ASP.NET Core support for validating data.

Selecting Model Properties in Razor Pages

The `asp-for` attribute for this and the other tag helpers described in this chapter can be used for Razor Pages, but the value for the `name` and `id` attributes in the transformed element includes the name of the page model property. For example, this element selects the `Name` property through the page model's `Product` property:

```
...
<input class="form-control" asp-for="Product.Name" />
...
```

The transformed element will have the following `id` and `name` attributes:

```
...
<input class="form-control" type="text" id="Product_Name"
    name="Product.Name" >
...
```

This difference is important when using the model binding feature to receive form data, as described in chapter 28.

27.4.1 *Transforming the input element type attribute*

The `input` element's `type` attribute tells the browser how to display the element and how it should restrict the values the user enters. The `input` element in listing 27.14 is configured to the `text` type, which is the default `input` element type and offers no restrictions. Listing 27.15 adds another `input` element to the form, which will provide a more useful demonstration of how the `type` attribute is handled.

Listing 27.15   Adding an input element in the Form.cshtml file in the Views/Form folder

```
@model Product
@{  Layout = "_SimpleLayout"; }

<h5 class="bg-primary text-white text-center p-2">HTML Form</h5>

<form asp-action="submitform" method="post" id="htmlform">
    <div class="form-group">
        <label>Id</label>
        <input class="form-control" asp-for="ProductId" />
    </div>
    <div class="form-group">
        <label>Name</label>
        <input class="form-control" asp-for="Name" />
    </div>
    <button type="submit" class="btn btn-primary mt-2">Submit</button>
</form>

<button form="htmlform" asp-action="submitform"
        class="btn btn-primary mt-2">
    Submit (Outside Form)
</button>
```

The new element uses the `asp-for` attribute to select the view model's `ProductId` property. Restart ASP.NET Core and a browser to request http://localhost:5000/controllers/form to see how the tag helper has transformed the element.

```
...
<div class="form-group">
    <label>Id</label>
    <input class="form-control" type="number" data-val="true"
        data-val-required="The ProductId field is required."
        id="ProductId" name="ProductId" value="1">
</div>
...
```

The value of the `type` attribute is determined by the type of the view model property specified by the `asp-for` attribute. The type of the `ProductId` property is the C# `long` type, which has led the tag helper to set the `input` element's type attribute to `number`, which restricts the element so it will accept only numeric characters. The `data-val` and `data-val-required` attributes are added to the `input` element to assist with validation, which is described in chapter 29. Table 27.5 describes how different C# types are used to set the `type` attribute of `input` elements.

NOTE   There is latitude in how the `type` attribute is interpreted by browsers. Not all browsers respond to all the `type` values that are defined in the HTML specification, and when they do, there are differences in how they are implemented. The `type` attribute can be a useful hint for the kind of data that you are expecting in a form, but you should use the model validation feature to ensure that users provide usable data, as described in chapter 29.

Table 27.5   C# property types and the input type elements they generate

C# Type	Input Element type Attribute
`byte`, `sbyte`, `int`, `uint`, `short`, `ushort`, `long`, `ulong`	`number`
`float`, `double`, `decimal`	`text`, with additional attributes for model validation, as described in chapter 29
`bool`	`checkbox`
`string`	`text`
`DateTime`	`datetime`

The `float`, `double`, and `decimal` types produce `input` elements whose `type` is `text` because not all browsers allow the full range of characters that can be used to express legal values of this type. To provide feedback to the user, the tag helper adds attributes to the `input` element that are used with the validation features described in chapter 29.

You can override the default mappings shown in table 27.5 by explicitly defining the `type` attribute on `input` elements. The tag helper won't override the value you define, which allows you to specify a `type` attribute value.

The drawback of this approach is that you must remember to set the `type` attribute in all the views where `input` elements are generated for a given model property. A more elegant—and reliable approach—is to apply one of the attributes described in table 27.6 to the property in the C# model class.

TIP The tag helper will set the `type` attribute of `input` elements to `text` if the model property isn't one of the types in table 27.5 and has not been decorated with an attribute.

Table 27.6 The input type elements attributes

Attribute	input Element type Attribute
[HiddenInput]	hidden
[Text]	text
[Phone]	tel
[Url]	url
[EmailAddress]	email
[DataType(DataType.Password)]	password
[DataType(DataType.Time)]	time
[DataType(DataType.Date)]	date

27.4.2 *Formatting input element values*

When the action method provides the view with a view model object, the tag helper uses the value of the property given to the `asp-for` attribute to set the `input` element's `value` attribute. The `asp-format` attribute is used to specify how that data value is formatted. To demonstrate the default formatting, listing 27.16 adds a new `input` element to the `Form` view.

Listing 27.16 Adding an element in the Form.cshtml file in the Views/Form folder

```
@model Product
@{  Layout = "_SimpleLayout"; }

<h5 class="bg-primary text-white text-center p-2">HTML Form</h5>

<form asp-action="submitform" method="post" id="htmlform">
    <div class="form-group">
        <label>Id</label>
        <input class="form-control" asp-for="ProductId" />
    </div>
    <div class="form-group">
        <label>Name</label>
```

```
        <input class="form-control" asp-for="Name" />
    </div>
    <div class="form-group">
        <label>Price</label>
        <input class="form-control" asp-for="Price" />
    </div>
    <button type="submit" class="btn btn-primary mt-2">Submit</button>
</form>

<button form="htmlform" asp-action="submitform"
        class="btn btn-primary mt-2">
    Submit (Outside Form)
</button>
```

Restart ASP.NET Core, use a browser to navigate to http://localhost:5000/controllers/
form/index/5, and examine the HTML the browser receives. By default, the `value` of
the `input` element is set using the value of the model property, like this:

```
...
<input class="form-control" type="text" data-val="true"
    data-val-number="The field Price must be a number."
    data-val-required="The Price field is required."
    id="Price" name="Price" value="79500.00">
...
```

This format, with two decimal places, is how the value is stored in the database. In
chapter 26, I used the `Column` attribute to select a SQL type to store `Price` values, like
this:

```
...
[Column(TypeName = "decimal(8, 2)")]
public decimal Price { get; set; }
...
```

This type specifies a maximum precision of eight digits, two of which will appear after
the decimal place. This allows a maximum value of 999,999.99, which is enough to
represent prices for most online stores. The `asp-format` attribute accepts a format
string that will be passed to the standard C# string formatting system, as shown in listing 27.17.

> **Listing 27.17   Formatting a data value in the Form.cshtml file in the Views/Form folder**

```
@model Product
@{ Layout = "_SimpleLayout"; }

<h5 class="bg-primary text-white text-center p-2">HTML Form</h5>

<form asp-action="submitform" method="post" id="htmlform">
    <div class="form-group">
        <label>Id</label>
        <input class="form-control" asp-for="ProductId" />
    </div>
    <div class="form-group">
        <label>Name</label>
        <input class="form-control" asp-for="Name" />
```

```
        </div>
        <div class="form-group">
            <label>Price</label>
            <input class="form-control"
                asp-for="Price" asp-format="{0:#,###.00}" />
        </div>
        <button type="submit" class="btn btn-primary mt-2">Submit</button>
    </form>

    <button form="htmlform" asp-action="submitform"
            class="btn btn-primary mt-2">
        Submit (Outside Form)
    </button>
```

The attribute value is used verbatim, which means you must include the curly brace characters and the 0: reference, as well as the format you require. Refresh the browser, and you will see that the value for the input element has been formatted, like this:

```
...
<input class="form-control" type="text" data-val="true"
    data-val-number="The field Price must be a number."
    data-val-required="The Price field is required."
    id="Price" name="Price" value="79,500.00">
...
```

This feature should be used with caution because you must ensure that the rest of the application is configured to support the format you use and that the format you create contains only legal characters for the input element type.

Applying Formatting via the Model Class

If you always want to use the same formatting for a model property, then you can decorate the C# class with the DisplayFormat attribute, which is defined in the System.ComponentModel.DataAnnotations namespace. The DisplayFormat attribute requires two arguments to format a data value: the DataFormatString argument specifies the formatting string, and setting the ApplyFormatInEditMode to true specifies that formatting should be used when values are being applied to elements used for editing, including the input element. Listing 27.18 applies the attribute to the Price property of the Product class, specifying a different formatting string from earlier examples.

> **Listing 27.18 Applying a formatting attribute to the Product.cs file in the Models folder**

```
using System.ComponentModel.DataAnnotations;
using System.ComponentModel.DataAnnotations.Schema;
using System.Text.Json.Serialization;

namespace WebApp.Models {
    public class Product {

        public long ProductId { get; set; }
```

```
        public required string Name { get; set; }
        [Column(TypeName = "decimal(8, 2)")]
        [DisplayFormat(DataFormatString = "{0:c2}",
            ApplyFormatInEditMode = true)]
        public decimal Price { get; set; }

        public long CategoryId { get; set; }
        public Category? Category { get; set; }

        public long SupplierId { get; set; }

        [JsonIgnore(Condition = JsonIgnoreCondition.WhenWritingNull)]
        public Supplier? Supplier { get; set; }
    }
}
```

The `asp-format` attribute takes precedence over the `DisplayFormat` attribute, so I have removed the attribute from the view, as shown in listing 27.19.

> **Listing 27.19   Removing an attribute in the Form.cshtml file in the Views/Form folder**

```
@model Product
@{ Layout = "_SimpleLayout"; }

<h5 class="bg-primary text-white text-center p-2">HTML Form</h5>

<form asp-action="submitform" method="post" id="htmlform">
    <div class="form-group">
        <label>Id</label>
        <input class="form-control" asp-for="ProductId" />
    </div>
    <div class="form-group">
        <label>Name</label>
        <input class="form-control" asp-for="Name" />
    </div>
    <div class="form-group">
        <label>Price</label>
        <input class="form-control" asp-for="Price" />
    </div>
    <button type="submit" class="btn btn-primary mt-2">Submit</button>
</form>

<button form="htmlform" asp-action="submitform"
        class="btn btn-primary mt-2">
    Submit (Outside Form)
</button>
```

Restart ASP.NET Core and use a browser to request http://localhost:5000/controllers/ form/index/5, and you will see that the formatting string defined by the attribute has been applied, as shown in figure 27.6.

Figure 27.6 Formatting data values

I chose this format to demonstrate the way the formatting attribute works, but as noted previously, care must be taken to ensure that the application is able to process the formatted values using the model binding and validation features described in chapters 28 and 29.

27.4.3 Displaying values from related data in input elements

When using Entity Framework Core, you will often need to display data values that are obtained from related data, which is easily done using the `asp-for` attribute because a model expression allows the nested navigation properties to be selected. First, listing 27.20 includes related data in the view model object provided to the view.

Listing 27.20 Including related data in the FormController.cs file in the Controllers folder

```
using Microsoft.AspNetCore.Mvc;
using WebApp.Models;
using Microsoft.EntityFrameworkCore;

namespace WebApp.Controllers {

    public class FormController : Controller {
        private DataContext context;

        public FormController(DataContext dbContext) {
            context = dbContext;
        }

        public async Task<IActionResult> Index(long id = 1) {
            return View("Form", await context.Products
                .Include(p => p.Category)
                .Include(p => p.Supplier)
                .FirstAsync(p => p.ProductId == id)
```

```
                ?? new() { Name = string.Empty });
        }

        [HttpPost]
        public IActionResult SubmitForm() {
            foreach (string key in
                    Request.Form.Keys.Where(k => !k.StartsWith("_"))) {
                TempData[key] = string.Join(", ",
                    (string?)Request.Form[key]);
            }
            return RedirectToAction(nameof(Results));
        }

        public IActionResult Results() {
            return View();
        }
    }
}
```

Notice that I don't need to worry about dealing with circular references in the related data because the view model object isn't serialized. The circular reference issue is important only for web service controllers. In listing 27.21, I have updated the Form view to include input elements that use the asp-for attribute to select related data.

Listing 27.21   Displaying related data in the Form.cshtml file in the Views/Form folder

```
@model Product
@{ Layout = "_SimpleLayout"; }

<h5 class="bg-primary text-white text-center p-2">HTML Form</h5>

<form asp-action="submitform" method="post" id="htmlform">
    <div class="form-group">
        <label>Id</label>
        <input class="form-control" asp-for="ProductId" />
    </div>
    <div class="form-group">
        <label>Name</label>
        <input class="form-control" asp-for="Name" />
    </div>
    <div class="form-group">
        <label>Price</label>
        <input class="form-control" asp-for="Price" />
    </div>
    <div class="form-group">
        <label>Category</label>
        @{ #pragma warning disable CS8602 }
        <input class="form-control" asp-for="Category.Name" />
        @{ #pragma warning restore CS8602 }
    </div>
    <div class="form-group">
        <label>Supplier</label>
        @{ #pragma warning disable CS8602 }
        <input class="form-control" asp-for="Supplier.Name" />
        @{ #pragma warning restore CS8602 }
```

```
    </div>
    <button type="submit" class="btn btn-primary mt-2">Submit</button>
</form>

<button form="htmlform" asp-action="submitform"
        class="btn btn-primary mt-2">
    Submit (Outside Form)
</button>
```

The value of the `asp-for` attribute is expressed relative to the view model object and can include nested properties, allowing me to select the `Name` properties of the related objects that Entity Framework Core has assigned to the `Category` and `Supplier` navigation properties.

As I explained in chapter 25, the null conditional operator cannot be used in model expressions. This presents a problem when selecting nullable-related data properties, such as the `Product.Category` and `Product.Supplier` properties. In chapter 25, I addressed this limitation by changing the type of a property so that it was not nullable, but this isn't always possible, especially when a nullable property has been used to indicate a specific condition.

In listing 27.21, I used the `#pragma warning` expression to disable code analysis for warning `CS8602`, which is the warning generated when a nullable value isn't accessed safely. The tag helper is able to deal with `null` values when processing the `asp-for` attribute, which means that the warning doesn't indicate a potential problem.

TIP You can elect to simply ignore the warnings the compiler produces, but I prefer to either address the underlying issue or explicitly disable the warning so that it is obvious that the warning has been investigated and deliberately ignored, rather than not noticed.

The same technique is used in Razor Pages, except that the properties are expressed relative to the page model object, as shown in listing 27.22.

> **Listing 27.22 Displayed related data in the FormHandler.cshtml file in the Pages folder**

```
@page "/pages/form/{id:long?}"
@model FormHandlerModel
@using Microsoft.AspNetCore.Mvc.RazorPages
@using Microsoft.EntityFrameworkCore

<div class="m-2">
    <h5 class="bg-primary text-white text-center p-2">HTML Form</h5>
    <form asp-page="FormHandler" method="post" id="htmlform">
        <div class="form-group">
            <label>Name</label>
            <input class="form-control" asp-for="Product.Name" />
        </div>
        <div class="form-group">
            <label>Price</label>
            <input class="form-control" asp-for="Product.Price" />
        </div>
```

```
        <div class="form-group">
            <label>Category</label>
            @{ #pragma warning disable CS8602 }
            <input class="form-control" asp-for="Product.Category.Name" />
            @{ #pragma warning restore CS8602 }
        </div>
        <div class="form-group">
            <label>Supplier</label>
            @{ #pragma warning disable CS8602 }
            <input class="form-control" asp-for="Product.Supplier.Name" />
            @{ #pragma warning restore CS8602 }
        </div>
        <button type="submit" class="btn btn-primary mt-2">Submit</button>
    </form>
    <button form="htmlform" asp-page="FormHandler"
            class="btn btn-primary mt-2">
        Submit (Outside Form)
    </button>
</div>

@functions {

    [IgnoreAntiforgeryToken]
    public class FormHandlerModel : PageModel {
        private DataContext context;

        public FormHandlerModel(DataContext dbContext) {
            context = dbContext;
        }

        public Product Product { get; set; }
            = new() { Name = string.Empty };

        public async Task OnGetAsync(long id = 1) {
            Product = await context.Products
                .Include(p => p.Category)
                .Include(p => p.Supplier)
                .FirstAsync(p => p.ProductId == id);
        }

        public IActionResult OnPost() {
            foreach (string key in Request.Form.Keys
                    .Where(k => !k.StartsWith("_"))) {
                TempData[key] = string.Join(", ",
                    (string?)Request.Form[key]);
            }
            return RedirectToPage("FormResults");
        }
    }
}
```

To see the effect, restart ASP.NET Core so the changes to the controller take effect, and use a browser to request http://localhost:5000/controllers/form, which produces the response shown on the left of figure 27.7. Use the browser to request http://localhost:5000/pages/form, and you will see the same features used by the Razor Page, as shown on the right of figure 27.7.

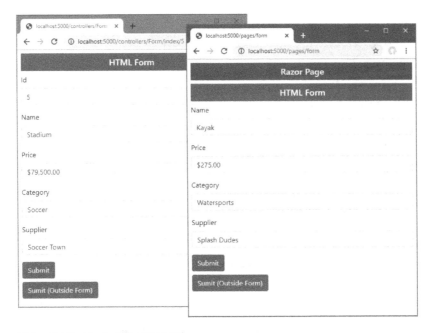

Figure 27.7 Displaying related data

27.5 *Working with label elements*

The LabelTagHelper class is used to transform label elements so the for attribute is set consistently with the approach used to transform input elements. Table 27.7 describes the attribute supported by this tag helper.

Table 27.7 The built-in tag helper attribute for label elements

Name	Description
asp-for	This attribute is used to specify the view model property that the label element describes.

The tag helper sets the content of the label element so that it contains the name of the selected view model property. The tag helper also sets the for attribute, which denotes an association with a specific input element. This aids users who rely on screen readers and allows an input element to gain the focus when its associated label is clicked.

Listing 27.23 applies the asp-for attribute to the Form view to associate each label element with the input element that represents the same view model property.

Listing 27.23   Transforming label elements in the Form.cshtml file in the Views/Form folder

```
@model Product
@{ Layout = "_SimpleLayout"; }

<h5 class="bg-primary text-white text-center p-2">HTML Form</h5>

<form asp-action="submitform" method="post" id="htmlform">
    <div class="form-group">
        <label asp-for="ProductId"></label>
        <input class="form-control" asp-for="ProductId" />
    </div>
    <div class="form-group">
        <label asp-for="Name"></label>
        <input class="form-control" asp-for="Name" />
    </div>
    <div class="form-group">
        <label asp-for="Price"></label>
        <input class="form-control" asp-for="Price" />
    </div>
    <div class="form-group">
        @{ #pragma warning disable CS8602 }
        <label asp-for="Category.Name">Category</label>
        <input class="form-control" asp-for="Category.Name" />
        @{ #pragma warning restore CS8602 }
    </div>
    <div class="form-group">
        @{ #pragma warning disable CS8602 }
        <label asp-for="Supplier.Name">Supplier</label>
        <input class="form-control" asp-for="Supplier.Name" />
        @{ #pragma warning restore CS8602 }
    </div>
    <button type="submit" class="btn btn-primary mt-2">Submit</button>
</form>

<button form="htmlform" asp-action="submitform"
        class="btn btn-primary mt-2">
    Submit (Outside Form)
</button>
```

You can override the content for a `label` element by defining it yourself, which is what I have done for the related data properties in listing 27.23. The tag helper would have set the content for both these `label` elements to be `Name`, which is not a useful description. Defining the element content means the `for` attribute will be applied, but a more useful name will be displayed to the user. Restart ASP.NET Core and use a browser to request http://localhost:5000/controllers/form to see the names used for each element, as shown in figure 27.8.

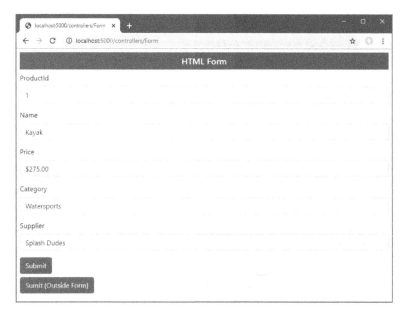

Figure 27.8 Transforming label elements

27.6 *Working with select and option elements*

The `select` and `option` elements are used to provide the user with a fixed set of choices, rather than the open data entry that is possible with an `input` element. The `SelectTagHelper` is responsible for transforming `select` elements and supports the attributes described in table 27.8.

Table 27.8 The built-in tag helper attributes for select elements

Name	Description
asp-for	This attribute is used to specify the view or page model property that the `select` element represents.
asp-items	This attribute is used to specify a source of values for the option elements contained within the `select` element.

The `asp-for` attribute sets the value of the `for` and `id` attributes to reflect the model property that it receives. In listing 27.24, I have replaced the `input` element for the category with a `select` element that presents the user with a fixed range of values.

Listing 27.24 Using a select element in the Form.cshtml file in the Views/Form folder

```
@model Product
@{ Layout = "_SimpleLayout"; }

<h5 class="bg-primary text-white text-center p-2">HTML Form</h5>
```

```
<form asp-action="submitform" method="post" id="htmlform">
    <div class="form-group">
        <label asp-for="ProductId"></label>
        <input class="form-control" asp-for="ProductId" />
    </div>
    <div class="form-group">
        <label asp-for="Name"></label>
        <input class="form-control" asp-for="Name" />
    </div>
    <div class="form-group">
        <label asp-for="Price"></label>
        <input class="form-control" asp-for="Price" />
    </div>
    <div class="form-group">
        @{ #pragma warning disable CS8602 }
        <label asp-for="Category.Name">Category</label>
        @{ #pragma warning restore CS8602 }
        <select class="form-control" asp-for="CategoryId">
            <option value="1">Watersports</option>
            <option value="2">Soccer</option>
            <option value="3">Chess</option>
        </select>
    </div>
    <div class="form-group">
        @{ #pragma warning disable CS8602 }
        <label asp-for="Supplier.Name">Supplier</label>
        <input class="form-control" asp-for="Supplier.Name" />
        @{ #pragma warning restore CS8602 }
    </div>
    <button type="submit" class="btn btn-primary mt-2">Submit</button>
</form>

<button form="htmlform" asp-action="submitform"
        class="btn btn-primary mt-2">
    Submit (Outside Form)
</button>
```

I have manually populated the select element with option elements that provide a range of categories for the user to choose from. If you use a browser to request http://localhost:5000/controllers/form/index/5 and examine the HTML response, you will see that the tag helper has transformed the select element like this:

```
...
<div class="form-group">
    <label for="Category_Name">Category</label>
    <select class="form-control" data-val="true"
            data-val-required="The CategoryId field is required."
            id="CategoryId" name="CategoryId">
        <option value="1">Watersports</option>
        <option value="2" selected="selected">Soccer</option>
        <option value="3">Chess</option>
    </select>
</div>
...
```

Notice that selected attribute has been added to the option element that corresponds to the view model's CategoryId value, like this:

```
...
<option value="2" selected="selected">Soccer</option>
...
```

The task of selecting an option element is performed by the OptionTagHelper class, which receives instructions from the SelectTagHelper through the TagHelper-Context.Items collection, described in chapter 25. The result is that the select element displays the name of the category associated with the Product object's CategoryId value.

27.6.1 Populating a select element

Explicitly defining the option elements for a select element is a useful approach for choices that always have the same possible values but doesn't help when you need to provide options that are taken from the data model or where you need the same set of options in multiple views and don't want to manually maintain duplicated content.

The asp-items attribute is used to provide the tag helper with a list sequence of SelectListItem objects for which option elements will be generated. Listing 27.25 modifies the Index action of the Form controller to provide the view with a sequence of SelectListItem objects through the view bag.

> **Listing 27.25 Providing a sequence in the FormController.cs file in the Controllers folder**

```
using Microsoft.AspNetCore.Mvc;
using WebApp.Models;
using Microsoft.EntityFrameworkCore;
using Microsoft.AspNetCore.Mvc.Rendering;

namespace WebApp.Controllers {

    public class FormController : Controller {
        private DataContext context;

        public FormController(DataContext dbContext) {
            context = dbContext;
        }

        public async Task<IActionResult> Index(long id = 1) {
            ViewBag.Categories = new SelectList(context.Categories,
                "CategoryId", "Name");
            return View("Form", await context.Products
                .Include(p => p.Category)
                .Include(p => p.Supplier)
                .FirstAsync(p => p.ProductId == id)
                ?? new() { Name = string.Empty });
        }

        [HttpPost]
        public IActionResult SubmitForm() {
```

```
                foreach (string key in
                        Request.Form.Keys.Where(k => !k.StartsWith("_"))) {
                    TempData[key] = string.Join(", ",
                        (string?)Request.Form[key]);
                }
                return RedirectToAction(nameof(Results));
            }

        public IActionResult Results() {
            return View();
        }
    }
}
```

SelectListItem objects can be created directly, but ASP.NET Core provides the
SelectList class to adapt existing data sequences. In this case, I pass the sequence of
Category objects obtained from the database to the SelectList constructor, along
with the names of the properties that should be used as the values and labels for option
elements. In listing 27.26, I have updated the Form view to use the SelectList.

Listing 27.26   Using a SelectList in the Form.cshtml file in the Views/Form folder

```
@model Product
@{ Layout = "_SimpleLayout"; }

<h5 class="bg-primary text-white text-center p-2">HTML Form</h5>

<form asp-action="submitform" method="post" id="htmlform">
    <div class="form-group">
        <label asp-for="ProductId"></label>
        <input class="form-control" asp-for="ProductId" />
    </div>
    <div class="form-group">
        <label asp-for="Name"></label>
        <input class="form-control" asp-for="Name" />
    </div>
    <div class="form-group">
        <label asp-for="Price"></label>
        <input class="form-control" asp-for="Price" />
    </div>
    <div class="form-group">
        @{ #pragma warning disable CS8602 }
        <label asp-for="Category.Name">Category</label>
        @{ #pragma warning restore CS8602 }
        <select class="form-control" asp-for="CategoryId"
            asp-items="@ViewBag.Categories">
        </select>
    </div>
    <div class="form-group">
        @{ #pragma warning disable CS8602 }
        <label asp-for="Supplier.Name">Supplier</label>
        <input class="form-control" asp-for="Supplier.Name" />
        @{ #pragma warning restore CS8602 }
    </div>
```

```
        <button type="submit" class="btn btn-primary mt-2">Submit</button>
    </form>

    <button form="htmlform" asp-action="submitform"
            class="btn btn-primary mt-2">
        Submit (Outside Form)
    </button>
```

Restart ASP.NET Core and use a browser to request http://localhost:5000/controllers/form/index/5. There is no visual change to the content presented to the user, but the `option` elements used to populate the `select` element have been generated from the database, like this:

```
...
<div class="form-group">
    <label for="Category_Name">Category</label>
    <select class="form-control" data-val="true"
            data-val-required="The CategoryId field is required."
            id="CategoryId" name="CategoryId">
        <option value="1">Watersports</option>
        <option selected="selected" value="2">Soccer</option>
        <option value="3">Chess</option>
    </select>
</div>
...
```

This approach means that the options presented to the user will automatically reflect new categories added to the database.

27.7 Working with text areas

The `textarea` element is used to solicit a larger amount of text from the user and is typically used for unstructured data, such as notes or observations. The `TextArea-TagHelper` is responsible for transforming `textarea` elements and supports the single attribute described in table 27.9.

Table 27.9 The built-in tag helper attributes for textarea elements

Name	Description
asp-for	This attribute is used to specify the view model property that the `textarea` element represents.

The `TextAreaTagHelper` is relatively simple, and the value provided for the `asp-for` attribute is used to set the `id` and `name` attributes on the `textarea` element. The value of the property selected by the `asp-for` attribute is used as the content for the `textarea` element. Listing 27.27 replaces the `input` element for the `Supplier.Name` property with a text area to which the `asp-for` attribute has been applied.

Listing 27.27   Using a text area in the Form.cshtml file in the Views/Form folder

```
@model Product
@{  Layout = "_SimpleLayout"; }

<h5 class="bg-primary text-white text-center p-2">HTML Form</h5>

<form asp-action="submitform" method="post" id="htmlform">
    <div class="form-group">
        <label asp-for="ProductId"></label>
        <input class="form-control" asp-for="ProductId" />
    </div>
    <div class="form-group">
        <label asp-for="Name"></label>
        <input class="form-control" asp-for="Name" />
    </div>
    <div class="form-group">
        <label asp-for="Price"></label>
        <input class="form-control" asp-for="Price" />
    </div>
    <div class="form-group">
        @{ #pragma warning disable CS8602 }
        <label asp-for="Category.Name">Category</label>
        @{ #pragma warning restore CS8602 }
        <select class="form-control" asp-for="CategoryId"
            asp-items="@ViewBag.Categories">
        </select>
    </div>
    <div class="form-group">
        @{ #pragma warning disable CS8602 }
        <label asp-for="Supplier.Name">Supplier</label>
        <textarea class="form-control" asp-for="Supplier.Name"></textarea>
        @{ #pragma warning restore CS8602 }
    </div>
    <button type="submit" class="btn btn-primary mt-2">Submit</button>
</form>

<button form="htmlform" asp-action="submitform"
        class="btn btn-primary mt-2">
    Submit (Outside Form)
</button>
```

Restart ASP.NET Core and use a browser to request http://localhost:5000/controllers/
form and examine the HTML received by the browser to see the transformation of the
`textarea` element.

```
...
<div class="form-group">
    <label for="Supplier_Name">Supplier</label>
    <textarea class="form-control" data-val="true"
            data-val-required="The Name field is required."
            id="Supplier_Name"
            name="Supplier.Name">
        Splash Dudes
    </textarea>
</div>
...
```

The `TextAreaTagHelper` is relatively simple, but it provides consistency with the rest of the form element tag helpers that I have described in this chapter.

27.8 *Using the anti-forgery feature*

When I defined the controller action method and page handler methods that process form data, I filtered out form data whose name begins with an underscore, like this:

```
...
[HttpPost]
public IActionResult SubmitForm() {
    foreach (string key in Request.Form.Keys
            .Where(k => !k.StartsWith("_"))) {
        TempData[key] = string.Join(", ", Request.Form[key]);
    }
    return RedirectToAction(nameof(Results));
}
...
```

I applied this filter to focus on the values provided by the HTML elements in the form. Listing 27.28 removes the filter from the action method so that all the data received from the HTML form is stored in temp data.

> **Listing 27.28   Removing a filter in the FormController.cs file in the Controllers folder**

```
using Microsoft.AspNetCore.Mvc;
using WebApp.Models;
using Microsoft.EntityFrameworkCore;
using Microsoft.AspNetCore.Mvc.Rendering;

namespace WebApp.Controllers {

    public class FormController : Controller {
        private DataContext context;

        public FormController(DataContext dbContext) {
            context = dbContext;
        }

        public async Task<IActionResult> Index(long id = 1) {
            ViewBag.Categories = new SelectList(context.Categories,
                "CategoryId", "Name");
            return View("Form", await context.Products
                .Include(p => p.Category)
                .Include(p => p.Supplier)
                .FirstAsync(p => p.ProductId == id)
            ?? new() { Name = string.Empty });
        }

        [HttpPost]
        public IActionResult SubmitForm() {
            foreach (string key in Request.Form.Keys) {
                TempData[key] = string.Join(", ",
                    (string?)Request.Form[key]);
            }
```

```
            return RedirectToAction(nameof(Results));
        }

        public IActionResult Results() {
            return View();
        }
    }
}
```

Restart ASP.NET Core and use a browser to request http://localhost:5000/controllers/ form. Click the Submit button to send the form to the application, and you will see a new item in the results, as shown in figure 27.9.

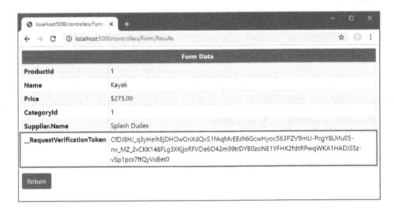

Figure 27.9   Showing all form data

The _RequestVerificationToken form value displayed in the results is a security feature that is applied by the FormTagHelper to guard against cross-site request forgery. Cross-site request forgery (CSRF) exploits web applications by taking advantage of the way that user requests are typically authenticated. Most web applications—including those created using ASP.NET Core—use cookies to identify which requests are related to a specific session, with which a user identity is usually associated.

CSRF—also known as *XSRF*—relies on the user visiting a malicious website after using your web application and without explicitly ending their session. The application still regards the user's session as being active, and the cookie that the browser has stored has not yet expired. The malicious site contains JavaScript code that sends a form request to your application to perform an operation without the user's consent—the exact nature of the operation will depend on the application being attacked. Since the JavaScript code is executed by the user's browser, the request to the application includes the session cookie, and the application performs the operation without the user's knowledge or consent.

TIP   CSRF is described in detail at http://en.wikipedia.org/wiki/Cross-site _request_forgery.

If a `form` element doesn't contain an `action` attribute—because it is being generated from the routing system with the `asp-controller`, `asp-action`, and `asp-page` attributes—then the `FormTagHelper` class automatically enables an anti-CSRF feature, whereby a security token is added to the response as a cookie. A hidden `input` element containing the same security token is added to the HTML form, and it is this token that is shown in figure 27.9.

27.8.1 *Enabling the anti-forgery feature in a controller*

By default, controllers accept POST requests even when they don't contain the required security tokens. To enable the anti-forgery feature, an attribute is applied to the controller class, as shown in listing 27.29.

> **Listing 27.29 Enabling the anti-forgery feature in the Controllers/FormController.cs file**

```
using Microsoft.AspNetCore.Mvc;
using WebApp.Models;
using Microsoft.EntityFrameworkCore;
using Microsoft.AspNetCore.Mvc.Rendering;

namespace WebApp.Controllers {

    [AutoValidateAntiforgeryToken]
    public class FormController : Controller {
        private DataContext context;

        public FormController(DataContext dbContext) {
            context = dbContext;
        }

        public async Task<IActionResult> Index(long id = 1) {
            ViewBag.Categories = new SelectList(context.Categories,
                "CategoryId", "Name");
            return View("Form", await context.Products
                .Include(p => p.Category)
                .Include(p => p.Supplier)
                .FirstAsync(p => p.ProductId == id)
            ?? new() { Name = string.Empty });
        }

        [HttpPost]
        public IActionResult SubmitForm() {
            foreach (string key in Request.Form.Keys) {
                TempData[key] = string.Join(", ",
                    (string?)Request.Form[key]);
            }
            return RedirectToAction(nameof(Results));
        }

        public IActionResult Results() {
            return View();
        }
    }
}
```

Not all requests require an anti-forgery token, and the `AutoValidateAntiforgery-Token` ensures that checks are performed for all HTTP methods except GET, HEAD, OPTIONS, and TRACE.

> **TIP**   Two other attributes can be used to control token validation. The `Ignore-ValidationToken` attribute suppresses validation for an action method or controller. The `ValidateAntiForgeryToken` attribute does the opposite and enforces validation, even for requests that would not normally require validation, such as HTTP GET requests. I recommend using the `AutoValidate-AntiforgeryToken` attribute, as shown in the listing.

Testing the anti-CSRF feature is a little tricky. I do it by requesting the URL that contains the form (http://localhost:5000/controllers/forms for this example) and then using the browser's F12 developer tools to locate and remove the hidden `input` element from the form (or change the element's value). When I populate and submit the form, it is missing one part of the required data, and the request will fail.

27.8.2   *Enabling the anti-forgery feature in a Razor Page*

The anti-forgery feature is enabled by default in Razor Pages, which is why I applied the `IgnoreAntiforgeryToken` attribute to the page handler method in listing 27.29 when I created the `FormHandler` page. Listing 27.30 removes the attribute to enable the validation feature.

Listing 27.30   Enabling Request Validation in the Pages/FormHandler.cshtml File

```
...
@functions {

    //[IgnoreAntiforgeryToken]
    public class FormHandlerModel : PageModel {
        private DataContext context;
...
```

Testing the validation feature is done in the same way as for controllers and requires altering the HTML document using the browser's developer tools before submitting the form to the application.

27.8.3   *Using anti-forgery tokens with JavaScript clients*

By default, the anti-forgery feature relies on the ASP.NET Core application being able to include an element in an HTML form that the browser sends back when the form is submitted. This doesn't work for JavaScript clients because the ASP.NET Core application provides data and not HTML, so there is no way to insert the hidden element and receive it in a future request.

For web services, the anti-forgery token can be sent as a JavaScript-readable cookie, which the JavaScript client code reads and includes as a header in its POST requests. Some JavaScript frameworks, such as Angular, will automatically detect the cookie and include a header in requests. For other frameworks and custom JavaScript code, additional work is required.

Listing 27.31 shows the changes required to the ASP.NET Core application to configure the anti-forgery feature for use with JavaScript clients.

> **Listing 27.31 Configuring the anti-forgery token in the WebApp/Program.cs file**

```
using Microsoft.EntityFrameworkCore;
using WebApp.Models;
using Microsoft.AspNetCore.Antiforgery;

var builder = WebApplication.CreateBuilder(args);

builder.Services.AddDbContext<DataContext>(opts => {
    opts.UseSqlServer(builder.Configuration[
        "ConnectionStrings:ProductConnection"]);
    opts.EnableSensitiveDataLogging(true);
});
builder.Services.AddControllersWithViews();
builder.Services.AddRazorPages();
builder.Services.AddSingleton<CitiesData>();

builder.Services.Configure<AntiforgeryOptions>(opts => {
    opts.HeaderName = "X-XSRF-TOKEN";
});

var app = builder.Build();

app.UseStaticFiles();

IAntiforgery antiforgery
    = app.Services.GetRequiredService<IAntiforgery>();
app.Use(async (context, next) => {
    if (!context.Request.Path.StartsWithSegments("/api")) {
        string? token =
            antiforgery.GetAndStoreTokens(context).RequestToken;
        if (token != null) {
            context.Response.Cookies.Append("XSRF-TOKEN",
                token,
                new CookieOptions { HttpOnly = false });
        }
    }
    await next();
});

app.MapControllerRoute("forms",
    "controllers/{controller=Home}/{action=Index}/{id?}");
app.MapRazorPages();

var context = app.Services.CreateScope().ServiceProvider
    .GetRequiredService<DataContext>();
SeedData.SeedDatabase(context);

app.Run();
```

The options pattern is used to configure the anti-forgery feature, through the `AntiforgeryOptions` class. The `HeaderName` property is used to specify the name of a header through which anti-forgery tokens will be accepted, which is `X-XSRF-TOKEN` in this case.

A custom middleware component is required to set the cookie, which is named `XSRF-TOKEN` in this example. The value of the cookie is obtained through the `IAntiForgery` service and must be configured with the `HttpOnly` option set to `false` so that the browser will allow JavaScript code to read the cookie.

> **TIP**   I have followed the names that are supported by Angular in this example. Other frameworks follow their own conventions but can usually be configured to use any set of cookie and header names.

To create a simple JavaScript client that uses the cookie and header, add a Razor Page named `JavaScriptForm.cshtml` to the `Pages` folder with the content shown in listing 27.32.

Listing 27.32   The contents of the JavaScriptForm.cshtml file in the Pages folder

```
@page "/pages/jsform"

<script type="text/javascript">
    async function sendRequest() {
        const token = document.cookie.replace(
            /(?:(?:^|.*;\s*)XSRF-TOKEN\s*\=\s*([^;]*).*$)|^.*$/, "$1");

        let form = new FormData();
        form.append("name", "Paddle");
        form.append("price", 100);
        form.append("categoryId", 1);
        form.append("supplierId", 1);

        let response = await fetch("@Url.Page("FormHandler")", {
            method: "POST",
            headers: { "X-XSRF-TOKEN": token },
            body: form
        });
        document.getElementById("content").innerHTML
            = await response.text();
    }

    document.addEventListener("DOMContentLoaded",
        () => document.getElementById("submit").onclick = sendRequest);
</script>

<button class="btn btn-primary m-2" id="submit">
    Submit JavaScript Form
</button>
<div id="content"></div>
```

The JavaScript code in this Razor Page responds to a button click by sending an HTTP POST request to the FormHandler Razor Page. The value of the XSRF-TOKEN cookie is read and included in the X-XSRF-TOKEN request header. The response from the FormHandler page is a redirection to the Results page, which the browser will follow automatically. The response from the Results page is read by the JavaScript code and inserted into an element so it can be displayed to the user. To test the JavaScript code, restart ASP.NET Core, use a browser to request http://localhost:5000/pages/ jsform, and click the button. The JavaScript code will submit the form and display the response, as shown in figure 27.10.

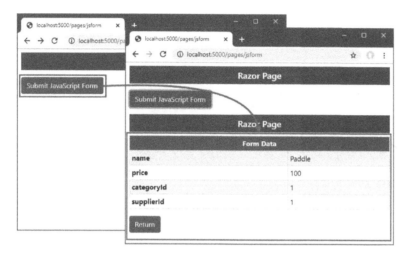

Figure 27.10 Using a security token in JavaScript code

Summary

- The FormTagHelper class transforms form elements so they target specific action methods or Razor pages.
- The InputTagHelper class transforms input elements, generating form content from model properties and their values.
- The LabelTagHelper class transforms label elements, setting their content from model property names.
- The TextAreaTagHelper transforms textarea elements.
- The AutoValidateAntiforgeryToken and IgnoreAntiforgeryToken attributes are used to control the anti-cross site request forgery feature.

Using model binding 28

This chapter covers

- Understanding how the ASP.NET Core model binder reads data values from HTTP requests
- Finding data values during model binding
- Customizing the model binding process and performing model binding manually

Model binding is the process of creating .NET objects using the values from the HTTP request to provide easy access to the data required by action methods and Razor Pages. In this chapter, I describe the way the model binding system works; show how it binds simple types, complex types, and collections; and demonstrate how you can take control of the process to specify which part of the request provides the data values your application requires. Table 28.1 puts model binding in context.

Table 28.1 Putting model binding in context

Question	Answer
What is it?	Model binding is the process of creating the objects that action methods and page handlers require using data values obtained from the HTTP request.
Why is it useful?	Model binding lets controllers or page handlers declare method parameters or properties using C# types and automatically receive data from the request without having to inspect, parse, and process the data directly.
How is it used?	In its simplest form, methods declare parameters, or classes define properties whose names are used to retrieve data values from the HTTP request. The part of the request used to obtain the data can be configured by applying attributes to the method parameters or properties.
Are there any pitfalls or limitations?	The main pitfall is getting data from the wrong part of the request. I explain the way that requests are searched for data in the "Understanding Model Binding" section, and the search locations can be specified explicitly using the attributes that I describe in the "Specifying a Model Binding Source" section.
Are there any alternatives?	Data can be obtained without model binding using context objects. However, the result is more complicated code that is hard to read and maintain.

Table 28.2 provides a guide to the chapter.

Table 28.2 Chapter guide

Problem	Solution	Listing
Binding simple types	Define method parameters with primitive types.	5–9
Binding complex types	Define method parameters with class types.	10
Binding to a property	Use the `BindProperty` attribute.	11, 12
Binding nested types	Ensure the form value types follow the dotted notation.	13–18
Selecting properties for binding	Use the `Bind` and `BindNever` attributes.	19–21
Binding collections	Follow the sequence binding conventions.	22–27
Specifying the source for binding	Use one of the source attributes.	28–33
Manually performing binding	Use the `TryUpdateModel` method.	34

28.1   *Preparing for this chapter*

This chapter uses the WebApp project from chapter 27. To prepare for this chapter, replace the contents of the Form.cshtml file in the Views/Form folder with the content shown in listing 28.1.

> **TIP**   You can download the example project for this chapter—and for all the other chapters in this book—from https://github.com/manningbooks/pro-asp .net-core-7. See chapter 1 for how to get help if you have problems running the examples.

Listing 28.1   The contents of the Form.cshtml file in the Views/Form folder

```
@model Product
@{ Layout = "_SimpleLayout"; }

<h5 class="bg-primary text-white text-center p-2">HTML Form</h5>

<form asp-action="submitform" method="post" id="htmlform">
    <div class="form-group">
        <label asp-for="Name"></label>
        <input class="form-control" asp-for="Name" />
    </div>
    <div class="form-group">
        <label asp-for="Price"></label>
        <input class="form-control" asp-for="Price" />
    </div>
    <button type="submit" class="btn btn-primary mt-2">Submit</button>
</form>
```

Next, comment out the DisplayFormat attribute that has been applied to the Product model class, as shown in listing 28.2.

Listing 28.2   Removing an attribute in the Product.cs file in the Models folder

```
using System.ComponentModel.DataAnnotations;
using System.ComponentModel.DataAnnotations.Schema;
using System.Text.Json.Serialization;

namespace WebApp.Models {
    public class Product {

        public long ProductId { get; set; }

        public required string Name { get; set; }

        [Column(TypeName = "decimal(8, 2)")]
        //[DisplayFormat(DataFormatString = "{0:c2}",
        //    ApplyFormatInEditMode = true)]
        public decimal Price { get; set; }

        public long CategoryId { get; set; }
        public Category? Category { get; set; }
```

```
        public long SupplierId { get; set; }

        [JsonIgnore(Condition = JsonIgnoreCondition.WhenWritingNull)]
        public Supplier? Supplier { get; set; }
    }
}
```

28.1.1 Dropping the database

Open a new PowerShell command prompt, navigate to the folder that contains the
WebApp.csproj file, and run the command shown in listing 28.3 to drop the database.

Listing 28.3   Dropping the database

```
dotnet ef database drop --force
```

28.1.2 Running the example application

Use the PowerShell command prompt to run the command shown in listing 28.4.

Listing 28.4   Running the example application

```
dotnet run
```

Use a browser to request http://localhost:5000/controllers/form, which will display
an HTML form. Click the Submit button, and the form data will be displayed, as shown
in figure 28.1.

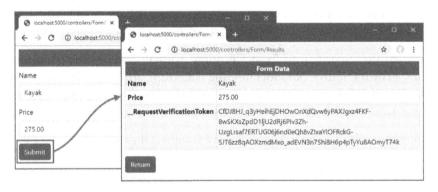

Figure 28.1   Running the example application

28.2   Understanding model binding

Model binding is an elegant bridge between the HTTP request and action or page handler methods. Most ASP.NET Core applications rely on model binding to some extent,
including the example application for this chapter.

You can see model binding at work by using the browser to request http://
localhost:5000/controllers/form/index/5. This URL contains the value of the
ProductId property of the Product object that I want to view, like this:

```
http://localhost:5000/controllers/form/index/5
```

This part of the URL corresponds to the `id` segment variable defined by the controller routing pattern and matches the name of the parameter defined by the `Form` controller's `Index` action:

```
...
public async Task<IActionResult> Index(long id = 1) {
...
```

A value for the `id` parameter is required before the MVC Framework can invoke the action method, and finding a suitable value is the responsibility of the *model binding* system. The model binding system relies on *model binders*, which are components responsible for providing data values from one part of the request or application. The default model binders look for data values in these four places:

- Form data
- The request body (only for controllers decorated with `ApiController`)
- Routing segment variables
- Query strings

Each source of data is inspected in order until a value for the argument is found. There is no form data in the example application, so no value will be found there, and the `Form` controller isn't decorated with the `ApiController` attribute, so the request body won't be checked. The next step is to check the routing data, which contains a segment variable named `id`. This allows the model binding system to provide a value that allows the `Index` action method to be invoked. The search stops after a suitable data value has been found, which means that the query string isn't searched for a data value.

> **TIP**   In the "Specifying a Model Binding Source" section, I explain how you can specify the source of model binding data using attributes. This allows you to specify that a data value is obtained from, for example, the query string, even if there is also suitable data in the routing data.

Knowing the order in which data values are sought is important because a request can contain multiple values, like this URL:

```
http://localhost:5000/controllers/Form/Index/5?id=1
```

The routing system will process the request and match the `id` segment in the URL template to the value 5, and the query string contains an `id` value of 1. Since the routing data is searched for data before the query string, the `Index` action method will receive the value 5, and the query string value will be ignored.

On the other hand, if you request a URL that doesn't have an `id` segment, then the query string will be examined, which means that a URL like this one will also allow the model binding system to provide a value for the `id` argument so that it can invoke the `Index` method.

```
http://localhost:5000/controllers/Form/Index?id=4
```

You can see the effect of both these URLs in figure 28.2.

Figure 28.2   The effect of model binding data source order

28.3   *Binding simple data types*

Request data values must be converted into C# values so they can be used to invoke action or page handler methods. *Simple types* are values that originate from one item of data in the request that can be parsed from a string. This includes numeric values, `bool` values, dates, and, of course, `string` values.

Data binding for simple types makes it easy to extract single data items from the request without having to work through the context data to find out where it is defined. Listing 28.5 adds parameters to the SubmitForm action method defined by the SubmitForm action method so that the model binder will be used to provide name and price values.

> **Listing 28.5   Adding parameters in the FormController.cs file in the Controllers folder**

```
using Microsoft.AspNetCore.Mvc;
using WebApp.Models;
using Microsoft.EntityFrameworkCore;
using Microsoft.AspNetCore.Mvc.Rendering;

namespace WebApp.Controllers {

    [AutoValidateAntiforgeryToken]
    public class FormController : Controller {
        private DataContext context;

        public FormController(DataContext dbContext) {
            context = dbContext;
        }

        public async Task<IActionResult> Index(long id = 1) {
            ViewBag.Categories = new SelectList(context.Categories,
                "CategoryId", "Name");
            return View("Form", await context.Products
                .Include(p => p.Category)
                .Include(p => p.Supplier)
                .FirstAsync(p => p.ProductId == id)
            ?? new() { Name = string.Empty });
        }
```

```
[HttpPost]
public IActionResult SubmitForm(string name, decimal price) {
    TempData["name param"] = name;
    TempData["price param"] = price.ToString();
    return RedirectToAction(nameof(Results));
}

public IActionResult Results() {
    return View();
}
    }
}
```

The model binding system will be used to obtain name and price values when ASP .NET Core receives a request that will be processed by the SubmitForm action method. The use of parameters simplifies the action method and takes care of converting the request data into C# data types so that the price value will be converted to the C# decimal type before the action method is invoked. (I had to convert the decimal back to a string to store it as temp data in this example. I demonstrate more useful ways of dealing with form data in chapter 31.) Restart ASP.NET Core and use a browser to request http://localhost:5000/controllers/form. Click the Submit button, and you will see the values that were extracted from the request by the model binding feature, as shown in figure 28.3.

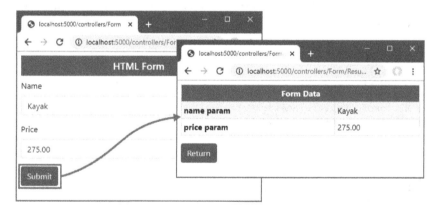

Figure 28.3 Model binding for simple types

28.3.1 Binding simple data types in Razor Pages

Razor Pages can use model binding, but care must be taken to ensure that the value of the form element's name attribute matches the name of the handler method parameter, which may not be the case if the asp-for attribute has been used to select a nested property. To ensure the names match, the name attribute can be defined explicitly, as shown in listing 28.6, which also simplifies the HTML form so that it matches the controller example.

```
@page "/pages/form/{id:long?}"
@model FormHandlerModel
@using Microsoft.AspNetCore.Mvc.RazorPages
@using Microsoft.EntityFrameworkCore

<div class="m-2">
    <h5 class="bg-primary text-white text-center p-2">HTML Form</h5>
    <form asp-page="FormHandler" method="post" id="htmlform">
        <div class="form-group">
            <label>Name</label>
            <input class="form-control" asp-for="Product.Name"
                name="name" />
        </div>
        <div class="form-group">
            <label>Price</label>
            <input class="form-control" asp-for="Product.Price"
                name="price" />
        </div>
        <button type="submit" class="btn btn-primary mt-2">Submit</button>
    </form>
</div>


@functions {

    public class FormHandlerModel : PageModel {
        private DataContext context;

        public FormHandlerModel(DataContext dbContext) {
            context = dbContext;
        }

        public Product Product { get; set; }
            = new() { Name = string.Empty };

        public async Task OnGetAsync(long id = 1) {
            Product = await context.Products
                .Include(p => p.Category)
                .Include(p => p.Supplier)
                .FirstAsync(p => p.ProductId == id);
        }

        public IActionResult OnPost(string name, decimal price) {
            TempData["name param"] = name;
            TempData["price param"] = price.ToString();
            return RedirectToPage("FormResults");
        }
    }
}
```

The tag helper would have set the name attributes of the input elements to `Product`
`.Name` and `Product.Price`, which prevents the model binder from matching the

values. Explicitly setting the name attribute overrides the tag helper and ensures the model binding process works correctly. Restart ASP.NET Core, use a browser to request http://localhost:5000/pages/form, and click the Submit button, and you will see the values found by the model binder, as shown in figure 28.4.

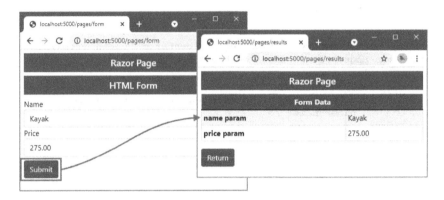

Figure 28.4   Model binding in a Razor Page

28.3.2 *Understanding default binding values*

Model binding is a best-effort feature, which means the model binder will try to get values for method parameters but will still invoke the method if data values cannot be located. You can see how this works by removing the default value for the id parameter in the Form controller's Index action method, as shown in listing 28.7.

Listing 28.7   Removing a parameter value in the Controllers/FormController.cs file

```
. . .
public async Task<IActionResult> Index(long id) {
    ViewBag.Categories = new SelectList(context.Categories,
        "CategoryId", "Name");
    return View("Form", await context.Products
        .Include(p => p.Category)
        .Include(p => p.Supplier)
        .FirstAsync(p => p.ProductId == id)
    ?? new() { Name = string.Empty });
}
. . .
```

Restart ASP.NET Core and request http://localhost:5000/controllers/form. The URL doesn't contain a value that the model binder can use for the id parameter, and there is no query string or form data, but the method is still invoked, producing the error shown in figure 28.5.

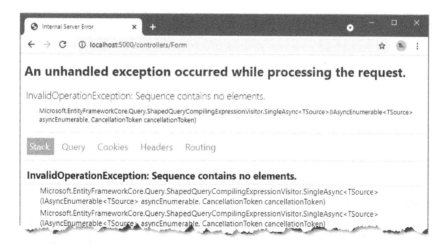

Figure 28.5 An error caused by a missing data value

This exception isn't reported by the model binding system. Instead, it occurred when the Entity Framework Core query was executed. The MVC Framework must provide *some* value for the id argument to invoke the Index action method, so it uses a default value and hopes for the best. For long arguments, the default value is 0, and this is what leads to the exception. The Index action method uses the id value as the key to query the database for a Product object, like this:

```
...
public async Task<IActionResult> Index(long id) {
    ViewBag.Categories = new SelectList(context.Categories,
        "CategoryId", "Name");
    return View("Form", await context.Products
        .Include(p => p.Category)
        .Include(p => p.Supplier)
        .FirstAsync(p => p.ProductId == id)
    ?? new() { Name = string.Empty });
}
...
```

When there is no value available for model binding, the action method tries to query the database with an id of zero. There is no such object, which causes the error shown in the figure when Entity Framework Core tries to process the result.

Applications must be written to cope with default argument values, which can be done in several ways. You can add fallback values to the routing URL patterns used by controllers (as shown in chapter 21) or pages (as shown in chapter 23). You can assign default values when defining the parameter in the action or page handler method, which is the approach that I have taken so far in this part of the book. Or you can simply write methods that accommodate the default values without causing an error, as shown in listing 28.8.

Listing 28.8   Avoiding a query error in the FormController.cs file in the Controllers folder

```
...
public async Task<IActionResult> Index(long id) {
    ViewBag.Categories = new SelectList(context.Categories,
        "CategoryId", "Name");
    return View("Form", await context.Products
        .Include(p => p.Category)
        .Include(p => p.Supplier)
        .FirstOrDefaultAsync(p => p.ProductId == id)
    ?? new() { Name = string.Empty });
}
...
```

The Entity Framework Core `FirstOrDefaultAsync` method will return `null` if there is no matching object in the database and won't attempt to load related data. The tag helpers cope with `null` values and display empty fields, which you can see by restarting ASP.NET Core and requesting http://localhost:5000/controllers/form, which produces the result shown in figure 28.6.

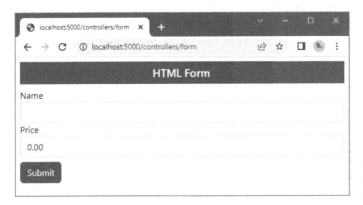

Figure 28.6 Avoiding an error

Some applications need to differentiate between a missing value and any value provided by the user. In these situations, a nullable parameter type can be used, as shown in listing 28.9.

Listing 28.9.   A nullable parameter in the FormController.cs file in the Controllers folder

```
...
public async Task<IActionResult> Index(long? id) {
    ViewBag.Categories = new SelectList(context.Categories,
        "CategoryId", "Name");
    return View("Form", await context.Products.Include(p => p.Category)
        .Include(p => p.Supplier)
        .FirstOrDefaultAsync(p => id == null || p.ProductId == id));
}
...
```

The `id` parameter will be `null` only if the request doesn't contain a suitable value, which allows the expression passed to the `FirstOrDefaultAsync` method to default to the first object in the database when there is no value and to query for any other value. To see the effect, restart ASP.NET Core and request http://localhost:5000/controllers/form and http://localhost:5000/controllers/form/index/0. The first URL contains no id value, so the first object in the database is selected. The second URL provides an id value of zero, which doesn't correspond to any object in the database. Figure 28.7 shows both results.

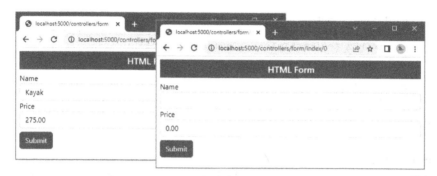

Figure 28.7 Using a nullable type to determine whether a request contains a value

28.4 Binding complex types

The model binding system shines when dealing with complex types, which are any type that cannot be parsed from a single string value. The model binding process inspects the complex type and performs the binding process on each of the public properties it defines. This means that instead of dealing with individual values such as name and price, I can use the binder to create complete Product objects, as shown in listing 28.10.

> **Listing 28.10. Binding a complex type in the Controllers/FormController.cs file**

```
using Microsoft.AspNetCore.Mvc;
using WebApp.Models;
using Microsoft.EntityFrameworkCore;
using Microsoft.AspNetCore.Mvc.Rendering;
using System.Text.Json;

namespace WebApp.Controllers {

    [AutoValidateAntiforgeryToken]
    public class FormController : Controller {
        private DataContext context;

        public FormController(DataContext dbContext) {
            context = dbContext;
        }

        public async Task<IActionResult> Index(long? id) {
            ViewBag.Categories = new SelectList(context.Categories,
```

```
            "CategoryId", "Name");
        return View("Form", await context.Products
            .Include(p => p.Category)
            .Include(p => p.Supplier)
            .FirstOrDefaultAsync(p => id == null || p.ProductId == id)
        ?? new() { Name = string.Empty });
    }

    [HttpPost]
    public IActionResult SubmitForm(Product product) {
        TempData["product"] = JsonSerializer.Serialize(product);
        return RedirectToAction(nameof(Results));
    }

    public IActionResult Results() {
        return View();
    }
    }
}
```

The listing changes the SubmitForm action method so that it defines a Product parameter. Before the action method is invoked, a new Product object is created, and the model binding process is applied to each of its public properties. The SubmitForm method is then invoked, using the Product object as its argument.

To see the model binding process, restart ASP.NET Core, navigate to http://localhost:5000/controllers/form, and click the Submit button. The model binding process will extract the data values from the request and produce the result shown in figure 28.8. The Product object created by the model binding process is serialized as JSON data so that it can be stored as temp data, making it easy to see the request data.

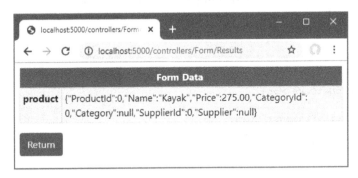

Figure 28.8   Data binding a complex type

The data binding process for complex types remains a best-effort feature, meaning that a value will be sought for each public property defined by the Product class, but missing values won't prevent the action method from being invoked. Instead, properties for which no value can be located will be left as the default value for the property type. The example provided values for the Name and Price properties, but the ProductId, CategoryId, and SupplierId properties are zero, and the Category and Supplier properties are null.

28.4.1 *Binding to a property*

Using parameters for model binding doesn't fit with the Razor Pages development style because the parameters often duplicate properties defined by the page model class, as shown in listing 28.11.

Listing 28.11   Binding a complex type in the FormHandler.cshtml file in the Pages folder

```
...
@functions {

    public class FormHandlerModel : PageModel {
        private DataContext context;

        public FormHandlerModel(DataContext dbContext) {
            context = dbContext;
        }

        public Product Product { get; set; }
            = new() { Name = string.Empty };

        public async Task OnGetAsync(long id = 1) {
            Product = await context.Products
                .Include(p => p.Category)
                .Include(p => p.Supplier)
                .FirstAsync(p => p.ProductId == id);
        }

        public IActionResult OnPost(Product product) {
            TempData["product"] =
                System.Text.Json.JsonSerializer.Serialize(product);
            return RedirectToPage("FormResults");
        }
    }
}
...
```

This code works, but the `OnPost` handler method has its own version of the `Product` object, mirroring the property used by the `OnGetAsync` handler. A more elegant approach is to use the existing property for model binding, as shown in listing 28.12.

Listing 28.12   Using a property for model binding in the Pages/FormHandler.cshtml file

```
@page "/pages/form/{id:long?}"
@model FormHandlerModel
@using Microsoft.AspNetCore.Mvc.RazorPages
@using Microsoft.EntityFrameworkCore

<div class="m-2">
    <h5 class="bg-primary text-white text-center p-2">HTML Form</h5>
    <form asp-page="FormHandler" method="post" id="htmlform">
        <div class="form-group">
            <label>Name</label>
            <input class="form-control" asp-for="Product.Name" />
```

```
        </div>
        <div class="form-group">
            <label>Price</label>
            <input class="form-control" asp-for="Product.Price" />
        </div>
        <button type="submit" class="btn btn-primary mt-2">Submit</button>
    </form>
</div>

@functions {

    public class FormHandlerModel : PageModel {
        private DataContext context;

        public FormHandlerModel(DataContext dbContext) {
            context = dbContext;
        }

        [BindProperty]
        public Product Product { get; set; }
            = new() { Name = string.Empty };

        public async Task OnGetAsync(long id = 1) {
            Product = await context.Products
                .Include(p => p.Category)
                .Include(p => p.Supplier)
                .FirstAsync(p => p.ProductId == id);
        }

        public IActionResult OnPost() {
            TempData["product"] =
                System.Text.Json.JsonSerializer.Serialize(Product);
            return RedirectToPage("FormResults");
        }
    }
}
```

Decorating a property with the BindProperty attribute indicates that its properties should be subject to the model binding process, which means the OnPost handler method can get the data it requires without declaring a parameter. When the Bind-Property attribute is used, the model binder uses the property name when locating data values, so the explicit name attributes added to the input element are not required. By default, BindProperty won't bind data for GET requests, but this can be changed by setting the BindProperty attribute's SupportsGet argument to true.

> **NOTE** The BindProperties attribute can be applied to classes that require the model binding process for all the public properties they define, which can be more convenient than applying BindProperty to many individual properties. Decorate properties with the BindNever attribute to exclude them from model binding.

28.4.2 *Binding nested complex types*

If a property that is subject to model binding is defined using a complex type, then the model binding process is repeated using the property name as a prefix. For example, the Product class defines the Category property, whose type is the complex Category type. Listing 28.13 adds elements to the HTML form to provide the model binder with values for the properties defined by the Category class.

> Listing 28.13 **Nested form elements in the Form.cshtml file in the Views/Form folder**

```
@model Product
@{  Layout = "_SimpleLayout"; }

<h5 class="bg-primary text-white text-center p-2">HTML Form</h5>

<form asp-action="submitform" method="post" id="htmlform">
    <div class="form-group">
        <label asp-for="Name"></label>
        <input class="form-control" asp-for="Name" />
    </div>
    <div class="form-group">
        <label asp-for="Price"></label>
        <input class="form-control" asp-for="Price" />
    </div>
    <div class="form-group">
        <label>Category Name</label>
        @{ #pragma warning disable CS8602 }
        <input class="form-control" name="Category.Name"
            value="@Model.Category.Name" />
        @{ #pragma warning restore CS8602 }
    </div>
    <button type="submit" class="btn btn-primary mt-2">Submit</button>
</form>
```

The name attribute combines the property names, separated by periods. In this case, the element is for the Name property of the object assigned to the view model's Category property, so the name attribute is set to Category.Name. The input element tag helper will automatically use this format for the name attribute when the asp-for attribute is applied, as shown in listing 28.14.

> Listing 28.14 **Using a tag helper in the Form.cshtml file in the Views/Form folder**

```
@model Product
@{  Layout = "_SimpleLayout"; }

<h5 class="bg-primary text-white text-center p-2">HTML Form</h5>

<form asp-action="submitform" method="post" id="htmlform">
    <div class="form-group">
        <label asp-for="Name"></label>
        <input class="form-control" asp-for="Name" />
    </div>
    <div class="form-group">
```

```
        <label asp-for="Price"></label>
        <input class="form-control" asp-for="Price" />
    </div>
    <div class="form-group">
        <label>Category Name</label>
        @{ #pragma warning disable CS8602 }
        <input class="form-control" asp-for="Category.Name" />
        @{ #pragma warning restore CS8602 }
    </div>
    <button type="submit" class="btn btn-primary mt-2">Submit</button>
</form>
```

The tag helper is a more reliable method of creating elements for nested properties and avoids the risk of typos producing elements that are ignored by the model binding process. To see the effect of the new elements, request http://localhost:5000/controllers/form and click the Submit button, which will produce the response shown in figure 28.9.

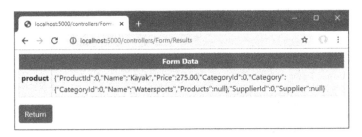

Figure 28.9
Model binding a
nested property

During the model binding process, a new `Category` object is created and assigned to the `Category` property of the `Product` object. The model binder locates the value for the `Category` object's `Name` property, which can be seen in the figure, but there is no value for the `CategoryId` property, which is left as the default value.

SPECIFYING CUSTOM PREFIXES FOR NESTED COMPLEX TYPES

There are occasions when the HTML you generate relates to one type of object but you want to bind it to another. This means that the prefixes containing the view won't correspond to the structure that the model binder is expecting, and your data won't be properly processed. Listing 28.15 demonstrates this problem by changing the type of the parameter defined by the controller's `SubmitForm` action method.

> **Listing 28.15   Changing a parameter in the Controllers/FormController.cs file**

```
...
[HttpPost]
public IActionResult SubmitForm(Category category) {
    TempData["category"] = JsonSerializer.Serialize(category);
    return RedirectToAction(nameof(Results));
}
...
```

The new parameter is a `Category`, which means that the model binder will look for form data using the category prefix. This process fails if the form data doesn't conform to that naming convention. To demonstrate, listing 28.16 overrides the name attribute input element that provides the category name.

```
...
@{ #pragma warning disable CS8602 }
<input class="form-control" asp-for="Category.Name" name="cat.name" />
@{ #pragma warning restore CS8602 }
...
```

This change creates a mismatch between the structure of the form data that is received by the application and the property names used by the model binder. The model binding process isn't able to identify the modified `input` element. Instead, the model binder will find the `Name` value for the `Product` object and use that instead, which you can see by restarting ASP.NET Core, requesting http://localhost:5000/controllers/form, and submitting the form data, which will produce the first response shown in figure 28.10.

This problem is solved by applying the `Bind` attribute to the parameter and using the `Prefix` argument to specify a prefix for the model binder, as shown in listing 28.17.

```
...
[HttpPost]
public IActionResult SubmitForm([Bind(Prefix ="cat")]Category category) {
    TempData["category"] = JsonSerializer.Serialize(category);
    return RedirectToAction(nameof(Results));
}
...
```

The syntax is awkward, but the attribute ensures the model binder can locate the data the action method requires. In this case, setting the prefix to `cat` ensures the correct data values are used to bind the `Category` parameter. Restart ASP.NET Core, request http://localhost:5000/controllers/form, and submit the form, which produces the second response shown in figure 28.10.

Figure 28.10　Specifying a model binding prefix

When using the `BindProperty` attribute, the prefix is specified using the `Name` argument, as shown in listing 28.18.

```
@page "/pages/form/{id:long?}"
@model FormHandlerModel
@using Microsoft.AspNetCore.Mvc.RazorPages
@using Microsoft.EntityFrameworkCore

<div class="m-2">
    <h5 class="bg-primary text-white text-center p-2">HTML Form</h5>
    <form asp-page="FormHandler" method="post" id="htmlform">
        <div class="form-group">
            <label>Name</label>
            <input class="form-control" asp-for="Product.Name" />
        </div>
        <div class="form-group">
            <label>Price</label>
            <input class="form-control" asp-for="Product.Price" />
        </div>
        <div class="form-group">
            <label>Category Name</label>
            @{ #pragma warning disable CS8602 }
            <input class="form-control" asp-for="Product.Category.Name"  />
            @{ #pragma warning restore CS8602 }
        </div>
        <button type="submit" class="btn btn-primary mt-2">Submit</button>
    </form>
</div>

@functions {

    public class FormHandlerModel : PageModel {
        private DataContext context;

        public FormHandlerModel(DataContext dbContext) {
            context = dbContext;
        }

        [BindProperty]
        public Product Product { get; set; }
            = new() { Name = string.Empty };

        [BindProperty(Name = "Product.Category")]
        public Category Category { get; set; }
            = new() { Name = string.Empty };

        public async Task OnGetAsync(long id = 1) {
            Product = await context.Products
                .Include(p => p.Category)
                .Include(p => p.Supplier)
                .FirstAsync(p => p.ProductId == id);
        }

        public IActionResult OnPost() {
            TempData["product"] =
                System.Text.Json.JsonSerializer.Serialize(Product);
```

```
        TempData["category"] =
            System.Text.Json.JsonSerializer.Serialize(Category);
        return RedirectToPage("FormResults");
        }
    }
}
```

This listing adds an `input` element that uses the `asp-for` attribute to select the `Product.Category` property. A page handler class defined a `Category` property that is decorated with the `BindProperty` attribute and configured with the `Name` argument. To see the result of the model binding process, restart ASP.NET Core, use a browser to request http://localhost:5000/pages/form, and click the Submit button. The model binding finds values for both the decorated properties, which produces the response shown in figure 28.11.

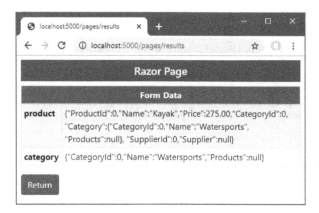

Figure 28.11
Specifying a
model binding
prefix in a Razor
Page

28.4.3 Selectively binding properties

Some model classes define properties that are sensitive and for which the user should not be able to specify values. A user may be able to change the category for a `Product` object, for example, but should not be able to alter the price.

You might be tempted to simply create views that omit HTML elements for sensitive properties but that won't prevent malicious users from crafting HTTP requests that contain values anyway, which is known as an *over-binding attack*. To prevent the model binder from using values for sensitive properties, the list of properties that should be bound can be specified, as shown in listing 28.19.

Listing 28.19 Selectively binding properties in the Controllers/FormController.cs file

```
using Microsoft.AspNetCore.Mvc;
using WebApp.Models;
using Microsoft.EntityFrameworkCore;
using Microsoft.AspNetCore.Mvc.Rendering;
using System.Text.Json;

namespace WebApp.Controllers {
```

```
[AutoValidateAntiforgeryToken]
public class FormController : Controller {
    private DataContext context;

    public FormController(DataContext dbContext) {
        context = dbContext;
    }

    public async Task<IActionResult> Index(long? id) {
        ViewBag.Categories = new SelectList(context.Categories,
            "CategoryId", "Name");
        return View("Form", await context.Products
            .Include(p => p.Category)
            .Include(p => p.Supplier)
            .FirstOrDefaultAsync(p => id == null || p.ProductId == id)
        ?? new() { Name = string.Empty });
    }

    [HttpPost]
    public IActionResult SubmitForm([Bind("Name", "Category")]
            Product product) {
        TempData["name"] = product.Name;
        TempData["price"] = product.Price.ToString();
        TempData["category name"] = product.Category?.Name;
        return RedirectToAction(nameof(Results));
    }

    public IActionResult Results() {
        return View();
    }
}
}
```

I have returned to the `Product` type for the action method parameter, which has been decorated with the `Bind` attribute to specify the names of the properties that should be included in the model binding process. This example tells the model binding feature to look for values for the `Name` and `Category` properties, which excludes any other property from the process.

Listing 28.20 removes the custom `name` attribute I added earlier so that the model binder can find the values it needs using the standard naming conventions.

Listing 28.20   Removing an attribute in the Form.cshtml file in the Views/Forms folder

```
...
@{ #pragma warning disable CS8602 }
<input class="form-control" asp-for="Category.Name" />
@{ #pragma warning restore CS8602 }
...
```

Restart ASP.NET Core, navigate to http://localhost:5000/controllers/form, and submit the form. Even though the browser sends a value for the `Price` property as part of the HTTP POST request, it is ignored by the model binder, as shown in figure 28.12.

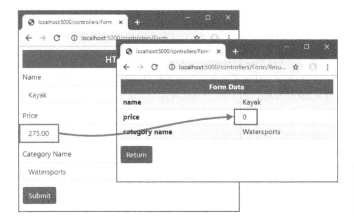

**Figure 28.12
Selectively
binding
properties**

SELECTIVELY BINDING IN THE MODEL CLASS

If you are using Razor Pages or you want to use the same set of properties for model binding throughout the application, you can apply the `BindNever` attribute directly to the model class, as shown in listing 28.21.

Listing 28.21 Decorating a property in the Product.cs file in the Models folder

```
using System.ComponentModel.DataAnnotations;
using System.ComponentModel.DataAnnotations.Schema;
using System.Text.Json.Serialization;
using Microsoft.AspNetCore.Mvc.ModelBinding;

namespace WebApp.Models {
    public class Product {

        public long ProductId { get; set; }

        public required string Name { get; set; }

        [Column(TypeName = "decimal(8, 2)")]
        [BindNever]
        public decimal Price { get; set; }

        public long CategoryId { get; set; }
        public Category? Category { get; set; }

        public long SupplierId { get; set; }

        [JsonIgnore(Condition = JsonIgnoreCondition.WhenWritingNull)]
        public Supplier? Supplier { get; set; }
    }
}
```

The `BindNever` attribute excludes a property from the model binder, which has the same effect as omitting it from the list used in the previous section. To see the effect, restart ASP.NET Core so the change to the `Product` class takes effect, request http://

localhost:5000/pages/form, and submit the form. Just as with the previous example, the model binder ignores the value for the `Price` property, as shown in figure 28.13.

> **TIP** There is also a `BindRequired` attribute that tells the model binding process that a request must include a value for a property. If the request doesn't have a required value, then a model validation error is produced, as described in chapter 29.

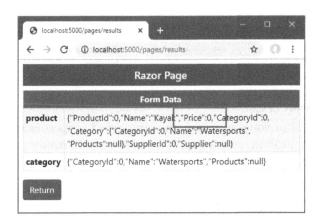

Figure 28.13 Excluding a property from model binding

28.5 Binding to arrays and collections

The model binding process has some nice features for binding request data to arrays and collections, which I demonstrate in the following sections.

28.5.1 Binding to arrays

One elegant feature of the default model binder is how it supports arrays. To see how this feature works, add a Razor Page named `Bindings.cshtml` to the `Pages` folder with the content shown in listing 28.22.

> **Listing 28.22   The contents of the Bindings.cshtml file in the Pages folder**

```
@page "/pages/bindings"
@model BindingsModel
@using Microsoft.AspNetCore.Mvc
@using Microsoft.AspNetCore.Mvc.RazorPages

<div class="container-fluid">
    <div class="row">
        <div class="col">
            <form asp-page="Bindings" method="post">
                <div class="form-group">
                    <label>Value #1</label>
                    <input class="form-control" name="Data"
                        value="Item 1" />
```

```
            </div>
            <div class="form-group">
                <label>Value #2</label>
                <input class="form-control" name="Data"
                    value="Item 2" />
            </div>
            <div class="form-group">
                <label>Value #3</label>
                <input class="form-control" name="Data"
                    value="Item 3" />
            </div>
            <button type="submit" class="btn btn-primary">
                Submit
            </button>
            <a class="btn btn-secondary" asp-page="Bindings">Reset</a>
        </form>
    </div>
    <div class="col">
        <ul class="list-group">
            @foreach (string s in Model.Data.Where(s => s != null)) {
                <li class="list-group-item">@s</li>
            }
        </ul>
    </div>
    </div>
</div>

@functions {

    public class BindingsModel : PageModel {

        [BindProperty(Name = "Data")]
        public string[] Data { get; set; } = Array.Empty<string>();
    }
}
```

Model binding for an array requires setting the `name` attribute to the same value for all the elements that will provide an array value. This page displays three `input` elements, all of which have a `name` attribute value of `Data`. To allow the model binder to find the array values, I have decorated the page model's `Data` property with the `BindProperty` attribute and used the `Name` argument.

> **TIP** Notice that the page model class in listing 28.22 defines no handler methods. This is unusual, but it works because there is no explicit processing required for any requests since requests only provide values for and display the `Data` array.

When the HTML form is submitted, a new array is created and populated with the values from all three `input` elements, which are displayed to the user. To see the binding process, restart ASP.NET Core, request http://localhost:5000/pages/bindings, edit the form fields, and click the Submit button. The contents of the `Data` array are displayed in a list using an `@foreach` expression, as shown in figure 28.14.

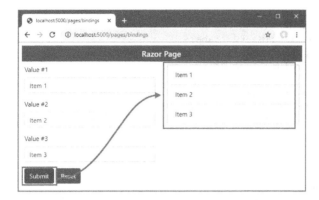

**Figure 28.14
Model binding for
array values**

Notice that I filter out `null` values when displaying the array contents.

```
...
@foreach (string s in Model.Data.Where(s => s != null)) {
    <li class="list-group-item">@s</li>
}
...
```

Empty form fields produce `null` values in the array, which I don't want to show in the results. In chapter 29, I show you how to ensure that values are provided for model binding properties.

SPECIFYING INDEX POSITIONS FOR ARRAY VALUES

By default, arrays are populated in the order in which the form values are received from the browser, which will generally be the order in which the HTML elements are defined. The `name` attribute can be used to specify the position of values in the array if you need to override the default, as shown in listing 28.23.

> **Listing 28.23   Specifying array position in the Bindings.cshtml file in the Pages folder**

```
@page "/pages/bindings"
@model BindingsModel
@using Microsoft.AspNetCore.Mvc
@using Microsoft.AspNetCore.Mvc.RazorPages

<div class="container-fluid">
    <div class="row">
        <div class="col">
            <form asp-page="Bindings" method="post">
                <div class="form-group">
                    <label>Value #1</label>
                    <input class="form-control" name="Data[1]"
                        value="Item 1" />
                </div>
                <div class="form-group">
                    <label>Value #2</label>
                    <input class="form-control" name="Data[0]"
                        value="Item 2" />
                </div>
                <div class="form-group">
```

```
                    <label>Value #3</label>
                    <input class="form-control" name="Data[2]"
                        value="Item 3" />
                </div>
                <button type="submit" class="btn btn-primary">
                    Submit
                </button>
                <a class="btn btn-secondary" asp-page="Bindings">Reset</a>
            </form>
        </div>
        <div class="col">
            <ul class="list-group">
                @foreach (string s in Model.Data.Where(s => s != null)) {
                    <li class="list-group-item">@s</li>
                }
            </ul>
        </div>
    </div>
</div>

@functions {

    public class BindingsModel : PageModel {

        [BindProperty(Name = "Data")]
        public string[] Data { get; set; } = Array.Empty<string>();
    }
}
```

The array index notation is used to specify the position of a value in the data-bound array. Restart ASP.NET Core, use a browser to request http://localhost:5000/pages/ bindings, and submit the form; you will see the items appear in the order dictated by the name attributes, as shown in figure 28.15. The index notation must be applied to all the HTML elements that provide array values, and there must not be any gaps in the numbering sequence.

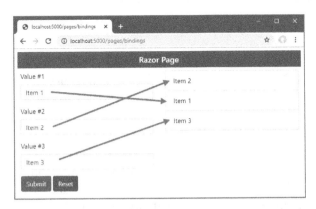

Figure 28.15
Specifying
array position

28.5.2 Binding to simple collections

The model binding process can create collections as well as arrays. For sequence collections, such as lists and sets, only the type of the property or parameter that is used by the model binder is changed, as shown in listing 28.24.

> **Listing 28.24   Binding to a list in the Bindings.cshtml file in the Pages folder**

```
...
@functions {

    public class BindingsModel : PageModel {

        [BindProperty(Name = "Data")]
        public SortedSet<string> Data { get; set; }
            = new SortedSet<string>();
    }
}
...
```

I changed the type of the Data property to SortedSet<string>. The model binding process will populate the set with the values from the input elements, which will be sorted alphabetically. I have left the index notation on the input element name attributes, but they have no effect since the collection class will sort its values alphabetically. To see the effect, restart ASP.NET Core, use a browser to request http://localhost:5000/pages/bindings, edit the text fields, and click the Submit button. The model binding process will populate the sorted set with the form values, which will be presented in order, as shown in figure 28.16.

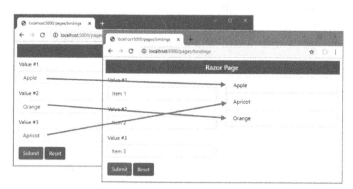

Figure 28.16
Model binding to a collection

28.5.3 Binding to dictionaries

For elements whose name attribute is expressed using the index notation, the model binder will use the index as the key when binding to a Dictionary, allowing a series of elements to be transformed into key-value pairs, as shown in listing 28.25.

Listing 28.25 Binding to a dictionary in the Bindings.cshtml file in the Pages folder

```
@page "/pages/bindings"
@model BindingsModel
@using Microsoft.AspNetCore.Mvc
@using Microsoft.AspNetCore.Mvc.RazorPages

<div class="container-fluid">
    <div class="row">
        <div class="col">
            <form asp-page="Bindings" method="post">
                <div class="form-group">
                    <label>Value #1</label>
                    <input class="form-control" name="Data[first]"
                        value="Item 1" />
                </div>
                <div class="form-group">
                    <label>Value #2</label>
                    <input class="form-control" name="Data[second]"
                        value="Item 2" />
                </div>
                <div class="form-group">
                    <label>Value #3</label>
                    <input class="form-control" name="Data[third]"
                        value="Item 3" />
                </div>
                <button type="submit" class="btn btn-primary">
                    Submit
                </button>
                <a class="btn btn-secondary" asp-page="Bindings">Reset</a>
            </form>
        </div>
        <div class="col">
            <table class="table table-sm table-striped">
                <tbody>
                    @foreach (string key in Model.Data.Keys) {
                        <tr>
                            <th>@key</th>
                            <td>@Model.Data[key]</td>
                        </tr>
                    }
                </tbody>
            </table>
        </div>
    </div>
</div>

@functions {

    public class BindingsModel : PageModel {

        [BindProperty(Name = "Data")]
        public Dictionary<string, string> Data { get; set; }
            = new Dictionary<string, string>();
    }
}
```

All elements that provide values for the collection must share a common prefix, which is Data in this example, followed by the key value in square brackets. The keys for this example are the strings first, second, and third, and they will be used as the keys for the content the user provides in the text fields. To see the binding process, restart ASP. NET Core, request http://localhost:5000/pages/bindings, edit the text fields, and submit the form. The keys and values from the form data will be displayed in a table, as shown in figure 28.17.

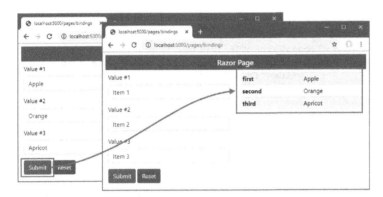

Figure 28.17   Model binding to a dictionary

28.5.4 Binding to collections of complex types

The examples in this section have all been collections of simple types, but the same process can be used for complex types, too. To demonstrate, listing 28.26 revises the Razor Page to gather details used to bind to an array of Product objects.

Listing 28.26   Binding to complex types in the Bindings.cshtml file in the Pages folder

```
@page "/pages/bindings"
@model BindingsModel
@using Microsoft.AspNetCore.Mvc
@using Microsoft.AspNetCore.Mvc.RazorPages

<div class="container-fluid">
    <div class="row">
        <div class="col">
            <form asp-page="Bindings" method="post">
                @for (int i = 0; i < 2; i++) {
                    <div class="form-group">
                        <label>Name #@i</label>
                        <input class="form-control" name="Data[@i].Name"
                            value="Product-@i" />
                    </div>
                    <div class="form-group">
                        <label>Price #@i</label>
                        <input class="form-control" name="Data[@i].Price"
                            value="@(100 + i)" />
                    </div>
```

```
            }
            <button type="submit" class="btn btn-primary">
                Submit
            </button>
            <a class="btn btn-secondary" asp-page="Bindings">Reset</a>
        </form>
    </div>
    <div class="col">
        <table class="table table-sm table-striped">
            <tbody>
                <tr><th>Name</th><th>Price</th></tr>
                @foreach (Product p in Model.Data) {
                    <tr>
                        <td>@p.Name</td>
                        <td>@p.Price</td>
                    </tr>
                }
            </tbody>
        </table>
    </div>
    </div>
</div>

@functions {

    public class BindingsModel : PageModel {

        [BindProperty(Name = "Data")]
        public Product[] Data { get; set; } = Array.Empty<Product>();
    }
}
```

The `name` attributes for the `input` elements use the array notation, followed by a period, followed by the name of the complex type properties they represent. To define elements for the `Name` and `Price` properties, this requires elements like this:

```
...
<input class="form-control" name="Data[0].Name" />
...
<input class="form-control" name="Data[0].Price" />
...
```

During the binding process, the model binder will attempt to locate values for all the `public` properties defined by the target type, repeating the process for each set of values in the form data.

This example relies on model binding for the `Price` property defined by the `Product` class, which was excluded from the binding process with the `BindNever` attribute. Remove the attribute from the property, as shown in listing 28.27.

Listing 28.27   Removing an attribute in the Product.cs file in the Models folder

```
using System.ComponentModel.DataAnnotations;
using System.ComponentModel.DataAnnotations.Schema;
using System.Text.Json.Serialization;
using Microsoft.AspNetCore.Mvc.ModelBinding;
```

```
namespace WebApp.Models {
    public class Product {

        public long ProductId { get; set; }

        public required string Name { get; set; }

        [Column(TypeName = "decimal(8, 2)")]
        //[BindNever]
        public decimal Price { get; set; }

        public long CategoryId { get; set; }
        public Category? Category { get; set; }

        public long SupplierId { get; set; }

        [JsonIgnore(Condition = JsonIgnoreCondition.WhenWritingNull)]
        public Supplier? Supplier { get; set; }
    }
}
```

Restart ASP.NET Core and use a browser to request http://localhost:5000/pages/
bindings. Enter names and prices into the text fields and submit the form, and you
will see the details of the Product objects created from the data displayed in a table, as
shown in figure 28.18.

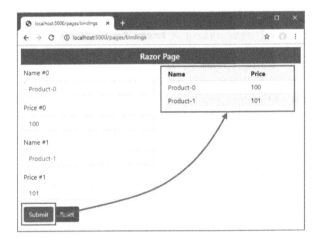

Figure 28.18
Binding to a
collection of
complex types

28.6   *Specifying a model binding source*

As I explained at the start of the chapter, the default model binding process looks for
data in four places: the form data values, the request body (for web service controllers
only), the routing data, and the request query string.

The default search sequence isn't always helpful, either because you always want data
to come from a specific part of the request or because you want to use a data source that
isn't searched by default. The model binding feature includes a set of attributes used to
override the default search behavior, as described in table 28.3.

TIP There is also the `FromService` attribute, which doesn't get a value from the request, but through the dependency injection feature described in chapter 14.

Table 28.3 The model binding source attributes

Name	Description
FromForm	This attribute is used to select form data as the source of binding data. The name of the parameter is used to locate a form value by default, but this can be changed using the `Name` property, which allows a different name to be specified.
FromRoute	This attribute is used to select the routing system as the source of binding data. The name of the parameter is used to locate a route data value by default, but this can be changed using the `Name` property, which allows a different name to be specified.
FromQuery	This attribute is used to select the query string as the source of binding data. The name of the parameter is used to locate a query string value by default, but this can be changed using the `Name` property, which allows a different query string key to be specified.
FromHeader	This attribute is used to select a request header as the source of binding data. The name of the parameter is used as the header name by default, but this can be changed using the `Name` property, which allows a different header name to be specified.
FromBody	This attribute is used to specify that the request body should be used as the source of binding data, which is required when you want to receive data from requests that are not form-encoded, such as in API controllers that provide web services.

The `FromForm`, `FromRoute`, and `FromQuery` attributes allow you to specify that the model binding data will be obtained from one of the standard locations but without the normal search sequence. Earlier in the chapter, I used this URL:

`http://localhost:5000/controllers/Form/Index/5?id=1`

This URL contains two possible values that can be used for the `id` parameter of the `Index` action method on the `Form` controller. The routing system will assign the final segment of the URL to a variable called `id`, which is defined in the default URL pattern for controllers, and the query string also contains an `id` value. The default search pattern means that the model binding data will be taken from the route data and the query string will be ignored.

In listing 28.28, I have applied the `FromQuery` attribute to the `id` parameter defined by the `Index` action method, which overrides the default search sequence.

Listing 28.28 Selecting the query string in the Controllers/FormController.cs file

```
using Microsoft.AspNetCore.Mvc;
using WebApp.Models;
using Microsoft.EntityFrameworkCore;
using Microsoft.AspNetCore.Mvc.Rendering;
using System.Text.Json;

namespace WebApp.Controllers {

    [AutoValidateAntiforgeryToken]
    public class FormController : Controller {
        private DataContext context;
```

```
        public FormController(DataContext dbContext) {
            context = dbContext;
        }

        public async Task<IActionResult> Index([FromQuery] long? id) {
            ViewBag.Categories = new SelectList(context.Categories,
                "CategoryId", "Name");
            return View("Form", await context.Products
                .Include(p => p.Category)
                .Include(p => p.Supplier)
                .FirstOrDefaultAsync(p => id == null || p.ProductId == id)
            ?? new() { Name = string.Empty });
        }

        [HttpPost]
        public IActionResult SubmitForm([Bind("Name", "Category")]
                Product product) {
            TempData["name"] = product.Name;
            TempData["price"] = product.Price.ToString();
            TempData["category name"] = product.Category?.Name;
            return RedirectToAction(nameof(Results));
        }

        public IActionResult Results() {
            return View();
        }
    }
}
```

The attribute specifies the source for the model binding process, which you can see by restarting ASP.NET Core and using a browser to request http://localhost:5000/controllers/form/index/5?id=1. Instead of using the value that has been matched by the routing system, the query string will be used instead, producing the response shown in figure 28.19. No other location will be used if the query string doesn't contain a suitable value for the model binding process.

> **TIP** You can still bind complex types when specifying a model binding source such as the query string. For each simple property in the parameter type, the model binding process will look for a query string key with the same name.

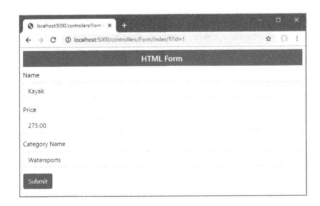

**Figure 28.19
Specifying a
model binding
data source**

28.6.1 Selecting a binding source for a property

The same attributes can be used to model bind properties defined by a page model or a controller, as shown in listing 28.29.

Listing 28.29 Selecting the query string in the Bindings.cshtml file in the Pages folder

```
...
@functions {

    public class BindingsModel : PageModel {

        //[BindProperty(Name = "Data")]
        [FromQuery(Name = "Data")]
        public Product[] Data { get; set; } = Array.Empty<Product>();
    }
}
...
```

The use of the `FromQuery` attribute means the query string is used as the source of values for the model binder as it creates the `Product` array, which you can see by starting ASP.NET Core and requesting http://localhost:5000/pages/bindings?data[0].name=Skis&data[0].price=500, which produces the response shown in figure 28.20.

NOTE In this example, I have used a GET request because it allows the query string to be easily set. Although it is harmless in such a simple example, care must be taken when sending GET requests that modify the state of the application. As noted previously, making changes in GET requests can lead to problems.

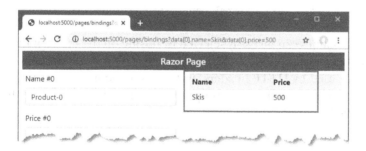

Figure 28.20 Specifying a model binding data source in a Razor Page

TIP Although it is rarely used, you can bind complex types using header values by applying the `FromHeader` attribute to the properties of a model class.

28.6.2 Using headers for model binding

The `FromHeader` attribute allows HTTP request headers to be used as the source for binding data. In listing 28.30, I have added a simple action method to the `Form` controller that defines a parameter that will be model bound from a standard HTTP request header.

```
using Microsoft.AspNetCore.Mvc;
using WebApp.Models;
using Microsoft.EntityFrameworkCore;
using Microsoft.AspNetCore.Mvc.Rendering;
using System.Text.Json;

namespace WebApp.Controllers {

    [AutoValidateAntiforgeryToken]
    public class FormController : Controller {
        private DataContext context;

        public FormController(DataContext dbContext) {
            context = dbContext;
        }

        // ...other actions omitted for brevity...

        public string Header([FromHeader] string accept) {
            return $"Header: {accept}";
        }
    }
}
```

The `Header` action method defines an `accept` parameter, the value for which will be taken from the `Accept` header in the current request and returned as the method result. Restart ASP.NET Core and request http://localhost:5000/controllers/form/header, and you will see a result like this:

```
Header: text/html,application/xhtml+xml,application/xml;q=0.9,image/webp,
    image/apng,*/*;q=0.8,application/signed-exchange;v=b3
```

Not all HTTP header names can be easily selected by relying on the name of the action method parameter because the model binding system doesn't convert from C# naming conventions to those used by HTTP headers. In these situations, you must configure the `FromHeader` attribute using the `Name` property to specify the name of the header, as shown in listing 28.31.

```
using Microsoft.AspNetCore.Mvc;
using WebApp.Models;
using Microsoft.EntityFrameworkCore;
using Microsoft.AspNetCore.Mvc.Rendering;
using System.Text.Json;

namespace WebApp.Controllers {

    [AutoValidateAntiforgeryToken]
    public class FormController : Controller {
        private DataContext context;
```

```
        public FormController(DataContext dbContext) {
            context = dbContext;
        }

        // ...other actions omitted for brevity...

        public string Header([FromHeader(Name = "Accept-Language")]
                string accept) {
            return $"Header: {accept}";
        }
    }
}
```

I can't use `Accept-Language` as the name of a C# parameter, and the model binder won't automatically convert a name like `AcceptLanguage` into `Accept-Language` so that it matches the header. Instead, I used the `Name` property to configure the attribute so that it matches the right header. If you restart ASP.NET Core and request http://localhost:5000/controllers/form/header, you will see a result like this, which will vary based on your locale settings:

```
Header: en-GB,en-US;q=0.9,en;q=0.8
```

28.6.3 *Using request bodies as binding sources*

Not all data sent by clients is sent as form data, such as when a JavaScript client sends JSON data to an API controller. The `FromBody` attribute specifies that the request body should be decoded and used as a source of model binding data. In listing 28.32, I have added a new action method to the `Form` controller with a parameter that is decorated with the `FromBody` attribute.

> **TIP** The `FromBody` attribute isn't required for controllers that are decorated with the `ApiController` attribute.

> **Listing 28.32   Adding an action method in the FormController.cs file in the Controllers folder**

```
using Microsoft.AspNetCore.Mvc;
using WebApp.Models;
using Microsoft.EntityFrameworkCore;
using Microsoft.AspNetCore.Mvc.Rendering;
using System.Text.Json;

namespace WebApp.Controllers {

    [AutoValidateAntiforgeryToken]
    public class FormController : Controller {
        private DataContext context;

        public FormController(DataContext dbContext) {
            context = dbContext;
        }
```

```
        // ...other actions omitted for brevity...

        [HttpPost]
        [IgnoreAntiforgeryToken]
        public Product Body([FromBody] Product model) {
            return model;
        }
    }
}
```

To test the model binding process, restart ASP.NET Core, open a new PowerShell command prompt, and run the command in listing 28.33 to send a request to the application.

> **NOTE** I added the `IgnoreAntiforgeryToken` to the action method in listing 28.32 because the request that I am going to send won't include an anti-forgery token, which I described in chapter 27.

Listing 28.33   Sending a request

```
Invoke-RestMethod http://localhost:5000/controllers/form/body -Method POST
➥-Body  (@{ Name="Soccer Boots"; Price=89.99} | ConvertTo-Json)
➥-ContentType "application/json"
```

The JSON-encoded request body is used to model bind the action method parameter, which produces the following response:

```
productId  : 0
name       : Soccer Boots
price      : 89.99
categoryId : 0
category   :
supplierId : 0
supplier   :
```

28.7   *Manual model binding*

Model binding is applied automatically when you define a parameter for an action or handler method or apply the `BindProperty` attribute. Automatic model binding works well if you can consistently follow the name conventions and you always want the process to be applied. If you need to take control of the binding process or you want to perform binding selectively, then you can perform model binding manually, as shown in listing 28.34.

Listing 28.34   Manually binding in the Bindings.cshtml file in the Pages folder

```
@page "/pages/bindings"
@model BindingsModel
@using Microsoft.AspNetCore.Mvc
@using Microsoft.AspNetCore.Mvc.RazorPages

<div class="container-fluid">
    <div class="row">
```

```
    <div class="col">
        <form asp-page="Bindings" method="post">
            <div class="form-group">
                <label>Name</label>
                <input class="form-control" asp-for="Data.Name" />
            </div>
            <div class="form-group">
                <label>Price</label>
                <input class="form-control" asp-for="Data.Price"
                    value="@(Model.Data.Price + 1)" />
            </div>
            <div class="form-check m-2">
                <input class="form-check-input" type="checkbox"
                    name="bind" value="true" checked />
                <label class="form-check-label">Model Bind?</label>
            </div>
            <button type="submit" class="btn btn-primary">
                Submit
            </button>
            <a class="btn btn-secondary" asp-page="Bindings">Reset</a>
        </form>
    </div>
    <div class="col">
        <table class="table table-sm table-striped">
            <tbody>
                <tr><th>Name</th><th>Price</th></tr>
                <tr>
                    <td>@Model.Data.Name</td>
                    <td>@Model.Data.Price</td>
                </tr>
            </tbody>
        </table>
    </div>
    </div>
</div>

@functions {

    public class BindingsModel : PageModel {

        public Product Data { get; set; }
            = new Product() { Name = "Skis", Price = 500 };

        public async Task OnPostAsync([FromForm] bool bind) {
            if (bind) {
                await TryUpdateModelAsync<Product>(Data,
                    "data", p => p.Name, p => p.Price);
            }
        }
    }
}
```

Manual model binding is performed using the `TryUpdateModelAsync` method, which is provided by the `PageModel` and `ControllerBase` classes, which means it is available for both Razor Pages and MVC controllers.

This example mixes automatic and manual model binding. The `OnPostAsync` method uses automatic model binding to receive a value for its `bind` parameter, which has been decorated with the `FromForm` attribute. If the value of the parameter is `true`, the `TryUpdateModelAsync` method is used to apply model binding. The arguments to the `TryUpdateModelAsync` method are the object that will be model bound, the prefix for the values, and a series of expressions that select the properties that will be included in the process, although there are other versions of the `TryUpdateModel-Async` method available.

The result is that the model binding process for the `Data` property is performed only when the user checks the checkbox added to the form in listing 28.34. If the checkbox is unchecked, then no model binding occurs, and the form data is ignored. To make it obvious when model binding is used, the value of the `Price` property is incremented when the form is rendered. To see the effect, restart ASP.NET Core, request http://localhost:5000/pages/bindings, and submit the form with the checkbox checked and then unchecked, as shown in figure 28.21.

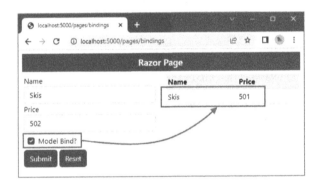

**Figure 28.21
Using manual
model binding**

Summary

- Model binding is the process by which request data is converted into parameters for action methods or page-handler methods.
- The model binder is integrated into ASP.NET Core and follows well-defined conventions to bind to simple and complex data types.
- ASP.NET Core provides attributes for fine-tuning the model binding process when the request data doesn't match the expected conventions.
- The model-binding process can read values from form data, the current route, the query string, the request header, and request body.
- Model binding is performed automatically but can be performed manually, which provides precise control over the binding process.

Using model validation

In the previous chapter, I showed you how the model binding process creates objects from HTTP requests. Throughout that chapter, I simply displayed the data that the application received. That's because the data that users provide should not be used until it has been inspected to ensure that the application is able to use it. The reality is that users will often enter data that isn't valid and cannot be used, which leads me to the topic of this chapter: model validation.

Model validation is the process of ensuring the data received by the application is suitable for binding to the model and, when this is not the case, providing useful information to the user that will help explain the problem.

The first part of the process, checking the data received, is one of the most important ways to preserve the integrity of an application's data. Rejecting data that cannot be used can prevent odd and unwanted states from arising in the application. The second part of the validation process is helping the user correct the problem and is equally important. Without the feedback needed to correct the problem, users become frustrated and confused. In public-facing applications, this means users will simply stop using the application. In corporate applications, this means the user's workflow will be hindered. Neither outcome is desirable, but fortunately, ASP.NET Core provides extensive support for model validation. Table 29.1 puts model validation in context.

Table 29.1   Putting model validation in context

Question	Answer
What is it?	Model validation is the process of ensuring that the data provided in a request is valid for use in the application.
Why is it useful?	Users do not always enter valid data, and using unvalidated data can produce unexpected and undesirable errors.
How is it used?	Controllers and Razor Pages check the outcome of the validation process, and tag helpers are used to include validation feedback in views displayed to the user. Validation can be performed automatically during the model binding process and can be supplemented with custom validation.
Are there any pitfalls or limitations?	It is important to test the efficacy of your validation code to ensure that it covers the full range of values that the application can receive.
Are there any alternatives?	Model validation is optional, but it is a good idea to use it whenever using model binding.

Table 29.2 provides a guide to the chapter.

Table 29.2   Chapter guide

Problem	Solution	Listing
Validating data	Manually use the `ModelState` features or apply validation attributes	5, 9, 14–22
Displaying validation messages	Use the classes to which form elements are assigned and the validation tag helpers	6–8, 10–13
Validating data before the form is submitted	Use client-side and remote validation	23–27

29.1 Preparing for this chapter

This chapter uses the WebApp project from chapter 28. To prepare for this chapter, change the contents of the `Form` controller's `Form` view so it contains `input` elements for each of the properties defined by the `Product` class, excluding the navigation properties used by Entity Framework Core, as shown in listing 29.1.

> **TIP** You can download the example project for this chapter—and for all the other chapters in this book—from https://github.com/manningbooks/pro-asp .net-core-7. See chapter 1 for how to get help if you have problems running the examples.

Listing 29.1 Changing elements in the Form.cshtml file in the Views/Form folder

```
@model Product
@{  Layout = "_SimpleLayout"; }

<h5 class="bg-primary text-white text-center p-2">HTML Form</h5>

<form asp-action="submitform" method="post" id="htmlform">
    <div class="form-group">
        <label asp-for="Name"></label>
        <input class="form-control" asp-for="Name" />
    </div>
    <div class="form-group">
        <label asp-for="Price"></label>
        <input class="form-control" asp-for="Price" />
    </div>
    <div class="form-group">
        <label>CategoryId</label>
        <input class="form-control" asp-for="CategoryId"  />
    </div>
    <div class="form-group">
        <label>SupplierId</label>
        <input class="form-control" asp-for="SupplierId"  />
    </div>
    <button type="submit" class="btn btn-primary mt-2">Submit</button>
</form>
```

Replace the contents of the `FormController.cs` file with those shown in listing 29.2, which adds support for displaying the properties defined in listing 29.1 and removes model binding attributes and action methods that are no longer required.

Listing 29.2 Replacing the FormController.cs file's contents in the Controllers folder

```
using Microsoft.AspNetCore.Mvc;
using WebApp.Models;
using Microsoft.EntityFrameworkCore;

namespace WebApp.Controllers {

    [AutoValidateAntiforgeryToken]
```

```
public class FormController : Controller {
    private DataContext context;

    public FormController(DataContext dbContext) {
        context = dbContext;
    }

    public async Task<IActionResult> Index(long? id) {
        return View("Form", await context.Products
            .OrderBy(p => p.ProductId)
            .FirstOrDefaultAsync(p => id == null
                || p.ProductId == id));
    }

    [HttpPost]
    public IActionResult SubmitForm(Product product) {
        TempData["name"] = product.Name;
        TempData["price"] = product.Price.ToString();
        TempData["categoryId"] = product.CategoryId.ToString();
        TempData["supplierId"] = product.SupplierId.ToString();
        return RedirectToAction(nameof(Results));
    }

    public IActionResult Results() {
        return View(TempData);
    }
}
```

29.1.1 *Dropping the database*

Open a new PowerShell command prompt, navigate to the folder that contains the
`WebApp.csproj` file, and run the command shown in listing 29.3 to drop the database.

Listing 29.3   Dropping the database

```
dotnet ef database drop --force
```

29.1.2 *Running the example application*

Use the PowerShell command prompt to run the command shown in listing 29.4.

Listing 29.4   Running the example application

```
dotnet run
```

Use a browser to request http://localhost:5000/controllers/form, which will display
an HTML form. Click the Submit button, and the form data will be displayed, as shown
in figure 29.1.

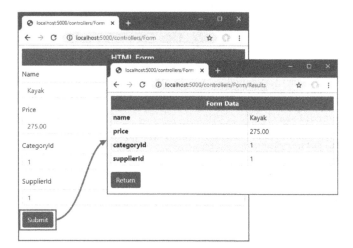

**Figure 29.1
Running the
example
application**

29.2 Understanding the need for model validation

Model validation is the process of enforcing the requirements that an application has for the data it receives from clients. Without validation, an application will try to operate on any data it receives, which can lead to exceptions and unexpected behaviors that appear immediately or long-term problems that appear gradually as the database is populated with bad, incomplete, or malicious data.

Currently, the action and handler methods that receive form data will accept any data that the user submits, which is why the examples just display the form data and don't store it in the database.

Most data values have constraints of some sort. This can involve requiring a value to be provided, requiring the value to be a specific type, and requiring the value to fall within a specific range.

Before I can safely store a `Product` object in the database, for example, I need to make sure that the user provides values for the `Name`, `Price`, `CategoryId`, and `SupplierId` properties. The `Name` value can be any valid string, the `Price` property must be a valid currency amount, and the `CategoryId` and `SupplierId` properties must correspond to existing `Supplier` and `Category` products in the database. In the following sections, I demonstrate how model validation can be used to enforce these requirements by checking the data that the application receives and providing feedback to the user when the application cannot use the data the user has submitted.

29.3 Validating data

Although it is not evident, ASP.NET Core is already performing some basic data validation during the model binding process, but the errors it detects are being discarded because ASP.NET Core hasn't been told how to respond to them. Listing 29.5 checks the outcome of the validation process so that the data values the user has provided will be used only if they are valid.

Listing 29.5   Checking the outcome in the FormController.cs file in the Controllers
                folder

```csharp
using Microsoft.AspNetCore.Mvc;
using WebApp.Models;
using Microsoft.EntityFrameworkCore;

namespace WebApp.Controllers {

    [AutoValidateAntiforgeryToken]
    public class FormController : Controller {
        private DataContext context;

        public FormController(DataContext dbContext) {
            context = dbContext;
        }

        public async Task<IActionResult> Index(long? id) {
            return View("Form", await context.Products
                .OrderBy(p => p.ProductId)
                .FirstOrDefaultAsync(p => id == null
                    || p.ProductId == id));
        }

        [HttpPost]
        public IActionResult SubmitForm(Product product) {
            if (ModelState.IsValid) {
                TempData["name"] = product.Name;
                TempData["price"] = product.Price.ToString();
                TempData["categoryId"] = product.CategoryId.ToString();
                TempData["supplierId"] = product.SupplierId.ToString();
                return RedirectToAction(nameof(Results));
            } else {
                return View("Form");
            }
        }

        public IActionResult Results() {
            return View(TempData);
        }
    }
}
```

I determine if the data provided by the user is valid using the ModelStateDictionary
object that is returned by the ModelState property inherited from the Controller-
Base class.

As its name suggests, the ModelStateDictionary class is a dictionary used to track
details of the state of the model object, with an emphasis on validation errors. Table
29.3 describes the most important ModelStateDictionary members.

Table 29.3 Selected ModelStateDictionary members

Name	Description
AddModelError(property, message)	This method is used to record a model validation error for the specified property.
GetValidationState(property)	This method is used to determine whether there are model validation errors for a specific property, expressed as a value from the ModelValidationState enumeration.
IsValid	This property returns true if all the model properties are valid and returns false otherwise.
Clear()	This property clears the validation state.

If the validation process has detected problems, then the IsValid property will return false. The SubmitForm action method deals with invalid data by returning the same view, like this:

```
...
if (ModelState.IsValid) {
    TempData["name"] = product.Name;
    TempData["price"] = product.Price.ToString();
    TempData["category name"] = product.Category?.Name;
    return RedirectToAction(nameof(Results));
} else {
    return View("Form");
}
...
```

It may seem odd to deal with a validation error by calling the View method, but the context data provided to the view contains details of the model validation errors; these details are used by the tag helper to transform the input elements.

To see how this works, restart ASP.NET Core and use a browser to request http://localhost:5000/controllers/form. Clear the contents of the Name field and click the Submit button. There won't be any visible change in the content displayed by the browser, but if you examine the input element for the Name field, you will see the element has been transformed. Here is the input element before the form was submitted:

```
<input class="form-control" type="text" data-val="true"
    data-val-required="The Name field is required." id="Name"
    name="Name" value="Kayak">
```

Here is the input element after the form has been submitted:

```
<input class="form-control input-validation-error" type="text"
    data-val="true" data-val-required="The Name field is required."
    id="Name" name="Name" value="">
```

The tag helper adds elements whose values have failed validation to the input -validation-error class, which can then be styled to highlight the problem to the user.

You can do this by defining custom CSS styles in a stylesheet, but a little extra work is required if you want to use the built-in validation styles that CSS libraries like Bootstrap provides. The name of the class added to the input elements cannot be changed, which means that some JavaScript code is required to map between the name used by ASP. NET Core and the CSS error classes provided by Bootstrap.

TIP Using JavaScript code like this can be awkward, and it can be tempting to use custom CSS styles, even when working with a CSS library like Bootstrap. However, the colors used for validation classes in Bootstrap can be overridden by using themes or by customizing the package and defining your own styles, which means you have to ensure that any changes to the theme are matched by corresponding changes to any custom styles you define. Ideally, Microsoft will make the validation class names configurable in a future release of ASP.NET Core, but until then, using JavaScript to apply Bootstrap styles is a more robust approach than creating custom stylesheets.

To define the JavaScript code so that it can be used by both controllers and Razor Pages, use the Razor View - Empty template in Visual Studio to add a file named _Validation.cshtml to the Views/Shared folder with the content shown in listing 29.6. Visual Studio Code doesn't require templates, and you can just add a file named _Validation.cshtml in the Views/Shared folder with the code shown in the listing.

Listing 29.6   The contents of the _Validation.cshtml file in the Views/Shared folder

```
<script type="text/javascript">
    window.addEventListener("DOMContentLoaded", () => {
        document.querySelectorAll("input.input-validation-error")
            .forEach((elem) => { elem.classList.add("is-invalid"); }
        );
    });
</script>
```

I will use the new file as a partial view, which contains a script element that uses the browser's JavaScript Document Object Model (DOM) API to locate input elements that are members of the input-validation-error class and adds them to the is-invalid class (which Bootstrap uses to set the error color for form elements). Listing 29.7 uses the partial tag helper to incorporate the new partial view into the HTML form so that fields with validation errors are highlighted.

Listing 29.7   Including a partial view in the Form.cshtml file in the Views/Form folder

```
@model Product
@{ Layout = "_SimpleLayout"; }

<h5 class="bg-primary text-white text-center p-2">HTML Form</h5>

<partial name="_Validation" />

<form asp-action="submitform" method="post" id="htmlform">
    <div class="form-group">
        <label asp-for="Name"></label>
        <input class="form-control" asp-for="Name" />
```

```
    </div>
    <div class="form-group">
        <label asp-for="Price"></label>
        <input class="form-control" asp-for="Price" />
    </div>
    <div class="form-group">
        <label>CategoryId</label>
        <input class="form-control" asp-for="CategoryId" />
    </div>
    <div class="form-group">
        <label>SupplierId</label>
        <input class="form-control" asp-for="SupplierId" />
    </div>
    <button type="submit" class="btn btn-primary mt-2">Submit</button>
</form>
```

The JavaScript code runs when the browser has finished parsing all the elements in the HTML document, and the effect is to highlight the `input` elements that have been assigned to the `input-validaton-error` class. You can see the effect by restarting ASP.NET Core, navigating to http://localhost:5000/controllers/form, clearing the contents of the Name field, and submitting the form, which produces the response shown in figure 29.2.

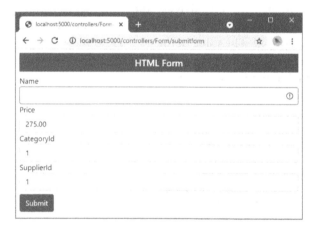

**Figure 29.2
Highlighting a
validation error**

29.3.1 *Displaying validation messages*

Figure 29.2 makes it clear that something is wrong with the `Name` field but doesn't provide any details about what problem has been detected. Providing the user with more information requires the use of a different tag helper, which adds a summary of the problems to the view, as shown in listing 29.8.

> **Listing 29.8   Displaying a summary in the Form.cshtml file in the Views/Form folder**

```
@model Product
@{  Layout = "_SimpleLayout"; }

<h5 class="bg-primary text-white text-center p-2">HTML Form</h5>
```

```
<partial name="_Validation" />

<form asp-action="submitform" method="post" id="htmlform">
    <div asp-validation-summary="All" class="text-danger"></div>
    <div class="form-group">
        <label asp-for="Name"></label>
        <input class="form-control" asp-for="Name" />
    </div>
    <div class="form-group">
        <label asp-for="Price"></label>
        <input class="form-control" asp-for="Price" />
    </div>
    <div class="form-group">
        <label>CategoryId</label>
        <input class="form-control" asp-for="CategoryId"  />
    </div>
    <div class="form-group">
        <label>SupplierId</label>
        <input class="form-control" asp-for="SupplierId"  />
    </div>
    <button type="submit" class="btn btn-primary mt-2">Submit</button>
</form>
```

The `ValidationSummaryTagHelper` class detects the `asp-validation-summary` attribute on `div` elements and responds by adding messages that describe any validation errors that have been recorded. The value of the `asp-validation-summary` attribute is a value from the `ValidationSummary` enumeration, which defines the values shown in table 29.4 and which I demonstrate shortly.

Table 29.4   The ValidationSummary values

Name	Description
`All`	This value is used to display all the validation errors that have been recorded.
`ModelOnly`	This value is used to display only the validation errors for the entire model, excluding those that have been recorded for individual properties, as described in the "Displaying Model-Level Messages" section.
`None`	This value is used to disable the tag helper so that it does not transform the HTML element.

Presenting error messages helps the user understand why the form cannot be processed. Restart ASP.NET Core, request http://localhost:5000/controllers/form, clear the Name field, and submit the form. As figure 29.3 shows, there is now an error message that explains the problem has been detected.

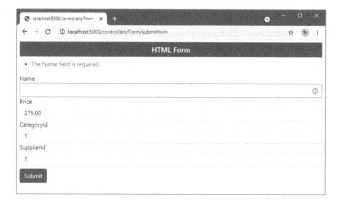

Figure 29.3 Displaying a validation message

29.3.2 Understanding the implicit validation checks

The error message displayed in figure 29.3 is generated by the implicit validation process, which is performed automatically during model binding.

Implicit validation is simple but effective, and there are two basic checks: the user must provide a value for all properties that are defined with a non-nullable type, and ASP.NET Core must be able to parse the `string` values received in the HTTP request into the corresponding property type.

As a reminder, here is the definition of the `Product` class, which is the class used to receive the form data:

```
using System.ComponentModel.DataAnnotations;
using System.ComponentModel.DataAnnotations.Schema;
using System.Text.Json.Serialization;
using Microsoft.AspNetCore.Mvc.ModelBinding;

namespace WebApp.Models {
    public class Product {

        public long ProductId { get; set; }

        public required string Name { get; set; }

        [Column(TypeName = "decimal(8, 2)")]
        //[BindNever]
        public decimal Price { get; set; }

        public long CategoryId { get; set; }
        public Category? Category { get; set; }

        public long SupplierId { get; set; }

        [JsonIgnore(Condition = JsonIgnoreCondition.WhenWritingNull)]
        public Supplier? Supplier { get; set; }
    }
}
```

The required keyword has been applied to the `Name` property, which is why a validation error was reported when the field was cleared in the previous section. There are no parsing issues for the `Name` property because the `string` value received from the HTTP request does not need any type conversion.

Enter `ten` into the `Price` field and submit the form; you will see an error that shows that ASP.NET Core cannot parse the string in the HTTP request into the `decimal` value required by the `Price` property, as shown in figure 29.4.

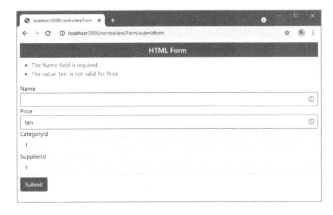

Figure 29.4 Displaying a parsing validation message

29.3.3 *Performing explicit validation*

Implicit validation takes care of the basics, but most applications require additional checks to ensure that they receive useful data. This is known as *explicit validation*, and it is done using the `ModelStateDictionary` methods described in table 29.4.

To avoid displaying conflicting error messages, explicit validation is typically done only when the user has provided a value that has passed the implicit checks. The `ModelStateDictionary.GetValidationState` method is used to see whether there have been any errors recorded for a model property. The `GetValidationState` method returns a value from the `ModelValidationState` enumeration, which defines the values described in table 29.5.

Table 29.5   The ModelValidationState values

Name	Description
Unvalidated	This value means that no validation has been performed on the model property, usually because there was no value in the request that corresponded to the property name.
Valid	This value means that the request value associated with the property is valid.
Invalid	This value means that the request value associated with the property is invalid and should not be used.
Skipped	This value means that the model property has not been processed, which usually means that there have been so many validation errors that there is no point continuing to perform validation checks.

Listing 29.9 defines explicit validation checks for some of the properties defined by the `Product` class.

Listing 29.9 Explicit validation in the FormController.cs file in the Controllers folder

```
using Microsoft.AspNetCore.Mvc;
using WebApp.Models;
using Microsoft.EntityFrameworkCore;
using Microsoft.AspNetCore.Mvc.ModelBinding;

namespace WebApp.Controllers {

    [AutoValidateAntiforgeryToken]
    public class FormController : Controller {
        private DataContext context;

        public FormController(DataContext dbContext) {
            context = dbContext;
        }

        public async Task<IActionResult> Index(long? id) {
            return View("Form", await context.Products
                .OrderBy(p => p.ProductId)
                .FirstOrDefaultAsync(p => id == null
                    || p.ProductId == id));
        }

        [HttpPost]
        public IActionResult SubmitForm(Product product) {

            if (ModelState.GetValidationState(nameof(Product.Price))
                    == ModelValidationState.Valid && product.Price <= 0) {
                ModelState.AddModelError(nameof(Product.Price),
                    "Enter a positive price");
            }

            if (ModelState.GetValidationState(nameof(Product.CategoryId))
                == ModelValidationState.Valid &&
                        !context.Categories.Any(c =>
                            c.CategoryId == product.CategoryId)) {
                ModelState.AddModelError(nameof(Product.CategoryId),
                    "Enter an existing category ID");
            }

            if (ModelState.GetValidationState(nameof(Product.SupplierId))
                    == ModelValidationState.Valid &&
                        !context.Suppliers.Any(s =>
                            s.SupplierId == product.SupplierId)) {
                ModelState.AddModelError(nameof(Product.SupplierId),
                    "Enter an existing supplier ID");
            }

            if (ModelState.IsValid) {
                TempData["name"] = product.Name;
```

```
                    TempData["price"] = product.Price.ToString();
                    TempData["categoryId"] = product.CategoryId.ToString();
                    TempData["supplierId"] = product.SupplierId.ToString();
                    return RedirectToAction(nameof(Results));
                } else {
                    return View("Form");
                }
            }

            public IActionResult Results() {
                return View(TempData);
            }
        }
    }
```

As an example of using the `ModelStateDictionary`, consider how the `Price` property is validated. One of the validation requirements for the `Product` class is to ensure the user provides a positive value for the `Price` property. This is something that ASP. NET Core cannot infer from the `Product` class and so explicit validation is required.

I start by ensuring that there are no existing validation errors for the `Price` property:

```
...
if (ModelState.GetValidationState(nameof(Product.Price))
        == ModelValidationState.Valid && product.Price <= 0) {
    ModelState.AddModelError(nameof(Product.Price),
        "Enter a positive price");
}
...
```

I want to make sure that the user provides a `Price` value that is greater than zero, but there is no point in recording an error about zero or negative values if the user has provided a value that the model binder cannot convert into a `decimal` value. I use the `GetValidationState` method to determine the validation status of the `Price` property before performing my own validation check:

```
...
if (ModelState.GetValidationState(nameof(Product.Price))
        == ModelValidationState.Valid && product.Price <= 0) {
    ModelState.AddModelError(nameof(Product.Price),
        "Enter a positive price");
}
...
```

If the user has provided a value that is less than or equal to zero, then I use the Add-ModelError method to record a validation error:

```
...
if (ModelState.GetValidationState(nameof(Product.Price))
        == ModelValidationState.Valid && product.Price <= 0) {
    ModelState.AddModelError(nameof(Product.Price),
        "Enter a positive price");
}
...
```

The arguments to the `AddModelError` method are the name of the property and a string that will be displayed to the user to describe the validation issue.

For the `CategoryId` and `SupplierId` properties, I follow a similar process and use Entity Framework Core to ensure that the value the user has provided corresponds to an ID stored in the database.

After performing the explicit validation checks, I use the `ModelState.IsValid` property to see whether there were errors, which means that implicit or explicit validation errors will be reported in the same way.

To see the effect of explicit validation, restart ASP.NET Core, request http://localhost:5000/controllers/form, and enter **0** into the `Price`, `CategoryId`, and `SupplierId` fields. Submit the form, and you will see the validation errors shown in figure 29.5.

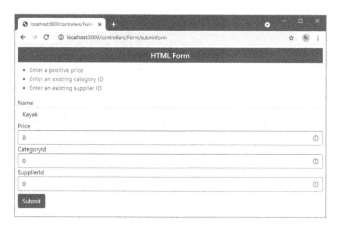

Figure 29.5 Explicit validation messages

29.3.4 *Configuring the default validation error messages*

The validation process has some inconsistencies when it comes to the validation messages that are displayed. Not all the validation messages produced by the model binder are helpful to the user, which you can see by clearing the Price field and submitting the form. The empty field produces the following message:

```
The value '' is invalid
```

This message is added to the `ModelStateDictionary` by the implicit validation process when it can't find a value for a property. A missing value for a `decimal` property, for example, causes a different—and less useful—message than a missing value for a `string` property. This is because of differences in the way that the validation checks are performed. The default messages for some validation errors can be replaced with custom messages using the methods defined by the `DefaultModelBindingMessage-Provider` class, the most useful of which are described in table 29.6.

Table 29.6   Useful DefaultModelBindingMessageProvider methods

Name	Description
`SetValueMustNotBeNullAccessor`	The function assigned to this property is used to generate a validation error message when a value is `null` for a model property that is non-nullable.
`SetMissingBindRequiredValueAccessor`	The function assigned to this property is used to generate a validation error message when the request does not contain a value for a required property.
`SetMissingKeyOrValueAccessor`	The function assigned to this property is used to generate a validation error message when the data required for dictionary model object contains null keys or values.
`SetAttemptedValueIsInvalidAccessor`	The function assigned to this property is used to generate a validation error message when the model binding system cannot convert the data value into the required C# type.
`SetUnknownValueIsInvalidAccessor`	The function assigned to this property is used to generate a validation error message when the model binding system cannot convert the data value into the required C# type.
`SetValueMustBeANumberAccessor`	The function assigned to this property is used to generate a validation error message when the data value cannot be parsed into a C# numeric type.
`SetValueIsInvalidAccessor`	The function assigned to this property is used to generate a fallback validation error message that is used as a last resort.

Each of the methods described in the table accepts a function that is invoked to get the validation message to display to the user. These methods are applied through the options pattern in the `Program.cs` file, as shown in listing 29.10, in which I have replaced the default message that is displayed when a value is null or cannot be converted.

Listing 29.10   Changing a validation message in the Program.cs file in the WebApp folder

```
using Microsoft.EntityFrameworkCore;
using WebApp.Models;
using Microsoft.AspNetCore.Antiforgery;
using Microsoft.AspNetCore.Mvc;

var builder = WebApplication.CreateBuilder(args);

builder.Services.AddDbContext<DataContext>(opts => {
    opts.UseSqlServer(builder.Configuration[
        "ConnectionStrings:ProductConnection"]);
    opts.EnableSensitiveDataLogging(true);
});
builder.Services.AddControllersWithViews();
builder.Services.AddRazorPages();
builder.Services.AddSingleton<CitiesData>();
```

```
builder.Services.Configure<AntiforgeryOptions>(opts => {
    opts.HeaderName = "X-XSRF-TOKEN";
});

builder.Services.Configure<MvcOptions>(opts =>
    opts.ModelBindingMessageProvider
    .SetValueMustNotBeNullAccessor(value => "Please enter a value"));

var app = builder.Build();

app.UseStaticFiles();

IAntiforgery antiforgery
    = app.Services.GetRequiredService<IAntiforgery>();
app.Use(async (context, next) => {
    if (!context.Request.Path.StartsWithSegments("/api")) {
        string? token =
            antiforgery.GetAndStoreTokens(context).RequestToken;
        if (token != null) {
            context.Response.Cookies.Append("XSRF-TOKEN",
                token,
                new CookieOptions { HttpOnly = false });
        }
    }
    await next();
});

app.MapControllerRoute("forms",
    "controllers/{controller=Home}/{action=Index}/{id?}");
app.MapRazorPages();

var context = app.Services.CreateScope().ServiceProvider
    .GetRequiredService<DataContext>();
SeedData.SeedDatabase(context);

app.Run();
```

The function that you specify receives the value that the user has supplied, although that is not especially useful when dealing with `null` values. To see the custom message, restart ASP.NET Core, use the browser to request http://localhost:5000/controllers/ form, and submit the form with an empty Price field. The response will include the custom error message, as shown in figure 29.6.

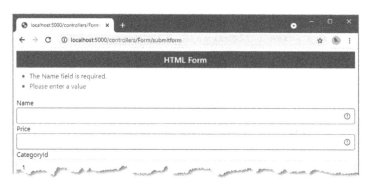

Figure 29.6 Changing the default validation messages

Figure 29.6 also shows the message displayed for a missing `Name` field, which isn't affected by the settings in table 29.6. This is a quirk of the way that non-nullable model properties are validated, which behaves as though the `Required` attribute has been applied to the non-nullable property. I describe the `Required` attribute later in this chapter and explain how it can be used to change the error message for non-nullable properties.

29.3.5 Displaying property-level validation messages

Although the custom error message is more meaningful than the default one, it still isn't that helpful because it doesn't clearly indicate which field the problem relates to. For this kind of error, it is more useful to display the validation error messages alongside the HTML elements that contain the problem data. This can be done using the `ValidationMessageTag` tag helper, which looks for `span` elements that have the `asp-validation-for` attribute, which is used to specify the property for which error messages should be displayed.

In listing 29.11, I have added property-level validation message elements for each of the `input` elements in the form.

> **Listing 29.11   Property-level messages in the Form.cshtml file in the Views/Form folder**

```
@model Product
@{
    Layout = "_SimpleLayout";
}

<h5 class="bg-primary text-white text-center p-2">HTML Form</h5>

<partial name="_Validation" />

<form asp-action="submitform" method="post" id="htmlform">
    <div asp-validation-summary="All" class="text-danger"></div>
    <div class="form-group">
        <label asp-for="Name"></label>
        <div>
            <span asp-validation-for="Name" class="text-danger">
            </span>
        </div>
        <input class="form-control" asp-for="Name" />
    </div>
    <div class="form-group">
        <label asp-for="Price"></label>
        <div>
            <span asp-validation-for="Price" class="text-danger">
            </span>
        </div>
        <input class="form-control" asp-for="Price" />
    </div>
    <div class="form-group">
        <label>CategoryId</label>
```

```
    <div>
        <span asp-validation-for="CategoryId" class="text-danger">
        </span>
    </div>
    <input class="form-control" asp-for="CategoryId" />
</div>
<div class="form-group">
    <label>SupplierId</label>
    <div>
        <span asp-validation-for="SupplierId" class="text-danger">
        </span>
    </div>
    <input class="form-control" asp-for="SupplierId" />
</div>
<button type="submit" class="btn btn-primary mt-2">Submit</button>
</form>
```

Since span elements are displayed inline, care must be taken to present the validation messages to make it obvious which element the message relates to. You can see the effect of the new validation messages by restarting ASP.NET Core, requesting http:// localhost:5000/controllers/form, clearing the Name and Price fields, and submitting the form. The response, shown in figure 29.7, includes validation messages alongside the text fields.

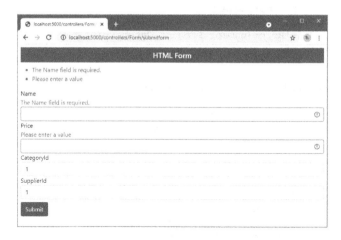

Figure 29.7
Displaying
property-level
validation
messages

29.3.6 *Displaying model-level messages*

It may seem that the validation summary message is superfluous because it duplicates the property-level messages. But the summary has a useful trick, which is the ability to display messages that apply to the entire model and not just individual properties. This means you can report errors that arise from a combination of individual properties, which would otherwise be hard to express with a property-level message.

In listing 29.12, I have added a check to the FormController.SubmitForm action that records a validation error when the Price value exceeds 100 at the time that the Name value starts with Small.

Listing 29.12   Model-level validation in the FormController.cs file in the Controllers folder

```
...
[HttpPost]
public IActionResult SubmitForm(Product product) {

    if (ModelState.GetValidationState(nameof(Product.Price))
            == ModelValidationState.Valid && product.Price <= 0) {
        ModelState.AddModelError(nameof(Product.Price),
            "Enter a positive price");
    }

    if (ModelState.GetValidationState(nameof(Product.Name))
            == ModelValidationState.Valid
        && ModelState.GetValidationState(nameof(Product.Price))
            == ModelValidationState.Valid
        && product.Name.ToLower().StartsWith("small")
        && product.Price > 100) {
            ModelState.AddModelError("",
                "Small products cannot cost more than $100");
    }

    if (ModelState.GetValidationState(nameof(Product.CategoryId))
            == ModelValidationState.Valid &&
                !context.Categories.Any(c =>
                    c.CategoryId == product.CategoryId)) {
        ModelState.AddModelError(nameof(Product.CategoryId),
            "Enter an existing category ID");
    }

    if (ModelState.GetValidationState(nameof(Product.SupplierId))
            == ModelValidationState.Valid &&
                !context.Suppliers.Any(s =>
                    s.SupplierId == product.SupplierId)) {
        ModelState.AddModelError(nameof(Product.SupplierId),
            "Enter an existing supplier ID");
    }

    if (ModelState.IsValid) {
        TempData["name"] = product.Name;
        TempData["price"] = product.Price.ToString();
        TempData["categoryId"] = product.CategoryId.ToString();
        TempData["supplierId"] = product.SupplierId.ToString();
        return RedirectToAction(nameof(Results));
    } else {
        return View("Form");
    }
}
...
```

If the user enters a Name value that starts with Small and a Price value that is greater than 100, then a model-level validation error is recorded. I check for the combination of values only if there are no validation problems with the individual property values, which ensures the user doesn't see conflicting messages. Validation errors that relate to the entire model are recorded using the AddModelError with the empty string as the first argument.

Listing 29.13 changes the value of the `asp-validation-summary` attribute to `ModelOnly`, which excludes property-level errors, meaning that the summary will display only those errors that apply to the entire model.

```
@model Product
@{
    Layout = "_SimpleLayout";
}

<h5 class="bg-primary text-white text-center p-2">HTML Form</h5>

<partial name="_Validation" />

<form asp-action="submitform" method="post" id="htmlform">
    <div asp-validation-summary="ModelOnly" class="text-danger"></div>
    <div class="form-group">
        <label asp-for="Name"></label>
        <div>
            <span asp-validation-for="Name" class="text-danger">
            </span>
        </div>
        <input class="form-control" asp-for="Name" />
    </div>
    <div class="form-group">
        <label asp-for="Price"></label>
        <div>
            <span asp-validation-for="Price" class="text-danger">
            </span>
        </div>
        <input class="form-control" asp-for="Price" />
    </div>
    <div class="form-group">
        <label>CategoryId</label>
        <div>
            <span asp-validation-for="CategoryId" class="text-danger">
            </span>
        </div>
        <input class="form-control" asp-for="CategoryId" />
    </div>
    <div class="form-group">
        <label>SupplierId</label>
        <div>
            <span asp-validation-for="SupplierId" class="text-danger">
            </span>
        </div>
        <input class="form-control" asp-for="SupplierId" />
    </div>
    <button type="submit" class="btn btn-primary mt-2">Submit</button>
</form>
```

Restart ASP.NET Core and request http://localhost:5000/controllers/form. Enter Small Kayak into the Name field and 150 into the Price field and submit the form. The response will include the model-level error message, as shown in figure 29.8.

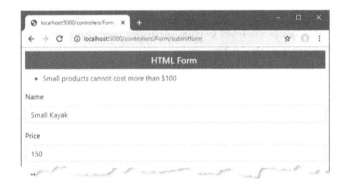

**Figure 29.8
Displaying a
model-level
validation
message**

29.4   *Explicitly validating data in a Razor Page*

Razor Page validation relies on the same features used in the controller in the previous section. Listing 29.14 adds explicit validation checks and error summaries to the `FormHandler` page.

Listing 29.14   Validating data in the FormHandler.cshtml file in the Pages folder

```
@page "/pages/form/{id:long?}"
@model FormHandlerModel
@using Microsoft.AspNetCore.Mvc.RazorPages
@using Microsoft.EntityFrameworkCore
@using Microsoft.AspNetCore.Mvc.ModelBinding

<partial name="_Validation" />

<div class="m-2">
    <h5 class="bg-primary text-white text-center p-2">HTML Form</h5>
    <form asp-page="FormHandler" method="post" id="htmlform">
        <div asp-validation-summary="ModelOnly" class="text-danger"></div>
        <div class="form-group">
            <label>Name</label>
            <div>
                <span asp-validation-for="Product.Name"
                    class="text-danger"></span>
            </div>
            <input class="form-control" asp-for="Product.Name" />
        </div>
        <div class="form-group">
            <label>Price</label>
            <div>
                <span asp-validation-for="Product.Price"
                    class="text-danger"></span>
            </div>
            <input class="form-control" asp-for="Product.Price" />
        </div>
        <div class="form-group">
            <label>CategoryId</label>
            <div>
                <span asp-validation-for="Product.CategoryId"
                    class="text-danger">
```

```
                </span>
            </div>
            <input class="form-control" asp-for="Product.CategoryId" />
        </div>
        <div class="form-group">
            <label>SupplierId</label>
            <div>
                <span asp-validation-for="Product.SupplierId"
                    class="text-danger">
                </span>
            </div>
            <input class="form-control" asp-for="Product.SupplierId" />
        </div>
        <button type="submit" class="btn btn-primary mt-2">Submit</button>
    </form>
</div>

@functions {

    public class FormHandlerModel : PageModel {
        private DataContext context;

        public FormHandlerModel(DataContext dbContext) {
            context = dbContext;
        }

        [BindProperty]
        public Product Product { get; set; }
            = new() { Name = string.Empty };

        //[BindProperty(Name = "Product.Category")]
        //public Category Category { get; set; } = new();

        public async Task OnGetAsync(long id = 1) {
            Product = await context.Products
                .OrderBy(p => p.ProductId)
                .FirstAsync(p => p.ProductId == id);
        }

        public IActionResult OnPost() {
            if (ModelState.GetValidationState("Product.Price")
                    == ModelValidationState.Valid && Product.Price < 1) {
                ModelState.AddModelError("Product.Price",
                    "Enter a positive price");
            }

            if (ModelState.GetValidationState("Product.Name")
                    == ModelValidationState.Valid
                && ModelState.GetValidationState("Product.Price")
                    == ModelValidationState.Valid
                && Product.Name.ToLower().StartsWith("small")
                && Product.Price > 100) {
                ModelState.AddModelError("",
                    "Small products cannot cost more than $100");
            }
```

```
    if (ModelState.GetValidationState("Product.CategoryId")
            == ModelValidationState.Valid &&
        !context.Categories
            .Any(c => c.CategoryId == Product.CategoryId)) {
                ModelState.AddModelError("Product.CategoryId",
                    "Enter an existing category ID");
    }

    if (ModelState.GetValidationState("Product.SupplierId")
            == ModelValidationState.Valid &&
        !context.Suppliers
            .Any(s => s.SupplierId == Product.SupplierId)) {
                ModelState.AddModelError("Product.SupplierId",
                    "Enter an existing supplier ID");
    }

    if (ModelState.IsValid) {
        TempData["name"] = Product.Name;
        TempData["price"] = Product.Price.ToString();
        TempData["categoryId"] = Product.CategoryId.ToString();
        TempData["supplierId"] = Product.SupplierId.ToString();
        return RedirectToPage("FormResults");
    } else {
        return Page();
    }
        }
    }
}
```

The `PageModel` class defines a `ModelState` property that is the equivalent of the one I used in the controller and allows validation errors to be recorded. The process for validation is the same, but you must take care when recording errors to ensure the names match the pattern used by Razor Pages. When I recorded an error in the controller, I used the `nameof` keyword to select the property to which the error relates, like this:

```
...
ModelState.AddModelError(nameof(Product.Price),"Enter a positive price");
...
```

This is a common convention because it ensures that a typo won't cause errors to be recorded incorrectly. This expression won't work in the Razor Page, where the error must be recorded against `Product.Price`, rather than `Price`, to reflect that `@Model` expressions in Razor Pages return the page model object, like this:

```
...
ModelState.AddModelError("Product.Price", "Enter a positive price");
...
```

To test the validation process, restart ASP.NET Core, use a browser to request http://localhost:5000/pages/form, and submit the form with empty fields or with values that cannot be converted into the C# types required by the `Product` class. The error messages are displayed just as they are for controllers, as shown in figure 29.9. (The values 1, 2, and 3 are valid for both the `CategoryId` and `SupplierId` fields.)

> **TIP** The methods described in table 29.6 that change the default validation messages affect Razor Pages as well as controllers.

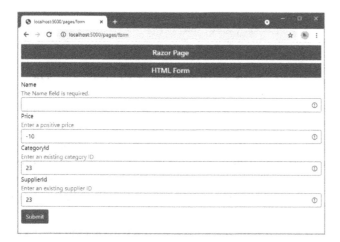

Figure 29.9
Validating data in
a Razor Page

29.5 Specifying validation rules using metadata

One problem with putting validation logic into an action method is that it ends up being duplicated in every action or handler method that receives data from the user. To help reduce duplication, the validation process supports the use of attributes to express model validation rules directly in the model class, ensuring that the same set of validation rules will be applied regardless of which action method is used to process a request. In listing 29.15, I have applied attributes to the `Product` class to describe the validation required for the `Name` and `Price` properties.

> **Listing 29.15 Applying validation attributes in the Product.cs file in the Models folder**

```
using System.ComponentModel.DataAnnotations;
using System.ComponentModel.DataAnnotations.Schema;
using System.Text.Json.Serialization;
using Microsoft.AspNetCore.Mvc.ModelBinding;

namespace WebApp.Models {
    public class Product {

        public long ProductId { get; set; }

        [Required(ErrorMessage = "Please enter a name")]
        public required string Name { get; set; }

        [Range(1, 999999, ErrorMessage = "Please enter a positive price")]
        [Column(TypeName = "decimal(8, 2)")]
        public decimal Price { get; set; }

        public long CategoryId { get; set; }
        public Category? Category { get; set; }

        public long SupplierId { get; set; }
```

```
    [JsonIgnore(Condition = JsonIgnoreCondition.WhenWritingNull)]
    public Supplier? Supplier { get; set; }
  }
}
```

I used two validation attributes in the listing: `Required` and `Range`. The `Required` attribute specifies that it is a validation error if the user doesn't submit a value for a property, which is useful when you have a nullable property but want to require a value from the user.

I used the `Required` attribute in listing 29.15 to change the error message that is displayed when the user doesn't provide a value for the `Name` property. As noted earlier, the implicit validation checks are inconsistent in the way that non-nullable properties are processed, but this can be corrected using the `ErrorMessage` argument that all of the validation attributes define.

I also applied the `Range` attribute in listing 29.15, which allows me to specify the set of acceptable values for the `Price` property. Table 29.7 shows the set of built-in validation attributes available.

Table 29.7   The Built-in Validation attributes

Attribute	Example	Description
Compare	[Compare ("OtherProperty")]	This attribute ensures that properties must have the same value, which is useful when you ask the user to provide the same information twice, such as an e-mail address or a password.
Range	[Range(10, 20)]	This attribute ensures that a numeric value (or any property type that implements `IComparable`) is not outside the range of specified minimum and maximum values. To specify a boundary on only one side, use a `MinValue` or `MaxValue` constant.
Regular-Expression	[RegularExpression ("pattern")]	This attribute ensures that a string value matches the specified regular expression pattern. Note that the pattern must match the *entire* user-supplied value, not just a substring within it. By default, it matches case sensitively, but you can make it case insensitive by applying the `(?i)` modifier—that is, `[RegularExpression("(?i)mypattern")]`.
Required	[Required]	This attribute ensures that the value is not empty or a string consisting only of spaces. If you want to treat whitespace as valid, use `[Required(Allow-EmptyStrings = true)]`.
String-Length	[StringLength(10)]	This attribute ensures that a string value is no longer than a specified maximum length. You can also specify a minimum length: `[StringLength(10, MinimumLength=2)]`.

The use of the validation attribute allows me to remove some of the explicit validation from the action method, as shown in listing 29.16.

```
...
[HttpPost]
public IActionResult SubmitForm(Product product) {

    //if (ModelState.GetValidationState(nameof(Product.Price))
    //        == ModelValidationState.Valid && product.Price <= 0) {
    //    ModelState.AddModelError(nameof(Product.Price),
    //        "Enter a positive price");
    //}

    if (ModelState.GetValidationState(nameof(Product.Name))
            == ModelValidationState.Valid
        && ModelState.GetValidationState(nameof(Product.Price))
            == ModelValidationState.Valid
        && product.Name.ToLower().StartsWith("small")
        && product.Price > 100) {
            ModelState.AddModelError("",
                "Small products cannot cost more than $100");
    }

    if (ModelState.GetValidationState(nameof(Product.CategoryId))
        == ModelValidationState.Valid &&
                !context.Categories.Any(c =>
                    c.CategoryId == product.CategoryId)) {
        ModelState.AddModelError(nameof(Product.CategoryId),
            "Enter an existing category ID");
    }

    if (ModelState.GetValidationState(nameof(Product.SupplierId))
            == ModelValidationState.Valid &&
                !context.Suppliers.Any(s =>
                    s.SupplierId == product.SupplierId)) {
        ModelState.AddModelError(nameof(Product.SupplierId),
            "Enter an existing supplier ID");
    }

    if (ModelState.IsValid) {
        TempData["name"] = product.Name;
        TempData["price"] = product.Price.ToString();
        TempData["categoryId"] = product.CategoryId.ToString();
        TempData["supplierId"] = product.SupplierId.ToString();
        return RedirectToAction(nameof(Results));
    } else {
        return View("Form");
    }
}
...
```

To see the validation attributes in action, restart ASP.NET Core MVC, request http://
localhost:5000/controllers/form, clear the Name and Price fields, and submit the
form. The response will include the validation errors produced by the attributes for
the Price field and the new message for the Name field, as shown in figure 29.10. The

validation attributes are applied before the action method is called, which means that I can still rely on the model state to determine whether individual properties are valid when performing model-level validation.

Validation work arounds

Getting the validation results you require can take some care when using the validation attributes. For example, you cannot use the `Required` attribute if you want to ensure that a user has checked a checkbox because the browser will send a `false` value when the checkbox is unchecked, which will always pass the checks applied by the `Required` attribute. Instead, use the `Range` attribute and specify the minimum and maximum values as `true`, like this:

```
...
[Range(typeof(bool), "true", "true",
    ErrorMessage="You must check the box")]
...
```

If this sort of workaround feels uncomfortable, then you can create custom validation attributes, as described in the next section.

To see the validation attributes in action, restart ASP.NET Core MVC, request http://localhost:5000/controllers/form, clear the Name and Price fields, and submit the form. The response will include the validation errors produced by the attributes, as shown in figure 29.10.

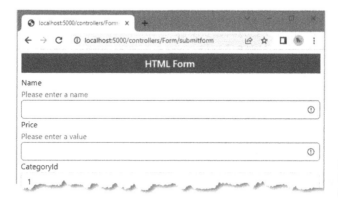

**Figure 29.10
Using validation attributes**

Understanding web service controller validation

Controllers that have been decorated with the `ApiController` attribute do not need to check the `ModelState.IsValid` property. Instead, the action method is invoked only if there are no validation errors, which means you can always rely on receiving validated objects through the model binding feature. If any validation errors are detected, then the request is terminated, and an error response is sent to the browser.

29.5.1 *Creating a custom property validation attribute*

The validation process can be extended by creating an attribute that extends the
`ValidationAttribute` class. To demonstrate, I created the `WebApp/Validation`
folder and added to it a class file named `PrimaryKeyAttribute.cs`, which I used to
define the class shown in listing 29.17.

> **Listing 29.17   The contents of the PrimaryKeyAttribute.cs file in the Validation folder**

```
using Microsoft.EntityFrameworkCore;
using System.ComponentModel.DataAnnotations;

namespace WebApp.Validation {
    public class PrimaryKeyAttribute : ValidationAttribute {

        public Type? ContextType { get; set; }

        public Type? DataType { get; set; }

        protected override ValidationResult? IsValid(object? value,
                ValidationContext validationContext) {
            if (ContextType != null && DataType != null) {
                DbContext? context =
                    validationContext.GetRequiredService(ContextType)
                        as DbContext;
                if (context != null
                        && context.Find(DataType, value) == null) {
                    return new ValidationResult(ErrorMessage ??
                        "Enter an existing key value");
                }
            }
            return ValidationResult.Success;
        }
    }
}
```

Custom attributes override the `IsValid` method, which is called with the value to
check, and a `ValidationContext` object that provides context about the validation
process and provides access to the application's services through its `GetService`
method.

In listing 29.17, the custom attribute receives the type of an Entity Framework Core
database context class and the type of a model class. In the `IsValid` method, the attribute obtains an instance of the context class and uses it to query the database to determine whether the value has been used as a primary key value.

> **Revalidating data**
>
> You may need to perform the validation process again if you modify the object received
> from the model binder. For these situations, use the `ModelState.Clear` method to
> clear any existing validation errors and call the `TryValidateModel` method.

29.5.2 *Creating a custom model validation attribute*

Custom validation attributes can also be used to perform model-level validation. To demonstrate, I added a class file named `PhraseAndPriceAttribute.cs` to the `Validation` folder and used it to define the class shown in listing 29.18.

> **Listing 29.18   The contents of the PhraseAndPriceAttribute.cs file in the Validation folder**

```
using System.ComponentModel.DataAnnotations;
using WebApp.Models;

namespace WebApp.Validation {
    public class PhraseAndPriceAttribute : ValidationAttribute {

        public string? Phrase { get; set; }

        public string? Price { get; set; }

        protected override ValidationResult? IsValid(object? value,
                ValidationContext validationContext) {

            if (value != null && Phrase != null && Price != null) {
                Product? product = value as Product;
                if (product != null
                    && product.Name.StartsWith(Phrase,
                        StringComparison.OrdinalIgnoreCase)
                    && product.Price > decimal.Parse(Price)) {
                        return new ValidationResult(ErrorMessage ??
                            $"{Phrase} products cannot cost more than $"
                            + Price);
                }
            }
            return ValidationResult.Success;
        }
    }
}
```

This attribute is configured with `Phrase` and `Price` properties, which are used in the `IsValid` method to check the `Name` and `Price` properties of the model object. Property-level custom validation attributes are applied directly to the properties they validate, and model-level attributes are applied to the entire class, as shown in listing 29.19.

> **Listing 29.19   Applying validation attributes in the Product.cs file in the Models folder**

```
using System.ComponentModel.DataAnnotations;
using System.ComponentModel.DataAnnotations.Schema;
using System.Text.Json.Serialization;
using Microsoft.AspNetCore.Mvc.ModelBinding;
using WebApp.Validation;

namespace WebApp.Models {

    [PhraseAndPrice(Phrase = "Small", Price = "100")]
    public class Product {
```

```
        public long ProductId { get; set; }

        [Required(ErrorMessage = "Please enter a name")]
        public required string Name { get; set; }

        [Range(1, 999999, ErrorMessage = "Please enter a positive price")]
        [Column(TypeName = "decimal(8, 2)")]
        public decimal Price { get; set; }

        [PrimaryKey(ContextType = typeof(DataContext),
            DataType = typeof(Category))]
        public long CategoryId { get; set; }
        public Category? Category { get; set; }

        [PrimaryKey(ContextType = typeof(DataContext),
            DataType = typeof(Supplier))]
        public long SupplierId { get; set; }

        [JsonIgnore(Condition = JsonIgnoreCondition.WhenWritingNull)]
        public Supplier? Supplier { get; set; }
    }
}
```

The custom attributes allow the remaining explicit validation statements to be removed
from the Form controller's action method, as shown in listing 29.20.

Listing 29.20 Removing explicit validation in the Controllers/FormController.cs file

```
using Microsoft.AspNetCore.Mvc;
using WebApp.Models;
using Microsoft.EntityFrameworkCore;
using Microsoft.AspNetCore.Mvc.ModelBinding;

namespace WebApp.Controllers {

    [AutoValidateAntiforgeryToken]
    public class FormController : Controller {
        private DataContext context;

        public FormController(DataContext dbContext) {
            context = dbContext;
        }

        public async Task<IActionResult> Index(long? id) {
            return View("Form", await context.Products
                .OrderBy(p => p.ProductId)
                .FirstOrDefaultAsync(p => id == null
                    || p.ProductId == id));
        }

        [HttpPost]
        public IActionResult SubmitForm(Product product) {
            if (ModelState.IsValid) {
                TempData["name"] = product.Name;
                TempData["price"] = product.Price.ToString();
                TempData["categoryId"] = product.CategoryId.ToString();
```

```
            TempData["supplierId"] = product.SupplierId.ToString();
            return RedirectToAction(nameof(Results));
        } else {
            return View("Form");
        }
    }

    public IActionResult Results() {
        return View(TempData);
    }
}
}
```

The validation attributes are applied automatically before the action method is invoked, which means that the validation outcome can be determined simply by reading the `ModelState.IsValid` property.

USING A CUSTOM MODEL VALIDATION ATTRIBUTE IN A RAZOR PAGE

An adaptation is required to support custom model validation attributes in Razor Pages. When the validation attribute is applied in a Razor Page, the errors it generates are associated with the `Product` property, rather than with the entire model, which means that the errors are not displayed by the validation summary tag helper.

To resolve this issue, add a class file named `ModelStateExtensions.cs` to the `WebApp/Validation` folder and use it to define the extension method shown in listing 29.21.

> **Listing 29.21   The contents of the ModelStateExtensions.cs file in the Validation folder**

```
using Microsoft.AspNetCore.Mvc.ModelBinding;

namespace WebApp.Validation {

    public static class ModelStateExtensions {

        public static void PromotePropertyErrors(
                this ModelStateDictionary modelState,
                string propertyName) {
            foreach (var err in modelState) {
                if (err.Key == propertyName && err.Value.ValidationState
                        == ModelValidationState.Invalid) {
                    foreach (var e in err.Value.Errors) {
                        modelState.AddModelError(string.Empty,
                            e.ErrorMessage);
                    }
                }
            }
        }
    }
}
```

The `PromotePropertyErrors` extension method locates validation errors associated with a specified property and adds corresponding model-level errors. Listing 29.22 removes the explicit validation from the Razor Page and applies the new extension method.

Listing 29.22   Removing explicit validation in the Pages/FormHandler.cshtml file

```
@page "/pages/form/{id:long?}"
@model FormHandlerModel
@using Microsoft.AspNetCore.Mvc.RazorPages
@using Microsoft.EntityFrameworkCore
@using Microsoft.AspNetCore.Mvc.ModelBinding
@using WebApp.Validation

<partial name="_Validation" />

<div class="m-2">

    <!-- ...markup omitted for brevity... -->

</div>

@functions {

    public class FormHandlerModel : PageModel {
        private DataContext context;

        public FormHandlerModel(DataContext dbContext) {
            context = dbContext;
        }

        [BindProperty]
        public Product Product { get; set; }
            = new() { Name = string.Empty };

        public async Task OnGetAsync(long id = 1) {
            Product = await context.Products
                .OrderBy(p => p.ProductId)
                .FirstAsync(p => p.ProductId == id);
        }

        public IActionResult OnPost() {
            if (ModelState.IsValid) {
                TempData["name"] = Product.Name;
                TempData["price"] = Product.Price.ToString();
                TempData["categoryId"] = Product.CategoryId.ToString();
                TempData["supplierId"] = Product.SupplierId.ToString();
                return RedirectToPage("FormResults");
            } else {
                ModelState.PromotePropertyErrors(nameof(Product));
                return Page();
            }
        }
    }
}
```

Expressing the validation through the custom attributes removes the code duplication between the controller and the Razor Page and ensures that validation is applied consistently wherever model binding is used for Product objects. To test the validation attributes, restart ASP.NET Core and navigate to http://localhost:5000/controllers/

form or http://localhost:5000/pages/form. Clear the form fields or enter bad key values and submit the form, and you will see the error messages produced by the attributes, some of which are shown in figure 29.11. (The values 1, 2, and 3 are valid for both the CategoryId and SupplierId fields.)

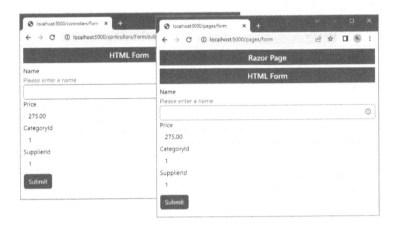

**Figure 29.11
Using custom
validation
attributes**

29.6 *Performing client-side validation*

The validation techniques I have demonstrated so far have all been examples of *server-side validation*. This means the user submits their data to the server, and the server validates the data and sends back the results of the validation (either success in processing the data or a list of errors that need to be corrected).

In web applications, users typically expect immediate validation feedback—without having to submit anything to the server. This is known as *client-side validation* and is implemented using JavaScript. The data that the user has entered is validated before being sent to the server, providing the user with immediate feedback and an opportunity to correct any problems.

ASP.NET Core supports *unobtrusive client-side validation*. The term *unobtrusive* means that validation rules are expressed using attributes added to the HTML elements that views generate. These attributes are interpreted by a JavaScript library distributed by Microsoft that, in turn, configures the jQuery Validation library, which does the actual validation work. In the following sections, I will show you how the built-in validation support works and demonstrate how I can extend the functionality to provide custom client-side validation.

The first step is to install the JavaScript packages that deal with validation. Open a new PowerShell command prompt, navigate to the `WebApp` project folder, and run the command shown in listing 29.23.

TIP   The core jQuery command was added to the project in chapter 26. Run the following command if you need to install it again: `libman install jquery@3.6.3 -d wwwroot/lib/jquery`.

Listing 29.23   Installing the validation packages

```
libman install jquery-validate@1.19.5 -d wwwroot/lib/jquery-validate
libman install jquery-validation-unobtrusive@4.0.0
    -d wwwroot/lib/jquery-validation-unobtrusive
```

Once the packages are installed, add the elements shown in listing 29.24 to the
_Validation.cshtml file in the Views/Shared folder, which provides a convenient
way to introduce the validation alongside the existing jQuery code in the application.

TIP   The elements must be defined in the order in which they are shown.

Listing 29.24   Adding elements in the _Validation.cshtml file in the Views/Shared folder

```
<script type="text/javascript">
    window.addEventListener("DOMContentLoaded", () => {
        document.querySelectorAll("input.input-validation-error")
            .forEach((elem) => { elem.classList.add("is-invalid"); }
        );
    });
</script>
<script src="/lib/jquery/jquery.min.js"></script>
<script src="/lib/jquery-validate/jquery.validate.min.js"></script>
<script src=
   "/lib/jquery-validation-unobtrusive/jquery.validate.unobtrusive.min.js">
</script>
```

The ASP.NET Core form tag helpers add data-val* attributes to input elements that
describe validation constraints for fields. Here are the attributes added to the input
element for the Name field, for example:

```
...
<input class="form-control input-validation-error is-invalid" type="text"
  data-val="true" data-val-required="Please enter a value" id="Name"
  name="Name" value="">
...
```

The unobtrusive validation JavaScript code looks for these attributes and performs validation in the browser when the user attempts to submit the form. The form won't be
submitted, and an error will be displayed if there are validation problems. The data
won't be sent to the application until there are no outstanding validation issues.

The JavaScript code looks for elements with the data-val attribute and performs
local validation in the browser when the user submits the form, without sending an
HTTP request to the server. You can see the effect by running the application and submitting the form while using the F12 tools to note that validation error messages are
displayed even though no HTTP request is sent to the server.

Avoiding conflicts with browser validation

Some of the current generation of browsers support simple client-side validation based on the attributes applied to `input` elements. The general idea is that, say, an `input` element to which the `required` attribute has been applied, for example, will cause the browser to display a validation error when the user tries to submit the form without providing a value.

If you are generating form elements using tag helpers, as I have been doing in this chapter, then you won't have any problems with browser validation because the elements that are assigned `data` attributes are ignored by the browser.

However, you may run into problems if you are unable to completely control the markup in your application, something that often happens when you are passing on content generated elsewhere. The result is that the jQuery validation and the browser validation can both operate on the form, which is just confusing to the user. To avoid this problem, ASP.NET Core adds the `novalidate` attribute to the `form` element to disable browser validation.

One of the nice client-side validation features is that the same attributes that specify validation rules are applied at the client *and* at the server. This means that data from browsers that do not support JavaScript are subject to the same validation as those that do, without requiring any additional effort.

To test the client-side validation feature, restart ASP.NET Core, request http://localhost:5000/controllers/form or http://localhost:5000/pages/form, clear the Name field, and click the Submit button.

The error message looks like the ones generated by server-side validation, but if you enter text into the field, you will see the error message disappear immediately as the JavaScript code responds to the user interaction, as shown in figure 29.12.

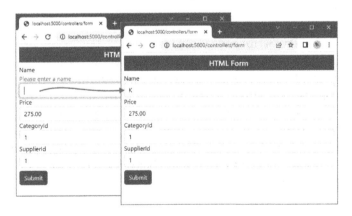

Figure 29.12   Performing client-side validation

Extending client-side validation

The client-side validation feature supports the built-in property-level attributes. The feature can be extended but requires fluency in JavaScript and requires working directly with the jQuery Validation package. See https://jqueryvalidation.org/documentation for details.

If you don't want to start writing JavaScript code, then you can follow the common pattern of using client-side validation for the built-in validation checks and server-side validation for custom validation.

29.7 *Performing remote validation*

Remote validation blurs the line between client- and server-side validation: the validation checks are enforced by the client-side JavaScript code, but the validation checking is performed by sending an asynchronous HTTP request to the application to test the value entered into the form by the user.

A common example of remote validation is to check whether a username is available in applications when such names must be unique, the user submits the data, and the client-side validation is performed. As part of this process, an asynchronous HTTP request is made to the server to validate the username that has been requested. If the username has been taken, a validation error is displayed so that the user can enter another value.

This may seem like regular server-side validation, but there are some benefits to this approach. First, only some properties will be remotely validated; the client-side validation benefits still apply to all the other data values that the user has entered. Second, the request is relatively lightweight and is focused on validation, rather than processing an entire model object.

The third difference is that the remote validation is performed in the background. The user doesn't have to click the submit button and then wait for a new view to be rendered and returned. It makes for a more responsive user experience, especially when there is a slow network between the browser and the server.

That said, remote validation is a compromise. It strikes a balance between client-side and server-side validation, but it does require requests to the application server, and it is not as quick to validate as normal client-side validation.

For the example application, I am going to use remote validation to ensure the user enters existing key values for the `CategoryId` and `SupplierId` properties. The first step is to create a web service controller whose action methods will perform the validation checks. I added a class file named `ValidationController.cs` to the `Controllers` folder with the code shown in listing 29.25.

Listing 29.25   The contents of the ValidationController.cs file in the Controllers folder

```
using Microsoft.AspNetCore.Mvc;
using WebApp.Models;

namespace WebApp.Controllers {

    [ApiController]
    [Route("api/[controller]")]
    public class ValidationController: ControllerBase {
        private DataContext dataContext;

        public ValidationController(DataContext context) {
            dataContext = context;
        }

        [HttpGet("categorykey")]
        public bool CategoryKey(string categoryId) {
            long keyVal;
            return long.TryParse(categoryId, out keyVal)
                && dataContext.Categories.Find(keyVal) != null;
        }

        [HttpGet("supplierkey")]
        public bool SupplierKey(string supplierId) {
            long keyVal;
            return long.TryParse(supplierId, out keyVal)
                && dataContext.Suppliers.Find(keyVal) != null;
        }
    }
}
```

Validation action methods must define a parameter whose name matches the field they will validate, which allows the model binding process to extract the value to test from the request query string. The response from the action method must be JSON and can be only true or false, indicating whether a value is acceptable. The action methods in listing 29.25 receive candidate values and check they have been used as database keys for Category or Supplier objects.

> **TIP**   I could have taken advantage of model binding so that the parameter to the action methods would be converted to a long value, but doing so would mean that the validation method wouldn't be called if the user entered a value that cannot be converted to the long type. If the model binder cannot convert a value, then the MVC Framework is unable to invoke the action method and validation can't be performed. As a rule, the best approach to remote validation is to accept a string parameter in the action method and perform any type conversion, parsing, or model binding explicitly.

To use the remote validation method, I apply the Remote attribute to the CategoryId and SupplierId properties in the Product class, as shown in listing 29.26.

Listing 29.26 Using the remote attribute in the Product.cs file in the Models folder

```
using System.ComponentModel.DataAnnotations;
using System.ComponentModel.DataAnnotations.Schema;
using System.Text.Json.Serialization;
using Microsoft.AspNetCore.Mvc.ModelBinding;
using WebApp.Validation;
using Microsoft.AspNetCore.Mvc;

namespace WebApp.Models {

    [PhraseAndPrice(Phrase = "Small", Price = "100")]
    public class Product {

        public long ProductId { get; set; }

        [Required(ErrorMessage = "Please enter a name")]
        public required string Name { get; set; }

        [Range(1, 999999, ErrorMessage = "Please enter a positive price")]
        [Column(TypeName = "decimal(8, 2)")]
        public decimal Price { get; set; }

        [PrimaryKey(ContextType = typeof(DataContext),
            DataType = typeof(Category))]
        [Remote("CategoryKey", "Validation",
            ErrorMessage = "Enter an existing key")]
        public long CategoryId { get; set; }
        public Category? Category { get; set; }

        [PrimaryKey(ContextType = typeof(DataContext),
            DataType = typeof(Supplier))]
        [Remote("SupplierKey", "Validation",
            ErrorMessage = "Enter an existing key")]
        public long SupplierId { get; set; }

        [JsonIgnore(Condition = JsonIgnoreCondition.WhenWritingNull)]
        public Supplier? Supplier { get; set; }
    }
}
```

The arguments to the `Remote` attribute specify the name of the validation controller and its action method. I have also used the optional `ErrorMessage` argument to specify the error message that will be displayed when validation fails. To see the remote validation, restart ASP.NET Core, navigate to http://localhost:5000/controllers/form, enter an invalid key value, and submit the form. You will see an error message, and the value of the `input` element will be validated after each key press, as shown in figure 29.13. (Only the values 1, 2, and 3 are valid for both the `CategoryId` and `SupplierId` fields.)

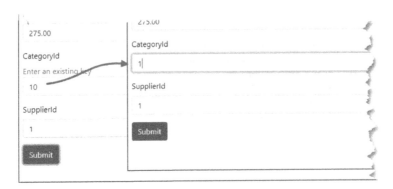

Figure 29.13 Performing remote validation

CAUTION   The validation action method will be called when the user first submits the form and again each time the data is edited. For text input elements, every keystroke will lead to a call to the server. For some applications, this can be a significant number of requests and must be accounted for when specifying the server capacity and bandwidth that an application requires in production. Also, you might choose *not* to use remote validation for properties that are expensive to validate (the example repeatedly queries the database for key values, which may not be sensible for all applications or databases).

29.7.1 *Performing remote validation in Razor Pages*

Remote validation works in Razor Pages, but attention must be paid to the names used in the asynchronous HTTP request used to validate values. For the controller example in the previous section, the browser will send requests to URLs like this:

`http://localhost:5000/api/Validation/categorykey?`**`CategoryId=1`**

But for the example Razor Page, the URL will be like this, reflecting the use of the page model:

`http://localhost:5000/api/Validation/categorykey?`**`Product.CategoryId=1`**

The way I prefer to address this difference is by adding parameters to the validation action methods that will accept both types of request, which is easy to do using the model binding features described in previous chapters, as shown in listing 29.27.

> **Listing 29.27 Adding parameters in the ValidationController.cs file in the Controllers folder**

```
using Microsoft.AspNetCore.Mvc;
using WebApp.Models;

namespace WebApp.Controllers {

    [ApiController]
    [Route("api/[controller]")]
    public class ValidationController : ControllerBase {
```

```
        private DataContext dataContext;

        public ValidationController(DataContext context) {
            dataContext = context;
        }

        [HttpGet("categorykey")]
        public bool CategoryKey(string? categoryId,
                [FromQuery] KeyTarget target) {
            long keyVal;
            return long.TryParse(categoryId ?? target.CategoryId,
                    out keyVal)
                && dataContext.Categories.Find(keyVal) != null;
        }

        [HttpGet("supplierkey")]
        public bool SupplierKey(string? supplierId,
                [FromQuery] KeyTarget target) {
            long keyVal;
            return long.TryParse(supplierId ?? target.SupplierId,
                    out keyVal)
                && dataContext.Suppliers.Find(keyVal) != null;
        }
    }

    [Bind(Prefix = "Product")]
    public class KeyTarget {
        public string? CategoryId { get; set; }
        public string? SupplierId { get; set; }
    }
}
```

The `KeyTarget` class is configured to bind to the `Product` part of the request, with properties that will match the two types of remote validation request. Each action method has been given a `KeyTarget` parameter, which is used if no value is received for existing parameters. This allows the same action method to accommodate both types of request, which you can see by restarting ASP.NET Core, navigating to http://localhost:5000/pages/form, entering a nonexistent key value, and clicking the Submit button, which will produce the response shown in figure 29.14.

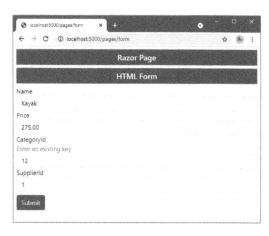

Figure 29.14 Performing remote validation using a Razor Page

Summary

- ASP.NET Core provides integrated support for validating data to ensure it can be used by the application.
- Validation messages can be displayed for the entire model or individual fields.
- Basic validation is performed automatically and can be complemented by explicit custom validation.
- Validation rules can be specified using attributes applied to model classes.
- Validation is usually performed when data is sent to the server, but there is support for client-side validation using a JavaScript library.
- Validation can also be performed by using JavaScript code to send individual data values to an ASP.NET Core controller for inspection.

Using filters

This chapter covers

- Injecting logic into request pipelines
- Understanding the different filter types and when each is executed
- Creating and applying filters
- Managing the filter lifecycle and execution order

Filters inject extra logic into request processing. Filters are like middleware that is applied to a single endpoint, which can be an action or a page handler method, and they provide an elegant way to manage a specific set of requests. In this chapter, I explain how filters work, describe the different types of filters that ASP.NET Core supports, and demonstrate the use of custom filters and the filters provided by ASP .NET Core. Table 30.1 provides a guide to the chapter.

Table 30.1   Chapter guide

Problem	Solution	Listing
Implementing a security policy	Use an authorization filter.	16, 17
Implementing a resource policy, such as caching	Use a resource filter.	18–20
Altering the request or response for an action method	Use an action filter.	21–24
Altering the request or response for a page handler method	Use a page filter.	25–27
Inspecting or altering the result produced by an endpoint	Use a result filter.	28–30
Inspecting or altering uncaught exceptions	Use an exception filter.	31, 32
Altering the filter lifecycle	Use a filter factory or define a service.	33–36
Applying filters throughout an application	Use a global filter.	37, 38
Changing the order in which filters are applied	Implement the `IOrdered-Filter` interface.	39–43

30.1   *Preparing for this chapter*

This chapter uses the WebApp project from chapter 29. To prepare for this chapter, open a new PowerShell command prompt, navigate to the `WebApp` project folder, and run the command shown in listing 30.1 to remove the files that are no longer required.

> **Listing 30.1   Removing files from the project**

```
Remove-Item -Path Controllers,Views,Pages -Recurse -Exclude _*,Shared
```

This command removes the controllers, views, and Razor Pages, leaving behind the shared layouts, data model, and configuration files.

> **TIP**   You can download the example project for this chapter—and for all the other chapters in this book—from https://github.com/manningbooks/pro-asp .net-core-7. See chapter 1 for how to get help if you have problems running the examples.

Create the `WebApp/Controllers` folder and add a class file named `HomeController` `.cs` to the `Controllers` folder with the code shown in listing 30.2.

> **Listing 30.2   The contents of the HomeController.cs file in the Controllers folder**

```
using Microsoft.AspNetCore.Mvc;

namespace WebApp.Controllers {
```

```
public class HomeController : Controller {

    public IActionResult Index() {
        return View("Message",
            "This is the Index action on the Home controller");
    }
}
}
```

The action method renders a view called `Message` and passes a string as the view data. I added a Razor view named `Message.cshtml` to the `Views/Shared` folder with the content shown in listing 30.3.

Listing 30.3 The contents of the Message.cshtml file in the Views/Shared folder

```
@{ Layout = "_SimpleLayout"; }

@if (Model is string) {
    @Model
} else if (Model is IDictionary<string, string>) {
    var dict = Model as IDictionary<string, string>;
    <table class="table table-sm table-striped table-bordered">
        <thead><tr><th>Name</th><th>Value</th></tr></thead>
        <tbody>
            @foreach (var kvp in dict ??
                    new Dictionary<string, string>()) {
                <tr><td>@kvp.Key</td><td>@kvp.Value</td></tr>
            }
        </tbody>
    </table>
}
```

Add a Razor Page named `Message.cshtml` to the `Pages` folder and add the content shown in listing 30.4.

Listing 30.4 The contents of the Message.cshtml file in the Pages folder

```
@page "/pages/message"
@model MessageModel
@using Microsoft.AspNetCore.Mvc.RazorPages

@if (Model.Message is string) {
    @Model.Message
} else if (Model.Message is IDictionary<string, string>) {
    var dict = Model.Message as IDictionary<string, string>;
    <table class="table table-sm table-striped table-bordered">
        <thead><tr><th>Name</th><th>Value</th></tr></thead>
        <tbody>
            @if (dict != null) {
                foreach (var kvp in dict) {
                    <tr><td>@kvp.Key</td><td>@kvp.Value</td></tr>
                }
            }
        </tbody>
    </table>
}
```

```
@functions {
    public class MessageModel : PageModel {

        public object Message { get; set; }
            = "This is the Message Razor Page";
    }
}
```

30.1.1 Enabling HTTPS Connections

Some of the examples in this chapter require the use of SSL. Add the configuration entries shown in listing 30.5 to the `launchSettings.json` file in the `Properties` folder to enable SSL and set the port to 44350.

Listing 30.5   Enabling HTTPS in the launchSettings.json file in the Properties folder

```
{
  "iisSettings": {
    "windowsAuthentication": false,
    "anonymousAuthentication": true,
    "iisExpress": {
      "applicationUrl": "http://localhost:5000",
      "sslPort": 0
    }
  },
  "profiles": {
    "WebApp": {
      "commandName": "Project",
      "dotnetRunMessages": true,
      "launchBrowser": false,
      "applicationUrl": "http://localhost:5000;https://localhost:44350",
      "environmentVariables": {
        "ASPNETCORE_ENVIRONMENT": "Development"
      }
    },
    "IIS Express": {
      "commandName": "IISExpress",
      "launchBrowser": true,
      "environmentVariables": {
        "ASPNETCORE_ENVIRONMENT": "Development"
      }
    }
  }
}
```

The .NET Core runtime includes a test certificate that is used for HTTPS requests. Run the commands shown in listing 30.6 in the `WebApp` folder to regenerate and trust the test certificate.

Listing 30.6   Regenerating the development certificates

```
dotnet dev-certs https --clean

dotnet dev-certs https --trust
```

Click Yes to the prompts to delete the existing certificate that has already been trusted and click Yes to trust the new certificate, as shown in figure 30.1.

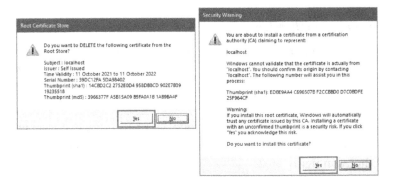

Figure 30.1 Regenerating the HTTPS certificate

Listing 30.7 replaces the contents of the `Program.cs` file to use the default controller routes and remove some of the services and components used in earlier chapters.

> **Listing 30.7 Configuring the platform in the Program.cs file in the WebApp folder**

```
using Microsoft.EntityFrameworkCore;
using WebApp.Models;

var builder = WebApplication.CreateBuilder(args);

builder.Services.AddDbContext<DataContext>(opts => {
    opts.UseSqlServer(builder.Configuration[
        "ConnectionStrings:ProductConnection"]);
    opts.EnableSensitiveDataLogging(true);
});
builder.Services.AddControllersWithViews();
builder.Services.AddRazorPages();

var app = builder.Build();

app.UseStaticFiles();
app.MapDefaultControllerRoute();
app.MapRazorPages();

var context = app.Services.CreateScope().ServiceProvider
    .GetRequiredService<DataContext>();
SeedData.SeedDatabase(context);

app.Run();
```

30.1.2 Dropping the database

Open a new PowerShell command prompt, navigate to the folder that contains the `WebApp.csproj` file, and run the command shown in listing 30.8 to drop the database.

Listing 30.8   Dropping the database

```
dotnet ef database drop --force
```

30.1.3 *Running the example application*

Use the PowerShell command prompt to run the command shown in listing 30.9.

Listing 30.9   Running the example application

```
dotnet run
```

Use a browser to request http://localhost:5000 and https://localhost:44350. Both URLs will be handled by the `Index` action defined by the `Home` controller, producing the responses shown in figure 30.2.

Figure 30.2   Responses from the Home controller

Request http://localhost:5000/pages/message and https://localhost:44350/pages/message to see the response from the `Message` Razor Page, delivered over HTTP and HTTPS, as shown in figure 30.3.

Figure 30.3   Responses from the Message Razor Page

30.2 *Using filters*

Filters allow logic that would otherwise be applied in a middleware component or action method to be defined in a class where it can be easily reused.

Imagine that you want to enforce HTTPS requests for some action methods. In chapter 16, I showed you how this can be done in middleware by reading the `IsHttps` property of the `HttpRequest` object. The problem with this approach is that the middleware would have to understand the configuration of the routing system to know how to intercept requests for specific action methods. A more focused approach would be to read the `HttpRequest.IsHttps` property within action methods, as shown in listing 30.10.

```
using Microsoft.AspNetCore.Mvc;

namespace WebApp.Controllers {

    public class HomeController : Controller {

        public IActionResult Index() {
            if (Request.IsHttps) {
                return View("Message",
                    "This is the Index action on the Home controller");
            } else {
                return new StatusCodeResult(
                    StatusCodes.Status403Forbidden);
            }
        }
    }
}
```

Restart ASP.NET Core and request http://localhost:5000. This method now requires HTTPS, and you will see an error response. Request https://localhost:44350, and you will see the message output. Figure 30.4 shows both responses.

> **TIP** Clear your browser's history if you don't get the results you expect from the examples in this section. Browsers will often refuse to send requests to servers that have previously generated HTTPS errors, which is a good security practice but can be frustrating during development.

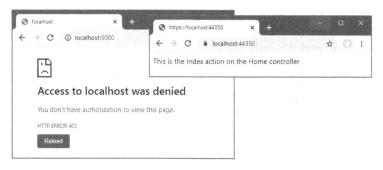

Figure 30.4 **Enforcing HTTPS in an action method**

This approach works but has problems. The first problem is that the action method contains code that is more about implementing a security policy than about handling the request. A more serious problem is that including the HTTP-detecting code within the action method doesn't scale well and must be duplicated in every action method in the controller, as shown in listing 30.11.

Listing 30.11   Adding actions in the HomeController.cs file in the Controllers folder

```
using Microsoft.AspNetCore.Mvc;

namespace WebApp.Controllers {

    public class HomeController : Controller {

        public IActionResult Index() {
            if (Request.IsHttps) {
                return View("Message",
                    "This is the Index action on the Home controller");
            } else {
                return new StatusCodeResult(
                    StatusCodes.Status403Forbidden);
            }
        }

        public IActionResult Secure() {
            if (Request.IsHttps) {
                return View("Message",
                    "This is the Secure action on the Home controller");
            } else {
                return new StatusCodeResult(
                    StatusCodes.Status403Forbidden);
            }
        }
    }
}
```

I must remember to implement the same check in every action method in every controller for which I want to require HTTPS. The code to implement the security policy is a substantial part of the—admittedly simple—controller, which makes the controller harder to understand, and it is only a matter of time before I forget to add it to a new action method, creating a hole in my security policy.

This is the type of problem that filters address. Listing 30.12 replaces my checks for HTTPS and implements a filter instead.

Listing 30.12   Applying a filter in the HomeController.cs file in the Controllers folder

```
using Microsoft.AspNetCore.Mvc;

namespace WebApp.Controllers {

    public class HomeController : Controller {

        [RequireHttps]
        public IActionResult Index() {
            return View("Message",
                "This is the Index action on the Home controller");
        }

        [RequireHttps]
        public IActionResult Secure() {
```

```
            return View("Message",
                "This is the Secure action on the Home controller");
        }
    }
}
```

The `RequireHttps` attribute applies one of the built-in filters provided by ASP.NET Core. This filter restricts access to action methods so that only HTTPS requests are supported and allows me to remove the security code from each method and focus on handling the successful requests.

> **NOTE** The `RequireHttps` filter doesn't work the same way as my custom code. For GET requests, the `RequireHttps` attribute redirects the client to the originally requested URL, but it does so by using the `https` scheme so that a request to http://localhost:5000 will be redirected to https://localhost:5000. This makes sense for most deployed applications but not during development because HTTP and HTTPS are on different local ports. The `RequireHttpsAttribute` class defines a protected method called `HandleNonHttpsRequest` that you can override to change the behavior. Alternatively, I re-create the original functionality from scratch in the "Understanding Authorization Filters" section.

I must still remember to apply the `RequireHttps` attribute to each action method, which means that I might forget. But filters have a useful trick: applying the attribute to a controller class has the same effect as applying it to each individual action method, as shown in listing 30.13.

> **Listing 30.13   Filtering all actions in the HomeController.cs file in the Controllers folder**

```
using Microsoft.AspNetCore.Mvc;

namespace WebApp.Controllers {

    [RequireHttps]
    public class HomeController : Controller {

        public IActionResult Index() {
            return View("Message",
                "This is the Index action on the Home controller");
        }

        public IActionResult Secure() {
            return View("Message",
                "This is the Secure action on the Home controller");
        }
    }
}
```

Filters can be applied with differing levels of granularity. If you want to restrict access to some actions but not others, then you can apply the `RequireHttps` attribute to just those methods. If you want to protect all the action methods, including any that you add to the controller in the future, then the `RequireHttps` attribute can be applied to the class. If you want to apply a filter to every action in an application, then you can use *global filters*, which I describe later in this chapter.

Filters can also be used in Razor Pages. To implement the HTTPS-only policy in the Message Razor Pages, for example, I would have to add a handler method that inspects the connection, as shown in listing 30.14.

Listing 30.14   Checking connections in the Message.cshtml file in the Pages folder

```
@page "/pages/message"
@model MessageModel
@using Microsoft.AspNetCore.Mvc.RazorPages

@if (Model.Message is string) {
    @Model.Message
} else if (Model.Message is IDictionary<string, string>) {
    var dict = Model.Message as IDictionary<string, string>;
    <table class="table table-sm table-striped table-bordered">
        <thead><tr><th>Name</th><th>Value</th></tr></thead>
        <tbody>
            @if (dict != null) {
                foreach (var kvp in dict) {
                    <tr><td>@kvp.Key</td><td>@kvp.Value</td></tr>
                }
            }
        </tbody>
    </table>
}

@functions {
    public class MessageModel : PageModel {

        public object Message { get; set; }
            = "This is the Message Razor Page";

        public IActionResult OnGet() {
            if (!Request.IsHttps) {
                return new StatusCodeResult(
                    StatusCodes.Status403Forbidden);
            } else {
                return Page();
            }
        }
    }
}
```

The handler method works, but it is awkward and presents the same problems encountered with action methods. When using filters in Razor Pages, the attribute can be applied to the handler method or, as shown in listing 30.15, to the entire class.

Listing 30.15   Applying a filter in the Message.cshtml file in the Pages folder

```
...
@functions {

    [RequireHttps]
```

```
public class MessageModel : PageModel {

    public object Message { get; set; }
        = "This is the Message Razor Page";

    //public IActionResult OnGet() {
    //    if (!Request.IsHttps) {
    //        return new StatusCodeResult(
    //            StatusCodes.Status403Forbidden);
    //    } else {
    //        return Page();
    //    }
    //}
}
}
...
```

You will see a normal response if you request https://localhost:44350/pages/message. If you request the regular HTTP URL, http://localhost:5000/pages/messages, the filter will redirect the request, and you will see an error (as noted earlier, the `RequireHttps` filter redirects the browser to a port that is not enabled in the example application).

30.3 *Understanding filters*

ASP.NET Core supports different types of filters, each of which is intended for a different purpose. Table 30.2 describes the filter categories.

Table 30.2 The filter types

Name	Description
Authorization filters	This type of filter is used to apply the application's authorization policy.
Resource filters	This type of filter is used to intercept requests, typically to implement features such as caching.
Action filters	This type of filter is used to modify the request before it is received by an action method or to modify the action result after it has been produced. This type of filter can be applied only to controllers and actions.
Page filters	This type of filter is used to modify the request before it is received by a Razor Page handler method or to modify the action result after it has been produced. This type of filter can be applied only to Razor Pages.
Result filters	This type of filter is used to alter the action result before it is executed or to modify the result after execution.
Exception filters	This type of filter is used to handle exceptions that occur during the execution of the action method or page handler.

Filters have their own pipeline and are executed in a specific order, as shown in figure 30.5.

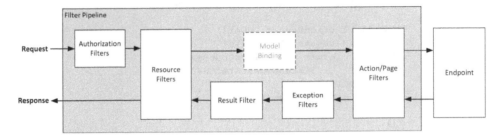

Figure 30.5 The filter pipeline

Filters can short-circuit the filter pipeline to prevent a request from being forwarded to the next filter. For example, an authorization filter can short-circuit the pipeline and return an error response if the user is unauthenticated. The resource, action, and page filters are able to inspect the request before and after it has been handled by the endpoint, allowing these types of filter to short-circuit the pipeline; to alter the request before it is handled; or to alter the response. (I have simplified the flow of filters in figure 30.5. Page filters run before and after the model binding process, as described in the "Understanding Page Filters" section.)

    Each type of filter is implemented using interfaces defined by ASP.NET Core, which also provides base classes that make it easy to apply some types of filters as attributes. I describe each interface and the attribute classes in the sections that follow, but they are shown in table 30.3 for quick reference.

Table 30.3 The filter types, interfaces, and attribute base classes

Filter Type	Interfaces	Attribute Class
Authorization filters	IAuthorizationFilter IAsyncAuthorizationFilter	No attribute class is provided.
Resource filters	IResourceFilter IAsyncResourceFilter	No attribute class is provided.
Action filters	IActionFilter IAsyncActionFilter	ActionFilterAttribute
Page filters	IPageFilter IAsyncPageFilter	No attribute class is provided.
Result filters	IResultFilter IAsyncResultFilter IAlwaysRunResultFilter IAsyncAlwaysRunResultFilter	ResultFilterAttribute
Exception Filters	IExceptionFilter IAsyncExceptionFilter	ExceptionFilterAttribute

30.4 Creating custom filters

Filters implement the `IFilterMetadata` interface, which is in the `Microsoft.Asp-NetCore.Mvc.Filters` namespace. Here is the interface:

```
namespace Microsoft.AspNetCore.Mvc.Filters {
    public interface IFilterMetadata { }
}
```

The interface is empty and doesn't require a filter to implement any specific behaviors. This is because each of the categories of filter described in the previous section works in a different way. Filters are provided with context data in the form of a `FilterContext` object. For convenience, Table 30.4 describes the properties that `FilterContext` provides.

Table 30.4 The FilterContext properties

Name	Description
ActionDescriptor	This property returns an `ActionDescriptor` object, which describes the action method.
HttpContext	This property returns an `HttpContext` object, which provides details of the HTTP request and the HTTP response that will be sent in return.
ModelState	This property returns a `ModelStateDictionary` object, which is used to validate data sent by the client.
RouteData	This property returns a `RouteData` object that describes the way that the routing system has processed the request.
Filters	This property returns a list of filters that have been applied to the action method, expressed as an `IList<IFilterMetadata>`.

30.4.1 Understanding authorization filters

Authorization filters are used to implement an application's security policy. Authorization filters are executed before other types of filter and before the endpoint handles the request. Here is the definition of the `IAuthorizationFilter` interface:

```
namespace Microsoft.AspNetCore.Mvc.Filters {

    public interface IAuthorizationFilter : IFilterMetadata {

        void OnAuthorization(AuthorizationFilterContext context);
    }
}
```

The `OnAuthorization` method is called to provide the filter with the opportunity to authorize the request. For asynchronous authorization filters, here is the definition of the `IAsyncAuthorizationFilter` interface:

```
using System.Threading.Tasks;

namespace Microsoft.AspNetCore.Mvc.Filters {

    public interface IAsyncAuthorizationFilter : IFilterMetadata {

        Task OnAuthorizationAsync(AuthorizationFilterContext context);
    }
}
```

The OnAuthorizationAsync method is called so that the filter can authorize the request. Whichever interface is used, the filter receives context data describing the request through an AuthorizationFilterContext object, which is derived from the FilterContext class and adds one important property, as described in table 30.5.

Table 30.5   The AuthorizationFilterContext property

Name	Description
Result	This IActionResult property is set by authorization filters when the request doesn't comply with the application's authorization policy. If this property is set, then ASP.NET Core executes the IActionResult instead of invoking the endpoint.

To demonstrate how authorization filters work, I created a Filters folder in the WebApp folder, added a class file called HttpsOnlyAttribute.cs, and used it to define the filter shown in listing 30.16.

Listing 30.16   The contents of the HttpsOnlyAttribute.cs file in the Filters folder

```
using Microsoft.AspNetCore.Mvc;
using Microsoft.AspNetCore.Mvc.Filters;

namespace WebApp.Filters {
    public class HttpsOnlyAttribute : Attribute, IAuthorizationFilter {

        public void OnAuthorization(AuthorizationFilterContext context) {
            if (!context.HttpContext.Request.IsHttps) {
                context.Result =
                    new StatusCodeResult(StatusCodes.Status403Forbidden);
            }
        }
    }
}
```

An authorization filter does nothing if a request complies with the authorization policy, and inaction allows ASP.NET Core to move on to the next filter and, eventually, to execute the endpoint. If there is a problem, the filter sets the Result property of the AuthorizationFilterContext object that is passed to the OnAuthorization method. This prevents further execution from happening and provides a result to return to the client. In the listing, the HttpsOnlyAttribute class inspects the IsHttps property of the `HttpRequest` context object and sets the `Result` property to interrupt execution if the request has been made without HTTPS. Authorization filters can be applied to controllers, action methods, and Razor Pages. Listing 30.17 applies the new filter to the `Home` controller.

Listing 30.17 Applying a filter in the HomeController.cs file in the Controllers folder

```
using Microsoft.AspNetCore.Mvc;
using WebApp.Filters;

namespace WebApp.Controllers {

    //[RequireHttps]
    [HttpsOnly]
    public class HomeController : Controller {

        public IActionResult Index() {
            return View("Message",
                "This is the Index action on the Home controller");
        }

        public IActionResult Secure() {
            return View("Message",
                "This is the Secure action on the Home controller");
        }
    }
}
```

This filter re-creates the functionality that I included in the action methods in listing 30.11. This is less useful in real projects than doing a redirection like the built-in `RequireHttps` filter because users won't understand the meaning of a 403 status code, but it does provide a useful example of how authorization filters work. Restart ASP.NET Core and request http://localhost:5000, and you will see the effect of the filter, as shown in figure 30.6. Request https://localhost:44350, and you will receive the response from the action method, also shown in the figure.

Figure 30.6 Applying a custom authorization filter

30.4.2 Understanding resource filters

Resource filters are executed twice for each request: before the ASP.NET Core model binding process and again before the action result is processed to generate the result. Here is the definition of the IResourceFilter interface:

```
namespace Microsoft.AspNetCore.Mvc.Filters {
    public interface IResourceFilter : IFilterMetadata {

        void OnResourceExecuting(ResourceExecutingContext context);

        void OnResourceExecuted(ResourceExecutedContext context);
    }
}
```

The OnResourceExecuting method is called when a request is being processed, and the OnResourceExecuted method is called after the endpoint has handled the request but before the action result is executed. For asynchronous resource filters, here is the definition of the IAsyncResourceFilter interface:

```
namespace Microsoft.AspNetCore.Mvc.Filters {
    public interface IAsyncResourceFilter : IFilterMetadata {

        Task OnResourceExecutionAsync(ResourceExecutingContext context,
            ResourceExecutionDelegate next);
    }
}
```

This interface defines a single method that receives a context object and a delegate to invoke. The resource filter is able to inspect the request before invoking the delegate and inspect the response before it is executed. The OnResourceExecuting method is provided with context using the ResourceExecutingContext class, which defines the properties shown in table 30.6 in addition to those defined by the FilterContext class.

Table 30.6   The properties defined by the ResourceExecutingContext class

Name	Description
Result	This IActionResult property is used to provide a result to short-circuit the pipeline.
ValueProviderFactories	This property returns an IList<IValueProviderFactory>, which provides access to the objects that provide values for the model binding process.

The OnResourceExecuted method is provided with context using the ResourceExecutedContext class, which defines the properties shown in table 30.7, in addition to those defined by the FilterContext class.

Table 30.7 The properties defined by the ResourceExecutedContext class

Name	Description
Result	This `IActionResult` property provides the action result that will be used to produce a response.
Canceled	This `bool` property is set to `true` if another filter has short-circuited the pipeline by assigning an action result to the `Result` property of the `Action-ExecutingContext` object.
Exception	This property is used to store an exception thrown during execution.
ExceptionDispatchInfo	This method returns an `ExceptionDispatchInfo` object that contains the stack trace details of any exception thrown during execution.
ExceptionHandled	Setting this property to `true` indicates that the filter has handled the exception, which will not be propagated any further.

CREATING A RESOURCE FILTER

Resource filters are usually used where it is possible to short-circuit the pipeline and provide a response early, such as when implementing data caching. To create a simple caching filter, add a class file called `SimpleCacheAttribute.cs` to the `Filters` folder with the code shown in listing 30.18.

Filters and dependency injection

Filters that are applied as attributes cannot declare dependencies in their constructors unless they implement the `IFilterFactory` interface and take responsibility for creating instances directly, as explained in the "Creating Filter Factories" section later in this chapter.

Listing 30.18 The contents of the SimpleCacheAttribute.cs file in the Filters folder

```
using Microsoft.AspNetCore.Mvc;
using Microsoft.AspNetCore.Mvc.Filters;

namespace WebApp.Filters {

    public class SimpleCacheAttribute : Attribute, IResourceFilter {
        private Dictionary<PathString, IActionResult> CachedResponses
            = new Dictionary<PathString, IActionResult>();

        public void OnResourceExecuting(
                ResourceExecutingContext context) {
            PathString path = context.HttpContext.Request.Path;
            if (CachedResponses.ContainsKey(path)) {
                context.Result = CachedResponses[path];
```

```
                    CachedResponses.Remove(path);

                }
            }

            public void OnResourceExecuted(ResourceExecutedContext context) {
                if (context.Result != null) {
                    CachedResponses.Add(context.HttpContext.Request.Path,
                        context.Result);
                }
            }
        }
    }
}
```

This filter isn't an especially useful cache, but it does show how a resource filter works. The `OnResourceExecuting` method provides the filter with the opportunity to short-circuit the pipeline by setting the context object's `Result` property to a previously cached action result. If a value is assigned to the `Result` property, then the filter pipeline is short-circuited, and the action result is executed to produce the response for the client. Cached action results are used only once and then discarded from the cache. If no value is assigned to the `Result` property, then the request passes to the next step in the pipeline, which may be another filter or the endpoint.

The `OnResourceExecuted` method provides the filter with the action results that are produced when the pipeline is not short-circuited. In this case, the filter caches the action result so that it can be used for subsequent requests. Resource filters can be applied to controllers, action methods, and Razor Pages. Listing 30.19 applies the custom resource filter to the `Message` Razor Page and adds a timestamp that will help determine when an action result is cached.

> **Listing 30.19   Applying a resource filter in the Message.cshtml file in the Pages folder**

```
@page "/pages/message"
@model MessageModel
@using Microsoft.AspNetCore.Mvc.RazorPages
@using WebApp.Filters

@if (Model.Message is string) {
    @Model.Message
} else if (Model.Message is IDictionary<string, string>) {
    var dict = Model.Message as IDictionary<string, string>;
    <table class="table table-sm table-striped table-bordered">
        <thead><tr><th>Name</th><th>Value</th></tr></thead>
        <tbody>
            @if (dict != null) {
                foreach (var kvp in dict) {
                    <tr><td>@kvp.Key</td><td>@kvp.Value</td></tr>
                }
            }
        </tbody>
    </table>
}
```

```
@functions {

    [RequireHttps]
    [SimpleCache]
    public class MessageModel : PageModel {

        public object Message { get; set; } =
            DateTime.Now.ToLongTimeString()
                + " This is the Message Razor Page";
    }
}
```

To see the effect of the resource filter, restart ASP.NET Core and request https://localhost:44350/pages/message. Since this is the first request for the path, there will be no cached result, and the request will be forwarded along the pipeline. As the response is processed, the resource filter will cache the action result for future use. Reload the browser to repeat the request, and you will see the same timestamp, indicating that the cached action result has been used. The cached item is removed when it is used, which means that reloading the browser will generate a response with a fresh timestamp, as shown in figure 30.7.

Figure 30.7 Using a resource filter

CREATING AN ASYNCHRONOUS RESOURCE FILTER

The interface for asynchronous resource filters uses a single method that receives a delegate used to forward the request along the filter pipeline. Listing 30.20 reimplements the caching filter from the previous example so that it implements the `IAsyncResourceFilter` interface.

Listing 30.20 An asynchronous filter in the Filters/SimpleCacheAttribute.cs file

```
using Microsoft.AspNetCore.Mvc;
using Microsoft.AspNetCore.Mvc.Filters;

namespace WebApp.Filters {

    public class SimpleCacheAttribute : Attribute, IAsyncResourceFilter {
        private Dictionary<PathString, IActionResult> CachedResponses
            = new Dictionary<PathString, IActionResult>();

        public async Task OnResourceExecutionAsync(
                ResourceExecutingContext context,
                ResourceExecutionDelegate next) {
            PathString path = context.HttpContext.Request.Path;
```

```
        if (CachedResponses.ContainsKey(path)) {
            context.Result = CachedResponses[path];
            CachedResponses.Remove(path);
        } else {
            ResourceExecutedContext execContext = await next();
            if (execContext.Result != null) {
                CachedResponses.Add(context.HttpContext.Request.Path,
                    execContext.Result);
            }
        }
    }
}
}
```

The `OnResourceExecutionAsync` method receives a `ResourceExecutingContext` object, which is used to determine whether the pipeline can be short-circuited. If it cannot, the delegate is invoked without arguments and asynchronously produces a `ResourceExecutedContext` object when the request has been handled and is making its way back along the pipeline. Restart ASP.NET Core and repeat the requests described in the previous section, and you will see the same caching behavior, as shown in figure 30.7.

> **CAUTION**   It is important not to confuse the two context objects. The action result produced by the endpoint is available only in the context object that is returned by the delegate.

30.4.3 *Understanding action filters*

Like resource filters, action filters are executed twice. The difference is that action filters are executed after the model binding process, whereas resource filters are executed before model binding. This means that resource filters can short-circuit the pipeline and minimize the work that ASP.NET Core does on the request. Action filters are used when model binding is required, which means they are used for tasks such as altering the model or enforcing validation. Action filters can be applied only to controllers and action methods, unlike resource filters, which can also be used with Razor Pages. (The Razor Pages equivalent to action filters is the page filter, described in the "Understanding Page Filters" section.) Here is the `IActionFilter` interface:

```
namespace Microsoft.AspNetCore.Mvc.Filters {

    public interface IActionFilter : IFilterMetadata {

        void OnActionExecuting(ActionExecutingContext context);

        void OnActionExecuted(ActionExecutedContext context);
    }
}
```

When an action filter has been applied to an action method, the `OnActionExecuting` method is called just before the action method is invoked, and the `OnActionExecuted` method is called just after. Action filters are provided with context data through two different context classes: `ActionExecutingContext` for the `OnActionExecuting` method and `ActionExecutedContext` for the `OnActionExecuted` method.

The `ActionExecutingContext` class, which is used to describe an action that is about to be invoked, defines the properties described in table 30.8, in addition to the `FilterContext` properties.

Table 30.8   The ActionExecutingContext properties

Name	Description
`Controller`	This property returns the controller whose action method is about to be invoked. (Details of the action method are available through the `ActionDescriptor` property inherited from the base classes.)
`ActionArguments`	This property returns a dictionary of the arguments that will be passed to the action method, indexed by name. The filter can insert, remove, or change the arguments.
`Result`	If the filter assigns an `IActionResult` to this property, then the pipeline will be short-circuited, and the action result will be used to generate the response to the client without invoking the action method.

The `ActionExecutedContext` class is used to represent an action that has been executed and defines the properties described in table 30.9, in addition to the `FilterContext` properties.

Table 30.9   The ActionExecutedContext properties

Name	Description
`Controller`	This property returns the `Controller` object whose action method will be invoked.
`Canceled`	This `bool` property is set to `true` if another action filter has short-circuited the pipeline by assigning an action result to the `Result` property of the `ActionExecutingContext` object.
`Exception`	This property contains any `Exception` that was thrown by the action method.
`ExceptionDispatchInfo`	This method returns an `ExceptionDispatchInfo` object that contains the stack trace details of any exception thrown by the action method.
`ExceptionHandled`	Setting this property to `true` indicates that the filter has handled the exception, which will not be propagated any further.
`Result`	This property returns the `IActionResult` produced by the action method. The filter can change or replace the action result if required.

Asynchronous action filters are implemented using the `IAsyncActionFilter` interface.

```
namespace Microsoft.AspNetCore.Mvc.Filters {

    public interface IAsyncActionFilter : IFilterMetadata {

        Task OnActionExecutionAsync(ActionExecutingContext context,
            ActionExecutionDelegate next);
    }
}
```

This interface follows the same pattern as the IAsyncResourceFilter interface described earlier in the chapter. The OnActionExecutionAsync method is provided with an ActionExecutingContext object and a delegate. The ActionExecutingContext object describes the request before it is received by the action method. The filter can short-circuit the pipeline by assigning a value to the ActionExecutingContext.Result property or pass it along by invoking the delegate. The delegate asynchronously produces an ActionExecutedContext object that describes the result from the action method.

CREATING AN ACTION FILTER

Add a class file called ChangeArgAttribute.cs to the Filters folder and use it to define the action filter shown in listing 30.21.

> **Listing 30.21   The contents of the ChangeArgAttribute.cs file in the Filters folder**

```
using Microsoft.AspNetCore.Mvc.Filters;

namespace WebApp.Filters {
    public class ChangeArgAttribute : Attribute, IAsyncActionFilter {

        public async Task OnActionExecutionAsync(
                ActionExecutingContext context,
                ActionExecutionDelegate next) {

            if (context.ActionArguments.ContainsKey("message1")) {
                context.ActionArguments["message1"] = "New message";
            }
            await next();
        }
    }
}
```

The filter looks for an action argument named message1 and changes the value that will be used to invoke the action method. The values that will be used for the action method arguments are determined by the model binding process. Listing 30.22 adds an action method to the Home controller and applies the new filter.

> **Listing 30.22   Applying a filter in the HomeController.cs file in the Controllers folder**

```
using Microsoft.AspNetCore.Mvc;
using WebApp.Filters;

namespace WebApp.Controllers {
```

```
[HttpsOnly]
public class HomeController : Controller {

    public IActionResult Index() {
        return View("Message",
            "This is the Index action on the Home controller");
    }

    public IActionResult Secure() {
        return View("Message",
            "This is the Secure action on the Home controller");
    }

    [ChangeArg]
    public IActionResult Messages(string message1,
            string message2 = "None") {
        return View("Message", $"{message1}, {message2}");
    }
}
}
```

Restart ASP.NET Core and request https://localhost:44350/home/messages ?message1=hello&message2=world. The model binding process will locate values for the parameters defined by the action method from the query string. One of those values is then modified by the action filter, producing the response shown in figure 30.8.

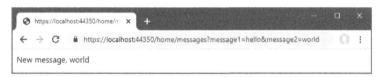

Figure 30.8 Using an action filter

IMPLEMENTING AN ACTION FILTER USING THE ATTRIBUTE BASE CLASS

Action attributes can also be implemented by deriving from the `ActionFilter-Attribute` class, which extends `Attribute` and inherits both the `IActionFilter` and `IAsyncActionFilter` interfaces so that implementation classes override just the methods they require. In listing 30.23, I have reimplemented the `ChangeArg` filter so that it is derived from `ActionFilterAttribute`.

Listing 30.23 Using a filter base class in the Filters/ChangeArgsAttribute.cs file

```
using Microsoft.AspNetCore.Mvc.Filters;

namespace WebApp.Filters {
    public class ChangeArgAttribute : ActionFilterAttribute {

        public override async Task OnActionExecutionAsync(
            ActionExecutingContext context,
                ActionExecutionDelegate next) {

                if (context.ActionArguments.ContainsKey("message1")) {
```

```
                context.ActionArguments["message1"] = "New message";
            }
            await next();
        }
    }
}
```

This attribute behaves in just the same way as the earlier implementation, and the use of the base class is a matter of preference. Restart ASP.NET Core and request https://localhost:44350/home/messages?message1=hello&message2=world, and you will see the response shown in figure 30.8.

USING THE CONTROLLER FILTER METHODS

The `Controller` class, which is the base for controllers that render Razor views, implements the `IActionFilter` and `IAsyncActionFilter` interfaces, which means you can define functionality and apply it to the actions defined by a controller and any derived controllers. Listing 30.24 implements the `ChangeArg` filter functionality directly in the `HomeController` class.

Listing 30.24   Using action filter methods in the Controllers/HomeController.cs file

```
using Microsoft.AspNetCore.Mvc;
using WebApp.Filters;
using Microsoft.AspNetCore.Mvc.Filters;

namespace WebApp.Controllers {

    [HttpsOnly]
    public class HomeController : Controller {

        public IActionResult Index() {
            return View("Message",
                "This is the Index action on the Home controller");
        }

        public IActionResult Secure() {
            return View("Message",
                "This is the Secure action on the Home controller");
        }

        //[ChangeArg]
        public IActionResult Messages(string message1,
                string message2 = "None") {
            return View("Message", $"{message1}, {message2}");
        }

        public override void OnActionExecuting(
                ActionExecutingContext context) {
            if (context.ActionArguments.ContainsKey("message1")) {
                context.ActionArguments["message1"] = "New message";
            }
        }
    }
}
```

The `Home` controller overrides the `Controller` implementation of the `OnAction-Executing` method and uses it to modify the arguments that will be passed to the execution method. Restart ASP.NET Core and request https://localhost:44350/home/messages?message1=hello&message2=world, and you will see the response shown in figure 30.8.

30.4.4 *Understanding page filters*

Page filters are the Razor Page equivalent of action filters. Here is the `IPageFilter` interface, which is implemented by synchronous page filters:

```
namespace Microsoft.AspNetCore.Mvc.Filters {

    public interface IPageFilter : IFilterMetadata {

        void OnPageHandlerSelected(PageHandlerSelectedContext context);

        void OnPageHandlerExecuting(PageHandlerExecutingContext context);

        void OnPageHandlerExecuted(PageHandlerExecutedContext context);
    }
}
```

The `OnPageHandlerSelected` method is invoked after ASP.NET Core has selected the page handler method but before model binding has been performed, which means the arguments for the handler method have not been determined. This method receives context through the `PageHandlerSelectedContext` class, which defines the properties shown in table 30.10, in addition to those defined by the `FilterContext` class. This method cannot be used to short-circuit the pipeline, but it can alter the handler method that will receive the request.

Table 30.10   The PageHandlerSelectedContext properties

Name	Description
`ActionDescriptor`	This property returns the description of the Razor Page.
`HandlerMethod`	This property returns a `HandlerMethodDescriptor` object that describes the selected handler method.
`HandlerInstance`	This property returns the instance of the Razor Page that will handle the request.

The `OnPageHandlerExecuting` method is called after the model binding process has completed but before the page handler method is invoked. This method receives context through the `PageHandlerExecutingContext` class, which defines the properties shown in table 30.11, in addition to those defined by the `PageHandlerSelected-Context` class.

Table 30.11   The PageHandlerExecutingContext properties

Name	Description
HandlerArguments	This property returns a dictionary containing the page handler arguments, indexed by name.
Result	The filter can short-circuit the pipeline by assigning an IActionResult object to this property.

The OnPageHandlerExecuted method is called after the page handler method has been invoked but before the action result is processed to create a response. This method receives context through the PageHandlerExecutedContext class, which defines the properties shown in table 30.12 in addition to the PageHandler-ExecutingContext properties.

Table 30.12   The PageHandlerExecutedContext properties

Name	Description
Canceled	This property returns true if another filter short-circuited the filter pipeline.
Exception	This property returns an exception if one was thrown by the page handler method.
ExceptionHandled	This property is set to true to indicate that an exception thrown by the page handler has been handled by the filter.
Result	This property returns the action result that will be used to create a response for the client.

Asynchronous page filters are created by implementing the IAsyncPageFilter inter-face, which is defined like this:

```
namespace Microsoft.AspNetCore.Mvc.Filters {
    public interface IAsyncPageFilter : IFilterMetadata {

        Task OnPageHandlerSelectionAsync(
            PageHandlerSelectedContext context);

        Task OnPageHandlerExecutionAsync(
            PageHandlerExecutingContext context,
            PageHandlerExecutionDelegate next);
    }
}
```

The OnPageHandlerSelectionAsync is called after the handler method is selected and is equivalent to the synchronous OnPageHandlerSelected method. The OnPage-HandlerExecutionAsync is provided with a PageHandlerExecutingContext object that allows it to short-circuit the pipeline and with a delegate that is invoked to pass on the request. The delegate produces a PageHandlerExecutedContext object that can be used to inspect or alter the action result produced by the handler method.

CREATING A PAGE FILTER

To create a page filter, add a class file named `ChangePageArgs.cs` to the `Filters` folder and use it to define the class shown in listing 30.25.

```
using Microsoft.AspNetCore.Mvc.Filters;

namespace WebApp.Filters {
    public class ChangePageArgs : Attribute, IPageFilter {

        public void OnPageHandlerSelected(
                PageHandlerSelectedContext context) {
            // do nothing
        }

        public void OnPageHandlerExecuting(
                PageHandlerExecutingContext context) {
            if (context.HandlerArguments.ContainsKey("message1")) {
                context.HandlerArguments["message1"] = "New message";
            }
        }

        public void OnPageHandlerExecuted(
                PageHandlerExecutedContext context) {
            // do nothing
        }
    }
}
```

The page filter in listing 30.25 performs the same task as the action filter I created in the previous section. In listing 30.26, I have modified the `Message` Razor Page to define a handler method and have applied the page filter. Page filters can be applied to individual handler methods or, as in the listing, to the page model class, in which case the filter is used for all handler methods. (I also disabled the `SimpleCache` filter in listing 30.26. Resource filters can work alongside page filters. I disabled this filter because caching responses makes some of the examples more difficult to follow.)

```
@page "/pages/message"
@model MessageModel
@using Microsoft.AspNetCore.Mvc.RazorPages
@using WebApp.Filters

@if (Model.Message is string) {
    @Model.Message
} else if (Model.Message is IDictionary<string, string>) {
    var dict = Model.Message as IDictionary<string, string>;
    <table class="table table-sm table-striped table-bordered">
        <thead><tr><th>Name</th><th>Value</th></tr></thead>
        <tbody>
            @if (dict != null) {
```

```
            foreach (var kvp in dict) {
                <tr><td>@kvp.Key</td><td>@kvp.Value</td></tr>
            }
        }
    </tbody>
    </table>
}

@functions {

    [RequireHttps]
    //[SimpleCache]
    [ChangePageArgs]
    public class MessageModel : PageModel {

        public object Message { get; set; } =
            DateTime.Now.ToLongTimeString()
                + " This is the Message Razor Page";

        public void OnGet(string message1, string message2) {
            Message = $"{message1}, {message2}";
        }
    }
}
```

Restart ASP.NET Core and request https://localhost:44350/pages/message-
?message1=hello&message2=world. The page filter will replace the value of the
`message1` argument for the `OnGet` handler method, which produces the response
shown in figure 30.9.

Figure 30.9   Using a page filter

USING THE PAGE MODEL FILTER METHODS

The `PageModel` class, which is used as the base for page model classes, implements
the `IPageFilter` and `IAsyncPageFilter` interfaces, which means you can add filter
functionality directly to a page model, as shown in listing 30.27.

Listing 30.27   Using the filter methods in the Message.cshtml file in the Pages folder

```
@page "/pages/message"
@model MessageModel
@using Microsoft.AspNetCore.Mvc.RazorPages
@using WebApp.Filters
@using Microsoft.AspNetCore.Mvc.Filters

@if (Model.Message is string) {
```

```
        @Model.Message
    } else if (Model.Message is IDictionary<string, string>) {
        var dict = Model.Message as IDictionary<string, string>;
        <table class="table table-sm table-striped table-bordered">
            <thead><tr><th>Name</th><th>Value</th></tr></thead>
            <tbody>
                @if (dict != null) {
                    foreach (var kvp in dict) {
                        <tr><td>@kvp.Key</td><td>@kvp.Value</td></tr>
                    }
                }
            </tbody>
        </table>
    }

@functions {

    [RequireHttps]
    //[SimpleCache]
    //[ChangePageArgs]
    public class MessageModel : PageModel {

        public object Message { get; set; } =
            DateTime.Now.ToLongTimeString()
                + " This is the Message Razor Page";

        public void OnGet(string message1, string message2) {
            Message = $"{message1}, {message2}";
        }

        public override void OnPageHandlerExecuting(
                PageHandlerExecutingContext context) {
            if (context.HandlerArguments.ContainsKey("message1")) {
                context.HandlerArguments["message1"] = "New message";
            }
        }
    }
}
```

Request https://localhost:44350/pages/message?message1=hello&message2=world.
The method implemented by the page model class in listing 30.27 will produce the
same result as shown in figure 30.9.

30.4.5 *Understanding result filters*

Result filters are executed before and after an action result is used to generate a
response, allowing responses to be modified after they have been handled by the endpoint. Here is the definition of the IResultFilter interface:

```
namespace Microsoft.AspNetCore.Mvc.Filters {
    public interface IResultFilter : IFilterMetadata {

        void OnResultExecuting(ResultExecutingContext context);
```

```
        void OnResultExecuted(ResultExecutedContext context);
    }
}
```

The `OnResultExecuting` method is called after the endpoint has produced an action result. This method receives context through the `ResultExecutingContext` class, which defines the properties described in table 30.13, in addition to those defined by the `FilterContext` class.

Table 30.13   The ResultExecutingContext class properties

Name	Description
`Controller`	This property returns the object that contains the endpoint.
`Cancel`	Setting this property to `true` will short-circuit the result filter pipeline.
`Result`	This property returns the action result produced by the endpoint.

The `OnResultExecuted` method is called after the action result has been executed to generate the response for the client. This method receives context through the `ResultExecutedContext` class, which defines the properties shown in table 30.14, in addition to those it inherits from the `FilterContext` class.

Table 30.14   The ResultExecutedContext class

Name	Description
`Canceled`	This property returns `true` if another filter short-circuited the filter pipeline.
`Controller`	This property returns the object that contains the endpoint.
`Exception`	This property returns an exception if one was thrown by the page handler method.
`ExceptionHandled`	This property is set to `true` to indicate that an exception thrown by the page handler has been handled by the filter.
`Result`	This property returns the action result that will be used to create a response for the client. This property is read-only.

Asynchronous result filters implement the `IAsyncResultFilter` interface, which is defined like this:

```
namespace Microsoft.AspNetCore.Mvc.Filters {

    public interface IAsyncResultFilter : IFilterMetadata {

        Task OnResultExecutionAsync(ResultExecutingContext context,
            ResultExecutionDelegate next);
    }
}
```

This interface follows the pattern established by the other filter types. The `OnResult-`
`ExecutionAsync` method is invoked with a context object whose `Result` property can
be used to alter the response and a delegate that will forward the response along the
pipeline.

UNDERSTANDING ALWAYS-RUN RESULT FILTERS

Filters that implement the `IResultFilter` and `IAsyncResultFilter` interfaces are
used only when a request is handled normally by the endpoint. They are not used if
another filter short-circuits the pipeline or if there is an exception. Filters that need to
inspect or alter the response, even when the pipeline is short-circuited, can implement
the `IAlwaysRunResultFilter` or `IAsyncAlwaysRunResultFilter` interface. These
interfaces derived from `IResultFilter` and `IAsyncResultFilter` but define no new
features. Instead, ASP.NET Core detects the always-run interfaces and always applies
the filters.

CREATING A RESULT FILTER

Add a class file named `ResultDiagnosticsAttribute.cs` to the `Filters` folder and
use it to define the filter shown in listing 30.28.

> **Listing 30.28 The contents of the ResultDiagnosticsAttribute.cs file in the Filters
> folder**

```
using Microsoft.AspNetCore.Mvc;
using Microsoft.AspNetCore.Mvc.Filters;
using Microsoft.AspNetCore.Mvc.ModelBinding;
using Microsoft.AspNetCore.Mvc.RazorPages;
using Microsoft.AspNetCore.Mvc.ViewFeatures;

namespace WebApp.Filters {

    public class ResultDiagnosticsAttribute :
            Attribute, IAsyncResultFilter {

        public async Task OnResultExecutionAsync(
                ResultExecutingContext context,
                ResultExecutionDelegate next) {

            if (context.HttpContext.Request.Query.ContainsKey("diag")) {
                Dictionary<string, string?> diagData =
                    new Dictionary<string, string?> {
                        {"Result type", context.Result.GetType().Name }
                    };
                if (context.Result is ViewResult vr) {
                    diagData["View Name"] = vr.ViewName;
                    diagData["Model Type"]
                        = vr.ViewData?.Model?.GetType().Name;
                    diagData["Model Data"]
                        = vr.ViewData?.Model?.ToString();
                } else if (context.Result is PageResult pr) {
                    diagData["Model Type"] = pr.Model.GetType().Name;
                    diagData["Model Data"]
                        = pr.ViewData?.Model?.ToString();
```

```
            }
            context.Result = new ViewResult() {
                ViewName = "/Views/Shared/Message.cshtml",
                ViewData = new ViewDataDictionary(
                                new EmptyModelMetadataProvider(),
                                new ModelStateDictionary()) {
                    Model = diagData
                }
            };
        }
        await next();
    }
}
```

This filter examines the request to see whether it contains a query string parameter named diag. If it does, then the filter creates a result that displays diagnostic information instead of the output produced by the endpoint. The filter in listing 30.28 will work with the actions defined by the Home controller or the Message Razor Page. Listing 30.29 applies the result filter to the Home controller.

TIP Notice that I use a fully qualified name for the view when I create the action result in listing 30.28. This avoids a problem with filters applied to Razor Pages, where ASP.NET Core tries to execute the new result as a Razor Page and throws an exception about the model type.

Listing 30.29   Applying a result filter in the Controllers/HomeController.cs file

```
using Microsoft.AspNetCore.Mvc;
using WebApp.Filters;
using Microsoft.AspNetCore.Mvc.Filters;

namespace WebApp.Controllers {

    [HttpsOnly]
    [ResultDiagnostics]
    public class HomeController : Controller {

        public IActionResult Index() {
            return View("Message",
                "This is the Index action on the Home controller");
        }

        public IActionResult Secure() {
            return View("Message",
                "This is the Secure action on the Home controller");
        }

        // [ChangeArg]
        public IActionResult Messages(string message1,
                string message2 = "None") {
            return View("Message", $"{message1}, {message2}");
        }
```

```
    public override void OnActionExecuting(
        ActionExecutingContext context) {
    if (context.ActionArguments.ContainsKey("message1")) {
        context.ActionArguments["message1"] = "New message";
    }
    }
    }
}
```

Restart ASP.NET Core and request https://localhost:44350/?diag. The query string parameter will be detected by the filter, which will generate the diagnostic information shown in figure 30.10.

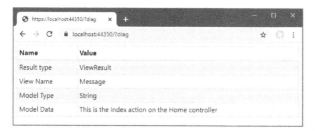

**Figure 30.10
Using a result
filter**

IMPLEMENTING A RESULT FILTER USING THE ATTRIBUTE BASE CLASS

The `ResultFilterAttribute` class is derived from `Attribute` and implements the `IResultFilter` and `IAsyncResultFilter` interfaces and can be used as the base class for result filters, as shown in listing 30.30. There is no attribute base class for the always-run interfaces.

Listing 30.30   Using the base class in the Filters/ResultDiagnosticsAttribute.cs file

```
using Microsoft.AspNetCore.Mvc;
using Microsoft.AspNetCore.Mvc.Filters;
using Microsoft.AspNetCore.Mvc.ModelBinding;
using Microsoft.AspNetCore.Mvc.RazorPages;
using Microsoft.AspNetCore.Mvc.ViewFeatures;

namespace WebApp.Filters {

    public class ResultDiagnosticsAttribute : ResultFilterAttribute {

        public override async Task OnResultExecutionAsync(
                ResultExecutingContext context,
                ResultExecutionDelegate next) {

            if (context.HttpContext.Request.Query.ContainsKey("diag")) {
                Dictionary<string, string?> diagData =
                    new Dictionary<string, string?> {
                        {"Result type", context.Result.GetType().Name }
                    };
                if (context.Result is ViewResult vr) {
                    diagData["View Name"] = vr.ViewName;
                    diagData["Model Type"]
                        = vr.ViewData?.Model?.GetType().Name;
```

```
                      diagData["Model Data"]
                          = vr.ViewData?.Model?.ToString();
                  } else if (context.Result is PageResult pr) {
                      diagData["Model Type"] = pr.Model.GetType().Name;
                      diagData["Model Data"]
                          = pr.ViewData?.Model?.ToString();
                  }
                  context.Result = new ViewResult() {
                      ViewName = "/Views/Shared/Message.cshtml",
                      ViewData = new ViewDataDictionary(
                                      new EmptyModelMetadataProvider(),
                                      new ModelStateDictionary()) {
                          Model = diagData
                      }
                  };
              }
              await next();
          }
      }
  }
```

Restart ASP.NET Core and request https://localhost:44350/?diag. The filter will produce the output shown in figure 30.10.

30.4.6 *Understanding exception filters*

Exception filters allow you to respond to exceptions without having to write `try...catch` blocks in every action method. Exception filters can be applied to controller classes, action methods, page model classes, or handler methods. They are invoked when an exception is not handled by the endpoint or by the action, page, and result filters that have been applied to the endpoint. (Action, page, and result filters can deal with an unhandled exception by setting the `ExceptionHandled` property of their context objects to `true`.) Exception filters implement the `IExceptionFilter` interface, which is defined as follows:

```
namespace Microsoft.AspNetCore.Mvc.Filters {

    public interface IExceptionFilter : IFilterMetadata {

        void OnException(ExceptionContext context);
    }
}
```

The `OnException` method is called if an unhandled exception is encountered. The `IAsyncExceptionFilter` interface can be used to create asynchronous exception filters. Here is the definition of the asynchronous interface:

```
using System.Threading.Tasks;

namespace Microsoft.AspNetCore.Mvc.Filters {

    public interface IAsyncExceptionFilter : IFilterMetadata {

        Task OnExceptionAsync(ExceptionContext context);
    }
}
```

The OnExceptionAsync method is the asynchronous counterpart to the OnException method from the IExceptionFilter interface and is called when there is an unhandled exception. For both interfaces, context data is provided through the ExceptionContext class, which is derived from FilterContext and defines the additional properties shown in table 30.15.

Table 30.15 The ExceptionContext properties

Name	Description
Exception	This property contains any Exception that was thrown.
ExceptionHandled	This bool property is used to indicate if the exception has been handled.
Result	This property sets the IActionResult that will be used to generate the response.

30.4.7 Creating an exception filter

Exception filters can be created by implementing one of the filter interfaces or by deriving from the ExceptionFilterAttribute class, which is derived from Attribute and implements both the IExceptionFilter and IAsyncException filters. The most common use for an exception filter is to present a custom error page for a specific exception type to provide the user with more useful information than the standard error-handling capabilities can provide.

To create an exception filter, add a class file named RangeExceptionAttribute.cs to the Filters folder with the code shown in listing 30.31.

Listing 30.31 The contents of the RangeExceptionAttribute.cs file in the Filters folder

```
using Microsoft.AspNetCore.Mvc;
using Microsoft.AspNetCore.Mvc.Filters;
using Microsoft.AspNetCore.Mvc.ModelBinding;
using Microsoft.AspNetCore.Mvc.ViewFeatures;

namespace WebApp.Filters {
    public class RangeExceptionAttribute : ExceptionFilterAttribute {

        public override void OnException(ExceptionContext context) {
            if (context.Exception is ArgumentOutOfRangeException) {
                context.Result = new ViewResult() {
                    ViewName = "/Views/Shared/Message.cshtml",
                    ViewData = new ViewDataDictionary(
                        new EmptyModelMetadataProvider(),
                        new ModelStateDictionary()) {
                        Model = @"The data received by the
                                application cannot be processed"
                    }
                };
            }
        }
```

```
            }
        }
    }
```

This filter uses the `ExceptionContext` object to get the type of the unhandled exception and, if the type is `ArgumentOutOfRangeException`, creates an action result that displays a message to the user. Listing 30.32 adds an action method to the `Home` controller to which I have applied the exception filter.

Listing 30.32   Applying an exception filter in the Controllers/HomeController.cs file

```
using Microsoft.AspNetCore.Mvc;
using WebApp.Filters;
using Microsoft.AspNetCore.Mvc.Filters;

namespace WebApp.Controllers {

    [HttpsOnly]
    [ResultDiagnostics]
    public class HomeController : Controller {

        public IActionResult Index() {
            return View("Message",
                "This is the Index action on the Home controller");
        }

        public IActionResult Secure() {
            return View("Message",
                "This is the Secure action on the Home controller");
        }

        //[ChangeArg]
        public IActionResult Messages(string message1,
                string message2 = "None") {
            return View("Message", $"{message1}, {message2}");
        }

        public override void OnActionExecuting(
                ActionExecutingContext context) {
            if (context.ActionArguments.ContainsKey("message1")) {
                context.ActionArguments["message1"] = "New message";
            }
        }

        [RangeException]
        public ViewResult GenerateException(int? id) {
            if (id == null) {
                throw new ArgumentNullException(nameof(id));
            } else if (id > 10) {
                throw new ArgumentOutOfRangeException(nameof(id));
            } else {
                return View("Message", $"The value is {id}");
            }
        }
    }
}
```

The `GenerateException` action method relies on the default routing pattern to receive a nullable `int` value from the request URL. The action method throws an `ArgumentNullException` if there is no matching URL segment and throws an `ArgumentOutOfRangeException` if its value is greater than 10. If there is a value and it is in range, then the action method returns a `ViewResult`.

Restart ASP.NET Core and request https://localhost:44350/Home/Generate-Exception/100. The final segment will exceed the range expected by the action method, which will throw the exception type that is handled by the filter, producing the result shown in figure 30.11. If you request /Home/GenerateException, then the exception thrown by the action method won't be handled by the filter, and the default error handling will be used.

Figure 30.11   Using an exception filter

30.5   *Managing the filter lifecycle*

By default, ASP.NET Core manages the filter objects it creates and will reuse them for subsequent requests. This isn't always the desired behavior, and in the sections that follow, I describe different ways to take control of how filters are created. To create a filter that will show the lifecycle, add a class file called `GuidResponseAttribute.cs` to the `Filters` folder, and use it to define the filter shown in listing 30.33.

Listing 30.33   The contents of the GuidResponseAttribute.cs file in the Filters folder

```
using Microsoft.AspNetCore.Mvc;
using Microsoft.AspNetCore.Mvc.Filters;
using Microsoft.AspNetCore.Mvc.ModelBinding;
using Microsoft.AspNetCore.Mvc.ViewFeatures;

namespace WebApp.Filters {

    [AttributeUsage(AttributeTargets.Method | AttributeTargets.Class,
        AllowMultiple = true)]
    public class GuidResponseAttribute
            : Attribute, IAsyncAlwaysRunResultFilter {
        private int counter = 0;
        private string guid = Guid.NewGuid().ToString();

        public async Task OnResultExecutionAsync(
            ResultExecutingContext context,
```

```
                    ResultExecutionDelegate next) {

                Dictionary<string, string> resultData;
                if (context.Result is ViewResult vr
                        && vr.ViewData.Model is Dictionary<string, string> data) {
                    resultData = data;
                } else {
                    resultData = new Dictionary<string, string>();
                    context.Result = new ViewResult() {
                        ViewName = "/Views/Shared/Message.cshtml",
                        ViewData = new ViewDataDictionary(
                                        new EmptyModelMetadataProvider(),
                                        new ModelStateDictionary()) {
                            Model = resultData
                        }
                    };
                }
                while (resultData.ContainsKey($"Counter_{counter}")) {
                    counter++;
                }
                resultData[$"Counter_{counter}"] = guid;
                await next();
            }
        }
    }
```

This result filter replaces the action result produced by the endpoint with one that will render the `Message` view and display a unique GUID value. The filter is configured so that it can be applied more than once to the same target and will add a new message if a filter earlier in the pipeline has created a suitable result. Listing 30.34 applies the filter twice to the `Home` controller. (I have also removed all but one of the action methods for brevity.)

Listing 30.34   Applying a filter in the HomeController.cs file in the Controllers folder

```
using Microsoft.AspNetCore.Mvc;
using WebApp.Filters;

namespace WebApp.Controllers {

    [HttpsOnly]
    [ResultDiagnostics]
    [GuidResponse]
    [GuidResponse]
    public class HomeController : Controller {

        public IActionResult Index() {
            return View("Message",
                "This is the Index action on the Home controller");
        }
    }
}
```

To confirm that the filter is being reused, restart ASP.NET Core and request https://
localhost:44350/?diag. The response will contain GUID values from the two `Guid-`
`Response` filter attributes. Two instances of the filter have been created to handle the
request. Reload the browser, and you will see the same GUID values displayed, indicating that the filter objects created to handle the first request have been reused (Figure
30.12).

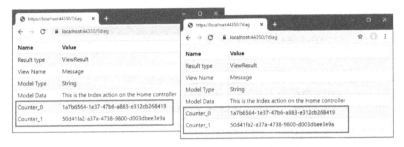

Figure 30.12 Demonstrating filter reuse

30.5.1 Creating filter factories

Filters can implement the `IFilterFactory` interface to take responsibility for creating instances of filters and specify whether those instances can be reused. The
`IFilterFactory` interface defines the members described in table 30.16.

Table 30.16 The IFilterFactory members

Name	Description
`IsReusable`	This `bool` property indicates whether instances of the filter can be reused.
`CreateInstance(serviceProvider)`	This method is invoked to create new instances of the filter and is provided with an `IServiceProvider` object.

Listing 30.35 implements the `IFilterFactory` interface and returns `false` for the
`IsReusable` property, which prevents the filter from being reused.

Listing 30.35 Implementing an interface in the Filters/GuidResponseAttribute.cs file

```
using Microsoft.AspNetCore.Mvc;
using Microsoft.AspNetCore.Mvc.Filters;
using Microsoft.AspNetCore.Mvc.ModelBinding;
using Microsoft.AspNetCore.Mvc.ViewFeatures;

namespace WebApp.Filters {

    [AttributeUsage(AttributeTargets.Method | AttributeTargets.Class,
        AllowMultiple = true)]
```

```
public class GuidResponseAttribute : Attribute,
        IAsyncAlwaysRunResultFilter, IFilterFactory {
    private int counter = 0;
    private string guid = Guid.NewGuid().ToString();

    public bool IsReusable => false;

    public IFilterMetadata CreateInstance(
            IServiceProvider serviceProvider) {
        return ActivatorUtilities
            .GetServiceOrCreateInstance
                <GuidResponseAttribute>(serviceProvider);
    }

    public async Task OnResultExecutionAsync(
            ResultExecutingContext context,
            ResultExecutionDelegate next) {

        Dictionary<string, string> resultData;
        if (context.Result is ViewResult vr
            && vr.ViewData.Model is Dictionary<string, string> data) {
            resultData = data;
        } else {
            resultData = new Dictionary<string, string>();
            context.Result = new ViewResult() {
                ViewName = "/Views/Shared/Message.cshtml",
                ViewData = new ViewDataDictionary(
                                new EmptyModelMetadataProvider(),
                                new ModelStateDictionary()) {
                    Model = resultData
                }
            };
        }
        while (resultData.ContainsKey($"Counter_{counter}")) {
            counter++;
        }
        resultData[$"Counter_{counter}"] = guid;
        await next();
    }
}
```

I create new filter objects using the `GetServiceOrCreateInstance` method, defined by the `ActivatorUtilities` class in the `Microsoft.Extensions.Dependency-Injection` namespace. Although you can use the `new` keyword to create a filter, this approach will resolve any dependencies on services that are declared through the filter's constructor.

To see the effect of implementing the `IFilterFactory` interface, restart ASP.NET Core and request https://localhost:44350/?diag. Reload the browser, and each time the request is handled, new filters will be created, and new GUIDs will be displayed, as shown in figure 30.13.

Figure 30.13 Preventing filter reuse

30.5.2 Using dependency injection scopes to manage filter lifecycles

Filters can be registered as services, which allows their lifecycle to be controlled through dependency injection, which I described in chapter 14. Listing 30.36 registers the `GuidResponse` filter as a scoped service.

> **Listing 30.36 Creating a filter service in the Program.cs file in the WebApp folder**

```
using Microsoft.EntityFrameworkCore;
using WebApp.Models;
using WebApp.Filters;

var builder = WebApplication.CreateBuilder(args);

builder.Services.AddDbContext<DataContext>(opts => {
    opts.UseSqlServer(builder.Configuration[
        "ConnectionStrings:ProductConnection"]);
    opts.EnableSensitiveDataLogging(true);
});
builder.Services.AddControllersWithViews();
builder.Services.AddRazorPages();

builder.Services.AddScoped<GuidResponseAttribute>();

var app = builder.Build();

app.UseStaticFiles();
app.MapDefaultControllerRoute();
app.MapRazorPages();

var context = app.Services.CreateScope().ServiceProvider
    .GetRequiredService<DataContext>();
SeedData.SeedDatabase(context);

app.Run();
```

By default, ASP.NET Core creates a scope for each request, which means that a single instance of the filter will be created for each request. To see the effect, restart ASP.NET Core and request https://localhost:44350/?diag. Both attributes applied to the Home controller are processed using the same instance of the filter, which means that both

GUIDs in the response are the same. Reload the browser; a new scope will be created, and a new filter object will be used, as shown in figure 30.14.

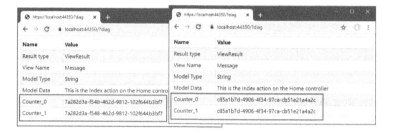

Figure 30.14   Using dependency injection to manage filters

Using filters as services without the IFilterFactory interface

The change in lifecycle took effect immediately in this example because I used the `ActivatorUtilities.GetServiceOrCreateInstance` method to create the filter object when I implemented the `IFilterFactory` interface. This method will check to see whether there is a service available for the requested type before invoking its constructor. If you want to use filters as services without implementing `IFilterFactory` and using `ActivatorUtilities`, you can apply the filter using the `ServiceFilter` attribute, like this:

```
...
[ServiceFilter(typeof(GuidResponseAttribute))]
...
```

ASP.NET Core will create the filter object from the service and apply it to the request. Filters that are applied in this way do not have to be derived from the `Attribute` class.

30.6 Creating global filters

Global filters are applied to every request that ASP.NET Core handles, which means they don't have to be applied to individual controllers or Razor Pages. Any filter can be used as a global filter; however, action filters will be applied to requests only where the endpoint is an action method, and page filters will be applied to requests only where the endpoint is a Razor Page.

Global filters are set up using the options pattern in the `Program.cs` file, as shown in listing 30.37.

Listing 30.37   Creating a global filter in the Program.cs file in the WebApp folder

```
using Microsoft.EntityFrameworkCore;
using WebApp.Models;
using WebApp.Filters;
```

```
using Microsoft.AspNetCore.Mvc;

var builder = WebApplication.CreateBuilder(args);

builder.Services.AddDbContext<DataContext>(opts => {
    opts.UseSqlServer(builder.Configuration[
        "ConnectionStrings:ProductConnection"]);
    opts.EnableSensitiveDataLogging(true);
});
builder.Services.AddControllersWithViews();
builder.Services.AddRazorPages();

builder.Services.AddScoped<GuidResponseAttribute>();
builder.Services.Configure<MvcOptions>(opts =>
    opts.Filters.Add<HttpsOnlyAttribute>());

var app = builder.Build();

app.UseStaticFiles();
app.MapDefaultControllerRoute();
app.MapRazorPages();

var context = app.Services.CreateScope().ServiceProvider
    .GetRequiredService<DataContext>();
SeedData.SeedDatabase(context);

app.Run();
```

The `MvcOptions.Filters` property returns a collection to which filters are added to apply them globally, either using the `Add<T>` method or using the `AddService<T>` method for filters that are also services. There is also an `Add` method without a generic type argument that can be used to register a specific object as a global filter.

The statement in listing 30.37 registers the `HttpsOnly` filter I created earlier in the chapter, which means that it no longer needs to be applied directly to individual controllers or Razor Pages, so listing 30.38 removes the filter from the `Home` controller.

NOTE Notice that I have disabled the `GuidResponse` filter in listing 30.38. This is an always-run result filter and will replace the result generated by the global filter.

Listing 30.38 Removing a filter in the HomeController.cs file in the Controllers folder

```
using Microsoft.AspNetCore.Mvc;
using WebApp.Filters;

namespace WebApp.Controllers {

    //[HttpsOnly]
    [ResultDiagnostics]
    //[GuidResponse]
    //[GuidResponse]
    public class HomeController : Controller {
```

```
        public IActionResult Index() {
            return View("Message",
                "This is the Index action on the Home controller");
        }
    }
}
```

Restart ASP.NET Core and request http://localhost:5000 to confirm that the HTTPS-only policy is being applied even though the attribute is no longer used to decorate the controller. The global authorization filter will short-circuit the filter pipeline and produce the response shown in figure 30.15.

**Figure 30.15
Using a global
filter**

30.7   *Understanding and changing filter order*

Filters run in a specific sequence: authorization, resource, action, or page, and then result. But if there are multiple filters of a given type, then the order in which they are applied is driven by the scope through which the filters have been applied.

To demonstrate how this works, add a class file named `MessageAttribute.cs` to the `Filters` folder and use it to define the filter shown in listing 30.39.

Listing 30.39   The contents of the MessageAttribute.cs file in the Filters folder

```
using Microsoft.AspNetCore.Mvc;
using Microsoft.AspNetCore.Mvc.Filters;
using Microsoft.AspNetCore.Mvc.ModelBinding;
using Microsoft.AspNetCore.Mvc.ViewFeatures;

namespace WebApp.Filters {

    [AttributeUsage(AttributeTargets.Method | AttributeTargets.Class,
        AllowMultiple = true)]
    public class MessageAttribute
            : Attribute, IAsyncAlwaysRunResultFilter {
        private int counter = 0;
        private string msg;

        public MessageAttribute(string message) => msg = message;

        public async Task OnResultExecutionAsync(
                ResultExecutingContext context,
```

```
            ResultExecutionDelegate next) {
        Dictionary<string, string> resultData;
        if (context.Result is ViewResult vr
            && vr.ViewData.Model is Dictionary<string, string> data) {
            resultData = data;
        } else {
            resultData = new Dictionary<string, string>();
            context.Result = new ViewResult() {
                ViewName = "/Views/Shared/Message.cshtml",
                ViewData = new ViewDataDictionary(
                                    new EmptyModelMetadataProvider(),
                                    new ModelStateDictionary()) {
                    Model = resultData
                }
            };
        }
        while (resultData.ContainsKey($"Message_{counter}")) {
            counter++;
        }
        resultData[$"Message_{counter}"] = msg;
        await next();
    }
}
}
```

This result filter uses techniques shown in earlier examples to replace the result from the endpoint and allows multiple filters to build up a series of messages that will be displayed to the user. Listing 30.40 applies several instances of the `Message` filter to the `Home` controller.

Listing 30.40   Applying a filter in the HomeController.cs file in the Controllers folder

```
using Microsoft.AspNetCore.Mvc;
using WebApp.Filters;

namespace WebApp.Controllers {

    [Message("This is the controller-scoped filter")]
    public class HomeController : Controller {

        [Message("This is the first action-scoped filter")]
        [Message("This is the second action-scoped filter")]
        public IActionResult Index() {
            return View("Message",
                "This is the Index action on the Home controller");
        }
    }
}
```

Listing 30.41 registers the `Message` filter globally.

Listing 30.41   Creating a global filter in the Program.cs file in the WebApp folder

```
using Microsoft.EntityFrameworkCore;
using WebApp.Models;
using WebApp.Filters;
using Microsoft.AspNetCore.Mvc;

var builder = WebApplication.CreateBuilder(args);

builder.Services.AddDbContext<DataContext>(opts => {
    opts.UseSqlServer(builder.Configuration[
        "ConnectionStrings:ProductConnection"]);
    opts.EnableSensitiveDataLogging(true);
});
builder.Services.AddControllersWithViews();
builder.Services.AddRazorPages();

builder.Services.AddScoped<GuidResponseAttribute>();
builder.Services.Configure<MvcOptions>(opts => {
    opts.Filters.Add<HttpsOnlyAttribute>();
    opts.Filters.Add(new MessageAttribute(
        "This is the globally-scoped filter"));
});

var app = builder.Build();

app.UseStaticFiles();
app.MapDefaultControllerRoute();
app.MapRazorPages();

var context = app.Services.CreateScope().ServiceProvider
    .GetRequiredService<DataContext>();
SeedData.SeedDatabase(context);

app.Run();
```

There are four instances of the same filter. To see the order in which they are applied, restart ASP.NET Core and request https://localhost:44350, which will produce the response shown in figure 30.16.

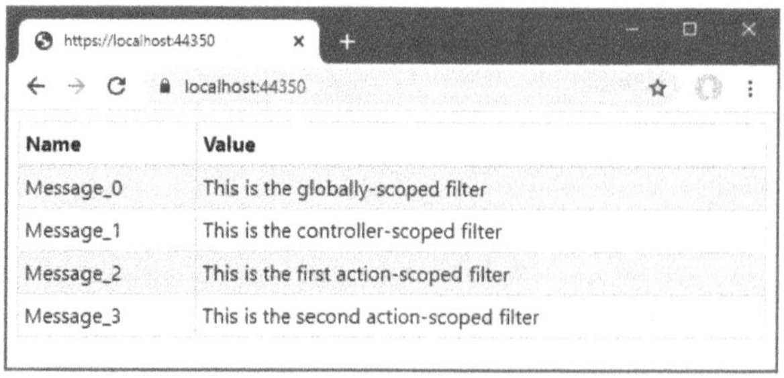

**Figure 30.16
Applying the
same filter in
different scopes**

Name	Value
Message_0	This is the globally-scoped filter
Message_1	This is the controller-scoped filter
Message_2	This is the first action-scoped filter
Message_3	This is the second action-scoped filter

By default, ASP.NET Core runs global filters, then filters applied to controllers or page model classes, and finally filters applied to action or handler methods.

The default order can be changed by implementing the `IOrderedFilter` interface, which ASP.NET Core looks for when it is working out how to sequence filters. Here is the definition of the interface:

```
namespace Microsoft.AspNetCore.Mvc.Filters {

    public interface IOrderedFilter : IFilterMetadata {
        int Order { get; }
    }
}
```

The `Order` property returns an `int` value, and filters with low values are applied before those with higher `Order` values. In listing 30.42, I have implemented the interface in the `Message` filter and defined a constructor argument that will allow the value for the `Order` property to be specified when the filter is applied.

> **Listing 30.42 Adding ordering in the MessageAttribute.cs file in the Filters folder**

```
using Microsoft.AspNetCore.Mvc;
using Microsoft.AspNetCore.Mvc.Filters;
using Microsoft.AspNetCore.Mvc.ModelBinding;
using Microsoft.AspNetCore.Mvc.ViewFeatures;

namespace WebApp.Filters {

    [AttributeUsage(AttributeTargets.Method | AttributeTargets.Class,
        AllowMultiple = true)]
    public class MessageAttribute : Attribute,
            IAsyncAlwaysRunResultFilter,
            IOrderedFilter {

        private int counter = 0;
        private string msg;

        public MessageAttribute(string message) => msg = message;

        public int Order { get; set; }

        public async Task OnResultExecutionAsync(
                ResultExecutingContext context,
                ResultExecutionDelegate next) {
            Dictionary<string, string> resultData;
            if (context.Result is ViewResult vr
                && vr.ViewData.Model is Dictionary<string, string> data) {
                resultData = data;
            } else {
                resultData = new Dictionary<string, string>();
                context.Result = new ViewResult() {
                    ViewName = "/Views/Shared/Message.cshtml",
                    ViewData = new ViewDataDictionary(
                                    new EmptyModelMetadataProvider(),
                                    new ModelStateDictionary()) {
                        Model = resultData
                }
```

```
            };
        }
        while (resultData.ContainsKey($"Message_{counter}")) {
            counter++;
        }
        resultData[$"Message_{counter}"] = msg;
        await next();
    }
}
```

In listing 30.43, I have used the constructor argument to change the order in which the filters are applied.

Listing 30.43　Setting filter order in the HomeController.cs file in the Controllers folder

```
using Microsoft.AspNetCore.Mvc;
using WebApp.Filters;

namespace WebApp.Controllers {

    [Message("This is the controller-scoped filter", Order = 10)]
    public class HomeController : Controller {

        [Message("This is the first action-scoped filter", Order = 1)]
        [Message("This is the second action-scoped filter", Order = -1)]
        public IActionResult Index() {
            return View("Message",
                "This is the Index action on the Home controller");
        }
    }
}
```

Order values can be negative, which is a helpful way of ensuring that a filter is applied before any global filters with the default order (although you can also set the order when creating global filters, too). Restart ASP.NET Core and request https://localhost:44350 to see the new filter order, which is shown in figure 30.17.

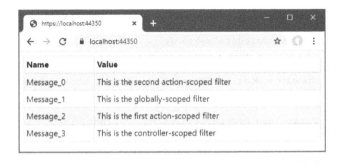

Figure 30.17 Changing filter order

Summary

- Filters allow request processing logic to be defined in a class where it can be applied to specific endpoints and easily reused.
- Filters have a well-defined lifecycle and can be used to perform the same tasks as middleware components.
- There are six types of filters: authorization, resource, action, page, result, and exception.
- Authorization filters are used to implement a security policy.
- Resource filters are executed before the model-binding process.
- Action and page filters are executed after the model-binding process.
- Result filters are executed before and after a result is used to generate a response.
- Exception filters are executed when an exception is thrown.

Creating form applications

31

This chapter covers

- Using ASP.NET Core form features with Entity Framework Core to create, read, update, and delete data
- Managing the use of related data in Entity Framework Core results

The previous chapters have focused on individual features that deal with one aspect of HTML forms, and it can sometimes be difficult to see how they fit together to perform common tasks. In this chapter, I go through the process of creating controllers, views, and Razor Pages that support an application with create, read, update, and delete (CRUD) functionality. There are no new features described in this chapter, and the objective is to demonstrate how features such as tag helpers, model binding, and model validation can be used in conjunction with Entity Framework Core.

31.1 Preparing for this chapter

This chapter uses the WebApp project from chapter 30. To prepare for this chapter, replace the contents of the `HomeController.cs` file in the `Controllers` folder with those shown in listing 31.1.

TIP You can download the example project for this chapter—and for all the other chapters in this book—from https://github.com/manningbooks/pro-asp .net-core-7. See chapter 1 for how to get help if you have problems running the examples.

Listing 31.1 The contents of the HomeController.cs file in the Controllers folder

```
using Microsoft.AspNetCore.Mvc;
using Microsoft.EntityFrameworkCore;
using WebApp.Models;

namespace WebApp.Controllers {

    [AutoValidateAntiforgeryToken]
    public class HomeController : Controller {
        private DataContext context;

        private IEnumerable<Category> Categories => context.Categories;
        private IEnumerable<Supplier> Suppliers => context.Suppliers;

        public HomeController(DataContext data) {
            context = data;
        }

        public IActionResult Index() {
            return View(context.Products.
                Include(p => p.Category).Include(p => p.Supplier));
        }
    }
}
```

Create the `Views/Home` folder and add to it a Razor View file named `Index.cshtml` files, with the content shown in listing 31.2.

Listing 31.2 The contents of the Index.cshtml file in the Views/Home folder

```
@model IEnumerable<Product>
@{
    Layout = "_SimpleLayout";
}

<h4 class="bg-primary text-white text-center p-2">Products</h4>
<table class="table table-sm table-bordered table-striped">
    <thead>
        <tr>
            <th>ID</th>
            <th>Name</th>
            <th>Price</th>
            <th>Category</th>
            <th></th>
        </tr>
    </thead>
    <tbody>
        @foreach (Product p in Model ?? Enumerable.Empty<Product>()) {
```

```
            <tr>
                <td>@p.ProductId</td>
                <td>@p.Name</td>
                <td>@p.Price</td>
                <td>@p.Category?.Name</td>
                <td class="text-center">
                    <a asp-action="Details" asp-route-id="@p.ProductId"
                            class="btn btn-sm btn-info">
                        Details
                    </a>
                    <a asp-action="Edit" asp-route-id="@p.ProductId"
                            class="btn btn-sm btn-warning">
                        Edit
                    </a>
                    <a asp-action="Delete" asp-route-id="@p.ProductId"
                            class="btn btn-sm btn-danger">
                        Delete
                    </a>
                </td>
            </tr>
        }
    </tbody>
</table>
<a asp-action="Create" class="btn btn-primary">Create</a>
```

Next, update the `Product` class as shown in listing 31.3 to change the validation constraints to remove the model-level checking and disable remote validation.

Listing 31.3   Changing validation in the Product.cs file in the Models folder

```
using System.ComponentModel.DataAnnotations;
using System.ComponentModel.DataAnnotations.Schema;
using System.Text.Json.Serialization;
using Microsoft.AspNetCore.Mvc.ModelBinding;
using WebApp.Validation;
using Microsoft.AspNetCore.Mvc;

namespace WebApp.Models {

    //[PhraseAndPrice(Phrase = "Small", Price = "100")]
    public class Product {

        public long ProductId { get; set; }

        [Required(ErrorMessage = "Please enter a name")]
        public required string Name { get; set; }

        [Range(1, 999999, ErrorMessage = "Please enter a positive price")]
        [Column(TypeName = "decimal(8, 2)")]
        public decimal Price { get; set; }

        [PrimaryKey(ContextType = typeof(DataContext),
            DataType = typeof(Category))]
        //[Remote("CategoryKey", "Validation",
        //    ErrorMessage = "Enter an existing key")]
```

```
        public long CategoryId { get; set; }
        public Category? Category { get; set; }

        [PrimaryKey(ContextType = typeof(DataContext),
            DataType = typeof(Supplier))]
        //[Remote("SupplierKey", "Validation",
        //    ErrorMessage = "Enter an existing key")]
        public long SupplierId { get; set; }

        [JsonIgnore(Condition = JsonIgnoreCondition.WhenWritingNull)]
        public Supplier? Supplier { get; set; }
    }
}
```

Finally, disable the global filters in the `Program.cs` file, as shown in listing 31.4. This listing also defines a route that makes it obvious when a URL targets a controller.

> **Listing 31.4 Disabling filters in the Program.cs file in the WebApp folder**

```
using Microsoft.EntityFrameworkCore;
using WebApp.Models;
using WebApp.Filters;
//using Microsoft.AspNetCore.Mvc;

var builder = WebApplication.CreateBuilder(args);

builder.Services.AddDbContext<DataContext>(opts => {
    opts.UseSqlServer(builder.Configuration[
        "ConnectionStrings:ProductConnection"]);
    opts.EnableSensitiveDataLogging(true);
});
builder.Services.AddControllersWithViews();
builder.Services.AddRazorPages();

builder.Services.AddScoped<GuidResponseAttribute>();
//builder.Services.Configure<MvcOptions>(opts => {
//    opts.Filters.Add<HttpsOnlyAttribute>();
//    opts.Filters.Add(new MessageAttribute(
//        "This is the globally-scoped filter"));
//});

var app = builder.Build();

app.UseStaticFiles();
app.MapDefaultControllerRoute();
app.MapControllerRoute("forms",
    "controllers/{controller=Home}/{action=Index}/{id?}");
app.MapRazorPages();

var context = app.Services.CreateScope().ServiceProvider
    .GetRequiredService<DataContext>();
SeedData.SeedDatabase(context);

app.Run();
```

31.1.1 Dropping the database

Open a new PowerShell command prompt, navigate to the folder that contains the `WebApp.csproj` file, and run the command shown in listing 31.5 to drop the database.

Listing 31.5   Dropping the database

```
dotnet ef database drop --force
```

31.1.2 Running the example application

Use the PowerShell command prompt to run the command shown in listing 31.6.

Listing 31.6   Running the example application

```
dotnet run
```

Use a browser to request http://localhost:5000/controllers, which will display a list of products, as shown in figure 31.1. There are anchor elements styled to appear as buttons, but these will not work until later when I add the features to create, edit, and delete objects.

Figure 31.1
Running the example application

31.2   Creating an MVC forms application

In the sections that follow, I show you how to perform the core data operations using MVC controllers and views. Later in the chapter, I create the same functionality using Razor Pages.

31.2.1 Preparing the view model and the view

I am going to define a single form that will be used for multiple operations, configured through its view model class. To create the view model class, add a class file named `ProductViewModel.cs` to the `Models` folder and add the code shown in listing 31.7.

```
namespace WebApp.Models {

    public class ProductViewModel {
        public Product Product { get; set; }
            = new () { Name = string.Empty };

        public string Action { get; set; } = "Create";

        public bool ReadOnly { get; set; } = false;

        public string Theme { get; set; } = "primary";

        public bool ShowAction { get; set; } = true;

        public IEnumerable<Category> Categories { get; set; }
            = Enumerable.Empty<Category>();

        public IEnumerable<Supplier> Suppliers { get; set; }
            = Enumerable.Empty<Supplier>();
    }
}
```

This class will allow the controller to pass data and display settings to its view. The `Product` property provides the data to display, and the `Categories` and `Suppliers` properties provide access to the `Category` and `Suppliers` objects when they are required. The other properties configure aspects of how the content is presented to the user: the `Action` property specifies the name of the action method for the current task, the `ReadOnly` property specifies whether the user can edit the data, the `Theme` property specifies the Bootstrap theme for the content, and the `ShowAction` property is used to control the visibility of the button that submits the form.

To create the view that will allow the user to interact with the application's data, add a Razor View named `ProductEditor.cshtml` to the `Views/Home` folder with the content shown in listing 31.8.

```
@model ProductViewModel
@{
    Layout = "_SimpleLayout";
}

<partial name="_Validation" />

<h5 class="bg-@Model?.Theme text-white text-center p-2">
    @Model?.Action
</h5>

<form asp-action="@Model?.Action" method="post">
    <div class="form-group">
        <label asp-for="Product.ProductId"></label>
        <input class="form-control"
```

```
                    asp-for="Product.ProductId" readonly />
    </div>
    <div class="form-group">
        <label asp-for="Product.Name"></label>
        <div>
            <span asp-validation-for="Product.Name" class="text-danger">
            </span>
        </div>
        <input class="form-control" asp-for="Product.Name"
            readonly="@Model?.ReadOnly" />
    </div>
    <div class="form-group">
        <label asp-for="Product.Price"></label>
        <div>
            <span asp-validation-for="Product.Price" class="text-danger">
            </span>
        </div>
        <input class="form-control" asp-for="Product.Price"
            readonly="@Model?.ReadOnly" />
    </div>
    <div class="form-group">
        <label asp-for="Product.CategoryId">Category</label>
        <div>
            <span asp-validation-for="Product.CategoryId"
                class="text-danger"></span>
        </div>
        <select asp-for="Product.CategoryId" class="form-control"
            disabled="@Model?.ReadOnly"
            asp-items="@(new SelectList(Model?.Categories,
                "CategoryId", "Name"))">
            <option value="" disabled selected>Choose a Category</option>
        </select>
    </div>
    <div class="form-group">
        <label asp-for="Product.SupplierId">Supplier</label>
        <div>
            <span asp-validation-for="Product.SupplierId"
                class="text-danger"></span>
        </div>
        <select asp-for="Product.SupplierId" class="form-control"
            disabled="@Model?.ReadOnly"
            asp-items="@(new SelectList(Model?.Suppliers,
                "SupplierId", "Name"))">
            <option value="" disabled selected>Choose a Supplier</option>
        </select>
    </div>
    @if (Model?.ShowAction == true) {
        <button class="btn btn-@Model?.Theme mt-2" type="submit">
            @Model?.Action
        </button>
    }
    <a class="btn btn-secondary mt-2" asp-action="Index">Back</a>
</form>
```

This view can look complicated, but it combines only the features you have seen in earlier chapters and will become clearer once you see it in action. The model for this view is a `ProductViewModel` object, which provides both the data that is displayed to the user and some direction about how that data should be presented.

For each of the properties defined by the `Product` class, the view contains a set of elements: a `label` element that describes the property, an `input` or `select` element that allows the value to be edited, and a `span` element that will display validation messages. Each of the elements is configured with the `asp-for` attribute, which ensures tag helpers will transform the elements for each property. There are `div` elements to define the view structure, and all the elements are members of Bootstrap CSS classes to style the form.

31.2.2 Reading data

The simplest operation is reading data from the database and presenting it to the user. In most applications, this will allow the user to see additional details that are not present in the list view. Each task performed by the application will require a different set of `ProductViewModel` properties. To manage these combinations, add a class file named `ViewModelFactory.cs` to the `Models` folder with the code shown in listing 31.9.

Listing 31.9 The contents of the ViewModelFactory.cs file in the Models folder

```
namespace WebApp.Models {

    public static class ViewModelFactory {

        public static ProductViewModel Details(Product p) {
            return new ProductViewModel {
                Product = p, Action = "Details",
                ReadOnly = true, Theme = "info", ShowAction = false,
                Categories = p == null || p.Category == null
                    ? Enumerable.Empty<Category>()
                    : new List<Category> { p.Category },
                Suppliers = p == null || p.Supplier == null
                    ? Enumerable.Empty<Supplier>()
                    : new List<Supplier> { p.Supplier },
            };
        }
    }
}
```

The `Details` method produces a `ProductViewModel` object configured for viewing an object. When the user views the details, the category and supplier details will be read-only, which means that I need to provide only the current category and supplier information.

Next, add an action method to the `Home` controller that uses the `ViewModel-Factory.Details` method to create a `ProductViewModel` object and display it to the user with the `ProductEditor` view, as shown in listing 31.10.

Listing 31.10   Adding an action in the HomeController.cs file in the Controllers folder

```
using Microsoft.AspNetCore.Mvc;
using Microsoft.EntityFrameworkCore;
using WebApp.Models;

namespace WebApp.Controllers {

    [AutoValidateAntiforgeryToken]
    public class HomeController : Controller {
        private DataContext context;

        private IEnumerable<Category> Categories => context.Categories;
        private IEnumerable<Supplier> Suppliers => context.Suppliers;

        public HomeController(DataContext data) {
            context = data;
        }

        public IActionResult Index() {
            return View(context.Products.
                Include(p => p.Category).Include(p => p.Supplier));
        }

        public async Task<IActionResult> Details(long id) {
            Product? p = await context.Products.
                Include(p => p.Category).Include(p => p.Supplier)
                .FirstOrDefaultAsync(p => p.ProductId == id)
                    ?? new () { Name = string.Empty };
            ProductViewModel model = ViewModelFactory.Details(p);
            return View("ProductEditor", model);
        }
    }
}
```

The action method uses the id parameter, which will be model bound from the routing data, to query the database and passes the Product object to the ViewModel-
Factory.Details method. Most of the operations are going to require the Category
and Supplier data, so I have added properties that provide direct access to the data.

To test the details feature, restart ASP.NET Core and request http://localhost:5000/
controllers. Click one of the Details buttons, and you will see the selected object presented in read-only form using the ProductEditor view, as shown in figure 31.2.

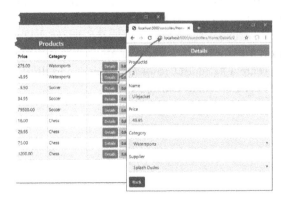

Figure 31.2
Viewing data

If the user navigates to a URL that doesn't correspond to an object in the database, such as http://localhost:5000/controllers/Home/Details/100, for example, then an empty form will be displayed.

31.2.3 *Creating data*

Creating data relies on model binding to get the form data from the request and relies on validation to ensure the data can be stored in the database. The first step is to add a factory method that will create the view model object for creating data, as shown in listing 31.11.

> **Listing 31.11 Adding a method in the ViewModelFactory.cs file in the Models folder**

```
namespace WebApp.Models {

    public static class ViewModelFactory {

        public static ProductViewModel Details(Product p) {
            return new ProductViewModel {
                Product = p, Action = "Details",
                ReadOnly = true, Theme = "info", ShowAction = false,
                Categories = p == null || p.Category == null
                    ? Enumerable.Empty<Category>()
                    : new List<Category> { p.Category },
                Suppliers = p == null || p.Supplier == null
                    ? Enumerable.Empty<Supplier>()
                    : new List<Supplier> { p.Supplier },
            };
        }

        public static ProductViewModel Create(Product product,
                IEnumerable<Category> categories,
                IEnumerable<Supplier> suppliers) {
            return new ProductViewModel {
                Product = product, Categories = categories,
                Suppliers = suppliers
            };
        }
    }
}
```

The defaults I used for the `ProductViewModel` properties were set for creating data, so the `Create` method in listing 31.11 sets only the `Product`, `Categories`, and `Suppliers` properties. Listing 31.12 adds the action methods that will create data to the `Home` controller.

> **Listing 31.12 Adding actions in the HomeController.cs file in the Controllers folder**

```
using Microsoft.AspNetCore.Mvc;
using Microsoft.EntityFrameworkCore;
using WebApp.Models;

namespace WebApp.Controllers {
```

```
[AutoValidateAntiforgeryToken]
public class HomeController : Controller {
    private DataContext context;

    private IEnumerable<Category> Categories => context.Categories;
    private IEnumerable<Supplier> Suppliers => context.Suppliers;

    public HomeController(DataContext data) {
        context = data;
    }

    public IActionResult Index() {
        return View(context.Products.
            Include(p => p.Category).Include(p => p.Supplier));
    }

    public async Task<IActionResult> Details(long id) {
        Product? p = await context.Products.
            Include(p => p.Category).Include(p => p.Supplier)
            .FirstOrDefaultAsync(p => p.ProductId == id)
                ?? new () { Name = string.Empty };
        ProductViewModel model = ViewModelFactory.Details(p);
        return View("ProductEditor", model);
    }

    public IActionResult Create() {
        return View("ProductEditor",
            ViewModelFactory.Create(new () { Name = string.Empty },
                Categories, Suppliers));
    }

    [HttpPost]
    public async Task<IActionResult> Create(
            [FromForm] Product product) {
        if (ModelState.IsValid) {
            product.ProductId = default;
            product.Category = default;
            product.Supplier = default;
            context.Products.Add(product);
            await context.SaveChangesAsync();
            return RedirectToAction(nameof(Index));
        }
        return View("ProductEditor",
            ViewModelFactory.Create(product, Categories, Suppliers));
    }
}
```

There are two Create methods, which are differentiated by the HttpPost attribute and method parameters. HTTP GET requests will be handled by the first method, which selects the ProductEditor view and provides it with a ProductViewModel object. When the user submits the form, it will be received by the second method, which relies on model binding to receive the data and model validation to ensure the data is valid.

If the data passes validation, then I prepare the object for storage in the database by resetting three properties, like this:

```
...
product.ProductId = default;
product.Category = default;
product.Supplier = default;
...
```

Entity Framework Core configures the database so that primary keys are allocated by the database server when new data is stored. If you attempt to store an object and provide a `ProductId` value other than zero, then an exception will be thrown.

I reset the `Category` and `Supplier` properties to prevent Entity Framework Core from trying to deal with related data when storing an object. Entity Framework Core is capable of processing related data, but it can produce unexpected outcomes. (I show you how to create related data in the "Creating New Related Data Objects" section, later in this chapter.)

Notice I call the `View` method with arguments when validation fails, like this:

```
...
return View("ProductEditor",
    ViewModelFactory.Create(product, Categories, Suppliers));
...
```

I do this because the view model object expected by the view isn't the same data type that I have extracted from the request using model binding. Instead, I create a new view model object that incorporates the model bound data and passes this to the `View` method.

Restart ASP.NET Core, request http://localhost:5000/controllers, and click Create. Fill out the form and click the Create button to submit the data. The new object will be stored in the database and displayed when the browser is redirected to the `Index` action, as shown in figure 31.3.

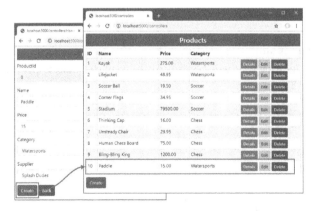

Figure 31.3 Creating a new object

Notice that `select` elements allow the user to select the values for the `CategoryId` and `SupplierId` properties, using the category and supplier names, like this:

```
...
<select asp-for="Product.SupplierId" class="form-control"
        disabled="@Model?.ReadOnly"
        asp-items="@(new SelectList(Model?.Suppliers,
            "SupplierId", "Name"))">
    <option value="" disabled selected>Choose a Supplier</option>
</select>
...
```

In chapter 30, I used `input` elements to allow the value of these properties to be set directly, but that was because I wanted to demonstrate different types of validation. In real applications, it is a good idea to provide the user with restricted choices when the application already has the data it expects the user to choose from. Making the user enter a valid primary key, for example, makes no sense in a real project because the application can easily provide the user with a list of those keys to choose from, as shown in figure 31.4.

> **TIP** I show you different techniques for creating related data in the "Creating new related data objects" section.

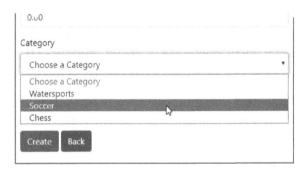

Figure 31.4
Presenting the user with a choice

31.2.4 *Editing data*

The process for editing data is similar to creating data. The first step is to add a new method to the view model factory that will configure the way the data is presented to the user, as shown in listing 31.13.

> **Listing 31.13   Adding a method in the ViewModelFactory.cs file in the Models folder**

```
namespace WebApp.Models {

    public static class ViewModelFactory {

        public static ProductViewModel Details(Product p) {
            return new ProductViewModel {
                Product = p, Action = "Details",
                ReadOnly = true, Theme = "info", ShowAction = false,
                Categories = p == null || p.Category == null
                    ? Enumerable.Empty<Category>()
```

```
                        : new List<Category> { p.Category },
                Suppliers = p == null || p.Supplier == null
                    ? Enumerable.Empty<Supplier>()
                    : new List<Supplier> { p.Supplier },
            };
        }

        public static ProductViewModel Create(Product product,
                IEnumerable<Category> categories,
                IEnumerable<Supplier> suppliers) {
            return new ProductViewModel {
                Product = product, Categories = categories,
                Suppliers = suppliers
            };
        }

        public static ProductViewModel Edit(Product product,
                IEnumerable<Category> categories,
                IEnumerable<Supplier> suppliers) {
            return new ProductViewModel {
                Product = product, Categories = categories,
                Suppliers = suppliers,
                Theme = "warning", Action = "Edit"
            };
        }
    }
}
```

The next step is to add the action methods to the Home controller that will display the current properties of a Product object to the user and receive the changes the user makes, as shown in listing 31.14.

Listing 31.14 Adding action methods in the HomeController.cs file in the Controllers folder

```
using Microsoft.AspNetCore.Mvc;
using Microsoft.EntityFrameworkCore;
using WebApp.Models;

namespace WebApp.Controllers {

    [AutoValidateAntiforgeryToken]
    public class HomeController : Controller {
        private DataContext context;

        private IEnumerable<Category> Categories => context.Categories;
        private IEnumerable<Supplier> Suppliers => context.Suppliers;

        public HomeController(DataContext data) {
            context = data;
        }

        // ...other action methods omitted for brevity...

        public async Task<IActionResult> Edit(long id) {
```

```
        Product? p = await context.Products.FindAsync(id);
        if (p != null) {
            ProductViewModel model =
                ViewModelFactory.Edit(p, Categories, Suppliers);
            return View("ProductEditor", model);
        }
        return NotFound();
    }

    [HttpPost]
    public async Task<IActionResult> Edit(
            [FromForm] Product product) {
        if (ModelState.IsValid) {
            product.Category = default;
            product.Supplier = default;
            context.Products.Update(product);
            await context.SaveChangesAsync();
            return RedirectToAction(nameof(Index));
        }
        return View("ProductEditor",
            ViewModelFactory.Edit(product, Categories, Suppliers));
    }
}
}
```

To see the editing feature at work, restart ASP.NET Core, navigate to http://
localhost:5000/controllers, and click one of the Edit buttons. Change one or more
property values and submit the form. The changes will be stored in the database and
reflected in the list displayed when the browser is redirected to the Index action, as
shown in figure 31.5.

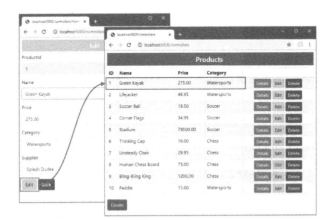

Figure 31.5
Editing a product

Notice that the ProductId property cannot be changed. Attempting to change the
primary key of an object should be avoided because it interferes with the Entity Framework Core understanding of the identity of its objects. If you can't avoid changing the
primary key, then the safest approach is to delete the existing object and store a new
one.

31.2.5 *Deleting data*

The final basic operation is removing objects from the database. By now the pattern will be clear, and the first step is to add a method to create a view model object to determine how the data is presented to the user, as shown in listing 31.15.

Listing 31.15 Adding a method in the ViewModelFactory.cs file in the Models folder

```
namespace WebApp.Models {

    public static class ViewModelFactory {

        // ...other methods omitted for brevity...

        public static ProductViewModel Delete(Product p,
                IEnumerable<Category> categories,
                IEnumerable<Supplier> suppliers) {
            return new ProductViewModel {
                Product = p, Action = "Delete",
                ReadOnly = true, Theme = "danger",
                Categories = categories, Suppliers = suppliers
            };
        }
    }
}
```

Listing 31.16 adds the action methods to the Home controller that will respond to the GET request by displaying the selected object and the POST request to remove that object from the database.

Listing 31.16 Adding action methods in the HomeController.cs file in the Controllers folder

```
using Microsoft.AspNetCore.Mvc;
using Microsoft.EntityFrameworkCore;
using WebApp.Models;

namespace WebApp.Controllers {

    [AutoValidateAntiforgeryToken]
    public class HomeController : Controller {
        private DataContext context;

        private IEnumerable<Category> Categories => context.Categories;
        private IEnumerable<Supplier> Suppliers => context.Suppliers;

        public HomeController(DataContext data) {
            context = data;
        }

        // ...other action methods removed for brevity...

        public async Task<IActionResult> Delete(long id) {
            Product? p = await context.Products.FindAsync(id);
```

```
        if (p != null) {
            ProductViewModel model = ViewModelFactory.Delete(
                p, Categories, Suppliers);
            return View("ProductEditor", model);
        }
        return NotFound();
    }

    [HttpPost]
    public async Task<IActionResult> Delete(Product product) {
        context.Products.Remove(product);
        await context.SaveChangesAsync();
        return RedirectToAction(nameof(Index));
    }
    }
}
```

The model binding process creates a `Product` object from the form data, which is passed to Entity Framework Core to remove from the database. Once the data has been removed from the database, the browser is redirected to the `Index` action, as shown in figure 31.6.

Figure 31.6
Deleting data

31.3 Creating a Razor Pages forms application

Working with Razor Forms relies on similar techniques as the controller examples, albeit broken up into smaller chunks of functionality. As you will see, the main difficulty is preserving the modular nature of Razor Pages without duplicating code and markup. The first step is to create the Razor Page that will display the list of `Product` objects and provide the links to the other operations. Add a Razor Page named `Index` `.cshtml` to the `Pages` folder with the content shown in listing 31.17.

> **Listing 31.17   The contents of the Index.cshtml file in the Pages folder**

```
@page "/pages/{id:long?}"
@model IndexModel
@using Microsoft.AspNetCore.Mvc.RazorPages
@using Microsoft.EntityFrameworkCore
```

```
<div class="m-2">
    <h4 class="bg-primary text-white text-center p-2">Products</h4>
    <table class="table table-sm table-bordered table-striped">
        <thead>
            <tr>
                <th>ID</th><th>Name</th><th>Price</th>
                <th>Category</th><th></th>
            </tr>
        </thead>
        <tbody>
            @foreach (Product p in Model.Products) {
                <tr>
                    <td>@p.ProductId</td>
                    <td>@p.Name</td>
                    <td>@p.Price</td>
                    <td>@p.Category?.Name</td>
                    <td class="text-center">
                        <a asp-page="Details" asp-route-id="@p.ProductId"
                            class="btn btn-sm btn-info">Details</a>
                        <a asp-page="Edit" asp-route-id="@p.ProductId"
                            class="btn btn-sm btn-warning">Edit</a>
                        <a asp-page="Delete" asp-route-id="@p.ProductId"
                            class="btn btn-sm btn-danger">Delete</a>
                    </td>
                </tr>
            }
        </tbody>
    </table>
    <a asp-page="Create" class="btn btn-primary">Create</a>
</div>

@functions {

    public class IndexModel: PageModel {
        private DataContext context;

        public IndexModel(DataContext dbContext) {
            context = dbContext;
        }

        public IEnumerable<Product> Products { get; set; }
            = Enumerable.Empty<Product>();

        public void OnGetAsync(long id = 1) {
            Products = context.Products
                .Include(p => p.Category).Include(p => p.Supplier);
        }
    }
}
```

This view part of the page displays a table populated with the details of the Product objects obtained from the database by the page model. Use a browser to request http://localhost:5000/pages, and you will see the response shown in figure 31.7.

Alongside the details of the `Product` objects, the page displays anchor elements that navigate to other Razor Pages, which I define in the sections that follow.

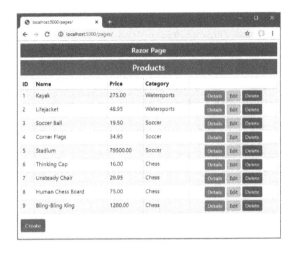

**Figure 31.7
Listing data
using a Razor
Page**

31.3.1 *Creating common functionality*

I don't want to duplicate the same HTML form and supporting code in each of the pages required by the example application. Instead, I am going to define a partial view that defines the HTML form and a base class that defines the common code required by the page model classes. For the partial view, add a Razor View named _Product-Editor.cshtml to the Pages folder with the content shown in listing 31.18.

Using multiple page handler methods

The `asp-page-handler` attribute can be used to specify the name of a handler method, which allows a Razor Page to be used for more than one operation. I don't like this feature because the result is too close to a standard MVC controller and undermines the self-contained and modular aspects of Razor Page development that I like.

The approach I prefer is, of course, the one that I have taken in this chapter, which is to consolidate common content in partial views and a shared base class. Either approach works, and I recommend you try both to see which suits you and your project.

Listing 31.18   The contents of the _ProductEditor.cshtml file in the Pages folder

```
@model ProductViewModel

<partial name="_Validation" />

<h5 class="bg-@Model?.Theme text-white text-center p-2">@Model?.Action</h5>

<form asp-page="@Model?.Action" method="post">
    <div class="form-group">
```

```
            <label asp-for="Product.ProductId"></label>
            <input class="form-control" asp-for="Product.ProductId"
                readonly />
        </div>
        <div class="form-group">
            <label asp-for="Product.Name"></label>
            <div>
                <span asp-validation-for="Product.Name" class="text-danger">
                </span>
            </div>
            <input class="form-control" asp-for="Product.Name"
                readonly="@Model?.ReadOnly" />
        </div>
        <div class="form-group">
            <label asp-for="Product.Price"></label>
            <div>
                <span asp-validation-for="Product.Price" class="text-danger">
                </span>
            </div>
            <input class="form-control" asp-for="Product.Price"
                readonly="@Model?.ReadOnly" />
        </div>
        <div class="form-group">
            <label asp-for="Product.CategoryId">Category</label>
            <div>
                <span asp-validation-for="Product.CategoryId"
                    class="text-danger">
                </span>
            </div>
            <select asp-for="Product.CategoryId" class="form-control"
                disabled="@Model?.ReadOnly"
                asp-items="@(new SelectList(Model?.Categories,
                    "CategoryId", "Name"))">
                <option value="" disabled selected>Choose a Category</option>
            </select>
        </div>
        <div class="form-group">
            <label asp-for="Product.SupplierId">Supplier</label>
            <div>
                <span asp-validation-for="Product.SupplierId"
                    class="text-danger">
                </span>
            </div>
            <select asp-for="Product.SupplierId" class="form-control"
                disabled="@Model?.ReadOnly"
                asp-items="@(new SelectList(Model?.Suppliers,
                    "SupplierId", "Name"))">
                <option value="" disabled selected>Choose a Supplier</option>
            </select>
        </div>
        @if (Model?.ShowAction == true) {
            <button class="btn btn-@Model.Theme mt-2" type="submit">
                @Model.Action
            </button>
        }
        <a class="btn btn-secondary mt-2" asp-page="Index">Back</a>
    </form>
```

The partial view uses the `ProductViewModel` class as its model type and relies on the built-in tag helpers to present `input` and `select` elements for the properties defined by the `Product` class. This is the same content used earlier in the chapter, except with the `asp-action` attribute replaced with `asp-page` to specify the target for the `form` and `anchor` elements.

To define the page model base class, add a class file named `EditorPageModel.cs` to the `Pages` folder and use it to define the class shown in listing 31.19.

Listing 31.19   The contents of the EditorPageModel.cs file in the Pages folder

```
using Microsoft.AspNetCore.Mvc.RazorPages;
using WebApp.Models;

namespace WebApp.Pages {

    public class EditorPageModel : PageModel {

        public EditorPageModel(DataContext dbContext) {
            DataContext = dbContext;
        }

        public DataContext DataContext { get; set; }

        public IEnumerable<Category> Categories => DataContext.Categories;
        public IEnumerable<Supplier> Suppliers => DataContext.Suppliers;

        public ProductViewModel? ViewModel { get; set; }
    }
}
```

The properties defined by this class are simple, but they will help simplify the page model classes of the Razor Pages that handle each operation.

All the Razor Pages required for this example depend on the same namespaces. Add the expressions shown in listing 31.20 to the `_ViewImports.cshtml` file in the `Pages` folder to avoid duplicate expressions in the individual pages.

TIP   Make sure you alter the `_ViewImports.cshtml` file in the `Pages` folder and not the file with the same name in the `Views` folder.

Listing 31.20   Adding namespaces in the _ViewImports.cshtml file in the Pages folder

```
@namespace WebApp.Pages
@using WebApp.Models
@addTagHelper *, Microsoft.AspNetCore.Mvc.TagHelpers
@addTagHelper *, WebApp
@using Microsoft.AspNetCore.Mvc.RazorPages
@using Microsoft.EntityFrameworkCore
@using System.Text.Json
@using Microsoft.AspNetCore.Http
```

31.3.2 Defining pages for the CRUD operations

With the partial view and shared base class in place, the pages that handle individual operations are simple. Add a Razor Page named `Details.cshtml` to the `Pages` folder with the code and content shown in listing 31.21.

Listing 31.21 The contents of the Details.cshtml file in the Pages folder

```
@page "/pages/details/{id}"
@model DetailsModel

<div class="m-2">
    <partial name="_ProductEditor" model="@Model.ViewModel" />
</div>

@functions {

    public class DetailsModel : EditorPageModel {

        public DetailsModel(DataContext dbContext) : base(dbContext) { }

        public async Task OnGetAsync(long id) {
            Product? p = await DataContext.Products.
                Include(p => p.Category).Include(p => p.Supplier)
                .FirstOrDefaultAsync(p => p.ProductId == id);
            ViewModel = ViewModelFactory.Details(p
                    ?? new () { Name = string.Empty});
        }
    }
}
```

The constructor receives an Entity Framework Core context object, which it passes to the base class. The handler method responds to requests by querying the database and using the response to create a `ProductViewModel` object using the `ViewModel-Factory` class.

Add a Razor Page named `Create.cshtml` to the `Pages` folder with the code and content shown in listing 31.22.

> **TIP** Using a partial view means that the `asp-for` attributes set element names without an additional prefix. This allows me to use the `FromForm` attribute for model binding without using the `Name` argument.

Listing 31.22 The contents of the Create.cshtml file in the Pages folder

```
@page "/pages/create"
@model CreateModel

<div class="m-2">
    <partial name="_ProductEditor" model="@Model.ViewModel" />
</div>

@functions {
```

```
public class CreateModel : EditorPageModel {

    public CreateModel(DataContext dbContext) : base(dbContext) { }

    public void OnGet() {
        ViewModel = ViewModelFactory.Create(
            new () { Name = string.Empty }, Categories, Suppliers);
    }

    public async Task<IActionResult> OnPostAsync(
            [FromForm] Product product) {
        if (ModelState.IsValid) {
            product.ProductId = default;
            product.Category = default;
            product.Supplier = default;
            DataContext.Products.Add(product);
            await DataContext.SaveChangesAsync();
            return RedirectToPage(nameof(Index));
        }
        ViewModel = ViewModelFactory.Create(product,
            Categories, Suppliers);
        return Page();
    }
}
}
```

Add a Razor Page named `Edit.cshtml` to the `Pages` folder with the code and content shown in listing 31.23.

Listing 31.23   The contents of the Edit.cshtml file in the Pages folder

```
@page "/pages/edit/{id}"
@model EditModel

<div class="m-2">
    <partial name="_ProductEditor" model="@Model.ViewModel" />
</div>

@functions {

    public class EditModel : EditorPageModel {

        public EditModel(DataContext dbContext) : base(dbContext) { }

        public async Task OnGetAsync(long id) {
            Product p = await this.DataContext.Products.FindAsync(id)
                ?? new () { Name = string.Empty };
            ViewModel = ViewModelFactory.Edit(p, Categories, Suppliers);
        }

        public async Task<IActionResult> OnPostAsync(
                [FromForm] Product product) {
            if (ModelState.IsValid) {
                product.Category = default;
                product.Supplier = default;
```

```
            DataContext.Products.Update(product);
            await DataContext.SaveChangesAsync();
            return RedirectToPage(nameof(Index));
        }
        ViewModel = ViewModelFactory.Edit(product,
            Categories, Suppliers);
        return Page();
    }
    }
}
```

Add a Razor Page named `Delete.cshtml` to the `Pages` folder with the code and content shown in listing 31.24.

Listing 31.24   The contents of the Delete.cshtml file in the Pages folder

```
@page "/pages/delete/{id}"
@model DeleteModel

<div class="m-2">
    <partial name="_ProductEditor" model="@Model.ViewModel" />
</div>

@functions {

    public class DeleteModel : EditorPageModel {

        public DeleteModel(DataContext dbContext) : base(dbContext) { }

        public async Task OnGetAsync(long id) {
            ViewModel = ViewModelFactory.Delete(
                await DataContext.Products.FindAsync(id)
                    ?? new () { Name = string.Empty },
                Categories, Suppliers);
        }

        public async Task<IActionResult> OnPostAsync(
                [FromForm] Product product) {
            DataContext.Products.Remove(product);
            await DataContext.SaveChangesAsync();
            return RedirectToPage(nameof(Index));
        }
    }
}
```

Restart ASP.NET Core and navigate to http://localhost:5000/pages, and you will be able to click the links to view, create, edit, and remove data, as shown in figure 31.8.

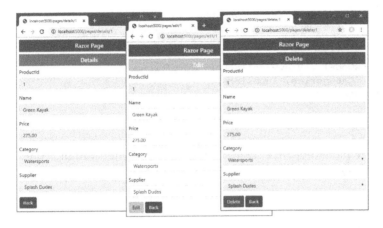

Figure 31.8   Using Razor Pages

31.4   Creating new related data objects

Some applications will need to allow the user to create new related data so that, for example, a new `Category` can be created along with a `Product` in that `Category`. There are two ways to approach this problem, as described in the sections that follow.

31.4.1   Providing the related data in the same request

The first approach is to ask the user to provide the data required to create the related data in the same form. For the example application, this means collecting details for a `Category` object in the same form that the user enters the values for the `Product` object.

This can be a useful approach for simple data types, where only a small amount of data is required to create the related object but is not well suited for types with many properties.

I prefer to define the HTML elements for the related data type in their own partial view. Add a Razor View named `_CategoryEditor.cshtml` to the `Pages` folder with the content shown in listing 31.25.

> **Listing 31.25   The contents of the _CategoryEditor.cshtml file in the Pages folder**

```
@model Product

<script type="text/javascript">
    window.addEventListener("DOMContentLoaded", () => {
        function setVisibility(visible) {
            document.getElementById("categoryGroup").hidden = !visible;
            input = document.getElementById("categoryInput")
            if (visible) {
                input.removeAttribute("disabled");
            } else {
                input.setAttribute("disabled", "disabled");
```

```
                }
            }
            setVisibility(false);
            document.querySelector("select[name='Product.CategoryId']")
                .addEventListener("change", (event) =>
                    setVisibility(event.target.value === "-1")
                );
    });
</script>

<div class="form-group bg-info mt-2 p-1" id="categoryGroup">
    @{ #pragma warning disable CS8602 }
    <label class="text-white" asp-for="Category.Name">
        New Category Name
    </label>
    <input class="form-control" asp-for="Category.Name" value=""
        id="categoryInput" />
    @{ #pragma warning restore CS8602 }
</div>
```

The Category type requires only one property, which the user will provide using a standard input element. The script element in the partial view contains JavaScript code that hides the new elements until the user selects an option element that sets a value of -1 for the Product.CategoryId property. (Using JavaScript is entirely optional, but it helps to emphasize the purpose of the new elements.)

Listing 31.26 adds the partial view to the editor, along with the option element that will display the elements for creating a new Category object.

Listing 31.26 Adding elements in the _ProductEditor.cshtml file in the Pages folder

```
...
<div class="form-group">
    <label asp-for="Product.CategoryId">Category</label>
    <div>
        <span asp-validation-for="Product.CategoryId"
            class="text-danger">
        </span>
    </div>
    <select asp-for="Product.CategoryId" class="form-control"
            disabled="@Model?.ReadOnly"
            asp-items="@(new SelectList(Model?.Categories,
                "CategoryId", "Name"))">
        <option value="-1">Create New Category...</option>
        <option value="" disabled selected>Choose a Category</option>
    </select>
</div>
<partial name="_CategoryEditor" for="Product" />
<div class="form-group">
    <label asp-for="Product.SupplierId">Supplier</label>
    <div>
        <span asp-validation-for="Product.SupplierId"
            class="text-danger">
        </span>
    </div>
```

```
        <select asp-for="Product.SupplierId" class="form-control"
                disabled="@Model?.ReadOnly"
                asp-items="@(new SelectList(Model?.Suppliers,
                    "SupplierId", "Name"))">
            <option value="" disabled selected>Choose a Supplier</option>
        </select>
    </div>
...
```

I need the new functionality in multiple pages, so to avoid code duplication, I have added a method that handles the related data to the page model base class, as shown in listing 31.27.

> **Listing 31.27   Adding a method in the EditorPageModel.cs file in the Pages folder**

```
using Microsoft.AspNetCore.Mvc.RazorPages;
using WebApp.Models;

namespace WebApp.Pages {

    public class EditorPageModel : PageModel {

        public EditorPageModel(DataContext dbContext) {
            DataContext = dbContext;
        }

        public DataContext DataContext { get; set; }

        public IEnumerable<Category> Categories => DataContext.Categories;
        public IEnumerable<Supplier> Suppliers => DataContext.Suppliers;

        public ProductViewModel? ViewModel { get; set; }

        protected async Task CheckNewCategory(Product product) {
            if (product.CategoryId == -1
                    && !string.IsNullOrEmpty(product.Category?.Name)) {
                DataContext.Categories.Add(product.Category);
                await DataContext.SaveChangesAsync();
                product.CategoryId = product.Category.CategoryId;
                ModelState.Clear();
                TryValidateModel(product);
            }
        }
    }
}
```

The new code creates a `Category` object using the data received from the user and stores it in the database. The database server assigns a primary key to the new object, which Entity Framework Core uses to update the `Category` object. This allows me to update the `CategoryId` property of the `Product` object and then re-validate the model data, knowing that the value assigned to the `CategoryId` property will pass validation because it corresponds to the newly allocated key. To integrate the new functionality into the `Create` page, add the statement shown in listing 31.28.

Listing 31.28 Adding a statement in the Create.cshtml file in the Pages folder

```
@page "/pages/create"
@model CreateModel

<div class="m-2">
    <partial name="_ProductEditor" model="@Model.ViewModel" />
</div>

@functions {

    public class CreateModel : EditorPageModel {

        public CreateModel(DataContext dbContext) : base(dbContext) { }

        public void OnGet() {
            ViewModel = ViewModelFactory.Create(
                new () { Name = string.Empty }, Categories, Suppliers);
        }

        public async Task<IActionResult> OnPostAsync(
                [FromForm] Product product) {
            await CheckNewCategory(product);
            if (ModelState.IsValid) {
                product.ProductId = default;
                product.Category = default;
                product.Supplier = default;
                DataContext.Products.Add(product);
                await DataContext.SaveChangesAsync();
                return RedirectToPage(nameof(Index));
            }
            ViewModel = ViewModelFactory.Create(product,
                Categories, Suppliers);
            return Page();
        }
    }
}
```

Add the same statement to the handler method in the Edit page, as shown in listing 31.29.

Listing 31.29 Adding a statement in the Edit.cshtml file in the Pages folder

```
@page "/pages/edit/{id}"
@model EditModel

<div class="m-2">
    <partial name="_ProductEditor" model="@Model.ViewModel" />
</div>

@functions {

    public class EditModel : EditorPageModel {

        public EditModel(DataContext dbContext) : base(dbContext) { }
```

```
public async Task OnGetAsync(long id) {
    Product p = await this.DataContext.Products.FindAsync(id)
        ?? new () { Name = string.Empty };
    ViewModel = ViewModelFactory.Edit(p, Categories, Suppliers);
}

public async Task<IActionResult> OnPostAsync(
        [FromForm] Product product) {
    await CheckNewCategory(product);
    if (ModelState.IsValid) {
        product.Category = default;
        product.Supplier = default;
        DataContext.Products.Update(product);
        await DataContext.SaveChangesAsync();
        return RedirectToPage(nameof(Index));
    }
    ViewModel = ViewModelFactory.Edit(product,
        Categories, Suppliers);
    return Page();
}
    }
}
```

Restart ASP.NET Core so the page model base class is recompiled and use a browser
to request http://localhost:5000/pages/edit/1. Click the Category select element
and choose Create New Category from the list of options. Enter a new category name
into the input element and click the Edit button. When the request is processed, a new
Category object will be stored in the database and associated with the Product object,
as shown in figure 31.9.

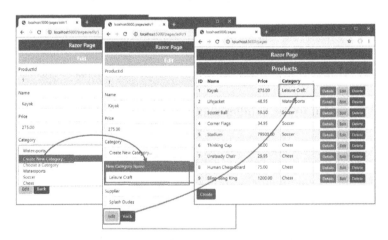

Figure 31.9   Creating related data

31.4.2 *Breaking out to create new data*

For related data types that have their own complex creation process, adding elements
to the main form can be overwhelming to the user; a better approach is to navigate

away from the main form to another controller or page, let the user create the new object, and then return to complete the original task. I will demonstrate this technique for the creation of Supplier objects, even though the Supplier type is simple and requires only two values from the user.

To create a form that will let the user create Supplier objects, add a Razor Page named SupplierBreakOut.cshtml to the Pages folder with the content shown in listing 31.30.

> **Listing 31.30   The contents of the SupplierBreakOut.cshtml file in the Pages folder**

```
@page "/pages/supplier"
@model SupplierPageModel

<div class="m-2">
    <h5 class="bg-secondary text-white text-center p-2">New Supplier</h5>
    <form asp-page="SupplierBreakOut" method="post">
        <div class="form-group">
            @{ #pragma warning disable CS8602 }
            <label asp-for="Supplier.Name"></label>
            <input class="form-control" asp-for="Supplier.Name"  />
            @{ #pragma warning restore CS8602 }
        </div>
        <div class="form-group">
            @{ #pragma warning disable CS8602 }
            <label asp-for="Supplier.City"></label>
            <input class="form-control" asp-for="Supplier.City"  />
            @{ #pragma warning restore CS8602 }
        </div>
        <button class="btn btn-secondary mt-2" type="submit">
            Create
        </button>
        <a class="btn btn-outline-secondary mt-2"
                asp-page="@Model.ReturnPage"
                asp-route-id="@Model.ProductId">
            Cancel
        </a>
    </form>
</div>

@functions {

    public class SupplierPageModel: PageModel {
        private DataContext context;

        public SupplierPageModel(DataContext dbContext) {
            context = dbContext;
        }

        [BindProperty]
        public Supplier? Supplier { get; set; }

        public string? ReturnPage { get; set; }
        public string? ProductId { get; set; }
```

```
public void OnGet([FromQuery(Name="Product")] Product product,
        string returnPage) {
    TempData["product"] = Serialize(product);
    TempData["returnAction"] =  ReturnPage = returnPage;
    TempData["productId"] = ProductId
        = product.ProductId.ToString();
}

public async Task<IActionResult> OnPostAsync() {
    if (ModelState.IsValid && Supplier != null) {
        context.Suppliers.Add(Supplier);
        await context.SaveChangesAsync();
        Product? product
            = Deserialize(TempData["product"] as string);
        if (product != null) {
            product.SupplierId = Supplier.SupplierId;
            TempData["product"] = Serialize(product);
            string? id = TempData["productId"] as string;
            return RedirectToPage(TempData["returnAction"]
                as string, new { id = id });
        }
    }
    return Page();
}

private string Serialize(Product p) =>
    JsonSerializer.Serialize(p);
private Product? Deserialize(string? json) =>
    json == null ? null
        : JsonSerializer.Deserialize<Product>(json);
    }
}
```

The user will navigate to this page using a GET request that will contain the details of the `Product` the user has provided and the name of the page that the user should be returned to. This data is stored using the temp data feature.

This page presents the user with a form containing fields for the `Name` and `City` properties required to create a new `Supplier` object. When the form is submitted, the POST handler method stores a new `Supplier` object and uses the key assigned by the database server to update the `Product` object, which is then stored as temp data again. The user is redirected back to the page from which they arrived.

Listing 31.31 adds elements to the `_ProductEditor` partial view that will allow the user to navigate to the new page.

Listing 31.31   Adding elements in the _ProductEditor.cshtml file in the Pages folder

```
...
<div class="form-group">
    <label asp-for="Product.SupplierId">
        Supplier
        @if (Model?.ReadOnly == false) {
            <input type="hidden" name="returnPage"
                value="@Model?.Action" />
```

```
            <button class="btn btn-sm btn-outline-primary ml-3 my-1"
                asp-page="SupplierBreakOut" formmethod="get"
                    formnovalidate>
                Create New Supplier
            </button>
        }
    </label>
    <div>
        <span asp-validation-for="Product.SupplierId"
            class="text-danger">
        </span>
    </div>
    <select asp-for="Product.SupplierId" class="form-control"
            disabled="@Model?.ReadOnly"
            asp-items="@(new SelectList(Model?.Suppliers,
                "SupplierId", "Name"))">
        <option value="" disabled selected>Choose a Supplier</option>
    </select>
</div>
...
```

The new elements add a hidden input element that captures the page to return to and a button element that submits the form data to the SupplierBreakOut page using a GET request, which means the form values will be encoded in the query string (and is the reason I used the FromQuery attribute in listing 31.30). Listing 31.32 shows the change required to the Create page to add support for retrieving the temp data and using it to populate the Product form.

Listing 31.32 Retrieving data in the Create.cshtml file in the Pages folder

```
@page "/pages/create"
@model CreateModel

<div class="m-2">
    <partial name="_ProductEditor" model="@Model.ViewModel" />
</div>

@functions {

    public class CreateModel : EditorPageModel {

        public CreateModel(DataContext dbContext) : base(dbContext) { }

        public void OnGet() {
            Product p = TempData.ContainsKey("product")
                ? JsonSerializer.Deserialize<Product>(
                        (TempData["product"] as string)!)!
                    : new () { Name = string.Empty };
            ViewModel = ViewModelFactory.Create(p, Categories, Suppliers);
        }

        public async Task<IActionResult> OnPostAsync(
                [FromForm] Product product) {
            await CheckNewCategory(product);
```

```
                if (ModelState.IsValid) {
                    product.ProductId = default;
                    product.Category = default;
                    product.Supplier = default;
                    DataContext.Products.Add(product);
                    await DataContext.SaveChangesAsync();
                    return RedirectToPage(nameof(Index));
                }
                ViewModel = ViewModelFactory.Create(product,
                    Categories, Suppliers);
                return Page();
            }
        }
    }
}
```

A similar change is required in the Edit page, as shown in listing 31.33. (The other pages do not require a change since the breakout is required only when the user is able to create or edit Product data.)

Listing 31.33   Retrieving data in the Edit.cshtml file in the Pages folder

```
@page "/pages/edit/{id}"
@model EditModel

<div class="m-2">
    <partial name="_ProductEditor" model="@Model.ViewModel" />
</div>

@functions {

    public class EditModel : EditorPageModel {

        public EditModel(DataContext dbContext) : base(dbContext) { }

        public async Task OnGetAsync(long id) {
            Product? p = TempData.ContainsKey("product")
                ? JsonSerializer.Deserialize<Product>(
                    (TempData["product"] as string)!)
                : await this.DataContext.Products.FindAsync(id);
            ViewModel = ViewModelFactory.Edit(p
                    ?? new () { Name = string.Empty },
                Categories, Suppliers);
        }

        public async Task<IActionResult> OnPostAsync(
                [FromForm] Product product) {
            await CheckNewCategory(product);
            if (ModelState.IsValid) {
                product.Category = default;
                product.Supplier = default;
                DataContext.Products.Update(product);
                await DataContext.SaveChangesAsync();
                return RedirectToPage(nameof(Index));
            }
            ViewModel = ViewModelFactory.Edit(product,
```

```
        Categories, Suppliers);
        return Page();
    }
  }
}
```

The effect is that the user is presented with a Create New Supplier button, which sends the browser to a form that can be used to create a `Supplier` object. Once the `Supplier` has been stored in the database, the browser is sent back to the originating page, and the form is populated with the data the user had entered, and the `Supplier` select element is set to the newly created object, as shown in figure 31.10.

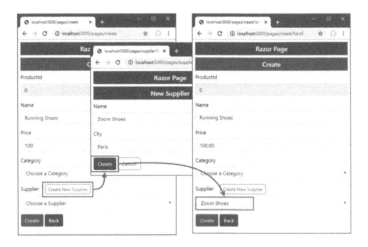

Figure 31.10 **Breaking out to create related data**

Summary

- The ASP.NET Core form-handling features can be combined with Entity Framework Core to perform CRUD operations.
- Forms can be created using Razor Views and Razor Pages.
- Care must be taken to ensure consistency when creating related data.

Part 4

32

Creating the example project

This chapter covers

- Creating an ASP.NET Core project
- Creating a simple data model
- Adding Entity Framework Core to the ASP.NET Core project
- Creating and applying an Entity Framework Core migration
- Adding the Bootstrap CSS package to the project
- Defining a simple request pipeline and services configuration
- Creating an MVC controller and Razor View
- Creating a Razor Page

In this chapter, you will create the example project used throughout this part of the book. The project contains a data model that is displayed using simple controllers and Razor Pages.

32.1   Creating the project

Open a new PowerShell command prompt from the Windows Start menu and run the commands shown in listing 32.1.

> **TIP** You can download the example project for this chapter—and for all the other chapters in this book—from https://github.com/manningbooks/pro-asp .net-core-7. See chapter 1 for how to get help if you have problems running the examples.

Listing 32.1   Creating the project

```
dotnet new globaljson --sdk-version 7.0.100 --output Advanced
dotnet new web --no-https --output Advanced --framework net7.0
dotnet new sln -o Advanced
dotnet sln Advanced add Advanced
```

If you are using Visual Studio, open the `Advanced.sln` file in the `Advanced` folder. If you are using Visual Studio Code, open the `Advanced` folder. Click the Yes button when prompted to add the assets required for building and debugging the project, as shown in figure 32.1.

**Figure 32.1
Adding project
assets**

Open the `launchSettings.json` file in the `WebApp/Properties` folder and change the HTTP port and disable automatic browser launching, as shown in listing 32.2.

Listing 32.2   Setting the HTTP port in the launchSettings.json file in the Properties folder

```
{
  "iisSettings": {
    "windowsAuthentication": false,
    "anonymousAuthentication": true,
    "iisExpress": {
      "applicationUrl": "http://localhost:5000",
      "sslPort": 0
    }
  },
  "profiles": {
    "WebApp": {
      "commandName": "Project",
      "dotnetRunMessages": true,
      "launchBrowser": false,
      "applicationUrl": "http://localhost:5000",
      "environmentVariables": {
        "ASPNETCORE_ENVIRONMENT": "Development"
      }
    },
    "IIS Express": {
```

```
      "commandName": "IISExpress",
      "launchBrowser": true,
      "environmentVariables": {
        "ASPNETCORE_ENVIRONMENT": "Development"
      }
    }
  }
}
}
```

32.1.1 Adding NuGet packages to the project

The data model will use Entity Framework Core to store and query data in a SQL Server LocalDB database. To add the NuGet packages for Entity Framework Core, use a PowerShell command prompt to run the commands shown in listing 32.3 in the `Advanced` project folder.

> **Listing 32.3 Adding packages to the project**

```
dotnet add package Microsoft.EntityFrameworkCore.Design --version 7.0.0
dotnet add package Microsoft.EntityFrameworkCore.SqlServer --version 7.0.0
```

If you have not followed the examples in earlier chapters, you will need to install the global tool package that is used to create and manage Entity Framework Core migrations. Run the commands shown in listing 32.4 to remove any existing version of the package and install the version required for this book.

> **Listing 32.4 Installing a global tool package**

```
dotnet tool uninstall --global dotnet-ef
dotnet tool install --global dotnet-ef --version 7.0.0
```

32.2 Adding a data model

The data model for this application will consist of three classes, representing people, the department in which they work, and their location. Create a `Models` folder and add to it a class file named `Person.cs` with the code in listing 32.5.

> **Listing 32.5 The contents of the Person.cs file in the Models folder**

```
namespace Advanced.Models {

    public class Person {

        public long PersonId { get; set; }
        public string Firstname { get; set; } = String.Empty;
        public string Surname { get; set; } = String.Empty;
        public long DepartmentId { get; set; }
        public long LocationId { get; set; }

        public Department? Department { get; set; }
        public Location? Location { get; set; }
    }
}
```

Add a class file named `Department.cs` to the `Models` folder and use it to define the class shown in listing 32.6.

Listing 32.6   The contents of the Department.cs file in the Models folder

```
namespace Advanced.Models {
    public class Department {

        public long Departmentid { get; set; }
        public string Name { get; set; } = String.Empty;

        public IEnumerable<Person>? People { get; set; }
    }
}
```

Add a class file named `Location.cs` to the `Models` folder and use it to define the class shown in listing 32.7.

Listing 32.7   The contents of the Location.cs file in the Models folder

```
namespace Advanced.Models {
    public class Location {

        public long LocationId { get; set; }
        public string City { get; set; } = string.Empty;
        public string State { get; set; } = String.Empty;

        public IEnumerable<Person>? People { get; set; }
    }
}
```

Each of the three data model classes defines a key property whose value will be allocated by the database when new objects are stored and defines foreign key properties that define the relationships between the classes. These are supplemented by navigation properties that will be used with the Entity Framework Core `Include` method to incorporate related data into queries.

To create the Entity Framework Core context class that will provide access to the database, add a file called `DataContext.cs` to the `Models` folder and add the code shown in listing 32.8.

Listing 32.8   The contents of the DataContext.cs file in the Models folder

```
using Microsoft.EntityFrameworkCore;

namespace Advanced.Models {
    public class DataContext : DbContext {

        public DataContext(DbContextOptions<DataContext> opts)
            : base(opts) { }

        public DbSet<Person> People => Set<Person>();
        public DbSet<Department> Departments => Set<Department>();
        public DbSet<Location> Locations => Set<Location>();
    }
}
```

The context class defines properties that will be used to query the database for `Person`, `Department`, and `Location` data.

32.2.1 *Preparing the seed data*

Add a class called `SeedData.cs` to the `Models` folder and add the code shown in listing 32.9 to define the seed data that will be used to populate the database.

Listing 32.9 The contents of the SeedData.cs file in the Models folder

```
using Microsoft.EntityFrameworkCore;

namespace Advanced.Models {
    public static class SeedData {

        public static void SeedDatabase(DataContext context) {
            context.Database.Migrate();
            if (context.People.Count() == 0
                    && context.Departments.Count() == 0
                    && context.Locations.Count() == 0) {

                Department d1 = new () { Name = "Sales" };
                Department d2 = new () { Name = "Development" };
                Department d3 = new () { Name = "Support" };
                Department d4 = new () { Name = "Facilities" };

                context.Departments.AddRange(d1, d2, d3, d4);
                context.SaveChanges();

                Location l1 = new () { City = "Oakland", State = "CA" };
                Location l2 = new () { City = "San Jose", State = "CA" };
                Location l3 = new () { City = "New York", State = "NY" };
                context.Locations.AddRange(l1, l2, l3);

                context.People.AddRange(
                    new Person {
                        Firstname = "Francesca", Surname = "Jacobs",
                        Department = d2, Location = l1
                    },
                    new Person {
                        Firstname = "Charles", Surname = "Fuentes",
                        Department = d2, Location = l3
                    },
                    new Person {
                        Firstname = "Bright", Surname = "Becker",
                        Department = d4, Location = l1
                    },
                    new Person {
                        Firstname = "Murphy", Surname = "Lara",
                        Department = d1, Location = l3
                    },
                    new Person {
                        Firstname = "Beasley", Surname = "Hoffman",
                        Department = d4, Location = l3
                    },
                    new Person {
```

```
            Firstname = "Marks", Surname = "Hays",
            Department = d4, Location = 11
        },
        new Person {
            Firstname = "Underwood", Surname = "Trujillo",
            Department = d2, Location = 11
        },
        new Person {
            Firstname = "Randall", Surname = "Lloyd",
            Department = d3, Location = 12
        },
        new Person {
            Firstname = "Guzman", Surname = "Case",
            Department = d2, Location = 12
        });
        context.SaveChanges();
    }
  }
 }
}
```

The static `SeedDatabase` method ensures that all pending migrations have been applied to the database. If the database is empty, it is seeded with data. Entity Framework Core will take care of mapping the objects into the tables in the database, and the key properties will be assigned automatically when the data is stored.

32.2.2 Configuring Entity Framework Core

Make the changes to the `Program.cs` file shown in listing 32.10, which configure Entity Framework Core and set up the `DataContext` services that will be used throughout this part of the book to access the database.

> **Listing 32.10   Configuring the application in the Program.cs file in the Advanced folder**

```
using Microsoft.EntityFrameworkCore;
using Advanced.Models;

var builder = WebApplication.CreateBuilder(args);

builder.Services.AddDbContext<DataContext>(opts => {
    opts.UseSqlServer(
        builder.Configuration["ConnectionStrings:PeopleConnection"]);
    opts.EnableSensitiveDataLogging(true);
});

var app = builder.Build();

app.MapGet("/", () => "Hello World!");

var context = app.Services.CreateScope().ServiceProvider
    .GetRequiredService<DataContext>();
SeedData.SeedDatabase(context);

app.Run();
```

To define the connection string that will be used for the application's data, add the configuration settings shown in listing 32.11 in the `appsettings.json` file. The connection string should be entered on a single line.

> **Listing 32.11 Defining a connection string in the Advanced/appsettings.json file**

```
{
  "Logging": {
    "LogLevel": {
      "Default": "Information",
      "Microsoft.AspNetCore": "Warning",
      "Microsoft.EntityFrameworkCore": "Information"
    }
  },
  "AllowedHosts": "*",
  "ConnectionStrings": {
    "PeopleConnection": "Server=(localdb)\\MSSQLLocalDB;Database=People;
MultipleActiveResultSets=True"
  }
}
```

In addition to the connection string, listing 32.11 increases the logging detail for Entity Framework Core so that the SQL queries sent to the database are logged.

32.2.3 *Creating and applying the migration*

To create the migration that will set up the database schema, use a PowerShell command prompt to run the command shown in listing 32.12 in the `Advanced` project folder.

> **Listing 32.12 Creating an Entity Framework Core migration**

```
dotnet ef migrations add Initial
```

Once the migration has been created, apply it to the database using the command shown in listing 32.13.

> **Listing 32.13 Applying the migration to the database**

```
dotnet ef database update
```

The logging messages displayed by the application will show the SQL commands that are sent to the database.

> **NOTE** If you need to reset the database, then run the `dotnet ef database drop --force` command and then the command in listing 32.13.

32.3 *Adding the Bootstrap CSS framework*

Following the pattern established in earlier chapters, I will use the Bootstrap CSS framework to style the HTML elements produced by the example application. To install the Bootstrap package, run the commands shown in listing 32.14 in the `Advanced` project folder. These commands rely on the Library Manager package.

Listing 32.14　Installing the Bootstrap CSS framework

```
libman init -p cdnjs
libman install bootstrap@5.2.3 -d wwwroot/lib/bootstrap
```

If you are using Visual Studio, you can install client-side packages by right-clicking the Advanced project item in the Solution Explorer and selecting Add > Client-Side Library from the pop-up menu.

32.4　*Configuring the services and middleware*

The example application in this part of the book will respond to requests using both MVC controllers and Razor Pages. Add the statements shown in listing 32.15 to the Program.cs file to configure the services and middleware the application will use.

Listing 32.15　Configuring the application in the Program.cs file in the Advanced folder

```
using Microsoft.EntityFrameworkCore;
using Advanced.Models;

var builder = WebApplication.CreateBuilder(args);

builder.Services.AddControllersWithViews();
builder.Services.AddRazorPages();

builder.Services.AddDbContext<DataContext>(opts => {
    opts.UseSqlServer(
        builder.Configuration["ConnectionStrings:PeopleConnection"]);
    opts.EnableSensitiveDataLogging(true);
});

var app = builder.Build();

//app.MapGet("/", () => "Hello World!");

app.UseStaticFiles();

app.MapControllers();
app.MapControllerRoute("controllers",
    "controllers/{controller=Home}/{action=Index}/{id?}");
app.MapRazorPages();

var context = app.Services.CreateScope().ServiceProvider
    .GetRequiredService<DataContext>();
SeedData.SeedDatabase(context);

app.Run();
```

In addition to mapping the controller route, I have added a route that matches URL paths that begin with controllers, which will make it easier to follow the examples in later chapters as they switch between controllers and Razor Pages. This is the same convention I adopted in earlier chapters, and I will route URL paths beginning with /pages to Razor Pages.

32.5 Creating a controller and view

To display the application's data using a controller, create a folder named `Controllers` in the `Advanced` project folder and add to it a class file named `HomeController.cs`, with the content shown in listing 32.16.

Listing 32.16 The contents of the HomeController.cs file in the Controllers folder

```csharp
using Advanced.Models;
using Microsoft.AspNetCore.Mvc;
using Microsoft.EntityFrameworkCore;

namespace Advanced.Controllers {
    public class HomeController : Controller {
        private DataContext context;

        public HomeController(DataContext dbContext) {
            context = dbContext;
        }

        public IActionResult Index([FromQuery] string selectedCity) {
            return View(new PeopleListViewModel {
                People = context.People
                    .Include(p => p.Department).Include(p => p.Location),
                Cities = context.Locations.Select(l => l.City).Distinct(),
                SelectedCity = selectedCity
            });
        }
    }

    public class PeopleListViewModel {

        public IEnumerable<Person> People { get; set; }
            = Enumerable.Empty<Person>();

        public IEnumerable<string> Cities { get; set; }
            = Enumerable.Empty<string>();

        public string SelectedCity { get; set; } = String.Empty;

        public string GetClass(string? city) =>
            SelectedCity == city ? "bg-info text-white" : "";
    }
}
```

To provide the controller with a view, create the `Views/Home` folder and add to it a Razor View named `Index.cshtml` with the content shown in listing 32.17.

Listing 32.17 The contents of the Index.cshtml file in the Views/Home folder

```html
@model PeopleListViewModel

<h4 class="bg-primary text-white text-center p-2">People</h4>

<table class="table table-sm table-bordered table-striped">
    <thead>
```

```
        <tr>
            <th>ID</th>
            <th>Name</th>
            <th>Dept</th>
            <th>Location</th>
        </tr>
    </thead>
    <tbody>
        @foreach (Person p in Model.People) {
            <tr class="@Model.GetClass(p.Location?.City)">
                <td>@p.PersonId</td>
                <td>@p.Surname, @p.Firstname</td>
                <td>@p.Department?.Name</td>
                <td>@p.Location?.City, @p.Location?.State</td>
            </tr>
        }
    </tbody>
</table>

<form asp-action="Index" method="get">
    <div class="form-group">
        <label for="selectedCity">City</label>
        <select name="selectedCity" class="form-control">
            <option disabled selected>Select City</option>
            @foreach (string city in Model.Cities) {
                <option selected="@(city == Model.SelectedCity)">
                    @city
                </option>
            }
        </select>
    </div>
    <button class="btn btn-primary mt-2" type="submit">Select</button>
</form>
```

To enable tag helpers and add the namespaces that will be available by default in views, add a Razor View Imports file named _ViewImports.cshtml to the Views folder with the content shown in listing 32.18.

> **Listing 32.18   The contents of the _ViewImports.cshtml file in the Views folder**

```
@addTagHelper *, Microsoft.AspNetCore.Mvc.TagHelpers
@using Advanced.Models
@using Advanced.Controllers
```

To specify the default layout for controller views, add a Razor View Start start file named _ViewStart.cshtml to the Views folder with the content shown in listing 32.19.

> **Listing 32.19   The contents of the _ViewStart.cshtml file in the Views folder**

```
@{
    Layout = "_Layout";
}
```

To create the layout, create the Views/Shared folder and add to it a Razor Layout named _Layout.cshtml with the content shown in listing 32.20.

```
<!DOCTYPE html>
<html>
<head>
    <title>@ViewBag.Title</title>
    <link href="/lib/bootstrap/css/bootstrap.min.css" rel="stylesheet" />
</head>
<body>
    <div class="m-2">
        @RenderBody()
    </div>
</body>
</html>
```

32.6 Creating a Razor Page

To display the application's data using a Razor Page, create the `Pages` folder and add to it a Razor Page named `Index.cshtml` with the content shown in listing 32.21.

```
@page "/pages"
@model IndexModel

<h4 class="bg-primary text-white text-center p-2">People</h4>

<table class="table table-sm table-bordered table-striped">
    <thead>
        <tr>
            <th>ID</th>
            <th>Name</th>
            <th>Dept</th>
            <th>Location</th>
        </tr>
    </thead>
    <tbody>
        @foreach (Person p in Model.People) {
            <tr class="@Model.GetClass(p.Location?.City)">
                <td>@p.PersonId</td>
                <td>@p.Surname, @p.Firstname</td>
                <td>@p.Department?.Name</td>
                <td>@p.Location?.City, @p.Location?.State</td>
            </tr>
        }
    </tbody>
</table>

<form asp-page="Index" method="get">
    <div class="form-group">
        <label for="selectedCity">City</label>
        <select name="selectedCity" class="form-control">
            <option disabled selected>Select City</option>
```

```
            @foreach (string city in Model.Cities) {
                <option selected="@(city == Model.SelectedCity)">
                    @city
                </option>
            }
        </select>
    </div>
    <button class="btn btn-primary mt-2" type="submit">Select</button>
</form>

@functions {

    public class IndexModel : PageModel {
        private DataContext context;

        public IndexModel(DataContext dbContext) {
            context = dbContext;
        }

        public IEnumerable<Person> People { get; set; }
            = Enumerable.Empty<Person>();

        public IEnumerable<string> Cities { get; set; }
            = Enumerable.Empty<string>();

        [FromQuery]
        public string SelectedCity { get; set; } = String.Empty;

        public void OnGet() {
            People = context.People.Include(p => p.Department)
                .Include(p => p.Location);
            Cities = context.Locations.Select(l => l.City).Distinct();
        }

        public string GetClass(string? city) =>
            SelectedCity == city ? "bg-info text-white" : "";
    }
}
```

To enable tag helpers and add the namespaces that will be available by default in the view section of the Razor Pages, add a Razor View imports file named `_ViewImports` `.cshtml` to the `Pages` folder with the content shown in listing 32.22.

```
@addTagHelper *, Microsoft.AspNetCore.Mvc.TagHelpers
@using Advanced.Models
@using Microsoft.AspNetCore.Mvc.RazorPages
@using Microsoft.EntityFrameworkCore
```

To specify the default layout for Razor Pages, add a Razor View start file named `_ViewStart.cshtml` to the `Pages` folder with the content shown in listing 32.23.

Listing 32.23   The contents of the _ViewStart.cshtml file in the Pages folder

```
@{
    Layout = "_Layout";
}
```

To create the layout, add a Razor Layout named `_Layout.cshtml` to the `Pages` folder with the content shown in listing 32.24.

Listing 32.24   The contents of the _Layout.cshtml file in the Pages folder

```html
<!DOCTYPE html>
<html>
<head>
    <title>@ViewBag.Title</title>
    <link href="/lib/bootstrap/css/bootstrap.min.css" rel="stylesheet" />
</head>
<body>
    <div class="m-2">
        <h5 class="bg-secondary text-white text-center p-2">Razor Page</h5>
        @RenderBody()
    </div>
</body>
</html>
```

32.7   *Running the example application*

Start the application by running the command shown in listing 32.25 in the `Advanced` project folder.

Listing 32.25   Running the example application

```
dotnet run
```

Use a browser to request http://localhost:5000/controllers and http://localhost:5000/pages. Select a city using the select element and click the Select button to highlight rows in the table, as shown in figure 32.2.

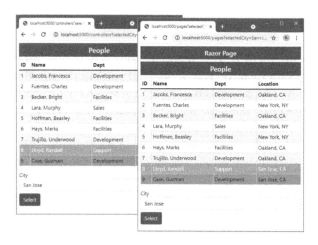

**Figure 32.2
Running the
example
application**

Using Blazor Server, part 1

This chapter covers

- Creating Razor Components to add client-side interactivity to ASP.NET Core applications
- Understanding how JavaScript events are used to respond to user interaction
- Managing event propagation in a Razor Component
- Understanding how to define Razor Components

Blazor adds client-side interactivity to web applications. There are two varieties of Blazor, and in this chapter, I focus on Blazor Server. I explain the problem it solves and how it works. I show you how to configure an ASP.NET Core application to use Blazor Server and describe the basic features available when using Razor Components, which are the building blocks for Blazor Server projects. I describe more advanced Blazor Server features in chapters 34–36, and in chapter 37, I describe Blazor WebAssembly, which is the other variety of Blazor. Table 33.1 puts Blazor Server in context.

Table 33.1 Putting Blazor Server in context

Question	Answer
What is it?	Blazor Server uses JavaScript to receive browser events, which are forwarded to ASP.NET Core and evaluated using C# code. The effect of the event on the state of the application is sent back to the browser and displayed to the user.
Why is it useful?	Blazor Server can produce a richer and more responsive user experience compared to standard web applications.
How is it used?	The building block for Blazor Server is the Razor Component, which uses a syntax similar to Razor Pages. The view section of the Razor Component contains special attributes that specify how the application will respond to user interaction.
Are there any pitfalls or limitations?	Blazor Server relies on a persistent HTTP connection to the server and cannot function when that connection is interrupted. Blazor Server is not supported by older browsers.
Are there any alternatives?	The features described in part 3 of this book can be used to create web applications that work broadly but that offer a less responsive experience. You could also consider a client-side JavaScript framework, such as Angular, React, or Vue.js.

Table 33.2 provides a guide to the chapter.

Table 33.2 Chapter guide

Problem	Solution	Listing
Configuring Blazor	Use the `AddServerSideBlazor` and `MapBlazorHub` methods to set up the required services and middleware and configure the JavaScript file.	3–6
Creating a Blazor Component	Create a `.blazor` file and use it to define code and markup.	7
Applying a component	Use a `component` element.	8, 9
Handling events	Use an attribute to specify the method or expression that will handle an event.	10–15
Creating a two-way relationship with an element	Create a data binding.	16–20
Defining the code separately from the markup	Use a code-behind class.	21–23
Defining a component without declarative markup	Use a Razor Component class.	24, 25

33.1 *Preparing for this chapter*

This chapter uses the Advanced project from chapter 32. No changes are required to prepare for this chapter.

> **TIP** You can download the example project for this chapter—and for all the other chapters in this book—from https://github.com/manningbooks/pro-asp .net-core-7. See chapter 1 for how to get help if you have problems running the examples.

Open a new PowerShell command prompt, navigate to the folder that contains the `Advanced.csproj` file, and run the command shown in listing 33.1 to drop the database.

Listing 33.1   Dropping the database

```
dotnet ef database drop --force
```

Use the PowerShell command prompt to run the command shown in listing 33.2.

Listing 33.2   Running the example application

```
dotnet run
```

Use a browser to request http://localhost:5000/controllers, which will display a list of data items. Pick a city from the drop-down list and click the Select button to highlight elements, as shown in figure 33.1.

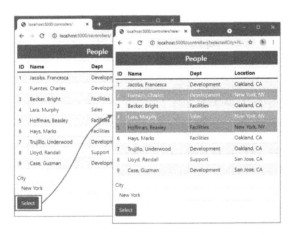

Figure 33.1 Running the example application

33.2 *Understanding Blazor Server*

Consider what happens when you choose a city and click the Select button presented by the example application. The browser sends an HTTP GET request that submits a form, which is received by either an action method or a handler method, depending on whether you use the controller or Razor Page. The action or handler renders its view, which sends a new HTML document that reflects the selection to the browser, as illustrated by figure 33.2.

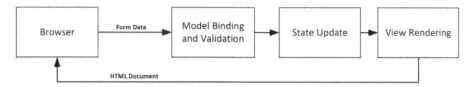

Figure 33.2 Interacting with the example application

This cycle is effective but can be inefficient. Each time the Submit button is clicked, the browser sends a new HTTP request to ASP.NET Core. Each request contains a complete set of HTTP headers that describe the request and the types of responses the browser is willing to receive. In its response, the server includes HTTP headers that describe the response and includes a complete HTML document for the browser to display.

The amount of data sent by the example application is about 3KB on my system, and almost all of it is duplicated between requests. The browser only wants to tell the server which city has been selected, and the server only wants to indicate which table rows should be highlighted; however, each HTTP request is self-contained, so the browser must parse a complete HTML document each time. The root issue that every interaction is the same: send a request and get a complete HTML document in return.

Blazor takes a different approach. A JavaScript library is included in the HTML document that is sent to the browser. When the JavaScript code is executed, it opens an HTTP connection back to the server and leaves it open, ready for user interaction. When the user picks a value using the select element, for example, details of the selection are sent to the server, which responds with just the changes to apply to the existing HTML, as shown in figure 33.3.

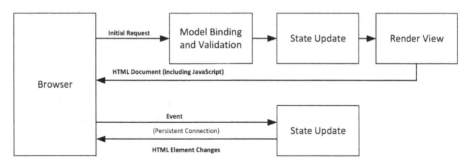

Figure 33.3 Interacting with Blazor

The persistent HTTP connection minimizes the delay, and replying with just the differences reduces the amount of data sent between the browser and the server.

33.2.1 *Understanding the Blazor Server advantages*

The biggest attraction of Blazor is that it is based on Razor Pages written in C#. This means you can increase efficiency and responsiveness without having to learn a new framework, such as Angular or React, and a new language, such as TypeScript or JavaScript. Blazor is nicely integrated into the rest of ASP.NET Core and is built on features described in earlier chapters, which makes it easy to use (especially when compared to a framework like Angular, which has a dizzyingly steep learning curve).

33.2.2 *Understanding the Blazor Server disadvantages*

Blazor requires a modern browser to establish and maintain its persistent HTTP connection. And, because of this connection, applications that use Blazor stop working if the connection is lost, which makes them unsuitable for offline use, where connectivity cannot be relied on or where connections are slow. These issues are addressed by Blazor WebAssembly, described in chapter 36, but, as I explain, this has its own set of limitations.

33.2.3 *Choosing between Blazor Server and Angular/React/Vue.js*

Decisions between Blazor and one of the JavaScript frameworks should be driven by the development team's experience and the users' expected connectivity. If you have no JavaScript expertise and have not used one of the JavaScript frameworks, then you should use Blazor, but only if you can rely on good connectivity and modern browsers. This makes Blazor a good choice for line-of-business applications, for example, where the browser demographic and network quality can be determined in advance.

If you have JavaScript experience and you are writing a public-facing application, then you should use one of the JavaScript frameworks because you won't be able to make assumptions about browsers or network quality. (It doesn't matter which framework you choose—I have written books about Angular, React, and Vue.js, and they are all excellent. My advice for choosing a framework is to create a simple app in each of them and pick the one whose development model appeals to you the most.)

If you are writing a public-facing application and you don't have JavaScript experience, then you have two choices. The safest option is to stick to the ASP.NET Core features described in earlier chapters and accept the inefficiencies this can bring. This isn't a terrible choice to make, and you can still produce top-quality applications. A more demanding choice is to learn TypeScript or JavaScript and one of Angular, React, or Vue.js—but don't underestimate the amount of time it takes to master JavaScript or the complexity of these frameworks.

33.3 *Getting started with Blazor*

The best way to get started with Blazor is to jump right in. In the sections that follow, I configure the application to enable Blazor and re-create the functionality offered by the controller and Razor Page. After that, I'll go right back to basics and explain how Razor Components work and the different features they offer.

33.3.1 *Configuring ASP.NET Core for Blazor Server*

Preparation is required before Blazor can be used. The first step is to add the services and middleware to the `Program.cs` file, as shown in listing 33.3.

Listing 33.3   Configuring the application in the Program.cs file in the Advanced folder

```
using Microsoft.EntityFrameworkCore;
using Advanced.Models;

var builder = WebApplication.CreateBuilder(args);

builder.Services.AddControllersWithViews();
builder.Services.AddRazorPages();
builder.Services.AddServerSideBlazor();

builder.Services.AddDbContext<DataContext>(opts => {
    opts.UseSqlServer(
        builder.Configuration["ConnectionStrings:PeopleConnection"]);
    opts.EnableSensitiveDataLogging(true);
});

var app = builder.Build();

app.UseStaticFiles();

app.MapControllers();
app.MapControllerRoute("controllers",
    "controllers/{controller=Home}/{action=Index}/{id?}");
app.MapRazorPages();
app.MapBlazorHub();

var context = app.Services.CreateScope().ServiceProvider
    .GetRequiredService<DataContext>();
SeedData.SeedDatabase(context);

app.Run();
```

The "hub" in the `MapBlazorHub` method relates to SignalR, which is the part of ASP. NET Core that handles the persistent HTTP request. I don't describe SignalR in this book because it is rarely used directly, but it can be useful if you need ongoing communication between clients and the server. See https://docs.microsoft.com/en-us/ aspnet/core/signalr for details. For this book—and most ASP.NET Core applications—it is enough to know that SignalR is used to manage the connections that Blazor relies on.

ADDING THE BLAZOR JAVASCRIPT FILE TO THE LAYOUT

Blazor relies on JavaScript code to communicate with the ASP.NET Core server. Add the elements shown in listing 33.4 to the `_Layout.cshtml` file in the `Views/Shared` folder to add the JavaScript file to the layout used by controller views.

Listing 33.4   Adding elements in the _Layout.cshtml file in the Views/Shared folder

```
<!DOCTYPE html>
<html>
<head>
    <title>@ViewBag.Title</title>
    <link href="/lib/bootstrap/css/bootstrap.min.css" rel="stylesheet" />
    <base href="~/" />
</head>
<body>
    <div class="m-2">
        @RenderBody()
    </div>
    <script src="_framework/blazor.server.js"></script>
</body>
</html>
```

The `script` element specifies the name of the JavaScript file, and requests for it are intercepted by the middleware added to the request pipeline in listing 33.3 so that no additional package is required to add the JavaScript code to the project. The `base` element must also be added to specify the root URL for the application. The same elements must be added to the layout used by Razor Pages, as shown in listing 33.5.

Listing 33.5   Adding elements in the _Layout.cshtml file in the Pages folder

```
<!DOCTYPE html>
<html>
<head>
    <title>@ViewBag.Title</title>
    <link href="/lib/bootstrap/css/bootstrap.min.css" rel="stylesheet" />
    <base href="~/" />
</head>
<body>
    <div class="m-2">
        <h5 class="bg-secondary text-white text-center p-2">
            Razor Page
        </h5>
        @RenderBody()
    </div>
    <script src="_framework/blazor.server.js"></script>
</body>
</html>
```

CREATING THE BLAZOR IMPORTS FILE

Blazor requires its own imports file to specify the namespaces that it uses. It is easy to forget to add this file to a project, but, without it, Blazor will silently fail. Add a file named _Imports.razor to the Advanced folder with the content shown in listing 33.6. (If you are using Visual Studio, you can use the Razor View imports template to create this file, but ensure you use the .razor file extension.)

Listing 33.6   The contents of the _Imports.razor file in the Advanced folder

```
@using Microsoft.AspNetCore.Components
@using Microsoft.AspNetCore.Components.Forms
@using Microsoft.AspNetCore.Components.Routing
@using Microsoft.AspNetCore.Components.Web
@using Microsoft.JSInterop
@using Microsoft.EntityFrameworkCore
@using Advanced.Models
```

The first five @using expressions are for the namespaces required for Blazor. The last two expressions are for convenience in the examples that follow because they will allow me to use Entity Framework Core and the classes in the Models namespace.

33.3.2 *Creating a Razor Component*

There is a clash in terminology: the technology is *Blazor*, but the key building block is called a *Razor Component*. Razor Components are defined in files with the .razor extension and must begin with a capital letter. Components can be defined anywhere, but they are usually grouped together to help keep the project organized. Create a Blazor folder in the Advanced folder and add to it a Razor Component named PeopleList.razor with the content shown in listing 33.7.

Listing 33.7   The contents of the PeopleList.razor file in the Blazor folder

```
<table class="table table-sm table-bordered table-striped">
    <thead>
        <tr>
            <th>ID</th>
            <th>Name</th>
            <th>Dept</th>
            <th>Location</th>
        </tr>
    </thead>
    <tbody>
        @foreach (Person p in People ?? Enumerable.Empty<Person>()) {
            <tr class="@GetClass(p?.Location?.City)">
                <td>@p?.PersonId</td>
                <td>@p?.Surname, @p?.Firstname</td>
                <td>@p?.Department?.Name</td>
                <td>@p?.Location?.City, @p?.Location?.State</td>
            </tr>
        }
    </tbody>
</table>

<div class="form-group">
    <label for="city">City</label>
    <select name="city" class="form-control" @bind="SelectedCity">
        <option disabled selected value="">Select City</option>
        @foreach (string city in Cities ?? Enumerable.Empty<string>()) {
            <option value="@city" selected="@(city == SelectedCity)">
                @city
            </option>
```

```
            }
        </select>
    </div>

    @code {

        [Inject]
        public DataContext? Context { get; set; }

        public IEnumerable<Person>? People =>
            Context?.People.Include(p => p.Department)
                .Include(p => p.Location);

        public IEnumerable<string>? Cities =>
            Context?.Locations.Select(l => l.City);

        public string SelectedCity { get; set; } = string.Empty;

        public string GetClass(string? city) =>
            SelectedCity == city ? "bg-info text-white" : "";
    }
```

Razor Components are similar to Razor Pages. The view section relies on the Razor features you have seen in earlier chapters, with @ expressions to insert data values into the component's HTML or to generate elements for objects in a sequence, like this:

```
...
@foreach (string city in Cities ?? Enumerable.Empty<string>()) {
    <option value="@city" selected="@(city == SelectedCity)">
        @city
    </option>
}
...
```

This @foreach expression generates option elements for each value in the Cities sequence and is identical to the equivalent expression in the controller view and Razor Page created in chapter 32.

Although Razor Components look familiar, there are some important differences. The first is that there is no page model class and no @model expression. The properties and methods that support a component's HTML are defined directly in an @code expression, which is the counterpart to the Razor Page @functions expression. To define the property that will provide the view section with Person objects, for example, I just define a People property in the @code section, like this:

```
...
public IEnumerable<Person>? People =>
    Context?.People.Include(p => p.Department)
        .Include(p => p.Location);
...
```

And, because there is no page model class, there is no constructor through which to declare service dependencies. Instead, the dependency injection sets the values of properties that have been decorated with the Inject attribute, like this:

```
...
[Inject]
public DataContext? Context { get; set; }
...
```

The most significant difference is the use of a special attribute on the `select` element.

```
...
<select name="city" class="form-control" @bind="SelectedCity">
    <option disabled selected value="">Select City</option>
...
```

This Blazor attribute creates a data binding between the value of the `select` element and the `SelectedCity` property defined in the `@code` section.

I describe data bindings in more detail in the "Working with Data Bindings" section, but for now, it is enough to know that the value of the `SelectedCity` will be updated when the user changes the value of the `select` element.

Razor components are delivered to the browser as part of a Razor Page or a controller view. Listing 33.8 shows how to use a Razor Component in a controller view.

> **Listing 33.8 Using a Razor Component in the Index.cshtml file in the Views/ Home folder**

```
@model PeopleListViewModel

<h4 class="bg-primary text-white text-center p-2">People</h4>

<component type="typeof(Advanced.Blazor.PeopleList)"
    render-mode="Server" />
```

Razor Components are applied using the `component` element, for which there is a tag helper. The `component` element is configured using the `type` and `render-mode` attributes. The `type` attribute is used to specify the Razor Component. Razor Components are compiled into classes just like controller views and Razor Pages. The `PeopleList` component is defined in the `Blazor` folder in the Advanced project, so the type will be `Advanced.Blazor.PeopleList`, like this:

```
...
<component type="typeof(Advanced.Blazor.PeopleList)"
    render-mode="Server" />
...
```

The `render-mode` attribute is used to select how content is produced by the component, using a value from the `RenderMode` enum, described in table 33.3.

Table 33.3 The RenderMode values

Name	Description
Static	The Razor Component renders its view section as static HTML with no client-side support.
Server	The HTML document is sent to the browser with a placeholder for the component. The HTML displayed by the component is sent to the browser over the persistent HTTP connection and displayed to the user.
ServerPrerendered	The view section of the component is included in the HTML and displayed to the user immediately. The HTML content is sent again over the persistent HTTP connection.

For most applications, the `Server` option is a good choice. The `ServerPrerendered` includes a static rendition of the Razor Component's view section in the HTML document sent to the browser. This acts as placeholder content so that the user isn't presented with an empty browser window while the JavaScript code is loaded and executed. Once the persistent HTTP connection has been established, the placeholder content is deleted and replaced with a dynamic version sent by Blazor. The idea of showing static content to the user is a good one, but it can be confusing because the HTML elements are not wired up to the server-side part of the application, and any interaction from the user either doesn't work or will be discarded once the live content arrives.

To see Blazor in action, restart ASP.NET Core and use a browser to request http://localhost:5000/controllers. No form submission is required when using Blazor because the data binding will respond as soon as the `select` element's value is changed, as shown in figure 33.4. (You may have to reload the browser to see the Blazor component in action.)

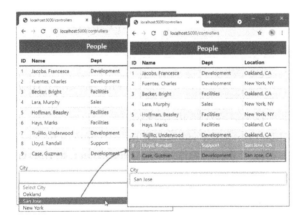

Figure 33.4
Using a Razor Component

When you use the `select` element, the value you choose is sent over the persistent HTTP connection to the ASP.NET Core server, which updates the Razor Component's `SelectedCity` property and re-renders the HTML content. A set of updates is sent to the JavaScript code, which updates the table.

Razor Components can also be used in Razor Pages. Add a Razor Page named `Blazor.cshtml` to the `Pages` folder and add the content shown in listing 33.9.

Listing 33.9   The contents of the Blazor.cshtml file in the Pages folder

```
@page "/pages/blazor"

<script type="text/javascript">
    window.addEventListener("DOMContentLoaded", () => {
        document.getElementById("markElems").addEventListener("click",
            () => {
                document.querySelectorAll("td:first-child")
                    .forEach(elem => {
                        elem.innerText = `M:${elem.innerText}`
```

```
                        elem.classList.add("border", "border-dark");
                });
        });
    });
</script>

<h4 class="bg-primary text-white text-center p-2">Blazor People</h4>

<button id="markElems" class="btn btn-outline-primary mb-2">
    Mark Elements
</button>

<component type="typeof(Advanced.Blazor.PeopleList)"
    render-mode="Server" />
```

The Razor Page in listing 33.9 contains additional JavaScript code that helps demonstrate that only changes are sent, instead of an entirely new HTML table. Restart ASP. NET Core and request http://localhost:5000/pages/blazor. Click the Mark Elements button, and the cells in the ID column will be changed to display different content and a border. Now use the `select` element to pick a different city, and you will see that the elements in the table are modified without being deleted, as shown in figure 33.5.

Understanding Blazor connection messages

When you stop ASP.NET Core, you will see an error message in the browser window, which indicates the connection to the server has been lost and prevents the user from interacting with the displayed component. Blazor will attempt to reconnect and pick up where it left off when the disconnection is caused by temporary network issues, but it won't be able to do so when the server has been stopped or restarted because the context data for the connection has been lost; you will have to explicitly request a new URL.

There is a default reload link in the connection message, but that goes to the default URL for the website, which isn't useful for this book where I direct you to specific URLs to see the effect of examples. See chapter 34 for details of how to configure the connection messages.

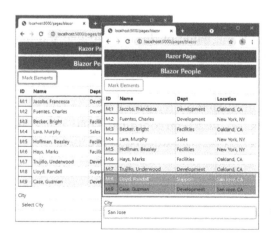

Figure 33.5 Demonstrating that only changes are used

33.4   *Understanding the basic Razor Component features*

Now that I have demonstrated how Blazor can be used and how it works, it is time to go back to the basics and introduce the features that Razor Components offer. Although the example in the previous section showed how standard ASP.NET Core features can be reproduced using Blazor, there is a much wider set of features available.

33.4.1   *Understanding Blazor events and data bindings*

Events allow a Razor Component to respond to user interaction, and Blazor uses the persistent HTTP connection to send details of the event to the server where it can be processed. To see Blazor events in action, add a Razor Component named `Events`
`.razor` to the `Blazor` folder with the content shown in listing 33.10.

> **Listing 33.10   The contents of the Events.razor file in the Blazor folder**

```
<div class="m-2 p-2 border">
    <button class="btn btn-primary" @onclick="IncrementCounter">
        Increment
    </button>
    <span class="p-2">Counter Value: @Counter</span>
</div>

@code {
    public int Counter { get; set; } = 1;

    public void IncrementCounter(MouseEventArgs e) {
        Counter++;
    }
}
```

You register a handler for an event by adding an attribute to an HTML element, where the attribute name is `@on`, followed by the event name. In the example, I have set up a handler for the `click` events generated by a `button` element, like this:

```
...
<button class="btn btn-primary" @onclick="IncrementCounter">
    Increment
</button>
...
```

The value assigned to the attribute is the name of the method that will be invoked when the event is triggered. The method can define an optional parameter that is either an instance of the `EventArgs` class or a class derived from `EventArgs` that provides additional information about the event.

For the `onclick` event, the handler method receives a `MouseEventArgs` object, which provides additional details, such as the screen coordinates of the click. Table 33.4 lists the event description events and the events for which they are used.

Table 33.4 The EventArgs classes and the events they represent

Class	Events
ChangeEventArgs	onchange, oninput
ClipboardEventArgs	oncopy, oncut, onpaste
DragEventArgs	ondrag, ondragend, ondragenter, ondragleave, ondragover, ondragstart, ondrop
ErrorEventArgs	onerror
FocusEventArgs	onblur, onfocus, onfocusin, onfocusout
KeyboardEventArgs	onkeydown, onkeypress, onkeyup
MouseEventArgs	onclick, oncontextmenu, ondblclick, onmousedown, onmouse-move, onmouseout, onmouseover, onmouseup, onmousewheel, onwheel
PointerEventArgs	ongotpointercapture, onlostpointercapture, onpointer-cancel, onpointerdown, onpointerenter, onpointerleave, onpointermove, onpointerout, onpointerover, onpointerup
ProgressEventArgs	onabort, onload, onloadend, onloadstart, onprogress, ontimeout
TouchEventArgs	ontouchcancel, ontouchend, ontouchenter, ontouchleave, ontouchmove, ontouchstart
EventArgs	onactivate, onbeforeactivate, onbeforecopy, onbeforecut, onbeforedeactivate, onbeforepaste, oncanplay, oncanplay-through, oncuechange, ondeactivate, ondurationchange, onemptied, onended, onfullscreenchange, onfullscreen-error, oninvalid, onloadeddata, onloadedmetadata, onpause, onplay, onplaying, onpointerlockchange, onpointerlock-error, onratechange, onreadystatechange, onreset, onscroll, onseeked, onseeking, onselect, onselection-change, onselectstart, onstalled, onstop, onsubmit, onsuspend, ontimeupdate, onvolumechange, onwaiting

The Blazor JavaScript code receives the event when it is triggered and forwards it to the server over the persistent HTTP connection. The handler method is invoked, and the state of the component is updated. Any changes to the content produced by the component's view section will be sent back to the JavaScript code, which will update the content displayed by the browser.

In the example, the click event will be handled by the IncrementCounter method, which changes the value of the Counter property. The value of the Counter property is included in the HTML rendered by the component, so Blazor sends the changes to the browser so that the JavaScript code can update the HTML elements displayed to the user. To display the Events component, replace the contents of the Blazor.cshtml file in the Pages folder, as shown in listing 33.11.

Listing 33.11   Using a new component in the Blazor.cshtml file in the Pages folder

```
@page "/pages/blazor"

<h4 class="bg-primary text-white text-center p-2">Events</h4>

<component type="typeof(Advanced.Blazor.Events)" render-mode="Server" />
```

Listing 33.11 changes the `type` attribute of the component element and removes the custom JavaScript and the `button` element I used to mark elements in the previous example. Restart ASP.NET Core and request http://localhost:5000/pages/blazor to see the new component. Click the Increment button, and the `click` event will be received by the Blazor JavaScript code and sent to the server for processing by the `IncrementCounter` method, as shown in figure 33.6.

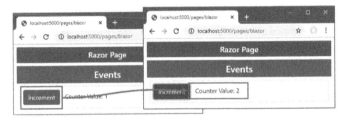

Figure 33.6 Handling an event

HANDLING EVENTS FROM MULTIPLE ELEMENTS

To avoid code duplication, elements from multiple elements can be received by a single handler method, as shown in listing 33.12.

Listing 33.12   Handling events in the Events.razor file in the Blazor folder

```
<div class="m-2 p-2 border">
    <button class="btn btn-primary"
            @onclick="@(e => IncrementCounter(e, 0))">
        Increment Counter #1
    </button>
    <span class="p-2">Counter Value: @Counter[0]</span>
</div>

<div class="m-2 p-2 border">
    <button class="btn btn-primary"
            @onclick="@(e => IncrementCounter(e, 1))">
        Increment Counter #2
    </button>
    <span class="p-2">Counter Value: @Counter[1]</span>
</div>

@code {
    public int[] Counter { get; set; } = new int[] { 1, 1 };

    public void IncrementCounter(MouseEventArgs e, int index) {
        Counter[index]++;
    }
}
```

Blazor event attributes can be used with lambda functions that receive the `EventArgs` object and invoke a handler method with additional arguments. In this example, I have added an `index` parameter to the `IncrementCounter` method, which is used to determine which counter value should be updated. The value for the argument is defined in the `@onclick` attribute, like this:

```
...
<button class="btn btn-primary" @onclick="@(e => IncrementCounter(e, 0))">
...
```

This technique can also be used when elements are generated programmatically, as shown in listing 33.13. In this example, I use an `@for` expression to generate elements and use the loop variable as the argument to the handler method. I have also removed the `EventArgs` parameter from the handler method, which isn't being used.

Avoiding the handler method name pitfall

The most common mistake when specifying an event handler method is to include parentheses, like this:

```
...
<button class="btn btn-primary" @onclick="IncrementCounter()">
...
```

The error message this produces will depend on the event handler method. You may see a warning telling you a formal parameter is missing or that `void` cannot be converted to an `EventCallback`. When specifying a handler method, you must specify just the event name, like this:

```
...
<button class="btn btn-primary" @onclick="IncrementCounter">
...
```

You can specify the method name as a Razor expression, like this:

```
...
<button class="btn btn-primary" @onclick="@IncrementCounter">
...
```

Some developers find this easier to parse, but the result is the same. A different set of rules applies when using a lambda function, which must be defined within a Razor expression, like this:

```
...
<button class="btn btn-primary" @onclick="@( ... )">
...
```

Within the Razor expression, the lambda function is defined as it would be in a C# class, which means defining the parameters, followed by the "goes to" arrow, followed by the function body, like this:

```
...
<button class="btn btn-primary" @onclick="@((e) => HandleEvent(e, local))">
...
```

(continued)

If you don't need to use the `EventArgs` object, then you can omit the parameter from the lambda function, like this:

```
...
<button class="btn btn-primary" @onclick="@(() =>
    IncrementCounter(local))">
...
```

You will quickly become used to these rules as you start to work with Blazor, even if they seem inconsistent at first.

Listing 33.13   Generating elements in the Events.razor file in the Blazor folder

```
@for (int i = 0; i < ElementCount; i++) {
    int local = i;
    <div class="m-2 p-2 border">
        <button class="btn btn-primary"
                @onclick="@(() => IncrementCounter(local))">
            Increment Counter #@(i + 1)
        </button>
        <span class="p-2">Counter Value: @GetCounter(i)</span>
    </div>
}

@code {
    public int ElementCount { get; set; } = 4;

    public Dictionary<int, int> Counters { get; }
        = new Dictionary<int, int>();

    public int GetCounter(int index) =>
        Counters.ContainsKey(index) ? Counters[index] : 0;

    public void IncrementCounter(int index) =>
        Counters[index] = GetCounter(index) + 1;
}
```

The important point to understand about event handlers is that the `@onclick` lambda function isn't evaluated until the server receives the `click` event from the browser. This means care must be taken not to use the loop variable `i` as the argument to the `IncrementCounter` method because it will always be the final value produced by the loop, which would be 4 in this case. Instead, you must capture the loop variable in a local variable, like this:

```
...
int local = i;
...
```

The local variable is then used as the argument to the event handler method in the attribute, like this:

```
...
<button class="btn btn-primary" @onclick="@(() => IncrementCounter(local))">
...
```

The local variable fixes the value for the lambda function for each of the generated elements. Restart ASP.NET Core and use a browser to request http://localhost:5000/pages/blazor, which will produce the response shown in figure 33.7. The `click` events produced by all the `button` elements are handled by the same method, but the argument provided by the lambda function ensures that the correct counter is updated.

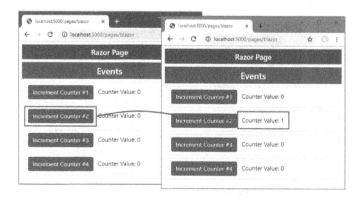

Figure 33.7 Handling events from multiple elements

PROCESSING EVENTS WITHOUT A HANDLER METHOD

Simple event handling can be done directly in a lambda function, without using a handler method, as shown in listing 33.14.

Listing 33.14   Handling events in the Events.razor file in the Blazor folder

```
@for (int i = 0; i < ElementCount; i++) {
    int local = i;
    <div class="m-2 p-2 border">
        <button class="btn btn-primary"
                @onclick="@(() => IncrementCounter(local))">
            Increment Counter #@(i + 1)
        </button>
        <button class="btn btn-info"
                @onclick="@(() => Counters.Remove(local))">
            Reset
        </button>
        <span class="p-2">Counter Value: @GetCounter(i)</span>
    </div>
}

@code {
    public int ElementCount { get; set; } = 4;

    public Dictionary<int, int> Counters { get; }
        = new Dictionary<int, int>();

    public int GetCounter(int index) =>
        Counters.ContainsKey(index) ? Counters[index] : 0;

    public void IncrementCounter(int index)  =>
        Counters[index] = GetCounter(index) + 1;
}
```

Complex handlers should be defined as methods, but this approach is more concise for simple handlers. Restart ASP.NET Core and request http://localhost:5000/pages/blazor. The Reset buttons remove values from the `Counters` collection without relying on a method in the `@code` section of the component, as shown in figure 33.8.

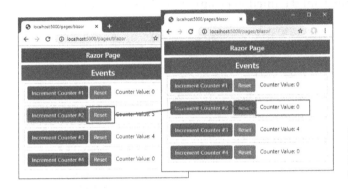

**Figure 33.8
Handling events
in a lambda
expression**

PREVENTING DEFAULT EVENTS AND EVENT PROPAGATION

Blazor provides two attributes that alter the default behavior of events in the browser, as described in table 33.5. These attributes, where the name of the event is followed by a colon and then a keyword, are known as *parameters*.

Table 33.5   The event configuration parameters

Name	Description
`@on{event}:preventDefault`	This parameter determines whether the default event for an element is triggered.
`@on{event}:stopPropagation`	This parameter determines whether an event is propagated to its ancestor elements.

Listing 33.15 demonstrates what these parameters do and why they are useful.

Listing 33.15   Overriding event defaults in the Events.razor file in the Blazor folder

```
<form action="/pages/blazor" method="get">
    @for (int i = 0; i < ElementCount; i++) {
        int local = i;
        <div class="m-2 p-2 border">
            <button class="btn btn-primary"
                    @onclick="@(() => IncrementCounter(local))"
                    @onclick:preventDefault="EnableEventParams">
                Increment Counter #@(i + 1)
            </button>
            <button class="btn btn-info"
                    @onclick="@(() => Counters.Remove(local))">
                Reset
            </button>
            <span class="p-2">Counter Value: @GetCounter(i)</span>
        </div>
    }
```

```
</form>

<div class="m-2" @onclick="@(() => IncrementCounter(1))">
    <button class="btn btn-primary"
            @onclick="@(() => IncrementCounter(0))"
            @onclick:stopPropagation="EnableEventParams">
        Propagation Test
    </button>
</div>

<div class="form-check m-2">
    <input class="form-check-input" type="checkbox"
            @onchange="@(() => EnableEventParams = !EnableEventParams)" />
    <label class="form-check-label">Enable Event Parameters</label>
</div>

@code {
    public int ElementCount { get; set; } = 4;

    public Dictionary<int, int> Counters { get; }
        = new Dictionary<int, int>();

    public int GetCounter(int index) =>
        Counters.ContainsKey(index) ? Counters[index] : 0;

    public void IncrementCounter(int index) =>
        Counters[index] = GetCounter(index) + 1;

    public bool EnableEventParams { get; set; } = false;
}
```

This example creates two situations in which the default behavior of events in the browser can cause problems. The first is caused by adding a form element. By default, button elements contained in a form will submit that form when they are clicked, even when the @onclick attribute is present. This means that whenever one of the Increment Counter buttons is clicked, the browser will send the form data to the ASP.NET Core server, which will respond with the contents of the Blazor.cshtml Razor Page.

The second problem is demonstrated by an element whose parent also defines an event handler, like this:

```
...
<div class="m-2" @onclick="@(() => IncrementCounter(1))">
    <button class="btn btn-primary" @onclick="@(() => IncrementCounter(0))"
...
```

Events go through a well-defined lifecycle in the browser, which includes being passed up the chain of ancestor elements. In the example, this means clicking the button will cause two counters to be updated, once by the @onclick handler for the button element and once by the @onclick handler for the enclosing div element.

To see these problems, restart ASP.NET Core and request http://localhost:5000/pages/blazor. Click an Increment Counter button; you will see that the form is submitted and the page is essentially reloaded. Click the Propagation Test button, and you will see that two counters are updated. Figure 33.9 shows both problems.

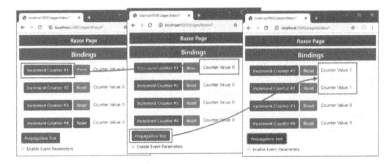

Figure 33.9   Problems caused by the default behavior of events in the browser

The checkbox in listing 33.15 toggles the property that applies the parameters described in table 33.5, with the effect that the form isn't submitted and only the handler on the button element receives the event. To see the effect, check the checkbox and then click an Increment Counter button and the Propagation Test buttons, which produces the result shown in figure 33.10.

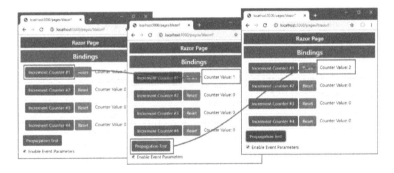

Figure 33.10   Overriding the default behavior of events in the browser

33.4.2 *Working with data bindings*

Event handlers and Razor expressions can be used to create a two-way relationship between an HTML element and a C# value, which is useful for elements that allow users to make changes, such as `input` and `select` elements. Add a Razor Component named `Bindings.razor` to the `Blazor` folder with the content shown in listing 33.16.

> **Listing 33.16   The contents of the Bindings.razor file in the Blazor folder**

```
<div class="form-group">
    <label>City:</label>
    <input class="form-control" value="@City" @onchange="UpdateCity" />
</div>
<div class="p-2 mb-2">City Value: @City</div>
<button class="btn btn-primary" @onclick="@(() => City = "Paris")">
    Paris
</button>
```

```
<button class="btn btn-primary" @onclick="@(() => City = "Chicago")">
    Chicago
</button>

@code {

    public string? City { get; set; } = "London";

    public void UpdateCity(ChangeEventArgs e) {
        City = e.Value as string;
    }
}
```

The @onchange attribute registers the UpdateCity method as a handler for the change event from the input element. The events are described using the ChangeEventArgs class, which provides a Value property. Each time a change event is received, the City property is updated with the contents of the input element.

The input element's value attribute creates a relationship in the other direction so that when the value of the City property changes, so does the element's value attribute, which changes the text displayed to the user. To apply the new Razor Component, change the component attribute in the Razor Page, as shown in listing 33.17.

> **Listing 33.17 Using a Razor Component in the Blazor.cshtml file in the Pages folder**

```
@page "/pages/blazor"

<h4 class="bg-primary text-white text-center p-2">Events</h4>

<component type="typeof(Advanced.Blazor.Bindings)" render-mode="Server" />
```

To see both parts of the relationship defined by the binding in listing 33.16, restart ASP.NET Core, navigate to http://localhost:5000/pages/blazor, and edit the content of the input element. The change event is triggered only when the input element loses the focus, so once you have finished editing, press the Tab key or click outside of the input element; you will see the value you entered displayed through the Razor expression in the div element, as shown on the left of figure 33.11. Click one of the buttons, and the City property will be changed to Paris or Chicago, and the selected value will be displayed by both the div element and the input element, as shown on the right of the figure.

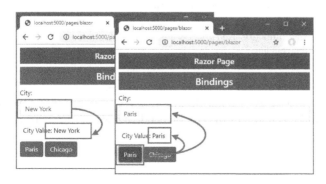

Figure 33.11 Creating a two-way relationship between an element and a property

Two-way relationships involving the change event can be expressed as data bindings, which allows both the value and the event to be configured with a single attribute, as shown in listing 33.18.

> **Listing 33.18   Using a data binding in the Bindings.razor file in the Blazor folder**

```
<div class="form-group">
    <label>City:</label>
    <input class="form-control" @bind="City" />
</div>
<div class="p-2 mb-2">City Value: @City</div>
<button class="btn btn-primary" @onclick="@(() => City = "Paris")">
    Paris
</button>
<button class="btn btn-primary" @onclick="@(() => City = "Chicago")">
    Chicago
</button>

@code {

    public string? City { get; set; } = "London";

    //public void UpdateCity(ChangeEventArgs e) {
    //    City = e.Value as string;
    //}
}
```

The @bind attribute is used to specify the property that will be updated when the change event is triggered and that will update the value attribute when it changes. The effect in listing 33.18 is the same as listing 33.16 but expressed more concisely and without the need for a handler method or a lambda function to update the property.

CHANGING THE BINDING EVENT

By default, the change event is used in bindings, which provides reasonable responsiveness for the user without requiring too many updates from the server. The event used in a binding can be changed by using the attributes described in table 33.6.

Table 33.6   The binding attributes for specifying an event

Attribute	Description
@bind-value	This attribute is used to select the property for the data binding.
@bind-value:event	This attribute is used to select the event for the data binding.

These attributes are used instead of @bind, as shown in listing 33.19, but can be used only with events that are represented with the ChangeEventArgs class. This means that only the onchange and oninput events can be used, at least in the current release.

Listing 33.19 Specifying an event in the Bindings.razor file in the Blazor folder

```
<div class="form-group">
    <label>City:</label>
    <input class="form-control" @bind-value="City"
           @bind-value:event="oninput" />
</div>
<div class="p-2 mb-2">City Value: @City</div>
<button class="btn btn-primary" @onclick="@(() => City = "Paris")">
    Paris
</button>
<button class="btn btn-primary" @onclick="@(() => City = "Chicago")">
    Chicago
</button>

@code {
    public string? City { get; set; } = "London";
}
```

This combination of attributes creates a binding for the `City` property that is updated when the `oninput` event is triggered, which happens after every keystroke, rather than only when the `input` element loses the focus. To see the effect, restart ASP.NET Core, navigate to http://localhost:5000/pages/blazor, and start typing into the `input` element. The `City` property will be updated after every keystroke, as shown in figure 33.12.

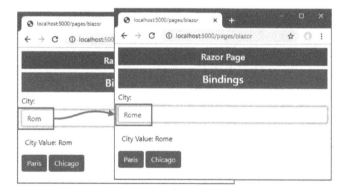

Figure 33.12 Changing the event in a data binding

CREATING DATETIME BINDINGS

Blazor has special support for creating bindings for `DateTime` properties, allowing them to be expressed using a specific culture or a format string. This feature is applied using the parameters described in table 33.7.

> **TIP** If you have used the `@bind-value` and `@bind-value:event` attributes to select an event, then you must use the `@bind-value:culture` and `@bind -value:format` parameters instead.

Table 33.7   The DateTime parameters

Name	Description
@bind:culture	This attribute is used to select a `Culture-Info` object that will be used to format the `DateTime` value.
@bind:format	This attribute is used to specify a data formatting string that will be used to format the `DateTime` value.

Listing 33.20 shows the use of these attributes with a `DateTime` property.

NOTE   The formatting strings used in these examples are described at https://docs.microsoft.com/en-us/dotnet/api/system.datetime.

Listing 33.20   Using a DateTime property in the Bindings.razor file in the Blazor folder

```
@using System.Globalization

<div class="form-group">
    <label>City:</label>
    <input class="form-control" @bind-value="City"
        @bind-value:event="oninput" />
</div>
<div class="p-2 mb-2">City Value: @City</div>
<button class="btn btn-primary" @onclick="@(() => City = "Paris")">
    Paris
</button>
<button class="btn btn-primary" @onclick="@(() => City = "Chicago")">
    Chicago
</button>

<div class="form-group mt-2">
    <label>Time:</label>
    <input class="form-control my-1" @bind="Time"
        @bind:culture="Culture" @bind:format="MMM-dd" />
    <input class="form-control my-1" @bind="Time"
            @bind:culture="Culture" />
    <input class="form-control" type="date" @bind="Time" />
</div>
<div class="p-2 mb-2">Time Value: @Time</div>

<div class="form-group">
    <label>Culture:</label>
    <select class="form-control" @bind="Culture">
        <option value="@CultureInfo.GetCultureInfo("en-us")">
            en-US
        </option>
        <option value="@CultureInfo.GetCultureInfo("en-gb")">
            en-GB
        </option>
        <option value="@CultureInfo.GetCultureInfo("fr-fr")">
```

```
                fr-FR
        </option>
    </select>
</div>

@code {
    public string? City { get; set; } = "London";

    public DateTime Time { get; set; }
        = DateTime.Parse("2050/01/20 09:50");

    public CultureInfo Culture { get; set; }
        = CultureInfo.GetCultureInfo("en-us");
}
```

There are three input elements that are used to display the same `DataTime` value, two of which have been configured using the attributes from table 33.7. The first element has been configured with a culture and a format string, like this:

```
...
<input class="form-control my-1" @bind="Time" @bind:culture="Culture"
    @bind:format="MMM-dd" />
...
```

The `DateTime` property is displayed using the culture picked in the `select` element and with a format string that displays an abbreviated month name and the numeric date. The second `input` element specifies just a culture, which means the default formatting string will be used.

```
...
<input class="form-control my-1" @bind="Time" @bind:culture="Culture" />
...
```

To see how dates are displayed, restart ASP.NET Core, request http://localhost:5000/pages/blazor, and use the `select` element to pick different culture settings. The settings available represent English as it is used in the United States, English as it used in the United Kingdom, and French as it is used in France. Figure 33.13 shows the formatting each produces.

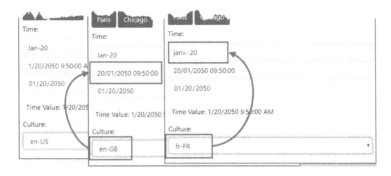

Figure 33.13   Formatting DateTime values

The initial locale in this example is en-US. When you switch to en-GB, the order in which the month and date appear changes. When you switch to en-FR, the abbreviated month name changes.

> **Letting the browser format dates**
>
> Notice that the value displayed by the third input element in listing 33.20 doesn't change, regardless of the locale you choose. This input element has neither of the attributes described in table 33.7 but does have its type attribute set to date, like this:
>
> ```
> ...
> <input class="form-control" type="date" @bind="Time" />
> ...
> ```
>
> You should not specify a culture or a format string when setting the type attribute to date, datetime-local, month, or time, because Blazor will automatically format date values into a culture-neutral format that the browser translates into the user's locale. Figure 33.11 shows how the date is formatted in the en-US locale, but the user will see the date expressed in their local convention.

33.5 *Using class files to define components*

If you don't like the mix of code and markup that Razor Components supports, you can use C# class files to define part, or all, of the component.

33.5.1 *Using a code-behind class*

The @code section of a Razor Component can be defined in a separate class file, known as a *code-behind class* or *code-behind file*. Code-behind classes for Razor Components are defined as partial classes with the same name as the component they provide code for.

Add a Razor Component named Split.razor to the Blazor folder with the content shown in listing 33.21.

> **Listing 33.21 The contents of the Split.razor file in the Blazor folder**

```
<ul class="list-group">
    @foreach (string name in Names) {
        <li class="list-group-item">@name</li>
    }
</ul>
```

This file contains only HTML content and Razor expressions and renders a list of names that it expects to receive through a Names property. To provide the component with its code, add a class file named Split.razor.cs to the Blazor folder and use it to define the partial class shown in listing 33.22.

Listing 33.22 The contents of the Split.razor.cs file in the Blazor folder

```
using Advanced.Models;
using Microsoft.AspNetCore.Components;

namespace Advanced.Blazor {

    public partial class Split {

        [Inject]
        public DataContext? Context { get; set; }

        public IEnumerable<string> Names =>
            Context?.People.Select(p => p.Firstname)
                ?? Enumerable.Empty<string>();
    }
}
```

The partial class must be defined in the same namespace as its Razor Component and have the same name. For this example, that means the namespace is `Advanced` `.Blazor`, and the class name is `Splt`. Code-behind classes do not define constructors and receive services using the `Inject` attribute. Listing 33.23 applies the new component.

Listing 33.23 Applying a new component in the Blazor.cshtml file in the Pages folder

```
@page "/pages/blazor"

<h4 class="bg-primary text-white text-center p-2">Code-Behind</h4>

<component type="typeof(Advanced.Blazor.Split)" render-mode="Server" />
```

Restart ASP.NET Core and request http://localhost:5000/pages/blazor, and you will see the response shown in figure 33.14.

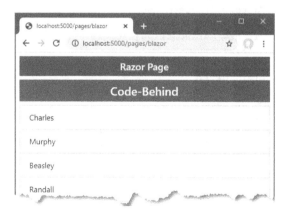

Figure 33.14 Using a code-behind class to define a Razor Component

33.5.2 Defining a Razor Component class

Razor Components can be defined entirely in a class file, although this can be less expressive than using Razor expressions. Add a class file named `CodeOnly.cs` to the `Blazor` folder and use it to define the class shown in listing 33.24.

> **Listing 33.24   The contents of the CodeOnly.cs file in the Blazor folder**

```csharp
using Advanced.Models;
using Microsoft.AspNetCore.Components;
using Microsoft.AspNetCore.Components.Rendering;
using Microsoft.AspNetCore.Components.Web;

namespace Advanced.Blazor {

    public class CodeOnly : ComponentBase {

        [Inject]
        public DataContext? Context { get; set; }

        public IEnumerable<string> Names =>
            Context?.People.Select(p => p.Firstname)
                ?? Enumerable.Empty<string>();

        public bool Ascending { get; set; } = false;

        protected override void BuildRenderTree(
            RenderTreeBuilder builder) {
                IEnumerable<string> data = Ascending
                    ? Names.OrderBy(n => n)
                    : Names.OrderByDescending(n => n);

            builder.OpenElement(1, "button");
            builder.AddAttribute(2, "class", "btn btn-primary mb-2");
            builder.AddAttribute(3, "onclick",
                EventCallback.Factory.Create<MouseEventArgs>(this,
                    () => Ascending = !Ascending));
            builder.AddContent(4, new MarkupString("Toggle"));
            builder.CloseElement();

            builder.OpenElement(5, "ul");
            builder.AddAttribute(6, "class", "list-group");
            foreach (string name in data) {
                builder.OpenElement(7, "li");
                builder.AddAttribute(8, "class", "list-group-item");
                builder.AddContent(9, new MarkupString(name));
                builder.CloseElement();
            }
            builder.CloseElement();
        }
    }
}
```

The base class for components is `ComponentBase`. The content that would normally be expressed as annotated HTML elements is created by overriding the `BuildRender-Tree` method and using the `RenderTreeBuilder` parameter. Creating content can be awkward because each element is created and configured using multiple code statements, and each statement must have a sequence number that the compiler uses to match up code and content. The `OpenElement` method starts a new element, which is configured using the `AddElement` and `AddContent` methods and then completed with the `CloseElement` method. All the features available in regular Razor Components are available, including events and bindings, which are set up by adding attributes to elements, just as if they were defined literally in a `.razor` file. The component in listing 33.24 displays a list of sorted names, with the sort direction altered when a `button` element is clicked. Listing 33.25 applies the component so that it will be displayed to the user.

Listing 33.25 Applying a new component in the Blazor.cshtml file in the Pages folder

```
@page "/pages/blazor"

<h4 class="bg-primary text-white text-center p-2">Class Only</h4>

<component type="typeof(Advanced.Blazor.CodeOnly)" render-mode="Server" />
```

Restart ASP.NET Core and request http://localhost:5000/pages/blazor to see the content produced by the class-based Razor Component. When you click the button, the sort direction of the names in the list is changed, as shown in figure 33.15.

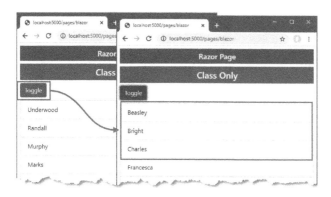

Figure 33.15 Defining a component entirely in code

Summary

- Blazor adds client-side interactivity to ASP.NET Core by introducing JavaScript to efficiently perform updates.
- Blazor functionality is created in Razor Components, which follow a similar syntax to Razor views and Razor Pages.
- Razor Components can respond to user interaction by handling JavaScript events, which are used to invoke server-side methods and generate selective updates.
- Razor Components are usually defined with the markup and code in a single file but can use a separate class file and even defined entirely in C#.

34

Using Blazor
Server, part 2

This chapter covers

- Composing elements to combine Blazor components
- Configuring components using attributes
- Displaying child content and creating templates
- Managing connection errors and application errors

In this chapter, I continue to describe Blazor Server, focusing on the way that Razor Components can be used together to create more complex features. Table 34.1 provides a guide to the chapter.

Table 34.1   Chapter guide

Problem	Solution	Listing
Creating complex features using Blazor	Combine components to reduce duplication.	3, 4
Configuring a component	Use the `Parameter` attribute to receive a value from an attribute.	5–10
Defining custom events and bindings	Use `EventCallbacks` to receive the handler for the event and follow the convention to create bindings.	11–14
Displaying child content in a component	Use a `RenderFragment` named `ChildContent`.	15, 16
Creating templates	Use named `RenderFragment` properties.	17, 25
Distributing configuration settings widely	Use a cascading parameter.	26, 27
Responding to connection errors	Use the connection element and classes.	28, 29
Responding to unhandled errors	Use the error element and classes or define an error boundary.	30–35

34.1   Preparing for this chapter

This chapter uses the Advanced project from chapter 33. No changes are required to prepare for this chapter.

> **TIP**   You can download the example project for this chapter—and for all the other chapters in this book—from https://github.com/manningbooks/pro-asp .net-core-7. See chapter 1 for how to get help if you have problems running the examples.

Open a new PowerShell command prompt, navigate to the folder that contains the `Advanced.csproj` file, and run the command shown in listing 34.1 to drop the database.

Listing 34.1   Dropping the database

```
dotnet ef database drop --force
```

Use the PowerShell command prompt to run the command shown in listing 34.2.

Listing 34.2   Running the example application

```
dotnet run
```

Use a browser to request http://localhost:5000/controllers, which will display a list of data items. Request http://localhost:5000/pages/blazor, and you will see the component from chapter 33 I used to demonstrate data bindings. Figure 34.1 shows both responses.

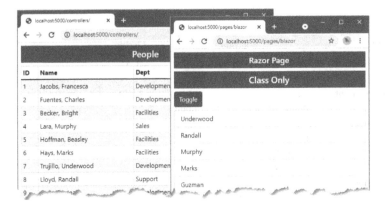

Figure 34.1   Running the example application

34.2   Combining components

Blazor components can be combined to create more complex features. In the sections that follow, I show you how multiple components can be used together and how components can communicate. To get started, add a Razor Component named `Select-Filter.razor` to the `Blazor` folder with the content shown in listing 34.3.

Listing 34.3   The contents of the SelectFilter.razor file in the Blazor folder

```
<div class="form-group">
    <label for="select-@Title">@Title</label>
    <select name="select-@Title" class="form-control"
            @bind="SelectedValue">
        <option disabled selected value="">Select @Title</option>
        @foreach (string val in Values) {
                <option value="@val" selected="@(val == SelectedValue)">
                @val
                </option>
        }
    </select>
</div>

@code {

    public IEnumerable<string> Values { get; set; }
        = Enumerable.Empty<string>();

    public string? SelectedValue { get; set; }

    public string Title { get; set; } = "Placeholder";
}
```

The component renders a `select` element that will allow the user to choose a city. In listing 34.4, I have applied the `SelectFilter` component, replacing the existing `select` element.

```
<table class="table table-sm table-bordered table-striped">
    <thead>
        <tr><th>ID</th><th>Name</th><th>Dept</th><th>Location</th></tr>
    </thead>
    <tbody>
        @foreach (Person p in People ?? Enumerable.Empty<Person>()) {
            <tr class="@GetClass(p?.Location?.City)">
                <td>@p?.PersonId</td>
                <td>@p?.Surname, @p?.Firstname</td>
                <td>@p?.Department?.Name</td>
                <td>@p?.Location?.City, @p?.Location?.State</td>
            </tr>
        }
    </tbody>
</table>

<div class="form-group">
    <label for="city">City</label>
    <select name="city" class="form-control" @bind="SelectedCity">
        <option disabled selected value="">Select City</option>
        @foreach (string city in Cities ?? Enumerable.Empty<string>()) {
            <option value="@city" selected="@(city == SelectedCity)">
                @city
            </option>
        }
    </select>
</div>

<SelectFilter />

@code {

    [Inject]
    public DataContext? Context { get; set; }

    public IEnumerable<Person>? People =>
        Context?.People.Include(p => p.Department)
            .Include(p => p.Location);

    public IEnumerable<string>? Cities =>
        Context?.Locations.Select(l => l.City);

    public string SelectedCity { get; set; } = string.Empty;

    public string GetClass(string? city) =>
        SelectedCity == city ? "bg-info text-white" : "";
}
```

When a component is added to the content rendered by a controller view or Razor Page, the `component` element is used, as shown in chapter 33. When a component is added to the content rendered by another component, then the name of the component is used as an element instead. In this case, I am adding the `SelectFilter` component to the content rendered by the PeopleList component, which I do with a SelectFilter element. It is important to pay close attention to the capitalization, which must match exactly.

When combining components, the effect is that one component delegates responsibility for part of its layout to another. In this case, I have removed the select element that the PeopleList component used to present the user with a choice of cities and replaced it with the SelectFilter component, which will provide the same feature. The components form a parent-child relationship; the PeopleList component is the parent, and the SelectFilter component is the child.

Additional work is required before everything is properly integrated, but you can see that adding the SelectFilter element displays the SelectFilter component by restarting ASP.NET Core and requesting http://localhost:5000/controllers, which produces the response shown in figure 34.2.

**Figure 34.2
Adding one
component to the
content rendered
by another**

34.2.1 *Configuring components with attributes*

My goal with the SelectList component is to create a general-purpose feature that I can use throughout the application, configuring the values it displays each time it is used. Razor Components are configured using attributes added to the HTML element that applies them. The values assigned to the HTML element attributes are assigned to the component's C# properties. The Parameter attribute is applied to the C# properties that a component allows to be configured, as shown in listing 34.5.

Listing 34.5   Configurable properties in the SelectFilter.razor file in the Blazor folder

```
<div class="form-group">
    <label for="select-@Title">@Title</label>
    <select name="select-@Title" class="form-control"
            @bind="SelectedValue">
        <option disabled selected value="">Select @Title</option>
        @foreach (string val in Values) {
                <option value="@val" selected="@(val == SelectedValue)">
                @val
                </option>
        }
    </select>
</div>

@code {
```

```
[Parameter]
public IEnumerable<string> Values { get; set; }
    = Enumerable.Empty<string>();

public string? SelectedValue { get; set; }

[Parameter]
public string Title { get; set; } = "Placeholder";
}
```

Components can be selective about the properties they allow to be configured. In this case, the `Parameter` attribute has been applied to two of the properties defined by the `SelectFilter` component. In listing 34.6, I have modified the element the `PeopleList` component uses to apply the `SelectFilter` component to add configuration attributes.

```
...
<SelectFilter values="@Cities" title="City" />
...
```

For each property that should be configured, an attribute of the same name is added to the parent's HTML element. The attribute values can be fixed values, such as the `City` string assigned to the `title` attribute, or Razor expressions, such as `@Cities`, which assigns the sequence of objects from the `Cities` property to the `values` attribute.

> **TIP** The `EditorRequired` attribute can be applied alongside the `Parameter` attribute to denote properties for which values are required. A warning will be produced if the component is used without the required attribute.

SETTING AND RECEIVING BULK CONFIGURATION SETTINGS

Defining individual properties to receive values can be error-prone if there are many configuration settings, especially if those values are being received by a component so they can be passed on, either to a child component or to a regular HTML element. In these situations, a single property can be designated to receive any attribute values that have not been matched by other properties, which can then be applied as a set, as shown in listing 34.7.

```
<div class="form-group">
    <label for="select-@Title">@Title</label>
    <select name="select-@Title" class="form-control"
            @bind="SelectedValue" @attributes="Attrs">
        <option disabled selected value="">Select @Title</option>
        @foreach (string val in Values) {
            <option value="@val" selected="@(val == SelectedValue)">
                @val
            </option>
        }
```

```
        </select>
</div>

@code {

    [Parameter]
    public IEnumerable<string> Values { get; set; }
        = Enumerable.Empty<string>();

    public string? SelectedValue { get; set; }

    [Parameter]
    public string Title { get; set; } = "Placeholder";

    [Parameter(CaptureUnmatchedValues = true)]
    public Dictionary<string, object>? Attrs { get; set; }
}
```

Setting the `Parameter` attribute's `CaptureUnmatchedValues` argument to `true` identifies a property as the catchall for attributes that are not otherwise matched. The type of the property must be `Dictionary<string, object>`, which allows the attribute names and values to be represented.

Properties whose type is `Dictionary<string, object>` can be applied to elements using the `@attribute` expression, like this:

```
...
<select name="select-@Title" class="form-control" @bind="SelectedValue"
    @attributes="Attrs">
...
```

This is known as *attribute splatting*, and it allows a set of attributes to be applied in one go. The effect of the changes in listing 34.7 means that the `SelectFilter` component will receive the `Values` and `Title` attribute values and that any other attributes will be assigned to the `Attrs` property and passed on to the `select` element. Listing 34.8 adds some attributes to demonstrate the effect.

> **Listing 34.8   Adding element attributes in the PeopleList.razor file in the Blazor folder**

```
...
<SelectFilter values="@Cities" title="City" autofocus="true" name="city"
    required="true" />
...
```

Restart ASP.NET Core and navigate to http://localhost:5000/controllers. The attributes passed on to the `select` element do not affect appearance, but if you right-click the `select` element and select Inspect from the pop-up menu, you will see the attributes added to the `SelectFilter` element in the `PeopleList` component have been added to the element rendered by the `SelectFilter` component, like this:

```
...
<select class="form-control" autofocus="true" name="city" required="true">
...
```

CONFIGURING A COMPONENT IN A CONTROLLER VIEW OR RAZOR PAGE

Attributes are also used to configure components when they are applied using the `component` element. In listing 34.9, I have added properties to the `PeopleList` component that specify how many items from the database should be displayed and a string value that will be passed on to the `SelectFilter` component.

Listing 34.9   Adding properties in the PeopleList.razor file in the Blazor folder

```
<table class="table table-sm table-bordered table-striped">
    <thead>
        <tr><th>ID</th><th>Name</th><th>Dept</th><th>Location</th></tr>
    </thead>
    <tbody>
        @foreach (Person p in People ?? Enumerable.Empty<Person>()) {
            <tr class="@GetClass(p?.Location?.City)">
                <td>@p?.PersonId</td>
                <td>@p?.Surname, @p?.Firstname</td>
                <td>@p?.Department?.Name</td>
                <td>@p?.Location?.City, @p?.Location?.State</td>
            </tr>
        }
    </tbody>
</table>

<SelectFilter values="@Cities" title="@SelectTitle" />

@code {

    [Inject]
    public DataContext? Context { get; set; }

    public IEnumerable<Person>? People => Context?.People
            .Include(p => p.Department)
            .Include(p => p.Location).Take(ItemCount);

    public IEnumerable<string>? Cities =>
        Context?.Locations.Select(l => l.City);

    public string SelectedCity { get; set; } = string.Empty;

    public string GetClass(string? city) =>
        SelectedCity == city ? "bg-info text-white" : "";

    [Parameter]
    public int ItemCount { get; set; } = 4;

    [Parameter]
    public string? SelectTitle { get; set; }
}
```

Values for the C# properties are provided by adding attributes whose name begins with `param-`, followed by the property name, to the `component` element, as shown in listing 34.10.

Listing 34.10   Adding attributes in the Index.cshtml file in the Views/Home folder

```
@model PeopleListViewModel

<h4 class="bg-primary text-white text-center p-2">People</h4>

<component type="typeof(Advanced.Blazor.PeopleList)" render-mode="Server"
    param-itemcount="5" param-selecttitle="@("Location")" />
```

The `param-itemcount` attribute provides a value for the `ItemCount` property, and the `param-selecttitle` attribute provides a value for the `SelectTitle` property.

When using the `component` element, attribute values that can be parsed into numeric or `bool` values are handled as literal values and not Razor expressions, which is why I am able to specify the value for the `ItemCount` property as 4. Other values are assumed to be Razor expressions and not literal values, even though they are not prefixed with `@`. This oddity means that since I want to specify the value for the `SelectTitle` property as a literal string, I need a Razor expression, like this:

```
...
<component type="typeof(Advanced.Blazor.PeopleList)" render-mode="Server"
    param-itemcount="5" param-selecttitle="@("Location")" />
...
```

To see the effect of the configuration attributes, restart ASP.NET Core and request http://localhost:5000/controllers, which will produce the response shown in figure 34.3.

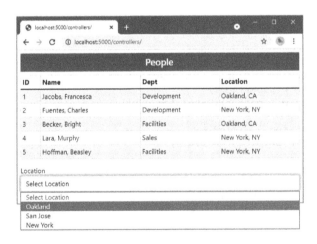

Figure 34.3 Configuring components with attributes

34.2.2 *Creating custom events and bindings*

The `SelectFilter` component receives its data values from its parent component, but it has no way to indicate when the user makes a selection. For this, I need to create a custom event for which the parent component can register a handler method, just as it would for events from regular HTML elements. Listing 34.11 adds a custom event to the `SelectFilter` component.

```
<div class="form-group">
    <label for="select-@Title">@Title</label>
    <select name="select-@Title" class="form-control"
            @onchange="HandleSelect" value="@SelectedValue">
        <option disabled selected value="">Select @Title</option>
        @foreach (string val in Values) {
            <option value="@val" selected="@(val == SelectedValue)">
                @val
            </option>
        }
    </select>
</div>

@code {

    [Parameter]
    public IEnumerable<string> Values { get; set; }
        = Enumerable.Empty<string>();

    public string? SelectedValue { get; set; }

    [Parameter]
    public string Title { get; set; } = "Placeholder";

    [Parameter(CaptureUnmatchedValues = true)]
    public Dictionary<string, object>? Attrs { get; set; }

    [Parameter]
    public EventCallback<string> CustomEvent { get; set; }

    public async Task HandleSelect(ChangeEventArgs e) {
        SelectedValue = e.Value as string;
        await CustomEvent.InvokeAsync(SelectedValue);
    }
}
```

The custom event is defined by adding a property whose type is EventCallback<T>. The generic type argument is the type that will be received by the parent's event handler and is string in this case. I have changed the select element so the @onchange attribute registers the HandleSelect method when the select element triggers its onchange event.

The HandleSelect method updates the SelectedValue property and triggers the custom event by invoking the EventCallback<T>.InvokeAsync method, like this:

```
...
await CustomEvent.InvokeAsync(SelectedValue);
...
```

The argument to the InvokeAsync method is used to trigger the event using the value received from the ChangeEventArgs object that was received from the select element. Listing 34.12 changes the PeopleList component so that it receives the custom event emitted by the SelectList component.

Listing 34.12 Handling an event in the PeopleList.razor file in the Blazor folder

```
<table class="table table-sm table-bordered table-striped">
    <thead>
        <tr><th>ID</th><th>Name</th><th>Dept</th><th>Location</th></tr>
    </thead>
    <tbody>
        @foreach (Person p in People ?? Enumerable.Empty<Person>()) {
            <tr class="@GetClass(p?.Location?.City)">
                <td>@p?.PersonId</td>
                <td>@p?.Surname, @p?.Firstname</td>
                <td>@p?.Department?.Name</td>
                <td>@p?.Location?.City, @p?.Location?.State</td>
            </tr>
        }
    </tbody>
</table>

<SelectFilter values="@Cities" title="@SelectTitle"
    CustomEvent="@HandleCustom" />

@code {

    [Inject]
    public DataContext? Context { get; set; }

    public IEnumerable<Person>? People => Context?.People
            .Include(p => p.Department)
            .Include(p => p.Location).Take(ItemCount);

    public IEnumerable<string>? Cities =>
        Context?.Locations.Select(l => l.City);

    public string SelectedCity { get; set; } = string.Empty;

    public string GetClass(string? city) =>
        SelectedCity == city ? "bg-info text-white" : "";

    [Parameter]
    public int ItemCount { get; set; } = 4;

    [Parameter]
    public string? SelectTitle { get; set; }

    public void HandleCustom(string newValue) {
        SelectedCity = newValue;
    }
}
```

To set up the event handler, an attribute is added to the element that applies the child component using the name of its `EventCallback<T>` property. The value of the attribute is a Razor expression that selects a method that receives a parameter of type `T`.

Restart ASP.NET Core, request http://localhost:5000/controllers, and select a value from the list of cities. The custom event completes the relationship between the parent and child components. The parent configures the child through its attributes to specify the title and the list of data values that will be presented to the user. The child component uses a custom event to tell the parent when the user selects a value, allowing the parent to highlight the corresponding rows in its HTML table, as shown in figure 34.4.

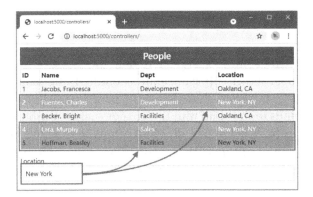

**Figure 34.4
Using a custom
event**

A parent component can create a binding on a child component if it defines a pair of properties, one of which is assigned a data value and the other of which is a custom event. The names of the property are important: the name of the event property must be the same as the data property plus the word `Changed`. Listing 34.13 updates the `SelectFilter` component so it presents the properties required for the binding.

Listing 34.13   Preparing for bindings in the SelectFilter.razor file in the Blazor folder

```
<div class="form-group">
    <label for="select-@Title">@Title</label>
    <select name="select-@Title" class="form-control"
            @onchange="HandleSelect" value="@SelectedValue">
        <option disabled selected value="">Select @Title</option>
        @foreach (string val in Values) {
            <option value="@val" selected="@(val == SelectedValue)">
                @val
            </option>
        }
    </select>
</div>

@code {

    [Parameter]
    public IEnumerable<string> Values { get; set; }
        = Enumerable.Empty<string>();

    [Parameter]
    public string? SelectedValue { get; set; }

    [Parameter]
    public string Title { get; set; } = "Placeholder";

    [Parameter(CaptureUnmatchedValues = true)]
    public Dictionary<string, object>? Attrs { get; set; }
```

```
    [Parameter]
    public EventCallback<string> SelectedValueChanged { get; set; }

    public async Task HandleSelect(ChangeEventArgs e) {
        SelectedValue = e.Value as string;
        await SelectedValueChanged.InvokeAsync(SelectedValue);
    }
}
```

Notice that the `Parameter` attribute must be applied to both the `SelectedValue` and `SelectedValueChanged` properties. If either attribute is omitted, the data binding won't work as expected.

The parent component binds to the child with the `@bind-<name>` attribute, where `<name>` corresponds to the property defined by the child component. In this example, the name of the child component's property is `SelectedValue`, and the parent can create a binding using `@bind-SelectedValue`, as shown in listing 34.14.

> **Listing 34.14   Using a custom binding in the PeopleList.razor file in the Blazor folder**

```
<table class="table table-sm table-bordered table-striped">
    <thead>
        <tr>
            <th>ID</th><th>Name</th><th>Dept</th><th>Location</th>
        </tr>
    </thead>
    <tbody>
        @foreach (Person p in People ?? Enumerable.Empty<Person>()) {
            <tr class="@GetClass(p?.Location?.City)">
                <td>@p?.PersonId</td>
                <td>@p?.Surname, @p?.Firstname</td>
                <td>@p?.Department?.Name</td>
                <td>@p?.Location?.City, @p?.Location?.State</td>
            </tr>
        }
    </tbody>
</table>

<SelectFilter values="@Cities" title="@SelectTitle"
    @bind-SelectedValue="SelectedCity" />

<button class="btn btn-primary mt-2"
    @onclick="@(() => SelectedCity = "Oakland")">
        Change
</button>

@code {

    [Inject]
    public DataContext? Context { get; set; }

    public IEnumerable<Person>? People => Context?.People
            .Include(p => p.Department)
            .Include(p => p.Location).Take(ItemCount);

    public IEnumerable<string>? Cities =>
```

```
        Context?.Locations.Select(l => l.City);

    public string SelectedCity { get; set; } = string.Empty;

    public string GetClass(string? city) =>
        SelectedCity == city ? "bg-info text-white" : "";

    [Parameter]
    public int ItemCount { get; set; } = 4;

    [Parameter]
    public string? SelectTitle { get; set; }

    //public void HandleCustom(string newValue) {
    //    SelectedCity = newValue;
    //}
}
```

Restart ASP.NET Core, request http://localhost:5000/controllers, and select New York from the list of cities. The custom binding will cause the value chosen in the `select` element to be reflected by the highlighting in the table. Click the Change button to test the binding in the other direction, and you will see the highlighted city change, as shown in figure 34.5.

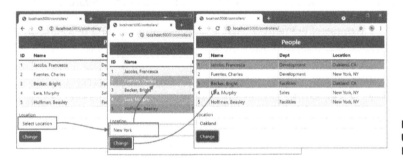

**Figure 34.5
Using a custom
binding**

34.3 *Displaying child content in a component*

Components that display child content act as wrappers around elements provided by their parents. To see how child content is managed, add a Razor Component named `ThemeWrapper.razor` to the `Blazor` folder with the content shown in listing 34.15.

> **Listing 34.15 The contents of the ThemeWrapper.razor file in the Blazor folder**

```
<div class="p-2 bg-@Theme border text-white">
    <h5 class="text-center">@Title</h5>
    @ChildContent
</div>

@code {
    [Parameter]
    public string? Theme { get; set; }

    [Parameter]
```

```
    public string? Title { get; set; }

    [Parameter]
    public RenderFragment? ChildContent { get; set; }
}
```

To receive child content, a component defines a property named `ChildContent` whose type is `RenderFragment` and that has been decorated with the `Parameter` attribute. The `@ChildContent` expression includes the child content in the component's HTML output. The component in the listing wraps its child content in a `div` element that is styled using a Bootstrap theme color and that displays a title. The name of the theme color and the text of the title are also received as parameters.

Restricting element reuse

When updating the content presented to the user, Blazor will reuse elements if it can because creating new elements is a relatively expensive operation. This is particularly true when displaying elements for a sequence of values, such as with `@for` or `@foreach` expressions. If the sequence changes, Blazor will reuse the elements it created for the old data values to display the new data.

This can cause problems if changes have been made to the elements outside of the control of Blazor, such as with custom JavaScript code. Blazor isn't aware of the changes, which will persist when the elements are reused. Although this is a rare situation, you can restrict the reuse of elements by using an `@key` attribute and providing an expression that associates the element with one of the data values in the sequence, like this:

```
...
@foreach (Person p in People ?? Enumerable.Empty<Person>()) {
    <tr @key="p.PersonId" class="@GetClass(p?.Location?.City)">
        <td>@p?.PersonId</td>
        <td>@p?.Surname, @p?.Firstname</td>
        <td>@p?.Department?.Name</td>
        <td>@p?.Location?.City, @p?.Location?.State</td>
    </tr>
}
...
```

Blazor will reuse an element only if there is a data item that has the same key. For other values, new elements will be created.

Child content is defined by adding HTML elements between the start and end tags when applying the component, as shown in listing 34.16.

Listing 34.16   Defining child content in the PeopleList.razor file in the Blazor folder

```
<table class="table table-sm table-bordered table-striped">
    <thead>
        <tr>
            <th>ID</th><th>Name</th><th>Dept</th><th>Location</th>
        </tr>
```

```
        </thead>
        <tbody>
            @foreach (Person p in People ?? Enumerable.Empty<Person>()) {
                <tr class="@GetClass(p?.Location?.City)">
                    <td>@p?.PersonId</td>
                    <td>@p?.Surname, @p?.Firstname</td>
                    <td>@p?.Department?.Name</td>
                    <td>@p?.Location?.City, @p?.Location?.State</td>
                </tr>
            }
        </tbody>
</table>

<ThemeWrapper Theme="info" Title="Location Selector">
    <SelectFilter values="@Cities" title="@SelectTitle"
        @bind-SelectedValue="SelectedCity" />

    <button class="btn btn-primary mt-2"
        @onclick="@(() => SelectedCity = "Oakland")">
            Change
    </button>
</ThemeWrapper>

@code {

    // ...statements omitted for brevity...
}
```

No additional attributes are required to configure the child content, which is processed and assigned to the `ChildContent` property automatically. To see how the `ThemeWrapper` component presents its child content, restart ASP.NET Core and request http://localhost:5000/controllers. You will see the configuration attributes that selected the theme and the title text used to produce the response shown in figure 34.6.

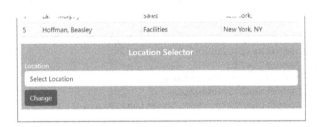

Figure 34.6
Using child content

34.3.1 *Creating template components*

Template components bring more structure to the presentation of child content, allowing multiple sections of content to be displayed. Template components are a good way of consolidating features that are used throughout an application to prevent the duplication of code and content.

To see how this works, add a Razor Component named `TableTemplate.razor` to the `Blazor` folder with the content shown in listing 34.17.

Listing 34.17   The contents of the TableTemplate.razor file in the Blazor folder

```
<table class="table table-sm table-bordered table-striped">
    @if (Header != null) {
        <thead>@Header</thead>
    }
    <tbody>@Body</tbody>
</table>

@code {
    [Parameter]
    public RenderFragment? Header { get; set; }

    [Parameter]
    public RenderFragment? Body { get; set; }
}
```

The component defines a `RenderFragment` property for each region of child content it supports. The `TableTemplate` component defines two `RenderFragment` properties, named `Header` and `Body`, which represent the content sections of a table. Each region of child content is rendered using a Razor expression, `@Header` and `@Body`, and you can check to see whether content has been provided for a specific section by checking to see whether the property value is `null`, which this component does for the `Header` section.

When using a template component, the content for each region is enclosed in an HTML element whose tag matches the name of the corresponding `RenderFragment` property, as shown in listing 34.18.

Listing 34.18   Applying a template component in the Blazor/PeopleList.razor file

```
<TableTemplate>
    <Header>
        <tr><th>ID</th><th>Name</th><th>Dept</th><th>Location</th></tr>
    </Header>
    <Body>
        @foreach (Person p in People ?? Enumerable.Empty<Person>()) {
            <tr class="@GetClass(p?.Location?.City)">
                <td>@p?.PersonId</td>
                <td>@p?.Surname, @p?.Firstname</td>
                <td>@p?.Department?.Name</td>
                <td>@p?.Location?.City, @p?.Location?.State</td>
            </tr>
        }
    </Body>
</TableTemplate>

<ThemeWrapper Theme="info" Title="Location Selector">
    <SelectFilter values="@Cities" title="@SelectTitle"
        @bind-SelectedValue="SelectedCity" />

    <button class="btn btn-primary mt-2"
        @onclick="@(() => SelectedCity = "Oakland")">
```

```
            Change
        </button>
</ThemeWrapper>

@code {

    [Inject]
    public DataContext? Context { get; set; }

    public IEnumerable<Person>? People => Context?.People
            .Include(p => p.Department)
            .Include(p => p.Location).Take(ItemCount);

    public IEnumerable<string>? Cities =>
        Context?.Locations.Select(l => l.City);

    public string SelectedCity { get; set; } = string.Empty;

    public string GetClass(string? city) =>
        SelectedCity == city ? "bg-info text-white" : "";

    [Parameter]
    public int ItemCount { get; set; } = 4;

    [Parameter]
    public string? SelectTitle { get; set; }
}
```

The child content is structured into sections that correspond to the template component's properties, `Header` and `Body`, which leaves the `TableTemplate` component responsible for the table structure and the `PeopleList` component responsible for providing the detail. Restart **ASP.NET Core** and request http://localhost:5000/controllers, and you will see the output produced by the template component, as shown in figure 34.7.

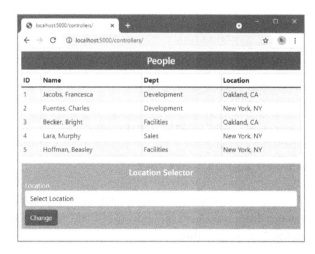

Figure 34.7
Using a template component

34.3.2 *Using generic type parameters in template components*

The template component I created in the previous section is useful, in the sense that it provides a consistent representation of a table that I can use throughout the example application. But it is also limited because it relies on the parent component to take responsibility for generating the rows for the table body. The template component doesn't have any insight into the content it presents, which means it cannot do anything with that content other than display it.

Template components can be made data-aware with the use of a generic type parameter, which allows the parent component to provide a sequence of data objects and a template for presenting them. The template component becomes responsible for generating the content for each data object and, consequently, can provide more useful functionality. As a demonstration, I am going to add support to the template component for selecting how many table rows are displayed and for selecting table rows. The first step is to add a generic type parameter to the component and use it to render the content for the table body, as shown in listing 34.19.

> **Listing 34.19   Adding a type parameter in the Blazor/TableTemplate.razor file**

```
@typeparam RowType

<table class="table table-sm table-bordered table-striped">
    @if (Header != null) {
        <thead>@Header</thead>
    }
    <tbody>
        @if (RowData != null && RowTemplate != null) {
            @foreach (RowType item in RowData) {
                <tr>@RowTemplate(item)</tr>
            }
        }
    </tbody>
</table>

@code {

    [Parameter]
    public RenderFragment? Header { get; set; }

    [Parameter]
    public RenderFragment<RowType>? RowTemplate { get; set; }

    [Parameter]
    public IEnumerable<RowType>? RowData { get; set; }
}
```

The generic type parameter is specified using the @typeparam attribute, and, in this case, I have given the parameter the name RowType because it will refer to the data type for which the component will generate table rows.

TIP Blazor generic type parameters can be constrained using the C# `where` keyword so that only types that have specified characteristics, such as classes that implement a particular interface, can be used. See https://docs.microsoft .com/en-us/dotnet/csharp/language-reference/keywords/where-generic-type-constraint for details.

The data the component will process is received by adding a property whose type is a sequence of objects of the generic type. I have named the property `RowData`, and its type is `IEnumerable<RowType>`. The content the component will display for each object is received using a `RenderFragment<T>` property. I have named this property `RowTemplate`, and its type is `RenderFragment<RowType>`, reflecting the name I selected for the generic type parameter.

When a component receives a content section through a `RenderFragment<T>` property, it can render it for a single object by invoking the section as a method and using the object as the argument, like this:

```
...
@foreach (RowType item in RowData) {
    <tr>@RowTemplate(item)</tr>
}
...
```

This fragment of code enumerates the `RowType` objects in the `RowData` sequence and renders the content section received through the `RowTemplate` property for each of them.

USING A GENERIC TEMPLATE COMPONENT

I have simplified the `PeopleList` component so it only uses the template component to produce a table of `Person` objects, and I have removed earlier features, as shown in listing 34.20.

> Listing 34.20   Using a generic template component in the Blazor/PeopleList.razor file

```
<TableTemplate RowType="Person" RowData="People">
    <Header>
        <tr><th>ID</th><th>Name</th><th>Dept</th><th>Location</th></tr>
    </Header>
    <RowTemplate Context="p">
        <td>@p.PersonId</td>
        <td>@p.Surname, @p.Firstname</td>
        <td>@p.Department?.Name</td>
        <td>@p.Location?.City, @p.Location?.State</td>
    </RowTemplate>
</TableTemplate>


@code {

    [Inject]
    public DataContext? Context { get; set; }

    public IEnumerable<Person>? People => Context?.People
            .Include(p => p.Department)
            .Include(p => p.Location);
}
```

The RowType attribute is used to specify the value for the generic type argument. The RowData attribute specifies the data the template component will process.

The RowTemplate element denotes the elements that will be produced for each data object. When defining a content section for a RenderFragment<T> property, the Context attribute is used to assign a name to the current object being processed. In this case, the Context attribute is used to assign the name p to the current object, which is then referred to in the Razor expressions used to populate the content section's elements.

The overall effect is that the template component is configured to display Person objects. The component will generate a table row for each Person, which will contain td elements whose content is set using the current Person object's properties.

Since I removed properties that were decorated with the Parameter attribute in listing 34.20, I need to remove the corresponding attributes from the element that applies the PeopleList component, as shown in listing 34.21.

> **Listing 34.21   Removing attributes in the Index.cshtml file in the Views/Home folder**

```
@model PeopleListViewModel

<h4 class="bg-primary text-white text-center p-2">People</h4>

<component type="typeof(Advanced.Blazor.PeopleList)"
    render-mode="Server" />
```

To see the generic template component, restart ASP.NET Core and request http://localhost:5000/controllers. The data and content sections provided by the PeopleList component have been used by the TableTemplate component to produce the table shown in figure 34.8.

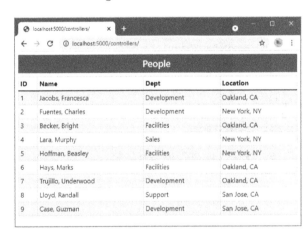

Figure 34.8
Using a generic template component

ADDING FEATURES TO THE GENERIC TEMPLATE COMPONENT

This may feel like a step backward, but, as you will see, giving the template component insight into the data it handles sets the foundation for adding features, as shown in listing 34.22.

Listing 34.22   Adding a feature in the TableTemplate.razor file in the Blazor folder

```razor
@typeparam RowType

<div class="container-fluid">
    <div class="row p-2">
        <div class="col">
            <SelectFilter Title="@("Sort")"
                Values="@SortDirectionChoices"
                @bind-SelectedValue="SortDirectionSelection" />
        </div>
        <div class="col">
            <SelectFilter Title="@("Highlight")"
                Values="@HighlightChoices()"
                @bind-SelectedValue="HighlightSelection" />
        </div>
    </div>
</div>

<table class="table table-sm table-bordered table-striped">
    @if (Header != null) {
        <thead>@Header</thead>
    }
    <tbody>
        @if (RowTemplate != null) {
            @foreach (RowType item in SortedData()) {
                <tr class="@IsHighlighted(item)">@RowTemplate(item)</tr>
            }
        }
    </tbody>
</table>

@code {

    [Parameter]
    public RenderFragment? Header { get; set; }

    [Parameter]
    public RenderFragment<RowType>? RowTemplate { get; set; }

    [Parameter]
    public IEnumerable<RowType> RowData { get; set; }
        = Enumerable.Empty<RowType>();

    [Parameter]
    public Func<RowType, string> Highlight { get; set; }
        = (row) => String.Empty;

    public IEnumerable<string> HighlightChoices() =>
        RowData.Select(item => Highlight(item)).Distinct();

    public string? HighlightSelection { get; set; }

    public string IsHighlighted(RowType item) =>
        Highlight(item) == HighlightSelection
            ? "table-dark text-white" : "";
```

```
    [Parameter]
    public Func<RowType, string> SortDirection { get; set; }
        = (row) => String.Empty;

    public string[] SortDirectionChoices =
        new string[] { "Ascending", "Descending" };

    public string SortDirectionSelection { get; set; } = "Ascending";

    public IEnumerable<RowType> SortedData() =>
        SortDirectionSelection == "Ascending"
            ? RowData.OrderBy(SortDirection)
            : RowData.OrderByDescending(SortDirection);
}
```

The changes present the user with two `select` elements via the `SelectFilter` component created earlier in the chapter. These new elements allow the user to sort the data in ascending and descending order and to select a value used to highlight rows in the table. The parent component provides additional parameters that give the template component functions that select the properties used for sorting and highlighting, as shown in listing 34.23.

Listing 34.23   Configuring component features in the Blazor/PeopleList.razor file

```
<TableTemplate RowType="Person" RowData="People"
        Highlight="@(p => p.Location?.City)"
        SortDirection="@(p => p.Surname)">
    <Header>
        <tr><th>ID</th><th>Name</th><th>Dept</th><th>Location</th></tr>
    </Header>
    <RowTemplate Context="p">
        <td>@p.PersonId</td>
        <td>@p.Surname, @p.Firstname</td>
        <td>@p.Department?.Name</td>
        <td>@p.Location?.City, @p.Location?.State</td>
    </RowTemplate>
</TableTemplate>


@code {

    [Inject]
    public DataContext? Context { get; set; }

    public IEnumerable<Person>? People => Context?.People
            .Include(p => p.Department)
            .Include(p => p.Location);
}
```

The `Highlight` attribute provides the template component with a function that selects the property used for highlighting table rows, and the `SortDirection` attribute provides a function that selects a property used for sorting. To see the effect, restart ASP .NET Core and request http://localhost:5000/controllers. The response will contain the new `select` elements, which can be used to change the sort order or select a city for filtering, as shown in figure 34.9.

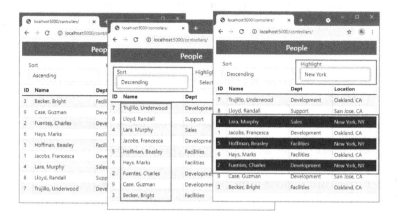

Figure 34.9 Adding features to a template component

REUSING A GENERIC TEMPLATE COMPONENT

The features added to the template component all relied on the generic type parameter, which allows the component to modify the content it presents without being tied to a specific class. The result is a component that can be used to display, sort, and highlight any data type wherever a table is required. Add a Razor Component named `DepartmentList.razor` to the `Blazor` folder with the content shown in listing 34.24.

Listing 34.24   The contents of the DepartmentList.razor file in the Blazor folder

```
<TableTemplate RowType="Department" RowData="Departments"
    Highlight="@(d => d.Name)"
    SortDirection="@(d => d.Name)">
    <Header>
        <tr><th>ID</th><th>Name</th><th>People</th><th>Locations</th></tr>
    </Header>
    <RowTemplate Context="d">
        <td>@d.Departmentid</td>
        <td>@d.Name</td>
        <td>@(String.Join(", ", d.People!.Select(p => p.Surname)))</td>
        <td>
            @(String.Join(", ", d.People!.Select(p =>
                p.Location!.City).Distinct()))
        </td>
    </RowTemplate>
</TableTemplate>

@code {
    [Inject]
    public DataContext? Context { get; set; }

    public IEnumerable<Department>? Departments => Context?.Departments?
        .Include(d => d.People!).ThenInclude(p => p.Location!);
}
```

The `TableTemplate` component is used to present the user with a list of the `Department` objects in the database, along with details of the related `Person` and `Location` objects, which are queried with the Entity Framework Core `Include` and `ThenInclude` methods. Listing 34.25 changes the Razor Component displayed by the Razor Page named `Blazor`.

> **Listing 34.25   Changing the component in the Blazor.cshtml file in the Pages folder**

```
@page "/pages/blazor"

<h4 class="bg-primary text-white text-center p-2">Departments</h4>

<component type="typeof(Advanced.Blazor.DepartmentList)"
    render-mode="Server" />
```

Restart ASP.NET Core and request http://localhost:5000/pages/blazor. The response will be presented using the templated component, as shown in figure 34.10.

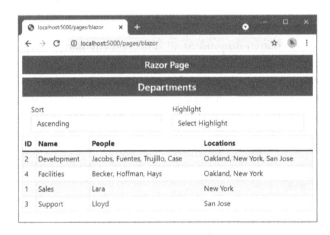

**Figure 34.10
Reusing a generic
template component**

34.3.3 *Cascading parameters*

As the number of components increases, it can be useful for a component to provide configuration data to descendants deep in the hierarchy of components. This can be done by having each component in the chain receive the data and pass it on to all of its children, but that is error-prone and requires every component to participate in the process, even if none of its descendants uses the data it passes on.

Blazor provides a solution to this problem by supporting *cascading parameters*, in which a component provides data values that are available directly to any of its descendants, without being relayed by intermediate components. Cascading parameters are defined using the `CascadingValue` component, which is used to wrap a section of content, as shown in listing 34.26.

```
<CascadingValue Name="BgTheme" Value="Theme" IsFixed="false">
    <TableTemplate RowType="Department" RowData="Departments"
                    Highlight="@(d => d.Name)"
                    SortDirection="@(d => d.Name)">
        <Header>
        <tr>
            <th>ID</th><th>Name</th><th>People</th><th>Locations</th>
        </tr>
        </Header>
        <RowTemplate Context="d">
            <td>@d.Departmentid</td>
            <td>@d.Name</td>
            <td>
                @(String.Join(", ", d.People!.Select(p => p.Surname)))
            </td>
            <td>
                @(String.Join(", ", d.People!.Select(p =>
                    p.Location!.City).Distinct()))
            </td>
        </RowTemplate>
    </TableTemplate>
</CascadingValue>

<SelectFilter Title="@("Theme")" Values="Themes"
            @bind-SelectedValue="Theme" />

@code {
    [Inject]
    public DataContext? Context { get; set; }

    public IEnumerable<Department>? Departments => Context?.Departments?
        .Include(d => d.People!).ThenInclude(p => p.Location!);

    public string Theme { get; set; } = "info";
    public string[] Themes =
        new string[] { "primary", "info", "success" };
}
```

The `CascadingValue` element makes a value available to the components it encompasses and their descendants. The `Name` attribute specifies the name of the parameter, the `Value` attribute specifies the value, and the `isFixed` attribute is used to specify whether the value will change. The `CascadingValue` element has been used in listing 34.26 to create a cascading parameter named `BgTheme`, whose value is set by an instance of the `SelectFilter` component that presents the user with a selection of Bootstrap CSS theme names.

> **TIP** Each `CascadingValue` element creates one cascading parameter. If you need to pass on multiple values, then you can nest the `CascadingValue` or create a simple parameter that provides multiple settings through a dictionary.

Cascading parameters are received directly by the components that require them with the CascadingParameter attribute, as shown in listing 34.27.

Listing 34.27   Receiving a cascading parameter in the SelectFilter.razor file in the Blazor folder

```
<div class="form-group p-2 bg-@Theme @TextColor()">
    <label for="select-@Title">@Title</label>
    <select name="select-@Title" class="form-control"
            @onchange="HandleSelect" value="@SelectedValue">
        <option disabled selected value="">Select @Title</option>
        @foreach (string val in Values) {
            <option value="@val" selected="@(val == SelectedValue)">
                @val
            </option>
        }
    </select>
</div>

@code {

    [Parameter]
    public IEnumerable<string> Values { get; set; }
        = Enumerable.Empty<string>();

    [Parameter]
    public string? SelectedValue { get; set; }

    [Parameter]
    public string Title { get; set; } = "Placeholder";

    [Parameter(CaptureUnmatchedValues = true)]
    public Dictionary<string, object>? Attrs { get; set; }

    [Parameter]
    public EventCallback<string> SelectedValueChanged { get; set; }

    public async Task HandleSelect(ChangeEventArgs e) {
        SelectedValue = e.Value as string;
        await SelectedValueChanged.InvokeAsync(SelectedValue);
    }

    [CascadingParameter(Name = "BgTheme")]
    public string Theme { get; set; } = "";

    public string TextColor() => String.IsNullOrEmpty(Theme)
        ? "text-dark" : "text-light";
}
```

The CascadingParameter attribute's Name argument is used to specify the name of the cascading parameter. The BgTheme parameter defined in listing 34.26 is received by the Theme property in listing 34.27 and used to set the background for the component. Restart ASP.NET Core and request http://localhost:5000/pages/blazor, which produces the response shown in figure 34.11.

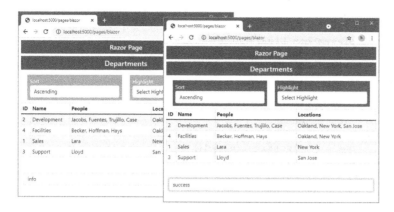

Figure 34.11   Using a cascading parameter

There are three instances of the SelectFilter component used in this example, but only two of them are within the hierarchy contained by the CascadingValue element. The other instance is defined outside of the CascadingValue element and does not receive the cascading value.

34.4   Handling errors

In the following sections, I describe the features Blazor provides for dealing with connection errors and unhandled application errors.

34.4.1   Handling connection errors

Blazor relies on its persistent HTTP connection between the browser and the ASP .NET Core server. The application cannot function when the connection is disrupted, and a modal error message is displayed that prevents the user from interacting with components.

Blazor allows the connection errors to be customized by defining an element with a specific id, as shown in listing 34.28.

Listing 34.28   A connection error element in the Blazor.cshtml file in the Pages folder

```
@page "/pages/blazor"

<h4 class="bg-primary text-white text-center p-2">Departments</h4>

<link rel="stylesheet" href="connectionErrors.css" />

<div id="components-reconnect-modal"
     class="h4 bg-dark text-white text-center my-2 p-2
            components-reconnect-hide">
    Blazor Connection Lost
    <div class="reconnect">
        Trying to reconnect...
    </div>
```

```
    <div class="failed">
        Reconnection Failed.
        <button class="btn btn-light btn-sm m-1"
                onclick="window.Blazor.reconnect()">
            Reconnect
        </button>
    </div>
    <div class="rejected">
        Reconnection Rejected.
        <button class="btn btn-light btn-sm m-1"
                onclick="location.reload()">
            Reload
        </button>
    </div>
</div>

<component type="typeof(Advanced.Blazor.DepartmentList)"
    render-mode="Server" />
```

The `id` attribute of the custom error element must be `components-reconnect-modal`. When there is a connection error, Blazor locates this element and adds it to one of four classes, described in table 34.2.

Table 34.2 The connection error classes

Name	Description
`components-reconnect-show`	The element is added to this class when the connection has been lost and Blazor is attempting a reconnection. The error message should be displayed to the user, and interaction with the Blazor content should be prevented.
`components-reconnect-hide`	The element is added to this class if the connection is reestablished. The error message should be hidden, and interaction should be permitted.
`components-reconnect-failed`	The element is added to this class if Blazor reconnection fails. The user can be presented with a button that invokes `window.Blazor.reconnect()` to attempt reconnection.
`components-reconnect-rejected`	The element is added to this class if Blazor is able to reach the server but the user's connection state has been lost. This typically happens when the server has been restarted. The user can be presented with a button that invokes `location.reload()` to reload the application and try again.

The element isn't added to any of these classes initially, so I have explicitly added it to the `components-reconnect-hide` class so that it isn't visible until a problem occurs.

I want to present specific messages to the user for each of the conditions that can arise during reconnection. To this end, I added elements that display a message for each condition. To manage their visibility, add a CSS stylesheet named `connection-Errors.css` to the `wwwroot` folder and use it to define the styles shown in listing 34.29.

```css
#components-reconnect-modal {
    position: fixed; top: 0; right: 0; bottom: 0;
    left: 0; z-index: 1000; overflow: hidden; opacity: 0.9;
}

.components-reconnect-hide { display: none; }
.components-reconnect-show { display: block; }

.components-reconnect-show > .reconnect { display: block; }
.components-reconnect-show > .failed,
.components-reconnect-show > .rejected {
    display: none;
}

.components-reconnect-failed > .failed {
    display: block;
}
.components-reconnect-failed > .reconnect,
.components-reconnect-failed > .rejected {
    display: none;
}

.components-reconnect-rejected > .rejected {
    display: block;
}
.components-reconnect-rejected > .reconnect,
.components-reconnect-rejected > .failed {
    display: none;
}
```

These styles show the `components-reconnect-modal` element as a modal item, with its visibility determined by the `components-reconnect-hide` and `components -reconnect-show` classes. The visibility of the specific messages is toggled based on the application of the classes in table 34.2.

To see the effect, restart ASP.NET Core and request http://localhost:5000/pages/ blazor. Wait until the component is displayed and then stop the ASP.NET Core server. You will see an initial error message as Blazor attempts to reconnect. After a few minutes, you will see the message that indicates that reconnection has failed.

Restart ASP.NET Core and request http://localhost:5000/pages/blazor. Wait until the component is displayed and then restart ASP.NET Core. This time Blazor will be able to connect to the server, but the connection will be rejected because the server restart has caused the connection state to be lost. Figure 34.12 shows both sequences of error messages.

TIP   It is not possible to test successful connection recovery with just the browser because there is no way to interrupt the persistent HTTP connection. I use the excellent Fiddler proxy, https://www.telerik.com/fiddler, which allows me to terminate the connection without stopping the ASP.NET Core server.

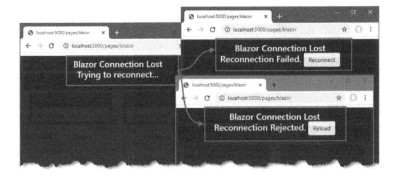

Figure 34.12   Handling connection errors

34.4.2 Handling uncaught application errors

Blazor does not respond well to uncaught application errors, which are almost always treated as terminal. To demonstrate the way that exceptions are handled, listing 34.30 introduces an exception that will be thrown when the user selects a specific value.

Listing 34.30   Introducing an exception in the SelectFilter.razor file in the Blazor folder

```
<div class="form-group p-2 bg-@Theme @TextColor()">
    <label for="select-@Title">@Title</label>
    <select name="select-@Title" class="form-control"
            @onchange="HandleSelect" value="@SelectedValue">
        <option disabled selected value="">Select @Title</option>
        @foreach (string val in Values) {
            <option value="@val" selected="@(val == SelectedValue)">
                @val
            </option>
        }
    </select>
</div>

@code {

    [Parameter]
    public IEnumerable<string> Values { get; set; }
        = Enumerable.Empty<string>();

    [Parameter]
    public string? SelectedValue { get; set; }

    [Parameter]
    public string Title { get; set; } = "Placeholder";

    [Parameter(CaptureUnmatchedValues = true)]
    public Dictionary<string, object>? Attrs { get; set; }

    [Parameter]
    public EventCallback<string> SelectedValueChanged { get; set; }
```

```
    public async Task HandleSelect(ChangeEventArgs e) {
        SelectedValue = e.Value as string;
        if (SelectedValue == "Sales") {
            throw new Exception("Sales cannot be selected");
        }
        await SelectedValueChanged.InvokeAsync(SelectedValue);
    }

    [CascadingParameter(Name = "BgTheme")]
    public string Theme { get; set; } = "";

    public string TextColor() => String.IsNullOrEmpty(Theme)
        ? "text-dark" : "text-light";
}
```

Restart ASP.NET Core, request http://localhost:5000/pages/blazor, and select Sales from the Highlight menu. There is no visible change in the browser, but the exception thrown at the server when the button was clicked has proved fatal: the user can still choose values using the select elements because these are presented by the browser, but the event handlers that respond to selections no longer work, and the application is essentially dead.

When there is an unhandled application error, Blazor looks for an element whose id is blazor-error-ui and sets its CSS display property to block. Listing 34.31 adds an element with this id to the Blazor.cshtml file styled to present a useful message.

Listing 34.31   Adding an error element in the Blazor.cshtml file in the Pages folder

```
@page "/pages/blazor"

<h4 class="bg-primary text-white text-center p-2">Departments</h4>

<link rel="stylesheet" href="connectionErrors.css" />

<div id="components-reconnect-modal"
     class="h4 bg-dark text-white text-center my-2 p-2
            components-reconnect-hide">
    Blazor Connection Lost
    <div class="reconnect">
        Trying to reconnect...
    </div>
    <div class="failed">
        Reconnection Failed.
        <button class="btn btn-light btn-sm m-1"
                onclick="window.Blazor.reconnect()">
            Reconnect
        </button>
    </div>
    <div class="rejected">
        Reconnection Rejected.
        <button class="btn btn-light btn-sm m-1"
                onclick="location.reload()">
            Reload
        </button>
    </div>
```

```
        </div>
    </div>

    <div id="blazor-error-ui"
        class="text-center bg-danger h6 text-white p-2 fixed-top w-100"
        style="display:none">
        An error has occurred. This application will not respond until reloaded.
        <button class="btn btn-sm btn-primary m-1" onclick="location.reload()">
            Reload
        </button>
    </div>

    <component type="typeof(Advanced.Blazor.DepartmentList)"
        render-mode="Server" />
```

When the element is shown, the user will be presented with a warning and a button that reloads the browser. To see the effect, restart ASP.NET Core, request http://localhost:5000/pages/blazor, and select Sales from the Highlight menu, which will display the message shown in figure 34.13.

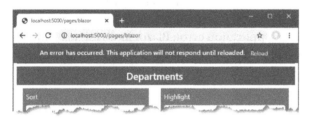

**Figure 34.13.
Displaying an
error message**

34.4.3 *Using error boundaries*

Error boundaries are used to contain errors within the component hierarchy so that a component can take responsibility for its own exceptions and the exceptions thrown by its child components. Listing 34.32 introduces an error boundary to contain the exception thrown by the SelectFilter component.

> **Listing 34.32   An error boundary in the TableTemplate.razor file in the Blazor folder**

```
...
@typeparam RowType

<link rel="stylesheet" href="errorBoundaries.css" />

<div class="container-fluid">
    <div class="row p-2">
        <div class="col">
            <SelectFilter Title="@("Sort")"
                Values="@SortDirectionChoices"
                @bind-SelectedValue="SortDirectionSelection" />
        </div>
        <div class="col">
            <ErrorBoundary>
                <SelectFilter Title="@("Highlight")"
```

```
                    Values="@HighlightChoices()"
                    @bind-SelectedValue="HighlightSelection" />
           </ErrorBoundary>
        </div>
     </div>
</div>

<table class="table table-sm table-bordered table-striped">
    @if (Header != null) {
        <thead>@Header</thead>
    }
    <tbody>
        @if (RowTemplate != null) {
            @foreach (RowType item in SortedData()) {
                <tr class="@IsHighlighted(item)">@RowTemplate(item)</tr>
            }
        }
    </tbody>
</table>
...
```

Error boundaries are defined using the `ErrorBoundary` component, which displays its child content normally until an exception is thrown, at which point the child content is removed and a `div` element assigned to a `blazor-error-boundary` class is displayed. To define the content and styles that will be displayed, add a CSS stylesheet named `errorBoundaries.css` to the `wwwroot` folder with the content shown in listing 34.33.

> **Listing 34.33   The contents of the errorBoundaries.css file in the wwwroot folder**

```
.blazor-error-boundary {
    background-color: darkred;
    color: white;
    padding: 1rem;
    text-align: center;
    vertical-align: middle;
    height: 100%;
    font-size: large;
    font-weight: bold;
}

.blazor-error-boundary::after {
    content: "Error: Sales selected"
}
```

The CSS in the stylesheet displays a basic error message, which is styled in white text on a red background. (Don't worry about how these styles work because there are easier ways to define error messages, as I explain shortly.)

To see the effect of the error boundary, restart ASP.NET Core, request http://localhost:5000/pages/blazor, and select Sales from the Highlight menu. An exception is thrown when the selection is made, which is contained by the error boundary, displaying the message shown in figure 34.14. Only the content contained within the `Error-Boundary` component is affected by the exception, which means that the rest of the application works as normal, which means that the user can still change the sort order.

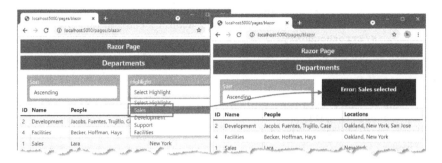

Figure 34.14   Using an error boundary

DEFINING ERROR CONTENT WITHIN THE BOUNDARY

Defining the error message in a CSS stylesheet is awkward, and I prefer to define the error content as part of the error boundary, as shown in listing 34.34.

Listing 34.34   Defining error content in the TableTemplate.razor file in the Blazor folder

```
...
<div class="container-fluid">
    <div class="row p-2">
        <div class="col">
            <SelectFilter Title="@("Sort")" Values="@SortDirectionChoices"
                @bind-SelectedValue="SortDirectionSelection" />
        </div>
        <div class="col">
            <ErrorBoundary>
                <ChildContent>
                    <SelectFilter Title="@("Highlight")"
                        Values="@HighlightChoices()"
                        @bind-SelectedValue="HighlightSelection" />
                </ChildContent>
                <ErrorContent>
                    <h4 class="bg-danger text-white text-center h-100 p-2">
                        Inline error: Sales Selected
                    </h4>
                </ErrorContent>
            </ErrorBoundary>
        </div>
    </div>
</div>
...
```

The `ChildContent` and `ErrorContent` tags are used to specify the content that will be displayed normally and when an exception has been thrown. Restart ASP.NET Core, request http://localhost:5000/pages/blazor, and select Sales from the Highlight menu to see the new error message, which is shown in figure 34.15.

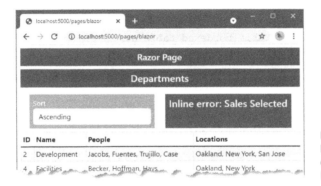

**Figure 34.15
Error content
defined within the
boundary**

RECOVERING FROM EXCEPTIONS

Error boundaries allow an application to recover from exceptions, as shown in listing 34.35, although care should be taken to ensure that whatever problem caused the issue originally has truly been resolved.

Listing 34.35   A recoverable error boundary in the Blazor/TableTemplate.razor file

```
@typeparam RowType

<link rel="stylesheet" href="errorBoundaries.css" />

<div class="container-fluid">
    <div class="row p-2">
        <div class="col">
            <SelectFilter Title="@("Sort")"
                Values="@SortDirectionChoices"
                @bind-SelectedValue="SortDirectionSelection" />
        </div>
        <div class="col">
            <ErrorBoundary @ref="boundary">
                <ChildContent>
                    <SelectFilter Title="@("Highlight")"
                        Values="@HighlightChoices()"
                        @bind-SelectedValue="HighlightSelection" />
                </ChildContent>
                <ErrorContent>
                    <h4 class="bg-danger text-white text-center h-100 p-2">
                        Inline error: Sales Selected
                        <div>
                            <button class="btn btn-light btn-sm m-1"
                                @onclick="@(() => boundary?.Recover())">
                                    Recover
                            </button>
                        </div>
                    </h4>
                </ErrorContent>
            </ErrorBoundary>
        </div>
    </div>
</div>
```

```
</div>

<table class="table table-sm table-bordered table-striped">
    @if (Header != null) {
        <thead>@Header</thead>
    }
    <tbody>
        @if (RowTemplate != null) {
            @foreach (RowType item in SortedData()) {
                <tr class="@IsHighlighted(item)">@RowTemplate(item)</tr>
            }
        }
    </tbody>
</table>

@code {

    ErrorBoundary? boundary;

    // ...other members omitted for brevity...
}
```

The @ref binding is used to obtain a reference to the ErrorBoundary, which defines a Recover method. The error content presented to the user contains a button that invokes the Recover method when clicked, allowing the user to recover from the error.

Restart ASP.NET Core, request http://localhost:5000/pages/blazor, and select Sales from the Highlight menu to trigger the error; then click the Recover button, which will display the child content once again, as shown in figure 34.16.

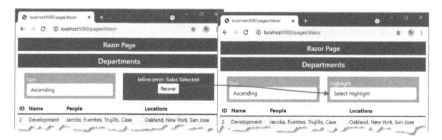

Figure 34.16   Recovering from an error

Summary

- Blazor components can be combined to present composite features to users.
- Components can be configured using attributes in markup, which are received by applying the `Parameter` attribute to code properties.
- Components can define custom events, which can be consumed in the parent component's markup.
- Components can also be wrappers around content, which is projected using the `@ChildContent` expression. Multiple sections of content can be presented by template components.
- Errors can be presented to the user by defining elements with specific classes, as described in table 34.2. These include connection errors and uncaught application errors.
- The effect of errors can be contained using error boundaries.

Advanced Blazor features

This chapter covers

- Creating routes that map requests to Blazor components
- Navigating between components and receiving route data in a component
- Using a layout with a routed component
- Implementing the component lifecycle methods
- Managing interaction between components and with JavaScript code

In this chapter, I explain how Blazor supports URL routing so that multiple components can be displayed through a single request. I show you how to set up the routing system, how to define routes, and how to create common content in a layout.

This chapter also covers the component lifecycle, which allows components to participate actively in the Blazor environment, which is especially important once you start using the URL routing feature. Finally, this chapter explains the different ways that components can interact outside of the parent-child relationships described in earlier chapters. Table 35.1 puts these features in context.

Table 35.1 Putting Blazor routing and lifecycle component interactions in context

Question	Answer
What are they?	The routing feature allows components to respond to changes in the URL without requiring a new HTTP connection. The lifecycle feature allows components to define methods that are invoked as the application executes, and the interaction features provide useful ways of communicating between components and with other JavaScript code.
Why are they useful?	These features allow the creation of complex applications that take advantage of the Blazor architecture.
How are they used?	URL routing is set up using built-in components and configured using `@page` directives. The lifecycle features are used by overriding methods in a component's `@code` section. The interaction features are used in different ways depending on what a component is interacting with.
Are there any pitfalls or limitations?	These are advanced features that must be used with care, especially when creating interactions outside of Blazor.
Are there any alternatives?	All the features described in this chapter are optional, but it is hard to create complex applications without them.

Table 35.2 provides a guide to the chapter.

Table 35.2 Chapter guide

Problem	Solution	Listing
Selecting components based on the current URL	Use URL routing.	6–12
Defining content that will be used by multiple components	Use a layout.	13, 14
Responding to the stages of the component's lifecycle	Implement the lifecycle notification methods.	15–17
Coordinating the activities of multiple components	Retain references with the `@ref` expression.	18, 19
Coordinating with code outside of Blazor	Use the interoperability features.	20–35

35.1 Preparing for this chapter

This chapter uses the Advanced project from chapter 35. No changes are required for this chapter.

> **TIP** You can download the example project for this chapter—and for all the other chapters in this book—from https://github.com/manningbooks/pro-asp .net-core-7. See chapter 1 for how to get help if you have problems running the examples.

Open a new PowerShell command prompt, navigate to the folder that contains the `Advanced.csproj` file, and run the command shown in listing 35.1 to drop the database.

Listing 35.1 Dropping the database

```
dotnet ef database drop --force
```

Use the PowerShell command prompt to run the command shown in listing 35.2.

Listing 35.2 Running the example application

```
dotnet run
```

Use a browser to request http://localhost:5000/controllers, which will display a list of data items. Request http://localhost:5000/pages/blazor, and you will see the component from chapter 34 that I used to demonstrate bindings. Figure 35.1 shows both responses.

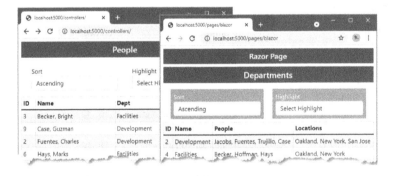

Figure 35.1 Running the example application

35.2 Using component routing

Blazor includes support for selecting the components to display to the user based on the ASP.NET Core routing system so that the application responds to changes in the URL by displaying different Razor Components. To get started, add a Razor Component named `Routed.razor` to the `Blazor` folder with the content shown in listing 35.3.

Listing 35.3 The contents of the Routed.razor file in the Blazor folder

```
<Router AppAssembly="typeof(Program).Assembly">
    <Found>
        <RouteView RouteData="@context" />
    </Found>
    <NotFound>
        <h4 class="bg-danger text-white text-center p-2">
            No Matching Route Found
        </h4>
    </NotFound>
</Router>
```

The `Router` component is included with ASP.NET Core and provides the link between Blazor and the ASP.NET Core routing features. `Router` is a generic template component that defines `Found` and `NotFound` sections.

The `Router` component requires the `AppAssembly` attribute, which specifies the .NET assembly to use. For most projects this is the current assembly, which is specified like this:

```
...
<Router AppAssembly="typeof(Program).Assembly">
...
```

The type of the `Router` component's `Found` property is `RenderFragment<Route-Data>`, which is passed on to the `RouteView` component through its `RouteData` property, like this:

```
...
<Found>
    <RouteView RouteData="@context" />
</Found>
...
```

The `RouteView` component is responsible for displaying the component matched by the current route and, as I explain shortly, for displaying common content through layouts. The type of the `NotFound` property is `RenderFragment`, without a generic type argument, and displays a section of content when no component can be found for the current route.

35.2.1 Preparing the Razor Page

Individual components can be displayed in existing controller views and Razor Pages, as previous chapters have shown. But when using component routing, it is preferable to create a set of URLs that are distinct to working with Blazor because the way that URLs are supported is limited and leads to tortured workarounds. Add a Razor Page named `_Host.cshtml` to the `Pages` folder and add the content shown in listing 35.4.

Listing 35.4 The contents of the _Host.cshtml file in the Pages folder

```
@page "/"
@{ Layout = null; }

<!DOCTYPE html>
```

```
<html>
<head>
    <title>@ViewBag.Title</title>
    <link href="/lib/bootstrap/css/bootstrap.min.css" rel="stylesheet" />
    <base href="~/" />
</head>
<body>
    <div class="m-2">
        <component type="typeof(Advanced.Blazor.Routed)"
            render-mode="Server" />
    </div>
    <script src="_framework/blazor.server.js"></script>
</body>
</html>
```

This page contains a `component` element that applies the `Routed` component defined in listing 35.4 and a `script` element for the Blazor JavaScript code. There is also a `link` element for the Bootstrap CSS stylesheet. Alter the configuration for the example application to use the `_Host.cshtml` file as a fallback when requests are not matched by the existing URL routes, as shown in listing 35.5.

> **Listing 35.5   Adding the fallback in the Progam.cs file in the Advanced folder**

```
using Microsoft.EntityFrameworkCore;
using Advanced.Models;

var builder = WebApplication.CreateBuilder(args);

builder.Services.AddControllersWithViews();
builder.Services.AddRazorPages();
builder.Services.AddServerSideBlazor();

builder.Services.AddDbContext<DataContext>(opts => {
    opts.UseSqlServer(
        builder.Configuration["ConnectionStrings:PeopleConnection"]);
    opts.EnableSensitiveDataLogging(true);
});

var app = builder.Build();

app.UseStaticFiles();

app.MapControllers();
app.MapControllerRoute("controllers",
    "controllers/{controller=Home}/{action=Index}/{id?}");
app.MapRazorPages();
app.MapBlazorHub();
app.MapFallbackToPage("/_Host");

var context = app.Services.CreateScope().ServiceProvider
    .GetRequiredService<DataContext>();
SeedData.SeedDatabase(context);

app.Run();
```

The `MapFallbackToPage` method configures the routing system to use the `_Host` page as a last resort for unmatched requests.

35.2.2 Adding routes to components

Components declare the URLs for which they should be displayed using `@page` directives. Listing 35.6 adds the `@page` directive to the `PeopleList` component.

Listing 35.6 Adding a directive in the PeopleList.razor file in the Blazor folder

```
@page "/people"

<TableTemplate RowType="Person" RowData="People"
        Highlight="@(p => p.Location?.City)"
        SortDirection="@(p => p.Surname)">
    <Header>
        <tr><th>ID</th><th>Name</th><th>Dept</th><th>Location</th></tr>
    </Header>
    <RowTemplate Context="p">
        <td>@p.PersonId</td>
        <td>@p.Surname, @p.Firstname</td>
        <td>@p.Department?.Name</td>
        <td>@p.Location?.City, @p.Location?.State</td>
    </RowTemplate>
</TableTemplate>


@code {

    [Inject]
    public DataContext? Context { get; set; }

    public IEnumerable<Person>? People => Context?.People
            .Include(p => p.Department)
            .Include(p => p.Location);
}
```

The directive in listing 35.6 means the `PeopleList` component will be displayed for the http://localhost:5000/people URL. Components can declare support for more than one route using multiple `@page` directives. Listing 35.7 adds `@page` directives to the `DepartmentList` component to support two URLs.

Listing 35.7 Adding a directive in the DepartmentList.razor file in the Blazor folder

```
@page "/departments"
@page "/depts"

<CascadingValue Name="BgTheme" Value="Theme" IsFixed="false">
    <TableTemplate RowType="Department" RowData="Departments"
                Highlight="@(d => d.Name)"
                SortDirection="@(d => d.Name)">
        <Header>
        <tr>
            <th>ID</th><th>Name</th><th>People</th><th>Locations</th>
```

```
        </tr>
      </Header>
      <RowTemplate Context="d">
          <td>@d.Departmentid</td>
          <td>@d.Name</td>
          <td>
              @(String.Join(", ", d.People!.Select(p => p.Surname)))
          </td>
          <td>
              @(String.Join(", ", d.People!.Select(p =>
                  p.Location!.City).Distinct()))
          </td>
      </RowTemplate>
    </TableTemplate>
</CascadingValue>

<SelectFilter Title="@("Theme")" Values="Themes"
            @bind-SelectedValue="Theme" />

@code {
    [Inject]
    public DataContext? Context { get; set; }

    public IEnumerable<Department>? Departments => Context?.Departments?
        .Include(d => d.People!).ThenInclude(p => p.Location!);

    public string Theme { get; set; } = "info";
    public string[] Themes =
        new string[] { "primary", "info", "success" };
}
```

Most of the routing pattern features described in chapter 13 can be used in @page expressions, except catchall segment variables and optional segment variables. Using two @page expressions, one with a segment variable, can be used to re-create the optional variable feature, as demonstrated in chapter 36, where I show you how to implement a CRUD application using Blazor.

To see the basic Razor Component routing feature at work, restart ASP.NET Core and request http://localhost:5000/people and http://localhost:5000/depts. Each URL displays one of the components in the application, as shown in figure 35.2.

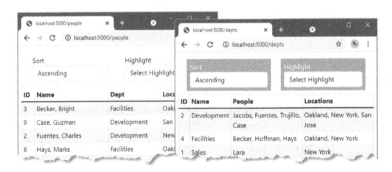

Figure 35.2 Enabling Razor Component routing in the example application

SETTING A DEFAULT COMPONENT ROUTE

The configuration change in listing 35.5 sets up the fallback route for requests. A corresponding route is required in one of the application's components to identify the component that should be displayed for the application's default URL, http://localhost:5000, as shown in listing 35.8.

> **Listing 35.8** Defining the default route in the PeopleList.razor file in the Blazor folder

```
@page "/people"
@page "/"

<TableTemplate RowType="Person" RowData="People"
        Highlight="@(p => p.Location?.City)"
        SortDirection="@(p => p.Surname)">
    <Header>
        <tr><th>ID</th><th>Name</th><th>Dept</th><th>Location</th></tr>
    </Header>
    <RowTemplate Context="p">
        <td>@p.PersonId</td>
        <td>@p.Surname, @p.Firstname</td>
        <td>@p.Department?.Name</td>
        <td>@p.Location?.City, @p.Location?.State</td>
    </RowTemplate>
</TableTemplate>


@code {

    [Inject]
    public DataContext? Context { get; set; }

    public IEnumerable<Person>? People => Context?.People
            .Include(p => p.Department)
            .Include(p => p.Location);
}
```

Restart ASP.NET Core and request http://localhost:5000, and you will see the content produced by the `PeopleList` component, as shown in figure 35.3.

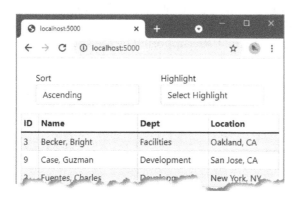

Figure 35.3 Displaying a component for the default URL

35.2.3   *Navigating between routed components*

The basic routing configuration is in place, but it may not be obvious why using routes offers any advantages over the independent components demonstrated in earlier chapters. Improvements come through the `NavLink` component, which renders anchor elements that are wired into the routing system. Listing 35.9 adds `NavLink` to the `PeopleList` component.

> **Listing 35.9   Adding navigation in the PeopleList.razor file in the Blazor folder**

```
@page "/people"
@page "/"

<TableTemplate RowType="Person" RowData="People"
        Highlight="@(p => p.Location?.City)"
        SortDirection="@(p => p.Surname)">
    <Header>
        <tr><th>ID</th><th>Name</th><th>Dept</th><th>Location</th></tr>
    </Header>
    <RowTemplate Context="p">
        <td>@p.PersonId</td>
        <td>@p.Surname, @p.Firstname</td>
        <td>@p.Department?.Name</td>
        <td>@p.Location?.City, @p.Location?.State</td>
    </RowTemplate>
</TableTemplate>

<NavLink class="btn btn-primary" href="/depts">Departments</NavLink>

@code {

    [Inject]
    public DataContext? Context { get; set; }

    public IEnumerable<Person>? People => Context?.People
            .Include(p => p.Department)
            .Include(p => p.Location);
}
```

Unlike the anchor elements used in other parts of ASP.NET Core, `Navlink` components are configured using URLs and not component, page, or action names. The `NavLink` in this example navigates to the URL supported by the `@page` directive of the `DepartmentList` component.

Navigation can also be performed programmatically, which is useful when a component responds to an event and then needs to navigate to a different URL, as shown in listing 35.10.

> **Listing 35.10.   Navigating in the DepartmentList.razor file in the Blazor folder**

```
@page "/departments"
@page "/depts"
```

```
<CascadingValue Name="BgTheme" Value="Theme" IsFixed="false">
    <TableTemplate RowType="Department" RowData="Departments"
                   Highlight="@(d => d.Name)"
                   SortDirection="@(d => d.Name)">
        <Header>
        <tr>
            <th>ID</th><th>Name</th><th>People</th><th>Locations</th>
        </tr>
        </Header>
        <RowTemplate Context="d">
            <td>@d.Departmentid</td>
            <td>@d.Name</td>
            <td>
                @(String.Join(", ", d.People!.Select(p => p.Surname)))
            </td>
            <td>
                @(String.Join(", ", d.People!.Select(p =>
                    p.Location!.City).Distinct()))
            </td>
        </RowTemplate>
    </TableTemplate>
</CascadingValue>

<SelectFilter Title="@("Theme")" Values="Themes"
    @bind-SelectedValue="Theme" />

<button class="btn btn-primary" @onclick="HandleClick">People</button>

@code {
    [Inject]
    public DataContext? Context { get; set; }

    public IEnumerable<Department>? Departments => Context?.Departments?
        .Include(d => d.People!).ThenInclude(p => p.Location!);

    public string Theme { get; set; } = "info";
    public string[] Themes =
        new string[] { "primary", "info", "success" };

    [Inject]
    public NavigationManager? NavManager { get; set; }

    public void HandleClick() => NavManager?.NavigateTo("/people");
}
```

The NavigationManager class provides programmatic access to navigation. Table 35.3 describes the most important members provided by the NavigationManager class.

Table 35.3 Useful NavigationManager members

Name	Description
NavigateTo(url)	This method navigates to the specified URL without sending a new HTTP request.
ToAbsoluteUri(path)	This method converts a relative path to a complete URL.
ToBaseRelativePath(url)	This method gets a relative path from a complete URL.
LocationChanged	This event is triggered when the location changes.
Uri	This property returns the current URL.

The NavigationManager class is provided as a service and is received by Razor Components using the Inject attribute, which provides access to the dependency injection features described in chapter 14.

The NavigationManager.NavigateTo method navigates to a URL and is used in this example to navigate to the /people URL, which will be handled by the People-List component.

To see why routing and navigation are important, restart ASP.NET Core and request http://localhost:5000/people. Click the Departments link, which is styled as a button, and the DepartmentList component will be displayed. Click the People link, and you will return to the PeopleList component, as shown in figure 35.4.

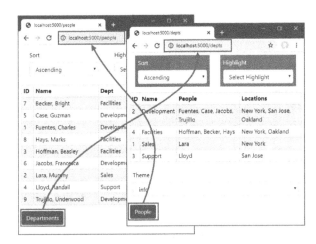

Figure 35.4 Navigating between routed components

If you perform this sequence with the F12 developer tools open, you will see that the transition from one component to the next is done without needing a separate HTTP request, even though the URL displayed by the browser changes. Blazor delivers the content rendered by each component over the persistent HTTP connection that is established when the first component is displayed and uses a JavaScript API to navigate without loading a new HTML document.

TIP The `NavigationManager.NavigateTo` method accepts an optional argument that, when `true`, forces the browser to send a new HTTP request and reload the HTML document.

35.2.4 Receiving routing data

Components can receive segment variables by decorating a property with the `Parameter` attribute. To demonstrate, add a Razor Component named `PersonDisplay.razor` to the `Blazor` folder with the content shown in listing 35.11.

Listing 35.11 The contents of the PersonDisplay.razor file in the Blazor folder

```
@page "/person"
@page "/person/{id:long}"

<h5>Editor for Person: @Id</h5>

<NavLink class="btn btn-primary" href="/people">Return</NavLink>

@code {

    [Parameter]
    public long Id { get; set; }
}
```

This component doesn't do anything other than displaying the value it receives from the routing data until I add features later in the chapter. The `@page` expression includes a segment variable named `id`, whose type is specified as `long`. The component receives the value assigned to the segment variable by defining a property with the same name and decorating it with the `Parameter` attribute.

TIP If you don't specify a type for segment variables in the `@page` expression, then you must set the type of the property to be `string`.

Listing 35.12 uses the `NavLink` component to create navigation links for each of the `Person` objects displayed by the `PeopleList` component.

Listing 35.12 Adding navigation links in the PeopleList.razor file in the Blazor folder

```
@page "/people"
@page "/"

<TableTemplate RowType="Person" RowData="People"
        Highlight="@(p => p.Location?.City)"
        SortDirection="@(p => p.Surname)">
    <Header>
        <tr><th>ID</th><th>Name</th><th>Dept</th><th>Location</th>
            <td></td>
        </tr>
    </Header>
    <RowTemplate Context="p">
```

```
        <td>@p.PersonId</td>
        <td>@p.Surname, @p.Firstname</td>
        <td>@p.Department?.Name</td>
        <td>@p.Location?.City, @p.Location?.State</td>
        <td>
            <NavLink class="btn btn-sm btn-info"
                    href="@GetEditUrl(p.PersonId)">
                Edit
            </NavLink>
        </td>
    </RowTemplate>
</TableTemplate>

<NavLink class="btn btn-primary" href="/depts">Departments</NavLink>

@code {

    [Inject]
    public DataContext? Context { get; set; }

    public IEnumerable<Person>? People => Context?.People
            .Include(p => p.Department)
            .Include(p => p.Location);

    public string GetEditUrl(long id) => $"/person/{id}";
}
```

Razor Components do not support mixing static content and Razor expressions in attribute values. Instead, I have defined the GetEditUrl method to generate the navigation URLs for each Person object, which is called to produce the value for the NavLink href attributes.

Restart ASP.NET Core, request http://localhost:5000/people, and click one of the Edit buttons. The browser will navigate to the new URL without reloading the HTML document and display the placeholder content generated by the PersonDisplay component, as shown in figure 35.5, which shows how a component can receive data from the routing system.

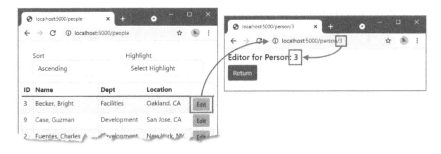

Figure 35.5   Receiving data from the routing system in a Razor Component

35.2.5 Defining common content using layouts

Layouts are template components that provide common content for Razor Components. To create a layout, add a Razor Component called `NavLayout.razor` to the `Blazor` folder and add the content shown in listing 35.13.

Listing 35.13　The contents of the NavLayout.razor file in the Blazor folder

```
@inherits LayoutComponentBase

<div class="container-fluid">
    <div class="row">
        <div class="col-3">
            <div class="d-grid gap-2">
                @foreach (string key in NavLinks.Keys) {
                    <NavLink class="btn btn-outline-primary"
                            href="@NavLinks[key]"
                            ActiveClass="btn-primary text-white"
                            Match="NavLinkMatch.Prefix">
                        @key
                    </NavLink>
                }
            </div>
        </div>
        <div class="col">
            @Body
        </div>
    </div>
</div>

@code {

    public Dictionary<string, string> NavLinks
        = new Dictionary<string, string> {
            {"People", "/people" },
            {"Departments", "/depts" },
            {"Details", "/person" }
        };
}
```

Layouts use the `@inherits` expression to specify the `LayoutComponentBase` class as the base for the class generated from the Razor Component. The `LayoutComponent-Base` class defines a `RenderFragment` class named `Body` that is used to specify the content from components within the common content displayed by the layout. In this example, the layout component creates a grid layout that displays a set of `NavLink` components for each of the components in the application. The `NavLink` components are configured with two new attributes, described in table 35.4.

Table 35.4   The NavLink configuration attributes

Name	Description
ActiveClass	This attribute specifies one or more CSS classes that the anchor element rendered by the NavLink component will be added to when the current URL matches the href attribute value.
Match	This attribute specifies how the current URL is matched to the href attribute, using a value from the NavLinkMatch enum. The values are Prefix, which considers a match if the href matches the start of the URL, and All, which requires the entire URL to be the same.

The NavLink components are configured to use Prefix matching and to add the anchor elements they render to the Bootstrap btn-primary and text-white classes when there is a match.

APPLYING A LAYOUT

There are three ways that a layout can be applied. A component can select its own layout using an @layout expression. A parent can use a layout for its child components by wrapping them in the built-in LayoutView component. A layout can be applied to all components by setting the DefaultLayout attribute of the RouteView component, as shown in listing 35.14.

Listing 35.14   Applying a layout in the Routed.razor file in the Blazor folder

```
<Router AppAssembly="typeof(Program).Assembly">
    <Found>
        <RouteView RouteData="@context"
            DefaultLayout="typeof(NavLayout)" />
    </Found>
    <NotFound>
        <h4 class="bg-danger text-white text-center p-2">
            No Matching Route Found
        </h4>
    </NotFound>
</Router>
```

Restart ASP.NET Core and request http://localhost:5000/people. The layout will be displayed with the content rendered by the PeopleList component. The navigation buttons on the left side of the layout can be used to navigate through the application, as shown in figure 35.6.

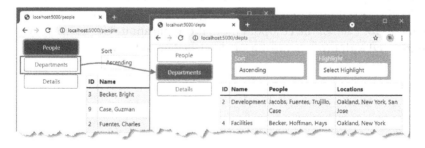

Figure 35.6   Using a layout component

NOTE   If you request http://localhost:5000, you will see the content from the `PeopleList` component, but the corresponding navigation button will not be highlighted. I show you how to resolve this problem later in the chapter.

35.3   *Understanding the component lifecycle methods*

Razor Components have a well-defined lifecycle, which is represented with methods that components can implement to receive notifications of key transitions. Table 35.5 describes the lifecycle methods.

Table 35.5   The Razor Component lifecycle methods

Name	Description
`OnInitialized()` `OnInitializedAsync()`	These methods are invoked when the component is first initialized.
`OnParametersSet()` `OnParametersSetAsync()`	These methods are invoked after the values for properties decorated with the `Parameter` attribute have been applied.
`ShouldRender()`	This method is called before the component's content is rendered to update the content presented to the user. If the method returns `false`, the component's content will not be rendered, and the update is suppressed. This method does not suppress the initial rendering for the component.
`OnAfterRender(first)` `OnAfterRenderAsync(first)`	This method is invoked after the component's content is rendered. The `bool` parameter is `true` when Blazor performs the initial render for the component.

Using either the `OnInitialized` or `OnParameterSet` method is useful for setting the initial state of the component. The layout defined in the previous section doesn't deal with the default URL because the `NavLink` component matches only a single URL. The same issue exists for the `DepartmentList` component, which can be requested using the `/departments` and `/depts` paths.

> **Understanding lifecycles for routed components**
>
> When using URL routing, components can be removed from the display when the URL changes. Components can implement the `System.IDisposable` interface, and Blazor will call the method when the component is removed.

Creating a component that matches multiple URLs requires the use of lifecycle methods. To understand why, add a Razor Component named `MultiNavLink.razor` to the `Blazor` folder with the content shown in listing 35.15.

Listing 35.15   The contents of the MultiNavLink.razor file in the Blazor folder

```
<a class="@ComputedClass" @onclick="HandleClick"  href="">
    @ChildContent
</a>

@code {

    [Inject]
    public NavigationManager? NavManager { get; set; }

    [Parameter]
    public IEnumerable<string> Href { get; set; }
        = Enumerable.Empty<string>();

    [Parameter]
    public string Class { get; set; } = string.Empty;

    [Parameter]
    public string ActiveClass { get; set; } = string.Empty;

    [Parameter]
    public NavLinkMatch? Match { get; set; }

    public NavLinkMatch ComputedMatch { get =>
            Match ?? (Href.Count() == 1
                ? NavLinkMatch.Prefix : NavLinkMatch.All); }

    [Parameter]
    public RenderFragment? ChildContent { get; set; }

    public string ComputedClass { get; set; } = string.Empty;


    public void HandleClick() {
        NavManager?.NavigateTo(Href.First());
    }

    private void CheckMatch(string currentUrl) {
        string path = NavManager!.ToBaseRelativePath(currentUrl);
        path = path.EndsWith("/")
            ? path.Substring(0, path.Length - 1) : path;
        bool match = Href.Any(href => ComputedMatch == NavLinkMatch.All
                ? path == href : path.StartsWith(href));
        ComputedClass = match ? $"{Class} {ActiveClass}" : Class;
    }

    protected override void OnParametersSet() {
        ComputedClass = Class;
        NavManager!.LocationChanged +=
            (sender, arg) => CheckMatch(arg.Location);
        Href = Href.Select(h => h.StartsWith("/") ? h.Substring(1) : h);
        CheckMatch(NavManager!.Uri);
    }
}
```

This component works in the same way as a regular `NavLink` but accepts an array of paths to match. The component relies on the `OnParametersSet` lifecycle method because some initial setup is required that cannot be performed until after values have been assigned to the properties decorated with the `Parameter` attribute, such as extracting the individual paths.

This component responds to changes in the current URL by listening for the `LocationChanged` event defined by the `NavigationManager` class. The event's `Location` property provides the component with the current URL, which is used to alter the classes for the anchor element. Listing 35.16 applies the new component in the layout.

> **TIP** Notice that I have removed the `Match` attribute in listing 35.14. The new component supports this attribute but defaults to matching based on the number of paths that it receives through the `href` attribute.

> **Listing 35.16 Applying a new component in the NavLayout.razor file in the Blazor folder**

```
@inherits LayoutComponentBase

<div class="container-fluid">
    <div class="row">
        <div class="col-3">
            <div class="d-grid gap-2">
                @foreach (string key in NavLinks.Keys) {
                    <MultiNavLink
                        class="btn btn-outline-primary btn-block"
                        href="@NavLinks[key]"
                        ActiveClass="btn-primary text-white">
                            @key
                    </MultiNavLink>
                }
            </div>
        </div>
        <div class="col">
            @Body
        </div>
    </div>
</div>

@code {
    public Dictionary<string, string[]> NavLinks
        = new Dictionary<string, string[]> {
            {"People", new string[] {"/people", "/" } },
            {"Departments", new string[] {"/depts", "/departments" } },
            {"Details", new string[] { "/person" } }
        };
}
```

Restart ASP.NET Core and request http://localhost:5000/people and http://localhost:5000/departments. Both URLs are recognized, and the corresponding navigation buttons are highlighted, as shown in figure 35.7.

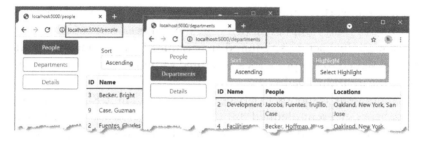

Figure 35.7   Using the lifecycle methods

35.3.1 *Using the lifecycle methods for asynchronous tasks*

The lifecycle methods are also useful for performing tasks that may complete after the initial content from the component has been rendered, such as querying the database. Listing 35.17 replaces the placeholder content in the `PersonDisplay` component and uses the lifecycle methods to query the database using values received as parameters.

Listing 35.17   Querying for data in the PersonDisplay.razor file in the Blazor folder

```
@page "/person"
@page "/person/{id:long}"

@if (Person == null) {
    <h5 class="bg-info text-white text-center p-2">Loading...</h5>
} else {
    <table class="table table-striped table-bordered">
        <tbody>
            <tr><th>Id</th><td>@Person.PersonId</td></tr>
            <tr><th>Surname</th><td>@Person.Surname</td></tr>
            <tr><th>Firstname</th><td>@Person.Firstname</td></tr>
        </tbody>
    </table>
}

<button class="btn btn-outline-primary"
        @onclick="@(() => HandleClick(false))">
    Previous
</button>
<button class="btn btn-outline-primary"
        @onclick="@(() => HandleClick(true))">
    Next
</button>

@code {

    [Inject]
    public DataContext? Context { get; set; }

    [Inject]
    public NavigationManager? NavManager { get; set; }
```

```
[Parameter]
public long Id { get; set; } = 0;

public Person? Person { get; set; }

protected async override Task OnParametersSetAsync() {
    await Task.Delay(1000);
    if (Context != null) {
        Person = await Context.People
            .FirstOrDefaultAsync(p => p.PersonId == Id)
            ?? new Person();
    }
}

public void HandleClick(bool increment) {
    Person = null;
    NavManager?.NavigateTo(
        $"/person/{(increment ? Id + 1 : Id - 1)}");
}
}
}
```

The component can't query the database until the parameter values have been set and so the value of the Person property is obtained in the OnParametersSetAsync method. Since the database is running alongside the ASP.NET Core server, I have added a one-second delay before querying the database to help emphasize the way the component works.

The value of the Person property is null until the query has completed, at which point it will be either an object representing the query result or a new Person object if the query doesn't produce a result. A loading message is displayed while the Person object is null.

Restart ASP.NET Core and request http://localhost:5000. Click one of the Edit buttons presented in the table, and the PersonDisplay component will display a summary of the data. Click the Previous and Next buttons to query for the objects with the adjacent primary key values, producing the results shown in figure 35.8.

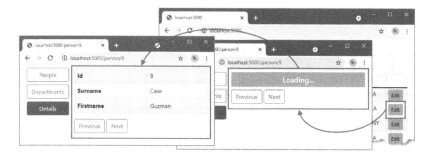

Figure 35.8 Performing asynchronous tasks in a component

Notice that Blazor doesn't wait for the Task performed in the OnParametersSetAsync method to complete before displaying content to the user, which is why a loading message is useful when the Person property is null. Once the Task is complete and a value has been assigned to the `Person` property, the component's view is automatically re-rendered, and the changes are sent to the browser over the persistent HTTP connection to be displayed to the user.

35.4 *Managing component interaction*

Most components work together through parameters and events, allowing the user's interaction to drive changes in the application. Blazor also provides advanced options for managing interaction with components, which I describe in the following sections.

35.4.1 *Using references to child components*

A parent component can obtain a reference to a child component and use it to consume the properties and methods it defines. In preparation, listing 35.18 adds a disabled state to the `MultiNavLink` component.

> **Listing 35.18   Adding a feature in the MultiNavLink.razor file in the Blazor folder**

```
<a class="@ComputedClass" @onclick="HandleClick"  href="">
    @if (Enabled) {
        @ChildContent
    } else {
        @("Disabled")
    }
</a>

@code {

    [Inject]
    public NavigationManager? NavManager { get; set; }

    [Parameter]
    public IEnumerable<string> Href { get; set; }
        = Enumerable.Empty<string>();

    [Parameter]
    public string Class { get; set; } = string.Empty;

    [Parameter]
    public string ActiveClass { get; set; } = string.Empty;

    [Parameter]
    public string DisabledClasses { get; set; } = string.Empty;

    [Parameter]
    public NavLinkMatch? Match { get; set; }

    public NavLinkMatch ComputedMatch { get =>
            Match ?? (Href.Count() == 1
                ? NavLinkMatch.Prefix : NavLinkMatch.All); }

    [Parameter]
    public RenderFragment? ChildContent { get; set; }
```

```
public string ComputedClass { get; set; } = string.Empty;


public void HandleClick() {
    NavManager?.NavigateTo(Href.First());
}

private void CheckMatch(string currentUrl) {
    string path = NavManager!.ToBaseRelativePath(currentUrl);
    path = path.EndsWith("/")
        ? path.Substring(0, path.Length - 1) : path;
    bool match = Href.Any(href => ComputedMatch == NavLinkMatch.All
            ? path == href : path.StartsWith(href));
    if (!Enabled) {
        ComputedClass = DisabledClasses;
    } else {
        ComputedClass = match ? $"{Class} {ActiveClass}" : Class;
    }
}

protected override void OnParametersSet() {
    ComputedClass = Class;
    NavManager!.LocationChanged +=
        (sender, arg) => CheckMatch(arg.Location);
    Href = Href.Select(h => h.StartsWith("/") ? h.Substring(1) : h);
    CheckMatch(NavManager!.Uri);
}

private bool Enabled { get; set; } = true;

public void SetEnabled(bool enabled) {
    Enabled = enabled;
    CheckMatch(NavManager!.Uri);
}
}
```

In listing 35.19, I have updated the shared layout so that it retains references to the
MultiNavLink components and a button that toggles their Enabled property value.

> **Listing 35.19** **Retaining references in the NavLayout.razor file in the Blazor folder**

```
@inherits LayoutComponentBase

<div class="container-fluid">
    <div class="row">
        <div class="col-3">
            <div class="d-grid gap-2">
                @foreach (string key in NavLinks.Keys) {
                    <MultiNavLink class="btn btn-outline-primary btn-block"
                        href="@NavLinks[key]"
                        ActiveClass="btn-primary text-white"
                        DisabledClasses="btn btn-dark text-light
                          btn-block disabled"
                         @ref="Refs[key]">
                        @key
```

```
            </MultiNavLink>
        }
        <button class="btn btn-secondary btn-block mt-5"
                @onclick="ToggleLinks">
            Toggle Links
        </button>
        </div>
    </div>
    <div class="col">
        @Body
    </div>
    </div>
</div>

@code {

    public Dictionary<string, string[]> NavLinks
        = new Dictionary<string, string[]> {
            {"People", new string[] {"/people", "/" } },
            {"Departments", new string[] {"/depts", "/departments" } },
            {"Details", new string[] { "/person" } }
        };

    public Dictionary<string, MultiNavLink?> Refs
        = new Dictionary<string, MultiNavLink?>();

    private bool LinksEnabled = true;

    public void ToggleLinks() {
        LinksEnabled = !LinksEnabled;
        foreach (MultiNavLink? link in Refs.Values) {
            link?.SetEnabled(LinksEnabled);
        }
    }
}
```

References to components are created by adding an `@ref` attribute and specifying the name of a field or property to which the component should be assigned. Since the MultiNavLink components are created in a `@foreach` loop driven by a Dictionary, the simplest way to retain references is also in a Dictionary, like this:

```
...
<MultiNavLink class="btn btn-outline-primary btn-block"
    href="@NavLinks[key]" ActiveClass="btn-primary text-white"
    DisabledClasses="btn btn-dark text-light btn-block disabled"
    @ref="Refs[key]">
...
```

As each MultiNavLink component is created, it is added to the Refs dictionary. Razor Components are compiled into standard C# classes, which means that a collection of MultiNavLink components is a collection of MultiNavlink objects.

```
...
public Dictionary<string, MultiNavLink> Refs
        = new Dictionary<string, MultiNavLink>();
...
```

Restart ASP.NET Core, request http://localhost:5000, and click the Toggle Links button. The event handler invokes the `ToggleLinks` method, which sets the value of the `Enabled` property for each of the `MultiNavLink` components, as shown in figure 35.9.

> **CAUTION**   References can be used only after the component's content has been rendered and the `OnAfterRender`/`OnAfterRenderAsync` lifecycle methods have been invoked. This makes references ideal for use in event handlers but not the earlier lifecycle methods.

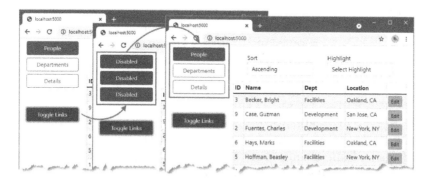

Figure 35.9   Retaining references to components

35.4.2 *Interacting with components from other code*

Components can be used by other code in the ASP.NET Core application, allowing a richer interaction between parts of complex projects. Listing 35.20 alters the method in the `MultiNavLink` component so it can be invoked by other parts of the ASP.NET Core application to enable and disable navigation.

Listing 35.20   Replacing a method in the MultiNavLink.razor file in the Blazor folder

```
<a class="@ComputedClass" @onclick="HandleClick"  href="">
    @if (Enabled) {
        @ChildContent
    } else {
        @("Disabled")
    }
</a>

@code {

    // ...other properties and methods omitted for brevity...

    private bool Enabled { get; set; } = true;

    public void SetEnabled(bool enabled) {
        InvokeAsync(() => {
            Enabled = enabled;
```

```
            CheckMatch(NavManager!.Uri);
            StateHasChanged();
        });
    }
}
```

Razor Components provide two methods that are used in code that is invoked outside of the Blazor environment, as described in table 35.6.

Table 35.6   The Razor component external invocation methods

Name	Description
InvokeAsync(func)	This method is used to execute a function inside the Blazor environment.
StateHasChanged()	This method is called when a change occurs outside of the normal lifecycle, as shown in the next section.

The `InvokeAsync` method is used to invoke a function within the Blazor environment, ensuring that changes are processed correctly. The `StateHasChanged` method is invoked when all the changes have been applied, triggering a Blazor update and ensuring changes are reflected in the component's output.

To create a service that will be available throughout the application, create the `Advanced/Services` folder and add to it a class file named `ToggleService.cs`, with the code shown in listing 35.21.

Listing 35.21   The contents of the ToggleService.cs file in the Services folder

```
using Advanced.Blazor;

namespace Advanced.Services {
    public class ToggleService {
        private List<MultiNavLink> components = new List<MultiNavLink>();
        private bool enabled = true;

        public void EnrolComponents(IEnumerable<MultiNavLink> comps) {
            components.AddRange(comps);
        }

        public bool ToggleComponents() {
            enabled = !enabled;
            components.ForEach(c => c.SetEnabled(enabled));
            return enabled;
        }
    }
}
```

This service manages a collection of components and invokes the `SetEnabled` method on all of them when its `ToggleComponents` method is called. There is nothing specific to Blazor in this service, which relies on the C# classes that are produced when Razor Component files are compiled. Listing 35.22 updates the application configuration to configure the `ToggleService` class as a singleton service.

Listing 35.22 Configuring a service in the Program.cs file in the Advanced folder

```
using Microsoft.EntityFrameworkCore;
using Advanced.Models;

var builder = WebApplication.CreateBuilder(args);

builder.Services.AddControllersWithViews();
builder.Services.AddRazorPages();
builder.Services.AddServerSideBlazor();

builder.Services.AddDbContext<DataContext>(opts => {
    opts.UseSqlServer(
        builder.Configuration["ConnectionStrings:PeopleConnection"]);
    opts.EnableSensitiveDataLogging(true);
});

builder.Services.AddSingleton<Advanced.Services.ToggleService>();

var app = builder.Build();

app.UseStaticFiles();

app.MapControllers();
app.MapControllerRoute("controllers",
    "controllers/{controller=Home}/{action=Index}/{id?}");
app.MapRazorPages();
app.MapBlazorHub();
app.MapFallbackToPage("/_Host");

var context = app.Services.CreateScope().ServiceProvider
    .GetRequiredService<DataContext>();
SeedData.SeedDatabase(context);

app.Run();
```

Listing 35.23 updates the Blazor layout so that references to the `MultiNavLink` components are retained and registered with the new service.

Listing 35.23 Using the service in the NavLayout.razor file in the Blazor folder

```
@inherits LayoutComponentBase
@using Advanced.Services

<div class="container-fluid">
    <div class="row">
        <div class="col-3">
            <div class="d-grid gap-2">
                @foreach (string key in NavLinks.Keys) {
                    <MultiNavLink class="btn btn-outline-primary btn-block"
                        href="@NavLinks[key]"
                        ActiveClass="btn-primary text-white"
                        DisabledClasses="btn btn-dark text-light
                            btn-block disabled"
                        @ref="Refs[key]">
```

```
                    @key
                </MultiNavLink>
            }
        <button class="btn btn-secondary btn-block mt-5"
                @onclick="ToggleLinks">
            Toggle Links
        </button>
        </div>
    </div>
    <div class="col">
        @Body
    </div>
    </div>
</div>

@code {

    [Inject]
    public ToggleService? Toggler { get; set; }

    public Dictionary<string, string[]> NavLinks
        = new Dictionary<string, string[]> {
            {"People", new string[] {"/people", "/" } },
            {"Departments", new string[] {"/depts", "/departments" } },
            {"Details", new string[] { "/person" } }
        };

    public Dictionary<string, MultiNavLink?> Refs
        = new Dictionary<string, MultiNavLink?>();

    //private bool LinksEnabled = true;

    protected override void OnAfterRender(bool firstRender) {
        if (firstRender && Toggler != null) {
            Toggler.EnrolComponents(
                Refs.Values as IEnumerable<MultiNavLink>);
        }
    }

    public void ToggleLinks() {
        Toggler?.ToggleComponents();
    }
}
```

As noted in the previous section, component references are not available until after the content has been rendered. Listing 35.23 uses the OnAfterRender lifecycle method to register the component references with the service, which is received via dependency injection.

The final step is to use the service from a different part of the ASP.NET Core application. Listing 35.24 adds a simple action method to the Home controller that invokes the ToggleService.ToggleComponents method every time it handles a request.

Listing 35.24   Adding an action in the HomeController.cs file in the Controllers folder

```csharp
using Advanced.Models;
using Microsoft.AspNetCore.Mvc;
using Microsoft.EntityFrameworkCore;
using Advanced.Services;

namespace Advanced.Controllers {
    public class HomeController : Controller {
        private DataContext context;
        private ToggleService toggleService;

        public HomeController(DataContext dbContext, ToggleService ts) {
            context = dbContext;
            toggleService = ts;
        }

        public IActionResult Index([FromQuery] string selectedCity) {
            return View(new PeopleListViewModel {
                People = context.People
                    .Include(p => p.Department).Include(p => p.Location),
                Cities = context.Locations.Select(l => l.City).Distinct(),
                SelectedCity = selectedCity
            });
        }

        public string Toggle() =>
            $"Enabled: {toggleService.ToggleComponents()}";
    }
}

public class PeopleListViewModel {

    public IEnumerable<Person> People { get; set; }
        = Enumerable.Empty<Person>();

    public IEnumerable<string> Cities { get; set; }
        = Enumerable.Empty<string>();

    public string SelectedCity { get; set; } = String.Empty;

    public string GetClass(string? city) =>
        SelectedCity == city ? "bg-info text-white" : "";
}
```

Restart ASP.NET Core and request http://localhost:5000. Open a separate browser window and request http://localhost:5000/controllers/home/toggle. When the second request is processed by the ASP.NET Core application, the action method will use the service, which toggles the state of the navigation button. Each time you request /controllers/home/toggle, the state of the navigation buttons will change, as shown in figure 35.10.

Figure 35.10   Invoking component methods

35.4.3 *Interacting with components using JavaScript*

Blazor provides a range of tools for interaction between JavaScript and server-side C# code, as described in the following sections.

INVOKING A JAVASCRIPT FUNCTION FROM A COMPONENT

To prepare for these examples, add a JavaScript file named `interop.js` to the `wwwroot` folder and add the code shown in listing 35.25.

Listing 35.25   The contents of the interop.js file in the wwwroot folder

```javascript
function addTableRows(colCount) {
    let elem = document.querySelector("tbody");
    let row = document.createElement("tr");
    elem.append(row);
    for (let i = 0; i < colCount; i++) {
        let cell = document.createElement("td");
        cell.innerText = "New Elements"
        row.append(cell);
    }
}
```

The JavaScript code uses the API provided by the browser to locate a `tbody` element, which denotes the body of a table and adds a new row containing the number of cells specified by the function parameter.

To incorporate the JavaScript file into the application, add the element shown in listing 35.26 to the `_Host` Razor Page, which was configured as the fallback page that delivers the Blazor application to the browser.

Listing 35.26   Adding an element in the _Host.cshtml file in the Pages folder

```
@page "/"
@{ Layout = null; }

<!DOCTYPE html>
<html>
<head>
    <title>@ViewBag.Title</title>
```

```
    <link href="/lib/bootstrap/css/bootstrap.min.css" rel="stylesheet" />
    <base href="~/" />
</head>
<body>
    <div class="m-2">
        <component type="typeof(Advanced.Blazor.Routed)"
            render-mode="Server" />
    </div>
    <script src="_framework/blazor.server.js"></script>
    <script src="~/interop.js"></script>
</body>
</html>
```

Listing 35.27 revises the `PersonDisplay` component so that it renders a button that invokes the JavaScript function when the `onclick` event is triggered. I have also removed the delay that I added earlier to demonstrate the use of the component lifecycle methods.

Listing 35.27   Invoking a function in the PersonDisplay.razor file in the Blazor folder

```
@page "/person"
@page "/person/{id:long}"

@if (Person == null) {
    <h5 class="bg-info text-white text-center p-2">Loading...</h5>
} else {
    <table class="table table-striped table-bordered">
        <tbody>
            <tr><th>Id</th><td>@Person.PersonId</td></tr>
            <tr><th>Surname</th><td>@Person.Surname</td></tr>
            <tr><th>Firstname</th><td>@Person.Firstname</td></tr>
        </tbody>
    </table>
}

<button class="btn btn-outline-primary" @onclick="@HandleClick">
    Invoke JS Function
</button>

@code {

    [Inject]
    public DataContext? Context { get; set; }

    [Inject]
    public NavigationManager? NavManager { get; set; }

    [Inject]
    public IJSRuntime? JSRuntime { get; set; }

    [Parameter]
    public long Id { get; set; } = 0;

    public Person? Person { get; set; }
```

```
protected async override Task OnParametersSetAsync() {
    //await Task.Delay(1000);
    if (Context != null) {
        Person = await Context.People
            .FirstOrDefaultAsync(p => p.PersonId == Id)
            ?? new Person();
    }
}

public async Task HandleClick() {
    await JSRuntime!.InvokeVoidAsync("addTableRows", 2);
}
}
```

Invoking a JavaScript function is done through the IJSRuntime interface, which components receive through dependency injection. The service is created automatically as part of the Blazor configuration and provides the methods described in table 35.7.

Table 35.7   The IJSRuntime methods

Name	Description
InvokeAsync<T>(name, args)	This method invokes the specified function with the arguments provided. The result type is specified by the generic type parameter.
InvokeVoidAsync(name, args)	This method invokes a function that doesn't produce a result.

In listing 35.27, I use the InvokeVoidAsync method to invoke the addTableRows JavaScript function, providing a value for the function parameter. Restart ASP.NET Core, navigate to http://localhost:5000/person/1, and click the Invoke JS Function button. Blazor will invoke the JavaScript function, which adds a row to the end of the table, as shown in figure 35.11.

Figure 35.11   Invoking a JavaScript function

Retaining References to HTML Elements

Razor Components can retain references to the HTML elements they create and pass those references to JavaScript code. Listing 35.28 changes the JavaScript function from the previous example so that it operates on an HTML element it receives through a parameter.

> Listing 35.28   Defining a parameter in the interop.js file in the wwwroot folder

```javascript
function addTableRows(colCount, elem) {
    //let elem = document.querySelector("tbody");
    let row = document.createElement("tr");
    elem.parentNode.insertBefore(row, elem);
    for (let i = 0; i < colCount; i++) {
        let cell = document.createElement("td");
        cell.innerText = "New Elements"
        row.append(cell);
    }
}
```

In listing 35.29, the `PersonDisplay` component retains a reference to one of the HTML elements it creates and passes it as an argument to the JavaScript function.

> Listing 35.29   Retaining a reference in the PersonDisplay.razor file in the Blazor folder

```razor
@page "/person"
@page "/person/{id:long}"

@if (Person == null) {
    <h5 class="bg-info text-white text-center p-2">Loading...</h5>
} else {
    <table class="table table-striped table-bordered">
        <tbody>
            <tr><th>Id</th><td>@Person.PersonId</td></tr>
            <tr @ref="RowReference">
                <th>Surname</th><td>@Person.Surname</td>
            </tr>
            <tr><th>Firstname</th><td>@Person.Firstname</td></tr>
        </tbody>
    </table>
}

<button class="btn btn-outline-primary" @onclick="@HandleClick">
    Invoke JS Function
</button>


@code {

    [Inject]
    public DataContext? Context { get; set; }

    [Inject]
    public NavigationManager? NavManager { get; set; }
```

```
[Inject]
public IJSRuntime? JSRuntime { get; set; }

[Parameter]
public long Id { get; set; } = 0;

public Person? Person { get; set; }

protected async override Task OnParametersSetAsync() {
    if (Context != null) {
        Person = await Context.People
            .FirstOrDefaultAsync(p => p.PersonId == Id)
            ?? new Person();
    }
}

public ElementReference RowReference { get; set; }

public async Task HandleClick() {
    await JSRuntime!.InvokeVoidAsync("addTableRows", 2, RowReference);
}
}
```

The `@ref` attribute assigns the HTML element to a property, whose type must be `ElementReference`. Restart ASP.NET Core, request http://localhost:5000/person/1, and click the Invoke JS Function button. The value of the `ElementReference` property is passed as an argument to the JavaScript function through the `InvokeVoidAsync` method, producing the result shown in figure 35.12.

NOTE   The only use for a reference to a regular HTML element is to pass it to a JavaScript function. Use the binding and event features described in earlier chapters to interact with the elements rendered by a component.

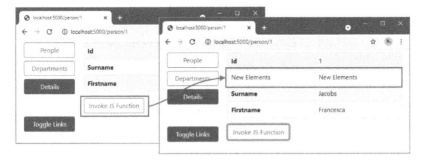

Figure 35.12   Retaining a reference to an HTML element

INVOKING A COMPONENT METHOD FROM JAVASCRIPT

The basic approach for invoking a C# method from JavaScript is to use a `static` method. Listing 35.30 adds a static method to the `MultiNavLink` component that changes the enabled state.

Listing 35.30   Introducing static members in the MultiNavLink.razor file in the Blazor folder

```
<a class="@ComputedClass" @onclick="HandleClick"  href="">
    @if (Enabled) {
        @ChildContent
    } else {
        @("Disabled")
    }
</a>

@code {

    // ...other methods and properties omitted for brevity...

    [JSInvokable]
    public static void ToggleEnabled() =>
        ToggleEvent?.Invoke(null, new EventArgs());

    private static event EventHandler? ToggleEvent;

    protected override void OnInitialized() {
        ToggleEvent += (sender, args) => SetEnabled(!Enabled);
    }
}
```

Static methods must be decorated with the JSInvokable attribute before they can be invoked from JavaScript code. The main limitation of using static methods is that it makes it difficult to update individual components, so I have defined a static event that each instance of the component will handle. The event is named ToggleEvent, and it is triggered by the static method that will be called from JavaScript. To listen for the event, I have used the OnInitialized lifecycle event. When the event is received, the enabled state of the component is toggled through the instance method Set-Enabled, which uses the InvokeAsync and StateHasChanged methods required when a change is made outside of Blazor.

Listing 35.31 adds a function to the JavaScript file that creates a button element that invokes the static C# method when it is clicked.

Listing 35.31   Adding a function in the interop.js file in the wwwroot folder

```
function addTableRows(colCount, elem) {
    //let elem = document.querySelector("tbody");
    let row = document.createElement("tr");
    elem.parentNode.insertBefore(row, elem);
    for (let i = 0; i < colCount; i++) {
        let cell = document.createElement("td");
        cell.innerText = "New Elements"
        row.append(cell);
    }
}

function createToggleButton() {
```

```
    let sibling = document.querySelector("button:last-of-type");
    let button = document.createElement("button");
    button.classList.add("btn", "btn-secondary", "btn-block");
    button.innerText = "JS Toggle";
    sibling.parentNode.insertBefore(button, sibling.nextSibling);
    button.onclick = () => DotNet.invokeMethodAsync("Advanced",
        "ToggleEnabled");
}
```

The new function locates one of the existing `button` elements and adds a new button after it. When the button is clicked, the component method is invoked, like this:

```
...
button.onclick = () => DotNet.invokeMethodAsync("Advanced",
    "ToggleEnabled");
...
```

It is important to pay close attention to the capitalization of the JavaScript function used for C# methods: it is `DotNet`, followed by a period, followed by `invokeMethodAsync`, with a lowercase `i`. The arguments are the name of the assembly and the name of the static method. (The name of the component is not required.)

The `button` element that the function in listing 35.31 looks for isn't available until after Blazor has rendered content for the user. For this reason, listing 35.32 adds a statement to the `OnAfterRenderAsync` method defined by the `NavLayout` component to invoke the JavaScript function only when the content has been rendered. (The `NavLayout` component is the parent to the `MultiNavLink` components that will be affected when the `static` method is invoked and allows me to ensure the JavaScript function is invoked only once.)

> **Listing 35.32** Invoking a JavaScript function in the NavLayout.razor file in the Blazor folder

```
...
@code {

    [Inject]
    public ToggleService? Toggler { get; set; }

    [Inject]
    public IJSRuntime? JSRuntime { get; set; }

    public Dictionary<string, string[]> NavLinks
        = new Dictionary<string, string[]> {
            {"People", new string[] {"/people", "/" } },
            {"Departments", new string[] {"/depts", "/departments" } },
            {"Details", new string[] { "/person" } }
        };

    public Dictionary<string, MultiNavLink?> Refs
        = new Dictionary<string, MultiNavLink?>();

    //private bool LinksEnabled = true;

    protected async override Task OnAfterRenderAsync(bool firstRender) {
```

```
        if (firstRender && Toggler != null) {
            Toggler.EnrolComponents(
                Refs.Values as IEnumerable<MultiNavLink>);
            await JSRuntime!.InvokeVoidAsync("createToggleButton");
        }
    }

    public void ToggleLinks() {
        Toggler?.ToggleComponents();
    }
}
...
```

Restart ASP.NET Core and request http://localhost:5000. Once Blazor has rendered its content, the JavaScript function will be called and creates a new button. Clicking the button invokes the `static` method, which triggers the event that toggles the state of the navigation buttons and causes a Blazor update, as shown in figure 35.13.

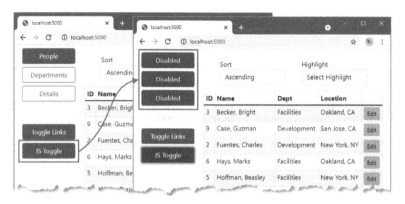

Figure 35.13 Invoking a component method from JavaScript

INVOKING AN INSTANCE METHOD FROM A JAVASCRIPT FUNCTION

Part of the complexity in the previous example comes from responding to a `static` method to update the Razor Component objects. An alternative approach is to provide the JavaScript code with a reference to an instance method, which it can then invoke directly.

The first step is to add the `JSInvokable` attribute to the method that the JavaScript code will invoke. I am going to invoke the `ToggleComponents` methods defined by the `ToggleService` class, as shown in listing 35.33.

Listing 35.33 Applying an attribute in the ToggleService.cs file in the Services folder

```
using Advanced.Blazor;
using Microsoft.JSInterop;

namespace Advanced.Services {
    public class ToggleService {
```

```
        private List<MultiNavLink> components = new List<MultiNavLink>();
        private bool enabled = true;

        public void EnrolComponents(IEnumerable<MultiNavLink> comps) {
            components.AddRange(comps);
        }

        [JSInvokable]
        public bool ToggleComponents() {
            enabled = !enabled;
            components.ForEach(c => c.SetEnabled(enabled));
            return enabled;
        }
    }
}
```

The next step is to provide the JavaScript function with a reference to the object whose method will be invoked, as shown in listing 35.34.

> **Listing 35.34   Providing an instance in the NavLayout.razor file in the Blazor folder**

```
...
protected async override Task OnAfterRenderAsync(bool firstRender) {
    if (firstRender && Toggler != null) {
        Toggler.EnrolComponents(
            Refs.Values as IEnumerable<MultiNavLink>);
        await JSRuntime!.InvokeVoidAsync("createToggleButton",
            DotNetObjectReference.Create(Toggler));
    }
}
...
```

The `DotNetObjectReference.Create` method creates a reference to an object, which is passed to the JavaScript function as an argument using the `JSRuntime.Invoke-VoidAsync` method. The final step is to receive the object reference in JavaScript and invoke its method when the button element is clicked, as shown in listing 35.35.

> **Listing 35.35   Invoking a C# method in the interop.js file in the wwwroot folder**

```
function addTableRows(colCount, elem) {
    //let elem = document.querySelector("tbody");
    let row = document.createElement("tr");
    elem.parentNode.insertBefore(row, elem);
    for (let i = 0; i < colCount; i++) {
        let cell = document.createElement("td");
        cell.innerText = "New Elements";
        row.append(cell);
    }
}

function createToggleButton(toggleServiceRef) {
    let sibling = document.querySelector("button:last-of-type");
    let button = document.createElement("button");
    button.classList.add("btn", "btn-secondary", "btn-block");
```

```
    button.innerText = "JS Toggle";
    sibling.parentNode.insertBefore(button, sibling.nextSibling);
    button.onclick = () =>
        toggleServiceRef.invokeMethodAsync("ToggleComponents");
}
```

The JavaScript function receives the reference to the C# object as a parameter and invokes its methods using `invokeMethodAsync`, specifying the name of the method as the argument. (Arguments to the method can also be provided but are not required in this example.)

Restart ASP.NET Core, request http://localhost:5000, and click the JS Toggle button. The result is the same as shown in figure 35.13, but the change in the components is managed through the `ToggleService` object.

Summary

- The component used to handle a request can be selected using routes, which are defined using the `@page` expression.

- The `NavLink` component is used to navigate between components with routes.

- Components have a well-defined lifecycle, through which methods are invoked at key moments, including initialization, configuration, and content rendering.

- Parent components can obtain references to child components using the `@ref` expression.

- Blazor supports interaction with JavaScript code running the browser. Components can invoke JavaScript functions and JavaScript code can invoke C# component methods.

Blazor forms and data

In this chapter, I describe the features that Blazor provides for dealing with HTML forms, including support for data validation. I describe the built-in components that Blazor provides and show you how they are used. In this chapter, I also explain how the Blazor model can cause unexpected results with Entity Framework Core and show you how to address these issues. I finish the chapter by creating a simple form application for creating, reading, updating, and deleting data (the CRUD operations) and explain how to extend the Blazor form features to improve the user's experience. Table 36.1 puts the Blazor form features in context.

Table 36.1   Putting Blazor form features in context

Question	Answer
What are they?	Blazor provides a set of built-in components that present the user with a form that can be easily validated.
Why are they useful?	Forms remain one of the core building blocks of web applications, and these components provide functionality that most projects will require.
How are they used?	The `EditForm` component is used as a parent for individual form field components.
Are there any pitfalls or limitations?	There can be issues with the way that Entity Framework Core and Blazor work together, and these become especially apparent when using forms.
Are there any alternatives?	You could create your own form components and validation features, although the features described in this chapter are suitable for most projects and, as I demonstrate, can be easily extended.

Table 36.2 provides a guide to the chapter.

Table 36.2   Chapter guide

Problem	Solution	Listing
Creating an HTML form	Use the `EditForm` and `Input*` components.	7-9, 13
Validating data	Use the standard validation attributes and the events emitted by the `EditForm` component.	10-12
Discarding unsaved data	Explicitly release the data or create new scopes for components.	14-16
Avoiding repeatedly querying the database	Manage query execution explicitly.	17-19

36.1   *Preparing for this chapter*

This chapter uses the Advanced project from chapter 35. To prepare for this chapter, create the `Blazor/Forms` folder and add to it a Razor Component named `Empty-Layout.razor` with the content shown in listing 36.1. I will use this component as the main layout for this chapter.

> **TIP**   You can download the example project for this chapter—and for all the other chapters in this book—from https://github.com/manningbooks/pro-asp .net-core-7. See chapter 1 for how to get help if you have problems running the examples.

```
@inherits LayoutComponentBase

<div class="m-2">
    @Body
</div>
```

Add a `RazorComponent` named `FormSpy.razor` to the `Blazor/Forms` folder with the content shown in listing 36.2. This is a component I will use to display form elements alongside the values that are being edited.

```
<div class="container-fluid no-gutters">
    <div class="row">
        <div class="col">
            @ChildContent
        </div>
        <div class="col">
            <table class="table table-sm table-striped table-bordered">
                <thead>
                    <tr>
                        <th colspan="2" class="text-center">
                            Data Summary
                        </th>
                    </tr>
                </thead>
                <tbody>
                    <tr>
                        <th>ID</th><td>@PersonData?.PersonId</td>
                    </tr>
                    <tr>
                        <th>Firstname</th><td>@PersonData?.Firstname</td>
                    </tr>
                    <tr>
                        <th>Surname</th><td>@PersonData?.Surname</td>
                    </tr>
                    <tr>
                        <th>Dept ID</th>
                        <td>@PersonData?.DepartmentId</td>
                    </tr>
                    <tr>
                        <th>Location ID</th>
                        <td>@PersonData?.LocationId</td>
                    </tr>
                </tbody>
            </table>
        </div>
    </div>
</div>

@code {

    [Parameter]
```

```
public RenderFragment? ChildContent { get; set; }

    [Parameter]
    public Person PersonData { get; set; } = new();
}
```

Next, add a component named `Editor.razor` to the `Blazor/Forms` folder and add the content shown in listing 36.3. This component will edit existing `Person` objects and create new ones.

> **CAUTION** Do not use the `Editor` and `List` components in real projects until you have read the rest of the chapter. I have included common pitfalls that I explain later in the chapter.

Listing 36.3 **The contents of the Editor.razor file in the Blazor/Forms folder**

```
@page "/forms/edit/{id:long}"
@layout EmptyLayout

<h4 class="bg-primary text-center text-white p-2">Edit</h4>

<FormSpy PersonData="PersonData">
    <h4 class="text-center">Form Placeholder</h4>
    <div class="text-center">
        <NavLink class="btn btn-secondary mt-2" href="/forms">
            Back
        </NavLink>
    </div>
</FormSpy>

@code {

    [Inject]
    public NavigationManager? NavManager { get; set; }

    [Inject]
    DataContext? Context { get; set; }

    [Parameter]
    public long Id { get; set; }

    public Person PersonData { get; set; } = new();

    protected async override Task OnParametersSetAsync() {
        if (Context != null) {
            PersonData = await Context.People.FindAsync(Id)
                ?? new Person();
        }
    }
}
```

The component in listing 36.3 uses an `@layout` expression to override the default layout and select `EmptyLayout`. The side-by-side layout is used to present the `Person-Table` component alongside a placeholder, which is where I will add a form.

Finally, create a component named `List.razor` in the `Blazor/Forms` folder and add the content shown in listing 36.4 to define a component that will present the user with a table that lists `Person` objects.

Listing 36.4   The contents of the List.razor file in the Blazor/Forms folder

```
@page "/forms"
@page "/forms/list"
@layout EmptyLayout

<h5 class="bg-primary text-white text-center p-2">People</h5>

<table class="table table-sm table-striped table-bordered">
    <thead>
        <tr>
            <th>ID</th>
            <th>Name</th>
            <th>Dept</th>
            <th>Location</th>
            <th></th>
        </tr>
    </thead>
    <tbody>
        @if (People.Count() == 0) {
            <tr>
                <th colspan="5" class="p-4 text-center">
                    Loading Data...
                </th>
            </tr>
        } else {
            @foreach (Person p in People) {
                <tr>
                    <td>@p.PersonId</td>
                    <td>@p.Surname, @p.Firstname</td>
                    <td>@p.Department?.Name</td>
                    <td>@p.Location?.City</td>
                    <td>
                        <NavLink class="btn btn-sm btn-warning"
                          href="@GetEditUrl(p.PersonId)">
                            Edit
                        </NavLink>
                    </td>
                </tr>
            }
        }
    </tbody>
</table>

@code {

    [Inject]
    public DataContext? Context { get; set; }

    public IEnumerable<Person> People { get; set; }
```

```
            = Enumerable.Empty<Person>();

    protected override void OnInitialized() {
        People = Context?.People?.Include(p => p.Department)
            .Include(p => p.Location)
                ?? Enumerable.Empty<Person>();
    }

    string GetEditUrl(long id) => $"/forms/edit/{id}";
}
```

36.1.1 Dropping the database and running the application

Open a new PowerShell command prompt, navigate to the folder that contains the `Advanced.csproj` file, and run the command shown in listing 36.5 to drop the database.

Listing 36.5 Dropping the database

```
dotnet ef database drop --force
```

Use the PowerShell command prompt to run the command shown in listing 36.6.

Listing 36.6 Running the example application

```
dotnet run
```

Use a browser to request http://localhost:5000/forms, which will produce a data table. Click one of the Edit buttons, and you will see a placeholder for the form and a summary showing the current property values of the selected `Person` object, as shown in figure 36.1.

Figure 36.1   Running the example application

36.2   Using the Blazor form components

Blazor provides a set of built-in components that are used to render form elements, ensuring that the server-side component properties are updated after user interaction and integrating validation. Table 36.3 describes the components that Blazor provides.

Table 36.3   The Blazor form components

Name	Description
EditForm	This component renders a `form` element that is wired up for data validation.
InputText	This component renders an `input` element that is bound to a C# `string` property.
InputCheckbox	This component renders an input element whose `type` attribute is `checkbox` and that is bound to a C# `bool` property.
InputDate	This component renders an input element those `type` attribute is `date` and that is bound to a C# `DateTime` or `DateTimeOffset` property.
InputNumber	This component renders an input element those `type` attribute is `number` and that is bound to a C# `int`, `long`, `float`, `double`, or `decimal` value.
InputTextArea	This component renders a `textarea` component that is bound to a C# `string` property.

The `EditForm` component must be used for any of the other components to work. In listing 36.7, I have added an `EditForm`, along with `InputText` components that represent two of the properties defined by the `Person` class.

Listing 36.7   Using form components in the Editor.razor file in the Blazor/Forms folder

```
@page "/forms/edit/{id:long}"
@layout EmptyLayout

<h4 class="bg-primary text-center text-white p-2">Edit</h4>

<FormSpy PersonData="PersonData">
    <EditForm Model="PersonData">
        <div class="form-group">
            <label>Person ID</label>
            <InputNumber class="form-control"
                @bind-Value="PersonData.PersonId" disabled />
        </div>
        <div class="form-group">
            <label>Firstname</label>
            <InputText class="form-control"
                @bind-Value="PersonData.Firstname" />
        </div>
        <div class="form-group">
            <label>Surname</label>
            <InputText class="form-control"
                @bind-Value="PersonData.Surname" />
        </div>
        <div class="form-group">
            <label>Dept ID</label>
            <InputNumber class="form-control"
                    @bind-Value="PersonData.DepartmentId" />
        </div>
```

```
        <div class="text-center">
            <NavLink class="btn btn-secondary" href="/forms">
                Back
            </NavLink>
        </div>
    </EditForm>
</FormSpy>

@code {

    [Inject]
    public NavigationManager? NavManager { get; set; }

    [Inject]
    DataContext? Context { get; set; }

    [Parameter]
    public long Id { get; set; }

    public Person PersonData { get; set; } = new();

    protected async override Task OnParametersSetAsync() {
        if (Context != null) {
            PersonData = await Context.People.FindAsync(Id)
                ?? new Person();
        }
    }
}
```

The EditForm component renders a form element and provides the foundation for the validation features described in the "Validating Form Data" section. The Model attribute provides the EditForm with the object that the form uses to edit and validate.

The components in table 36.3 whose names begin with Input are used to display an input or textarea element for a single model property. These components define a custom binding named Value that is associated with the model property using the @bind-Value attribute. The property-level components must be matched to the type of the property they present to the user. It is for this reason that I have used the InputText component for the Firstname and Surname properties of the Person class, while the InputNumber component is used for the PersonId and DepartmentId properties. If you use a property-level component with a model property of the wrong type, you will receive an error when the component attempts to parse a value entered into the HTML element.

Restart ASP.NET Core and request http://localhost:5000/forms/edit/2, and you will see the three input elements displayed. Edit the values and move the focus by pressing the Tab key, and you will see the summary data on the right of the window update, as shown in figure 36.2. The built-in form components support attribute splatting, which is why the disabled attribute applied to the InputNumber component for the PersonId property has been applied to the input element.

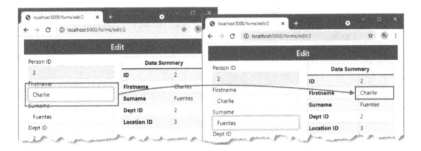

Figure 36.2   Using the Blazor form elements

36.2.1 Creating custom form components

Blazor provides built-in components for only `input` and `textarea` elements. Fortunately, creating a custom component that integrates into the Blazor form features is a simple process. Add a Razor Component named `CustomSelect.razor` to the `Blazor/Forms` folder and use it to define the component shown in listing 36.8.

Listing 36.8   The contents of the CustomSelect.razor file in the Blazor/Forms folder

```
@typeparam TValue
@inherits InputBase<TValue>
@using System.Diagnostics.CodeAnalysis

<select class="form-control @CssClass" value="@CurrentValueAsString"
        @onchange="@(ev => CurrentValueAsString = ev.Value as string)">
        @ChildContent
        @foreach (KeyValuePair<string, TValue> kvp in Values) {
            <option value="@kvp.Value">@kvp.Key</option>
        }
</select>

@code {

    [Parameter]
    public RenderFragment? ChildContent { get; set; }

    [Parameter]
    public IDictionary<string, TValue> Values { get; set; }
        = new Dictionary<string, TValue>();

    [Parameter]
    public Func<string, TValue>? Parser { get; set; }

    protected override bool TryParseValueFromString(string? value,
            [MaybeNullWhen(false)] out TValue? result,
            [NotNullWhen(false)] out string? validationErrorMessage) {
        try {
            if (Parser != null && value != null) {
                result = Parser(value);
                validationErrorMessage = null;
```

```
            return true;
        }
        result = default(TValue);
        validationErrorMessage = "Value or parser not defined";
        return false;
    } catch {
        result = default(TValue);
        validationErrorMessage = "The value is not valid";
        return false;
    }
  }
 }
}
```

The base class for form components is `InputBase<TValue>`, where the generic type argument is the model property type the component represents.

The base class takes care of most of the work and provides the `CurrentValueAsString` property, which is used to provide the current value in event handlers when the user selects a new value, like this:

```
...
<select class="form-control @CssClass" value="@CurrentValueAsString"
        @onchange="@(ev => CurrentValueAsString = ev.Value as string)">
...
```

In preparation for data validation, which I describe in the next section, this component includes the value of the `CssClass` property in the `select` element's `class` attribute, like this:

```
...
<select class="form-control @CssClass" value="@CurrentValueAsString"
        @onchange="@(ev => CurrentValueAsString = ev.Value as string)">
...
```

The abstract `TryParseValueFromString` method has to be implemented so that the base class is able to map between string values used by HTML elements and the corresponding value for the C# model property. I don't want to implement my custom `select` element to any specific C# data type, so I have used an `@typeparam` expression to define a generic type parameter.

> **NOTE**   At the time of writing, typing override and selecting the `TryParse ValueFromString` from the list of options in Visual Studio creates a method with the wrong signature. It is important to pay close attention to the parameters, especially when the code analysis attributes, described in chapter 5, are used.

The `Values` property is used to receive a dictionary mapping string values that will be displayed to the user and `TValue` values that will be used as C# values. The method receives two `out` parameters that are used to set the parsed value and a parser validation error message that will be displayed to the user if there is a problem. Since I am working with generic types, the `Parser` property receives a function that is invoked to parse a string value into a `TValue` value.

Listing 36.9 applies the new form component so the user can select values for the `DepartmentId` and `LocationId` properties defined by the `Person` class.

Listing 36.9   Using a custom element in the Editor.razor file in the Blazor/Forms folder

```
@page "/forms/edit/{id:long}"
@layout EmptyLayout

<h4 class="bg-primary text-center text-white p-2">Edit</h4>

<FormSpy PersonData="PersonData">
    <EditForm Model="PersonData">
        <div class="form-group">
            <label>Person ID</label>
            <InputNumber class="form-control"
                        @bind-Value="PersonData.PersonId" disabled />
        </div>
        <div class="form-group">
            <label>Firstname</label>
            <InputText class="form-control"
                        @bind-Value="PersonData.Firstname" />
        </div>
        <div class="form-group">
            <label>Surname</label>
            <InputText class="form-control"
                        @bind-Value="PersonData.Surname" />
        </div>
        <div class="form-group">
            <label>Dept ID</label>
            <CustomSelect TValue="long" Values="Departments"
                        Parser="@((string str) => long.Parse(str))"
                        @bind-Value="PersonData.DepartmentId">
                <option selected disabled value="0">
                    Choose a Department
                </option>
            </CustomSelect>
        </div>
        <div class="form-group">
            <label>Location ID</label>
            <CustomSelect TValue="long" Values="Locations"
                        Parser="@((string str) => long.Parse(str))"
                        @bind-Value="PersonData.LocationId">
                <option selected disabled value="0">
                    Choose a Location
                </option>
            </CustomSelect>
        </div>
        <div class="text-center">
            <NavLink class="btn btn-secondary mt-2" href="/forms">
                Back
            </NavLink>
        </div>
    </EditForm>
</FormSpy>

@code {

    [Inject]
```

```
public NavigationManager? NavManager { get; set; }

[Inject]
DataContext? Context { get; set; }

[Parameter]
public long Id { get; set; }

public Person PersonData { get; set; } = new();

public IDictionary<string, long> Departments { get; set; }
    = new Dictionary<string, long>();

public IDictionary<string, long> Locations { get; set; }
    = new Dictionary<string, long>();

protected async override Task OnParametersSetAsync() {
    if (Context != null) {
        PersonData = await Context.People.FindAsync(Id)
            ?? new Person();
        Departments = await Context.Departments
            .ToDictionaryAsync(d => d.Name, d => d.Departmentid);
        Locations = await Context.Locations
            .ToDictionaryAsync(l => $"{l.City}, {l.State}",
                l => l.LocationId);
    }
}
}
```

I use the Entity Framework Core `ToDictionaryAsync` method to create collections of values and labels from the `Department` and `Location` data and use them to configure the `CustomSelect` components. Restart ASP.NET Core and request http://localhost:5000/forms/edit/2; you will see the `select` elements shown in figure 36.3. When you pick a new value, the `CustomSelect` component will update the `Current-ValueAsString` property, which will result in a call to the `TryParseValueFromString` method, with the result used to update the `Value` binding.

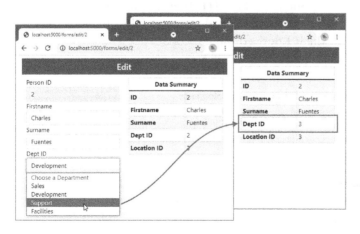

Figure 36.3 Using a custom form element

36.2.2 *Validating form data*

Blazor provides components that perform validation using the standard attributes. Table 36.4 describes the validation components.

Table 36.4   The Blazor validation components

Name	Description
DataAnnotationsValidator	This component integrates the validation attributes applied to the model class into the Blazor form features.
ValidationMessage	This component displays validation error messages for a single property.
ValidationSummary	This component displays validation error messages for the entire model object.

The validation components generate elements assigned to classes, described in table 36.5, which can be styled with CSS to draw the user's attention.

Table 36.5   The classes used by the Blazor validation components

Name	Description
validation-errors	The ValidationSummary component generates a ul element that is assigned to this class and is the top-level container for the summary of validation messages.
validation-message	The ValidationSummary component populates its ul element with li elements assigned to this class for each validation message. The ValidationMessage component renders a div element assigned to this class for its property-level messages.

The Blazor Input* components add the HTML elements they generate to the classes described in table 36.6 to indicate validation status. This includes the InputBase-<TValue> class from which I derived the CustomSelect component and is the purpose of the CssClass property in listing 36.8.

Table 36.6   The validation classes added to form elements

Name	Description
modified	Elements are added to this class once the user has edited the value.
valid	Elements are added to this class if the value they contain passes validation.
invalid	Elements are added to this class if the value they contain fails validation.

This combination of components and classes can be confusing at first, but the key is to start by defining the CSS styles you require based on the classes in table 36.5 and 36.6. Add a CSS Stylesheet named `blazorValidation.css` to the `wwwroot` folder with the content shown in listing 36.10.

Listing 36.10   The Contents of the blazorValidation.css File in the wwwroot Folder

```
.validation-errors {
    background-color: rgb(220, 53, 69); color: white; padding: 8px;
    text-align: center; font-size: 16px; font-weight: 500;
}
div.validation-message { color: rgb(220, 53, 69); font-weight: 500 }
.modified.valid { border: solid 3px rgb(40, 167, 69); }
.modified.invalid { border: solid 3px rgb(220, 53, 69); }
```

These styles format error messages in red and apply a red or green border to individual form elements. Listing 36.11 imports the CSS stylesheet and applies the Blazor validation components.

Listing 36.11   Applying validation in the Editor.razor file in the Blazor/Forms folder

```
@page "/forms/edit/{id:long}"
@layout EmptyLayout

<link href="/blazorValidation.css" rel="stylesheet" />
<h4 class="bg-primary text-center text-white p-2">Edit</h4>

<FormSpy PersonData="PersonData">
    <EditForm Model="PersonData">
        <DataAnnotationsValidator />
        <ValidationSummary />
        <div class="form-group">
            <label>Person ID</label>
            <InputNumber class="form-control"
                        @bind-Value="PersonData.PersonId" disabled />
        </div>
        <div class="form-group">
            <label>Firstname</label>
            <ValidationMessage For="@(() => PersonData.Firstname)" />
            <InputText class="form-control"
                @bind-Value="PersonData.Firstname" />
        </div>
        <div class="form-group">
            <label>Surname</label>
            <ValidationMessage For="@(() => PersonData.Surname)" />
            <InputText class="form-control"
                @bind-Value="PersonData.Surname" />
        </div>
        <div class="form-group">
            <label>Dept ID</label>
            <ValidationMessage For="@(() => PersonData.DepartmentId)" />
            <CustomSelect TValue="long" Values="Departments"
```

```
                        Parser="@((string str) => long.Parse(str))"
                        @bind-Value="PersonData.DepartmentId">
                    <option selected disabled value="0">
                        Choose a Department
                    </option>
                </CustomSelect>
            </div>
            <div class="form-group">
                <label>Location ID</label>
                <ValidationMessage For="@(() => PersonData.LocationId)" />
                <CustomSelect TValue="long" Values="Locations"
                            Parser="@((string str) => long.Parse(str))"
                            @bind-Value="PersonData.LocationId">
                    <option selected disabled value="0">
                        Choose a Location
                    </option>
                </CustomSelect>
            </div>
            <div class="text-center">
                <NavLink class="btn btn-secondary mt-2" href="/forms">
                    Back
                </NavLink>
            </div>
        </EditForm>
    </FormSpy>

@code {

    // ...members omitted for brevity...
}
```

The `DataAnnotationsValidator` and `ValidationSummary` components are applied without any configuration attributes. The `ValidationMessage` attribute is configured using the `For` attribute, which receives a function that returns the property the component represents. For example, here is the expression that selects the `Firstname` property:

```
...
<ValidationMessage For="@(() => PersonData.Firstname)" />
...
```

The expression defines no parameters and selects the property from the object used for the `Model` attribute of the `EditForm` component and not the model type. For this example, this means the expression operates on the `PersonData` object and not the `Person` class.

> **TIP** Blazor isn't always able to determine the type of the property for the `ValidationMessage` component. If you receive an exception, then you can add a `TValue` attribute to set the type explicitly. For example, if the type of the property the `ValidationMessage` component represents is `long`, then add a `TValue="long"` attribute.

The final step for enabling data validation is to apply attributes to the model class, as shown in listing 36.12.

Listing 36.12 Applying validation attributes in the Person.cs file in the Models folder

```
using System.ComponentModel.DataAnnotations;

namespace Advanced.Models {

    public class Person {

        public long PersonId { get; set; }

        [Required(ErrorMessage = "A firstname is required")]
        [MinLength(3, ErrorMessage
            = "Firstnames must be 3 or more characters")]
        public string Firstname { get; set; } = String.Empty;

        [Required(ErrorMessage = "A surname is required")]
        [MinLength(3, ErrorMessage
            = "Surnames must be 3 or more characters")]
        public string Surname { get; set; } = String.Empty;

        [Range(1, long.MaxValue,
            ErrorMessage = "A department must be selected")]
        public long DepartmentId { get; set; }

        [Range(1, long.MaxValue,
            ErrorMessage = "A location must be selected")]
        public long LocationId { get; set; }

        public Department? Department { get; set; }
        public Location? Location { get; set; }
    }
}
```

To see the effect of the validation components, restart ASP.NET Core and request http://localhost:5000/forms/edit/2. Clear the `Firstname` field and move the focus by pressing the Tab key or clicking on another field. As the focus changes, validation is performed, and error messages will be displayed. The `Editor` component shows both summary and per-property messages, so you will see the same error message shown twice. Delete all but the first two characters from the Surname field, and a second validation message will be displayed when you change the focus, as shown in figure 36.4. (There is validation support for the other properties, too, but the `select` element doesn't allow the user to select an invalid valid. If you change a value, the `select` element will be decorated with a green border to indicate a valid selection, but you won't be able to see an invalid response until I demonstrate how the form components can be used to create new data objects.)

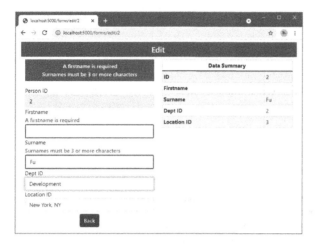

Figure 36.4
Using the Blazor
validation
features

36.2.3 *Handling form events*

The `EditForm` component defines events that allow an application to respond to user action, as described in table 36.7.

Table 36.7   The EditForm events

Name	Description
`OnValidSubmit`	This event is triggered when the form is submitted and the form data passes validation.
`OnInvalidSubmit`	This event is triggered when the form is submitted and the form data fails validation.
`OnSubmit`	This event is triggered when the form is submitted and before validation is performed.

These events are triggered by adding a conventional submit button within the content contained by the `EditForm` component. The `EditForm` component handles the `onsubmit` event sent by the `form` element it renders, applies validation, and triggers the events described in the table. Listing 36.13 adds a submit button to the `Editor` component and handles the `EditForm` events.

Listing 36.13   Handling events in the Editor.razor file in the Blazor/Forms folder

```
@page "/forms/edit/{id:long}"
@layout EmptyLayout

<link href="/blazorValidation.css" rel="stylesheet" />
<h4 class="bg-primary text-center text-white p-2">Edit</h4>
<h6 class="bg-info text-center text-white p-2">@FormSubmitMessage</h6>
```

```
<FormSpy PersonData="PersonData">
    <EditForm Model="PersonData" OnValidSubmit="HandleValidSubmit"
            OnInvalidSubmit="HandleInvalidSubmit">
        <DataAnnotationsValidator />
        <ValidationSummary />
        <div class="form-group">
            <label>Person ID</label>
            <InputNumber class="form-control"
                        @bind-Value="PersonData.PersonId" disabled />
        </div>
        <div class="form-group">
            <label>Firstname</label>
            <ValidationMessage For="@(() => PersonData.Firstname)" />
            <InputText class="form-control"
                @bind-Value="PersonData.Firstname" />
        </div>
        <div class="form-group">
            <label>Surname</label>
            <ValidationMessage For="@(() => PersonData.Surname)" />
            <InputText class="form-control"
                @bind-Value="PersonData.Surname" />
        </div>
        <div class="form-group">
            <label>Dept ID</label>
            <ValidationMessage For="@(() => PersonData.DepartmentId)" />
            <CustomSelect TValue="long" Values="Departments"
                        Parser="@((string str) => long.Parse(str))"
                        @bind-Value="PersonData.DepartmentId">
                <option selected disabled value="0">
                    Choose a Department
                </option>
            </CustomSelect>
        </div>
        <div class="form-group">
            <label>Location ID</label>
            <ValidationMessage For="@(() => PersonData.LocationId)" />
            <CustomSelect TValue="long" Values="Locations"
                        Parser="@((string str) => long.Parse(str))"
                        @bind-Value="PersonData.LocationId">
                <option selected disabled value="0">
                    Choose a Location
                </option>
            </CustomSelect>
        </div>
        <div class="text-center">
            <button type="submit" class="btn btn-primary mt-2">
                Submit
            </button>
            <NavLink class="btn btn-secondary mt-2" href="/forms">
                Back
            </NavLink>
        </div>
    </EditForm>
</FormSpy>

@code {
```

```
    // ...members omitted brevity...

    public string FormSubmitMessage { get; set; }
        = "Form Data Not Submitted";

    public void HandleValidSubmit() => FormSubmitMessage
        = "Valid Data Submitted";

    public void HandleInvalidSubmit() => FormSubmitMessage
        = "Invalid Data Submitted";
}
```

Restart ASP.NET Core and request http://localhost:5000/forms/edit/2. Clear the Firstname field, and click the Submit button. In addition to the validation error, you will see a message indicating that the form was submitted with invalid data. Enter a name into the field and click Submit again, and the message will change, as shown in figure 36.5.

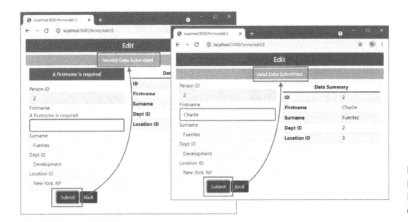

Figure 36.5 Handling EditForm events

36.3   *Using Entity Framework Core with Blazor*

The Blazor model changes the way that Entity Framework Core behaves, which can lead to unexpected results if you are used to writing conventional ASP.NET Core applications. In the sections that follow, I explain the issues and how to avoid the problems that can arise.

36.3.1   *Understanding the EF Core context scope issue*

To see the first issue, request http://localhost:5000/forms/edit/4, clear the Firstname field, change the contents of the Surname field to La, and press Tab to change the focus.

Neither of the new values passes validation, and you will see error messages as you move between the form elements. Click the Back button, and you will see that the data table reflects the changes you made, as shown in figure 36.6, even though they were not valid.

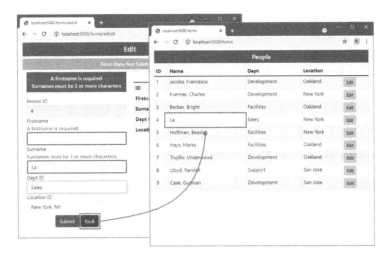

Figure 36.6
The effect of
editing data

In a conventional ASP.NET Core application, written using controllers or Razor Pages, clicking a button triggers a new HTTP request. Each request is handled in isolation, and each request receives its own Entity Framework Core context object, which is configured as a scoped service. The result is that the data created when handling one request affects other requests only once it has been written to the database.

In a Blazor application, the routing system responds to URL changes without sending new HTTP requests, which means that multiple components are displayed using only the persistent HTTP connection that Blazor maintains to the server. This results in a single dependency injection scope being shared by multiple components, as shown in figure 36.7, and the changes made by one component will affect other components even if the changes are not written to the database.

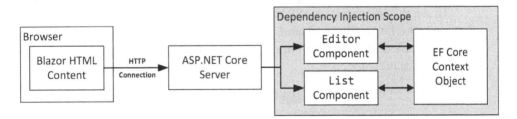

Figure 36.7   The use of an Entity Framework Core context in a Blazor application

Entity Framework Core is trying to be helpful, and this approach allows complex data operations to be performed over time before being stored (or discarded). Unfortunately, much like the helpful approach Entity Framework Core takes to dealing with related data, which I described in chapter 35, it presents a pitfall for the unwary developer who expects components to handle data like the rest of ASP.NET Core.

DISCARDING UNSAVED DATA CHANGES

If sharing a context between components is appealing, which it will be for some applications, then you can embrace the approach and ensure that components discard any changes when they are destroyed, as shown in listing 36.14.

> **Listing 36.14   Discarding unsaved data in the Editor.razor file in the Blazor/Forms folder**

```
@page "/forms/edit/{id:long}"
@layout EmptyLayout
@implements IDisposable

<!-- ...elements omitted for brevity... -->

@code {

    // ...members omitted for brevity...

    public void HandleInvalidSubmit() => FormSubmitMessage
        = "Invalid Data Submitted";

    public void Dispose() {
        if (Context != null) {
            Context.Entry(PersonData).State = EntityState.Detached;
        }
    }
}
```

As I noted in chapter 35, components can implement the System.IDisposable interface, and the Dispose method will be invoked when the component is about to be destroyed, which happens when navigation to another component occurs. In listing 36.14, the implementation of the Dispose method tells Entity Framework Core to disregard the PersonData object, which means it won't be used to satisfy future requests. To see the effect, restart ASP.NET Core, request http://localhost:5000/forms/edit/4, clear the Firstname field, and click the Back button. The modified Person object is disregarded when Entity Framework Core provides the List component with its data, as shown in figure 36.8.

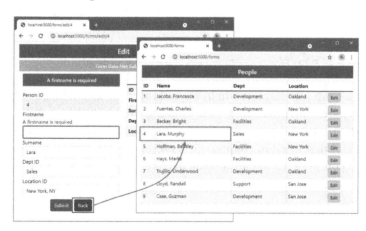

**Figure 36.8
Discarding data
objects**

CREATING NEW DEPENDENCY INJECTION SCOPES

You must create new dependency injection scopes if you want to preserve the model used by the rest of ASP.NET Core and have each component receive its own Entity Framework Core context object. This is done by using the `@inherits` expression to set the base class for the component to `OwningComponentBase` or `OwningComponentBase<T>`.

The `OwningComponentCase` class defines a `ScopedServices` property that is inherited by the component and that provides an `IServiceProvider` object that can be used to obtain services that are created in a scope that is specific to the component's lifecycle and will not be shared with any other component, as shown in listing 36.15.

Listing 36.15 Using a new scope in the Editor.razor file in the Blazor/Forms folder

```
@page "/forms/edit/{id:long}"
@layout EmptyLayout
@inherits OwningComponentBase
@using Microsoft.Extensions.DependencyInjection

<!-- ...elements omitted for brevity... -->

@code {

    [Inject]
    public NavigationManager? NavManager { get; set; }

    //[Inject]
    DataContext? Context => ScopedServices.GetService<DataContext>();

    [Parameter]
    public long Id { get; set; }

    // ...members omitted for brevity...

    public void HandleInvalidSubmit() => FormSubmitMessage
        = "Invalid Data Submitted";

    //public void Dispose() {
    //    if (Context != null) {
    //        Context.Entry(PersonData).State = EntityState.Detached;
    //    }
    //}
}
```

In the listing, I commented out the `Inject` attribute and set the value of the `Context` property by obtaining a `DataContext` service. The `Microsoft.Extensions.DependencyInjection` namespace contains extension methods that make it easier to obtain services from an `IServiceProvider` object, as described in chapter 14.

NOTE Changing the base class doesn't affect services that are received using the `Inject` attribute, which will still be obtained within the request scope. Each service that you require in the dedicated component's scope must be obtained through the `ScopedServices` property, and the `Inject` attribute should not be applied to that property.

The `OwningComponentBase<T>` class defines an additional convenience property that provides access to a scoped service of type `T` and that can be useful if a component requires only a single scoped service, as shown in listing 36.16 (although further services can still be obtained through the `ScopedServices` property).

Listing 36.16 Using the typed base in the Editor.razor file in the Blazor/Forms folder

```
@page "/forms/edit/{id:long}"
@layout EmptyLayout
@inherits OwningComponentBase<DataContext>

<link href="/blazorValidation.css" rel="stylesheet" />
<h4 class="bg-primary text-center text-white p-2">Edit</h4>
<h6 class="bg-info text-center text-white p-2">@FormSubmitMessage</h6>

<!-- ...elements omitted for brevity... -->

@code {

    [Inject]
    public NavigationManager? NavManager { get; set; }

    //[Inject]
    DataContext? Context => Service;

    [Parameter]
    public long Id { get; set; }

    // ...statements omitted for brevity...
}
```

The scoped service is available through a property named `Service`. In this example, I specified `DataContext` as the type argument for the base class.

Regardless of which base class is used, the result is that the `Editor` component has its own dependency injection scope and its own `DataContext` object. The `List` component has not been modified, so it will receive the request-scoped `DataContext` object, as shown in figure 36.9.

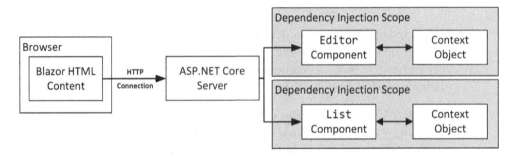

Figure 36.9 Using scoped services for components

Restart ASP.NET Core, navigate to http://localhost:5000/forms/edit/4, clear the Firstname field, and click the Back button. The changes made by the Editor component are not saved to the database, and since the `Editor` component's data context is separate from the one used by the `List` component, the edited data is discarded, producing the same response as shown in figure 36.8.

36.3.2 Understanding the repeated query issue

Blazor responds to changes in state as efficiently as possible but still has to render a component's content to determine the changes that should be sent to the browser.

One consequence of the way that Blazor works is that it can lead to a sharp increase in the number of queries sent to the database. To demonstrate the issue, listing 36.17 adds a button that increments a counter to the `List` component.

Listing 36.17 Adding a button in the List.razor file in the Blazor/Forms folder

```
@page "/forms"
@page "/forms/list"
@layout EmptyLayout

<h5 class="bg-primary text-white text-center p-2">People</h5>

<table class="table table-sm table-striped table-bordered">
    <thead>
        <tr>
            <th>ID</th><th>Name</th><th>Dept</th><th>Location</th><th></th>
        </tr>
    </thead>
    <tbody>
        @if (People.Count() == 0) {
            <tr>
                <th colspan="5" class="p-4 text-center">
                    Loading Data...
                </th>
            </tr>
        } else {
            @foreach (Person p in People) {
                <tr>
                    <td>@p.PersonId</td>
                    <td>@p.Surname, @p.Firstname</td>
                    <td>@p.Department?.Name</td>
                    <td>@p.Location?.City</td>
                    <td>
                        <NavLink class="btn btn-sm btn-warning"
                            href="@GetEditUrl(p.PersonId)">
                            Edit
                        </NavLink>
                    </td>
                </tr>
            }
        }
    </tbody>
</table>
```

```
<button class="btn btn-primary" @onclick="@(() => Counter++)">
    Increment
</button>
<span class="h5">Counter: @Counter</span>

@code {

    [Inject]
    public DataContext? Context { get; set; }

    public IEnumerable<Person> People { get; set; }
        = Enumerable.Empty<Person>();

    protected override void OnInitialized() {
        People = Context?.People?.Include(p => p.Department)
            .Include(p => p.Location)
                ?? Enumerable.Empty<Person>();
    }

    string GetEditUrl(long id) => $"/forms/edit/{id}";

    public int Counter { get; set; } = 0;
}
```

Restart ASP.NET Core and request http://localhost:5000/forms. Click the `Increment`
button and watch the output from the ASP.NET Core server. Each time you click the
button, the event handler is invoked, and a new database query is sent to the database,
producing logging messages like these:

```
...
info: Microsoft.EntityFrameworkCore.Database.Command[20101]
      Executed DbCommand (0ms) [Parameters=[], CommandType='Text',
      CommandTimeout='30']
      SELECT [p].[PersonId], [p].[DepartmentId], [p].[Firstname],
        [p].[LocationId], [p].[Surname], [d].[Departmentid],
        [d].[Name], [l].[LocationId], [l].[City], [l].[State]
      FROM [People] AS [p]
      INNER JOIN [Departments] AS [d] ON [p].[DepartmentId]
        = [d].[Departmentid]
      INNER JOIN [Locations] AS [l] ON [p].[LocationId] = [l].[LocationId]
info: Microsoft.EntityFrameworkCore.Database.Command[20101]
      Executed DbCommand (0ms) [Parameters=[], CommandType='Text',
       CommandTimeout='30']
      SELECT [p].[PersonId], [p].[DepartmentId], [p].[Firstname],
        [p].[LocationId], [p].[Surname], [d].[Departmentid], [d].[Name],
        [l].[LocationId], [l].[City], [l].[State]
      FROM [People] AS [p]
      INNER JOIN [Departments] AS [d] ON [p].[DepartmentId] = [d].
[Departmentid]
      INNER JOIN [Locations] AS [l] ON [p].[LocationId] = [l].[LocationId]
...
```

Each time the component is rendered, Entity Framework Core sends two identical
requests to the database, even when the Increment button is clicked where no data
operations are performed.

This issue can arise whenever Entity Framework Core is used and is exacerbated by Blazor. Although it is common practice to assign database queries to `IEnumerable<T>` properties, doing so masks an important aspect of Entity Framework Core, which is that its LINQ expressions are expressions of queries and not results, and each time the property is read, a new query is sent to the database. The value of the `People` property is read twice by the `List` component: once by the `Count` property to determine whether the data has loaded and once by the `@foreach` expression to generate the rows for the HTML table. When the user clicks the Increment button, Blazor renders the `List` component again to figure out what has changed, which causes the `People` property to be read twice more, producing two additional database queries.

Blazor and Entity Framework Core are both working the way they should. Blazor must rerender the component's output to figure out what HTML changes need to be sent to the browser. It has no way of knowing what effect clicking the button has until after it has rendered the elements and evaluated all the Razor expressions. Entity Framework Core is executing its query each time the property is read, ensuring that the application always has fresh data.

This combination of features presents two issues. The first is that needless queries are sent to the database, which can increase the capacity required by an application (although not always because database servers are adept at handling queries).

The second issue is that changes to the database will be reflected in the content presented to the user after they make an unrelated interaction. If another user adds a `Person` object to the database, for example, it will appear in the table the next time the user clicks the Increment button. Users expect applications to reflect only their actions, and unexpected changes are confusing and distracting.

MANAGING QUERIES IN A COMPONENT

The interaction between Blazor and Entity Framework Core won't be a problem for all projects, but if it is, then the best approach is to query the database once and requery only for operations where the user might expect an update to occur. Some applications may need to present the user with an explicit option to reload the data, especially for applications where updates are likely to occur that the user will want to see, as shown in listing 36.18.

> **Listing 36.18 Controlling queries in the List.razor file in the Blazor/Forms folder**

```
@page "/forms"
@page "/forms/list"
@layout EmptyLayout

<h5 class="bg-primary text-white text-center p-2">People</h5>

<table class="table table-sm table-striped table-bordered">
    <thead>
        <tr>
            <th>ID</th>
            <th>Name</th>
            <th>Dept</th>
```

```
                <th>Location</th>
                <th></th>
            </tr>
        </thead>
        <tbody>
            @if (People.Count() == 0) {
                <tr>
                    <th colspan="5" class="p-4 text-center">
                        Loading Data...
                    </th>
                </tr>
            } else {
                @foreach (Person p in People) {
                    <tr>
                        <td>@p.PersonId</td>
                        <td>@p.Surname, @p.Firstname</td>
                        <td>@p.Department?.Name</td>
                        <td>@p.Location?.City</td>
                        <td>
                            <NavLink class="btn btn-sm btn-warning"
                             href="@GetEditUrl(p.PersonId)">
                                Edit
                            </NavLink>
                        </td>
                    </tr>
                }
            }
        </tbody>
</table>

<button class="btn btn-danger" @onclick="UpdateData">Update</button>

<button class="btn btn-primary" @onclick="@(() => Counter++)">
    Increment
</button>
<span class="h5">Counter: @Counter</span>

@code {

    [Inject]
    public DataContext? Context { get; set; }

    public IEnumerable<Person> People { get; set; }
        = Enumerable.Empty<Person>();

    protected async override Task OnInitializedAsync() {
        await UpdateData();
    }

    private async Task UpdateData() {
        if (Context != null) {
            People = await Context.People.Include(p => p.Department)
                .Include(p => p.Location).ToListAsync<Person>();
        } else {
            People = Enumerable.Empty<Person>();
        }
```

```
    }

    string GetEditUrl(long id) => $"/forms/edit/{id}";

    public int Counter { get; set; } = 0;
}
```

The `UpdateData` method performs the same query but applies the `ToListAsync` method, which forces evaluation of the Entity Framework Core query. The results are assigned to the `People` property and can be read repeatedly without triggering additional queries. To give the user control over the data, I added a button that invokes the `UpdateData` method when it is clicked. Restart ASP.NET Core, request http://localhost:5000/forms, and click the Increment button. Monitor the output from the ASP.NET Core server, and you will see that there is a query made only when the component is initialized. To explicitly trigger a query, click the Update button.

Some operations may require a new query, which is easy to perform. To demonstrate, listing 36.19 adds a sort operation to the `List` component, which is implemented both with and without a new query.

Listing 36.19   Adding operations to the List.razor file in the Blazor/Forms folder

```
@page "/forms"
@page "/forms/list"
@layout EmptyLayout

<h5 class="bg-primary text-white text-center p-2">People</h5>

<table class="table table-sm table-striped table-bordered">
    <thead>
        <tr>
            <th>ID</th>
            <th>Name</th>
            <th>Dept</th>
            <th>Location</th>
            <th></th>
        </tr>
    </thead>
    <tbody>
        @if (People.Count() == 0) {
            <tr>
                <th colspan="5" class="p-4 text-center">
                    Loading Data...
                </th>
            </tr>
        } else {
            @foreach (Person p in People) {
                <tr>
                    <td>@p.PersonId</td>
                    <td>@p.Surname, @p.Firstname</td>
                    <td>@p.Department?.Name</td>
                    <td>@p.Location?.City</td>
                    <td>
                        <NavLink class="btn btn-sm btn-warning"
```

```
                    href="@GetEditUrl(p.PersonId)">
                        Edit
                    </NavLink>
                </td>
            </tr>
        }
    }
    </tbody>
</table>

<button class="btn btn-danger my-2" @onclick="@(() => UpdateData())">
    Update
</button>
<button class="btn btn-info my-2" @onclick="SortWithQuery">
    Sort (With Query)
</button>
<button class="btn btn-info my-2" @onclick="SortWithoutQuery">
    Sort (No Query)
</button>

<button class="btn btn-primary" @onclick="@(() => Counter++)">
    Increment
</button>
<span class="h5">Counter: @Counter</span>

@code {

    [Inject]
    public DataContext? Context { get; set; }

    public IEnumerable<Person> People { get; set; }
        = Enumerable.Empty<Person>();

    protected async override Task OnInitializedAsync() {
        await UpdateData();
    }

    private IQueryable<Person> Query =>
        Context!.People.Include(p => p.Department)
            .Include(p => p.Location);


    private async Task UpdateData(IQueryable<Person>? query = null) =>
        People = await (query ?? Query).ToListAsync<Person>();

    public async Task SortWithQuery() {
        await UpdateData(Query.OrderBy(p => p.Surname));
    }

    public void SortWithoutQuery() {
        People = People.OrderBy(p => p.Firstname).ToList<Person>();
    }

    string GetEditUrl(long id) => $"/forms/edit/{id}";

    public int Counter { get; set; } = 0;
}
```

Entity Framework Core queries are expressed as `IQueryable<T>` objects, allowing the query to be composed with additional LINQ methods before it is dispatched to the database server. The new operations in the example both use the LINQ `OrderBy` method, but one applies this to the `IQueryable<T>`, which is then evaluated to send the query with the `ToListAsync` method. The other operation applies the `OrderBy` method to the existing result data, sorting it without sending a new query. To see both operations, restart ASP.NET Core, request http://localhost:5000/forms, and click the Sort buttons, as shown in figure 36.10. When the Sort (With Query) button is clicked, you will see a log message indicating that a query has been sent to the database.

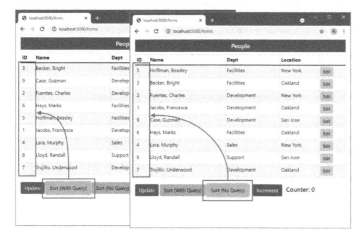

**Figure 36.10
Managing
component queries**

Avoiding the overlapping query pitfall

You may encounter an exception telling you that "a second operation started on this context before a previous operation completed." This happens when a child component uses the `OnParametersSetAsync` method to perform an asynchronous Entity Framework Core query and a change in the parent's data triggers a second call to `OnParametersSetAsync` before the query is complete. The second method call starts a duplicate query that causes the exception. This problem can be resolved by performing the Entity Framework Core query synchronously. You can see an example in listing 36.23, where I perform queries synchronously because the parent component will trigger an update when it receives its data.

36.4 Performing CRUD operations

To show how the features described in previous sections fit together, I am going to create a simple application that allows the user to perform create, read, update, and delete (CRUD) operations on `Person` objects.

36.4.1 *Creating the list component*

The List component contains the basic functionality I require. Listing 36.20 removes some of the features from earlier sections that are no longer required and adds buttons that allow the user to navigate to other functions.

Listing 36.20   Preparing the component in the List.razor file in the Blazor/Forms folder

```
@page "/forms"
@page "/forms/list"
@layout EmptyLayout
@inherits OwningComponentBase<DataContext>

<h5 class="bg-primary text-white text-center p-2">People</h5>

<table class="table table-sm table-striped table-bordered">
    <thead>
        <tr>
            <th>ID</th><th>Name</th><th>Dept</th><th>Location</th><th></th>
        </tr>
    </thead>
    <tbody>
        @if (People.Count() == 0) {
            <tr>
                <th colspan="5" class="p-4 text-center">
                    Loading Data...
                </th>
            </tr>
        } else {
            @foreach (Person p in People) {
                <tr>
                    <td>@p.PersonId</td>
                    <td>@p.Surname, @p.Firstname</td>
                    <td>@p.Department?.Name</td>
                    <td>@p.Location?.City</td>
                    <td class="text-center">
                        <NavLink class="btn btn-sm btn-info"
                                href="@GetDetailsUrl(p.PersonId)">
                            Details
                        </NavLink>
                        <NavLink class="btn btn-sm btn-warning"
                                href="@GetEditUrl(p.PersonId)">
                            Edit
                        </NavLink>
                        <button class="btn btn-sm btn-danger"
                                @onclick="@(() => HandleDelete(p))">
                            Delete
                        </button>
                    </td>
                </tr>
            }
        }
    </tbody>
</table>
```

```
<NavLink class="btn btn-primary" href="/forms/create">Create</NavLink>

@code {

    //[Inject]
    public DataContext? Context => Service;

    public IEnumerable<Person> People { get; set; }
        = Enumerable.Empty<Person>();

    protected async override Task OnInitializedAsync() {
        await UpdateData();
    }

    private IQueryable<Person> Query =>
        Context!.People.Include(p => p.Department)
            .Include(p => p.Location);


    private async Task UpdateData(IQueryable<Person>? query = null) =>
        People = await (query ?? Query).ToListAsync<Person>();

    public async Task SortWithQuery() {
        await UpdateData(Query.OrderBy(p => p.Surname));
    }

    public void SortWithoutQuery() {
        People = People.OrderBy(p => p.Firstname).ToList<Person>();
    }

    string GetEditUrl(long id) => $"/forms/edit/{id}";

    string GetDetailsUrl(long id) => $"/forms/details/{id}";

    public async Task HandleDelete(Person p) {
        if (Context != null) {
            Context.Remove(p);
            await Context.SaveChangesAsync();
            await UpdateData();
        }
    }
}
```

The operations for creating, viewing, and editing objects navigate to other URLs, but the delete operations are performed by the List component, taking care to reload the data after the changes have been saved to reflect the change to the user.

36.4.2 *Creating the details component*

The details component displays a read-only view of the data, which doesn't require the Blazor form features or present any issues with Entity Framework Core. Add a Blazor Component named Details.razor to the Blazor/Forms folder with the content shown in listing 36.21.

Listing 36.21   The contents of the Details.razor file in the Blazor/Forms folder

```
@page "/forms/details/{id:long}"
@layout EmptyLayout
@inherits OwningComponentBase<DataContext>

<h4 class="bg-info text-center text-white p-2">Details</h4>

<div class="form-group">
    <label>ID</label>
    <input class="form-control" value="@PersonData.PersonId" disabled />
</div>
<div class="form-group">
    <label>Firstname</label>
    <input class="form-control" value="@PersonData.Firstname" disabled />
</div>
<div class="form-group">
    <label>Surname</label>
    <input class="form-control" value="@PersonData.Surname" disabled />
</div>
<div class="form-group">
    <label>Department</label>
    <input class="form-control" value="@PersonData.Department?.Name"
        disabled />
</div>
<div class="form-group">
    <label>Location</label>
    <input class="form-control"
        value="@($"{PersonData.Location?.City}, "
            + PersonData.Location?.State)"
        disabled />
</div>
<div class="text-center p-2">
    <NavLink class="btn btn-info" href="@EditUrl">Edit</NavLink>
    <NavLink class="btn btn-secondary" href="/forms">Back</NavLink>
</div>

@code {

    [Inject]
    public NavigationManager? NavManager { get; set; }

    DataContext Context => Service;

    [Parameter]
    public long Id { get; set; }

    public Person PersonData { get; set; } = new();

    protected async override Task OnParametersSetAsync() {
        if (Context != null) {
            PersonData = await Context.People
                .Include(p => p.Department)
                .Include(p => p.Location)
                .FirstOrDefaultAsync(p => p.PersonId == Id)
```

```
                          ?? new();
            }
      }

      public string EditUrl => $"/forms/edit/{Id}";
}
```

All the `input` elements displayed by this component are disabled, which means there is no need to handle events or process user input.

36.4.3 *Creating the editor component*

The remaining features will be handled by the `Editor` component. Listing 36.22 removes the features from earlier examples that are no longer required and adds support for creating and editing objects, including persisting the data.

> **Listing 36.22 Adding features in the Editor.razor file in the Blazor/Forms folder**

```
@page "/forms/edit/{id:long}"
@page "/forms/create"
@layout EmptyLayout
@inherits OwningComponentBase<DataContext>

<link href="/blazorValidation.css" rel="stylesheet" />

<h4 class="bg-@Theme text-center text-white p-2">@Mode</h4>

<EditForm Model="PersonData" OnValidSubmit="HandleValidSubmit" >
    <DataAnnotationsValidator />
    @if (Mode == "Edit") {
        <div class="form-group">
            <label>ID</label>
            <InputNumber class="form-control"
                @bind-Value="PersonData.PersonId" readonly />
        </div>
    }
    <div class="form-group">
        <label>Firstname</label>
        <ValidationMessage For="@(() => PersonData.Firstname)" />
        <InputText class="form-control"
            @bind-Value="PersonData.Firstname" />
    </div>
    <div class="form-group">
        <label>Surname</label>
        <ValidationMessage For="@(() => PersonData.Surname)" />
        <InputText class="form-control"
            @bind-Value="PersonData.Surname" />
    </div>
    <div class="form-group">
        <label>Deptartment</label>
        <ValidationMessage For="@(() => PersonData.DepartmentId)" />
        <CustomSelect TValue="long" Values="Departments"
                      Parser="@((string str) => long.Parse(str))"
                      @bind-Value="PersonData.DepartmentId">
            <option selected disabled value="0">
```

```
                    Choose a Department
                </option>
            </CustomSelect>
    </div>
    <div class="form-group">
        <label>Location</label>
        <ValidationMessage For="@(() => PersonData.LocationId)" />
        <CustomSelect TValue="long" Values="Locations"
                      Parser="@((string str) => long.Parse(str))"
                      @bind-Value="PersonData.LocationId">
            <option selected disabled value="0">Choose a Location</option>
        </CustomSelect>
    </div>
    <div class="text-center">
        <button type="submit" class="btn btn-@Theme mt-2">Save</button>
        <NavLink class="btn btn-secondary mt-2" href="/forms">
            Back
        </NavLink>
    </div>
</EditForm>

@code {

    [Inject]
    public NavigationManager? NavManager { get; set; }

    //[Inject]
    DataContext? Context => Service;

    [Parameter]
    public long Id { get; set; }

    public Person PersonData { get; set; } = new();

    public IDictionary<string, long> Departments { get; set; }
        = new Dictionary<string, long>();

    public IDictionary<string, long> Locations { get; set; }
        = new Dictionary<string, long>();

    protected async override Task OnParametersSetAsync() {
        if (Context != null) {
            if (Mode == "Edit") {
                PersonData = await Context.People.FindAsync(Id)
                    ?? new Person();
            }
            Departments = await Context.Departments
                .ToDictionaryAsync(d => d.Name, d => d.Departmentid);
            Locations = await Context.Locations
                .ToDictionaryAsync(l => $"{l.City}, {l.State}",
                    l => l.LocationId);
        }
    }

    public string Theme => Id == 0 ? "primary" : "warning";
    public string Mode => Id == 0 ? "Create" : "Edit";
```

```
public async Task HandleValidSubmit()  {
    if (Context != null) {
        if (Mode == "Create") {
            Context.Add(PersonData);
        }
        await Context.SaveChangesAsync();
        NavManager?.NavigateTo("/forms");
    }
}
}
```

I added support for a new URL and used Bootstrap CSS themes to differentiate between creating a new object and editing an existing one. I removed the validation summary so that only property-level validation messages are displayed and added support for storing the data through Entity Framework Core. Unlike form applications created using controllers or Razor Pages, I don't have to deal with model binding because Blazor lets me work directly with the object that Entity Framework Core produces from the initial database query. Restart ASP.NET Core and request http://localhost:5000/forms. You will see the list of `Person` objects shown in figure 36.11, and clicking the Create, Details, Edit, and Delete buttons will allow you to work with the data in the database.

> **TIP** Open a command prompt and run `dotnet ef database drop --force` in the `Advanced` project folder if you need to reset the database to undo the changes you have made. The database will be seeded again when you restart ASP .NET Core, and you will see the data shown in the figure.

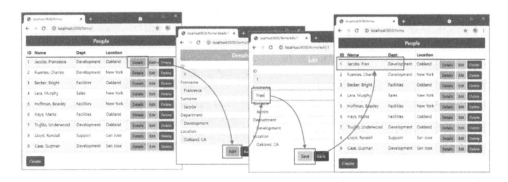

Figure 36.11 Using Blazor to work with data

36.5 *Extending the Blazor form features*

The Blazor form features are effective but have the rough edges that are always found in new technology. I expect future releases to round out the feature set, but, in the meantime, Blazor makes it easy to enhance the way that forms work. The `EditForm` component defines a cascading `EditContext` object that provides access to form validation and makes it easy to create custom form components through the events, properties, and methods described in table 36.8.

Table 36.8   The EditContext features

Name	Description
OnFieldChanged	This event is triggered when any of the form fields are modified.
OnValidationRequested	This event is triggered when validation is required and can be used to create custom validation processes.
OnValidationStateChanged	This event is triggered when the validation state of the overall form changes.
Model	This property returns the value passed to the EditForm component's Model property.
Field(name)	This method is used to get a FieldIdentifier object that describes a single field.
IsModified()	This method returns true if any of the form fields have been modified.
IsModified(field)	This method returns true if the field specified by the FieldIdentifier argument has been modified.
GetValidationMessages()	This method returns a sequence containing the validation error messages for the entire form.
GetValidationMessages (field)	This method returns a sequence containing the validation error messages for a single field, using a FieldIdentifier object obtained from the Field method.
MarkAsUnmodified()	This method marks the form as unmodified.
MarkAsUnmodified(field)	This method marks a specific field as unmodified, using a FieldIdentifer object obtained from the Field method.
NotifyValidationStateChanged()	This method is used to indicate a change in validation status.
NotifyFieldChanged(field)	This method is used to indicate when a field has changed, using a FieldIdentifer object obtained from the Field method.
Validate()	This method performs validation on the form, returning true if all the form fields pass validation and false otherwise.

36.5.1   *Creating a custom validation constraint*

You can create components that apply custom validation constraints if the built-in validation attributes are not sufficient. This type of component doesn't render its own content, and it is more easily defined as a class. Add a class file named DeptState-Validator.cs to the Blazor/Forms folder and use it to define the component class shown in listing 36.23.

Listing 36.23   The contents of the DeptStateValidator.cs file in the Blazor/Forms folder

```
using Advanced.Models;
using Microsoft.AspNetCore.Components;
using Microsoft.AspNetCore.Components.Forms;
```

```
namespace Advanced.Blazor.Forms {

    public class DeptStateValidator : OwningComponentBase<DataContext> {

        public DataContext Context => Service;

        [Parameter]
        public long DepartmentId { get; set; }

        [Parameter]
        public string? State { get; set; }

        [CascadingParameter]
        public EditContext? CurrentEditContext { get; set; }

        private string? DeptName { get; set; }
        private IDictionary<long, string>? LocationStates { get; set; }

        protected override void OnInitialized() {
            if (CurrentEditContext != null) {
                ValidationMessageStore store =
                    new ValidationMessageStore(CurrentEditContext);
                CurrentEditContext.OnFieldChanged += (sender, args) => {
                    string name = args.FieldIdentifier.FieldName;
                    if (name == "DepartmentId" || name == "LocationId") {
                        Validate(CurrentEditContext.Model as Person,
                            store);
                    }
                };
            }
        }

        protected override void OnParametersSet() {
            DeptName = Context.Departments.Find(DepartmentId)?.Name;
            LocationStates = Context.Locations
                .ToDictionary(l => l.LocationId, l => l.State);
        }

        private void Validate(Person? model,
                ValidationMessageStore store) {
            if (model?.DepartmentId == DepartmentId
                    && LocationStates != null
                    && CurrentEditContext != null
                    && (!LocationStates.ContainsKey(model.LocationId)
                        || LocationStates[model.LocationId] != State)) {
                store.Add(CurrentEditContext.Field("LocationId"),
                    $"{DeptName} staff must be in: {State}");
            } else {
                store.Clear();
            }
            CurrentEditContext?.NotifyValidationStateChanged();
        }
    }
}
```

This component enforces a restriction on the state in which departments can be defined so that, for example, locations in California are the valid options only when the `Development` department has been chosen, and any other locations will produce a validation error.

The component has its own scoped `DataContext` object, which it receives by using `OwningComponentBase<T>` as its base class. The parent component provides values for the `DepartmentId` and `State` properties, which are used to enforce the validation rule. The cascading `EditContext` property is received from the `EditForm` component and provides access to the features described in table 36.8.

When the component is initialized, a new `ValidationMessageStore` is created. This object is used to register validation error messages and accepts the `EditContext` object as its constructor argument, like this:

```
...
ValidationMessageStore store =
    new ValidationMessageStore(CurrentEditContext);
...
```

Blazor takes care of processing the messages added to the store, and the custom validation component only needs to decide which messages are required, which is handled by the `Validate` method. This method checks the `DepartmentId` and `LocationId` properties to make sure that the combination is allowed. If there is an issue, then a new validation message is added to the store, like this:

```
...
store.Add(CurrentEditContext.Field("LocationId"),
    $"{DeptName} staff must be in: {State}");
...
```

The arguments to the `Add` method are a `FieldIdentifier` that identifies the field the error relates to and the validation message. If there are no validation errors, then the message store's `Clear` method is called, which will ensure that any stale messages that have been previously generated by the component are no longer displayed.

The `Validation` method is called by the handler for the `OnFieldChanged` event, which allows the component to respond whenever the user makes a change.

```
...
CurrentEditContext.OnFieldChanged += (sender, args) => {
    string name = args.FieldIdentifier.FieldName;
    if (name == "DepartmentId" || name == "LocationId") {
        Validate(CurrentEditContext.Model as Person, store);
    }
};
...
```

The handler receives a `FieldChangeEventArgs` object, which defines a `FieldIdentifer` property that indicates which field has been modified. Listing 36.24 applies the new validation to the `Editor` component.

> **Listing 36.24 Applying validation in the Editor.razor file in the Blazor/Forms folder**

```
@page "/forms/edit/{id:long}"
@page "/forms/create"
@layout EmptyLayout
```

```
@inherits OwningComponentBase<DataContext>

<link href="/blazorValidation.css" rel="stylesheet" />

<h4 class="bg-@Theme text-center text-white p-2">@Mode</h4>

<EditForm Model="PersonData" OnValidSubmit="HandleValidSubmit" >
    <DataAnnotationsValidator />
    <DeptStateValidator DepartmentId="2" State="CA" />
    @if (Mode == "Edit") {
        <div class="form-group">
            <label>ID</label>
            <InputNumber class="form-control"
                @bind-Value="PersonData.PersonId" readonly />
        </div>
    }

    <!-- ...elements omitted for brevity... -->

</EditForm>

@code {

    // ...statements omitted for brevity...
}
```

The `DepartmentId` and `State` attributes specify the restriction that only locations in California can be selected for the Development department. Restart ASP.NET Core and request http://localhost:5000/forms/edit/4. Choose Development for the Department field, and you will see a validation error because the location for this `Person` is New York. This error will remain visible until you select a location in California or change the department, as shown in figure 36.12.

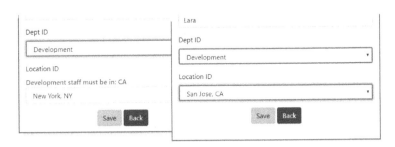

Figure 36.12   Creating a custom validation component

36.5.2 *Creating a valid-only submit button component*

To finish this chapter, I am going to create a component that will render a submit button for the form that is enabled only when the data is valid. Add a Razor Component named `ValidButton.razor` to the `Blazor/Forms` folder with the contents shown in listing 36.25.

Listing 36.25   The contents of the ValidButton.razor file in the Blazor/Forms folder

```
<button class="@ButtonClass" @attributes="Attributes"
        disabled="@Disabled">
    @ChildContent
</button>

@code {

    [Parameter]
    public RenderFragment? ChildContent { get; set; }

    [Parameter]
    public string BtnTheme { get; set; } = "primary";

    [Parameter]
    public string DisabledClass { get; set; }
        = "btn-outline-dark disabled";

    [Parameter(CaptureUnmatchedValues = true)]
    public IDictionary<string, object>? Attributes { get; set; }

    [CascadingParameter]
    public EditContext? CurrentEditContext { get; set; }

    public bool Disabled { get; set; }

    public string ButtonClass =>
        Disabled ? $"btn btn-{BtnTheme} {DisabledClass} mt-2"
                 : $"btn btn-{BtnTheme} mt-2";

    protected override void OnInitialized() {
        SetButtonState();
        if (CurrentEditContext != null) {
            CurrentEditContext.OnValidationStateChanged +=
                (sender, args) => SetButtonState();
            CurrentEditContext.Validate();
        }
    }

    public void SetButtonState() {
        if (CurrentEditContext != null) {
            Disabled = CurrentEditContext.GetValidationMessages().Any();
        }
    }
}
```

This component responds to the `OnValidationStateChanged` method, which is triggered when the validation state of the form changes. There is no `EditContext` property that details the validation state, so the best way to see if there are any validation issues is to see whether there are any validation messages. If there are, there are validation issues. If there are no validation messages, the form is valid. To ensure the button state is displayed correctly, the `Validation` method is called so that a validation check is performed as soon as the component is initialized.

Listing 36.26 uses the new component to replace the conventional button in the `Editor` component.

Listing 36.26 Applying a component in the Editor.razor file in the Blazor/Forms folder

```
...
<div class="text-center">
    <ValidButton type="submit" BtnTheme="@Theme">Save</ValidButton>
    <NavLink class="btn btn-secondary mt-2" href="/forms">Back</NavLink>
</div>
...
```

Restart ASP.NET Core and request http://localhost:5000/forms/create; you will see the validation messages displayed for each form element, with the Save button disabled. The button will be enabled once each validation issue has been resolved, as shown in figure 36.13.

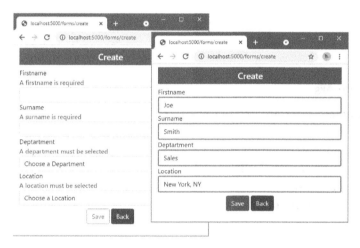

Figure 36.13 Creating a custom form button

Summary

- Blazor provides built-in components for common HTML form elements, including `form`, `input`, and `textarea` elements.
- Form events are presented through the `EditForm` component.
- Entity Framework Core context scopes must be carefully managed to avoid stale data. Scopes can be managed through the `IDisposable` interface, or through automatic dependency injection.
- Take care with data read from Entity Framework Core to avoid repeated queries.

Using Blazor WebAssembly

This chapter covers

- Using WebAssembly to create self-contained client-side applications
- Creating WebAssembly components
- Navigating between components in a WebAssembly application
- Creating a forms application using WebAssembly components

In this chapter, I demonstrate the use of Blazor WebAssembly, which is an implementation of Blazor written for WebAssembly.

WebAssembly is a virtual machine running inside the browser. High-level languages are compiled into low-level language-neutral assembler format that can be executed at close to native performance. WebAssembly provides access to the APIs available to JavaScript applications, which means that WebAssembly applications can access the domain object model, use cascading style sheets, and initiate asynchronous HTTP requests.

Blazor WebAssembly breaks the dependency on the server and executes the Blazor application entirely in the browser. The result is a true client-side application, with access to all the same features of Blazor Server but without the need for a persistent HTTP connection.

It is early days for both WebAssembly and Blazor WebAssembly, and there are some serious restrictions. WebAssembly is a new technology and is supported only by the latest browser versions. You will not be able to use WebAssembly if your project needs to support legacy browsers—or even older versions of modern browsers. Blazor WebAssembly applications are restricted to the set of APIs the browser provides, which means that not all .NET features can be used in a WebAssembly application. This doesn't disadvantage Blazor when compared to client-side frameworks like Angular, but it does mean that features such as Entity Framework Core are not available because browsers restrict WebAssembly applications to making HTTP requests.

Still, despite the limitations of Blazor WebAssembly, it is an exciting technology, and it offers the promise of being able to write true client-side applications using C# and ASP.NET Core, without the need for a JavaScript framework. Table 37.1 puts Blazor WebAssembly in context.

Table 37.1 Putting Blazor WebAssembly in context

Question	Answer
What is it?	Blazor WebAssembly is an implementation of Blazor that runs in the browser using WebAssembly.
Why is it useful?	Blazor WebAssembly allows client-side applications to be written in C# without server-side execution or the persistent HTTP connection required by Blazor Server.
How is it used?	Blazor components are added to a project that is dedicated to Blazor WebAssembly.
Are there any pitfalls or limitations?	Not all browsers support WebAssembly. A larger download is required to provide the browser with the code it requires, and not all ASP.NET Core features are available in Blazor WebAssembly components.
Are there any alternatives?	Blazor WebAssembly is the only combination of true client-side applications written using ASP.NET Core. Blazor Server can be used if server-side support is acceptable; otherwise, a JavaScript framework, such as Angular, React, or Vue.js, should be used.

37.1 Preparing for this chapter

This chapter uses the Advanced project from chapter 36. To prepare for this chapter, add a class file named `DataController.cs` to the `Controllers` folder and use it to define the web service controller shown in listing 37.1.

> **TIP** You can download the example project for this chapter—and for all the other chapters in this book—from https://github.com/manningbooks/pro-asp .net-core-7. See chapter 1 for how to get help if you have problems running the examples.

Listing 37.1 The contents of the DataController.cs file in the Controllers folder

```
using Advanced.Models;
using Microsoft.AspNetCore.Mvc;
using Microsoft.EntityFrameworkCore;
```

```csharp
namespace Advanced.Controllers {

    [ApiController]
    [Route("/api/people")]
    public class DataController : ControllerBase {
        private DataContext context;

        public DataController(DataContext ctx) {
            context = ctx;
        }

        [HttpGet]
        public IEnumerable<Person> GetAll() {
            IEnumerable<Person> people
                = context.People
                    .Include(p => p.Department)
                    .Include(p => p.Location);
            foreach (Person p in people) {
                if (p.Department?.People != null) {
                    p.Department.People = null;
                }
                if (p.Location?.People != null) {
                    p.Location.People = null;
                }
            }
            return people;
        }


        [HttpGet("{id}")]
        public async Task<Person> GetDetails(long id) {
            Person p = await context.People
                .Include(p => p.Department)
                .Include(p => p.Location)
                .FirstAsync(p => p.PersonId == id);
            if (p.Department?.People != null) {
                p.Department.People = null;
            }
            if (p.Location?.People != null) {
                p.Location.People = null;
            }
            return p;
        }

        [HttpPost]
        public async Task Save([FromBody] Person p) {
            await context.People.AddAsync(p);
            await context.SaveChangesAsync();
        }

        [HttpPut]
        public async Task Update([FromBody] Person p) {
            context.Update(p);
            await context.SaveChangesAsync();
        }

        [HttpDelete("{id}")]
```

```
    public async Task Delete(long id) {
        context.People.Remove(new Person() { PersonId = id });
        await context.SaveChangesAsync();
    }

    [HttpGet("/api/locations")]
    public IAsyncEnumerable<Location> GetLocations() =>
        context.Locations.AsAsyncEnumerable();

    [HttpGet("/api/departments")]
    public IAsyncEnumerable<Department> GetDepts() =>
        context.Departments.AsAsyncEnumerable();
    }
}
```

This controller provides actions that allow `Person` objects to be created, read, updated, and deleted. I have also added actions that return the `Location` and `Department` objects. I usually create separate controllers for each type of data, but these actions are required only in support of the `Person` features, so I have combined all the operations into a single controller.

37.1.1 *Dropping the database and running the application*

Open a new PowerShell command prompt, navigate to the folder that contains the `Advanced.csproj` file, and run the command shown in listing 37.2 to drop the database.

Listing 37.2 Dropping the database

```
dotnet ef database drop --force
```

Use the PowerShell command prompt to run the command shown in listing 37.3.

Listing 37.3 Running the example application

```
dotnet run
```

Use a browser to request http://localhost:5000/api/people, which will produce a JSON representation of the `Person` objects from the database, as shown in figure 37.1.

Figure 37.1 Running the example application

37.2   Setting Up Blazor WebAssembly

Blazor WebAssembly requires a separate project so that Razor Components can be compiled ready to be executed by the browser. The compiled components can be delivered to the browser by a standard ASP.NET Core server, which can also provide data through web services. To make it easy for the Blazor WebAssembly components to consume the data provided by the ASP.NET Core server, a third project is required that contains those items that are shared between them.

The process for creating the three projects is involved, partly because I am going to move some of the existing classes from the Advanced project into the data model project. Although it is possible to perform some of the steps using the Visual Studio wizards, I have set out the steps using the command-line tools to minimize errors.

> **NOTE**   If you have problems following the steps, you can download all three projects from the GitHub repository for this book, at https://github.com/ manningbooks/pro-asp.net-core-7.

37.2.1   Creating the shared project

Make sure Visual Studio or Visual Studio Code is closed before you start. Open a new PowerShell command prompt and navigate to the `Advanced` project folder, which is the one that contains the `Advanced.csproj` file, and run the commands shown in listing 37.4.

Listing 37.4   Preparing the project for Blazor

```
dotnet new classlib -o ../DataModel -f net7.0
Move-Item -Path @("Models/Person.cs", "Models/Location.cs",
    "Models/Department.cs") ../DataModel
```

These commands create a new project named `DataModel` and move the data model classes to the new project.

37.2.2   Creating the Blazor WebAssembly project

I usually prefer to start with an empty project and add the packages and configuration files that the application requires. Use the PowerShell command prompt to run the commands shown in listing 37.5 from within the `Advanced` project folder (the folder that contains the `Advanced.csproj` file).

Listing 37.5   Creating the Blazor WebAssembly project

```
dotnet new blazorwasm -o ../BlazorWebAssembly -f net7.0
dotnet add ../BlazorWebAssembly reference ../DataModel
```

These commands create a Blazor WebAssembly project named `BlazorWebAssembly` and add a reference to the `DataModel` project, which makes the `Person`, `Department`, and `Location` classes available.

37.2.3 *Preparing the ASP.NET Core project*

Use the PowerShell command prompt to run the commands shown in listing 37.6 in the `Advanced` project folder.

```
dotnet add reference ../DataModel ../BlazorWebAssembly
dotnet add package Microsoft.AspNetCore.Components.WebAssembly.Server
    --version 7.0.0
```

These commands create references to the other projects so that the data model classes and the components in the Blazor WebAssembly project can be used.

37.2.4 *Adding the solution references*

Run the command shown in listing 37.7 in the `Advanced` folder to add references to the new project to the solution file.

```
dotnet sln add ../DataModel ../BlazorWebAssembly
```

37.2.5 *Opening the projects*

Once you have set up all three projects, start Visual Studio or Visual Studio Code. If you are using Visual Studio, open the `Advanced.sln` file in the `Advanced` folder. All three projects are open for editing, as shown in figure 37.2. If you are using Visual Studio Code, open the folder that contains all three projects, as shown in figure 37.2.

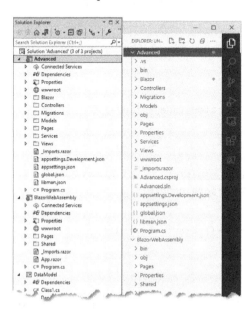

Figure 37.2
Opening the three projects

37.2.6 Completing the Blazor WebAssembly configuration

The next step is to configure the ASP.NET Core project so that it can deliver the contents of the Blazor WebAssembly project to clients. Add the statements shown in listing 37.8 to the `Program.cs` file in the `Advanced` folder.

> **CAUTION**   It is important to pay close attention to which files you are editing. Files with the same name exist in multiple projects, and if you don't follow the examples closely, you won't end up with a working application. Future versions of Blazor may be easier to work with, but for the moment, the details are important.

Listing 37.8   Configuring the application in the Program.cs file in the Advanced project

```
using Microsoft.EntityFrameworkCore;
using Advanced.Models;

var builder = WebApplication.CreateBuilder(args);

builder.Services.AddControllersWithViews();
builder.Services.AddRazorPages();
builder.Services.AddServerSideBlazor();

builder.Services.AddDbContext<DataContext>(opts => {
    opts.UseSqlServer(
        builder.Configuration["ConnectionStrings:PeopleConnection"]);
    opts.EnableSensitiveDataLogging(true);
});

builder.Services.AddSingleton<Advanced.Services.ToggleService>();

var app = builder.Build();

app.UseStaticFiles();

app.MapControllers();
app.MapControllerRoute("controllers",
    "controllers/{controller=Home}/{action=Index}/{id?}");
app.MapRazorPages();
app.MapBlazorHub();
app.MapFallbackToPage("/_Host");

app.UseBlazorFrameworkFiles("/webassembly");
app.MapFallbackToFile("/webassembly/{*path:nonfile}",
    "/webassembly/index.html");

var context = app.Services.CreateScope().ServiceProvider
    .GetRequiredService<DataContext>();
SeedData.SeedDatabase(context);

app.Run();
```

These statements configure the ASP.NET Core request pipeline so that requests for `/webassembly` are handled by Blazor WebAssembly using the contents of the `Blazor-WebAssembly` project.

SETTING THE BASE URL

The next step is to modify the HTML file that will be used to respond to requests for the `/webassembly` URL. Apply the change shown in listing 37.9 to the `index.html` file in the `wwwroot` folder of the `BlazorWebAssembly` folder.

CAUTION Make sure there are forward-slash (/) characters before and after `webassembly` in the `href` attribute of the `base` element. If you omit either character, then Blazor WebAssembly will not work.

Listing 37.9 Setting the URL in the index.html file in the wwwroot folder of the BlazorWebAssembly project

```
<!DOCTYPE html>
<html lang="en">

<head>
    <meta charset="utf-8" />
    <meta name="viewport" content="width=device-width, initial-scale=1.0,
        maximum-scale=1.0, user-scalable=no" />
    <title>BlazorWebAssembly</title>
    <base href="/webassembly/" />
    <link href="css/bootstrap/bootstrap.min.css" rel="stylesheet" />
    <link href="css/app.css" rel="stylesheet" />
    <link rel="icon" type="image/png" href="favicon.png" />
    <link href="BlazorWebAssembly.styles.css" rel="stylesheet" />
</head>

<body>
    <div id="app">
        <svg class="loading-progress">
            <circle r="40%" cx="50%" cy="50%" />
            <circle r="40%" cx="50%" cy="50%" />
        </svg>
        <div class="loading-progress-text"></div>
    </div>

    <div id="blazor-error-ui">
        An unhandled error has occurred.
        <a href="" class="reload">Reload</a>
        <a class="dismiss"> </a>
    </div>
    <script src="_framework/blazor.webassembly.js"></script>
</body>
```

The `base` element sets the URL from which all relative URLs in the document are defined and is required for the correct operation of the Blazor WebAssembly routing system.

SETTING THE STATIC WEB ASSET BASE PATH

If you are using Visual Studio, right-click the BlazorWebAssembly project in the Solution Explorer, select Edit Project File from the pop-up menu, and add the configuration element shown in listing 37.10. If you are using Visual Studio Code, open the

`BlazorWebAssembly.csproj` file in the `BlazorWebAssembly` folder and add the configuration element shown in listing 37.10.

```
...
<PropertyGroup>
    <TargetFramework>net6.0</TargetFramework>
    <Nullable>enable</Nullable>
    <ImplicitUsings>enable</ImplicitUsings>
    <StaticWebAssetBasePath>/webassembly/</StaticWebAssetBasePath>
</PropertyGroup>
...
```

The element tag name is `StaticWebAssetBasePath`, and the content is `/webassembly/`, which starts and ends with a `/` character.

> **CAUTION**   Make sure there are forward-slash (`/`) characters before and after `webassembly` in the `StaticWebAssetBasePath` attribute of the `base` element. If you omit either character, then Blazor WebAssembly will not work.

37.2.7 *Testing the placeholder components*

Start ASP.NET Core by selecting Start Without Debugging or Run Without Debugging from the Debug menu. If you prefer to use the command prompt, run the command shown in listing 37.11 in the `Advanced` project folder.

```
dotnet run
```

Use a browser to request http://localhost:5000/webassembly, and you will see the placeholder content added by the template used to create the `BlazorWebAssembly` project.

Using the PowerShell command prompt, run the following commands from within the `Advanced` project folder. Click the Counter and Fetch Data links, and you will see different content displayed, as shown in figure 37.3.

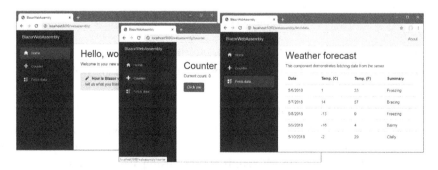

Figure 37.3   The Blazor WebAssembly placeholder content

37.3 Creating a Blazor WebAssembly component

Blazor WebAssembly uses the same approach as Blazor Server, relying on components as building blocks for applications, connected through the routing system, and displaying common content through layouts. In this section, I show how to create a Razor Component that works with Blazor WebAssembly, and then I'll re-create the simple forms application from chapter 36.

37.3.1 Importing the data model namespace

The components I will create in this chapter all use the classes in the shared `Data-Model` project. Rather than add `@using` expressions to each component, add the namespace for the data model classes to the `_Imports.razor` file in the root folder of the `BlazorWebAssembly` project, as shown in listing 37.12.

> **Listing 37.12 Adding a namespace in the _Imports.razor file in the BlazorWebAssembly project**

```
@using System.Net.Http
@using System.Net.Http.Json
@using Microsoft.AspNetCore.Components.Forms
@using Microsoft.AspNetCore.Components.Routing
@using Microsoft.AspNetCore.Components.Web
@using Microsoft.AspNetCore.Components.Web.Virtualization
@using Microsoft.AspNetCore.Components.WebAssembly.Http
@using Microsoft.JSInterop
@using BlazorWebAssembly
@using BlazorWebAssembly.Shared
@using Advanced.Models
```

Notice that although I moved the model classes to the `DataModel` project, I have specified the `Advanced.Models` namespace. This is because the class files I moved all have `namespace` declarations that specify `Advanced.Models`, which means that moving the files hasn't changed the namespace in which the classes exist.

37.3.2 Creating a component

In earlier chapters, I defined my Razor Components in a `Blazor` folder to keep the new content separate from the other parts of ASP.NET Core. There is only Blazor content in the `BlazorWebAssembly` project, so I am going to follow the convention adopted by the project template and use the `Pages` and `Shared` folders.

Add a Razor Component named `List.razor` to the `Pages` folder of the `Blazor-WebAssembly` project and add the content shown in listing 37.13.

> **Listing 37.13 The contents of the List.razor File in the Pages folder of the BlazorWebAssembly project**

```
@page "/forms"
@page "/forms/list"

<h5 class="bg-primary text-white text-center p-2">
```

```
        People (WebAssembly)
</h5>

<table class="table table-sm table-striped table-bordered">
    <thead>
        <tr>
            <th>ID</th>
            <th>Name</th>
            <th>Dept</th>
            <th>Location</th>
            <th></th>
        </tr>
    </thead>
    <tbody>
        @if (People.Count() == 0) {
            <tr>
                <th colspan="5" class="p-4 text-center">
                    Loading Data...
                </th>
            </tr>
        } else {
            @foreach (Person p in People) {
                <tr>
                    <td>@p.PersonId</td>
                    <td>@p.Surname, @p.Firstname</td>
                    <td>@p.Department?.Name</td>
                    <td>@p.Location?.City</td>
                    <td class="text-center">
                        <NavLink class="btn btn-sm btn-info"
                         href="@GetDetailsUrl(p.PersonId)">
                            Details
                        </NavLink>
                        <NavLink class="btn btn-sm btn-warning"
                         href="@GetEditUrl(p.PersonId)">
                            Edit
                        </NavLink>
                        <button class="btn btn-sm btn-danger"
                        @onclick="@(() => HandleDelete(p))">
                            Delete
                        </button>
                    </td>
                </tr>
            }
        }
    </tbody>
</table>

<NavLink class="btn btn-primary" href="forms/create">Create</NavLink>

@code {

    [Inject]
    public HttpClient? Http { get; set; }

    public Person[] People { get; set; } = Array.Empty<Person>();
```

```
protected async override Task OnInitializedAsync() {
    await UpdateData();
}

private async Task UpdateData() {
    if (Http != null) {
        People = await Http.GetFromJsonAsync<Person[]>("/api/people")
            ?? Array.Empty<Person>();
    }
}

string GetEditUrl(long id) => $"forms/edit/{id}";
string GetDetailsUrl(long id) => $"forms/details/{id}";

public async Task HandleDelete(Person p) {
    if (Http != null) {
        HttpResponseMessage resp =
            await Http.DeleteAsync($"/api/people/{p.PersonId}");
        if (resp.IsSuccessStatusCode) {
            await UpdateData();
        }
    }
}
}
```

If you compare this component with the Blazor Server equivalent from chapter 36, you will see that they are largely the same. Both types of Blazor use the same set of core features, which is why the content uses the same Razor directives, handles events with the @onclick attributes, and uses the same @code section for C# statements. A Blazor WebAssembly component is compiled into a C# class, just like its Blazor Server counterpart. The key difference is, of course, that the C# class that is generated is executed in the browser—and that's the reason for the differences from the component in chapter 36.

NAVIGATING IN A BLAZOR WEBASSEMBLY COMPONENT

Notice that the URLs that are used for navigation are expressed without a leading forward-slash character, like this:

```
...
<NavLink class="btn btn-primary" href="forms/create">Create</NavLink>
...
```

The root URL for the application was specified using the base element in listing 37.13, and using relative URLs ensures that navigation is performed relative to the root. In this case, the relative forms/create URL is combined with the /webassembly/ root specified by the base element, and navigation will be to /webassembly/forms/create. Including a leading forward slash would navigate to /forms/create instead, which is outside the set of URLs that are being managed by the Blazor WebAssembly part of the application. This change is required only for navigation URLs. URLs specified with the @page directive, for example, are not affected.

GETTING DATA IN A BLAZOR WEBASSEMBLY COMPONENT

The biggest change is that Blazor WebAssembly can't use Entity Framework Core. Although the runtime may be able to execute the Entity Framework Core classes, the browser restricts WebAssembly applications to HTTP requests, preventing the use of SQL. To get data, Blazor WebAssembly applications consume web services, which is why I added the API controller to the Advanced project at the start of the chapter.

As part of the Blazor WebAssembly application startup, a service is created for the `HttpClient` class, which components can receive using the standard dependency injection features. The `List` component receives an `HttpClient` component through a property that has been decorated with the `Inject` attribute, like this:

```
...
[Inject]
public HttpClient? Http { get; set; }
...
```

The `HttpClient` class provides the methods described in table 37.2 to send HTTP requests.

Table 37.2   The methods defined by the HttpClient class

Name	Description
GetAsync(url)	This method sends an HTTP GET request.
PostAsync(url, data)	This method sends an HTTP POST request.
PutAsync(url, data)	This method sends an HTTP PUT request.
PatchAync(url, data)	This method sends an HTTP PATCH request.
DeleteAsync(url)	This method sends an HTTP DELETE request.
SendAsync(request)	This method sends an HTTP, configured using an HttpRequestMessage object.

The methods in table 37.2 return a `Task<HttpResponseMessage>` result, which describes the response received from the HTTP server to the asynchronous request. Table 37.3 shows the most useful `HttpResponseMessage` properties.

Table 37.3   Useful HttpClient properties

Name	Description
Content	This property returns the content returned by the server.
HttpResponseHeaders	This property returns the response headers.
StatusCode	This property returns the response status code.
IsSuccessStatusCode	This property returns `true` if the response status code is between 200 and 299, indicating a successful request.

The List component uses the DeleteAsync methods to ask the web service to delete objects when the user clicks a Delete button.

```
...
public async Task HandleDelete(Person p) {
    if (Http != null) {
        HttpResponseMessage resp =
            await Http.DeleteAsync($"/api/people/{p.PersonId}");
        if (resp.IsSuccessStatusCode) {
            await UpdateData();
        }
    }
}
...
```

These methods are useful when you don't need to work with the data the web service sends back, such as in this situation where I check to see only if the DELETE request has been successful. Notice that I specify the path for the request URL only when using the HttpClient service because the web service is available using the same scheme, host, and port as the application.

For operations where the web service returns data, the extension methods for the HttpClient class described in table 37.4 are more useful. These methods serialize data into JSON so it can be sent to the server and parse JSON responses into C# objects. For requests that return no result, the generic type argument can be omitted.

Table 37.4   The HttpClient extension methods

Name	Description
GetFromJsonAsync<T>(url)	This method sends an HTTP GET request and parses the response to type T.
PostJsonAsync<T>(url, data)	This method sends an HTTP POST request with the serialized data value of T.
PutJsonAsync<T>(url, data)	This method sends an HTTP PUT request with the serialized data value of T.

The List component uses the GetJsonAsync<T> method to request data from the web service.

```
...
private async Task UpdateData() {
    if (Http != null) {
        People = await Http.GetFromJsonAsync<Person[]>("/api/people")
            ?? Array.Empty<Person>();
    }
}
...
```

Setting the generic type argument to Person[] tells HttpClient to parse the response into an array of Person objects.

NOTE The `HttpClient` class doesn't present any scope or lifecycle issues and sends requests only when one of the methods described in table 37.2 or table 37.4 is invoked. Some thought is required, however, about when to request new data. In this example, I requery the web service after an object has been deleted, rather than simply remove the object from the data that was requested when the component was initialized. This may not be suitable for all applications because it will reflect any changes to the database that have been made by other users.

37.3.3 *Creating a layout*

The template used to create the Blazor WebAssembly project includes a layout that presents the navigation features for the placeholder content. I don't want these navigation features, so the first step is to create a new layout. Add a Razor Component named `EmptyLayout.razor` to the `Shared` folder of the `BlazorWebAssembly` project with the content shown in listing 37.14.

> **Listing 37.14   The EmptyLayout.razor file in the Shared folder of the BlazorWebAssembly project**

```
@inherits LayoutComponentBase

<div class="m-2">
    @Body
</div>
```

I could apply the new layout with `@layout` expressions, as I did in chapter 36, but I am going to use this layout as the default by changing the routing configuration, which is defined in the `App.razor` file in the `BlazorWebAssembly` project, as shown in listing 37.15.

> **Listing 37.15   Applying the layout in the App.razor file in the BlazorWebAssembly project**

```
<Router AppAssembly="@typeof(App).Assembly">
    <Found Context="routeData">
        <RouteView RouteData="@routeData"
            DefaultLayout="@typeof(EmptyLayout)" />
        <FocusOnNavigate RouteData="@routeData" Selector="h1" />
    </Found>
    <NotFound>
        <PageTitle>Not found</PageTitle>
        <LayoutView Layout="@typeof(EmptyLayout)">
            <p role="alert">Sorry, there's nothing at this address.</p>
        </LayoutView>
    </NotFound>
</Router>
```

Chapter 35 describes the `Router`, `RouteView`, `Found`, and `NotFound` components.

37.3.4 Defining CSS styles

The template created the Blazor WebAssembly project with its own copy of the Bootstrap CSS framework and with an additional stylesheet that combines the styles required to configure the Blazor WebAssembly error and validation elements and manage the layout of the application. Replace the link elements in the HTML file as shown in listing 37.16 and apply styles directly to the error element. This has the effect of removing the styles used by the Microsoft layout and using the Bootstrap CSS stylesheet that was added to the Advanced project.

> **Listing 37.16** Modifying the index.html file in the wwwroot folder in the BlazorWebAssembly project

```
<!DOCTYPE html>
<html lang="en">

<head>
    <meta charset="utf-8" />
    <meta name="viewport" content="width=device-width, initial-scale=1.0,
        maximum-scale=1.0, user-scalable=no" />
    <title>BlazorWebAssembly</title>
    <base href="/webassembly/" />
    <!--<link href="css/bootstrap/bootstrap.min.css" rel="stylesheet" />-->
    <!--<link href="css/app.css" rel="stylesheet" />-->
    <link href="/lib/bootstrap/css/bootstrap.min.css" rel="stylesheet" />
    <link rel="icon" type="image/png" href="favicon.png" />
    <link href="BlazorWebAssembly.styles.css" rel="stylesheet" />
</head>

<body>
    <div id="app">
        <svg class="loading-progress">
            <circle r="40%" cx="50%" cy="50%" />
            <circle r="40%" cx="50%" cy="50%" />
        </svg>
        <div class="loading-progress-text"></div>
    </div>

    <div id="blazor-error-ui"
        class="text-center bg-danger h6 text-white p-2 fixed-top w-100"
        style="display:none">
        An unhandled error has occurred.
        <a href="" class="reload">Reload</a>
        <a class="dismiss"></a>
    </div>
    <script src="_framework/blazor.webassembly.js"></script>
</body>

</html>
```

To see the new component, restart ASP.NET Core and request http://localhost:5000/webassembly/forms, which will produce the response shown in figure 37.4.

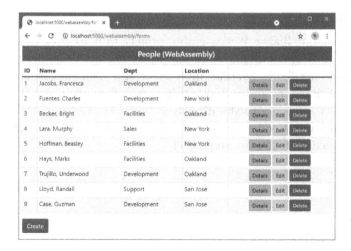

**Figure 37.4.
A Blazor
WebAssembly
component**

Blazor WebAssembly components follow the standard Blazor lifecycle, and the component displays the data it receives from the web service.

37.4 *Completing the Blazor WebAssembly Form application*

Only the Delete button displayed by the List component works currently. In the sections that follow, I complete the Blazor WebAssembly form application by creating additional components.

37.4.1 *Creating the details component*

Add a Razor Component named Details.razor to the Pages folder of the Blazor-WebAssembly project with the content shown in listing 37.17.

> **Listing 37.17   The contents of the Details.razor file in the Pages folder of the BlazorWebAssembly Project**

```
@page "/forms/details/{id:long}"

<h4 class="bg-info text-center text-white p-2">Details (WebAssembly)</h4>

<div class="form-group">
    <label>ID</label>
    <input class="form-control" value="@PersonData.PersonId" disabled />
</div>
<div class="form-group">
    <label>Firstname</label>
    <input class="form-control" value="@PersonData.Firstname" disabled />
</div>
<div class="form-group">
    <label>Surname</label>
    <input class="form-control" value="@PersonData.Surname" disabled />
</div>
<div class="form-group">
    <label>Department</label>
```

```
    <input class="form-control" value="@PersonData.Department?.Name"
        disabled />
</div>
<div class="form-group">
    <label>Location</label>
    <input class="form-control"
            value="@($"{PersonData.Location?.City}, "
                + PersonData.Location?.State)"
            disabled />
</div>
<div class="text-center p-2">
    <NavLink class="btn btn-info" href="@EditUrl">Edit</NavLink>
    <NavLink class="btn btn-secondary" href="forms">Back</NavLink>
</div>

@code {

    [Inject]
    public NavigationManager? NavManager { get; set; }

    [Inject]
    public HttpClient? Http { get; set; }

    [Parameter]
    public long Id { get; set; }

    public Person PersonData { get; set; } = new Person();

    protected async override Task OnParametersSetAsync() {
        if (Http != null) {
            PersonData = await Http.GetFromJsonAsync<Person>(
                $"/api/people/{Id}")
                    ?? new();
        }
    }

    public string EditUrl => $"forms/edit/{Id}";
}
```

The `Details` component has only two differences from its Blazor Server counterpart, following the pattern established by the `List` component: the data is obtained through the `HttpClient` service, and navigation targets are expressed using relative URLs. In all other regards, such as obtaining parameters from routing data, Blazor WebAssembly works just the same way as Blazor Server.

37.4.2 *Creating the editor component*

To complete the forms application, add a Razor Component named `Editor.razor` to the `Pages` folder of the `BlazorWebAssembly` project with the content shown in listing 37.18.

```
@page "/forms/edit/{id:long}"
@page "/forms/create"

<link href="/blazorValidation.css" rel="stylesheet" />

<h4 class="bg-@Theme text-center text-white p-2">@Mode (WebAssembly)</h4>

<EditForm Model="PersonData" OnValidSubmit="HandleValidSubmit">
    <DataAnnotationsValidator />
    @if (Mode == "Edit") {
        <div class="form-group">
            <label>ID</label>
            <InputNumber class="form-control"
                    @bind-Value="PersonData.PersonId" readonly />
        </div>
    }
    <div class="form-group">
        <label>Firstname</label>
        <ValidationMessage For="@(() => PersonData.Firstname)" />
        <InputText class="form-control"
            @bind-Value="PersonData.Firstname" />
    </div>
    <div class="form-group">
        <label>Surname</label>
        <ValidationMessage For="@(() => PersonData.Surname)" />
        <InputText class="form-control"
            @bind-Value="PersonData.Surname" />
    </div>
    <div class="form-group">
        <label>Department</label>
        <ValidationMessage For="@(() => PersonData.DepartmentId)" />
        <select @bind="PersonData.DepartmentId" class="form-control">
            <option selected disabled value="0">
                Choose a Department
            </option>
            @foreach (var kvp in Departments) {
                <option value="@kvp.Value">@kvp.Key</option>
            }
        </select>
    </div>
    <div class="form-group">
        <label>Location</label>
        <ValidationMessage For="@(() => PersonData.LocationId)" />
        <select @bind="PersonData.LocationId" class="form-control">
            <option selected disabled value="0">Choose a Location</option>
            @foreach (var kvp in Locations) {
                <option value="@kvp.Value">@kvp.Key</option>
            }
        </select>
    </div>
    <div class="text-center p-2">
        <button type="submit" class="btn btn-@Theme">Save</button>
```

```
            <NavLink class="btn btn-secondary" href="forms">Back</NavLink>
        </div>
    </EditForm>

    @code {

        [Inject]
        public HttpClient? Http { get; set; }

        [Inject]
        public NavigationManager? NavManager { get; set; }

        [Parameter]
        public long Id { get; set; }

        public Person PersonData { get; set; } = new Person();

        public IDictionary<string, long> Departments { get; set; }
            = new Dictionary<string, long>();
        public IDictionary<string, long> Locations { get; set; }
            = new Dictionary<string, long>();

        protected async override Task OnParametersSetAsync() {
            if (Http != null) {
                if (Mode == "Edit") {
                    PersonData = await Http.GetFromJsonAsync<Person>(
                            $"/api/people/{Id}")
                        ?? new();
                }
                var depts = await Http.GetFromJsonAsync<Department[]>(
                        "/api/departments");
                Departments = (depts ?? Array.Empty<Department>())
                    .ToDictionary(d => d.Name, d => d.Departmentid);

                var locs = await Http.GetFromJsonAsync<Location[]>(
                    "/api/locations");
                Locations = (locs ?? Array.Empty<Location>())
                    .ToDictionary(l => $"{l.City}, {l.State}",
                        l => l.LocationId);
            }
        }

        public string Theme => Id == 0 ? "primary" : "warning";
        public string Mode => Id == 0 ? "Create" : "Edit";

        public async Task HandleValidSubmit() {
            if (Http != null) {
                if (Mode == "Create") {
                    await Http.PostAsJsonAsync("/api/people", PersonData);
                } else {
                    await Http.PutAsJsonAsync("/api/people", PersonData);
                }
                NavManager?.NavigateTo("forms");
            }
        }
    }
}
```

This component uses the Blazor form features described in chapter 36 but uses HTTP requests to read and write data to the web service created at the start of the chapter. The `GetFromJsonAsync<T>` method is used to read data from the web service, and the `PostAsJsonAsync` and `PutAsJsonAsync` methods are used to send POST or PUT requests when the user submits the form.

Notice that I have not used the custom `select` component or validation components I created in chapter 36. Sharing components between projects—especially when Blazor WebAssembly is introduced after development has started—is awkward. I expect the process to improve in future releases, but for this chapter, I have simply done without the features. As a consequence, the `select` elements do not trigger validation when a value is selected, the submit button isn't automatically disabled, and there are no restrictions on the combination of department and location.

Restart ASP.NET Core and request http://localhost:5000/webassembly/forms, and you will see the Blazor WebAssembly version of the form application. Click the Details button for the first item in the table, and you will see the fields for the selected object. Click the Edit button, and you will be presented with an editable form. Make a change and click the Save button, and the changes will be sent to the web service and displayed in the data table, as shown in figure 37.5.

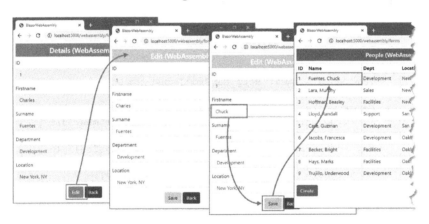

Figure 37.5 The completed Blazor WebAssembly form application

Summary

- Blazor WebAssembly creates client-side applications that do not need to maintain a persistent connection to the ASP.NET Core server.

- Creating an application with WebAssembly builds on the features described in earlier chapters for Blazor Server.

- Data access in a WebAssembly application must be performed through the `HttpClient` object received via dependency injection.

Using ASP.NET
Core Identity

38

This chapter covers

- Setting up ASP.NET Core Identity in an ASP.NET Core project
- Creating the ASP.NET Core Identity database
- Managing user accounts and roles

ASP.NET Core Identity is an API from Microsoft to manage users in ASP.NET Core applications and includes support for integrating authentication and authorization into the request pipeline.

ASP.NET Core Identity is a toolkit with which you create the authorization and authentication features an application requires. There are endless integration options for features such as two-factor authentication, federation, single sign-on, and account self-service. There are options that are useful only in large corporate environments or when using cloud-hosted user management.

ASP.NET Core Identity has evolved into its own framework and is too large for me to cover in detail in this book. Instead, I have focused on the parts of the Identity API that intersect with web application development, much as I have done with Entity Framework Core. In this chapter, I show you how to add ASP.NET Core Identity to a project and explain how to consume the ASP.NET Core Identity API to create tools to perform basic user and role management. In chapter 39, I show you how to use ASP.NET Core Identity to authenticate users and perform authorization. Table 38.1 puts ASP.NET Core Identity in context.

Table 38.1   Putting ASP.NET Core Identity in context

Question	Answer
What is it?	ASP.NET Core Identity is an API for managing users.
Why is it useful?	Most applications have some features that should not be available to all users. ASP.NET Core Identity provides features to allow users to authenticate themselves and gain access to restricted features.
How is it used?	ASP.NET Core Identity is added to projects as a package and stores its data in a database using Entity Framework Core. Management of users is performed through a well-defined API, and its features are applied as attributes, as I describe in chapter 39.
Are there any pitfalls or limitations?	ASP.NET Core Identity is complex and provides support for a wide range of authentication, authorization, and management models. It can be difficult to understand all the options, and documentation can be sparse.
Are there any alternatives?	There is no sensible alternative to ASP.NET Core Identity if a project needs to restrict access to features.

Table 38.2 provides a guide to the chapter.

Table 38.2   Chapter guide

Problem	Solution	Listing
Preparing the application for Identity	Create the context class and use it to prepare a migration that is applied to the database.	4–7
Managing user accounts	Use the `UserManager<T>` class.	8–12, 15, 16
Setting a username and password policy	Use the options pattern to configure Identity.	13, 14
Managing roles	Use the `RoleManager<T>` class to manage the roles and use the `UserManager<T>` class to assign users to roles.	17–20

38.1   Preparing for this chapter

This chapter uses the Advanced, DataModel, and BlazorWebAssembly projects from chapter 37. If you are using Visual Studio, open the `Advanced.sln` file you created in the previous chapter to open all three projects. If you are using Visual Studio Code, open the folder that contains the three projects.

> **TIP**   You can download the example project for this chapter—and for all the other chapters in this book—from https://github.com/manningbooks/pro-asp .net-core-7. See chapter 1 for how to get help if you have problems running the examples.

Open a new PowerShell command prompt, navigate to the folder that contains the `Advanced.csproj` file, and run the command shown in listing 38.1 to drop the database.

> **Listing 38.1　Dropping the database**

```
dotnet ef database drop --force
```

Use the PowerShell command prompt to run the command shown in listing 38.2.

> **Listing 38.2　Running the example application**

```
dotnet run
```

Use a browser to request http://localhost:5000, which will produce the response shown in figure 38.1.

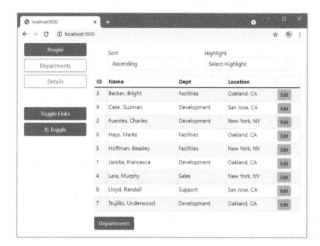

Figure 38.1 Running the example application

38.2　Preparing the project for ASP.NET Core Identity

The process for setting up ASP.NET Core Identity requires adding a package to the project, configuring the application, and preparing the database. To get started, use a PowerShell command prompt to run the command shown in listing 38.3 in the `Advanced` project folder, which installs the ASP.NET Core Identity package. If you are using Visual Studio, you can install the package by selecting Project > Manage NuGet Packages.

> **Listing 38.3　Installing ASP.NET Core Identity packages**

```
dotnet add package Microsoft.AspNetCore.Identity.EntityFrameworkCore
    --version 7.0.0
```

38.2.1 *Preparing the ASP.NET Core Identity database*

ASP.NET Identity requires a database, which is managed through Entity Framework Core. To create the Entity Framework Core context class that will provide access to the Identity data, add a class file named `IdentityContext.cs` to the `Advanced/Models` folder with the code shown in listing 38.4.

Listing 38.4   The IdentityContext.cs File in the Models Folder of the Advanced Project

```
using Microsoft.AspNetCore.Identity;
using Microsoft.AspNetCore.Identity.EntityFrameworkCore;
using Microsoft.EntityFrameworkCore;

namespace Advanced.Models {
    public class IdentityContext: IdentityDbContext<IdentityUser> {

        public IdentityContext(DbContextOptions<IdentityContext> options)
            : base(options) { }
    }
}
```

The ASP.NET Core Identity package includes the `IdentityDbContext<T>` class, which is used to create an Entity Framework Core context class. The generic type argument `T` is used to specify the class that will represent users in the database. You can create custom user classes, but I have used the basic class, called `IdentityUser`, which provides the core Identity features.

> **NOTE**   Don't worry if the classes used in listing 38.4 don't make sense. If you are unfamiliar with Entity Framework Core, then I suggest you treat the class as a black box. Changes are rarely required once the building blocks for ASP.NET Core Identity have been set up, and you can copy the files from this chapter into your own projects.

CONFIGURING THE DATABASE CONNECTION STRING

A connection string is required to tell ASP.NET Core Identity where it should store its data. In listing 38.5, I added a connection string to the `appsettings.json` file, alongside the one used for the application data.

Listing 38.5   Adding a connection in the appsettings.json file in the Advanced project

```
{
  "Logging": {
    "LogLevel": {
      "Default": "Information",
      "Microsoft.AspNetCore": "Warning",
      "Microsoft.EntityFrameworkCore": "Information"
    }
  },
  "AllowedHosts": "*",
  "ConnectionStrings": {
```

```
    "PeopleConnection": "Server=(localdb)\\MSSQLLocalDB;Database=People;
MultipleActiveResultSets=True",
    "IdentityConnection": "Server=(localdb)\\MSSQLLocalDB;Database=Identity
;MultipleActiveResultSets=True"
  }
}
```

The connection string specifies a LocalDB database named `Identity`.

> **NOTE** The width of the printed page doesn't allow for sensible formatting of the connection string, which must appear in a single unbroken line. When you add the connection string to your own project, make sure that it is on a single line.

38.2.2 Configuring the application

The next step is to configure ASP.NET Core so the Identity database context is set up as a service, as shown in listing 38.6.

Listing 38.6 Configuring identity in the Program.cs file in the Advanced project

```
using Microsoft.EntityFrameworkCore;
using Advanced.Models;
using Microsoft.AspNetCore.Identity;

var builder = WebApplication.CreateBuilder(args);

builder.Services.AddControllersWithViews();
builder.Services.AddRazorPages();
builder.Services.AddServerSideBlazor();

builder.Services.AddDbContext<DataContext>(opts => {
    opts.UseSqlServer(
        builder.Configuration["ConnectionStrings:PeopleConnection"]);
    opts.EnableSensitiveDataLogging(true);
});

builder.Services.AddSingleton<Advanced.Services.ToggleService>();

builder.Services.AddDbContext<IdentityContext>(opts =>
    opts.UseSqlServer(builder.Configuration[
        "ConnectionStrings:IdentityConnection"]));
builder.Services.AddIdentity<IdentityUser, IdentityRole>()
    .AddEntityFrameworkStores<IdentityContext>();

var app = builder.Build();

app.UseStaticFiles();

app.MapControllers();
app.MapControllerRoute("controllers",
    "controllers/{controller=Home}/{action=Index}/{id?}");
app.MapRazorPages();
app.MapBlazorHub();
app.MapFallbackToPage("/_Host");
```

```
app.UseBlazorFrameworkFiles("/webassembly");
app.MapFallbackToFile("/webassembly/{*path:nonfile}",
    "/webassembly/index.html");

var context = app.Services.CreateScope().ServiceProvider
    .GetRequiredService<DataContext>();
SeedData.SeedDatabase(context);

app.Run();
```

38.2.3   Creating and applying the identity database migration

The remaining step is to create the Entity Framework Core database migration and apply it to create the database. Open a new PowerShell window, navigate to the `Advanced` project folder, and run the commands shown in listing 38.7.

> **Listing 38.7   Creating and applying the database migration**

```
dotnet ef migrations add --context IdentityContext Initial
dotnet ef database update --context IdentityContext
```

As I explained in earlier chapters, Entity Framework Core manages changes to database schemas through a feature called *migrations*. Now that there are two database context classes in the project, the Entity Framework Core tools require the `--context` argument to determine which context class is being used. The commands in listing 38.7 create a migration that contains the ASP.NET Core Identity schema and apply it to the database.

> **Resetting the ASP.NET Core Identity database**
>
> If you need to reset the database, run the `dotnet ef database drop --force --context IdentityContext` command in the `Advanced` folder and then run the `dotnet ef database update --context IdentityContext` command. This will delete the existing database and create a new—and empty—replacement. Do not use these commands on production systems because you will delete user credentials. If you need to reset the main database, then run the `dotnet ef database drop --force --context DataContext` command, followed by `dotnet ef database update --context DataContext`.

38.3   Creating user management tools

In this section, I am going to create the tools that manage users through ASP.NET Core Identity. Users are managed through the `UserManager<T>` class, where `T` is the class chosen to represent users in the database. When I created the Entity Framework Core context class, I specified `IdentityUser` as the class to represent users in the database. This is the built-in class that is provided by ASP.NET Core Identity, and it provides the core features that are required by most applications. table 38.3 describes the most useful `IdentityUser` properties. (There are additional properties defined by the

`IdentityUser` class, but these are the ones required by most applications and are the ones I use in this book.)

Scaffolding the Identity management tools

Microsoft provides a tool that will generate a set of Razor Pages for user management. The tool adds generic content—known as *scaffolding*—from templates to a project, which you then tailor to the application. I am not a fan of scaffolding or templates, and this is not an exception. The Microsoft Identity templates are well thought out, but they are of limited use because they focus on self-management, allowing users to create accounts, change passwords, and so on, without administrator intervention. You can adapt the templates to restrict the range of tasks that users perform, but the premise behind the features remains the same.

If you are writing the type of application where users manage their own credentials, then the scaffolding option may be worth considering and is described at https://docs. microsoft.com/en-us/aspnet/core/security/authentication/scaffold-identity. For all other approaches, the user management API provided by ASP.NET Core Identity should be used.

Table 38.3   Useful IdentityUser properties

Name	Description
`Id`	This property contains the unique ID for the user.
`UserName`	This property returns the user's username.
`Email`	This property contains the user's e-mail address.

Table 38.4 describes the `UserManagement<T>` members I use in this section to manage users.

Table 38.4   Useful UserManager<T> members

Name	Description
`Users`	This property returns a sequence containing the users stored in the database.
`FindByIdAsync(id)`	This method queries the database for the user object with the specified ID.
`CreateAsync(user, password)`	This method stores a new user in the database using the specified password.
`UpdateAsync(user)`	This method modifies an existing user in the database.
`DeleteAsync(user)`	This method removes the specified user from the database.

38.3.1 *Preparing for user management tools*

In preparation for creating the management tools, add the expressions shown in listing 38.8 to the `_ViewImports.cshtml` file in the `Pages` folder of the Advanced project.

> **Listing 38.8   Adding expressions in the _ViewImports.cshtml file in the Pages folder of the Advanced project**

```
@addTagHelper *, Microsoft.AspNetCore.Mvc.TagHelpers
@using Advanced.Models
@using Microsoft.AspNetCore.Mvc.RazorPages
@using Microsoft.EntityFrameworkCore
@using System.ComponentModel.DataAnnotations
@using Microsoft.AspNetCore.Identity
@using Advanced.Pages
```

Next, create the `Pages/Users` folder in the Advanced project and add to it a Razor Layout named `_Layout.cshtml` to the `Pages/Users` folder with the content shown in listing 38.9.

> **Listing 38.9   The _Layout.cshtml file in the Pages/Users folder in the Advanced project**

```
<!DOCTYPE html>
<html>
<head>
    <title>Identity</title>
    <link href="/lib/bootstrap/css/bootstrap.min.css" rel="stylesheet" />
</head>
<body>
    <div class="m-2">
        <h5 class="bg-info text-white text-center p-2">
            User Administration
        </h5>
        @RenderBody()
    </div>
</body>
</html>
```

Add a class file named `AdminPageModel.cs` to the `Pages` folder and use it to define the class shown in listing 38.10.

> **Listing 38.10   The AdminPageModel.cs file in the Pages folder in the Advanced project**

```
using Microsoft.AspNetCore.Mvc.RazorPages;

namespace Advanced.Pages {
    public class AdminPageModel : PageModel {

    }
}
```

This class will be the base for the page model classes defined in this section. As you will see in chapter 39, a common base class is useful when it comes to securing the application.

38.3.2 Enumerating user accounts

Although the database is currently empty, I am going to start by creating a Razor Page that will enumerate user accounts. Add a Razor Page named `List.cshtml` to the `Pages/Users` folder in the Advanced project with the content shown in listing 38.11.

```
@page
@model ListModel

<table class="table table-sm table-bordered">
    <tr><th>ID</th><th>Name</th><th>Email</th><th></th></tr>
    @if (Model.Users.Count() == 0) {
        <tr><td colspan="4" class="text-center">No User Accounts</td></tr>
    } else {
        foreach (IdentityUser user in Model.Users) {
            <tr>
                <td>@user.Id</td>
                <td>@user.UserName</td>
                <td>@user.Email</td>
                <td class="text-center">
                    <form asp-page="List" method="post">
                        <input type="hidden" name="Id" value="@user.Id" />
                        <a class="btn btn-sm btn-warning"
                            asp-page="Editor" asp-route-id="@user.Id"
                            asp-route-mode="edit">
                                Edit
                        </a>
                        <button type="submit"
                                class="btn btn-sm btn-danger">
                            Delete
                        </button>
                    </form>
                </td>
            </tr>
        }
    }
</table>

<a class="btn btn-primary" asp-page="create">Create</a>

@functions {

    public class ListModel : AdminPageModel {
        public UserManager<IdentityUser> UserManager;

        public ListModel(UserManager<IdentityUser> userManager) {
            UserManager = userManager;
        }

        public IEnumerable<IdentityUser> Users { get; set; }
            = Enumerable.Empty<IdentityUser>();
```

```
        public void OnGet() {
            Users = UserManager.Users;
        }
    }
}
```

The UserManager<IdentityUser> class is set up as a service so that it can be consumed via dependency injection. The Users property returns a collection of IdentityUser objects, which can be used to enumerate the user accounts. This Razor Page displays the users in a table, with buttons that allow each user to be edited or deleted, although this won't be visible initially because a placeholder message is shown when there are no user objects to display. There is a button that navigates to a Razor Page named Create, which I define in the next section.

Restart ASP.NET and request http://localhost:5000/users/list to see the (currently empty) data table, which is shown in figure 38.2.

**Figure 38.2
Enumerating
users**

38.3.3 *Creating users*

Add a Razor Page named Create.cshtml to the Pages/Users folder with the content shown in listing 38.12.

> **Listing 38.12   The Create.cshtml file in the Pages/Users folder of the Advanced project**

```
@page
@model CreateModel

<h5 class="bg-primary text-white text-center p-2">Create User</h5>
<form method="post">
    <div asp-validation-summary="All" class="text-danger"></div>
    <div class="form-group">
        <label>User Name</label>
        <input name="UserName" class="form-control"
                value="@Model.UserName" />
    </div>
    <div class="form-group">
        <label>Email</label>
        <input name="Email" class="form-control"
                value="@Model.Email" />
    </div>
    <div class="form-group">
```

```
            <label>Password</label>
            <input name="Password" class="form-control"
                    value="@Model.Password" />
        </div>
        <div class="py-2">
            <button type="submit" class="btn btn-primary">Submit</button>
            <a class="btn btn-secondary" asp-page="list">Back</a>
        </div>
    </form>

    @functions {

        public class CreateModel : AdminPageModel {
            public UserManager<IdentityUser> UserManager;

            public CreateModel(UserManager<IdentityUser> usrManager) {
                UserManager = usrManager;
            }

            [BindProperty]
            public string UserName { get; set; } = string.Empty;

            [BindProperty]
            [EmailAddress]
            public string Email { get; set; } = string.Empty;

            [BindProperty]
            public string Password { get; set; } = string.Empty;

            public async Task<IActionResult> OnPostAsync() {
                if (ModelState.IsValid) {
                    IdentityUser user =
                        new IdentityUser {
                            UserName = UserName,
                            Email = Email
                        };
                    IdentityResult result =
                        await UserManager.CreateAsync(user, Password);
                    if (result.Succeeded) {
                        return RedirectToPage("List");
                    }
                    foreach (IdentityError err in result.Errors) {
                        ModelState.AddModelError("", err.Description);
                    }
                }
                return Page();
            }
        }
    }
```

Even though ASP.NET Core Identity data is stored using Entity Framework Core, you don't work directly with the database context class. Instead, data is managed through the methods provided by the UserManager<T> class. New users are created using the CreateAsync method, which accepts an IdentityUser object and a password string as arguments.

This Razor Page defines three properties that are subject to model binding. The UserName and Email properties are used to configure the IdentityUser object, which is combined with the value bound to the Password property to call the CreateAsync method. These properties are configured with validation attributes, and values will be required because the property types are non-nullable.

The result of the CreateAsync method is a Task<IdentityResult> object, which indicates the outcome of the create operation, using the properties described in table 38.5.

Table 38.5   The properties defined by the IdentityResult class

Name	Description
Succeeded	Returns true if the operation succeeded.
Errors	Returns a sequence of IdentityError objects that describe the errors encountered while attempting the operation. Each IdentityError object provides a Description property that summarizes the problem.

I inspect the Succeeded property to determine whether a new user has been created in the database. If the Succeeded property is true, then the client is redirected to the List page so that the list of users is displayed, reflecting the new addition.

```
...
if (result.Succeeded) {
    return RedirectToPage("List");
}
foreach (IdentityError err in result.Errors) {
    ModelState.AddModelError("", err.Description);
}
...
```

If the Succeeded property is false, then the sequence of IdentityError objects provided by the Errors property is enumerated, with the Description property used to create a model-level validation error using the ModelState.AddModelError method.

To test the ability to create a new user account, restart ASP.NET Core and request http://localhost:5000/users/list. Click the Create button and fill in the form with the values shown in table 38.6.

> **TIP**   There are domains reserved for testing, including example.com. You can see a complete list at https://tools.ietf.org/html/rfc2606.

Table 38.6   The values for creating an example user

Field	Description
Name	Joe
Email	joe@example.com
Password	Secret123$

Once you have entered the values, click the Submit button. ASP.NET Core Identity will create the user in the database, and the browser will be redirected, as shown in figure 38.3. (You will see a different ID value because IDs are randomly generated for each user.)

> **NOTE** I used a regular `input` element for the `Password` field to make it easier to follow the examples in this chapter. For real projects, it is a good idea to set the `input` element's `type` attribute to `password` so that the characters entered cannot be seen.

Figure 38.3 Creating a new user

Click the Create button again and enter the same details into the form, using the values in table 38.6. This time you will see an error reported through the model validation summary when you click the Create button, as shown in figure 38.4. This is an example of an error returned through the `IdentityResult` object produced by the `CreateAsync` method.

**Figure 38.4
An error when
creating a new
user**

VALIDATING PASSWORDS

One of the most common requirements, especially for corporate applications, is to enforce a password policy. You can see the default policy by navigating to http://localhost:5000/Users/Create and filling out the form with the data shown in table 38.7.

Table 38.7 The values for creating an example user

Field	Description
Name	Alice
Email	alice@example.com
Password	secret

When you submit the form, ASP.NET Core Identity checks the candidate password and generates errors if it doesn't match the password, as shown in figure 38.5.

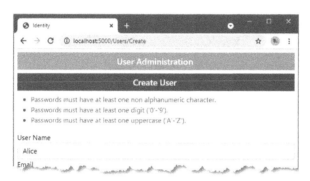

Figure 38.5
Password
validation
errors

The password validation rules are configured using the options pattern, as shown in listing 38.13.

Listing 38.13 Configuring validation in the Program.cs file in the Advanced project

```
using Microsoft.EntityFrameworkCore;
using Advanced.Models;

using Microsoft.AspNetCore.Identity;

var builder = WebApplication.CreateBuilder(args);

builder.Services.AddControllersWithViews();
builder.Services.AddRazorPages();
builder.Services.AddServerSideBlazor();

builder.Services.AddDbContext<DataContext>(opts => {
    opts.UseSqlServer(
        builder.Configuration["ConnectionStrings:PeopleConnection"]);
    opts.EnableSensitiveDataLogging(true);
});

builder.Services.AddSingleton<Advanced.Services.ToggleService>();

builder.Services.AddDbContext<IdentityContext>(opts =>
    opts.UseSqlServer(builder.Configuration[
        "ConnectionStrings:IdentityConnection"]));
builder.Services.AddIdentity<IdentityUser, IdentityRole>()
    .AddEntityFrameworkStores<IdentityContext>();
```

```
builder.Services.Configure<IdentityOptions>(opts => {
    opts.Password.RequiredLength = 6;
    opts.Password.RequireNonAlphanumeric = false;
    opts.Password.RequireLowercase = false;
    opts.Password.RequireUppercase = false;
    opts.Password.RequireDigit = false;
});

var app = builder.Build();

app.UseStaticFiles();

app.MapControllers();
app.MapControllerRoute("controllers",
    "controllers/{controller=Home}/{action=Index}/{id?}");
app.MapRazorPages();
app.MapBlazorHub();
app.MapFallbackToPage("/_Host");

app.UseBlazorFrameworkFiles("/webassembly");
app.MapFallbackToFile("/webassembly/{*path:nonfile}",
    "/webassembly/index.html");

var context = app.Services.CreateScope().ServiceProvider
    .GetRequiredService<DataContext>();
SeedData.SeedDatabase(context);

app.Run();
```

ASP.NET Core Identity is configured using the `IdentityOptions` class, whose `Password` property returns a `PasswordOptions` class that configures password validation using the properties described in table 38.8.

Table 38.8   The PasswordOptions properties

Name	Description
RequiredLength	This `int` property is used to specify the minimum length for passwords.
RequireNonAlphanumeric	Setting this `bool` property to `true` requires passwords to contain at least one character that is not a letter or a digit.
RequireLowercase	Setting this `bool` property to `true` requires passwords to contain at least one lowercase character.
RequireUppercase	Setting this `bool` property to `true` requires passwords to contain at least one uppercase character.
RequireDigit	Setting this `bool` property to `true` requires passwords to contain at least one numeric character.

In the listing, I specified that passwords must have a minimum length of six characters and disabled the other constraints. This isn't something that you should do without careful consideration in a real project, but it allows for an effective demonstration. Restart ASP.NET Core, request http://localhost:5000/users/create, and fill out the form using the details from table 38.7. When you click the Submit button, the password will be accepted by the new validation rules, and a new user will be created, as shown in figure 38.6.

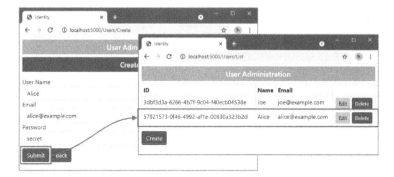

Figure 38.6   Changing the password validation rules

Validating user details

Validation is also performed on usernames and e-mail addresses when accounts are created. To see how validation is applied, request http://localhost:5000/users/create and fill out the form using the values shown in table 38.9.

Table 38.9   The values for creating an example user

Field	Description
Name	Bob!
Email	alice@example.com
Password	secret

Click the Submit button, and you will see the error message shown in figure 38.7.

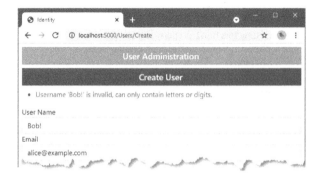

**Figure 38.7
A user details
validation error**

Validation can be configured with the options pattern, using the `User` property defined by the `IdentityOptions` class. This class returns a `UserOptions` class, whose properties are described in table 38.10.

Table 38.10   The UserOptions properties

Name	Description
AllowedUserNameCharacters	This `string` property contains all the legal characters that can be used in a username. The default value specifies a–z, A–Z, and 0–9 and the hyphen, period, underscore, and @ characters. This property is not a regular expression, and every legal character must be specified explicitly in the string.
RequireUniqueEmail	Setting this `bool` property to `true` requires new accounts to specify e-mail addresses that have not been used previously.

In listing 38.14, I have changed the configuration of the application so that unique e-mail addresses are required and so that only lowercase alphabetic characters are allowed in usernames.

Listing 38.14   Changing validation in the Program.cs file in the Advanced project

```
...
builder.Services.Configure<IdentityOptions>(opts => {
    opts.Password.RequiredLength = 6;
    opts.Password.RequireNonAlphanumeric = false;
    opts.Password.RequireLowercase = false;
    opts.Password.RequireUppercase = false;
    opts.Password.RequireDigit = false;
    opts.User.RequireUniqueEmail = true;
    opts.User.AllowedUserNameCharacters = "abcdefghijklmnopqrstuvwxyz";
});
...
```

Restart ASP.NET Core, request http://localhost:5000/users/create, and fill out the form with the values in table 38.9. Click the Submit button, and you will see that the e-mail address now causes an error. The username still contains illegal characters and is also flagged as an error, as shown in figure 38.8.

**Figure 38.8
Validating user
detail**

38.3.4 Editing users

To add support for editing users, add a Razor Page named `Editor.cshtml` to the `Pages/Users` folder of the Advanced project with the content shown in listing 38.15.

Listing 38.15   The Editor.cshtml file in the Pages/Users folder of the Advanced project

```
@page "{id}"
@model EditorModel

<h5 class="bg-warning text-white text-center p-2">Edit User</h5>
<form method="post">
    <div asp-validation-summary="All" class="text-danger"></div>
    <div class="form-group">
        <label>ID</label>
        <input name="Id" class="form-control" value="@Model.Id"
            disabled />
        <input name="Id" type="hidden" value="@Model.Id" />
    </div>
    <div class="form-group">
        <label>User Name</label>
        <input name="UserName" class="form-control"
            value="@Model.UserName" />
    </div>
    <div class="form-group">
        <label>Email</label>
        <input name="Email" class="form-control" value="@Model.Email" />
    </div>
    <div class="form-group">
        <label>New Password</label>
        <input name="Password" class="form-control"
            value="@Model.Password" />
    </div>
    <div class="py-2">
        <button type="submit" class="btn btn-warning">Submit</button>
        <a class="btn btn-secondary" asp-page="list">Back</a>
    </div>
</form>

@functions {

    public class EditorModel : AdminPageModel {
        public UserManager<IdentityUser> UserManager;

        public EditorModel(UserManager<IdentityUser> usrManager) {
            UserManager = usrManager;
        }

        [BindProperty]
        public string Id { get; set; } = string.Empty;

        [BindProperty]
        public string UserName { get; set; } = string.Empty;

        [BindProperty]
```

```
    [EmailAddress]
    public string Email { get; set; } = string.Empty;

    [BindProperty]
    public string? Password { get; set; }

    public async Task OnGetAsync(string id) {
        IdentityUser? user = await UserManager.FindByIdAsync(id);
        if (user != null) {
            Id = user.Id;
            UserName = user.UserName ?? string.Empty;
            Email = user.Email ?? string.Empty;
        }
    }

    public async Task<IActionResult> OnPostAsync() {
        if (ModelState.IsValid) {
            IdentityUser? user = await UserManager.FindByIdAsync(Id);
            if (user != null) {
                user.UserName = UserName;
                user.Email = Email;

                IdentityResult result =
                    await UserManager.UpdateAsync(user);
                if (result.Succeeded
                        && !String.IsNullOrEmpty(Password)) {
                    await UserManager.RemovePasswordAsync(user);
                    result = await UserManager.AddPasswordAsync(user,
                        Password);
                }
                if (result.Succeeded) {
                    return RedirectToPage("List");
                }
                foreach (IdentityError err in result.Errors) {
                    ModelState.AddModelError("", err.Description);
                }
            }
        }
        return Page();
    }
  }
}
```

The `Editor` page uses the `UserManager<T>.FindByIdAsync` method to locate the user, querying the database with the `id` value received through the routing system and received as an argument to the `OnGetAsync` method. The values from the `Identity-User` object returned by the query are used to populate the properties that are displayed by the view part of the page, ensuring that the values are not lost if the page is redisplayed due to validation errors.

When the user submits the form, the `FindByIdAsync` method is used to query the database for the `IdentityUser` object, which is updated with the `UserName` and `Email` values provided in the form. Passwords require a different approach and must be removed from the `user` object before a new password is assigned, like this:

```
...
await UserManager.RemovePasswordAsync(user);
result = await UserManager.AddPasswordAsync(user, Password);
...
```

The `Editor` page changes the password only if the form contains a `Password` value and if the updates for the UserName and Email fields have been successful. Errors from ASP.NET Core Identity are presented as validation messages, and the browser is redirected to the `List` page after a successful update. Request http://localhost:5000/Users/List, click the Edit button for Joe, and change the UserName field to bob, with all lowercase characters. Click the Submit button, and you will see the change reflected in the list of users, as shown in figure 38.9.

> **NOTE**   You will see an error if you click the Edit button for the Alice account and click Submit without making changes. This is because the account was created before the validation policy was changed. ASP.NET Core Identity applies validation checks for updates, leading to the odd situation where the data in the database can be read—and used—but cannot be updated.

Figure 38.9
Editing a user

38.3.5 Deleting users

The last feature I need for my basic user management application is the ability to delete users, as shown in listing 38.16.

> **Listing 38.16   Deleting users in the List.cshtml file in the Pages/Users folder in the Advanced project**

```
...
@functions {

    public class ListModel : AdminPageModel {
        public UserManager<IdentityUser> UserManager;

        public ListModel(UserManager<IdentityUser> userManager) {
            UserManager = userManager;
```

```
        }

        public IEnumerable<IdentityUser> Users { get; set; }
            = Enumerable.Empty<IdentityUser>();

        public void OnGet() {
            Users = UserManager.Users;
        }

        public async Task<IActionResult> OnPostAsync(string id) {
            IdentityUser? user = await UserManager.FindByIdAsync(id);
            if (user != null) {
                await UserManager.DeleteAsync(user);
            }
            return RedirectToPage();
        }
    }
}
...
```

The List page already displays a Delete button for each user in the data table, which
submits a POST request containing the Id value for the IdentityUser object to be
removed. The OnPostAsync method receives the Id value and uses it to query Identity using the FindByIdAsync method, passing the object that is returned to the
DeleteAsync method, which deletes it from the database. To check the delete functionality, request http://localhost:5000/Users/List and click Delete for the Alice
account. The user object will be removed, as shown in figure 38.10.

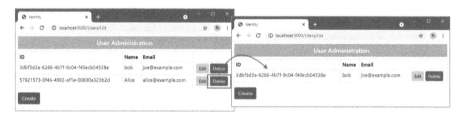

Figure 38.10   Deleting a user

38.4   Creating role management tools

Some applications enforce only two levels of authorization: authenticated users are
allowed access to all the application's features, while unauthenticated users have less—
or no—access. The SportsStore application in part 1 followed this approach: there
was one user, and once authenticated, they had access to all the application's features,
including administration tools, while unauthenticated users were restricted to the public store features.

ASP.NET Core Identity supports *roles* for applications that require more granular
authorization. Users are assigned to one or more roles, and their membership of those
roles determines which features are accessible. In the sections that follow, I show you
how to build tools to create and manage roles.

Roles are managed through the RoleManager<T> class, where T is the representation of roles in the database. When I configured ASP.NET Core Identity at the start of the chapter, I selected IdentityRole, which is the built-in class that Identity provides to describe a role, which means that I will be using the RoleManager<IdentityRole> class in these examples. The RoleManager<T> class defines the methods and properties shown in table 38.11 that allow roles to be created and managed.

Table 38.11   The members defined by the RoleManager<T> class

Name	Description
CreateAsync(role)	Creates a new role
DeleteAsync(role)	Deletes the specified role
FindByIdAsync(id)	Finds a role by its ID
FindByNameAsync(name)	Finds a role by its name
RoleExistsAsync(name)	Returns true if a role with the specified name exists
UpdateAsync(role)	Stores changes to the specified role
Roles	Returns an enumeration of the roles that have been defined

Table 38.12 describes the key properties defined by the IdentityRole class.

Table 38.12   Useful IdentityRole properties

Name	Description
Id	This property contains the unique ID for the role.
Name	This property returns the role name.

Although roles are managed through the RoleManager<T> class, membership of roles is managed through the methods provided by UserManager<T> described in table 38.13.

Table 38.13   The UserManager<T> methods for managing role membership

Name	Description
AddToRoleAsync(user, role)	This method adds a user to a role.
RemoveFromRoleAsync(user, role)	This method removes a user from a role.
GetRolesAsync(user)	This method returns the roles for which the user is a member.
GetUsersInRoleAsync(role)	This method returns users who are members of the specified role.
IsInRoleAsync(user, role)	This method returns true if the user is a member of the specified role.

38.4.1 *Preparing for role management tools*

To prepare for the role management tools, create the `Pages/Roles` folder in the Advanced project and add to it a Razor Layout named `_Layout.cshtml` with the content shown in listing 38.17.

Listing 38.17   The _Layout.cshtml file in the Pages/Roles folder in the Advanced project

```
<!DOCTYPE html>
<html>
<head>
    <title>Identity</title>
    <link href="/lib/bootstrap/css/bootstrap.min.css" rel="stylesheet" />
</head>
<body>
    <div class="m-2">
        <h5 class="bg-secondary text-white text-center p-2">
            Role Administration
        </h5>
        @RenderBody()
    </div>
</body>
</html>
```

This layout will ensure there is an obvious difference between the user and role management tools.

38.4.2 *Enumerating and deleting roles*

Add a Razor Page named `List.cshtml` to the `Pages/Roles` folder in the Advanced project with the content shown in listing 38.18.

Listing 38.18   The List.cshtml file in the Pages/Roles folder in the Advanced project

```
@page
@model ListModel

<table class="table table-sm table-bordered">
    <tr><th>ID</th><th>Name</th><th>Members</th><th></th></tr>
    @if (Model.Roles.Count() == 0) {
        <tr><td colspan="4" class="text-center">No Roles</td></tr>
    } else {
        foreach (IdentityRole role in Model.Roles) {
            <tr>
                <td>@role.Id</td>
                <td>@role.Name</td>
                <td>@(await Model.GetMembersString(role.Name))</td>
                <td class="text-center">
                    <form asp-page="List" method="post">
                        <input type="hidden" name="Id" value="@role.Id" />
                        <a class="btn btn-sm btn-warning"
                            asp-page="Editor"
                            asp-route-id="@role.Id"
                            asp-route-mode="edit">Edit</a>
```

```
                        <button type="submit"
                                class="btn btn-sm btn-danger">
                            Delete
                        </button>
                    </form>
                </td>
            </tr>
        }
    }
</table>
<a class="btn btn-primary" asp-page="create">Create</a>

@functions {

    public class ListModel : AdminPageModel {
        public UserManager<IdentityUser> UserManager;
        public RoleManager<IdentityRole> RoleManager;

        public ListModel(UserManager<IdentityUser> userManager,
                RoleManager<IdentityRole> roleManager) {
            UserManager = userManager;
            RoleManager = roleManager;
        }

        public IEnumerable<IdentityRole> Roles { get; set; }
            = Enumerable.Empty<IdentityRole>();

        public void OnGet() {
            Roles = RoleManager.Roles;
        }

        public async Task<string> GetMembersString(string? role) {
        IEnumerable<IdentityUser> users
                = (await UserManager.GetUsersInRoleAsync(role!));
            string result = users.Count() == 0
                ? "No members"
                : string.Join(", ",
                    users.Take(3).Select(u => u.UserName).ToArray());
            return users.Count() > 3
                ? $"{result}, (plus others)" : result;
        }

        public async Task<IActionResult> OnPostAsync(string id) {
            IdentityRole? role = await RoleManager.FindByIdAsync(id);
            if (role != null) {
                await RoleManager.DeleteAsync(role);
            }
            return RedirectToPage();
        }
    }
}
```

The roles are enumerated, along with the names of up to three of the role members or a placeholder message if there are no members. There is also a Create button, and each role is presented with Edit and Delete buttons, following the same pattern I used for the user management tools.

The Delete button sends a POST request back to the Razor Page. The `OnPostAsync` method uses the `FindByIdAsync` method to retrieve the role object, which is passed to the `DeleteAsync` method to remove it from the database.

38.4.3 Creating roles

Add a Razor Page named `Create.cshtml` in the `Pages/Roles` folder in the Advanced project with the contents shown in listing 38.19.

> **Listing 38.19** The Create.cshtml file in the Pages/Roles folder in the Advanced project

```
@page
@model CreateModel

<h5 class="bg-primary text-white text-center p-2">Create Role</h5>
<form method="post">
    <div asp-validation-summary="All" class="text-danger"></div>
    <div class="form-group">
        <label>Role Name</label>
        <input name="Name" class="form-control" value="@Model.Name" />
    </div>
    <div class="py-2">
        <button type="submit" class="btn btn-primary">Submit</button>
        <a class="btn btn-secondary" asp-page="list">Back</a>
    </div>
</form>

@functions {

    public class CreateModel : AdminPageModel {
        public RoleManager<IdentityRole> RoleManager;

        public CreateModel(UserManager<IdentityUser> userManager,
                RoleManager<IdentityRole> roleManager) {
            RoleManager = roleManager;
        }

        [BindProperty]
        public string Name { get; set; } = string.Empty;

        public async Task<IActionResult> OnPostAsync() {
            if (ModelState.IsValid) {
                IdentityRole role =
                    new IdentityRole { Name = Name };
                IdentityResult result =
                    await RoleManager.CreateAsync(role);
                if (result.Succeeded) {
                    return RedirectToPage("List");
                }
                foreach (IdentityError err in result.Errors) {
                    ModelState.AddModelError("", err.Description);
```

```
            }
        }
        return Page();
        }
    }
}
```

The user is presented with a form containing an `input` element to specify the name of the new role. When the form is submitted, the `OnPostAsync` method creates a new `IdentityRole` object and passes it to the `CreateAsync` method.

38.4.4 Assigning role membership

To add support for managing role memberships, add a Razor Page named `Editor` `.cshtml` to the `Pages/Roles` folder in the Advanced project, with the content shown in listing 38.20.

> **Listing 38.20**   The Editor.cshtml file in the Pages/Roles folder in the Advanced project

```html
@page "{id}"
@model EditorModel

<h5 class="bg-primary text-white text-center p-2">
    Edit Role: @Model.Role?.Name
</h5>

<form method="post">
    <input type="hidden" name="rolename" value="@Model.Role?.Name" />
    <div asp-validation-summary="All" class="text-danger"></div>
    <h5 class="bg-secondary text-white p-2">Members</h5>
    <table class="table table-sm table-striped table-bordered">
        <thead><tr><th>User</th><th>Email</th><th></th></tr></thead>
        <tbody>
            @if ((await Model.Members()).Count() == 0) {
                <tr>
                    <td colspan="3" class="text-center">No members</td>
                </tr>
            }
            @foreach (IdentityUser user in await Model.Members()) {
                <tr>
                    <td>@user.UserName</td>
                    <td>@user.Email</td>
                    <td>
                        <button asp-route-userid="@user.Id"
                            class="btn btn-primary btn-sm" type="submit">
                            Change
                        </button>
                    </td>
                </tr>
            }
        </tbody>
    </table>

    <h5 class="bg-secondary text-white p-2">Non-Members</h5>
```

```html
<table class="table table-sm table-striped table-bordered">
    <thead><tr><th>User</th><th>Email</th><th></th></tr></thead>
    <tbody>
        @if ((await Model.NonMembers()).Count() == 0) {
            <tr>
                <td colspan="3" class="text-center">
                    No non-members
                </td>
            </tr>
        }
        @foreach (IdentityUser user in await Model.NonMembers()) {
            <tr>
                <td>@user.UserName</td>
                <td>@user.Email</td>
                <td>
                    <button asp-route-userid="@user.Id"
                        class="btn btn-primary btn-sm" type="submit">
                        Change
                    </button>
                </td>
            </tr>
        }
    </tbody>
</table>
</form>

<a class="btn btn-secondary" asp-page="list">Back</a>

@functions {

    public class EditorModel : AdminPageModel {
        public UserManager<IdentityUser> UserManager;
        public RoleManager<IdentityRole> RoleManager;

        public EditorModel(UserManager<IdentityUser> userManager,
                RoleManager<IdentityRole> roleManager) {
            UserManager = userManager;
            RoleManager = roleManager;
        }

        public IdentityRole? Role { get; set; } = new();

        public Task<IList<IdentityUser>> Members() {
            if (Role?.Name != null) {
                return UserManager.GetUsersInRoleAsync(Role.Name);
            }

            return Task.FromResult(new List<IdentityUser>()
                as IList<IdentityUser>);
        }

        public async Task<IEnumerable<IdentityUser>> NonMembers() =>
                UserManager.Users.ToList().Except(await Members());

        public async Task OnGetAsync(string id) {
```

```
                Role = await RoleManager.FindByIdAsync(id);
            }

            public async Task<IActionResult> OnPostAsync(string userid,
                    string rolename) {
                Role = await RoleManager.FindByNameAsync(rolename);
                IdentityUser? user = await UserManager.FindByIdAsync(userid);
                if (user != null) {
                    IdentityResult result;
                    if (await UserManager.IsInRoleAsync(user, rolename)) {
                        result = await UserManager.RemoveFromRoleAsync(user,
                            rolename);
                    } else {
                        result =
                            await UserManager.AddToRoleAsync(user, rolename);
                    }
                    if (result.Succeeded) {
                        return RedirectToPage();
                    } else {
                        foreach (IdentityError err in result.Errors) {
                            ModelState.AddModelError("", err.Description);
                        }
                        return Page();
                    }
                }
                return Page();
            }
        }
    }
```

The user is presented with a table showing the users who are members of the role and with a table showing nonmembers. Each row contains a Change button that submits the form. The `OnPostAsync` method uses the `UserManager.FindByIdAsync` method to retrieve the user object from the database. The `IsInRoleAsync` method is used to determine whether the user is a member of the role, and the `AddToRoleAsync` and `RemoveFromRoleAsync` methods are used to add and remove the user, respectively.

Restart ASP.NET Core and request http://localhost:5000/roles/list. The list will be empty because there are no roles in the database. Click the Create button, enter Admins into the text field, and click the Submit button to create a new role. Once the role has been created, click the Edit button, and you will see the list of users who can be added to the role. Clicking the Change button will move the user in and out of the role. Click back, and the list will be updated to show the users who are members of the role, as shown in figure 38.11.

CAUTION   ASP.NET Core Identity revalidates user details when changing role assignments, which will result in an error if you try to modify a user whose details do not match the current restrictions, which happens when restrictions are introduced after the application has been deployed and the database is already populated with users created under the old roles. It is for this reason that the Razor Page in listing 38.20 checks the result from the operations to add or remove users from a role and displays any errors as validation messages.

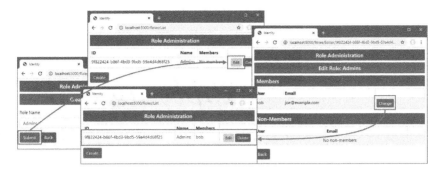

Figure 38.11   Managing roles

Summary

- The ASP.NET Core Identity framework is used to authenticate users.
- User data can be stored in an relational database, but there are other authentication mechanisms available, although some of them can be complex to set up.
- User identities are managed and authenticated using the `UserManager<T>` class, where `T` is the class used to represent users in the application.
- Roles are managed and applied using the `RoleManager<T>` class, where `T` is the class used to represent roles in the application.
- Account administration tools can be created using the standard ASP.NET Core features.

Applying ASP.NET Core Identity

In this chapter, I explain how ASP.NET Core Identity is applied to authenticate users and authorize access to application features. I create the features required for users to establish their identity, explain how access to endpoints can be controlled, and demonstrate the security features that Blazor provides. I also show two different ways to authenticate web service clients. Table 39.1 provides a guide to the chapter.

Table 39.1 Chapter guide

Problem	Solution	Listing
Authenticating users	Use the `SignInManager<T>` class to validate the credentials users provide and use the built-in middleware to trigger authentication.	3–8
Restricting access to endpoints	Use the `Authorize` attribute and the built-in middleware to control access.	9–13
Restricting access to Blazor components	Use the `Authorize` attribute and the built-in Razor Components to control access.	14–17
Restricting access to web services	Use cookie authentication or bearer tokens.	18–30

39.1 *Preparing for this chapter*

This chapter uses the projects from chapter 38. To prepare for this chapter, I am going to reset both the application data and ASP.NET Core Identity databases and create new users and roles. Open a new command prompt and run the commands shown in listing 39.1 in the `Advanced` project folder, which contains the `Advanced.csproj` file. These commands remove the existing databases and re-create them.

> **TIP** You can download the example project for this chapter—and for all the other chapters in this book—from https://github.com/manningbooks/pro-asp .net-core-7. See chapter 1 for how to get help if you have problems running the examples.

Listing 39.1 Re-creating the project databases

```
dotnet ef database drop --force --context DataContext
dotnet ef database drop --force --context IdentityContext
dotnet ef database update --context DataContext
dotnet ef database update --context IdentityContext
```

Now that the application contains multiple database context classes, the Entity Framework Core commands require the `--context` argument to select the context that a command applies to. Use the PowerShell command prompt to run the command shown in listing 39.2.

Listing 39.2 Running the example application

```
dotnet run
```

Use a browser to request http://localhost:5000/controllers, which will produce the response shown in figure 39.1.

**Figure 39.1
Running the
example
application**

The main application database is automatically reseeded when the application starts.
There is no seed data for the ASP.NET Core Identity database. Request http://
localhost:5000/users/list and http://localhost:5000/roles/list, and you will see the
responses in figure 39.2, which show the database is empty.

Figure 39.2   The empty ASP.NET Core Identity database

39.2 *Authenticating users*

In the sections that follow, I show you how to add authentication features to the example project so that users can present their credentials and establish their identity to the
application.

Authentication vs. authorization

It is important to understand the difference between authentication and authorization
when working with ASP.NET Core Identity. *Authentication*, often referred to as *AuthN*, is
the process of establishing the identity of a user, which the user does by presenting their
credentials to the application. In the case of the example application, those credentials
are a username and a password. The username is public information, but the password

(continued)

is known only by the user, and when the correct password is presented, the application is able to authenticate the user.

Authorization, often referred to as *AuthZ*, is the process of granting access to application features based on a user's identity. Authorization can be performed only when a user has been authenticated because an application has to know the identity of a user before deciding whether they are entitled to use a specific feature.

39.2.1 Creating the login feature

To enforce a security policy, the application must allow users to authenticate themselves, which is done using the ASP.NET Core Identity API. Create the `Pages/Account` folder and add to it a Razor layout named `_Layout.cshtml` with the content shown in listing 39.3. This layout will provide common content for authentication features.

> **Listing 39.3   The _Layout.cshtml file in the Pages/Account folder in the Advanced project**

```
<!DOCTYPE html>
<html>
<head>
    <title>Identity</title>
    <link href="/lib/bootstrap/css/bootstrap.min.css" rel="stylesheet" />
</head>
<body>
    <div class="m-2">
        @RenderBody()
    </div>
</body>
</html>
```

Add a Razor Page named `Login.cshtml` to the `Pages/Account` folder in the Advanced project with the content shown in listing 39.4.

> **Listing 39.4   The Login.cshtml file in the Pages/Account folder of the Advanced project**

```
@page
@model LoginModel

<div class="bg-primary text-center text-white p-2"><h4>Log In</h4></div>

<div class="m-1 text-danger" asp-validation-summary="All"></div>

<form method="post">
    <input type="hidden" name="returnUrl" value="@Model.ReturnUrl" />
    <div class="form-group">
        <label>UserName</label>
        <input class="form-control" asp-for="UserName" />
    </div>
    <div class="form-group">
```

```
            <label>Password</label>
            <input asp-for="Password" type="password" class="form-control" />
        </div>
        <button class="btn btn-primary mt-2" type="submit">Log In</button>
</form>

@functions {

    public class LoginModel : PageModel {
        private SignInManager<IdentityUser> signInManager;

        public LoginModel(SignInManager<IdentityUser> signinMgr) {
            signInManager = signinMgr;
        }

        [BindProperty]
        public string UserName { get; set; } = string.Empty;

        [BindProperty]
        public string Password { get; set; } = string.Empty;

        [BindProperty(SupportsGet = true)]
        public string? ReturnUrl { get; set; }

        public async Task<IActionResult> OnPostAsync() {
            if (ModelState.IsValid) {
                Microsoft.AspNetCore.Identity.SignInResult result =
                    await signInManager.PasswordSignInAsync(UserName,
                        Password, false, false);
                if (result.Succeeded) {
                    return Redirect(ReturnUrl ?? "/");
                }
                ModelState.AddModelError("",
                    "Invalid username or password");
            }
            return Page();
        }
    }
}
```

ASP.NET Core Identity provides the `SigninManager<T>` class to manage logins, where the generic type argument T is the class that represents users in the application, which is `IdentityUser` for the example application. Table 39.2 describes the `Signin-Manager<T>` members I use in this chapter.

Table 39.2   Useful SigninManager<T> members

Name	Description
PasswordSignInAsync(name, password, persist, lockout)	This method attempts authentication using the specified username and password. The `persist` argument determines whether a successful authentication produces a cookie that persists after the browser is closed. The `lockout` argument determines whether the account should be locked if authentication fails.
SignOutAsync()	This method signs out the user.

The Razor Page presents the user with a form that collects a username and a password, which are used to perform authentication with the `PasswordSignInAsync` method, like this:

```
...
Microsoft.AspNetCore.Identity.SignInResult result =
    await signInManager.PasswordSignInAsync(UserName,
        Password, false, false);
...
```

The result from the `PasswordSignInAsync` methods is a `SignInResult` object, which defines a `Suceeded` property that is `true` if the authentication is successful. (There is also a `SignInResult` class defined in the `Microsoft.AspNetCore.Mvc` namespace, which is why I used a fully qualified class name in the listing.)

Authentication in an ASP.NET Core application is usually triggered when the user tries to access an endpoint that requires authorization, and it is convention to return the user to that endpoint if authentication is successful, which is why the `Login` page defines a `ReturnUrl` property that is used in a redirection if the user has provided valid credentials.

```
...
if (result.Succeeded) {
    return Redirect(ReturnUrl ?? "/");
}
...
```

If the user hasn't provided valid credentials, then a validation message is shown, and the page is redisplayed.

Protecting the authentication cookie

The authentication cookie contains the user's identity, and ASP.NET Core trusts that requests containing the cookie originate from the authenticated user. This means you should use HTTPS for production applications that use ASP.NET Core Identity to prevent the cookie from being intercepted by an intermediary. See part 2 for details of enabling HTTPS in ASP.NET Core.

39.2.2 *Inspecting the ASP.NET Core Identity cookie*

When a user is authenticated, a cookie is added to the response so that subsequent requests can be identified as being already authenticated. Add a Razor Page named `Details.cshtml` to the `Pages/Account` folder of the Advanced project with the content shown in listing 39.5, which displays the cookie when it is present.

> Listing 39.5 The Details.cshtml file in the Pages/Account folder of the Advanced folder

```
@page
@model DetailsModel

<table class="table table-sm table-bordered">
    <tbody>
```

```
        @if (Model.Cookie == null) {
            <tr><th class="text-center">No Identity Cookie</th></tr>
        } else {
            <tr>
                <th>Cookie</th>
                <td class="text-break">@Model.Cookie</td>
            </tr>
        }
    </tbody>
</table>

@functions {

    public class DetailsModel : PageModel {

        public string? Cookie { get; set; }

        public void OnGet() {
            Cookie = Request.Cookies[".AspNetCore.Identity.Application"];
        }
    }
}
```

The name used for the ASP.NET Core Identity cookie is `.AspNetCore.Identity` `.Application`, and this page retrieves the cookie from the request and displays its value or a placeholder message if there is no cookie.

39.2.3 Creating a Sign-Out page

It is important to give users the ability to sign out so they can explicitly delete the cookie, especially if public machines may be used to access the application. Add a Razor Page named `Logout.cshtml` to the `Pages/Account` folder of the `Advanced` folder with the content shown in listing 39.6.

> **Listing 39.6   The Logout.cshtml file in the Pages/Account folder in the Advanced project**

```
@page
@model LogoutModel

<div class="bg-primary text-center text-white p-2"><h4>Log Out</h4></div>
<div class="m-2">
    <h6>You are logged out</h6>
    <a asp-page="Login" class="btn btn-secondary">OK</a>
</div>

@functions {

    public class LogoutModel : PageModel {
        private SignInManager<IdentityUser> signInManager;

        public LogoutModel(SignInManager<IdentityUser> signInMgr) {
            signInManager = signInMgr;
        }

        public async Task OnGetAsync() {
```

```
            await signInManager.SignOutAsync();
        }
    }
}
```

This page calls the `SignOutAsync` method described in table 39.2 to sign the application out of the application. The ASP.NET Core Identity cookie will be deleted so that the browser will not include it in future requests (and invalidated the cookie so that requests will not be treated as authenticated even if the cookie is used again anyway).

39.2.4 *Testing the authentication feature*

Restart ASP.NET Core and request http://localhost:5000/users/list. Click the Create button and fill out the form using the data shown in table 39.3. Click the Submit button to submit the form and create the user account.

Table 39.3   **The data values to create a user**

Field	Description
UserName	bob
Email	bob@example.com
Password	secret

Navigate to http://localhost:5000/account/login and authenticate using the username and password from table 39.3. No return URL has been specified, and you will be redirected to the root URL once you have been authenticated. Request http://localhost:5000/account/details, and you will see the ASP.NET Core Identity cookie. Request http://localhost:5000/account/logout to log out of the application and return to http://localhost:5000/account/details to confirm that the cookie has been deleted, as shown in figure 39.3.

Figure 39.3   **Authenticating a user**

39.2.5 *Enabling the Identity authentication middleware*

ASP.NET Core Identity provides a middleware component that detects the cookie created by the `SignInManager<T>` class and populates the `HttpContext` object with details of the authenticated user. This provides endpoints with details about the user without needing to be aware of the authentication process or having to deal directly with the cookie created by the authentication process. Listing 39.7 adds the authentication middleware to the example application's request pipeline.

Listing 39.7   Enabling middleware in the Program.cs file in the Advanced folder

```
using Microsoft.EntityFrameworkCore;
using Advanced.Models;
using Microsoft.AspNetCore.Identity;

var builder = WebApplication.CreateBuilder(args);

builder.Services.AddControllersWithViews();
builder.Services.AddRazorPages();
builder.Services.AddServerSideBlazor();

builder.Services.AddDbContext<DataContext>(opts => {
    opts.UseSqlServer(
        builder.Configuration["ConnectionStrings:PeopleConnection"]);
    opts.EnableSensitiveDataLogging(true);
});

builder.Services.AddSingleton<Advanced.Services.ToggleService>();

builder.Services.AddDbContext<IdentityContext>(opts =>
    opts.UseSqlServer(builder.Configuration[
        "ConnectionStrings:IdentityConnection"]));
builder.Services.AddIdentity<IdentityUser, IdentityRole>()
    .AddEntityFrameworkStores<IdentityContext>();

builder.Services.Configure<IdentityOptions>(opts => {
    opts.Password.RequiredLength = 6;
    opts.Password.RequireNonAlphanumeric = false;
    opts.Password.RequireLowercase = false;
    opts.Password.RequireUppercase = false;
    opts.Password.RequireDigit = false;
    opts.User.RequireUniqueEmail = true;
    opts.User.AllowedUserNameCharacters = "abcdefghijklmnopqrstuvwxyz";
});

var app = builder.Build();

app.UseStaticFiles();

app.UseAuthentication();

app.MapControllers();
app.MapControllerRoute("controllers",
    "controllers/{controller=Home}/{action=Index}/{id?}");
app.MapRazorPages();
app.MapBlazorHub();
app.MapFallbackToPage("/_Host");

app.UseBlazorFrameworkFiles("/webassembly");
app.MapFallbackToFile("/webassembly/{*path:nonfile}",
    "/webassembly/index.html");
```

```
var context = app.Services.CreateScope().ServiceProvider
    .GetRequiredService<DataContext>();
SeedData.SeedDatabase(context);

app.Run();
```

The middleware sets the value of the `HttpContext.User` property to a `Claims-Principal` object. *Claims* are pieces of information about a user and details of the source of that information, providing a general-purpose approach to describing the information known about a user.

The `ClaimsPrincipal` class is part of .NET Core and isn't directly useful in most ASP.NET Core applications, but there are two nested properties that are useful in most applications, as described in table 39.4.

Table 39.4 Useful Nested ClaimsPrincipal Properties

Name	Description
`ClaimsPrincipal.Identity.Name`	This property returns the username, which will be `null` if there is no user associated with the request.
`ClaimsPrincipal.Identity.IsAuthenticated`	This property returns `true` if the user associated with the request has been authenticated.

The username provided through the `ClaimsPrincipal` object can be used to obtain the ASP.NET Core Identity user object, as shown in listing 39.8.

Listing 39.8 User details in the Details.cshtml file in the Pages/Account folder of the Advanced project

```
@page
@model DetailsModel

<table class="table table-sm table-bordered">
    <tbody>
        @if (Model.IdentityUser == null) {
            <tr><th class="text-center">No User</th></tr>
        } else {
            <tr><th>Name</th><td>@Model.IdentityUser.UserName</td></tr>
            <tr><th>Email</th><td>@Model.IdentityUser.Email</td></tr>
        }
    </tbody>
</table>

@functions {

    public class DetailsModel : PageModel {
        private UserManager<IdentityUser> userManager;

        public DetailsModel(UserManager<IdentityUser> manager) {
            userManager = manager;
        }
```

```
        public IdentityUser? IdentityUser { get; set; }

        public async Task OnGetAsync() {
            if (User.Identity != null
                    && User.Identity.Name != null
                    && User.Identity.IsAuthenticated) {
                IdentityUser = await
                    userManager.FindByNameAsync(User.Identity.Name);
            }
        }
    }
}
```

The `HttpContext.User` property can be accessed through the `User` convenience property defined by the `PageModel` and `ControllerBase` classes. This Razor Page confirms that there is an authenticated user associated with the request and gets the `IdentityUser` object that describes the user.

Restart ASP.NET Core, request http://localhost:5000/account/login, and authenticate using the details in table 39.3. Request http://localhost:5000/account/details, and you will see how the ASP.NET Core Identity middleware enabled in listing 39.7 has processed the cookie to associate user details with the request, as shown in figure 39.4.

Considering two-factor authentication

I have performed single-factor authentication in this chapter, which is where the user authenticates using a single piece of information known to them in advance: the password.

ASP.NET Core Identity also supports two-factor authentication, where the user needs something extra, usually something that is given to the user at the moment they want to authenticate. The most common examples are a value from a hardware token or smartphone app or an authentication code that is sent as an email or text message. (Strictly speaking, the two factors can be anything, including fingerprints, iris scans, and voice recognition, although these are options that are rarely required for most web applications.)

Security is increased because an attacker needs to know the user's password *and* have access to whatever provides the second factor, such as an e-mail account or cell phone.

I don't show two-factor authentication in the book for two reasons. The first is that it requires a lot of preparatory work, such as setting up the infrastructure that distributes the second-factor e-mails and texts and implementing the validation logic, all of which is beyond the scope of this book.

The second reason is that two-factor authentication forces the user to remember to jump through an additional hoop to authenticate, such as remembering their phone or keeping a security token nearby, something that isn't always appropriate for web applications. I carried a hardware token of one sort or another for more than a decade in various jobs, and I lost count of the number of times that I couldn't log in to an employer's system because I left the token at home. If you are considering two-factor authentication, then I recommend using one of the many hosted providers that will take care of distributing and managing the second factors for you.

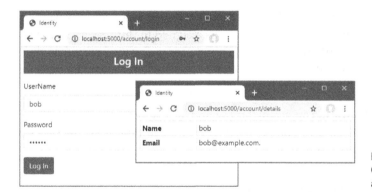

Figure 39.4
Getting details of an
authenticated user

39.3 *Authorizing access to endpoints*

Once an application has an authentication feature, user identities can be used to restrict access to endpoints. In the sections that follow, I explain the process for enabling authorization and demonstrate how an authorization policy can be defined.

39.3.1 *Applying the authorization attribute*

The Authorize attribute is used to restrict access to an endpoint and can be applied to individual action or page handler methods or to controller or page model classes, in which case the policy applies to all the methods defined by the class. I want to restrict access to the user and role administration tools created in chapter 38. When there are multiple Razor Pages or controllers for which the same authorization policy is required, it is a good idea to define a common base class to which the Authorize attribute can be applied because it ensures that you won't accidentally omit the attribute and allow unauthorized access. It is for this reason that I defined the AdminPageModel class and used it as the base for all the administration tool page models in chapter 38. Listing 39.9 applies the Authorize attribute to the AdminPageModel class to create the authorization policy.

> **Listing 39.9 Applying an attribute in the AdminPageModel.cs file in the Pages folder in the Advanced project**

```
using Microsoft.AspNetCore.Mvc.RazorPages;
using Microsoft.AspNetCore.Authorization;

namespace Advanced.Pages {

    [Authorize(Roles="Admins")]
    public class AdminPageModel : PageModel {

    }
}
```

The Authorize attribute can be applied without arguments, which restricts access to any authenticated user. The Roles argument is used to further restrict access to users who are members of specific roles, which are expressed as a comma-separated list. The attribute in this listing restricts access to users assigned to the Admins role. The authorization restrictions are inherited, which means that applying the attribute to the base class restricts access to all the Razor Pages created to manage users and roles in chapter 38.

> **NOTE** If you want to restrict access to most, but not all, of the action methods in a controller, then you can apply the Authorize attribute to the controller class and the AllowAnonymous attribute to just the action methods for which unauthenticated access is required.

39.3.2 *Enabling the authorization middleware*

The authorization policy is enforced by a middleware component, which must be added to the application's request pipeline, as shown in listing 39.10.

> **Listing 39.10   Adding middleware in the Program.cs file in the Advanced project**

```
...
app.UseStaticFiles();

app.UseAuthentication();
app.UseAuthorization();

app.MapControllers();
...
```

The UseAuthorization method must be called between the UseRouting and UseEndpoints methods and after the UseAuthentication method has been called. This ensures that the authorization component can access the user data and inspect the authorization policy after the endpoint has been selected but before the request is handled.

39.3.3 *Creating the access denied endpoint*

The application must deal with two different types of authorization failure. If no user has been authenticated when a restricted endpoint is requested, then the authorization middleware will return a challenge response, which will trigger a redirection to the login page so the user can present their credentials and prove they should be able to access the endpoint.

But if an authenticated user requests a restricted endpoint and doesn't pass the authorization checks, then an access denied response is generated so the application can display a suitable warning to the user. Add a Razor Page named AccessDenied.cshtml to the Pages/Account folder of the Advanced folder with the content shown in listing 39.11.

Listing 39.11 The AccessDenied.cshtml file in the Pages/Account folder of the Advanced project

```
@page

<h4 class="bg-danger text-white text-center p-2">Access Denied</h4>

<div class="m-2">
    <h6>You are not authorized for this URL</h6>
    <a class="btn btn-outline-danger" href="/">OK</a>
    <a class="btn btn-outline-secondary" asp-page="Logout">Logout</a>
</div>
```

This page displays a warning message to the user, with a button that navigates to the root URL. There is typically little the user can do to resolve authorization failures without administrative intervention, and my preference is to keep the access denied response as simple as possible.

39.3.4 *Creating the seed data*

In listing 39.9, I restricted access to the user and role administration tools so they can be accessed only by users in the Admin role. There is no such role in the database, which creates a problem: I am locked out of the administration tools because there is no authorized account that will let me create the role.

I could have created an administration user and role before applying the Authorize attribute, but that complicates deploying the application, when making code changes should be avoided. Instead, I am going to create seed data for ASP.NET Core Identity to ensure there will always be at least one account that can be used to access the user and role management tools. Add a class file named IdentitySeedData.cs to the Models folder in the Advanced project and use it to define the class shown in listing 39.12.

Listing 39.12 The IdentitySeedData.cs file in the Models folder of the Advanced project

```
using Microsoft.AspNetCore.Identity;

namespace Advanced.Models {
    public class IdentitySeedData {

        public static void CreateAdminAccount(
                IServiceProvider serviceProvider,
                IConfiguration configuration) {

            CreateAdminAccountAsync(serviceProvider, configuration)
                .Wait();
        }

        public static async Task CreateAdminAccountAsync(IServiceProvider
                serviceProvider, IConfiguration configuration) {

            serviceProvider =
                serviceProvider.CreateScope().ServiceProvider;
```

```
UserManager<IdentityUser> userManager = serviceProvider
    .GetRequiredService<UserManager<IdentityUser>>();
RoleManager<IdentityRole> roleManager = serviceProvider
    .GetRequiredService<RoleManager<IdentityRole>>();

string username = configuration["Data:AdminUser:Name"]
    ?? "admin";
string email = configuration["Data:AdminUser:Email"]
    ?? "admin@example.com";
string password = configuration["Data:AdminUser:Password"]
    ?? "secret";
string role = configuration["Data:AdminUser:Role"]
    ?? "Admins";

if (await userManager.FindByNameAsync(username) == null) {
    if (await roleManager.FindByNameAsync(role) == null) {
        await roleManager.CreateAsync(new IdentityRole(role));
    }

    IdentityUser user = new IdentityUser {
        UserName = username,
        Email = email
    };

    IdentityResult result = await userManager
        .CreateAsync(user, password);
    if (result.Succeeded) {
        await userManager.AddToRoleAsync(user, role);
    }
    }
   }
  }
}
```

The `UserManager<T>` and `RoleManager<T>` services are scoped, which means I need to create a new scope before requesting the services since the seeding will be done when the application starts. The seeding code creates a user account that is assigned to a role. The values for the seed data are read from the application's configuration with fallback values, making it easy to configure the seeded account without needing a code change. Listing 39.13 adds a statement to the `Program.cs` file so that the database is seeded when the application starts.

CAUTION   Putting passwords in code files or plain-text configuration files means you must make it part of your deployment process to change the default account's password when you deploy the application and initialize a new database for the first time. You can also use the user secrets feature to keep sensitive data outside of the project.

```
...
var context = app.Services.CreateScope().ServiceProvider
    .GetRequiredService<DataContext>();
SeedData.SeedDatabase(context);
IdentitySeedData.CreateAdminAccount(app.Services, app.Configuration);

app.Run();
...
```

39.3.5 *Testing the authentication sequence*

Restart ASP.NET Core and request http://localhost:5000/account/logout to ensure that no user is logged in to the application. Without logging in, request http://localhost:5000/users/list. The endpoint that will be selected to handle the request requires authentication, and the login prompt will be shown since there is no authenticated user associated with the request. Authenticate with the username `bob` and the password `secret`. This user doesn't have access to the restricted endpoint, and the access denied response will be shown, as illustrated by figure 39.5.

**Figure 39.5
A user without
authorization**

Click the Logout button and request http://localhost:5000/users/list again, which will lead to the login prompt being displayed. Authenticate with the username `admin` and the password `secret`. This is the user account created by the seed data and that is a member of the role specified by the `Authorize` attribute. The user passes the authorization check, and the requested Razor Page is displayed, as shown in figure 39.6.

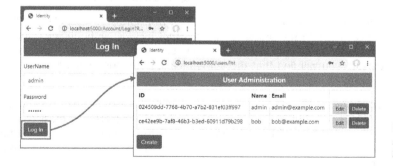

**Figure 39.6.
A user with
authorization**

Changing the authorization URLs

The `/Account/Login` and `/Account/AccessDenied` URLs are the defaults used by ASP.NET Core authorization files. These can be changed in the `Program.cs` file using the options pattern, like this:

```
...
builder.Services.Configure<CookieAuthenticationOptions>(
    IdentityConstants.ApplicationScheme,
  opts => {
     opts.LoginPath = "/Authenticate";
     opts.AccessDeniedPath = "/NotAllowed";
  });
...
```

Configuration is performed using the `CookieAuthenticationOptions` class, defined in the `Microsoft.AspNetCore.Authentication.Cookies` namespace. The `LoginPath` property is used to specify the path to which browsers will be redirected when an unauthenticated user attempts to access a restricted endpoint. The `Access-DeniedPath` property is used to specify the path when an authenticated user attempts to access a restricted endpoint and does not have authorization.

39.4 *Authorizing access to Blazor applications*

The simplest way to protect Blazor applications is to restrict access to the action method or Razor Page that acts as the entry point. In listing 39.14, I added the `Authorize` attribute to the page model class for the `_Host` page, which is the entry point for the Blazor application in the example project.

Understanding OAuth and IDENTITYSERVER

If you read the Microsoft documentation, you will be left with the impression that you need to use a third-party server called `IdentityServer` (https://duendesoftware .com) to authenticate web services.

`IdentityServer` is a high-quality open-source package that provides authentication and authorization services, with paid-for options for add-ons and support. `Identity-Server` provides support for `OAuth`, which is a standard for managing authentication and authorization and provides packages for a range of client-side frameworks.

What the Microsoft documentation is saying—albeit awkwardly—is that Microsoft has used `IdentityServer` in the project templates that include authentication for web services. If you create an Angular or React project using an ASP.NET Core template provided by Microsoft, you will find that the authentication has been implemented using `IdentityServer`.

Authentication is complex, and `IdentityServer` can be difficult to set up correctly. I like `IdentityServer`, but it is not essential and is not required by most projects. `IdentityServer` may be useful if your project needs to support complex authentication scenarios, but my advice is not to rush into using third-party authentication servers until they are essential.

Listing 39.14 Applying an attribute in the _Host.cshtml file in the Pages folder of the Advanced project

```
@page "/"
@{ Layout = null; }
@model HostModel
@using Microsoft.AspNetCore.Authorization

<!DOCTYPE html>
<html>
<head>
    <title>@ViewBag.Title</title>
    <link href="/lib/bootstrap/css/bootstrap.min.css" rel="stylesheet" />
    <base href="~/" />
</head>
<body>
    <div class="m-2">
        <component type="typeof(Advanced.Blazor.Routed)"
            render-mode="Server" />
    </div>
    <script src="_framework/blazor.server.js"></script>
    <script src="~/interop.js"></script>
</body>
</html>

@functions {

    [Authorize]
    public class HostModel : PageModel { }
}
```

This has the effect of preventing unauthenticated users from accessing the Blazor application. Request http://localhost:5000/account/logout to ensure the browser doesn't have an authentication cookie and then request http://localhost:5000. This request will be handled by the _Host page, but the authorization middleware will trigger the redirection to the login prompt. Authenticate with the username bob and the password secret, and you will be granted access to the Blazor application, as shown in figure 39.7.

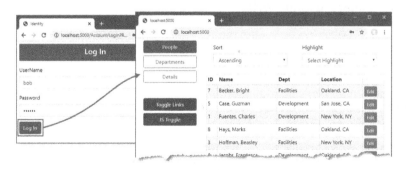

Figure 39.7   Restricting access to the Blazor endpoint

39.4.1 *Performing authorization in Blazor components*

Restricting access to the endpoint is an effective technique, but it applies the same level of authorization to all the Blazor functionality. For applications that require more granular restrictions, Blazor provides the `AuthorizeRouteView` component, which allows different content to be displayed for authorized and unauthorized when components are managed using URL routing. Listing 39.15 adds the `AuthorizeRouteView` to the routing component in the example application.

> **Listing 39.15   Adding a component in the Routed.razor file in the Blazor folder of the Advanced project**

```
@using Microsoft.AspNetCore.Components.Authorization

<Router AppAssembly="typeof(Program).Assembly">
    <Found>
        <AuthorizeRouteView RouteData="@context"
                DefaultLayout="typeof(NavLayout)">
            <NotAuthorized Context="authContext">
                <h4 class="bg-danger text-white text-center p-2">
                    Not Authorized
                </h4>
                <div class="text-center">
                    You may need to log in as a different user
                </div>
            </NotAuthorized>
        </AuthorizeRouteView>
    </Found>
    <NotFound>
        <h4 class="bg-danger text-white text-center p-2">
            No Matching Route Found
        </h4>
    </NotFound>
</Router>
```

The `NotAuthorized` section is used to define the content that will be presented to users when they attempt to access a restricted resource. To demonstrate this feature, I am going to restrict access to the `DepartmentList` component to users assigned to the `Admins` role, as shown in listing 39.16.

> **Listing 39.16   Restricting access in the DepartmentList.cshtml file in the Blazor folder in the Advanced project**

```
@page "/departments"
@page "/depts"
@using Microsoft.AspNetCore.Authorization
@attribute [Authorize(Roles = "Admins")]

<CascadingValue Name="BgTheme" Value="Theme" IsFixed="false">
    <TableTemplate RowType="Department" RowData="Departments"
                Highlight="@(d => d.Name)"
                SortDirection="@(d => d.Name)">
```

```
            <Header>
            <tr>
                <th>ID</th><th>Name</th><th>People</th><th>Locations</th>
            </tr>
            </Header>
            <RowTemplate Context="d">
                <td>@d.Departmentid</td>
                <td>@d.Name</td>
                <td>
                    @(String.Join(", ", d.People!.Select(p => p.Surname)))
                </td>
                <td>
                    @(String.Join(", ", d.People!.Select(p =>
                        p.Location!.City).Distinct()))
                </td>
            </RowTemplate>
        </TableTemplate>
    </CascadingValue>
</CascadingValue>

<SelectFilter Title="@("Theme")" Values="Themes"
            @bind-SelectedValue="Theme" />

<button class="btn btn-primary" @onclick="HandleClick">People</button>

@code {
    [Inject]
    public DataContext? Context { get; set; }

    public IEnumerable<Department>? Departments => Context?.Departments?
        .Include(d => d.People!).ThenInclude(p => p.Location!);

    public string Theme { get; set; } = "info";
    public string[] Themes =
        new string[] { "primary", "info", "success" };

    [Inject]
    public NavigationManager? NavManager { get; set; }

    public void HandleClick() => NavManager?.NavigateTo("/people");
}
```

I have used the @attribute directive to apply the Authorize attribute to the component. Restart ASP.NET Core and request http://localhost:5000/account/logout to remove the authentication cookie and then request http://localhost:5000. When prompted, authenticate with the username bob and the password secret. You will see the Blazor application, but when you click the Departments button, you will see the authorization content defined in listing 39.15, as shown in figure 39.8. Log out again and log in as admin with the password secret, and you will be able to use the restricted component.

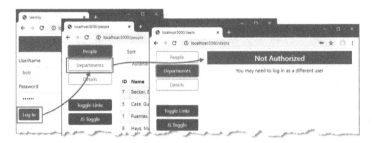

Figure 39.8
Using authorization in
a Blazor application

39.4.2 *Displaying content to authorized users*

The `AuthorizeView` component is used to restrict access to sections of content rendered by a component. In listing 39.17, I have changed the authorization for the `DepartmentList` component so that any authenticated user can access the page and use the `AuthorizeView` component so that the contents of the `Locations` column in the table is shown only to users assigned to the `Admins` group.

> **Listing 39.17   Selective content in the DepartmentList.razor file in the Blazor folder in the Advanced project**

```
@page "/departments"
@page "/depts"
@using Microsoft.AspNetCore.Authorization
@using Microsoft.AspNetCore.Components.Authorization
@attribute [Authorize]

<CascadingValue Name="BgTheme" Value="Theme" IsFixed="false">
    <TableTemplate RowType="Department" RowData="Departments"
                Highlight="@(d => d.Name)"
                SortDirection="@(d => d.Name)">
        <Header>
        <tr>
            <th>ID</th><th>Name</th><th>People</th><th>Locations</th>
        </tr>
        </Header>
        <RowTemplate Context="d">
            <td>@d.Departmentid</td>
            <td>@d.Name</td>
            <td>
                @(String.Join(", ", d.People!.Select(p => p.Surname)))
            </td>
            <td>
                <AuthorizeView Roles="Admins">
                    <Authorized>
                        @(String.Join(", ",d.People!
                            .Select(p => p.Location!.City).Distinct()))
                    </Authorized>
                    <NotAuthorized>
                        (Not authorized)
                    </NotAuthorized>
                </AuthorizeView>
            </td>
```

```
                </RowTemplate>
        </TableTemplate>
</CascadingValue>

<SelectFilter Title="@("Theme")" Values="Themes"
              @bind-SelectedValue="Theme" />

<button class="btn btn-primary" @onclick="HandleClick">People</button>

@code {
    [Inject]
    public DataContext? Context { get; set; }

    public IEnumerable<Department>? Departments => Context?.Departments?
        .Include(d => d.People!).ThenInclude(p => p.Location!);

    public string Theme { get; set; } = "info";
    public string[] Themes =
        new string[] { "primary", "info", "success" };

    [Inject]
    public NavigationManager? NavManager { get; set; }

    public void HandleClick() => NavManager?.NavigateTo("/people");
}
```

The `AuthorizeView` component is configured with the `Roles` property, which accepts a comma-separated list of authorized roles. The `Authorized` section contains the content that will be shown to authorized users. The `NotAuthorized` section contains the content that will be shown to unauthorized users.

TIP You can omit the `NotAuthorized` section if you don't need to show content to unauthorized users.

Restart ASP.NET Core and authenticate as `bob`, with password `secret`, before requesting http://localhost:5000/depts. This user is not authorized to see the contents of the `Locations` column, as shown in figure 39.9. Authenticate as `admin`, with password `secret`, and request http://localhost:5000/depts again. This time the user is a member of the `Admins` role and passes the authorization checks, also shown in figure 39.9.

Figure 39.9 Selectively displaying content based on authorization

39.5   *Authenticating and authorizing web services*

The authorization process in the previous section relies on being able to redirect the client to a URL that allows the user to enter their credentials. A different approach is required when adding authentication and authorization to a web service because there is no option to present the user with an HTML form to collect their credentials. The first step in adding support for web services authentication is to disable the redirections so that the client will receive HTTP error responses when attempting to request an endpoint that requires authentication. Add a class file named `Cookie-AuthenticationExtensions.cs` to the `Advanced` folder and use it to define the extension method shown in listing 39.18.

> **Listing 39.18   The CookieAuthenticationExtensions.cs file in the Advanced folder**

```
using System.Linq.Expressions;

namespace Microsoft.AspNetCore.Authentication.Cookies {
    public static class CookieAuthenticationExtensions {

        public static void DisableRedirectForPath(
            this CookieAuthenticationEvents events,
            Expression<Func<CookieAuthenticationEvents,
                Func<RedirectContext<CookieAuthenticationOptions>,
                Task>>> expr,
            string path, int statuscode) {

            string propertyName
                = ((MemberExpression)expr.Body).Member.Name;
            var oldHandler = expr.Compile().Invoke(events);

            Func<RedirectContext<CookieAuthenticationOptions>, Task>
                newHandler = context => {
                    if (context.Request.Path.StartsWithSegments(path)) {
                        context.Response.StatusCode = statuscode;
                    } else {
                        oldHandler(context);
                    }
                    return Task.CompletedTask;
                };

            typeof(CookieAuthenticationEvents).GetProperty(propertyName)?
                .SetValue(events, newHandler);
        }
    }
}
```

This code is hard to follow. ASP.NET Core provides the `CookieAuthentication-Options` class, which is used to configure cookie-based authentication. The `Cookie-AuthenticationOptions.Events` property returns a `CookieAuthenticationEvents` object, which is used to set the handlers for the events triggered by the authentication system, including the redirections that occur when the user requests unauthorized content. The extension methods in listing 39.18 replaces the default handler for an event with one that performs redirection only if the request doesn't start with a specified path string. Listing 39.19 uses the extension method to replace the `OnRedirectToLogin` and `OnRedirectToAccessDenied` handlers so that redirections are not performed when the request path starts with `/api`.

> **Listing 39.19** **Preventing redirection in the Program.cs file in the Advanced folder**

```
using Microsoft.EntityFrameworkCore;
using Advanced.Models;
using Microsoft.AspNetCore.Identity;
using Microsoft.AspNetCore.Authentication.Cookies;

var builder = WebApplication.CreateBuilder(args);

builder.Services.AddControllersWithViews();
builder.Services.AddRazorPages();
builder.Services.AddServerSideBlazor();

builder.Services.AddDbContext<DataContext>(opts => {
    opts.UseSqlServer(
        builder.Configuration["ConnectionStrings:PeopleConnection"]);
    opts.EnableSensitiveDataLogging(true);
});

builder.Services.AddSingleton<Advanced.Services.ToggleService>();

builder.Services.AddDbContext<IdentityContext>(opts =>
    opts.UseSqlServer(builder.Configuration[
        "ConnectionStrings:IdentityConnection"]));
builder.Services.AddIdentity<IdentityUser, IdentityRole>()
    .AddEntityFrameworkStores<IdentityContext>();

builder.Services.Configure<IdentityOptions>(opts => {
    opts.Password.RequiredLength = 6;
    opts.Password.RequireNonAlphanumeric = false;
    opts.Password.RequireLowercase = false;
    opts.Password.RequireUppercase = false;
    opts.Password.RequireDigit = false;
    opts.User.RequireUniqueEmail = true;
    opts.User.AllowedUserNameCharacters = "abcdefghijklmnopqrstuvwxyz";
});

builder.Services.AddAuthentication(opts => {
    opts.DefaultScheme =
        CookieAuthenticationDefaults.AuthenticationScheme;
    opts.DefaultChallengeScheme =
        CookieAuthenticationDefaults.AuthenticationScheme;
}).AddCookie(opts => {
    opts.Events.DisableRedirectForPath(e => e.OnRedirectToLogin,
        "/api", StatusCodes.Status401Unauthorized);
    opts.Events.DisableRedirectForPath(e => e.OnRedirectToAccessDenied,
        "/api", StatusCodes.Status403Forbidden);
});
```

```
var app = builder.Build();

app.UseStaticFiles();

app.UseAuthentication();
app.UseAuthorization();

app.MapControllers();
app.MapControllerRoute("controllers",
    "controllers/{controller=Home}/{action=Index}/{id?}");
app.MapRazorPages();
app.MapBlazorHub();
app.MapFallbackToPage("/_Host");

app.UseBlazorFrameworkFiles("/webassembly");
app.MapFallbackToFile("/webassembly/{*path:nonfile}",
    "/webassembly/index.html");

var context = app.Services.CreateScope().ServiceProvider
    .GetRequiredService<DataContext>();
SeedData.SeedDatabase(context);
IdentitySeedData.CreateAdminAccount(app.Services, app.Configuration);

app.Run();
```

The `AddAuthentication` method is used to select cookie-based authentication and is chained with the `AddCookie` method to replace the event handlers that would otherwise trigger redirections.

39.5.1 *Building a simple JavaScript client*

To demonstrate how to perform authentication with web services, I am going to create a simple JavaScript client that will consume data from the `Data` controller in the example project.

> **TIP** You don't have to be familiar with JavaScript to follow the examples in this part of the chapter. It is the server-side code that is important and the way it supports authentication by the client so that it can access the web service.

Add an HTML Page called `webclient.html` to the `wwwroot` folder of the `Advanced` project with the elements shown in listing 39.20.

> **Listing 39.20   The contents of the webclient.html file in the wwwroot folder of the Advanced project**

```
<!DOCTYPE html>
<html>
<head>
    <title>Web Service Authentication</title>
    <link href="/lib/bootstrap/css/bootstrap.min.css" rel="stylesheet" />
    <script type="text/javascript" src="webclient.js"></script>
</head>
<body>
```

```
    <div id="controls" class="m-2"></div>
    <div id="data" class="m-2 p-2">
        No data
    </div>
</body>
</html>
```

Add a JavaScript file named `webclient.js` to the `wwwroot` of the Advanced project with the content shown in listing 39.21.

Listing 39.21   The webclient.js file in the wwwroot folder of the Advanced project

```javascript
const username = "bob";
const password = "secret";

window.addEventListener("DOMContentLoaded", () => {
    const controlDiv = document.getElementById("controls");
    createButton(controlDiv, "Get Data", getData);
    createButton(controlDiv, "Log In", login);
    createButton(controlDiv, "Log Out", logout);
});

function login() {
    // do nothing
}

function logout() {
    // do nothing
}

async function getData() {
    let response = await fetch("/api/people");
    if (response.ok) {
        let jsonData = await response.json();
        displayData(...jsonData.map(item => `${item.surname},
            ${item.firstname}`));
    } else {
        displayData(`Error: ${response.status}: ${response.statusText}`);
    }
}

function displayData(...items) {
    const dataDiv = document.getElementById("data");
    dataDiv.innerHTML = "";
    items.forEach(item => {
        const itemDiv = document.createElement("div");
        itemDiv.innerText = item;
        itemDiv.style.wordWrap = "break-word";
        dataDiv.appendChild(itemDiv);
    })
}

function createButton(parent, label, handler) {
    const button = document.createElement("button");
    button.classList.add("btn", "btn-primary", "m-2");
```

```
        button.innerText = label;
        button.onclick = handler;
        parent.appendChild(button);
}
```

This code presents the user with Get Data and Log In and Log Out buttons. Clicking the Get Data button sends an HTTP request using the Fetch API, processes the JSON result, and displays a list of names. The other buttons do nothing, but I'll use them in later examples to authenticate with the ASP.NET Core application using the hardwired credentials in the JavaScript code.

> **CAUTION** This is just a simple client to demonstrate server-side authentication features. If you need to write a JavaScript client, then consider a framework such as Angular or React. Regardless of how you build your clients, do not include hardwired credentials in the JavaScript files.

Request http://localhost:5000/webclient.html and click the Get Data button. The JavaScript client will send an HTTP request to the `Data` controller and display the results, as shown in figure 39.10.

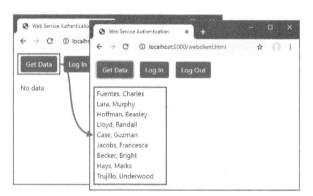

Figure 39.10 A simple web client

39.5.2 Restricting access to the web service

The standard authorization features are used to restrict access to web service endpoints, and in listing 39.22, I have applied the `Authorize` attribute to the `DataController` class.

> **Listing 39.22 Applying an attribute in the DataController.cs file in the Controllers folder of the Advanced project**

```
using Advanced.Models;
using Microsoft.AspNetCore.Mvc;
using Microsoft.EntityFrameworkCore;
using Microsoft.AspNetCore.Authorization;

namespace Advanced.Controllers {

    [ApiController]
```

```
[Route("/api/people")]
[Authorize]
public class DataController : ControllerBase {
    private DataContext context;

    // ...methods omitted for brevity...
}
}
```

Restart ASP.NET Core and request http://localhost:5000/account/logout to ensure that the JavaScript client doesn't use an authentication cookie from a previous example. Request http://localhost:5000/webclient.html to load the JavaScript client and click the Get Data button to send the HTTP request. The server will respond with a 401 Unauthorized response, as shown in figure 39.11.

**Figure 39.11
An unauthorized
request**

39.5.3 *Using cookie authentication*

The simplest way to implement authentication is to rely on the standard ASP.NET Core cookies demonstrated in previous sections. Add a class file named ApiAccount-Controller.cs to the Controllers folder of the Advanced project and use it to define the controller shown in listing 39.23.

> **Listing 39.23   The ApiAccountController.cs file in the Controllers folder of the
>   Advanced project**

```
using Microsoft.AspNetCore.Identity;
using Microsoft.AspNetCore.Mvc;

namespace Advanced.Controllers {

    [ApiController]
    [Route("/api/account")]
    public class ApiAccountController : ControllerBase {
        private SignInManager<IdentityUser> signinManager;

        public ApiAccountController(SignInManager<IdentityUser> mgr) {
            signinManager = mgr;
        }

        [HttpPost("login")]
        public async Task<IActionResult> Login([FromBody]
```

```
                    Credentials creds) {
            Microsoft.AspNetCore.Identity.SignInResult result
                = await signinManager.PasswordSignInAsync(creds.Username,
                    creds.Password, false, false);
            if (result.Succeeded) {
                return Ok();
            }
            return Unauthorized();
        }

        [HttpPost("logout")]
        public async Task<IActionResult> Logout() {
            await signinManager.SignOutAsync();
            return Ok();
        }

        public class Credentials {

            public string Username { get; set; } = string.Empty;

            public string Password { get; set; } = string.Empty;
        }
    }
}
```

This web service controller defines actions that allow clients to log in and log out. The response for a successful authentication request will contain a cookie that the browser will automatically include in requests made by the JavaScript client.

Listing 39.24 adds support to the simple JavaScript client for authenticating using the action methods defined in listing 39.23.

Listing 39.24   Adding authentication in the webclient.js file in the wwwroot folder of the Advanced project

```
const username = "bob";
const password = "secret";

window.addEventListener("DOMContentLoaded", () => {
    const controlDiv = document.getElementById("controls");
    createButton(controlDiv, "Get Data", getData);
    createButton(controlDiv, "Log In", login);
    createButton(controlDiv, "Log Out", logout);
});

async function login() {
    let response = await fetch("/api/account/login", {
        method: "POST",
        headers: { "Content-Type": "application/json" },
        body: JSON.stringify({ username: username, password: password })
    });
    if (response.ok) {
        displayData("Logged in");
    } else {
        displayData(`Error: ${response.status}: ${response.statusText}`);
```

```
        }
    }

    async function logout() {
        let response = await fetch("/api/account/logout", {
            method: "POST"
        });
        if (response.ok) {
            displayData("Logged out");
        } else {
            displayData('Error: ${response.status}: ${response.statusText}');
        }
    }

    async function getData() {
        let response = await fetch("/api/people");
        if (response.ok) {
            let jsonData = await response.json();
            displayData(...jsonData.map(item => `${item.surname},
                ${item.firstname}`));
        } else {
            displayData(`Error: ${response.status}: ${response.statusText}`);
        }
    }

    function displayData(...items) {
        const dataDiv = document.getElementById("data");
        dataDiv.innerHTML = "";
        items.forEach(item => {
            const itemDiv = document.createElement("div");
            itemDiv.innerText = item;
            itemDiv.style.wordWrap = "break-word";
            dataDiv.appendChild(itemDiv);
        })
    }

    function createButton(parent, label, handler) {
        const button = document.createElement("button");
        button.classList.add("btn", "btn-primary", "m-2");
        button.innerText = label;
        button.onclick = handler;
        parent.appendChild(button);
    }
```

Restart ASP.NET Core, request http://localhost:5000/webclient.html, and click the Login In button. Wait for the message confirming authentication and then click the Get Data button. The browser includes the authentication cookie, and the request passes the authorization checks. Click the Log Out button and then click Get Data again. No cookie is used, and the request fails. Figure 39.12 shows both requests.

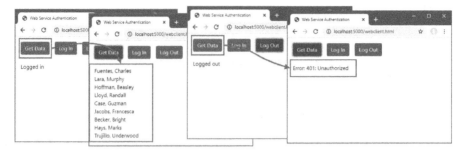

Figure 39.12   Using cookie authentication

39.5.4 *Using bearer token authentication*

Not all web services will be able to rely on cookies because not all clients can use then. An alternative is to use a bearer token, which is a string that clients are given and is included in the requests they send to the web service. Clients don't understand the meaning of the token—which is said to be *opaque*—and just use whatever token the server provides.

I am going to demonstrate authentication using a JSON Web Token (JWT), which provides the client with an encrypted token that contains the authenticated username. The client is unable to decrypt or modify the token, but when it is included in a request, the ASP.NET Core server decrypts the token and uses the name it contains as the identity of the user. The JWT format is described in detail at https://tools.ietf.org/html/rfc7519.

> **CAUTION**   ASP.NET Core will trust that any request that includes the token originates from the authenticated user. Just as when using cookies, production applications should use HTTPS to prevent tokens from being intercepted and reused.

Open a new PowerShell command prompt, navigate to the `Advanced` project folder, and run the commands shown in listing 39.25 to add the packages for JWT to the project.

Listing 39.25   Installing the NuGet package

```
dotnet add package System.IdentityModel.Tokens.Jwt --version 6.25.0
dotnet add package Microsoft.AspNetCore.Authentication.JwtBearer
    --version 7.0.0
```

JWT requires a key that is used to encrypt and decrypt tokens. Add the configuration setting shown in listing 39.26 to the `appsettings.json` file. If you use JWT in a real application, ensure you change the key or use a secret to store the key outside of the project.

Listing 39.26   Adding a setting in the appsettings.json file in the Advanced project

```
{
  "Logging": {
    "LogLevel": {
      "Default": "Information",
      "Microsoft.AspNetCore": "Warning",
      "Microsoft.EntityFrameworkCore": "Information"
    }
  },
  "AllowedHosts": "*",
  "ConnectionStrings": {
    "PeopleConnection": "Server=(localdb)\\MSSQLLocalDB;...
Database=People;MultipleActiveResultSets=True",
    "IdentityConnection": "Server=(localdb)\\MSSQLLocalDB;Database=Identity
;MultipleActiveResultSets=True"
  },
  "jwtSecret": "jwt_secret"
}
```

39.5.5 *Creating tokens*

The client will send an HTTP request that contains user credentials and will receive a
JWT in response. Listing 39.27 adds an action method to the ApiAccount controller
that receives the credentials, validates them, and generates tokens.

**Listing 39.27   Generating tokens in the ApiAccountController.cs file in the Controllers
folder of the Advanced project**

```
using Microsoft.AspNetCore.Identity;
using Microsoft.AspNetCore.Mvc;
using Microsoft.IdentityModel.Tokens;
using System.IdentityModel.Tokens.Jwt;
using System.Text;
using System.Security.Claims;

namespace Advanced.Controllers {

    [ApiController]
    [Route("/api/account")]
    public class ApiAccountController : ControllerBase {
        private SignInManager<IdentityUser> signinManager;
        private UserManager<IdentityUser> userManager;
        private IConfiguration configuration;

        public ApiAccountController(SignInManager<IdentityUser> mgr,
                UserManager<IdentityUser> usermgr,
                IConfiguration config) {
            signinManager = mgr;
            userManager = usermgr;
            configuration = config;
        }

        [HttpPost("login")]
```

```csharp
public async Task<IActionResult> Login(
        [FromBody] Credentials creds) {
    Microsoft.AspNetCore.Identity.SignInResult result
        = await signinManager.PasswordSignInAsync(creds.Username,
            creds.Password, false, false);
    if (result.Succeeded) {
        return Ok();
    }
    return Unauthorized();
}

[HttpPost("logout")]
public async Task<IActionResult> Logout() {
    await signinManager.SignOutAsync();
    return Ok();
}

[HttpPost("token")]
public async Task<IActionResult> Token(
        [FromBody] Credentials creds) {
    if (await CheckPassword(creds)) {
        JwtSecurityTokenHandler handler =
            new JwtSecurityTokenHandler();
        byte[] secret =
            Encoding.ASCII.GetBytes(configuration["jwtSecret"]!);
        SecurityTokenDescriptor descriptor =
            new SecurityTokenDescriptor {
                Subject = new ClaimsIdentity(new Claim[] {
                    new Claim(ClaimTypes.Name, creds.Username)
                }),
                Expires = DateTime.UtcNow.AddHours(24),
                SigningCredentials = new SigningCredentials(
                    new SymmetricSecurityKey(secret),
                        SecurityAlgorithms.HmacSha256Signature)
            };
        SecurityToken token = handler.CreateToken(descriptor);
        return Ok(new {
            success = true,
            token = handler.WriteToken(token)
        });
    }
    return Unauthorized();
}

private async Task<bool> CheckPassword(Credentials creds) {
    IdentityUser? user
        = await userManager.FindByNameAsync(creds.Username);
    if (user != null) {
        return (await signinManager.CheckPasswordSignInAsync(user,
            creds.Password, true)).Succeeded;
    }
    return false;
}

public class Credentials {
```

```
            public string Username { get; set; } = string.Empty;

            public string Password { get; set; } = string.Empty;
        }
    }
}
```

When the `Token` action method is invoked, it passes the credentials to the `Check-Password` method, which enumerates the `IPasswordValidator<T>` objects to invoke the `ValidateAsync` method on each of them. If the password is validated by any of the validators, then the Token method creates a token.

The JWT specification defines a general-purpose token that can be used more broadly than identifying users in HTTP requests, and many of the options that are available are not required for this example. The token that is created in listing 39.27 contains a payload like this:

```
. . .
{
  "unique_name": "bob",
  "nbf": 1579765454,
  "exp": 1579851854,
  "iat": 1579765454
}
. . .
```

The `unique_name` property contains the name of the user and is used to authenticate requests that contain the token. The other payload properties are timestamps, which I do not use.

The payload is encrypted using the key defined in listing 39.27 and returned to the client as a JSON-encoded response that looks like this:

```
. . .
{
    "success":true,
    "token":"eyJhbGciOiJIUzI1NiIsInR5cCI6IkpXVCJ9..."
}
. . .
```

I have shown just the first part of the token because they are long strings and it is the structure of the response that is important. The client receives the token and includes it in future requests using the `Authorization` header, like this:

```
. . .
Authorization: Bearer eyJhbGciOiJIUzI1NiIsInR5cCI6IkpXVCJ9
. . .
```

The server receives the token, decrypts it using the key, and authenticates the request using the value of the `unique_name` property from the token payload. No further validation is performed, and requests with a valid token will be authenticated using whatever username is contained in the payload.

39.5.6 *Authenticating with tokens*

The next step is to configure the application to receive and validate the tokens, as shown in listing 39.28.

> **Listing 39.28   Authenticating tokens in the Program.cs file in the Advanced project**

```
using Microsoft.EntityFrameworkCore;
using Advanced.Models;
using Microsoft.AspNetCore.Identity;
using Microsoft.AspNetCore.Authentication.Cookies;
using Microsoft.IdentityModel.Tokens;
using System.Text;
using System.Security.Claims;
using Microsoft.AspNetCore.Authentication.JwtBearer;

var builder = WebApplication.CreateBuilder(args);

builder.Services.AddControllersWithViews();
builder.Services.AddRazorPages();
builder.Services.AddServerSideBlazor();

builder.Services.AddDbContext<DataContext>(opts => {
    opts.UseSqlServer(
        builder.Configuration["ConnectionStrings:PeopleConnection"]);
    opts.EnableSensitiveDataLogging(true);
});

builder.Services.AddSingleton<Advanced.Services.ToggleService>();

builder.Services.AddDbContext<IdentityContext>(opts =>
    opts.UseSqlServer(builder.Configuration[
        "ConnectionStrings:IdentityConnection"]));
builder.Services.AddIdentity<IdentityUser, IdentityRole>()
    .AddEntityFrameworkStores<IdentityContext>();

builder.Services.Configure<IdentityOptions>(opts => {
    opts.Password.RequiredLength = 6;
    opts.Password.RequireNonAlphanumeric = false;
    opts.Password.RequireLowercase = false;
    opts.Password.RequireUppercase = false;
    opts.Password.RequireDigit = false;
    opts.User.RequireUniqueEmail = true;
    opts.User.AllowedUserNameCharacters = "abcdefghijklmnopqrstuvwxyz";
});

builder.Services.AddAuthentication(opts => {
    opts.DefaultScheme =
        CookieAuthenticationDefaults.AuthenticationScheme;
    opts.DefaultChallengeScheme =
        CookieAuthenticationDefaults.AuthenticationScheme;
}).AddCookie(opts => {
    opts.Events.DisableRedirectForPath(e => e.OnRedirectToLogin,
        "/api", StatusCodes.Status401Unauthorized);
    opts.Events.DisableRedirectForPath(e => e.OnRedirectToAccessDenied,
```

```
                "/api", StatusCodes.Status403Forbidden);
}).AddJwtBearer(opts => {
    opts.RequireHttpsMetadata = false;
    opts.SaveToken = true;
    opts.TokenValidationParameters = new TokenValidationParameters {
        ValidateIssuerSigningKey = true,
        IssuerSigningKey = new SymmetricSecurityKey(
            Encoding.ASCII.GetBytes(builder.Configuration["jwtSecret"]!)),
        ValidateAudience = false,
        ValidateIssuer = false
    };

    opts.Events = new JwtBearerEvents {
        OnTokenValidated = async ctx => {
            var usrmgr = ctx.HttpContext.RequestServices
                .GetRequiredService<UserManager<IdentityUser>>();
            var signinmgr = ctx.HttpContext.RequestServices
                .GetRequiredService<SignInManager<IdentityUser>>();
            string? username =
                ctx.Principal?.FindFirst(ClaimTypes.Name)?.Value;
            if (username != null) {
                IdentityUser? idUser =
                    await usrmgr.FindByNameAsync(username);
                if (idUser != null) {
                    ctx.Principal =
                        await signinmgr.CreateUserPrincipalAsync(idUser);
                }
            }
        }
    };
});

var app = builder.Build();

app.UseStaticFiles();

app.UseAuthentication();
app.UseAuthorization();

app.MapControllers();
app.MapControllerRoute("controllers",
    "controllers/{controller=Home}/{action=Index}/{id?}");
app.MapRazorPages();
app.MapBlazorHub();
app.MapFallbackToPage("/_Host");

app.UseBlazorFrameworkFiles("/webassembly");
app.MapFallbackToFile("/webassembly/{*path:nonfile}",
    "/webassembly/index.html");

var context = app.Services.CreateScope().ServiceProvider
    .GetRequiredService<DataContext>();
SeedData.SeedDatabase(context);

IdentitySeedData.CreateAdminAccount(app.Services, app.Configuration);
app.Run();
```

The `AddJwtBearer` adds support for JWT to the authentication system and provides the settings required to decrypt tokens. I have added a handler for the `OnToken-Validated` event, which is triggered when a token is validated so that I can query the user database and associate the `IdentityUser` object with the request. This acts as a bridge between the JWT tokens and the ASP.NET Core Identity data, ensuring that features like role-based authorization work seamlessly.

39.5.7 *Restricting access with tokens*

To allow a restricted endpoint to be accessed with tokens, I have modified the `Authorize` attribute applied to the `Data` controller, as shown in listing 39.29.

> **Listing 39.29   Enabling tokens in the DataController.cs file in the Controllers folder of the Advanced project**

```
using Advanced.Models;
using Microsoft.AspNetCore.Mvc;
using Microsoft.EntityFrameworkCore;
using Microsoft.AspNetCore.Authorization;

namespace Advanced.Controllers {

    [ApiController]
    [Route("/api/people")]
    [Authorize(AuthenticationSchemes = "Identity.Application, Bearer")]
    public class DataController : ControllerBase {
        private DataContext context;

        // ...methods omitted for brevity...
    }
}
```

The `AuthenticationSchemes` argument is used to specify the types of authentication that can be used to authorize access to the controller. In this case, I have specified that the default cookie authentication and the new bearer tokens can be used.

39.5.8 *Using tokens to request data*

The final step is to update the JavaScript client so that it obtains a token and includes it in requests for data, as shown in listing 39.30.

> **Listing 39.30   Using tokens in the webclient.js file in the wwwroot folder of the Advanced project**

```
const username = "bob";
const password = "secret";
let token;

window.addEventListener("DOMContentLoaded", () => {
    const controlDiv = document.getElementById("controls");
    createButton(controlDiv, "Get Data", getData);
    createButton(controlDiv, "Log In", login);
```

```
        createButton(controlDiv, "Log Out", logout);
});

async function login() {
    let response = await fetch("/api/account/token", {
        method: "POST",
        headers: { "Content-Type": "application/json" },
        body: JSON.stringify({ username: username, password: password })
    });
    if (response.ok) {
        token = (await response.json()).token;
        displayData("Logged in", token);
    } else {
        displayData(`Error: ${response.status}: ${response.statusText}`);
    }
}

async function logout() {
    token = "";
    displayData("Logged out");
}

async function getData() {
    let response = await fetch("/api/people", {
        headers: { "Authorization": 'Bearer ${token}' }
    });
    if (response.ok) {
        let jsonData = await response.json();
        displayData(...jsonData.map(item =>
            `${item.surname}, ${item.firstname}`));
    } else {
        displayData(`Error: ${response.status}: ${response.statusText}`);
    }
}

function displayData(...items) {
    const dataDiv = document.getElementById("data");
    dataDiv.innerHTML = "";
    items.forEach(item => {
        const itemDiv = document.createElement("div");
        itemDiv.innerText = item;
        itemDiv.style.wordWrap = "break-word";
        dataDiv.appendChild(itemDiv);
    })
}

function createButton(parent, label, handler) {
    const button = document.createElement("button");
    button.classList.add("btn", "btn-primary", "m-2");
    button.innerText = label;
    button.onclick = handler;
    parent.appendChild(button);
}
```

The client receives the authentication response and assigns the token so it can be used by the `GetData` method, which sets the `Authorization` header. Notice that no logout request is required, and the variable used to store the token is simply reset when the user clicks the Log Out button.

> **CAUTION**   It is easy to end up authenticating with a cookie when attempting to test tokens. Make sure you clear your browser cookies before testing this feature to ensure that cookies from previous tests are not used.

Restart ASP.NET Core and request http://localhost:5000/webclient.html. Click the Log In button, and a token will be generated and displayed. Click the Get Data button, and the token will be sent to the server and used to authenticate the user, producing the results shown in figure 39.13.

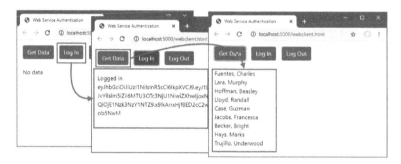

Figure 39.13   Using a token for authentication

Summary

- User credentials are validated using the `SignInManager` service and successful authentications usually generate a cookie that will be included in subsequent requests.

- Identity supports alternatives to cookies, including bearer tokens for use with web services and JavaScript clients.

- Access controls are applied to ensure that only authorized users can request restricted actions, pages, or components. Authorization policies are specified using attributes.

index

S